Fodor's 2002

Mexico

D0839657

Fodor's Travel Publications • New York, Toronto, London, Sydney, Auckland
www.fodors.com

CONTENTS

MAPS

Circled letters in text correspond to letters on the photographs. For more information on the sights pictured, turn to the indicated page number (A)> on each photograph.

DESTINATION MEXICO

It could happen while you're climbing the Pyramid of the Magician at the magnificent Maya ruins of Uxmal in the Yucatán, descending into the formidable Barranca del Cobre (Copper Canyon), strolling through the shady plaza of a colonial Heartland town in the heat and torpor of siesta time, lolling on the beach in glittering Acapulco, snorkeling off Quintana Roo in the waters of the Caribbean, or gawking at the variety of chilies in Oaxaca's Central de Abastos market. And you won't be in Mexico too long before it does happen—you realize that what makes this country so alluring is its diversity. Mexico is a blend—of peoples, of cultures, of landscapes, of worlds new and old, of the legacies of the vanquished and the conqueror—and the mix is so enchanting that you'll hardly even notice that you're falling under its spell.

MEXICO CITY
AND SIDE TRIPS

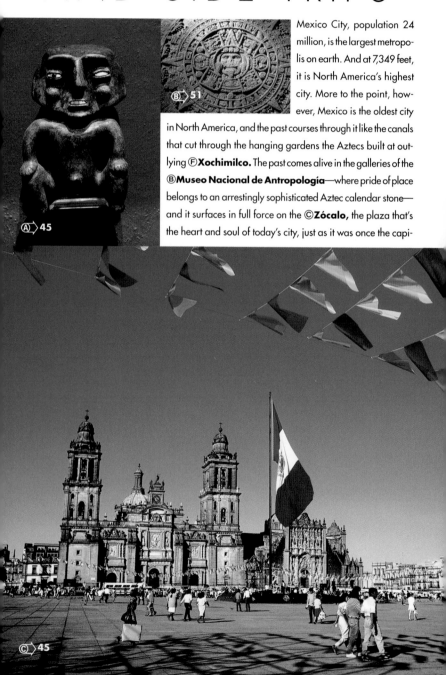

Mexico City, population 24 million, is the largest metropolis on earth. And at 7,349 feet, it is North America's highest city. More to the point, however, Mexico is the oldest city in North America, and the past courses through it like the canals that cut through the hanging gardens the Aztecs built at outlying ⓕ**Xochimilco.** The past comes alive in the galleries of the Ⓑ**Museo Nacional de Antropología**—where pride of place belongs to an arrestingly sophisticated Aztec calendar stone—and it surfaces in full force on the ⓒ**Zócalo,** the plaza that's the heart and soul of today's city, just as it was once the capi-

Ⓐ 45

Ⓑ 51

Ⓒ 45

Ⓔ 104

tal of the Aztec empire, Tenochtitlán. A stroll through this square takes you past the 16th-century Catedral Metropolitana, Latin America's oldest and largest cathedral, to the ruined Ⓐ**Templo Mayor,** the ceremonial Aztec center of human sacrifice. An adjacent museum displays the treasures unearthed during its excavation. Southeast of the city the gilded carvings in Ⓓ**Iglesia de Santo Domingo,** one of 224 churches the Spanish built in the valley of Puebla, hover over the faithful as if to promise a glittering life after death. Looming above the city and the Valley of Mexico, the rumbling 17,887-foot volcano Ⓔ**Popocatépetl** is a constant reminder of forces mightier than any civilization, past or present, and an opportunity to hike off last night's rich chicken mole dinner beneath the crater, so long as you don't pass the 12,000-foot danger point.

Ⓕ 99

BAJA

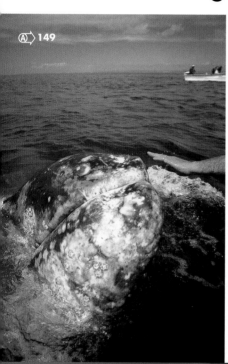

Ⓐ 149

Lively border traffic colors the culture of the upper reaches of Baja Norte, the half of the peninsula attached to the state of California, where Tijuana keeps right on living up to its raucous and rowdy reputation. Down the coast Rosarito and Puerto Nuevo open their doors for weekending Californians, likewise Ⓓ**Ensenada,** which also has a busy fishing port and fish market to show for it. But you can't say you've really experienced the 1,000-mile-long finger of land that is Baja California until you head south, off the beaten path. Here, in some of the most beautiful terrain on earth, quiet

Ⓑ 168

©⟩170   ⒹⰪ133

fishing villages and pristine beaches punctuate two coast-lines. On the Sea of Cortez you can kayak in protected Bahía Concepción—or on the Pacific coast, in the Ⓐ**Laguna de San Ignacio,** pull up within petting distance of migrating gray whales. Inland, boulder-strewn deserts are dotted with cacti, mountain peaks soar to 10,000 feet, and the high sierra yields its wonders as you hike through Parque Nacional San Pedro Mártir. Caves near Misión San Javier display an-cient paintings left by Baja's earliest inhabitants. In their wake, explorers, missionaries, pirates, and movie stars have made their way here, trying to get away from it all. The silhouettes of golfers, anglers, and sunseekers stand out in today's crowds, which flock to the elegant hostelries of that still wonderfully natural area at Baja California's tip known as Los Cabos. And with secluded coves like Playa de Amor and a spectacular land's end at ©**El Arco,** it's no wonder that newlyweds are among the Los Cabos pilgrims—the hacienda-style Ⓑ**Palmilla** even has its own adobe wedding chapel.

SONORA

Ⓐ 198

Imagine Arizona a hundred years ago, when cowboys drove cattle across wide-open ranges and lined up along the bars of saloons to sing *rancheras,* ballads right out of the storybooks of the Old West. Then add a coastline—a fringe of beach washed by a balmy turquoise sea—and you've conjured up Sonora, Mexico's northernmost state. South of Nogales, a sometimes-rowdy border town, relatively unspoiled coastal towns like Bahía Kino and Guaymas keep company with quiet, undiscovered seaside ⒷⒸ**San Carlos,** for example. And arid coffee-colored hills tumble into the Sea of

Ⓑ 195

Cortés in a profusion of creosote bushes, saguaro, and organ-pipe cacti. Offshore, dolphins, pelicans, sea lions, and migrating whales thrive—as do swimmers, snorkelers, sea kayakers, and enthusiasts of just about every other aquatic

Ⓒ 195

stripe. Inland, Father Eusebio Francisco Kino's missions populate towns such as Magdalena, and deserts give way to stands of cottonwoods and evergreens rising into the foothills of the Sierra Madre. Their hidden treasures include Ⓐ**Alamos,** a former silver-mining center that is one of Mexico's loveliest and best-preserved colonial towns.

(A) 217

The high desert of the Sierra Madre gives way to high drama when it plunges into the four gorges known as the Barranca del Cobre—the Copper Canyon—a mile deep, a mile wide, and four times the size of the Grand Canyon. Most people see it from the Chihuahua al Pacífico railroad on its run between Los

COPPER CANYON

Mochis and Chihuahua City. From whistle-stops like the one at ©**Divisadero,** you'll see how this difficult terrain has pushed its resident Tarahumara Indians to master extraordinary skills—like super-long-distance running. Tarahumara ancestors left marks all around the Paquimé Ruins at Ⓐ**Casas Grandes.** Of the priests who worked among the tribes, creating missions like the one at Ⓑ**Cusárare,** Father Miguel Hidalgo began preaching Mexican independence in 1810. A hundred years later General Pancho Villa launched Mexico's civil war from his home in lively Chihuahua City.

(B) 213

(C) 212

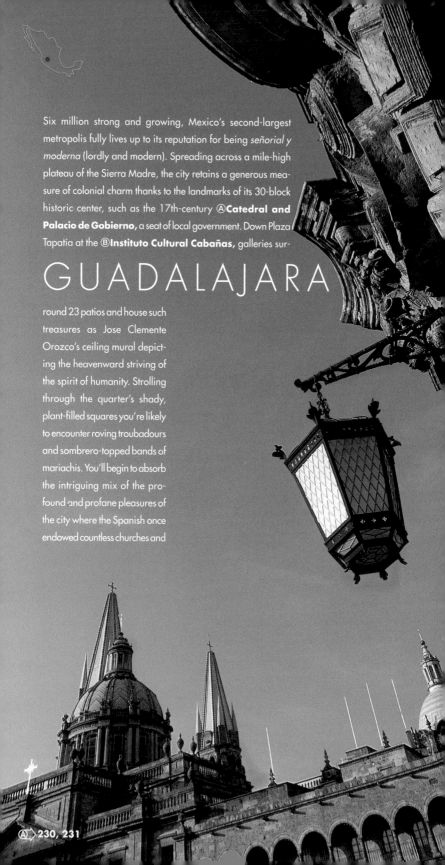

Six million strong and growing, Mexico's second-largest metropolis fully lives up to its reputation for being *señorial y moderna* (lordly and modern). Spreading across a mile-high plateau of the Sierra Madre, the city retains a generous measure of colonial charm thanks to the landmarks of its 30-block historic center, such as the 17th-century Ⓐ**Catedral and Palacio de Gobierno,** a seat of local government. Down Plaza Tapatía at the Ⓑ**Instituto Cultural Cabañas,** galleries sur-

GUADALAJARA

round 23 patios and house such treasures as Jose Clemente Orozco's ceiling mural depicting the heavenward striving of the spirit of humanity. Strolling through the quarter's shady, plant-filled squares you're likely to encounter roving troubadours and sombrero-topped bands of mariachis. You'll begin to absorb the intriguing mix of the profound and profane pleasures of the city where the Spanish once endowed countless churches and monuments with vast sums—and invented such traditional Mexican mainstays as *el jarabe tapatío* (the hat dance) and *charreadas* (rodeos), in which cowboys still compete weekly. In the ⒟**Mercado Libertad,** one of Latin America's largest enclosed markets, with its thousand-odd stalls, you can haggle with local vendors for a piece of fruit or a gold watch. Locally made handicrafts are the reward for a

Ⓑ 230

Ⓒ 248

trip across the cactus-studded plains surrounding Guadalajara. In Tlaquepaque and nearby ⒞**Tonalá** thousands of artisans fashion artful ceramics and glassware, from the Baroque to the whimsical and contemporary. It's all sold in outdoor markets, studios in old adobe houses, and shops along pedestrian malls and plazas. The dusty cobblestone streets of these towns and their air of old-time Mexico make a refreshing antidote to Guadalajara's urban bustle. Nearby at Tequila you can drink at the source of Mexico's famous firewater.

Ⓓ 245

In this fertile swath of farm country, traditions cling as tenaciously as the prickly pear and other cacti that spring from the rolling landscape. On Ⓑ**Lake Pátzcuaro,** Purépecha Indians fish and ply their canoes as they have for hundreds of years. Even in

THE HEARTLAND

Ⓐ▷ 295

mountainous San Miguel de Allende, known for its substantial English-speaking community, local women still gather at the public *lavandería* for laundry and gossip. These connections with the past keep the Heartland's turbulent history alive, as do a wealth of monuments, museums, and landmarks. In Ⓐ**Querétaro,** handsome mansions bespeak civic pride that stems in no small measure from the city's status as an eyewitness to history—it was here that Mexico's short-term Emperor Maximilian was executed and the Mexican constitution signed. In Ⓒ**Guanajuato,** musicians

Ⓑ▷ 312

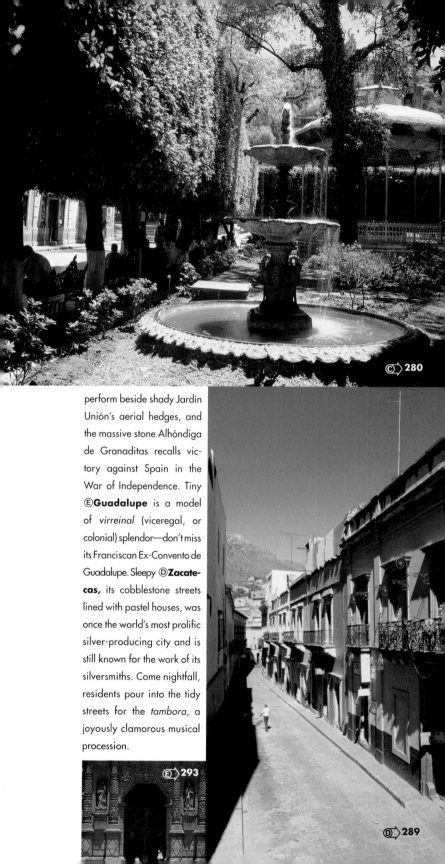

perform beside shady Jardín Unión's aerial hedges, and the massive stone Alhóndiga de Granaditas recalls victory against Spain in the War of Independence. Tiny ⒺGuadalupe is a model of *virreinal* (viceregal, or colonial) splendor—don't miss its Franciscan Ex-Convento de Guadalupe. Sleepy ⒹZacatecas, its cobblestone streets lined with pastel houses, was once the world's most prolific silver-producing city and is still known for the work of its silversmiths. Come nightfall, residents pour into the tidy streets for the *tambora,* a joyously clamorous musical procession.

©⟩280

Ⓔ⟩293

Ⓓ⟩289

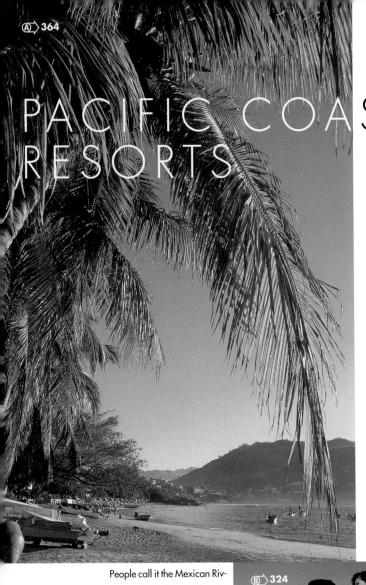

Ⓐ 364

PACIFIC COAST RESORTS

Ⓑ 324

People call it the Mexican Riviera and Gold Coast, but the most apt way to refer to this jungle-backed coastline might just be Tropical Paradise. Historical landmarks like the colonial church of Nuestra Señora

de Guadalupe in the once-sleepy fishing village—now glittering resort—of ©**Puerto Vallarta** are few and far between. But the 900 miles of cove-scalloped white strands edging the Pacific provide more-than-ample diversion for sun worshippers and water-sports lovers, from angling in Ⓑ**Mazatlán,** to snorkeling off the white- or black-sand beaches of Manzanillo, to simply feeling sand between your toes in low-key Ⓐ**Zihuatanejo** or its glitzy neighbor, Ixtapa.

© 338

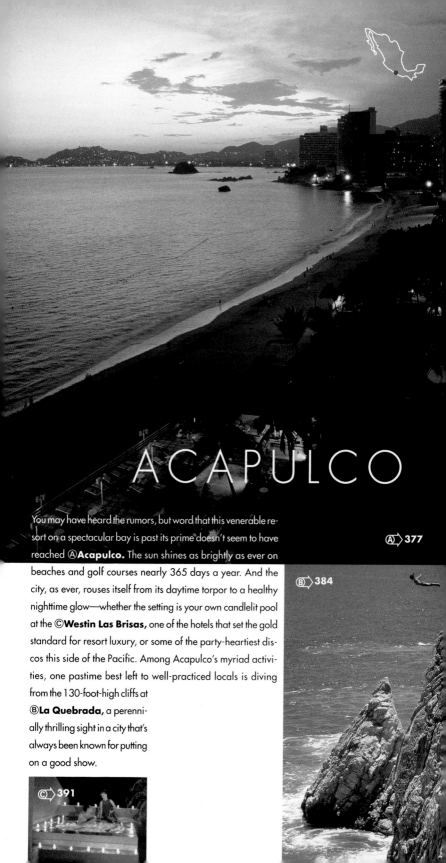

ACAPULCO

You may have heard the rumors, but word that this venerable resort on a spectacular bay is past its prime doesn't seem to have reached Ⓐ**Acapulco.** The sun shines as brightly as ever on beaches and golf courses nearly 365 days a year. And the city, as ever, rouses itself from its daytime torpor to a healthy nighttime glow—whether the setting is your own candlelit pool at the ©**Westin Las Brisas,** one of the hotels that set the gold standard for resort luxury, or some of the party-heartiest discos this side of the Pacific. Among Acapulco's myriad activities, one pastime best left to well-practiced locals is diving from the 130-foot-high cliffs at Ⓑ**La Quebrada,** a perennially thrilling sight in a city that's always been known for putting on a good show.

Ⓐ⟩377

Ⓑ⟩384

©⟩391

OAXACA

Ⓐ➤426

Ⓑ➤420

Surfers and beach lovers know Oaxaca for its more than 300 miles of lush coastline, washed by the warm Pacific. Zicatela, pounded by the so-called Mexican Pipeline, is one of the world's top surfing beaches. But the prime appeal of Oaxaca state and its eponymous colonial capital is the old and the older. Brilliantly ornamented Baroque monuments from the Spanish conquest, including the color- fully tile-domed Ⓑ**Catedral Metropolitana de Oaxaca,** pass almost for new, when magnificent remnants of civi- lizations long past are so near at hand. Mountaintop Ⓐ**Monte Albán,** with its still-intact ball court, temples, and observatory, was already a thriving city of 40,000 more than 2,500 years ago. A full millennium of civilization passed before the original Zapotec people were surpassed by the Mixtec, who turned the site into a rich necropolis that has yielded some of North America's greatest archaeological treasures. Today the descendants of both peoples enrich life in Oaxaca City. Festivals are lavish and intense, none more so than the macabre celebrations leading up to the Ⓒ**Día de Muertos** (Day of the Dead/All Souls' Day). Elegantly singsong native languages lend a distinctly musical note to the commotion in Saturday's Central de Abastos, Mexico's largest Indian market. Here and elsewhere, vendors sell everything from herbs and chilies to baskets, rugs, tin toys, and *huipiles* (embroidered tunics). After dark, strings of lights deck the 19th-century Ⓓ**Palacio de Gobierno** for no special reason. Every turn of a corner is likely to deliver a dose of local color that will etch itself into your memory.

Ⓒ▷417

Ⓓ▷421

These less-developed southern states are at the heart of Maya and Lacandon Indian country and are for most people a gateway to Guatemala. But if you linger here you'll discover what is arguably Mexico's most authentic culture, in

CHIAPAS AND TABASCO

Ⓐ 467

Ⓑ 463

colonial San Cristóbal de las Casas and traditional villages around it such as Ⓑ **San Juan Chamula,** whose daily life turns on centuries-old rituals. Make your way from the city through jungles and sinuous mountainscapes to verdant Ⓐ **Sumidero Canyon,** a 4,000-foot-deep near-vertical gash carved by the Grijalva River. In all of Mexico there is nothing like the mesmerizing power of the 2,000-year-old Maya city of Ⓒ **Palenque** rising out of the lush forests, echoing in its stone-capped tower and temples the spirit of the surrounding hills.

Ⓒ 468

VERACRUZ AND THE NORTHEAST

Ⓐ 492

Ⓑ 498

Ⓒ 506

If you were to work your way south from the Texas border, from souvenir-choked Nuevo Laredo through the mountain city of Saltillo and low-profile coastal Tampico, you'd get a taste of Mexico as heady as the brew from the coffee beans harvested in the tropical highlands outside the raffish city of Ⓐ **Veracruz.** In the antique city itself the diverse citizenry takes to the streets for entertainment and exuberant self-expression: trios slap away at tiny guitars and portable harps, singers belt out that famed local song, *La Bamba*, and, most alluring of all, evening strollers pause in the Ⓑ **Plaza de Armas** for a little *danzón*—the sensuous, once-scandalous dance brought to Mexico by 19th-century Cubans. Elegance of movement is an aerial affair in colonial Ⓒ **Papantla de Olarte,** where four *voladores* (fliers) enact the ancient Totonac Indian calendrical cycle, diving backwards while tethered to an 82-foot pole and circling it upside down 52 times. The sublime Pyramid of the Niches at El Tajín, nearby, is the architectural flower of the ancient Indian civilizations that once dominated the coast.

YUCATÁN

Ⓐ❯599

Beaches and ruins, beaches and ruins, beaches and ruins: Mexico's most-visited region will reward you with an embarrassment of both riches, sometimes simultaneously—on Ⓒ**Playa Chacmool** in Cancún, the Chichén Maya rain god Chac looks as much like a beachgoer as he does like the sacrificial altar he once was. Ⓓ**Tulum** may well be the most satisfying spot in the Yucatán (in spite of the crowds). Here, alongside the Caribbean, the local limestone of the temples has mellowed

©>530

in the salt air, and you can go for a swim from the perfect slip of sand where the ancients beached their canoes. But it was the sky, not the sea, upon which the Maya builders set their sights, and in their displays of might they erected monumental temple-pyramids to soar above their now-deserted cities. The enormous Ⓐ**Chichén Itzá,** which once dominated the Yucatán, is populated with hundreds of structures. Elegant, refined Uxmal is exceptional in another way—for the grace of its pyramids, courtyards, and relief carvings. And along the Puuc Route, satellite cities like Kabah, Sayil, and Labná help color the picture of one of the Americas' most intriguing civilizations. These cities once hummed with activity, but today many are quiet: at Ⓑ**Cobá,** the lonely silence is broken only by the shrieks of spider monkeys from the encroaching jungle. And Ⓔ**Cenote Dzitnup,** the swimmable, skylit sinkhole near colonial Valladolid, is as eerily mysterious as ever.

Ⓓ>584

Ⓔ>603

YUCATÁN

(F) 553

Ruins of Maya civilizations may beckon, remnants of Spanish colonialism, like quirky Mérida and fortified Campeche and the formidable ⑥**Convento de San Antonio de Padua** at Izamal, may cry out to be explored, but let's face it—the reason you're thinking about the Yucatán is its irresistible mix of sun, sand, and sea. On much of the Quintana Roo coast between Cancún and Tulum, luxury hotel strips like those at Playa del Carmen preside over balmy, crystalline waters and unbroken beaches as white as alabaster. The world's second-largest barrier reef lies just off the island of Cozumel, luring divers and snorkelers, and nature reserves farther south at Sian Ka'an and Boca Paila and north at Parque Natural Río Lagartos attract migrating flamingos, herons, and other birds, as well as their binocular-toting admirers. To the west, along the shores of the Golfo de México, temperatures hover appealingly at 80 degrees, and the sun shines 240-plus days a year—even more than on the Caribbean—and you'll find relaxed coastal villages like ①**Celestún.** The epicenter of the peninsula, where your every whim can be satisfied both by day and by night, is ⑭**Cancún,** hacked out of the jungle three decades ago and purpose-built for pleasure. The let-the-good-

(G) 599

(H) 533

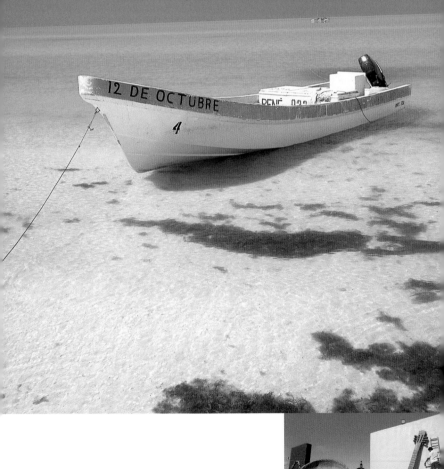

times-roll attitude of Mexico's top resort is so entrenched that even roadside art aims to amuse. For a bit more quiet— and more beach life than nightlife—tiny fish-shaped ⒻIsla **Mujeres** is just the thing, a mere half hour by boat across the bay from Cancún. Or head down the coast to laid-back Paamul for great beachcombing, the midsummer hatching of sea turtles, and a lagoon that's ideal for snorkeling. Whatever your passion, you'll find a place to pursue it under the Yucatán sun—and you don't have to set your sights any farther than that point out there where the blue-green sea meets the cloudless sky.

GREAT ITINERARIES

Ⓐ⏵ 162

Canyons and Coasts
8 to 12 days

Natural wonders never cease in northern and western Mexico. From the heart-stopping views and hikes into the Barranca del Cobre—the Copper Canyon—to Baja Sur's inland deserts, its annual migrations of whales, and the beaches of Los Cabos, opportunities for adventure and relaxation are everywhere.

THE COPPER CANYON
3 to 4 days. Riding the Chihuahua al Pacífico rail line from west to east affords the most stunning views of the Copper Canyon. So start off in Los Mochis and make the mountain village of Cerocahui your first stop. From here, views of Urique Canyon— and the cave paintings at the Cueva de las Cruces—are superb. Head up the line to

Divisadero, *the* place for sunset views and horseback trips to the Tarahumara village of Bacajipare. Farther on, the 806-foot Basaseachi Falls are one of North America's highest cascades. If a dose of urban life feels like the appropriate tonic after taking in the canyons, spend the night in Chihuahua before catching a plane for La Paz. ☞ *Chapter 5*

LA PAZ
1 to 2 days. Begin with a kayaking, snorkeling, or diving trip to Isla Espíritu Santo or Isla Partida in the Sea of Cortez—you're almost guaranteed to spot sea lions and whales. Spend the rest of the day in town, at the Plaza Constitución, Catedral de Nuestra Señora de la Paz, and the Museum of Anthropology. At sunset nears, head for the seaside malecón where couples and families stroll beside playgrounds on the sand. If you're here in the winter, join a tour to Bahía Magdalena, where migrating gray whales give birth. ☞ *La Paz in Chapter 3*

LORETO
1 to 2 days. Visitors to Loreto are largely intent on fishing in the rich waters off nearby islands, and even nonanglers enjoy a boat ride at dawn,

when the rising sun casts a glow over the Sierra Gigante. Loreto's laid-back hotels are also the perfect base for exploring the nearby mountains and coast. Drive about two hours past cattle ranches and boulder-strewn hills to the well-preserved Misión San Javier, set amid citrus trees in a tiny mountain village. Or drive a couple of hours north to the incomparably picturesque Bahía Concepción and the town of Mulegé, in an oasis by the sea. ☞ *Loreto in Chapter 3*

LOS CABOS
3 to 4 days. Spend your first day in Ⓐ Los Cabos fishing for marlin, golfing at a championship course on the Sea of Cortez, or swimming and sunbathing at Playa Médano. Sample Cabo San Lucas's theme restaurants and trendy cafés that night. Begin day two with breakfast at one of the Corridor's lavish resorts and snorkeling at Bahía Chileno. Stroll through San José del Cabo's plazas and galleries in the evening, and end the day dining on fresh fish. Spend the rest of your days exploring Baja's incomparable desert and sea scenery: head for the artsy enclave of Todos Santos, or to the East Cape for long drives on sandy desert roads beside the sea. ☞ *Los Cabos in Chapter 3*

PACIFIC OCEAN

By Public Transportation
Distances here demand a fair amount of air travel: first from Mexico City to Los Mochis, then from Chihuahua to La Paz—which flies you over the canyons. The entire rail trip from Los Mochis to Chihuahua is a 15-hour proposition, but it's best to stop at towns along the way and reboard later in the day or the next day, or even the next. From La Paz, tour companies will take you to Bahía Magdalena to see whales. To get to Loreto (3 hrs north of La Paz), the East Cape (1 hr south), and Los Cabos (2 hrs south), rent a car so you can explore the quieter coastal stretches on your own. Buses also run throughout Baja Sur.

Colonial Mexico
7 to 10 days

Remarkably well-preserved, these colonial cities are full of atmospheric haciendas and richly decorated cathedrals—along with intriguing juxtapositions of the colonial and the indigenous that are classic Mexico.

QUERÉTARO
1 day. This Heartland city has been called the cradle of independence. Its restored Plaza de la Independencia is filled with grand mansions once belonging to titled friends of the Crown. Amble around the square and nearby streets to see the baroque Ⓑ Museo de Arte de Querétaro, housed in an 18th-century monastery, the Palacio del Gobierno del Estado, and the Jardín de la Corregidora.
☞ *Querétaro in Chapter 7*

SAN MIGUEL DE ALLENDE
1 to 2 days. A cultural hub of the region, this friendly city is full of bookstores, art galleries, coffee shops, and American expats. Take time to visit churches—the Gothic Revival Parroquia, the churrigueresque Iglesia de San Francisco, and the unique Oratorio de San Felipe Neri. San Miguel's historic inns are perfect for soaking up more local ambiance. Consider a side trip to the historic village of Dolores Hidalgo, home of the insurgent priest whose cry for independence started the 1810 war.
☞ *San Miguel de Allende in Chapter 7*

GUANAJUATO
2 to 3 days. Splendid buildings rising above labyrinthine streets give Guanajuato its medieval appearance. Make your way to the main square and the impressive Teatro Juárez, headquarters of the annual Cervantes Festival (October). El Museo Casa Diego Rivera, birthplace of the famed muralist, and the hulking Alhóndiga de Granaditas fortress are nearby. On day two, visit the Basílica Colegiata de Nuestra Señora de Guanajuato and La Valenciana—the former for its 8th-century statue of the Virgin, the latter for its elaborately carved pink facade and gilded altars.
☞ *Guanajuato in Chapter 7*

SAN CRISTÓBAL DE LAS CASAS
1 to 2 days. San Cristóbal is a walking city, and on foot you encounter the same mix of colonial and indigenous cultures—from the iconic ochre-colored *catedral* to the *mercado municipal* bustling with Lacandon Maya merchants—that exists between the city and the surrounding Indian villages. One of them, San Juan Chamula, is known for its colorfully trimmed white stucco church and its devout syncretism of traditional Maya rituals and Spanish Catholicism.
☞ *San Cristóbal de las Casas in Chapter 11*

MÉRIDA
2 days. No city in Mexico has anything like Mérida's quirky self-confidence and cosmopolitan flair. At the same time the jaunty metropolis is just as Maya as San Cristóbal. Urbane streets like Paseo de Montejo are offset by the chilies-to-crafts *mercado*. And the cathedral, built with stone from a Maya temple, contains a dark-skinned Christ that aimed to reconcile people of Maya and Spanish descent. Mérida, the Yucatán's largest city, is at heart a typical Yucatecan town.
☞ *Mérida in Chapter 13*

By Public Transportation
The easiest way to get to and between Querétaro, San Miguel de Allende, and Guanajuato is by luxury bus. From Mexico City the bus from the Observatorio or Northern bus terminals to Querétaro takes about two hours. From Querétaro it's another two hours to San Miguel. San Miguel to Guanajuato is a 2½-hour ride. Nearby León's airport has flights to Mexico City (1 hr), from which you can fly to Tuxtla Gutiérrez (2 hrs), an hour west of San Cristóbal by bus. Then fly out of Tuxtla straight to Mérida (1 hr).

Léon
100 km Dolores Hidalgo
Guanajuato   San Miguel de Allende
GUANAJUATO 53 km Querétaro
220 km HIDALGO
Tula
Teotihuacán
Mexico City
Cuernavaca   Puebla

La Cocina Mexicana
8 to 11 days

Considering the poor representation that Mexican food gets in the United States, savoring the true flavors of Mexico can only deepen your appreciation of the country and its culture. By necessity—Mexico is a vast country—this gastronomic tour is limited to a few cities, but keep in mind that every region has its own excellent cuisine.

© 96

MEXICO CITY
2 to 4 days. Mexico City chefs turn out everything from colonial to *cocina Mexicana moderna* (modern Mexican cuisine) to pre-Hispanic dishes like chilied maguey worms for their *chilango* (Mexico City) clientele. Many restaurants focus on some regional cuisine, which means that you'll find the best of Veracruz seafood, Yucatecan *pibil*, Tampico *carne asada*, and Chihuahua *carnitas* within the capital. And luxury hotels often invite regional chefs to oversee gastronomic festivals in their restaurants. Take advantage of the city's

dining options—from quaint fondas to colonial mansions and elegant old haciendas.
☞ *Dining in Chapter 1*

PUEBLA
2 days. From Mexico City, make your way out to colonial convents like the Ex-Convento de Santa Rosa, where nuns invented the city's most famous dishes—mole and *chiles en nogadas*. Then tuck into the food itself in restaurants in Puebla's historic district, most of which are lavishly decorated with Talavera tile, for which Puebla is famous. Visit the Calle de los Dulces (Sweets Street), filled with shops selling the nuns' fruit, coconut, and sweet-potato candies. And don't miss the town's fruit wines.
☞ *Puebla in Chapter 2*

VERACRUZ
2 to 3 days. The transit from inland Puebla to coastal Veracruz will take you to the home of that notorious chili, Jalapa's jalapeño, and to the source of a dish that appears on menus throughout Mexico—*huachinango á la veracruzana* (red snapper covered in tomatoes, onions, olives, and herbs) In Veracruz City seafood is a way of life,

and you can expect stunning sea bass, prawns, and lobster and dishes like crab *salpicón*—finely chopped with onion, cilantro, and lime. Coffee grown in the highlands around Jalapa, the famous Mexican *altura*, fuels a café society in

Veracruz—look for Gran Café del Portal, a local stronghold of *café lechero* (coffee with hot milk).
☞ *The State of Veracruz in Chapter 12*

OAXACA CITY
2 days. Several native cultures merge in exotic Oaxaca City, where you can feast on the seven types of mole the city is known for, or taste its sweet and salty tamales. Try one of the traditional fondas under the *portales* (arcades) in the main square. You'll also find *quesillo*, Oaxaca's special cheese, as well as table chocolate and giant *totopos* (baked tortillas) in regional dishes and piled in heaps at the local mercado, an essential stop for its symphony of colors and smells. Mountaintop Monte Albán, where archaeologists found royal tombs full of splendid gold jewelry, makes an easy day trip from the city.
☞ *Oaxaca City in Chapter 10*

By Public Transportation
The best way to get from Mexico City to Puebla is by luxury bus (2 hrs), from the TAPO terminal or the international airport. The bus from Puebla over the mountains and into Veracruz City takes four hours. From Veracruz to Oaxaca it's best to fly: back to Mexico City (1½ hrs), then on to Oaxaca (2 hrs).

Léon

100 km Dolores Hidalgo

VERACRUZ

Guanajuato

San Miguel de Allende

53 km

Querétaro

HIDALGO

220 km Tula

53 km Teotihuacán

MEXICO CITY

Mexico City

TLAXCALA

MEXICO

133 km

Cuernavaca

Puebla

PUEBLA

150 km

Orizaba

Córdoba

151 km

Veracruz

68 km

Jalapa

GULF OF MEXICO

124 km

Tuxtepec

218 km

Monte Albán

Oaxaca City

OAXACA

Puerto Escondido

Tehuantepec

Puerto Ángel

PACIFIC OCEAN

The Lost Cities of Ancient Mexico
9 to 11 days

Inhabited by numerous cultures in pre-Columbian days, Mexico has one of the world's most impressive collections of archaeological sites. The monumental Maya cities, the standout, are at their finest on the Yucatán Peninsula and in jungly Tabasco and mountainous Chiapas.

TEOTIHUACÁN
1 day. For the 14th- to 16th-century Aztecs, this was the birthplace of the gods. At its 8th-century peak © Teotihuacán hummed with as many as 250,000 people, its massive, spellbinding pyramids symbolizing the ordered lives of people in the ancient Valley of Mexico. Just an hour outside of Mexico City by bus, these ruins are an essential first site.
☞ *Teotihuacán in Chapter 2*

VILLAHERMOSA
2 to 3 days. The banana and oil capital of Mexico, Villahermosa is roughly at the midpoint between ancient culture and modern development. Head for the Parque Museo La Venta, with its enormous Olmec stone heads, for an in-depth look at a culture that preceded the Maya by several centuries. Later in the day, swing north out of town to Comalcalco, a Maya site with giant stucco masks and the only known brick temples in the Maya world. Save the best for last and make your way to Chiapas to see Palenque. Its classicism is akin to that of Greek architecture, and it is both ethereal and bewitching.
☞ *Villahermosa, Comalcalco, and Palenque in Chapter 11*

MÉRIDA
6 or 7 days. A capital city of the Yucatán and the most Maya of all Yucatecan cities, Mérida is a perfect base for seeing the region's ruins. Take in the Museum of Anthropology to preview Maya art, and walk around the lively main square to view its colonial mansions, cathedral, small churches, and shady plazas. On your second day, head to Chichén Itzá, an extensive site built by two different Maya empires. Climb to the top of the Temple of the Warriors for a glimpse of its famous Chacmool and a bird's-eye view. Later in the afternoon visit the Cave of Balancanchén, with its ceremonial artifacts, and the Maya village of Izamal, on the way back to Mérida. Spend all of day three at beautiful Uxmal, the sterling example of the graceful Puuc architectural style. Optional overnights are possible at hotels near Chichén Itzá and Uxmal, which has an evening sound-and-light show. If time permits, you can spend a day at the smaller Puuc ruins of Kabah, Sayil, and Labná. Consider planning your trip around a local Maya festival to see the intriguing blend of pre-Hispanic beliefs and Catholic rituals.
☞ *The State of Yucatán in Chapter 13*

By Public Transportation
In Villahermosa you can take a cab to the Parque Museo La Venta but need to book an excursion to Comalcalco. Buses are unreliable. To get to Palenque you can catch a luxury bus from the ADO terminal; the trip takes about 2½ hours. There are also full-day excursions to Palenque from Villahermosa. From Tuxtla Gutiérrez there is a one-hour flight to Mérida. You can take day trips to the major Yucatán sites from Mérida. Second-class buses do run to Chichén Itzá and Uxmal from Mérida's main bus terminal, but they have no air-conditioning and are a bit uncomfortable.

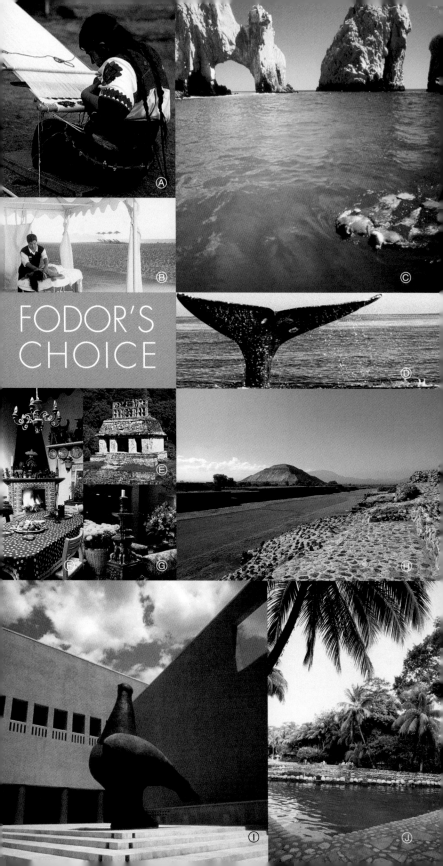

FODOR'S
CHOICE

Even with so many special places in Mexico, Fodor's writers and editors have their favorites. Here are a few that stand out.

ARCHAEOLOGICAL SITES

El Tajín. The Pyramid of the Niches rises out of the jungle like the fantasy of a lost world. ☞ p. 505

Ⓔ **Palenque.** Nestled in a rain forest in Chiapas, these Maya ruins have a magical quality, perhaps because of their intimacy. The most magnificent royal tomb in the Maya empire was uncovered here. ☞ p. 468

Ⓗ **Teotihuacán.** Predating the Aztecs and believed by them to be the birthplace of the gods, this pyramid complex outside Mexico City was one of the largest cities in the ancient world. ☞ p. 97

BEACHES

Ⓒ **Playa de Amor, Cabo San Lucas.** From this secluded cove at the very tip of Baja California you can see the Sea of Cortés on one side, the Pacific Ocean on the other. ☞ p. 170

Playa Norte (Playa Cocoteros), Isla Mujeres. This beach on sleepy Isla Mujeres is ideal for water sports and lounging under grass-roofed *palapas.* ☞ p. 557

Zicatela, Oaxaca Coast. A long stretch of cream-color sand, Zicatela is one of the top 10 surfing beaches in the world. ☞ p. 432

SPECIAL MOMENTS

A *calesa* (horse-drawn carriage) ride through Mérida. Discover Old World graciousness by trotting slowly through the wide streets and French-style neighborhoods of Yucatán's capital. ☞ p. 591

Don Porfirio's Bar, Querétaro. After a day of exploring, stop in at the bar of the Casa de la Marquesa hotel for a drink, and to drink in the Old World elegance of this 18th-century house. ☞ p. 297

Ⓓ **Whale-watching, Baja.** Go out on a boat for the best views of the great gray mammals, who pass through Scammon's and San Ignacio lagoons en route from Alaska each winter. ☞ p. 149

MUSEUMS

Ⓘ **Museo de Arte Contemporaneo, Monterrey.** The best of postmodern Latin American art is gathered at this gallery. A chic coffeehouse attracts the city's intellectuals. ☞ p. 518

Museo de Frida Kahlo, Mexico City. The former home of the now-fashionable Kahlo is filled with her disturbing, surrealistic paintings and those of friends such as Klee and Duchamp. ☞ p. 59

Museo Na Bolom, San Cristóbal de las Casas. Franz and Gertrude Blom lived in a lovely, rambling home surrounded by gardens. Their former residence contains displays reflecting their extensive archaeological, ethnological, and ecological interests. ☞ p. 453

SHOPPING

Ⓐ **Casa de las Artesanías and Sna Jolobil, San Cristóbal de las Casas.** Stop here for some of Mexico's most striking Indian weavings, hand-embroidered blouses and tunics, multicolored *fajas* (sashes), and beribboned hats. ☞ p. 459

Old Town, Puerto Vallarta. Few Mexican cities have a collection of native crafts, among them clothing and household goods, as representative as that of Puerto Vallarta. ☞ p. 339

Zona Rosa, Mexico City. Antiques, crafts, and the latest fashions are abundant in this tony neighborhood. ☞ p. 82

FLAVORS

Cicero Centenario, Mexico City. The setting, in a restored 17th-century mansion, is superb, and the menu is enticing, featuring inventive versions of authentic colonial dishes. $$$ ☞ p. 66

La Cocay, Cozumel. The name is Maya for firefly and, like its namesake, this restaurant is a bit magical. Meals here are some of the most innovative and flavorful on Cozumel. $$$ ☞ p. 569

La Estancia de los Tecajetes, Jalapa. Local *cocina Mexicana* doesn't get much better than the enchiladas or *crepa consentida*—chicken crepes doused with a poblano-and-cheese sauce—served here. $$ ☞ p. 502

COMFORTS

Ⓕ **La Casa de Espiritus Alegres Bed and Breakfast, Guanajuato.** This renovated hacienda filled with folk-art paradise filled with whimsical treasures from every state in Mexico. $$$$ ☞ p. 285

Ⓖ **Quinta Real, Guadalajara.** Colonial architecture and Spanish-style furnishings distinguish this luxury hotel in a quiet residential neighborhood. $$$$ ☞ p. 238

Ⓑ **Las Ventanas al Paraíso, Cabo San Lucas.** This waterside architectural wonder is the last word in earthy elegance—and reason enough to hop on the next plane to the southern tip of the Baja Peninsula. $$$$ ☞ p. 169

Ⓙ **Chan Kah, Palenque.** A resident monkey is among the charms of this jungle retreat near the Maya ruins; accommodations are in comfortable bungalows. $$$ ☞ p. 473

AFTER HOURS

Zucca and Enigma discos, Acapulco. Two standouts in a city where Saturday-night fever still rages, Fantasy attracts an older crowd, and Enigma's great light-and-sound show comes with drop-dead views of Acapulco Bay. ☞ p. 397

Gran Café del Portal, Veracruz. People-watch into the wee hours over a cup of *café con leche* at this renowned coffeehouse. ☞ p. 496

Joe's Lobster House, Cozumel. Beginning after 10 PM, live rollicking reggae and hot salsa spice up the music menu here. This quaint nightspot, popular with locals, hops into the wee hours. ☞ p. 572

1 MEXICO CITY

Two volcanoes and a pyramid complex flank Mexico's capital, once the center of Aztec civilization and now the country's cosmopolitan business, art, and culinary hub. From the Alameda, a leafy center of activity since Aztec times, to the Zona Rosa, a chic shopping neighborhood, Mexico City offers endless options to urban adventurers.

Updated by
Barbara
Kastelein

MEXICO CITY is a city of superlatives. It is both the oldest (675 years) and the highest (7,349 ft) metropolis on the North American continent. And with nearly 24 million inhabitants, it's the most populous city in the world. It is Mexico's cultural, political, and financial core—at the dawn of the 21st century but clinging to its deeply entrenched Aztec heritage.

As the gargantuan pyramids of Teotihuacán attest—the name is Aztec, meaning "the place of the gods"—the area around Mexico City was occupied from early times by a great civilization, probably Nahuatl in origin. The founding of the Aztec capital nearby did not occur until more than 600 years after Teotihuacán was abandoned, around 750. As the story goes, the nomadic Aztecs were searching for a promised land in which to settle. Their prophecies said they would recognize the spot when they encountered an eagle, perched on a prickly pear cactus, holding a snake in its beak. In 1325, the disputed date of Tenochtitlán's founding, the Aztecs discovered this eagle in the valley of Mexico. They built Tenochtitlán on what was then an island in shallow Lake Texcoco and connected it to lakeshore satellite towns by a network of *calzadas* (canals and causeways, now freeways). Even then it was the largest city in the Western hemisphere and, according to historians, one of the three largest cities on earth. When he first laid eyes on Tenochtitlán in the early 16th century, Spanish conquistador Hernán Cortés was dazzled by the glistening metropolis, which reminded him of Venice.

A combination of factors made the Spanish conquest possible. The superstitious Aztec emperor Moctezuma II believed the white, bearded Cortés on horseback to be the mighty plumed serpent-god Quetzalcóatl, who, according to a tragically ironic prophecy, was supposed to arrive from the east in the year 1519 to rule the land. Moctezuma therefore welcomed the foreigner with gifts of gold and palatial accommodations.

In return, Cortés initiated the bloody massacre of Tenochtitlán, which lasted almost two years. Joining forces with him was a massive army of Indians from other settlements such as Cholula and Tlaxcala, who were fed up with the Aztec empire's domination and with paying tribute, especially sending warriors and maidens to be sacrificed. With the strength of their numbers—along with the European tactical advantages of brigantines, horses, firearms, armor, and inadvertently, the introduction of smallpox and the common cold—Cortés succeeded in devastating Tenochtitlán. Only two centuries after it was founded, the young Aztec capital lay in ruins, about half its population dead from battle, starvation, and European diseases against which they had no immunity.

Cortés began building the capital of what he patriotically dubbed New Spain, the Spanish empire's colony that would spread north to cover what is now the United States's southwest, and south to Panama. *Mexico* comes from the word *Mexica* (pronounced *meh*-shee-ka), which is the Aztecs' name for themselves. Aztec is the Spaniards' name for the Mexica. At the site of the demolished Aztec ceremonial center—now the 10-acre Zócalo—Cortés started building a church (the precursor of the gigantic Metropolitan Cathedral), mansions, and government buildings. He utilized the slave labor—and artistry—of the vanquished native Mexicans. On top of the ruins of their city, and using rubble from it, they were forced to build what became the most European-style city in North America. But instead of having the random layout of contemporary medieval European cities, it followed the sophisticated grid pattern of the Aztecs. For much of the construction material the Spaniards quarried the local porous, volcanic reddish stone called *tezontle*. The Spaniards also drained Lake Texcoco and filled it with earth, preferring wheels and horses (which they introduced to Mexico) over canals and canoes for transport. The land-filled lake bed turned out to be a soggy support for the immense buildings that have been slowly sinking into it since they were built.

The city grew during the colonial period, and the Franciscans and Dominicans converted the Aztecs to Christianity. In 1571 the Spaniards established the Inquisition in New Spain and burned heretics at its palace headquarters, which still stands in Plaza de Santo Domingo.

It took more than 200 years for Mexicans to successfully rise up against Spain. The historic downtown street 16 de Septiembre commemorates the "declaration" of the War of Independence. On that date in 1810, Miguel Hidalgo, Father of the Catholic Church—and of a couple of illegitimate daughters—rang a church bell and cried out his history-making *grito* (shout): "Death to the *gachupines* (wealthy Spaniards living in Mexico)! Long live the Virgin of Guadalupe!" Excommunicated and executed the following year, Hidalgo is one of many independence heroes who fostered a truly popular movement, culminating in Mexico's independence in 1821. The liberty bell which now hangs above the main entrance to the National Palace is rung on every eve of September 16 by the president of the republic, who then shouts a revised version of the patriot's cry: "Viva Mexico! Viva Mexico! Viva Mexico!"

Flying in or out of Mexico City, you get an aerial view of the remaining part of Lake Texcoco on the eastern outskirts of the city. At night the expanse of city lights abruptly ends at a black void that appears to be an ocean. In daylight you can also see the sprawling flatness of the 1,482-square-km (572-square-mi) Meseta de Anáhuac (Valley of Mexico), completely surrounded by mountains. On its south side, two usually snowcapped volcanoes, Popocatépetl and Iztaccíhuatl, are both well over 17,000 ft high. After a period of relative tranquility, Popocatépetl awakened and began spewing smoke, ash, and even some lava in 1994—and then again on the heels of President Vicente Fox's inauguration in 2000—and has remained active on and off since then.

Unfortunately, the single most widely known fact about Mexico City is that its air is polluted. So you might picture the city, its streets packed with vehicles, wrapped daily in a cloak of black smog. In reality, in spite of the capital's serious pollution problem, it also has some of the clearest, bluest skies anywhere, especially in summer and autumn. At 7,556 ft, it often has mild daytime weather perfect for sightseeing and cool evenings comfortable for sleeping. Mornings can be glorious—chilly and bright with the promise of the warming sun.

If Mexico City's smog brings Los Angeles to mind, so might the fault line that runs through the valley. In 1957 a major earthquake took a tragic toll, which was exceeded by the devastating 1985 earthquake—8.1 on the Richter scale—whose scars are still visible. The government reported 10,000 deaths, but locally it's said to be closer to 50,000.

Growing nonstop, Mexico City—which goes by just "Mexico" in Mexico—covers a 1,480-square-km (570-square-mi) area of the valley. The city is surrounded on three sides by the state of Mexico and bordered on the south by the state of Morelos. Glossy magazine ads usually tout Mexico's paradisiacal beach resorts and ancient ruins, but cosmopolitan, historic Mexico City is a vital destination in itself—more and fascinating than many major capitals on faraway continents.

Pleasures and Pastimes

Dining

Mexico City has been a culinary capital ever since the time of Moctezuma. Chronicles tell of the extravagant daily banquets prepared for the slender Aztec emperor by his palace chefs. More than 300 different dishes were served for every meal—vast assortments of meat and fowl seasoned in dozens of ways; limitless fruit, vegetables, and herbs; freshwater fish; and, one report has it, even fresh seafood that was rushed to Tenochtitlán from both seacoasts by sprinting relay runners.

Until the 15th century, Europeans had never seen indigenous Mexican edibles such as corn, chilies of all varieties, tomatoes, potatoes, pumpkin, squash, avocado, turkey, cocoa, and vanilla. In turn, the colonization brought European gastronomic influence and ingredients—wheat, onions, garlic, olives, citrus fruit, cattle, sheep, goats, chickens, domesticated pigs (and lard for frying)—and ended up broadening the already complex pre-Hispanic cuisine into one of the most multifaceted and exquisite in the world: traditional Mexican.

Today's cosmopolitan Mexico City is a gastronomic melting pot with some 15,000 restaurants. You'll find everything from simple family-style eateries to five-star world-class restaurants. And international restaurants serve foods from around the world—although Spanish, Italian, and Argentine are dominant.

In the past decade or so a renaissance of Mexican cooking has brought about a new wave known as *nueva cocina mexicana* (nouvelle Mexican cuisine), served by many of the finer Mexico City restaurants. Emphasis is on presentation, the delicate tastes of traditional regional dishes gleaned from colonial cookbooks, and ancient indigenous cooking techniques such as steaming and baking, which used a lot less fat, as there were no pigs for lard. Also, items such as crunchy fried grasshoppers and cooked *maguey* (cactus) worms have become fashionable in some restaurants in town.

Lodging

As might be expected of a megalopolis, Mexico City has more than 25,000 hotel rooms—enough to accommodate every taste and budget. You can lodge in the quaint or the colonial, the smoked-glass-and-steel high-rise, or the elegant replica of an Italianate palace.

Museums

Mexico City is the cultural as well as political capital of the country, as evidenced by its 80-plus museums—some of the finest in Latin America. In buildings of architectural merit, you can see the sweeping murals of such native sons as Diego Rivera, José Clemente Orozco, David Alfaro Siqueiros, and Juan O'Gorman; the haunting paintings of Frida Kahlo; stunning pre-Hispanic ceremonial pieces; and outstanding collections of religious art.

Nightlife and the Arts

Mexico City is the cultural capital of Latin America and, with the exception of Río de Janiero (or maybe São Paolo), has the liveliest nightlife of the region. There's something for every taste, from opera and symphonies to a renowned folklore ballet and a lively square where mariachi play. You'll also find discos and offbeat places where salsa and *danzón* (elegant Cuban dance music) are headliners.

Shopping

Native crafts and specialties from all over Mexico are available in the capital, as are designer clothes. You'll also find contemporary art by some of Mexico's best painters and sculptors. And of course Mexican goods are a far better deal here than they are in overseas outlets.

Sports and the Outdoors

Latin sports such as the *fiesta brava* (bullfighting)—brought to Mexico by the conquistadores—have enjoyed popularity for more than four centuries in the capital, which attracts the country's best athletes. And although the roots of soccer ("fútbol") are probably English, a weekend afternoon game at Mexico City's giant Estadio Azteca leaves no question that this is the sport Mexicans are craziest about. Ecotourism and adventure-travel agencies have also opened in Mexico City to offer great weekend getaways such as white-water rafting in nearby Veracruz. Tennis, golf, running—even rowing a boat in a park—are other outdoor pursuits to engage in while in town.

EXPLORING MEXICO CITY

Most of Mexico City is aligned on two major intersecting thoroughfares: Paseo de la Reforma and Avenida Insurgentes—at 34 km (21 mi), the longest avenue in the city. Administratively, Mexico City is divided into 16 *delegaciones* (districts) and about 400 *colonias* (neighborhoods), each with street names fitting a given theme, such as a river, philosopher, doctor, or revolutionary hero. The same street can change names as it goes through different colonias. Hence, most street addresses include their colonia (abbreviated as Col.). Unless you're going to an obvious place, it's important to tell your taxi driver the name of the colonia.

The principal sights of Mexico City fall into three areas. Allow a full day to cover each thoroughly, although you could race through them in four or five hours apiece. You can cover the first two areas—the Zócalo and Alameda Central, and Zona Rosa and Bosque de Chapultepec (Chapultepec Park)—on foot. Getting around Coyoacán and San Angel in southern Mexico City will require a taxi ride or two.

Numbers in the text correspond to numbers in the margin and on the Zócalo and Alameda Central; Zona Rosa, Bosque de Chapultepec, and Condesa; and San Angel and Coyoacán maps.

Great Itineraries

You can spend a month in Mexico City and just begin to grasp the tip of its iceberg of sights, sounds, and tastes. For stays shorter than this, here are some highlights.

IF YOU HAVE 3 DAYS

Start with the **Casa de los Azulejos** ⑬ for a Mexican breakfast, which you can digest with a stroll around the **Alameda Central** ⑱; visit the **Palacio de Bellas Artes** ⑮ and then wind your way through the historic center on Calle Tacuba to have lunch in the historic Café de Tacuba; here, you are right on the corner of the **Zócalo** ①, with its exotic ruins, museums, and public buildings, and you could end your day overlooking it all from the bars in either the Hotel Majestic or the Holiday Inn Zócalo. Day 2, head for the **Museo Nacional de Antropología** ㉖ in the morning and enjoy lunch in one one the many swank eateries in the Polanco neighborhood; head to the **Zona Rosa** in the afternoon, when it starts to come alive. Visit the **Mercado Insurgentes** for some fun shopping, or any of the stores on our list. Consider an evening in the pleasant **Colonia Condesa** for dinner. Day 3, go to **Bosque de Chapultepec** ㉑ to stroll the green pathways past the rowing lake and visit the **Castillo de Chapultepec** ㉒, the **Museo de Arte Moderno** ㉔, **Museo Rufino Tamayo** ㉕, and, of course, the **Zoológico** ㉗ to see the pandas. Visit downtown's

Mexico City Orientation *(Boxes Refer to Detail Maps)*

San Angel and Coyoacán

Mexico City Subways

Plaza Garibaldi on your last night in town for a rousing mariachi send-off. If the Classic period site of **Teotihuacán** intrigues you, however, you could spend the third day there.

IF YOU HAVE 5 DAYS

Follow the three-day itinerary, going to **Bosque de Chapultepec** ㉑ on Day 3. On Day 4 spend time in **San Angel**—start with the Bazar Sábado (if your plans bring you here on a Saturday) and lunch in the San Angel Inn—and in **Coyoacán**, with its lovely casa-museums, especially the **Museo de Frida Kahlo** ㊲ and **Museo de Leon Trotsky** ㊳. On Day 5 take an excursion to the **Basílica of the Virgin of Guadalupe**, Latin America's holiest shrine, and if you are back by midday you could just make it to the pyramids of **Teotihuacán**, where a powerful regime held sway over the region more than a millennium before the arrival of the Spanish. Climb at least one pyramid, visit the museum, and head back to Mexico City.

IF YOU HAVE 10 DAYS

Follow the five-day option and add a visit to the resort town of **Cuernavaca**, just over an hour's drive southeast of Mexico City. Spend the day in its museums and browsing its pretty main square, then overnight at one of the town's converted mansions. On Day 7 head back to Mexico City via Highway 95 and stop in **Xochimilco**, where you can ride through the floating gardens on a gondola-like boat and view an outstanding private collection of works by Diego Rivera and Frida Kahlo at the Dolores Olmedo Patino Museum. On Day 8 drive to the ancient Toltec ruins at **Tula** and continue to the village of **Tepotzotlán**, which has a beautiful Jesuit church. The next day, head to **Puebla** for a two-hour tour, including the main square and the fine Amparo Museum, then pop over to the nearby town of **Cholula**, once a sacred ceremonial site. Climb to the top of the church built over a pyramid, and return to Puebla for the night. En route back to Mexico City on the last day, drive to **Cacaxtla** to see some of the best-preserved Mesoamerican murals in Mexico.

The Zócalo and Alameda Central

This area is all about history: the Zócalo, its surrounding Centro Histórico, and Alameda Park were the heart of both the Aztec and Spanish cities. Several streets in the downtown area have been converted into pedestrian-only thoroughfares.

A Good Walk

An excellent point of departure for any tour of the city's center is the **Zócalo** ①, the heart and soul of old downtown. From here you can literally see the layers of history in the buildings around you. On the north side of this huge square you'll see the tilting **Catedral Metropolitana** ② and adjacent to it the comparatively small 18th-century Sagrario Chapel, even more angled than the cathedral. The **Templo Mayor** ③, ruins from the Aztec capital, with its superb museum, is northeast of the cathedral, across the pedestrian plaza. If you're interested in modern art, walk south about a half block from the Templo Mayor to the end of Calle Seminario, then go two blocks east on Calle Moneda to Academia to find the **Museo José Luis Cuevas** ④. Take Moneda back (west) to the Zócalo. The building on your left is the massive **Palacio Nacional** ⑤, covering two city blocks. Its interior is lined with Diego Rivera's profound story of Mexican history. Walk south past the palacio to the corner and turn right, crossing the street to get to the section of the Zócalo occupied by the 1722 **Ayuntamiento** ⑥. Recross the street and walk northwest through the open square to Calle Cinco de Mayo and the National Pawn Shop in the **Monte de Piedad** ⑦. Three-

42

The Zócalo and Alameda Central

and-a-half blocks north is the historic **Plaza de Santo Domingo** ⑧. Walk one block east along Calle República de Cuba and one block south on Calle República de Argentina to get to Calle Justo Sierra and the **Antiguo Colegio de San Idelfonso** ⑨, now an art and history museum. Turn west and follow Calle Justo Sierra three blocks—it will change into Calle Donceles—to Calle República de Chile, then turn left (south) a block to Calle Tacuba. Turn right and walk one block to have a scrumptious lunch at the Café de Tacuba on the right side of the street. Or, you can continue west on Tacuba 1½ blocks to the **Museo Nacional de Arte** ⑩ in the colonial Plaza Manuel Tolsa.

From Calle Tacuba, head two short blocks south to Calle Madero, one of the city's most architecturally varied streets. On the south side of Madero, between Bolivar and Gante, is the 1780 Baroque **Palacio de Iturbide** ⑪. Go west along on the south side of Madero; less than a block past the palacio you'll come to the **Iglesia de San Francisco** ⑫, with its beautifully painted walls. The stunning tilework of the **Casa de los Azulejos** ⑬ will draw your eye across Calle Madero.

The ultimate goals of the remainder of this walk are an antiques museum and a Diego Rivera mural museum. From Calle Madero, walk less than a half block west to Eje Central Lázaro Cárdenas, a wide four-lane avenue. At the corner and on your left, you can't miss the 1950s-style skyscraper, the **Torre Latinoamericana** ⑭, which has one of the best aerial views of the city as well as a sky-high aquarium. Cross the avenue and turn right (north) to explore the beautiful **Palacio de Bellas Artes** ⑮ opera house, the long side of which skirts Lázaro Cárdenas (its entrance is on Juárez). The 1908 post office building of **Dirección General de Correos** ⑯ is up Lázaro Cárdenas another 150 ft across from Bellas Artes.

Pass the post office to Calle Tacuba and cross Lázaro Cárdenas one last time, where Calle Tacuba turns into Avenida Hidalgo. One block west, you'll come to the antiques-filled **Museo Franz Mayer** ⑰, which often hosts world-class art and photography exhibitions. Across Avenida Hidalgo is the north end of the leafy park **Alameda Central** ⑱. At its south end, on Avenida Juárez, **Fonart** is a government-owned handicrafts store. To get to the **Museo Mural Diego Rivera** ⑲, take Juárez west to Calle Balderas, about 3½ blocks from Fonart. Turn right and walk a short block to Calle Colón.

TIMING

The Zócalo area will be quietest on Sunday, when bureaucrats have their day of rest. But Alameda Park will be jumping with children and their parents enjoying a Sunday outing. The park will be particularly festive during December, when dozens of "Santas" will appear with plastic reindeer to take wish lists from long lines of children. Although Mexicans celebrate on the night of Dec. 24, the tradition of giving presents, especially to children, kicks in January 5, the eve of the Day of the Three Kings, and the Three Wise Men of biblical lore replace the Santas in the Alameda. Gorgeous Christmas paintings-in-lights deck the Zócalo from end to end and stream up Calle Madero past Alameda Park to Paseo de la Reforma beyond the museums in Bosque de Chapultepec.

During the daytime, the downtown area is filled with people and vibrant with activity. As in any big city, watch out for pickpockets, especially on crowded buses and subways, and avoid dark, deserted streets at night.

The streets in the walking tour are fairly close to one another and can be covered in a day if you're short on time; otherwise, a couple days will make for a more leisurely tour. The National Palace, Templo Mayor and its museum, and Franz Mayer Museum are worth an hour each of your time; you can cover the Palace of Fine Arts in a half hour unless you stumble upon one of its marvelous and epic temporary exhibitions.

Sights to See

THE ZÓCALO

❻ **Ayuntamiento** (City Hall). The two buildings of Mexico's city hall stand on the south side of the Zócalo; colonial tiles of the arms of Cortés and other conquistadores decorate the one on the west. Originally built in 1532, it was destroyed by fire in 1692 and rebuilt in 1722. In 1935 the Distrito Federal needed more office space, and to maintain the architectural integrity of the Zócalo, the "matching" structure across the street (20 de Noviembre) was built. In 1997, for the first time in 70 years, Mexico City residents were allowed to elect their own mayor (the post had previously been appointed by the president). Thus did the city's first leftist administration begin, first under Cuauhtémoc Cárdenas, son of Mexico's populist president Lázaro Cárdenas, and then, to much acclaim, came feminist Rosario Robles, the first woman to hold such a powerful post in Mexico. Still under leftist auspices, Manuel López Obrador followed her in clearing up city corruption.

❷ **Catedral Metropolitana** (Metropolitan Cathedral). Construction on this oldest and largest cathedral in Latin America began in 1573 on the north side of the Zócalo and continued intermittently throughout the next three centuries. The result is a medley of Baroque and neoclassical touches. Inside are four identical domes, their airiness grounded by rows of supportive columns. There are five altars and 14 chapels, mostly in the churrigueresque style, an ornate Baroque style named for

Spanish architect José Churriguera (d. 1725). Like most Mexican churches, the cathedral itself is all but overwhelmed by the innumerable paintings, altarpieces, and statues—in graphic color—of Christ and the saints. Over the centuries, this cathedral has sunk alarmingly into the spongy subsoil, but a major engineering project to stabilize the structure has recently been declared successful.

❼ Monte de Piedad (Mountain of Pity). This structure from the late 18th century houses the National Pawn Shop. It's on the northwest corner of the Zócalo, on what was once the site of an Aztec palace. ☎ 5278–1800, WEB *www.nmp.org.mx*. ☉ *Mon.–Sat. about 10–5*.

❹ Museo José Luis Cuevas. One of the newer museums downtown, installed in a refurbished former convent, it displays contemporary art, as well as work by Mexico's enfant terrible, José Luis Cuevas, one of the country's best-known contemporary artists. The museum's highlight is the sensational *La Giganta* (*The Giantess*), Cuevas's 8-ton bronze sculpture in the central patio. Up-and-coming Latin American artists appear in temporary exhibitions throughout the year. ✉ *Academia 13*, ☎ *5522–0156*. ▨ *90¢, free Sun*. ☉ *Tues.–Sun. 10–5:30*.

★ ❺ Palacio Nacional (National Palace). This grand government building was initiated by Cortés on the site of Moctezuma's home and remodeled by the viceroys. Its current form dates from 1693, although a third floor was added in 1926. Now the seat of government, it has always served as a public-function site. In fact, during colonial times, the first bullfight in New Spain took place in the inner courtyard.

Diego Rivera's sweeping, epic murals on the second floor of the main courtyard have the power to mesmerize. For more than 16 years (1929–45), he and his assistants mounted scaffolds day and night, perfecting techniques adapted from Renaissance Italian frescoes. The result, nearly 1,200 square feet of vividly painted wall space, is grandiosely entitled *Epic of the Mexican People in Their Struggle for Freedom and Independence*. The larger-than-life paintings represent two millennia of Mexican history, filtered through Rivera's imagination. He painted pre-Hispanic times in innocent, almost sugary scenes of Tenochtitlán. Only a few vignettes—a man offering a human arm for sale, and the carnage of warriors—acknowledge the darker aspects of ancient life. As you walk around the floor, you'll pass images of the savagery of the conquest and the hypocrisy of the Spanish priests, the noble independence movement, and the bloody revolution. Marx appears amid scenes of class struggle, toiling workers, industrialization (which Rivera idealized), bourgeois decadence, and nuclear holocaust. These are among Rivera's finest—as well as most accessible and probably most visited—paintings. The palace also houses a minor museum that focuses on 19th-century president Benito Juárez and the Mexican Congress; it also contains some pleasant gardens.

The liberty bell rung by Padre Hidalgo to proclaim independence in 1810 hangs high on the central facade. It chimes every eve of September 16, while from the balcony the president repeats the historic shout of independence to throngs of *chilangos* (Mexico City residents) below. Usually the people demand that the chief executive continue shouting until he loses his voice. ✉ *East side of the Zócalo*, ☎ *5542–6466*. ▨ *Free (you'll be asked to leave an I.D. at the front desk)*. ☉ *Mon.–Sat. 9–6, Sun. 9–2*.

❽ Plaza de Santo Domingo (Santo Domingo Plaza). The Aztec emperor Cuauhtémoc built a palace here, where heretics were later burned at the stake in the Spanish Inquisition. The plaza was the intellectual hub of the city during the colonial era. Today, its most colorful feature is the **Portal de los Evangelistas** (Portal of the Evangelists), filled with scribes at old-fashioned typewriters who are most likely composing letters for love-stricken swains. This age-old custom, which originated when quill pens were in vogue, has successfully launched quite a few of Cupid's arrows.

The gloomy-looking **Palacio de la Escuela de Medicina Mexicana** (Palace of Medicine; ☎ 5529–7543, ☒ Free, ☉ Daily 9–6), once the headquarters for the Inquisition, is catercorner to the lively portal. Founded by the Catholic Church in 1571 (50 years after the conquest) and closed by government decree in 1820, it was a medical school for many years. Now it serves as a museum portraying the history of both the Inquisition and medicine. The 18th-century Baroque **Santo Domingo church,** slightly north of the portal, is all that remains of the first Dominican convent in New Spain. The convent building was demolished in 1861 under the Reform laws that forced clerics to turn over all religious buildings not used for worship to the government. Today, you can still see white-robed Dominican nuns visiting the church. ☒ *Between República de Cuba, República de Brasil, República de Venezuela, and Palma.*

❸ **Templo Mayor** (Great Temple). The ruins of the ancient hub of the Aztec empire were unearthed accidentally in 1978 by telephone repairmen and have since been turned into a vast and historically significant archaeological site and museum. At this temple, dedicated to the Aztec cult of death, captives from rival tribes—as many as 10,000 at a time— were sacrificed to the bloodthirsty god of war, Huitzilopochtli. Seven rows of leering stone skulls adorn one side of the structure.

The adjacent **Museo del Templo Mayor** contains 3,000 pieces unearthed from the site and from other ruins in central Mexico; they include ceramic warriors, stone carvings and knives, skulls of sacrificial victims, a rare gold ingot, models and scale reproductions, and a room on the Spaniards' destruction of Tenochtitlán. The centerpiece is an 8-ton disk discovered at the Templo Mayor. It depicts the moon goddess Coyolxauhqui, who, according to myth, was decapitated and dismembered by her brother Huitzilopochtli; she had tried to persuade her 400 other brothers to murder their mother for her unfaithfulness. Call 6 weeks ahead to schedule free English-language tours by museum staff; you can also hire a freelance guide outside the museum. ☒ *Seminario 8, at República de Guatemala (entrance on the plaza, near Catedral Metropolitana),* ☎ *5542–4784, 5542–4785, or 5542–4786.* ☒ *$3, free Sun. ☉ Tues.–Sun. 9–5.*

❶ **Zócalo** (formal name: Plaza de la Constitución). Mexico City's historic plaza and the buildings around it were built by the Spaniards, using local slave labor. This enormous paved square, the largest in the Western Hemisphere, occupies the site of the ceremonial center of Tenochtitlán, the capital of the Aztec empire, which once comprised 78 buildings. Throughout the 16th, 17th, and 18th centuries, the Spaniards and their descendants constructed elaborate churches and convents, elegant mansions, and stately public edifices around the square, many of which have long since been converted to other uses. There is an air of Old Europe in this part of the city, which, in its entirety (the Centro Histórico), is a national monument that has undergone major refurbishing. Imposing buildings are constructed with the reddish volcanic tezontle stone and the quarry stones that the Spaniards recycled from the rubble of the Aztec temples they razed. Clusters of small shops, eateries, cantinas, street vendors, and a few women in native Indian dress contribute to an inimitably Mexican flavor and exuberance.

Zócalo literally means "pedestal" or "base": in the mid-19th century, an independence monument was planned for the square, but it was never built. The term stuck, however, and now the word "zócalo" is applied to the main plazas of most Mexican cities. Mexico City's Zócalo (because it's the original, it is always capitalized) is used for government rallies, protest marches, sit-ins, and festive events. It is the focal point for Independence Day celebrations on the eve of September 16 and is spectacularly festooned during the Christmas season. Flag-raising and -lowering ceremonies take place here in the early morning and late afternoon. ⊠ *Bounded on the south by 16 de Septiembre, north by 5 de Mayo, east by Pino Suárez, and west by Monte de Piedad.*

ALAMEDA CENTRAL

⑱ Alameda Central (Alameda Park). This has been one of the capital's oases of greenery and centers of activity since Aztec times, when the Indians held their *tianguis* (market) on the site. In the early days of the Viceroyalty, the Inquisition burned its victims at the stake here. Later, national leaders, from 18th-century viceroys to Emperor Maximilian and President Porfirio Díaz, clearly envisioned the park as a symbol of civic pride and prosperity: over the centuries, it has been endowed with fountains, railings, a Moorish kiosk imported from Paris, and ash, willow, and poplar trees. Its most conspicuous man-made structure is the semicircular, white-marble **Hemiciclo a Benito Juárez** (monument to Juárez) on the Avenida Juárez side of the park. It's a fine place for strolling, relaxing, and listening to live music on Sunday and holidays.

❾ Antiguo Colegio de San Idelfonso (College of San Idelfonso). This colonial building with lovely patios started out as a Jesuit school for the sons of wealthy Mexicans in the 18th century, then took life as a medical college, and finally became a public preparatory school. After a complete renovation, it reopened in 1992 as a museum with "Splendors of Mexico: 30 Centuries of Art" and has been showcasing outstanding traveling regional exhibitions ever since. The interior contains murals by Diego Rivera, José Clemente Orozco, and Fernando Leal. ⊠ *Justo Sierra 16, almost at the corner of República de Argentina, 2 blocks north of the Zócalo,* ☎ *5789–0485.* ⊡ *$2.50, free Tues.* ☉ *Tues.– Sun. 10–6.*

⑬ Casa de los Azulejos (House of Tiles). Built as the palace of the counts of the Valle de Orizaba, an aristocratic family from the early period of Spanish rule, this 17th-century masterpiece acquired its name from the tilework installed by a later descendant, a ne'er-do-well scion who married a rich woman. In addition to its well-preserved white, blue, and yellow tiles, the facade also has iron grillwork balconies and gray stonework. One of the prettiest Baroque structures in the country, it is currently occupied by Sanborns, a chain store–restaurant. The dazzling interior, which includes a Moorish patio, a monumental staircase, and a mural by Orozco, is worth seeing. If you have plenty of time— service is slow—this is a good place to stop for breakfast, lunch, or dinner. ⊠ *Calle Madero 4, at Callejón de la Condesa,* ☎ *5512–9820 ext. 103.* ☉ *Daily 7 AM–1 AM.*

⑯ Dirección General de Correos (General Post Office). Mexico City's main post office building is a fine example of Renaissance revival architecture. Constructed of cream-color sandstone in 1908, it epitomizes the grand imitations of European architecture common in Mexico during the Porfiriato—the rather long dictatorship of Porfirio Díaz (1876–1911). Upstairs, the **Museo del Palacio Postal** shows Mexico's postal history. ⊠ *Calle Tacuba and Eje Central Lázaro Cárdenas,* ☎ *5510–2999 museum; 5521–7394 post office.* ⊡ *Free.* ☉ *Museum weekdays 9–4, weekends 10–2; post office weekdays 8–8, Sat. 9–1.*

⑫ **Iglesia de San Francisco.** On the site of Mexico's first convent (1524)—and supposedly the site of Moctezuma's zoo before that—this church's current 18th-century French Gothic incarnation is one of the newest buildings on the street. ⊠ *Calles Madero and 16 de Septiembre,* ☎ *no phone.* ⊙ *Daily 7 AM–8:30 PM.*

⑰ **Museo Franz Mayer.** Opened in 1986 in the 16th-century Hospital de San Juan de Dios, this museum has exhibitions that include 16th- and 17th-century antiques, such as wooden chests inlaid with ivory, tortoiseshell, and ebony; tapestries, paintings, and lacquerware; rococo clocks, glassware, and architectural ornamentation; and an unusually large assortment of Talavera ceramics and *azulejos,* or tiles. The museum also has an impressive collection of more than 700 editions of Cervantes's *Don Quixote.* The old hospital building is faithfully restored, with pieces of the original frescoes peeking through. ⊠ *Av. Hidalgo 45, at Plaza Santa Veracruz,* ☎ *5518–2267.* ⊡ *$2, free Tues.* ⊙ *Tues.–Sun. 10–5. Call 1 wk ahead for an English-speaking guide.*

⑲ **Museo Mural Diego Rivera.** Diego Rivera's controversial mural, *Sunday Afternoon Dream in the Alameda Park,* originally was painted on a lobby wall of the Hotel Del Prado in 1947–48. Its controversy grew out of Rivera's Marxist inscription, "God does not exist," which the artist later replaced with the bland "Conference of San Juan de Letrán" to placate Mexico's dominant Catholic population. The 1985 earthquake destroyed the hotel but not the poetic mural. This museum was built across the street from the hotel to house the work. ⊠ *Calles Balderas and Colón,* ☎ *5510–2329.* ⊡ *$1, free Sun.* ⊙ *Tues.–Sun. 10–6.*

⑩ **Museo Nacional de Arte** (National Art Museum). This neoclassical building, built during the Porfiriato, turned into a museum in 1982, and restored in 2000, contains examples of nearly every school of Mexican art, with a concentration on work made between 1810 to 1950. Works include Diego Rivera's portrait of Adolfo Best Maugard, José María Velasco's *Vista del Valle de México desde el Cerro de Santa Isabel (View of the Valley of Mexico from the Hill of Santa Isabel),* and Ramón Cano Manilla's *El Globo (The Balloon). El Caballito (The Horsey),* a statue of Spain's Carlos V on horseback, stands out front. ⊠ *Calle Tacuba 8,* ☎ *5512–3224.* ⊡ *$2, free Sun.* ⊙ *Tues.–Sun. 10–5:30.*

★ ⑮ **Palacio de Bellas Artes** (Fine Arts Palace). Construction on this colossal white-marble opera house was begun in 1904 by Porfirio Díaz, who wanted to add yet another ornamental building to his accomplishments. He was ousted seven years later after winning yet another rigged election. He died in 1915, and the building wasn't finished until 1934. Today the theater serves as a handsome venue for international and national artists, including such groups as the Ballet Folklórico de México. The palace is indeed renowned for its architecture, the work of Italian Adamo Boari, who also designed the post office; it includes an art deco facade trimmed in pre-Hispanic motifs. Inside are a Tiffany stained-glass curtain depicting the two volcanoes outside Mexico City and paintings by several celebrated Mexican artists, including Rufino Tamayo and Mexico's trio of muralists: Rivera, Orozco, and Siqueiros. Temporary art exhibitions are also held here. ⊠ *Eje Central Lázaro Cárdenas and Av. Juárez,* ☎ *5512–3633.* ⊡ *$2.50 for exhibitions, free Sun. (no charge to look at the building and gift shops inside).* ⊙ *Building Tues.–Sun. 10–9, exhibits Tues.–Sun. 10–6.*

OFF THE BEATEN PATH

TLATELOLCO – At Paseo de la Reforma's northern end, about 2 km (1 mi) north of the Palacio de Bellas Artes, the area known as Tlatelolco (pronounced tla-tel-*ohl*-coh) was the domain of Cuauhtémoc (pronounced kwa-oo-*teh*-mock)—the last Aztec emperor before the conquest—and the sister city of Tenochtitlán. In modern times its name makes residents shudder, because it was here that the Mexican army massacred several hundred protesting students in 1968. In addition, the 1985 earthquake destroyed several high-rise apartments in Tlatelolco, killing hundreds. The center of Tlatelolco is the **Plaza de las Tres Culturas,** so named because Mexico's three cultural eras—pre-Hispanic, colonial, and contemporary—are represented on the plaza in the form of the small ruins of a pre-Hispanic ceremonial center (visible from the roadway); the Iglesia de Santiago Tlatelolco (1609) and Colegio de la Santa Cruz de Tlatelolco (1535–36); and the modern Ministry of Foreign Affairs (1970). The *colegio* (college), founded by the Franciscans after the conquest, was once attended by the sons of the Aztec nobility. ⊠ *The plaza is bounded on the north by Manuel González, on the west by Av. San Juan de Letrán Nte., and on the east by Paseo de la Reforma, between Glorietas de Peralvillo and Cuitláhuac.*

⓫ **Palacio de Iturbide** (Emperor Iturbide's Palace). Built in 1780, this handsome Baroque structure—note the imposing door and its carved-stone trimmings—became the residence of Iturbide in 1822. One of the heroes of the independence movement, the misguided Iturbide proclaimed himself emperor of a country that had thrown off the imperial yoke of the Hapsburgs only a year before. His own empire, needless to say, was short-lived. Now his home is owned by Banamex (Banco Nacional de México), which sponsors cultural exhibitions in the atrium. ⊠ *Calle Madero 17,* ☎ *5225–0281.* ☞ *Free.* ☉ *Inner atrium daily 10–7.*

⓮ **Torre Latinoamericana** (Latin American Tower). This 47-story skyscraper, the second-tallest building in the capital, was completed in 1956. On clear days the observation deck and café on the top floors afford fine views of the city. The **Fantastic World of the Sea,** a sky-high aquarium, miraculously transported small sharks and crocodiles to the 38th floor. ⊠ *Calle Madero and Eje Central Lázaro Cárdenas,* ☎ *5521–0844 observation deck; 5521–7455 aquarium.* ☞ *Deck $3.50, aquarium $2.20.* ☉ *Deck daily 9:30 AM–11 PM; aquarium daily 9:30 AM–10 PM.*

Zona Rosa, Bosque de Chapultepec, and Colonia Condesa

Bosque de Chapultepec, originally called Cerro de Chapultepec, is the largest park in the city, a great green refuge from gray urban living. Housing five world-class museums, a castle, a lake, an amusement park, and the Mexican president's official residence, Chapultepec is a saving grace for visitors and locals. If you pick only one of these museums to visit, make it the Museo Nacional de Antropología—you won't find the likes of its exhibits anywhere else.

The Zona Rosa, once a cultural center of Mexico City, is now a first stop for shopping, where stores, hotels, travel agencies, and restaurants line the avenues. Nearby Colonia Condesa is the newcomer on foreigners' itineraries. This tranquil neighborhood is filled with casual cafés and eateries for the city's young and trendy.

A Good Walk

Emperor Maximilian built the Paseo de la Reforma in 1865, modeling it after the Champs-Elysées in Paris. Its purpose was to connect the Palacio Nacional with his residence, the Castillo de Chapultepec. At the northeastern end of Reforma are Tlatelolco, the Lagunilla Market, and Plaza Garibaldi, where the mariachis gather. To the west, Reforma winds its leisurely way west into the wealthy neighborhoods of Lomas de Chapultepec, where most of the houses and estates sit behind stone walls.

Start your exploration of the Zona Rosa at the junction of Reforma, Avenida Juárez, and Bucareli, just west of the Alameda Central. Along the stretch of Reforma west of this intersection are a number of statues erected at the request of former Mexican president Porfirio Díaz to honor illustrious men, including Simón Bolívar, Columbus, Pasteur, and the Aztec emperor Cuauhtémoc. The best known, the **Monumento a la Independencia** ⑳, also known as The Angel, marks the western edge of the Zona Rosa. To get the best of the area's sights, walk along Hamburgo, Londres, and Copenhague streets—like others in the Zona, named for Continental cities. There is a crafts market, Mercado Zona Rosa, on Londres.

Four blocks southwest of the Zona Rosa, at Avenida Chapultepec, you'll come to the main entrance of **Bosque de Chapultepec** ㉑, or Chapultepec Park. Uphill from the entrance is the **Castillo de Chapultepec** ㉒ and its National History Museum. Heading downhill again after leaving the Castillo, you'll go past the much smaller, also historical, **Museo del Caracol** ㉓. North of the Castillo on the near side of Paseo de la Reforma is the **Museo de Arte Moderno** ㉔. Almost directly across Paseo de la Reforma on its north side and west of Calle Gandhi, you'll see the **Museo Rufino Tamayo** ㉕, in which you'll find Tamayo's works as well as those of other outstanding modern artists. West of the Museo Tamayo on the same side of Reforma is the **Museo Nacional de Antropología** ㉖, with its world-renowned collections of Mesoamerican art and artifacts. Cross Reforma again and you'll come to the entrance to the **Zoológico** ㉗.

Southeast of Bosque de Chapultepec, **Colonia Condesa** ㉘ is a tree-lined neighborhood where meandering streets make for pleasant strolling, especially in spring when jacaranda blossoms color the colonia. From the Bosque de Chapultepec, take a *pesero* (minibus) from beside the Chapultepec metro or a five-minute taxi ride to the buzzing restaurant zone of Calle Michoacán. If you choose to walk, it'll take 20–25 minutes: walk along Calle Veracruz going away from the park, turn right on Avenida Mazatlán, then left onto Calle Michoacán.

TIMING

You can easily spend an hour at each Bosque de Chapultepec museum, with the exception of the National Museum of Anthropology, which is huge compared with its sister institutions. You can have a quick go-through in two hours, but to really appreciate the fine exhibits, anywhere from a half-day to two full days is more appropriate. Tuesday to Saturday are good days to visit the museums and stroll around the park. On Sunday and Mexican holidays, when museum entry is free, the park and museums are packed with families. Adding Colonia Condesa to the end of a day of museum visits will make for a delightful evening.

Sights to See
BOSQUE DE CHAPULTEPEC

㉑ **Bosque de Chapultepec** ("The Woods of Chapultepec," or Chapultepec Park). This 1,600-acre green space, divided into three sections, draws families on weekend outings, cyclists, and joggers. And its museums—including the Museo Nacional de Antropología—are among the finest in Mexico. This is one of the oldest parts of Mexico City, having been inhabited by the Mexica (Aztec) tribe as early as the 13th century. The Mexica poet-king Nezahualcoyotl had his palace here and ordered construction of the aqueduct that brought water to Tenochtitlán. Ahuehuete trees (Moctezuma cypress) still stand from that era, when the woods were used as hunting preserves.

At the park's principal entrance, one block west of the Chapultepec metro station, the **Monumento a los Niños Héroes** (Monument to the Boy Heroes) consists of six marble columns adorned with eaglets. Supposedly buried in the monument are the young cadets who, it is said, wrapped themselves in the Mexican flag and jumped to their deaths rather than surrender to the Americans during the U.S. invasion of 1847. To Mexicans, that war is still a troubling symbol of their neighbor's aggressive dominance: the war cost Mexico almost half of its national territory—the present states of Texas, California, Arizona, New Mexico, and Nevada.

Other sights in the first section of Bosque de Chapultepec include three small boating lakes, a botanical garden, and the Casa del Lago cultural center, which hosts free plays, cultural events, and live music on weekends. **Los Pinos,** the residential palace of the president of Mexico, is on a small highway called Avenida Constituyentes, which cuts through the park. This is heavily guarded and cannot be visited.

The less crowded second and third sections of Bosque de Chapultepec contain a fancy restaurant; **La Feria de Chapultepec** (**El Papalote, Museo de Niño;** the national cemetery; and the Lienzo Charro (Mexican rodeos), held on Sunday afternoon.

★ ㉒ **Castillo de Chapultepec** (Chapultepec Castle). On Cerro del Chapulín (Grasshopper Hill), the Castillo has borne witness to all the turbulence and grandeur of Mexican history. In its earliest permutations, it was a Mexica palace, where the Indians made one of their last stands against the Spaniards. Later it was a Spanish hermitage, gunpowder plant, and military college. Emperor Maximilian used the castle, parts of which date from 1783, as his residence, and his example was followed by various presidents from 1872 to 1940, when Lázaro Cárdenas decreed that it be turned into the **Museo Nacional de Historia** (National History Museum).

Displays on the museum's ground floor cover Mexican history from the conquest to the revolution. The bathroom, bedroom, tea salon, and gardens were used by Maximilian and his wife, Carlotta, during the 19th century. The ground floor also contains works by 20th-century muralists O'Gorman, Orozco, and Siqueiros, while the upper floor is devoted to temporary exhibitions, Porfirio Díaz's malachite vases, and religious art. A 40¢ shuttle bus runs between this museum and the Museo del Caracol. ⊠ *Section 1 of Bosque de Chapultepec,* ☎ *5553–6224 or 5286–9920.* ☜ *$3, free Sun.* ⊙ *Tues.–Sun. 9–4.*

Ⓒ **La Feria de Chapultepec.** This children's amusement park has various games and more than 50 rides, including a truly hair-raising haunted house and a *montaña rusa*—"Russian mountain," or roller coaster. The admission price varies, depending on which rides are covered and whether or not meals are included. ⊠ *Section 2 of Bosque de Chapultepec,* ☎ *5230–2112.* ☜ *$7–$15.* ⊙ *Tues.–Fri. 11–6, weekends 10–9.*

★ ㉔ **Museo de Arte Moderno** (Museum of Modern Art). One room here is devoted to Mexican plastic arts from the 1930s to the 1960s; four others feature revolving exhibitions of contemporary painters, sculptors, lithographers, and photographers from around the world. ⊠ *Paseo de la Reforma and Calle Gandhi, Section 1 of Bosque de Chapultepec,* ☎ *5553–9394.* ☜ *$1.50, free Sun.* ⊙ *Tues.–Sun. 10–5:45.*

Ⓒ ㉓ **Museo del Caracol.** Officially it's the Galería de la Lucha del Pueblo Mexicano por su Libertad, but most people refer to it by the more fanciful name Museum of the Snail because of its spiral shape. The gallery concentrates on the 400 years from the establishment of the Viceroyalty to the Constitution of 1917, using dioramas and light-and-sound displays that children can appreciate. ⊠ *Section 1 of Bosque de Chapultepec, on the ramp up to the Castillo,* ☎ *5553–6285.* ☜ *$2.50, free Sun..* ⊙ *Tues.–Sun. 9–5:30.*

★ ㉖ **Museo Nacional de Antropología** (National Museum of Anthropology). Newly remodeled, this is the greatest museum in the country—and arguably one of the finest archaeological museums in the world. Even its architectural design, by Pedro Ramírez Vázquez, is distinguished. The museum is arranged on two floors, surrounded by salons, each displaying artifacts from a particular geographic region and/or culture. The collection is so extensive—covering some 100,000 square ft—that you could easily spend a day here, and that might be barely adequate. Labels and explanations are in Spanish and English and free tours are available at set times between 3 and 6. You can also reserve a special tour with an English-speaking guide by calling the museum one week in advance, or hire an unofficial bilingual guide outside the museum for about $10. The museum has English audio guides for rent ($3.50), and English-language guidebooks are available in the bookshop.

A good place to start is in the Orientation Room, where a film is shown in Spanish nearly every hour on the hour during the week and every two hours on the weekends. The film traces the course of Mexican prehistory and the pre-Hispanic cultures of Mesoamerica. The 12 ground-floor rooms treat pre-Hispanic cultures by region—such as Sala Teotihuacána, Sala Tolteca, Sala Oaxaca (Zapotec and Mixtec peoples), Sala Maya (Maya groups from many areas, including Guatemala), and so on. The famous Aztec calendar stone, the original *Piedra del Sol* (Stone of the Sun) is found in Room 7, the Sala Mexica, which describes Aztec life. A copy of the Aztec ruler Moctezuma's feathered headdress is displayed nearby in the same salon—strangely, the original headdress is in Vienna. An original stela from Tula, near Mexico City, massive Olmec heads from Veracruz, and vivid reproductions of Maya murals in a reconstructed temple are some of the other highlights. The magnificent tomb of the 8th-century Maya ruler Pacal, which was discovered in the ruins of Palenque, is another must to explore (Sala Maya). The perfectly preserved skeletal remains lie in state in an immense stone chamber, and the stairwell walls leading to it are beautifully decorated with bas-relief scenes of the underworld. Pacal's jade death mask is also on display nearby. The ground floor is filled with everything from the early remnants of nomadic societies to the statuary, jewelry, weapons, figurines, and pottery that evoke the intriguing, complex, and frequently bloodthirsty civilizations that peopled Mesoamerica for the 3,000 years that preceded the Spanish invasion.

The nine rooms on the upper floor contain faithful ethnographic displays of current indigenous peoples, using maps, photographs, household objects, folk art, clothing, and religious articles. When leaving the museum, take a rest and watch the famous Voladores de Papantla (flyers of Papantla) as they swing by their feet down an incredibly high maypolelike structure. ⊠ *Paseo de la Reforma at Calle Gandhi, Section 1 of Bosque de Chapultepec,* ☎ *5286–2923; 5553–6381; 5553–6386 for a guide.* ☒ *$3, free Sun.* ☉ *Tues.–Sun. 9–7.*

★ ㉕ **Museo Rufino Tamayo** (Rufino Tamayo Museum). Within its modernist shell, this sleek museum contains the paintings of the noted Mexican artist, works from his private collection, and temporary exhibitions of pieces by contemporary artists from around the world. The majority of paintings are by Tamayo; those from his collection, which demonstrate his unerring eye for great art, include a Picasso and a few works by Joan Miró, René Magritte, Francis Bacon, and Henry Moore. ⊠ *Paseo de la Reforma at Calle Gandhi, Section 1 of Bosque de Chapultepec,* ☎ *5286–6519.* ☒ *$1.50, free Sun.* ☉ *Tues.–Sun. 10–6.*

☾ **El Papalote, Museo del Niño** (The Butterfly/Kite, Children's Museum). Five theme sections compose this excellent interactive museum: *Our World; The Human Body; Con-Sciencia,* with exhibits relating to both consciousness and science; *Communication,* on topics ranging from language to computers; and *Expression,* which includes art, music, theater, and literature. There are also workshops, an IMAX theater, a store, and a restaurant. ⊠ *Av. Constituyentes 268, Section 2 of Bosque de Chapultepec,* ☎ *5237–1781.* ☒ *$4.50.* ☉ *Weekdays 9–1 and 2–6; weekends 10–2 and 3–7.*

☾ **Ripley's Museo de lo Increíble** (Ripley's Museum of the Incredible) and the Museo de Cera de la Ciudad de Mexico (Mexico City Wax Museum). Although these museums lack the polish of their equivalents in, say, Hollywood, they are nonetheless fun for children of all ages. The Ripley's museum has 14 exhibit rooms chockablock with believe-it-or-not items, and in the wax museum, Placido Domingo and Mexican politicians come to life. ⊠ *Londres 4 (east of Zona Rosa),* ☎ *5546–3784.* ☒ *$3 each museum or $5 for both.* ☉ *Weekdays 11–7, weekends 10–7.*

☾ ㉗ **Zoológico.** During the early 16th century, Mexico City's zoo housed a small private collection of animals belonging to Moctezuma II; it became quasi-public when he allowed favored subjects to visit it. The current zoo opened on this site in the 1920s and has the usual suspects as well as some superstar pandas. A gift from China, the original pair—Pepe and Ying Ying—produced the world's first panda baby born in captivity (much to competitive China's chagrin). The zoo also produced the first spectacled bears in captivity in 1998, the same year officials added the Moctezuma Aviary. The zoo is surrounded by a miniature train depot, botanical gardens, and lakes where you can go rowing. You'll see the entrance on Paseo de la Reforma, across from the Museo Nacional de Antropología. ⊠ *Section 1 of Bosque de Chapultepec,* ☎ *5553–6263 or 5256–4104.* 🖃 *Free; English audio guide $3.50.* ☉ *Tues.–Sun. 9–4.*

COLONIA CONDESA

㉘ Colonia Condesa. The neighborhood sprang up in the early 1900s around the city's elite, who quickly abandoned it in the '40s for more fashionable areas, leaving decaying mansions and parks behind. In the last decade, the neighborhood has been spruced up by an influx of new residents, mostly young artists, entrepreneurs, and foreigners. Restaurants have sprung up everywhere in the colonia, making Condesa a place to eat and be seen.

Condesa doesn't have much in the way of museums or monuments, but it is the perfect place to break from a hectic day of sightseeing— just sit back in one of the neighborhood's relaxed sidewalk cafés and watch the hip young world go by. The main drag is Avenida Michoacán, from which restaurants radiate out in every direction. Avenida México loops the main park in the area, Parque México, and Avenida Amsterdam makes another loop around the area. The park area used to be a racetrack, which explains the circular roads.

There is also an abundance of fashionable clothing shops in the area. The best-known are on Michoacán. **Soho** (☎ 5553–1730) is a clothing store whose name refers to the somewhat hopeful comparison of Condesa to New York's Soho neighborhood in the 1950s. The trendy **La Esquina** clothing store (☎ 5211–2951) down the street is similar. A great shop to browse through is **El Péndulo** (⊠ Nuevo León 115, ☎ 5286–9493), a sort of cultural center. It has a large selection of Spanish books and an international collection of CDs, and the restaurant has a great breakfast menu, with classical guitarists playing on Saturday and Sunday from 11 to 1. El Péndulo often hosts other performers—jazz, classical, folk, or rock bands—on weekends.

Farther east on Michoacán, you can head to the Parque México or the smaller Parque España for a picnic or a stroll. There's a great movie theater right on the Parque España that shows American and Mexican films, the **Plaza Condesa** (☎ 5286–4973); it has waiters who will serve you popcorn and drinks during the flick. From Michoacán, take Tamaulipas north about four blocks to arrive at the park and theater.

ZONA ROSA

For years the touristic Zona Rosa has been a favorite part of the city because of its plethora of restaurants, cafés, art and antiques galleries, hotels, discos, and shops. With the mushrooming of fast-food places and some tacky bars and stores, however, the area has lost some of its former gloss; it nonetheless still draws the faithful. Most of the buildings in the Zona Rosa are on a very human scale, at two or three stories high: they were originally private homes built in the 1920s for the wealthy. All the streets are wistfully named after European cities; some, such as Génova, are garden-lined pedestrian malls accented with contemporary bronze statuary.

To enjoy the Zona Rosa, just walk the lengths of Hamburgo and Londres and some of the side streets, especially Copenhague—a veritable restaurant row. The large crafts market on Londres is officially Mercado Insurgentes, although most people call it either Mercado Zona Rosa or Mercado Londres. Just opposite the market's Londres entrance is Plaza del Angel, a small upscale shopping mall, the halls of which are crowded by antiques vendors on weekends.

⓴ Monumento a la Independencia (Independence Monument). A Corinthian column topped by a gold-covered angel is the city's most beautiful monument, built to celebrate the 100th anniversary of Mexico's War of Independence. Beneath the pedestal lie the remains of the principal heroes of the independence movement; an eternal flame burns in their honor. ⊠ *Traffic circle between Calle Río Tiber, Paseo de la Reforma, and Calle Florencia.*

San Angel and Coyoacán

Originally separate colonial towns and then suburbs of Mexico City, San Angel and Coyoacán were both absorbed by the ever-growing capital. In the process they've managed to retain their original pueblo charm and tranquility.

San Angel is a little colonial enclave of cobblestone streets, stone walls, pastel houses, and gardens drenched in bougainvillea. It became a haven for wealthy Spaniards during the Viceroyalty period, around the time of the construction of the Ex-Convento del Carmen. The elite were drawn to the area because of its rivers, pleasant climate, and rural ambience, and proceeded to build haciendas and mansions that, for many, were country homes.

Coyoacán means "Place of the Coyotes." According to local legend, a coyote used to bring chickens to a friar who had saved the coyote from being strangled by a snake. Coyoacán was founded by Toltecs in the 10th century and later settled by the Aztecs, or Mexica. Bernal Díaz Castillo, a Spanish chronicler, wrote that there were 6,000 houses at the time of the conquest. Cortés set up headquarters in Coyoacán during his siege of Tenochtitlán and at one point considered making it his capital. He changed his mind for political reasons, but many of the Spanish buildings left from the two-year period during which Mexico City was built still stand.

Coyoacán has had many illustrious residents from Mexico's rich and intellectual elite, including Miguel de la Madrid, president of Mexico from 1982 to 1988; artists Diego Rivera, Frida Kahlo, and José Clemente Orozco; Gabriel Figueroa, cinematographer for Luis Buñuel and John Huston; film star Dolores del Río; film director El Indio Fernández; and writers Carlos Monsiváis, Jorge Ibargüengoitia, and Nobel laureate Octavio Paz before his death in 1998. It is also the neighborhood where Leon Trotsky in exile met his violent death. Although superficially it resembles San Angel, Coyoacán has a more animated street life. Most of the houses and other buildings honor the traditions of colonial Mexican architecture, and the neighborhood is well kept by residents, many of whose families have lived here for generations.

A Good Tour

Weekends are best for exploring the southern part of the city. Take a taxi or pesero down Avenida Insurgentes and get off at Avenida de la Paz where you'll find many fine restaurants. On the east side of Insurgentes is the **Monumento al General Alvaro Obregón** ㉙. Cross Insurgentes on Avenida de la Paz, and take the southern fork off Avenida de la Paz (Calle Madero) until you come to San Angel's center, **Plaza San Jacinto** ㉚. Stroll to the **Casa del Risco** ㉛ on the north side of the plaza and, if it's a Saturday, head for the **Bazar Sábado** on the north end.

Retrace your steps on Avenida La Paz, to Avenida Revolución and Plaza del Carmen, which lies at the corner of Calle Monasterio. Inside is the colonial **Ex-Convento del Carmen** ㉜, interesting as an example of sacred architecture and for its religious artifacts. Now take Avenida Revolución one long block north to see the modern Mexican and European works at the **Museo Alvar y Carmen T. de Carrillo Gil** ㉝ (known as the Carrillo Gil). Unless you have plenty of energy, get a taxi to take

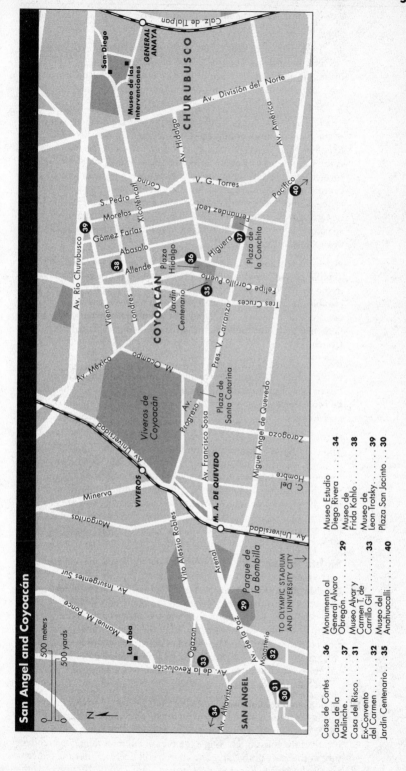

San Angel and Coyoacán

you up Altavista to the **Museo Estudio Diego Rivera** ㉞, (and to an elegant lunch in the San Angel Inn or Il Fornaio).

The next part of the tour goes to Coyoacán, which extends east of Avenida Insurgentes about 1 km (½ mi) from San Angel. You're best off taking a taxi to the **Plaza de Santa Catarina** on Avenida Francisco Sosa, about halfway into the center of Coyoacán, because the tour involves a lot of walking.

The pretty 16th-century Iglesia de Santa Catarina dominates this tiny plaza. It also contains a bust of Mexican historian Francisco Sosa, who lived here and wrote passionately about Coyoacán. Across the street is the **Casa de Jesús Reyes Heroles** (Avenida Francisco Sosa 202); the former home of the ex-minister of education is a fine example of 20th-century architecture on the colonial model. It's now used as a cultural center. Continue east on Francisco Sosa and you'll pass Casa de Diego de Ordaz at the corner of Tres Cruces. This *mudéjar* (Spanish-Arabic) structure, adorned with inlaid tiles, was the home of a former captain in Cortés's army.

Now you're standing at the entrance of the **Jardín Centenario** ㉟. The Templo de San Juan Bautista and the picturesque **Casa de Cortés** ㊱ sit in the small Plaza Hidalgo adjacent to and north of the garden. Walk two blocks southeast of Plaza Hidalgo on Calle Higuera to the corner of Calle Vallarta, where you'll find the **Casa de la Malinche** ㊲. The house, darkened with age, faces an attractive cobbled park called Plaza de la Conchita.

Return to Plaza Hidalgo and walk five blocks north on Calle Allende to the corner of Calle Londres and the **Museo de Frida Kahlo** ㊳. It is linked both historically and romantically with the fortresslike **Museo de Leon Trotsky** ㊴, east of it on Londres, then two long blocks north on Morelos.

TIMING

You're likely to want to linger in these elegant and beautiful sections of town, especially in Coyoacán. The Frida Kahlo and Leon Trotsky museums give intense, intimate looks at the lives of two famous people who were friends and lovers, and who breathed their personalities into the places where they lived. Allow at least an hour at each. The other museums are much smaller and merit less time. Weekends are liveliest at the Plaza Hidalgo and its neighboring Jardín Centenario, where street life explodes into a fiesta.

Sights to See
SAN ANGEL

㉛ **Casa del Risco** (Risco House). This 1681 mansion is one of the prettiest houses facing the Plaza San Jacinto. A huge free-form fountain sculpture—exploding with colorful porcelain, tiles, shells, and mosaics—covers the entire eastern wall of its patio. Although it's not ranked among the city's top museums, the **Museo de la Casa del Risco** houses a splendid collection of 17th- and 18th-century European and colonial Mexican paintings as well as period furnishings. ✉ *Plaza San Jacinto 15,* ☎ *5616–2711.* 🎫 *Free.* 🕐 *Tues.–Sun. 10–5.*

㉜ **Ex-Convento del Carmen** (Carmelite Convent and Church). Erected by Carmelite friars with the help of an Indian chieftain between 1615 and 1628, this cloister, with its tile-covered domes, fountains, and gardens, is one of the most interesting examples of colonial religious architecture in this part of the city. The church still operates, but the convent is now the **Museo Regional del Carmen,** with a fine collection of 16th- to 18th-century religious paintings and icons. It's worth visiting the

12 mummified corpses tucked away in the crypt. ⊠ *Av. Revolución 4, at Monasterio,* ☎ *5616–2816 or 5616–1177.* 🖾 *$2.50, free Sun.* ⊙ *Tues.–Sun. 10–4:45.*

㉙ Monumento al General Alvaro Obregón. This somber gray granite monument marks the spot where reformer and national hero Obregón was gunned down by a religious zealot in a restaurant in 1928, soon before he was to begin his second term as president. It used to house a gruesome display of the General's hand, which he lost in battle, but it was removed in the interest of good taste. ⊠ *Parque de la Bombilla, east of Av. La Paz at Av. Insurgentes.*

㉝ Museo Alvar y Carmen T. de Carrillo Gil. Considerably superior in design and natural lighting to the city's Museo de Arte Moderno, this private collection contains early murals by Orozco, Rivera, and Siqueiros; works by modern European artists such as Klee and Picasso; and temporary expositions of young Mexican artists. ⊠ *Av. Revolución 1608, at Altavista,* ☎ *5550–1254.* 🖾 *$1.* ⊙ *Tues.–Sun. 10–6.*

㉞ Museo Estudio Diego Rivera. Some of Diego's last paintings are still resting here on ready easels, and his denim jacket and shoes sit on a wicker chair, waiting. The museum that once was home to Diego Rivera and his artist wife, Frida Kahlo, appears as if the two could return at any moment to continue work. Juan O'Gorman, a famous architect and close friend of Rivera, designed the house in the functionalist spirit, with an intent to economize space. ⊠ *Diego Rivera 2, at Altavista,* ☎ *5616–0996.* 🖾 *$1.50.* ⊙ *Tues.–Sun. 10–6.*

★ ㉚ Plaza San Jacinto. This cozy plaza with a grisly history is the center of San Angel. In 1847 about 50 Irish soldiers of St. Patrick's Battalion, who had sided with the Mexicans in the Mexican-American War, had their foreheads branded here with the letter *D*—for deserter—and were then hanged by the Americans. These men had been enticed to swim the Rio Grande, deserting the ranks of U.S. General Zachary Taylor, by pleas to the historic and religious ties between Spain and Ireland. As settlers in Mexican Texas, they felt their allegiance lay with Catholic Mexico, and they were among the bravest fighters in the war. They met their end when the American flag flew over Castillo de Chapultepec after the death of the *niños héroes.* A memorial plaque (on a building on the plaza's west side) lists their names and expresses Mexico's gratitude for their help in the "unjust North American invasion." Off to one side of the plaza, the excellent handicrafts market, Bazar Sábado, is held on Saturday. ⊠ *Between Miramon, Cda. Santisima, Dr. Galvez, and Madero.*

COYOACÁN

㊱ Casa de Cortés (Cortés's House). The place where the Aztec emperor Cuauhtémoc was held prisoner by Cortés is reputed to have been rebuilt in the 18th century from the stones of his original house by one of Cortés's descendants; the municipal government now has offices here. Dominating the little square on which it sits, this was almost the city's first city hall, but Cortés decided to rebuild Tenochtitlán instead. The two-story, deep-red house, with its wide arches and tile patio, is gorgeous. The house is not open to the public, but there is a tourist-information booth in the front room that's staffed by friendly employees eager to tell you about Coyoacán. ⊠ *Plaza Hidalgo between Calles Carillo Puerto and Caballo Calco.*

㊲ Casa de la Malinche. One of the most powerful symbols of the conquest is located in Coyoacán but, significantly perhaps, is not even marked. It's the somber-looking, fortresslike residence of Malinche, Cortés's Indian mistress and interpreter, whom the Spaniards called Doña

FRIDA KAHLO: A RIBBON AROUND A BOMB

"**O**F COURSE, he does pretty well for a little boy, but it is I who am the big artist."

Frida Kahlo's tongue-in-cheek comment about her husband to the *Detroit News* in 1933 seems less and less a joke as the years go by. This petite painter, who has gained international recognition since the 1980s for her colorful but pained self-portraits, has begun to overshadow the massive muralist, Diego Rivera. Considered one of the last century's major artistic figures, Rivera created images—especially those rounded peasant women with braided hair, arms brim-full of creamy lilies—that have typified this country for more than a half century. The bizarre Beauty-and-the-Beast dynamics and sordid drama of the couple's relationship ensure the popularity of many of Mexico's museums and murals. But, if Diego dwarfed Frida in stature, he no longer does in fame.

Now, Kahlo's hauntingly beautiful face, broken body, and bright Tehuana costumes, along with a few exotic accessories such as monkeys, parrots, and hairless dogs, have become the trademark of Mexican femininity. Life-size cardboard cutouts with her bat-wing brows, moustache, and clunky ethnic earrings are as familiar here as Marilyn's pout and puffed-up white dress are in the United States.

In fact, Frida didn't even need to paint to make it into the history books. The controversy and scandal that surrounded her two marriages to Diego include his affair with her younger sister—the same year Frida suffered a third miscarriage and had toes removed from her right foot—and her affair with Communist exile Leon Trotsky. It's hard not to become mired in the tragic twists and turns of her life—from childhood polio to a tram accident that smashed her pelvis, a gangrenous foot that resulted in the amputation of a leg, as well as bouts of anorexia and alcoholism.

But she was also a groundbreaking artist who pioneered a new expressivism, and her unique iconography of suffering transcended self-pity to create an existential art. Kahlo was the first Latin American woman to have a painting in the Louvre; her work caused a storm in Paris in 1939 (at an exhibition entitled "Mexique"), and the Surrealists claimed it as supremely illustrative of their ideas. It was André Breton who described her art as "a ribbon around a bomb."

Frida, who was always frank about her start in painting—she did it to kill time in one of her many convalescences—had doubts that her paintings were Surrealist, saying, "they are the most frank expression of myself." Later she expressed unease with her art for not being suitable to serve the aims of the Communist Party, of which she and Diego were avid supporters. Her gargantuan husband was more generous, emphasizing how the influence of the religious retablo (ex-voto) that Frida collected was transformed in her art to an exploration of the permanent miracle of life. "Frida . . . tore open her chest and heart to reveal the biological truth of her feelings," he wrote.

And Frida tried hard to be as much the comrade and revolutionary as the icon of long-suffering Mexican femininity. Her last public appearance was 11 days before her death, in a wheelchair at Diego's side, protesting the intervention of the United States in Guatemala.

— Barbara Kastelein

María and the Indians called Malintzín. Malinche aided the conquest by enabling Cortés to communicate with the Nahuatl-speaking tribes he met en route to Tenochtitlán. Today she is a much-reviled Mexican symbol of a traitorous xenophile—hence the term *malinchista*, used to describe a Mexican who prefers things foreign. Legend says that Cortés's wife died in this house, poisoned by the conquistador. ⊠ *2 blocks east of Plaza Hidalgo on Calle Higuera at Vallarta.*

㉟ Jardín Centenario (Centenary Gardens). Small fairs, amateur musical performances, and poetry and palm readings are frequent occurrences in this large park surrounded by outdoor cafés. At the far end of the Jardín you'll see **Templo de San Juan Bautista**, one of the first churches to be built in New Spain. It was completed in 1582, and its door has a Baroque arch. ⊠ *Between Calle Centenario, Av. Hidalgo, and Caballo Calco.*

★ ㊳ Museo de Frida Kahlo. Kahlo has become a sort of cult figure, not only because of her paintings—55 of 143 are self-portraits—but also because of her bohemian lifestyle and flamboyant individualism. The "Blue House" where Kahlo was born in 1907 (not 1910, as she wanted people to believe) and died 47 years later, is both museum and shrine. Kahlo's astounding vitality and originality are reflected in the house, from the giant papier-mâché skeletons outside and the painted tin *retablos* (ex-votos) on the staircase to the gloriously decorated kitchen and the bric-a-brac in her bedroom. Feminists and fetishists alike can admire her early sketches, diary entries, tiny outfits, wheelchair at the easel, plus painted corsets and four-poster bed conveniently fitted with mirror above. Even if you know nothing about Kahlo, a visit to the museum will leave you with a strong, visceral impression of this pivotal feminist artist. ⊠ *Londres 247, at Allende,* ☎ *5554–5999.* ⊠ *$2.* ☉ *Tues.–Sun. 10–5:45.*

㊴ Museo de Leon Trotsky. Resembling an anonymous and forbidding fortress, with turrets for armed guards, this is where Leon Trotsky lived and was murdered. It is difficult to believe that it's the final resting place for the ashes of one of the most important figures of the Russian Revolution, but that only adds to the allure of the house, which is owned by Trotsky's grandson.

This is a modest, austere dwelling. Anyone taller than 5 ft must stoop to pass through doorways to Trotsky's bedroom—with bullet holes still in the walls from the first assassination attempt, in which the muralist Siqueiros was implicated—his wife's study, the dining room, and the study where the Mexican communist Ramón Mercader finally drove an ice pick into Trotsky's head. On his desk, cluttered with writing paraphernalia and an article he was revising in Russian, the calendar is open to that fateful day, August 20, 1940. The volunteers will tell you how Trotsky's teeth left a permanent scar on Mercader's hand, how he clung to life for 26 hours, what his last words were, and how his death was sponsored by the United States (others would say Stalin). Not all the volunteers, however, speak English. ⊠ *Río Churubusco 410,* ☎ *5658–8732.* ⊠ *$1.* ☉ *Tues.–Sun. 10–5.*

㊵ Museo del Anahuacalli. Diego Rivera built his own museum for the thousands of pre-Columbian artifacts he collected over the years. The third-floor studio that Rivera did not live long enough to use displays sketches for some of his most controversial murals. The huge dark-gray building, constructed in the 1950s from volcanic rock, resembles an aboveground tomb. If you visit between October and the end of December you'll see one of the city's finest altars to the dead in honor of Rivera himself. ⊠ *Calle del Museo 150,* ☎ *5617–4310 or 5617–3797.* ⊠ *$1.* ☉ *Tues.–Sun. 10–6.*

OFF THE
BEATEN PATH

SIX FLAGS OF MÉXICO — This 100-acre theme park on the southern edge of the city comprises seven "villages": Mexican, French, Swiss, Polynesian, Moroccan, the Wild West, and Children's World. Shows include performances by trained dolphins. ⊠ *Southwest of Coyoacán on Carretera Picacho a Ajusco at Km 1.5,* ☎ *5645–5434 or 5728–7200.* ▦ *$20 includes entrance and all rides.* ☉ *Tues.–Thurs. 10–6, Fri.– Sun. 10–7.*

DINING

Mexico City restaurants open 7–11 AM for breakfast (*desayuno*) and 1:30–5 for lunch (*comida*)—although it's rare for Mexicans to eat lunch before 3. Most locals start out at 9 PM for dinner (*cena*); restaurants stay open till midnight during the week and a little later on weekends. At deluxe restaurants, dress is generally formal (jacket and tie), and reservations are almost always required; see reviews for details. (Even if a deluxe restaurant doesn't *require* a jacket and tie, men are likely to feel out-of-place if not well dressed.) If you're short on time, there are American-style coffee shops (VIPS, Denny's, Shirley's, and Sanborns) all over the city; some are open 24 hours.

Colonia Polanco is an attractive, upscale neighborhood on the edge of Chapultepec Park that has some of the best and most expensive dining (and lodging) in the city. Zona Rosa restaurants get filled pretty quickly on Saturday night, especially the Saturday coinciding with most people's payday, which falls on the 1st and 15th of each month.

CATEGORY	COST*
$$$$	over $40
$$$	$25–$40
$$	$15–$25
$	under $15

*per person for a main course at dinner

Argentine

$$$ ✕ **Cambalache.** Before entering this ever-busy beef-lover's dream, you can see the chefs preparing their thick cuts in the window. If you come with a few people, try the Super Lomo Cambalache, a steak big enough for three–four people. If you're not in the mood for beef, there are several chicken dishes on the menu, such as the Don Ignacio: a boneless chicken breast served in a mushroom sauce with pineapple and fresh sweet peppers. Vegetables *do* come with menu items, and potatoes, particularly the soufflé, are a specialty. ⊠ *Arquímedes 85, Col. Polanco,* ☎ *5280–2080 or 5280–2957,* ℻ *5280–1979. AE, MC, V.*

$$$ ✕ **Rincon Argentino.** This established Argentine restaurant is known as much for its decor as for its exquisitely prepared cuts of beef. The ceiling here is painted like a sky, the bar is covered by a thatch roof, and the dining areas are made to resemble a stone-and-wood lodge. Most Argentines prefer their beef *bien cocida* (well-done), but you can have it any way you like. ⊠ *Presidente Masarik 177, Col. Polanco,* ☎ *5531–8617 or 5254–8775. MC, V.*

$$ ✕ **La Taba.** This smart, yet unpretentious, restaurant in the south of the city is characterized by its generous portions of top-quality beef, done perfectly to your choice of five options—from blue to well done. A delectable butter bean and parsley salad is free while you browse the expanded menu, which caters adequately to those who avoid red meat. Even vegetarians will be content with the variety of soups, pastas, and salads. The *bife de chorizo* is superb, and big eaters might find room for one of the traditional Argentine desserts. ⊠ *Revolución*

LA COCINA MEXICANA

TO ENTERTAIN THE NOTION that Mexican food is little more than tacos, enchiladas, and burritos—or Tex-Mex or Taco Bell—would be culinary blasphemy to native gastronomes. Regional cooking is the heart and soul of Mexico, multiplied by the republic's 32 states and the provinces within them. Fresh ingredients abound, recipes are passed down through generations (think *Like Water for Chocolate*), and preparation requires much patience and loving care. With the staples—rice, beans, chilies, and corn—chefs are turning out ever more sophisticated variations on national dishes. But in terms of the Mexican chef's arsenal of ingredients, they're only the beginning.

Maize was sacred to the Indians, who have innumerable ways of preparing it—from faithful tortillas and tamales (cornmeal wrapped in banana leaves or corn husks) to tostadas (lightly fried, open tortillas topped with meat, lettuce, and the like) and tacos (tortillas briefly heated, filled, and wrapped into slim cylinders). *Pozole* (made with hominy) is a delicious pork-based soup. The sweet, corn-based drink *atole,* similar in consistency to hot chocolate, is a favorite breakfast or before-bed treat.

You'll find fish not just on the coasts but also in the lake regions around Guadalajara and in the state of Michoacán. *Huachinango* (red snapper), abalone, crab, and swordfish are all popular. And ceviche—raw *mariscos* (shellfish) marinated in lime juice then topped with chopped chilies, onions, and cilantro—is almost a national dish; just make sure it's fresh. Shrimp, lobster, and oysters can be huge and succulent; bear in mind the folk adage and eat oysters only in months with names that contain the letter *r.* Likewise avoid raw shellfish wherever cholera or water pollution might be a risk.

Mexicans love beef, pork, and *barbacoa* (barbecued lamb) with a variety of sauces. The complex, spicy mole—its ingredients can number more than 100, among them many kinds of chilies, and in one mole, chocolate—is one of Mexico's proudest culinary inventions. It is usually served over chicken or turkey. Chicken is often roasted, served in sauces like mole, or tucked in enchiladas, tacos, or burritos.

Fresh fruits and vegetables are another Mexican pleasure. Jicama, papaya, mamey, avocado, mango, guayaba, squash, and tomatoes are just some of the produce native to Mexico. (All fresh produce should be washed in water with a commercial disinfectant—bacteria exist in Mexico that your stomach might not be happy with. For this reason, avoid eating at street stalls and beware of uncooked herbs such as cilantro).

Other Mexican specialties are less common abroad: *antojitos* or *botanas* (appetizers), *chilaquiles* (breakfast dishes made with tortilla strips scrambled with chilies, tomatoes, onions, cream, and cheese), and *chiles en nogada* (a large poblano chili stuffed with beef or cheese, raisins, onion, olives, and almonds and topped with a creamy walnut sauce and pomegranate seeds). Soups are hearty—particularly pozole, *sopa azteca* (avocado, chicken chunks, and tortilla in a broth), and don't forget to try the lighter *sopa de flor de calabaza* (zucchini-flower soup) or, if you get a chance, *sopa de colorin,* made from a bright red flower.

The astonishing assortment of breads, sweets, beers, wines (which are fast improving), and agave- (related to the cactus) based liquors goes on and on. Sadly, shortage of the blue agave has caused tequila prices to soar, so watch out for cheap varieties which add sugar cane liquor or less-digestible substances. Freshly squeezed fruit juices and fruit shakes (*licuados*) are safe to drink—if ordered in a restaurant with hygienic practices—and taste heavenly. And coffee ranges from Americano (black) to organic varieties to sweet *café de olla,* which is laced with spices.

62

Mexico City Dining

COLEGIO MILITAR

Ricardeo Flores Magon

TLATELOLCO

Plaza de la
Tres Culturas

Calle Allende

NORMAL

Mosqueta

GUERRERO

Rayón
Rep. de Costa Rica

SAN COSME

Violeta

Rep. de Chile

Rivera de San Cosme

REVOLUCIÓN

Paseo de la Reforma

Cárdenas

36

HIDALGO

BELLAS
ARTES

Rep.
de Cuba

37

Rep. de
Bolivia

35

Tacuba

Plaza de la
Republica

Alameda
Central

ALLENDE
5 de Mayo

38

39

Moneda

M. María Contreras

Antonio Caso

Sullivan

34

JUÁREZ

Av. Juárez

Madero

ZÓCALO

Av. Parque Via

Independencia

Eje Central

CENTRO

Villalongin

Río Rhin

Insurgentes Centro

Av. Bucareli

Revillagigedo

Ayuntamiento

Rep. del Salvador

Río Tíber

14

R-Sena

Guadalquivir

de la Reforma

ZONA
ROSA

Luis
Moya

BALDERAS

SALTO DEL AGUA

40

Paseo

31

33

CUAUHTÉMOC

I. LA CATOLICA

PINO
SUÁREZ

Londres

Dr. Río de la Loza

15

30

32

Bolívar

ILLA

Av. Chapultepec

INSURGENTES

Puebla

29

Plaza
Río de
Janeiro

Av. Oaxaca

ROMA

Av. Cuauhtémoc

Av. Dr. Vertiz

L. Boturini

S. Antonio Abad

Av. Durango

Av. Insurgentes Sur

Obregón

Ortiz Iba

NIÑOS HÉROES

Dr. Claudio Bernard

SAN ANTONIO
ABAD

Av. México

Av. Yucatán

San Luis Potosí

Eje Central Lázaro Cárdenas

Laredo

Medellin

Monterrey

HOSPITAL GENERAL

Cuauhtémoc

Manzanillo

19

21

22

CENTRO
MÉDICO

23

28

CHABACANO

1398, Col. Guadalupe Inn, ☎ *5662–3165 or 5662–2670,* FAX *5662–2670. AE, MC, V.*

$ ✕ **Fonda Garufa.** Its tables spilling out onto a Condesa sidewalk, this is a perfect place for a relaxed meal after a day of sightseeing. Filet mignon, served with mushrooms and watercress, is especially delicious. There's also an extensive list of innovative pastas. A favorite with regulars is fettuccine Hindú: half a chicken breast bathed in a yogurt sauce laced with cilantro, ginger, onion, and chili, over fresh fettuccine. ✉ *Michoacán 93, Col. Condesa,* ☎ *5286–8295. MC, V.*

French

$$$$ ✕ **Fouquet's de Paris.** In the Camino Real hotel, this branch of the
★   renowned Parisian restaurant is an elegant haven of peace and tranquillity. The best pâtés in Mexico and tender, juicy lamb chops are part of the diverse and stylish menu. Desserts are in a class of their own: sorbets, such as the delicately flavored passion fruit, are outstanding, and the cakes, mousses, and pastries are light and delicious. Gastronomic festivals are held here throughout the year. ✉ *Hotel Camino Real, Mariano Escobedo 700, Col. Polanco,* ☎ *5263–8888 or 5263–8823,* FAX *5263–8889. Reservations essential. Jacket and tie. AE, DC, MC, V. Closed Sun. No lunch Sat.*

$$$ ✕ **Au Pied de Cochon.** Tucked on the ground floor inside the Hotel Presidente, this fashionable bistro was an immediate hit when it opened in
★   2000, stunning the capital with everything from oysters to offal. The roasted leg of pork with béarnaise sauce is the signature dish, and you'll find traditional French onion soup, fillet mignon with pepper sauce and tartare de boeuf haché done to perfection. Options also include smoked salmon with blini and a delectable mille-feuille with crab and artichoke heart. For dessert, a green-apple sorbet with calvados comes highly recommended. Even though celebrities come here to dine, the daily three-course set menu—which may include seafood, a perfect crème brûlée, as well as a glass of house wine—is only $15. ✉ *Campos Elíseos 218, Col. Polanco,* ☎ *5327–7700 or 5327–7776,* FAX *5327–7767. Reservations essential. AE, MC, V.*

$$$ ✕ **Champs Élysées.** Commanding a superb view of the Independence
★   Monument is one of the bastions of haute cuisine in Mexico City. The variety of sauces served with both meat and fish dishes is impressive—tarragon sauce over salmon, or sea urchin over bass take top honors. The cheese board is particularly generous. ✉ *Paseo de la Reforma 316, at Estocolmo, Zona Rosa,* ☎ *5525–7259,* FAX *5208–2302. AE, DC, MC, V. Closed Sun.*

Greek

$ ✕ **Agapi Mu** (My Love). This 20-table Greek bistro tucked in a converted Colonia Condesa home with a Greek flag out front and snug rooms inside attracts its share of actors, singers, and artists. Come for authentic Greek food in a casual, intimate setting and rambunctious Greek song and dance Thursday through Saturday nights. The menu includes *paputsáka* (stuffed eggplant), *kalamárea* (fried squid Greek style), and *dolmádes* (stuffed grape leaves). Wash it all down with a Hungarian Sangre de Toro wine, and finish it off with a smooth, sweet Greek coffee. ✉ *Alfonso Reyes 96, Col. Condesa,* ☎ *5286–1384,* FAX *5286–1942. AE, MC, V.*

International

$$$$ ✕ **Maxim's de Paris.** Under the auspices of the original Parisian Maxim's, this spacious but intimate art deco restaurant sits under a stained-glass

ceiling and serves classic Gallic cuisine spiced up with the best of Mexican ingredients. Try such delicacies as tender veal in its juice accented with truffles and asparagus, and fresh Dover sole in white butter sauce studded with bits of lobster. The pastry chef's desserts include mouthwatering soufflés. The wine cellar is nonpareil, and the service impeccable. ⊠ *Hotel Presidente Inter-Continental México, Campos Elíseos 218, Col. Polanco,* ☎ *5327–7700,* FAX *5327–7767. Reservations essential. Jacket and tie. AE, DC, MC, V. Closed Sun. No lunch Sat.*

$$$–$$$$ ✕ **Les Célébrités.** In addition to its superb French Basque fare, this el-
★ egant hotel restaurant has refreshed the menu with Mediterranean selections. The sunny yellow decor and a profusion of flowers enhance the pleasing, light-filled ambience. The restaurant is known for its one-of-a-kind combinations, such as an appetizer of king crab with asparagus cream, sauce of caviar, and passion-fruit vinaigrette. For dessert, there's a sinfully rich chocolate mousse cake and a light, flaky hazelnut pastry with profiteroles in a chocolate-coriander sauce. The restaurant is open for breakfast as well. ⊠ *Nikko México hotel, Campos Elíseos 204, Col. Polanco,* ☎ *5280–1111. Reservations essential. Jacket and tie. AE, DC, MC, V. Closed weekends.*

$$$–$$$$ ✕ **Estoril.** In an exquisitely furnished 1930s town house in fashionable
★ Colonia Polanco, Rosa Martin serves French cuisine with a Mexican flair. *Perejil frito* (fried parsley) is a popular starter, and main dishes offer some unusual combinations: giant prawns in Chablis or curry sauce, and sea bass in fresh coriander sauce. If you have a sweet tooth, try either the delicious tart Tatin—an upside-down apple tart with caramel— or the homemade mint sorbet. ⊠ *Alejandro Dumas 24, Col. Polanco,* ☎ *5280–9828,* FAX *5280–9311. AE, DC, MC, V. Closed Sun.*

$$$–$$$$ ✕ **Hacienda de los Morales.** This Mexican institution, set in a former hacienda that dates back to the 16th century, is grandly colonial in style, with dark-wood beams, huge terra-cotta expanses, and dramatic torches. The menu combines international and Mexican cuisines with imaginative variations on both. Walnut soup is delicate and unusual. Fish is seemingly unlimited, from sea bass *marinière* (in a white-wine sauce) to a mixed seafood gratin. The charcoal-broiled grain-fed chicken has a distinct flavor and the duck in raspberry sauce is a highlight. Live trio music (three voices and guitars that play melodic traditional Mexican ballads) completes the atmosphere. ⊠ *Vázquez de Mella 525, Col. Chapultepec Morales,* ☎ *5281–4554 or 5281–4703. AE, DC, MC, V. No dinner Sun.*

$$$ ✕ **Bellini.** While its great turntable slowly revolves on the 45th floor of the World Trade Center, executives from surrounding offices pack Bellini at lunch. While the view of the city by night is romantic, the view by day—when it's clear and you can see the volcanoes—is truly breathtaking. The majority of the dishes here aren't Italian but Mexican and international. The house special is a lobster of your choosing from a tank brought tableside; it's prepared to your taste. Other favorites are filet mignon and homemade pastas served with classic Italian sauces. Finish with a flambéed dessert, such as strawberries jubilee or crêpes suzette. ⊠ *Av. de las Naciones 1, World Trade Center Tower, Col. Napoles, 20 mins by car south of Zona Rosa,* ☎ *5628–8305,* FAX *5628–8325. Jacket and tie. AE, DC, MC, V.*

$$ ✕ **Bellinghausen.** This is one of the most beloved lunch spots in the Zona Rosa and practically a landmark of good eating for the locals. The partially covered hacienda-style courtyard at the back, set off by an ivy-laden wall, is a midday magnet for executives and tourists. A veritable army of waiters scurries back and forth serving such tried-and-true favorites as *sopa de hongos mexicana* (mushroom soup) and *filete chemita* (broiled steak with mashed potatoes). The *huachinango a la parrilla* (grilled red snapper) with a side order of sautéed spinach

is another winning dish. The restaurant is open until 7 PM. ⊠ *Londres 95, Zona Rosa,* ☎ *5207–6149. AE, DC, MC, V. No dinner.*

$ ✗ **Los Arroces.** The name means "rices," and at this trendy spot in Colonia Condesa, rice is exactly what you'll get—from 50 different places around the world, in soups, salads, and main dishes. There's *pastel de arroz,* for example, which is white Mexican rice prepared with *rajas* (poblano chili strips), *flor de calabaza* (zucchini blossom), corn, and bacon; Maya rice, served with squid, chopped red onion, sour oranges, and beans; and Spanish paella with rice from Valencia. ⊠ *Michoacán 126, Col Condesa,* ☎ *5286–4287. AE, MC, V.*

Italian

$$$–$$$$ ✗ **Il Fornaio.** The first Latin American branch of this prestigious Milan chain attracts a steady stream of well-heeled diners. In a tranquil and inviting atmosphere, you can taste *carpaccio di salmone* dressed with Belgian endive, grapefruit, cress, and a lightly citric vinegar, or enjoy an excellent *linguine ai sapori di mare* (linguine with seafood). The chef refuses to use anything but Italian ingredients; notice the authentic cheeses (as in the succulent veal in Gorgonzola sauce). The desserts, such as the sweet crepes *crespelle al caffe,* are unforgettable. ⊠ *Altavista 192, Col. San Angel,* ☎ *5616–5985. AE, DC, MC, V. No dinner Sun.*

$–$$ ✗ **La Lanterna.** The Petterino family has run this two-story restaurant for more than three decades. The downstairs has the rustic feel of a northern-Italian trattoria, with the cramped seating adding to the intimacy. Upstairs is more spacious. All pastas are made on the premises; the Bolognese sauce, in particular, is a favorite. Raw artichoke salad, *conejo al Salmi* (rabbit in a wine sauce), and *filete al burro nero* (steak in black butter) are all worthy dishes. Seasonal presentations include fungi in a variety of dishes plus homegrown arugula for salads and carpaccio. ⊠ *Paseo de la Reforma 458, Col. Juárez,* ☎ *5207–9969. AE, DC, MC, V. Closed Sun. and Dec. 25–Jan. 1.*

Japanese

$$$ ✗ **Suntory.** This main branch of the Suntory restaurants in Mexico welcomes you with a Japanese garden at the entryway. In this enchanted world you are not absolved of the difficulty of choice, however. Will it be the teppanyaki room to watch your fresh meat or fish prepared with a variety of vegetables? Or perhaps the sushi bar—or maybe you'll end up in the shabu-shabu room, with its wafer-thin sashimi and a copper pot of steaming vegetable broth for cooking wafer-thin slices of beef. Prices are high, but the ingredients are of the best quality. ⊠ *Torres Adalid 14, Col. del Valle,* ☎ *5536–9432,* 𝙵𝙰𝚇 *5687–1912. Reservations essential. AE, DC, MC, V. No dinner Sun.*

Mexican

$$$ ✗ **Cicero Centenario.** This thoroughly Mexican restaurant occupies a
★   restored 17th-century mansion in the heart of the historic downtown. Elegant colonial antiques are strikingly posed against folk art and pastel walls, and the bar has an outstanding collection of tin ex-votos and other religious memorabilia. The enticing menu includes excellent versions of authentic colonial dishes such as *crepas de huitlacoche* (corn fungus crepes). Try the *chicharrón* (crispy pork rind) and guacamole appetizer, but be sure to leave room for dessert, such as rose-petal ice cream. An ebullient street-level cantina has afternoon serenades by a folk trio. ⊠ *República de Cuba 79,* ☎ *5512–1510 or 5512–6868. Reservations essential. AE, DC, MC, V. No dinner Sun.*

$$$ ✕ San Angel Inn. In the south of the city, this magnificent old hacienda
★ and ex-convent, with elegant grounds and immaculately tended gardens, is a joy to the eye. Dark mahogany furniture, crisp white table
linens, and beautiful blue-and-white Talavera place settings strike a note
of restrained opulence. Many dishes are recommended, especially the
classic *huitlacoche* (corn fungus) served in crepas de huitlacoche, as
well as *sopa de tortilla* (tortilla soup). The *puntas de filete* (sirloin tips)
are liberally laced with chilies, and the *huachinango* (red snapper) is
offered in a variety of ways. Desserts—from light and crunchy meringues
to pastries bulging with cream—can be rich to the point of surfeit. ⊠
Calle Diego Rivera 50, at Altavista, Col. San Angel, ☎ *5616–0537,
5616–2222, or 5616–1402. Jacket required. AE, DC, MC, V.*

$$–$$$ ✕ El Arroyo. This dining complex, complete with its own bullring, is
an attraction in itself. At the south end of town near the beginning of
the highway to Cuernavaca, it was founded more than 50 years ago
by the Arroyo family and is now run by jovial Jesús ("Chucho") Arroyo. His loyal following includes celebrities, dignitaries, and bullfighters,
along with local families, groups, and tourists; more than 2,600 people can dine simultaneously in a labyrinth of 11 picturesque dining areas.
Typical Mexican specialties—chicken mole, a dozen types of tacos, and
much more—are prepared in open kitchens. There's jarocho music from
Veracruz and the full gamut of Mexican drinks, including *pulque,* a
classic alcoholic Aztec beverage made from the maguey cactus. The small
bullring is the forum for *novilleros,* or young bullfighters just beginning their careers, during the season (about May through September).
Breakfast starts at 8 AM, and lunch is served until 8 PM. ⊠ *Av. Insurgentes Sur 4003, Col. Tlalpán, a 30–40-min drive south of Zona Rosa,*
☎ *5573–4344. AE, DC, MC, V. No dinner.*

$$–$$$ ✕ Fonda El Refugio. Since it opened in 1954, this Zona Rosa restaurant in a converted two-story town house has served the best dishes
from each major region of the country. Atmosphere is casual but elegant in the intimate colonial-decor dining rooms (the one downstairs
is the prettiest). Along with a varied regular menu, there's a daily selection of appetizers and entrées; you might find a mole made with pumpkin seeds or *albóndigas en chile chipotle* (meatballs in chipotle sauce).
Try the refreshing *aguas* (fresh-fruit and seed juices) with your meal
and the *café de olla* (clove-flavored coffee sweetened with brown
sugar) after dessert. ⊠ *Liverpool 166, Zona Rosa,* ☎ *5207–2732 or
5525–8128,* ﬀX *5207–8802. AE, DC, MC, V. No dinner Sun.*

$$–$$$ ✕ Isadora. Some of Mexico City's most inventive cooking takes place
in this converted private house in Polanco. The three smallish dining
rooms have deco elements and vibrant paintings on display. The management sponsors cooking festivals, and every three months the kitchen
produces dishes from a different country. The basic menu changes regularly, and includes Mexican food fests that may feature a superb *sopa
de lima* (lime soup) and beef fillet dressed in corn fungus sauce (huitlacoche). The focus on the set menu is seafood: don't miss the *calamares a los tres chiles secos* (squid flavored with three dried chilies) or
the white tuna with artichokes. You'll be delighted to wrap up with a
teardrop chocolate mousse. ⊠ *Moliere 50, Col. Polanco,* ☎ *5280–1586,*
ﬀX *5280–7372. Jacket and tie. AE, DC, MC, V. Closed Sun.*

$$–$$$ ✕ El Tajín. Named after El Tajín Pyramid in Veracruz, this eatery serves
innovative Mexican cooking that has taken the metropolis by storm.
El Tajín adds zest and style to many well-known dishes: dazzling main
dishes include soft-shell crab accented by sesame seeds and a tad of
chipotle. This lovely restaurant is hidden behind the functional facade
of the Veracruz Cultural Center in Colonia Coyoacán. Ancient Huastecan faces grinning from a splashing fountain add a bit of levity to the

dining experience. ⊠ *Miguel Angel de Quevedo 687, Col. Coyoacán,* ☎ *5659–4447 or 5659–5759. AE, MC, V. No dinner.*

$$ ✕ **Los Almendros.** If you can't make it to the Yucatán, try the peninsula's unusual and lively food at one of this restaurant's two locations. If the spacious, cool white interior and bubbling fountain don't transport you, then the habañero chilies, red onions, and other native Yucatecan ingredients will. Traditional dishes, such as a refreshing lime soup or *frijol con puerco* (tender pork pieces with black beans), share the menu with impossible-to-pronounce Maya cuisine. Especially worth trying is the *pescado tikinxic*—white fish in a mild red marinade of achiote seed and juice of bitter orange. This is a good place to sample a wide array of fine tequila, served with sliced jicama and a tangy tomato-juice chaser called sangrita. ⊠ *Campos Elíseos 164, Col. Polanco,* ☎ *5531–6646. Insurgentes Sur 1759,* ☎ *5663–5151.*

$$ ✕ **Fonda del Recuerdo.** A popular family restaurant, the *fonda* (mod-
★   est restaurant) also has a solid reputation among tourists and anyone celebrating anything. Every day from 1 to 10, five lively jarocho and mariachi groups provide festive music. The place made its name with its fish and seafood platters from the gulf state of Veracruz, and the house special is huachinango *à la Veracruzano* (a whole red snapper in a succulent, mildly spiced sauce of tomato, chopped onion, and olives). Sharing its fame is the *torito*, a potent drink made from sugarcane liquor, and exotic tropical fruit juices. Meat from the kitchen's own *parillas* (grills) is always first-rate. Portions are huge, but if you have room for dessert, try *crepas de cajeta al tequila* (milk-caramel crepes lightly sauced with tequila). ⊠ *Bahía de las Palmas 37, Col. Veronica Anzures,* ☎ *5260–7339 or 5260–1292. Reservations essential. AE, DC, MC, V.*

$$ ✕ **Los Girasoles.** Two prominent Mexico City society columnists own this downtown spot. Los Girasoles (which means sunflowers) is on a lovely old square in a restored three-story colonial home and serves light, tasty, and innovative nueva cocina Mexicana. Meat, fish, and seafood dishes are blended with exotic herbs and spices. There are also pre-Hispanic delicacies such as *escamoles* (ant roe), *gusanos de maguey* (chilied worms), and *mini chapulines* (tiny crispy fried grasshoppers). Among the desserts are such creations as *nieve de guanábana* (sour-sop sorbet) and *nieve de tequila* (an original tequila sorbet). One of the most attractive places for dining is the room overlooking the square. ⊠ *Plaza Manuel Tolsa on Xicoténcatl 1,* ☎ *5510–0630 or 5510–3281,* FAX *5510–0630. AE, MC, V. No dinner Sun.*

$$ ✕ **Los Irabien.** This beautiful dining area filled with plants and the owner's impressive art collection is a worthwhile stop for foodies and culture vultures. Featuring Mexican traditional and international cuisine, the *filete de res en salsa de fresas* triumphs as a blend of beef with peppered strawberry sauce. Los Irabien is one of the city's breakfast spots par excellence—tempting you with *huevos de codorniz huitzilopochtli*—quail eggs with tortilla in a zucchini-blossom sauce. ⊠ *Av. de la Paz 45, Col. San Angel,* ☎ *5616–0014. Jacket and tie. AE, DC, MC, V. No dinner Sun.*

$$ ✕ **Tecla.** This see-and-be-seen eatery is an established (five-year) vet-
★   eran of Mexico City's growing nueva cocina Mexicana scene. Named after an old-fashioned typesetting key, the restaurant's locations and newsprint collage set a hip tone. The appetizers are especially intriguing, including squash flowers stuffed with goat cheese in a chipotle sauce and a spicy crab-stuffed chili. The house-special beef dish, *filete Tecla,* shows a flair for sauces, in this case combining Roquefort with huitlacoche. Best of all, the prices are still unpretentious. ⊠ *Moliere 56, Col. Polanco,* ☎ *5282–0010;* ⊠ *Durango 186A, Col. Roma,* ☎ *5525–4920. AE, MC, V. No dinner Sun.*

$ ✗ **Bajío.** Decorated in bright colors, Bajío attracts Mexican families and is run by vivacious Carmen "Titita" Ramírez—a chef and culinary expert who has been featured in various food and lifestyle magazines. The restaurant specializes in classic Mexican regional cooking. The 30-ingredient mole, a Bajío signature dish, is to die for; also excellent are *empanadas de platano rellenos de frijol* (tortilla turnovers filled with bananas and beans) and *carnitas* (roast pork). You may have to go a little off the beaten track to get here, but it's worth it. ✉ *Cuitláhuac 2709, Col. Azcapotzalco, about a 20-min ride north of Zona Rosa,* ☎ *5341–9889. AE, MC, V. No dinner.*

$ ✗ **Café de Tacuba.** An essential breakfast, lunch, dinner, or snack stop downtown, this Mexican classic has been charming all comers since it opened in 1912 in a section of an old convent. At the entrance to the atmospheric main dining room are huge 18th-century oil paintings depicting the invention of *mole poblano,* a complex sauce with a variety of chilies and chocolate that was created by the nuns in the Santa Rosa Convent of Puebla. Along with mole poblano, look for delicious tamales made fresh every morning. There are also pastries galore. A student group dressed in medieval capes and hats serenades Thursday–Sunday 3:30–11:30; mariachis play during dinner on other days. ✉ *Tacuba 28, Col. Centro,* ☎ *5518–4950. AE, MC, V.*

$ ✗ **Casa de la Sirena.** Dining is picturesque here at the foot of the Templo Major ruins, which supplied some of the building blocks for this 16th-century mansion. A wandering Spanish monk named the home after a mermaid (*sirena*) carved into the facade of a nearby building. The atmospheric second-floor terrace is within sight and sound of numerous Indian dances honoring the spirits of the crumbling Aztec temples below. At night, it's utterly romantic dining under the stars. The cuisine is nouvelle with such specialties as Cornish hen in mango mole sauce and a plethora of other innovative meat and fish dishes. If you've never tried it, order a smooth tequila liqueur as an after-dinner digestive. ✉ *Guatemala 32, Zócalo,* ☎ *5704–3225,* FAX *5704–3465. AE, MC, V. No dinner Sun.*

$ ✗ **Las Cazuelas.** Traditional Mexican cooking at its best is the word
★ at one of the most famous of the capital's fondas. The large dining area is brightened by hand-painted chairs from Michoacán and blue-and-white table linens. Ideal Mexican appetizers to share are *carnitas rancheras* (pork morsels in red sauce). The tortilla soup, with its dash of *pasilla* chili and bits of cheese, makes another excellent starter. Main courses center on various moles or the piquant sesame-flavored pipián sauce with pork or chicken. Finish with a café de olla and a domestic brandy. ✉ *San Antonio 143, at Illinois, Col. Napoles,* ☎ *5563–4118. AE, MC, V. No dinner.*

$ ✗ **Fonda Chon.** This unpretentious family-style restaurant, deep in a downtown working-class neighborhood, is famed for its pre-Hispanic Mexican dishes. A knowledge of zoology, Spanish, and Nahuatl helps in making sense of a menu that takes in a gamut of ingredients—no processed foods among them—from throughout the republic. *Escamoles de hormiga* (red-ant roe), 97% protein, is known as the "caviar of Mexico" for its costliness, but you may have to acquire a taste for it. Among the exotic dishes are armadillo in mango sauce, fillet of wild boar, crackling crisp fried grasshoppers with guacamole and ostrich in plum and tequila sauce. The zapote (a sticky, sweet fruit) flan is also worth a try. ✉ *Regina 160, near La Merced market, Col. Centro,* ☎ *5542–0873. Reservations not accepted. MC, V. Closed Sun. No dinner.*

$ ✗ **Hosteria de Santo Domingo.** This genteel institution near downtown's Plaza Santo Domingo has been serving *authentico* colonial dishes for more than a century in an atmospheric late-19th-century town house. Feast on tried-and-true favorites such as stuffed cactus paddles, thousand-flower soup, pot roast, and a stunning array of quesadillas. Among what may be the best homemade Mexican desserts in town are the comforting flan and *arroz con leche* (rice pudding). The place is open for breakfast and is always full at lunch. Get there early to avoid standing in line. ⊠ *Belisario Dominguez 72, Col. Centro,* ☎ *5510–1434 or 5526–5276. AE, DC, MC, V. Closes 9:30 PM Sun.*

Spanish

$$ ✕ **Loyola.** A Basque tour de force, the ample menu with unpronounceable but delicious items includes *kokotxas* (fish cheeks), tapas, black rice simmered in squid ink, oxtail, and many other such regional delicacies. Great salads and wines are another welcome feature. Courteous service surrounded by stained glass, Basque coats of arms, and the cozy hum of conversation from contented connoisseurs make this an excellent and authentic dining experience. ⊠ *Aristóteles 239, Col. Polanco,* ☎ *5250–6756 or 5250–9097. AE, MC, V. No dinner.*

$$ ✕ **Tezka.** This Zona Rosa restaurant specializing in nueva cocina Basque was created by famous Basque chef Arzac, who transposed many of his best dishes to Mexico from his restaurant in San Sebastían, Spain. (It's often packed with a Spanish clientele.) Feast on yellow tuna in a fluffy sweet and spicy sauce, or liver prepared with beer, green pepper, and malt. The starters are exquisite, both to look at and taste; the *caldo de xipiron* (broth of baby squid) is the best in the city. There are tempting and original desserts, and the servings are small enough that you'll have room. A decent list of Spanish wines includes Cune, Vina Ardanza, and Reserva 904. ⊠ *Royal Hotel, Amberes 78, at Liverpool,* ☎ *5228–9918,* ℻ *5514–3330. AE, DC, MC, V. Closed Sun. No dinner Sat.*

$–$$ ✕ **Meson El Cid.** This charming *meson* (tavern) exudes an atmosphere of Old Spain. During the week, classic dishes such as paella, spring lamb, suckling baby pig, and Cornish hens with truffles keep customers happy, but on Saturday night this place really comes into its own with a medieval banquet. The fun unfolds with a procession of costumed waiters carrying huge trays of steaming hot viands. A caged cat—the grandson of the first feline to play this role, the waiters will tell you—heads the parade as in olden days, when a king's food was tested for poisoning by letting a cat nose around in it first (cats being keen enough not to touch the stuff if it had been tampered with). Entertainment is provided by a student singing group dressed in medieval Spanish capes and hats. ⊠ *Humboldt 61, Col. Centro,* ☎ *5521–1940, 5512–8881, or 5512–7629. AE, MC, V. No dinner Sun.*

Vegetarian

$ ✕ **Las Fuentes.** About three blocks north of the U.S. Embassy on Calle Río Tiber, Las Fuentes has a huge salad bar and a range of soups and keeps its prices low. A sample meal might be tacos stuffed with carrots and potatoes accompanied by apple salad and followed by whole-grain cookies made with honey. Don't be put off by the sterile Formica tables. The office and embassy workers who pack the place at lunchtime come for the food rather than the ambience. ⊠ *Río Panuco 127, at Calle Río Tiber, Col. Cuauhtémoc,* ☎ *5525–0843. MC, V.*

LODGING

Although the city is huge and spread out, most hotels are within a relatively manageable group of neighborhoods. Stylish Colonia Polanco and Bosque de Chapultepec are on the west side of the city. Paseo de la Reforma runs from Chapultepec, northeast through "midtown," and intersects with Avenida Juárez at the beginning of the downtown area.

Mexico City Lodging

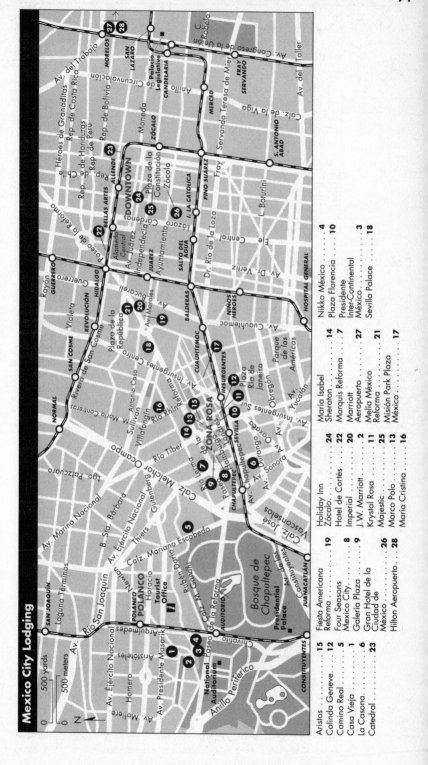

Aristos	15
Calinda Geneve	12
Camino Real	5
Casa Vieja	1
La Casona	6
Catedral	23
Fiesta Americana Reforma	19
Four Seasons	8
Mexico City	9
Galería Plaza	9
Gran Hotel de la Ciudad de México	26
Hilton Aeropuerto	28
Holiday Inn Zócalo	24
Hotel de Cortés	22
Imperial	20
J.W. Marriott	2
Krystal Rosa	11
Majestic	25
Marco Polo	13
Maria Cristina	16
Maria Isabel Sheraton	14
Marquis Reforma	7
Marriott Aeropuerto	27
Melia México Reforma	21
Misión Park Plaza México	17
Nikko México	4
Plaza Florencia	10
Presidente Inter-Continental México	3
Sevilla Palace	18

Juárez becomes Calle Madero, which continues east to the downtown historic district and its very core, the Zócalo. The Zona Rosa, replete with boutiques, cafés, restaurants, and nightspots, is literally across Reforma (south), in the western midtown area.

Business travelers tend to fill up deluxe hotels during the week; some major hotels discount their weekend rates. If you reserve through the toll-free reservations numbers, you may find rates as much as 50% off during special promotions. You can expect hotels in the $$$ and $$$$ categories to have purified water, air-conditioning, cable TV, radio, minibars, and extended (often 24-hour) room service.

CATEGORY	COST*
$$$$	over $250
$$$	$175–$250
$$	$110–$175
$	under $110

All prices are for a standard double room, excluding service charge and tax.

Colonia Polanco and Bosque de Chapultepec

$$$$ 🏨 **Casa Vieja.** This classically elegant, sumptuously decorated Colonia Polanco mansion is the dream-come-true of a local businessman who took his love of things Mexican and expressed it in his all-suites (one and two bedrooms) hotel. Tastefully selected folk art, handsomely hand-carved furniture, and gilded wall trimmings complement patios and splashing fountains. Lively Mexican colors are a light-hearted touch in the 10 suites, all of them different. All have a full kitchen, fax machine, CD and video-cassette players, hot tub, and picture window overlooking an inside garden. The hotel's Mexican restaurant is named after its huge floor-to-ceiling *Arbol de la Vida (Tree of Life)* sculpture. Rates include breakfast. ✉ *Eugenio Sue 45, Col. Polanco, 11560,* ☎ *5282–0067,* FAX *5281–3780,* WEB *www.casavieja.com. 10 suites. Restaurant, bar, concierge, free parking. AE, MC, V.*

$$$$ 🏨 **J. W. Marriott.** In posh Colonia Polanco, this hotel was designed as a boutique property with personalized service and small, clubby public areas; nothing overwhelms here. Rooms are done with plenty of wood and warm colors but are otherwise unremarkable in decor. Each has a work desk with an outlet for a personal computer and modem. The hotel has the best-equipped business center in the city, open 24 hours. Executive floors come with extra amenities. ✉ *Andrés Bello 29, at Campos Elíseos, Col. Polanco, 11560,* ☎ *5282–8888 or 800/228–9290,* FAX *5282–8811,* WEB *www.marriott.com. 311 rooms. 2 restaurants, bar, coffee shop, pool, exercise room, business services, meeting room, travel services, car rental. AE, DC, MC, V.*

$$$$ 🏨 **Nikko México.** Part of the Japanese Nikko chain, this glistening, 42-floor high-rise occupies a prime Polanco position: adjacent to Bosque de Chapultepec, just a five-minute walk from the Anthropology Museum. It has signage and menus in Japanese, English, and Spanish. Although it's the second-largest hotel in the city and has marvelous views from the top floor, its standard rooms are a little claustrophobic; executive floors have better rooms and extra facilities. Four top restaurants excel in their gastronomic specialties: Les Célébrités, Teppan Grill and Benkay (both Japanese), and El Jardín (international). ✉ *Campos Elíseos 204, 11560,* ☎ *5280–1111, 01–800/908–8800, or 800/ 645–5687,* FAX *5280–9191,* WEB *www.nikkohotels.com. 724 rooms, 24 suites. 4 restaurants, 2 bars, indoor pool, 4 tennis courts, gym, jogging, dance club, business services, meeting room, travel services, car rental. AE, DC, MC, V.*

$$$ 🏨 **Camino Real.** About the size of Teotihuacán's Pyramid of the Sun,
★ this sleek, minimalist, bright pink and yellow, 8-acre city-within-a-city was designed by Mexico's modern master, Legorreta. A firm favorite with dignitaries whose portraits you'll see splashed immodestly about the reception area, the Camino Real really is as regal as you can hope to get in Mexico, and stylish to boot. Impressive works of art embellishing the endless corridors and lounges include Rufino Tamayo's mural *Man Facing Infinity* and a Calder sculpture. The fifth-floor executive level has 100 extra-large guest rooms with special amenities. Fouquet's de Paris restaurant holds culinary events, and the airy Azulejos serves Mexican fare and Sunday buffet brunches. ⊠ *Mariano Escobedo 700, Col. Polanco, 11590,* ☎ *5263–8888 or 800/722–6466,* FAX *5263–8898,* WEB *www.caminoreal.com/mexico. 678 rooms, 36 suites. 3 restaurants, 3 bars, pool, 4 tennis courts, gym, business services. AE, DC, MC, V.*

$$–$$$ 🏨 **Presidente Inter-Continental México.** This 42-story Inter-Continental, adjacent to Bosque de Chapultepec in Colonia Polanco, has a dramatic five-story atrium lobby—a hollow pyramid of balconies—with music performed daily at the lively lobby bar. Rooms are spacious, and all have work areas. On clear days, the top two floors have views of the nearby snowcapped volcanoes. The executive floors have a lounge, concierge, and extra amenities. A number of smart stores and six eateries are on the premises, including branches of Maxim's de Paris and Au Pied de Cochon. ⊠ *Campos Elíseos 218, 11560,* ☎ *5327–7700 or 800/344–0548,* FAX *5327–7730,* WEB *www.interconti.com. 629 rooms, 32 suites. 6 restaurants, coffee shop, lobby lounge, exercise room, baby-sitting, business services, meeting room, travel services, car rental, parking (fee). AE, DC, MC, V.*

Zona Rosa

$$$ 🏨 **Galería Plaza.** Part of the Westin Hotel deluxe chain, this ultramodern
★ property is on a quiet street in elegant Zona Rosa—ideal for shopping, enjoying nightlife, and dining out. Standard rooms are relatively small, but service and facilities are faultless. Rooms on the executive floor, where a special concierge desk provides personalized service and easy checkout, are larger. Other advantages include voice mail in all rooms, a heated rooftop pool with sundeck, a secure underground parking lot, and a 24-hour restaurant, which has a popular buffet breakfast. ⊠ *Hamburgo 195, at Varsovia, 06600,* ☎ *5208–0370 or 800/228–3000,* FAX *5207–5867,* WEB *www.westin.com. 420 rooms, 19 suites. 3 restaurants, lobby lounge, room service, pool, exercise room, concierge, travel services, parking (fee). AE, DC, MC, V.*

$$ 🏨 **Calinda Geneve.** A Quality Inn, referred to locally as El Génova, this five-story 1906 hotel is fitted with traditional colonial-style carved-wood chairs and tables in the pleasant lobby; guest rooms are smallish but comfortable. The attractive Salón Jardín has been taken over by the popular Sanborns restaurant chain. ⊠ *Londres 130, 06600,* ☎ *5211–0071 or 800/228–5151,* FAX *5207–4160,* WEB *www.hotelescalinda.com.mx. 300 rooms. Restaurant, bar, café, room service, exercise room, coin laundry, business services. AE, DC, MC, V.*

$$ 🏨 **La Casona.** This charming 30-room hotel is an elegant, understated former mansion, registered as an artistic monument by Mexico's Institute of Fine Arts. Filled with sunny patios and sitting rooms, the hotel is finely decorated with antiques, hardwood floors, and accessories in the spirit of the days of the Porfiriato, when the house was built. No two rooms are alike, but all have hair dryers, fluffy bathrobes and slippers, and good-size bathtubs. There's a small restaurant that serves old-style country cooking. The two-story hotel building, with its demure

salmon facade, looks out on a tree-lined street in Colonia Roma, about a 10-minute walk south of the Zona Rosa and in easy reach of museums, restaurants, and Paseo de la Reforma. A Continental breakfast is included in the price of a room. ✉ *Durango 280, at Cozumel,* ☎ *5286–3001 or 800/223–5652,* FAX *5211–0871,* WEB *www.srs-worldhotels. com/mexico/mexico_city/hotel_mexcas.html. 30 rooms. Restaurant, bar, room service, exercise room. AE, DC, MC, V.*

$$ 🏨 **Krystal Rosa.** Part of the Mexican Krystal Hotel chain, this superbly run high-rise hotel is in the heart of the Zona Rosa and has an excellent view of the city from the rooftop pool terrace. There is a stylish lobby cocktail lounge, a bar with local entertainers, and a restaurant, Hacienda del Mortero, that serves excellent classic Mexican cuisine. Two club floors have VIP check-in and service, complimentary Continental buffet breakfast, and rooms with extra amenities. ✉ *Liverpool 155, 06600,* ☎ *5228–9928,* FAX *5228–9929,* WEB *www.krystal.com.mx. 267 rooms, 35 suites. 2 restaurants, 2 bars, pool, concierge, business services, parking (fee). AE, DC, MC, V.*

$$ 🏨 **Marco Polo.** Ultramodern and intimate, the central Zona Rosa all-
★ suites Marco Polo has the amenities and outstanding personalized service often associated with a small European hotel. All rooms have climate control, cable TV, FM radio, minibar, and work desks; some suites have hot tubs. North-facing top-floor rooms have excellent views of Paseo de la Reforma and the Angel monument—the four penthouse suites have terraces—and the U.S. Embassy is close by. In the street-level restaurant called Amberes 27, you can listen to sophisticated piano music evenings 7–9. ✉ *Amberes 27, 06600,* ☎ *5207–1893,* FAX *5533–3727,* WEB *www.marcopolo.com.mx. 60 suites, 4 penthouse suites, 9 long-stay apartments. Restaurant, bar, business services. AE, DC, MC, V.*

$$ 🏨 **Plaza Florencia.** This modern hotel is on a busy avenue that borders the Zona Rosa. The lobby's heavy furniture and dark colors make it feel more like a lodge, in which guests relax after a day of exploring. Rooms are well furnished in hotel-modern style—cheerfully decorated, and soundproofed against the location's heavy traffic noise; higher floors have views of the Angel monument. Some large family suites are available. All rooms have air-conditioning, heat, color TV, and a phone. A business center offers fax, copy, computer, and Internet-access services. ✉ *Florencia 61, 06600,* ☎ *5242–4700,* FAX *5242–4785,* WEB *www.florencia.web.com.mx. 130 rooms, 12 suites. Restaurant, bar, coffee shop, business services. AE, DC, MC, V.*

$ 🏨 **Aristos.** On bustling Paseo de la Reforma a few blocks east of the U.S. Embassy and near the Mexican Stock Exchange, this 15-story Zona Rosa–fringe hotel wears its age well (it was one of the first luxury hotels in the area). Rooms are well supplied and attractively decorated in shades of peach and mauve, with brass and wood accents. The business center has a bilingual staff and a message service. ✉ *Paseo de la Reforma 276, 06600,* ☎ *5211–0112,* FAX *5514–3543,* WEB *www.aristoshotels. com.mx. 320 rooms, 25 suites. 4 restaurants, bar, beauty salon, sauna, exercise room, travel services, parking (fee). AE, DC, MC, V.*

$ 🏨 **Misión Park Plaza México.** A part of the Misión chain, this very comfortable hotel a few blocks from the Zona Rosa's eastern end is well placed for shopping and sightseeing. Mirrors, good light, and like-new bathrooms make the rooms more pleasant; all have air-conditioning and color TV with U.S. channels. Sixteen rooms have been converted into executive units that have work areas, and Internet connection has been added to an office off the lobby for guests' use. Staff is friendly and accommodating, and breakfast is included in the room rates. ✉ *Napoles 62, 06600,* ☎ *5533–0535,* FAX *5533–1589,* WEB *www.hotelesmision.com.mx. 50 rooms. Coffee shop, lobby lounge, exercise room, meeting room. AE, MC, V.*

Midtown and along the Reforma

$$$$ ⊞ **Four Seasons Mexico City.** This is—perhaps by definition—one of
★ the most luxurious hotels in the capital and accordingly has won the
AAA Five Diamond Award three years running. Surrounding a traditional courtyard with a fountain, the eight-story building was modeled after the 18th-century Iturbide Palace downtown. Half the rooms
overlook the lush inner courtyard garden. Huge bowls of flowers and
lovely European furnishings fill the spacious marble lobby. Geared for
business travelers, rooms have data ports and all the amenities you'd
expect at a Four Seasons hotel. There's also a boardroom on the
premises and a full-service business center with even a reference library.
A well-stocked tequila bar off the lobby is a perfect pre-dinner option.
Excellent cultural tours of the city are offered free to guests on weekends. ⊠ *Paseo de la Reforma 500, 06600,* ☎ *5230–1818 or 800/332–
3442,* FAX *5230–1808,* WEB *www.fourseasons.com. 200 rooms, 40 suites.
2 restaurants, bar, in-room data ports, pool, exercise room, gym, business services, meeting room. AE, DC, MC, V.*

$$$$ ⊞ **María Isabel Sheraton.** Don Antenor Patiño, the Bolivian "Tin
King," inaugurated this Mexico City classic in 1969 and named it after
his granddaughter, socialite Isabel Goldsmith. The hotel is constantly
being remodeled, but the glistening brown marble and art deco details
in the lobby and other public areas remain. All guest and public rooms
are impeccably maintained; penthouse suites in the 22-story tower section are extra-spacious and exceptionally luxurious. The location—across
from the Angel monument and the Zona Rosa, with Sanborns next door
and the U.S. Embassy a half block away—is prime. It has the largest
conference room (for 1,500) in town. ⊠ *Paseo de la Reforma 325,
06500,* ☎ *5242–5555 or 800/334–8484,* FAX *5207–0684,* WEB *www.
sheraton.com. 681 rooms, 74 suites. 3 restaurants, 2 bars, room service, pool, massage, sauna, gym, concierge floor, business services, meeting room, parking (fee). AE, DC, MC, V.*

$$$$ ⊞ **Marquis Reforma.** This plush, privately owned member of the Lead-
★ ing Hotels of the World, and 1999 recipient of the Five Stars and Five
Diamonds Award given by the Mexican government, is within walking distance of the Zona Rosa. It has a striking pink-stone and curved-
glass art nouveau facade, and its seventh-floor suites afford picture-perfect
views of the Castillo de Chapultepec. The elegant lobby is fitted in a
classic European style, with paintings, sculpture, and palatial furniture.
Guest-room furniture and decor are art deco–inspired. The La Jolla
restaurant serves Mexican cuisine. The fully staffed corporate center
has state-of-the-art computer services, and guest-room phones feature
a second plug for your modem. The health club has hard-to-find holis-
tic, stress-busting massages. ⊠ *Paseo de la Reforma 465, 06500,* ☎
5211–3600; 800/235–2387; 877/818–5011 in Canada, FAX *5211–5561,*
WEB *www.hotelmarquisrsma.com.mx. 133 rooms, 84 suites. 2 restaurants, bar, in-room data ports, gym, business services, meeting room.
AE, DC, MC, V.*

$$$ ⊞ **Melía México Reforma.** Perched at the junction of Paseo de la Re-
forma, Juárez, and Bucareli—convenient to downtown, the Zona
Rosa, and the Stock Exchange—this flashy 22-story smoked-glass be-
hemoth looks quite spectacular in its otherwise nondescript sur-
roundings. It touts the ultimate in high-tech amenities for business
travelers: a stock-market indicator, computers, cellular phones, and sec-
retarial, translation, messenger, and shipping services. Executive rooms
have PC- and fax-modem outlets and three telephone lines. Public
areas include a coffee bar with 20 java concoctions, an oyster-and-jazz
bar, and a French restaurant. The hotel also has limousine rental, a phar-
macy, and boutiques. ⊠ *Paseo de la Reforma 1, Col. Tabacalera,*

06030, ☎ 5128–5000 or 800/336–3542, FAX 5128–5050, WEB *www. solmelia.com. 424 rooms, 30 suites. 2 restaurants, 2 bars, in-room data ports, room service, beauty salon, shops, business services, travel services, car rental. AE, DC, MC, V.*

$$ 🏨 **Fiesta Americana Reforma.** This immense hotel, built in the 1970s by a Mexican chain that billed it a "bar with a hotel," may be past its prime, but the business travelers and large groups that parade in and out of the lobby still keep it lively. There isn't much Mexican atmosphere except for the live Mexican music in the lobby bar, but there's something to say for being able to get a good tan on the sundeck, work out in the gym, and choose from two restaurants, one of which offers breakfast and lunch buffets. ⊠ *Paseo de la Reforma 80, 06600, ☎ 5140–4100 or 800/343–7821, FAX 5140–4140, WEB www.fiestamericana.com. 610 rooms. 2 restaurants, 2 bars, exercise room, business services, free parking. AE, DC, MC, V.*

$$ 🏨 **Sevilla Palace.** This glistening modern showplace has five panoramic elevators for its 23 floors, a covered rooftop pool with hot tub, a health club, a top-floor supper club with entertainment, a terraced rooftop lounge with a city view, and convention halls with capacities of up to 1,000. It's near the Columbus traffic circle and attracts lots of tourists from Spain. ⊠ *Paseo de la Reforma 105, 06030, ☎ 5705–2800 or 800/732–9488, FAX 5703–1521, WEB www.sevillapalace.com.mx. 413 rooms. 2 restaurants, 3 bars, pool, gym, nightclub, meeting room. AE, MC, V.*

$ 🏨 **Imperial.** The Imperial occupies a stately late-19th-century European-style building right on the Reforma alongside the Columbus Monument. Quiet elegance and personal service are keynotes of this privately owned property. The hotel's Restaurant Gaudí has an understated, tony atmosphere and serves Continental cuisine with some classic Spanish selections. ⊠ *Paseo de la Reforma 64, 06600, ☎ 5705–4911, FAX 5703–3122, WEB www.hotelimperial.com.mx. 50 rooms, 10 junior suites, 5 master suites. Restaurant, bar, café, in-room safes, business services, meeting room, travel services. AE, DC, MC, V.*

$ 🏨 **María Cristina.** Full of old-world charm, this Spanish colonial–style
★ gem is a Mexico City classic. Impeccably maintained since it was built in 1937, the building surrounds a delightful garden courtyard—the setting for its El Retiro bar. Three tastefully decorated apartment-style master suites come complete with hot tubs. All rooms have safes. Located in a quiet residential setting near Parque Sullivan, the hotel is a block from the Paseo de la Reforma and close to the Zona Rosa. ⊠ *Río Lerma 31, 06500, ☎ 5566–9688, FAX 5566–9194. 140 rooms, 8 suites. Bar, in-room safes, room service, beauty salon, travel services. MC, V.*

Downtown

$$ 🏨 **Majestic.** The atmospheric, colonial-style Majestic, built in 1937, is perfectly located if you're interested in exploring the historic downtown: on the Zócalo at the corner of Madero. This Best Western property is also perfect for viewing the Independence Day (September 16) celebrations, which draw hundreds of thousands of people to this square, and many people reserve a room a year in advance of the festivities. Rooms are decorated in the style of the 1940s and have no air-conditioning but are kept cool by high ceilings and the fact that you are in a high-mountain city; each has a remote-control color TV and a minibar. Although the front units have balconies and a charming view, they can be noisy with car traffic until about 11 at night. Service is efficient and courteous. The terrace of the seventh-floor La Terraza restaurant—which serves international and Mexican specialties—has marvelous panoramas of the Zócalo. Live Mexican music accompanies the Sunday buffet (1–5). The fun El Campanario piano bar welcomes anyone who wants to make a singing debut, and has become a favorite with locals. ⊠ *Madero 73, 06000, ☎ 5521–8600 or 800/528–1234,* 🖷 *5512–6262,* 🕸 *www.majestic.com.mx. 85 rooms. Restaurant, bar, coffee shop, travel services. AE, DC, MC, V.*

$ 🏨 **Catedral.** In the heart of historic downtown, this refurbished older
★ hotel is a bargain, with many of the amenities of the more upscale hotels at less than half the price. Public areas sparkle with marble and glass. Guest rooms are done in a generic but cheerful contemporary fashion, and all have color TVs (local channels only) and phones; suites have king-size beds, in-room safes, and hot tubs. You can get a room with a view of the namesake Catedral, but keep in mind that its bells chime every 15 minutes late into the night. Service is friendly, the hotel restaurant is excellent, and El Retiro bar attracts a largely Mexican clientele to hear live Latin music. ⊠ *Donceles 95, 06000, ☎ 5512–8581,* 🖷 *5512–4344,* 🕸 *www.hotelcatedral.com.mx. 120 rooms, 8 suites. Restaurant, bar, coffee shop, room service, nightclub, laundry service, dry cleaning, business services, travel services, free parking. AE, MC, V.*

$ 🏨 **Gran Hotel de la Ciudad de México.** Ensconced in a former 19th-century department store, this more traditional hotel has contemporary rooms. Its central location—adjacent to the Zócalo and near the Templo Mayor—makes it a good choice for local sightseeing. Its distinctive Belle Epoque lobby—with a striking stained-glass Tiffany dome, chandeliers, gilded birdcages, and 19th-century wrought-iron elevators—is worth a visit in its own right. The Mirador breakfast restaurant overlooks the Zócalo. The Del Centro restaurant-bar run by Delmónicos is one of Mexico City's best—a great place to stop for a drink while exploring nearby. The hotel has been undergoing a long-term, gradual refurbishing; be sure to request a renovated room that does not look out onto a brick wall. ⊠ *16 de Septiembre 82, 06000,* ☎ 🖷 *5510–4040. 124 rooms. 2 restaurants, bar, concierge, travel services, parking (fee). AE, DC, MC, V.*

$ 🏨 **Holiday Inn Zócalo.** This hotel couldn't have a better location—on the Zócalo and close to a gaggle of museums, restaurants, and historic buildings. It's actually in a historic building that dates back to colonial times. The interior is modern and has the feel of a Holiday Inn. Although the glass-front lobby lacks personality, there's more flavor to the terrace restaurant, which is set with old-fashioned wrought-iron tables and has an amazing view of the Metropolitan Cathedral and National Palace. Rooms are small but well-equipped with closet safe, coffeemaker, air-conditioning and heat, iron and ironing board, and bathroom amenities. All suites have data ports; five have Jacuzzi bathtubs. ⊠ *5 de Mayo at Zócalo, Centro Histórico, 06000, ☎ 5521–2121 or 800/465–4329,* 🖷 *5521–2122,* 🕸 *www.holidayinnzocalo.com.mx. 100 rooms, 15 suites. 2 restaurants, bar, in-room safes, room service, exercise room, meeting room, travel services, parking (fee). AE, MC, V.*

$ 🏨 **Hotel de Cortés.** This delightful small hotel, managed by Best Western, is housed in a 1780 colonial building that's also a national monument. Rooms, in colonial decor, are small and simply furnished; they open onto an enclosed central courtyard. Two comfortable soundproof suites overlook Alameda Park across the busy street. A restaurant also looks onto the park, and a friendly bar opens to the tree-shaded central courtyard and fountain, a lovely setting for tea or cocktails. Friday evening at 7:30, there's a Mexican folkloric show with music and dance. The Franz Mayer Museum is just a block away, and it's an easy walk to Palacio de Bellas Artes. Loyal guests reserve many months in advance. ⊠ *Av. Hidalgo 85, 06000, ☎ 5518–2184 or 800/334–7234,* 🖷 *5512–1863,* 🕸 *www.albec.net.mx/hoteldecortes. 19 rooms, 10 suites. Restaurant, bar. AE, DC, MC, V.*

Airport

$$$ 🏨 **Hilton Aeropuerto.** This luxury oasis opened in 1998, marking the arrival of the only hotel *inside* the airport. Cool and compact, with a distinctive gray marble lobby and a wide-angle view from the bar of landing planes, the hotel feels like a private club with its subdued elegance and attentive but unobtrusive staff. Rooms come with full working gear for a traveling executive: two phone lines, modem connection, ergonomic chairs, and coffeemaker. Rooms have four different views—airstrip, street, atrium, or garden (bamboo plants set along a concrete ledge). All units wrap around one floor. ⊠ *Benito Juárez International Airport, international terminal, 15520,* ☎ *5133–0505 or 800/445–8667,* FAX *5133–0500,* WEB *www.hilton.com. 129 rooms. Restaurant, bar, in-room data ports, exercise room, business services, meeting room, parking (fee). AE, DC, MC, V.*

$$ 🏨 **Marriott Aeropuerto.** Just over a short covered footbridge from the airport terminal is this deluxe hotel that's sleek and modern as well as comfortable. There's a pool on the eighth floor. Even if you're only between flights and don't overnight, you can sit in one of the overstuffed chairs in the soothing lobby to get away from the frantic energy of the airport, or catch a meal in the restaurant. ⊠ *Benito Juárez International Airport, 15520,* ☎ *5133–0033 or 800/228–9290,* FAX *5133–0030,* WEB *www.marriott.com. 600 rooms, 8 suites. Restaurant, bar, coffee shop, pool, sauna, gym, meeting room, car rental, free parking. AE, DC, MC, V.*

NIGHTLIFE AND THE ARTS

Good places to check for current events include the Friday edition of *The News,* a daily English-language newspaper, and *Tiempo Libre,* a weekly magazine listing activities and events in Spanish. All are available at newsstands.

Citywide festivals with free music, dance, and theater performances by local groups take place all year long but especially in July and August. A three-week spring cultural and gastronomic festival with international headliners takes place in the Historic Center between March and April. Check with the Mexico City Tourist Office for dates and details.

The Arts

Dance

The world-renowned **Ballet Folklórico de México,** directed by Amalia Hernández, presents stylized Mexican regional folk dances and is one of the most popular shows in Mexico. Performances Wednesday at 8:30 PM and Sunday at 9:30 AM and 8:30 PM are at the beautiful Palacio de Bellas Artes (Palace of Fine Arts; ⊠ Av. Juárez at Eje Central Lázaro Cárdenas)—it's a treat to see its Tiffany-glass curtain lowered. Call the Palacio de Bellas Artes box office (☎ 5512–3633) or Ticketmaster (☎ 5325–9000) for information on prices and for reservations. Hotels and travel agencies can also secure tickets.

The **National Dance Theater** (☎ 5280–8771), behind the National Auditorium on Paseo de la Reforma, and the **Miguel Covarrubias Hall** (⊠ National Autonomous University of Mexico [UNAM], Av. Insurgentes Sur 3000, Ciudad Universitaria, ☎ 5622–7051 for university's dance department) frequently sponsor modern-dance performances.

Music

The primary venue for classical music is the **Palacio de Bellas Artes** (⊠ Eje Central Lázaro Cárdenas and Av. Juárez, ☎ 5512–3633), which has a main auditorium and the smaller Manuel Ponce concert hall. The National Opera has performances from February through November at the palace. The National Symphony Orchestra stages classical and modern pieces at the palace in the spring and fall.

The top concert hall, often touted as the best in Latin America, is **Ollin Yolitzli** (⊠ Periférico Sur 5141, ☎ 5606–0016 or 5606–4958); it hosts the Mexico City Philharmonic several times a year. The National Autonomous University of Mexico's Philharmonic orchestra performs at **Nezahualcoyotl Hall** (⊠ National Autonomous University of Mexico, Av. Insurgentes Sur 3000, Ciudad Universitaria, ☎ 5622–7112 or 5606–8933).

For pop and rock music stars such as Lou Reed, Luis Miguel, Kiss, and Cafe Tacuba, check newspapers for attractions. The **Auditorio Nacional** (⊠ Paseo de la Reforma 50, across from Nikko México hotel, ☎ 5280–9234 or 5280–9979) is smart and modern, with great acoustics. Though it's in need of an overhaul, the ambience is good at the **Teatro Metropolitano** (⊠ Independencia 90, downtown, ☎ 5510–1035 or 5510–1045). **Palacio de los Deportes** (⊠ Av. Río Churubusco and Calle Añil, ☎ 5237–9999 ext. 4264), is nicknamed the *Palacio de los Rebotes* (Echo Palace), which says it all. A choice venue, the **Hard Rock Cafe** (⊠ Campos Elíseos 278, Col. Chapultepec Polanco, ☎ 5327–7171) is intimate with state-of-the-art sound.

Theater

You might find some English-language plays by checking listings in *The News*. However, if you understand Spanish (or are content to watch), you'll be able to enjoy a wider range of theatrical entertainment in Mexico City, including recent Broadway hits. Prices are reasonable compared with those for stage productions of similar caliber in the United States. Although Mexico City has no central theater district, most theaters are within a 15- to 30-minute taxi ride from the major hotels. The top venues include **Hidalgo** (⊠ Av. Hidalgo 23, at Eje Central Lázaro Cárdenas, ☎ 5521–5859), **Insurgentes** (⊠ Av. Insurgentes Sur 1587, ☎ 5598–6894), **Silvia Pinal** (⊠ Yucatán 160, at Coahuila, Col. Roma, ☎ 5264–1172), **Teatros Alameda** (⊠ Av. Cuauhtémoc at Av. Chapultepec, Col. Roma, ☎ 5207–1498), and **Manolo Fabregas** (⊠ Joaquín Velázquez de León 31, Col. San Rafael, ☎ 5566–4321). Theater tickets are available through **Ticketmaster** (☎ 5325–9000).

Nightlife

Night is the key word to understanding the timing of going out in Mexico City. People generally have cocktails at 7 or 8, take in dinner and a show at 10 or 11, head to discos at midnight, then find a spot for a nightcap or tacos somewhere around 3 AM. The easiest way to do this if you don't speak Spanish is on a nightlife tour. If you set off on your own you should have no trouble getting around, but for personal safety absolutely avoid taking taxis off the street—take official hotel taxis or call a *sitio* (stationed) taxi.

Niza and Florencia streets in the Zona Rosa are practically lined with nightclubs, bars, and discos that are especially lively Friday and Saturday nights. Big hotels have both bars and places to dance or be entertained, and they are frequented by locals. Outside the Zona Rosa, Paseo de la Reforma and Avenida Insurgentes Sur have the greatest concentration of nightspots. Mexico City has something for everyone in the way of night entertainment, but remember that the capital's high altitude makes liquor extremely potent, even jolting. Imported booze is expensive, so you may want to stick with what the Mexicans order: tequila, *cerveza* (beer), and rum, usually as a *cuba libre* (with Coke).

Dancing

Dance emporiums in the capital run the gamut from cheek-to-cheek romantic to throbbing strobe lights and ear-splitting music. Most places have a cover charge, but it is rarely more than $10. Some of the clubs require that reservations be made one to two days beforehand for Thursday through Saturday nights, if you want a table.

To really experience the nightlife Mexico has to offer, it's imperative to visit a dance club. **Bar León** (⊠ República de Brasil 5, Col. Centro, behind the Catedral Metropolitana in the Zócalo, ☎ 5510–2979) is a traditional salsa bar with great live music and a kitschy feel. **Salón Los Ángeles** (⊠ Lerdo 206, Col. Guerrero, ☎ 5597–5181) takes you back in time to the 1930s, with decor straight out of a movie. The grand, open dance floor swings to the rhythms of danzón and salsa. When renowned Latin musicians such as Celia Cruz come to town, this is often where they perform. The spectacular **Salón México** (⊠ 2do Callejón San Juan de Dios 25, ☎ 5518–0931) is a Colonia Guerrero dance hall built in a converted factory. **Meneo** (⊠ Nueva York 315, Col. Napoles, just off Av. Insurgentes Sur, ☎ 5523–9448) is a modern dance hall for live salsa and merengue with two dance floors. So popular it recently opened a branch in the south is **Mama Rumba** (⊠ Querétaro 230, at Medellín, Col. Roma, ☎ 5564–6920; ⊠ Plaza San Jacinto 23, Col. San Angel, ☎ 5550–8099), a 10-minute cab ride from the Zona Rosa. A nondescript Cuban restaurant during the day, it turns on the heat Wednesday through Saturday nights, when the top-rate Cuban house band takes the stand. Both Bar León and Mama Rumba are great if you aren't an expert dancer because the tiny dance floors are so packed that no one will notice mistakes.

If Latin music isn't your thing, two of the hippest discos in the city stand close to each other in the center. The **Pervert Lounge** (⊠ Uruguay 70½, Col. Centro, ☎ 5518–0976) and **Colmillo** (Fang; ⊠ Versailles 52, Col. Juárez, ☎ 5553–0262) are swank, upscale places where the young and beautiful come to see and be seen while shaking their things on the dance floor. The Colmillo spins techno music downstairs and has an exclusive jazz bar upstairs.

Bars

Nice bars to sit and have a few drinks in are hard to come by in Mexico City. Often they are either too noisy (the rougher cantina variety) or too seedy. Bars are usually open Tuesday–Saturday 8–3 and generally don't charge a cover.

Bar Mata (⊠ Filomeno Mata 11, at 5 de Mayo, ☎ 5518–0237) is on the fourth and fifth floors of a colonial building near Palacio de Bellas Artes in the centro. The atmosphere is conducive to dancing and mingling, especially in the rooftop (fifth-floor) bar, which has great views of the night-lit city and is a place to escape the cigarette smoke. **Bar Milán** (⊠ Milán 18, at General Prim, Col. Juárez, ☎ 5592–0031) is a local favorite with the young and hip; the music is good but very loud. Upon entering you need to change pesos into *milagros* (miracles), which are notes necessary to buy drinks throughout the night. The catch is to remember to change them back for pesos before last call. A sophisticated crowd and mellow music set the scene at the **Camino Real** bar (⊠ Mariano Escobedo 700, Col. Nueva Anzures, ☎ 5263–8888). **La Guadalupana** (⊠ Higuera 14, Coyoacán, ☎ 5554–6253), a famous

Coyoacán cantina dating from 1932, is always packed and heavy on local color. The crowd is overwhelmingly male, so unaccompanied women will be showered with attention.

Students and hip intellectuals of all ages pack **El Hijo del Cuervo** (✉ Jardín Centenario 17, Coyoacán, ☎ 5658–5306) for an interesting mix of rock and nueva canción, and the occasional theater show. Cover varies (up to $7), depending on the show. **El Nivel** (✉ Calle de Moneda, near the Templo Mayor, ☎ 5522–9755) Mexico City's first cantina, opened in 1855, is right off the Zócalo. It's a small traditional cantina where you can get a cheap beer or tequila and be served free appetizers like peanuts and chicharron as long as you keep ordering drinks. The bar got its name because of a water marker outside (called "el nivel") that warned of the city of imminent floods during the last century. **La Nueva Ópera** (✉ 5 de Mayo 10, at Filomeno Mata, downtown, ☎ 5512–8959) is one of the city's most elegant watering holes, and it's brought in top personalities since it opened in 1870. The bar provides a relaxing atmosphere, Mexican appetizers and entrées, and an expansive drink list. Don't forget to have your waiter point out the bullet hole allegedly left in the ceiling by Mexican revolutionary hero Pancho Villa.

Dinner Shows

The liveliest shows are in clubs downtown and in the Zona Rosa. The **Feria de México** (✉ Paseo de la Reforma 28, across from Melía México Reforma hotel, ☎ 5535–1065) is the newest venue for enjoying traditional Mexican music and dance over dinner. Show times at this rustic dinner club are 4 and 10:30 daily, with an additional 6:30 show Thursday through Saturday. The show is free, but you pay for your meal (varied Mexican–American fare) à la carte. At **Focolare** (✉ Hamburgo 87, at Río Niza, ☎ 5207–8257), you can watch a cock fight, mariachi singers, and traditional folk dancers Thursday through Saturday nights. The show costs $8.50; Mexican dinner and drinks are separate. At the **Hotel de Cortés** (✉ Hidalgo 85, downtown, ☎ 5518–2184) you can take in the strains of marimba and mariachi players as well as watch traditional dancers on the beautiful patio. The show goes on Friday night only and for $20 includes a full meal.

Mariachi Music

The traditional last stop for nocturnal Mexicans is **Plaza Garibaldi** (✉ east of Eje Central Lázaro Cárdenas, between República de Honduras and República de Perú), where exuberant mariachis gather to unwind after evening performances—by performing even more. There are roving mariachis, as well as *norteño* (country-style) music and white-clad *jarocho* bands (Veracruz-style), peddling songs in the outdoor plaza, where you can also buy beer and shots of tequila. Well-to-do Mexicans park themselves inside one of the cantinas or clubs surrounding the plaza and belt out their favorite songs with the hired musicians.

Tenampa (☎ 5526–6341) is one of the better cantinas with some great paintings on the walls. Order a tequila and the musicians will be around shortly offering to serenade you (a song costs about $5, though Mexicans typically haggle for a dozen), so the bar is rarely without the wailing mariachis for more than 10 minutes. These places stay open Sunday through Thursday until at least 2 AM, and even later Friday and Saturday.

Note: The square was spruced up in the early '90s to rid it of its seedy image, but things still get raucous late at night. Furthermore, leaving Plaza Garibaldi can be dangerous—be sure to arrange for transportation ahead of time. You may call a travel agency, drive your car and park in the well-lit ramp below the plaza, or call a safe sitio taxi.

OUTDOOR ACTIVITIES AND SPORTS

Adventure Sports

A number of adventure-travel agencies have sprouted up to entice both tourists and natives out of the smog and chaos of Mexico City for a weekend of white-water rafting, rappelling, or biking. One of the best is **México Verde Expeditions** (✉ Homero 526, Int. 801, Col. Polanco, ☎ 5255–4400 or 5255–4465), whose guides speak English and lead tours to the pristine areas of such nearby states as Veracruz and Morelos. Call a week in advance to make reservations and bring a sleeping bag and sunblock.

Bullfighting

The main season for bullfighting is the dry season, around November through March, when celebrated *matadores* appear at **Plaza México** (✉ Calle Agusto Rodín 241, at Holbein, Col. Ciudad de los Deportes, ☎ 5563–3959), the world's largest bullring (it seats 40,000). Tickets, about $2–$25, can be purchased at hotel travel desks or at the bullring's ticket booths weekends 9:30–2 and 3:30–7. The ring is next to the Ciudad de los Deportes sports complex, and the show goes on at 4 Sunday.

Golf

All golf courses are private in Mexico City, but you can play if you are the guest of a member. If you stay at the Camino Real hotel, you can have the hotel arrange admittance to the **Bella Vista Golf Club** (☎ 5360–3501), off the Querétaro Highway. Greens fees Tuesday through Friday are $100; weekends, $200.

Soccer

Fútbol is the sport that Mexicans are most passionate about, which is evident in the size of their soccer stadium, **Estadio Azteca** (✉ Calzada de Tlalpan 3465), the second largest in Latin America. The World Cup Finals were held here in 1970 and 1986. You can buy tickets outside the stadium in the south of the city on the same day of any minor game. For more-important games, buy tickets a week in advance. The Pumas, a popular university-sponsored team, play at **Estadio Olímpica** (✉ Av. Insurgentes Sur at Universidad Nacional Autónoma de México).

Tennis

Tennis clubs are private in Mexico, so if you want to play, consider staying at a hotel that has courts on site.

Water Sports

The best place for swimming is your hotel pool. If you're desperate to row a boat, however, you can rent one in the lakes of Bosque de Chapultepec, near the Zoológico.

SHOPPING

The finest, most-concentrated shopping area is the **Zona Rosa,** a 29-square-block area bounded by Paseo de la Reforma on the north, Niza on the east, Avenida Chapultepec on the south, and Varsovia on the west. It's chock-full of boutiques, jewelry stores, leather-goods shops, antiques stores, and art galleries, as well as dozens of restaurants and coffee shops. Day or night, the Zona Rosa is always lively.

Polanco, a choice residential neighborhood along the northeast perimeter of Bosque de Chapultepec, has blossomed into a more upscale shopping area with exclusive stores and boutiques. Many are in such malls as the huge ultramodern **Plaza Polanco** (✉ Jaime Balmes 11), the upscale **Plaza Moliere** (✉ Moliere between Calles Horacio and

Homero), and the **Plaza Masarik** (⊠ Presidente Masarik and Anatole France).

There are hundreds of shops with more modest trappings and better prices spread along the length of Avenida Insurgentes, as well as along Avenida Juárez and in the old downtown area.

Department Stores, Malls, and Shopping Arcades

Department stores are generally open Monday, Tuesday, Thursday, and Friday 10–7, and Wednesday and Saturday 10–8.

Bazar del Centro (⊠ Isabel la Católica 30, just below Calle Madero, downtown) is a restored, late-17th-century noble mansion built around a garden courtyard that houses several chic boutiques and prestigious jewelers such as **Aplijsa** (☎ 5521–1923), known for its fine gold, silver, pearls, and gemstones, and **Ginza** (☎ 5518–6453), which has Japanese pearls, including the prized cultured variety. Other shops sell Taxco silver, Tonalá stoneware, and Mexican tequilas and liqueurs. This complex is elegant and also has a congenial bar.

Liverpool (⊠ Av. Insurgentes Sur 1310; ⊠ Mariano Escobedo 425; and in the Plaza Satélite and Perisur shopping centers) often has bargains on clothes.

El Palacio de Hierro (⊠ Calles Durango and Salamanca, Col. Condesa; in the Plaza Moliere in Col. Polanco, and in the Plaza Coyoacán in Col. Xoco) is noted for items by well-known designers and seductive advertising campaigns.

Perisur shopping mall (⊠ Periférico Sur), on the southern edge of the city, near where the Periférico Expressway meets Avenida Insurgentes, is posh and pricey.

Plaza La Rosa, a modern shopping arcade (⊠ between Amberes and Génova, Zona Rosa), has 72 prestigious shops and boutiques, including Aldo Conti and Diesel. It spans the depth of the block between Londres and Hamburgo, with entrances on both streets.

Portales de los Mercaderes (Merchants' Arcade; ⊠ extending the length of the west side of the Zócalo between Calles Madero and 16 de Septiembre) has attracted merchants since 1524. It's lined with jewelry shops selling gold (often by the gram) and authentic Taxco silver at prices lower than those in Taxco itself, where the overhead is higher. In the middle of the Portales de los Mercaderes is **Tardán** (⊠ Plaza de la Constitución 7, ☎ 5512–2459), an unusual shop specializing in fashionable men's hats of every shape and style.

Sanborns is a chain of mini–department stores with some 65 branches in Mexico City. The most convenient are at Madero 4 (its original store in the House of Tiles, downtown); several along Paseo de la Reforma (including one at the Angel monument and another four blocks west of the Diana Fountain); and in the Zona Rosa (one at the corner of Niza and Hamburgo and another at Londres 130 in the Hotel Calinda Geneve). They carry quality ceramics and crafts (and can ship anywhere), and most have restaurants or coffee shops, a pharmacy, ATMs, and periodical and book departments with English-language publications.

Santa Fe (⊠ Salida a Toluca) is the largest mall in Latin America, with 285 stores, a movie theater, and several restaurants. It's in the wealthy Santa Fe district, which in recent years has become the favored office real-estate property in the city. To get here, take the Periférico Expressway south to the exit marked CENTRO SANTA FE.

Markets

A "must"—even for browsers—is a visit to the **Bazar Sábado** (Saturday Bazaar) at Plaza San Jacinto in the southern San Angel district. It's been selling unique handicrafts, some at excellent prices, for more than three decades. Outside, vendors sell embroidered clothing, leather goods, wooden masks, beads, *amates* (bark paintings), and trinkets. Inside the bazaar building, a renovated two-story colonial mansion, are the better-quality—and higher-priced—goods, including *alebrijes* (painted wooden animals from Oaxaca), glassware, pottery, jewelry, and papier-mâché flowers. There is an indoor restaurant as well. Market and restaurant are open 10–7.

Sunday 10–4, more than 100 artists exhibit and sell their painting and sculpture at the **Jardín del Arte** (Garden of Art) in Parque Sullivan, just northeast of the Reforma–Insurgentes intersection. Along the west side of the park, a colorful weekend mercado with scores of food stands is also worth a visit.

The **Mercado Insurgentes** (also called Mercado Zona Rosa) is an entire block deep, with entrances on both Londres and Liverpool (⊠ between Florencia and Amberes). This is a typical neighborhood public market with one big difference: most of the stalls (222 of them) sell crafts. You can find all kinds of handmade items—including serapes and ponchos, baskets, pottery, silver, pewter, fossils, and onyx, as well as regional Mexican dresses and costumes.

The Zona Rosa's pink neocolonial Plaza del Angel (⊠ Londres 161) has a **Centro de Antigüedades** (antiques center) with several fine shops. On Saturday, together with other vendors, the dealers set up a flea market in the arcades and patios. On Sunday, bibliophiles join the antiques vendors to sell, peruse, and buy collectors' books and periodicals.

The Zócalo and Alameda Park areas have interesting markets for browsing and buying handicrafts and curios; polite bargaining is customary. **Centro Artesanal Buenavista** (⊠ Aldama 187, by the Buenavista train station, about 1½ km [1 mi] northwest of downtown) is the biggest market in the area. **La Lagunilla** market (⊠ Libertad, between República de Chile and Calle Allende) has been a site for local trade and bartering for over five centuries. The best day is Sunday, when flea-market and antiques stands are set up outside. Dress down and watch out for pickpockets; it's known affectionately as the Thieves' Market—local lore says you can buy back on Sunday what was stolen from your home Saturday. Within the colonial walls of **La Ciudadela** market (⊠ Balderas and Ayuntamiento, about 4 blocks south of Av. Juárez), more than 300 artisans' stalls display a variety of good handicrafts from all over the country, at better prices than you can find at the rest of the markets.

Specialty Shops

Antiques

Antigüedades Coloniart (⊠ Estocolmo 37, Zona Rosa, ☎ 5514–4799) has good-quality antique paintings, furniture, and sculpture. The store is open weekdays noon–3 and 4–7, Saturday 10–2. **Antigüedades Imperio** (⊠ Hamburgo 149, Zona Rosa, ☎ 5525–5798) specializes in 19th-century European furniture, paintings, glass, and vases. It's open weekdays 11–2 and 4–7, Saturday 11:30–3.

Art

The **Juan Martín Gallery** (⊠ Dickens 33-B, Col. Polanco, ☎ 5280–0277) is an avant-garde studio. The store and gallery of the renowned **Sergio Bustamante** (⊠ Nikko México hotel, Campos Elíseos 204, Col. Polanco, ☎ 5282–2638; ⊠ Amberes 13, Zona Rosa, ☎ 5525–9059; ⊠ Camino Real hotel, Mariano Escobedo 700, Col. Polanco, ☎ 5254–7372) displays and sells the artist's wild sculpture, jewelry, and interior-design pieces. The **Oscar Roman Gallery** (⊠ Julio Verne 14, Col. Polanco, ☎ 5280–0436) is packed with work by good Mexican painters with a contemporary edge. The **Nina Menocal de Rocha Gallery** (⊠ Zacatecas 93, Col. Roma, ☎ 5564–7209) specializes in up-and-coming Cuban painters. **Misrachi** (⊠ Presidente Masarik 523, Col. Polanco, ☎ 5250–4105), a long-standing gallery, promotes well-known Mexican and international artists.

Candy

Celaya (⊠ 5 de Mayo 39, ☎ 5521–1787), in the downtown historic section, is a decades-old haven for those with a sweet tooth. It specializes in candied pineapple, sweet potato, guava, and other exotic fruit; almond-paste; candied walnut rolls; and *cajeta,* a typical Mexican dessert of thick caramelized milk.

Clothing

The Spanish designer store **Zara** (⊠ Londres 102, Zona Rosa, ☎ 5525–1516; ⊠ Presidente Masarik 332, at Tennyson, Col. Polanco, ☎ 5280–1529; ⊠ Plaza Coyoacán, Col. Xoco, ☎ 5605–7944; and other locations) has sleek women's fashions. **Guess** (⊠ Presidente Masarik 326, Col. Polanco, ☎ 5282–0133) sells chic denim sportswear.

Designer Items

Cartier (⊠ Amberes 9, Zona Rosa, ☎ 5207–6109; ⊠ Presidente Masarik 438, Col. Polanco, ☎ 5281–5528) sells genuine designer jewelry and clothes, under the auspices of the French Cartier. **Gucci** (⊠ Hamburgo 136, Zona Rosa, ☎ 5207–9997) has no connection with the European store of the same name; nevertheless, it has a fine selection of shoes, gloves, and handbags.

Jewelry

The owner of **Los Castillo** (⊠ Amberes 41, Zona Rosa, ☎ 5511–8396) developed a unique method of melding silver, copper, and brass, and is considered by many to be Taxco's top silversmith. His daughter Emilia Castillo displays fine ceramic dishes with tiny inlaid silver figures, such as fish and birds. Taxco silver of exceptional style is sold at **Arte en Plata** (⊠ Londres 162-A, Zona Rosa, ☎ 5511–1422), with many designs inspired by pre-Columbian art. **Pelletier** (⊠ Torcuato Caso 237, Col. Polanco, ☎ 5250–8600) sells fine jewelry and watches. **Tane** (⊠ Amberes 70, Zona Rosa, ☎ 5511–9429; ⊠ Presidente Masarik 430, Col. Polanco, ☎ 5281–4775; ⊠ Santa Catarina 207, Col. San Angel Inn, ☎ 5616–0165; and other locations) is a treasure trove of perhaps the best silver work in Mexico—jewelry, flatware, candelabra, museum-quality reproductions of archaeological finds, and bold new designs by young Mexican silversmiths.

Leather

For leather goods you have a few choices in Mexico City. **Aries** (⊠ Florencia 14, Zona Rosa, ☎ 5533–2509) is Mexico's finest purveyor of leather goods, with a superb selection of bags and accessories for men and women; prices are high. **Gaitán** (⊠ Calle Sarasete 95-B, at Tetracini, Col. Peralvillo downtown, ☎ 5759–3393) carries an extensive array of leather coats, luggage, golf bags, and saddles. **Las Bolsas de Coyoacán** (⊠ Carrillo Puerto 9, Col. Coyoacán, ☎ 5554–2010) specializes in high-quality leather goods.

Mexican Crafts

Browse for folk art, sculpture, and furniture in the gallery **Artesanos de México** (⊠ Londres 117, Zona Rosa, ☎ 5514–7455). Handwoven wool rugs, tapestries, and fabrics with original and unusual designs can be found at **Tamacani** (⊠ Av. Insurgentes Sur 1748B, Col. Florida, ☎ 5662–7133). **Arte Popular en Miniatura** (⊠ Hamburgo 85, Col. Juárez, ☎ 5525–8145) is a tiny shop filled with tiny things, from dollhouse furniture and lead soldiers to miniature Nativity scenes. **Flamma** (⊠

Hamburgo 167, Zona Rosa, ☎ 5511–8499 or 5511–0266) is a town
house that sells beautiful handmade candles.

Under the auspices of the National Council for Culture and Arts,
Fonart (National Fund for Promoting Handicrafts) operates two stores
in Mexico City, and others around the country. Prices are fixed (and
high), but the diverse, top-quality folk art and hand-crafted furnishings from all over Mexico represent the best artisans. The best location is downtown (⊠ Juárez 89, ☎ 5521–0171), just west of Alameda
Park. Major sales at near wholesale prices are held from time to time
at the main store–warehouse (⊠ Av. Patriotismo 691, Col. Mixcoac,
☎ 5563–4060).

MEXICO CITY A TO Z

To research prices, get advice from other travelers, and book travel ar-
rangements, visit www.fodors.com.

AIR TRAVEL
Mexico City's airport, Aeropuerto Internacional Benito Juárez, is the
main gateway to the country. Many American carriers fly direct to Mexico City, and most Mexican carriers have flights there from elsewhere
in the country.

CARRIERS
Major North American carriers, including Air Canada, Alaska Airlines,
American, America West, Canadian, Continental, Delta, Northwest,
Trans World Airlines, United, and US Airways–Air France fly nonstop
between Houston and Mexico City.

Mexicana has scheduled service from Chicago, Denver, Las Vegas, Los
Angeles, Miami, New York, Orlando, San Antonio, San Francisco, and
San Jose. It has direct or connecting service at 30 locations throughout
the country. Aeroméxico serves Mexico City daily from Dallas, Hous-
ton, Los Angeles, Miami, Orlando, New Orleans, Atlanta, New York,
Phoenix, San Antonio, San Diego, and Tucson (as well as Tijuana).
Aeroméxico serves some 35 cities within Mexico. Aerolitoral, a subsidiary
of Aeroméxico based in Monterrey, serves north-central cities as well as
San Antonio, Texas, via Monterrey from Mexico City.
➤ AIRLINES AND CONTACTS: **Mexicana** (☎ 5448–0990, www.mexicana.
com.mx). **Aeroméxico** (☎ 5133–4000, www.aeromexico.com.mx).
Aerolitoral (☎ 5133–4000).

AIRPORTS AND TRANSFERS
The newest wing of Mexico City's Aeropuerto Internacional Benito Juárez
is a high-tech elongation of the east end of the airport. It has four
banks and seven currency exchanges (*casas de cambio*); Cirrus and Plus
ATMs that disburse pesos; places to rent cellular phones; an Internet
room; and a food court, pharmacy, bookstore, and pricey shops. A multilevel parking garage charges $2 an hour for short-term parking.

Porters and free carts are available in the baggage-retrieval areas. Banks
and currency exchanges rotate their schedules to provide around-the-clock
service. You can also use your ATM card to take pesos directly out of
your U.S. account at ATMs (called *cajero automático* locally) here and
throughout the city—and you'll get an even better exchange rate. Just
remember that your home bank may charge $3 or more for the trans-
action. The Mexico City Tourist Office, Mexican Ministry of Tourism
(Sectur), and the Hotel Association have stands in the arrival areas that
can provide information and find visitors a room for the night.
➤ AIRPORT INFORMATION: **Aeropuerto Internacional Benito Juárez** (☎
5571–3600, www.asa.gob.mx).

AIRPORT TRANSFERS

If you're taking a taxi, purchase your ticket at one of the official air-port taxi counters marked Transportación Terrestre (ground trans-portation), located in the baggage-carousel areas as well as in the concourse area and curbside; avoid *pirata* taxis (taxi drivers offering their services). Government-controlled fares are based on which colo-nia you are going to and are usually about $8–$10 (per car, not per person) to most hotels. A 10% tip is customary for airport drivers if they help with baggage. All major car-rental agencies have booths at both arrival areas.

BUS TRAVEL TO AND FROM MEXICO CITY

Greyhound buses make connections to major U.S. border cities, from which Mexican bus lines depart throughout the day. Reserved seating is available on first-class coaches, which are comfortable but not nearly as plush as the intercity buses. If you plan stopovers en route, make sure in advance that your ticket is written up accordingly. In Mexico, platform announcements are in Spanish only.

Within Mexico, buses are becoming the most popular way to travel: you can board ultramodern, superdeluxe motor coaches that show U.S. movies and serve soft drinks and coffee. ETN (Enlaces Terrestres Na-cionales) serves cities to the west and northwest, such as Guadalajara, Morelia, Querétaro, Guanajuato, San Miguel de Allende, and Toluca. ADO buses depart southeast to such places as Puebla, Oaxaca, Ver-acruz, Mérida, and Cancún. Reserved-seat tickets can be purchased at Mexico City travel agencies.

Various other classes of intercity bus tickets can be purchased at vir-tually any travel agency in the city (there's an especially large number in the Zona Rosa). Buses depart from four outlying stations (*termi-nales de autobuses*), where tickets can also be purchased: Central de Autobuses del Norte, going north; Central de Autobuses del Sur, going south; Central de Autobuses del Oriente, going east; and Terminal de Autobuses del Poniente, going west.

➤ BUS INFORMATION: **ADO** (☎ 5133–2424, 5133–2444, or 01–800/ 702–8000). **Central de Autobuses del Norte** (✉ Av. Cién Metros 4907, ☎ 5587–1552). **Central de Autobuses del Sur** (✉ Tasqueña 1320, ☎ 5689–9745). **Central de Autobuses del Oriente** (✉ Ignacio Zaragoza 200, ☎ 5762–5977). **ETN** (☎ 5577–6529, 5271–1262, or 5277– 6529). **Greyhound** (☎ 5669–1287, 5669–0986, or 01–800/010–0600, www.greyhound.com.mx). **Terminal de Autobuses del Poniente** (✉ Río Tacubaya and Sur 122, ☎ 5271–4519).

BUS TRAVEL WITHIN MEXICO CITY

The Mexico City bus system is used by millions of commuters because it's cheap and goes everywhere. Buses are packed during rush hours so, as in all big cities, you should be wary of pickpockets. One of the principal bus routes runs along Paseo de la Reforma, Avenida Juárez, and Calle Madero. This west–east route connects Bosque de Chapul-tepec with the Zócalo. A southbound bus may be taken along Avenida Insurgentes Sur to San Angel and University City, or northbound along Avenida Insurgentes Norte to the Guadalupe Basilica. Mexico City tourism offices provide free bus-route maps. The price is between 1 and 3.50 pesos (about 35¢), depending on how far you're going.

CAR TRAVEL

Major arteries into Mexico City include Highway 57 to the north, which starts at Laredo, Texas, and goes through Monterrey and Querétaro. High-way 95 comes in from Cuernavaca to the south, and Highway 190D from Puebla to the east. Highway 15 via Toluca is the main western route.

Millions of intrepid drivers brave Mexico City's streets every day and survive, but for out-of-towners the experience can be frazzling. One-way streets are confusing, rush-hour traffic is nightmarish, and parking places can be hard to come by. Police tow trucks haul away illegally parked vehicles, and the owner is heavily fined. Getting your car back here is a tedious process. Locatel is an efficient 24-hour service for tracing vehicles that are towed, stolen, or lost (in case you forgot where you parked). There's a chance an operator on duty may speak English, but the service is primarily in Spanish. Visitors can hire a chauffeur for their cars through a hotel concierge or travel service such as American Express.

Also keep in mind that the strictly enforced law *Hoy No Circula* (Today My Car Can't Circulate) applies to all private vehicles, including your own. One of several efforts to reduce smog and traffic congestion, this law prohibits every privately owned vehicle (including out-of-state, foreign, and rental cars) from being used on one designated weekday. All cars in the city without a Verification "0" rating (usually those built before 1994) are prohibited from driving one day a week (two days a week during alert periods, which are usually in December and January). Cars in violation are inevitably impounded by the police. Expect a hefty fine as well.

The weekday you can't drive is specified by the last number or letter of the license plate: on a nonemergency week, 5–6 are prohibited on Monday; 7–8 on Tuesday; 3–4 on Wednesday; 1–2 on Thursday; and 9–0 on Friday. For further information, contact the Mexican Government Tourism Office nearest you, and by all means plan your schedule accordingly.

➤ CONTACT: **Locatel** (☎ 5658–1111).

EMBASSIES

The U.S. Embassy is open weekdays 9–5, but is closed for American and Mexican holidays; however, there's always a duty officer to take emergency calls on holidays and after closing hours. The embassy keeps a list of English-speaking local doctors on hand if you need to consult one. The Canadian Embassy is open weekdays 9–1 and 2–5 and is closed for Canadian and Mexican holidays. The British Embassy is open weekdays 8:30–3:30.

➤ CONTACTS: **U.S. Embassy** (✉ Paseo de la Reforma 305, Col. Juárez, ☎ 5209–9100, www.usembassy-mexico.gob). **Canadian Embassy** (✉ Schiller 529, Col. Polanco, ☎ 5724–7900, www.canada.org.mx). **British Embassy** (✉ Río Lerma 71, Col. Cuauhtémoc, ☎ 5207–2449, www.embajadabritanica.com.mx).

EMERGENCIES

Dial 060 or 080 for police, Red Cross, ambulance, fire, or other emergency situations. If you are not able to reach an English-speaking operator, call the Sectur hot line. For missing persons or cars call Locatel. You'll find English-speaking staff at both the American British Cowdray Hospital and the Hospital Espanol.

➤ HOSPITALS: **American British Cowdray Hospital** (✉ Calle Sur 136–116, corner of Observatorio, Col. las Américas, ☎ 5230–8161 for emergencies; 5230–8000 switchboard). **Hospital Espanol** (✉ Ejercito Nacional 613, Col. Granada, ☎ 5203–3735).

ENGLISH-LANGUAGE MEDIA

The best place for English- and foreign-language newspapers and magazines is Casa de la Prensa, which has two locations in the Zona Rosa. Sanborns carries a limited number of U.S. newspapers but an ample supply of magazines, paperbacks, and guidebooks. The American Book Store has an extensive selection of publications. A daily English-language newspaper, *The News,* is available at hotels and at newsstands in the tourist areas; it provides a summary of what is happening in Mexico and the rest of the world with cultural and entertainment listings and daily stock-market reports. Remember that most U.S. or foreign-published publications are about double the price you'd pay for them at home.

The Benjamin Franklin Library, actually a part of the U.S. Embassy, was instituted to create greater understanding and cultural exchange between the United States and Mexico. The library, open weekdays noon–7, has a substantial collection of English novels, a good reference section, and many U.S. periodicals. You must be at least 20 years old, fill out an application, and have a Mexican resident sign it in order to check out books, but anyone can browse through the stacks.

➤ ENGLISH-LANGUAGE MEDIA OUTLETS: **American Book Store** (✉ Bolivar 23). **Benjamin Franklin Library** (✉ Londres 16, Zona Rosa, ☎ 5209–9100 ext. 3482 or 3483). **Casa de la Prensa** (✉ Florencia 57; ✉ Hamburgo 141).

MAIL AND SHIPPING

Many hotels have complimentary e-mail service for guests. There is also a proliferation of Internet cafés in areas such as the Colonia Condesa and Coyoacán, as well as the Zona Rosa, that charge as little as $3.50 an hour for access. At Bits Café, you can have a cappuccino and cheesecake, or a beer and a sandwich, while you catch up on your electronic correspondence. It's open Monday–Saturday 10–10. Open 10–10 daily, JavaChat offers free bottomless coffee while you're on the computers.

➤ INTERNET SERVICES: **Bits Café** (✉ Hamburgo 165-C, at Florencia, 1 block south of the Angel monument, ☎ 5525–0144). **JavaChat** (✉ Génova 44-K, next to McDonald's, ☎ 5514–6856 or 5525–6853).

PESERO TRAVEL

Originally six-passenger sedans, then vans, and now minibuses, peseros operate on a number of fixed routes and charge a flat rate (a peso once upon a time, hence the name). They're a good alternative to buses and taxis; however, be prepared for a jolting ride because many drivers like to turn their buses into bucking broncos. Likely routes for tourists are along the city's major west–east axis (Bosque de Chapultepec–Paseo de la Reforma–Avenida Juárez–Zócalo) and north–south along Avenida Insurgentes, between the Guadalupe Basilica and San Angel–University City. Peseros pick up passengers at bus stops and outside almost all metro stations. Just stand on the curb, check the route sign on the oncoming pesero's windshield, and hold out your hand. Tell the driver where to stop, or press the button by the back door. If it's really crowded and you can't reach the back door in time, just bang on the ceiling and yell, "Baja," which means "getting down." Base fares are 2 pesos (about 20¢) with the price going up to 3.50 pesos (about 35¢) according to how far you travel. Exact change is appreciated by drivers. Peseros are also known as "combis," "micros," and "rutas."

SIGHTSEEING TOURS

Various travel agencies run tourist-friendly, English-guided tours of Mexico City and surrounding areas. The basic city tour ($39) lasts eight hours and takes in the Zócalo, Palacio Nacional, Catedral Metropolitana, and Bosque de Chapultepec. A four-hour pyramid tour costs around $23 and covers the Basílica de Nuestra Señora de Guadalupe and the major ruins at Teotihuacán. Except for the Tren Turístico, the tours described below can be booked through the agents listed in Travel Agencies (☞ *below*); most agencies offer some version of each tour.

CULTURAL TOUR

A seven-hour cultural tour is run Sunday morning only and usually includes a performance of the folkloric dances at the Palacio de Bellas Artes, a gondola ride in the canals of Xochimilco's floating gardens, and a visit to the modern campus of the National University.

BULLRING TOUR

There are trips to the bullring on Sunday with a guide who will explain the finer points of this spectacle. This three-hour afternoon tour can usually be combined with the Ballet Folklórico–Xochimilco trip.

NIGHTLIFE TOUR

Nightlife tours are among the most popular tours of Mexico City. The best are scheduled to last five hours and include transfers by private car rather than bus; dinner at an elegant restaurant (frequently Bellini or at the Del Lago); a drink and a show at the Plaza Garibaldi, where mariachis play; and a nightcap at one of the cantinas around the square, which features Mexican folk dancers.

TROLLEY TOUR

A good way to see the historic downtown—if you know some Spanish—is on Tren Turístico's charming replicas of 20-passenger trolleys from the 1920s. The 50-minute narrated tour ($3.50) includes the Zócalo, Colegio de San Idelfonso, Plaza de Santo Domingo, Plaza Manuel Tolsá (location of the Palacio de Minería and Museo Nacional de Arte), Plaza de la Santa Veracruz (Museo Franz Mayer), and the Palacio de Iturbide. Trolleys depart hourly 10–5 daily from the train's offices in front of Alameda Park.

➤ CONTACTS: **Tren Turístico's** (✉ Av. Juárez 66, at Revillagigedo, ☎ 5512–1013).

SUBWAY TRAVEL

Transporting 5 million passengers daily, Mexico City's metro is one of the world's best, busiest, and cheapest transportation systems—a ride costs 1.50 pesos (about 15¢). The impeccably clean marble-and-onyx stations are brightly lit, and modern French-designed trains run quietly on rubber tires. Some stations, such as Insurgentes, are shopping centers. Even if you don't take a ride, visit the Zócalo station, which has large models of central Mexico City during three historic periods. Many stations have temporary cultural displays ranging from archaeological treasures to contemporary art; the Pino Suárez station has a small Aztec pyramid inside, a surprise discovery during construction.

There are 10 intersecting metro lines covering more than 160 km (100 mi). It's a bit confusing: the number 8 previously had been assigned to a line whose construction was canceled because it would have destroyed unearthed Aztec ruins. Line 9 was subsequently built. Now number 8 designates the newest (10th) line. The ninth line was A. Segments of Lines 1 and 2 cover most points of interest to foreigners, including the Zona Rosa, Bellas Artes, and the Centro Histórico. At the southern edge of the city, the Tasqueña station (Line 2) connects with the electric train (*tren eléctrico*) that continues south to Xochimilco. To the southeast, the Tren Ligero from the Pantitlán station (Lines 1, 5, and 9) heads east to Chalco in the state of Mexico. The various lines also serve all four bus stations, the Buenavista train station, and the airport; however, only light baggage is allowed on board during rush hours. User-friendly, color-coded maps are sometimes available free at metro-station information desks (if there's an attendant) and at Mexico City tourism offices; color-keyed signs and maps are posted all around.

Trains run frequently (about two minutes apart) and are least crowded 10–4 and at night. To reduce incidences of harassment during crowded rush hours, regulations (not strictly enforced) require men to ride separate cars from women and children. Hours vary somewhat according to the line, but service is essentially 5 AM–midnight weekdays; 6 AM–2 AM Saturday; 6 AM–1 AM Sunday and holidays.

TAXIS

The Mexico City variety comes in several colors, types, and sizes. Unmarked, or *turismo,* sedans with hooded meters are usually stationed outside major hotels and in tourist areas; however, they are uneconomical for short trips. Their drivers are almost always English-speaking guides and can be hired for sightseeing on a daily or hourly basis (always negotiate the price in advance). Sitio taxis operate out of stands, take radio calls, and are authorized to charge a small premium. Among these, Servi-Taxis, Radio-Taxi, and Taxi-Mex, which accepts American Express, offer 24-hour service.

Serious dangers to your safety come from unauthorized cab drivers (often criminals who have stolen the cabs they drive). While the situation has improved slightly, tourists are especially vulnerable to their assaults, and many have been robbed or forced to withdraw money from ATMs. Take only registered hotel taxis or have a hotel concierge call a sitio cab—do not hail taxis on the street under any circumstances. Be sure to establish the fare in advance.

Taxi drivers are authorized to charge 10% more at night, usually after 10. Taking a taxi in Mexico City is extremely inexpensive and tips are not expected unless you have luggage—then 10% is sufficient.
➤ TAXI SERVICES: **Servi-Taxis** (☎ 5271–2560). **Radio-Taxi** (☎ 5566–0077). **Taxi-Mex** (☎ 5538–0912 or 5538–0573).

TRAIN TRAVEL

The train system in Mexico is in the process of being privatized and is badly in need of refurbishing. Currently, trains are mostly used for cargo, and the very few existing passenger services take at least twice as long as road transportation. We don't recommend it, but if you're determined to go by rail, you can get information from English-speaking operators about schedules and prices from Ferrocarriles Nacionales de Mexico in Mexico City.
➤ TRAIN INFORMATION: **Ferrocarriles Nacionales de Mexico** (National Mexican Railways; ☎ 5547–9317).

TRANSPORTATION AROUND MEXICO CITY

You can get around Mexico City in the popular public buses, the subway, taxis, or the idiosyncratic peseros—minibuses which follow designated routes through the city. The subway is cheap, fast, and efficient, and routes are easy to understand. Along with taxis (which are of course more expensive), it's the best option for those who don't speak much Spanish. Buses and peseros are something of a nightmare for those who don't speak the language (and confusing and hectic even for most of those who do). Note that peseros can also be unsafe.

TRAVEL AGENCIES

➤ LOCAL AGENT REFERRALS: **Grey Line Tours** (✉ Londres 166, ☎ 5208–1163, www.greyline.com.mx). **American Express** (✉ Paseo de la Reforma 234, ☎ 5326–3521, www.vacaciones.amex.com). **Mexico Travel Advisors** (MTA; ✉ Génova 30, ☎ 5525–7520 or 5525–7534).

VISITOR INFORMATION

The Mexico City Tourist Office (Departamento de Turismo del Distrito Federal, or DDF) maintains information booths at both the international and domestic arrival areas at the airport. In town, visit the city's tourism module in the Zona Rosa. This office also provides information by phone with its Infotur service 9–7 daily. Multilingual operators are available and have access to an extensive data bank.

The Secretariat of Tourism (Sectur) operates a 24-hour multilingual hot line that provides information on both Mexico City and the entire country. If lines are busy, keep trying. Outside Mexico City, call the Sectur Tourist Information Center in Colonia Polanco toll-free weekdays 8–8.

➤ TOURIST INFORMATION: **Mexico City Tourist Office** (✉ Amberes 54, at the corner of Londres, Zona Rosa, ☎ 5525–9380, WEB www.mexicocity.gob.mx). **Secretariat of Tourism** (✉ Presidente Masarik 172, Colonia Polanco, ☎ 5250–0123, 5250–0493, 5250–0027, 5250–0589, 5250–0151, 5250–0292, or 5250–0741, WEB www.mexico-travel.com; outside Mexico City, ☎ 01–800/903–9200, 800/482–9832).

2 SIDE TRIPS FROM MEXICO CITY

If the pace—or smog—of the megalopolis begins to run you down, just an hour or two outside Mexico City lies a plethora of towns and archaeological sites guaranteed to make you feel that you've turned back the clock on the concrete jungle. Take a deep breath of fresh air while you hike up the Tepozteco mountain or water ski at Valle de Bravo, relax amid the bougainvillea in the perennial spring of Cuernavaca, or marvel at the spectacular pyramids at Teotihuacán.

Updated by
Barbara
Kastelein

A**LTHOUGH THE URBAN** lifestyle in Mexico City is steeped in U.S. culture, you'll be pleasantly surprised to find that just a short drive or bus ride can place you in a traditional small-town church, in the middle of a gorgeous national park, or on top of breathtaking ancient ruins. Quaint towns such as Cholula or Tepoztlán give a taste of what life might have been like in Mexico City earlier last century, well before its population began exploding with industrial growth in the 1960s and '70s. Cholula is famous for its friendly townsfolk and colonial churches. Tepoztlán has a curious cultural mix of its indigenous community and the New Age proselytes drawn by the town's mystic reputation. Just an hour north of the city, you can climb the famous pyramids of the sun and the moon in the mammoth and mysterious ruins of Teotihuacán. Other historically significant pyramids can be seen in the former Toltec capital of Tula and the splendid ruins at Cacaxtla and Xochicalco to the southeast.

Two nearby state capitals, the cities of Cuernavaca and Puebla, are windows on the diversity of Mexican life. Cuernavaca's deliciously warm climate and abundance of flowers have made it a favorite weekend getaway for *chilangos* (Mexico City residents), as well as a center for Spanish-language schools that draw people from around the world. Puebla, on the other hand, is a beautifully preserved and conservative colonial city, surrounded by important agricultural valleys and populated with an abundance of churches, chapels, ex-convents, and monasteries.

NORTH OF MEXICO CITY

Hugging the roads to the north of Mexico City are several of the country's most celebrated pre-Columbian and colonial monuments. The Basílica de Guadalupe, a church dedicated to Mexico's patron saint, and the pyramids of Teotihuacán can be enjoyed in a day tour if you get an early start, as can the combination of the ex-convent (now a magnificent museum of the viceregal period) at Tepotzotlán and the ruins at Tula, also to the north but in a slightly different direction.

There are no tourist offices in the area, but a good English-language guidebook to Teotihuacán is sold at the site.

La Villa de Guadalupe

"La Villa"—the local moniker of the site of the two basilicas of the Virgin of Guadalupe—is Mexico's holiest shrine. Its importance derives from the miracle that the devout believe transpired here on December 12, 1531: an Indian named Juan Diego received from the Virgin a cloak permanently imprinted with her image so he could prove to the priests that he had had a holy vision. On that date each year millions of pilgrims arrive, many crawling on their knees for the last few hundred yards, praying for cures and other divine favors. When Pope John Paul II visited Mexico in 1999, he blessed the new statue of Juan Diego located outside the **Antigua Basílica** (Old Basilica). The Antigua Basílica dates from 1536; various additions have been made since then. The altar was executed by sculptor Manuel Tolsá. The basilica now houses a museum of ex-votos (hand-painted depictions of miracles, dedicated to Mary or a saint in thanks) and popular religious art, paintings, sculpture, and decorative and applied arts from the 15th through the 18th centuries.

Because the structure of the Antigua Basílica had weakened over the years and the building was no longer large enough or safe enough to

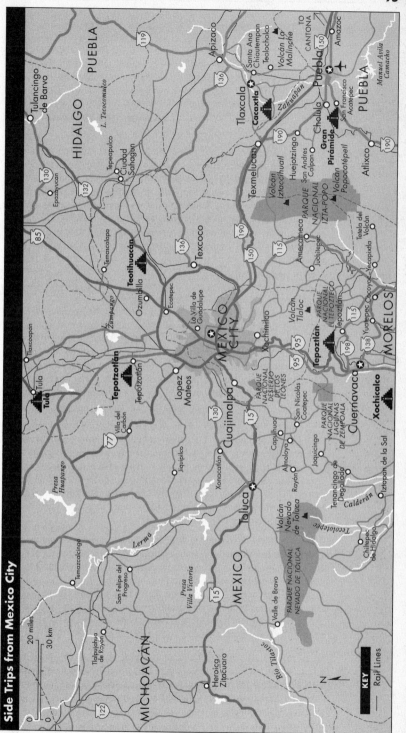

Side Trips from Mexico City

PUEBLA

HIDALGO

Tulancingo de Barvo

119

Apizaco

136

Tlaxcala

Cacaxtla

Santa Ana Chiautempan
Teolochoco
Volcán La Malinche

TO CANTONA

150

Amazoc

Puebla

PUEBLA

Manuel Avila Camacho

San Francisco Acatepec

Cholula
Gran Pirámide

San Andrés Calpan

Huejotzingo

Atlixco

190

190

I. Tecocamalco

Tepeapulco

Ciudad Sahagún

130

132

Epazoyucan

85

Temascalapa

Texmelucan

Volcán Iztaccíhuatl

PARQUE NACIONAL IZTA-POPO

Volcán Popocatépetl

Tetela del Volcán

190

Texcoco

136

Amecameca

115

Juchitepec

Teotihuacán

Zumpango

Ozumbilla

Ecatepec

La Villa de Guadalupe

MEXICO CITY

Xochimilco

Volcán Tláloc

PARQUE NACIONAL EL TEPOZTECO

115

Yautepec

Cocoyoc

Yecapixtla

MORELOS

198

138

Tlaxcoapan

Zimpango

Tepotzotlán

Tepotzotlán

Lopez Mateos

Cuajimalpa

15

130

PARQUE NACIONAL DESIERTO DE LOS LEONES

San Nicolas Coatepec

95

95

Tepoztlán

Cuernavaca

Tula
Tula

77

Villa del Carbón

Jiquipilco

Xonacatlán

Capulhuac

Almoloya

PARQUE NACIONAL LAGUNAS DE ZEMPOALA

Xochicalco

Presa Huapango

Jocotitlán

Toluca

Joquicingo

Rayón

Tenancingo de Degollado

Iztapan de la Sal

Calderón

Temazcalcingo

San Felipe del Progreso

MEXICO

Volcán Nevado de Toluca

Tecolotepec

Chiltepec de Hidalgo

Lerma

15

Presa Villa Victoria

Valle de Bravo

PARQUE NACIONAL NEVADO DE TOLUCA

Tlalpujahua de Rayón

Río Tilo

MICHOACÁN

Heroica Zitácuaro

122

20 miles

30 km

0

KEY

Rail Lines

N

accommodate all the worshipers, Pedro Ramírez Vázquez, the architect responsible for Mexico City's splendid National Museum of Anthropology, was commissioned to design a new shrine; it was consecrated in 1976. In this case, alas, the architect's inspiration failed him: the **Nueva Basílica** is a bizarre and rather unspiritual mass of steel, wood, resinous fibers, and polyethylene. The famous cloak is enshrined in its own altar and can be viewed from a moving sidewalk that passes below it.

Teotihuacán

★ This Mesoamerican Giza is one of the most powerful sites in Mexico; from its size and scale, there's no doubting Teotihuacán's (*teh*-oh-tee-wa-*can*) monumental place in history. It was likely a small town already by 100 BC; four centuries later it had reached its zenith. At the time of its decline in the 8th century, it was one of the largest cities in the world, with possibly as many as 250,000 people. The sacred metropolis lay in the midst of rich obsidian mines, which provided the means for its rise as a major regional trading power and center for the arts—its influence on Maya pottery stretched as far away as Tikal in present-day Guatemala. The glasslike obsidian is still being fashioned into animal figures, which are sold in market stalls on the site. Just who lived here isn't exactly clear—even the original name of the city is lost. It is believed that water shortages and crises caused by local deforestation contributed to Teotihuacán's downfall. It was set on fire and destroyed by raiders around AD 650. Centuries later, the Aztecs arrived in the Valley of Mexico. Because the memory of the grandeur of this city survived the passage of time, these new settlers named the site Teotihuacán, which meant "place of the gods." It was here, the Aztecs believed, that the gods created the universe.

The awesome **Pirámide del Sol** (Pyramid of the Sun), with a base as broad as that of the pyramid of Cheops in Egypt, is off the center of Teotihuacán's main axis. Estimated to have been built between AD 100 and AD 250, it is the site's oldest structure. Its planes and angles were precisely built in relation to the movement of the sun—marking the equinoxes, for example—and the Pleiades constellation. The 242 steps of the 215-ft pyramid face west, the cardinal point where it was believed that the sun was transformed into a jaguar in order to pass nightly through the darkness of death.

The most impressive sight in Teotihuacán is the 4-km- (2½-mi-) long **Calzada de los Muertos** (Avenue of the Dead), the main axis of the ancient city along which six major structures lie. The Aztecs gave the avenue this name because of the stepped platforms lining it, which they mistook for tombs. The graceful 126-ft-high **Pirámide de la Luna** (Pyramid of the Moon) dominates the northern end of the avenue, and the compact, square **Ciudadela** (Citadel) flanks the opposite end. More than 4,000 one-story dwellings constructed of adobe and stone and occupied by artisans, warriors, and tradesmen once surrounded the avenue. On the west side of the spacious plaza facing the Pyramid of the Moon are the **Palacio del Quetzalpápalotl** (Palace of the Plumed Butterfly), **Templo de las Conchas Emplumados** (Temple of Plumed Conch Shells), and **Palacio de los Jaguares** (Palace of Jaguars), which is where the priests resided. The palaces are best known for the spectacular bird and jaguar murals in their winding underground chambers.

The Ciudadela, with the decorative **Templo de Quetzalcóatl y Tlaloc** (Temple of the Plumed Serpent and Rain God), shows off the plastic arts of the time with its brawny toothed serpent heads jutting out of

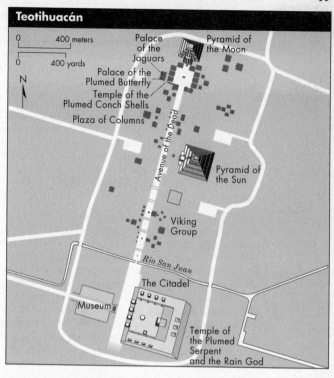

Teotihuacán

the temple facade. Quetzalcóatl and Tlaloc together represent the fusion of earth and sky.

Climbing one pyramid is probably enough for most people. The Pyramid of the Sun is the taller by 89 ft, and affords a spectacular view of the entire area. Wear comfortable clothes (especially shoes) and bring sunscreen or a visored hat when you visit.

Many of the artifacts uncovered at Teotihuacán are on display at the Museum of Anthropology in Mexico City. The **on-site museum,** opened in 1994 near the Pyramid of the Sun, contains fabulous pieces from the archaeological zone—such as the stone sculpture of Tlaloc, the goggle-eyed god of rain; black and green obsidian arrowheads; and simulated burial sites of exalted personages of the empire, their skeletons arranged as they were when discovered.

Seeing the ruins will take two–four hours, depending on how smitten you are by the place—or when your tour bus leaves. ☎ 595/60052 or 595/60276. ⌨ $3, free Sun. ☼ Daily 7–6.

Many tour buses to the ruins stop briefly in **San Agustín Acolmán,** about 20 km (12 mi) south of Teotihuacán, to see the outstanding plateresque (an ornate 16th-century Spanish style) church and ex-convent, now a museum. The original Augustinian church (1539) is noteworthy for its vaulted roof and pointed towers. The ornate cloister and plateresque facade, set off with candelabralike columns, were added a century later by the monks.

Dining and Lodging

For price categories, *see* Dining *and* Lodging *in* Chapter 1.

$ ✕🏨 **Villa Arqueológica.** If you'd like to overnight at the pyramids, this Club Med stands across the road from the fenced-off site. It has snug rooms and a huge garden and patio restaurant-bar surrounding a pool and tennis court. This is the only hotel that has permission to be in the area. ⊠ *Villa Arqueológica Teotihuacán, San Juan de Teotihuacán 55800,* ☎ *595/60909; 5203–3086 or 5254–7077 in Mexico City; 01-800/203–3086. 39 rooms. Restaurant, pool, tennis court. AE, MC, V.*

Tepotzotlán

The **Jesuit church** and **school of San Francisco Javier** at Tepotzotlán (pronounced teh-po-tzot-*lan*) rank among the masterpieces of Mexican churrigueresque architecture. The unmitigated Baroque facade of the church (1682) is the first thing to catch the eye, but inside and out, every square inch has been worked over, like an overdressed Christmas tree. Note the gilded, mirrored Chapel of the Virgin of Loreto.

In pre-Hispanic times, the settlement was an important stop along the salt route—salt was used as money—between Toluca and Texcoco (near Teotihuacán) and had a prestigious school of dance and art. In 1580, four Jesuit priests arrived, learned the native language, and turned the village into a center of evangelization by setting up a school for the young nobles of the conquered nation. The church, of course, was built with Indian slave labor, but as a concession to the slaves, many of the angels decorating the chambers have been painted with dark-skinned indigenous faces. This is probably the only church in Mexico where you'll find such paintings. There's also a museum of religious art in the complex. There are two notable restaurants for taking a light snack or lunch after viewing the Jesuit complex. One is the museum's coffee shop and the other is **Casa Mago,** directly across the square from the church. Casa Mago's owners will proudly recount how Elizabeth Taylor dropped by in 1963 to have a beer.

This village is also famous for its traditional Christmas *pastorela,* a charming and humorous morality play that has been taking place for more than 30 years, telling the story of the birth of Jesus Christ. Staged every year December 16–23 in the patio of the church at night, the cast includes a few professionals and loads of extras from the town who portray shepherds, angels, and, of course, the Devil. Tickets are a little pricey, but now include a meal and a tequila; they're available through Ticketmaster (☎ 5325–9000 in Mexico City).

Tula

Tula, capital of the Toltecs—whose name for it was Tollán—was founded around AD 1000 and abandoned two centuries later. Quetzalcóatl was born in Tula and became its priest-king. Under his rule, the Toltecs reached the pinnacle of their civilization, with art, science, and philosophy flourishing. According to myth, Quetzalcóatl went into exile in Yucatán but vowed to return—on a date (1519) that happened to coincide with the arrival of Hernán Cortés, whom the Aztecs therefore fatefully welcomed. The archaeological site includes the remains of a palace, two ball courts, and three temples shaped like truncated pyramids. However, visible from afar, Tula's 15-ft **warrior statues** (*atlantes*), rather than the ruins themselves, make the show. These basalt figures tower over Pyramid B, their strong geometrics looking vaguely totemic. Crocodiles, jaguars, coyotes, and eagles are also depicted in the carvings and represent the various warrior orders of the Toltecs. ⊠ *$2.50, free Sun. ☉ Tues.–Sun. 9:30–4:30.*

North of Mexico City A to Z

BUS TRAVEL

Buses run every 20 minutes between 7 AM and 3 PM from the Central de Autobuses del Norte to **Teotihuacán**; the trip takes about one hour. Tour companies also offer combination visits to Teotihuacán and La Villa de Guadalupe.

Buses to **Tula/Tepotzotlán** leave Mexico City every 20 minutes, also from the Central de Autobuses del Norte.

CAR TRAVEL

To get to **La Villa de Guadalupe,** take Paseo de la Reforma Norte until it forks into Calzada de Guadalupe, which leads directly to the shrine.

From the city, follow Periférico Norte to **Tepotzotlán.** After 41 km (25 mi), you'll come to the exit for Tepotzotlán. **Tula** is about 8 km (5 mi) north of Tepotzotlán.

SUBWAY TRAVEL

You can reach **La Villa de Guadalupe** by taking the No. 3 metro line from downtown to Deportivo 18 de Marzo. Here, change to line No. 6 in the direction Martin Carrera, getting off at La Villa–Basilica stop.

SOUTH OF MEXICO CITY

Xochimilco (pronounced kso-chee-*meel*-co) is famous for its floating gardens, where you can ride in gondolalike boats and get a fleeting sense of a pre-Hispanic Mexico City. Beyond Xochimilco, in the neighboring state of Morelos, Cuernavaca is a weekend retreat for wealthy chilangos and foreigners. From Cuernavaca, consider a detour to the town of Tepoztlán, which has a 16th-century Dominican convent, a lively weekend market, its own little pyramid, and plenty of New Age devotees.

Xochimilco

When the first nomadic settlers arrived in the Valley of Mexico, they found an enormous lake. As the years went by and their population grew, the land wasn't sufficient to satisfy their agricultural needs. They solved the problem by devising a system of *chinampas* (floating gardens), rectangular structures something like barges, which they filled with reeds, branches, and mud. They planted them with willows, whose roots anchored the floating gardens to the lake bed, making a labyrinth of small islands and canals, on which they carried the flowers and produce grown on the chinampas to market.

Today Xochimilco is the only place in Mexico where the gardens still exist. Go on a Saturday, when the *tianguis* (market) is most active, or on a Sunday. (Note that Xochimilco is popular among families on Sunday and can become crowded.) On weekdays the place is practically deserted, so it loses some of its charm. Hire a *trajinera* (flower-painted launch); an arch over each spells out its name in flowers. As you sail through the canals, you'll pass mariachis and women selling tacos from other trajineras.

★ People also flock to Xochimilco for the **Museo Dolores Olmedo Patino,** which holds a superb collection of paintings by Frida Kahlo and the largest private collection of works by Kahlo's husband, the flamboyant muralist Diego Rivera. It was put together by Olmedo, his lifelong model, patron, and onetime mistress. The lavish display of nearly 140 pieces from his cubist, post-cubist, and mural periods hangs in a magnificent 17th-century hacienda with beautiful gardens. Concerts and entertainment for children are held on weekends, while gaggles of geese and strutting peacocks add to the clamor. This is also the place to see the strange Mexican hairless dog: Ms. Olmedo shares Rivera's passion for these funny-looking creatures and keeps a few as pets on the grounds. The museum also has works by Rivera's common-law wife, Angelina Beloff. ✉ *Av. México 5843,* ☎ *5555–1016.* ◱ *$2.* ◷ *Tues.–Sun. 10–6.*

Cuernavaca

The climate in Cuernavaca, a trifling 85 km (53 mi) from Mexico City, changes dramatically to lush and semitropical as the altitude descends almost 2,500 ft. In fact, it was this balmy springlike temperature that first attracted the rich and famous to what has become a resort: Cortés built the first summer place—read palace—here in the 16th century and even the Aztec emperors kept botanical gardens in the area. There are spectacular restaurants and hotels, in addition to the beautiful Borda Gardens and Diego Rivera murals in the Palacio de Cortés. An overnight stay is recommended.

Cuernavaca is built on a series of small hills whose streets intertwine at a maddening pace. If you're not used to driving in San Francisco, say, it's better to get around by cab, especially on weekends, when the number of cars swells to disproportionate numbers.

Most sights are concentrated around the central **Plaza de Armas,** which is surrounded by crafts shops, sidewalk cafés, and government buildings. The square itself is filled with vendors from neighboring villages. Throughout the week they hawk local arts and crafts; on weekends, one side of the square is taken over by stalls in which you'll find silver and gold jewelry and leather goods from elsewhere in the country. **Jardín Juárez** (Juárez Gardens), a smaller square across the street from Plaza de Armas, puts on free band concerts Thursday evening at 6 under its colonial arcade. Either of these two squares is the perfect place for whiling away a pleasant afternoon after a visit to the tourist sights. After dark, the hip spot is the **Plazuela del Zacate** (✉ Galeana and Fray Bartolomé de Las Casas, 2 blocks from the Plaza de Armas), where sidewalk cafés and bars open every night and young people gather.

The **Palacio de Cortés** (Cortés's palace-cum-fortress) houses the **Museo de Cuauhnáhuac**—Cuauhnáhuac being the pre-Hispanic name for Cuernavaca—which focuses on Mexican history before and after the conquest. Diego Rivera painted some of his finest murals on the palace's top floor in 1930–32. Like those of Mexico City's National Palace, they dramatize the history and the horrors of the conquest, colonialism, and the revolution. Former U.S. Ambassador to Mexico Dwight Morrow commissioned Rivera to paint the murals for $30,000. ✉ *Juárez and Hidalgo,* ☎ *73/12–81–71.* ◱ *$1.60, free Sun.* ◷ *Tues.–Sun. 10–5.*

The beautiful, spacious **Jardín Borda** (Borda Gardens) is the most visited sight in Cuernavaca. The jardín was designed in the late 18th century by a member of the Borda family—rich miners of French extraction—for one of his relatives; Maximilian and Carlotta visited the gardens frequently. Here Maximilian had a dalliance with the gardener's wife, La India Bonita, who was immortalized in a portrait by a noted painter of the time. Novelist Malcolm Lowry turned the gardens into a sinister symbol in his 1947 *Under the Volcano.* ✉ *Av. Morelos 103, at Hidalgo, 3 blocks west of Palacio de Cortés,* ☎ *73/12–92–37.* ◱ *$1, free Sun.* ◷ *Tues.–Sun. 10–5:30.*

The **Catedral de la Asunción,** an eclectic structure begun in 1529 by Cortés, is noteworthy for the skull and crossbones over its main entrance and its 17th-century Japanese wall paintings. Paintings inside the **Palacio Municipal,** diagonally opposite the cathedral, depict pre-Hispanic city life. ✉ *Hidalgo and Av. Morelos, opposite Borda Gardens.*

Near Plaza de Armas, the **Robert Brady Museum** is a delightful restored colonial mansion housing a diverse collection of art and artifacts assembled by the late Brady—an artist, antiquarian, and decorator from Fort Dodge, Iowa. You can see ceramics, antique furniture, sculptures, paintings, and tapestries, all beautifully arranged in rooms painted with bright Mexican colors and more than a hint of kitsch. ✉ *Calle Netzahuacóyotl 4, between Hidalgo and Abasolo,* ☎ *73/18–85–54.* 🎟 *$2.* ☉ *Tues.–Sun. 10–6.*

★ ⛰ The beautifully restored ruins of **Xochicalco** ("place of flowers") are the most fascinating in Morelos state. They sit atop terraced hills overlooking a valley and include a pyramid, ball court, and underground observatory. Showing Maya, Toltec, and Zapotec influences, the ancient fortified city reached its peak between AD 700 and 900. It was of great astronomical significance for the whole region and seems to have been a ceremonial center where scholars met to calibrate their calendars. A solar-powered museum has six rooms of artifacts, including beautiful sculptures of Xochicalco deities found on site. Guides have an extensive knowledge of the site and its history, so feel free to ask questions. The museum has a café, bookstore, and gift shop. ✉ *23 mi southwest of Cuernavaca (take Hwy. 95D south; look for the sign for the turnoff).* ☎ *No phone, but information in Cuernavaca 73/12–59– 55.* 🎟 *$3, free Sun.* ☉ *Tues.–Sun. 10–5.*

Dining and Lodging

If you've missed getting invited to one of the wealthy weekenders' mansions set in the hills on the edge of town, not to worry: there are a number of remarkable hotels and restaurants with equally remarkable gardens—several of them in restored colonial mansions and even haciendas—where you can get a taste of the high life behind the high stone walls. Many people come here to do just that, and many Cuernavaca hostelries began as restaurants: they added on rooms to satisfy clients who felt too relaxed to drive back to Mexico City after their elaborate meals.

$$ ✕ **La Pancha.** Perched on the edge of a gulley, dining is picturesque as well as tasty. The fare is beautifully presented and has Italian leanings, but portions are on the small side. Salads are fresh and creative, and the lamb broth is exquisite. You can dine by the pool or in the garden, and the bar space is popular with a younger crowd. ✉ *Rufino Tamayo 26, Acapantzingo,* ☎ *73/12–81–86,* FAX *73/18–94–77. MC, V.*

$$ ✕ **La Strada.** For a change from Mexican food, come to this old-timer to enjoy a good Italian meal on a colonial candlelit patio. You can't go wrong with the fish dishes, pizzas (ask for the pizza menu), or the house beef specialty—*filete de Estrada,* served with homemade pasta. A guitarist plays Wednesday and Friday night, and the chef whips up weekend specials each Friday. ✉ *Salazar 3, around the corner from Palacio de Cortés,* ☎ *73/18–60–85. AE, MC, V.*

$$$–$$$$ ✕🛏 **Las Mañanitas.** Opened 41 years ago by an American expat, rooms and suites here are exquisitely decorated with traditional Mexican fireplaces, hand-carved bedsteads, hand-painted tiles in the bathrooms, and gilded handicrafts. Chilangos drive an hour on weekends just to dine at the restaurant, with its spectacular open-air terraces and garden inhabited by flamingos, peacocks, and African cranes. Portions are ample, as with the tried-and-true favorite Mexican Plate—enchilada, chile relleno, *carne asada* (thinly sliced oven-grilled beef), and tamale, served with side dishes of guacamole and refried beans. Don't

miss the black-bottom (chocolate) pie. ✉ *Ricardo Linares 107, 62000,* ☎ *73/14–14–66,* FAX *73/18–36–72,* WEB *www.lasmananitas.com.mx. 1 room, 21 suites. Restaurant, bar, pool. AE.*

$$$ 🛏 **Camino Real Sumiya.** The romantic hideaway, built by Woolworth heiress Barbara Hutton, was converted into a restaurant after she died. In 1993 new owners took over and turned it into a posh hotel. It's set amid formal Japanese gardens (including a contemplative rock garden) and contains an original Kabuki theater brought over from Kyoto. A concierge takes care of every need. The rooms, which are equipped with modern furniture, two queen-size beds, and color satellite TVs, are set in the far part of the garden for privacy. Nonguests can eat in the restaurant. ✉ *Morelos 62550, about 15 mins south of town at Interior del Fracc. Sumiya, Col. José Parres, Juitepec (take Civac exit on Acapulco Hwy.),* ☎ *73/20–91–99 or 800/722–6466,* FAX *73/20–91–42. 163 rooms. 2 restaurants, bar, coffee shop, 2 pools, 7 tennis courts. AE, DC, MC, V.*

$$ 🛏 **Clarion Cuernavaca Racquet Club.** This posh tennis club–turned–hotel is less expensive than most lodgings, and its appeal is in its beautiful gardens and spacious two-room suites equipped with romantic fireplaces. Families converge here on weekends. The restaurant admits nonguests. ✉ *Francisco Villa 100, Rancho Cortés, 62120,* ☎ *73/11–24–00,* FAX *73/17–54–83. 52 suites. Restaurant, bar, pool, 9 tennis courts. AE, DC, MC, V.*

$$ 🛏 **Hacienda de Cortés.** This old hacienda dates from the 16th century and *did* belong to the conquistador. Wandering at dusk around the secret gardens and discovering cascades, fountains, and sculptures is an enchanting experience. Rooms are decorated in traditional Mexican furnishings; they have lovely patios and gardens that will beckon you outdoors, as well as TVs and minibars inside. Nonguests can eat in the restaurant, and concerts of classical music are often held on weekends. ✉ *Plaza Kennedy 90, Col. Atlacomulco, 62250,* ☎ *73/15–88–44,* FAX *73/15–00–35,* WEB *www.haciendadecortes.com. 22 rooms. Restaurant, bar, pool. MC, V.*

$$ 🛏 **Hacienda San Gabriel de las Palmas.** A colorful history pervades the walls of this grand hacienda built under the orders of Cortés in 1529. A palm-lined promenade leads you into its luxury terraces, fountains, and orchards, while the pool is a haven surrounded by lush vegetation. Suites are laden with art objects and decorated with period furnishings. The restaurant offers three nooks for diners, including one by a waterfall, and makes an ideal lunch stop for those visiting the Xochicalco ruins. Its location in Morelos state but outside Cuernavaca facilitates visits to Taxco, the caves of Cacahuamilpa, and the lake of Tequesquitengo. ✉ *Km 41.8 Carretera Federal Cuernavaca–Chilpancingo, Amacuzac, Morelos 62642,* ☎ *73/48–06–36; 5616–6032 in Mexico City; 01–800/347–2642,* FAX *73/48–01–13,* WEB *www.hacienda-sangabriel.com.mx. 13 suites. Restaurant, bar, pool, tennis courts, squash. AE, MC, V.*

Tepoztlán

Tepoztlán, surrounded by beautiful sandstone monoliths that throw off a russet glow at sunset, is a magical place. It attracts practitioners of yoga, meditation, crystal healing, herbal medicine, astrology, and native sorcery and is a favorite for U.F.O. congresses. However, the New Age attractions have struck a comfortable balance with traditional Mexican life, and Tepoztlán boasts an gentle affluence that encompasses both Internet cafés and barefoot Indian women selling local produce and chatting in indigenous tongues. This town of 13,000, with a village atmosphere and cobblestone streets, is primarily known for its tiny **Tepozteco pyramid,** probably of Aztec origin, perched on top of a hill;

hundreds of people come each weekend to climb it. While steep, the hour-long trek is not arduous as long as you wear comfortable shoes. Near the summit, however, you have to scale a ladder, so it may not be appropriate for small children. The view over the valley is delightful. Just remember that it closes at 4:30 so set out no later than 3.

Other points of interest include the lively **weekend market,** with its fruits, vegetables, and handicrafts (a slightly smaller version is held on Wednesday), and the **dances** held during the pre-Lenten, or Mardi Gras, Carnival, when celebrants don bright masks depicting birds, animals, and Christian figures. Tepoztlán's landmark is the multibuttressed 1559 **Templo y Ex-Convento de la Natividad de la Virgen María** (Temple and Ex-Convent of the Birth of the Virgin Mary), its fine paneled doors adorned with Indian motifs. Yearly on September 8, the faithful assemble here to celebrate the birth of the Virgin Mary, the town's patron saint. The date also commemorates the baptism of the legendary ruler Tepoztecatl, for whom the pyramid is named; there's a colorful indigenous festival held at the ruins the day before. Both pyramid and convent are closed Monday.

Tepoztlán drew national attention in 1995, when townspeople stormed city hall and took government officials hostage to protest the proposed building of a mega–golf resort on their revered Tepozteco terrain. They eventually ousted the mayor and town police and continued protesting until the developers abandoned the project. In 1997 they finally elected a member of the Party of the Democratic Revolution, but for more than a year they governed themselves.

Dining and Lodging

$　✕ **Axitla.** Surrounded by ponds and bridges right in the skirts of the mountain, this smart establishment has the most attractive setting (though it can get chilly as the sun sets). The creations of amicable gringo William Grady, food has international leanings and is a step up from most local fare, with generous salads and superb baked bass *a la talla* (charcoal grilled, with a creamy sauce). ✉ *Av. del Tepozteco, at the road to the Pyramid,* ☎ *73/95–05–19 or 73/95–25–55. MC, V.*

$　✕ **Los Colorines.** Folksy and full of colored *papel picado* (frilly paper cut-outs), this popular fonda serves great bean soup, stuffed chilies, and grilled meat from an attractive open kitchen. Special dishes include *huauzontles* (a fine, broccoli-like vegetable you scrape from the stalk with your teeth) and *sopa de colorín,* a soup made from the red blossom of the flower that gives the cheerful family restaurant its name. ✉ *Av. del Tepozteco 13,* ☎ *73/95–01–98. No credit cards.*

$　✕ **La Luna Mextli.** Just over the road from the church, this is one of the oldest restaurants in the village. Its sunny patio is especially inviting for laid-back breakfasts while leafing through the newspaper. Wooden masks and flying mermaids provide the principal adornment, and local women patting fresh tortillas add to the ambience. ✉ *Av. Revolución 16,* ☎ *73/95–11–14 or 73/95–08–00. AE, MC, V.*

$$　🏨 **Posada del Tepozteco.** Two pools, a tennis court, and terraced gardens bursting with bougainvillea are perched here above the downtown area, providing splendid views of both the village and the pyramid. The restaurant offers an excellent variety of salads and adds a twist to traditional Mexican breakfasts. One can dine outside; in the evening, candlelight and large arched windows overlooking the glittering village make this a perfect spot for romance. A favorite for weddings and with honeymooners, it's also a good place for children, with trampoline, swings, a pair of rabbits discreetly tucked away in the lower garden, and a video room with giant-screen TV. Most rooms have balconies

and Jacuzzis, and a Temazcal steam room is now available. The staff speak English and offer tourist advice. Prime location and a series of distinguished guests have made this tranquil hotel a highly sought-after retreat; reservations for weekend stays should be made two weeks in advance. ⊠ *Calle del Paraíso 3, 62520,* ☎ *73/95–00–10,* FAX *73/95–03–23,* WEB *www.posadadeltepozteco.com.mx. 18 rooms. Restaurant, bar, 2 pools, massage, steam room, tennis court. AE, MC, V.*

South of Mexico City A to Z

BUS TRAVEL
Buses run every 15 minutes from Mexico City's Metro Taxqueña to Tepoztlán.

CAR TRAVEL
To get to Xochimilco by car, take Periférico Sur to the extension of División del Norte. Xochimilco is 21 km (13 mi) from the Zócalo in Mexico City; the trip should take between 45 minutes and one hour, depending on traffic. (If Xochimilco is your final stop, you're probably better off taking a taxi.)

To continue south by car, return to Periférico Sur, turn left (south) on Viaducto Tlalpán, and watch for signs to Cuernavaca in about a half hour. The *cuota* (toll road, Route 95D) costs about $10 but is much faster than the *carretera libre* (free road, Route 95). On Route 95D, it will take you about 1½ hours to cover 85 km (53 mi).

Tepoztlán is 26 km (16 mi) east of Cuernavaca via Route 95D.

SUBWAY TRAVEL
You can reach Xochimilco via metro line No. 2 to Taxqueña; here, catch any bus marked Xochimilco.

VISITOR INFORMATION
The Morelos State Tourist Office in Cuernavaca is open weekdays 8–3 and 6–9; weekends it holds a stand in the square opposite the Universal cafeteria.

➤ TOURIST INFORMATION: **Morelos State Tourist Office** (⊠ Av. Morelos Sur 187, Colonia Las Palmas, ☎ 73/14–38–72).

SOUTHEAST OF MEXICO CITY

Well-preserved colonial Puebla was once the center of the Spanish tile industry. Nearby Cholula is a sacred spot in ancient Mexico and home to an important pyramid and scores of churches. On the way you can size up the volcanoes, Popocatépetl (pronounced poh-poh-kah-*teh*-pettle) and Iztaccíhuatl (pronounced eesh-tah-*see*-wattle) which tower over the valley. On your way back to the capital, leave time—an entire day would be best—to visit the city of Tlaxcala, with its rare church and former convent, and an amazing archaeological site nearby.

The Volcanoes

Leaving Mexico City, you'll see **Popocatépetl** and **Iztaccíhuatl** to your right—if the clouds and smog allow. "Popo," 17,887 ft high, is the pointed volcano farther away, usually topped with a plume of smoke; "Izta" is the larger, rugged one covered with snow. Popo last erupted in 1802, but rumblings and bubblings in late 1994 were sufficiently strong to cause nearby villages to be evacuated temporarily. It continued to belch and spew large clouds of ash and rock during the following years—and even spit up some lava in 1998 and had a moderate eruption in 2000—but most seismologists have found little cause for alarm. Nevertheless, Popo is currently off-limits for climbing and Izta can only be explored up to the Paso de Cortes. Check with the U.S. State Department for the latest developments as even the Parque Nacional, a verdant pine forest, may no longer be recommended for picnics.

The legend states that Popocatépetl, an Aztec warrior, had been sent by the emperor—father of his beloved Iztaccíhuatl—to bring back the head of a feared enemy in order to win Iztaccíhuatl's hand. He returned triumphantly only to find that Iztaccíhuatl had killed herself, believing him dead. The grief-stricken Popo laid out her body on a small knoll and lit an eternal torch that he watches over, kneeling. Each of Iztaccíhuatl's four peaks is named for a different part of her body, and its silhouette conjures up its nickname, "Sleeping Woman."

Lodging

$ 🏨 **Los Volcanes.** This venerable hotel is about an hour from Popocatépetl and Iztaccíhuatl, but it's the closest hotel and has fine views of both volcanoes. It was still considered safe at time of publication and has 38 rustic rooms, all with potbellied stoves. ✉ *Blvd. Los Volcanes, at Km 66.5 on Carretera Mexico–Cuautla, Popo Park 56970,* ☎ *597/ 60294.*

Cholula

Before the Spanish Conquest, Cholula, 8 km (5 mi) west of Puebla, reportedly had hundreds of temples and rivaled Teotihuacán as a cultural and ceremonial center. The *mercado santuario* (market sanctuary) system was developed here in AD 1200, whereby satellite cities of Cholula exchanged cultural ideas and began trading with the Gulf region and Oaxaca. On his arrival, Cortés ordered every temple destroyed, and a church built in its place. The town fathers claim that Cholula has 365 church cupolas, one for every day in the year.

★ Alas, the 39 churches in Cholula—and the 128 in the surrounding area— are mostly in poor condition, especially after the 1999 earthquake. But 6½ km (4 mi) south of town, **San Francisco Acatepec** has one of the most stunning, well-preserved churches in the country. Covered with Puebla tiles, it's been called the most ornate rococo Poblano facade in Mexico. Equally unusual is **Santa María Tonantzintla**'s church interior, on the way to Cholula (about 5 km [3 mi] south of town). Its polychrome wood-and-stucco carvings—inset columns, altarpieces, and the main archway—are the essence of churrigueresque. Set off by ornate gold-leaf figures of plant forms, angels, and saints, the carvings were made by local craftspeople.

Thanks in part to the student presence at the respected Universidad de las Americas in Cholula, some pleasant eateries (with menus in English) have popped up downtown. The liveliest time to visit Cholula is Sunday and Wednesday, which are market days.

🏛 The **Gran Pirámide** (Great Pyramid) was the centerpiece of Olmec, Toltec, and Aztec religious centers and is, by volume, the largest pyramid in the world. It consists of seven superimposed structures (one for every tribe) connected by tunnels and stairways. The Spaniards, as they often did, built a chapel to **Nuestra Señora de los Remedios** (Our Lady of the Remedies) on top of it. Behind the pyramid is a vast 43-acre temple complex, once dedicated to Quetzalcóatl. From the top of the pyramid, or from the smaller, earth-covered pyramid in front of it, you have a clear view of the surrounding area. Note the many churches, color-coded by period: oxidized red was used in the 16th century, yellow in the 17th and 18th, and pastel colors in the 19th. ✉ *Calzada*

San Andreas at Calle 8 Nte., ☎ *22/47–90–81,* 💰 *$2.50 (includes museum), free Sun.* 🕐 *Daily 10–5, museum 10–6.*

Puebla

Maize was first cultivated in the Tehuacán Valley around 5000 BC. Later, the region was a crossroads for many ancient Mesoamerican cultures, including the Olmecs and Totonacs. The young Spanish colony Puebla had the first glass factory, the first textile mill, and the second hospital. The battle of May 5, 1862—resulting in a short-lived victory against French invaders—took place just north of town. The national holiday, Cinco de Mayo, is celebrated yearly on that date in its honor, and the battle is reenacted. Throughout the month of May bullfights are held in the city's quaint and intimate bullring.

Puebla (the fourth-largest city in Mexico) today retains a strong conservative religious element. Overflowing with religious structures, this city probably has more ex-convents and monasteries, chapels, and churches per square mile than anywhere else in the country. In fact, the valley of Puebla, which includes Cholula, was said to have 224 churches and 10 convents and monasteries in its heyday.

The city is full of idiosyncratic Baroque structures built with red bricks, gray stone, white stucco, and the beautiful Talavera tiles produced from local clay. Puebla is one of the few cities in Mexico declared a Patrimony of Humanities site by the United Nations because of the splendor of its colonial architecture. It remains a prosperous and civilized town, with textiles, ceramics, and a Volkswagen plant bolstering the local economy. Streets are safe and women will feel comfortable walking alone.

❹ **Barrio del Artista.** You can watch painters and sculptors working in the galleries here 10–6 daily. You may also purchase pieces, or continue walking down Calle 8 Norte and buy Talavera pottery, cheaper copies of Talavera, and other local handicrafts and souvenirs from the dozens of small stores and street vendors along the way. ✉ *Calle 8 Nte. and Av. 6 Ote.*

❻ **La Calle de las Dulces.** Puebla is famous for *camote,* a popular candy made from sweet potatoes and fruit. Sweets Street is lined with shops competing to sell a wide variety of freshly made camote. Don't fail to try the cookies you see in Puebla—they're even more delicious than they look. ✉ *Av. 6 Ote. between Av. 5 de Mayo and Calle 4 Nte.*

❾ **Callejón de los Sapos.** Toad Alley cuts diagonally behind the cathedral, and the attached square, Plazuela de los Sapos, is the up-and-coming antiques market and café area for the trendy. It brims with bright young things on Sunday.

❼ **Catedral.** The cathedral was partially financed by Puebla's most famous son, Bishop Juan de Palafox y Mendoza—who donated his personal fortune to build its famous tower, the second-largest church tower in the country. Palafox was the illegitimate son of a Spanish nobleman who grew up poor but inherited his father's wealth. Onyx, marble, and gold adorn the cathedral's high altar, designed by Mexico's most illustrious colonial architect, Manuel Tolsá. ✉ *Calle 2 Sur, south of the Zócalo.*

❶ **Ex-Convento Secreto de Santa Mónica.** Today a museum, the ex-convent originally opened in 1688 as a spiritual refuge for women whose husbands were away on business. Despite the Reform Laws of the 1850s, it functioned as a convent until 1934, requiring that the nuns withdraw completely from the outside world. You can see the peepholes through which the nuns watched mass in the church next door and tour the crypt where they are buried. Curiosities include the gruesome display of the preserved heart of the convent's founder, and the velvet painting in which the feet and faces seem to change position as you view them from different angles. ⊠ *Av. 18 Pte. 103, near 5 de Mayo,* ☎ *22/32–01–78.* ☞ *$2.*

② Ex-Convento de Santa Rosa. The colonial former convent is now a museum of crafts from the state's seven regions; wandering through the well-designed rooms will give you a good introduction to traditional Mexican arts. The museum also contains the intricately tiled kitchen where Puebla's renowned chocolate mole sauce is believed to have been invented—by the nuns as a surprise for their demanding gourmet bishop. ⊠ *Av. 14 Pte. between Calles 3 and 5 Nte.,* ☎ *22/46–22–71.* ☞ *40¢.*

③ Iglesia de Santo Domingo (Santo Domingo Church). The beautiful church is especially famous for its overwhelming Rosary Chapel, where almost every inch of the walls, ceilings, and altar is covered with gilded carvings and sculpture. Dominican friars arrived in Puebla as early as 1534, only 13 years after the conquest, and the chapel of La Tercera Orden (The Third Order) was originally called "the chapel of the dark-skinned," so designated for the mixed-race population that shortly ensued. ⊠ *Av. Cinco de Mayo at Av. 4 Pte.*

★ **⑧ Museo Amparo.** The private collection of pre-Columbian and Colonial art of Mexican banker and philanthropist Manuel Espinoza Yglesias, the museum was a pioneer in interactive information systems. Accessible (in four different languages) and modern, it displays unforgettable pieces from diverse regions of the country. Displays are organized clearly and artfully, and videos and ancient poems lend life to the exhibits. The museum has temporary exhibitions that often showcase current international work, as well as the museum's own collection of contemporary and Modern pieces. The museum is also a cultural center and library, hosting events and conferences. One of the most beautiful museums in Mexico, it does full justice to its philosophy that art is "an aesthetic through which humanity has endeavored to represent and understand the world." ⊠ *Calle 2 Sur at Av. 9 Ote.,* ☎ *22/46–46–46,* FAX *22/46–63–33,* WEB *www.museoamparo.com.* ⊠ *$1.75, free Mon.* ☉ *Wed.–Mon. 10–6.*

❺ Uriarte Talavera. This pottery factory was founded in 1824 and is one of the few authentic Talavera workshops left today. To be authentic, the pieces must be hand-painted in intricate designs with natural dyes derived from minerals, which is why only five colors are used: blue, black, yellow, green, and a reddish pink. There is a shop on site, and free tours of the factory are given Monday through Saturday 10–2. ⊠ *Av. 4 Pte. 911, between Avs. 9 and 11 Nte.,* ☎ *22/32–15–98.* ☉ *Weekdays 9–6:30, Sat. 10–6:30, Sun. 11–6.*

Dining and Lodging

Puebla is noted for its cuisine. Two of Mexico's most popular dishes were supposedly created here to celebrate special occasions: mole, a sauce made with as many as 100 ingredients, the best-known mole being one with bitter chocolate. The other local specialty, believed to have been initiated by the town's nuns, is *chiles en nogada*, a green poblano chili filled with ground meats, fruits, and nuts, then covered with a sauce of chopped walnuts and cream, and topped with red pomegranate seeds; the colors represent the red, green, and white of the Mexican flag.

$$ ✕ **Las Bodegas del Molino.** In a 16th-century hacienda at the edge of town, this elegant restaurant is notable for both its setting and its fine cuisine. If you're not sure about mole, give it a try here: the same woman has been making it for 18 years, and her seductive, fruity blend will probably win you over. Make time to request a tour (Matthijs de Kool speaks excellent English) of the fabulous premises, which are being renovated with admirable care. Romantics should book a private dinner in the "French Room." ⊠ *Molino de San José del Puente,* ☎ *22/49–04–83 or 22/49–03–99. AE, MC, V.*

$ ✕ **Fonda de Santa Clara.** Founded in 1965, this popular spot is a classic and now has branches in Puebla, Acapulco, and Mexico City. Typical regional fare is offered in a super setting in both Puebla locales. The original has a cozy and home-style atmosphere and is only a few blocks from the Zócalo; the larger newcomer (Paseo Bravo) has a shop and banquet hall attached, but still maintains a very attractive colonial flavor. It's open for breakfast, lunch, and dinner. ⊠ *Calle 3 Pte. 307,* ☎ *22/42–26–59,* FAX *22/32–76–74.* ⊠ *Paseo Bravo, Calle 3 Pte. 920,* ☎ *22/46–19–19,* FAX *22/32–05–03, AE, MC, V.*

$ ✕ **La Tecla.** Stylish decor and nouvelle Mexican cuisine has made this branch of the Mexico City restaurants a hit in Puebla. Try the duck tacos in green sauce, or fillet of veal bathed in corn fungus and roquefort. ⊠ *Avenida Juárez 1909, between 19 and 21 Sur,* ☎ *22/46–26–16,* FAX *22/46–60–66. AE, DC, MC, V.*

$$ ✕⊡ **Mesón Sacristia de la Compañia.** Each individually decorated room in this converted colonial mansion is outfitted with antiques that are also for sale. The rich colors of folk art pervade the cozy but stylish bar and restaurant, where excellent regional dishes are served; you can savor everything from steaks to the scrumptious "Grandma's enchiladas." Breakfast is included in the room rate. ⊠ *Calle 6 Sur 304, at Callejón de los Sapos, 72000,* ☎ *22/42–35–54,* FAX *22/32–45–13,* WEB *www.mesones-sacristia.com. 9 rooms. Restaurant, bar. AE, MC, V.*

$$$ 🏨 **Mesón Sacristía de Capuchinas.** Centrally located but very quiet, this elegant hotel is for those who want to rest without distractions or disturbances. The suites have thick walls and are decorated in a contemporary style. Staff are friendly and pride themselves on the designer restaurant's haute cuisine. ⊠ *Av. 9 Ote. 16, 72000,* ☎ *22/32–80–88 or 22/46–60–84,* WEB *www.g-networks.net/sacristia. 7 suites. Restaurant, bar. AE, MC, V.*

$$ 🏨 **Camino Real.** The accommodations are deluxe in this former 16th-
★ century convent, with luminous restored fresco murals and heaps of historical character. Each room is decorated differently, based on the original decor, which varied depending on each nun's donation to the order. (Mestizas whose sole contribution to the convent was their musical talent lived in the dorm—now the banquet hall.) The junior suite was once the convent's chapel, and the presidential suite has original 16th-century gilded furnishings and carpeting. The entire property has been sensitively and beautifully restored, and the staff is exceptionally warm and professional. ⊠ *Av. 7 Pte. 105, 72000,* ☎ *22/29–09–09, 22/29–09–10, or 01–800/901–2300,* FAX *22/32–92–51,* WEB *www.caminoreal.com/puebla. 81 rooms, 2 suites. 2 restaurants, bar, in-room data ports, business services. AE, DC, MC, V.*

$$ 🏨 **El Mesón del Angel.** At the city's entrance—a bit far from the attractions—is this quiet and cheery hotel with spacious and colorful gardens. The executive area is designed for business travelers; it consists of a separate building with 70 rooms and its own pool, restaurant, and business area. Breakfast is included in room rates. ⊠ *Av. Hermanos Serdan 807, 72100,* ☎ *22/23–83–00 or 01–800/223–3300,* FAX *22/23–83–01,* WEB *www.mesondelangel.com.mx. 192 rooms. Restaurants, bar, in-room safes, room service, 2 pools, business services, meeting rooms. AE, DC, MC, V.*

$ 🏨 **Royalty.** Small and well maintained, this hotel on the main square is one of the less expensive choices in Puebla. ⊠ *Portal Hidalgo 8, 72000,* ☎ *22/42–47–40,* FAX *22/42–47–43. 45 rooms. Restaurant, bar. AE, MC, V.*

Cantona

 Puebla state is home to the fascinating Cantona—opened to the public in 1995—which has 24 ball courts where a precursor to soccer was played. It's built into a hillock and is larger than Teotihuacán. It supposedly reached its pinnacle in AD 950, and we can judge its importance from the fact that around 500 cobblestone streets and lanes crisscross its 13-square-km (5-square-mi) area. Note that in the rainy season (Aug.–Oct.), you can only navigate the site with a four-wheel drive. ⊠ *107 km (66 mi) northeast of Puebla: take Hwy. 150 to Hwy. 129; turn off Hwy. 129 at Oriental.* 🎟 *$2.50.* ☉ *Tues.–Sun. 9–5.*

Tlaxcala

The warriors of the state of Tlaxcala (pronounced tlas-*ca*-la) played a pivotal role in the Spanish conquest by aligning themselves with Cortés against their enemy Aztecs, thus swelling the conqueror's military ranks by 5,000 men. The state capital, seat of the ancient nation with the same name, will interest both archaeology buffs and church lovers.

A former Franciscan church, now called the **Catedral de Nuestro Señora de la Asunción** (Our Lady of the Assumption Cathedral), with its adjoining **monastery** (1537–40), stands atop a hill one block from the handsome main square. This was the first permanent Catholic edifice in the New World. The most unusual feature of the church is its wood ceiling beams, carved and gilded with gold studs after the Moorish fashion. There are only three churches of this kind in Mexico. (Moorish, or mudéjar, architecture appeared in Mexico only during the very early years after the conquest, when the Moorish occupation was still recent enough to influence Spain with Arabic architectural styles.) The austere monastery, now a museum of history, displays 16th- and 18th-century religious paintings and a small collection of pre-Columbian pieces. A beautiful outdoor **chapel** near the monastery has notable Moorish and Gothic traces.

The **Palacio de Gobierno** (Government Palace), which occupies the north side of the Zócalo, was built about 1550. Inside are vivid epic murals of Tlaxcala before the conquest, painted in the 1960s by local artist Desiderio Hernández Xochitiotzin.

About 1 km (½ mi) west of Tlaxcala is the large, ornate **Santuario de la Virgen de Ocotlán** (Basilica of Our Lady of Ocotlán). The legend of the Virgin dates from 1541, when, during a severe epidemic, she appeared to a poor Indian and told him to take the water from a stream, which had miraculously appeared, to his people to cure them. The villagers recovered. The Virgin then asked for the Franciscan monks from a nearby monastery. When they arrived in her forest, they were temporarily blinded by the raging flames of a fire that didn't harm the trees. They returned the next day with an axe to cut open one particular pine (*ocotlán*) tree that had caught their attention. When they split it open, they discovered the wooden image of the Virgin, which they installed in the present basilica. Many miracles have been attributed to the Virgin since then. Noteworthy sights of the church are the churrigueresque white-plaster facade, which conjures up images of a wedding cake; the two white Poblano towers adorned with the apostles; and, inside, the brilliantly painted and gilded **Camarín de la Virgen** (Virgin's Dressing Room) with figures on each of its eight sides portraying the history of the Lady of Ocotlán.

Cacaxtla

 The archaeological site at Cacaxtla, accidentally discovered in 1975 by a *campesino* (peasant) working the land, contains a breathtaking series of murals (AD 650–700) depicting scenes of a fierce battle between Maya and Central Mexican warriors. It's considered a major breakthrough in tracing the immigration and trade patterns of pre-Hispanic Mexico. The site is thought to have been settled around 2000 BC by the Olmeca-Xicalancas, a transition culture between the Olmecs and the peoples of central Mexico. It reached its height between AD 600 and 900 and was abandoned by 1000. The vividly portrayed battle scenes with life-size figures show warriors in lofty bird headdresses and plumage being vanquished by victors wearing jaguar skins and wielding spears, obsidian knives, and lances. The murals—painted on the walls of a series of palaces built one on top of another—are protected under a huge roof. Give yourself at least three hours to see both Cacaxtla and Xochitécatl. ⊠ *About 19 km (12 mi) southwest of Tlaxcala,* ☎ *24/16–04–77.* ☞ *$3, free Sun.* ☉ *Tues.–Sun. 10–5.*

Xochitécatl

Dedicated to a bevy of important goddesses, little Xochitécatl is decidedly soft and feminine. Four Classic period **pyramids** are built on a hill that affords a spectacular view of the Tlaxcala and Puebla valleys. A small on-site **museum** has a good collection of sculpted stone heads and pregnant women. ⊠ *Less than 1½ km (1 mi) north of Cacaxtla.* ☞ *$2.50.* ☉ *Tues.–Sun. 10–5.*

Southeast of Mexico City A to Z

CAR TRAVEL

From Mexico City, head east on the Viaducto Miguel Aleman toward the airport and exit right onto Calzada Zaragoza, the last wide boulevard before arriving at the airport; this becomes the Puebla Highway at the tollbooth. Route 150D is the toll road straight to Puebla; Route 190 is the scenic—and bumpy—free road (the trip takes about 1½ hours on the former, three hours on the latter). To go directly to Cholula, take the exit at San Martín Texmelucan and follow the signs. From Puebla, Cholula is 8 km (5 mi) west. You'll need to go to Puebla to get to Tlaxcala; from there, take Highway 119 north.

INTERNET

The Cyberbyte Café on Calle 2 between Avs. 5 and 7 Ote. is open daily 10–9 and charges $2 an hour.
➤ CYBERCAFÉ: **Cyberbyte Café** (⊠ Calle 2 Sur 505B, Puebla, ☎ 22/17–55–23).

VISITOR INFORMATION

The Puebla Tourist Office is open Monday–Saturday 9–8, Sunday 9–2. Ask for Jorge Estrada or Jose Luis Hernández; both speak English and love to talk up their state. The Tlaxcala Tourist Office is open Monday–Friday 9–7, Saturday and Sunday 10–6.
➤ TOURIST INFORMATION: **Puebla Tourist Office** (⊠ Av. 5 Ote. 3, ☎ 22/46–12–85). **Tlaxcala Tourist Office** (⊠ Av. Juárez 18, corner with Lardizabal, ☎ 24/65–09–60 and 24/65–09–60, www.tlaxcala.gob/turismo.com).

WEST OF MEXICO CITY

Toluca, renowned for its Friday market, makes a good day trip from Mexico City. For a longer stay, stop over in Valle de Bravo, a lovely lakeside village popular with vacationing chilangos; it's often called Mexico's Switzerland because of its green, hilly setting. We suggest a quick trip into Parque Nacional Desierto de los Leones—a forested national park whose centerpiece is an intriguing Carmelite monastery—and making a detour from Toluca for a picnic at Parque Nacional Nevado de Toluca.

Parque Nacional Desierto de los Leones

Several walking trails crisscross this 5,000-acre national park's pine forest. Its focal point is the ruined 17th-century **ex-monastery of the Carmelites,** isolated amid an abundance of greenery. The park played a significant role in the War of Independence: in late October 1810, at a spot called **Las Cruces,** Father Hidalgo's troops trounced the Spaniards but resolved not to go on to attack Mexico City, an error that cost the insurgents 10 more years of fighting.

Toluca

The capital of the state of Mexico is an industrial town. Indians still come in from the surrounding villages on Friday to sell their produce and handicrafts at the huge municipal market, but it's mainly radios and CDs from Asia and denim jackets and jeans from the United States. For local crafts, your best bet is the **Casa de Artesanías** on Paseo Tolloca.

There are three main sights: The **Jardín Botánico Cosmovitral** (Cosmovitral Botanical Garden; ⊠ Calles Sebastian Lerdo de Tejada and

Benito Juárez, ☎ 72/14–67–85), open 10–5 Tuesday–Sunday, is in a
remodeled, art nouveau structure that once housed the public market.
Admission is $1. The **Iglesia de la Santa Veracruz** (✉ Av. Independencia
and Calle Constitución, next to Plaza Principal, ☎ 72/15–47–33) displays a rare black Christ statue. The church is open 9–8 daily.

The **Centro Cultural Mexiquense** (Mexican Cultural Center) is home
to the **Museo de Culturas Populares** (☎ 72/74–12–66 or 72/74–12–
77), which features indigenous crafts from the state of Mexico, including
ceramics, clothing, and wooden toys. The center also houses the **Museo
de Antropología e Historia** and the **Museo de Arte Moderno**. ✉ *Ex-
Hacienda la Pila, 8 km [5 mi] southeast of Toluca.* ☞ *$1 for all mu-
seums or 50¢ each.* ⊙ *Tues.–Sun. 10–6.*

Parque Nacional Nevado de Toluca

At 15,090 ft, the Nevado de Toluca, a now-extinct volcano, is Mexico's fourth-tallest mountain; on clear days its crater affords wonderful views of the valley. You can hire a guide at the entrance to go with
your car to the top of the crater and lead you down to its sandy floor,
which surrounds two lakes. Self-guided hiking trails are plentiful.

Valle de Bravo

In colonial Valle de Bravo, white stucco houses are trimmed with
wrought-iron balconies and red-tile roofs, and red-potted succulents
clutter the doorways. Valle and its suburb of Avandaro are enclaves
for artists and the wealthy, and the pines, clear air, and sparkling lake
make it very different from most people's idea—and experience—of
Mexico.

A hilly town that rises from the shores of Lake Avandaro and is surrounded by pines and mountains, Valle was founded in 1530 but has
no historical monuments to speak of other than the town church. The
area's geography lends itself to endless diversions: boating, waterskiing, and swimming in the lake and its waterfalls—and hang-gliding and
motocross for the adventurous. Valle also has a pleasant Sunday market, where exceptional pottery is the draw, vegetarian restaurants, and
jazz clubs.

But the area's main attraction is the migration of monarch butterflies
November through March, when you hike through the butterfly sanctuaries. Other sights in the area include the Hacienda Santa Maria Pi-
pioltepec, whose name means "hill of the bees"; Amanalco de Becerra
Parish, where there's a fine nursery; the Franciscan temple in Amanalco;
the San Lucas Waterfall; and the Carmel Maranatha prayer house and
retreat. Valle is a big weekend-vacation town for well-to-do Mexicans
(and foreigners) from Mexico City; locals like to keep a low profile,
and the population shrinks when the weekend is over.

Lodging

$$$ 🏨 **Avandaro Golf & Spa Resort.** For a weekend stay, head for this posh
former country club, where all the rooms have romantic fireplaces and
great views of the pine forest. In addition to its golf course, the resort
has a high-tech spa equipped with hot tubs and offering massage, fa-
cials, body toning, and aerobics and yoga classes. ✉ *Vega del Río, Fracc.
Avandaro, 52100,* ☎ *726/6–03–66; 726/6–03–03; 5280–1532 in Mex-
ico City; 800/223–6510,* 📠 *726/6–09–05. 66 rooms. Restaurant, bar,
2 pools, spa, 18-hole golf course, health club. AE, MC, V.*

West of Mexico City A to Z

CAR TRAVEL

By car from Mexico City, follow Paseo de la Reforma all the way west. It eventually merges with the Carretera Libre at Toluca, and after 20 km (12 mi), you'll see signs for the turnoff to the Parque Nacional Desierto de los Leones; it's another 10 km (6 mi) to the park. To go straight to Toluca, take the toll highway (expensive, but worth it); alternatively, buses depart Terminal Poniente every 20 minutes. To reach Parque Nacional Nevado de Toluca, make a 44-km (27-mi) detour south of Toluca on Route 130.

There are two choices for getting to Valle de Bravo: the winding, scenic route, which you pick up 3 km (2 mi) west of Zinacantepec, or Route 15. The former takes twice as much time but is worth it for the unspoiled mountain scenery.

VISITOR INFORMATION

The Mexico State Tourist Office in Toluca is open weekdays 9–6.
➤ TOURIST INFORMATION: **Mexico State Tourist Office** (✉ Urawa 100, Gate 110, Toluca, ☎ 72/19–51–90 or 72/19–61–58, www.gem. uaemex.mx/turismo).

3 BAJA CALIFORNIA

Separated from mainland Mexico by the Sea of Cortez, the Baja California peninsula stretches 1,625 km (1,000 mi) from Tijuana to Los Cabos. The desert landscape harbors isolated fishing retreats, Prohibition-era gambling palaces, world-class golf courses, and one of the busiest international borders in the world. Adventurers delight in kayaking alongside migrating gray whales, diving with hammerhead sharks, and hiking to hidden cave paintings.

By Maribeth
Mellin

BAJA (MEANING LOWER) CALIFORNIA is an arid stretch of land dipping southward from the international boundary that divides California and Mexico. The 240-km-wide (150-mi-wide) Sea of Cortez—also called the Gulf of California—separates Baja from the Mexican mainland. Both Baja and the Gulf of California are part of Mexico.

Although only 21 km (13 mi) across at one point and 193 km (120 mi) at its widest, Baja has one of the most varied and beautiful terrains on the planet. The peninsula's two coasts are separated by great mountain ranges, with one peak soaring more than 10,000 ft high. Countless bays and coves with pristine beaches indent both shores, and islands big and small—many inhabited only by sea lions—dot the 3,364 km (2,086 mi) of coastline. You'll find stretches of desert as dry as the Sahara, as well as cultivated farmlands, vineyards, and resorts lush with swaying palm trees.

Varied, too, is the demographic makeup of Baja. The border strip of northern Baja is densely populated. Tijuana is home to more than 2 million people, making it more populous than the entire remainder of the peninsula. La Paz, with about 170,000 residents, is the only city of any size south of Ensenada. The two towns at Los Cabos (The Capes) have yet to reach city status.

Baja is divided politically into two states—Baja California (also called Baja Norte, meaning North Baja) and Baja California Sur (South)—at the 28th parallel, about 710 km (440 mi) south of the border. Near the tip of the peninsula, a monument marks the spot where the Tropic of Cancer crosses the Transpeninsular Highway (Mexico Highway 1).

Baja travelers have traditionally been adventurous, and the peninsula has become a cult destination. Back in the days of Prohibition, when Hollywood was new, the movie crowd learned the joy of having an international border so near. John Steinbeck brought attention to La Paz when he made it a setting for his novella *The Pearl*. Erle Stanley Gardner took a break from writing to battle marlin off Los Cabos. Bing Crosby is said to have put up some of the money for the first resort hotel in San José del Cabo when the only way to get there was aboard a yacht or private plane.

Today you'll fly in on commercial jets and check into thoroughly modern hotels. The rich and famous still find Baja, particularly the southern tip, an ideal escape, and you can see them in secluded hotels along the Los Cabos Corridor. But Baja is no longer the exclusive turf of adventurers and the owners of private yachts and planes. Caravans of motor homes and pickups occasionally clog the Transpeninsular Highway, and flights into Loreto, La Paz, and Los Cabos are often packed with regular folks on their first forays into Mexico. Baja's resort towns have become mainstream, but you can still find adventure and sublime solitude at the peninsula's hidden beaches and bays.

Pleasures and Pastimes

Dining

Baja's cuisine highlights food from the sea. Fresh fish, lobster, shrimp, and abalone are particularly good. In both states, scores of restaurants and kitchens serve great authentic Mexican seafood dishes. Beef, pork, and local quail are also excellent, both grilled and marinated. Imported steak, lamb, and duck are popular in upscale places. Many restaurants serve regional Mexican cuisine, and plenty of spots throughout the peninsula combine U.S. and Mexican flavors in tacos, burritos, burgers, and pizza.

Two dishes originated in Baja and have become standard fare in southern California. Lobster Puerto Nuevo–style (shellfish grilled or boiled in oil and served with beans, rice, and tortillas) comes from the fishing settlement of the same name near Tijuana. Fish tacos (chunks of deep-fried fish wrapped with condiments in a corn tortilla) are said to have originated in the northern Baja town of San Felipe. Mexico's best domestic wines are nurtured in the vineyards and wineries in the Santo Tomás and Guadalupe valleys outside Ensenada, and one of the country's most popular beers, Tecate, comes from the Baja Norte town of the same name.

Restaurants as a rule are low-key, except in Tijuana, Ensenada, and Los Cabos, where dining options range from *taquerías* (taco stands) to upscale Continental dining rooms. Dress is accordingly casual at nearly all Baja restaurants, and reservations are not required unless otherwise noted. Moderate prices prevail even in city restaurants—except in Los Cabos, which can be surprisingly expensive. Some places add a 15% service charge to the bill.

CATEGORY	COST*
$$$	over $20
$$	$10–$20
$	under $10

per person for a three-course meal, excluding drinks and service

Fishing

Baja is considered one of the world's great sportfishing destinations. The fishing is best in the south, with large fishing fleets in Loreto, La Paz, and Los Cabos. Although the summer months bring the most fish, anglers are sure to catch something year-round. Fishing from Ensenada and San Quintín is best in the summer and early fall.

Golf

With well-established courses in Tijuana, Rosarito, and Ensenada, Baja is growing in popularity among golfers. Los Cabos has experienced a particular boom, with several excellent, championship-level courses opening in recent years.

Kayaking

Both the Pacific Ocean and the Sea of Cortez have isolated bays and coves ideal for kayaking. Some hotels and outfitters in Ensenada, Loreto, La Paz, and Los Cabos offer kayak rentals and excursions, and some U.S. companies offer kayaking trips to the Sea of Cortez.

Lodging

Baja lodging is mostly low-key—except world-class Los Cabos. Until the 1980s, Los Cabos's hotels were mostly fishing lodges where diehard sportsmen took refuge. Now the area draws golfers to deluxe hotels that front championship courses. In the rest of Baja, you can find great deals at small, one-of-a-kind hostelries.

Reservations are a must on holiday weekends for most of Baja's coastal towns; some hotels require a minimum two-night stay for a confirmed reservation. Several hotels in Baja have toll-free numbers that connect directly to the hotel; although the operator may answer in Spanish, there is usually someone who speaks English in the reservations office. Many hotels have fax numbers (a good way to confirm reservations), although you may have to ask them to turn on the fax machine when you call. A few of the out-of-the-way and budget-price hotels do not accept credit cards; some of the more lavish places add a 10%–20% service charge to your bill. Most properties also raise their rates for the December–

April high season (and raise them even higher for the days around Christmas). Rates here are based on high-season standards. Expect to pay 25% less during the off-season. Many hotels offer midweek discounts of 30%–50% off the weekend rates; always ask about special promotions.

Several agencies in the United States book reservations at Baja hotels, condos, and time-share resorts, which may actually cost less than hotel rooms if you are traveling with a group of four or more.

CATEGORY	COST*
$$$$	over $160
$$$	$90–$160
$$	$45–$90
$	under $45

*All prices are for a standard double room, excluding service charge and 12%–17% hotel occupancy tax.

Whale-Watching

Gray whales migrate to the Pacific coast of Baja from January through March. Whale-watching expeditions are available in Ensenada, Guerrero Negro, San Ignacio, Loreto, La Paz, and Los Cabos.

Exploring Baja California

The Baja Peninsula is made up of two Mexican states: Baja California, which begins at the U.S. border, and Baja California Sur.

The northern half of the Baja peninsula, Baja California, contains the largest cities and highest population. Tijuana, Tecate, and Mexicali—the peninsula's border cities—have close ties to the Southwestern United States. San Felipe, the northernmost town on the Sea of Cortez, is a popular weekend escape for Arizonans and southern Californians. Similarly, Rosarito and Ensenada, on Baja's northern Pacific coast, are practically extensions of the southern California coast, offering American visitors an experience both familiar and foreign. South of Ensenada the natural side of Baja appears in desolate mountain ranges and fields of cacti and boulders.

Baja California Sur is more remote, in spite of its strong American influences. The most populated areas lie on the Sea of Cortez coast. The Pacific side is more popular with migrating gray whales, who travel by the thousands every winter from the Bering Strait to isolated coves and lagoons along this coast. For those few months, people come from around the world to Guerrero Negro and a few bays and lagoons farther south. Loreto, on the Sea of Cortez, is beloved by sportfishers who find seclusion in this small, largely undiscovered town. La Paz is capital of Baja California Sur, the region's major port, and a busy center of commerce and government. Los Cabos, made up of the two towns of Cabo San Lucas and San José del Cabo, has become one of the fastest-growing resort areas in Mexico. Despite all the development and steep prices, it remains a mysteriously natural hideaway.

Numbers in the text correspond to numbers in the margin and on the Tijuana, Ensenada, La Paz, Los Cabos Coast, San José del Cabo, and Cabo San Lucas maps.

Great Itineraries

Baja aficionados will tell you that you haven't really explored the peninsula unless you've driven its entire length, stopping at small towns and secluded beaches along the way. That's a major journey, requiring at least 10 days of travel time—one way. If you plan to drive the peninsula, you must have Mexican auto insurance (about $18 per day) for the length of your drive. Always carry water, and make sure your vehicle is in good condition. Keep your gas tank at least half full at all times—remote gas stations may be out of gas just when you need it. For the most part, the Transpeninsular Highway is well maintained, although some areas are marred by potholes or gravel and rocks. In addition, it has only two lanes, and sharing them with semis and speeding buses can be somewhat unnerving.

Even if you don't have 10 days you can still see plenty of the peninsula's attractions by focusing on the area around where you enter Baja. A full week allows a quick jaunt through the peninsula or a more leisurely exploration of northern Baja or Baja Sur. If you have five days, you can see the most interesting towns in one state and still linger a bit. With three days you're best off staying within the immediate vicinity of your entry point.

IF YOU HAVE 3 DAYS
In northern Baja, you can explore Tijuana, Rosarito, and Ensenada. Start in **Tijuana** ①–⑪ at the **Centro Cultural** ⑧, then stroll down **Avenida Revolución** ②. Head south before nightfall to a hotel in **Rosarito** or **Puerto Nuevo.** Tour **Ensenada** ⑫–⑲ the next day, taking in the **Fish Market** ⑭, the **Riviera del Pacífico** ⑱, and the shops on **Paseo Calle Primera** ⑰. Take the third day in Rosarito.

In Baja Sur, you're best off staying in **Los Cabos,** allowing time for golf, sportfishing, and snorkeling at **Bahía Santa Maria** or **Bahía Chileno.**

IF YOU HAVE 5 DAYS
You can do a thorough tour of northern Baja, starting with a full day and overnight in **Tijuana** ①–⑪. From there head to the small town of **Tecate,** then on to **Mexicali** and **San Felipe.** Overnight in San Felipe, and spend Day 3 checking out the beaches before driving the backcountry to **Ensenada** ⑫–⑲. Devote Day 4 to exploring **La Bufadora** and downtown Ensenada; then head up the coast for a lobster feast at **Puerto Nuevo.** On Day 5, head back to Tijuana and the border.

If you'd rather tour Baja Sur, begin in **Los Cabos,** spending the night there and starting out early the next day for **La Paz** ⑳–㉘. Spend Day 2 exploring downtown La Paz, making sure to see the **malecón** ㉑, or boardwalk, and the **Plaza Constitución** ㉕. On Day 3, head up the coast to the small mission town of **Loreto.** Spend Days 4 and 5 making your way back to Los Cabos at a leisurely pace, stopping to explore the desert and coast along the way.

IF YOU HAVE 7 DAYS
If you want to cover great distances—and spend much time in the car— you could drive the length of the peninsula in a week, especially if you arrange to begin in the north and drop off your car in the south. Most rental-car agencies will charge you a whopping drop-off fee, however, and the terrain covered isn't always awe-inspiring. (A leisurely round-trip takes about 14 days, especially as many of Baja's treasures take some extra time and effort to reach.) Start in **Tijuana** ①–⑪ on Day 1, touring the **Centro Cultural** ⑧ and **Avenida Revolución** ②. Head south before nightfall to a hotel in **Rosarito** or **Puerto Nuevo.** On Day 2, move on to **Ensenada** ⑫–⑲ for a brief tour of the city; then head south to **San Quintín** and **Guerrero Negro.** If you're traveling between January and March, arrange for a whale-watching tour for the next day and spend Nights 2 and 3 in Guerrero Negro. If not, overnight in Guerrero Negro and then move on for a full day's trip to **Mulegé** on the Sea of Cortez. The drive between the two coasts, through stark desert scenery, is one of the most beautiful and desolate in Baja. Spend Night

3 or 4 in Mulegé. Move on to **Loreto,** stopping for a swim at **Bahía Concepción,** and spend the next night there. If you didn't stay in Guerrero Negro for whale-watching, spend an extra night in Loreto and arrange a boat tour of the Sea of Cortez. Devote Day 6 to the drive to **La Paz** ⑳–㉘, spending the evening strolling the waterfront **malecón** ㉑. On Day 7, continue on to **Los Cabos.**

When to Tour Baja

Baja's climate is extreme, thanks to its desert locale. Temperatures in Tijuana, Ensenada, and Rosarito are similar to those in southern California. Mexicali gets extremely hot in the summer. Northern Baja's resort cities are crowded on holiday weekends, and advance reservations are a must.

Baja Sur's winters are mild, but not warm; Loreto, La Paz, and Los Cabos can get downright chilly in the evening. Sportfishing aficionados prefer the summer months: although the temperatures are high, the fish are abundant. Loreto and La Paz tend to be crowded only on holiday weekends, but Los Cabos is crowded through much of the year, except at the height of the summer heat.

BAJA CALIFORNIA NORTE

The most densely populated area of the Baja California Peninsula, the state of Baja California begins at the U.S. border and extends 699 km (433 mi) to the border with Baja California Sur. Tijuana, just 29 km (18 mi) south of San Diego, is Baja's largest city. Its promoters like to call it "the most visited city in the world," and the border crossing to Tijuana is the busiest in the United States.

By comparison, the state's capital, Mexicali, has a population of only 850,000 residents and attracts few tourists. Tecate, located between Tijuana and Mexicali, is a typical village famous for its beer of the same name. Travelers who do pass through Tecate and Mexicali are usually en route to San Felipe, the northernmost town on the Sea of Cortez.

On Baja's Pacific coast, travelers stream down the Transpeninsular Highway (Highway 1) to the beach communities of Rosarito and Ensenada. English is spoken as freely as Spanish here, and the dollar is as readily accepted as the peso. Between Baja's towns, the landscape is unlike any other, with cacti growing beside the sea, and stark mountains and plateaus rising against clear blue skies.

Highway 3 runs east from Ensenada to San Felipe through the foothills of the Sierra San Pedro Mártir. The same highway runs north from Ensenada to Tecate through the Guadalupe Valley, where you'll find many of the area's vineyards and wineries. If you're traveling south, Ensenada is the last major city on the northern section of Mexico Highway 1. San Quintín, 184 km (114 mi) south of Ensenada, is an agricultural community said to be the windiest spot in Baja. Sportfishing is particularly good here. Farther south are turnoffs for a dirt road to San Felipe and a paved road to Bahía de los Angeles, a remote bay beloved by fishermen and naturalists.

At the end of the northern section of Baja, 595 km (369 mi) from Ensenada, stands a steel monument in the form of an eagle, 138 ft high. It marks the border between the states of Baja California and Baja California Sur, and the time changes from Pacific to Mountain as you cross that 28th parallel. Guerrero Negro, Baja Sur's northernmost town, with hotels and gas stations, is 2 km (1 mi) south.

Baja California Norte

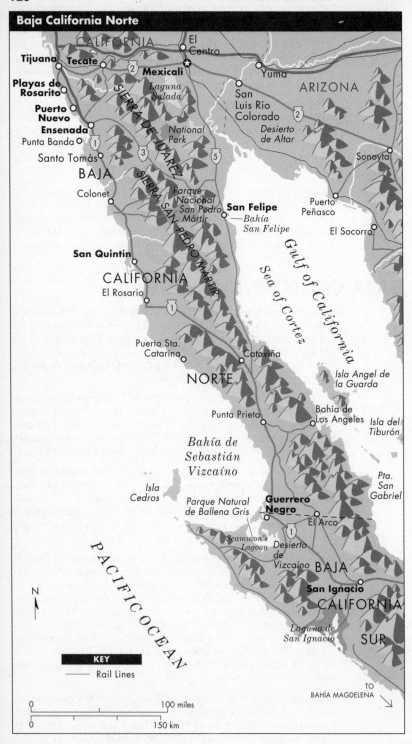

CALIFORNIA

El Centro

Tijuana
Tecate
(2)
Mexicali

Yuma

ARIZONA

Playas de Rosarito

San Luis Río Colorado

(2)

Laguna Salada

Puerto Nuevo
Ensenada
(1)

National Park

Desierto de Altar

Sonoyta

Punta Banda

(3)

(5)

Santo Tomás

SIERRA DE JUÁREZ

BAJA

Colonet

Parque Nacional San Pedro Mártir

San Felipe

Bahía San Felipe

Puerto Peñasco

El Socorro

SIERRA SAN PEDRO MÁRTIR

San Quintín

CALIFORNIA

El Rosario

(1)

Gulf of California

Sea of Cortez

Puerto Sta. Catarina

Cataviña

NORTE

Isla Angel de la Guarda

Punta Prieta

(1)

Bahía de Los Angeles

Isla del Tiburón

Bahía de Sebastián Vizcaíno

Isla Cedros

Parque Natural de Ballena Gris

Guerrero Negro

Pta. San Gabriel

El Arco

(1)

Scammon's Lagoon

Desierto de Vizcaíno

BAJA

PACIFIC OCEAN

N

San Ignacio

CALIFORNIA

Laguna de San Ignacio

SUR

KEY

—— Rail Lines

0 ————— 100 miles

0 ————— 150 km

TO BAHÍA MAGDELENA

Tijuana

29 km (18 mi) south of San Diego.

Tijuana is the only part of Mexico many people see—a distorted view of the country's many cultures. Before the city became a gigantic recreation center for southern Californians, it was a ranch populated by a few hundred Mexicans. In 1911 a group of Americans invaded the area and attempted to set up an independent republic; they were quickly driven out by Mexican soldiers. When Prohibition hit the United States in the 1920s and the Agua Caliente Racetrack and Casino opened (1929), Tijuana boomed. Americans seeking alcohol, gambling, and more fun than they could find back home flocked across the border, spending freely and fueling the region's growth. Tijuana became the entry port for what some termed a "sinful, steamy playground" frequented by Hollywood stars and the idle rich.

Then Prohibition was repealed, Mexico outlawed gambling, and Tijuana's fortunes declined. Although the flow of travelers from the north slowed to a trickle for a while, Tijuana still captivated those in search of the sort of fun that was not allowed back home. Drivers heading into Baja's wilderness passed through downtown Tijuana, stopping along Avenida Revolución and its side streets for supplies and souvenirs.

When the toll highway to Ensenada was finished in 1967, travelers bypassed the city and tourism dropped again. But Tijuana began attracting residents from throughout Latin America. The city's population mushroomed from a mere 300,000 in 1970 to more than 2 million today. The city has spread into canyons and dry riverbeds, over hillsides, and onto ocean cliffs. As the government struggles to keep up with the growth and demand for services, thousands live without electricity, running water, or adequate housing in squatters' villages along the border. Crime is now a significant problem in Tijuana. Poverty is vast, and petty crime is on the rise. Moreover, the area has become headquarters for serious drug cartels, and violent crime—reaching the highest levels of law enforcement and business—is booming. You're unlikely to witness a shooting or some other frightening situation, but be mindful of your surroundings and guard your belongings.

City leaders, realizing that tourism creates jobs and bolsters Tijuana's fragile economy, are working hard to attract visitors. Avenida Revolución, the main street, is lined with tourist-oriented shopping arcades, restaurants, and bars. The city has an international airport; a fine cultural center that presents international music, dance, and theater groups; and deluxe high-rise hotels. The demand for high-end accommodations has increased with the growth of *maquiladoras* (foreign manufacturing plants). Although it's no longer considered just a bawdy border town, the city remains best known as a place for an intense, somewhat exotic day-long adventure.

Tijuana's tourist attractions have remained much the same throughout the century. The impressive El Palacio Frontón (Jai Alai Palace) no longer hosts jai alai games but is occasionally used as a concert venue. Some of Mexico's greatest bullfighters appear at the oceanfront and downtown bullrings, and an extraordinary number of places in town serve up good food and drinks.

And then, of course, there's shopping. From the moment you cross the border, people will approach you or call out and insist that you look at their wares. If you drive, workers will run out from auto-body shops to place bids on new paint or upholstery for your car. All along Avenida Revolución and its side streets, shops sell everything from tequila

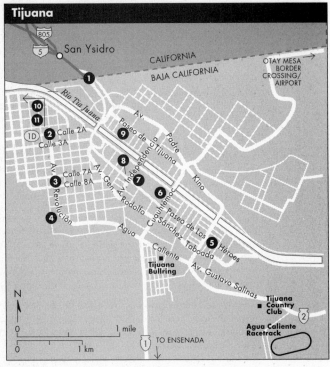

to Tiffany-style lamps. Serious shoppers can spend a full day searching and bargaining for their items of choice. If you intend to buy food
in Mexico, get the U.S. customs list of articles that are illegal to bring
back so that your purchases won't be confiscated.

② **Avenida Revolución.** This infamous strip, lined with an array of shops
and restaurants that cater to uninhibited travelers, has long been Tijuana's main tourism zone. Shopkeepers call out from their doorways,
offering low prices for an assortment of garish souvenirs and genuine
folk art treasures. Many shopping arcades open onto Avenida Revolución; inside the front doors are mazes of stands with low-priced pottery and other crafts.

⑧ **Centro Cultural.** The Cultural Center was designed by architects Manuel
Rosen and Pedro Ramírez Vásquez, who also created Mexico City's
famous Museum of Anthropology. The center's Museum of the Californias, which opened in 2000, provides an excellent overview of the
history, geography, and flora and fauna of Baja. Exhibits include replicas of several Baja missions and prehistoric cave paintings, along with
a nearly full-size sailing ship filled with interactive exhibits for children. The Omnimax Theater, with its curved 180-degree screen, shows
films on a rotating schedule; many are in English. Exhibitions on art
and culture change frequently, and the center's stage hosts musical and
dance performances by international groups. The center's bookstore
has an excellent selection on Mexican history, culture, and arts, mostly
in Spanish. ⊠ *Paseo de los Héroes and Av. Independencia,* ☎ *6/684-
1111 or 6/684-1125.* ☜ *Museum $2, museum and Omnimax The-
ater $4.* ☉ *Weekdays 10–6, weekends 10–8.*

④ **L.A. Cetto Winery.** Most of Baja's legendary wineries are in the Ensenada
region, but Tijuana does have this branch of one of Mexico's finest wineries. You can tour the bottling plant, sample the excellent wines while watch-

ing a video on the winery's operations in the Guadalupe Valley, and spend as long as you like in the gift and wine shop, where prices are far lower than in regular liquor stores. ⊠ *Cañon Johnson 8151, at Av. Constitución Sur,* ☎ *6/685–3031 or 6/685–1644.* ☞ *$2 for tour and tasting 4 wines; $6 for tour and tasting 11 wines.* ☉ *Mon.–Sat. 10–5.*

👶 ❺ **Mundo Divertido.** This popular amusement park in the Río zone includes a miniature golf course, batting cages, bumper boats, go-carts, a roller coaster, and a video-game parlor. A food court with hot dogs, burgers, and tacos will keep the kids happy. Admission is free, and the rides cost just a few pesos. ⊠ *Paseo de los Héroes at Calle Velasco,* ☎ *6/634–3213 or 6/634–3214.* ☉ *Weekdays noon–8:30, weekends 11–9:30.*

❸ **El Palacio Frontón.** For many years, the magnificent Moorish-style Jai Alai Palace hosted fast-paced jai alai games. The sport has declined in popularity, however, and the Palacio is now occasionally used for boxing contests and concerts. ⊠ *Av. Revolución at Calle 7,* ☎ *6/685–7833.*

❿ **Playas Tijuana.** Along the oceanfront is this mix of modest and expensive residential neighborhoods, with a few restaurants and hotels. The isolated beaches are visited mostly by residents.

⓫ **Plaza de Toros Monumental.** The "Bullring by the Sea" sits at the northwest corner of the beach area near the U.S. border. The bullring is occasionally used for summer concerts.

❼ **Plaza Río Tijuana.** The area's largest shopping complex has good restaurants, department stores, hundreds of shops, and a multiplex theater where several English-language films are usually shown. Shade trees and flowers line the sidewalks that lead from the shopping complex to the Cultural Center. ⊠ *Paseo de los Héroes, across from the Centro Cultural,* ☎ *6/684–0402.*

❾ **Pueblo Amigo.** This entertainment center was built to resemble a colonial Mexican village, replete with stucco facades and tree-lined pathways leading to a domed gazebo. The complex includes a hotel, several restaurants and clubs, a huge grocery store, and a large branch of the Caliente Race Book, where gambling on televised races and sporting events is legal. ⊠ *Paseo de Tijuana between Puente Mexico and Av. Independencia.*

❶ **San Ysidro Border Crossing.** Locals and tourists jostle each other along the pedestrian walkway through the Viva Tijuana dining and shopping center and into the center of town. Artisans' stands line the walkway and adjoining streets, offering a quick overview of the wares to be found all over town.

❻ **Zona Río.** The section that runs along Avenida Paseo de los Héroes, parallel to the dry Tia Juana River, is one of the city's main thoroughfares, with large statues of historical figures, including Abraham Lincoln. With its impressive **Centro Cultural**, several shopping complexes, fine restaurants, and fashionable discos, this part of town rivals Avenida Revolución for tourists' as well as locals' attention. A massive 10-story-high cathedral dedicated to the Virgin of Guadalupe is under construction in this neighborhood; when completed it will surely be a city landmark. ⊠ *Paseo de los Héroes between Blvd. Sanchez Taboada and the border.*

Dining and Lodging

$$$ ✕ **Cien Años.** Mexican haute cuisine is all the rage on the mainland but has been slow to appear in Baja. This gracious Spanish colonial–style restaurant has met the need with aplomb, offering *crepas de huitlacoche* (a mushroomlike corn delicacy), beet salad, shrimp with nopal cactus, and tender beef covered with avocado and cheese. Each dish has an unusual blend of flavors—tamarind, Mexican oregano, mango,

poblano chilies—that elevates the taste of even common appetizers such as *queso fundido* (melted cheese wrapped in tortillas). The soothing decor and service make for a special night out. ⊠ *Av. José María 1407, in the Zona Río,* ☎ *6/634–3039. MC, V.*

$$$ ✕ **Villa Saverios.** Well-dressed Tijuanans and their guests dine on exceptional pastas, gourmet pizzas, and unusual entrées in this elegant dining room reminiscent of a Mediterranean café. Starters include foie gras, carpaccio, sashimi, lobster taquitos, and tiny mesquite-grilled quail with a tamarind glaze. Canneloni is stuffed with eggplant, spinach, and mushrooms, duck is marinated with raspberry liqueur, and Calvados scents the sweetbreads. The menu is successfully ambitious, and the service attentive. Diners from both sides of the border make regular pilgrimages to sample the chef's latest creations. ⊠ *Blvd. Sánchez Taboada at Escuadrón 201,* ☎ *6/686–6502. AE, MC, V.*

$$ ✕ **El Faro de Mazatlán.** Fresh fish prepared simply is the hallmark of one of Tijuana's best seafood restaurants. This is the place to try ceviche, abalone, squid, and lobster without spending a fortune. Meals start with savory soup and crusty rolls. Frequented by professionals from nearby offices, the dining room is a peaceful spot for a long, leisurely lunch. Appetizers and soup are included in the price of the meal. ⊠ *Blvd. Sanchez Taboada 9542,* ☎ *6/684–8883. MC, V.*

$$ ✕ **La Fonda de Roberto.** Roberto's is the best restaurant in Tijuana for traditional cuisine from the diverse culinary regions of Mexico. Try the *chiles en nogada* (chilies stuffed with raisins and meat and topped with cream and pomegranate seeds), meats with spicy *achiote* (a blend of seasonings) sauce, and many varieties of mole. Portions are small, so order liberally and share samples of many dishes. ⊠ *La Siesta Motel, Blvd. Cuauhtémoc Suroeste 2800 (also called Old Ensenada Hwy.), near Blvd. Agua Caliente,* ☎ *6/686–4687. MC, V.*

$$ ✕ **La Taberna Española.** A mainstay of Plaza Fiesta's multiethnic cafés, this Spanish tapas bar attracts a youthful, sophisticated crowd. The menu is printed in Spanish, but with a bit of luck you should be able to select an interesting sampling, such as octopus basted in its own ink, spicy sausages, and Spanish tortilla with potatoes, eggs, and fava beans. The café is smoky and invariably crowded; outdoor tables have excellent people-watching. ⊠ *Plaza Fiesta, Paseo de los Héroes 1001,* ☎ *6/684–9401. No credit cards.*

$ ✕ **Carnitas Uruapan.** You'll need to take a cab to either location of this festive restaurant, where patrons mingle at picnic tables and toast one another to live mariachi music. The main attraction here is *carnitas* (marinated pork roasted over an open pit), sold by weight and served with homemade tortillas, salsa, cilantro, guacamole, and onions. ⊠ *Blvd. Díaz Ordaz 550,* ☎ *6/681–6181;* ⊠ *Paseo de los Héroes at Av. Rodríguez,* ☎ *no phone. No credit cards.*

$ ✕ **La Especial.** At the foot of the stairs leading to an underground shopping arcade, this place serves up home-style Mexican cooking at low
★ prices. The gruff, efficient waiters, decked out in black slacks and vests, shuttle platters of *carne asada* (grilled strips of marinated meat), enchiladas, and burritos, all with a distinctive flavor found only at this busy, cavernous basement dining room. ⊠ *Av. Revolución 718,* ☎ *6/685–6654. No credit cards.*

$$$$ ⌂ **Camino Real.** Elegant and fashionable, this modernistic purple and yellow hotel near the Centro Cultural is the most prestigious hotel in town. Business guests abound, but tourists are also happy with the plush rooms decorated in browns and gold, the direct-dial phones, excellent restaurant, and perfect location. ⊠ *Paseo de los Héroes 10305, 22320,* ☎ *6/633–4000 or 800/722–6466,* ℻ *6/633–4001,* ⓦⒺⒷ *www.camino-real.com. 235 rooms, 15 suites. Restaurant, 2 bars, room service, laundry service, gym. AE, MC, V.*

$$$ 🏨 **Fiesta Inn Agua Caliente.** It's hard to resist this quirky hotel, despite its odd location. Set between two major boulevards on a landscaped island, the building stands beside the underground thermal spring that fed the pools at the 1920s-era Agua Caliente Spa. Today's rooms aren't as luxurious as they once were, although they're modern and comfortable. The star of the property is the Vita Spa, with individual and couples' hot tubs fed from the healing spring. Facials, massage, soothing mud wraps, and a cozy relaxation room make the spa—which is also open to nonguests—a perfect weekend retreat. ⊠ *Paseo de los Héroes 18818, Zona Río 22320,* ☎ *6/634–6901 or 800/343–7821 for the hotel; 888/848–2928 for the spa,* FAX *6/634–6912,* WEB *www.fiestamericana.com, www.sdro.com/vitaspa. 122 rooms, 5 suites. Restaurant, pool, spa. AE, MC, V.*

$$$ 🏨 **Grand Hotel.** The twin, mirrored towers of the hotel and a high-rise office building are Tijuana's most ostentatious landmarks. The hotel's atrium restaurant is a favorite lunch and Sunday brunch spot. The rooms used to be the nicest in town, but new hotels have upped the standards. Still, it's a good spot for business travelers and anyone looking for moderately priced luxury. The hotel mall has an Internet café. ⊠ *Blvd. Agua Caliente 4500, 22420,* ☎ *6/681–7000,* FAX *6/681–7016. 422 rooms. Restaurant, pool, 2 tennis courts, exercise room, shops, nightclub, travel services. AE, MC, V.*

$$$ 🏨 **Lucerna.** Once one of the most charming hotels in Tijuana, the Lucerna is now showing its age. Still, the lovely gardens, large pool surrounded by palms, touches of tile work, and folk art lend the hotel a distinct Mexican character. ⊠ *Paseo de los Héroes 10902, at Av. Rodríguez, 22320,* ☎ *6/633–3900 or 800/582–3762,* FAX *6/634–2400,* WEB *www.hotel-lucerna.com.mx. 167 rooms, 11 suites. Restaurant, coffee shop, pool, nightclub, travel services. MC, V.*

$$ 🏨 **Bugambilias.** Proximity to the Tijuana airport makes this modest hotel a great find. The pink three-story building has motel-like rooms; suites have kitchenettes. The hotel offers free transportation to and from the Tijuana airport. ⊠ *Ave. Tijuana 1600, 22450,* ☎ *6/623–7600 or 800/472–1153. 132 rooms, 9 suites. Restaurant, bar, pool, exercise room. MC, V.*

$$ 🏨 **La Villa de Zaragoza.** Some rooms in this brown stucco motel have kitchenettes, and all offer air-conditioning and cable TV. The location, near the Jai Alai Palace and one block from Avenida Revolución, is ideal. The neighborhood can be noisy, and it's best to choose a room at the back. The guarded parking lot is a major plus, although you won't need a car if you stay here. The motel is used by tour groups, so book ahead for holidays and weekends. ⊠ *Av. Madero 1120, 22000,* ☎ *6/685–1832,* FAX *6/685–1837. 66 rooms. Restaurant, free parking. MC, V.*

$ 🏨 **Hotel Nelson.** Were it better cared for, the Nelson's pale pink, five-story corner building might be considered a historic landmark. It feels like an older downtown inn, with a barber shop, somewhat noisy bar, and coffee shop on the ground floor. The rooms are serviceable and clean; the best have air-conditioning, heat, and cable TV. ⊠ *Ave. Revolución 721, 22000,* ☎ *6/685–4302,* FAX *6/685–4304. 92 rooms. Restaurant, bar, parking (fee). MC, V.*

Nightlife and the Arts

Tijuana has toned down its Sin City image, but there are still plenty of raucous bars on Avenida Revolución. Locals, however, prefer the classier nightclubs in the Zona Río. Tijuana's discos usually have strict dress codes—no T-shirts, jeans, or sandals allowed.

Tijuana now has its own brand name beer, thanks to the Czech brewmaster at **Tijuana Brewery Company/La Cerveceria** (⊠ Blvd. Fundadores 2951, ☎ 6/638–8662). The European-style pub serves only two drinks–Tijuana Claro and Tijuana Oscura, the light and dark beers brewed in the glassed-in brewery beside the bar. Botanes, or appetizers, include chiles rellenos, queso fundido, and smoked tuna, and live music is offered some nights. The bar is a popular after-work spot, and is usually crowded by 7 PM. **Hard Rock Cafe** (⊠ Av. Revolución 520, between Calles 1 and 2, ☎ 6/685–0206) has the same menu and decor as other branches of the ubiquitous club. This one, too, is popular with families and singles. **Baby Rock** (⊠ Calle Diego Rivera 1482, Zona Río, ☎ 6/634–2406), an offshoot of a popular Acapulco disco, attracts a young, hip crowd. **Rodeo de Santa Fe** (⊠ Pueblo Amigo center, Paseo Tijuana, Zona Río, ☎ 6/682–4969) features live *norteño* bands at the dance floor and an indoor rodeo at midnight. One of the hottest night spots with the fashionable set is **Zka** (⊠ Blvd. Paseo de los Heroes, at Ave. Diego Rivera, ☎ 6/634–7140). Dancers take a break from the action on the large disco floor by settling in on comfy couches in the quieter cocktail lounge. Businessmen (there's a definite shortage of women here) favor **Maria Bonita** (⊠ Camino Real hotel, Paseo de los Héroes 10305, ☎ 6/633–4000). Designed after the famed L'Opera bar in Mexico City, this small clublike tavern serves several brands of fine tequila along with beer and mixed drinks, and patrons are encouraged to play dominoes, chess, and card games at the tables.

Outdoor Activities and Sports

BULLFIGHTING

Bullfights feature skilled matadors from throughout Mexico and Spain. Fights are held at **El Toreo de Tijuana** (⊠ Blvd. Agua Caliente, outside downtown, ☎ 6/686–1510) Sunday at 4:30, May through October. In July and August you can see bullfights at the **Plaza de Toros Monumental** (⊠ Playas Tijuana area, Ensenada Hwy., ☎ 6/685–2210) Sunday at 4:30. Admission to bullfights varies, depending on the fame of the matador and the location of your seat.

GOLF

The **Tijuana Country Club** (⊠ Blvd. Agua Caliente, east of downtown, ☎ 6/681–7855) is open to the public. You can rent clubs, electric and hand carts, and caddies for the 18-hole course.

Shopping

The Avenida Revolución shopping area spreads across Calle 1 to the pedestrian walkway leading from the border. Begin by checking out the stands along the border-crossing walkway, comparing prices as you travel toward Avenida Revolución. You may find that the best bargains are closer to the border; you can pick up your piñatas and serapes on your way out of town. The traditional shopping strip is Avenida Revolución between Calles 1 and 8; it's lined with shops and arcades that display a wide range of crafts and curios. Bargaining is expected on the streets and in the arcades, but not in the finer shops.

The shops in **Plaza Revolución** (⊠ Calle 1 and Av. Revolución) sell quality crafts. **Bazar de Mexico** (⊠ Av. Revolución at Calle 7, ☎ 6/638–4737) is a huge complex of shops and stalls carrying the full gamut of Tijuana treasures. The **Mexicoach Terminal** (⊠ Av. Revolución between Calles 6 and 7, ☎ 6/685–1470) is a one-stop center. **La Piel** (⊠ Av. Revolución between Calles 4 and 5, ☎ 6/687–2398) has dependable quality in its leather jackets, backpacks, and luggage.

Sanborns (⊠ Av. Revolución at Calle 8, ☎ 6/688–1462) has beautiful crafts from throughout Mexico, an excellent bakery, and chocolates from Mexico City. **Importaciones Sara** (⊠ Av. Revolución at Calle 4, ☎ 6/688–0482), one of the best department stores in Tijuana, features a wide selection of imported perfumes and fine clothing at attractive prices. The nicest folk-art store, **Tolan** (⊠ Av. Revolución between Calles 7 and 8, ☎ 6/688–3637), carries everything from antique, carved wooden doors to tiny, ceramic miniature village scenes.

MARKET

The **Mercado Hidalgo** (✉ Av. Independencia at Av. Sanchez Taboada, 2 blocks south of Paseo de los Héroes) is Tijuana's municipal market, with rows of fresh produce, grains, herbs, some souvenirs, and the best selection of piñatas in Baja.

SHOPPING CENTERS

Plaza Fiesta (✉ Paseo de los Héroes, across from Plaza Río Tijuana) has a collection of boutiques, jewelry stores, and stained-glass shops. You can find great buys on fashionable clothing and shoes at **Plaza Río Tijuana** (✉ Paseo de los Héroes).

Playas de Rosarito

29 km (18 mi) south of Tijuana.

For better or worse, Rosarito has seen a transformation during the past few decades. The one-time small seaside community, once part of the municipality of Tijuana, had been an overlooked suburb on the way to the port city of Ensenada. But as the roads improved—and particularly after the 1973 completion of Baja's Transpeninsular Highway— Rosarito began to flower. Cityhood didn't come until 1995, when a group of residents finally succeeded in its years-long campaign for the town's self-governance. The following year, Rosarito attracted considerable attention when 20th Century Fox built a permanent movie-production studio on the coastline south of town; the mega-success *Titanic* was shot here in 1996 and 1997. Today, the studio is home to an exciting theme park. Rosarito's leaders had hoped their town would become a cruise ship port, and funded construction of a long pier at the Rosarito Beach Hotel. Unfortunately, the sea is too rough and shallow for the ships, and the pier has become an outdoor café. Still, tourism continues to boom.

Meanwhile, Rosarito's population, now about 110,000, has been growing steadily. The city's main drag, alternately known as the Old Ensenada Highway and Boulevard Benito Juárez, reflects the unrestrained growth and speculation that have both helped and harmed Rosarito. The street is packed with restaurants, bars, and shops in a jarring juxtaposition of building styles. Fortunately, the building boom has slowed and the town's boosters are attempting to beautify the boulevard.

Southern Californians have made Rosarito their weekend getaway, and the crowd is far from subdued. Surfers, swimmers, and sunbathers come here to enjoy the beach, which stretches from the power plant at the north end of town to about 8 km (5 mi) south. Horseback riding, jogging, and strolling are popular along this uninterrupted strand, where whales swim within viewing distance on their winter migration and dolphins and sea lions frequent the shoreline.

Rosarito has always attracted a varied group. These days it's made up of prosperous young Californians building villas and vacation developments, retired Americans and Canadians homesteading in gated communities, and an abundance of young adults seeking cheap food, drink, and an escape from supervision. It often seems that spring break is a year-round event here, with much of the action centered on the Festival Plaza hotel. The police do their best to control the revelers, but spring and summer weekend nights can be outrageously noisy. If you're here to relax in peace, choose a hotel room far from any bars or restaurants.

Hedonism and health get equal billing in Rosarito. Seafood is a favorite here, especially lobster, shrimp, and abalone, and visiting Americans act as if they've been dry for months—margaritas and beer are the favored thirst quenchers. People throw off their inhibitions, at least to the degree permitted by local constables. A typical Rosarito day might begin with a breakfast of eggs, refried beans, and tortillas, followed by a few hours of horseback riding on the beach. Lying in the sun or browsing in shops takes care of midday. Siestas are imperative and are usually followed by more shopping, strolling, or sunbathing before a night of dinner and dancing.

Rosarito has few historic or cultural attractions, beaches and bars being the main draws. Sightseeing consists of strolling along the beach or down **Boulevard Benito Juárez,** which runs parallel to it. An immense Pemex gasoline installation and electric plant anchor the northern end of Boulevard Juárez, which then runs along a collection of shopping arcades, restaurants, and motels.

Museo Wa-Kuatay. Rosarito's history is illustrated in exhibits on the Kumiai indians, the early missions, and ranching in the region at this small museum. ⊠ *Blvd. Juárez next to the Rosarito Beach Hotel,* ☎ *no phone.* ☺ *Free.* ☾ *Closed Tues.*

Foxploration. Fox Studios has expanded its operation to include a film-oriented theme park. Guests learn how films are made by visiting a set resembling a New York street scene, and another filled with props from *Titanic.* Exhibits on filming, sound and light effects, and animation are both educational and entertaining, and Fox's most famous films are shown in the large state-of-the-art theater. The park includes a children's playroom where kids can shoot thousands of foam balls out of air cannons, a food court with U.S. franchises including Subway and Starbucks, and a large retail area. ⊠ *Old Ensenada Hwy. Km 32.8, Poptla,* ☎ *6/614–9499,* WEB *www.foxploration.com.* ☺ *$9–$12.*

Galeria Giorgio Santini. Baja's finest painters and sculptors now have a worthwhile venue for their works, which are handsomely displayed in this architecturally stunning gallery. Stop by for a glass of wine or an espresso in the coffeeshop, and learn something about Baja's vibrant art scene. ⊠ *Old Ensenada Hwy. Km 40,* ☎ *6/614–1459,* WEB *www.giorgiosantini.com.* ☺ *Free.* ☾ *Closed Wed.*

Dining and Lodging

$$$ ✕ **Calafia.** This restaurant, a 10-minute car ride south of Rosarito, is part of a whitewashed stucco complex that houses an eclectic array of attractions—all perched above the crashing sea. The walls are a nascent museum dedicated to the missionary conquests in Baja. Featuring fresh seafood and creative Mexican cuisine, Calafia is a unique place to enjoy a meal by the sea. Hotel rooms are available in a variety of buildings and trailers packed tightly by the restaurant. ⊠ *Old Ensenada Hwy. Km 35.5,* ☎ *6/612–1581 or 877/700–2342,* FAX *6/612–0296,* WEB *www.calafia.com.mx. MC, V.*

$$–$$$ ✕ **El Patio.** Calm amid the bustle of the Festival Plaza complex, this tasteful, colonial-style restaurant is the best spot for a relaxed, authentic Mexican meal. Umbrella-covered tables are framed by soft-blue and azure walls, and the aromas of chilies, mole, and grilled meats spark the appetite. The menu favors dishes like savory grilled quail, shrimp crepes, and chicken with poblano sauce. The bar is peaceful as well—a good place to enjoy a cocktail away from the streetside crowds. ⊠ *Festival Plaza, Blvd. Juárez,* ☎ *6/612–2950. AE, MC, V.*

$$ ✕ **La Leña.** The cornerstone restaurant of the Quinta Plaza shopping
★   center, La Leña is spacious and impeccably clean, with the tables spread far enough apart for privacy. Try any of the beef dishes, espe-

cially the tender carne asada with tortillas and guacamole. ⊠ *Quinta Plaza, Blvd. Juárez,* ☎ *6/612–0826. MC, V.*

$$ ✕ **El Nido.** A dark, wood-paneled restaurant with leather booths and a large central fireplace, this is one of the oldest eateries in Rosarito. Diners unimpressed with newer, fancier places come here for mesquite-grilled steaks and for grilled quail from the owner's farm in the Baja wine country. ⊠ *Blvd. Juárez 67,* ☎ *6/612–1430. MC, V.*

$ ✕ **La Flor de Michoacán.** Michoacán-style carnitas, served with home-made tortillas, guacamole, and salsa, are featured at this rustic Rosarito landmark, established in 1950. The tacos, *tortas* (sandwiches), and tostadas are great. Takeout is available. ⊠ *Blvd. Juárez 291,* ☎ *6/612–1858. No credit cards. Closed Wed.*

$ ✕ **Tacos El Yaqui.** For true downhome Mexican cooking, nothing beats this clean taco stand. Their carne asada tacos wrapped in fresh corn tortillas are superb, and are the perfect fix for late-night munchies. The stand is clean and the cooks use purified water. ⊠ *Calle de la Palma off Blvd. Juárez across from the Rosarito Beach Hotel,* ☎ *no phone. No credit cards.*

$$$–$$$$ ✕☷ **Rosarito Beach Hotel and Spa.** In the heart of Rosarito, this resort is a piece of local history. Built during the Prohibition, it has huge ballrooms, tiled fountains and stairways, murals, and a glassed-in pool deck overlooking the sea. A wooden pier stretches over the ocean; on calm days, there's no better place to watch the sunset than from the café tables along its glassed-in edges. The rooms suffer from age, but have a certain weary charm. Those in the oldest section have hand-painted wooden beams and heavy dark furnishings. Those in the tower have air-conditioning and more modern pastel decor. Reduced midweek rates and special packages are often available. A refurbished 1930s mansion next door houses Casa Playa Spa, with massage, beauty treatments, exercise equipment, and hot tubs. Chabert's, the resort's French restaurant, is filled with European antiques. It's open for dinner only. Azteca, the main restaurant, is a good place to stop for Sunday brunch or a light meal when you're exploring the area. ⊠ *Blvd. Juárez, south end of town, 22710 (Box 430145, San Diego, CA 22710),* ☎ *6/612–0144 or 800/343–8582,* 𝔽𝔸𝕏 *6/612–1125,* 𝚆𝙴𝙱 *www.rosaritobeachhotel.com. 180 rooms, 100 suites. 3 restaurants, bar, 2 pools, spa, tennis court, exercise room, beach, playground. MC, V.*

$$$ ✕☷ **Marriott Real Del Mar Residence Inn.** Golfers and escapists relish
★ their privacy at this cliffside all-suites hotel with faraway views of the sea. Standard accommodations have living rooms with vaulted brick ceilings, fireplaces, kitchens, and two double beds. Larger units come with one or two bedrooms. Greens fees at the on-site golf course are included in packages. The hotel, 19 km (12 mi) south of downtown Tijuana and 10 km (6 mi) north of Rosarito Beach, is completely removed from the action. Both restaurants attract diners from Tijuana and Rosarito for their fresh seafood and nouvelle Mexican preparations. ⊠ *Ensenada toll road Km 19.5, 22710,* ☎ *6/631–3670 or 800/ 331–3131,* 𝔽𝔸𝕏 *6/631–3677,* 𝚆𝙴𝙱 *www.realdelmar.com.mx. 75 suites. 2 restaurants, bar, snack bar, pool, spa, 18-hole golf course, exercise room. AE, MC, V.*

$$$–$$$$ ☷ **Las Rocas.** This white hotel with blue-tile domes is the prettiest and
★ most romantic in the area—which explains the many weddings held on the ocean-facing lawns. The building sits atop a hillside, giving all the rooms ocean views. The least expensive ones are small, but recently renovated. The most expensive suites are larger and have fireplaces and microwaves. The pool and whirlpool seem to spill over the cliffs into the ocean. A full spa offers massage, facials, wraps, and other treatments in serene treatment rooms with full ocean views. The restaurant is quite good, and the low-cal spa offerings include a tasty turkey and

spinach roll. Ask about spa packages and midweek specials. ⊠ *Old Ensenada Hwy. Km 38.5, 22710 (⊠ Box 189003 HLR, Coronado, CA 92178),* ☎ FAX *6/612–2140,* ☎ *619/234–9810 in CA; 888/527–7622,* WEB *www.lasrocas.com 40 rooms, 34 suites. Restaurant, 2 bars, 2 pools, hot tub, spa, beach. AE, MC, V.*

$$ ⊞ **Festival Plaza.** Designed with unrestrained fun in mind, Festival Plaza is geared toward a youthful crowd. The motel-like rooms are in an eight-story building with a facade resembling a roller coaster. The casitas close to the beach are the quietest accommodations and have small hot tubs, separate living rooms with foldout couches, and private garages, but no kitchen facilities. The hotel also operates a complex of 13 villas just south of Rosarito; these have full kitchens. Within the hotel complex are several bars and good restaurants—try the traditional Mexican dishes at El Patio—and the central courtyard serves as a con-cert stage, children's playground, and party headquarters. Rooms in the newest section face patio bars where revelers tend to be wildly noisy. Discounted room rates are often available, especially in winter. ⊠ *Blvd. Juárez 11, 22710,* ☎ *6/612–0842, 6/612–2950, or 800/453–8606,* FAX *6/612–0124,* WEB *www.festivalbaja.com. 217 rooms, 5 suites, 7 casitas, 13 villas. 4 restaurants, 6 bars, pool, dance club. AE, MC, V.*

$ ⊞ **Brisas del Mar.** A modern motel (built in 1992), the Brisas del Mar is especially good for families—the large pastel rooms comfortably ac-commodate four people. A few of the suites on the second story have hot tubs and ocean views; all have air-conditioning and TV. The motel is on the inland side of Boulevard Juárez, and traffic noise can be a problem. ⊠ *Blvd. Juárez 22, 22710 (Box 18903, Coronado, CA 92178-9003),* ☎ FAX *6/612–2547 or 888/871–3605. 69 rooms, 2 suites. Bar, coffee shop, pool. AE, MC, V.*

Nightlife and the Arts

Rosarito's many restaurants keep customers entertained with live music, piano bars, or *folklórico* (folk music and dance) shows, and the bar scene is hopping as well. Drinking-and-driving laws are stiff; the police will fine you no matter how little you've had. If you drink, take a cab or assign a designated driver. The police are also enforcing laws that prohibit drinking in the streets: confine your revelry to the bars.

There's a lot going on at night at the **Rosarito Beach Hotel** (⊠ Blvd. Juárez, ☎ 6/612–0144): live music at the ocean-view **Beachcomber Bar**; a Mexican Fiesta on Friday and Saturday nights; and occasional live bands and dances in the cavernous ballroom. **Papas and Beer** (⊠ on the beach off Blvd. Juárez near Rosarito Beach Hotel, ☎ 6/612–0444) draws a young, energetic crowd for drinking and dancing. The **Festi-val Plaza** (⊠ Blvd. Juárez 11, ☎ 6/612–0842) has become party cen-tral for Rosarito's younger crowd and presents live concerts on the hotel's courtyard stage most weekends. In the hotel complex are El **Museo Cantina Tequila** (☎ 6/612–2950), dedicated to the art of imbibing tequila and stocked with more than 130 brands of the fiery drink—including the house rattlesnake tequila, said to be an aphrodisiac. Also at Festi-val Plaza, **Rock & Roll Taco** is a taco stand and boisterous bar with several sections, including an outdoor area backed by hotel rooms. It's the largest (and probably the most rambunctious) dancing and drink-ing hangout in town. **Señor Frog's** (⊠ Blvd. Juárez 1 block north of the Festival Plaza) offers a raucous blend of tequila and loud music.

Rene's Sports Bar (⊠ Carretera Transpeninsular Km 28, ☎ 6/612–1061) draws a somewhat quieter, older crowd; the restaurant isn't great, but a few pool tables, TVs broadcasting sporting events, and a convivial gaggle of gringos make the bar a great hangout. **Chabert's Lounge** (⊠ Rosarito Beach Hotel, Blvd. Juárez, ☎ 6/612–0144) is by far the classiest place for a grownup cocktail accompanied by the pianist's romantic ballads.

Outdoor Activities and Sports

GOLF

The **Real del Mar Golf Club** (⌧ 18 km [11 mi] south of the border on Ensenada toll road, ☎ 6/631–3401) has 18 holes overlooking the ocean. Golf packages are available at some Rosarito Beach hotels.

HORSEBACK RIDING

You can hire horses at the north and south ends of Boulevard Juárez and on the beach south of the Rosarito Beach Hotel for $10 per hour. If you're a dedicated equestrian, ask about tours into the countryside, which can be arranged with the individual owners.

SURFING

The waves are particularly good at **Popotla** (Km 33), **Calafia** (Km 35.5), and **Costa Baja** (Km 36) on the Old Ensenada Highway.

Shopping

Shopping is far better in Rosarito than in most Baja cities, especially for pottery, wood furniture, and high-end household items favored by condo-owners in nearby expat clusters. Curio stands and open-air artisans' markets line Boulevard Juárez both north and south of town. Major hotels have shopping arcades with restaurants, taco stands, and some decent crafts stores.

Apisa (⌧ Blvd. Juarez 2400, ☎ 6/612–0125) is said to be the finest home-decor shop in town, and sells contemporary furnishings and iron sculptures from Guadalajara.

Casa la Carreta (⌧ Old Ensenada Hwy. Km 29, ☎ 6/612–0502), one of Rosarito's best furniture shops, keeps expanding and is worth a visit just to see the wood-carvers shaping elaborate desks, dining tables, and armoires. **Don Quijote Furniture** (⌧ Blvd. Juárez s/n, across from Quinta Plaza, ☎ no phone) is a great outlet for custom furnishings and wrought iron. Resembling a colonial church with its facade of hand-painted tiles, **La Misión** (⌧ Blvd. Juárez s/n, across from Ortega's, ☎ 6/612–1576) displays hand-carved chairs, tin lamps shaped like stars, and glazed pottery. **Casa Torres** (⌧ Rosarito Beach Hotel Shopping Center, Blvd. Juárez, ☎ 6/612–1008) carries a wide array of imported perfumes. There are several shops in this center by the hotel's parking lot, along with an Internet café. The **Calimax** grocery store on Boulevard Juárez is a good place to stock up on necessities.

Puerto Nuevo (Newport)

Old Ensenada Hwy. Km 44, 12 km (7½ mi) south of Rosarito.

Southern Californians regularly cross the border to indulge in the classic Puerto Nuevo meal: grilled lobster, refried beans, rice, homemade tortillas, butter, salsa, and lime. At least 30 restaurants are packed into this small village; nearly all offer the identical menu. An artisans' market sits at the entrance to the restaurant row, and stands selling pottery, serapes, and T-shirts line the highway. Several longtime favorite inns and restaurants line the road south to Ensenada. A new marina is under construction at Puerto Salina south of Puerto Nuevo; when completed, it will allow private boaters to anchor and refuel before reaching Ensenada.

Dining and Lodging

Don't expect much variety in the food at any of the Puerto Nuevo restaurants: people come here for the classic lobster meal. Some places have full bars; others serve only wine and beer. **Ortega's,** with several branches in Puerto Nuevo and Rosarito, is the most crowded; **Ponderosa** is smaller and quieter and is run by a gracious family; **Puerto Nuevo II** offers unusual preparations of scallops and abalone (when it's available); and **La Casa de la Langosta** serves grilled fish along with lobster and shrimp. Lobsters in most places are priced as small, medium, and large—medium is about $15. Most of the lobster comes from the waters 1½ km (1 mi) or so off Baja's shores (where pollution is not a concern), and is frozen when not in season (October through March). Most places are open for lunch and dinner on a first-come, first-served basis. Some take credit cards.

$$ ✕🏨 **La Fonda.** A longtime favorite with beachgoers, La Fonda has well-
★ worn rooms decorated with carved-wood furniture, old bullfighting posters, and local folk art; most rooms have great views of the ocean. There are no phones or televisions, just the sound of the surf and miles of empty beach to keep you entertained. At the restaurant you can sit on an outdoor patio and sip potent margaritas served with fresh lobster, grilled steaks, prime rib, and traditional Mexican dishes. The bar is packed on weekend nights, and the patrons boisterous. If you plan on getting any sleep, ask for a room as close to the sounds of the surf as possible. Credit cards are accepted at the restaurant and to reserve rooms, but accommodations have to be paid for in cash. ✉ *Old Ensenada Hwy. Km 59, 22710 (Box 430268, San Ysidro, CA 92143),* ☎ *615/5–0307. 26 rooms. Restaurant, bar, beach. MC, V.*

$$$$ 🏨 **Hacienda Bajamar.** On the grounds of the Bajamar golf resort, south of Puerto Nuevo and about halfway between Rosarito and Ensenada, this hacienda-style hotel surrounds a central courtyard. Rooms have hand-carved furnishings and French doors leading to landscaped patios. Private condos (some for rent) edge the golf course and the cliffs overlooking the ocean. ✉ *Old Ensenada Hwy., Km 77.5, Ensenada 22800,* ☎ *615/5–0151, 619/299–1112, or 800/225–2418,* 🖷 *615/5–0150,* 🌐 *www.bajamar.com. 81 rooms. Restaurant, bar, pool, golf, 2 tennis courts. AE, MC, V.*

$$ 🏨 **New Port Beach Hotel.** The closest accommodations to the lobster restaurants are in this sand-color complex with ocean views. Rooms don't have air-conditioning, but they do have heaters for chilly winter nights, along with cable TV, small balconies, and simple blue-gray and white furnishings. The hotel has dance bands in the upstairs lounge, marimba music on the weekend in the lobby bar, and classical music on Sunday. ✉ *Old Ensenada Hwy. Km 45, 22712,* ☎ *6/614–1166 or 800/582–1018,* 🖷 *6/614–1174,* 🌐 *www.newportbeachhotel.com. 147 rooms. Restaurant, bar, pool, 2 tennis courts, exercise room. MC, V.*

Outdoor Activities and Sports

GOLF

Bajamar (✉ Old Ensenada Hwy. Km 77.5, ☎ 615/5–0151; 615/5–0161 for tee times) has 18 holes of championship-level golf on the cliffs above the ocean and another nine holes near the beach.

En Route   Open views of pounding surf and jagged cliffs are interspersed with one-of-a-kind hotels and restaurants along the coastline between Rosarito and Ensenada. The paved highway (Mexico Highway 1) between the two cities often cuts a path between low mountains and high oceanside cliffs. Exits lead to rural roads, oceanfront campgrounds, and an ever-increasing number of resort communities. The small fishing villages of **San Miguel** and **El Sauzal** sit off the highway to the north of Ensenada, and you can see the **Coronado Islands** clearly off the coast.

Ensenada

104 km (65 mi) south of Tijuana, 75 km (47 mi) south of Rosarito.

In 1542 Juan Rodríguez Cabrillo first discovered the seaport that Sebastián Vizcaino named Ensenada-Bahía de Todos Santos (All Saints' Bay) in 1602. Since then the town has drawn a steady stream of explorers and developers. First ranchers made their homes on large plots along the coast and into the mountains. Gold miners followed, turning the area into a boomtown in the late 1800s. After mine stocks were depleted, the area settled back into a pastoral state, but the harbor gradually grew into a major port for shipping agricultural goods from the nearby ranches and farms. Today, with a population of some 369,000, it's one of Mexico's largest seaports and has a thriving fishing fleet and fish-processing industry. The smell of fish from the canneries lining the north and south sides of the city can be overpowering at times.

There are no beaches in Ensenada proper, but beaches north and south of town are satisfactory for swimming, sunning, surfing, and camping. On summer and holiday weekends the population swells, but the town rarely feels overcrowded. Whereas the hotels and resorts along the coast, especially around Rosarito, attract the bulk of the weekend escapists, Ensenada tends to draw those who want to explore a more traditional Mexican city.

Ensenada, the third-largest city in Baja, hugs the harbor of Bahía de Todos Santos. The city is undergoing a boom, thanks in part to the cruise-ship industry. A new cruise port was completed in 2000, with space for three ships. A hotel and shopping center in a complex to be called Cruise Port Village are in the planning stages. At this time, ships call several days a week, bringing shoppers and diners to the city. Both the waterfront and downtown's main street have been renovated, and the main entrance into downtown has been diverted to avoid traffic around the commercial port area.

⑬ **Las Bodegas de Santo Tomás.** Baja's oldest winery gives tours and tastings at its downtown winery and bottling plant. The restaurant in the winery, La Embotelladora Vieja, is one of Baja's finest. The winery also operates La Esquina de Bodegas, a café, shop, and gallery in a bright-blue building across Avenida Miramar. ⊠ *Av. Miramar 666,* ☎ *6/174–0836, 858/454–7166, or 800/336–5454.* 🖅 *$2.* ☉ *Tours, tastings daily at 11, 1, and 3.*

⑭ **Fish Market.** At the northernmost point of Boulevard Costero, the main street along the waterfront, is an indoor-outdoor market where row after row of counters display piles of shrimp, tuna, dorado, marlin, snapper, and dozens of other species of fish caught off Baja's coasts. Outside, stands sell grilled or smoked fish, seafood cocktails, and fish tacos. Browsers can pick up some standard souvenirs, eat well for very little money, and take some great photographs. The original fish taco stands line the dirt path to the fish market. If your stomach is on the delicate side, try the fish tacos at the cleaner, quieter **Plaza de Mariscos** in the shadow of the giant beige **Plaza de Marina** that blocks the view of the traditional fish market from the street.

⑲ **Our Lady of Guadalupe.** The city's largest cathedral is the heart of Ensenada for many residents. ⊠ *Av. Floresta at Av. Juárez.*

⑫ **Parque Revolución.** Revolution Park is the most traditional plaza in Ensenada, with a bandstand, playground, and plenty of benches in the shade. The plaza takes on a festive feeling Saturday and Sunday evenings, when neighbors congregate on the benches and children chase seagulls down the pathways. ⊠ *Av. Juárez at Av. Obregón.*

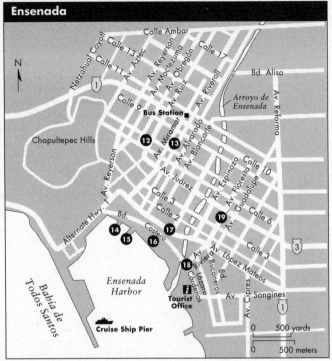

Ensenada

⑰ **Paseo Calle Primera.** The renamed Avenida López Mateos is the center of Ensenada's traditional tourist zone. High-rise hotels, souvenir shops, restaurants, and bars line the avenue for eight blocks, from its beginning at the foot of the Chapultepec Hills to the dry channel of the Arroyo de Ensenada. Tourist promoters have sponsored a beautification project along the avenue, which now has sidewalks, outdoor cafés, and restored storefronts. Businesses use one or both street names for their addresses, though must stick with López Mateos. Locals shop for furniture, clothing, and other necessities a few blocks inland on **Avenida Juárez**, in Ensenada's downtown area.

⑯ **Plaza Cívica.** The block-long concrete park has sculptures of Mexican heroes Benito Juárez, Miguel Hidalgo, and Venustiano Carranza. ⊠ *Blvd. Costero at Av. Riveroll.*

⑱ **Riviera del Pacífico.** Officially called the Centro Social, Cívico y Cultural de Ensenada (Social, Civic and Cultural Center of Ensenada), the Riviera is a rambling white, hacienda-style mansion built in the 1920s. An enormous gambling palace, hotel, restaurant, and bar, the glamorous Riviera was frequented by wealthy U.S. citizens and Mexicans, particularly during Prohibition. When gambling was outlawed in Mexico and Prohibition ended in the United States, the palace lost its raison d'être. You can tour some of the elegant ballrooms and halls, which occasionally host art shows and civic events. Many of the rooms are locked; check at the main office to see if there is someone available to show you around. The gardens alone are worth visiting, and the building now houses the **Museo de Historia de Ensenada**, a museum on Baja's history. ⊠ *Blvd. Costero and Av. Riviera,* ☎ *6/176–4233; 6/177–0594 for museum.* ▨ *Building and gardens free, museum donations requested.* ☉ *Daily 9:30–2 and 3–5.*

⑮ **Sportfishing Pier.** Fishing and whale-watching boats depart from the pier. The area around the pier has been remodeled, and a broad malecón (seaside walkway) with park benches and palms runs along the waterfront. ⊠ *Blvd. Costero at Av. Alvarado.*

OFF THE
BEATEN PATH

LA BUFADORA – Seawater splashes up to 75 ft in the air, spraying sightseers standing near this impressive tidal blowhole (*la bufadora* means the buffalo snort) in the coastal cliffs at Punta Banda. Legend has it that the blowhole was created by a whale or sea serpent trapped in an undersea cave; both these stories, and the less romantic scientific facts, are posted on a roadside plaque here. The road to La Bufadora along Punta Banda, an isolated, mountainous point that juts into the sea, is lined with stands selling olives, tamales, strands of chilies and garlic, and terracotta planters. The drive gives short-term visitors a sampling of Baja's wilderness and is well worth a half-day excursion. Public rest rooms are available. There is a small fee to park near the blowhole. From the lot, you file through a row of permanent vendors' stands en route to the cliff. There's a public bus that runs from the downtown Ensenada bus station to Maneadero, the nearest town on the highway to La Bufadora. There, you can catch a minibus labeled Punta Banda that goes to La Bufadora. ⊠ *Hwy. 23, 31 km (19 mi) south of Ensenada.*

Beaches

The waterfront in Ensenada proper is taken up by fishing boats, repair yards, and commercial shipping. The best swimming beaches are south of town. **Estero Beach** is long and clean, with mild waves; the Estero Beach Hotel takes up much of the oceanfront, but the beach is public. Surfers populate the beaches off Highway 1 north and south of Ensenada, particularly **San Miguel, California, Tres Marías,** and **La Joya;** scuba divers prefer **Punta Banda,** by La Bufadora. Lifeguards are rare, so swimmers should be cautious. The tourist office in Ensenada has a map that shows safe diving and surfing beaches.

Dining and Lodging

$$$ ✕ **La Embotelladora Vieja.** The most elegant restaurant in Ensenada
★ is this converted wine-aging room at the Santo Tomás winery. The decor is classic French country. The Baja French menu includes appetizers of smoked tuna and French pâté; among the most sublime entrées are the grilled lobster in cabernet sauvignon sauce and quail with sauvignon blanc sauce. Teetotalers, note: Nearly every dish is prepared with wine, although much of the alcohol evaporates during cooking. You can order some dishes without alcohol-enhanced sauces. All of Baja's wineries are represented on the extensive wine list. ⊠ *Av. Miramar 666,* ☎ *6/174–0807. MC, V. Closed Tues.*

$$$ ✕ **El Rey Sol.** From its chateaubriand *bouquetière* (garnished with a
★ bouquet of vegetables) to the savory chicken chipotle, this family-owned French restaurant sets the standard for fine dining in Baja. The decor at El Rey Sol, open since 1947, is comfortable and elegant, with Louis XIV–style furnishings, and the service is attentive. The sidewalk tables are also a perfect place to dine and enjoy the fresh air. Pastries, all made on the premises, can be bought to go from the small café in the front. ⊠ *Av. López Mateos 1000,* ☎ *6/178–1733. AE, MC, V.*

$$ ✕ **Bronco's Steak House.** A great find near the Riviera del Pacífico, Bronco's serves exceptional steaks and Mexican specialties. Try the Boca del Río, a New York steak stuffed with grilled onions and fiery serrano chilies. Tripe appears frequently on the menu, satisfying the cravings of the local diners gathered at many of the wood tables. Brick walls, wood-plank floors, and hanging spurs and chaps give the place a Wild West feel, but the mood is subdued and relaxed. Locals rave about the weekend breakfast buffet. ⊠ *Av. López Mateos 1525,* ☎ *6/176–4900. MC, V.*

$$ ✕ **Las Cazuelas.** Begin the day with a shrimp omelette or end it with tender abalone at this locally popular dining room. The seafood feast is a bountiful spread of fish and shellfish bound to please; beef and chicken entrées satisfy those who prefer turf over surf. ⊠ *Av. Sangines 6,* ☎ *6/176–1044. MC, V.*

$ ✕ **El Charro.** You can find less (and more) expensive rotisserie chicken,
★ beans, rice, and tortillas at other places downtown, but El Charro still attracts a steady stream of locals and tourists. Hungry patrons hover over platters of *chiles rellenos* (cheese-stuffed chilies deep-fried in batter), enchiladas, and fresh chips and guacamole at heavy wooden picnic tables. Plump chickens slowly turn over a wood fire by the front window, and the aroma of mesquite and simmering beans fills the air. Similarly named restaurants have opened on the same block; stick with the original to avoid disappointment. ⊠ *Av. López Mateos 475,* ☎ *6/178–3881. No credit cards.*

$ ✕ **Mariscos de Bahía de Ensenada.** Red lights flicker around the front
★ door, making this popular seafood house just off the main drag easy to spot. The place is packed on weekends; tables are easier to come by weeknights. Clams, shrimp, lobster, red snapper, squid, and other fresh seafood are fried, baked, broiled, or grilled, and served with a basic iceberg-lettuce salad, white rice, and tortillas made fresh at the window-front tortilleria. A few canopied sidewalk tables allow for outdoor dining. ⊠ *Av. Riveroll 109,* ☎ *6/178–1015. MC, V.*

$$$–$$$$ ▥ **Hotel Coral & Marina.** The largest resort on the Baja Norte coast fea-
★ tures a marina with slips for 600 boats and customs-clearing facilities. All rooms here are suites. Those in two eight-story towers are decorated in burgundy and dark green; most have waterfront balconies, seating areas, cable TV, and international phone service. Conventions, fishing and golf tournaments, and boat races fill the hotel on weekends; rates are often 30%–50% lower on winter weekdays. ⊠ *Carretera Transpeninsular Tijuana–Ensenada Km 103, No. 3421, Zona Playitas,* ☎ *6/175–0000 or 877/233–5839,* ℻ *6/175–0005,* 🆆🅴🅱 *www.hotelcoral.com. 147 suites. Restaurant, 1 indoor pool, 2 outdoor pools, hot tub, spa, 2 tennis courts, exercise room, boating, fishing. MC, V.*

$$$–$$$$ ▥ **Punta Morro.** Just five minutes from Ensenada, this secluded all-suites
★ hotel is a great place to relax. The Punta Morro is popular with newlyweds, and, with its romantic-getaway package (which includes champagne and roses), it's known as a great place to pop the question. The restaurant, perched just above the crashing waves, has an excellent combination of Continental cuisine and fresh seafood; Continental breakfast is included and delivered to your door. All rooms have seaside terraces and fireplaces. Two- and three-bedroom suites are available for groups and families. ⊠ *Mexico Hwy. 1, 3 km (2 mi) north of town, Apdo. 2891, 22800 (Box 43-4263, San Ysidro, CA 92143),* ☎ *6/178–3507 or 800/526–6676,* ℻ *6/174–4490,* 🆆🅴🅱 *www.punta-morro.com. 30 suites. Restaurant, bar, pool, hot tub, beach. MC, V.*

$$$ ▥ **Las Rosas.** This elegant all-suites hotel just north of Ensenada is both
★ intimate and upscale. The atrium lobby has marble floors, mint-green-and-pink couches that look out at the sea, and a glass ceiling that glows at night. All rooms face the ocean and pool; some have fireplaces and hot tubs, and even the least expensive are lovely. Las Rosas is booked solid most weekends—make reservations far in advance. *Mexico Hwy. 1, north of Ensenada (⊠ 374 East H St., Suite A–455, Chula Vista, CA 91910),* ☎ *6/174–4360,* ℻ *6/174–4595,* 🆆🅴🅱 *www.lasrosas.com. 32 suites. Restaurant, bar, pool, hot tub. AE, MC, V.*

$$ ▥ **Estero Beach Resort.** Families settle in for a week or more at this long-standing resort on Ensenada's best beach. The rooms (some with kitchenettes) are housed in several mint-green buildings. The best are those right by the sand; the worst (and cheapest) are in the oldest section, by

the parking lot. Guests spend their days swimming, fishing, riding horses, playing volleyball, and generally hanging out with friends. Nights are spent at the casual restaurant and bar. Nonguests should stop by and check out the resort's small museum with an outstanding collection of Mexican folk art and artifacts. Midweek winter rates are a real bargain, and the resort feels almost deserted at this time. ⊠ *Mexico Hwy. 1, between Ensenada and Maneadero, 10 km (6 mi) south of Ensenada, 22810 (482 San Ysidro Blvd., Suite 1186, San Ysidro, CA 92173),* ☎ *6/176–6225,* FAX *6/176–6925. 106 rooms, 2 suites. Restaurant, bar, kitchenettes, pool, 4 tennis courts, horseback riding, volleyball, shops, playground, water sports, equipment, museum. MC, V.*

$ 🏨 **Hotel del Valle.** Fishermen and budget travelers frequent the clean, basic rooms in this small hotel on a relatively quiet side street. Although the rooms lack air-conditioning, they're well maintained and have fans, phones, and TVs (with local stations only). Guests have use of a coffeemaker in the lobby and parking spaces in front of the rooms. As always, ask about rate discounts—those posted behind the front desk are about 40% higher than guests in the know normally pay. ⊠ *Av. Riveroll 367, 22800,* ☎ *6/178–2224,* FAX *6/174–0466. 42 rooms. MC, V.*

$ 🏨 **Joker Hotel.** A bizarre, colorful mishmash of styles makes it hard to miss the Joker, which is conveniently located for those traveling south of Ensenada. Spacious rooms have private balconies, satellite TV, and phones. Traffic noise from the highway and from guests leaving at the crack of dawn can be a problem; try to stay away from the road and the busiest parts of the parking lot. ⊠ *Mexico Hwy. 1 Km 12.5, 22800,* ☎ FAX *6/176–7201. 40 rooms. Pool, hot tub. MC, V.*

Nightlife and the Arts

Ensenada is a party town for college students, surfers, and other young tourists. **Hussong's Cantina** (⊠ Av. Ruíz 113, ☎ 6/178–3210) has been an Ensenada landmark since 1892 and has changed little since then. A security guard stands by the front door to handle the often rowdy crowd—a mix of locals and tourists of all ages over 18. The noise is usually deafening, pierced by mariachi and ranchera musicians and the whoops and hollers of the inebriated. **Papas and Beer** (⊠ Av. Ruíz at López Mateos, ☎ 6/178–0145) attracts a collegiate crowd. **La Capilla** (⊠ Hotel El Cid, Blvd. López Mateos 993, ☎ 6/174–2401) is better suited to an older crowd who enjoy live Cuban music in a relaxed setting.

Outdoor Activities and Sports

FISHING

Boats leave the Ensenada **Sportfishing Pier** regularly. The best angling is from April through November, with bottom fishing good in the winter. Charter vessels and party boats are available from several outfitters along Avenida López Mateos and Boulevard Costero and off the sportfishing pier. Trips on group boats cost about $35 for a half day or $100 for a full day. Licenses are available at the tourist office or from charter companies.

Ensenada Clipper Fleet (⊠ Sportfishing Pier, Blvd. Costero at Av. Alvarado, ☎ 6/178–2185) has charter and group boats. **Sergio's Sportfishing** (⊠ Sportfishing Pier, Blvd. Costero at Av. Alvarado, ☎ 6/178–2185, FAX 6/178–2377), one of the best sportfishing companies in Ensenada, has charter and group boats, and slips for guests' boats. You can book sportfishing packages including transportation, accommodations, and fishing through **Baja California Tours** (☎ 858/454–7166 or 800/336-5454 in the U.S., FAX 858/454–2703).

GOLF

The **Baja Country Club** (⊠ Mexico Hwy. 1 south of Ensenada at Maneadero, ☎ 6/177–5523) has a secluded 18-hole course in a resort development.

KAYAKING

Estero Beach and Punta Banda (en route to La Bufadora south of Ensenada) are both good kayaking areas, although facilities are limited. **Dale's La Bufadora Shop** (⊠ Rancho La Bufadora at Punta Banda, ☎ 6/154–2092) offers kayak rentals. The shop is open on weekends or by advance reservation. **Expediciones de Turismo Ecológico y Aventura** (⊠ Blvd. Costero 1094-14, ☎ 6/178–3704) runs kayaking trips and other adventure tours in the region.

WHALE-WATCHING

Boats leave the Ensenada **Sportfishing Pier** for whale-watching trips from December through February. The gray whales migrating from the north to bays and lagoons in southern Baja pass through Todos Santos Bay, often close to shore. There are restrictions on how close the boats can get to the whales, but you should be able to get good photos. Binoculars and telephoto camera lenses come in handy. The trips last about three hours. Vessels and tour boats are available from several outfitters, including Sergio's, along Avenida López Mateos and Boulevard Costero and off the sportfishing pier. You can book whale-watching packages, which include transportation, accommodations, and the boat trips, through the American company **Baja California Tours** (☎ 800/336–5454; 858/454–7166 in the U.S., FAX 858/454–2703).

Shopping

Most of the tourist shops are located along Avenida López Mateos beside the hotels and restaurants. There are several two-story shopping arcades, many with empty shops. Dozens of curio shops line the street, all selling similar selections of pottery, woven blankets and serapes, embroidered dresses, and onyx chess sets.

Bazar Casa Ramirez (⊠ Av. López Mateos 510, ☎ 6/178–8209) sells high-quality Talavera pottery and other ceramics, wrought-iron lamps and household accoutrements, and papier-mâché figurines. **Artes Don Quijote** (⊠ Av. López Mateos 503, ☎ 6/176–9476) has an impressive array of carved wood doors, huge terra-cotta pots, and crafts from Oaxaca. **Mario's Silver** (⊠ Calle Primera 1090-6, ☎ 6/178–2451) has several branches along the main street tempting shoppers with displays of silver and gold jewelry and leather handbags. At **Los Castillo** (⊠ Av. López Mateos 815, ☎ 6/176–1187), the display of silver jewelry from Taxco is limited but of excellent quality. **La Mina de Salomón** (⊠ Av. López Mateos 1000, ☎ 6/178–2836) carries elaborate jewelry in a tiny gallery next to El Rey Sol restaurant.

The **Centro Artesenal de Ensenada** has a smattering of galleries and shops. By far, the best shop at the Centro Artesenal is **Galería de Pérez Meillón** (⊠ Blvd. Costera 1094–39, ☎ 6/174–0394), with its museum-quality Casas Grandes pottery and varied folk art by indigenous northern Mexican peoples. **La Esquina de Bodegas** (⊠ Av. Miramar at Calle 6, ☎ 6/178–3557) is an innovative gallery, shop, and café in a century-old winery building. Baja's finest wines are sold here at reasonable prices, and an upstairs gallery sells glassware, pottery, and books. The café at the back of the building serves coffee, wine, and a small menu of soups and entrées. Bargain hunters are delighted with **Los Globos** (⊠ Calle 9, three blocks east of Reforma, ☎ no phone), a daily open-air swap meet. Vendors and shoppers are most abundant on weekends.

Side Trip to the Guadalupe Valley

Most of Baja's wineries are located in the Guadalupe Valley northeast of Ensenada on Highway 3 to Tecate. The valley, originally settled by Russian immigrants, is one of the loveliest parts of the state, with vast vineyards and rambling hacienda-style estates. A few of the wineries are open to the public; **Baja California Tours** (☎ 800/336–5454; 858/454–7166 in the U.S., ℻ 858/454–2703) frequently offers winery tours, which include visits to several wineries, a historical overview of the valley, transportation from the border, and lunch.

Domecq (✉ Hwy. 3 Km 73, ☎ 6/155–2264) offers wine tastings and tours weekdays 10–2 and Sat. 10–1:30. **L.A. Cetto** (✉ Hwy. 3 Km 73.5, ☎ 6/155–2264) has wine tastings and tours daily 10–4. Several other wineries give tours by appointment.

The **Museo Comunitario del Valle de Guadalupe** (✉ Hwy 3 Km 70, ☎ 615/5–2030), open Tues.–Sun. 9–5, contains a display of Russian household items and artifacts from the local indigenous settlements in a 1905 Russian home.

Tecate

32 km (20 mi) east of Tijuana, 112 km (69 mi) northeast of Ensenada.

Tecate is a quiet border community with a population of about 100,000 and the pleasant ambience of a small Mexican town. Visitors stop by on day trips from Tijuana, Ensenada, or San Diego to shop for tiles, furnishings, and pottery and to have lunch at modest cafés facing the pleasant Parque Hidalgo. Tecate's most famous attraction is Rancho la Puerta.

Lodging

$$$$ 🏨 **Rancho la Puerta.** This peaceful, isolated health spa just west of Tecate is an idyllic resort. Spanish-style buildings with red-tile roofs and modern glass-and-wood structures are spread throughout the sprawling ranch. Hiking trails lead into scrub-pine hills and on Kuchuma Mountain, and a large bright-blue pool is a central gathering spot. Guests stay in luxurious private cottages and usually check in for at least a week to indulge in the resort's perfect blend of exercise, diet, and pampering. Advance reservations are essential. Transportation is available to and from the San Diego airport. ✉ *Hwy. 2, 5 km (3 mi) west of Tecate, 21275,* ☎ *6/654–1155; 800/443–7565; 760/744–4222 in the U.S.,* ℻ *6/654–1108; 760/744–5007 in the U.S.,* 🌐 *www.rancholapuerta.com 80 rooms. Restaurant, pool, beauty salon, spa, 4 tennis courts, 2 health clubs. AE, MC, V.*

Mexicali

136 km (84 mi) east of Tijuana.

Mexicali, with a population of about 850,000, shares the Imperial Valley farmland and the border crossing with Calexico, a small California city. The capital of Baja California, Mexicali sees a great deal of government activity and a steady growth of maquiladoras. Most visitors come to town on business, and the city's sights are few and far between. A tourist-oriented strip of curio shops, restaurants, and bars is located along Avenida Francisco Madero, a block south of the border.

Dining and Lodging

$$$ ✕🏨 **La Lucerna.** The prettiest hotel in Mexicali, the colonial-style Lucerna has plenty of palms and fountains around the pools and carved-wood furnishings in the dark, somber rooms. A newer section has suites with separate seating areas and more-modern furnishings. The three restaurants have local decor and good Mexican meals. Conventions and business meetings sometimes fill the hotel; advance reservations are advised. ✉ *Av. Benito Juárez 2151, 21270,* ☎ *6/564–7000, 800/582–3762,* ℻ *6/566–4706,* 🌐 *www.hotel-lucerna.com.mx. 175 rooms, 28 cabins, 4 suites. 2 restaurants, bar, 2 pools. MC, V.*

$$ ✕ **La Misión Dragon.** Chinese laborers came to Mexicali in the early 20th century to work on irrigation and railroad projects. As a result, the city has one of the largest Chinese populations (and some of the best Chinese restaurants) in Mexico. The most famous one is housed in an old hacienda, and is renowned for its crispy special duck and suckling pig in plum sauce. ✉ *Lázaro Cárdenas 555,* ☎ *6/566–4400. MC, V.*

En Route   **Parque Nacional San Pedro Mártir.** Baja's interior mountain ranges are filled with hidden caves and mountain hideaways. This park is more accessible than most, and even a short drive or hike up its rough trails offers a new perspective on Baja. As long as it hasn't been raining, a regular car can handle the dirt road into the park. ✉ *140 km (87 mi) south of Ensenada, turn off Hwy. 1 south of Colonet and drive 98 km (61 mi) east to the park.*

San Quintín

191 km (118 mi) south of Ensenada.

Agricultural fields line the highway as you enter San Quintín, the largest producer of tomatoes in Baja. The Oaxacan migrant workers who plant and pick the fertile valley's produce live in squalid camps out of the view of travelers. **Bahía de San Quintín,** which fronts a few small hotels, is among northern Baja's best fishing grounds, along with **Bahía Falsa** and **Bahía Santa Maria,** and the area's few hostelries tend to cater to anglers. Pismo clams collected at water's edge along San Quintín's bays are considered a local delicacy; roadside stands sell them fresh and cooked. Travelers often stop here for essentials en route farther south; this is the last major outpost until Guerrero Negro (a drive of about six hours).

Lodging

$ 🏨 **Old Mill.** Anglers ease their boats into the sheltered bay at this long-time favorite hideaway and set up housekeeping in a variety of rooms, some with kitchens and fireplaces. The lodge-style bar with its huge fireplace is filled with locals and travelers on weekend nights, and the restaurant serves hearty meals. ✉ *South of San Quintín on a dirt road leading to the bay,* 🌐 *www.oldmillbaja.com,* ☎ 📠 *6/165–3376, 800/ 479–7962, or 877/800–4081 30 rooms, 2 suites. Restaurant, bar, camping, fishing. No credit cards.*

San Felipe

198 km (123 mi) south of Mexicali, 244 km (151 mi) southeast of Ensenada.

San Felipe (pop. 20,000) is the quintessential fishing village with one main street (two if you count the highway into town). It sits at the edge of the northern Sea of Cortez, which is protected as an ecological reserve in this region. The **malecón** runs along a broad beach with a swimming area and public changing rooms. Taco stands, bars, and restaurants line the sidewalk across the street from the beach. The main landmark in town is the **shrine of the Cerro de la Virgen** (Virgin of Guadalupe), at the north end of the malecón on a hill overlooking the sea.

In 1948 the first paved road from Mexicali was extended into town, at which point San Felipe became significant. Prior to that time only a few fishermen and their families lived along the coast; now there are impressive fishing and shrimping fleets. The **Bahía San Felipe** has dramatic changes in its tides. They crest at 20 ft, and because the beach is so broad, the waterline can move in and out up to 1 km (about ½ mi). Local fishermen are well aware of the peculiarities of this section of the Sea of Cortez; many of them visit the shrine of the Cerro de la Virgen before setting sail.

A getaway spot for years, San Felipe has several campgrounds and a dozen hotels, which fill up quickly during winter and spring holidays. At times, up to 5,000 visitors wander the beaches, fill the few restaurants, and enjoy the sun. On holiday weekends San Felipe can be boisterous—dune buggies, motorcycles, and off-road vehicles abound—but most of the time it's a quiet, relaxing place. The town also appeals to sportfishermen, especially in spring. Launches, bait, and supplies are readily available.

Dining and Lodging

$$ ✕ **George's.** A favorite with resident Americans, George's has comfy padded red Naugahyde booths, powerful margaritas, and very good chiles rellenos, carne asada, and seafood. ⊠ *Av. Mar de Cortés 336,* ☎ *6/577–10–57. MC, V.*

$ ✕ **El Toro.** Open for breakfast only, El Toro is renowned among locals and San Felipe regulars for its chorizo, *machaca* (marinated shredded beef), *huevos rancheros* (fried eggs served on a corn tortilla and covered with a tomato, onion, and green-pepper sauce), and American-style breakfasts. ⊠ *Calzada Chetumal Norte,* ☎ *6/577–1032. No credit cards.*

$ ✕ **Tony's Tacos.** The most popular of the many taco stands along the waterfront, Tony's is a simple spot with sidewalk picnic tables and a counter lined with condiments for the house specialty—cheap, delicious fish tacos. ⊠ *Malecón at Av. Chetumal,* ☎ *no phone. No credit cards.*

$ ✕ **Viva Mexico.** This family-run operation (formerly called Juan's Place) two blocks east of the waterfront offers consistently excellent home-style cooking at reasonable prices. The catch of the day and grilled meats come with boiled vegetables—ask for beans, rice, and the delicious homemade tortillas instead. ⊠ *Mar Baltico between calles Ensenada and Calzada Chetumal,* ☎ *no phone. No credit cards.*

$$–$$$ ▥ **El Cortez.** Easily the most popular hotel in San Felipe, El Cortez has several types of accommodations, including moderate-price bungalows and modern hotel rooms with white walls, pastel bedspreads and drapes, and white-tile floors. The hotel's beachfront and second-story bars are both enduringly beloved, and the restaurant is the nicest water-view dining spot in town. The hotel is a five-minute walk from the malecón. ⊠ *Av. Mar de Cortés s/n, 21850 (Box 1227, Calexico, CA 92232),* ☎ *6/577–1055,* 𝖥𝖠𝖷 *6/577–1056. 77 rooms, 4 suites, 24 bungalows. Restaurant, 2 bars, pool. MC, V.*

$$–$$$ ▥ **San Felipe Marina Resort.** Most rooms at this low-slung terra-cotta building facing the sea have kitchens, woven rugs on white-tile floors, folk-art decorations, and balconies or patios with sea views. The least-expensive rooms lack kitchens and ocean views. The pool sits above the beach next to a *palapa* (thatch-roof) bar; a second, indoor pool is a delight on cold winter days. The resort is a five-minute drive south of town and has an RV campground next door. ⊠ *Carretera San Felipe Aeropuerto, Km 4.5, 21850,* ☎ *6/577–1455 or 800/291–5397,* 𝖥𝖠𝖷 *6/577–1568. 60 rooms and 123 RV spaces. Restaurant, bar, indoor pool, pool, 2 tennis courts, exercise room, shops. AE, MC, V.*

$$ ▥ **Las Misiones.** A pretty oasis of blue pools and green palms by the beach, this resort is big with group tours. It's also a good choice if you want to get away from it all—but you'll need a car or cab to get to town. A building just down the street from the hotel contains suites that have kitchens. ⊠ *Av. Misión de Loreto 148, 21850,* ☎ *6/577–1280 or 800/ 298–4105,* 𝖥𝖠𝖷 *6/577–1283,* 𝖶𝖤𝖡 *www.hotellasmisiones.com. 185 rooms, 32 suites. Restaurant, bar, 2 pools, 2 tennis courts. MC, V.*

Outdoor Activities and Sports

FISHING

The northern part of the Sea of Cortez offers plentiful sea bass, snapper, corbina, halibut, and other game fish. Clamming is good here as well. It's important to use a well-established company when fishing off san Felipe, as there have been several serious incidents involving anglers lost at sea. **Tony Reyes Sportfishing** (☎ 6/577–1120; 714/538–9300 in the U.S., FAX 714/538–1368 in the U.S.) is one of the most reputable companies offering multiday trips, and uses a U.S.-based company to organize their trips. **Alex Sportfishing** (☎ 6/577–1052), runs day trips on small skiffs.

BAJA NORTE A TO Z

To research prices, get advice from other travelers, and book travel arrangements, visit www.fodors.com.

AIR TRAVEL

There are few international flights into Baja Norte; most travelers access the area from the border at San Diego. Several airlines offer flights between mainland Mexico and Tijuana or Mexicali, which currently have the only commercial flights in the region. Tijuana's Aeropuerto Alberado Rodriguez is on the eastern edge of the city, near the Otay Mesa border crossing. The Tijuana airport is served from cities in Baja and mainland Mexico and from L.A. Mexicali's international airport, Aeropuerto Internacional General Rodolfo Sánchez Taboada, is about 11 km (7 mi) east of the city.

CARRIERS

Mexicana flies to Hermosillo, Monterrey, Mexico City, and Guadalajara, connecting with other national and international flights. Aeroméxico flies to Los Cabos, La Paz, and Mexicali on the Baja Peninsula and to several cities in mainland Mexico. AeroCalifornia is the only airline with flights between Los Angeles and Tijuana, and also flies to La Paz.

➤ AIRLINES AND CONTACTS: **Mexicana** (☎ 6/634–6596 in Tijuana; 6/552–9391 in Mexicali). **Aeroméxico** (☎ 6/686–5588 in Tijuana; 6/557–2551 in Mexicali). **AeroCalifornia** (☎ 6/684–2100 or 6/684–2876 in Tijuana).

BUS TRAVEL

Greyhound serves the border from San Diego several times daily. Buses to San Diego and Los Angeles depart from the Greyhound terminal in Tijuana at Avenida Mexico at Madero. Mexicoach runs buses from the trolley depot and the large parking lot on the U.S. side of the border to its depot on Avenida Revolución. Buses also run from Tijuana to Rosarito several times daily.

Buses connect all the towns in Baja Norte and are easy to use; stations are in Ensenada, Mexicali, San Felipe, Tecate, and Tijuana. Buses traveling to Rosarito no longer stop in town, but instead stop at the Rosarito exit on the toll road where taxis wait to transport passengers to town. There is no official bus station here; check at the hotels for bus-schedule information.

Autotransportes de Baja California covers the entire Baja route and connects in Mexicali with buses to Guadalajara and Mexico City. Elite has first-class service to mainland Mexico. Transportes del Pacífico goes to Mexico City and other points on the mainland from Mexicali; Transportes Norte de Sonora frequents border towns in Baja and on mainland Mexico.

➤ Bus Information: **Greyhound** (☎ 6/621–2951; 6/686–0695 in Tijuana; 619/239–3266 in the U.S.; 800/231–2222). **Mexicoach** (☎ 6/685–1470; 619/428–9517 in the U.S.).

➤ Bus Stations: **Ensenada bus station** (✉ Av. Riveroll 1075 between Calles 10 and 11, Ensenada, ☎ 6/178–6680). **Mexicali bus station** (✉ Centro Cívico, Av. Independencia, Mexicali, ☎ 6/557–2410). **San Felipe bus station** (✉ Av. Mar Caribe at Av. Manzanillo, San Felipe, ☎ 6/577–1516). **Tecate bus station** (✉ Av. Benito Juárez and Calle Abelardo Rodríguez, Tecate, ☎ 6/654–1221). **Tijuana bus station** (✉ Calzada Lázaro Cárdenas and Blvd. Arroyo Alamar, Tijuana, ☎ 6/621–2982).

TIJUANA BUS TRAVEL

The downtown station for buses within the city is at Calle 1a and Avenida Madero (☎ 6/686–9515). Most city buses at the border will take you downtown; look for the ones marked CENTRO CAMIONERA. To catch the bus back to the border from downtown, go to Calle Benito Juárez (also called Calle 2a) between Avenidas Revolución and Constitución. *Colectivos* (small vans often painted white with colored stripes) cover neighborhood routes in most Baja cities and towns. The destination is usually painted on the windshield; look for them on main streets.

CAR RENTAL

Many U.S. car-rental companies do not allow you to drive their cars into Mexico. Avis permits its cars to go from San Diego into Baja as far as 724 km (450 mi) south of the border. Cars must be returned by the renter to San Diego, and you must declare your intention to take the car into Mexico and purchase Mexican auto insurance. Southwest Car Rentals allows its cars as far as Ensenada. You must purchase Mexican insurance when you rent the car. California Baja Rent-A-Car rents four-wheel-drive vehicles, convertibles, and sedans for use throughout Mexico (the only company to do this). If you plan to rent your car in Tijuana or San Diego and drop it in Los Cabos, be prepared to pay a hefty sum (up to $900) on top of the rental price.

Fiesta Rent-a-Car and Hertz have offices in Ensenada. The larger U.S. rental agencies have offices at the Tijuana International Airport (Aeropuerto Alberado Rodriguez), and Avis and Budget have offices in downtown Tijuana.

➤ Major Agencies: **Avis** (✉ Av. Agua Caliente 3310, Tijuana, ☎ 6/686–4004, 6/686–3718, or 800/331–1212). **Budget** (✉ Paseo de los Héroes 77, Tijuana, ☎ 6/634–3303). **California Baja Rent-A-Car** (✉ 9245 Jamacha Blvd., Spring Valley, CA 91977, ☎ 619/470–7368 or 888/470–7368). **Fiesta Rent-a-Car** (Hotel Corona, at Boulevard Costero, Ensenada, ☎ 6/176–3344). **Hertz** (Avenida Blancarte between Calles 1 and 2, Ensenada, ☎ 6/178–2982). **Southwest Car Rentals** (✉ 2975 Pacific Hwy., San Diego, CA 92101, ☎ 619/497–4800).

CAR TRAVEL

The best way to tour Baja Norte is by car, although the driving can be difficult and confusing. If you're just visiting Tijuana, Tecate, or Mexicali, it's easiest to park on the U.S. side of the border and walk across.

From San Diego, U.S. 5 and I–805 end at the San Ysidro border crossing; Highway 905 leads from I–5 and I–805 to the Tijuana border crossing at Otay Mesa. U.S. 94 from San Diego connects with U.S. 188 to the border at Tecate, 57 km (35 mi) east of San Diego. I–8 from San Diego connects with U.S. 111 at Calexico—203 km (126 mi) east—and the border crossing to Mexicali. San Felipe lies on the coast, 200 km (124 mi) south of Mexicali via Highway 5.

To head south into Baja from Tijuana, follow the signs for Ensenada Cuota, the toll road (also called Highway 1 and, on newer signs, the Scenic Highway) that runs south along the coast. There are two clearly marked exits for Rosarito, and one each for Puerto Nuevo, Bajamar, and Ensenada. The road is excellent, although it has some hair-raising curves atop the cliffs and is best driven in daylight (the stretch from Rosarito to Ensenada is one of the most scenic drives in Baja). Tollbooths accept U.S. and Mexican currency; tolls are usually about $2.15. Rest rooms are available near toll stations. The alternative free road—Highway 1D or Ensenada Libre—has been vastly improved, but it's difficult for the first-timer to navigate. Highway 1 continues south of Ensenada through San Quintín to Guerrero Negro, at the border between Baja California and Baja Sur, and on to the southernmost tip of Baja; there are no tolls past Ensenada.

Mexico Highway 2 runs east from Tijuana to Tecate and Mexicali. A toll road between Tijuana and Tecate opened in 1994, and another was completed between Tecate and Mexicali in 1995. The 134-km (83-mi) journey from Tecate east to Mexicali on La Rumorosa, as the road is known, is as exciting as a roller-coaster ride, with the highway twisting and turning down steep mountain grades and over flat, barren desert.

If you're traveling only as far as Ensenada or San Felipe, you do not need a tourist card, unless you stay longer than 72 hours. If you know you'll be traveling south of Ensenada, you can get the form at the Mexican Customs Office. You must have Mexican auto insurance, available at agencies near the border.

The combination of overpopulation, lack of infrastructure, and heavy winter rains makes many of Tijuana's streets difficult to navigate by automobile. It's always best to stick to the main thoroughfares. There are parking lots along Avenida Revolución and at most major attractions. Most of Rosarito proper can be explored on foot, which is a good idea on weekends, when Boulevard Juárez has bumper-to-bumper traffic. To reach Puerto Nuevo and other points south, continue on Boulevard Juárez (also called Old Ensenada Highway and Ensenada Libre) through town. Most of Ensenada's attractions are within five blocks of the waterfront; it's easy to take a long walking tour of the city. A car is necessary to reach La Bufadora and most of the beaches.

When driving farther south to San Quintín, Guerrero Negro, and Baja Sur, be sure to fill up your gas tank when it's half full. Few towns appear on the highway, and you quickly have the feeling you are headed into the unknown (unless you're following a caravan of RVs). Don't drive at night, and watch your speed. You never know when a pothole or arroyo will challenge your driving skills.

➤ CONTACT: **Mexican Customs Office** (✉ inside San Ysidro border crossing, ☎ 6/682–3439 or 6/684–7790).

EMBASSIES
➤ UNITED STATES: **U.S. Consulate** (☎ 6/681–7400 Tapachula 96, Tijuana).

EMERGENCIES
In an emergency anywhere in Baja Norte, dial **060** for the police, **066** for Red Cross, and **068** for the fire department.

Tijuana operates a bilingual Tourist Assistance Hot Line, and the city's Tourist Assistance Office takes calls on weekdays to help with tourist complaints and problems.

➤ CONTACTS: **Tourist Assistance Hot Line** (☎ 078). **Tourist Assistance Office** (☎ 6/688–0555).

LANGUAGE

A great way to get to know Ensenada and improve your Spanish is to attend weekend or weeklong classes at the International Spanish Institute of Ensenada.

➤ SPANISH CLASSES: **International Spanish Institute of Ensenada** (☎ 6/176–0109; 858/755–7044 in the U.S.).

LODGING

RESERVING A ROOM

Several companies specialize in arranging hotel reservations in northern Baja. Baja Information is one of the oldest and best agencies working with Baja hotels and tourism departments. Baja California Tours books hotel rooms in the cities and outlying areas. Mexico Condo Reservations books hotel and condo accommodations and represents La Pinta Hotels, a chain with several hotels on the peninsula.

➤ CONTACTS: **Baja Information** (✉ 7860 Mission Center Ct., Suite 202, San Diego, CA 92108, ☎ 619/298–4105; 800/522–1516 in CA, NV, AZ; 800/225–2786 elsewhere, FAX 619/294–7366). **Baja California Tours** (✉ 7734 Herschel Ave., Suite O, La Jolla, CA 92037, ☎ 858/454–7166 or 800/336-5454 in the U.S., FAX 858/454–2703, WEB www.bajatours.signonsandiego.com). **Mexico Condo Reservations** (✉ 4420 Hotel Circle Ct., Suite 230, San Diego, CA 92108, ☎ 619/275–4500 or 800/262–4500, FAX 619/456–1350. WEB www.gobaja.com).

TOURS AND PACKAGES

Baja California Tours (☞ *above*) has comfortable, informative bus trips throughout northern Baja. Seasonal day and overnight trips focus on whale-watching, fishing, shopping, wineries, sports, dude ranches, and art and cultural events in Tijuana, Rosarito, Ensenada, and San Felipe.

TROLLEY TRAVEL

The San Diego Trolley travels from the Santa Fe Depot in San Diego, at Kettner Boulevard and Broadway, to within 100 ft of the border every 15 minutes from 5 AM to midnight. The 45-minute trip costs $2.

➤ CONTACT: **San Diego Trolley** (☎ 619/595–4949).

VISITOR INFORMATION

Baja tours, Mexican auto insurance, a monthly newsletter, and workshops are available through Discover Baja, which is a membership club for Baja travelers.

Baja's largest cities have several tourism offices operated by different agencies. These regional tourist offices are usually open weekdays 9–7 (although some may close in early afternoon for lunch) and weekends 9–1. Some of the smaller areas do not have offices. The excellent Baja California State Secretary of Tourism distributes information on the entire state.

Ensenada's most comprehensive office is at Blvd. Costera 1477. A second office is on Blvd. Costera at the entrance to town. Mexicali has both a Convention and Tourism Bureau, and a State Secretary of Tourism office, as does Tijuana. Tijuana Convention and Tourism Bureau has two offices, one within the San Ysidro border crossing, and one on Av. Revolución. The Tijuana Tourist Board operates an office in the Zona Río. Rosarito, San Felipe and Tecate also each have a tourist office.

➤ TOURIST INFORMATION: **Baja California State Secretary of Tourism** (✉ Paseo de los Héroes 10289, Tijuana, ☎ 6/634–6330, FAX 6/634–7157, WEB www.turismobc.gob.mx). **Discover Baja** (✉ 3089 Clairemont Dr., San Diego, CA 92117, ☎ 619/275–4225 or 800/727–2252, FAX 619/275–1836). **Ensenada Tourism** (✉ Blvd. Costera 1477, ☎ 6/172–

3022, 6/172–3081, or 6/178–2411, ⓦⒺⒷ www.ensenada-tourism.com; ⊠ Blvd. Costera, at the entrance to town, ☎ 6/178–2411). **Mexicali Convention and Tourism Bureau** (⊠ Calzada López Mateos at Calle Compresora, ☎ 6/552–2376, ☎ ⒻⒶⓍ 6/557–2561). **Mexicali State Secretary of Tourism Office** (⊠ Calle Calafia at Calzada Independencia, ☎ 6/566–1277). **Rosarito Convention & Visitors Bureau Office** (⊠ Blvd. Juárez, Oceana Plaza Shopping Center #14, ☎ 6/612–3078 or 800/962–2252, ⓦⒺⒷ www.rosaritobch.com). **San Felipe Tourist Information Office** (⊠ Av. Mar de Cortés, ☎ 6/577–1155 or 6/577–1865, ⓦⒺⒷ www.sanfelipe.com.mx). **Tecate Tourist Information** (⊠ Callejón Libertad, ☎ 6/654–1095). **State Secretary of Tourism Office** (⊠ Av. Revolución and Calle 1, ☎ 6/688–1685). **Tijuana Convention and Tourism Bureau** (⊠ inside the San Ysidro border crossing, ☎ 6/684–0481 or 6/684–0537; ⊠ Av. Revolución between Calles 3 and 4, ☎ 6/684–0481, 6/684–7790). **Tijuana Tourist Board** (⊠ Paseo de los Héroes 9365-201, in the Zona Río, ☎ 6/684–2854 or 888/775–2417, ⓦⒺⒷ www.seetijuana.com).

BAJA CALIFORNIA SUR

With the completion in 1973 of the Transpeninsular Highway, also called Mexico Highway 1, travelers gradually started finding their way down the 1,708-km (1,059-mi) road, drawn by the wild terrain and the pristine beaches of both coastlines. Baja California Sur became Mexico's 30th state in 1974, and the population and tourism have been growing. Still, Baja Sur remains a rugged and largely undeveloped land. Many people opt to fly to the region rather than brave Highway 1. The road is in fairly good repair, but there are potholes in some stretches and services (gas, rest rooms) may not be available. Those venturing on the Transpeninsular Highway should be well prepared with water and other provisions for a long drive in desolate but beautiful country.

Whale-watching in Guerrero Negro, Scammon's Lagoon, San Ignacio Lagoon, and Magdalena Bay is a main attraction in winter. History buffs enjoy Loreto, where the first mission in the Californias was established. La Paz, today a busy governmental center and sportfishing city, was the first Spanish settlement in Baja. At the southernmost tip of the peninsula, where the Pacific Ocean and the Sea of Cortez merge, fishing aficionados, golfers, and sun worshippers gather in Los Cabos, one of Mexico's most popular and most expensive coastal resorts.

Guerrero Negro and Scammon's Lagoon

720 km (446 mi) south of Tijuana, 771 km (478 mi) north of La Paz.

Every December through March, thousands of gray whales swim 8,000 km (5,000 mi) south from Alaska's Bering Strait to the tip of the Baja Peninsula. Up to 6,000 whales swim past and stop close to the shore at several spots along the Baja coast—including Scammon's Lagoon near **Guerrero Negro**—to give birth to their calves. These newborns each weigh about half a ton and consume nearly 50 gallons of milk a day. In the past, Guerrero Negro was the headquarters for whale-watching trips, but many of the whale-watching operators have moved farther south, to Laguna de San Ignacio and Bahía Magdalena. Still, it's easiest to spot whales from shore or to arrange for a boat in Guerrero Negro.

If it weren't for the whales and the Transpeninsular Highway, which passes near town, few would venture to Guerrero Negro, a town of 10,000. Those traveling south can easily bypass the town. The name Guerrero Negro, which means Black Warrior, was derived from a whaling ship that ran aground in Scammon's Lagoon in 1858. Near

Baja California Sur

Isla Angel de la Guarda

Isla del Tiburón

Hermosillo

Mazatán

Pta. San Gabriel

San Rafael

Tecoripa

Cieneguita

El Arco

(1)

Guaymas

(15)

San Ignacio

Isla Lobos

Ciudad Obregón

Santa Rosalia
Mulegé

Pta. Concepción

Navajoa

TO GUERRERO NEGRO

Laguna de San Ignacio

(1)

Bahía Concepción

Huatabampo

(15)

BAJA

Isla Carmen

Gulf of California

Sea of Cortez

Loreto

Las Grullas Márgen Derecha

La Poza

Misión San Javier

CALIFORNIA

SIERRA GIGANTA

Topolobampo

TO LOS MOCHIS

Insurgentes

Constitución

Isla San José

SUR

Isla Partida

Bahía Magdalena

Santa Rita

Bahía la Paz

Pichilingue

TO MAZATLÁN

Isla Santa Margarita

(1)

Isla Cerralvo

La Paz

Bahía de los Muertos

El Triunfo

Punta Pescadero

Los Barriles

Buenavista

La Ribera

Todos Santos

SIERRA DE LA LAGUNA

Santiago

Cabo Pulmo

(19)

(1)

San José del Cabo

Cabo San Lucas

N

PACIFIC OCEAN

KEY

—— Rail Lines

🚢 Ferry Lines

0 ————————— 100 miles

0 ————————— 150 km

the Desierto de Vizcaíno (Vizcaíno Desert), on the Pacific Ocean, the area is best known for its salt pans, which provide work for much of the town's population and produce one-third of the world's salt supply. Saltwater collects in some 780 square km (300 square mi) of sea-level ponds and evaporates quickly in the desert heat, leaving great blocks of salt. The town is dusty, windy, and generally unpleasant, but it happens to be a favored roosting spot for osprey, which build huge nests on power poles around town.

Scammon's Lagoon is about 27 km (17 mi) south of Guerrero Negro, down a rough but passable sand road that crosses the salt flats. The lagoon got its name from U.S. explorer Charles Melville Scammon of Maine, who came here in the mid-1800s. On his first expedition to the lagoon, Scammon and his crew collected more than 700 barrels of valuable whale oil, and the whale rush was on. Within 10 years, nearly all the whales in the lagoon had been killed, and it took almost a century for the whale population to increase to what it had been before Scammon arrived. It wasn't until the 1940s that the U.S. and Mexican governments took measures to protect the whales and banned the whalers from the lagoon.

These days, whale-watching boats—most of them *pangas* (small skiffs)—must get permission from the Mexican government to enter Scammon's Lagoon, now a national park called **Parque Natural de Ballenas Gris** (Gray Whale Natural Park). The other major whale-watching spots (also protected by the government) are farther south, at Laguna de San Ignacio and Bahía Magdalena, both on the Pacific coast. If traveling on your own, you can reach Laguna de San Ignacio from the town of San Ignacio. Bahía Magdalena—regulars call it "Mag Bay"—is about a four-hour drive across the peninsula from La Paz. Fishermen will take you out in their boats to get closer to the whales at both places. But for a better view, and an easier stay in this rugged country, travel with an outfitter who will arrange your transportation, accommodations, and time on the water. Whales will come close to your boat, rising majestically from the water, and sometimes swim close enough to be patted on the back.

Dining and Lodging

There are several hotels in Guerrero Negro, none of which is worth visiting for its own sake. Double-occupancy rooms cost from about $25 to $70 a day; rates tend to increase during the peak whale-watching season from January through March. None of the hotels has heat, and winter nights can be downright frigid. Credit cards aren't normally accepted, but the hotels do take traveler's checks. The food in the hotel restaurants recommended below is far from haute cuisine, but it's about as good as you're going to get in the area.

$ ✕ **La Espinitá.** This small restaurant serves good home-style Mexican and American breakfasts, along with standard enchiladas, tacos, and fish for lunch and dinner. The market next door has cold drinks, purified water, and snacks. ⊠ *Hwy. 1 at 28th parallel next to La Pinta, Domicilio Conocido, 23940,* ☎ *no phone. No credit cards.*

$ ✕▥ **Malarrimo.** This trailer park and Mexican and seafood restaurant has a 10-room motel—Cabañas San Miguelito—with private baths and TV. It fills up quickly and is one of the best deals in town. The restaurant is a favorite spot for caravans heading farther south. The grilled or steamed fresh fish, lobster, and clams are legendary, and the dining-room walls are covered with maps and photos of Baja. Whale-watching excursions from the hotel are also immensely popular and are run by knowledgeable local guides. ⊠ *Blvd. Zapata, 23940,* ☎ *1/157–0250,* FAX *1/157–0100. 10 rooms. Restaurant. No credit cards.*

$$ ▦ **La Pinta.** A few kilometers outside of town, looking like an oasis of palms in the desert, La Pinta is the largest hotel in the area. The clean, functional rooms are dependable, the setting more attractive than that of other local lodgings, and the American–Mexican restaurant decent, but the rates are high for the area. Package deals are sometimes available if you plan to use La Pinta hotels throughout the peninsula. Whale-watching excursions can be arranged here. ✉ *La Pinta Hwy. 1 at 28th parallel, Domicilio Conocido, 23940,* ☎ *1/157–1301; 800/ 800–9632; 619/275–4500 in the U.S.,* ℻ *1/157–1306,* ☒ *www.lap- intahotels.com. 26 rooms. Restaurant. MC, V.*

Outdoor Activities and Sports
WHALE-WATCHING
The gray whales that migrate from the Bering Strait are Guerrero Negro's biggest attraction. With a sturdy vehicle, you can drive the 24-km (15-mi) washboard dirt and sand road to Scammon's Lagoon and arrange a trip with the boat captains who await passengers there. Trips usually cost $25 per person and boats stay on the water for about an hour. Start early to take advantage of the calmest water and best viewing conditions. Whale-watching from the shores of the lagoon can be disappointing without binoculars. But it is still an impressive sight to see the huge mammals spouting water high into the air, their 12-ft-wide tails flailing.

Eco-Tours Malarrimo (✉ Blvd. Zapata, 23940, ☎ 1/157–0250) is the best tour operator in the area. It offers four-hour trips with bus transportation to and from the lagoon (about 75% of the trip is spent in small skiffs among the whales with English-speaking guides) and lunch for $40 per person. Reserve several months in advance, especially for February, when whales appear in abundance.

San Ignacio

227 km (141 mi) southeast of Guerrero Negro.

San Ignacio is an oasis amid the Desierto de Vizcaíno. Date palms, planted by Jesuit missionaries in the late 1700s, sway gently, in sync with the town's laid-back air. San Ignacio is primarily a place to organize whale-watching and cave-painting tours or to stop and cool off in the shady *zócalo* (town square).

Lodging
$$ ▦ **La Pinta.** This simple, functional hotel is a pleasant place to stay on your transpeninsular journey—although you may wish for a bit more for the money. White arches frame the courtyard and pool, and the rooms are decorated with folk art and wood furnishings. Both the river and town are within walking distance. The hotel staff can set up whale-watching trips with local guides. ✉ *2 km (1 mi) west of Hwy. 1 on an unnamed road into town, Apdo. 37, 23943,* ☎ *1/154–0300; 800/ 800–9632; 619/275–4500 in the U.S.,* ☒ *www.lapintahotels.com 28 rooms. Restaurant, bar, pool. No credit cards.*

Outdoor Activities and Sports
WHALE-WATCHING
San Ignacio is the base for trips to Laguna de San Ignacio, 59 km (35 miles) from San Ignacio on the Pacific Coast. The lagoon is one of the best places to watch the gray-whale migration, and local boat captains will usually take you close enough to pet the new baby whales. **Eco-turísticos Kuyima** (☎ 1/154–0026 or 1/154–0070) in San Ignacio offers transport between town and the lagoon and uses local guides as boat captains. Tours arranged through **Baja Discovery** (✉ Box 152527,

San Diego, CA 92195, ☎ 619/262–0700; 800/829–2252, WEB www.ba-jadiscovery.com) include round-trip transport from San Diego to San Ignacio, by van and private plane, with hotel stays en route to the lagoon. The company operates a comfortable camp at the lagoon with solar-heated showers and private tents facing the water. **Baja Expeditions** (✉ 2625 Garnet Ave., San Diego, CA 92109, ☎ 858/581–3311 or 800/843–6967, FAX 858/581–6542) also operates a camp at the lagoon and offers tours including air transportation from San Diego.

Santa Rosalia

77 km (48 mi) southeast of San Ignacio.

You'll find a fascinating mix of French, Mexican, and American Old West–style architecture in this dusty mining town. Santa Rosalia is known for its **Iglesia Santa Barbara,** a prefabricated iron church designed by Alexandre-Gustave Eiffel, creator of the Eiffel Tower. Be sure to stop by **El Boleo** (✉ Av. Obregón at Calle 4), where fresh breads bring a lineup of eager bakery customers weekday mornings at 10.

Lodging

$ 🏨 **Hotel Frances.** The former glory of this 1886 French mansion shines through despite its modest furnishings. The Frances sits on a steep hill, and many of its refurbished rooms open onto a second-story porch with views of town and the sea. There's a small pool in the courtyard and a charming restaurant. ✉ *Av. 11 de Julio at Calle Jean M. Cousteau, 23920,* ☎ FAX *1/152–2052. 17 rooms. Pool. MC, V.*

$ 🏨 **El Morro.** Santa Rosalia's best hotel is on the waterfront a bit south of town. Rooms, in a series of one-story buildings connected by rock arches and tile mosaics, are large and comfortable; some have terraces and tile bathrooms. The rooms are a bit worn, but the reasonable price and the proximity of the sea even the score. The restaurant serves bountiful Mexican combo plates, imported steak, and local seafood. The bar is a popular gathering spot for travelers. ✉ *1½ km (1 mi) south of Santa Rosalia on Hwy. 1, 23900,* ☎ FAX *1/152–0414. 39 rooms. Restaurant, bar, pool. MC, V.*

Mulegé

64 km (40 mi) south of Santa Rosalia.

Mulegé has become a popular base for exploring the nearby **Sierra de Guadalupe** mountains, the site of several prehistoric rock paintings, and for kayaking in **Bahía Concepción,** the largest protected bay in Baja. Once a mission settlement, this charming tropical town of some 3,500 residents swells in winter, when Americans and Canadians fleeing the cold arrive in motor homes. There are several campgrounds outside town and a few good hotels and restaurants in town and on the coast.

Lodging

$$ 🏨 **Hotel Serenidad.** A Mulegé mainstay for Baja aficionados since the late 1960s, the Serenidad is owned by the Johnson family, longtime Baja residents. The hotel is a delightful escape, with simple rooms in brick and stucco buildings scattered under bougainvillea vines and fruit trees. Some rooms have fireplaces and/or air-conditioning; all have private baths. The Saturday night pig roast is a Baja tradition. Note that the restaurant is closed in September. ✉ *2½ km (1½ mi) south of Mulegé, Hwy. 1, 23900,* ☎ *1/153–0530 or 800/346–3942,* FAX *1/153–0311. 29 rooms. Restaurant, bar, pool, private airstrip. AE, MC, V.*

$ 🏨 **Hacienda.** Guests read and lounge in rocking chairs by the pool or along the bar at this small, comfortable hotel steps from the town plaza. Kayak trips and tours to cave paintings in the mountains can be arranged, and special fiestas are planned for groups. Rooms are spartan but work fine for a night or two. Even when other hotels in the area are nearly empty, the Hacienda is filled with Europeans attracted by the ambience and moderate room rates. ⊠ *Calle Madero 3, 23900,* ☎ 🖷 *1/153–0021 or 800/ 346–3942. 24 rooms. Restaurant, bar, pool, travel services. MC, V.*

Outdoor Activities and Sports

DIVING

Cortez Explorers (⊠ Calle Moctezuma 75A 23900, ☎ 1/153–0500, 🖷 1/153–0500) conducts dive trips to the rocky reefs off the Santa Inez Islands in the Sea of Cortez. They rent dive equipment, mountain bikes, and ATVs, and offer resort courses and snorkeling trips.

KAYAKING

Baja Tropicales (⊠ Apdo. 60, 23900, ☎ 1/153–0409, 🖷 1/153–0190) rents kayaks, wet suits, and other gear and has several types of kayaking tours, including day and overnight trips in the area of Mulegé. Whale-watching trips on the Pacific coast are also available.

Seafaris (⊠ 5095 Comanche Dr, La Mesa CA 91941, ☎ 🖷 619/462– 3761) operates eight-day kayaking trips between Mulegé and Loreto from October through April. The trips include gear, meals, and accommodations in camps along the way. Clients are responsible for their travel to Mulegé or Loreto.

Loreto

134 km (83 mi) south of Mulegé.

Loreto's setting on the Sea of Cortez is truly spectacular: the gold and green hills of the Sierra Gigante seem to tumble into the cobalt water. According to local promoters, the skies are clear 360 days of the year, and the desert climate harbors few bothersome insects.

The Kikiwa, Cochimi, Cucapa, and Kumyaii Indian tribes first inhabited the barren lands of Baja. Jesuit priest Juan María Salvatierra founded the first California mission at Loreto in 1697, and not long after, the indigenous populations were nearly obliterated by disease and war. Seventy-two years later, a Franciscan monk from Mallorca, Spain— Father Junípero Serra—set out from here to establish a chain of missions from San Diego to San Francisco, in the land then known as Alta California.

In 1821 Mexico achieved independence from Spain, which ordered all missionaries home. Loreto's mission was abandoned and fell into disrepair. Then in 1829, a hurricane swept through the remains, virtually destroying the settlement, capital of the Californias at the time. The capital was moved to La Paz, and Loreto languished for a century. In 1976, when oil revenue filled government coffers, the area was tapped for development. Streets were paved, and phone service, electricity, potable water, and sewage systems were installed in both the town and the surrounding area. Even an international airport was built. A luxury hotel and tennis center were opened in nearby Nopoló. Eventually, the pace of development slowed as the money dried up.

With a population of 10,000, Loreto is a good place to escape the crowds, relax, and go fishing. The fears of sports enthusiasts that the town would be spoiled have thus far been largely unfounded, although the residential trailer parks are filling up and private homes are clustered in secluded enclaves. For the most part, however, Loreto still stands quietly by the sea.

The **malecón,** built in 1991, is a pleasant place for a stroll along downtown's waterfront. A marina shelters yachts and the panga fleet; the adjoining beach is a popular gathering spot for locals, especially on

Sunday afternoon, and the playground has an assortment of play equipment for children.

Loreto's main historic sight is **La Misión de Nuestra Señora de Loreto.** The stone walls, gilded altar, and primitive-style portraits of its priests are worth seeing.

El Museo de los Misiones, also called the Museum of Anthropology and History, contains religious relics, tooled leather saddles used in the 19th century, and displays of Baja's history. ⊠ *Next door to La Misión de Nuestra Señora de Loreto,* ☎ *1/135–0441.* ▣ *$2.* ⊙ *Tues.–Sun. 9–1 and 2–6.*

Nopoló, an area being developed for luxury resorts, is about 8 km (5 mi) south of Loreto. There's a nine-court tennis complex and an 18-hole golf course, and private homes have sprung up, but Nopoló has yet to become a major resort area.

Puerto Escondido, 16 km (10 mi) down the road from Nopoló, has an RV park, Tripui, with a good restaurant, a few motel rooms, a snack shop, bar, stores, showers, laundry, a pool, and tennis courts. A boat ramp has been completed at the marina; to pay the fee required to launch here, go to the port captain's offices (☎ 1/135–0656, FAX 1/135–0465) just south of the ramp; the offices are open weekdays 8–3.

Isla Danzante, 5 km (3 mi) southeast of Puerto Escondido, has good reefs and diving opportunities. Picnic trips to **Coronado Island,** inhabited only by sea lions, may be arranged in Loreto, Nopoló, or Puerto Escondido. The snorkeling and scuba diving on the island are excellent. Danzante and other islands off Loreto are now part of the Parque Marítmo Nacional Bahía de Loreto. Commercial fishing boats are not allowed within the 60-square-km (23-square-mi) park.

A trip to **Misión San Javier,** 32 km (20 mi) southwest of Loreto, is one of the best ways to see Baja at its most picturesque. A high-clearance vehicle is essential for the three-hour drive to the mission—and don't even try getting here if the dirt and gravel road is muddy. The road climbs past small ranches, palm groves, and the steep cliffs of the Cerro de la Giganta. Unmarked trails lead off the road to caves and remnants of **Indian cave paintings.** The mission village is a remote community of some 300 residents, many of whom come outdoors when visitors arrive. The church, built in 1699, is impressive and well preserved, set amid fruit orchards. It's often locked; ask anyone hanging about to find the person with the keys, and you'll be allowed to go inside to look at the stained-glass windows and ornate altar. Slip a few pesos into the contribution box as a courtesy to the village's inhabitants, who need all the help they can get to keep the church well maintained. Although you can drive to San Javier on your own, it helps to have a guide along to lead you to the caves and Indian paintings. Most hotels, or the tour companies listed below, can arrange tours.

Dining and Lodging

$$$ ✕ **El Nido.** If you're hungry for steak, chicken, and hearty Mexican combo plates, then this is your place. As close as you'll get to a steak house in these parts, El Nido caters to a meat-and-potatoes crowd. The wood and brass decor and courteous waiters make up for prices that seem outrageously high for the neighborhood. ⊠ *Calle Salvatierra s/n,* ☎ *1/135–0284. No credit cards.*

$$ ✕ **Chile Willie.** A convivial crowd, eclectic menu, and sea views make this a popular hangout from breakfast through sunset. Seafood omelets, burritos, burgers, pastas, and several preparations of fresh fish provide enough variety that diners return frequently. Proud anglers share

fish tales during sunset happy hour. ✉ *Playa Loreto north of the boat ramp,* ☎ *1/135–0677. No credit cards.*

$$ ✕ **La Palapa.** A favorite with kayakers and travelers, this thatch-roof restaurant one block from the waterfront serves up a good combination of Mexican plates. This is the only place in town to get fried red snapper, the house specialty. Try the delicious mesquite-grilled steaks and seafood. ✉ *Paseo Hidalgo between Calle Francisco Madero and the malecón,* ☎ *1/135–1101. No credit cards.*

$ ✕ **Café Olé.** This local and gringo hangout is the best taquería in town, but it also serves good burgers, ice cream, and french fries. ✉ *Calle Francisco Madero,* ☎ *1/135–0496. No credit cards.*

$$$–$$$$ 🛏 **Hotel Posada de los Flores.** The overwhelming charm and attention to detail set this gorgeous hotel apart from other accommodations in the area. Exposed beams and locally crafted tile adorn every room of the remodeled colonial mansion in Loreto's historical center. A rooftop garden provides beautiful views. Above the hotel's atrium lobby sits a crystal-bottom pool, so be sure to look up. Two restaurants serve up Loreto's finest Mexican and Italian fare, and breakfast is included in the room rate. Smoking is not allowed in the rooms. Note that the hotel may not be suitable for children. ✉ *Calle Salvatierra at Calle Francisco Madero, 23880.* ☎ *1/135–1162; 877/245–2860 in the U.S.,* WEB *www.posadalasflores.com. 10 rooms, 5 junior suites. 2 restaurants, 2 bars, snack bar, pool, car rental. AE, MC, V.*

$$ 🛏 **Oasis.** One of the original fishing camps, Oasis remains a favorite with those who want to spend as much time as possible on the water. Many of the rooms, set amid an oasis of palms, have a view of the water and hammocks on the front terraces. The hotel has its own fleet of skiffs. The hotel offers rates with and without meal plans. ✉ *Calle de la Playa at Zaragoza, Apdo. 17, 23880,* ☎ *1/135–0112 or 800/662–7476,* FAX *1/135–0795. 39 rooms. Restaurant, bar, pool, boating, fishing. MC, V.*

$$ 🛏 **La Pinta.** Part of a Baja California hotel chain, La Pinta is a collection of pastel brick buildings right on the beach. The rooms are spacious but unremarkable, with air-conditioning and satellite TVs, and there's a large pool. ✉ *Blvd. Misión de Loreto, 23880,* ☎ *1/135–0025; 800/800–9632; 619/275–4500 in the U.S.,* FAX *1/135–0026,* WEB *www.lapintahotels.com. 48 rooms. Restaurant, bar, pool, tennis court, fishing. MC, V.*

$$ 🛏 **Villas de Loreto.** This is one of Loreto's nicest hideaways, just south of town. There are 10 large rooms with refrigerators and front porches, along with a large pool. An RV campground is behind the hotel buildings. Bikes are available for guests' use (free), and horseback riding, kayaking (for experienced paddlers), and fishing tours can be arranged. Smoking isn't permitted in the rooms or on the property. Continental breakfast is included in the room rate. To get here, turn right off Calle Salvatierra onto Calle Francisco Madero and drive across the dry riverbed to signs for the hotel. ✉ *Antonio Mijares at beach, 23880,* ☎ FAX *1/135–0586. 10 rooms. Pool, laundry service. MC, V.*

$–$$ 🛏 **Plaza Loreto.** Since its opening in 1992, the Plaza Loreto has garnered a loyal following of Loreto regulars who appreciate the prime downtown location near the old mission. The two-story hotel has an upstairs bar overlooking the street. Rooms aren't consistently maintained—the best of the lot have TVs and huge showers. Check a few before choosing one. ✉ *Paseo Hidalgo, 23880,* ☎ *1/135–0280,* FAX *1/135–0855. 25 rooms. Bar, restaurant. MC, V.*

Outdoor Activities and Sports

FISHING

Fishing put Loreto on the map, especially for American sports enthusiasts. Cabrillo and snapper are caught year-round; yellowtail in the spring; and dorado, marlin, and sailfish in the summer. If you plan to fish, bring tackle, as top-notch gear can be difficult to find, although some sportfishing fleets do update their equipment regularly. All Loreto-area hotels can arrange fishing, and many own skiffs. Local fishermen congregate with their small boats on the beach at the north and south ends of town. **Alfredo's Sportfishing** (✉ Blvd. Mateos at Juárez, across from the marina, ☎ 1/135–0132, ☒ 1/135–0590) has good fishing guides. **Arturo's Fishing Fleet** (✉ Calle Hidalgo between the plaza and the marina, ☎ 1/135–0409, ☒ 1/135–0022) has several types of boats and fishing packages. **The Baja Big Fish Company** (✉ Paseo Hidalgo 19, by the plaza, ☎ 1/135–0448 or 888/533–2252, ☒ 1/135–0078) has full fishing packages from the United States, which include air and hotel, as well as fishing trips from Loreto. Baja Big Fish specializes in tag-and-release and in light tackle and fly-fishing.

GOLF

The 18-hole **Loreto Campo de Golf** (☎ 1/135–0788 or 1/133–0554) is along Nopoló Bay at the south side of the Fonatur resort. Several hotels in Loreto have golf packages and reduced or free greens fees.

KAYAKING

There are some ideal sites for kayakers off Loreto's shores. Tours and rentals can be arranged through the **Baja Outpost** (✉ Blvd. Mateos near the Oasis Hotel, ☎ 1/135–1134 or 888/649–5951). Loreto outdoor specialists **Las Parras Tours** (✉ Calle Salvatierra at Madero, ☎ 1/135–1010, ☒ 1/135–0900) provides experienced local guides for kayaking, as well as for whale-watching, scuba diving, visiting San Javier, and hiking to cave paintings in the mountains.

SCUBA DIVING

The **Baja Outpost** (✉ Blvd. Mateos near the Oasis Hotel, ☎ 1/135–1134 or 888/649–5951), has scuba certification courses, dive trips to the islands, gear rental, and guest rooms for clients. **Las Parras Tours** (☎ 1/135–1010, ☒ 1/135–0900) offers certification courses, guided tours, and gear rental.

TENNIS

The **Loreto Tennis Center** (☎ 1/135–0408), 8 km (5 mi) south of town, has nine courts open, for a fee, to the public.

Shopping

There are few opportunities for shopping in Loreto. **El Alacran,** in the small complex behind the church on Calle Salvatierra, has remarkable folk art, jewelry, and sportswear. You can also find some nice silver shops in this complex. Groceries and ice are available on Calle Salvatierra at **El Pescador,** the town's only supermarket.

La Paz

354 km (220 mi) south of Loreto.

La Paz is one of those cities that makes you wish you'd been here 30 years ago. In the slowest of times, in late summer when the heat is oppressive, you can easily see how it must have been when it was a quiet place, living up to its name: "Peace." Today the city has a population of 180,000, with a large contingent of retirees from the United States and Canada. Travelers use La Paz as both a destination in itself and a stopping-off point en route to Los Cabos. Some call it the most traditional city on the peninsula, with the feel of a mainland community that has adapted to tourism while retaining its character. There's always excellent scuba diving and sportfishing in the gulf—La Paz is the stop-off for divers and fishermen headed for **Cerralvo, La Partida,** and the **Espíritu Santo** islands, where parrot fish, manta rays, neons, and angels blur the clear waters by the shore, and marlin, dorado, and yellowtail leap out of the sea.

Hernán Cortés and his soldiers were drawn to La Paz in 1535 by stories of magnificent pearls and women. In 1720 the Jesuits arrived to deliver their message of salvation to the indigenous Pericú people. Instead, they inadvertently introduced smallpox, which decimated the local populace within 30 years.

La Paz became the capital of the Californias in 1829 after a hurricane nearly leveled Loreto. In 1853 a group of U.S. Southerners, led by William Walker, tried to make La Paz a slave state, but Mexicans quickly banished them. Peace reigned for the next century. In 1940 disease wiped out the oyster beds, and with the pearls gone, La Paz no longer attracted prospectors.

La Paz officially became the capital of Baja California Sur in 1974, and is now the state's largest settlement. The city underwent considerable restoration in the late 1990s, with the main road between the airport and town enlarged to four lanes and construction of new residential areas constantly under way. It is the site of the governor's house and the state's bureaucracy, jail, and power plant, as well as the ferry port to Mazatlán.

Sights to See

⓴ At La Paz's west end is the construction zone for the 500-acre **Fidepaz Marina,** a long-term development that has yet to reach comple-
㉑ tion. There is a resort hotel by the waterfront. The **malecón** is La Paz's seawall, tourist zone, and main drag rolled into one. As you enter town from the southwest (near Fidepaz Marina), Paseo Alvaro Obregón turns into the malecón at a cluster of high-rise condos. **Marina La Paz,** at the southwest end of the malecón, is an ever-growing development with condominiums, vacation homes, and a pleasant walkway lined with casual cafés.

㉒ **Malecón Plaza.** A two-story white gazebo is the focus at this small cement square where musicians sometimes appear on weekend nights. The tourist-information center sits beside the gazebo. Across the street, Calle 16 de Septiembre leads inland to the city center. Around the plaza and all along the malecón, a steady stream of teens cruises through town, red and yellow car lights twinkling around their license plates and radios blaring.

㉓ The **Biblioteca de las Californias,** a library specializing in the history of Baja California, has reproductions of local prehistoric cave paintings, oil paintings of the missions, and the best collection of historical documents on the peninsula. Films and lectures are sometimes presented in the evening. Check the bulletin board outside the library or ask the librarian for information. ⊠ *Madero at 5 de Mayo,* ☎ *1/122–0162.* ☉ *Weekdays 9–6.*

La Paz's downtown is the busiest in Baja Sur, with shops crammed to-
㉔ gether on narrow streets. Downtown's big attraction is **La Catedral de Nuestra Señora de La Paz** (Our Lady of La Paz Cathedral). It was built in 1860 near the site of La Paz's first mission, which was established that same year by Jesuit Jaime Bravo. You'll see it just across from the
㉕ town's main square. The zócalo also goes by the names **Plaza Constitución** and Jardín Velazco.

㉖ **Museum of Anthropology.** La Paz's culture and heritage is well represented here, with re-creations of Comondo and Las Palmas Indian villages, photos of cave paintings found in Baja, and copies of Cortés's writings on first sighting La Paz. Many exhibit descriptions are written only in Spanish, but the museum's staff will help you translate. ✉ *Altamirano and 5 de Mayo,* ☎ *1/122–0162.* 🖃 *Donation.* ☉ *Weekdays 9–5, Sat. 9–2.*

Northeast of town, Paseo Alvaro Obregón, or the malecón, becomes what is commonly known as the **Pichilingue Road.** It curves northeast along the bay about 16 km (10 mi) to the terminals where the ferries from Mazatlán and Topolobampo arrive and many of the sportfishing boats depart. The warehouselike **Ferry Terminal** is a busy spot with a large parking lot. Roadside stands serving oysters and grilled fish line the highway across the street.

Pichilingue. Since the time of pirate ships and Spanish invaders, Pichilingue was known for its preponderance of oysters bearing black pearls. In 1940 an unknown disease killed them off, leaving the beach deserted. Today it's a pleasant place for sunbathing and watching sportfishing boats bring in their hauls. Palapa restaurants on the beach serve cold beer and oysters *diablo* (raw oysters steeped in a fiery-hot sauce), as well as some of the freshest and least expensive grilled fish in town.

Beaches

Off a dirt road just past Pichilingue, **Playa Tecolote** and **Playa Coyote** are adjacent crystal-blue coves with clean beaches. Both have restaurants, water-sports equipment rentals, and palapas for shade. This is a good place to test your kayaking skills, and rentals are available on site. Camping is allowed in the parking lots. **Playa Balandra,** on a side road between Pichilingue and Tecolote, is a peaceful cove favored by kayak and snorkeling operations from town. There are no facilities or rentals at this beach. Make arrangements in advance in town.

Dining and Lodging

$$$ ✕ **El Bismark.** You've got to go a bit out of your way for a local home-
★ style Mexican restaurant. Specialties include carne asada served with
beans, guacamole, and homemade tortillas; and enormous grilled lob-
sters. Seafood cocktails are huge, too, and fish fillets are always fresh
from the sea. You'll see families settle down for hours at long wood
tables, while waitresses divide their attention between patrons and soap
operas on the TV above the bar. The desultory service is a drawback.
⊠ *Santos Degollado and Av. Altamirano,* ☎ *1/122–4854. MC, V.*

$$ ✕ **Carlos 'n' Charlie's.** The noise level here is deafening, but it's a fun
place, with a wide-screen TV in the bar and waiters so jolly you ex-
pect them to break into song. The food—basic beef, chicken, fish, and
Mexican selections—is good and plentiful. Live bands appear weekend evenings on the back patio and attached dance club, one of the
hottest nightlife spots in town. ⊠ *Paseo Obregón at Calle 16 de Septiembre,* ☎ *1/122–9290. MC, V.*

$$ ✕ **La Pazta.** Locals who crave international fare rave about this trat-
toria with sleek black-and-white decor and excellent homemade pasta.
Imported cheeses and wines, fresh herbs and vegetables, and bracing
espresso and cappuccino are all welcome changes from the local seafood
and taco fare. ⊠ *Allende 36,* ☎ *1/125–1195. MC, V.*

$ ✕ **El Quinto Sol Restaurante Vegetariano.** El Quinto's brightly painted
exterior walls are covered with Indian snake symbols and smiling
suns. The all-vegetarian menu can be a nice change of pace, and there's
a wide selection of fresh juices and herbal elixirs. The four-course
prix-fixe dinner (5–7 PM) is a bargain. The back half of the space is a
bare-bones natural-foods store offering grains, fresh breads, soaps, oils,
bulk herbs, and homeopathic remedies. ⊠ *Belisario Domínguez and
Independencia,* ☎ *1/122–1692. No credit cards.*

$ ✕ **Taco Hermanos Gonzalez.** La Paz has plenty of great taco stands,
but the Gonzalez brothers still corner the market with their hunks of
fresh fish wrapped in corn tortillas. Bowls of condiments line the small
stand, and the best fast food in town draws crowds of sidewalk munch-
ers. ⊠ *Mutualismo and Esquerro,* ☎ *no phone. No credit cards.*

$$$ ✕🏠 **Crowne Plaza Resort.** By far the most modern resort in La Paz,
this hacienda-style inn sits beside the Fidepaz Marina. Its suites range
in size and style; the largest have two bedrooms and a kitchenette. The
pool flows through several levels in the courtyard, and there's a children's playground. The restaurant, with its cordial service, serene ambience, and excellent cuisine, has become a favorite among local
executives. The fitness center has a sauna and steam baths and a
squash court. ⊠ *Lote A, Marina Fidepaz, Apdo. 482, 23000,* ☎ *1/
124–0830 or 800/227–6963,* FAX *1/124–0837,* WEB *www.crowneplaza.
com. 54 suites. Restaurant, bar, pool, gym, nightclub, business services,
travel services. AE, MC, V.*

$$ ✕🏠 **El Angél Azul.** La Paz's historic center has finally attracted en-
trepreneurs. The city's historic courthouse has been converted into a
charming hotel, restaurant, and art gallery. The rooms frame a central
courtyard and are simply decorated with original artworks (which also
fill the walls in the restaurant). Breakfast is the restaurant's best meal,
drawing rave reviews from locals. Try the eggs with mole, or the home-
made yogurt and muesli. Light meals and snacks are served the rest of
the day. ⊠ *Independencia 518, at Guillermo Prieto,* ☎ *1/125–5130,*
WEB *www.elangelazul.com. 11 rooms. Restaurant, bar, air-condition-
ing, no-smoking rooms. MC, V. Restaurant closed Mon.*

$$$ 🏠 **Hotel Marina.** From the lush gardens surrounding the pool and
Jacuzzi to its seaside promenade along the marina walls, there are plenty
of ways to spend your day at the Hotel Marina. The full-service marina offers fishing, scuba diving, and kayaking. Private charters are avail-

able. Most rooms have terraces with water views and are airy, clean, and functional. ⊠ *Carretera a Pichilingue, Km 2.5, 23000,* ☎ *1/121–6254 or 800/250–3186,* 𝔽𝔸𝕏 *1/121–2177,* 𝕎𝔼𝔹 *www.trybaja.com/hotelmarina. 70 rooms, 18 junior suites, 5 master suites. Restaurant, bar, pool, hot tub, tennis court, marina. MC, V.*

$$ 🏨 **Los Arcos.** The colonial-style architecture and classic Baja hospitality make this 1950s hotel a La Paz landmark. The lobby is open and bright, and leads to the central courtyard, where the rush of water in the fountain drowns out the music from the street and other noise. Most rooms have balconies, some facing the bay. The coffee shop opens early, so you can have breakfast and pick up a box lunch if you're going fishing. The Cabañas de Los Arcos next door consists of several small brick cottages surrounded by gardens and a small hotel with a pool. ⊠ *Paseo Obregón 498, between Rosales and Allende, 23000 (6 Jenner St., No. 120, Irvine, CA 92618),* ☎ *1/122–2744; 800/347–2252; 949/450–9000 in the U.S.,* 𝔽𝔸𝕏 *1/125–4313; 949/450–9010 in the U.S.,* 𝕎𝔼𝔹 *www.losarcos.com 130 rooms and suites at the hotel, 30 bungalows and rooms at Cabañas. Restaurant, bar, coffee shop, 2 pools, sauna, fishing. MC, V.*

$$ 🏨 **Club Hotel Cantamar.** Fernando Aguilar, the most famous scuba diving master in the area, has expanded his operation to include this small sports lodge beside a private marina, 14 km (9 mi) north of town. Rooms have balconies that look out on the pool and the sea. The restaurant is in the clubhouse beside the dive boats. This is the ideal hangout for divers, who have easy access to some of the best diving in the Sea of Cortez. ⊠ *Carretera a Pichilingue (Calle Obregon 1665, Apdo. 782) 23000.* ☎ *1/122–1826 or 1/122–7010,* 𝔽𝔸𝕏 *1/122–8644. 18 rooms. Restaurant, bar, pool, dive shop, snorkeling, kayak rental, fishing. MC, V.*

$$ 🏨 **La Concha Beach Resort.** Come to La Concha for its clean private
★   beach, modern rooms, complete water-sports center, and very good restaurant. All rooms have tile floors, TVs, phones, and small refrigerators. Guests gather at the pool and the Cortez Club, a full-scale water-sports center with a bar, equipment rental, and scuba, snorkeling, kayaking, and sportfishing tours. Whale-watching trips are extremely popular in winter. The scuba operation is one of the best in La Paz, and you can arrange tours and rentals through the club even if you're not staying here. A separate building houses condos with kitchenettes, living rooms, and bedrooms ($$$), and has its own pool. Another section, in town, has six suites for long-term rental. There is a shuttle to town and back. ⊠ *Carretera a Pichilingue, Km 5, 23010,* ☎ *1/121–6344, 1/121–6161, or 800/999–2252,* 𝔽𝔸𝕏 *1/121–6218; 619/294–7366 in the U.S.,* 𝕎𝔼𝔹 *www.laconcha.com 107 rooms. Restaurant, 3 bars, pool, water sports, shops, travel services, car rental. AE, MC, V.*

$$ 🏨 **Hotel Suites Club El Moro.** A vacation-ownership resort with suite rentals on a nightly and weekly basis, El Moro has a garden of lush palms and a densely landscaped pool area. You can recognize the building by its stark-white turrets and domes. Rooms are Mediterranean in style and decor, with arched windows, Mexican tiles, and private balconies. Some rooms have kitchens and can sleep up to five people. A small café serves light fare. ⊠ *Carretera a Pichilingue Km 2, Apdo. 357, 23010,* 𝕎𝔼𝔹 *www.clubelmoro.com,* ☎ 𝔽𝔸𝕏 *1/122–4084 or 1/125–2828. 21 suites. Café, bar, pool. AE, MC, V.*

$$ 🏨 **La Perla.** This brown low-rise hotel has a long-standing reputation
★   as one of the best places to stay in La Paz. Rooms have white walls and light-wood furnishings; some have king-size beds. The pool is on a second-story sundeck away from main street traffic. Noise is a factor in the oceanfront rooms; the trade-off is wonderful sunset views over the malecón. ⊠ *Paseo Obregón 1570, 23010,* ☎ *1/122–0777,* 𝔽𝔸𝕏 *1/125–5363. 101 rooms. Restaurant, bar, pool, shops. AE, MC, V.*

$ ⊡ **Pensión California.** This run-down hacienda still has clean blue-and-white rooms with baths and draws backpackers and low-budget travelers. The courtyard has picnic tables and a TV. A laid-back camaraderie prevails. ⊠ *Av. Degollado 209, 23000,* ☎ *1/122–2896. 25 rooms. No credit cards.*

Nightlife and the Arts

El Teatro de la Ciudad (⊠ Av. Navarro 700, ☎ 1/125–0004) is La Paz's cultural center. The theater seats 1,500 and stages shows by visiting performers as well as by local ensembles. **La Terraza** (⊠ La Perla hotel, Paseo Obregón 1570, ☎ 1/122–0777) is the best spot for both sunset- and people-watching along the malecón. The hotel also has a disco open on weekend nights.

Outdoor Activities and Sports

BOATING AND FISHING

The considerable fleet of private boats in La Paz now has room for docking at three marinas: **Fidepaz Marina** at the north end of town, and the **Marina Palmira** and **Marina La Paz** south of town. Most hotels can arrange sportfishing trips. Tournaments are held in August and November. The **Dorado Velez Fleet** (⊠ Apdo. 402, 23000, ☎ 1/122–2744 ext. 608, FAX 1/125–5313), operated by Jack Velez in Los Arcos hotel, has cabin cruisers; charters start around $240 per day.

KAYAKING

The calm waters off La Paz are perfect for kayaking, and novice and experienced kayakers enjoy multiday trips along the coast to Loreto or out to the nearby islands. **Baja Expeditions** (⊠ 2625 Garnet Ave., San Diego, CA 92109, ☎ 800/843–6967; 858/581–3311 in the U.S., FAX 858/581–6542) is one of the oldest outfitters working in Baja, offers several options for kayaking tours. **Baja Quest** (⊠ Sonora 174, ☎ 1/123–5320, FAX 1/123–5321) has day and overnight trips. **Mar y Aventuras** (⊠ Calle Topete 564, ☎ FAX 1/123–0559, ☎ 800/355–7140 in the U.S., FAX 1/123–5321) offers group tours and customized trips and kayak rentals.

SCUBA DIVING

Popular diving spots include the white coral banks off Isla Espíritu Santo, the sea lion colony off Isla Partida, and the seamount 14 km (9 mi) farther north. Conveniently, almost every hotel has arrangements with a dive outfitter. **Baja Diving & Service** (⊠ Paseo Obregón 1665-2, ☎ 1/122–1826, FAX 1/122–8644) rents equipment and operates diving, snorkeling, and tours to Espíritu Santo, the wreck of the ferryboat *Salvatierra,* and a seamount where you can observe schools of hammerhead sharks. They are affiliated with the Club Hotel Cantamar. **Scuba Baja Joe** (⊠ Calle Obregón at Ocampo, ☎ 1/122–4006, FAX 1/122–4000), offers full equipment rentals and guided tours. **Baja Quest** (⊠ Sonora 174, ☎ 1/123–5320, FAX 1/123–5321) has day trips and liveaboard dive cruises during the summer months. The Cortez Club at **La Concha Beach Resort** (⊠ Carretera a Pichilingue, Km 5, ☎ 1/121–6344 or 1/121–6161) offers dive trips. **Baja Expeditions** (⊠ 2625 Garnet Ave., San Diego, CA 92109, ☎ 800/843–6967; 858/581–3311 in the U.S., FAX 858/581–6542 in the U.S.) runs multiday live-aboard dive trips as well as day trips.

WHALE-WATCHING

La Paz has become a center for whale-watching expeditions to Magdalena Bay on the Pacific coast. Most hotels can make all the arrangements, but keep in mind that any whaling trip will entail about six hours' transportation from La Paz and back for two–three hours on the water. Serious whale fans with extra time overnight in San Carlos, the small town by the bay. You can do the trip on your own by taking a public bus from La Paz to San Carlos and then hiring a boat captain to take you into the bay. Check with the tourist office before starting your trip; they'll help with hotel arrangements. In La Paz, you can arrange a trip through **Baja Quest** (✉ Sonora 174, ☎ 1/123–5320, FAX 1/123–5321). **Discover Baja** (☎ 800/727–2252) has guided camping tours and whale-watching trips to Bahía Magdalena. **Baja Expeditions** (✉ 2625 Garnet Ave., San Diego, CA 92109, ☎ 800/843–6967; 858/581–3311 in the U.S., FAX 858/581–6542) also runs whale-watching trips to the bay.

Shopping

Shops carrying a predictable assortment of sombreros, onyx chess sets, and painted plaster curios are scattered along Avenida Obregón across from the malecón. **Artesanías la Antigua California** (✉ Av. Obregón 220, ☎ 1/125–5230) has the nicest selection of Mexican folk art in La Paz, including wooden masks and lacquered boxes from Guerrero, along with a good supply of English-language books on Baja. **Artesanía Cuauhtémoc** (✉ Av. Abasolo between Calles Nayarit and Oaxaca, ☎ no phone) is the workshop of weaver Fortunado Silva, who creates and sells cotton place mats, rugs, and tapestries. **La Tiendita** (✉ Los Arcos hotel, Av. Obregón 498, ☎ 1/125–2744) has embroidered guayabera shirts and dresses, tin ornaments and picture frames, and some black pottery from Oaxaca.

Los Barriles and the East Cape

105 km (65 mi) south of La Paz.

The Sea of Cortez coast north of Los Cabos has long been a favored hideaway for anglers and adventurers. The area known as the East Cape consists of a string of settlements and fishing villages between La Paz and San José del Cabo—including Los Barriles, Buena Vista, and La Ribera, all accessible from Highway 1. From Punta Pescadero in the north to Cabo Pulmo in the south, the cape is renowned for its rich fishing grounds, top-notch diving, and, when the wind kicks up, excellent windsurfing. Moderately developed but growing, the cape makes a great day trip or, if you want more time away from the glitz (and prices) of Los Cabos, a nice place to overnight. Food and lodging tend to be modest affairs; most hotels have meal plans—a good idea since fine dining is scarce.

There's an outback feel to the East Cape, with a robust group of American "settlers" making their presence known and creating a real-estate market out of thin air. Many of the communities are accessible via paved road from Los Cabos. For the intrepid traveler, a three-hour drive on a dirt washboard takes you along the coast to La Ribera, Punta Colorado, and Cabo Pulmo—the latter a superb dive site within a national marine reserve. (This route is *not* recommended for those bothered by dust or long stretches of precipitous driving conditions.)

Windsurfers take over the East Cape in January, when stiff breezes provide ideal conditions. Water-sports equipment and boat trips are available through area hotels, although regulars tend to bring their own gear and rent cars for getting to isolated spots. The nearest airport is at San José del Cabo, about a two-hour drive from the farthest East Cape hotels; several car rental agencies have desks at the airport. Expensive shuttle service can be arranged through most hotels, and there are plenty of cabs in the area.

Dining and Lodging

$$ ✕ **Otra Vez.** Whether you're in the mood for some simple grilled seafood, an omelet, or lobster New Orleans, this great little California-style café is sure to please. This may be the only time you see sprouts in Baja, so stock up. The clientele largely consists of expat retirees and tourists who gossip freely while listening to the Beach Boys. Live music and theme nights are featured. ✉ *Calle 20 de Noviembre, Los Barriles,* ☎ *1/142–0249. MC, V.*

$$$–$$$$ ☷ **Rancho Leonero.** Diehard anglers love this casual seaside hotel. Thatch-roof bungalows are scattered about the landscaped property. Although far from fancy, the rooms are serviceable, with tile floors, hard mattresses, and powerful showers. Meals (included in the room rate) are served family-style in the large dining room, the ambience of which depends on the guests, who can tend toward the rowdy side. In the afternoon the pool fills with sunburned boaters and their fish-story boasting. The fishing fleet, diving at nearby Cabo Pulmo's reefs, and use of kayaks are other pluses. Credit cards are not accepted at the hotel, but can be used for room reservations in advance. ✉ *Carretera Transpeninsular Km 103, Buena Vista (22603 La Palma Ave., Suite 307, Yorba Linda, CA 92887), 32 km (20 mi) north of San José del Cabo,* ☎ *1/141–0216 or 800/334–2252,* ꜰᴀx *1/141–0216. 34 rooms. Restaurant, pool, beach, fishing. AE, MC, V for advance payment.*

$$$ ☷ **Hotel Buena Vista Beach Resort.** The most pleasant surroundings on the coast are at this old-time resort built around a 1940s private mansion. Sixty tile-roof bungalows are set along flower-lined paths next to swimming pools and lawns. Some rooms have private terraces. The fishing fleet is one of the best in the area, and there are plenty of other diversions, including scuba diving, snorkeling, kayaking, horseback riding, trips to natural springs and caves, and tours into Los Cabos and La Paz. Airport shuttle service can be arranged in advance. Room rates include all meals. ✉ *Carretera Transpeninsular Km 105, Buena Vista 23500 (130 27th St., Chula Vista, CA 91911),* ☎ *1/141–0033; 800/752–3555; 619/429–8079 in the U.S.,* ꜰᴀx *1/141–0133; 619/429–7924 in the U.S.,* ᴡᴇʙ *www.hotelbuenavista.com. 60 rooms. Restaurant, 2 pools, hot tub, massage, tennis court, horseback riding, beach, fishing. AE, MC, V.*

$$$ ☷ **Hotel Palmas de Cortés.** A long-standing favorite with anglers, this casual lodge is often featured on sportfishing shows. It's near the famed Cortez banks, where marlin and tuna abound. The rooms and suites are sparsely furnished, with the basic comforts, and have few frills beyond powerful air-conditioners and hot showers. Caged parrots and macaws hang about the gardens among hammocks. Food is hearty and abundant and is included in your room rate. ✉ *On the beach (take the road north through Los Barriles and continue to the beach), Los Barriles (Box 9016, Calabasas, CA 91372),* ☎ *1/141–0050; 818/591–9463 in the U.S.,* ꜰᴀx *1/141–0046. 30 rooms, 10 suites, 10 condos. Restaurant, pool, tennis court, gym, squash, fishing. MC, V.*

$$$ ☷ **Hotel Punta Pescadero.** Despite the many vacation homes sprouting up in the area, this secluded resort is one of the most peaceful spots in Baja. Rooms have private waterfront terraces and are reserved far in advance by regulars (some 75% of the clientele is made up of returnees). They brave the half-hour drive along a hilly rock-strewn dirt road to the hotel for the sense of complete escape—miles of windswept beach and calm coves with superb snorkeling—and the camaraderie of the staff and guests. Transportation from the Los Cabos airport is available for a fee and must be arranged in advance. The hotel can also arrange for tours to local sights. ✉ *Camino de los Barriles a El Cardonal, Punta Pescadero, 23000, 12 km (7 mi) north of Los Barriles,* ☎ *1/121–0101 or 888/765–0653,* ꜰᴀx *1/126–1771 or 1/142–4626,* ᴡᴇʙ

www.puntapescadero.com. 22 rooms. Restaurant, refrigerators, pool, beach, snorkeling, dive shop, fishing, private airstrip. MC, V.

Shopping

The **Plaza Del Pueblo** (⊠ Hwy. 1, Los Barriles) is just about the area's only shopping opportunity. At the **East Cape Smoke House** (☎ 1/141–0294), you can sample and purchase freshly smoked seafood, and get a report on the local fishing conditions. The Smoke House also specializes in custom smoking and vacuum-packing your fresh catch. The small shopping center also includes an Internet shop, a tackle store, an ice cream parlor, and a bakery.

Los Cabos

195 km (121 mi) south of La Paz.

At the southern tip of the 1,625-km (1,000-mi) Baja California peninsula, the land ends in a rocky point called El Arco (The Arch), a place of stark beauty. The warm waters of the Sea of Cortez swirl into the Pacific Ocean's rugged surf as marlin and sailfish leap out of the waves. The desert ends in sandy coves, with cactus standing at their entrances like sentries under the soaring palm trees.

The conquistadores focused their attention on La Paz during expeditions from mainland Mexico in the mid-1500s, but pirates found the tip of the Baja peninsula ideal for spotting Spanish galleons traveling from the Philippines to Spain's empire in central Mexico. In their turn missionaries came to convert the few thousand local Indians who lived off the sea. The Jesuits established the mission of **San José del Cabo** in the mid-1700s, but their settlements didn't last long. The missionaries (and other Europeans) had brought syphilis and smallpox along with their preachings, and, like elsewhere on the peninsula, the indigenous population was nearly wiped out after a few decades.

Anglers rediscovered this remote region in the 20th century. When pilots flew over Baja during World War II, they spotted the swirling waters and fertile fishing grounds from the air, and word soon spread. Wealthy adventurers with private planes and boats created a demand for fishing lodges, airstrips, and other services, and the region became a cult destination. By the 1960s a half-dozen exclusive resorts were thriving on the cliffs and shores amid the barren landscape.

Connected by a 32-km (20-mi) stretch of highway called the **Corridor,** the two towns of Cabo San Lucas and San José del Cabo were distinct until the late 1970s, when the Mexican government's office of tourism development (Fonatur) targeted the southern tip of Baja as a major resort and dubbed the area Los Cabos. The destination now consists of three major areas: San José del Cabo, Cabo San Lucas, and the Corridor.

In the process Los Cabos has become one of Mexico's most popular and most expensive coastal getaways, with deluxe hotels, championship golf courses, and some of the best sportfishing in the world. The population growth rate is among the fastest in Mexico, and the inadequate infrastructure is becoming a problem. But despite all the development that has taken place, and the steep prices that have come along with it, the area remains a mysteriously natural hideaway.

San José del Cabo

San José del Cabo is the municipal headquarters for the two Los Cabos towns and has a population of about 25,000. The hotel zone faces a long stretch of waterfront on the Sea of Cortez, and several large hotels and timeshare projects are under construction. A nine-hole golf course and private residential community are well established south of the town

Los Cabos Coast

center. The downtown area with its adobe houses and jacaranda trees has become the loveliest part of Los Cabos as entrepreneurs convert old homes into stylish restaurants and shops. Unfortunately, bumper-to-bumper traffic often clogs the streets during weekday business hours. Despite the development, San José remains the more peaceful of the two towns—the one to come to for a quiet escape. Those seeking exciting nightlife and a rowdy beach scene are better off staying in Cabo San Lucas, since it costs nearly $20 to take a taxi between the two towns.

㉚ Boulevard Mijares. The south end of the main street in San José del Cabo has been designated a tourist zone, with the Los Cabos Club de Golf as its centerpiece. A few reasonably priced hotels are situated perpendicular to the boulevard on a beautiful long beach where the surf, unfortunately, is too dangerous for swimming. Several new hotels are emerging on this beach.

㉛ City Hall. The modest yellow municipal building is near Avenida Zaragoza, where Boulevard Mijares ends—a spot marked by a long fountain. There is a small, shaded plaza here with a few café tables in front of restaurants.

㉙ Estero de San José. The spot where the freshwater Río San José flows into the sea is at the end of the tourist strip, on Paseo San José by the Presidente Inter-Continental. The estuary is a natural preserve closed to boats, but supervision of the reserve is slack. More than 200 species of birds can be spotted here, and anglers enjoy fishing from shore where the river meets the sea.

㉝ Iglesia San José. The town's church looms above the plaza. Be sure to walk up to the front and see the tile mural of a captured priest being dragged toward a fire by Indians.

㉜ Plaza Mijares. Locals and travelers mingle at the large central plaza, which has a white wrought-iron gazebo and green benches set in the shade.

BEACHES

Playa Hotelera is the stretch of beach that most of the finer hotels use. It's beautiful, but the current is dangerously rough, and swimming is not advised. At the east end of the beach, near the Presidente Inter-Continental, there's a freshwater lagoon filled with tropical birds and plants. If you plan to spend time here, be sure to douse yourself with insect repellent. The best swimming beach near San José is **Playa Palmilla**, which is protected by a rocky point just south of town. The northern part of the beach is cluttered with boats and shacks, but if you walk south you'll reach the Hotel Palmilla beach, a long stretch of white sand and calm sea.

164

San José del Cabo

0 _____ 500 meters
0 _____ 500 yards

↑ TO LA PAZ AND AIRPORT
Ignacio Comonfort

Av. Zaragoza **33** ✉ **32** **31**

Av. Manuel Doblado
M. Castro
Coronado
Margarita Maza de Juárez

Cerro de la Cruz

Valerio Gonzalez Canseco

Morelos
Miguel Hidalgo

Carretera Transpeninsular

Cerro de El Vigia

Club de Golf

30

Blvd. Mijares

29

Playa Hotelera

Sea of Cortez

1 TO CABO SAN LUCAS →

DINING AND LODGING

$$$ ✕ **Da Antonio.** Overlooking the estuary, this subdued Italian trattoria
★ serves an antipasto tower on a multitiered silver platter that alone is
worth the price of a meal. The restaurant is part of the all-inclusive
Presidente, but is open to the public for a set price four-course meal
worth savoring. Choices include red snapper with asparagus in a
tomato and black olive sauce, beef tenderloin with Chianti sauce, veal
scallopini, and several homemade pastas. The wine list includes im-
ports from Italy, Chile, and the Napa Valley. ✉ *Paseo San José, at the
end of the hotel zone,* ☎ *1/142–0211. Reservations essential. AE,
MC, V. Closed Mon.*

$$$ ✕ **Damiana.** For a special night out, come to this small hacienda
★ tucked beside the plaza, past the center of town. Bougainvilleas wrap
around the tall pines shading the wrought-iron tables, and the pink adobe
walls glow in the candlelight. Start with fiery oysters diablo, then
move on to the tender chateaubriand, charbroiled lobster, or the restaurant's signature shrimp steak, made with ground shrimp. You'll find
the setting so relaxing and charming that you might want to linger well
into the night. ✉ *Blvd. Mijares 8,* ☎ *1/142–0499. AE, MC, V.*

$$$ ✕ **Fandango.** This quirky restaurant has an excellent reputation among
longtime residents, and its eclectic menu should please almost every-
one. Interesting dishes include Chilean seafood stew, grilled sea bass,
wild-mushroom pizza, and Thai chicken. The decor is as diverse as the
menu: there's a festive mural, Chinese umbrellas, and a candlelit patio.
✉ *Obregón 19 at Morelos,* ☎ *1/142–2226. MC, V. Closed Sun.*

$$$ ✕ **Floriska.** An international fusion menu—which includes such savory
dishes as coconut shrimp with mango sauce, lobster in a Grand Marnier
vinaigrette, and lamb with a spicy sauce—is complemented by the elegant decor and fine tableware. Be sure to save room for dessert; the
fruit sabayon is a divine way to end your meal. Jazz guitarists perform

some nights on the outdoor patio. ⊠ *Blvd. Mijares 16-1, Col. Centro,* ☎ *1/142–4600. AE, MC, V.*

$$$ ✕ **Tequila Restaurante.** An old adobe home serves as the setting for the classiest restaurant in town. The lengthy tequila list gives you a chance to savor the finer brands of Mexico's national drink, and the menu challenges you to decide between excellent regional dishes and innovative Pacific Rim spring rolls, salads, and seafood with mango, ginger, and citrus sauces. Take your time and sample all you can. ⊠ *Manuel Doblado s/n,* ☎ *1/142–1155. AE.*

$$ ✕ **Tropicana Bar and Grill.** Start the day with coffee and French toast at the sidewalk tables in front of this enduringly popular restaurant. Later, as the temperature rises, it's more comfortable to sit inside the large, air-conditioned bar over an ice-cold lemonade, watching sporting events and music videos on TV. In the evening the back patio quickly fills with a loyal clientele who enjoy the garden setting and decent cooking. The menu has grown over the years to include U.S. cuts of beef and imported seafood along with fajitas, chiles rellenos, and lobster, always in demand. The nightly dinner special is usually a good deal. ⊠ *Blvd. Mijares 30,* ☎ *1/142–1580. AE, MC, V.*

$ ✕ **Baja Natural.** Tucked down a flight of steps away from the busy streets, this is a good place to cool off. The menu features dozens of fresh-fruit smoothies and juices, shakes, and power drinks, as well as hamburgers, hot dogs, and veggie burgers. The decor is sparse, but you're not here to be impressed with the surroundings, just refreshed. Kids will like it. ⊠ *Manuel Oblado between Morelos and Hidalgo,* ☎ *1/142–3105. No credit cards. Closed Sun.*

$ ✕ **Restaurant La Playita.** A longtime local secret, this small, out-of-the-way restaurant has undergone several changes in owners and chefs but always draws dedicated locals and tourists. The main attraction is the seafood brought in daily by fishermen who beach their boats just a few yards away. The fish is prepared according to the whims of the cook and available ingredients; you can't go wrong if you stick with the catch of the day grilled with oil and garlic. Lunch here is a nice midday outing, especially when followed by a long walk down the largely deserted beach. ⊠ *Pueblo la Playa, 2 km (1 mi) south of San José,* ☎ *1/142–3774. MC, V.*

$ ✕ **Caffé Gourmet.** This art gallery, coffeehouse, and café fills a large room in a converted building near the plaza. The sounds of soft jazz accompany the groups of stylish locals and tourists sipping lattes and nibbling on flaky apple strudel and dense cheesecake. Local artists display their works on the walls; local musicians perform on weekends. ⊠ *Manuel Doblado at Hidalgo,* ☎ *1/142–5522. MC, V.*

$$$$ 🏨 **Casa Natalia.** Standing gracefully at the north end of San José's most charming street and public plaza is this beautiful hotel, a husband-and-wife effort opened in 1999. The bright, airy rooms, among the most private and well appointed in Los Cabos, are decorated in regional Mexican motifs and have California king-size beds, European linens, remote-control air-conditioning, and sliding glass doors that lead to a private patio. From your hammock you can enjoy the view of the garden, pool, and regal palms. The restaurant, presided over by owner-chef Luïc Tenoux, features a delicious blend of traditional Mexican and European cuisine. ⊠ *Blvd. Mijares 4, 23400,* ☎ *1/142–5100 or 888/277–3814,* FAX *1/142–5110,* WEB *www.casanatalia.com. 16 rooms, 2 suites. Restaurant, bar, pool, massage. AE, MC, V.*

$$$$ 🏨 **Presidente Inter-Continental Los Cabos.** Greatly expanded from its former subdued state, the all-inclusive Presidente has become the largest resort in San José. The hotel sits amid cactus gardens next to the estuary, and has three sections centered by pools and lounging areas. The quietest area is by the estuary; volleyball games, aerobics classes, and other fun take place at the main pool. The newest wing faces the largest pool with a swim-up bar. Guests choose between three gourmet restaurants and themed buffets at dinner (the restaurants are far better than the buffets), order 24-hour room service, or opt for fast-food nachos, hot dogs, and fries at several food carts. The open bars include mixed drinks as well as wine and beer, and amenities include a fitness center, putting green, tennis center, and children's programs. The rooms are not equal, however: Those on the first floor have terraces, and those on the third floor have balconies. But the windows in rooms on the second floor don't even open. ⊠ *Paseo San José, at the end of the hotel zone, 23400,* ☎ *1/142–0211 or 800/327–0200,* FAX *1/142–0232,* WEB *www.loscabosinterconti.com. 400 rooms. 6 restaurants, 4 bars, 5 snack bars, air-conditioning, room service, 3 pools, 3 tennis courts, horseback riding, beach, fishing, children's programs, playground, meeting room. AE, MC, V.*

$$$ ☷ **Tropicana Inn.** This small hotel is a great option if you aren't desperate to be on the beach. The stucco buildings decorated with tile murals of Diego Rivera paintings frame a pool and palapa bar in a quiet enclave behind San José's main boulevard. Rooms are air-conditioned, have satellite TV, and are maintained to look brand new. Book in advance in high season. ⊠ *Blvd. Mijares 30, 23400,* ☎ *1/142–0907,* FAX *1/142–1590. 39 rooms, 2 suites. Restaurant, bar, air-conditioning, room service, pool. AE, MC, V.*

$$ ☷ **Posada Terranova.** San José's best inexpensive hotel is a friendly place where guests return so frequently they're almost part of the family. The large, air-conditioned rooms are painted bright white and have two double beds and tile bathrooms. The hotel has expanded in recent years. Even so, when guests congregate at the front patio tables or in the restaurant, it still feels like a private home. ⊠ *Calle Degollado at Zaragoza, 23400,* ☎ *1/142–0534,* FAX *1/142–0902,* WEB *www.hterranova.com.mx. 25 rooms. Restaurant, bar. AE, MC, V.*

NIGHTLIFE AND THE ARTS

The hottest nightspot in town is **Iguana Bar** (⊠ Blvd. Mijares 24, ☎ 1/142–0266), a local hangout with live rock and roll on weekend nights during the high season. **Kitsch Café and Gallery** (⊠ Blvd. Mijares 29–1, ☎ 1/142–4767), a gallery and coffee shop by day, draws a young crowd on weekends with open-mike poetry, tarot readings, and late-night dancing.

OUTDOOR ACTIVITIES AND SPORTS

Fishing. Most hotels in San José can arrange trips. As there is no marina in town, you'll board your boat at the marina in Cabo San Lucas—hotels will also set up transportation to the marina and prepare lunches. Pangas depart from the sand at La Playita; you can arrange trips through hotels.

Kayaking. Kayak tours and rentals are available through **Los Lobos del Mar** (⊠ Brisas del Mar RV park, on the south side of San José, ☎ 1/142–2983). The tours paddle along the Corridor's peaceful bays and are especially fun in the winter months when gray whales pass by offshore.

Surfing. The **Killer Hook Surf Shop** (⊠ Av. Hidalgo, ☎ 1/142–2430) sells and rents snorkeling gear, along with surfboards and boogie boards.

SHOPPING

San José's shops and galleries carry a gorgeous array of high-quality folk art, jewelry, and housewares. In fact, serious shoppers staying elsewhere should plan on splurging here. **ADD** (⊠ Av. Zaragoza at Hidalgo, ☎ 1/143–2055), an interior-design shop, sells gorgeous hand-painted dishes from Guanajuato and carved wood furniture from Michoacán. **Copal** (⊠ Plaza Mijares, ☎ 1/142–3070) has a nice array of carved animals from Oaxaca, masks from Guerrero, and heavy wooden furnishings. **Daniel Espinosa Studio** (⊠ Blvd. Mijares 2, ☎ 1/142–4696) displays handcrafted silver jewelry from some of the country's finest artists.

Veryka (⊠ Blvd. Mijares 6B, ☎ 1/142–0575) is associated with galleries in San Miguel de Allende and Oaxaca, two of the finest art centers in Mexico. This shop's selection of huipiles, masks, tapestries, and pottery is coveted by collectors. At **Kitsch Café and Gallery** (⊠ Blvd. Mijares 29–1, ☎ 1/142–4767), you can relax with a cappuccino or cocktail while surrounded by paintings by the owner and a wide selection of traditional crafts from around Mexico. Across from City Hall is **Almacenes Goncanseco** (⊠ Blvd. Mijares 18, ☎ no phone), where you can get film, postcards, groceries, and liquor. For fresh produce, flowers, meat, fish, and a sampling of local life in San José, visit the **Mercado Municipal,** off Calle Doblado.

The Corridor

Many of the legendary fishing lodges and exclusive resorts built before the government stepped in were located along the wild cliffs between San José del Cabo and Cabo San Lucas. Since the mid-1980s, the area has developed as a destination unto itself. It has several private communities and large-scale resorts, and three championship golf courses. Much of the development is centered on two major areas—Cabo Real and Cabo del Sol—both containing hotels, private homes, restaurants, and golf courses. The highway along the Corridor has been widened to four lanes. The road is in good shape most of the time, but tends to flood during heavy rains, especially between August and November.

BEACHES

Costa Azul is the most popular surfing beach in Los Cabos. A few small campgrounds and casual restaurants line the beach. **Playa Palmilla** is one of the Corridor's best swimming beaches.

Two bays, **Bahía Chileno** and **Bahía Santa María,** are terrific for diving and snorkeling.

DINING AND LODGING

$$$ ✕ **Pitahayas.** This elegant restaurant has found its niche in a lovely spot just above the beach at Cabo del Sol. The wide-ranging menu features Pacific Rim cuisine, blending touches of Thai, Polynesian, and Chinese cooking in unusual recipes. Lobster appears in the form of gourmet hash, duckling is served with a plum-tangerine sauce, and fresh organic vegetables are lightly stir-fried and served while still crisp. Soft jazz plays in the background, and the setting is decidedly romantic. ⊠ *Hwy. 1, Km 10,* ☎ *1/145–8010. AE, MC, V.*

$$ ✕ **Da Giorgio II.** The best sunset-watching in all of Los Cabos is at the cliffside tables outside this restaurant. Staggered along the cliffs and poised beside a small pond with a waterfall, the tables have great views of the arch at land's end. The menu focuses on pastas and pizza, and the salad bar has an abundance of fresh veggies. ⊠ *Hwy. 1, Km 5,* ☎ *1/145–8160. MC, V.*

$ ✕ **Zippers.** Home of the surfing crowd and those who like a bit of sand in their burgers, this casual palapa-roof restaurant sits on Costa Azul beach just south of San José. Burgers, ribs, and chicken are all decent, but it's the crowd that makes the place fun. ⊠ *Hwy. 1, Km 18.5,* ☎ *no phone. No credit cards.*

$$$$ ✕🔟 **Twin Dolphin.** Sleek and Japanese-modern, with an austere air, the Twin Dolphin has been a hideaway for the rich and famous since

1977. Guest rooms are in low-lying casitas along a seaside cliff and are furnished in minimalist style, without TVs or phones. The hotel is worth a visit if only for the reproductions of Baja's cave paintings on the lobby wall. The restaurant has been updated and chef Michael Richards uses homemade goat cheese, homegrown organic vegetables and herbs, and local seafood for his creations. The Saturday-night fiesta buffet has become legendary, and reservations are a must. ⊠ *Carretera Transpeninsular Km 11.5, Cabo San Lucas 23410 (1625 W. Olympic Blvd., Suite 1005, Los Angeles, CA 90015),* ☎ *1/145–8190 or 800/421–8925,* 𝗙𝗔𝗫 *1/143–0496; 213/380–1302 in the U.S.,* 𝗪𝗘𝗕 *www.twindolphin.com. 44 rooms, 6 suites. Restaurant, bar, pool, massage, 2 tennis courts, beach, fishing. MC, V.*

$$$$ 🏨 **Casa Del Mar.** One of the smallest properties in the area, this hacienda-style hotel is all about luxurious privacy. An antique hand-carved wooden door leads into the courtyard-lobby with stone fountains and stairways that curve up to the rooms, spa, and library. Rooms are designed with pampering in mind—the bathrooms with whirlpool bathtubs and shower and separate toilet stalls are set a few steps above the main bedroom, where cushy beds covered in satiny soft sheets have sea views. A series of flowing streams, fountains, and gardens leads around the pool to a wide stretch of beach where you can leave footprints in the untrammeled sand. The restaurant is excellent. ⊠ *Carretera Transpeninsular Km 19.5, Cabo San Lucas 23410,* ☎ *1/144–0030 or 800/221–8808,* 𝗙𝗔𝗫 *1/144–0034,* 𝗪𝗘𝗕 *www.casadelmarresort.com. 25 rooms, 31 suites. Restaurant, pool, spa, beach. AE, MC, V.*

$$$$ 🏨 **Hotel Cabo San Lucas.** Looking like a mountain lodge nearly buried in palms, this long-standing Corridor hotel is a favorite of Baja devotees. The rooms are furnished with cheery yellow and blue fabrics and light-wood pieces; suites and villas are more luxurious. The hacienda-style buildings are located right above Chileno Beach, one of the best diving spots in Los Cabos. The restaurant has been cited one of the region's best by *Gourmet* magazine. ⊠ *Carretera Transpeninsular Km 14.5, Cabo San Lucas 23410,* ☎ *1/144–0014 or 877/733–2226,* 𝗙𝗔𝗫 *1/144–0015; 323/655–3243 in the U.S.,* 𝗪𝗘𝗕 *www.hotelcabo.com. 68 rooms, 7 villas. Restaurant, pool, beach, dive shop, fishing. AE, MC, V.*

$$$$ 🏨 **Meliá Cabo Real.** The Meliá sprawls over a hilltop with a crystal-blue pool, fountains, waterfalls, white canopies shading rest areas, and a private beach created by a small jetty jutting from the rocky hillside. Maya carvings and bas-reliefs adorn the walls in the rooms, which all have landscaped terraces. The Cabo Real resort development around the hotel is ongoing, and now includes two golf courses. Meliá guests can use it for a fee. Meliá also has another hotel in the Cabo Real development, and a shuttle runs to its sister property in Cabo San Lucas. ⊠ *Carretera Transpeninsular Km 19.5, Cabo San Lucas 23400,* ☎ *1/144–0000 or 800/336–3542,* 𝗙𝗔𝗫 *1/144–0101,* 𝗪𝗘𝗕 *www.solmelia.com. 287 rooms, 15 suites. 4 restaurants, café, pool, 2 tennis courts, exercise room, beach, dive shop, fishing. AE, MC, V.*

$$$$ 🏨 **Palmilla.** One of the original hotels in Los Cabos, the Palmilla is a
★   gracious, sprawling, hacienda-style resort with a small white adobe chapel. Tile stairways lead up from flower-lined paths to large modernized suites with hand-carved furniture, French doors opening onto private patios, and tile baths; all rooms have TVs and phones. There's also a swimming pool with fountains and a swim-up bar. The buildings are spread along a hillside overlooking the beach, the service is delightfully personalized, and the hotel's La Paloma restaurant is excellent. A 27-hole Jack Nicklaus–designed golf course and a condo resort development surrounds the hotel, which still manages to feel secluded and serene. ⊠ *Carretera Transpeninsular Km 1 (about 8 km [5 mi] from San José), 23400* ☎ *1/144–5000 or 800/637–2226,* 𝗙𝗔𝗫 *1/144–5100,* 𝗪𝗘𝗕

www.palmillaresort.com. 24 rooms, 91 suites, 1 villa. Restaurant, bar, pool, golf privileges, 2 tennis courts, beach. AE, MC, V.

$$$$ ★ 🖫 **Las Ventanas al Paraíso.** Las Ventanas set the standard for luxury, privacy, and amenities in Los Cabos. All suites have individual hot tubs, wood-burning fireplaces, and telescopes for viewing whales at sea and stars at night. The service is sublime—courteous staff seem to pop out of nowhere to offer anything from a beach towel to a cool drink. A sort-of handbook on contemporary seaside elegance, the hotel is filled with handcrafted lamps and doors, sculpture, and paintings, and the stone walkways were patterned by hand. The outstanding restaurants are worth a visit for the chef's home-baked breads and innovative recipes, and the spa offers the latest luxurious treatments. Guests have access to off-property golf and tennis facilities nearby. ⊠ *Carretera Transpeninsular Km 19.5, Cabo San Lucas 23400,* ☎ *1/144–0300; 888/525–0483; 214/880–4200 in the U.S.,* 𝖥𝖠𝖷 *1/144–0301,* 𝖶𝖤𝖡 *www.lasventanas.com. 61 suites. 2 restaurants, 2 bars, 2 pools, spa, hot tub, massage, steam room, golf privileges, fitness center, gym, beach, fishing. AE, MC, V.*

OUTDOOR ACTIVITIES AND SPORTS

Diving and Snorkeling. Bahía Chileno, an underwater preserve, teems with marine life and is a wonderful place for snorkeling and diving. You'll need to bring your own equipment. **Bahía Santa María,** a white-sand cove protected by towering brown cliffs, has superb snorkeling, with hundreds of colorful fish swarming through chunks of white coral. There is a concession stand on the beach with snorkeling-gear rental; its hours are erratic.

Fishing. Most Corridor hotels have excellent fishing fleets, with the boats anchored at the marina in Cabo San Lucas. Hotels typically can set up the trips and provide transportation to the marina and box lunches. **Victor's Aquatics** (☎ 1/142–1092, 𝖥𝖠𝖷 1/142–1093) has a fleet of pangas on the Palmilla resort's beach. **Jig Stop Tours** (☎ 800/521–2281) books fishing trips for several Los Cabos fleets.

Golf. Los Cabos is a hot spot for golf, hosting tournaments including the PGA Senior Grand Slam. The courses that have brought so much attention this way are all in the Corridor and serve as the centerpieces for megaresort developments. If you aren't staying at a hotel associated with one of the courses, reserve a tee time a week in advance. Expect to pay exorbitant greens fees—nearly $200 in winter, and $140 in summer. Among the most spectacular golf courses is the 27-hole Jack Nicklaus–designed course at the **Palmilla Golf Club** (⊠ Palmilla resort, Carretera Transpeninsular Km 1, ☎ 1/144–5250 or 800/386–2465). **Cabo del Sol** (☎ 1/145–8200; 800/386–2465, a resort development in the Corridor, has an 18-hole Jack Nicklaus course. Ultimately, the development will have three 18-hole courses (the second one will be designed by Tom Weiskopf). The Robert Trent Jones–designed **Cabo Real Golf Club** (⊠ Meliá Cabo Real Hotel, ☎ 1/144–0040) has 36 holes. The **El Dorado** (☎ 1/144–5440) is the latest 18-hole course from Jack Nicklaus and covers rough seaside terrain in Cabo Real.

Cabo San Lucas

Cabo San Lucas, once an unsightly fishing town with dusty streets and smelly canneries, has become Los Cabos's center of tourism activity. The sportfishing fleet is headquartered here, and cruise ships anchored off the marina disperse passengers into town. Trendy restaurants and bars line the streets, and massive hotels have risen on every available plot of waterfront turf—alas, a five-story condo-hotel complex along the bay blocks the view from the town's older hotels. Cabo San Lucas is decidedly *in*—for its rowdy nightlife, its slew of restaurants, and its shopportunities.

The main downtown street, Avenida Lázaro Cárdenas, passes the
(34) pretty **Plaza San Lucas** with its white wrought-iron gazebo. Buildings
around the plaza house galleries and restaurants. Most of the shops,
services, and restaurants are located between Avenida Cárdenas and
the waterfront.

Boulevard Marina has been transformed from a dusty main drag into
a busy thoroughfare lined with hotels and cafés. Paved walkways now
run from here to the hotels and beaches on the east end of town and
(35) west to the **Handicrafts Market** at the Cabo San Lucas marina. The sport-
(36) fishing fleet is docked in the **Bahía de Cabo San Lucas,** and there are
glass-bottom boats available at the water's edge.

(37) **El Arco.** The most spectacular sight in Cabo San Lucas, this natural rock
arch is visible from the marina and from some of the hotels but is more
impressive from the water. You should take at least a short boat ride
out to the arch and Playa de Amor, the beach underneath, to fully appreciate Cabo.

(38) **El Faro de Cabo Falso.** The Lighthouse of the False Cape, built in 1890
and set amid sand dunes, is on the cliffs above the Pacific Coast. You
need a four-wheel-drive vehicle to reach the lighthouse by land; most
hotels can arrange off-road-vehicle tours.

BEACHES

Playa de Amor consists of a secluded cove at the very end of the peninsula, with the Sea of Cortez on one side and the Pacific Ocean on the
other. The contrast between the peaceful azure cove on the Sea of Cortez
and the pounding white surf of the Pacific is dramatic. **Playa Hacienda,** in the inner harbor by the Hacienda Hotel, has the calmest waters of any beach in town and good snorkeling around the rocky point.
Playa Médano, just north of Cabo San Lucas, is the most popular stretch
in Los Cabos (and possibly in all Baja) for sunbathing and people-watching. The 3-km (2-mi) span of white sand is always crowded, especially
on weekends. **Playa Solmar,** fringing the Solmar Hotel, is a beautiful
wide beach at the base of the mountains leading into the Pacific, but
it has dangerous surf with a swift undertow. Stick to sunbathing here.

DINING AND LODGING

$$$ ✕ **El Galeón.** Considered by some to be the most distinguished dining
room in town, El Galeón is across from the marina. The choice seats are
on the outside terraces facing the water; the inside is decorated with heavy
wooden furniture. Traditional Italian, Mexican, and American dishes are
prepared expertly, with an emphasis on thick, tender cuts of beef. The
piano bar is a nice setting for a late-night brandy. ✉ *Across from ma-
rina by the road to the Finisterra Hotel,* ☎ *1/143–0443. AE, MC, V.*

$$$ ✕ **Mi Casa.** One of Cabo's best restaurants is in a cobalt-blue build-
★ ing painted with a mural of a burro, just across the street from the main
plaza. Mexican cuisine reaches gourmet status here with fresh tuna and
dorado served with tomatillo salsa or Yucatecan achiote, or with so-
phisticated dishes such as chili en nogada. The large back courtyard
is especially nice at night, illuminated by candlelight and the moon. ✉
Av. Cabo San Lucas, ☎ *1/143–1933. No lunch Sun. MC, V.*

$$$ ✕ **Peacocks.** This classy and casually sophisticated dining room is
★ known for its ambitious list of imported wines and its innovative cui-
sine. The ubiquitous dorado is coated with a crust of chopped pecans,
and the shrimp masterfully tossed with spinach fettuccine. The chef is
known for his home-baked breads and incredible desserts—if you miss
dinner, be sure to stop by for a cappuccino and a tequila mousse or prof-
iterole. The candlelit two-level dining room has an open kitchen and is
topped by an enormous palapa; you can also dine on an outdoor patio.
✉ *Paseo Pescador near Playa Médano,* ☎ *1/143–1858. AE, MC, V.*

$$ ✕ **Edith's Café.** Calm and romantic by local standards, this small café
starts out with live jazz and blues in the background and views of the
sea. Lobster and other seafood, an excellent wine list, and good cof-
fees and desserts fill out the picture of a long, romantic dinner here.
✉ *Paseo del Pescador near Playa Médano,* ☎ *1/143–0801. MC, V.*

$$ ✕ **Mocambo.** Veracruz (known for its regional seafood preparations)
★ meets Los Cabos in an enormous dining room packed with locals. The
menu features hard-to-find regional dishes including octopus ceviche,
shrimp empanadas, and a heaping mixed seafood platter that includes
sea snails, clams, and octopus with the more standard lobster and shrimp.
Musicians stroll among the tables and the chatter is somewhat ca-
cophonous, but you're sure to have a great dining experience here. ✉
Leona Vicario at 20 de Noviembre, ☎ *1/143–2122. AE, MC, V.*

$$ ✕ **Las Palmas.** Slip off your sandals and wiggle your toes in the sand
at the beach tables, or gather around a linen-draped table in the open-
air dining room. Either way, you'll enjoy the mixed seafood grill served
atop a clay hibachi, or selections from the full sushi bar. Have your
catch of the day grilled and served with garlic, butter, and mango sal-
sas. ✉ *Playa Médano,* ☎ *1/143–04–47. MC, V.*

$$ ✕ **Pancho's.** This festive restaurant, a favorite among locals in the know,
has an enormous collection of tequilas (almost 500 labels); take ad-
vantage of owner John Bragg's encyclopedic knowledge of tequila and
sample a few. Oaxacan tablecloths, murals, painted chairs, and stream-
ers add to the fun atmosphere. The menu offers a variety of delicious
seafood and regional Mexican specialties; try the tortilla soup, chiles
rellenos, or stuffed bacon-wrapped shrimp. Pancho's is also open for
breakfast. ✉ *Hidalgo between Zapata and Serdan,* ☎ *1/143–0973,* FAX
1/143–5095. AE, MC, V.

$$ ✕ **El Shrimp Bucket.** This is the calmest of the three Carlos Anderson
restaurants in Cabo San Lucas. A few tables are set out on the walk-
way that runs along the marina in front of the Marina Fiesta Hotel, a
good spot to relax and watch the boats rock on the water. The indoor
dining room has the chain's typical mishmash decor and quirky adorn-
ments. The food—barbecued ribs and chicken, burgers, piles of fried
shrimp—is dependable and abundant. ✉ *Blvd. Marina in Marina Fi-
esta complex,* ☎ *1/143–2598. AE, MC, V.*

$ ✕ **The Office.** Playa Médano is lined with cafés on the sand, some with
lounge chairs, others with more formal settings. All serve the same ba-
sics—cold beer, snacks, fish tacos, french fries—and most accompany
the meal with loud American rock. The Office, which has provided per-
fect vacation photo opportunities for more than a decade, is the best,
serving ample portions of excellent salads, sandwiches, and tacos. ✉
Playa Médano, ☎ *1/143–3464. MC, V.*

$ ✕ **Señor Greenberg's Mexicatessen.** Pastrami, chopped liver, knishes, bagels, lox, cheesecake—such wonders one finds behind the glass counters at this decent Mexican incarnation of a New York deli. It's open 24 hours; the tables, air-conditioning, stacks of newspapers, and soft music encourage frequent visits. Stop in the day before your fishing trip and order a gourmet box lunch; they'll deliver it to the marina in the morning. ⊠ *Plaza Nautica on Blvd. Marina,* ☎ *1/143–5630. AE, MC, V.*

$$$$ ⊡ **Finisterra.** One of the oldest hotels in Cabo, the Finisterra is also one of the most modern, with its two towers rising directly from the beach. An eight-story-high palapa covers the restaurant and bar on the beach next to two free-form swimming pools. Rooms in the newer buildings, with oceanfront balconies, are by far the nicest; some have king-size beds. Longtime guests favor the less expensive older section of the hotel, with its stone buildings that have a fishing-lodge feel. The restaurant is only fair, but the Whale Watcher bar atop a high cliff has the best view in town. ⊠ *Blvd. Marina, 23410,* ☎ *1/143–3333; 800/347–2252; 949/450–9000 in the U.S.,* FAX *1/143–0590; 949/450–9010 in the U.S.,* WEB *www.bajahotels.com. 287 rooms. 2 restaurants, 2 bars, 3 pools, travel services. AE, MC, V.*

$$$$ ⊡ **Hotel Hacienda Beach Resort.** Set on the tip of a tree-filled point jutting into Bahía San Lucas, the Hacienda resembles a Spanish colonial inn with its white arches and bell towers, stone fountains, and statues of Indian gods set amid scarlet hibiscus and bougainvillea. The bar is a veritable museum of Indian artifacts. The white rooms have red-tile floors, tile baths, and folk art on the walls. The water-sports center is on the calmest beach in town and has kayaks, Jet Skis, snorkeling equipment, and any other gear you might need. The hotel has a three-night minimum stay on weekdays, and a four-night minimum on weekends in the high season. ⊠ *Playa Médano, 23410,* ☎ *1/143–2062, 1/143–0122, or 800/733–2226,* FAX *1/143–0666,* WEB *www.haciendacabo.com. 51 rooms, 12 suites, 10 town houses, 9 garden patio rooms, 30 beachfront cabañas. Restaurant, bar, pool, beach, dive shop, snorkeling, surfing, jet skiing. MC, V.*

$$$$ ⊡ **Meliá San Lucas.** From the moment you enter the Meliá and spot
★ El Arco framed by the lobby's arches, you know you're at a hotel where details are important. The blue walls and linens in the rooms complement the views of the aquamarine sea; the outer adobe walls of the terraced hotel buildings glow orange and gold with the changing sunlight. The Meliá has a long beach with calm waters, a spacious hot tub under the palms, and all the equipment you could need for playing on and in the water. Early reservations are essential. ⊠ *Playa Médano, 23410,* ☎ *1/143–4444 or 800/336–3542,* FAX *1/143–0418,* WEB *www.solmelia.com. 144 rooms, 6 suites. 3 restaurants, 2 pools, hot tub, beach, snorkeling, jet skiing. AE, MC, V.*

$$$$ ⊡ **Pueblo Bonito Rosé.** Soft-pink Mediterranean-style buildings surround lush gardens populated with strolling peacocks at this Playa Médano resort. Waterfalls, fountains, and a hot tub separate the pool area into several sections so serious swimmers have room for laps while kids have their own area for splashing about. Many of the commodious suites have kitchenettes, and the restaurants are worth checking out. ⊠ *Playa Médano, 23410,* ☎ *1/143–5500 or 800/990–8250,* FAX *1/143–5979. 260 suites. 2 restaurants, pool, beach, snorkeling, jet skiing. MC, V.*

$$$$ ⊡ **Solmar Suites.** From afar, the Solmar looks like a space colony, set
★ against granite cliffs at the tip of Land's End, facing the wild Pacific. The rooms, decorated in Mexico–Santa Fe style, have separate sitting areas and tile baths; the best ones are set up against the rocks right over the beach. The adjacent time-share and condo units have kitchenettes and a private pool area. The surf here is far too dangerous for

swimming, but don't miss a stroll along the wide strip of beach. Most visitors hang out around the main pools and swim-up bar (though there are two other pools for those who prefer solitude). The Solmar's sport-fishing fleet is first-rate. The good restaurant hosts a Saturday night Mexican fiesta and buffet dinner. ✉ *Av. Solmar at Blvd. Marina, Apdo. 8, 23410 (Box 383, Pacific Palisades, CA 90272),* ☎ *1/143–3535; 800/344–3349; 310/459–9861 in the U.S.,* FAX *1/143–0410; 310/454–1686 in the U.S. 82 junior suites, 55 condos, 37 studios. Restaurant, bar, 3 pools, beach, fishing. AE, MC, V.*

$$–$$$ ⊡ **The Bungalows Breakfast Inn.** If solitude and a reasonable room rate are more important than being in the center of the action, this is your place, 10 blocks from the beach. Several two-story buildings frame a small, heated pool. Rooms are beautifully decorated with Mexican textiles and art. Breakfast is included in the rates; smoking is not permitted. ✉ *Calle Constitución (5 blocks from main plaza), 23410,* WEB *www.cabobungalows.com,* ☎ FAX *1/143–5035. 16 suites. Breakfast room, pool. AE.*

$$ ⊡ **Siesta Suites.** The least expensive rooms lack air-conditioning, but even those are large and immaculate with kitchenettes and televisions. The three-story hotel sits just two blocks from the marina, and the proprietors are the friendliest in town. Music from nearby bars might bother some. ✉ *Calle Zapata, Apdo. 310, 23410,* ☎ FAX *1/143–2773, 602/331–1354 in the U.S.,* WEB *www.loscabosguide.com. 5 rooms, 15 suites. Kitchenettes. No credit cards.*

$ ⊡ **Las Villas Turismo Juvenil.** Cabo's youth hostel (for young and old) is about 10 blocks from the waterfront in a quiet neighborhood. Two dormitory rooms have bunk beds and shelves, and there are several private rooms with shared baths. In the courtyard, you can use sinks and counters to fix meals and wash clothes. ✉ *Av. de la Juventud, 23410,* ☎ *1/143–0148. 2 dorms, 11 private rooms. No credit cards.*

NIGHTLIFE AND THE ARTS

Some travelers choose Cabo San Lucas for its nightlife, which consists mainly of noisy bars with blaring music and plenty of dancing, flirting, and imbibing. The latest U.S. rock plays over an excellent sound system at **Cabo Wabo** (✉ Calle Guerrero, ☎ 1/143–1198), but the impromptu jam sessions with appearances by Sammy Hagar—an owner—and his many music-business friends are the real highlight. **Squid Roe** (✉ Av. Cárdenas, ☎ 1/143–0655) is the rowdiest spot in town, packed with young foreigners who work in the local tourist industry and know how to party. **The Hard Rock Cafe** (✉ Plaza Bonita, Blvd. Marina, ☎ 1/143–3779) offers a familiar ambience for those intimidated by the rowdier bars. **Giggling Marlin** (✉ Blvd. Marina, ☎ 1/143–1182) seems to have been around forever as the favorite watering hole for fishermen. **El Galeón** (✉ Blvd. Marina, ☎ 1/143–0443) is a welcome refuge for the quieter crowd, who sip brandy by the piano bar. **Edith's** (✉ Paseo del Pescador at Playa Médano, ☎ 1/143–0801) presents live jazz in a tasteful garden setting. **Sancho Panza Wine Bistro** (✉ Blvd. Marina in the Plaza las Glorias Hotel, ☎ 1/143–3212) is the place to sip imported wines served by the glass while listening to live soft jazz.

OUTDOOR ACTIVITIES AND SPORTS

Diving. El Arco is a prime diving and snorkeling area, as are several rocky points off the coast. Divers consider the sandfalls, an underwater cascade of sand that flows from 90 to 1200 ft below sea level, an essential experience; many also undertake the two-hour boat trip to the coral reefs off Cabo Pulmo, located off the East Cape. Most hotels can arrange diving trips and equipment rental. The oldest and most complete dive shop in the area is **Amigos del Mar** (✉ Blvd. Marina across from the sportfishing docks at the marina, ☎ 1/143–0505 or 800/344–

3349, ℻ 1/143–0887). **Cabo Acuadeportes** (⊠ Hotel Hacienda, Playa Médano, ☎ 1/143–0117) offers diving trips along with all other imaginable water sports. **The Activity Center** (⊠ Playa Médano, ☎ 1/143–03093) has every type of water and land sports equipment, including diving gear, wave runners, wind surfers, and parasails. The *Solmar V* (⊠ Solmar Suites Hotel, Blvd. Marina, ☎ 1/143–0022 or 800/344–3349), a live-aboard dive boat, takes weeklong trips to the islands of Socorro, San Benedicto, and Clarion, and the coral reefs at Cabo Pulmo. It has 12 cabins with private baths (maximum 24 passengers).

Fishing. There are more than 800 species of fish in the waters off Los Cabos. Most hotels will arrange fishing charters, which include a captain and mate, tackle, bait, licenses, and drinks. Prices start at $295 per day for a 25-ft cruiser. Some charters provide lunch, and most can arrange to have your catch mounted, frozen, or smoked. Most of the boats leave from the sportfishing docks in the Cabo San Lucas marina. Usually there are a fair number of pangas for rent at about $30 per hour with a five-hour minimum. Dependable companies include the following: **Gaviota Fleet** (⊠ Bahía Condo Hotel, Playa Médano, ☎ 1/143–0430 or 800/932–5599); **Minerva's** (⊠ Madero between Blvd. Marina and Guerrero, ☎ 1/143–1282, ℻ 1/143–0440); **Pisces Sportfishing Fleet** (⊠ Cabo Maritime Center on Blvd. Marina, ☎ 1/143–1288); and **Solmar Fleet** (⊠ Blvd. Marina across from the sportfishing dock, ☎ 1/143–0646, 1/143–4542, or 800/344–3349, ℻ 1/143–0410; 310/454–1686 in the U.S.).

Horseback Riding. Cantering down an isolated beach or up a desert trail is one of the great pleasures of Baja (as long as the sun isn't beating down on your head). Horses are available for rent in a shady grove in front of the Playa Médano hotels; contact **Rancho Collins Horses** (☎ 1/143–3652). **Red Rose Riding Stables** (⊠ Hwy. 1, Km 4, ☎ 1/143–4826) has healthy horses for all levels of riders and an impressive array of tack. The **Cuadra San Francisco Equestrian Center** (⊠ on Corridor highway across from Cabo Real development, ☎ 1/144–0260) is a professional center with training and trail rides.

Whale-Watching. The gray whale migration doesn't end at Baja's Pacific lagoons. Plenty of whales of all sizes make it down to the warmer waters off Los Cabos and into the Sea of Cortez. Several companies run whale-watching trips from Cabo San Lucas. Check with **Cabo Acuadeportes** or any of the fishing companies. **Cabo Expeditions** (⊠ Plaza las Glorias hotel, Blvd. Marina, ☎ 1/143–2700) offers snorkeling and whale-watching tours in rubber boats. To watch whales from shore, go to the beach at the Solmar Suites or any Corridor hotel, or the lookout points along the Corridor highway.

SHOPPING

Some of the nicest shops in Cabo San Lucas are in **Plaza Bonita** on the waterfront at the beginning of Boulevard Marina. **Cartes** (⊠ Plaza Bonita, Blvd. Marina, ☎ 1/143–1770) is the best of Los Cabos's many home-furnishing stores, with an irresistible array of hand-painted pottery and tableware, pewter frames, handblown glass, and carved furniture. **Dos Lunas** (⊠ Plaza Bonita, Blvd. Marina, ☎ 1/143–1969) has a trendy selection of colorful sportswear and straw hats. **Francisco's Café del Mundo** (⊠ Plaza Bonita, Blvd. Marina, ☎ 1/143–2366) is the place to take an espresso or cappuccino break.

Boulevard Marina and the side streets between the waterfront and the main plaza are filled with an ever-changing parade of small shops. **Libros** (⊠ Blvd. Marina 20, ☎ 1/143–3172) carries a good selection of books on Baja and some English-language novels and magazines. **J&J**

Habanos (⊠ Madero between Blvd. Marina and Guerrero, ☎ 1/143–6160) is a cigar aficionado's heaven, with a walk-in humidor stocked with pricy cigars. The shop also sells expensive tequilas. **Necri** (⊠ Blvd. Marina between Madero and Ocampo, ☎ 1/143–0283) has an excellent selection of folk art and furnishings. **El Callejon** (⊠ Guerrero between Cárdenas and Madero, ☎ 1/143–1139) has multiple showrooms with gorgeous furniture, lamps, dishes, and pottery. **Magic of the Moon** (⊠ Hidalgo near Blvd. Marina, ☎ 1/143–3161) has long been known as the place to shop for handmade women's sundresses, skirts, and lingerie in fashionable fabrics and styles. **Mama Eli's** (⊠ Av. San Lucas, ☎ 1/143–1616) is a three-story gallery with fine furnishings, ceramics, appliquéd clothing, and children's toys. **Galeria Gatemelatta** (⊠ on dirt road to Hotel Hacienda, ☎ 1/143–1166) specializes in colonial furniture and antiques.

At the **Handicrafts Market** in the marina, you can pose for a photo with an iguana, plan a ride in a glass-bottom boat, or browse to your heart's content through stalls packed with blankets, sombreros, and pottery.

Todos Santos

30 km (19 mi) north of Cabo San Lucas.

The Pacific side of the tip of Baja has remained largely undeveloped. The exception is the small agricultural town of Todos Santos, which has become a haven for artists, architects, and speculators who have contributed to a rapid rise in real estate prices. The town sits a bit inland from the rugged coast and is classically charming with its 19th-century brick-and-stucco buildings and small central plaza. It's an ideal haven for those who deplore the overdevelopment of Baja's tip, since both Los Cabos and La Paz are within easy driving distance (for shopping, dining, and taking care of business). Todos Santos also benefits from cooling breezes from the Pacific and fresh water from underground springs. New neighborhoods are rising in the outskirts of town, usually before electricity, telephone lines, and water pipes are installed. Entrepreneurs have turned some of the plaza-front buildings into galleries and cafés, and there is always something new to check out. Business hours are erratic, especially in summer.

Los Cabos regulars typically drive up the coast to Todos Santos on day trips, stopping to watch surfers at Playa Migrio, Playa los Cerritos, and Punta Gaspareo. El Pescadero is the largest settlement before Todos Santos, populated by ranchers and farmers who grow herbs and vegetables for the restaurants in Los Cabos. Seasonal produce is sold at small stands by the side of the road. Dirt roads intersect the highway at several points along the way to Todos Santos, but you should attempt these roads only with four-wheel-drive vehicles—sands on the beach or in the desert will stop conventional vehicles in their tracks.

During high season, you may find tour buses clogging the streets around the plaza in Todos Santos; it is a pit stop on tours between Cabo San Lucas and La Paz. When the buses leave, the town is a pleasant and peaceful place to wander through shops and galleries. If you drive to Todos Santos on your own, head back to Cabo before dark; Highway 19 between the two towns is unlit and is prone to high winds and flooding. When you get to town, be sure to pick up *El Calendario de Todos Santos,* a free monthly guide with the most current happenings and developments.

Dining and Lodging

$$ ✕ **Cafe Santa Fe.** Owners Paula and Ezio Colombo can be credited with much of their town's popularity since their Italian restaurant is a des-

tination in its own right. And many Cabo residents lunch here weekly. The setting, with tables amid herb gardens in an overgrown courtyard, is part of the appeal, but the reason you can't get a table on weekends is the food—salads and soups made from homegrown organic vegetables and herbs, homemade pastas and calzone, and fresh fish with light herbal sauces. It's tempting to linger for hours over a bottle of Chianti, but make sure you've got an alert designated driver to get you home. ⊠ *Calle Centenario,* ☎ *1/145–0340. No credit cards. Closed Tues. and parts of Sept. and Oct.*

$$ ✕ **Caffé Todos Santos.** Omelets, bagels, granola, and delicious whole-grain breads delight the breakfast crowd at this small café, known to have the best Mexican food in town; deli sandwiches, fresh salads, and an array of tamales, *flautas* (tortillas rolled around savory fillings), and combo plates are lunch and dinner highlights. Check for fresh seafood on the daily specials board, and pick up a loaf of bread for the road. You'll enjoy the high ceilings and quirky charm of the main dining room or the shady calm of the outdoor patio. ⊠ *Calle Centenario 33,* ☎ *1/ 145–0300. No credit cards.*

$$$ ▦ **Todos Santos Inn.** The four guest rooms in this converted 19th-cen-
  ★ tury house are unparalleled in design and comfort. Gorgeous antiques are set against stone walls under brick ceilings. Ceiling fans and the shade from garden trees keep the rooms cool and breezy. The absence of telephones and TVs makes a perfect foil for the conceits of Los Cabos. And good restaurants are within easy walking distance. The whole house can be booked by vacationing families. ⊠ *Calle Legaspi, 23300,* ☎ 𝖥𝖠𝖷 *1/145–0040. 4 rooms. No credit cards.*

$ ▦ **Hosteria Las Casitas.** If Los Cabos has got you feeling like turning down the volume (and the cash flow), this B&B in a lush garden set-ting might give you the quiet you're looking for—and great breakfasts to start the day. The buildings' traditional Mexican architecture makes for cool accommodations. Owner Wendy Faith's art-glass studio is also on site. ⊠ *Calle Rangel at Obregón and Hidalgo, A.P. 73, 23300,* ☎ 𝖥𝖠𝖷 *1/145–0255. 3 rooms with private ½ bath and shared showers, 2 suites with bath. No credit cards.*

$ ▦ **Hotel Misión del Pilar.** Offering comfortable but spartan accom-modations, this hotel is fine for those who don't mind close quarters with no frills. The hotel is down the street from Pilar's Taco Stand, the town bus stop. ⊠ *Colegio Militar and Hidalgo, 23300,* ☎ *1/145–0114. 12 rooms. No credit cards.*

BAJA SUR A TO Z

AIR TRAVEL
Baja Sur has three airports—in La Paz, Los Cabos, and Loreto—and is serviced by many domestic and international airlines.

CARRIERS
AeroCalifornia serves the La Paz airport from Tijuana and Los Ange-les, has daily flights from Los Angeles to Loreto's airport, and flies to Los Cabos from Los Angeles and Tijuana. Aeroméxico flies to La Paz from Los Angeles, Tucson, Tijuana, Mexico City, and other cities within Mexico; it flies to Los Cabos from San Diego and Mexico City. Aerolitoral has daily flights to La Paz from Loreto. Mexicana has flights to the Los Cabos airport from Guadalajara, Mexico City, and Los Angeles. Alaska Airlines operates its own terminal at the Los Cabos airport and has flights from Anchorage, Fairbanks, Portland, Phoenix, San Francisco, San Diego, Los Angeles, and Seattle. Amer-ica West flies into Los Cabos from Phoenix, Continental from Hous-ton. Other international airlines may have service in winter.

> ➤ AIRLINES AND CONTACTS: **AeroCalifornia** (☎ 1/125–1023 in La Paz; 1/143–3700 in Los Cabos; 1/135–0555 in Loreto; 800/237–6225). **Aeroméxico** (☎ 1/122–0091 in La Paz; 1/146–5097 in Los Cabos; 800/237–6639). **Aerolitoral** (☎ 1/135–0999 in Loreto). **Alaska Airlines** (☎ 1/146–5210 in Los Cabos; 800/426–0333). **America West** (☎ 1/142–2882 or 1/142–2880 in Los Cabos; 800/235–9292). **Continental** (☎ 1/142–3880 in Los Cabos; 800/525–0280). **Mexicana** (☎ 1/146–5001 in Los Cabos).

AIRPORTS

The La Paz airport is about 16 km (10 mi) north of town. Loreto's airport is 7 km (4½ mi) southwest of town. The Los Cabos International Airport is about 11 km (7 mi) north of San José del Cabo and about 48 km (30 mi) from Cabo San Lucas.

> ➤ AIRPORT INFORMATION: **Los Cabos International Airport** (☎ 1/146–5111). **Loreto Airport** (☎ 1/135–0565). **La Paz Airport** (☎ 1/112–0082).

BOAT AND FERRY TRAVEL

The ferry system connecting Baja to mainland Mexico is constantly undergoing changes in rates and schedules. Currently there are Sematur ferries from La Paz to Mazatlán (an 18-hour trip) every day except Saturday. There are also ferries from La Paz to Topolobampo, the port at Los Mochis, every day except Sunday. Tickets are available at the La Paz Terminal at the dock on the road to Pichilingue. Tickets are also available at the Sematur Office. The Sematur Web site *should* have the most up-to-date information, but isn't always accurate. Purchase your ticket in advance of your trip—it's probably best to use a Mexican travel agent for this—and expect confusion. Continuous changes in Sematur procedure and pricing make it difficult for even ferry personnel to keep up with the latest policy. If you plan to take a car or a motor home on the ferry to the mainland, you must obtain a vehicle permit before boarding the ferry and must have Mexican auto-insurance papers; everyone crossing to the mainland also needs a tourist card. Tourism officials in La Paz strongly suggest that you obtain the vehicle permit when crossing the U.S. border into Baja; although permits are not needed in Baja, offices at the border are better equipped to handle the paperwork than those in La Paz. Tourist cards also are available at the border. It would be wise to take copies of the following, in triplicate, plus the original: passport, tourist card, birth certificate, and vehicle registration.

Ferries travel from Santa Rosalia to Guaymas on the mainland Pacific coast. They depart for the six-hour trip to the mainland at 9 AM on Thursday and arrive in Santa Rosalia at 3 PM Tuesday. Buy tickets in advance at the Santa Rosalia ferry terminal, just south of town on Highway 1. Schedules are often erratic.

> ➤ BOAT AND FERRY INFORMATION: **La Paz Terminal** (☎ 1/125–4666, FAX 1/125–6588). **Santa Rosalia ferry terminal** (☎ 1/152–0014, FAX 1/152–0013). **Sematur Office** (✉ Calle 5 de Mayo 502, ☎ 1/125–3833, FAX 1/125–6588, WEB www.ferrysematur.com.mx).

BUS TRAVEL TO AND FROM BAJA SUR

The Autotransportes de Baja California bus line runs the length of the peninsula from Tijuana to Los Cabos, stopping at towns en route; the peninsula-long trip takes 22 hours. It also has a route from La Paz to Guerrero Negro (the bus stops at the highway entrance to town) and a daily one between Cabo San Lucas and San José. Loreto is serviced by both Autotransportes de Baja California and Aguila. The Loreto bus terminal sits at the entrance to town. The Aguila bus line runs from Santa Rosalia to Los Cabos. Aguila runs along the Transpeninsular Highway to the border and to Los Cabos.

➤ Bus Information: **Aguila** (☎ 1/122–4270 or 1/122–7898). **Auto-transportes de Baja California** (☎ 1/122–6476, 1/122–7094, or 1/142–0200). **Loreto bus terminal** (✉ Salvatierra and Tamaral, ☎ 1/135–0767).

BUS TRAVEL WITHIN BAJA SUR

In La Paz it's fairly easy to get around by bus: city buses run along the malecón and into downtown. Buses run between Cabo San Lucas and San José del Cabo, and will stop along the Corridor if you ask the driver.

CAR RENTAL

California Baja Rent-A-Car rents four-wheel-drive vehicles, convertibles, and sedans for use throughout Mexico; you can pick up a car in San Diego and drop it off in Los Cabos, but expect to pay a hefty additional charge.

Thrifty has an office south of Loreto in Nopoló. They'll deliver your car to town. Budget in Loreto has a few four-wheel drive vehicles available.

Avis and Hertz have desks at the La Paz airport. Hertz has an additional office on Av. Obregon in town.

Several car-rental agencies have desks at the airport and in San José or Cabo San Lucas. Reserve a car in advance during high season, especially if you want a van, four-wheel-drive, or air-conditioning. Most agencies rent VW bugs and topless VW bugs, which seem like fun until you're under the blazing sun for several hours. Avis has a desk at the airport and desks in several hotels. Dollar has a desk at the airport and at the Presidente Inter-Continental Hotel in San José. Hertz has a desk at the airport.

➤ Major Agencies: **Avis** (✉ ☎ 1/122–1813; 1/122–2651 in La Paz; 1/146–0388 at the Los Cabos airport). **Budget** (✉ Paseo Hidalgo at the malecón, Loreto, ☎ 1/135–1090; ✉ Paseo Obregón at Hidalgo La Paz, ☎ 1/122–1097 or 1/122–7655). **California Baja Rent-A-Car** (✉ 9245 Jamacha Blvd., Spring Valley, CA 91977, ☎ 888/470–7368; 619/470–8368 in the U.S.). **Dollar** (☎ 1/142–0100 or 1/143–1250 in Los Cabos). **Hertz** (☎ 1/122–0919 at the La Paz airport; 1/142–0375 at the Los Cabos airport; ✉ Av. Obregon 2130, La Paz, ☎ 1/122–5300; 1/122–0919 at the La Paz airport). **Thrifty** (✉ Hotel Eden, Nopoló, ☎ 1/133–0612).

CAR TRAVEL

Mexico Highway 1, also known as the Transpeninsular Highway, runs the entire 1,700 km (1,060 mi) from Tijuana to Cabo San Lucas. The highway's condition varies depending on the weather and intervals between road repairs. Don't drive it at high speeds or at night—it's not lighted. There are exits for all the principal towns in Baja Sur.

The road between San José del Cabo and Cabo San Lucas was widened to four lanes and is in good condition, although dips and bridges become flooded in heavy rains.

CRUISE TRAVEL

Several cruise lines use Cabo San Lucas as a port of call. Carnival makes a short stop during its cruise between Los Angeles and Mexico's mainland Pacific Coast. Princess has cruises to Los Cabos and the Mexican Riviera from Los Angeles and San Francisco. Royal Caribbean stops off during its Panama Canal and Mexican Riviera cruises.

➤ Cruise Lines: **Carnival** (☎ 800/327–9501). **Princess** (☎ 800/421–0522). **Royal Caribbean** (☎ 800/327–6700)

EMERGENCIES

➤ Contacts: **Police** (☎ 1/122–6610 in La Paz; 1/143–3977 in Cabo San Lucas; 1/142–0361 in San José del Cabo). **Fire** (☎ 1/122–7474 in

La Paz). **Hospital** (☎ 1/143–1594 in Cabo San Lucas; 1/142–0013 in San José del Cabo). **Red Cross** (☎ 1/122–1111 in La Paz; 1/143–3300 in Cabo San Lucas; 1/142–0316 in San José del Cabo).

INTERNET

Dr. Z's Internet Café and Bar in Cabo San Lucas has a full bar and casual menu, and charges $9 an hour for Internet access. The fastest connections are at Quik Internet. Cabocafe in San José del Cabo offers access for $9 an hour.

➤ INTERNET CAFÉS: **Dr. Z's Internet Café and Bar** (⊠ Blvd. Cárdenas across from Pemex, ☎ 1/143–5390). **Quik Internet** Blvd. Marina 19, ☎ no phone. **Cabocafe** (⊠ Plaza José Green, Suite 3, Blvd. Mijares, ☎ 1/142–5250).

TAXIS

In Loreto, taxis are in good supply and fares are inexpensive. There are two gas stations in Loreto; be sure to fill your tank before heading out on any long jaunts. Taxi fares in Los Cabos are steep.

A car isn't necessary if you plan to stay in La Paz; taxis are readily available and inexpensive. If you'd like to explore the remote beaches, however, *see* Car Rental, *above*.

TOURS AND PACKAGES

Eco-Tours Malarrimo is the best tour operator in Guerrero Negro. The company runs four-hour tours ($40 per person) by bus to and from Scammon's Lagoon, three hours in small skiffs among whales with English-speaking guides, and lunch. Reserve several months in advance, especially for February, when whales appear in abundance.

There are several options for tours from Loreto, including trips inland to Misión San Javier and prehistoric rock paintings, as well as kayaking, sportfishing, diving, and day trips north to Mulegé. Las Parras Tours has the most options for local-guided adventure tours focusing on natural history and conservation.

The Cortez Club at La Concha Beach Resort has diving, fishing, whale-watching, and cruising tours and is the most complete tour facility in La Paz.

With the water as the main attraction in Los Cabos, most tours involve getting into a boat and diving or fishing. It's a must to take a ride to El Arco, the natural rock arches at Land's End, and Playa de Amor (Lovers' Beach), where the Sea of Cortez merges with the Pacific. Nearly all hotels have frequent boat trips to these destinations; the fare depends on how far your hotel is from the point. Tour boats dock by the arts-and-crafts market in the Cabo San Lucas marina, and the sidewalk along the water is lined with salesmen offering boat rides. Check out the boat before you pay, and make sure there are life jackets on board.

Contactours has land and sea tours of Los Cabos for groups, and booking agents at several hotels. TourCabos runs boat trips, offer horseback riding, and can provide information on water sports. Nomadas de Baja offers hiking, snorkeling, and kayaking tours of Los Cabos with an ecological bent. Pez Gato, on marina near Plaza Las Glorias hotel in Los Cabos, has sailing and sunset cruises on a 46-ft catamaran, with live music as well as snorkeling and sailing tours. All trips depart from the marina in Cabo San Lucas; call or stop by the booth at the marina for further information.

➤ TOUR OPERATOR RECOMMENDATIONS: **Baja Expeditions** (⊠ 2625 Garnet Ave., San Diego, CA 92109, ☎ 800/843–6967; 858/581–3311 in the U.S., FAX 858/581–6542). **Baja California Tours** (⊠ 7734 Herschel

Ave., Suite O, La Jolla, CA 92037, ☎ 858/454–7166, FAX 858/454–2703).
Contactours (✉ Finisterra Hotel, Blvd. Marina, Los Cabos, ☎ 1/143–
3333 or 1/143–2499). **Discover Baja** (✉ 3089 Clairemont Dr., San Diego,
CA 92117, ☎ 800/727–2252; 619/275–4225 in the U.S., FAX 619/
275–1836 WEB www.discoverbaja.com). **Eco-Tours Malarrimo** (✉ Blvd.
Zapata, Guerrero Negro 23940, ☎ 1/157–0250). **Las Parras Tours** (✉
Salvatierra at Madero, Loreto, ☎ 1/135–1010, FAX 1/135–0900). **Lind-
blad Special Expeditions** (✉ 720 Fifth Ave., New York, NY 10019,
☎ 800/397–3348; 212/765–7740 in the U.S.). **Nomadas de Baja** (☎
1/148–1468 in Los Cabos, ☎ FAX 1/142–4388). **Pez Gato** (☎ 1/143–
3797 in Los Cabos). **TourCabos** (✉ Plaza los Cabos, Paseo San José,
☎ 1/142–4040 in Los Cabos, FAX 1/142–0782).

TRANSPORTATION AROUND LOS CABOS

The best way to see the sights of Los Cabos is on foot. Downtown San
José and Cabo San Lucas are compact, with the plaza, church, shops,
and restaurants within a few blocks of one another. Bus service runs
between the towns, although buses might not stop along the Corridor.
If you plan to dine at the Corridor hotels or travel frequently between
the two towns, it's a good idea to rent a car for a few days.

VISITOR INFORMATION

The Baja California Sur State Tourist Office has two locations in La
Paz—one at Mariano Abasolo s/n, and a more convenient location on
the malecón near Calle 16 de Septiembre.

The Loreto Tourist Information Office is located in the Municipal
Building on the main plaza. The hours are erratic, at best.

There are no official tourist-information offices in Los Cabos; hotel
tour desks are the best sources of information. Avoid tour stands on
the streets; they are usually associated with time-share operations.
➤ TOURIST INFORMATION: **Baja California Sur State Tourist Office** (✉
Mariano Abasolo s/n, ☎ 1/124–0100; 1/122–5939; 1/124–0100; 1/
122–5939 at the malecón, FAX 1/124–0722). **Loreto Tourist Information Office** (✉ Municipal Building on the main plaza, ☎ 1/135–0411).

4 SONORA

Cowboys still ride the range in Mexican ranch country, but beaches have upstaged beef as this northwestern state's economic indicator. Along with relatively unspoiled and inexpensive coastal towns such as Bahía Kino and San Carlos, Sonora's lures include colonial Alamos, a sprinkling of Spanish missions, and an immaculate former silver-mining center with cobblestone streets and restored haciendas that evoke the spirit of Old Mexico.

ONORA, Mexico's second-largest, second-richest state, is a vacationland with its own band of devoted followers. Many are from Arizona, for whom the beaches of Sonora, its sister state, are closer, cheaper, and more interesting than those of southern California; and this stretch of the Mexican northwest is reminiscent of the old Wild West in the United States. *Rancheras,* ballads not unlike country-and-western songs, blare from saloons and radios. Irrigated ranch lands feed Mexico's finest beef cattle, and rivers flowing westward from the Sierra Madre are diverted by giant dams to irrigate a low rainfall area that now produces cotton, sugarcane, and vegetables. Hermosillo, Sonora's capital, bustles with agricultural commerce in the midst of the fertile lands that turn dry again toward the coast.

Mexico Highway 15 begins at the border town of Nogales, Sonora, adjacent to the U.S. town of Nogales, Arizona. It passes south through Hermosillo and reaches the Sea of Cortez (also called the Gulf of California) at Guaymas, 418 km (259 mi) from the Arizona border. The Sonoran desert dominates the landscape through northern Sonora, as it does in southern Arizona. Long stretches of flat scrub are punctuated by brown hills and mountains, towering saguaros, and organ-pipe cacti. Highway 15 continues southward after Guaymas, as the landscape gradually takes on a more tropical aspect, and finally enters the state of Sinaloa just north of the city of Los Mochis. Except in the mountains, the entire region is uncomfortably warm between May and late September, with afternoon temperatures sometimes exceeding 120°F.

In 1540 Francisco Vázquez de Coronado, governor of the provinces to the south, became the first Spanish leader to walk the plains of Sonora. More than a century later, Father Eusebio Francisco Kino led a missionary expedition to Sonora and what is now southern Arizona—an area referred to historically as the Pimería Alta—founding several towns and missions there. Although Alamos, in the south of Sonora, boomed with silver-mining wealth in the late 17th century, no one paid much attention to the northern part of the region for the next three centuries. It was not part of the Mexican territory ceded to the U.S. after the War of 1847. Sonora became a haven for Arizona outlaws, and international squabbles bloomed and faded over the next decades as officials argued over issues such as the right to pursue criminals across the border. During the last quarter of the 19th century, Porfirio Díaz, dictator of Mexico for most of the years between 1876 and 1911, finally moved to secure the state by settling it.

For Don Porfirio, however, developing Sonora may have been a mistake: the revolutionaries who later overthrew him came from here. In fact, Mexico was ruled by the Sonora dynasty for nearly a quarter century and, until the 1994 assassination of Sonora native son Luis Donaldo Colosio, the ruling-party candidate for president, it appeared likely that a Sonoran would control the destiny of the country again. The Mexican Revolution brought prosperity to the state. With irrigation from the state's dams, inhabitants have been able to grow enough wheat not only for Mexico but also for export.

Pleasures and Pastimes

Beaches

Lively hotels and restaurants line the coastal areas around San Carlos, Guaymas, and Puerto Peñasco, but if you are willing to take more time for travel and forgo facilities, you'll find miles and miles of more-secluded beaches that run along the Sea of Cortés. Most of Sonora's main beaches have paved access roads, but some of the best—like pristine Playa San Nicolás just south of Bahía Kino (Kino Bay)—await the adventurous at the end of rutted, washed-out dirt tracks.

Dining

Sonoran cuisine is distinguished by the high quality of its steaks and the freshness of its fish. Sonora is also the home of the giant flour tortilla and bean burritos. There are no five-star restaurants in the state, but shrimp lovers will find plenty to like in Sonora, especially in Guaymas. Traditional-Mexican foodies will be contented as well, with an abundance of dishes such as enchiladas, tamales, and some of the best *carne asada* (grilled marinated meat) in Mexico. Indeed, the style of Mexican cooking with which most Americans are familiar derives from this region. Casual dress (but not beachwear) is always acceptable, and reservations are rarely needed.

CATEGORY	COST*
$$$$	over $20
$$$	$15–$20
$$	$10–$15
$	under $10

*per person for a main course at dinner

Lodging

In Sonora you might find yourself sleeping in a converted convent in fashionable Alamos, growing a Hemingway beard in a beach bungalow at Bahía Kino, or luxuriating in a five-star resort in San Carlos. Lodging in Sonora is no longer the bargain it once was, but prices are still lower here than for comparable accommodations in the better-known vacation spots in other parts of Mexico.

CATEGORY	COST*
$$$$	over $150
$$$	$100–$150
$$	$60–$100
$	under $60

*All prices are for a standard double room, excluding tax.

Missions

Nestled among Sonora's hills and river valleys are a handful of almost forgotten missions that were founded by Jesuit fathers in the 17th and early 18th centuries and completed by the Franciscans in the late-18th and 19th centuries. Some of the churches, such as San Ignacio, still serve the small agricultural communities around them, whereas others, like Cocospera, are mostly shadows of their remarkable past.

Exploring Sonora

Sonoran landscapes are as varied as the state is vast. From the seemingly endless tracts of desert that tumble into the Sea of Cortés to the mountains of the Sierra Madre and the fields and valleys that nurture its produce and livestock, Sonora is a place of dramatic contrasts.

Mexico Highway 2 enters Sonora's far northwest from Baja California, paralleling the U.S. border. There are several crossing points, but most people entering Sonora from the United States do so at Nogales, south of Tucson, Arizona. It is also a point of entry for winter fruit and vegetables exported to the United States.

Numbers in the text correspond to numbers in the margin and on the Sonora map.

Sonora

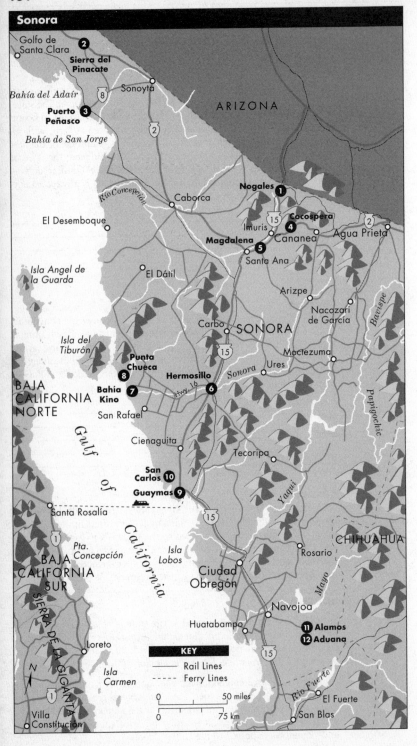

Great Itineraries

Because it is so diverse, the state of Sonora demands eight days or more to really do it justice. With less time, you'll have to decide whether seashore, mountains, or missions are most important.

IF YOU HAVE 3 DAYS

Take Highway 15 south from Nogales to **Magdalena** ⑤ and stop to see the plaza and church, and the bones of missionary explorer Eusebio Francisco Kino. If you're interested in churches, you might spend the night in this area—nine missions founded by Father Kino are accessible from here by car. Then continue south on the same highway to the state capital, **Hermosillo** ⑥, where you will find a variety of good hotels and restaurants. Overnight here and spend the next morning touring the city or browsing through the Centro Ecologico, which is of special interest to children. After lunch, drive west on Highway 16 to **Bahía Kino** ⑦, a perfect beach for a one- or two-night retreat. The drive back to the Arizona border from Kino Bay is about six hours.

An alternative three-day itinerary is to cross the U.S. border at Lukeville-Sonoyta, explore the lunarlike regions of the **Sierra del Pinacate** ②, and then cool off on the beaches of **Puerto Peñasco** ③ for the rest of the first day and the next. Then take Highway 2 about 2¾ hours to **Magdalena** ⑤ and stop for lunch and a visit to the Kino shrine before heading north on Highway 15 to **Nogales** ①. Spend an afternoon shopping there before you cross the U.S. border.

IF YOU HAVE 5 DAYS

Take Highway 15 from **Nogales** ① to **Guaymas** ⑨; the drive will take six or seven hours. Exploring the town of Guaymas and the adjacent resort area of **San Carlos** ⑩ will give you plenty to do for two days and nights. Continue south and then east for 3½ hours to charming colonial **Alamos** ⑪, in the foothills of the Sierra Madre. After one or two nights in Alamos, head back north. You might consider spending the night along the tranquil shores of **Bahía Kino** ⑦ on your way home.

IF YOU HAVE 8 DAYS

Combine the second of the three-day itineraries with the five-day itinerary, but stop off at **Hermosillo** ⑥ on the way down to **Guaymas** ⑨. If you have extra time, you might want to take a short side trip from Alamos to **Aduana** ⑫, former site of a thriving silver mine and current location of a thriving gourmet restaurant.

When to Tour

Summer temperatures in Sonora are as high as they are in southern Arizona, so unless you are prepared to broil, plan your trip for sometime between October and April.

Nogales

❶ *100 km (62 mi) south of Tucson via Highway 19, on the Arizona-Mexico border.*

Bustling Nogales can become fairly rowdy on weekend evenings, when under-age Tucsonans head south of the border to drink. It has some good restaurants, however, and visitors can find fine-quality crafts and furnishings in addition to the usual made-for-tourists souvenirs. If you're just coming for the day, it's best to park on the Arizona side of the border—you'll see many guarded lots that cost about $8 for the day—and walk across. Most of the good shopping is within easy strolling distance of the border.

THE MAQUILA'S MARCH TO MODERNITY

WHEN MEXICO BEGAN its Border Industrialization Program in 1965, few could have imagined the social and environmental ills that open markets and prosperous free-trade deals would spawn three decades later. Mexico's *maquiladoras* (also known as *maquilas*) are foreign-owned assembly plants that produce cars, electronics, and garments for export to the First World; the passage of the North American Free Trade Agreement (NAFTA), which relaxed tariffs on goods moving across North American borders, made the maquila a profitable tool in getting cheap products to the United States. Even prior to NAFTA, repeated recessions and peso devaluations in the '80s, combined with drought and chronic poverty in many of the northern and central agricultural states, brought both multinational companies and desperate migrant workers to Tijuana and Ensenada, in Baja California, Nogales in Sonora, Matamoros in Tamaulipas, and above all, Ciudad Juárez in the state of Chihuahua.

Shanty towns sprung up, most of which are still lacking in clean water, sanitation, schools, electricity, and other basic infrastructure; companies and city governments have had no legal obligation, no financial incentive, and in the case of the local governments, no tax revenue, to provide for inhabitants. With time, the living conditions have improved marginally in some areas, but even with the meager allowances for housing or health care, workers here are still exploited by American labor standards. And because NAFTA has only an impotent Commission on Environmental Cooperation (CEC) to evaluate, but not enforce, the safe environmental procedures outlined in the agreement, hundreds of maquilas regularly dump hazardous waste along the border. It's estimated that less than half of American maquilas follow Mexican law

and return their toxic waste to the United States. Many maquila workers live with contaminated water as a result.

But the maquila industry also created hundreds of thousands of jobs, gave a new impetus to Mexico's economy, and effectively threw a grenade in the midst of rural Mexico's family mores and values—for better and worse. Academic studies chart devastating social disintegration and the heartbreaking effect on young children; but Mexican women—who for the first time earn a wage and decide what to do with it—are viewed by many to have finally found liberation from rural, macho servitude.

Ciudad Juárez sits above anonymous swathes of the huge state of Chihuahua, just over the Río Bravo (or Rio Grande) from El Paso, Texas. Over the last three decades nearly a million have come to toil in the maquilas, assembling televisions, clothes, car parts, calculators, telephones, and other appliances for the wealthiest market in the world. Juárez became a magnet for young women, lured from the interior of the country by plentiful jobs. As it turned out, though, not only was their labor cheap, but so were their lives: at the end of the 1990s, over 200 female corpses were found in the desert around town. Murders of women in Juárez (most of whom worked in the maquilas) has become a scandal of international proportions, and most cases remain unsolved.

The maquila zone poses profound questions with no easy answers, but it still looks a long way from resolution as a quick drive into the hills reveals the squalor in which people live. Hopeful young men and women are carted in from their rank little huts every day to make gadgets for others, before they can make a life for themselves.

— Barbara Kastelein

The shopping area centers mainly on Avenida Obregón, which begins a few blocks west of the border entrance and runs north–south; just follow the crowds. Most of the good restaurants near the border are also on Obregón. Take Obregón as far south as you like; you'll know you have entered workaday Mexico when the shops are no longer fronted by smiling, English-speaking hustlers trying to lure you in the door.

Dining

$$$–$$$$ ✕ **La Roca.** This elegant restaurant on the sprawling second floor of a
★ stately old stone house has great beamed ceilings, fireplaces, and a variety of dining rooms. The best place for a margarita is on the balcony overlooking a charming patio with magnolia trees and a gurgling fountain. Among the excellent meat and seafood dishes is *carne tampiqueña*, an assortment of grilled meats that comes with a *chile relleno* (a chili pepper stuffed with cheese, batter-dipped, and fried) and an enchilada. The *queso la Roca* (seasoned potato slices covered with melted cheese) makes a fine starter. ⊠ *Calle Elias 91,* ☎ *631/2–08–91. MC, V.*

$$ ✕ **El Cid.** This clean, festive restaurant has something for everyone. The menu features a variety of sandwiches, burgers, fresh seafood, and traditional Mexican specialties such as *camarones ajo* (grilled garlic shrimp) and carne asada. Be sure to wash it all down with a house-special margarita. ⊠ *Av. Obregón 124,* ☎ *631/2–11–13. MC, V.*

$$ ✕ **Elvira.** The free shot of tequila that comes with each meal complements Elvira's fine fish dishes, chicken mole, or chiles rellenos. This large, friendly restaurant, which is divided into intimate dining areas, is at the very end of Avenida Obregón, next to the border. ⊠ *Av. Obregón 1,* ☎ *631/2–47–73. MC, V.*

Shopping

Nogales's wide selection of handicrafts, furnishings, and jewelry makes for some of Sonora's best shopping. At more-informal shops, bargaining is not only acceptable but expected. The following shops tend to have fixed prices. East of the railroad tracks and off the beaten tourist path, **El Changarro** (⊠ Calle Elias 93, ☎ 631/2–05–45) carries high-quality furniture, antiques, pottery, and handwoven rugs. **Mickey** (⊠ Av. Obregón 128–130, ☎ 631/2–22–99) has two floors of handcrafted Mexican treasures, *equipale* (pigskin) furniture, Talavera ceramic dishes, pottery, glassware, and liquors. **El Sarape** (⊠ Av. Obregón 161, ☎ 631/2–03–09) specializes in sterling-silver jewelry from Taxco and designer clothing for women.

Sierra del Pinacate

❷ *50 km (31 mi) west of Lukeville-Sonoyta.*

Midway between the Arizona border and the beach town of Puerto Peñasco, Sierra del Pinacate is a Biosphere Reserve International Park best known for its volcanic rock formations and craters so moonlike that they were used for training the Apollo astronauts. The diversity of the lava flows makes Pinacate unique, as does the striking combination of Sonoran desert and volcanic field. Highlights of the area include **Santa Clara peak**, a little more than 4,000 ft high and 2.5 million years old, and **El Elegante crater**, 1½ km (1 mi) across and 750 ft deep, created by a giant steam eruption 150,000 years ago.

There are no facilities of any kind at Pinacate. You'll need to bring your own water—take plenty of it—food, and extra gasoline, as well as a good map, which you can get in Arizona at Si Como No bookstore in Ajo or at Tucson's Map and Flag Center, or in Mexico at the Intercultural Center for the Study of Desert and Oceans (CEDO). A high-clearance vehicle is strongly advised, and four-wheel drive is recommended. Camping is allowed with a permit obtainable from the Oficina Sierra del Pinacate in Sonoyta, a block south of the border crossing on the west side of the street. You must register at the park entrance.

Summer temperatures can be blistering. The best time to visit is between November and March, when daytime temperatures range between 60°F and 90°F. Tours can be arranged through the tourism office in Puerto Peñasco. An excellent naturalist-led tour in English is available from **Ajo Stage Lines** (✉ 1041 Solana St., Ajo, AZ 85321, ☎ 520/387–6559 or 800/942–1981).

Puerto Peñasco

❸ *104 km (65 mi) south of the Arizona border at Lukeville on Mexico Highway 8.*

The real appeal of Puerto Peñasco, at the north end of the Sea of Cortés, is the miles of sandy beaches, often punctuated by stretches of black, volcanic rock that get inundated at high tide. Puerto Peñasco, or Rocky Point, has a remarkably high tide change—as much as 23 ft, depending on the season. At low tide the cragged stretches of coastline are great for poking among countless shallow tidal pools inhabited by such local marine life as octopus, shrimp, and starfish.

This coastline is rapidly changing. A number of major projects have been under construction—including a complex with a shopping center, luxury hotel, condos and villas, a yacht club, a golf course, and a marina—all designed to attract an upscale clientele.

The town was established about 1927, when Mexican fishermen found abundant shrimp beds in the area and American John Stone built the first hotel; Al Capone was a frequent visitor during the Prohibition era, when he was hiding from U.S. law. Puerto Peñasco is rather faceless, but the "old town" has a number of interesting shopping stalls, fish markets, and restaurants.

Puerto Peñasco was dubbed Rocky Point by British explorers in the 18th century, and that's the name most Americans know it by today. For now it is a popular wintering spot for American RVers and retirees, and a favorite weekend getaway for beach-seeking Arizonans—especially college kids during spring break. Thanks to a special program, Mexican immigration laws—as well as vehicle-import laws—are relaxed for tourists crossing into this so-called free zone. Simply tell the border guards that you are heading for Puerto Peñasco as you drive through—but don't neglect to get Mexican auto insurance.

The northern Gulf area forms a desert-coast ecosystem unmatched in the Western Hemisphere, and scientists from both the United States and Mexico conduct research programs at the **Intercultural Center for the Study of Desert and Oceans** (known as CEDO, its acronym in Spanish), about 3 km (2 mi) east of town on Fremont Boulevard, in the Las Conchas housing development. You can take a tour of the facility (Tuesday at 2, Saturday at 4) to learn about its history and current projects, or just pick up a tide calendar—useful if you're planning beach activities—or field guide from the gift shop. Don't forget to stop in at the small **CETMAR Aquarium** (☎ 638/2–00–10, ◻ $2, ◷ Mon.–Sat. 9–2) next door, which is an especially kid-friendly, hands-on experience. Talks are offered sporadically on a wide range of topics. ✉ *Turn east at municipal building and follow signs for Caborca Rd., where there will be signs for Las Conchas Beach and CEDO,* ☎ *638/2–01–13.* ◻ *Free.* ◷ *Mon.–Sat. 9–5, Sun. 10–2.*

Dining and Lodging

$$-$$$ ✕ **La Casa del Capitán.** Perched atop Rocky Point's tallest "rock," this restaurant has the best views over the bay and the town below. There's inside dining, but the long outdoor porch overlooking the sea is the place to be. A wide-ranging menu includes everything from nachos and quesadillas to flaming brandied jumbo shrimp. ⊠ *Follow Blvd. Benito Juárez to* LA CASA DEL CAPITÁN *sign and head up the steep hill,* ☎ *638/3–60–27. MC, V.*

$$-$$$ ✕ **Costa Brava.** In town, this small, split-level restaurant has excellent service and a great view of the Gulf. For four, try the excellent *marinera de la casa,* a combination of octopus, shrimp, sea snails, and clams. The house specialty is a dish of succulent prawns, done any way you like, and the seafood soup is also good. Hundreds of business cards on the wall testify to this place's popularity with Americans. ⊠ *Blvd. Kino 41, at Paseo Estrella,* ☎ *638/3–31–30. MC, V.*

$$ ✕ **Friendly Dolphin.** You'll recognize this charming downtown spot by the bright blue dolphins on its doorway. Inside, the place feels like a wealthy Mexican family home, with nicely stuccoed ceilings, wood-paneled windows, and exquisite hand-painted tiles. Interesting old photographs, including some of Emiliano Zapata and Pancho Villa, line the hallways. Gaston, the owner, can often be found on the premises singing in an operatic baritone as rich and robust as the food he serves. Unique family recipes include foil-wrapped shrimp or fish prepared *estilo delfin*—steamed in orange juice, herbs, and spices. An upstairs porch overlooks the harbor. ⊠ *Av. Alcantar 44,* ☎ *638/3–26–08. MC, V.*

$$ ✕ **Puesta del Sol.** As the name ("setting of the sun") implies, this is a
★ perfect place to see the sun set, with plenty of outdoor seating on a patio overlooking the beach. The menu features such seafood dishes as fish Mornay (with a creamy cheese sauce) and grilled lobster, with appetizers to appeal to American tastes. Don't miss the margaritas—they're to die for. ⊠ *Hotel Playa Bonita, Paseo Balboa,* ☎ *638/3–25–86. MC, V.*

$-$$ ✕ **La Curva.** This friendly family restaurant with great Mexican food is easy to spot if you look for the mermaid on the sign. The menu lists more than 100 items, including shrimp cooked 20 ways. Turn east where the railroad tracks cross the main road into town. ⊠ *Blvd. Kino and Comonfort,* ☎ *638/3–34–70. MC, V.*

$$$ ⛾ **Plaza Las Glorias.** One of a chain of hotels in Mexico, Plaza Las Glorias is the first lodging of its kind at Puerto Peñasco. Changing the face of the town, this soaring monument to Mexico's desire to promote tourism at any cost sits like a sand-color fortress overlooking the beach. The open, marble-floor lobby with its towering quadrangular ceiling and bamboo-covered skylights draws gasps of admiration from the busloads of tourists who flock to the hotel. Rooms are well appointed, many of them with kitchenettes; suites offer ocean views. ⊠ *Paseo Las Glorias, Las Explanadas 83550,* ☎ *638/3–60–10, 01–800/342–2644, or 800/515–4321,* ℻ *638/3–60–15. 210 rooms. Restaurant, 2 bars, pool, hot tub, beach, snorkeling, shops. AE, MC, V.*

$$ ⛾ **Playa Bonita.** One of the first three hotels in Rocky Point, Playa Bonita offers clean, comfortable rooms; ask for one facing the hotel's broad, sandy beach. This place is very popular with Americans, who also enjoy the Puesta del Sol restaurant. An RV park offers 300 hookups at $17–$20 a day. ⊠ *Paseo Balboa 100, 85550,* ☎ *638/3–21–86; 638/3–25–96 for RV Park. 120 rooms, 6 suites. Restaurant, bar, pool, hot tub, beach. MC, V.*

$ ▥ **Costa Brava.** All the rooms in this small, clean, and economical downtown hotel overlook the Gulf. Down the street are the fish markets, popular with those who bring the catch of the day back across the border. ⊠ *Malecón Kino and Paseo Estrella, 83550,* ☎ *638/3–41–00 or 638/3–41–01,* ☏ *638/3–36–21. 25 rooms. Restaurant, bar. MC, V.*

Nightlife and the Arts

Nightlife tends to be spontaneous and informal in Puerto Peñasco. All ages congregate along the beaches near **Manny's Beach Club** (⊠ Avs. Coahuila and Primera, ☎ no phone), where recorded music is always blaring. Manny's is the place for those who don't want to put too much distance between the water's edge and their next margarita; it's right on the beach, with signs like NO SHOES, NO SHIRT, NO PROBLEM. The food is nothing special, but as the quintessential beach hangout, Manny's is not to be missed.

Outdoor Activities and Sports

WATER SPORTS

At **Sun and Fun Dive Shop** (⊠ Av. Benito Juárez and Parque Industrial, ☎ 638/3–54–50) you can rent diving or snorkeling equipment or receive PADI and NAUI scuba instruction. Sunset cruises, fishing charters, and snorkeling trips can all be booked here.

Cocospera

❹ *104 km (65 mi) southeast of Nogales, between Imuris and Cananea.*

Cocospera is one of the two dozen churches established in the state of Sonora and Arizona by Father Eusebio Francisco Kino between 1687 and 1711. The crumbling adobe mission sits on a bluff above an oak forest and farmlands in a mountain pass in the Sierra Madre Occidental. To get here from Nogales, take Highway 15 Libre to Highway 2.

Magdalena

❺ *25 km (16 mi) south of Imuris, 96 km (60 mi) from Nogales.*

The grave of Father Eusebio Francisco Kino was discovered in Magdalena in 1966. His remains are in a mausoleum across the plaza from Santa Maria Magdalena de Buquivaba, the cathedral that stands on one of the missions he founded. A $1 million monument to the memory of this pioneer priest also stands here. A number of shops surround the plaza, selling curios, blankets, and religious artifacts; stop in at the bakery for some excellent sweet rolls and bread. Magdalena is now also known as the final resting place of its beloved native son, slain presidential candidate Luis Donaldo Colosio, whose statue also presides over the plaza.

If you're really interested in Spanish missions and in rural Mexican life as it has been lived for centuries, drive just a few kilometers north of Magdalena on a clearly marked dirt road to San Ignacio, another of Father Kino's churches, still in use in a tiny Mexican farming village.

Hermosillo

❻ *185 km (115 mi) south of Magdalena on Highway 15.*

Hermosillo (pop. 850,000) is the capital of Sonora, a status it has held on and off since 1831. It is the seat of the state university and benefits from that institution's cultural activities. If you know a bit of Spanish, you might think the city's name means "little beauty." In fact, it honors José Mariá González Hermosillo, one of the leaders in Mexico's War of Independence.

Settled in 1742 by Captain Augustín de Vildosola and a contingent of 50 soldiers, Hermosillo was originally called Pitic, the Pima Indian name for "the place where two rivers meet." The city's most prestigious neighborhood—home to the governor and U.S. consul, among other prominent citizens—still bears the name Pitic. Located immediately north of the highway into town and just behind the Hotel Bugambilia, the area is worth an hour's stroll to view the creative handling of concrete, tile, and other materials in the homes of Hermosillo's affluent residents.

A business center for the state of Sonora, Hermosillo is largely modern, but some lovely plazas and parks hark back to a more graceful past. Although Hermosillo is usually just considered a jumping-off point for Bahía Kino or Guaymas, it has a number of attractions in its own right, as well as the best accommodations and restaurants until you reach Guaymas or San Carlos.

The city's main boulevard is lined with monuments to Sonora's famous sons: Adolfo de la Huerta, Alvaro Obregón, Plutarco Elías Calles, and Abelardo Rodríguez (after whom the boulevard is named)—all presidents of the country after the revolution (Rodríguez also served as governor of Sonora). At the center of town, look for the **Plaza Zaragoza** and the standout **Catedral de San Agustín** (1878), which has been regilded at great expense. Across from the cathedral is the **Palacio de Gobierno del Estado,** its graceful courtyard surrounded by somewhat disjunctive modern murals depicting Sonoran history. Between the two buildings sits an ornate Victorian gazebo. On the south edge of town, the **Plaza de los Tres Pueblos** marks the original settlement.

Overlooking the city on the Cerro la Campana (Hill of Bells), the **Museo de Sonora,** a former penitentiary, has regional history displays; you can also tour the tiny, dark prison cells. ⊠ *Calle California,* ☎ *62/17–27–14.* ⊠ *$2.20, free Sun.* ⊙ *Tues.–Sat. 10–5, Sun. 9–4.*

View 500-year-old Pima mummies and other fascinating pre-Columbian artifacts at the **Museo de la Universidad de Sonora.** ⊠ *Blvds. Luis Encinas and Rosales,* ☎ *62/12–06–09.* ⊠ *Free.* ⊙ *Mon.–Sat. 9–5.*

On the highway south of town, stop at the **Centro Ecologico,** an environmental and ecological park (read: zoo) with more than 500 species of plants and animals—both native to Sonora as well as exotic. It's modeled after the Arizona–Sonora Desert Museum in Tucson and is best visited November through March because of the heat and lack of shade the rest of the year. ⊠ *Hwy. 15, 5 km (3 mi) south of Hermosillo,* ☎ *62/50–12–25 or 62/50–84–90.* ⊠ *$2.* ⊙ *Daily 8–5.*

Dining and Lodging

$$ ✕ **Sonora Steak.** Here in a restored old house you can enjoy the finest cuts of the famous Sonoran beef at reasonable prices. An organist plays mellow music to help digest that steak. The restaurant also serves seafood and is a good spot for a late-night meal—it's open until 2 AM. ⊠ *Blvd. Kino 914,* ☎ *62/10–03–13. MC, V.*

$$ ✕ **Xochimilco.** Dine inside or choose a spot outdoors in the deep shade of large fiddle-leaf figs and yucateca trees at this large and friendly place on a narrow side street in the southern part of town (from Blvd. Rosales, follow the sign near the Oxxo store). Popular with locals and regulars from across the border, Xochimilco serves well-prepared typical Sonoran dishes. ⊠ *Av. Obregón 51,* ☎ *62/50–40–89. MC, V.*

$$$$ 🏨 **Fiesta Americana.** Hermosillo's only five-star hotel, this full-service property is the largest in town and popular among business travelers. The decor is predictable, but some rooms have excellent views, and the beds are large and firm. ⊠ *Blvd. Kino 369, 83010,* ☎ *62/59–60–00 or 800/343–7821,* FAX *62/59–60–60,* WEB *www.fiestaamericana.com. 221 rooms. Restaurant, cafeteria, lobby lounge, pool, tennis court, gym, dance club, business services, travel services. AE, MC, V.*

$$$ 🏨 **Holiday Inn Hermosillo.** Two-thirds of the attractive rooms in this contemporary Spanish-style hotel look out on extensive, well-kept gardens and a good-size pool. The staff is geared toward accommodating the many Mexican business travelers who stay here. ⊠ *Blvd. Kino and Ramón Corral 1110, 83010,* ☎ *62/14–45–70 or 800/623–3330,* FAX *62/14–64–73. 132 rooms. Restaurant, bar, pool, exercise room. AE, MC, V.*

$$ 🏨 **Hotel Bugambilia.** This green oasis on the boulevard into Hermosillo is one of the first motels in town. Here you will find a more personal atmosphere than at some of the faceless chain hotels around it. Rates include breakfast. ⊠ *Blvd. Kino 712, 83010,* ☎ *62/14–50–50,* FAX *62/14–52–52. 104 rooms. Restaurant, pool. AE, MC, V.*

$$ 🏨 **Hotel Gandara.** One of the old traditional spots in Hermosillo, this hotel, with its palm trees, gardens, and colonnades, has the charm of Old Spain. You can stay in bungalows or in conventional-style hotel rooms; all offer cable TV. ⊠ *Blvd. E. Kino 1000, 83150,* ☎ *62/14–44–14 or 01–800/623–4400,* FAX *62/14–99–26. 141 rooms, 8 suites. Restaurant, bar, pool. AE, MC, V.*

$ 🏨 **Hotel Washington.** Though not sparse by budget Mexican standards, the hotel's facilities are limited to two vending machines. The central location, however, only four blocks from the buses to Bahía Kino, makes this an excellent base to avoid the expensive beds on the beach. ⊠ *Calle Dr. Noriega 68, between Matamoros and Guerrero, 83010,* ☎ *62/13–11–83. 40 rooms. No credit cards.*

Nightlife and the Arts

Hermosillo is home to several lively night spots. **Bar Freedom** (⊠ Blvd. Kino 1012, ☎ 62/15–13–40) is a popular upscale joint. **Joy's** (⊠ Fiesta Americana, Blvd. Kino 369, ☎ 62/59–60–00) attracts an affluent clientele. **Marco n' Charlie's** (⊠ Blvd. Rodríguez at Calle San Luis Potosí, ☎ 62/15–30–61) is a watering hole for young locals. **La Trova** (⊠ Calle Guerrero and Tamaulipas, ☎ 62/14–28–61) has live Latin-style music and dancing Wednesday through Saturday.

Shopping

In the downtown markets of Hermosillo, particularly along Avenidas Serdán and Monterrey, you can buy anything from blankets and candles to wedding attire, as well as a selection of *charro* (Mexican cowboy) items. The variety of goods concentrated in this area equals what you'll find in Nogales, and the prices are better.

Bahía Kino

❼ *116 km (72 mi) west of Hermosillo on Highway 16.*

On the shore of the Sea of Cortés lies Bahía Kino, home to some of the prettiest beaches in northwest Mexico. For many years, Bahía Kino was undiscovered except by RV owners and other aficionados of the unspoiled. In the past decade or so, great change has come at the hands of North Americans who have been plopping down trailers and building condos and beach houses here. Bahía Kino itself is divided into Kino Viejo (Old Kino, the Mexican village) and Kino Nuevo

(New Kino), where the beaches, condos, RV sites, and other tourist facilities are.

Consider taking a run across the narrow channel to **Isla del Tiburón** (Shark Island), which is being developed into one of the finest wildlife and game refuges in North America. Permission to visit Tiburón may be obtained from the Port Captain, at the end of the main street in Kino Viejo. Ask at any of the area hotels or RV parks where to find a reliable guide. Only the Seri Indians, for whom Isla del Tiburón is a traditional fishing ground, need no permit. For a crash ethnography of the Seri, poke around the hodgepodge of a collection in the **Museo de los Seris.** You can buy their fine ironwood animal carvings, tightly woven and prized baskets, as well as other crafts in the gift shop. ⊠ *Blvd. Mar de Cortés at Calle Progreso.* ☎ *30¢.* ⊘ *Weekdays 8–3.*

Note: Be sure to ask permission before photographing the Seri.

Dining and Lodging

$$ ✕ **La Palapa.** This thatch-roof restaurant, with a casual interior and a small balcony overlooking the beach, has great seafood. The shrimp brochette with green chilies is memorable, especially with a glass of some very palatable Mexican wine. ⊠ *Blvd. Mar de Cortés and Wellington, on the way into Kino Nuevo,* ☎ *624/2–02–10. AE, MC, V.*

$$ ✕ **El Pargo Rojo.** The best-known restaurant in town has fish and fishnets decorating its two rooms (with a small bandstand for musicians). The catch of the day varies, but you can depend on consistent quality, including such classics as a brimming shrimp cocktail for starters and fresh lobster any way you want it. Fine cuts of meat are available and, depending on your luck, you'll either be serenaded by Mexican musicians or by the ceaseless wailing of recorded, polkalike *norteña* music. ⊠ *Blvd. Mar de Cortés 1426, Kino Nuevo,* ☎ *624/2–02–05. MC, V.*

$$ ✕ **Restaurant Marlin.** This restaurant in Kino Viejo is only hard to find the first time; after that, you will return frequently, drawn by the clean, unpretentious atmosphere and congenial service—not to mention margaritas as big as fishbowls. After serving you superb seafood dishes such as *sopa de siete mares* (soup of the seven seas) or *jaiba a la diabla* (deviled crab), your waiter might produce a guitar and serenade you free of charge. ⊠ *Calles Tastiota and Guaymas,* ☎ *624/2–01–11. Reservations not accepted. MC, V.*

$ ✕ **Restaurant Kino Bay.** Owned by an American, this clean, comfortable family restaurant overlooks the bay. One of the few places serving breakfast, lunch, and dinner, it's a perfect spot for coffee, morning pancakes, and pelican viewing. ⊠ *Near the end of Blvd. Mar de Cortés at Alecantres,* ☎ *624/2–00–49. No credit cards.*

$$$ ⚏ **Posada Santa Gemma.** On a beautiful strip of beach, these eclectically furnished two-story bungalows with kitchenettes, fireplaces, and spectacular views of the sea are ideal for families. Each has two bedrooms and sleeps four or five comfortably. Bring your own cooking utensils and settle in. ⊠ *Blvd. Mar de Cortés, Kino Nuevo 83340,* ☎ *624/2–00–26,* ℻ *624/14–55–79. 14 bungalows. Beach. MC, V.*

$ ⚏ **Posada del Mar.** Across the street from the beach and set back from a rambling garden with a small pool and winding walkways hewn from rock, this mission-style hotel was one of the first in Kino Nuevo. Antiques and Mexican art lend an old-world charm. ⊠ *Blvd. Mar de Cortés and Creta, Apdo. 132, Kino Nuevo 83340,* ☎ *624/2–01–55. 42 rooms, 2 suites, 4 bungalows. Restaurant, bar, pool. MC, V.*

Punta Chueca

❽ *27 km (17 mi) north of Bahía Kino.*

This rustic Seri fishing village perches at the end of a bumpy, winding dirt road. You'll pass exquisite vistas of the bay, distant empty beaches, and rolling mountains. The inhabitants of this community live a subsistence lifestyle, relying on the sea and desert much as they have for hundreds of years.

With fewer than 1,000 Seris in existence, this tribe represents an ancient culture on the verge of extinction. The Seris' love for their natural surroundings is evident in the necklaces that they have traditionally worn and now create to sell. Pretty little shells are wound into the shape of flowers and strung with wild desert seeds and tiny bleached snake vertebrae to result in delicate necklaces. Seri women weave elaborate *canastas* (baskets) of torote grass, which have become highly prized and expensive.

As you get out of your car and head toward the only "store" in town, be prepared to encounter an entourage of Seri women dressed in colorful ankle-length skirts, their heads covered with scarves and their eager outstretched arms laden with necklaces for sale. The Seri are also known for their carved ironwood figurines that represent the animal world around them, including dolphins, turtles, and pelicans. Note: In recent years, many Mexican merchants have taken to machine-making large figures out of ironwood for the tourist trade, thereby seriously depleting the supply of the unique tree that grows only in the Sonoran desert. Make sure the ones you buy are made by the Seri.

Guaymas

❾ *128 km (79 mi) south of Hermosillo.*

The buzz and bustle of Guaymas—Mexico's seventh-largest port—has a pleasant backdrop of rusty red, saguaro-speckled mountains that nudge the deep-blue waters of a sprawling bay on the Sea of Cortés. The Spanish arrived in this "port of ports" as early as the mid-16th century. In 1701, two Jesuit priests, Father Francisco Eusebio Kino and his colleague Juan María Salvatierra, erected a mission base here intended to convert the native Guaimas, Seri, and Yaqui Indians.

Guaymas was officially declared a port in 1814 and became an important center of trade with Europe as well as within Mexico. In 1847, during the Mexican–American War, U.S. naval forces attacked and occupied the town for a year. Bumbling filibuster William Walker also managed to take Guaymas for a short time in 1853, and, in 1866, during Maximilian's brief reign, the French took control. Today, foreign invaders in Guaymas are mostly travelers passing through on their way somewhere else. Given its proximity to the beaches of San Carlos and Mazatlán, as well as the twice-weekly ferry that travels between Guaymas and Santa Rosalía on the Baja peninsula, modern Guaymas is more a stepping stone than a destination. That said, there is plenty to do here to put together a pleasant day in this congenial seaside town.

After the throngs at the *mercado,* a daily municipal market, you'll find quiet at the 19th-century **Catedral de San Fernando.** Or you might relax in the typical Mexican park across the street from the church, **Plaza 13 de Julio,** with its white, Moorish-style, lacy wrought-iron bandstand and time-worn, tree-shaded benches. **Plaza de los Tres Presidentes** is within walking distance of Plaza 13 de Julio. In front of the 1899 **Palacio Municipal** (City Hall) loom imposing statues of the three Sonora-born presidents of Mexico: Plutarco Elías Calles, Adolfo de la Huerta, and Abelardo Rodríguez.

Dining and Lodging

$$$ ✕ **Los Barcos.** Across the street from the harbor, Los Barcos offers a predictable seafood-and-steak menu. The main room is large and pseudo-beach casual, with picnic tables and overhead palm fronds and nets; there are also two smaller, more traditional dining rooms. The crab tostadas are especially good. ⊠ *Calle 22 and Malecón,* ☎ *622/2–76–50. AE, MC, V.*

$ ✕ **Los Delfines.** At the end of the harbor, this spacious restaurant offers a variety of no-frills fresh seafood and a postcard-perfect view of the water. Popular with the locals, who enjoy the *ambiente familiar* (family atmosphere), Los Delfines has a festive air; a band plays weekend afternoons. ⊠ *At end of Blvd. Sanchez Taboada,* ☎ *622/4–05–95. Reservations not accepted. No credit cards.*

$$ 🏠 **Hotel Armida.** Close to the shops and restaurants of downtown Guaymas, this sand-color hotel has a large, well-kept pool; a good coffee shop where locals gather for power breakfasts; and an excellent steak house, El Oeste. Rooms in the hotel's old section are dark, with ill-matched furnishings. The larger, brighter accommodations in the newest section, done in light wood, are worth the higher rates; many have balconies overlooking the pool. ⊠ *Carretera Internacional, Salida Norte, Apdo. 296, 85400,* ☎ *622/4–30–35 or 800/716–4705,* 𝖥𝖠𝖷 *622/2–04–48. 125 rooms. Restaurant, bar, coffee shop, room service, pool, laundry service. AE, MC, V.*

$$ 🏠 **Playa de Cortés.** This fine, sprawling old hotel overlooking Bacochibampo Bay resembles a Spanish colonial hacienda, with towering wooden beam ceilings and a lavish fireplace in the reception room. With tropical landscaping and a sweeping view of the bay, this hotel evokes its genteel past before condos and time-shares. The rooms are furnished with hand-carved antiques; many have fireplaces and balconies. Some private casitas are available, too. To get here from the highway, take the turnoff for Colonia Miramar. ⊠ *Bahía Bacochibampo, San Carlos 85506 (A.P. 66, Guaymas 85400),* ☎ *622/1–12–24, 01–800/623–4400, or 800/782–7608,* 𝖥𝖠𝖷 *622/1–01–35. 89 rooms, 22 suites, 9 bungalows. Restaurant, bar, pool, tennis court, beach. AE, MC, V.*

Nightlife and the Arts

The younger set heads to **Charles Baby** (⊠ Av. Serdán and Malecón, ☎ no phone). Another gathering spot is the disco **Xanadu** (⊠ Malecón Malpica, ☎ no phone).

Shopping

In Guaymas, the **Mercado Publico** is the best place for *artesanías* (crafts) such as baskets, hats, necklaces, and other trinkets. **Plaza el Vigía,** a huge shopping center on the main road from the north into Guaymas, has everything from groceries, film, toiletries, and clothes to household wares.

San Carlos

❿ *32 km (20 mi) northwest of Guaymas.*

Long considered an extension of Guaymas, this resort town—on the other side of the rocky peninsula that separates Bacochibampo Bay from San Carlos Bay—has a personality of its own. Whitewashed houses with red-tile roofs snuggle together along the water where countless yachts and motorboats are docked. The town is a laid-back favorite among professional anglers, North American tourists, and the time-share crowd, as well as wealthy Mexican families from Guaymas. There is a growing assortment of hotels, motels, and condominiums, as well as a country club with an 18-hole golf course.

The overlapping of desert and tropical flora and fauna has created a fascinating diversity of species along this coast. Among marine life, more than 650 species of fish exist here; red snapper, marlin, corbina, yellowtail, sea bass, and flounder are commonly caught. Whales have been spotted in San Carlos Bay, and there is an abundance of dolphins and pelicans. The water is calm and warm enough through October for the whole family to enjoy excellent swimming. Scuba, snorkeling, fishing, and boat excursions are popular, too.

The quiet 5-km (3-mi) stretch of sandy beach at **Los Algodones,** where the San Carlos Plaza Hotel and Club Med are now, was in the 1960s a location site for the film *Catch 22.* Mexico's first man-made marina lies in the shadow of the jagged twin-peak **Tetakawi mountain,** once a sacred site where Indian warriors gathered to gain spiritual strength. An interesting day trip can be made by boat out to the pristine **San Pedro Island,** where sea lions frolic on the rocks.

To reach San Carlos from Guaymas, take Mexico 15 north for about 8 km (5 mi) to the well-marked turnoff for San Carlos. Continue for 24 km (15 mi) on the four-lane **Corredor Escénico** (Scenic Corridor), which was completed in 1995 to replace an infamously bumpy road.

Dining and Lodging

$$ ✕ **Bananas.** American food (BLTs, burgers, fries), Mexican fare—try "shrimp bananas," wrapped in bacon with barbecue sauce—and even sushi are served in a single large room with a peaked ceiling lined with palm fronds. There are a few seats in the entrance patio as well. A copy of Charlie Chaplin's 1924 marriage license hangs on the wall by the rest rooms. ⊠ *Av. San Carlos 345,* ☎ *622/6–06–10. Reservations not accepted. MC, V.*

$$ ✕ **El Pueblito.** This is San Carlos's most sophisticated eatery, although all the "authentic" Mexican decor is a bit excessive. You'll be treated to creative international cuisine, as well as regional favorites. The Tetakawi prawns, stuffed with other shellfish and served in a rich and creamy béchamel sauce, are a heavenly indulgence. ⊠ *San Carlos Plaza Hotel, Paseo Mar Barmejo Nte., Los Algodones, Apdo. 441,* ☎ *622/6–07–77, ext. 510. AE, MC, V.*

$$ ✕ **Rosa's Cantina.** Bearing little resemblance to the saloon in M. Robbins's song "El Paso," this cozy, pink, laid-back restaurant has picnic tables that fill two large dining rooms. Come to feast on ample breakfasts of *huevos rancheros* (eggs with chorizo). The tortilla soup is great for lunch or dinner, and the homemade salsa is divine. ⊠ *Calle Aurora 297,* ☎ *622/6–10–00. Reservations not accepted. MC, V.*

$$$$ ☷ **San Carlos Plaza Hotel and Resort.** Rising from San Carlos Bay en route to Club Med, this huge structure is thoroughly and strikingly pink. It's the most luxurious hotel in Sonora, with a marble-floor atrium lobby that opens onto a large pool and beach. Rooms are done in an attractive contemporary style. All have safes and minibars, and rooms on the first two floors have balconies overlooking the sea. Children love the swimming-pool slide and horseback riding on the beautiful beach. ⊠ *Paseo Mar Barmejo Nte. 4, Los Algodones, Apdo. 441, 85506,* ☎ *622/7–00–77 or 800/854–2320,* FAX *622/7–00–98. 148 rooms, 25 suites. 3 restaurants, 2 bars, snack bar, 2 pools, hot tub, 2 tennis courts, exer-*

cise room, horseback riding, volleyball, beach, travel services, car rental. AE, MC, V.

$$$ ⊞ **Club Med Sonora Bay.** Although San Carlos is expanding rapidly in its direction, this Club Med is still secluded from the main tourist area, its verdant 42-acre complex spreading fortresslike behind a large gate fronted by saguaros. Accommodations are tasteful but plain, and the range of available activities is as great as one would expect from the chain. All meals, soft drinks, and tips—and many sports, such as sailing and scuba diving—are included. It's worth paying extra for the dawn horseback ride to the foothills of the nearby Sierra Madre. ⊠ *Playa de los Algodones, 85400,* ☎ *622/7–00–05 or 800/258–2633,* FAX *622/7–00–02,* WEB *www.clubmed.com. 375 rooms. 2 restaurants, 2 bars, pool, sauna, golf course, 28 tennis courts, horseback riding, beach, windsurfing, boating. AE, MC, V. Closed Nov.–mid-Mar.*

$$$ ⊞ **Plaza Las Glorias.** This condo-hotel complex overlooks the San Carlos marina. It's smaller than the San Carlos Plaza Hotel but nearly as impressive. Subtle pastels set a tasteful tone in the comfortable rooms. Most accommodations have a tiny kitchenette. The few rooms with hot tubs go for the same rate, so request one when you reserve. ⊠ *Plaza Comercial San Carlos 10, Planta Baja, 85006,* ☎ *622/6–10–21 or 622/ 6–10–34,* FAX *622/6–10–35. 105 rooms. Restaurant, snack bar, 2 pools, baby-sitting, travel services, car rental. AE, MC, V.*

$$ ⊞ **Hacienda Tetakawi.** This hotel and trailer park across from the beach on the main street of town is a Best Western. Rooms are generic but clean, and each has a balcony, a few with a view of the sea. ⊠ *Carretera Escénico San Carlos Km 10, 85000,* ☎ *622/6–02–48. 22 rooms. Restaurant, bar. AE, MC, V.*

$ ⊞ **Fiesta San Carlos.** This small hotel on the bay has a lot of charm and is clean and comfortable. Some rooms with kitchens are available, though none have TVs or phones. Breakfast is included. ⊠ *Carretera Escénico San Carlos Km 8.5, 85506,* ☎ *622/6–02–29. 31 rooms. Restaurant, bar, pool. AE, MC, V.*

Nightlife and the Arts

For a feast of artwork by a variety of Mexican and foreign artists, stop by the two floors at the **Galería Bellas Artes** (⊠ Villa Hermosa 111, ☎ 622/60–07–3), where their work is for sale. It's open Monday–Saturday 9:30–5. One favorite gathering spot in the area is **Ranas Ranas** (⊠ Carretera San Carlos Km 9.5, ☎ 622/6–06–10), from which you can enjoy a view of the beach.

Outdoor Activities and Sports

GOLF

Most hotels in the Guaymas–San Carlos area can arrange for temporary membership at the **San Carlos Country Club,** which has an 18-hole golf course.

HORSEBACK RIDING

You can inquire at the **San Carlos Plaza Hotel** (⊠ Paseo Mar Barmejo Nte. 4, Los Algodones, Apdo. 441, ☎ 622/7–00–77 or 800/854–2320) about horses for hire.

WATER SPORTS

Gary's Dive Shop (⊠ Blvd. Beltrones Km 10, San Carlos, ☎ 622/6–00–49 or 622/6–00–24 after hours, WEB www.garysdivemexico.com) runs fishing, snorkeling, and PADI-certified diving excursions. You can also book sunset cruises, and whale-watching and customized expeditions.

Shopping

Kiamy's Gift Shop (✉ Carretera San Carlos Km 10, ☎ 622/6–04–00) is like a bazaar, with something for everyone, at a reasonable price; silver jewelry, earrings, leather bags, Yaqui Indian masks, T-shirts, and caps, as well as a variety of ceramics, can be found here. **Sagitario's Gift Shop** (✉ Carretera San Carlos 132, ☎ 622/6–00–90), across from the entrance to the San Carlos Country Club, features clothing and a variety of crafts, including wood carvings, baskets, high-quality rugs, and Talavera tile.

Alamos

⓫ *257 km (160 mi) southeast of Guaymas.*

With its cobblestone streets, charming central plaza, 200-year-old mission church, and a large number of thoughtfully restored haciendas, Alamos is the most authentic colonial-style town in Sonora. Set in the ecologically rich zone where the Sonoran desert meets a dry tropical forest (also called the thorn forest) in the foothills of the Sierra Madre, the entire town is designated a national monument, and it manages to consistently maintain the dignified side of the early days of Mexico.

Coronado camped here in 1540, and a Jesuit mission was established in 1630, but the town really boomed when silver was discovered in the area during the 1680s. Wealth from the mines financed Spanish expeditions to the north—as far as Los Angeles and San Francisco during the 1770s and '80s—and the town became the capital of the state of Occidente, which combined the provinces of Sinaloa and Sonora, from 1827 to 1832. A government mint was established here in 1864. The mines closed by the end of the 19th century, and the town went into decline.

These days, Alamos is reinventing itself as a tourist spot. Leading the movement are a growing number of expats who have been buying and restoring sprawling haciendas near the center of town, turning some into hotels. So far, the foreigners' efforts to keep the town producing magical, postcard moments seem to be successful.

Points of interest include the impressive **cathedral** on the central Plaza las Armas, begun in 1787 on the site of a 17th-century Jesuit adobe church and completed in 1894. It is fronted by an ornate Moorish-style wrought-iron gazebo, brought from Mazatlán in 1904. To the west of the square, on Guadalupe Hill, is the old Alamos **jail**, built around the turn of the 20th century; it is now a private home, but visitors may tour the structure on occasional Saturdays when tours of the many beautiful **restored colonial houses** in town are also held. The tourist office and all the local hotels have listings of the times and rates.

Not to be missed, the **Museo Costumbrista de Sonora** gives an excellent overview of the cultural history of the entire state of Sonora. The numerous well-marked (but only in Spanish) displays include artifacts from the nearby silver mines and coins from the mints of Alamos and Hermosillo, as well as typical examples of the clothing and furnishings of prominent local families. ✉ *Calle Guadalupe Victoria 1, on Plaza las Armas,* ☎ *642/8–00–53.* ▣ *$1.* ☼ *Wed.–Sun. 9–6.*

Dining and Lodging

✕ **Los Sabinos.** This small, unpretentious café, with indoor and outdoor seating, offers house specials of beef tips and ranch-style shrimp, along with fried fillet of sole in garlic butter as well as several types of tacos and hamburgers. ✉ *Calle 2 de Abril No. 5,* ☎ *642/8–05–98. Reservations not accepted. No credit cards.*

$ ★ **✗ Las Palmeras.** This Mexican family restaurant is crammed onto the sidewalk across the street from the Museo Costumbrista de Sonora and right on the main square. Here you might get homemade *rosca* bread (a sweet, round loaf) with your coffee and an assortment of daily specials. The corn tamales are hard to beat; other specialties include the chile relleno and the carne Milanese. ⊠ *Lázaro Cárdenas 9,* ☎ *642/8–00–65. Reservations not accepted. No credit cards.*

$ **✗ Polo's.** One of the few hangouts for locals, this place is not unfriendly to the many gringos who flock to this beautiful colonial town—but it's not the most welcoming either. That said, Polo's does have many loyal gringo customers. The food is simple but very good: sandwiches and shish kebab. Sonoran steaks are the specialty. ⊠ *Calle Zaragosa 4,* ☎ *642/8–00–01. No credit cards.*

$$$$ ★ **🏨 Hacienda de los Santos.** Owned by a Californian couple, Alamos's most opulent hotel rambles across the lushly landscaped grounds of four restored and linked colonial mansions. Filling every room and lining the long porticos around the many courtyards are centuries-old *santos, retablos,* and other religious art; hand-carved antique wooden furniture; huge and inviting leather sofas; and scores of other old Mexican and Southwest treasures. Spacious bedrooms are appointed with beautiful Spanish colonial furnishings, gigantic tile baths, and fireplaces. The attentive, sometimes bubbly staff knows how to pamper. For those who fly in style, an on-site airplane hangar accommodates six planes. ⊠ *Calle Molina 8, 85763,* ☎ *642/8–02–22,* FAX *642/8–03–67. 8 rooms, 5 suites. Restaurant, bar, 3 pools, spa. MC, V.*

$$ **🏨 Casa de los Tesoros.** This hotel, the House of Treasures, is a picturesque and romantic converted 18th-century convent. The rooms are former nuns' cells and have fireplaces, tile baths, antique furnishings, and high-quality handicrafts on the walls. Room rates include breakfast, and the restaurant is excellent. ⊠ *Av. Obregón 10, Apdo. 12, 85763,* ☎ *642/8–00–10,* FAX *642/8–04–00. 13 rooms, 2 suites. Restaurant, bar, pool. MC, V.*

$$ **🏨 Casa Encantada.** Just off the main square, this lovely B&B owned by a California couple is the converted 250-year-old mansion of one of Alamos's former Spanish mine owners. Rooms retain a colonial character, with high-beamed ceilings, fireplaces, and carved-wood furnishings; all have tile baths and good lighting. ⊠ *Calle Juárez 20, 85760,* ☎ *642/8–04–82,* FAX *642/8–00–04. 10 rooms. Pool. MC, V.*

$ **🏨 Casa Obregón Dieciocho.** This sprawling 275-year-old casa owned by artist and chef Roberto Bloor has two suites, both with a bedroom, sitting room, fireplace, coffeemaker, bath, and private patio. Guests can sit out in a lovely, lush garden; inside, colorful crafts and paintings abound. Write for reservations or (at a slightly extra expense) book almost any accommodation in town through Fraser & Pratt Real Estate in Alamos (☎ *642/8–07–90* or *642/8–01–18*). ⊠ *Av. Obregón 18, 85760. 2 suites. No credit cards.*

Shopping

It's worth a peek into the three crowded rooms of **El Nicho Curios** (⊠ Calle Juárez 15, ☎ no phone), filled with treasures ranging from Mexican religious paintings to old jewelry and regional pottery. In addition, small stores lining **Plaza Alameda** (northwest of the central plaza) sell Mexican sweets, fabrics, belts, and hats, among other items.

Aduana

⑫ *8 km (5 mi) west of Alamos.*

Aduana was formerly the site of one of the richest mines in the district. Today it is the unlikely location of one of Sonora's best restaurants, **Casa la Aduana.** Mexican tourists and expats living in Alamos spill from the nondescript dining room onto the patio of this gourmet eatery run by California exile Samuel Beardsley. A four-course, prix-fixe menu ($17 to $25) is served at both lunch and dinner, and entrée selections might include chicken in apple–chipotle cream or grilled Norwegian salmon.

Across the plaza from Casa la Aduana is the **Iglesia de Nuestra Señora de Balvanere.** A cactus that grows out of one of the church's walls is said to mark the spot where the Virgin appeared to the Yaqui Indians in the late 17th century, an event that is celebrated by a procession every November 21.

SONORA A TO Z

To research prices, get advice from other travelers, and book travel arrangements, visit www.fodors.com.

AIR TRAVEL
AeroCalifornia offers daily nonstop jet service from Los Angeles and Tucson to Hermosillo. Aeroméxico and its subsidiary Aero Litoral has daily flights to Hermosillo from Tucson, and flights from Los Angeles to Hermosillo. Aeroméxico has direct flights to Hermosillo from many cities in Mexico—including Mexico City, Tijuana, Chihuahua, and Guadalajara—and from La Paz and Mexico City to Guaymas; connections to other U.S. cities can be made from these points. America West Express has daily flights to Hermosillo from Phoenix.

CARRIERS
➤ AIRLINES AND CONTACTS: **America West Express** (☎ 01–800/23–59–292 or 800/363–2597). **AeroCalifornia** (☎ 62/60–25–55 or 800/237–6225). **Aeroméxico** (☎ 622/2–01–23, 01–800/02–14–000, or 800/237–6639).

BOAT AND FERRY TRAVEL
Ferries from Guaymas to Santa Rosalía on the Baja coast leave Monday and Thursday at 11 AM and are scheduled to arrive at 6:30 PM. You can buy tickets the day before or the morning of the day you plan to travel unless you have a car, for which you must make reservations three weeks in advance. Fares are about $30 for a reclining seat and $90 for a cabin. Car transportation is priced by car size, with the smallest cars costing $288. Purchase tickets at the Sematur ferry terminal, just east of the center of Guaymas. Check with the Guaymas tourist office for the latest information and schedules.
➤ BOAT AND FERRY INFORMATION: **Sematur ferry terminal** (✉ Av. Serdán, ☎ 622/2–23–24 or 01–800/69–69–600).

BUS TRAVEL
Frequent buses travel to Hermosillo and Guaymas from Nogales, Tijuana, and Mexicali via Tres Estrellas de Oro. Golden State Buses makes daily trips between Tucson, Arizona, and Alamos, with stops at major points along the way. ABC Bus Service travels between Puerto Peñasco and Cabo San Lucas, with plenty of stops en route.
➤ BUS INFORMATION: **ABC Bus Service** (☎ 01–800/621–3623). **Golden State Buses** (☎ 520/623–1675 in the U.S.). **Tres Estrellas de Oro** (☎ 621/3–24–16).

CAR RENTAL
In Guaymas, the agencies to contact are Budget and Hertz, both on the main highway. Budget and Hertz are also in Hermosillo.

➤ Major Agencies: **Budget** (✉ Carmendia 46, at Tamaulipas, Guaymas, ☎ 62/14–30–33 in Hermosillo; ☎ 622/2–14–50 in Guaymas). **Hertz** (✉ Blvds. Rodríguez and Guerrero, ☎ 62/14–85–00 in Hermasillo; 622/2–10–00 in Guaymas).

CAR TRAVEL

Many visitors to Sonora travel by car from Tucson via I–19 to the border in Nogales, Arizona, and then pick up Mexico's Highway 15, which begins in Nogales, Sonora. Highway 15 is now a divided four-lane road, making the ride much quicker and easier than it used to be. This convenience, however, comes at a cost: drivers heading south to Alamos can expect to pay approximately $35 in tolls. The alternative "Libre" (free) routes are much slower and often poorly maintained.

There are two points of entry into Nogales. Most drivers take U.S. I–19 to the end and then follow the signs to the border crossing. This route, however, will take you through the busiest streets of Nogales. It's better to take the Mariposa exit west from I–19, which leads to the international truck crossing and joins a small periphery highway that connects with Highway 15 after skirting the worst traffic.

The official checkpoint for entering Mexico is 21 km (13 mi) south of Nogales. It is here that you have to buy insurance and complete paperwork to bring in your car if you haven't already done so in Tucson at either Sanborn's Mexico Insurance or the Arizona Automobile Association.

As a result of the Sonora Only program, if you are not planning to go farther into Mexico, you do not have to leave a credit-card imprint or pay a deposit (though insurance is still required). Stop at the "Sonora Only" booth at the Km 21 checkpoint.

➤ Contacts: **Arizona Automobile Association** (✉ 8204 E. Broadway, Tucson, AZ, ☎ 520/296–7461; ✉ 6950 N. Oracle Rd., Phoenix, AZ, ☎ 520/885–0694 or 800/352–5382). **Sanborn's Mexico Insurance** (✉ 105 W. Grant, Tucson, AZ, ☎ 520/327–1255).

CONSULATES

There is a U.S. consulate in Hermosillo, in back of Hotel Calinda near downtown.

➤ United States: **U.S. consulate** (✉ Calle Monterrey 140, ☎ 62/17–23–75).

EMERGENCIES

In case of an emergency, contact the police, Red Cross, or a hospital at one of the local numbers listed below.

The Green Angels in Hermosillo is a very helpful state-run road service for travelers.

➤ Emergency Contacts: **Hospitals** (☎ 62/13–25–56 in Hermosillo; 622/2–01–22 in Guaymas). **Police** (☎ 62/12–59–05 or 62/13–27–01 in Hermosillo; 622/4–01–05 in Guaymas). **Red Cross** (☎ 638/3–22–66 in Puerto Peñasco; 62/14–07–69 in Hermosillo; 622/3–05–87 in Guaymas). **Green Angels** (☎ 62/69–27–14).

TOURS

Arizona Coach Tours runs mostly senior-citizen package tours to Alamos, San Carlos, Puerto Peñasco, and the Copper Canyon. Mexico Tours offers package tours to San Carlos and Puerto Peñasco.

➤ Tour Operator Recommendations: **Arizona Coach Tours** (✉ 200 E. 35th St., Tucson, AZ, ☎ 520/791–0210). **Mexico Tours** (✉ 1604 E. Seneca, Tucson, AZ, ☎ 520/325–3284 or 800/347–4731).

TRANSPORTATION AROUND SONORA

By far the easiest way to get around is by automobile—Guaymas and San Carlos are particularly spread out. Most hotels have car-rental agencies. Buses between towns are frequent and inexpensive.

VISITOR INFORMATION

In addition to the tourism offices listed below—which are better to visit than to try to reach by phone—the Sonora Department of Tourism will send you mounds of information and a helpful, full-color magazine.

➤ TOURIST INFORMATION: **Alamos** (✉ Main Plaza, Calle Juárez 6, ☎ 642/8–04–50). **Guaymas** (✉ Calle 19 and Av. 6, ☎ 622/6–03–13 or 888/800–3866). **Hermosillo** (✉ Centro de Gobierno, 3rd floor, Paseo Canal and Comonfort, ☎ 62/17–00–76). **Puerto Peñasco** (✉ Blvds. Juárez and V. Estrella, ☎ 638/3–36–22). **San Carlos** (✉ Corredor Escénico San Carlos, Edificio Bella Mar, ☎ 622/6–02–02). **Sonora Department of Tourism** (☎ 800/476–6672).

5 THE COPPER CANYON: FROM LOS MOCHIS TO CHIHUAHUA CITY

In the heart of the scenic, rugged Sierra Madre, the Copper Canyon—a series of gorges, some deeper than the Grand Canyon in the United States—is known for hikes that range from pleasant walks to thigh-busting descents to the canyon floor. These gorges are home to the largely reclusive Tarahumara Indians. One of North America's most spectacular train trips snakes its way through this magnificent, mostly uncharted region, usually beginning or ending in the lively city of Chihuahua.

THE MAGNIFICENT series of gorges known collectively as Barranca del Cobre—the Copper Canyon—is the real hidden treasure of the Sierra Madre. Inaccessible to the casual visitor until the early 1960s and still largely uncharted, the canyons may now be explored by taking one of the most breathtaking rides in North America: the Chihuahua al Pacífico railroad whistles down 661 km (410 mi) of track, passing through 87 tunnels and crossing 35 bridges through rugged country as rich in history and culture as in physical beauty.

The *barrancas* (canyons) of the Sierra Tarahumara, as this portion of the Sierra Madre Occidental is known, are on the eastern edge of the Pacific "Ring of Fire." Seismic and volcanic activity set the stage, in the process hurling a good quantity of the earth's buried mineral wealth to the surface. The canyons were then carved over eons by the Urique, Septentrión, Batopilas, and Chínipas rivers and further defined by wind erosion. Totaling more than 1,452 km (900 mi) in length and capable of enveloping four times the area of the Arizona Grand Canyon, the gorges are nearly a mile deep and wide in places. The average height of the peaks is 8,000 ft, and some rise to more than 12,000 ft. Four of the major barrancas—Copper, Urique, Sinforosa, and Batopilas—descend deeper than the Grand Canyon, Urique by nearly 1,500 ft.

The idea of building a rail line to cross this region was first conceived in 1872 by Albert Kinsey Owen, an idealistic American socialist. Owen met with some success initially. More than 1,500 people came from the states to join him in Topolobampo, his utopian colony on the Mexican west coast, and in 1881 he obtained a concession from Mexican president General Manuel Gonzáles to build the railroad. Construction on the flat stretches near Los Mochis and Chihuahua presented no difficulties, but eventually the huge mountains of the Sierra Madre got in the way of Owen's dream, along with the twin scourges of typhoid and disillusionment within the community.

Owen abandoned the project in 1893, but it was taken up in 1900 by American railroad magnate and spiritualist Edward Arthur Stilwell. One of Stilwell's contractors in western Chihuahua was Pancho Villa, who ended up tearing up his own work during the Mexican Revolution in order to impede the movement of government troops. By 1910, when the Mexican Revolution started, the Mexican government had taken charge of building the railroad line. But progress was very slow until 1940, when surveying the difficult Sierra Madre stretch finally began in earnest. Some 90 years and more than $100 million after it was started, the Ferrocarril Chihuahua al Pacífico was dedicated on November 23, 1961.

The railroad no longer starts at Topolobampo but at nearby Los Mochis, and Chihuahua City—capital of the eponymous state—is at the other end of the line. The city was established in 1709, after the Spanish discovered silver in the area around 1649. Chihuahua still derives its wealth from mining, as well as ranching, agriculture, and lumber.

Closely related to the Pima Indians of southern Arizona, the Tarahumara Indians once occupied the entire state of Chihuahua. They are renowned for their running ability—Tarahumara is a Spanish corruption of their word Rarámuri, which means "running people"; it's said that in earlier times the Tarahumara hunted deer by chasing them to the point of collapse. Like so many native groups, the Tarahumara were totally disrupted by the European arrival in the area. The Spanish made them serve in the mines, then the Mexicans and Americans put them to work on the railroads. The threat of slavery and the series of wars that began in the 1600s and continued until the 20th century forced them to retreat deeper into the canyons, where they are still subject to having their lands taken over by loggers and drug lords. Many are semi-nomadic, roaming the high plateaus of the Sierra Madre in summer and moving down to the warmer canyon floor in winter. Their population, ravaged over the years by disease, drought, and poverty, is estimated at around 50,000.

Pleasures and Pastimes

Dining

Throughout the canyons you'll encounter relatively undeveloped areas where there are few eateries besides those connected with lodges. In Los Mochis and Topolobampo your best bet is seafood. At the hotels in Cerocahui, Divisadero, and Posada Barrancas, hearty meals are generally included in room rates. There are a few more dining options in Creel, where, in addition to hotel dining rooms, you'll find small cafés along the town's main street, Avenida López Mateos.

You'll have the greatest choice of restaurants in Chihuahua City. The state is a large producer of beef, so upscale steak houses and places serving *carne asada* (charbroiled strips of marinated beef) abound, but Mexican specialties and seafood flown in from the coast are also available. Many of Chihuahua's well-appointed international restaurants are in the Zona Dorada, on Calle Juárez starting at its intersection with Calle Colón.

Dress is casual everywhere except at some of Chihuahua's pricier restaurants. Unless otherwise indicated, reservations aren't necessary.

CATEGORY	COST*
$$$$	over $20
$$$	$15–$20
$$	$8–$15
$	under $8

per person for a main course at dinner

Hiking

Hiking in the Copper Canyon is fantastic if you take the proper precautions. *Mexico's Copper Canyon Country,* by M. John Fayhee, is a good source of information. But even the most experienced trekkers should enlist the help of local guides, who can be contacted through all the hotels in the area or through travel agents in Los Mochis and Chihuahua. Few adequate maps are available for even the so-called marked trails, and many of the better-worn routes into the canyon are made by the Tarahumara, whose prime concern is getting from one habitable area to the next rather than getting to the bottom.

Urique Canyon is most easily reached from Cerocahui. The Copper Canyon proper is most accessible from Divisadero. Trails range from easy rim walks to a 27-km (17-mi) descent to the bottom. If you're in Creel, a gentle and rewarding hike is the 6-km (4-mi) walk from the Copper Canyon Lodge to 100-ft-high Cusárare Falls. More difficult but equally scenic is the trek to the base of Basaseachi Falls—a full-day outing. The descent into Batopilas Canyon from Creel—a not-for-the-faint-of-heart affair—requires an overnight stay.

Horseback Riding

Most hotels in the canyon area can arrange for local guides with gentle horses, but most trips aren't for couch potatoes. The trails into the canyon are badly defined and can be rocky as well as slippery if the weather is icy or wet. At rough spots you might be asked to dismount and walk part of the way. A fairly easy and inexpensive ride is to Wicochic Falls at Cerocahui, about two hours round-trip, including a half-hour hike at the end, where the trail is too narrow for the horses. From Divisadero, the four-hour round-trip to Bacajipare, a Tarahumara village in the Copper Canyon, has stunning vistas, but it's not for the faint-hearted.

Lodging

Accommodations in this area tend to fall into two categories: comfortable but characterless in the cities, and charming but rustic in the villages. In Cerocahui, Divisadero, Posada Barrancas (*posada* means "inn"), and Creel, all the hotels send buses or cars to meet the train. If you don't have a reservation, you'll have to make a quick decision and then hop on the hotel vehicle of your choice. In summer, October, and around Christmas and Easter, it's important to book in advance. Where indicated, rates for hotels include meals.

CATEGORY	COST*
$$$$	over $170
$$$	$120–$170
$$	$60–$120
$	under $60

All prices are for a standard double room, excluding 15% tax.

Nightlife

Conversing with fellow guests in your lodge or stargazing from a rooftop balcony are about the extent of nighttime activities in the heart of Sierra country, although occasionally one of the larger hotels will have performances in the evening by Tarahumara dancers or Mexican musicians. Entertainment is considerably less rural in Los Mochis, and Chihuahua is a typically bustling, late-night Mexican city.

Shopping

A main source of cash income for the Tarahumara is their crafts, including lovely handwoven baskets made from sotol (an agavelike plant) or pine needles, carved wooden dolls, rustic pottery, roughly carved wooden masks, brightly colored woven belts and sashes made on back-strap looms, and wooden fiddles decorated with faces from which the men produce haunting music. The Tarahumara women, who are generally shy about talking with tourists, sell their wares throughout the Copper Canyon area. Their prices are fair, so bargaining is unnecessary. Tarahumara wares are sold at the Divisadero train station and at shops in Creel and Chihuahua. Chihuahua is known for affordable cowboy boots, and *bota* (boot) shops proliferate downtown.

Exploring the Copper Canyon

Imagine visiting the Grand Canyon in the days before it was tamed by tourist facilities and you'll have some sense of what a trip through the Copper Canyon will be like—for better and for worse. That is, with the opportunity to encounter a relatively untouched natural site come some of the discomforts of the rustic experience. But if you are careful in your choice of time to visit and are properly prepared, the trip's myriad rewards should far outstrip any temporary inconveniences.

Numbers in the text correspond to numbers in the margin and on the Copper Canyon map.

Great Itineraries

You'll see some beautiful scenery even if you only ride the railroad—including a panoramic look into the canyons during a 15-minute stop at Divisadero—but you'll take in only a fraction of what the canyons

Copper Canyon

have to offer if you don't get off the train. If possible, plan on a night in Cerocahui (Bahuichivo stop), one at Posada Barrancas or Divisadero (the train stations are five minutes apart), and one or two at Creel.

Most people make their way into the Copper Canyon via Los Mochis, which is the easiest route if you're coming from California or Arizona. On top of that, some of the best scenery is at the western end of the ride, and you're likely to miss it if you approach Los Mochis in the evening. Train delays of three hours or more are not unusual, so even during the extended daylight hours of summer, you can't count on reaching the scenic end of the route before dark.

Even if you drive down to either Los Mochis or Chihuahua, your itinerary will be largely dependent on the schedule of the Chihuahua al Pacífico train: it runs in each direction only once a day, so you must plan the time spent in each stop accordingly. The following itineraries assume you will add on a day's train ride to return to your starting point—unless you catch one of the Aerolitoral flights between Los Mochis and Chihuahua. The small turboprops fly low over the mountains and canyons, providing magnificent views.

Note: The Sinaloa-Chihuahua state border divides two time zones: Mountain Time to the west and Central Time to the east.

IF YOU HAVE 3 DAYS

Departing from **Los Mochis** ①, take the 6 AM Chihuahua al Pacífico train and get off at Bahuichivo, where you can explore the mission at **Cerocahui** ③ and the overlook into Urique Canyon. The next day, continue to **Divisadero** ④, where it's practically impossible not to get a room with a view. Spend your last day exploring **Creel** ⑤ and taking a short hike to the falls near Cusárare. If you begin the trip in **Chihuahua City** ⑧, make Cerocahui your final stop.

IF YOU HAVE 5 DAYS

Starting in the west, consider spending a day in the old colonial town of **El Fuerte** ②, then catching the train through the canyons at 7:30 the next morning. Follow the three-day itinerary, above, and use the last day and night to extend your time in **Creel** ⑤, with a visit to the Tarahumara community of San Ignacio or a drive to Basaseachi Falls. If you start in the east, you might take the extra day to explore **Chihuahua City** ⑧. Don't miss Pancho Villa's home, now a museum.

IF YOU HAVE 8 OR MORE DAYS

Spend a day each in **El Fuerte** ②, **Cerocahui** ③, and **Divisadero** ④, then extend your stay in **Creel** ⑤ to include a trip down to the former silver mining town of **Batopilas** ⑥. It's six to eight hours each way by car (preferably four-wheel drive) or bus, so you'll want to spend at least two nights. You'll be ready for modern conveniences after that, so plan to enjoy the restaurants and museums of **Chihuahua City** ⑧ for an additional day. Another option would be to visit the Mennonite community near **Cuauhtémoc** ⑦ before going on to Chihuahua.

When to Tour

Unless you're planning to head deep into the barrancas, winter—December through February—is not the best time to come. Some of the hotels in the region are inadequately prepared for the cold, and the minor rainy season in January renders some of the roads for side excursions impassable. The warm months are May through September. The rainy season, late June through September, brings precipitation for a short period every day, but this shouldn't interfere with your enjoyment in any way. It's temperate in the highlands during the summer. If you're planning to hike down into the canyons, however, remember that the deeper you go, the hotter it will get. The best months to visit are October and November, when the weather is still warm and rains have brought out all the colors in the Sierra Tarahumara.

Many people come during Easter and Christmas, specifically to see the Tarahumaras' colorful take on church holidays. On these and other religious feast days, Tarahumara villages challenge one another in races that can go for days. The men run in small groups, upward of 161 km (100 mi) or more, all the while kicking a wooden ball. It's not *just* fun and games—each village places a huge communal wager for this winner-take-all event.

Los Mochis

❶ *763 km (473 mi) south of Nogales on the Arizona-Mexico border.*

At the western end of the rail line, Los Mochis (population 331,000) is an agricultural boomtown. The rail terminus and the city's location about 19 km (12 mi) from the harbor at Topolobampo make it the export center of the state of Sinaloa. You can tour Benjamin Johnston's sugar refinery, the **Ingenio Azucarero,** around which the town grew. Near Johnston's estate you can still see the American colony—the group of brick bungalows that housed his associates.

The **Museo Regional del Valle del Fuerte** rotates work by local, regional, national, and international artists, and has a didactic exhibit on the area's history. A replica of a railroad steam engine is on permanent display. Labels are in Spanish only. ✉ *Obregón and Mina,* ☎ *68/12–46– 92.* 🎟 *$1.* 🕒 *Mon.–Sat. 9–1 and 4–7.*

Cottonwood trees and bougainvillea line the highway from Los Mochis to **Topolobampo.** Fields en route are planted with crops ranging from sugarcane to marigolds and mangoes. Once the site of Albert Owen's utopian colony and the center of the railroad-building activity in the area, it is now a suburb of Los Mochis. **Isla El Farallón,** off the coast, is a breeding ground for the sea lions that gave the town its name: in the language of the Mayo Indians who once dominated the area, *Topolobampo* means "watering place of the sea lions."

Dining and Lodging

$$ ✕ **El Farallón.** Nautical decor and murals set the tone for the excellent fish served at this simple restaurant. Sushi and sashimi are especially good, as is the *pitalla* (cactus fruit with brightly colored flesh) ice cream. ✉ *Obregón 593, at Ángel Flores,* ☎ *68/12–14–28 or 68/12–12–73. AE, MC, V.*

$$ ✕ **Restaurante España.** This slightly upscale restaurant in downtown Los Mochis is popular with the local business crowd. Good seafood, U.S. cuts of beef, and Spanish dishes are served around an indoor fountain. ✉ *Obregón 525,* ☎ *68/12–22–21 or 68/12–23–35. AE, MC, V.*

$ ✕ **Las Fuentes.** This unpretentious, colonial-style restaurant specializes in Sinaloan and U.S. beef cuts. Try the local favorite, *cabreria*—a thinly cut fillet. ✉ *Calzada López Mateos 1070 Nte., at Jiquilpan,* ☎ *68/12–47–70. AE, MC, V.*

$$ ⊞ **Corintios Hotel.** This modern-style dwelling with a dark-glass facade has a bit more class than the other reasonable hotels in town and is a good deal in this price category. Rooms have diffused lighting, with both carpeted and tile floors. The hotel has no elevator. ✉ *Obregón 580 Pte., 82000,* ☎ *68/18–23–00,* FAX *68/18–22–24. 34 rooms, 1 suite, 6 junior suites. Restaurant, bar, hot tub, exercise room, travel services. AE, DC, MC, V.*

$$ ✕⊞ **Hotel Plaza Inn.** Los Mochis's only five-star hotel caters to businesspeople and tourists with luxuries that you won't necessarily find elsewhere: three phones (one in the bathroom) in each room, tubs, card keys, and locks and security safes. Furniture is sturdy but rather standard; beds are covered with floral spreads. There's a small club for duck hunters and fishermen. The restaurant here, Mr. Owen's, on the ground floor, is reliable. ✉ *Av. Leyva and Cárdenas, 81200,* ☎ *68/18–10–42 or 800/862–9026,* FAX *68/12–15–90. 100 rooms, 25 suites. 2 restaurants, bar, nightclub, travel services. AE, DC, MC, V.*

$$ ✕⊞ **Hotel Santa Anita.** The central reservations link of the Balderrama chain, this downtown hotel is also an informal information center for what's happening along the Chihuahua al Pacífico route and a place to book tours. Built in 1959, the property has midsize rooms fitted with tasteful and comfortable modern furniture. All have cable TVs, and many have hair dryers and scalloped onyx sinks. The restaurant is one of the best in town. ✉ *Av. Leyva and Hidalgo, 81200,* ☎ *68/18–70–46 or 800/862–9026,* FAX *68/12–00–46. 116 rooms. Restaurant, bar, travel services. AE, MC, V.*

$ ⊞ **Villa Cahita.** The main attraction to this rustic hotel two blocks from El Dorado is its expansive lobby and restaurant area with comfortable *equipale* (tree-branch-and-pigskin) chairs and high ceilings. The junior suites are a good deal, and secure parking is available. ✉ *Ignacio Ramirez 400 Pte., 81200,* ☎ *68/12–12–00,* FAX *68/12–63–35. 50 rooms, 16 junior suites. Restaurant, bar, travel services. AE, DC, MC, V.*

Nightlife

Locals kick up their heels at **Fantasy Laser Club** (✉ Hotel Plaza Inn, Av. Leyva and Cárdenas, ☎ 68/18–70–46). **Morocco** (✉ Av. Leyva and Rendon, ☎ 68/12–13–88) is a disco downtown. **Yesterday** (✉ Obregón and Guerrero, ☎ 68/15–38–10) has live bands for an over-30 audience.

Shopping

If you're headed to Divisadero, Creel, or beyond, snacks and reading material can help pass the nine-hour-plus journey. **Libreria Los Mochis** (⊠ Calle Madero Pte. 402, at Av. Leyva) has a limited selection of English-language magazines and plenty of Spanish-language daily newspapers. **La Cava Deli** (⊠ Av. Leyva 425, ☎ 14/10–99–40) sells American and Mexican beers, a good selection of wines and liquors, Cuban cigars, and snack foods. If a celebration is in order, you can pick up **piñatas** for $5–$10 at the small family business at Callejón Guadalupe Victoria 43.

El Fuerte

❷ *80 km (50 mi) northeast of Los Mochis.*

If you're ready for old Mexico, take a bus to El Fuerte (instead of the train that leaves at the crack of dawn), stay the night, and sleep in an hour longer before grabbing the 7:30 train to points east. A bus with comfortable seats leaves from **Mercado Independencia** (⊠ Avs. Independencia and Degollado) every half hour 7:30 AM–8:30 PM for the two-hour trip. Fresh foods are available at the mercado.

The small colonial town of El Fuerte was named after the 17th-century fort built by the Spaniards to protect against attacks by the local Mayo, Sinaloa, Zuaque, and Tehueco Indians. Conquistador Don Francisco de Ibarra and a small group of soldiers founded it in 1564, and they called their town San Juan de Carapoa. Located on the central El Camino Real route, El Fuerte was at one time the frontier outpost from which the Spanish set out to explore and settle New Mexico and California. For three centuries, it was a major trading post for gold and silver miners from the nearby Sierras and the most important commercial and farming center of the area. It was chosen as Sinaloa's capital in 1824 and remained so for several years.

Now a rather sleepy town of 25,000, El Fuerte has intact colonial mansions, one of the best being the Posada del Hidalgo. Most of the historic houses are set off the cobblestone streets leading from the central plaza.

Dining and Lodging

$$ ✕ **El Mesón del General.** Just a block off the main plaza, this is the best bet in town for good freshwater fish and crayfish caught in a nearby lake. A varied menu includes Mexican fare, *langostino caque* (local river crawfish) and *lobina* (black bass), and tasty steaks. ⊠ *Benito Juárez 202, ☎ 68/93–02–60. MC, V.*

$$ ⊡ **El Fuerte Lodge.** Longtime hunting guide Robert Brand expanded
★ his lodge in the restored 380-year-old mansion of Spanish explorer Francisco Ibarra situated on the old Camino Real—two blocks off the town square—and now offers it to canyon travelers. A flower-filled courtyard has been fitted with a waterfall and hidden Jacuzzi, and some of Mexico's best *artesanía* (folk art) adorns the rooms and common areas. ⊠ *Montesclaro 37, 81820, ☎ 68/93–02–26. 31 rooms. Bar, dining room, air-conditioning, hot tub. MC, V.*

$$ ⊡ **Posada del Hidalgo.** You'll be transported back to a more gracious
★ era at this restored hacienda, with its gardens and cobblestone paths, built in 1895 by Rafael Almada, the richest man in nearby Alamos. It's difficult to choose between the larger rooms with balconies, set off a lobby filled with period artifacts, and those that open onto the gardens. All are decorated with rough-hewn handcrafted furniture. *Langostino* (crawfish) is a specialty of the dining room. ⊠ *Hidalgo 101, ☎ 68/93–02–42. Reservations: Hotel Santa Anita, Av. Leyva and Hi-*

dalgo, Apdo. 159, Los Mochis 81200, ☎ *68/18–70–46, ext. 432, or 800/896–8196,* FAX *68/12–00–46. 50 rooms, 2 suites. Bar, dining room, air-conditioning, pool, dance club. AE, MC, V.*

$ ☆ 🏨 **Mirador de Montesclaros.** On the Cerro de las Pilas, the highest spot in El Fuerte, with a commanding view, is this small, adobe-and-wood posada owned by local guide Eleazar Gamez. Rooms are rustic but very creatively decorated with family heirlooms and antiques from friends in town, each piece with its own story that the owner gladly shares. Continental breakfast and a tour of El Fuerte are included in the room price. ✉ *Cerro de las Pilas,* ☎ *68/93–04–13. 9 rooms. Bar. No credit cards.*

En Route As the train ascends almost 5,906 ft from El Fuerte to Bahuichivo, it passes through 87 tunnels and over 24 bridges, including the longest and highest ones of the rail system. The scenery shifts from Sinaloan thorn forest, with cactus and scrublike vegetation; to the pools, cascades, and tropical trees of the Río Septentrión canyon; to the oak and pine forest that begins to take over past Temoris, where a plaque marks the 1961 dedication of the railroad by President López Mateos.

Cerocahui

❸ *160 km (100 mi) northeast of El Fuerte.*

The quiet mountain village of Cerocahui, just inside the Sinaloa state border, is a good place to get a sense of how people live in the canyon area. Next door to the Hotel Misión is a **Jesuit mission,** established around 1680 by Juan María de Salvatierra, who proselytized widely in the region. It is said that because the Tarahumara were the most difficult Indians to convert, he considered this mission his favorite among the many he founded. Nearby, the church operates a boarding school for Tarahumara children. From the train station at Bahuichivo, two hotels have buses that make the 45-minute ride up the bumpy, unpaved road to Cerocahui.

The prime reason to come to Cerocahui is its accessibility to **Urique Canyon.** It's a kidney-crunching ride to the **Cerro del Gallego** lookout, where amid mountains spread against the horizon you can make out the slim thread of the Urique River and the old mining town of Urique, a dot on the distant canyon bottom. On the way up you'll pass a Tarahumara cave where women sell baskets. Nearby, a shrine to the Virgin of Fatima is strikingly set against a spring in the mountainside. From Cerro del Gallego the road continues down the canyon into Urique, which has a few basic hotels and restaurants. A public bus makes the trip from Cerocahui a few times a week, but many people opt for the local hotels' round-trip, full-day tours.

Dining and Lodging

$$$$ ✕ 🏨 **Hotel Misión.** Part of the Balderrama chain—the Copper Canyon's equivalent of the Grand Canyon's Fred Harvey hotel empire—this is the only accommodation in Cerocahui itself. The main house, which looks like a combination ski lodge and hacienda, contains the hotel's office, small shops, and a dining room, bar, and lounge. There are two large fireplaces around which to huddle in winter: Cerocahui isn't wired for electricity, and the hotel uses its generator for only a few hours. The plain rooms have beam ceilings, Spanish colonial–style furnishings, wood-burning stoves, and kerosene lamps. Rates include meals. ✉ *Cerocahui. Reservations: Hotel Santa Anita, Av. Leyva and Hidalgo, Apdo. 159, Los Mochis 81200,* ☎ *68/18–70–46, ext. 432, or 800/896–8196,* FAX *68/12–00–46. 38 rooms. Restaurant, bar, lounge, shops. AE, DC, MC, V.*

$$$ ✕⊡ **Paraíso del Oso Lodge.** Doug "Diego" Rhodes runs a lodge near
★   Cerocahui that's known as a base camp for the great horseback rides
      he leads through the Urique Canyon to Batopilas and beyond. The rooms
      are plain, with simple handmade wood furniture. You have to stoke
      the wood-burning stove for heat at night, as there is no electricity here.
      A huge window-filled lobby affords excellent views of the cliffs above
      the lodge. A gift shop carries local crafts as well as wares from other
      parts of Mexico. Rates include meals. *5 km (3 mi) outside of Ceroc-
      ahui. Reservations: ⊠ Box 31089, El Paso, TX 79931, ☎ FAX 14/21–
      33–72 in Chihuahua City. 21 rooms. Dining room. MC, V.*

Divisadero

❹ *80 km (50 mi) northeast of Cerocahui, in the state of Chihuahua.*

There's little to do in Divisadero, a postage stamp of a place on the
Continental Divide, but it's impossible to be unmoved by its Copper
Canyon vistas—don't miss the canyon at sunset. You can also glimpse
a bit of the distant Urique and Tararecua canyons from here. A pop-
ular excursion that takes about five hours round-trip on foot or on horse-
back is to Bacajipare, a Tarahumara village in the canyon; the Hotel
Cabañas Divisadero-Barrancas has a $65 guided trip.

Dining and Lodging

$$$$ ✕⊡ **Hotel Cabañas Divisadero-Barrancas.** The dining room and Rooms
       1–10 in the old section and 35–52 in the newer section of this canyon-
       rim hotel have panoramic views. Food and service get mixed reviews
       from the international visitors who sign the guest log, but you're not
       likely to notice what you're eating when you look out the window. The
       Sandoval family has owned the vast tract of land surrounding the
       hotel since the former mayor of Batopilas, Indalecio Sandoval, bought
       it to escape the summer heat of that town, and later to hide himself
       and his family from Pancho Villa's revolutionaries. Rates include
       meals. ⊠ *Divisadero stop on Chihuahua al Pacífico train. Reservations:
       ⊠ Av. Mirador 4516, Apdo. 661, Col. Residencial Campestre, Chi-
       huahua, Chihuahua 31000, ☎ 14/15–11–99, FAX 14/15–65–75. 48
       rooms. Restaurant, bar. AE, MC, V.*

$$$$ ✕⊡ **Hotel Posada Barrancas Mirador.** This beautiful pink hotel—an-
★   other link in the Balderrama chain—perches on the edge of the Cop-
       per Canyon. The dining room and all the guest rooms have spectacular
       views; balconies seem to hang right over the abyss. Accommodations
       are bright, with custom-made furniture, hand-loomed textiles, and
       heat from fireplaces. Plentiful and tasty meals are included in the rates.
       The hotel can organize day trips to Creel and the surrounding area.
       ⊠ *Posada Barrancas stop on Chihuahua al Pacífico train. Reservations:
       ⊠ Hotel Santa Anita, Av. Leyva and Hidalgo, Apdo. 159, Los Mochis
       81200, ☎ 68/18–70–46 or 800/862–9026, FAX 68/12–00–46. 51 rooms.
       Restaurant, bar, meeting room. AE, MC, V.*

$$$ ✕⊡ **Hotel Mansion Tarahumara.** It's a bit disconcerting to come across
★   a red-turreted, medieval-style "castle" out in barranca country, but
       somehow this whimsical fancy works. All rooms (15 in separate cab-
       ins) have Spanish contemporary-style light-pine furniture, plus fire-
       places and individual heaters. The newest units have pine-log walls. Older
       rooms have gray cobblestone walls that match the lodge's exterior. The
       large dining hall is hard to keep warm in winter but has wonderful views
       of the Sierra Madre. All meals are included. ⊠ *Posada Barrancas.
       Reservations: Av. Juárez 1602-A, Col. Centro, Chihuahua, Chihuahua
       31000, ☎ 14/15–47–21, FAX 14/16–54–44. 57 rooms, 1 suite. Restau-
       rant, bar, pool, tennis court, dance club, meeting room, travel services.
       AE, DC, MC, V.*

$$ ✕🏨 **Rancho Posada Hotel.** This is a good base from which to explore the Barranca del Cobre. The 14 remodeled rooms have ocher stucco walls, ceramic-tile floors, and colonial-style, hand-painted furniture; all but six have cozy fireplaces. The older accommodations, also slated for remodeling, have plain, contemporary-style furnishings of dark wood. The lobby–dining room has a massive stone fireplace, beamed ceiling, and wood furniture. Rates include meals. ✉ *Posada Barrancas stop on Chihuahua al Pacífico train. Reservations:* ✉ *Hotel Santa Anita, Av. Leyva and Hidalgo, Apdo. 159, Los Mochis 81200,* ☎ *68/18–70–46, ext. 432, or 800/896–8196,* 🗚 *68/12–00–46. 38 rooms. Restaurant, bar. AE, MC, V.*

Creel

❺ *60 km (37 mi) northeast of Divisadero.*

Nestled in pine-covered mountains, Creel is a rugged mining, ranching, and logging town that grew up around the railroad station. The largest settlement in the area, it's also a gathering place for Tarahumara Indians seeking supplies and markets for their crafts. It's easy to imagine American frontier towns at the turn of the 20th century looking like Creel—without, of course, the international backpacking contingent that makes this town its base.

It's 19 km (12 mi) from Creel to **Cusárare,** a Tarahumara village with a 300-year-old Jesuit mission. En route you'll pass limpid-blue Lake Arareco and the turnoff for the strange volcanic-rock formations of the Valley of the Mushrooms. An impressive waterfall can be reached by an easy 6-km (4-mi) hike from town through a lovely piñon forest.

If the unpaved roads are passable, consider taking the longer trips to the **Recohuata Hot Springs,** a fairly strenuous hike down from the rim of the Tararecua Canyon, and to **El Tejaban,** a spectacular overlook at the Copper Canyon. Among several worthwhile day trips along the way to the colonial town of Batopilas are **Basihuare,** where wide horizontal bands of color cross huge vertical outcroppings of rock; the **Urique Canyon overlook,** a perspective that differs from the one at Divisadero; and **La Bufa,** site of a former Spanish silver mine. Seventy-three kilometers (45 miles) northwest of Creel, along an unpaved, winding road, the 806-ft **Basaseachi Falls** are among the highest cascades in North America.

Dining and Lodging

$ ✕ **Tío Molcas.** Furnished with chunky wooden tables and chairs, this small, cheerful restaurant dishes up delicious Mexican food, especially the cheese enchiladas topped with a zesty red-pepper sauce. ✉ *Av. López Mateos 35,* ☎ *145/6–00–33. No credit cards.*

$ ✕ **Veronica's.** This clean, simple eatery on the main street is popular with locals and tourists for its variety of tasty and economical meals. *Comidas corridas*—set meals with soup, main course, and dessert—are available, or you can order à la carte. Try the *sopa de verduras* (vegetable soup) or the vegetarian tacos. The salsa is sublime. ✉ *Av. López Mateos 34,* ☎ *145/6–06–31. No credit cards.*

$$ 🏨 **Best Western: The Lodge at Creel.** At the other end of town from the plaza, this lodge is actually several log buildings with four rooms each. The spacious, well-lighted, comfortable quarters exude rustic-chic charm with their pine floors and walls, high double beds with thick coverlets, Tarahumara artifacts, and old-fashioned "wood stoves" that are really gas-log heaters controlled by wall thermostats. The main lodge building has a small bar–dining area with leather-and-wood furniture. ✉ *Av. López Mateos 61, 33200,* ☎ *145/6–00–71 or 888/879–4071,* 🗚 *145/6–00–82. 27 rooms. Restaurant, bar. AE, MC, V.*

$$ ☎ **Motel Parador de la Montaña.** This clean, well-run motel has large, comfortable, no-frills rooms with private, hot-water baths and a secure parking area. In the cozy wood-paneled lounge, the warmth radiating from the huge stone fireplace beckons you to plop down on the funky, handmade pine furniture and relax. ⊠ *Av. López Mateos 41, 33200,* ☎ *145/6–00–75. 50 rooms. Restaurant, bar. AE, MC, V.*

$ ☎ **Copper Canyon Sierra Lodge.** About 24 km (15 mi) from Creel, set
★ in a peaceful piñon forest near Cusárare Falls, this hotel is an incredibly successful blend of elegant and rustic. Adjacent to a Tarahumara village, the lodge gives guests a closer look at the daily lives of these very private cave-dwelling natives. There's no electricity in the lodge itself, but the pine-paneled rooms with antique furnishings and tile, hot-water baths are romantically equipped with kerosene lamps and wood stoves. People usually book rooms here as part of an all-inclusive package deal with a sister lodge in Batopilas, but the lodge will accept walk-ins if space permits. ⊠ *Cusárare,* FAX *145/6–00–36,* WEB *www.sierratrail.com. (Copper Canyon Lodges, 2741 Paldan, Auburn Hills, MI 48326,* ☎ *248/340–7230 or 800/776–3942.) 14 rooms. Restaurant, bar. AE, D, MC, V.*

$ ☎ **Margarita's.** If a small boy at the train station offers to take you to
★ Margarita's, and the prospect of hanging out with a motley neo-beatnik crowd appeals, go with him for one of the best deals in town. Even if you follow directions (it's between the two churches facing the plaza), and though there's a small sign above the door, you may think you're walking into a private kitchen when you enter. At this gathering spot for backpackers, you can get anything from a bunk bed in a dorm room (less than $6) to a double room with two beds and a private bathroom (around $25 per person). Prices include breakfast and dinner. The rooms—with wrought-iron lamps, light-wood furnishings, and clean, modern baths—are as pleasant as anything you'll find for three times the price. ⊠ *Av. López Mateos 11, 33200,* ☎ *145/6–00–45 or 145/6–02–45. 17 rooms, 1 dorm. Restaurant. No credit cards.*

$ ☎ **Margarita's Plaza Mexicana.** This pretty hotel with two floors of rooms around a private courtyard is one of the town bargains, serving up solid meals and honest hospitality at low prices. The rooms, with private baths, individual heat, and plenty of hot water, are decorated with locally crafted pine furniture and charming murals depicting Tarahumara activities. Two complaints often heard about the Plaza Mexicana are that it's too aggressive in soliciting guests to go on its tours and that the nightly tequila parties it throws for its two properties—Margarita's is the other one—can get quite noisy. Rates include breakfast and dinner. ⊠ *Calle Chapultepec, 1 block off Av. López Mateos, 33200,* ☎ *145/6–02–45 or 145/6–00–45. 26 rooms. Restaurant, bar. No credit cards.*

Nightlife

When the sun goes down in Creel, head to **Laylo's Lounge** (⊠ Av. López Mateos, at the west end of town, ☎ no phone), next to El Caballo Bayo restaurant. Although it stays open only until 9 PM, the **Sierra Tropico** ice-cream parlor (⊠ Av. López Mateos 27, ☎ no phone), in the middle of town, is worth a visit.

Shopping

For Tarahumara dolls and handiwork, check out **Artesanías Misión,** on the town plaza. At the west end of Avenida López Mateos, **Artesanías Victoria** sells huge Tarahumara pots and handmade wood furniture. The gift shop in **Casa de las Artesanías,** an excellent museum (on the plaza) focusing on traditional Tarahumara life, including a beautiful exhibit of black-and-white photographs, has Tarahumara crafts and dolls.

Batopilas

❻ *80 km (50 mi) southeast of Creel.*

This remote village of about 800 people was once one of the wealthiest towns in Mexico because of the nearby veins of silver mined on and off from the time of the conquistadores. At one time it was the only place in the country besides Mexico City that had electricity. The hair-raising, 80-km (50-mi) ride down dusty, unpaved roads to the now-sleepy town at the bottom of Batopilas Canyon takes about 5½ hours by car from Creel (closer to seven hours on the local bus, which runs back and forth every day except Sunday). Sights in this lush, flower-filled oasis include the ruined **hacienda of Alexander Shepherd,** built in the late 1800s by one of the town's wealthiest mine owners; the original **aqueduct,** which still services the town (it's set along the Camino Real); and a triple-dome 17th-century **cathedral,** mysteriously isolated in the Satevo Valley on a scenic 6½-km (4-mi) hike from town. Because it takes much of a day to get down to Batopilas, you'll need to stay overnight at one of the town's modest posadas or at the quirkily opulent Copper Canyon Riverside Lodge.

Lodging

$ ☒ **Copper Canyon Riverside Lodge.** The sprawling grounds of three
★ connected and restored late-19th-century haciendas are filled with all sorts of delicious nooks and crannies to explore. Each of the high-ceiling rooms is individually decorated, but all have spacious private baths and huge feather duvets. Only partially wired for electricity, the accommodations have an odd mix of kerosene reading lamps and electrical outlets for hair dryers. The gourmet meals are excellent. Rooms are usually booked as part of an all-inclusive package deal with a sister lodge in Cusárare, but walk-ins are welcome when space permits. Rates include all meals. ✉ *Batopilas,* FAX *145/6–00–36. (Copper Canyon Lodges, 2741 Paldan, Auburn Hills, MI 48326,* ☎ *248/340–7230 or 800/776–3942,* WEB *www.sierratrail.com.) 14 rooms. Restaurant. No credit cards.*

Cuauhtémoc

❼ *128 km (79 mi) northeast of Creel, 105 km (65 mi) southwest of Chihuahua.*

A rather anomalous experience in Mexico is a visit to **Campos Menonitas,** a large Mennonite community in Cuauhtémoc. Some 20,000 Mennonites came to the San Antonio Valley in 1922 at the invitation of President Alvaro Obregón, who gave them the right to live freely and autonomously in return for farming the 247,000 acres of land.

You can set up a tour in Cuauhtémoc at Mennonite David Friesen's travel agency, Cumbres Friesen (✉ Calle 3A No. 466, ☎ 158/2–54–57, FAX 158/2–40–60), or in Chihuahua.

Chihuahua City

❽ *375 km (233 mi) south of the El Paso–Ciudad Juárez border, 1,440 km (893 mi) northwest of Mexico City.*

If you're arriving from the peaceful Copper Canyon, the sprawling city of Chihuahua with nearly 1 million inhabitants might come as a bit of a jolt. But, then, the city is known for its jolting nature—two of Mexico's most famous revolutionaries are closely tied to Chihuahua. The father of Mexican independence, Father Miguel Hidalgo, and his co-conspirators were executed here by the Spanish in 1811. And Chihuahua was home to General Pancho Villa. His revolutionary army, the División del Norte (Army of the North), was decisive in overthrowing dictator Porfirio Díaz in 1910 and securing victory in the ensuing civil war. A half-century earlier, Benito Juárez, known as the Abraham Lincoln of Mexico, made Chihuahua his base when the French invaded the country in 1865.

Whatever you do, don't miss the Museo Histórico de la Revolución en el Estado de Chihuahua, better known as **Pancho Villa's House.** Villa lived in this 1909 mansion, also called the "Quinta Luz" (*quinta* can mean "mansion"), with his second wife, Luz Corral. She stayed here until her death on June 6, 1981, willing the residence to the government. The 50 small rooms that used to board Villa's bodyguards now house a vast array of artifacts of Chihuahua's cultural and revolutionary history. Parked in the museum's courtyard is the bullet-ridden 1919 Dodge in which Villa was assassinated in 1923 at the age of 45. ⊠ *Calle Décima 3010,* ☎ *14/16–29–58.* 🎫 *$1.* ☉ *Tues.–Sat. 9–1 and 3–7, Sun. 9–5.*

The **Catedral,** on the town's central square, is also worth a visit. Construction on this beautiful baroque structure was started by the Jesuits in 1726 and not completed until 1825 because of local Indian uprisings. The opulent church has Carrara marble altars, a 24-karat solid-gold ceiling, a cedar-and-brass depiction of Saints Peter and Paul, and a huge German-made organ. In the back of the cathedral, the **Museum of Sacred Art** displays the work of seven local artists of the 18th-century Mexican baroque tradition. ⊠ *Plaza de la Constitución,* ☎ *no phone.* 🎫 *50¢.* ☉ *Weekdays 10–2 and 4–6.*

The **Palacio de Gobierno** (State Capitol) was built by the Jesuits as a convent in 1882. Converted into government offices in 1891, it was destroyed by a fire in the early 1940s and rebuilt in 1947. Murals around the patio depict famous episodes from the history of the state of Chihuahua. A plaque commemorates the spot where Father Hidalgo was executed on the morning of July 30, 1811. ⊠ *Plaza Hidalgo,* ☎ *14/10–63–24.* 🎫 *Free.* ☉ *Daily 8–8.*

The **Palacio Federal** (Federal Building) houses the city's main post office and telegraph office, as well as the dungeon where Hidalgo was imprisoned before he was executed by the Spanish. His pistols, traveler's trunk, crucifix, and reproductions of his letters are on display here. ⊠ *Calle Libertad around the corner from Plaza Hidalgo,* ☎ *no phone.* 🎫 *Free.* ☉ *Tues.–Sun. 9–7.*

The 1721 **Iglesia de San Francisco** (San Francisco Church) is the oldest church built in Chihuahua that is still standing. Father Hidalgo's decapitated body was interred in the chapel of this simple church from 1811 to 1827, when it was sent to Mexico City. His head was publicly displayed for 10 years by Spanish Royalists in Guanajuato on the Alhóndiga de Granaditas. ⊠ *Av. Libertad at Calle 15,* ☎ *no phone.* 🎫 *Free.* ☉ *Daily 7–7.*

Slightly outside the center of town but well worth a visit is the Cultural Center of the University of Chihuahua, known as **Quinta Gameros.** This hybrid French Second Empire–Art Nouveau mansion, with stained-glass windows, ornate wooden staircases, rococo plaster wall panels, and lavish ironwork, was built in 1910 by Julio Corredor, a Colombian architect, for Manuel Gameros, a wealthy mining engineer. Here you'll see European art of the past two centuries as well as changing exhibitions ranging from Mennonite crafts to contemporary art. ⊠ *Calle Bolívar 401,* ☎ *14/16–66–84.* 🎫 *About $2.* ☉ *Tue.–Sun. 10–2 and 4–7.*

Not to be confused with the University Cultural Center, the **Chihuahua Cultural Center** displays exquisite Paquimé ceramics from the pre-

Columbian settlement of Casas Grandes northwest of Chihuahua. ✉ *Aldama and Ocampo,* ☎ *14/16–13–36.* ✆ *Free.* ☉ *Tues.–Sun. 10–2 and 4–7.*

A restoration project has made the site of the town's original settlement, **Santa Eulalia,** particularly appealing. The 30-minute drive southeast of town, about $10 one-way by taxi (less by bus), is repaid by the colonial architecture and cobblestone streets of this village, which was founded in 1652. Tours of local silver mines can be arranged by guides in town. The religious artwork in the 18th-century cathedral is noteworthy.

OFF THE
BEATEN PATH

CASAS GRANDES – Some 350 km (161 mi) northwest of Chihuahua, the twin towns of Nuevo Casas Grandes and Casas Grandes are the gateways to the ancient area known as Paquimé, recently declared a UNESCO World Heritage site. Nuevo Casas Grandes, a two-horse town with wide, dusty streets and cowboys en regalia, has the hotels and most of the local restaurants. Sleepy Casas Grandes, 8 km (5 mi) away, occupies a single square block.

Near the aspen-lined Casas Grandes River, sheltered by the burnt-sienna peaks of the Sierra Madre Occidental, Paquimé was inhabited by Pima, Concho, and Tolima peoples between AD 700 and 1500. A key site poised between the Pueblo cultures of the now-American southwest and their Mesoamerican neighbors—with architecture borrowed from each—Paquimé was a cosmopolitan center for trade whose residents raised fowl and manufactured jewelry. Evidence of their worldliness still stands, in the form of heat-shielding walls and intricate indoor plumbing systems. The high-tech museum on site houses Paquimé artifacts and ceramics and has bilingual descriptions of local cultural, religious, and economic practices. ✆ *Museum $1.* ☉ *Tues.–Sat. 10–6, Sun. 11–5.*

In Nuevo Casas Grandes, **Restaurante Constantino** (✉ Juárez, across from Hotel Paquimé, ☎ 169/4–10–05) makes great enchiladas and has a full breakfast menu. In Casas Grandes, **El Pueblo** (✉ off Juárez, ☎ no phone) draws residents from all around with great food (no breakfast) and a full bar. **Motel Piñon** (✉ Juárez 605, Nuevo Casas Grandes, ☎ 169/4–06–55) has a swimming pool and a private collection of ancient *ollas* (clay pots) from Paquimé. **Motel Hacienda** (✉ Juárez 2603, Nuevo Casas Grandes, ☎ 169/4–10–46) has 124 rooms and is considered one of the best places to stay in the city.

Omnibus de México makes the 5½-hour trip from Chihuahua to Nuevo Casas Grandes (about $15). To get to the ruins, hop a blue-and-gold CASAS GRANDES bus (30¢) at Constitución and 16 de Septiembre. After 15 minutes, get off at Casas Grandes' *zócalo* (main square). Paquimé is a 10-minute walk from town—follow the PAQUIMÉ sign on Constitución. The last bus returns to Nuevo Casas Grandes at 9 PM.

Dining and Lodging

$$$ ✕ **La Calesa.** A large, dimly lit room with wood paneling and red tablecloths and curtains, this looks like the classic steak house it is. The filet mignon and rib-eye steaks from the area are particularly recommended as entrées; try the former cooked with mushrooms. ✉ *Av. Juárez 3300,* ☎ *14/10–10–38 or 14/16–02–22. AE, MC, V.*

$$ ✕ **Rincon Mexicano.** The folks who run the Mesón de Santa Eulalia restaurant in Santa Eulalia also serve some of the best Mexican food in Chihuahua and always have mariachi musicians to serenade you. ✉ *Av. Cuauhtémoc 224,* ☎ *14/11–14–27. AE, MC, V.*

$ ✕ **Ah Chiles.** If you like it hot, this is the spot. A block from Plaza Hidalgo, this Chihuahua chain serves *norteño* (northern Mexican) food and dishes out a dozen different salsas. It also has foot-long hot dogs, hot wings, stuffed baked potatoes, and shrimp burgers. Ah Chiles is next to three other worthy, modestly priced restaurants: Ricky's Tacos, 1000 Tortas, and El Burro Seguido. ⊠ *Aldama 712, corner of Guerrero,* ☎ *14/37–09–77. No credit cards.*

$ ✕ **La Casa de Los Milagros.** According to locals, this blue house with frilly white trim was once the favorite "Casa de Muñecas" (dollhouse) of Pancho Villa and his compañeros. Today it's the happening place for light Mexican snacks, drinks, and music after 9 PM, when the courtyard and rooms of this rambling abode start to fill with well-heeled, twentysomething Chihuahuans. ⊠ *Victoria 812, near Ocampo,* ☎ *14/37–06–93. AE, MC, V.*

$$$ ☷ **Holiday Inn Hotel & Suites.** This appealing property combines com-
★   fort, style, and convenience: 10 minutes from the downtown sights, Chihuahua's first all-suites hotel is decorated in contemporary style. Each room has a kitchenette with stove, dishwasher, and coffeemaker, as well as a VCR. A complimentary Continental breakfast buffet is served at the Clubhouse. The English-speaking staff is friendly and helpful. ⊠ *Escudero 702, 31000,* ☎ *14/39–00–00 or 01–800/009–9900,* 𝔽𝔸𝕏 *14/14–33–13. 74 suites. Restaurant, 2 pools, spa, basketball, exercise room. AE, DC, MC, V.*

$$$ ☷ **Westin Soberano Chihuahua.** At the edge of town atop a rise that has magnificent views of the city and surrounding mountains, Chihuahua's first *gran turismo* (Mexico's highest quality level) hotel sparkles with fountains and marble. Designed around an atrium with a several-story waterfall cascading down one wall, the hotel is a contemporary palace of sorts in contrast to the rustic accommodations of the Copper Canyon. Rooms are plush, with richly patterned textiles, comfortable furniture, TV in a tall chest, and bath with both tub and shower. ⊠ *Barranca del Cobre 3211, Fracc. Barrancas, 31125,* ☎ *14/29–29–29 or 01–888/625–5144,* 𝔽𝔸𝕏 *14/29–29–00. 194 rooms, 10 suites. 2 restaurants, bar, pool, health club, tennis court, meeting room, car rental. AE, DC, MC, V.*

$$ ☷ **Hotel San Francisco.** A favorite of Mexican business travelers, this modern five-story hotel has a prime location right next to the Catedral and Plaza de Armas. Its clean and comfortable if rather bland rooms are equipped with color TVs and phones. The lobby, somewhat gloomy during the day, can be lively at night. ⊠ *Victoria 409, 31000,* ☎ *14/16–75–50, 01–800/71–41–107, or 800/847–2546,* 𝔽𝔸𝕏 *14/15–35–38. 111 rooms, 20 suites. Restaurant, bar. AE, MC, V.*

$$ ☷ **Palacio del Sol.** This five-star hotel, just two blocks from the cathe-
★   dral, is set up for businesspeople staying long term: all rooms include such luxuries as computer ports and a radio. Although convenient to downtown and very comfortable, it lacks the Mexican charm of some lesser-quality hotels. ⊠ *Independencia 116,* ☎ *14/16–60–00, 01–800/71–14–007, or 800/852–4049,* 𝔽𝔸𝕏 *14/16–08–66. 152 rooms, 26 suites. 2 restaurants, lobby bar, exercise room, coin laundry, laundry service, meeting room, car rental. AE, DC, MC, V.*

$ ☷ **Posada Tierra Blanca.** Across the street from the Palacio del Sol but considerably less expensive, this modern motel-style property is convenient to downtown sights. Rooms, decorated in red and black with pseudo-antique furnishings, are large and well heated in winter; all have TVs. ⊠ *Niños Heroes 102,* ☎ *14/15–00–00,* 𝔽𝔸𝕏 *14/16–00–63. 98 rooms, 5 suites. Restaurant, piano bar, pool. AE, MC, V.*

Nightlife and the Arts

Chihuahua has the most nightlife options in the Copper Canyon area. **La Casa de Los Milagros** starts to groove after 9 PM. At **Hotel Sicomoro** (✉ Blvd. Ortiz Mena 411, ☎ 14/13–54–45), there's live entertainment nightly in the lobby bar. Compared with dance clubs, **El Leñador** (✉ Avs. Tecnologico and Pascual Orozco, ☎ no phone) offers a more tranquil scene, with Mexican and Cuban folksingers.

The hotel **Posada Tierra Blanca** has a piano bar. **La Reggae** (✉ Blvd. Ortiz Mena and Bosque de la Reina, ☎ 14/15–47–55) draws a dancing crowd with its rock-and-roll bands. **Taberna La Cerveceria** (✉ Av. Juárez 3333, ☎ 14/15–83–80) is a glass-encased, neon-laced restaurant and bar in a four-story former brewery where you can play pool or dance to a DJ.

Shopping

Across the street from the *calabozo* (calaboose) where Father Hidalgo was jailed, the **Casa de las Artesanías del Estado de Chihuahua** (✉ Av. Juárez 705, ☎ 14/37–12–92) carries the best selection of Tarahumara and regional crafts in the state. **Mercado de Artesanías** (✉ Calle Victoria 506 and Aldama 511, ☎ 14/15–34–62), a block wide with two entrances, sells everything from jewelry, candy, and T-shirts to crafts from all over the region. In addition to selling gems and geodes from the area, the **Rock Shop** (✉ Calle Décima, directly across from Pancho Villa's home, ☎ 14/15–28–82) carries a wide variety of crafts.

COPPER CANYON/CHIHUAHUA A TO Z

To research prices, get advice from other travelers, and book travel arrangements, visit www.fodors.com.

AIR TRAVEL

You can either fly into Chihuahua or Los Mochis from Los Angeles, Tuscon, Mexico City, or other major U.S. and Mexican cities.

CARRIERS

Aeroméxico and its feeder airline, Aerolitoral, have daily flights to Chihuahua from Los Angeles, Phoenix, and Tucson, and from San Antonio and El Paso. Within Mexico, the airlines have daily flights from Mexico City, Monterrey, Guadalajara, and Tijuana.

AeroCalifornia has daily flights to Los Mochis from Los Angeles, Tucson, Tijuana, Mexico City, and Guadalajara. Aeroméxico and Aerolitoral fly from Los Angeles, Phoenix, Tucson, San Antonio, El Paso, Mexico City, La Paz, and Chihuahua.

➤ AIRLINES AND CONTACTS: **AeroCalifornia** (☎ 68/18–16–16 in Los Mochis). **Aeroméxico** (✉ Paseo Bolívar 405, next to Quinta Gameros, Chihuahua, ☎ 14/15–63–03 in Chihuahua; 68/15–25–70 in Los Mochis).

BOAT AND FERRY TRAVEL

The Sematur car ferry runs Monday, Wednesday, and Friday from La Paz to Topolobampo, depending on the weather. It leaves La Paz at 10 PM and arrives in Topolobampo at approximately 8 AM. The return trip leaves at 10 PM and arrives in La Paz at 7 AM. In Los Mochis, contact the travel agency Festival Tour for information and reservations. In Topolobampo, contact Sematur.

➤ BOAT AND FERRY INFORMATION: **Festival Tour** (✉ Allende Sur 655, below Hotel Americas, Los Mochis, ☎ 68/18–39–86). **Sematur** (☎ 12/5–23–66, 12/5–88–99, 12/5–23–46, or 800/696–9600, FAX 68/62–00–35).

BUS TRAVEL

The Chihuahuenses and Omnibus de México lines run clean, air-conditioned buses from Ciudad Juárez to Chihuahua. These leave approximately every hour from 7 AM to 8 PM. The cost of the 4½-hour trip is approximately $20 for first class. Buses shuttle between El Paso and Ciudad Juárez every two hours; the price is $5.

The Elite and TUFESA bus lines leave every two hours from Nogales, Sonora, to Los Mochis; both charge about $35. Transportes del Pacífico leaves hourly and charges $30. With luck, the trip should take about 12 hours.

➤ BUS INFORMATION: **Chihuahuenses** (☎ 14/29–02–42 or 14/29–02–40). **Elite** (☎ 63/13–16–03 in Nogales; 68/15–00–62 in Los Mochis). **Omnibus de México** (☎ 14/20–15–80). **Transportes del Pacífico** (☎ 63/13–16–06 in Nogales; 68/12–03–41 in Los Mochis). **TUFESA** (☎ 63/13–38–62 in Nogales).

CAR RENTAL

Avis, Budget, and Hertz all have offices at the airport in Chihuahua. Car companies at the airport in Los Mochis and in town include AGA, Budget, and Hertz.

➤ MAJOR AGENCIES: **AGA** (✉ Av. Leyva and Callejón Municipal, Los Mochis, ☎ 68/12–53–60). **Avis** (✉ Av. Universidad 1703, Chihuahua, ☎ 14/14–19–99). **Budget** (✉ Ortiz Mena 3322, Chihuahua, ☎ 14/14–21–71; ✉ G. Prieto 850 Nte., Los Mochis, ☎ 68/15–83–00, FAX 68/15–84–00). **Hertz** (✉ Av. Revolución 514, Chihuahua, ☎ 14/16–64–73; ✉ Av. Leyva 171 Nte., Los Mochis, ☎ 68/12–11–22, FAX 68/15–19–29).

CAR TRAVEL

Most U.S. and Canadian visitors drive to Chihuahua via Mexico Highway 45 from the El Paso–Ciudad Juárez border, a distance of 375 km (233 mi), or up from Mexico City, 1,440 km (893 mi). The drive down to Los Mochis from Nogales on the Arizona border via Mexico Highway 15, four lanes much of the way, is 763 km (473 mi).

Paved roads connect Chihuahua to Creel and Divisadero: take Mexico Highway 16 west to San Pedro, then State Highway 127 south to Creel. The 300-km (186-mi) trip takes 3½–4 hours in good weather. This drive, through the pine forests of the Sierra Madre foothills, is more scenic than the railroad route via the plains area. Driving is a good option if you have a four-wheel-drive vehicle, because there are many worthwhile, if difficult, excursions into the canyons from Creel. From Divisadero to Bahuichivo, the dirt road is full of potholes and especially dangerous in rain or snow.

EMERGENCIES

To contact the police in Chihuahua or Los Mochis dial 06. In case of a medical emergency, contact the Red Cross (*Cruz Roja*) or the local hospital or clinic in Chihuahua. In case of a fire, contact the local fire department *Bomberos*.

Chihuahua has an abundance of pharmacies with late-night service in the city center. Farmacia Mendoza is open 24 hours. Farmacia San Jorge has two stores in Los Mochis that are open 24 hours.

➤ CONTACTS: **Bomberos** (☎ 68/12–01–00 in Los Mochis; 14/10–07–70 in Chihuahua). **Cruz Roja** (✉ Guillermo Prieto and Tenochtitlán, Los Mochis, ☎ 68/15–08–08 or 68/18–64–64 in Los Mochis; 14/11–14–84 or 14/11–22–11 in Chihuahua).

➤ HOSPITALS: **Clínica del Parque** (✉ Calle de la Llave and Leal Rodriguez, Chihuahua, ☎ 14/15–74–11 or 14/15–73–39). **Hospital del Centro del**

Estado (✉ Calle 33 and Rosales, Chihuahua, ☎ 14/15–47–20 or 14/15–90–00).

➤ 24-HOUR PHARMACIES: **Farmacia Mendoza** (✉ Calle Aldama 1901, Chihuahua, ☎ 14/16–44–14 or 14/10–27–96). **Farmacia San Jorge** (✉ Av. Independencia and Angel Flores, Los Mochis, ☎ 68/15–74–74; ✉ Degollado and Juárez, Los Mochis, ☎ 68/18–18–19).

MONEY MATTERS

Be sure to change money before you get into real barranca country: there are no banks in Cerocahui, Divisadero, or Posada Barrancas, and no guarantee that the hotels in those places will have enough cash to accommodate you. A bank in the main plaza at Creel transacts foreign exchanges from 10:30 to noon only, though it is equipped with a cash machine. In Los Mochis, most banking hours are weekdays between 8:30 and 4:30; some banks open Saturday morning. In Chihuahua, most banks open weekdays from 9 to 1:30 and from 3:30 to 7:30, and Saturday from 9 to 1:30. Banco Bital in downtown Chihuahua is open Monday through Saturday 8–8. The Casa de Cambio Rachasa, open Monday through Saturday 9–9, Sunday 9–2, has good exchange rates and quick service. In El Fuerte, Bancomer is open Monday through Saturday 8:30–3. In Creel, there's a Serfín just across from the train station. It's open weekdays 9–3 and, more importantly, it has a 24-hour ATM that accepts Cirrus and Plus system cards. Hotels have slightly lower exchange rates but charge no commission, and you normally won't have to wait in line.

➤ BANKS: **Banco Bital** (✉ Libertad 1922, Chihuahua, ☎ 14/16–08–80). **Bancomer** (✉ Constitución and Juárez, El Fuerte). **Casa de Cambio Rachasa** (✉ Av. Ocampo and Niños Heroes, Chihuahua, ☎ 14/10–03–33). **Serfín** (✉ Creel, ☎ 145/6–00–71).

TAXIS

In Chihuahua and Los Mochis, taxis are easy to find and can be engaged at hotels or hailed on the street. The trip from the airport into town costs about $6 in Chihuahua and $12 in Los Mochis. Always agree on a price before getting into the cab.

TOURS

Most large hotels in Los Mochis and Chihuahua have in-house travel agencies that arrange city tours and tours of the Copper Canyon area, as well as hiking, hunting, and fishing expeditions. In Los Mochis, the Hotel Santa Anita offers city tours for about $29 per person. In Chihuahua, independent travel agencies include the American Express agent, Rojo y Casavantes, and, particularly recommended, Turismo Al Mar. In Cuauhtémoc, Cumbres Friesen, owned by Mennonite David Friesen, can arrange Mennonite tours.

From the United States, the oldest operator in the area is Pan American Tours. Prices for tailor-made tours between Los Mochis and Chihuahua range from about $300 to $700 per person, depending on length of stay and number of stops made. Synergy Tours runs individual and group trips about 10 times a year, including off-the-beaten-path treks. California Native runs a seven-day escorted trip through the Copper Canyon every month that starts at $1,690, and also has deluxe excursions. A good tour operator who will book horseback-riding tours through the Copper Canyon is Native Trails.

➤ TOUR OPERATOR RECOMMENDATIONS: **California Native** (✉ 6701 W. 87th Pl., Los Angeles, CA 90045, ☎ 800/926–1140). **Cumbres Friesen** (✉ Calle 3A No. 466, Cuauhtémoc, ☎ 158/2–54–57, FAX 158/2–40–60). **Native Trails** (✉ 6440 Airport Rd., Suite C, El Paso, TX 79925, ☎ 800/884–3107). **Pan American Tours** (✉ Box 9401, El Paso, TX

79984, ☎ 915/778–5395 or 800/876–3942). **Rojo y Casavantes** (⊠ Calle Vincent Guerrero 1207, ☎ 14/15–58–58 or 14/15–74–70, FAX 14/15–53–84). **Synergy Tours** (⊠ 7336 E. Shoeman La., Suite 120, Scottsdale, AZ 85251, ☎ 800/569–1797, FAX 602/994–4439). **Turismo Al Mar** (⊠ Calle Verna 2202, ☎ FAX 14/16–65–89, ☎ 14/16–59–50).

TRAIN TOURS

Sierra Madre Express of Tucson runs its own deluxe trains (with dome/dining and Pullman cars) to the Copper Canyon from Tucson on eight-day, seven-night trips about four times a year. Its trips combine the charm of sleeping on the train with first-class accommodations. The luxury train South Orient Express offers all-inclusive "rail cruises"—in dome, dining/lounge, and Pullman cars—from Chihuahua and Los Mochis in spring and fall (and from Fort Worth twice a year), starting at $1,599 per person for a five-day trip. The company also has individual trips year-round on its slightly less luxurious "VSP" train, ranging from transportation only ($175 one-way between Chihuahua and Los Mochis with unlimited stops) to packages with lodging, meals, and sightseeing.

➤ FEES AND SCHEDULES: **Sierra Madre Express of Tucson** (⊠ Box 26381, Tucson, AZ 85726, ☎ 520/747–0346 or 800/666–0346, WEB www.sierramadreexpress.com). **South Orient Express** (⊠ 16800 Greenspoint Park Dr., Suite 245 N, Houston, TX 77060, ☎ 800/659–7602, WEB www.southorientexpress.com).

TRAIN TRAVEL

There is no first-class service from any U.S. border city to either Los Mochis or Chihuahua. Some luxury trains go directly from the United States to the Copper Canyon.

The Ferrocarril Chihuahua al Pacífico line (*Che'Pa'*, as it is affectionately called by locals) runs a first-class and a second-class train daily in each direction from Chihuahua and Los Mochis through the Copper Canyon. For long-term reservations and price information, your best bet may be using one of the private train companies or tour operators.

The first-class train departs from Los Mochis at 6 AM (sit on the right side of the train for the best views) and arrives in Chihuahua 15 hours later. Westbound, it departs from Chihuahua at 6 AM and arrives in Los Mochis around 8 PM (most of the time, but delays of three hours or more are not unusual). You can buy tickets at the train station or at almost any hotel in Los Mochis or Chihuahua. The price is about $100 each way, plus a 15% charge for up to two stopovers en route, which you should arrange when you buy tickets. Make reservations at least a week in advance during the busy months of July, August, and October, and around Christmas and Easter. It's best to book through a hotel, tour company, or travel agency, as the phones in the local train stations are rarely answered. Keep in mind that it's the scenery, not the vehicle, that continues to draw passengers. Guards armed with automatic weapons often patrol the passenger cars to discourage robberies. Exercise caution by carrying passports and cash in a money belt and leaving your jewelry at home. Bring your own food and drink, as there is no guarantee that even on the first-class train there will be any for sale.

The second-class train, *El Pollero,* leaves an hour later from each terminus but makes many stops and is scheduled to arrive 3½ hours later in both directions than the first-class train. Although it is less comfortable, this train is a good way to meet local residents and their poultry. No reservations are needed; prices are approximately $9 each way.

If you're driving down to Los Mochis, you're better off leaving your car there and taking the train round-trip. If you're coming via Chihuahua, however, consider driving to Creel or Divisadero and doing a round-trip from there.

➤ TRAIN INFORMATION: **Ferrocarril Chihuahua al Pacífico** (☎ 14/39–72–10 in Chihuahua; 68/24–11–67 in Los Mochis; 01–800/367–3900 for general information; 888/416–5420, FAX 14/10–90–59 in Chihuahua; 68/15–77–75 in Los Mochis).

VISITOR INFORMATION

The Government Tourist Office in Chihuahua is open weekdays 9–4, and the Oficina de Información is open Monday through Saturday 9–4. At the Oficina, Sonia Estrada, who speaks fluent English, will answer questions and help visitors (in person or over the phone) make travel arrangements all over the state.

The Oficina de Turismo in Los Mochis is in the Unidad Administrativa del Gobierno del Estado building, on the first floor, in the back.

➤ TOURIST INFORMATION: **Government Tourist Office** (✉ Av. Libertad and Calle 13, 1st floor, Chihuahua, ☎ 14/29–34–21 or 14/29–33–00, ext. 4511 or 4512). **Oficina de Información** (✉ Central patio of Palacio de Gobierno in Plaza Hidalgo, Chihuahua, ☎ 14/29–33–00, ext. 1061, or 14/10–10–77). **Oficina de Turismo** (✉ Allende and Ordoñez, Los Mochis, ☎ 68/15–10–90).

6 GUADALAJARA

INCLUDING TLAQUEPAQUE, TONALÁ, AND LAKE CHAPALA

Colonial architecture that dates to the city's heyday as the center of regional commerce is among the lures of Guadalajara, which introduced the world to mariachis, tequila, and the Mexican hat dance. On the city's outskirts, Tlaquepaque has some of Mexico's finest crafts, as does Tonalá. A near-perfect semitropical climate and proximity to the Pacific Ocean—240 km (149 mi) away—ensure warm, sunny days and cool, clear nights.

T RADITIONS ARE PRESERVED and customs perpetuated in Guadalajara; it's a place where the siesta is an institution and the fiesta an art form. Mexico's second-largest city, and the capital of the state of Jalisco, Guadalajara is engaged in a struggle to retain its provincial ambience and colonial charm as its population surpasses 7 million. Émigrés from Mexico City after the devastating 1985 earthquake and staggering numbers of the rural poor seeking employment created a population explosion that continues to strain public services and the city's often outdated infrastructure. Visitors can enjoy the tree-lined boulevards, parks, plazas, and stately churrigueresque architecture, but recent years have brought traffic jams and increasingly heavy pollution.

Updated by
Jane Onstott

Guadalajara has always been one of the most socially traditional and politically conservative cities in Mexico. It has also been a seat of Christian fundamentalism and was one of the strategic areas of the *cristeros,* a movement of Catholic zealots in western Mexico in the 1920s. Tapatíos, as the city's residents are called (the name may come from *tlapatiotl,* three units or purses of cacao or other commodities used as currency by the Indians of the area), even seem to take a certain amount of pride in their rather straight and narrow outlook.

Still, Tapatíos are historically accustomed to challenge and change. Within 10 years of its founding in 1531, the location of the city changed three times. In 1542 the City Council followed the advice of Doña Beatriz Hernández to build the city in the center of the Atemajac Valley, where it could expand. Thus Guadalajara was placed on a mile-high plain of the Sierra Madre, bounded on three sides by rugged cliffs and on the fourth by the spectacular Barranca de Oblatos (Oblatos Canyon).

Geographically remote from the rest of the republic during the nearly 300 years of Spanish rule, the city cultivated and maintained a political and cultural autonomy. By the end of the 16th century, money was flowing into Guadalajara from the rich farms and silver mines in the region, creating the first millionaires of what was then known as New Galicia. Under orders from Spain, much of the wealth was lavished on magnificent churches, residences, and monuments. Many of these reminders of the golden era still stand in downtown Guadalajara.

The suburbs of Tlaquepaque (pronounced tla-kay-*pah*-kay) and Tonalá (pronounced toe-na-*la*) produce some of Mexico's finest and most popular traditional crafts and folk art. Lake Chapala—Mexico's largest body of fresh water—and the nearby towns Chapala and Ajijic have lured retirees from the United States and Canada, who enjoy most of the amenities they were accustomed to north of the border.

Pleasures and Pastimes

Arts and Architecture

You can find all kinds of Mexican and international arts in Guadalajara—from the traditional Ballet Folklórico at the Teatro Degollado to rock groups at the Instituto Cultural Cabañas. Galleries and museums around town also offer the best of modern and traditional work. Numerous 16th-century colonial buildings fill the downtown area, connected by a series of large, Spanish-style plazas.

Churches

Guadalajara seems to have a church every block or two—there are 15 in the downtown area alone, all dating from the colonial era. Some have elaborately carved facades, and others conceal ornate Baroque altars and priceless colonial oil paintings behind sober stone exteriors.

Dining

The variety of Guadalajara's restaurants includes classic Mexican dishes, Continental delicacies, Argentine-style steaks, and fresh seafood. Savory regional specialties—often served in simpler places—include *birria,* a spicy stew prepared with goat, lamb, or beef in a light tomato broth; *pozole,* a thick pork and hominy soup; and *carne en su jugo,* consisting of steak bits in a clear spicy broth with bacon, beans, and cilantro, usually served with a side of tiny, grilled whole onions.

Lodging

Hotels run the gamut from older establishments in the downtown historic district—including one finely restored building that has been a hotel since 1610—to representatives of the large chains, most of which are on or near Avenida López Mateos Sur, a 16-km (10-mi) strip extending from the Minerva Fountain to the Plaza del Sol shopping center. In the mid-1990s several hotels were built close to the Expo-Guadalajara convention center, which opened in 1987.

Shopping

Blown glass, hand-carved wood furniture, fine leatherwork, and hand-glazed pottery are local traditions. Two of the most common ceramic techniques are *barro bruñido,* in which the pieces are hand-burnished to a soft sheen, and *petatillo,* in which glaze is applied to earthenware in a fine crosshatch pattern. Guadalajara is also home to a thriving shoe industry. At sprawling markets you can bargain for anything from embroidered shirts to huaraches, and sleek shopping malls have full-service department stores and trendy boutiques.

Sports

Highly stylized *charreadas,* traditional equestrian events with teams of elegantly clad women and men, are presented weekly, and there are bullfights in October and November. Late August through May, soccer fans crowd Estadio Jalisco (Jalisco Stadium).

EXPLORING GUADALAJARA

Metropolitan Guadalajara consists of a historic city center and nearby urban districts, including Tlaquepaque, Tonalá, and Zapopan. Just outside are the tranquil villages on Lake Chapala's receding shores.

Numbers in the text correspond to numbers in the margin and on the Downtown Guadalajara, Tlaquepaque, Tonalá, and Lake Chapala Area maps.

Great Itineraries

It's not surprising that Guadalajara has been described as *señorial y moderna* (lordly and modern). In fact, although the graciousness of colonial Mexico is still readily apparent, it now takes a back seat to 20th-century culture, for both better and worse. The once-separate satellite pueblos of Tonalá and Tlaquepaque are now the best places to feel the pulse of traditional pueblo life. Ten days would allow you to fully explore the city and villages surrounding Lago de Chapala, as well as to take an excursion or two to points farther afield. With five days to spend, you'll have time to see most of the city's highlights and to get to know Tlaquepaque, Tonalá, and the Lake Chapala area. In three days, you can take in the historic center and make day trips to Tlaquepaque and Tonalá.

IF YOU HAVE 3 DAYS

Spend your first day in the historic **centro** ①–⑪ (town center). The next day, spend the morning and have lunch in **Tlaquepaque** ㉓–㉜, and visit **Tonalá** ㉝–㉟ in the afternoon. These two towns are the best places in

Guadalajara to shop. On your third day, see more of the city sights, including an evening performance of theater or dance, or head to one of the thermal spas southwest of town.

IF YOU HAVE 5 DAYS

See **el centro** ①–⑪ on your first day, and then consider your interests. If traditional crafts or outstanding furniture and housewares lure you, devote a day to **Tlaquepaque** ㉓–㉜ and Day 3 to **Tonalá** ㉝–㉟. Alternatively, explore the two towns in one day, and leave a day to spend around **Lake Chapala** ㊵–㊹. Spend your final day back in Guadalajara in museums and the **Basílica de la Virgen de Zapopan** ⑱, for which you'll need several hours, or even the **Zoológico Guadalajara** ⑯. Plan an afternoon of strolling past the mansions that were built by Guadalajara's upper classes in the glorious twilight before the 1910 revolution; the best area is in a six-block radius around Avenida Vallarta west of Avenida Chapultepec. If you'd like to get your feet on the ground in more natural surroundings, hike in the nearby **Barranca de Oblatos.**

IF YOU HAVE 7 DAYS

You will be able to cover all of **el centro** ①–⑪ plus the other city sights, and **Tlaquepaque** ㉓–㉜, **Tonalá** ㉝–㉟, and the **Lake Chapala** area ㊵–㊹. Fill in the gaps with a visit to Tequila and a soak in the soothing thermal waters of **San Juan Cosalá,** on the shores of Lake Chapala, or one of the thermal pools around **Villa Corona,** southwest of Guadalajara.

Guadalajara

Beginning around 1960, 20th-century architecture started to threaten the aesthetic of this provincial state capital. In the early 1980s the city declared a 30-square-block area in the heart of downtown a cultural sanctuary, and in the late 1990s private-sector groups formed a trust to continue spiffing up **el centro.** The 16th-century buildings here are connected by a series of large Spanish-style plazas where children chase balloons, young lovers coo on tree-shaded park benches, and grandparents stroll hand in hand past vendors and marble fountains. At nearby **Plaza de los Mariachis,** the nostalgic songs and music of sombrero-topped troubadours fill the air.

Outside the historic center, most tourist sights and large hotels are located in three areas: near Avenida Chapultepec, near the Minerva Fountain and Los Arcos monument, and near the Plaza del Sol shopping mall and ExpoGuadalajara convention center.

A Good Walk

Guadalajara's 17th-century **Catedral** ①, on the north side of Plaza de Armas, is the place to start exploring downtown. After you've marveled at the interior, exit through the main doors and cross Avenida Alcalde to Plaza de la Ciudad de Guadalajara, with its large fountain, outdoor café, and benches scattered beneath square-cut laurel trees. To your right (with your back toward the cathedral) across Avenida Hidalgo is the **Palacio Municipal** ②, built in the mid-20th century to match surrounding buildings. The second-floor Salón Guadalajara often features cultural exhibits.

From the corner of Avenidas Alcalde and Hidalgo, head one block east to Calle Liceo, where you'll see the **Museo Regional de Guadalajara** ③. You'll pass the Rotonda de Hombres Ilustres de Jalisco, a tree-shaded square whose central colonnaded rotunda covers a mausoleum containing the remains of 17 of the state of Jalisco's most illustrious people.

After you leave the museum, you can turn either way on Calle Liceo: three blocks to your right is the **Casa-Museo López Portillo** ④ and,

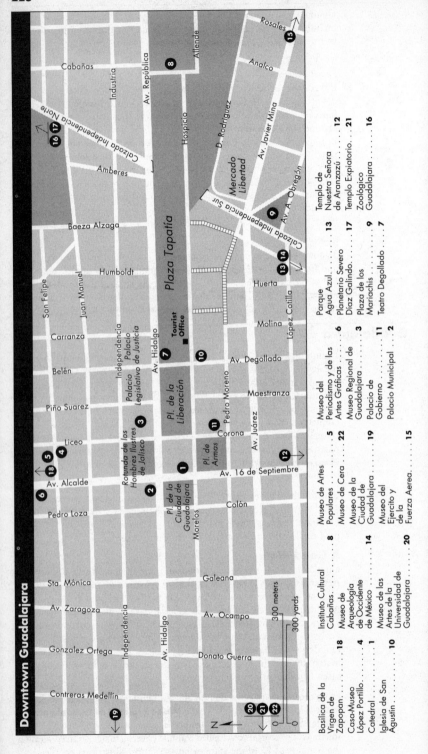

Downtown Guadalajara

Virgen de
Zopopan. **18**

Casa-Museo
López Portillo. **4**

Catedral **1**

Iglesia de San
Agustín **10**

Instituto Cultural
Cabañas. **8**

Museo de
Arqueología
de Occidente
de México **14**

Museo de las
Artes de la
Universidad de
Guadalajara **20**

Museo de Artes
Populares **5**

Museo de Cera **22**

Museo de la
Ciudad de
Guadalajara **19**

Museo del
Ejército y
de la
Fuerza Aerea. **15**

Museo del
Periodismo y de las
Artes Gráficas **6**

Museo Regional de
Guadalajara **3**

Palacio de
Gobierno **11**

Palacio Municipal . . **2**

Parque
Agua Azul. **13**

Planetario Severo
Díaz Galindo. **17**

Plaza de los
Mariachis **9**

Teatro Degollado . . **7**

Templo de
Nuestra Señora
de Aranzazú **12**

Templo Expiatorio. . **21**

Zoológico
Guadalajara **16**

around the corner on San Felipe, the **Museo de Artes Populares** ⑤, a museum of regional arts and crafts. North and west of that, on Avenida Alcalde, is the fascinating **Museo del Periodismo y de las Artes Gráficas** ⑥. Around the corner to the left of the Museo Regional, on Avenida Hidalgo, are the Palacio Legislativo—a former customs house, tobacco warehouse, and inn that today houses Jalisco's state legislature—and the Palacio de Justícia, which was built in 1588 as part of Guadalajara's first convent and now is the state courthouse. Across Avenida Hidalgo on your right sprawls the Plaza de la Liberación, at the east end of which rises the spectacular **Teatro Degollado** ⑦. Behind it begins the Plaza Tapatía, a five-block-long pedestrian mall lined with shops, trees, and whimsical sculpture. At the end, visit the **Instituto Cultural Cabañas** ⑧. Then proceed back west to the modernistic Quetzalcóatl Fountain in the center. (Too heavy for its base, the statue's 5-ton serpent head lies in one of the patios of the Instituto Cabaas.) Turn left and walk down the stairs to the sprawling **Mercado Libertad.** Turn left again when you leave the market and cross the pedestrian bridge over Avenida Javier Mina to the **Plaza de los Mariachis** ⑨.

Return to Plaza Tapatía by heading right to the intersection of Calzada Independencia Sur and Avenida Javier Mina, in front of the Iglesia de San Juan de Dios. Continue two blocks past the church and go back up the stairs. Turn left and walk west four blocks (so you can see the stores on this side of the plaza) to the **Iglesia de San Agustín** ⑩.

As you leave the church, turn left down Calle Morelos to Avenida Corona. Turn left again and walk a half block to the main entrance of the **Palacio de Gobierno** ⑪ to see two of José Clemente Orozco's murals. Exit the palacio back onto Avenida Corona (the way you came in) and cross the street to the Plaza de Armas, where you can rest on a wrought-iron bench, imagining yourself in the Porfiriato—Mexico's Victorian period—when wealthy *dons* and *doñas* strolled amid the trees and flower beds around the ornately sculpted kiosk, a gift from France in 1910. With the cathedral to your right, you've come full circle back to the north side of the plaza.

TIMING

You can take in most of downtown Guadalajara in a day or two. The sights outside of the center can easily take a half or full day each. Most museums, the zoo, and the planetarium are closed Monday. In early September Guadalajara hosts the international mariachi and tequila festival, bringing traditional troubadours from as far away as Japan and running daily train trips to Tequila, home of the fiery elixir of the same name. In October the city puts on the Fiestas de Octubre, a monthlong cultural festival that exudes a county fair–like atmosphere and is sprinkled with top-flight international entertainment.

Sights to See

⑱ **Basílica de la Virgen de Zapopan.** This vast church, with an ornate plateresque facade and *mudéjar* (Moorish) tile dome, was consecrated in 1730. It is known throughout Mexico as the home of La Zapopanita, Our Lady of Zapopan. The 10-inch-high statue is venerated as the source of many miracles in and around Guadalajara. Every October 12, more than a million people crowd the streets leading to the basilica to which the Virgin is returned after a five-month tour of parish churches throughout the state. In the right side of the basilica is the **Museo Huichol** (✉ Avs. Avila Camacho and de las Américas, ☎ no phone), a small gallery and shop with exquisite beadwork and other handicrafts by the Huichol Indians of northern Jalisco and neighboring states Zacatecas and Nayarit; it's open Mon.–Sat. 10–2 and 4–6, and Sun. 10–2. The basilica is 7 km (4½ mi) northwest of downtown. ⊠ *Av. Hidalgo at Morelos.*

④ Casa-Museo López Portillo. Guadalajara's illustrious López Portillo family included prominent writers and politicians, such as an early-20th-century Jalisco governor and his Mexico City–born grandson, José López Portillo, president of Mexico in 1976–82. As is typical of homes built by Mexico's 19th-century upper class, the plain stucco exterior belies the rich interior, where French Baroque–style rooms ring a spacious interior patio. ⊠ *Liceo 177, at San Felipe,* ☎ *3613–2411.* 🎫 *Free.* ☉ *Mon.–Sat. 9–5.*

★ **❶ Catedral.** Consecrated in 1618, this focal point of downtown is an intriguing mélange of Baroque, Gothic, and other styles, the result of design and structural modifications during its 57 years of construction. Its emblematic twin towers replaced the originals, which fell in the earthquake of 1818. Ten of the silver-and-gold altars were gifts from King Fernando VII, in appreciation of Guadalajara's financial support of Spain during the Napoleonic Wars; the 11th, of white marble, was carved in Italy in 1863. On the walls of the cathedral hang some of the world's most beautiful *retablos* (altarpieces); above the sacristy (often closed to the public) is the priceless 17th-century painting by Bartolomé Esteban Murillo, *The Assumption of the Virgin.* In a loft high above the main entrance is a magnificent late-19th-century French organ, which is played during the afternoon mass on the third Sunday of the month, and in May's organ festival. ⊠ *Av. Alcalde between Av. Hidalgo and Calle Morelos.* ☉ *Daily 8–7.*

⑩ Iglesia de San Agustín. The venerable St. Augustine Church is one of the oldest churches in the city. It has been remodeled many times since its consecration in 1574, but the sacristy is original. The building to the left of the church, originally an Augustinian cloister, is now the **Escuela de Música** (School of Music) of the University of Guadalajara. Free recitals and concerts are held on its patio. ⊠ *Calle Morelos at Av. Degollado,* ☎ *3614–5365.* ☉ *Daily 8–1 and 5–8.*

★ **❽ Instituto Cultural Cabañas.** This landmark neoclassical-style cultural center was designed by the famous Spanish architect–sculptor Manuel Tolsá. Originally a shelter for widows, the elderly, and orphans, the building was later home to 400 indigent children, until the 1970s, when the orphanage moved. The rooms, which surround 23 flower-filled patios, contain permanent and revolving art exhibitions. The central dome and walls of the main chapel display a series of murals painted by José Clemente Orozco in 1938–39, including *The Man of Fire,* widely considered to be his finest work. Room 33 has a permanent exhibition of Orozco's paintings, cartoons, and drawings. Ask the attendant at the front desk for an English-speaking guide. ⊠ *Calle Cabañas 8, at Plaza Tapatía,* ☎ *3617–4322 or 3617–4440.* 🎫 *About $1, free Sun.* ☉ *Tues.–Sat. 10–6, Sun. 10–3.*

⑭ Museo de Arqueología de Occidente de México. The Archaeological Museum of Western Mexico houses pottery and other artifacts used by ancient peoples of what are now the states of Colima, Jalisco, and Nayarit. It's across from the entrance to Parque Agua Azul. ⊠ *Av. 16 de Septiembre 889,* ☎ *3619–0104.* 🎫 *30¢.* ☉ *Daily 10–2 and 4–7.*

⑳ Museo de las Artes de la Universidad de Guadalajara. The University of Guadalajara's impressive contemporary-art museum is housed in an exquisite early-20th-century building. In addition to its permanent collection of 20th-century drawings and paintings, the museum shows revolving exhibitions of contemporary Latin American, U.S., and European work. Look for the murals Orozco painted upon returning to

Guadalajara at age 53. ⊠ *Lopez Cotilla 930 at Diaz de Leon,* ☎ *3826–6114.* 🎟 *$1.* ☯ *Tues.–Sun. 10:30–6:30.*

⑤ Museo de Artes Populares. Regional folk art and handmade housewares are displayed and sold in this new museum behind the López Portillo family museum. ⊠ *San Felipe, between Liceo and Av. Alcalde,* ☎ *3614–3891.* 🎟 *50¢.* ☯ *Tues.–Sun. 11–5.*

👆 ㉒ Museo de Cera. At Guadalajara's 120-figure wax museum, now in the historic downtown area across from Plaza de la Liberación, go eye-to-eye with Madonna, Mahatma Gandhi, beloved Mexican comic Cantinflas, and a host of other Mexican and international political and artistic luminaries. Visit the underground Aztec sacrificial chamber and a chamber of horrors. A wax mariachi, playing "Guadalajara Guadalajara," greets you at the door. Next door, with the same phone and address, is the Ripley's Believe-It-Or-Not Museum. ⊠ *Calle Morelos 217,* ☎ *3614–8487.* 🎟 *$2.* ☯ *Daily 11–8.*

⑲ Museo de la Ciudad de Guadalajara. In a series of rooms surrounding the tranquil interior patio of this spacious remodeled colonial home, you'll find informative artwork, artifacts, and reproductions of documents about the city's development from pre-Hispanic times through the 20th century. ⊠ *Calle Independencia 684, between Contreras Medellín and Mariano Bárcenas,* ☎ *3658–2531 or 3658–3706.* 🎟 *30¢, free Sun.* ☯ *Wed.–Sat. 10–5:30, Sun. 10–2:30.*

⑮ Museo del Ejercito y de la Fuerza Aerea. Housed in *el Cuartel Colorado,* an old army barracks, this army and air force museum has photos and relics from Mexican wars dating back to the Aztec conquest. The collection of six old planes includes those entirely or partially built in Mexico. Exhibits are labeled in Spanish only. ⊠ *Gómez Farias 600, between Calzada del Ejercito and Riva Palacio,* ☎ *3618–3974.* 🎟 *Free.* ☯ *Tues.–Sat. 10–6, Sun. 10–4.*

⑥ Museo del Periodismo y de las Artes Gráficas. In 1792 Guadalajara's first printing press was set up on this site, where today you can see displays of historic newspapers, printing presses, recording equipment, and a complete television studio. The building, a fine old mansion, has long been known as the Casa de los Perros because of the two wrought-iron dogs (*perros*) "guarding" the roof. ⊠ *Av. Alcalde 225, between Reforma and San Felipe,* ☎ *3613–9286.* 🎟 *About 50¢.* ☯ *Tues.–Sat. 10–6, Sun. 10:30–5.*

★ ③ Museo Regional de Guadalajara. Constructed as a seminary and public library in 1701, this distinguished building has been home to the Regional Museum (also known as the State Museum) since 1918. The first-floor galleries, which surround a garden courtyard, contain artifacts and memorabilia that trace the history of western Mexico from prehistoric times through the Spanish conquest; there are also revolving exhibitions of art and crafts. On the second-floor balcony are five 19th-century carriages; the galleries here offer an impressive collection of paintings by European and Mexican artists, including Bartolomé Esteban Murillo. ⊠ *Liceo 60,* ☎ *3614–9957.* 🎟 *About $1.60, free Tues.* ☯ *Tues.–Sat. 9–5:45, Sun. 9–3:45.*

⑪ Palacio de Gobierno. Built first of adobe in 1643, this churrigueresque and neoclassical stone structure was begun in the 18th century. Within are Jalisco's state government offices and two of José Clemente Orozco's most passionate murals. The mural just past the entrance, in the stairwell to the right, depicts a gigantic Father Miguel Hidalgo looming amid shadowy figures—including the Pope, Hitler, and Mussolini—representing oppression and slavery. The other mural, in the former state-legislature quarters on the upper level, portrays Juárez and other figures of the 1850s Reform era. ✉ *Av. Corona between Calle Morelos and Pedro Moreno.* ⊙ *Daily 9–8:45.*

② **Palacio Municipal.** Guadalajara's city hall was designed and built in 1952 with an arched facade and interior patios to fit in with neighboring buildings. Inside are colorful murals of the city's founding, painted by Guadalajara native Gabriel Flores. ✉ *Av. Hidalgo at Av. Alcalde.* ⊙ *Daily 9–8.*

⑬ **Parque Agua Azul.** Amid acres of trees and flowers, this popular park has carnival rides, tropical birds in cages, an orchid house, and a geodesic dome covering a semitropical garden. Next to the park entrance, the small **Teatro Experimental** (☎ 3619–1176) is a venue for plays in Spanish for adolescents and adults, as well as for chamber music and other cultural events. The **Museo de la Paleontología** (✉ Dr. R. Michel 520 at González Gallo, ☎ 3619–7043), on the southeast side of the park, displays regional animal and plant fossils and mammoth bones as well as exhibits—some hands-on for kids—on the origin of the planet. Free guided tours are offered at 11, 12:30, and 4:30; with advance notice English-language guides are available. ✉ *Calzada Independencia Sur, between González Gallo and Las Palmas,* ☎ *3619–0328 or 3619–0332.* 🎟 *60¢.* ⊙ *Tues.–Sat. 10–6, Sun. 11–6.*

⑰ **Planetario Severo Díaz Galindo.** A modern facility with astronomy shows and aeronautical displays, the planetarium also has exhibits that allow children to test the forces and laws of nature, and a new display of some 40 antique cars. Six km (4 mi) northeast of downtown, it's part of the zoo complex. ✉ *Anillo Periférico Manuel Gómez Morín 401, east of Calzada Independencia,* ☎ *3674–4106 or 3674–3978.* 🎟 *Museum 20¢, astronomy show and movie 40¢.* ⊙ *Wed.–Sun. 10–7.*

★ ⑨ **Plaza de los Mariachis.** Experience the most Mexican of music in this picturesque little plaza surrounded by honky-tonks, where strolling mariachi groups perform for paying customers. Mariachi serenades are about $4 a song. Although the action lasts all night, it's safer to visit during the day or early evening. Use the pedestrian overpass from the Mercado Libertad to avoid the heavy traffic. ✉ *Calzada Independencia Sur, between Av. Javier Mina and Alvaro Obregón.*

★ ⑦ **Teatro Degollado.** Inaugurated in 1866, this magnificent theater was modeled after Milan's La Scala. Above the Corinthian columns gracing the entrance is a relief depicting Apollo and the nine Muses. Inside, the recently refurbished theater has kept its traditional red-and-gold color scheme, and the balconies ascend to a multitier dome adorned with Gerardo Suárez's depiction of Dante's *Divine Comedy.* The theater is the permanent home for the Jalisco Philharmonic and the Ballet Folklórico of the University of Guadalajara and hosts visiting orchestras, plays, and numerous other performances.

According to tradition, Guadalajara was founded on the site of what is now the **Plaza de los Fundadores,** which flanks the east side of the theater. A sculpted frieze on the rear wall of the Teatro Degollado depicts the historic event. ✉ *Av. Degollado, between Av. Hidalgo and Calle Morelos,* ☎ *3614–4773 or 3613–1115.* ⊙ *Weekdays 10–2.*

NEED A
BREAK?
A signature pink-and-white color scheme heralds the city's most popular ice-cream chain. A stop at **Helados Bing** (✉ on the north side of Plaza Tapatía, east of the Quetzalcóatl Fountain) provides a welcome respite from an afternoon of sightseeing. Choose from more than 20 flavors of pasteurized ice cream and ices, and relax on a shaded bench.

⑫ **Templo de Nuestra Señora de Aranzazú.** Don't be fooled by Our Lady of Aranzazú's drab brown stone exterior: inside is a spectacular Baroque gilt altar whose 14 niches contain life-size statues of saints. The walls' and ceilings' intricate floral details are painted in various hues and shades of blues, reds, and greens. The church is on the west side of Parque San Francisco, a small green oasis that draws food vendors, families, and senior citizens. ⊠ *Av. 16 de Septiembre and Prisciliano Sánchez,* ☎ *3614–4083.* ☉ *Weekdays 10–2 and 4–7, Sat. 10–2, Sun. 11:30–8:30.*

㉑ **Templo Expiatorio.** Behind the museum, on Avenida Lopez Cotilla, the Church of Atonement is a striking Gothic structure. Modeled after the Orvieto Cathedral in Italy, it has a beautiful rose window above the choir and pipe organ, and lovely stained glass throughout. ⊠ *Calle Diaz de Leon at Escorza.*

🐣 ⑯ **Zoológico Guadalajara.** On the edge of the jagged Barranca Huentitán (Huentitán Canyon), the impressive zoo has more than 1,500 animals representing some 360 species. There's a kid's zoo, two aviaries, and a herpetarium with 130 species of reptiles, amphibians, and fish. For 50¢ you can take a guided train tour around part of the 40-hectare grounds. The adjacent **Selva Mágica**, or Magic Jungle amusement park, has carnival rides and attractions for about $1.30. Spanish speakers will enjoy the comical trained-animal shows, usually at 2 PM. The complex is 6 km (nearly 4 mi) northeast of downtown, near the planetarium. ⊠ *Paseo del Zoológico 600,* ☎ *3674–4488.* 🎫 *$2.50.* ☉ *Daily 10–6.*

OFF THE
BEATEN PATH

BARRANCA DE OBLATOS – A spectacular 2,000-ft-deep gorge, Oblatos Canyon also has hiking trails and the narrow Cola de Caballo waterfall, named for its horse-tail shape. You can see the falls from the zoo, or better yet, catch an Ixcantantus-bound bus from Glorieta La Normal, 10 blocks north of the cathedral. Ask to be let off at the view point, *mirador de la cascada.* You'll have about 20 minutes to view the falls before catching the bus upon its return to Guadalajara. ⊠ *10 km (6 mi) northeast of downtown Guadalajara via Calzada Independencia Nte.*

DINING

Guadalajara eateries continue to be very affordable. Most are open throughout the evening, although seafood restaurants often close earlier. A number of places listed below have branches elsewhere in the city; our choices are either the most colorful, original locations or those most convenient to the hotel areas. Because Guadalajara is a big, business-oriented city, it is advisable to dress well for $$$ restaurants.

CATEGORY	COST*
$$$	$15–$25
$$	$10–$15
$	under $10

per person for a three-course meal, excluding drinks, service, and 15% sales tax

$$$ ✕ **Santo Coyote.** At this *nouvelle* Mexican eatery in the former U.S.
★ Consul General's residence, murals of goddesses adorn one dining area, waterfalls flow, and candles burn at a huge shrine to Mexico's patron saint—the Virgin of Guadalupe. Look on the menu for wood-fired roast or grilled *cabrito* (goat)—a house specialty—or baby back ribs topped with a tamarind and pepper sauce, or marrow soup. Service and presentation are excellent. ⊠ *Lerdo de Tejada 2379,* ☎ *3616–6978. AE, MC, V.*

$$–$$$ ✗ **La Rinconada.** Popular for its old Guadalajara charm, La Rinconada
★   has appeared in numerous Mexican movies and TV comedies. The heart
     of an 1897 farm, its dining area has arched pillars and high vaulted
     ceilings. Local businesspeople in search of excellent steak and other
     international and Mexican dishes fill the colonial dining room, which
     feels equally welcoming to casually dressed tourists. There's breakfast
     daily beginning at 8; later on, try the *plato Mexicano*: strips of steak
     served with an enchilada, quesadilla, guacamole, rice, and beans. Piano
     music plays between 2 and 6:30. ⊠ *Calle Morelos 86, at Plaza Tap-
     atía,* ☎ *3613–9914 or 3613–9925. AE, MC, V.*

$$–$$$ ✗ **La Trattoria.** Guadalajara's top Italian restaurant has retained its rep-
     utation as a family place committed to good value. Pictures of Italian
     piazzas decorate the dining room, which has closely spaced tables. The
     menu's best options include *spaghetti frutti di mari* (seafood spaghetti)
     and *scaloppine alla Marsala* (beef medallions with Marsala and mush-
     rooms). The homemade bread is delicious, and all meals include the
     salad bar. ⊠ *Av. Niños Héroes 3051,* ☎ *3122–1817. AE, MC, V.*

$$ ✗ **Casa Bariachi.** This grand mariachi restaurant and bar is a favorite
     among locals, a place to celebrate with friends and enjoy some of
     Guadalajara's finest mariachi bands. Expect waiters as well as diners
     to sing along. The menu highlights steaks and alcoholic drinks, and
     the fiesta continues until 3 AM. ⊠ *Av. Vallarta 2221,* ☎ *3615–0029
     or 3616–9900. AE, MC, V. Closed Sun.*

$$ ✗ **La Destilería.** If you can't make it to the village of Tequila, here's
     the next best thing: a restaurant-cum-tequila-museum that serves novel
     Mexican specialties and 240 varieties of the fiery liquor. Antique pho-
     tos of tequila distilleries and bilingual plaques explaining tequila's his-
     tory line the brick walls. ⊠ *Av. México 2916,* ☎ *3640–3110. AE, MC,
     V. No dinner Sun.*

$$ ✗ **La Estancia Gaucha.** In a town that loves Argentine cuisine, this no-
     nonsense steak establishment is considered by many to be the cream
     of the crop. Among the best cuts here are the *churrasco estancia* (rib
     eye) and the *bife de chorizo* (essentially New York strip). The empanadas
     and the *parillada* (a mixed grill that often includes beef, sausages, and
     selected organ meats) are also delicious. Piano music accompanies
     dinner Wednesday through Saturday. ⊠ *Av. Niños Héroes 2860,* ☎
     3122–6565. AE, MC, V.

$$ ✗ **El Farallón de Tepic.** Set underneath a bright-blue awning, this
     open-air establishment is reminiscent of beach restaurants in the
     nearby state of Nayarit. Order fresh *pescado*—usually red snapper or
     an equally mild fish—grilled with garlic or butter, in classic tomato
     sauce, breaded, or stuffed with seafood and cheese. Pescado *saran-
     deado* (Jalisco-style whole barbecued fish stuffed with vegetables) is
     worth every second of the 30-minute wait. Try the homemade flan
     for dessert. ⊠ *Av. Niño Obrero 566,* ☎ *3121–2616 or 3121–9616.
     MC, V. No dinner.*

$$ ✗ **La Feria.** Boasting the most festive atmosphere of any restaurant down-
★   town, La Feria offers spectacular entertainment: mariachis, *charros* (tal-
     ented, elegantly suited equestrians performing rope tricks), and traditional
     Mexican folkloric dances. Come for a late lunch or appetizers to catch
     the afternoon show, or for a late-night dinner to catch the evening show.
     The shrimp tacos are scrumptious, and meat lovers will want to share
     the parillada for two. After the show, play *lotería* (a type of bingo) for
     a bottle of tequila or have a parakeet choose your fortune. ⊠ *Av. Corona
     291,* ☎ *3613–1812 or 3613–1839. AE, MC, V.*

$$ ✗ **Formosa Gardens.** For a taste of home, it's no wonder Guadalajara's
     Asian residents visit Formosa Gardens, which has sister restaurants in
     Beijing and Taiwan. Peking duck is crisp and tasty here, but go for the

deep-fried orange beef—sweet and tangy. This beautiful mansion opens onto a garden dining area, where each table is set with crisp linens. ⊠ *Av. Union 322,* ☎ *3615–7415. MC, V.*

$$ ✕ **Pierrot.** This quiet French dining room offers mouthwatering pâtés
★ followed by seafood, chicken, and beef entrées—among them trout almondine, osso buco, and pâté-stuffed chicken breast in tarragon sauce. Wall-mounted lamps with fringed velvet shades and fresh flowers on each table lend a gracious touch. ⊠ *Justo Sierra 2355,* ☎ *3630–2087 or 3615–4758. AE, MC, V. Closed Sun.*

$ ✕ **La Chata.** Black-and-white photos of old Guadalajara and exquisitely glazed plates adorn the white walls of this popular, casual downtown eatery. Start off with guacamole and then savor the zesty *chiles rellenos* (stuffed peppers). Or try one of the spicy roasted meat dishes, such as *carne tampiqueña,* served with rice, beans, taco, guacamole, and enchilada. Complement your meal with a tangy *jugo de lima,* the distinctive lime juice popular throughout Jalisco. Breakfast is served as well. ⊠ *Av. Corona 126, between Avs. López Cotilla and Juárez,* ☎ *3613–0588. AE, MC, V.*

$ ✕ **Karne Garibaldi.** According to the *Guinness Book of World Records,* this Tapatío institution has the fastest service in the world—at 13.5 seconds. This lightning service is possible because there's only one thing on the menu: carne in su jugo, a tasty combination of finely diced beef and bacon simmered in a rich beef broth. Served with grilled onions, tortillas, and refried beans mixed with corn, it's a great down-home meal. ⊠ *Garibaldi 1306,* ☎ *3826–1286. AE, MC, V.*

$ ✕ **Mondo Cafe.** The alluring fragrance from Mondo's coffee roaster wafts into wide, tree-lined Avenida Chapultepec. Foreign and local students frequent this favorite coffee house for its large picture-window views onto the busy avenue and for various blends of fresh-roasted coffee. Hearty breakfasts are served daily beginning at 7, along with mixed fruit and vegetable juices and flavored coffees. A former manager of Starbucks in Seattle, the American owner offers beer and wine as well. ⊠ *Av. Chapultepec 48 at Pedro Moreno,* ☎ *3616–2709. V.*

$ ✕ **La Pianola.** The entrance—through what looks like an open-air
★ kitchen where costumed women are making tortillas—may be misleading to first-timers: in back is a large restaurant and garden with an excellent, varied Mexican menu. Specialties include pozole and chilies *en nogada,* spicy stuffed chili peppers in a walnut cream sauce. The signature player-piano music accompanies the meal. ⊠ *Av. México 3220,* ☎ *3813–1385 or 3813–2412. AE, MC, V.*

LODGING

Guadalajara has a variety of hotels in all price ranges. Call ahead if you're apprehensive about noise levels outside your hotel room; many hotels are on busy intersections, in which case rooms higher up or in the back tend to be less noisy. If fresh air is important to you, ask if there are windows or balconies, as some of the most exclusive hotels have windows that won't open.

The rates given are based on the year-round or peak-season price; promotional rates may be lower, and business-oriented hotels may offer lower rates on weekends. You can expect hotels in the $$$ and $$$$ categories to have purified-water systems, English-language TV channels, concierge, and laundry and dry cleaning service. Many hotels now offer in-room data ports and room safes.

Guadalajara Dining & Lodging

Dining

Casa Bariachi **9**	La Estancia Gaucha . . .**11**	Karne Garibaldi **19**	La Rinconada **23**
La Chata **25**	El Farallón de Tepic . .**7**	Mondo Cafe **20**	Santo Coyote **16**
La Destilería **13**	La Feria **27**	La Pianola **8**	La Trattoría **10**
	Formosa Gardens . . .**17**	Pierrot **18**	

Lodging

CATEGORY	COST*
$$$$	over $160
$$$	$90–$160
$$	$40–$90
$	under $40

*All prices are for a standard double room, excluding 15% VAT and 2% hotel tax.

$$$$ **Camino Real.** A 15-minute cab ride from downtown will bring you to the first of Guadalajara's luxury hotels. Although its five stars are likely posted more for reputation and atmosphere than for actual creature comforts, guest rooms are large and well-decorated, with many surrounding the hotel pool and gardens, where trios serenade during the excellent Sunday morning buffet brunch. Rooms in the rear face noisy Avenida Vallarta. ☒ *Av. Vallarta 5005, 45040,* ☎ *3121–8000, 01–800/901–2300, or 800/722–6466,* FAX *3134–2404,* WEB *www.caminoreal.com/guadalajara. 195 rooms, 10 suites. 3 restaurants, bar, coffee shop, in-room data ports, no-smoking rooms, 4 pools, putting green, tennis court, baby-sitting, playground, concierge, free parking. AE, DC, MC, V.*

$$$$ **Quinta Real.** Stone and brick walls, colonial arches, and objets
★   d'art highlight public areas of this luxury hotel on the city's west side. Suites are plush and intimate, with select neocolonial furnishings, including glass-top writing tables with carved-stone pedestals and fireplaces with marble mantelpieces. Tile bathrooms have marble sinks and bronze fixtures; some suites have sunken hot tubs. Deluxe tower accommodations are the most lavish, although removed from the gardens below. ☒ *Av. México 2727, at Av. López Mateos Norte, 44680,* ☎ *3615–0000, 01–800/713–1966, or 800/457–4000,* FAX *3630–1797,* WEB *www.quintareal.com. 76 suites. Restaurant, bar, in-room data ports, no-smoking rooms, pool, baby-sitting, concierge, meeting rooms, car rental, free parking. AE, MC, V.*

$$$ **Crowne Plaza Guadalajara.** Expansive, shaded, well-tended gardens and towering trees with nests of chirping birds surround a large pool, bringing a bit of nature to this hotel near the convention center. The hotel's public areas are tastefully decorated with antiques and reproductions; rooms have marble baths, upholstered furniture (some rather worn), carpeting, and lots of natural light. Tower rooms have city views; those in the two-story building surround the pool and gardens, but beware of rooms in the back near the children's play area and caged, shrieking macaws. ☒ *Av. López Mateos Sur 2500, 45050,* ☎ *3634–1034, 01–800/365–5500, or 800/227–6963,* FAX *3631–9393,* WEB *www.basshotels.com/crowneplaza. 380 rooms, 4 suites. 3 restaurants, bar, in-room data ports, no-smoking floor, pool, beauty salon, miniature golf, 2 tennis courts, exercise room, shops, baby-sitting, playground, concierge floor, business services, airport shuttle, car rental, free parking. AE, DC, MC.*

$$$ **Fiesta Americana.** The dramatic glass facade of this luxury high-
★   rise faces the Minerva Fountain, on the city's west side. Four glass-enclosed elevators ascend above the 14-story atrium lobby to the city's largest guest rooms, which have modern furnishings, marble bathrooms, and panoramic views. The business center is one of the best-equipped in the city. ☒ *Aurelio Aceves 225, 44100,* ☎ *3825–3434, 01–800/504–5000, or 800/343–7821,* FAX *3630–3725. 352 rooms, 39 suites. Restaurant, bar, coffee shop, in-room data ports, no-smoking floor, pool, beauty salon, 2 tennis courts, gym, shops, baby-sitting, concierge, business services, meeting room, car rental, free parking. AE, DC, MC, V.*

$$$ **Hilton.** Adjacent to the Guadalajara World Trade Center and Expo, the Hilton is a premier business destination. Although the hotel lacks character, it has modern furnishings and considerable business services,

including a multilingual staff, a private executive floor, and a well-equipped business center. The hotel caters to convention goers. ⊠ *Av. de las Rosas 2933, 44540,* ☎ *3678–0505, 01–800/003–1400, or 800/445–8667,* FAX *3678–0511,* WEB *www.guadalajara.hilton.com. 402 rooms, 20 suites. 2 restaurants, bar, in-room data ports, no-smoking room, pool, beauty salon, massage, exercise room, concierge floor, business services, meeting room. AE, DC, MC, V.*

$$$ 🏨 **Presidente Inter-Continental.** A modern hotel with a multiplane mirrored facade and a 12-story atrium lobby, the Inter-Continental attracts a sophisticated business clientele. For the best city view, request a room on an upper floor facing the Plaza del Sol shopping center. There's a Tane silver shop on the premises, and guests can use nearby golf and tennis facilities. The hotel's health club is the best in the city. ⊠ *Av. López Mateos Sur and Moctezuma, 45050,* ☎ *3678–1234, 01–800/904–4400, or 800/327–0200,* FAX *3678–1222,* WEB *www.interconti.com. 381 rooms, 30 suites. Restaurant, bar, coffee shop, in-room data ports, pool, massage, sauna, spa, steam room, health club, shops, baby-sitting, concierge floor, business services, meeting room, airport shuttle, car rental, free parking. AE, DC, MC, V.*

$$$ 🏨 **Vista Plaza Del Sol.** Location and price bring families, visiting soccer teams, and tour groups to this two-building hotel at the south end of the Plaza del Sol shopping center. Rooms and public areas are painted glossy white; accommodations in the cylindrical tower are a bit larger and have views of the shopping center. The popular restaurant has piping hot coffee and buffet or à la carte dining for all three meals. ⊠ *Avs. López Mateos Sur 2375 at Mariano Otero, 45050,* ☎ *3647–8790 or 01–800/368–8000, or 888/300–6394,* FAX *3122–9685,* WEB *www.vistahotel.com. 341 rooms, 16 suites. Restaurant, bar, coffee shop, pool, hair salon, shop, baby-sitting, concierge floor, meeting rooms, travel services, car rental, free parking. AE, DC, MC, V.*

$$ 🏨 **De Mendoza.** This downtown hotel is convenient—on a quiet side
★ street a block from the Teatro Degollado—and elegant, with its impressive postcolonial architecture and refined atmosphere. Low, beamed ceilings, hand-carved furniture and doors, and wrought-iron railings decorate public areas and the clean, comfortable rooms. Twenty rooms have balconies with tables and chairs overlooking the small but inviting courtyard pool, just outside the hotel's acclaimed international restaurant. ⊠ *Calle Venustiano Carranza 16, 44100,* ☎ *3613–4646, 3614–2621, or 01–800/361–2600,* FAX *3613–7310,* WEB *www.demendoza.com.mx. 87 rooms, 17 suites. Restaurant, in-room data ports, no-smoking room, pool, meeting rooms, free parking. AE, DC, MC, V.*

$$ 🏨 **Diana.** Mexican and European travelers favor this hotel two blocks from the Minerva Fountain. The white stucco lobby adjoins a small lounge and busy restaurant. Standard-size rooms have white-on-white walls and ceilings and brightly patterned curtains and bedspreads; the quietest rooms are on the upper floors in the rear. Some suites have private saunas. The small Internet center has three computers. ⊠ *Circunvalación Agustín Yáñez 2760, 44100,* ☎ *3615–5510, 3615–6428, or 01–800/024–8181,* FAX *3630–3685. 134 rooms, 15 suites. Restaurant, bar, coffee shop, pool, airport shuttle, free parking. AE, DC, MC, V.*

$$ 🏨 **Francés.** Guadalajara's oldest hotel, dating from 1610, is also a na-
★ tional monument. Stone columns and colonial arches surround a three-story enclosed atrium lobby with a polished marble fountain and cut-crystal chandeliers. On Friday, loud live music is played at the bar there until midnight; other days there's more tranquil piano playing 2–8 and a trio 8–10:30. Rooms vary in size, and the authentic colonial ambience—with white stucco walls, polished wood floors, and high-beam ceilings—seems a bit stiff and spare by modern standards. Rooms facing Calle Maestranza have tiny 17th-century balconies, but also street

noise. The location in the historic center is a plus. ✉ *Calle Maestranza 35, 44100,* ☎ *3613–1190, 3613–0936, or 01–800/718–5309,* FAX *3658–2831. 50 rooms, 10 suites. Restaurant, bar, fans, dance club, car rental, free parking. AE, MC, V.*

$$ 🏨 **Misión Carlton.** This modern 20-story tower hotel on the edge of downtown has oversize rooms; those on the upper floors have spectacular city views and provide a retreat from the horrendous street noise. Ivy-draped walls surround the rear gardens and fountain. Although the hotel is convenient for tourists, it caters to the business traveler. ✉ *Av. Niños Héroes 125, at Av. 16 de Septiembre, 44100,* ☎ *3614–7272 or 01–800/967–6400,* FAX *3613–5539. 193 rooms, 1 suite. Restaurant, 2 bars, no-smoking floor, pool, hair salon, shop, baby-sitting, concierge, meeting rooms, free parking. AE, MC, V.*

$$ 🏨 **Posada Guadalajara.** Rooms in this colonial-style hotel open onto airy, wrought-iron-rail hallways overlooking the small patio and its enormous stone fountain. Accommodations are clean and comfortable and have carved-wood furniture. In addition to its loyal international patrons, the Posada welcomes visiting sports teams, so evenings here can be festive or raucous. The hotel is south of Calzada Lázaro Cárdenas, about 1½ km (1 mi) northeast of Plaza del Sol. ✉ *Av. López Mateos Sur 1280, 45040,* ☎ *3121–2022 or 3121–2424,* FAX *3122–1834. 170 rooms, 3 suites. Restaurant, bar, pool, baby-sitting, free parking. AE, DC, MC, V.*

$$ 🏨 **Santiago de Compostela.** This cozy downtown hotel in a converted 19th-century building is across from the Parque San Francisco and offers simple, modern accommodations. More expensive rooms overlooking the park—where you can watch worshipers file into the two colonial churches—have tall, narrow windows with iron balconies. Inside rooms open onto an atrium. All the bathrooms here have tubs, and the suites—only slightly more expensive and worth it—have Jacuzzis. The open-air pool and sunning area on the fifth floor overlook the park. A drawback is that there is one small elevator to service the six floors. ✉ *Colón 272, 44100,* ☎ *3613–8880 or 01–800/ 365–5300,* FAX *3658–1925. 91 rooms, 4 suites. Restaurant, bar, pool, shop, free parking. AE, DC, MC, V.*

$$ 🏨 **La Villa del Ensueño.** If you prefer a hotel out of the fray and near the region's fabulous shopping, choose this intimate B&B in the heart of Tlaquepaque, about 20 minutes outside downtown Guadalajara. The restored 19th-century hacienda maintains a rustic air, with thick white adobe walls, exposed beam ceilings, and plants in huge unglazed pots. Smokers should request a room with private balcony, as no smoking is allowed inside the hotel. ✉ *Florida 305, 45500,* ☎ *3635–8792,* FAX *3659–6152,* WEB *www.bestinns.net/mexico/ensueno. 4 suites, 14 rooms. Bar, 2 pools, no-smoking rooms, parking.*

$ 🏨 **San Francisco Plaza.** On a quiet downtown side street in the historic district, this attractive two-story colonial-style building is easy to spot with its pale orange facade. Potted palms and geraniums surround a gurgling stone fountain in the pleasant courtyard sitting area, and copper wall lamps lend an old-fashioned air to the sparely furnished rooms, with somewhat threadbare furnishings. ✉ *Calle Degollado 267, 44100,* ☎ *3613–8954,* FAX *3613–3257. 74 rooms, 2 suites. Restaurant, laundry service, free parking. AE, MC, V.*

NIGHTLIFE AND THE ARTS

Guadalajara is an active cultural and performing-arts center, with excellent local talent and well-known artists and entertainers from abroad. The U.S. and Canadian communities around Lake Chapala have also developed a schedule of English-language cultural events. During the afternoon and evening, many cafés along Avenida Chapultepec also have live music.

The Arts

DANCE

Ballet Folklórico of the University of Guadalajara. The university's internationally acclaimed troupe offers traditional Mexican folkloric dances and music in the Teatro Degollado every Sunday at 10 AM. ☎ 3614–4773. ☞ $2.50–$11.

PERFORMANCE VENUES

Cine Cinematógrafo I, II, and III. Founded by two Guadalajara-area movie buffs, these theaters present mostly art-house variety films—often in English with Spanish subtitles. ⊠ *Av. Vallarta 1102,* ☎ 3825–0514; ⊠ *Av. México 2222, at Plaza Amistad,* ☎ 3630–1208; ⊠ *Av. Patria 600,* ☎ 3629–4780.

Ex-Convento del Carmen. Classical music performances are held in the former convent of Our Lady of Mt. Carmel during "Martes Musical," Tuesdays at 8:30 PM; literature-oriented Wednesdays are dedicated to book presentations or poetry readings. Fridays and Saturdays at 8:30 PM and Sundays at 6 PM different theatrical presentations are the norm. There's also a spacious art gallery and bookshop. It's 6½ blocks west of Avenida 16 de Septiembre. ⊠ *Av. Juárez 638,* ☎ 3614–7184.

Instituto Cultural Cabañas. Large-scale theater, dance, and musical performances take place on a patio here. The Tolsá Chapel hosts more intimate events, and subtitled English-language films are often shown in the theater. Exhibitions of both Mexican and foreign art are on display, and free art classes are given. ⊠ *Calle Cabañas 8, at Plaza Tapatía,* ☎ 3617–4322 or 3617–4440.

Plaza de Armas. The State Band of Jalisco, the Municipal Band, and sometimes even the Philharmonic plays at the bandstand on Tuesday, Thursday, and Sunday evenings around 6:30. ⊠ *Av. Corona between Calle Morelos and Pedro Moreno, across from Palacio de Gobierno.*

Teatro Degollado. Nationally and internationally famous artists perform here year-round. The refurbished velvet seats are comfortable, the acoustics are excellent, and the central air-conditioning can be a treat. ⊠ *Calle Degollado, between Av. Hidalgo and Calle Morelos,* ☎ 3614–4773 or 3613–1115. ☞ $3–$40 per performance.

SYMPHONY

Orquesta Filarmónica de Jalisco. Conducted by Maestro Guillermo Salvador, performances take place Sunday at 12:30 PM and Friday night at 8:30 at the Teatro Degollado. ☎ 3658–3812 or 3658–3819. ☞ $2–$12.

Nightlife

A string of Guadalajara night spots generally geared to the under-30 crowd lines Avenida Vallarta and the centro area. Live tropical tunes Wednesday through Saturday after 10 draw crowds to **Cubilete** (⊠ General Río Seco 9, in the Nine Corners area of downtown, ☎ 3613–2096). For a bit of local color, stop downtown at **La Maestranza** (⊠ Calle Maestranza 179, downtown, ☎ 3613–5878), a renovated 1940s cantina chock-full of bullfighting memorabilia. The Fiesta Americana hotel's sleek **Lobby Bar** has live but low-key entertainment, with jazz most nights after 8. The Crowne Plaza's jungle-theme **Manglar** (⊠ Av. López Mateos Sur 2500, ☎ 3634–1034) has a game room and large-screen TV in addition to live Latin music.

El Archivo (⊠ Madero 111, downtown, ☎ 3613-9758) is an atmospheric turn-of-the-20th-century house-cum-cantina featuring mainly Mexican rock music. Nightly after 9 (except Monday), patrons cluster around the small stage at **La Peña Cuicacalli** (⊠ Av. Niños Héroes 1988, at the traffic circle of the same name, ☎ 3825–4690). There's *rock en español* on Tuesday, and folk music from Mexico, Latin America, and Spain most other nights.

DANCE CLUBS AND DISCOS

A hot spot in town is the 94th **Hard Rock Cafe** (⊠ Av. Vallarta 2125, ☎ 3616–4560), in the Centro Magno mall. Live bands play rock, naturally, Wednesday through Saturday from 10 PM on. Well-dressed professional types 25 and older like the classic rock at **El Mito** (⊠ Vallarta 2425, Centro Magno shopping center, ☎ 3615–7246). You can dance most of the night to popular Latin and European music at the multilevel **Tropigala** (⊠ Av. López Mateos Sur 2188, across from Plaza del Sol shopping center, ☎ 3122–5553 or 3122–7903). **Co-Co & Co-Co** (⊠ Av. Corona 160, ☎ 3614–5714, closed Mon.), at the Fenix hotel downtown, has tropical tunes after 9 PM.

Salón Veracruz (⊠ Manzano 486, behind the Hotel Carlton, ☎ 3613–4422) is a spartan, old-style dance hall where a 15-piece band keeps hundreds of hoofers moving to Colombian cumbias, Dominican merengue, and danzón, a waltzlike dance invented in Cuba and favored in Veracruz. It's open Wednesday through Sunday 10 PM–3:30 AM. **Copacabana** (⊠ Av. López Mateos Sur and Las Aguilas, not far from La Plaza del Sol, ☎ 3631–4596, ☼ open Wed.–Sat.) plays oldies and current dance music between sets of live Latin tunes. **Maxim's** (⊠ Calle Maestranza 35, ☎ 3613–1190, 3613–0936, or 01–800/718–5309) in the Hotel Francés, is one of the better downtown discos.

OUTDOOR ACTIVITIES AND SPORTS

Participant Sports

Amusement Parks

The **Go Kartmania** go-cart racetrack park, in a tree-lined former city park, has four tracks of varying difficulty. Budding Mario Andrettis from 8 to 80 can race around on tracks that have banked curves, trees, and landscaping. A cafeteria and arcade are also on site. ⊠ *Av. Avila Camacho 2700, across from Plaza Patria,* ☎ *3854–2894.* ☜ *Entrance 50¢, plus about $2 for 5 minutes of track time.* ☼ *Daily 11–8.*

WATER PARKS

Approximately 50 km (31 mi) from Guadalajara are two water parks with thermal pools and lots of entertainment for both adults and children. They can be reached most easily by taxi, or by bus from the old or new bus terminals to Villa Corona. **Agua Caliente** (⊠ Carretera a Barra de Navidad Km 56, Villa Corona, ☎ 3778-0022 or 3778–0784, ☜ $2) has a large artificial wave pool and large water slides as well as thermal pools, gardens, and restaurants. All of the pools and facilities are open on weekends; some are closed midweek. Nearby, **Chimulco** (⊠ Camino Real Km. ½, in the village of Villa Corona, ☎ 3778–0014, ☜ $4), in a more intimate setting, serves hot food and has a thermal pool, water slides, boat rides, and a large children's play area.

Fitness Clubs

The health club at the **Presidente Inter-Continental** (☎ 3678–1227) is open 5:30 AM–11 PM to nonguests for about $12 a day. It includes a fitness center, heated pool, massage, and spa. Celebrities visit **Gold's Gym** (⊠ Av. Xóchitl 4203, ☎ 3647–0420) for its unique amenities, such as a climbing wall, a full basketball court, and Tae Kwon Do lessons. Guest passes are available for about $7 a day.

Golf

Several golf clubs admit nonmembers upon payment of a greens fee of $40–$100. **El Palomar** (✉ Paseo del Palomar 220, ☎ 3684–4434 or 3684–4436), is the most exclusive country club in Guadalajara. Across from Montenegro Park is the **Atlas Chapalita Golf Club** (✉ Carretera Guadalajara-Chapala Km. 6.5, El Salto, ☎ 3689–2620 or 3689–0240, ⊠ $47, closed Mon.). Tuesday and Thursday are the least-crowded nights at **Las Cañadas Country Club** (✉ Av. Bosques San Isidro 777, ☎ 3685–0285 or 3685–0412, ⊠ $50–$55, ☉ closed Mon.). As is the case at most courses, rates rise on weekends at the **Club de Golf Santa Anita** (✉ Carretera a Morelia Km 6.5, ☎ 3686–0321).

Ice-Skating

The **Iceland Pista de Hielo** has daily one-hour public ice-skating sessions. There's also a restaurant and ice-cream parlor. ✉ *Av. México 2582,* ☎ *3615–4438 or 3615–7876.* ⊠ *$4.50 an hour, including skates.* ☉ *8:30–6.*

Tennis

The **Crowne Plaza Guadalajara** (✉ Av. López Mateos Sur 2500, ☎ 3634–1034) allows nonguests to use its two courts, open 7 AM–dark, for a fee. Nonguests are allowed to use the **Camino Real** court (✉ Av. Vallarta 5005, ☎ 3134–2424) for a fee. It's open 7 AM–10 PM. English is spoken at the **Club de Tenis Royal** (✉ San Ignacio 316, ☎ 3647–5348), where you can take lessons. It's open weekdays 7 AM–10 PM, Saturday 7–7, and Sunday 7–3.

Spectator Sports

Bullfighting

Corridas (bullfights) are held Sunday at 4:30 PM at **Plaza Nuevo Progreso.** Tickets are sold for either the *sol* (sunny) or *sombra* (shady) side of the bullring. You can buy tickets at the bullring (about 5 km [3 mi] northeast of downtown) or at the bullring's booth in Plaza México. *Novilleros* (apprentice matadors) work the cape many mornings between 7 AM and 1 PM, and it doesn't cost anything to watch them practice. ✉ *M. Pirineos 1930 and Calzada Independencia Nte., across from Estadio Jalisco,* ☎ *3637–9982 or 3651–8378.* ⊠ *$9.50–$65.*

Charreadas

Charreadas take place year-round at the **Lienzo Charros de Jalisco** Sunday at noon. The competitors participate in 10 equestrian and roping events, mariachis or *bandas* (brass bands) perform during breaks, and food and drinks are available. ✉ *Av. Dr. R. Michel 577, next to Parque Agua Azul,* ☎ *3619–3232.* ⊠ *About $2.*

Soccer

Two professional teams (and a university team) play at **Estadio Jalisco,** including one of Mexico's favorite teams, Las Chivas ("the she-goats") de Guadalajara, who generally play on Sunday. The two regular seasons run January through April or May and July through December. ✉ *Siete Colinas 1772 and Calzada Independencia Nte., across from the bullring,* ☎ *3637–0301 or 3637–0299.* ⊠ *$1.50–$26.*

SHOPPING

Guadalajara has a great variety of high-quality merchandise at low prices, although you also can find high-priced low-quality items. Store hours tend to be Monday through Saturday 9 or 10 until 8, and Sunday 10–2; some shops close during lunch, usually 2–4 or 2–5, and others close all day on Sunday. In Guadalajara, shopping malls are springing up everywhere: the metropolitan area now has more than 50. Shopping-mall stores generally stay open at lunch and weekends. *Tianguis* (street markets) run every day throughout the Guadalajara area; you never know what you'll find. If you're interested in traditional arts and crafts, the best stores are found in Tlaquepaque and Tonalá.

Malls and Shops

Centro Magno. A number of upscale boutiques and bistros, along with a large cineplex and a Hard Rock Cafe, make this a trendy shopping and dining spot. It's just a few blocks from the Minerva. ⊠ *Av. Vallarta 2425,* ☎ *3630–1113 or 3630–1776.* ☉ *Daily 10–10.*

El Charro, an excellent leather-goods store, has branches in Plaza del Sol (☎ 3122–5148 and 3647–5731) as well as downtown (⊠ Av. Juárez 148, ☎ 3614–7599 or 3614–9743).

Galería del Calzado. The 60 stores in this westside complex all sell shoes. Guadalajara is one of Mexico's leading shoe centers, and high-quality footwear and accessories are available here, many at lower prices than you find in the States. ⊠ *Avs. México 3225,* ☎ *3647–6422.* ☉ *Mon.–Sat. 11–9, Sun. 11–8:30.*

La Gran Plaza. A sleek glass-and-steel exterior houses 334 commercial spaces and a 14-plex cinema, surrounded by a large food court and some quality restaurants. It's east of the Guadalajara Chamber of Commerce and the Camino Real hotel. ⊠ *Av. Vallarta 3959,* ☎ *3122–3004.* ☉ *Daily 10–9:30.*

Plaza del Sol. The city's largest mall sprawls like a park, with 270 commercial spaces, outdoor patios, trees and garden areas, and parking for 2,100 cars. It's across from the Presidente Inter-Continental hotel. ⊠ *Avs. López Mateos Sur 2375, at Mariano Otero,* ☎ *3121–5950.* ☉ *Weekdays 10–8, Sat. 10–9, Sun. 10–7.*

Plaza México. There are about 120 stores in the city's second most popular shopping mall (after Centro Magno), seven blocks west of the Plaza Galería del Calzado. ⊠ *Av. México 3300,* ☎ *3813–2488.* ☉ *Daily 10–8.*

Markets and Handicrafts

While the shops listed below are great for shopping for crafts from the area and from throughout Mexico, the best shops—for crafts, fine furniture, and home furnishings, are found in the satellite towns of Tlaquepaque and Tonalá.

El Baratillo. This is one of the world's largest flea markets. Thirty city blocks are lined with stalls, tents, and blankets piled high with new, used, and antique merchandise. ⊠ *On and around Calle Esteban Loera, some 15 blocks east of Mercado Libertad.* ☉ *Sun. 7–5.*

Bazar Capitán. Serious art-, crafts-, and antiques-lovers may want to consult with Roberto Alvarado, who has 30 years in the art and antiques business. Alvarado runs personalized buying tours, scheduling appointments in private homes depending on clients' interests. One month's advance notice is requested, although visits can sometimes be accommodated at shorter notice. His bilingual *El Antiquario* magazine promotes local antiquities dealers. ⊠ *Argentina 73, ½ block off Av. Vallarta,* ☎ *3827–1990,* FAX *3640–1292.*

Calle Esteban Alatorre. Several blocks of stores selling shoes and leather goods—all reasonably priced—line this street. ⊠ *East of Calzada Independencia Nte. and 4 blocks north of Av. Hidalgo.*

El Festival Dominical de Arte. Fine art is sold *al aire libre* here Sunday 10–6. ⊠ *Glorieta Chapalita, Avs. Tepeyac and De las Rosas.*

Instituto de Artesanías Jaliscienses. Run by the state government, this store has a wide selection of the exquisite blown glass and hand-glazed pottery typical of Jalisco artisans. Merchandise—including belts, wood furniture, silver, and Huichol art—is sold at fixed prices. ⊠ *Calzadas González Gallo 20 and Independencia Sur, next to Parque Agua Azul,* ☎ *3619–4664.* ☉ *Weekdays 10–6, Sat. 10–5, Sun. 10–3.*

Mercado Libertad. Also known as the Mercado San Juan de Dios, the Liberty Market is one of Latin America's largest enclosed markets. Within a three-square-block area, you can browse through more than 1,000 stalls selling everything from clothing and crafts to live animals and gold watches. It's a good place to shop for typical silver jewelry. ⊠ *Calzada Independencia Sur between Dionísio Rodríguez and Av. Javier Mina.* ☉ *Daily 10–8.*

SIDE TRIPS FROM GUADALAJARA

No trip to Guadalajara is complete without an excursion out of the city, whether you're into shopping for crafts in Tlaquepaque and Tonalá, taking in the towns surrounding Lake Chapala, or unlocking the secrets of Mexican fire water in Tequila.

Tlaquepaque and Tonalá

For inveterate shoppers, a combined visit to the crafts meccas of Tlaquepaque and Tonalá makes a perfect day trip from Guadalajara. There's at least one good bed-and-breakfast in Tlaquepaque if you really want to shop until you drop, or if you'd just like to relax in a charming town that's reminiscent of Guadalajara, but is less congested and more picturesque. Those preferring a more intimate, tranquil base of operations might even consider staying in Tlaquepaque and taking one or more day trips into Guadalajara, only 15–20 minutes away by cab.

Tlaquepaque

7 km (4½ mi) southeast of downtown Guadalajara.

Tlaquepaque is known throughout Mexico as an arts-and-crafts center. Among its offerings are intricate blown-glass miniatures; exquisite pottery; jewelry, silver, and copperware; leather and hand-carved wood furniture; and handwoven clothing. More than 300 shops—many of which are run by families with centuries-old traditions of workmanship—line pedestrian malls and plazas in this charming town.

Tlaquepaque's craft heritage began with the distinctive decorated pottery fashioned by the Tonaltecan Indians, who lived in the area in the mid-16th century. After local authorities met here to sign a regional proclamation of independence from Spain in 1821, the village emerged from obscurity as wealthy Guadalajara residents began to build palatial summer houses—many of which have been restored and now house shops and restaurants. As more people came to purchase the pottery and intricate glass creations (glass-blowing was introduced from Europe in 1870), weavers, jewelers, and wood-carvers also arrived and built workshops. In 1973 downtown Tlaquepaque underwent a major renovation, the highlight of which was the creation of a wide pedestrian mall, Calle Independencia. More shops line Calle Juárez, a block south, as well as the many side streets.

A GOOD WALK

Begin your walking and shopping tour near the west end of pedestrian-only Calle Independencia, at **La Casa Canela** ㉓, a pretty venue with plenty of handicrafts for sale. A half block west, the modest but worthwhile **Museo Regional de la Cerámica** ㉔ shows the different styles of regional pottery through the ages, while across the street, **Galería Sergio Bustamante** ㉕ sells contemporary ceramics and folk art. Turn left at the next street, Contreras Medellín, and after several blocks, right

on Florida and right again on Prisciliano Sánchez to see the prize-winning pottery at the **Museo Municipal del Premio Nacional de la
Cerámica** ㉖. Continuing south on this street and returning to Calle Independencia you'll find exquisite Baroque-style statues, wood-and-gilt
altarpieces, and other treasures for sale at **Agustín Parra Diseño Barroco** ㉗. One block west, on the lively main plaza, is tiny **Templo Parroquial de San Pedro** ㉘. After visiting the parish church, walk north
on Madero from the northeast corner of the square to **Cerámica de
Ken Edwards** ㉙, the town's first stoneware workshop. Two and a half
blocks southwest, on Juárez, the shopping opportunities continue at
Plaza de Artesanías ㉚ and **Bazar Hecht** ㉛. You can now celebrate your
fine purchases (or your admirable restraint) with a drink and appetizer
at the festive **El Parián** ㉜, catercorner from the Plaza Hidalgo, at Independencia near Calle Progreso.

㉗ **Agustín Parra Diseño Barroco.** Step through the doors of this shop into
a mystical 18th-century land. Spiritual music accompanies your scrutiny
of virgins, angels, saints, cherubs, and other wonderful wood and ceramic sculptures. ⊠ *Calle Independencia 158,* ☎ *3657–8530 or 3657–
0316.* ⊙ *Weekdays 10–2 and 3–7, Sat. 10–7, Sun. 10–4.*

㉛ **Bazar Hecht.** Housewares and hacienda-style furniture and antiques
fill this two-story shop. The Hecht family is known throughout Mexico for its high-quality, ornately sculpted tables, armoires, and chairs.
⊠ *Juárez 162,* ☎ *3659–0205.* ⊙ *Weekdays 10–2:30 and 3:30–7, Sat.
10:30–2:30 and 3:30–7.*

㉓ **La Casa Canela.** Color seems to explode in the extensive shop's more
than 24 rooms, each exquisitely decorated with vivid papier-mâché flowers, finely glazed pottery, and elegant furniture. All surround a courtyard blooming with tropical plants. Free tequila and snacks are served
on Saturday. ⊠ *Calle Independencia 258,* ☎ *3635–3717 or 3657–1343.*
⊙ *Weekdays 10–2 and 3–7, Sat. 10–6, Sun. 11–3.*

㉙ **Cerámica de Ken Edwards.** In 1959 Ken Edwards introduced more
durable stoneware (which is by nature lead-free) into the Tonalá pottery vernacular—the original local earthenware is more fragile. His store
is filled with brightly colored, hand-decorated plates, cups, and vases.
Ask to see the seconds; some are real bargains. Edwards also has a store
in Tonalá. ⊠ *Francisco Madero 70,* ☎ *3635–5456.* ⊙ *Mon.–Sat.
10:30–6:30.*

㉕ **Galería Sergio Bustamante.** Sergio Bustamante's work is found in galleries throughout the world, but you can purchase his whimsical sculpture or silver- and gold-plated jewelry for less here. At the back of the
store is an art gallery featuring work by Mexican artists. The flamingos under the waterfall in the rear are real. ⊠ *Calle Independencia 238,*
☎ *3639–5519 or 01-800/024–2727.* ⊙ *Mon.–Sat. 10–7, Sun. 11–4.*

㉖ **Museo Municipal del Premio Nacional de la Cerámica.** Prize-winning
entries in traditional, contemporary, and miniature categories of its annual competitions become property of the museum and comprise the
collection. The ceramic works come from all across Mexico. ⊠ *Prisciliano Sánchez 191 between Donato Guerra and Florida,* ☎ *3639–
5646.* 🎟 *Free.* ⊙ *Tues.–Sat. 10–6, Sun. 10–3.*

★ ㉔ **Museo Regional de la Cerámica.** Housed in a colonial mansion, the
museum covers the evolution of ceramic wares in the Atemajac Valley during the past century. Free guided tours in Spanish or English
will enrich your visit and make for more-enlightened shopping. ⊠
Calle Independencia 237, ☎ *3635–5404.* 🎟 *Free.* ⊙ *Tues.–Sat. 10–
6, Sun. 10–3.*

Tlaquepaque

0 — 350 meters
0 — 350 yards

㉜ **El Parián.** When you're ready for lunch or simply a drink, head for the 120-year-old former handicrafts market south of Calle Independencia that's now an enormous cantina (some say the biggest in Mexico). Mariachis stroll through in the afternoons and—although the food is only average—the margaritas slide down well. Use the arcade shops here only to compare prices; *shop* on Calle Independencia or another main street. ⊠ *Jardín Hidalgo,* ☎ *3659–2362.*

㉚ **Plaza de Artesanías.** Browse through boutiques selling high-quality leather goods, embroidered clothing, ceramics, and blown glass. Some shops close on weekends. ⊠ *Juárez 145.*

㉘ **Templo Parroquial de San Pedro.** The Franciscan friars who founded this tiny parish church during the Spanish conquest named it after San Pedro de Analco. In keeping with the Mexican custom of adding to the town's name the name of its patron saint, Tlaquepaque was officially changed to San Pedro Tlaquepaque in 1915. The altars of Our Lady of Guadalupe and the Sacred Heart of Jesus are intricately carved in silver and gilt. ⊠ *In square at Calles Guillermo Prieto and Morelos.* ☉ *Daily 7 AM–9 PM.*

DINING

$$ ✕ **Casa Fuerte.** Dine on such gourmet Mexican dishes as chicken stuffed with *huitlacoche* (a corn fungus known as Mexico's answer to the truffle) and shrimp in tamarind sauce. There are tables on the front sidewalk or in the verdant patio garden, decorated with palms and a fountain. ⊠ *Calle Independencia 224,* ☎ *3639–6481. AE, MC, V.*

$$ ✕ **Restaurant sin Nombre.** The "Restaurant with No Name" serves Mexican cuisine, a combination of pre-Hispanic and modern recipes. High adobe walls surround the 18th-century colonial building and interior gardens. Afternoon entertainment includes jazz and traditional Mexican music. ⊠ *Francisco Madero 80,* ☎ *3635–4520. Closed Mon. AE, MC, V.*

$ ✗ **El Abajeño.** Quality Mexican specialties are served on the outdoor patio of this converted hacienda, including *carnitas* (shredded pork) or *filete tapado* (cheese-topped fillet of beef) for two. Mexican dance performances and mariachi music take place weekends at 4:30. ⊠ *Juárez 231,* ☎ *3635–9015 or 3635–9097. MC, V.*

Tonalá
8 km (5 mi) east of Tlaquepaque.

Tonalá is 10 minutes away but centuries removed from its more tourist-oriented, spruced-up neighbor, Tlaquepaque. One of the region's oldest pueblos, Tonalá is a quiet but prosperous village with dusty, cobblestone streets and adobe houses covered in stucco. The village was both the pre-Hispanic capital of the Atemajac Valley Indians and the capital of New Spain when Captain Juan de Oñate moved Guadalajara here in 1532. Within three years, however, Indians and a lack of water forced the Spaniards out.

While it's been swallowed by the ever-expanding city of Guadalajara, Tonalá preserves the character of a small town. It's homey, independent, and industrious. Municipal officials estimate that more than 6,000 artisans live and work here. Indeed, much of the ceramics and pottery sold in Tlaquepaque (and in many other parts of the world) are made in Tonalá. In small home studios, families create the lovely pieces, cobalt-blue glassware, and playful animals with the same materials and techniques their ancestors used. More than 20 techniques of producing barro are used in the village. You can visit many home studios on free tours offered by the Tonalá municipal tourist office, beginning from the Casa de Artesanos, with a minimum of one-day advance notice.

On Thursday, much Tonalá merchandise is sold at bargain prices at one of the best tianguis in all of Mexico. Most stores are open Monday through Saturday 10–2 and 4–7; some are open Sunday 10–2. As opposed to Tlaquepaque, where shops line up shoulder to shoulder along pedestrian-only Calle Independencia and surrounding streets, Tonalá's shops and factories are spread throughout the area, with a special concentration on Avenida Tonalteca, the main street into town.

A GOOD WALK
Begin your tour at the many different workshops comprising la **Casa de los Artesanos** ㉝, on Av. Tonaltecas between 16 de Septiembre and Matamoros. From there you'll pass scores of stores and workshops as you cruise north along the broad, busy avenue. Turn right onto Juárez and enter the downtown area where the town church, the **Santuario** ㉞, the municipal palace, and the tourism office surround the open plaza. Walk several blocks north on Morelos to **Erandi** ㉟ and **Galería José Bernabe** ㊱, both specializing in typical local ceramics. One block farther north on López Cotilla at Morelos is store and workshop **Cerámica de Ken Edwards** ㊲. Continue north on Morelos several long blocks, turning east (right) on La Paz and left onto Privado Obregón to see handmade wooden masks at **El 7** ㊳. Return the way you came, this time turning west (right) onto López Cotilla. Not far past Av. Tonaltecas is la **Casa de Salvador Vásquez Carmona** ㊴, where the owner sells his fanciful ceramic pottery.

❸❽ **El 7.** Tonalá native J. Cruz Coldívar Lucano, who signs his work and named his shop El 7 (el see-*ey*-tey), makes striking hand-painted masks, as well as decorative plates and other wall hangings. He has exhibited throughout Mexico, and also in North and South America and Europe. The Spanish Crown owns a number of his works. ⊠ *Alvaro Obregón 28,* ☎ *3683–1122.* ⊙ *Weekdays 9–6, Sat. 9–2.*

Tonalá

🟢**33** **Casa de los Artesanos.** This virtual department store of Mexican folk art and crafts displays an excellent selection of works by the best of Tonalá's artisans. The work of generations is here, including items made from wood, glass, wrought iron, brass, and of course clay. Prices are reasonable, and the staff can direct you to local artisans' studios. ⊠ *Av. de los Tonaltecas Sur 140,* ☎ *3683–0590.* ⊙ *Weekdays 9–7, weekends 9–3.*

🟢**37** **Cerámica de Ken Edwards.** At this workshop, you can view Edwards's trademark stoneware, lead-free pottery based on centuries-old designs. Although Edwards has moved on to Guatemala, his quality ceramics live on. ⊠ *Morelos 184,* ☎ *3683–0313.* ⊙ *Weekdays 9–6, Sat. 8–1.*

🟢**35** **Erandi.** One of Tonalá's largest exporters of hand-painted ceramics abroad has its exhibition center in founder Jorge Wilmot's former workshop. To see artisans in action, stop by their factory three blocks away. ⊠ *Calle Morelos 86,* ☎ *3683–0101.* ⊙ *Mon.–Sat. 9–6 (Thurs. 9–2 only), Sat. 9–2. Factory:* ⊠ *López Cotilla 118,* ☎ *3683–0253.* ⊙ *Weekdays 9:30–6, Sat. 9:30–2.*

🟢**36** **Galería José Bernabe.** The Bernabe family has made exquisite petatillo ceramics for generations, as well as simpler stoneware. The sprawling workshop in back of the gallery is open to visitors. ⊠ *Hidalgo 83, between Zapata and Constitución,* ☎ *3683–0040.* ⊙ *Weekdays 10–3 and 4–7, weekends 10–3. Workshop closed weekends.*

🟢**39** **Casa de Salvador Vásquez Carmona.** On a small patio behind his home, molds enormous ceramic pots and glazes them with intricate designs. Numerous awards certificates hang in his living room. Call before visiting. ⊠ *Av. de los Maestros 328, west of Av. de los Tonaltecas,* ☎ *3683–2896.*

③④ **Santuario.** In the parish church, paintings of the 14 stations of the cross fill the walls. Next door is the simple **Palacio Municipal,** or City Hall. The **Plaza Principal** is across the street. ⊠ *Juárez at Hidalgo.*

DINING

$$ ✕ **El Rincón del Sol.** A peaceful covered patio invites you to sip margaritas while listening to live guitar music that begins around 3:30. Try the chilis en nogada or one of the steak or chicken dishes. Hours are about 8:30 AM to 8 PM. ⊠ *Av. 16 de Septiembre 61,* ☎ *3683–1989. AE, MC, V.*

$ ✕ **Restaurant Jalapeños.** Steaks are the house specialty in this small but clean and tastefully appointed restaurant decorated with bright *papel picado* (cut paper streamers). Come for a late breakfast or reasonably early (9 PM) dinner, or enjoy the daily lunch special, with soup, main dish, drink, and dessert for under $5. ⊠ *Madero 23, ½ block from town hall,* ☎ *3683–0344. MC, V.*

$ ✕ **Restaurant Trópico de Tonalá.** Although it has virtually no aesthetic appeal, this plain six-table luncheonette with counter area is frequented for its tasty, fresh sandwiches, soups, and chicken and meat dishes. ⊠ *Madero 15,* ☎ *3683–0689. No credit cards.*

Tlaquepaque and Tonalá A to Z

BUS TRAVEL

There is frequent public bus service from downtown Guadalajara to Tlaquepaque and Tonalá. The trips take around 30 and 45 minutes, respectively. You can also catch the number 707 bus to Tonalá from the Plaza del Sol mall.

CAR TRAVEL

From Guadalajara, take Avenida Revolución southeast. At the Plaza de la Bandera, jog right onto Boulevard General Marcelino García Barragán, which becomes Boulevard Tlaquepaque as it leads into town. When you reach the *glorieta* (traffic circle), follow the circle around to Avenida Niños Héroes. The first intersection is Calle Independencia, the pedestrian mall. From the Plaza del Sol area, take Calzada Lázaro Cárdenas southeast to the Alamo traffic circle. Fork off to the north onto Avenida Niños Héroes. Both routes take around 20 minutes.

To get from Tlaquepaque to Tonalá, take Avenida Río Nilo southeast directly into town, to the intersection of Avenida de los Tonaltecas.

TAXIS

The fare from downtown Guadalajara to Tlaquepaque comes to about $4–$6, a bit more to Tonalá. A cab from Tlaquepaque to Tonalá runs about $4.

VISITOR INFORMATION

Both the Tlaquepaque and Tonalá tourist office will cheerfully dispense maps and whatever brochures are available. At least one of the attendants usually speaks some English.
➤ CONTACT INFORMATION: **Tlaquepaque municipal tourist office** (⊠ Morelos 288, Tlaquepaque, ☎ 3635–5756 or 3657–3846; ☉ weekdays 9–7). **Tonalá municipal tourist office** (⊠ Av. Hidalgo 21, Tonalá, ☎ 3683–0047 or 3683–0048; ☉ weekdays 9–3).

Around Lake Chapala

The jagged mountains that ring Lake Chapala, Mexico's largest inland lake, make it seem a world away from Guadalajara; and the tranquility of lakeshore towns offers a welcome contrast to the bustling city. Sunsets are spectacular, and there's just enough humidity to keep the abundant bougainvillea blooming.

In the 1960s, Mexico's favorable rate of exchange and the springlike climate around Lake Chapala began to woo U.S. and Canadian retirees to the area. Today the community numbers nearly 35,000 and proffers music and arts events that entertain expats, snowbirds, and visitors. Since 1995, however, the lake's shrinking parameters and the metropolitan area's pollution have made it less scenic and desirable. Chapala has been declared part of Mexico's national heritage, and steps have allegedly been taken to find alternative water sources and to protect the lake from further industrial dumping. Nonetheless, the lake, and its formerly prestigious lakeshore villages, have gone downhill.

Spanish settlement in the area dates from 1538, when Franciscan friar Miguel de Bolonio arrived to convert the Taltica Indians to Christianity. Their chief was named Chapalac, from which the name Chapala may have originated. Today, Chapala is the area's largest settlement; although 8 km (5 mi) to the west, Ajijic is now the more vital and attractive. The latter has been home to expat artists and writers since the 1920s. The towns and villages along the lake are linked by one highway with multiple names, such as Carretera Chapala–Ajijic or Carretera Ajijic–Jocotepec.

Chapala
45 km (28 mi) south of Guadalajara.

With Chapala's proximity to rapidly growing Guadalajara, as well as its comfortable climate, it is surprising that tourists didn't frequent the area until the late 19th century. Then-president Porfirio Díaz heard that aristocrats had discovered this ideal place for weekend getaways, and he began spending holidays here in 1904. Soon summer homes were built, and in 1910 the Chapala Yacht Club opened. Word of the town, with its lavish lawn parties and magnificent estates, spread quickly to the United States and Europe. Along the main street, Avenida Madero, you can see the still-functioning (but now rather decrepit) Hotel Nido, built in the early 1900s to accommodate President Porfirio Díaz and his entourage. In the 1940s, Mexican film star María Félix spent the first of her numerous honeymoons there.

Nowadays the town of Chapala attracts a less influential but equally fun-loving assortment of visitors. On weekends the town still fills with Mexican families, although the once-bustling promenade is a shadow of its former self. Vendors sell refreshments and souvenirs, while dilapidated buses carry visitors across mud flats to the lake's edge—now nearly a half mile away. American and Canadian retirees still frequent area restaurants and play golf. And everyone hopes for a series of good rainy seasons—and miracles of ecological and governmental action—to restore the lake, and subsequently the town, to its former glory.

Avenida Madero, the town's main drag, is lined with restaurants, shops, and cafés. On Madero, three blocks north of the promenade, **40** the **plaza,** at the corner of López Cotilla, is a relaxing spot to sit and read the paper, or to succumb to ice cream or doughnuts from the sur- **41** rounding shops. Two blocks south of the plaza, the **Iglesia de San Francisco** is easy to spot by the blue neon crosses on its twin steeples. The church was built in 1528 and reconstructed in 1580. On weekends, **42** the rather forlorn **Parque la Cristianía,** on the south side of the *malecón* (boardwalk), fills with Tapatíos taking a respite from the city and browsing the remaining souvenir booths. Boys compete in energetic games of volleyball, while kids play on jungle gyms and swings. Indoor/outdoor cafés at the end of the promenade serve up seafood (but no longer the native white fish, *pescado blanco*).

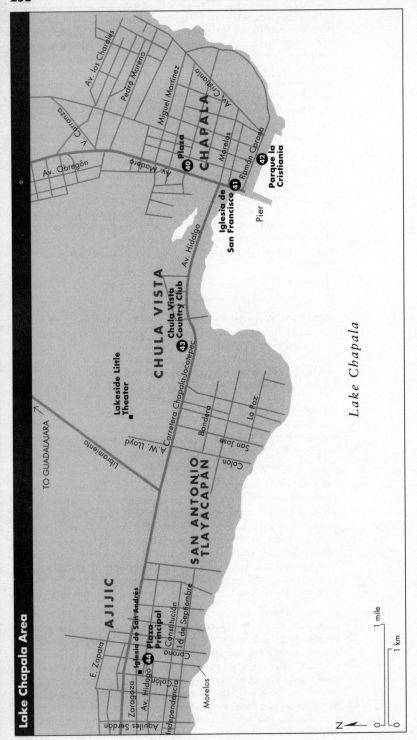

Lake Chapala Area

TO GUADALAJARA

Libramiento

AJIJIC

E. Zapata

Zaragoza

Av. Hidalgo

Colón

Independencia

Aquiles Serdán

Morelos

Iglesia de San Andrés

44 Plaza Principal

Corona

Constitución

16 de Septiembre

SAN ANTONIO TLAYACAPAN

Colón

San José

Bandera

La Paz

A.W. Lloyd

Carretera Chapala-Jocotepec

Lakeside Little Theater

CHULA VISTA

43 Chula Vista Country Club

Av. Hidalgo

Av. los Charales

Pedro Moreno

Av. Carranza

Av. Obregón

Av. Madero

Miguel Martínez

Av. Cristiania

CHAPALA

40 Plaza

Morelos

Ramón Corona

42 Parque la Cristiania

41 Iglesia de San Francisco

Pier

Lake Chapala

N

1 mile

1 km

DINING AND LODGING

$$ ✕ **Cozumel.** Ajijic residents regularly drive over to Chapala for the Wednesday Chicken Cordon Bleu special, which includes wine or a margarita in addition to an opening cocktail and nachos. Other days choose from seafood and international dishes (you still get the free wine), and listen to a mini mariachi band on Wednesday and Friday. Cozumel is open from 9 AM to midnight. Reservations are essential for Wednesday night. ✉ *Paseo Corona 22-A,* ☎ *3765–4606. MC, V. Closed Mon.*

$$ ✕ **Mariscos Guicho's.** The best of the waterfront seafood joints, Guicho's serves savory caviar tostadas, frog legs, garlic shrimp, and spicy seafood soup. The bright gold and green walls and tomato-red tablecloths lend an authentic Mexican charm. ✉ *Paseo Ramón Corona 20,* ☎ *3765–3232. No credit cards. Closed Tues.*

$ ✕ **Restaurant Cazadores.** This grandly turreted brick building was once the summer home of the Braniff family, owners of the now-defunct airline. The food is nothing special—just come for a cool drink and watch the street action from the covered outdoor patio. ✉ *Av. Madero and Paseo Ramón Corona, northeast corner,* ☎ *376/5–21–62. AE, MC, V. Closed Mon.*

$$ ⌂ **Lake Chapala Inn.** It's a pity this charming inn was built just about the time the lake began to recede. Three of the four rooms in this renovated mansion face the dusty lakebed; all have whitewashed oak furniture, TVs, and phones. A dining room, library, large garden terrace, and kitchen are on site, and an English-style breakfast is included in the rate (with a Continental breakfast on Sunday). The family-run hotel caters to American and Canadian tourists. ✉ *Paseo Ramón Corona 23, 45900,* ☎ FAX *3765–4786. 4 rooms. Pool, laundry service, free parking. No credit cards.*

OUTDOOR ACTIVITIES AND SPORTS

The **Chapala Country Club** (✉ Vista del Lago 1, San Nicholás Ibarra, ☎ 3763–5136) is open daily to nonmembers from dawn to dusk, except Tues. and Wed., when it's open to nonmembers after noon. Fees are $22–$38.

Chula Vista
3 km (2 mi) west of Chapala.

Chula Vista, one of the most American neighborhoods in Mexico, lies between Chapala and Ajijic. Dozens of condos dot the hillside north ❹❸ of the road. The **Chula Vista Country Club** (✉ Paseo de Golf 5, ☎ 3766–2515, 💳 $22 weekdays, $33 on weekends and holidays) is a favorite of the local foreign community. The "billy-goat" (hilly) golf course here—open to nonmembers—offers a real workout, as the rugged terrain cannot be negotiated by golf cart.

DINING

$ ✕ **Chicken Little.** As its name suggests, this restaurant and deli serves roast chicken (Tuesday and Saturday only), but you'll also find homemade soups, salads, sandwiches, and American-style pies and cakes. Takeout is available. ✉ *Av. Hidalgo 101-B, in Riberas del Pilar,* ☎ *3765–4399. No credit cards. Closed Sun. No dinner.*

NIGHTLIFE AND THE ARTS

Just west of Chula Vista, above the PAL RV Resort and next to Oak Hill High School, the 112-seat **Lakeside Little Theater** (☎ 3765–3479) stages English-language musicals and plays throughout the year. Box-office hours are 10 AM–1 PM starting three days before performances and one hour before curtain. To find out what's playing, look in *The Guadalajara Reporter* or the *Lake Chapala Review.*

Banana's Night Club has a live house band weekends and has become a favorite of North Americans and locals who have a beer mug with their name at the bar. ⊠ *Carretera Chapala–Jocotepec 159, San Antonio Tlayacapán,* ☎ *3766–0935. No credit cards. Closed Sun.–Tues.*

Ajijic
8 km (5 mi) west of Chapala.

Despite blocks of galleries and crafts shops, Ajijic's small-town ambience is still defined by its narrow cobblestone streets, whitewashed buildings, and gentle pace. Still, the foreign influence is unmistakable: English is spoken almost as widely here as Spanish, and license plates run the gamut from Alaska to Texas. Although Lago de Chapala has receded here also, the change is less dramatic and desultory than in nearby Chapala, and the arts scene gives Ajijic a raison d'etre independent of the lake's existence.

❹❹ The **Plaza Principal** (also called the Plaza de Armas or el jardín) is a tree- and flower-filled central square at the corner of Avenidas Colón and Hidalgo. The **Iglesia de San Andrés** (Church of St. Andrew) sits on the Jardín's north side, shaded by laurel and tulip trees and brightened with roses, lilies, and hibiscus bushes in the courtyard. In late November the plaza fills for the saint's nine-day fiesta.

Walk down Calle Morelos (the continuation of Avenida Colón) toward the lake and you'll find stores and boutiques that sell everything from designer fashions to traditional arts and crafts. Turn left onto Independencia to find about a dozen art galleries and studios.

Another area of activity centers around the soccer field, just northeast of the plaza, which doubles as a venue for bullfights and concerts. Locals and visitors frequent the movie theater, cybercafé, athletic club, and Salvador's restaurant, a local institution.

DINING AND LODGING
In addition to the establishments listed below, there are other good-quality lodgings in the area. Consult the tourist office in Chapala, the *Ojo del Lago* newspaper, or *The Guadalajara Colony Reporter.* Note that restaurants in Ajijic seem to come and go frequently.

$$ ✕ **Ajijic Grill.** Although the hot-pink tablecloths and *equipale* furniture
★ don't exactly scream Nippon, this simple establishment indeed specializes in Japanese cuisine, and a sushi bar has been added. There are grilled meats, seafood, and fresh salads. The patio is prettiest at night, when it is softly lit by tiny white lights. ⊠ *Calle Morelos 5,* ☎ *3766–2458. MC, V. Closed Tues.*

$$ ✕ **Johanna's.** If you tire of Mexican or Continental cuisine, come to this intimate bit of Bavaria on the lake. The authentic German cuisine includes a variety of excellent sausages and homemade goose or duck pate. Main dishes come with soup or salad as well as applesauce and cooked red cabbage. For dessert indulge in plum strudel or blackberry-topped torte. ⊠ *Blvd. Ajijic 118A, in front of the La Floresta Auditorium,* ☎ *3766–0437. No credit cards. Closed Mon.*

$ ✕ **La Casa del Waffle.** Stop in this bright cheery spot on the outskirts of town for breakfast and choose from 12 varieties of waffles and numerous other favorites. ⊠ *Carretera Chapala–Jocotepec Pte. 75, on the highway west of Ajijic,* ☎ *3766–2301. No credit cards. Closed Tues. No dinner.*

$ ✕ **Salvador's.** An afternoon hangout for local expats looking for a great value, this restaurant has a well-kept salad bar and specialties from both south and north of the border. A musician tickles the ivories during the fabulous Sunday brunch, as well as during Wednesday lunch. On

Friday locals come in droves for the well-loved fish and chips lunch special. ⊠ *Carretera Chapala–Jocotepec Oriente 56, in Plaza Bugambilias,* ☎ *3766–2301.* ◷ *Closed Sat. No credit cards.*

$$ **✕🏨 La Nueva Posada.** Luxuriant gardens framed in bougainvillea de-
★ fine this charming inn. Rooms are perfectly adequate, but it's the public areas that truly shine. There is fine entertainment most evenings (typically a jazz trio or tropical music) in the cozy bar, with its brick domed ceilings, hanging reed lamps, and leather chairs surrounding custom-made tables. Out in the garden restaurant, strands of tiny white lights set the mood for an evening meal, where anything from chef Lorraine Rousseau's eclectic menu is recommended. ⊠ *Donato Guerra 9, Apdo. 30, 45920,* ☎ *3766–1444,* FAX *3766–2049,* WEB *www.mexconnect.com. 19 rooms, 4 suites. Restaurant, bar, fans, pool, laundry service, free parking. MC, V.*

$$ **🏨 Los Artistas.** This cozy inn is surrounded by an acre of splendidly landscaped gardens. Each room—with white textured walls and red tile floors—is uniquely decorated with colorful handwoven Mexican bedspreads, wrought iron or carved wood bedframes, and fresh-cut bouquets; most have patios made intimate by bowers of blooming things; four have fireplaces. Rates include a generous breakfast of egg dishes, local fruits and fresh homemade yogurt, granola, and breads. ⊠ *Constitución 105, 45920,* ☎ *3766–1027,* FAX *3766–1762. 7 rooms. Pool, free parking. No credit cards.*

$$ **🏨 Real de Chapala.** Airy and ample yet somewhat impersonal rooms look out over soccer fields once covered by Lake Chapala in its grander days. The hotel's Mexican clientele—especially city-dwellers escaping from nearby Guadalajara—loves the Sunday mariachi lunch served on the covered patio. ⊠ *Paseo del Prado 20, 45920,* ☎ *376/6–00–14 or 376/6–00–21,* FAX *376/6–00–25. 80 rooms, 5 suites. Restaurant, bar, fans, pool, wading pool, 2 tennis courts, volleyball, billiards, laundry service, meeting rooms, free parking. AE, MC, V.*

$ **🏨 Inn at San Andres.** This small B&B integrates hand-painted tiles and rustic furniture in each one-of-a-kind suite. ⊠ *Galeana 22-A, on block off plaza, 45920,* ☎ *3766–1250; 703/830–8398 in the U.S.,* FAX *3766–1250. 5 suites. Pool. No credit cards.*

NIGHTLIFE AND THE ARTS

The rambling, hacienda-style **Posada Ajijic** (⊠ Calle Morelos, facing the lake, ☎ 3766–0744 or 3766–0430) is a restaurant, bar, and popular weekend dance place with an unobstructed view of the lakebed. A cozy, candlelit nightclub, **Viva María** (⊠ Donato Guerra 20-A, ☎ 3766–0984), presents an eclectic range of live musical offerings Wednesday through Saturday. Art classes, exhibitions, and informal gallery space characterize **CABA** (⊠ Colón 43, ☎ FAX 3766–1920). Initiated in 1999, the **Festival Internacional de Cine,** held in November, showcases international films and organizes art and cultural events related to filmmaking.

SHOPPING

Along the shores of Lake Chapala are workshops creating export-quality crafts. Although Ajijic doesn't have as many boutiques and crafts shops as inhabitants, it sometimes seems that way. **La Casa de las Artesanías Ajijik** (⊠ Carretera Chapala-Jocotepec Km 6.5, ☎ 3766–0548) is a branch of the state-run Instituto de Artesanías Jaliscienses crafts shop. It's open weekdays 10–6, Saturday 10–4, and Sunday 10–2. **La Colección Bárbara** (⊠ Av. Independencia 7A–9A, ☎ 3766–1824), open Friday 9–5:30, Sat. 9–4, sells traditional crafts, antiques, jewelry, and fine furniture. You can find exhibitions of sculpture, paintings, prints, photography, pottery, and other artworks by local and Guadalajara artists at **Galería Américas** (⊠ Ramón Corona 11, across from the Lake

Chapala Society, ☎ 3766–1292, ☉ Mon.–Sat. 10–4). Local artists' works are on offer at **Galería Daniel Palma** (✉ Ocampo 30, ☎ 3766–1688, ☉ Weekdays 10–2 and 4–7, Sat. 10–3). The **Mi México** (✉ Morelos 8, ☎ 3766–0133, ☉ Mon.–Sat. 10–2 and 3–6, Sun. 11–3) boutique sells women's clothing and jewelry as well as pottery, blown glass, and other crafts and gifts.

OUTDOOR ACTIVITIES AND SPORTS

Take a break with the kids—or pretend you are one again—and explore the **Tobolandia** water park. ✉ *Blvd. Ajijic 57, Fracc. La Floresta, Chapala,* ☎ *3766–2120.* 🎟 *$4.50.* ☉ *Daily 10–6.*

Lively horses are rented (about $2.50 an hour) at a narrow grassy plaza shaded by oak trees in Ajijic at **Caballos.** ✉ *Paseo Delgado and Camino Real,* ☎ *3766–1319.*

San Juan Cosalá

10 km (6 mi) west of Chapala.

San Juan Cosalá is known for its natural thermal-water spas on the shores of Lake Chapala, with the mountains rising to the north. The **Hotel Balneario San Juan Cosalá** (✉ La Paz 420, ☎ 3761–0222, 🎟 $5.50) welcomes both day-trippers and overnight guests to its four large swimming pools and two wading pools. A restaurant with international fare is on the premises. Although **Villas Buenaventura Cosalá** (✉ Km. 13.5 Carr. Chapala–Jocotepec, ☎ 3761–0202) doesn't accept day-trippers, guests can enjoy thermal waters in their hotel suite's bathtubs as well as in the property's hot tubs and swimming pools. Facilities include six one-bedroom suites and 11 with two bedrooms; most have kitchenettes. There is a two-night minimum on weekends.

Lake Chapala A to Z

BUS TRAVEL

Autotransportes Guadalajara Chapala and other bus lines have frequent service to Chapala, Ajijic, and other lakeside towns from Guadalajara's Antigua Central Camionera (Old Bus Station). It's about 45 minutes to Chapala and another 10–15 minutes to Ajicic. Make sure you ask for the *directo* (direct) as opposed to *clase segunda* (second class), which stops at every little pueblo en route.

➤ BUS INFORMATION: **Autotransportes Guadalajara Chapala** (☎ 3619–5365).

CAR TRAVEL

From downtown Guadalajara take Calzada Independencia Sur to Dr. R. Michel, turn left, and follow the signs to Chapala and the other lakeside towns. The trip takes 40 minutes.

ENGLISH-LANGUAGE MEDIA

The *Ojo del Lago* monthly newspaper is available free throughout Chapala and Ajijic. The monthly *Lake Chapala Review* sells for less than a dollar. *The Guadalajara Reporter* weekly newspaper devotes a section to lakeside news and events. Libros de Chapala, open daily 9–2 and 3–6, has an extensive range of English-language magazines, U.S. and Canadian newspapers, and a large selection of books on Mexico in English.

➤ BOOKSTORES: **Libros de Chapala** (✉ Av. Madero, across from the plaza, Chapala, ☎ no phone).

VISITOR INFORMATION

The Jalisco tourism office in Chapala is open weekdays 9–7, and weekends 9–5. In Ajijic, the nonprofit Lake Chapala Society, open Monday–Saturday 10–1, provides information about the area.

➤ TOURIST INFORMATION: **Jalisco state tourism office** (✉ Madero 407-A, 2nd floor, ☎ FAX 3765–3141). **Lake Chapala Society** (✉ Av. 16 de Septiembre 16, ☎ no phone).

Tequila

56 km (35 mi) northwest of Guadalajara.

For a close look at how Mexico's most famous liquor is made from the spiny blue agave plant that grows in the fields alongside the highway, spend part or all of a day in this tidy village, about 59 km (37 miles) from outside the city of Guadalajara. It's said that centuries ago, the Tiquilas, a small Nahuatl-speaking tribe, discovered the heart of the agave produced a juice that could be fermented to make intoxicating drinks. When distilled (an innovation introduced after the arrival of the Spanish in the 16th century), the fermented liquid turns into the heady liquor which in this and only a few other regions can be rightfully labeled tequila.

You can tour the famous Sauza Distillery or one of the other modern tequila distilleries here—it's best to make reservations ahead of time or to take a tour. Most distilleries prefer to receive visitors weekdays between 10 AM and 1 PM. Bus service is available from Guadalajara's Old Bus Station, and various Guadalajara tour companies offer guided excursions. Each Saturday the Tequila Express leaves Guadalajara on a 10-hour trip that includes a tour of the Hacienda San José del Refugio distillery, in Amatitlán, a satisfying lunch, a folkloric ballet performance serenaded by mariachis, and an unlimited supply of Mexico's most famous liquor. Tickets are available through Guadalajara's **Chamber of Commerce** (☎ 3880–9099).

GUADALAJARA A TO Z

To research prices, get advice from other travelers, and book travel arrangements, visit www.fodors.com.

AIR TRAVEL

The main gateway to Guadalajara is Los Angeles, but you can also fly direct from Dallas, Houston, or Atlanta on some airlines.

CARRIERS

Aero California serves Tuscon and Los Angeles as well as many Mexican cities. Aeroméxico has nonstop service to Guadalajara from Los Angeles and extensive internal flights. Mexicana has direct flights from Chicago, Los Angeles, San Francisco, and San José. Through Dallas, American Airlines provides service to Guadalajara from all cities in its system. Flights on Continental are routed through the Houston hub. Delta Air Lines flies direct from Los Angeles and Atlanta.

➤ AIRLINES AND CONTACTS: **Aero California** (☎ 3616–2525). **Aeroméxico** (☎ 3669–0202). **Mexicana** (☎ 3678–7676). **American Airlines** (☎ 3616–4090 or 3688–5518). **Continental** (☎ 3688–5141 or 3647–4251). **Delta Air Lines** (☎ 3630–3530).

AIRPORTS AND TRANSFERS

Libertador Miguel Hidalgo International Airport is 16½ km (10 mi) south of Guadalajara, en route to Chapala. A new international terminal is planned in the next decade to help meet the demands of increased air service to the area.

➤ AIRPORT INFORMATION: **Libertador Miguel Hidalgo International Airport** (✉ Av. Solidaridad Iberoamericana Km 17.5, ☎ 3688–5248 or 3688–5127).

The Chapala Highway stretches north from the airport to the city. The 30-minute trip can be delayed by slow-moving caravans of trucks and weekend recreational traffic.

Autotransportaciones Aeropuerto is 24-hour airport taxi service that goes anywhere in the Guadalajara area in VW buses (*combis*). Fares, based on distance, range from $8 to $12 for up to three people going in the same part of the city. At the airport, buy a ticket from the booth outside the terminal exit. To the airport, hotel taxis have set rates, as do regular city taxis.

➤ TAXI AND SHUTTLES: **Autotransportaciones Aeropuerto** (☎ 3812–4278 or 3812–4308).

BUS TRAVEL TO AND FROM GUADALAJARA
First-class, air-conditioned buses with rest rooms run daily to Guadalajara from most major cities on the border. Greyhound has schedule and fare information for service into Mexico, although you will have to change to a Mexican carrier at the border. Guadalajara's Nueva Central Camionera (New Bus Station) is 10 km (6 mi) southeast of downtown Guadalajara on the highway to Zapotlanejo. Elite has first-class service to Mexico City and many other destinations. One of the most reliable lines is ETN. Primera Plus has first- and second-class buses serving mainly central and western Mexico. Omnibus de México serves the U.S. border and intermediate destinations.

Buses to and from such nearby destinations as Chapala, Ajijic, and Tequila depart from the Antigua Central Camionera, just northeast of the Parque Agua Azul on Avenida Dr. R. Michel, between Calles Los Angeles and 5 de Febrero.

➤ BUS INFORMATION: **Greyhound** (☎ 01–800/712–8819 or 800/231–2222). **Elite** (☎ 3679–0404). **ETN** (☎ 3600–0477 or 01–800/360–4200). **Primera Plus** (☎ 3600–0398). **Omnibus de México** (☎ 3600–0469).

BUS TRAVEL WITHIN GUADALAJARA
Buses run every few minutes between 6 AM and 11 PM to all local attractions, including Tlaquepaque, Tonalá, and Zapopan. Fares are roughly 30¢, making buses the preferred mode of transportation for Guadalajara natives, so expect to stand during daytime. Various "luxury" buses—which run on some of the main routes through the city, including out to Tlaquepaque and Tonalá—cost 55¢ and are much less crowded and vastly more comfortable.

CAR RENTAL
All the major international players, including Avis, Hertz, Dollar, and Budget have offices in Guadalajara's airport. Downtown, you can walk into Budget or the local agency, Express.

➤ MAJOR AGENCIES: **Avis** (☎ 3688–5528 or 3688–5656). **Budget** (✉ Av. Niños Héroes 934, at Av. 16 de Septiembre, ☎ 3613–0027). **Dollar** (✉ Av. Federalismo Sur 540A at Av. de la Paz, ☎ 3826–7959). **Hertz** (☎ 3688–5403 [airport]; ✉ Av. 16 de Septiembre 738-B, ☎ 3614–6162). **Express Rent a Car** (✉ Manzano 444, ☎ 3614–1465 or 3614–1865).

CAR TRAVEL
Major routes include Highway 54, which leads south to Colima (220 km [136 mi]) and north to Zacatecas (320 km [198 mi]). Highway 15 hugs the southern shore of Lake Chapala before continuing southeast to Morelia (255 km [58 mi]) and Mexico City (209 km [130 mi]). Highway 15-D is the toll road to Mexico City. Heading northwest from

Guadalajara, both Highways 15 and 15D pass through some of the most beautiful country in Jalisco and neighboring Nayarit state. If you have a choice between a free or toll road, remember that the latter tend to be quite expensive and have fewer opportunities to exit the highway, but tend to be in better condition than their free counterparts.

In Guadalajara, beware of heavy traffic and *topes* (speed bumps). Traffic circles are common at many busy intersections. Parking in the city center can be scarce, so take a taxi or bus if you're not staying nearby; otherwise, try the underground lots across from the Palacio Municipal (✉ Av. Hidalgo and Calle Pedro Loza) and below the Plaza de la Liberación (✉ Av. Hidalgo and Calle Belén, in front of the Teatro Degollado). If you park illegally, the police may tow your vehicle: you'll have to go to the municipal transit office to pay a fine and then to a *correlones* (holding areas) to pay the tow charge (around $15) and retrieve your car.

EMBASSIES

For information about consulates other than those listed below, call Guadalajara's consular association, open weekdays 9–3 and 5–8.

The U.S. Consulate is open weekday mornings 8:30–11:30. The Canadian Consulate is open weekdays 8:30–2 and 3–5. The U.K. Consulate is open only by appointment.

➤ CONSULAR INFORMATION: **Asociación Consular de Guadalajara** (☎ 3616–0629).

➤ CONSULATES: **Canadian Consulate** (✉ Fiesta Americana, Aurelio Aceves 225, ☎ 3616–5642; 01–800/706–2900 after-hours emergency). **British Consulate** (✉ Eulogio Parra 2539, ☎ 3616–0629). **American Consulate** (✉ Progreso 175, between Av. López Cotilla and Libertad, ☎ 3825–2700; 3825–1717; 3826–5553 after-hours emergency).

EMERGENCIES

Dialing 080 will connect you with a central emergency system (for all of the organizations listed below and other metro-area police stations). Ask for an English-speaking operator.

➤ EMERGENCY SERVICES: **Guadalajara City police** (☎ 3668–0800). **State police** (☎ 3617–0770 or 3614–7374). **Theft Line** (☎ 3618–2539). **Highway patrol** (☎ 3629–5082 or 3629–5085). **Cruz Roja** (Red Cross; ☎ 3614–5600 or 3614–2707). **Cruz Verde** (Green Cross municipal emergency medical service; ☎ 3812–5143 or 3614–5252).

➤ HOSPITALS: **Hospital del Carmen** (✉ Tarascos 3435, ☎ 3813–1224 or 3813–0025). **Hospital México-Americano** (✉ Colomos 2110, ☎ 3641–3141). **Hospital San Javier** (✉ Av. Pablo Casals 640, Col. Providencia, ☎ 3669–0222).

ENGLISH-LANGUAGE MEDIA

Sandi Bookstore, open weekdays 9:30–2:30 and 3:30–7 and Saturday 9:30–2, sells many newspapers, magazines, and books. Sanborn's has a good selection of books, periodicals, and music.

The Guadalajara Reporter, a weekly newspaper sold for 90¢ at newsstands and hotels, includes excellent community and cultural listings. The monthly newspaper *Ojo del Lago* covers the Lake Chapala area. An excellent source of information on the Lake Chapala area as well as 40 different day excursions from Guadalajara is *Outdoors in Western Mexico* by John and Susana Pint (Editoriales Agata, 1998).

➤ BOOKSTORES: **Sandi Bookstore** (✉ Av. Tepeyac 718, Chapala, ☎ 3121–0863). **Sanborn's** (✉ Av. 16 de Septiembre 127, centro, ☎ 3613–6693; ✉ Av. López Mateos 2718, Plaza del Sol mall, ☎ 3647–2510).

HEALTH

DOCTORS AND DENTISTS

The U.S. Consulate maintains a list of English-speaking doctors and dentists. All major hotels have the names of doctors who are on 24-hr call.

HOSPITALS

Hospital del Carmen is near the Plaza México mall on the west side of the city. Hospital México-Americano is southeast of the Colón Monument, just off Av. de las Américas. Hospital San Javier in the northwest sector, is considered the best in the city.

PHARMACIES

Several branches of Farmacias Guadalajara are open 24 hours. Benavides is another ubiquitous drugstore chain. Convenient branches are located downtown, and in Zapopan.

➤ PHARMACY INFORMATION: **Farmacias Guadalajara** (⊠ Av. Javier Mina 221, between Calle Cabañas and Vicente Guerrero, ☎ 3618–3767). **Benavides** (⊠ Morelos 468, near el Palacio Municipal, ☎ 3614–7676; ⊠ Hidalgo 307-A, ☎ 3633–2510).

MAIL AND SHIPPING

The main post office is open weekdays 8–7.

Sending e-mail from an Internet café is an increasingly popular alternative to Mexico's slow postal service. Both CCCP and Cybercentro are inexpensive, and Cybercentro also serves coffee.

➤ POST OFFICE: **Post Office** (⊠ Administración de Correos 1, ☎ 3614–8125).

➤ INTERNET CAFÉS: **CCCP** (⊠ Av. Alcade 159, ☎ 3614–5311). **Cybercentro** (⊠ Santa Mónica 208 near San Felipe, ☎ 3613–4259).

MONEY MATTERS

The most convenient places to change currency are *casas de cambio*, generally open weekdays 9–7 and Saturday until 1 PM. Many of them are on Calle López Cotilla downtown and in the Plaza del Sol area. Banks tend to have more limited hours, longer waits, and a similar rate of exchange.

SIGHTSEEING TOURS

Most tour operators in Guadalajara have guided city tours and excursions to Tequila, Lake Chapala, Tlaquepaque, and Tonalá. Free three-hour guided bus and walking tours are offered periodically by the tourist office. They usually leave from the Municipal Palace Saturday at 10 AM. Call 3616–3333 to confirm. Free guided trolley tours of Zapopan are offered for groups by the Zapopan Tourist Board; call 3110–0754 for information and reservations.

You can hire a horse-drawn carriage (calandrias) in front of the Museo Regional, the Mercado Libertad, or Parque San Francisco. The charge is about $16 for an hour-long tour for up to five passengers. Few drivers speak English.

Panoramex offers lake tours and arranges bus tickets and excursions to Tequila. The bilingual guides of Ajijic's Charter Club Tours lead tours to Guadalajara, shopping and factory tours to Tlaquepaque and Tonalá, and to lesser known yet scenic towns throughout the state of Jalisco. Sonrisa Tours is another established, reliable tour operator.

➤ TOUR INFORMATION: **Panoramex** (⊠ Av. Federalismo Sur 944, ☎ 3810–5057, 3810–5005). **Charter Club Tours** (⊠ Carretera Oriente 1, Ajijic, Plaza Moñana mall, ☎ 3766–1777). **Sonrisa Tours** (⊠

Paseo del Hospicio 63, Plaza Tapatía, ☎ 3618–9601, 3617–2511, or 3617–2590).

SUBWAY TRAVEL

Guadalajara's underground *tren ligero* (light train) system is clean, safe, and efficient. Line 1 runs north–south along Avenida Federalismo from the Periférico (city beltway) Sur to Periférico Norte, near the Benito Juárez Auditorium. The central terminal is at Parque Revolución. Line 2 runs east–west along Avenida Javier Mina (which becomes Avenida Juárez at Calzada Independencia) from Tetlán in eastern Guadalajara to Avenida Federalismo. Trains run about every 15 minutes from 6 AM to 11 PM; a token for one trip costs about 30¢. Juárez Station, where Lines 1 and 2 meet, serves as a public art gallery, with changing exhibits of works by Mexican artists.

TAXIS

Taxis are readily available and reasonably economical. Although all cabs are supposed to use meters, many do not, in which case you should agree on a fare before you enter the cab. Schedules listing fares to downtown and all major attractions are posted in most hotel lobbies, and cab drivers should produce a copy upon request. *Sitios* (cab stands) are near all hotels and attractions. Fares go up about 25% after 10 PM.

TRAIN TRAVEL

Train tickets for a full-day, round-trip Saturday excursion to Tequila are available from the Cámera de Comercio (Chamber of Commerce) for $40. The trip runs from 10:30 AM to 8:30 PM.
➤ TRAIN INFORMATION: **Cámera de Comercio** (☎ 3122–9020).

TRANSPORTATION AROUND GUADALAJARA

Guadalajara's major attractions are best seen on foot. For points outside the city center, Guadalajara has an inexpensive, well-organized public-transportation system.

Buses are without a doubt the cheapest and most efficient—but sometimes least comfortable—means of traversing the city.

TRAVEL AGENCIES

Many of the city's 100-plus travel agencies are in the two hotel zones, el centro and Avenida López Mateos Sur, on the city's southwest side. Near the Minerva Fountain you'll find American Express. Copenhagen Tours sells bus and plane tickets.
➤ LOCAL AGENT REFERRALS: **American Express** (✉ Av. Vallarta 2440, ☎ 3818–2323 or 3818–2325). **Copenhagen Tours** (✉ Av. J. Manuel Clouthier 156, Col. Prados Vallarta, ☎ 3629–7957 or 3629–4758).

VISITOR INFORMATION

The Jalisco state tourist offices have information about Guadalajara and other parts of Mexico.

Guadalajara's Municipal Tourist Office, in front of the Municipal Palace, also has kiosks downtown in the Plaza Guadalajara, in Los Arcos monument on Avenida Vallarta just east of the Minerva Fountain, in Parque San Francisco, in front of the Instituto Cultural Cabañas, in front of Mercado Libertad, at Vicente Guerrero 233 (open weekdays only), and at the airport.

The Tourist Board of Zapopan provides information and maps about metropolitan Guadalajara, including Zapopan, Tonalá, and Tlaquepaque.

➤ Tourist Information: **Jalisco state tourist offices** (✉ Calle Morelos 102, in Plaza Tapatía, ☎ 3668–1600, 3613–0306, or 01–800/363–2200; ☉ weekdays 9–8, weekends 9–1; ✉ Palacio de Gobierno ☎ no phone; ☉ weekdays 8:30–7:30, Sat. 10–1). **Municipal Tourist Office** (☎ 3616–3333 or 3616–3300; ☉ Mon.–Sat. 9–7). **Tourist Board of Zapopan** (✉ Av. Vallarta 6501, Ciudad Granja, ☎ 3110–0754; ☉ weekdays 9–7:30).

7 THE HEARTLAND

Rich with the history of Mexico's revolution, the heartland is a treasury of colonial towns—Guanajuato, Zacatecas, Querétaro, Morelia, and Pátzcuaro, among others— whose residents lead quiet, largely traditional lives. Even in San Miguel de Allende, an American art colony and home to a well-known language institute, women wash their clothes and gossip at the local lavandería as they have for hundreds of years.

MEXICO'S HEARTLAND, so named for its central position in the country, is known for its well-preserved colonial architecture, its fertile farmland and surrounding mountains, and its leading role in Mexican history, particularly during the War of Independence (1810–21). The Bajío (ba-*hee*-o), as it is also called, corresponds roughly to the states of Guanajuato and parts of Querétaro and Michoacán. In the hills surrounding the cities of Guanajuato, Zacatecas, Querétaro, and San Miguel de Allende, the Spanish found silver in the 1500s, leading them to colonize the area heavily.

Updated by
Amy Mansell

Three centuries later, wealthy Creoles (Mexicans of Spanish descent) in Querétaro and San Miguel took the first audacious steps toward independence from Spain. When their clandestine efforts were discovered, two of the early insurgents, Ignacio Allende and Father Miguel Hidalgo, began in earnest the War of Independence.

When Allende and Hidalgo were executed in 1811, another native son, José María Morelos, picked up the independence banner. This mestizo (mixed race) mule skinner–turned–priest–turned–soldier, with his army of 9,000, came close to gaining control of the land before he was killed in 1815. Thirteen years later, the city of Valladolid was renamed Morelia in his honor.

Long after the War of Independence ended in 1821, the cities of the Bajío continued to play a prominent role in Mexico's history. Three major events took place in Querétaro alone: in 1848 the Mexican-American War ended with the signing of the Treaty of Guadalupe Hidalgo; in 1867 Austrian Maximilian of Hapsburg, crowned Emperor of Mexico by Napoleon III of France, was executed in the hills north of town; and in 1917 the Mexican Constitution was signed here.

The heartland honors the events and people that helped shape modern Mexico. In ornate cathedrals or bucolic plazas, down narrow alleyways or atop high hillsides, you'll find monuments—and remnants—of a heroic past. During numerous fiestas, you can savor the region's historic spirit. On a night filled with fireworks, off-key music, and tireless celebrants, it's hard not to be caught up in the vital expression of national pride.

Tourism is welcomed in the heartland, especially in these hard economic times, and, for the most part, it doesn't disrupt the normal routines of residents. Families visit parks for Sunday picnics, youngsters tussle in school courtyards, old men chat in shaded plazas, and Purépecha women in traditional garb sell their wares in crowded *mercados* (markets). Unlike areas where attractions have been specifically designed for tourism, the Bajío relies on its historic ties and the architectural integrity of its cities to appeal to travelers. Although this is an interesting area to tour by car, there is frequent inexpensive bus service from one city to the next throughout the Bajío.

Pleasures and Pastimes

Architecture

Financed largely by the region's fabulously wealthy silver mines, the cities of the heartland are architectural masterpieces full of buildings richly worked with curvaceous lines, human, animal, plant, and geometric motifs, and sculptural depth that accents the play of light and shadow. From the stately, almost European grandeur of Morelia to the steep, labyrinthine allure of Guanajuato and the sandstone pink splendor of Zacatecas, no two towns are alike. San Miguel de Allende's

ZACATECAS

Ojuelos de
Jalisco

Villa de
Reyes

Santa María
del Río

JALISCO

Ocampo

KEY

Rail Lines

0   20 miles
0   30 km

Lagos de
Moreno

80

San Luis
de la Paz

León

SIERRA
DE
GUANAJUATO

Dolores
Hidalgo

110

45

✈
☆ **Guanajuato**

**San Miguel
de Allende**

XILITLA

Silao

111

QUERÉ-
TARO

Manuel
Doblado

GUANAJUATO

Irapuato

51

Querétaro ☆

45
D

Salamanca

45
D

Celaya

57

45

TO
SAN JUAN DEL RÍO,
TEQUISQUIAPAN

La Piedad
de Cabadas

Lago
Yuriria

15

Moroleón

Lerma

Acámbaro

51

43

Lago de
Cuitzeo

ZAMORA/GUADALAJARA

15

Isla Yunueo

Morelia ✈

Ciudad
Hidalgo

Quiroga ☆

TO
PARICUTÍN VOLCANO

Lake
Pátzcuaro

Tzintzuntzan

51

15

14

Isla
Janitzio

Pátzcuaro

✈
Uruapan

Zitácuaro

Parque
Nacional
Eduardo
Ruíz

Santa Clara
del Cobre

MICHOACÁN

Tuzantla

120

Nueva
Italia

La Huacana

Nocupétaro

Bejucos

134

Presa del
Infiernillo

Huetamo

Balsas

Gothic-style parish church puts a Gallic touch on an otherwise very Mexican skyline. And in Pátzcuaro and Querétaro, the ornate 16th-century colonial mansions surrounding the city squares have been converted into hotels and government offices, making their interior patios accessible to the public.

Dining

It's no surprise that culinary tastes vary widely in the heartland, which spans a large area across central Mexico. In the state of Michoacán, Purépecha Indian influences predominate. The tomato-based *sopa tarasca* (a soup with cheese, cream, and tortillas) is one of the best-known regional specialties. Because of the numerous lakes and rivers in the state, several types of freshwater fish are often served in Michoacán restaurants.

At the northern end of the heartland, in Zacatecas, the hearty, meat-eating tastes of the *norteños* (northerners) rule the dinner table. Although beef is the favored dish, other specialties include *asado de boda* (wedding barbecue), pork in a spicy but semisweet sauce. The region is also known for its cheese and wine. And because of San Miguel's expatriate community, the city has a wealth of worthy eateries.

CATEGORY	COST*
$$$$	over $15
$$$	$10–$15
$$	$5–$10
$	under $5

per person for a main course at dinner

Hiking and Walking

With its rolling farmland, lofty volcanoes, lakes, and Indian villages, Michoacán is a perfect area for day hikes. Trails near Pátzcuaro wind up to nearby hilltops for great views across town and the surrounding countryside, and in Uruapan—64 km (40 mi) away and 2,000 ft lower in elevation—you can walk along a lush river valley. And no tour of the heartland would be complete without a few days of leisurely strolling on the avenues and back streets of colonial cities and towns.

Lodging

In many of the heartland's colonial cities, restored haciendas of the fabulously rich residents of centuries past make the best lodgings. Often near the center of town, sometimes facing directly onto plazas, some of these mansions date from the 16th century. There are also deluxe modern high-rises and functional, low-cost hotels. Except for five-star hotels, most properties in the region aren't heated; you may want to bring warm, comfortable clothes for indoor wear, or to inquire in advance if heating is important to you. In restored colonial properties, rooms often vary dramatically as to size and furnishings, so if you aren't satisfied with the one you are shown, ask to see another. High season, for the most part, is limited to specific dates surrounding Christmas, Easter, and regional festivals. Most moderate and inexpensive hotels quote prices with 15% value-added tax already included.

CATEGORY	COST*
$$$$	over $200
$$$	$100–$200
$$	$50–$100
$	under $50

All prices are for a standard double room, excluding 15% tax.

Exploring the Heartland

Many travelers barrel past the heartland to points north or west of Mexico City, but there are plenty of reasons to stop here: browsing in the shops of San Miguel or Guanajuato for bargains in silver and other local crafts, or heading to the state of Michoacán, renowned for its folklore and folk crafts, especially ceramics and lacquerware. Stay longer to linger over the wealth of architectural styles that each of the colonial cities has to offer.

Numbers in the text correspond to numbers in the margin and on the San Miguel de Allende, Guanajuato, Zacatecas, Querétaro, Morelia, and Pátzcuaro maps.

Great Itineraries

If you have only a couple of days to spare, stop in any of several colonial cities for a taste of life in the heartland—each one has its own particular flavor. If you happen to fall under the heartland's peaceful, friendly spell, you'll want a week to 10 days to give yourself time to drink in the atmosphere of two or three of the region's cities.

IF YOU HAVE 3 DAYS

Head to **Guanajuato** ⑫–㉒ (365 km [226 mi] from Mexico City), the most architecturally dramatic of the heartland cities. Make a day trip from here to the picturesque town of **San Miguel de Allende** ①–⑪, 90 minutes away by car or bus, to shop for crafts.

Another option is to go from Mexico City to the Michoacán capital of **Morelia** ㊵–㊾ (about four hours by car) and spend a day taking in its stately architecture and café-lined plaza. The next day, drive on to **Pátzcuaro** ㊿–�56, set among volcanoes in the center of Purépecha Indian country. Spend the morning in the bustling market or strolling in the surrounding countryside before making a late-afternoon return to Mexico City.

IF YOU HAVE 5 DAYS

Make **Guanajuato** ⑫–㉒ your base and allow an extra day to see its churches and museums—perhaps even the gruesome Mummy Museum. Stop off at the town of Dolores Hidalgo, home of Mexican independence, on your way to a day of shopping in San Miguel. Overnight in San Miguel and the next morning head for **Querétaro** ㉜–㉝, 63 km (39 mi) away. This quiet colonial city is considered the capital of the Bajío. After a night in a downtown hotel, return to Mexico City (three hours) or to the airport outside Guanajuato (2½ hours).

If you decide to spend several days in Michoacán, you can easily fill your time exploring the state's colonial towns and enjoying the lush, mountainous countryside. After three days in **Morelia** ㊵–㊾ and **Pátzcuaro** ㊿–�56, take a day trip to explore the crater on an extinct volcano in **San Juan Parangaricútiro** or the ruins of an ancient Purépecha Indian capital, **Tzintzuntzan** (both are easy day trips from Pátzcuaro), before returning on the final day to Morelia and Mexico City.

IF YOU HAVE 7 DAYS

From your base in **Guanajuato** ⑫–㉒, consider adding to the first of the five-day itineraries a round-trip flight from León's Guanajuato International Airport to **Zacatecas** ㉓–㉛. This would give you a day and a half to explore the northern colonial mining city. Because it lies off the main tourist track, Zacatecas has a refreshingly un-self-conscious mood. Another possibility for a week in the heartland would be to make a loop from Mexico City that includes both Morelia and Guanajuato. You'd have time for leisurely side trips to **Pátzcuaro** ㊿–�56 and **San Miguel de Allende** ①–⑪ and a stop in **Querétaro** ㉜–㉝. When in Pátzcuaro, be sure to take a boat out to the island town of **Janítzio** on nearby Lake Pátzcuaro, home of Mexico's most famous Day of the Dead festival (lasting up to two days), or to the island of **Yunuen,** which isn't as yet besieged by tourists.

When to Tour the Heartland

One of the most pleasing aspects of the heartland is its superb climate— it rarely gets overly hot, even in the middle of summer, and although winter days can get nippy, especially in northern Zacatecas, they are generally temperate. Average temperatures in the southern city of Morelia range from 20°C (68°F) in May to just under 10°C (49°F) in January. Zacatecas is more extreme, with winter temperatures as low as 0°C (32°F) and snow flurries every several years, and summer highs of 28°C–30°C (81°F–85°F). Nights are cool all year in most of the region's cities. The rainy season across the heartland hits between June and October and is generally strongest in July and August.

Consider going to the heartland for cultural festivals or religious events: in October Guanajuato's three-week-long International Cervantes Festival, which brings actors, musicians, painters, and hundreds of thousands of visitors to town; in late November San Miguel's Jazz Festival International; and November 1–2 on the island of Janítzio, where local Purépecha (also called Tarascan) Indians hold a Day of the Dead in honor of their ancestors. Of ecological interest is the arrival of millions of monarch butterflies near Morelia between early November and early March.

SAN MIGUEL DE ALLENDE

San Miguel de Allende first began luring foreigners in the late 1930s when American Stirling Dickinson and prominent local residents founded an art school in this mountainous settlement. The school, now called the Instituto Allende, has grown in stature over the years—as has the city's reputation as a writers' and artists' colony. Walk down any cobblestone street and you're likely to see residents of a variety of national origins. Some come to study at the Instituto Allende or the Academia Hispano-Americana, some to escape the harsh northern winters, and still others to retire.

Cultural offerings in this town of about 110,000 reflect its large American and Canadian community. There are literary readings, art shows, a yearly jazz festival, psychic fairs, aerobics and past-life regression classes, and a lending library. International influence notwithstanding, San Miguel, declared a national monument in 1926, retains its Mexican characteristics. Wandering down streets lined with 18th-century mansions, you'll also discover fountains, monuments, and churches—all reminders of the city's illustrious, and sometimes notorious, past. The onetime headquarters of the Spanish Inquisition in New Spain, for example, is located at the corner of Calles Hernández Macías and Pila Seca. The former Inquisition jail stands across the way. Independence Day is celebrated with exceptional fervor in San Miguel, with fireworks, dances, and parades September 15 and 16, and bullfights and cultural events for the remainder of the month, including the running of the bulls.

Exploring San Miguel de Allende

You'll find most of San Miguel's sights in a cluster downtown, which you can visit in a couple of hours.

A Good Walk

Begin at the main plaza, otherwise known as **El Jardín** ①. After you get a feel for the square, stop into **La Parroquia** ②, the sandstone

San Miguel de Allende

church on its south side. Three blocks northeast of La Parroquia (take Calle San Francisco, on the north side of El Jardín, to Calle Juárez) is the **Iglesia de San Francisco** ③, with a fine churrigueresque (heavily ornamented) facade. Take a few steps north on Calle Juárez to Calle Mesones, then east to Calle Colegio, where the colorful **Mercado Ignacio Ramírez** occupies a cavernous structure off the west side of the street. The dome of the **Oratorio de San Felipe Neri** ④ is visible just before the market.

A block west of the church on Calle Insurgentes, **La Biblioteca Pública** ⑤ is a great place to catch up on town events. Continue west from the library two blocks to Calle Hernández Macías, then head south to the **Bellas Artes** ⑥ cultural center at No. 75 and the ornate **Iglesia de la Concepción** ⑦ behind it. Take Hernández Macías south for a block and turn left on Calle Umarán to reach the **Casa de Ignacio Allende** ⑧, birthplace of the Mexican national hero. You've circled back to the southwest corner of El Jardín.

After making your way around the center of town, consider a leisurely stroll to sights a bit farther afield. From the south side of the plaza (by La Parroquia), head west four blocks on Calle Umarán until you reach Calle Zacateros. Turn south on this narrow cobblestone street for some of the town's most interesting crafts shops—stocked with everything from silver jewelry to Mexican ceremonial masks.

Past the shops, Calle Zacateros becomes Ancha de San Antonio. On your left at No. 20 is the renowned **Instituto Allende** ⑨, where many of San Miguel's foreign visitors come to study. From the institute, continue south on Ancha de San Antonio until you reach Callejón del Cardo on your left. Continue past St. Paul's Episcopal Church, an expat house of worship, until you arrive at the cobblestone Calle Aldama on your left. Head downhill and walk briefly through a neighborhood of whitewashed houses before reaching the north entrance to the 5-acre Parque Benito Juárez, an oasis of evergreens, palm trees, and gardens.

From the north edge of the park, follow Calle Diezmo Viejo to the terra-cotta–color mansion known as La Huerta Santa Elena. From here turn left and walk one block uphill to the **Lavaderos Publicos** ⑩, San Miguel's outdoor laundry and a favorite gathering spot for local women. Calle Recreo, above the Lavandería, heads north back toward the plaza: follow Recreo until reaching Calle Correo, turn left, and walk three blocks to return to El Jardín.

Sights to See

❻ **Bellas Artes.** This impressive cloister across the street from the U.S. Consulate was once the Royal Convent of the Conception. Since 1938 it has been an institute for the study of music, dance, and the visual arts. There are rotating exhibits and a cafeteria on the patio. A bulletin board at the entrance lists cultural events. ⊠ *Calle Hernández Macías 75,* ☎ *4/152–0289.* ☞ *Free.* ☉ *Mon.–Sat. 9–8, Sun. 10–2.*

❺ **La Biblioteca Pública.** Notices—about such things as literary readings or yoga and aerobics classes—are posted on the bulletin board in the entranceway to the library. There is a lovely courtyard café inside, as well as the offices of the English-language newspaper *Atención San Miguel* and reading rooms with back issues of popular publications and books in English. It's a great place to take a breather from sightseeing. On Sunday a two-hour house-and-garden tour (about $15) of San Miguel leaves the library at noon. ⊠ *Calle Insurgentes 25,* ☎ *4/ 152–0293,* FAX *4/152–7048.* ☉ *Weekdays 10–2 and 4–7, Sat. 10–2.*

❽ **Casa de Ignacio Allende.** Now housing a museum and gallery, this is the birthplace of Ignacio Allende, one of Mexico's great independence heroes. Allende was a Creole aristocrat who, along with Father Miguel Hidalgo, plotted in the early 1800s to overthrow the Spanish regime. At clandestine meetings held in San Miguel and nearby Querétaro, the two discussed strategies, organized an army, gathered weapons, and enlisted the support of clerics for the struggle ahead.

Spanish Royalists learned of their plot and began arresting conspirators in Querétaro on September 13, 1810. Allende and Hidalgo received word of these actions and hastened their plans. At dawn on September 16, they rang out the cry for independence, and the fighting began. Allende was captured and executed by the Royalists the following year. As a tribute to his brave efforts, San Miguel El Grande was renamed San Miguel de Allende in the 20th century. ⊠ *Calle Cuna de Allende 1,* ☎ *4/152–2499.* ☞ *$3.* ☉ *Tues.–Sun. 10–4.*

El Charco del Ingenio. Founded in 1991 northeast of the city center, San Miguel's botanical garden is an enjoyable place to walk, particularly in the early morning or late afternoon. Its five-odd miles of pathways wind past more than 1,500 species of cacti and succulents. ⊠ *1½ km (1 mi) northeast of El Jardín; signs point the way off Cuesta de San Jose.* ☞ *$1.* ☉ *Sunrise–sunset.*

❼ **Iglesia de la Concepción.** Just behind the Bellas Artes cultural center, this church has one of the largest domes in Mexico. The two-story dome (completed in 1891) and the elegant Corinthian columns and pilasters gracing its drum are said to have been inspired by the dome of the Hôtel des Invalides in Paris. Ceferino Gutiérrez (of La Parroquia fame) is credited with its design. ⊠ *Calle Canal between Calles Hernández Macías and Zacateros.*

❸ **Iglesia de San Francisco.** The San Francisco Church has one of the finest churrigueresque facades in the state of Guanajuato. This term for the style refers to José Churriguera, a 17th-century (baroque) Spanish architect, noted for his extravagant surface decoration. Built in the late 18th century, it was financed by donations from wealthy patrons and by revenue from bullfights. Topping the elaborately carved exterior is the image of Saint Francis of Assisi. Below, along with a crucifix, are sculptures of Saint John and Our Lady of Sorrows. ⊠ *Calle Juárez between Calles San Francisco and Mesones.*

9 **Instituto Allende.** The school is set in the former country estate of the Count of Canal. Since its founding in 1951, thousands of students from around the world have come to learn Spanish and to take classes in social studies and the arts here. Courses last from a couple of weeks to a month or longer. Lush with bougainvillea, rosebushes, and ivy vines, the grounds provide a quiet refuge for students and visitors alike. ⊠ *Ancha de San Antonio 20,* ☎ *4/152–0190,* FAX *4/152–4538,* WEB *www.instituto-allende.edu.mx.* ⊙ *Weekdays 8–6, Sat. 9–1.*

1 **El Jardín** (The Garden). The heart of San Miguel is the plaza commonly known as El Jardín. Seated on one of its wrought-iron benches, you'll quickly get a feel for the town: old men with canes exchange tales, young lovers smooch, fruit vendors hawk their wares, and bells from nearby La Parroquia pierce the thin mountain air at each quarter hour. At dusk thousands of grackles make a fantastic ruckus as they return to roost in the laurel trees. ⊠ *Bounded by Calle Correo on the south, Calle San Francisco on the north, Portal Allende on the west, and Portal Guadalupe on the east.*

NEED A BREAK? On the southwest corner of the main plaza is **Café del Jardín** (⊠ Portal Allende 2, ☎ 4/152–5006). This unassuming little café has excellent coffee, cappuccino, hot chocolate, and, in the evening, pizza. Breakfasts are tasty and inexpensive. There's friendly service and, best of all—it's that American influence—free coffee refills.

10 **Lavaderos Publicos.** At this outdoor public laundry—a collection of red cement tubs set above Parque Benito Juárez—local women gather daily to wash clothes and chat as their predecessors have done for centuries. Although some women claim to have more-efficient washing facilities at home, the lure of the spring-fed troughs—not to mention the chance to catch up on the news—brings them to this shaded courtyard. ⊠ *Calle Diezmo Viejo at Calle Recreo.*

11 **El Mirador.** Climb El Mirador (The Lookout) for a panorama of the city, mountains, and reservoir below. The vista is great at sunset, and chances are you won't be alone. Locals and tourists like to join Pedro Vargas, whose bronze image commands this spot. ⊠ *1 block before town turn right off Calle Recreo onto Calle Hospicio, follow Hospicio 3 blocks to Calle Pedro Vargas, turn right, and head uphill to the overlook.*

4 **Oratorio de San Felipe Neri.** Built by local Indians in 1712, the original chapel can still be glimpsed in the eastern facade, made of pink stone and adorned with a figure of Our Lady of Solitude. The newer, southern front was built in an ornate baroque style. In 1734 the wealthy Count of Canal paid for an addition to the Oratorio. His **Templo de Santa Casa de Loreto,** dedicated to the Virgin of Loreto, is just behind the Oratorio. Its main entrance, now blocked by a grille, is on the Oratorio's left rear side. Peer through the grille to see the heavily gilded altars and effigies of the count and his wife, under which they are buried. ⊠ *Calles Insurgentes and Loreto.*

❷ **La Parroquia.** This towering Gothic Revival parish church, made of
local *cantera* sandstone, was designed in the late 19th century by self-
trained Indian mason Ceferino Gutiérrez, who sketched his designs in
the sand with a stick. Gutiérrez was purportedly inspired by postcards
of European Gothic cathedrals. Since the postcards gave no hint of what
the back of those cathedrals looked like, the posterior of La Parroquia
was done in quintessential Mexican style.

La Parroquia still functions as a house of worship, although its interior has been changed over the years. Gilded wood altars, for example, were replaced with neoclassical stone altars. The original bell, cast
in 1732, still calls parishioners to mass several times daily. ⊠ *South
side of El Jardín on Calle Correo.*

Dining

For its size, San Miguel has a surprisingly large number of international
restaurants. The recent influx of Americans and Canadians has given
rise to new Tex-Mex and health-food places. A European influence has
contributed to variations on French, Italian, and Spanish themes.

$$$$ ✕ **El Market Bistro.** Fine French cuisine is served in a lush, stone-paved
★   garden equipped with a piano or in a private dining room charged with
     original art and enhanced by a roaring fire. For a special evening try the
     tournedos rossini, a marinated sirloin smothered in foie gras, red wine
     sauce, and mushrooms. The leek and potato soup and goat cheese salad
     are delectable. ⊠ *Hernandez Macias 95,* ☎ *4/152–3229. AE, MC, V.*

$$$ ✕ **Bugambilia.** Founded in 1945, Mercedes Arteaga Tovar's restaurant
     has a well-earned reputation for serving fine traditional Mexican cui-
     sine. Try such classic specialties as *pollo en mole poblano* (chicken
     coated in a traditional mole sauce—made with more than 25 ingredi-
     ents) and *sopa azteca* (classic tortilla soup served with a variety of top-
     pings). The candlelit, tree-filled colonial courtyard and live classical
     guitarist make for a romantic setting. ⊠ *Calle Hidalgo 42,* ☎ *4/152–
     0127. AE, MC, V.*

$$$ ✕ **L'Invito.** Indulge in Sylvia's authentic Italian cuisine beneath the soft
     lights of a romantic courtyard. Begin with a glass of wine and sample
     the prosciutto and mozzarella cheese panini. Select from a menu of tra-
     ditional pastas, Italian meat dishes, and side vegetables like the car-
     rots flambeéd in cognac. The daily special includes soup, meat,
     vegetables, and homemade dessert; the peanut ice cream is delicious.
     Portions are designed to leave you satisfied, not stuffed. ⊠ *Correo 24,*
     ☎ *4/152–7333. AE, MC, V.*

$$$ ✕ **Tio Lucas.** Possibly the most popular restaurant in San Miguel as much
     for the nightly jazz music and covered-patio ambience as for the grilled
     fare. Share an *ensalada César,* created at your table by one of the tal-
     ented and friendly waiters. The sumptuous house specialty, *filete
     Chemita,* is a thick-cut fillet crowned in a secret recipe garlic sauce. ⊠
     Mesones 103, ☎ *4/152–4996. AE, MC, V.*

$$ ✕ **Fonda Mesón de San José.** On an umbrella-shaded cobblestone
★   patio inside a complex of small shops, this well-established restaurant
     serves German, Mexican, and vegetarian dishes. Locals wax enthusi-
     astic about owner-chef Angela Merkel's roulade, potato pancakes,
     and German chocolate cake, as well as her *chile en nogada,* a mild chili
     stuffed with ground meat and raisins and topped with cream sauce and
     pomegranate seeds. The sunny patio is great for lunch, less popular
     for dinner. ⊠ *Calle Mesones 38,* ☎ *4/152–3848. MC, V.*

$ ✕ **The Bagel Café.** A popular hangout for breakfast and lunch, The
     Bagel Café has patio or indoor (art-gallery) dining near El Jardín.
     Healthy lunch fare includes a variety of homemade soups, sandwiches,

salads, and daily specials. Revive with a fresh-baked bagel and lox, or the chicken breast sandwich on rosemary-and-sun-dried-tomato sourdough bread. ☒ *Correo 19,* ☎ *4/152–2497. No credit cards.*

$ ✕ **La Buena Vida.** Don't miss this fabulous bakery and tiny coffee shop and its mouthwatering orange scones, chocolate-chip cookies, and light breakfasts. If the few patio tables are full, take your treats to the plaza. ☒ *Hernández Macías 72–5,* ☎ *4/152–2211. No credit cards.*

Lodging

San Miguel has a wide selection of lodging, from cozy bed-and-breakfasts to elegant all-suites properties. Rooms fill up quickly during summer and winter seasons, when northern tourists migrate here in droves. Make reservations several months in advance if you plan to visit at these times or during the September Independence Day festivities.

$$$$ 🏨 **Casa de Sierra Nevada.** Built in 1580 as the residence of the arch-
★ bishop of Guanajuato, this elegant country-style inn still attracts ambassadors, diplomats, film stars, and other luminaries; children under 16 aren't admitted, however, and the formerly attentive service has fallen dramatically, leaving guests at the mercy of chance. Its complex of eight colonial buildings, all located within a few blocks of the main plaza, contains 20 individually decorated suites and 17 deluxe rooms. Lace curtains, handwoven rugs, and chandeliers adorn some rooms; fireplaces, cozy private terraces, and skylights enhance others. The international cuisine at the hotel's original restaurant is delicately prepared and beautifully presented. The hotel runs the separate **Casa de Sierra Nevada en el Parque** (☒ Santa Elena 2), an exquisitely restored 18th-century ex-hacienda with just five guest rooms. Its restaurant serves refined versions of traditional Mexican dishes and has a wonderful view of Parque Benito Juárez. ☒ *Calle Hospicio 35, 37700,* ☎ *4/152–7040,* 𝖥𝖠𝖷 *4/152–7040. 17 rooms, 20 suites. 2 restaurants, bar, pool, massage, spa, horseback riding. AE, MC, V.*

$$$$ 🏨 **La Puertecita Boutique Hotel.** Set in a secluded, wooded canyon in the tony Atascadero neighborhood, this luxury no-smoking hotel has uniquely decorated rooms with rustic Mexican furnishings, domed vaulted ceilings, and in many cases private patios, fireplaces, and bathrooms with small indoor gardens. Customized vacation packages including room, meals, mountain biking, horseback riding, hot-springs excursions, and yoga, cooking, art, or Spanish classes are available. Guests can use the golf and tennis facilities at Club Malanquin. ☒ *Santo Domingo 75, 37740,* ☎ *4/152–5011 or 4/152–2250,* 𝖥𝖠𝖷 *4/152–5505,* 𝖶𝖤𝖡 *www.lapuertecita.com. 18 rooms, 6 suites. Restaurant, bar, 2 pools, massage, billiards. AE, MC, V.*

$$$ 🏨 **Casa Luna.** In a restored 300-year-old Spanish colonial house, this
★ lovely B&B has 2-ft-thick walls, 20-ft-high ceilings, and tranquil fountain- and flower-filled patios. The luxurious rooms have antiques, fireplaces, featherbeds, and bathtubs. The rooftop honor bar is spectacular at night, lighted by some two dozen miniature tin star lights. A three-night minimum stay is required; children are allowed only when the entire house is rented to one party. ☒ *Pila Seca 11, 37700,* ☎ 𝖥𝖠𝖷 *4/152–1117. 8 rooms, 1 suite. Dining room, massage, shop. AE, MC, V.*

$$$ 🏨 **Villa Jacaranda.** Near the Parque Benito Juárez, the Villa Jacaranda has a full range of amenities. Rooms, although unimaginatively decorated, have space heaters (not something to be taken for granted in these parts) and cable TV. The hotel's Cine/Bar shows American movies daily at 7:30 PM. The price of admission—roughly $5—includes a drink. The restaurant serves international and Mexican cuisine in the homey dining room or in a stained-glass gazebo, and there's a delicious Sunday champagne brunch for about $8. ☒ *Calle Aldama 53, 37700,* ☎ *4/*

152–1015, 4/152–0811, or 800/310–9688, FAX *4/152–0883,* WEB *www. villajacaranda.com. 5 rooms, 11 suites. Restaurant, bar, hot tub, cinema, free parking. AE, MC, V.*

$$$ 🏨 **Villas Mirasol.** Each of this lodge's rooms is tastefully decorated with original prints, oil paintings, pastels, or small sculptures. Most rooms are flooded with sunlight during the day. All have either a private or shared terrace. In 1999, the owner opened a second branch in a cozy house near the Mercado Ignacio Ramírez (⊠ Callejón del Pueblito 4–A). Both locations are on quiet streets, each about a 10-minute walk from the main plaza. Villa Mirasol includes in its price a rich breakfast. The hotels may not be suitable for children under 12. ⊠ *Pila Seca 35, Apdo. 409, 37700,* ☎ *4/152–6685 or 4/154–5113,* FAX *4/152–1564,* WEB *www.infosma.com/villamirasol. 13 rooms, 6 suites. Dining room. AE, MC, V.*

$$ 🏨 **Casa Carmen.** Run by a friendly San Miguel family, this pension is an oasis of peace in the center of town. The 200-year-old house two blocks from El Jardín has large, clean rooms, each with desk or writing table and portable gas heater, and two small patios. The large suite on the top floor has a great view of the city for the same price, but is often booked far in advance. Rates include breakfast and lunch. ⊠ *Calle Correo 31, 37700,* ☎ *4/152–0844. 12 rooms. Dining room. No credit cards.*

$$ 🏨 **Villa Scorpio al Puente.** Located next to the Heroes Bridge (where couples meet to enjoy enchanting sunsets), this cozy B&B boasts a stunning rooftop-patio view of San Miguel and the surrounding countryside. A well-stocked library, three gardens, and an elegant salon provide comfortable places to visit with friends or enjoy a quiet afternoon. You'll find a fresh bouquet of flowers, down bedding, and a fireplace in every room. The 250-year-old house was connected to an underground tunnel system used during the revolution. ⊠ *Quebrada 93, 37700,* ☎ FAX *4/152–7575. 4 rooms. Bar, dining room. No credit cards.*

$ 🏨 **Posada de las Monjas.** This 19th-century inn has been operating as a hotel for more than 50 years. Rooms are simply furnished in a colonial style. Some in the old wing are uncomfortably dark and cramped. The rooftop public terrace has tables and lounge chairs and offers commanding views of mountains and city. Some rooms have fireplaces, and there's a communal TV in the lobby, which looks like a formal Mexican living room. ⊠ *Calle Canal 37, 37700,* ☎ *4/152–0171,* FAX *4/152–6227. 65 rooms. Restaurant, bar, laundry service, free parking. MC, V.*

$ 🏨 **Quinta Loreto.** Clean, plain, comfortable rooms, shady and pleasantly kept grounds, and excellent *comida casera* (home cooking) make this inexpensive hotel a favorite with snowbirds and other San Miguel aficionados. Each room has a gas heater, TV, and phone. There is a dilapidated tennis court and an unheated pool, which is uninvitingly dirty. The hotel is about a 10-minute walk north of the main plaza, near the market. Many nonguests take their meals in the unpretentious dining room, especially the diet-defying *comida corrida* (fixed-menu lunch), served daily. ⊠ *Calle Loreto 15, 37700,* ☎ *4/152–0042,* FAX *4/152–3616. 40 rooms. Restaurant, pool, tennis court. AE, MC, V.*

Nightlife and the Arts

The Arts

San Miguel, long known as an artists' colony, continues to nurture that image today. Galleries, museums, and arty shops line the streets near El Jardín, and two government-run salons—at **Bellas Artes** and **Instituto Allende**—feature the work of Mexican artists. For a sampling of both regional and international talent, visit **Galería Atenea** (⊠ Jesús 2, ☎ 4/152–0785), **Galería de Arte Contemporáneo** (⊠ Plaza Principal 14, ☎ 4/152–0454), **Galería Duo Duo** (⊠ Pila Seca 3, ☎ 4/152–

6211), **Galería del Pueblo** (✉ Calle Correo 12A, ☎ 4/152–1448), **Galería San Miguel** (✉ Plaza Principal 14, ☎ 4/152–0454), or **Kligerman Gallery** (✉ Calle San Francisco 11, ☎ 4/152–0951). Most close weekdays between 2 and 4 and are open Sunday 10 or 11 to 2 or 3.

For more than 20 years, San Miguel has played host to the world-class **Festival de Música de Cámara** in August, a feast of classical chamber music that in past years has included the illustrious Tokyo String Quartet. The **Jazz Festival International** takes place around the last week in November. There is live jazz, workshops, and after-hour jam sessions. Tickets may be purchased individually or for the series. Call the tourist office for dates and details.

Nightlife

On most evenings in San Miguel you can readily satisfy a whim for a literary reading, an American movie, a theatrical production, or a turn on a disco dance floor. The most up-to-date listings of events can be found in the English-language paper *Atención San Miguel,* published every Sunday. The bulletin board at the public library (✉ Calle Insurgentes 25) is also a good source of current events.

Agave Azul (✉ Calle Mesones 99, ☎ 4/152–1958) draws a crowd for live music and, of course, tequila. **Mama Mia** (✉ Calle Umarán 8, ☎ 4/152–2063) presents everything from Peruvian folk music, classical guitar, and flamenco to salsa and rock. The rotating art exhibitions and comfortable leather chairs at **El Petit Bar** (✉ Hernandez Macias 95, ☎ 4/152–3229) attract an eclectic mix of locals, tourists, and ex-patriots. Jazz and blues reign every night at **Tío Lucas** (✉ Calle Mesones 103, ☎ 4/152–4996), a favorite hangout of Instituto Allende art students.

Outdoor Activities and Sports

The **Club de Golf Malanquin** (✉ Celaya Hwy., Km 3, ☎ 4/152–0516) has a heated pool, steam baths, tennis courts, and nine holes of golf, all of which are open to the public for a guest fee of $45 on weekdays or $70 on weekends; it's closed Monday. The exclusive **Hotel Hacienda Taboada** (✉ Dolores Hidalgo Hwy., Km 8, ☎ 4/152–0888, FAX 4/152–1798) has several geothermal pools, manicured grounds, and tennis courts. It's open to the public for about $15, which includes lunch; closed Wednesday. **Taboada** (✉ Dolores Hidalgo Hwy., Km 8) has three outdoor geothermally heated pools, one of which is Olympic-size and good for doing laps. They are open to the public for $3.50; closed Tuesday.

Ballooning

Gone with the Wind Balloon Adventures (✉ Calle Recreo 68, ☎ 4/152–6735) offers hot-air balloon rides over town and the surrounding countryside with licensed/certified pilots from Napa Valley, California. The one-hour flights depart at 6 or 7 AM, depending on the season. The $150 cost includes breakfast upon landing.

Biking

Aventuras San Miguel (✉ Calle Recreo 10, ☎ FAX 4/152–6406) rents bicycles at reasonable prices. **Bici-Burro** (✉ Calle Hospicio 1, esq. Barranca, ☎ 4/152–1526) rents and services bikes for exploring San Miguel and environs.

Bullfights

To witness the pageantry of a traditional Mexican bullfight, go to the **Plaza de Toros Oriente** (✉ off Calle Recreo), which has events several times a year. The most important contest takes place in the last week of September during *la fiesta de San Miguel.* Call the tourist office for more information.

Horseback Riding

Aventuras San Miguel rents horses at reasonable rates. The equestrian center of the **Casa de Sierra Nevada** offers riding lessons, carriage rides, and horse rental at its 500-acre ranch for about $50 per hour.

Spas

Jasmine Day Spa (✉ Jesus 25-A, ☎ 4/152–7973) offers a variety of treatments including Swedish massage, aromatherapy, reflexology, salt scrubs, manicures, and pedicures.

Shopping

For centuries San Miguel's artisans have been creating crafts ranging from straw products to metalwork. Although some boutiques in town may be a bit pricey, you can find good buys on silver, brass, tin, woven-cotton goods, and folk art. Store hours tend to be erratic, but most stores open daily at around 9, shut their doors for the traditional afternoon siesta (2 to 4 or 5), then reopen in the afternoon until 7 or 8, and open for just a half day on Sunday. Most San Miguel shops accept MasterCard and Visa.

Markets

Mercado Ignacio Ramírez, a traditional Mexican covered market off Calle Colegio, one block north of Calle Mesones, is a colorful jumble of fresh fruits and vegetables, flowers, bloody butchers' counters, inexpensive plastic toys, taco stands, and Mexican-made cassettes. Spilling out for several blocks behind the Mercado Ignacio Ramírez, the **Mercado de Artesanías** (artisans' market) is where you'll find vendors of local work—glass, tin, and papier mâché—as well as some of the best prices on silver jewelry in town.

Specialty Shops

FOLK ART

Artes de México (✉ Calzada Aurora 47, at Dolores Hidalgo exit, ☎ 4/152–0764) has been producing and selling traditional crafts, including furniture, metalwork, and ceramics, for more than 40 years. **La Calaca** (✉ Calle Mesones 93, ☎ 4/152–3954) focuses on quality antique and contemporary Latin American folk and ceremonial art. Although the inventory at the **Casa Maxwell** (✉ Calle Canal 14, ☎ 4/152–0247) has slipped in quality, there is still a reasonable selection of folk art. **La Guadalupana** (✉ Jesus 25-A, inside Jasmine Day Spa, ☎ 4/152–7973) sells all manner of items adorned with images of Mexico's beloved Virgin of Guadalupe—from temporary tattoos to coffee mugs. **Talisman Boutique 2** (✉ San Franscisco 7, ☎ 4/152–0438) sells beautiful embroidered *huipiles* (tunics or blouses) from southern Mexico and Guatemala. **Tonatiu Metzli** (✉ Calle Juárez 7, ☎ 4/152–0869) has a wonderful selection of both antique and contemporary masks from all over Mexico. **Veryka** (✉ Zacateros 6-A, ☎ 4/152–2114), whose emphasis is on Latin American folk art, has a particularly fine selection of *muertos* (skeleton figurines for the Day of the Dead) from Puebla.

HOUSEWARES

Casa Canal (✉ Calle Canal 3, ☎ 4/152–0479), in a beautiful old hacienda, sells new furniture, much of it in traditional styles. **Casa María Luisa** (✉ Calle Canal 40, ☎ 4/152–0130) has a fantastic jumble of furniture, glassware, wall hangings, and lamps, as well as an enormous selection of collectibles made of tin, iron, wood, and glass. **Casa Vieja** (✉ Calle Mesones 83, ☎ 4/152–1284) has tons of glassware and ceramics, decorative and functional housewares, picture frames, furniture, and more. **CLAN destino** (✉ Zacateros 19, ☎ FAX 4/152–1623) features an eclectic international mix of antiques, contemporary art,

MÉXICO: HECHO A MANO

HANDMADE IN MEXICO: Some of the world's finest *artesanías* (handicrafts) come from this country. Artisanal work is varied, original, colorful, and inexpensive, and it supports millions of families who are carrying on ancient and more recent traditions. Although cheap, shoddy items masquerading as "native crafts" are certainly common, careful shoppers who take their time can come away with real works of folk art. Also keep in mind that many items are exempt from duty.

The crafts to look for are ceramics, woodwork, lacquerware, leather, weaving and textiles, and silver, gold, and semiprecious stone jewelry. Each region has its specialty. Cities that are noted for the quality of their crafts are Puebla (Chapter 2); Nogales in Sonora (Chapter 4); Guadalajara, Tlaquepaque, and Tonalá in Jalisco (Chapter 6); San Miguel de Allende, Guanajuato, and Pátzcuaro in the heartland (Chapter 7); Taxco in Morelos (Chapter 9); Oaxaca City in Oaxaca (Chapter 10); San Cristóbal de las Casas in Chiapas (Chapter 11); and Mérida in Yucatán (Chapter 13).

Ceramics. Talavera-style tiles (blue majolica) and other ceramic ware are at their best in Puebla. Oaxaca state is known for its unglazed, burnished black pottery. Inventive masks and figurines come from Valle de Bravo, Pátzcuaro in the state of Michoacán, Tonalá outside of Guadalajara, Taxco, and Chiapas.

Jewelry. Silver is best in Taxco, San Miguel de Allende, and Oaxaca; be sure purchases are stamped "925," which means 92.5% pure silver. You can find gold filigree in Guanajuato and Oaxaca. Oaxaca and Chiapas are also known for their amber, but be aware that much of what is sold as amber is in fact glass or plastic. Good rules of thumb: don't buy amber off the street; and if it seems like

a great bargain, it's probably fake. For semiprecious stones, go to jewelers' shops in Puebla and Querétaro. Coral jewelry is sold in the Yucatán and other coastal areas, but because of the massive ecological damage caused by coral harvesting, the practice around it is environmentally unsensible.

Leather. The key places to find quality leatherwork are Guadalajara, Oaxaca (for sandals), Chiapas (for belts and purses), and the Yucatán (for bags).

Metalwork. Look for copper in Santa Clara del Cobre in Michoacán, and tin in San Miguel de Allende and Oaxaca.

Weavings and Textiles. Fabric work is quite varied: you'll find *rebozos* (shawls) and blankets around Oaxaca, Guadalajara, Jalapa, and Pátzcuaro; *huipiles* (heavily embroidered tunics worn by Indian women) and other embroidered clothing in Michoacán, Oaxaca state, Chiapas, and the Yucatán; masterfully woven rugs, some colored with natural dyes, in Oaxaca; hammocks and baskets in Oaxaca and the Yucatán; lace in the colonial cities of the heartland area; *guayaberas* (comfortable, embroidered and/or pleated men's dress shirts, now usually mass-produced) along the Gulf coast; and reed mats in Oaxaca and Valle de Bravo. The Mezquital region east of Querétaro can also be rewarding, as can shopping for Huichol Indian yarn paintings and embroidery near Puerto Vallarta.

Woodwork. Look for masks in Mexico City; *alebrijes* (painted wooden animals) in Oaxaca; furniture in Cuernavaca, Guadalajara, San Miguel de Allende, Querétaro, Tequisquiapan, and Pátzcuaro; lacquerware in Uruapan and Pátzcuaro in Michoacán, Chiapa de Corzo in Chiapas, and Puerto Vallarta for pieces from Olinalá in Guerrero state; and guitars in Paracho, Michoacán.

and jewelry. **México Lindo** (⊠ Calle Mesones 85, ☎ 4/152–0730) sells a good selection of hand-painted tiles and ceramics from Dolores Hidalgo. **La Zandunga** (⊠ Calle Hernández Macías 129, ☎ 4/152–4608) sells high-quality, 100% wool rugs from Oaxaca.

JEWELRY

Established in 1963, **Joyería David** (⊠ Calle Zacateros 53, ☎ 4/152–0056) has an extensive selection of gold, silver, copper, and brass jewelry, all made on the premises. A number of pieces contain Mexican opals, amethysts, topaz, malachite, and turquoise. **Platería Cerroblanco** (⊠ Calle Canal 17, ☎ 4/152–0502) creates and crafts its own silver and gold jewelry and will arrange a visit to its *taller* (workshop) on request. The reputable **7th Heaven** (⊠ Sollano 31, ☎ 4/154–4677) designs and creates its own silver, gold, and carved amber pieces.

Side Trip to Dolores Hidalgo

50 km (31 mi) north of San Miguel via Rte. 51.

Dolores Hidalgo played an important role in the fight for independence. It was here, before dawn on September 16, 1810, that Father Miguel Hidalgo—the local priest—gave an impassioned sermon to his clergy that ended with the *grito* (cry), "Death to bad government!" At 11 PM on September 15, politicians throughout the land repeat a revised version of the grito—"Viva Mexico! Viva Mexico! Viva Mexico!"—signaling the start of Independence Day celebrations. On September 16 (and only on this day), the bell in Hidalgo's parish church is rung.

Casa Hidalgo, the house where Father Hidalgo lived, is now a museum. It contains copies of important letters Hidalgo sent or received, and other independence memorabilia. ⊠ *Calle Morelos 1,* ☎ *4/182–0171.* 🎟 *About $3, free Sun.* ⊙ *Tues.–Sat. 10–5:45, Sun. 10–4:45.*

Dolores Hidalgo is famous for its lovely hand-glazed Talavera-style ceramics, most notably tiles and tableware. There are good prices at the town's many stores and factories. After shopping, head for the plaza for some of the most exotic ice creams you'll taste—flavors such as mole, avocado, beer, and corn. The town is an easy one-hour bus ride from San Miguel de Allende's Central de Autobuses.

San Miguel de Allende A to Z

AIR TRAVEL

Many international airlines fly into León's Guanajuato International Airport, which is about 1½ hours from San Miguel. Aeroméxico flies from Los Angeles. American travels from Dallas–Fort Worth. Continental has service from Houston. Mexicana comes from Chicago. Taxis from León's Guanajuato International Airport to downtown San Miguel cost about $60.

➤ AIRLINES AND CONTACTS: **Aeroméxico** (☎ 47/14–05–74). **American** (☎ 47/16–05–02). **Continental** (☎ 47/14–71–10). **Mexicana** (☎ 47/13–45–50).

BUS TRAVEL

Daily buses run direct from Mexico City's Central del Norte (North Bus Station) to the Central de Autobuses in San Miguel. Several major lines have frequent service. They include ETN, Flecha Amarilla, Primera Plus, Herradura de Plata, and Pegasso Plus. Travel time is about four hours.

➤ BUS INFORMATION: **ETN** (☎ 4/154–5135 or 4/152–6407). **Flecha Amarilla** (☎ 4/152–7323). **Herradura de Plata** (☎ 4/152–0725). **Pegasso Plus** (☎ 4/152–0725). **Primera Plus** (☎ 4/152–0084).

CAR RENTAL

Hola Rent a Car has a limited selection of manual-transmission compacts available.

➤ LOCAL AGENCIES: **Hola Rent a Car** (⊠ Plaza Principal 2, Int. 5, ☎ 4/152–0198).

CAR TRAVEL

Driving time from Mexico City to San Miguel is roughly four hours via Route 57 (to Querétaro) then Route 111. Traveling on Route 45 from Mexico City, a road connecting to Routes 57 and 111 bypasses Querétaro, saving a half hour. Guanajuato is 100 km (62 mi), about 1½ hours, west of San Miguel.

EMBASSIES

The U.S. Consulate is open weekdays 9–1.

➤ UNITED STATES: **U.S. Consulate** (⊠ Calle Hernández Macías 72, ☎ 4/152–2357 during office hours; 4/152–0068 and 4/152–0653 for emergencies).

EMERGENCIES

The staff at Hospital de la Fé can refer you to an English-speaking doctor.

San Miguel has many pharmacies. American residents recommend Botica Agundis, where English speakers are often on hand. It's open daily 10:30 AM–11 PM.

➤ EMERGENCY CONTACTS: **Ambulance–Red Cross** (☎ 4/152–4121 or 4/152–4225). **Fire Department** (☎ 4/152–2888). **Police** (☎ 4/152–0022). **Traffic Police** (☎ 4/152–0538).

➤ HOSPITAL: **Hospital de la Fé** (⊠ Libramiento a Dolores Hidalgo 43, ☎ 4/152–2233 or 4/152–2320).

➤ PHARMACY: **Botica Agundis Pharmacy** (⊠ Calle Canal 26, ☎ 4/152–1198).

ENGLISH-LANGUAGE MEDIA

El Colibrí has a good selection of paperback novels, magazines, and a few art supplies. Libros el Tecolote has a great selection of new and used books on Mexican art, history, literature, and cooking.

➤ BOOKSTORES: **El Colibrí** (⊠ Sollano 30, ☎ 4/152–0751). **Libros el Tecolote** (⊠ Calle Jesús 11, ☎ FAX 4/152–7395).

MAIL, INTERNET, AND SHIPPING

Border Crossings offers 24-hour answering and fax service, a Mexico address for receiving mail, packing and shipping, e-mail, a gift shop and art gallery, and other services. Internet San Miguel charges $5 an hour for the fastest Internet access in town. Coffee and fresh juices are available.

➤ CONTACTS: **Border Crossings** (⊠ Correo 19 Int. 2, ☎ 4/152–2497, FAX 4/152–3672.) **Internet San Miguel** (⊠ Mesones 27, or side entrance at Reloj, ☎ 4/152–4634, WEB www.internetsanmiguel.com).

MONEY MATTERS

A better bet for money exchange than the slow-moving bank lines is Deal Casa de Cambio, open weekdays 9–6, Saturday 9–2.

➤ EXCHANGE SERVICES: **Deal Casa de Cambio** (⊠ Calles San Francisco 4, Correo 15, or Juárez 27, ☎ 4/152–2932).

TAXIS

You can easily hail a taxi on the street or find one at taxi stands—Sitio Allende in the main plaza, Sitio San Francisco on Calle Mesones, or

Sitio San Felipe on Calle Juárez. Flat rates to the bus terminal, train station, and other parts of the city apply.

➤ TAXI COMPANIES: **Sitio Allende** (☎ 4/152–0192).

TOURS

Aventuras San Miguel has off-the-beaten-track mountain-bike treks, "ghost town" trips, even nighttime full-moon excursions. Colonial México Tours runs historical tours to Guanajuato, Querétaro, and Dolores Hidalgo. Recommended for local tours is PMC (Promotion of Mexican Culture).

➤ TOUR OPERATOR RECOMMENDATIONS: **Aventuras San Miguel** (✉ Calle Recreo 10, ☎ 𝙵𝙰𝚇 4/152–6406). **Colonial México Tours** (✉ Plaza Portal Allende 4, 2nd floor, ☎ 𝙵𝙰𝚇 4/152–5794). **PMC** (✉ Calle Cuna de Allende 11, ☎ 4/152–1630, 𝙵𝙰𝚇 4/152–0121).

TRANSPORTATION AROUND SAN MIGUEL DE ALLENDE

San Miguel de Allende is best covered on foot, keeping in mind two pieces of advice. The city is more than a mile above sea level, so you might tire quickly during your first few days here if you aren't accustomed to high altitudes. Streets are paved with rugged cobblestones, and some have no sidewalks. Sturdy footwear, such as athletic or other rubber-sole walking shoes, is recommended.

TRAVEL AGENCIES

Viajes Vértiz is the American Express representative in San Miguel.

➤ LOCAL AGENT REFERRALS: **Viajes Vértiz** (✉ Calle Hidalgo 1A, ☎ 4/152–1856 or 4/152–1695, 𝙵𝙰𝚇 4/152–0499).

VISITOR INFORMATION

Delegación de Turismo, on the southeast corner of El Jardín, in a glassed-in office next to la Terraza restaurant, is open weekdays 10–3 and 5–7, Saturday 10–2.

➤ TOURIST INFORMATION: **Delegación de Turismo** (☎ 4/152–6565).

GUANAJUATO

100 km (62 mi) west of San Miguel de Allende, 365 km (226 mi) northwest of Mexico City.

Once Mexico's most prominent silver-mining city, Guanajuato is a colonial gem, tucked into the mountains at 6,700 ft. This provincial state capital is distinguished by twisting cobblestone alleyways, colorful houses, 15 shaded plazas, and a vast subterranean roadway where a rushing river once coursed. In the center of town is **Alhóndiga de Granaditas,** an 18th-century grain-storage facility that was the site of Mexico's first major victory in its War of Independence from Spain.

The city fills to overflowing in mid-October with the International Cervantes Festival, a three-week celebration of the arts. During the rest of the year, things regain a semblance of normalcy. Students rush to class with books tucked under their arms, women eye fresh produce at the Mercado Hidalgo, and old men utter greetings from behind whitewashed doorways. On weekend nights, *estudiantinas* (student minstrels dressed as medieval troubadours) serenade the public in the city squares.

Exploring Guanajuato

Although Guanajuato's many plazas and labyrinthine streets may seem confusing at first, this is not a bad city in which to get lost. The center is small, and there are wonderful surprises around every corner. Remember that the top of the Alhóndiga (which you can see from many

Guanajuato

250 meters
250 yards

Teatro Principal

Cantarranas

Sopeña

Calvario

San Antonio

Tourist Office

San Miguel

Plaza de la Paz

Alonso

Pocitos

Plaza de Los Angeles

Juan Valle

El Subterráneo

Plaza de San Fernando

Plaza de San Roque

Pocitos

Reforma

Av. Juárez

Jardín Reforma

Grasero

Chilito

Mendizábal

Terremoto

28 de Septiembre

5 de Mayo

Pósitos

Av. Juárez

La Alhóndiga

El Apartado

Insurgencia

de Salgado

Jardín del Cantador

Llanitos

MINERAL DE CATA

GRITERIA

Av. Juárez

Bus Station

Railroad Station

Alhóndiga de
Granaditas **17**
Basílica Colegiata
de Nuestra
Señora de
Guanajuato **20**
Jardín Unión **12**
Mansión del
Conde de Rul **19**
Mercado Hidalgo . . . **18**

El Museo Casa
Diego Rivera **16**
Museo de las
Momias **22**
El Pípila **14**
Teatro Juárez **13**
University of
Guanajuato **15**
La Valenciana **21**

spots in town) points north, and the spires of the Basílica Colegiata Nuestra Señora de Guanajuato, at Plaza de la Paz, point south.

A Good Walk

The tourist office, at Plaza de la Paz 14, is a good place to begin a walking tour. Turn right and walk up Avenida Juárez to reach **Jardín Unión** ⑫, Guanajuato's central square. The ornate **Teatro Juárez** ⑬ is just past the Jardín to your right on Calle Sopeña. The hardy might want to make a detour and take a half-hour climb to **El Pípila** ⑭, a monument to a hero of the War of Independence of 1810 that looms over the center of the city. If you're interested, bear right on Calle Sopeña just past the Teatro Juárez. A sign marked EL PÍPILA will direct you onto Callejón de Calvario, which eventually leads to the hillside memorial.

Head back into town on Calle Cantarranas, a main street that winds down the hill and around the Jardín Unión. Just before Calle Cantarranas changes its name to Calle Pocitos, you'll see the **University of Guanajuato** ⑮. A short way down from where Calle Cantarranas becomes Calle Pocitos is **El Museo Casa Diego Rivera** ⑯, birthplace of Mexico's famous muralist. Calle Pocitos weaves past more residences and eventually becomes Calle 28 de Septiembre. On the left, just past the junction with Mendizabal, is the **Alhóndiga de Granaditas** ⑰, a former fortress converted into a state museum. Head one block south to return to Avenida Juárez and the glassed-in **Mercado Hidalgo** ⑱.

Turn right on Juárez as you leave the market and continue until the road splits near the Jardín Reforma. Bear left and cut down Calle Reforma, a short alleyway lined with shops. Keep right at the end of the street and you'll come to two pleasant courtyards: Plaza de San Roque, which hosts outdoor performances during the Cervantes Festival, and Plaza de San Fernando, a shady square where many book fairs are held. After the Plaza de San Roque continue southeast and this short detour will return you to Avenida Juárez, where it's a slight climb up to Plaza de la Paz, a square built from 1895 to 1898 and surrounded by some of the city's finest colonial buildings, including the 18th-century **Mansión del Conde de Rul** ⑲. The bright-yellow 17th-century baroque **Basílica Colegiata de Nuestra Señora de Guanajuato** ⑳ dominates the plaza. If you continue up Avenida Juárez about a half block past the plaza, you'll pass the tourist office again and arrive back at the Jardín Unión.

Sights to See

⑰ **Alhóndiga de Granaditas.** A massive stone structure with horizontal slit windows, this 18th-century grain-storage facility served as a jail under Emperor Maximilian and as a fortress during the War of Independence, where El Pípila committed his courageous act. It is now a state museum with exhibits on local history, archaeology, and crafts. The hooks on which the Spanish Royalists hung the severed heads of Father Hidalgo, Ignacio Allende, and two other independence leaders still dangle on the exterior. ⊠ *Calle 28 de Septiembre 6,* ☎ *4/732–1112.* ☞ *About $2, free Sun.* ◷ *Tues.–Sat. 10–1:30 and 4–5:30, Sun. 10–2:30.*

⑳ **Basílica Colegiata de Nuestra Señora de Guanajuato.** A 17th-century baroque church painted a striking shade of yellow, the Basílica dominates Plaza de la Paz. Inside is the oldest Christian statue in Mexico, a bejeweled 8th-century statue of the Virgin. The highly venerated figure was a gift from King Philip II of Spain in 1557. On the Friday preceding Good Friday, miners, accompanied by floats and mariachi bands, parade to the Basílica to pay homage to the Lady of Guanajuato. ⊠ *Plaza de la Paz.* ◷ *Daily 9–8.*

⑫ **Jardín Unión.** This tree-lined, wedge-shape plaza is Guanajuato's central square. All three sides of the wedge are pedestrian walkways.

Tuesday, Thursday, and Sunday evenings, musical performances take place in the band shell here; at other times, groups of musicians break into impromptu song along the plaza's shaded tile walkways.

NEED A
BREAK?
For alfresco dining at the Jardín, try the terrace at the **Hotel Museo Posada Santa Fé** (⊠ Jardín Unión 12, ☎ 4/732–0084). You can order a cappuccino and a slice of cake, or a full meal. Try the *pozole estilo Guanajuato* (hominy soup into which you spoon, or squeeze, the desired amounts of onions, radishes, lettuce, lime, and chili peppers).

El Cafe (⊠ Calle Sopeña 10, ☎ 4/732–2566) has indoor and outdoor tables next to Teatro Juárez and serves good soups and sandwiches, as well as an interesting assortment of spiked specialty coffees—among them *cafe diable* (coffee, rum, and lemon juice).

⑲ **Mansión del Conde de Rul.** This 18th-century residence, now a government office, housed the count of Rul and Valenciana, who owned La Valenciana, which was then the country's richest silver mine. The two-story structure was designed by famed Mexican architect Eduardo Tresguerras. ⊠ *Plaza de la Paz at Av. Juárez and Callejón del Estudiante,* ☎ *no phone.* 🎫 *Free.* ⊙ *Weekdays 8–3.*

⑱ **Mercado Hidalgo.** You can't miss this 1910 cast-iron-and-glass structure, designed by the one-and-only Gustave Eiffel. Though the balcony stalls are filled with T-shirts and cheap plastic toys, the lower level is full of authentic local wares and colorful basketry, as well as fresh produce, peanuts, and honey-drenched nut candies shaped like mummies. ⊠ *Calle Juárez near Mendizabal.* ⊙ *Daily 8–8.*

⑯ **El Museo Casa Diego Rivera.** This museum, birthplace of Mexico's best-known muralist, Diego Rivera, contains family portraits and furniture as well as works by the master, among them his studies for the controversial mural commissioned for New York City's Rockefeller Center. Completed in 1933, the mural contained a portrait of Lenin and had a decidedly Communist bent, which caused it to be removed immediately after it was displayed. The museum's upper galleries show revolving contemporary art exhibitions. ⊠ *Calle Pocitos 47,* ☎ 4/732–1197. 🎫 *$1.* ⊙ *Tues.–Sat. 10–2:30 and 4–6:30, Sun. 10–2:30.*

㉒ **Museo de las Momias.** For a macabre thrill, check out this unique museum located at the municipal cemetery off Calzada del Panteón, at the west end of town. In the museum, mummified human corpses—once buried in the cemetery—are on display. Until the law was amended in 1858, if a grave site hadn't been paid for after five years, the corpse was removed to make room for new arrivals. Because of the mineral properties of the local soil, these cadavers (the oldest is more than 130 years old) were in astonishingly good condition upon exhumation. Some of them are exhibited in glass cases. ⊠ *Panteón Municipal,* ☎ 4/732–0639. 🎫 *$2.* ⊙ *Daily 10–6:30.*

⑭ **El Pípila.** A half-hour's climb from downtown is the monument to Juan José de los Reyes Martínez, a young miner and hero of the War of Independence of 1810. Nicknamed El Pípila, De los Reyes crept into the Alhóndiga de Granaditas, where Spanish Royalists were hiding. With a stone shield strapped to his back, he set the front door ablaze. The Spanish troops were captured by Father Hidalgo's army in this early battle, giving the independence forces their first major military victory. There's a splendid view of the city from the monument. It's easiest to take a taxi or a bus (marked PÍPILA) from the Jardín. ⊠ *Carretera Panorámica, on bluff above south side of Jardín Unión.*

⑬ **Teatro Juárez.** Adorned with bronze lion sculptures and a line of large Greek muses overlooking the Jardín Unión from the roof, the theater was inaugurated by Mexican dictator Porfirio Díaz in 1903 with a performance of *Aïda*. It now serves as the principal venue of the annual International Cervantes Festival. A brief tour of the art deco interior is available. ✉ *Calle Sopeña s/n*, ☎ *4/732–0183.* 🎫 *$1.20.* ☉ *Tues.– Sun. 9–1:45 and 5–7:45.*

⑮ **University of Guanajuato.** Founded in 1732, the university was formerly a Jesuit seminary. The original churrigueresque church, **La Compañía**, still stands next door. The facade of the university building, built in 1955, was designed to blend in with the town's architecture. If you do wander inside, check out the bulletin boards for notices of cultural events in town. ✉ *Calle Lascurain de Retana 5, ½ block north of Plaza de la Paz*, ☎ *4/732–0006.* ☉ *Weekdays 8–3:30.*

㉑ **La Valenciana.** Officially called La Iglesia de San Cayetano, this is one of the best-known colonial churches in all of Mexico. The mid- to late-18th-century pink stone facade is brilliantly ornate. Inside are three altars, each hand-carved in wood and gilded, in different styles: plateresque, churrigueresque, and baroque. There are also fine examples of religious painting from the viceregal period. The silver mine near the church, also called La Valenciana, was discovered in 1760 and is still in operation today. Although you can't descend into the 1,650-ft-deep mine shaft, if the caretaker is around he'll usually let you take a peek down. The mine and the church are included in any guided tour of Guanajuato, and there are also frequent buses (marked LA VALEN-CIANA) from the city center. ✉ *Carretera Guanajuato–Dolores Hidalgo, Km 2.* ☉ *Daily 9–6.*

OFF THE **MINERAL DE CATA** – The modest church at Mineral de Cata, officially
BEATEN PATH called Señor de Villaseca, is a moving testament to religious faith. Since its founding in 1725, silver miners and their families have come here to offer heartfelt *ex-votos* (also called *retablos*)—folk paintings with text about prayer and gratitude. The church is now covered floor to ceiling with these remarkable offerings. Those near the ceiling are a couple hundred years old, painted on tin. The recent, lower ones deal with contemporary issues, such as immigration. It is best to take a taxi here and have the driver wait (which will run you about $8 an hour) while you look inside. ✉ *Callejón del Quijote.*

Dining

Guanajuato's better restaurants are located in hotels near the Jardín Unión and on the highway to Dolores Hidalgo. For simpler fare, private eateries around town offer a good variety of Mexican and international dishes. Dress tends to be casual.

$$$ ✕ **El Comedor Real.** Continental cuisine served in a medieval environment
★   defines this bright whitewashed restaurant in the Hotel Castillo Santa Cecilia. It serves such specialties as *filete pimienta* (steak with peppercorns) and fish soup with vegetables. Troubadours perform every Friday and Saturday at 10:30 PM at La Cava, the bar next door. ✉ *Camino a la Valenciana s/n, Km 1*, ☎ *4/732–0485. AE, MC, V.*

$$ ✕ **Casa del Conde de la Valenciana.** Come to this refurbished 18th-
★   century home across the street from La Iglesia de San Cayetano (La Valenciana) for superbly prepared traditional Mexican and international fare. Fresh gazpacho comes in a bowl made of ice, and the tender *lomo en salsa de ciruela pasa* (pork shoulder in prune sauce) and *pollo a la flor de calabaza* (chicken with poblano chili slices and squash-blossom

sauce) are delicious. ⊠ *Carretera Guanajuato–Dolores Hidalgo, Km 5,* ☎ *4/732–2550. MC, V. Closed Sun. No dinner.*

$$ ✕ **El Gallo Pitagórico.** Prevail over the 100-plus steps that lead to the threshold of El Gallo Pitagórico and bask in the exceptional view of downtown Guanajuato. Your efforts are further rewarded by a plate of the house specialty, *Filetto Claudio,* (Italian-style fillet marinated in olive oil, capers, parsley, and garlic). The salmon fettuccine is savory, but make room for dessert—a velvety tiramisu. If the evening is fair, ask to have your aperitif in the top-story bar, which offers a view surpassing that of the restaurant. ⊠ *Constancia 10, behind the Teatro Juárez,* ☎ *4/732–9498. MC, V.*

$$ ✕ **Tasca de los Santos.** This cozy restaurant, across the street from the Basílica, specializes in Spanish and international fare. Recommended dishes include the *sopa de mariscos* (a rich broth with shrimp, mussels, clams, and crabs, all in their shells) and *filete parrilla* (grilled beef with baked potatoes and spinach). Dine inside or out under umbrellas on the plaza, with a view of the fountain. A variety of music, ranging from French to Russian, enhances the cosmopolitan mood. ⊠ *Plaza de la Paz 28,* ☎ *4/732–2320. AE, MC, V.*

$ ✕ **El Pingüis Cafeteria.** Cheap and plentiful food attracts the university crowd to this spartan eatery decorated with Mexican art posters. For about $2.50, a midday meal consists of soup, Mexican rice, a chicken or beef dish, dessert, and coffee. *Consumé de verduras* (vegetable soup) is good, as is the *café americano.* Service can be slow, but vibrant music and a lively crowd will keep you entertained. ⊠ *Jardín Unión at Allende 3,* ☎ *4/732–1414. No credit cards.*

$ ✕ **Truco 7.** Red-tile floors, *equipale* (pigskin) chairs, and original art
★ enliven this cozy coffeehouse and restaurant. In the morning, serious students hunch over coffee and textbooks. Later in the day locals and savvy tourists pile in for the inexpensive comida corrida, sandwiches, or grilled chicken. The atmosphere is also lively at night, when Mexican wines are served by the glass. ⊠ *Calle Truco 7,* ☎ *4/732–8374. No credit cards.*

$ ✕ **El Unicorno Azul.** If you're growing weary of heavy meat dishes, stop by this food counter just behind Jardín Unión: it serves fruit drinks, yogurt, and vegetarian burgers and sandwiches. The owner will cheerfully recommend other health-food places and yoga classes. ⊠ *Plaza del Baratillo 2,* ☎ *4/732–0700. No credit cards. Closed Sun.*

Lodging

Guanajuato's less-expensive hotels are along Avenida Juárez and Calle de la Alhóndiga. Moderately priced and upscale properties are near the Jardín Unión and on the outskirts of town. It's best to secure reservations at least six months in advance if you plan to attend the Cervantes Festival, which usually runs from mid- to late October.

$$$ ▦ **La Casa de Espiritus Alegres Bed and Breakfast.** A paradise for folk-
★ art lovers, this "house of good spirits" is filled with extraordinary crafts from every state in Mexico. Owned by a California artist, the lovingly restored hacienda (circa 1700) has thick stone walls and serene grounds lush with bougainvillea, banana trees, and calla lilies. All rooms have hand-glazed tile baths, fireplaces, and a private terrace, patio, or balcony. Rates include a sumptuous breakfast served in a glassed-in atrium overlooking the garden. Children under 13 are not admitted. Marfil is about a 15-minute drive from the center of town—frequent bus service is available. ⊠ *La Ex-Hacienda La Trinidad 1, Marfil 36250,* ☎ FAX *4/733–1013. 5 rooms, 3 suites. Bar, shop, library, free parking. No credit cards.*

$$ 🏨 **Hostería del Frayle.** A half block off Jardín Unión, this quiet four-story lodging was once the Casa de Moneda, where ore was taken to be refined after it was brought out of the mines. Built in 1673 and turned into a hotel in the mid-1960s, it has whitewashed plaster and wood-beam rooms (which nonetheless are somewhat dark), arranged around a small maze of stairways, landings, and courtyards. All have phones and cable TV, and some have excellent views of the Pípila, Teatro Juárez, and Jardín Unión. The staff is extremely friendly and helpful. ⊠ *Calle Sopeña 3, 36000,* ☎ FAX *4/732–1179. 32 rooms, 5 suites. Restaurant, bar. MC, V.*

$$ 🏨 **Hotel Museo Posada Santa Fé.** This colonial-style inn, at the Jardín Unión, has been in operation since 1862. Large historic paintings by local artist Don Manuel Leal hang in the wood-paneled lobby. A sweeping, if tattered, carpeted stairway leads to second-floor quarters. Each room has cable TV and a phone. Rooms facing the plaza can be noisy; quieter rooms face narrow alleyways. ⊠ *Plaza Principal at Jardín Unión 12, 36000,* ☎ *4/732–0084,* FAX *4/732–4653. 47 rooms, 9 suites. 2 restaurants, bar, free parking. AE, MC, V.*

$$ 🏨 **Parador San Javier.** This immaculately restored hacienda was converted into a hotel in 1971. A safe from the Hacienda San Javier and old wood trunks still decorate the large, plant-filled lobby. Rooms are clean and spacious with inviting blue-and-white-tile baths. A few of the 16 colonial-style rooms reached via a stone archway have fireplaces. Newer rooms in the adjoining high-rise have satellite TVs. A word of caution: large convention groups sometimes crowd the facility. ⊠ *Plaza Aldama 92, 36000,* ☎ *4/732–0626,* FAX *4/732–3114. 100 rooms, 12 suites. 2 restaurants, bar, café, pool, dance club, free parking. AE, MC, V.*

$ 🏨 **Hotel Socavón.** One of Guanajuato's newer hotels, this modest five-story property was built in 1981. Don't be put off by the gloomy, tunnel-like entrance: open-air walkways, with views of surrounding mountains, lead to guest quarters. Each small room—simply furnished with a bed, desk, and tiny TV—has a wood-beam ceiling and a modern bath. Fourth-floor corner rooms have some good views. ⊠ *Calle de la Alhóndiga 41A, 36000,* ☎ *4/732–6666,* ☎ FAX *4/732–4885. 40 rooms. Restaurant, bar. AE, MC, V.*

Nightlife and the Arts

Guanajuato, on most nights a somnolent provincial capital, awakens each fall for the **International Cervantes Festival.** For three weeks in October world-renowned actors, musicians, and dance troupes (which have included the Bolshoi Ballet) perform nightly at the Teatro Juárez and other venues in town. Plaza San Roque, a small square near the Jardín Reforma, hosts a series of *Entremeses Cervantinos*—swashbuckling one-act farces by classical Spanish writers. Grandstand seats require advance tickets, but crowds often gather by the edge of the plaza and watch for free. Hundreds of thousands of people attend the festivities, a fact that those who abhor crowds should take into account. If you plan to be in Guanajuato for the festival, contact the Festival Internacional Cervantino office (⊠ Plaza de San Francisquito 1, ☎ 4/731–1150 or 4/731–1161, FAX 4/732–6775) or Ticketmaster (☎ 5/325–9000) at least six months in advance for top-billed events.

At other times of the year, nightlife in Guanajuato mostly consists of dramatic, dance, and musical performances at the **Teatro Juárez** (⊠ Calle de Sopeña s/n, ☎ 4/732–0183). Friday and Saturday at 8 PM, *callejoneadas* (mobile musical parties) begin in front of the Teatro Juárez and meander through town (don't forget to tip the musicians). The **Castillo Santa Cecilia** (⊠ Camino a la Valenciana s/n, Km 1, ☎ 4/732–0485) offers live music on Friday and Saturday nights. You'll find several nightclubs in or near the downtown area, including **Discoteque El Pequeño Juan** (⊠ Panorámica Al Pípila at Callejón de Guadalupe, ☎ 4/732–2308). Its panoramic view of the city at night is stunning. For evening musical entertainment try the **Parador San Javier.** The **Teatro Principal** (⊠ Calle Hidalgo, ☎ 4/732–1523) shows American movies several times a week.

Shopping

Artesanías Vázques (⊠ Cantarranas 8, ☎ FAX 4/732–5231) carries Talavera ceramics from Dolores Hidalgo. You'll find painterly, old-style majolica ceramics at **Capelo** (⊠ Cerro de la Cruz s/n, a dirt road off the Guanajuato–Dolores Hidalgo Hwy., past La Valenciana, ☎ 4/732–8964). Next to the Casa del Conde de la Valencia restaurant, **Casa del Conde de la Valenciana** (⊠ Carretera Guanajuato–Dolores Hidalgo, Km 5, ☎ 4/732–2550) specializes in brass, tin, ceramic, and wrought-iron home decorations from Mexico and Africa. The **Gorky González Workshop** (⊠ Pastita Ex-huerta de Montenegro s/n, past the baseball stadium, ☎ 4/731–0389) offers higher-quality ceramics (at a higher price). Both venerable studios now use lead-safe glazes. Some jewelry and regional knickknacks are sold at the **Mercado Hidalgo.** Other shops around Plaza de la Paz and Jardín Unión sell ceramics and woolen shawls and sweaters. Silver is available from street vendors and shops clustered near La Valenciana and El Pípila.

Side Trip to León

56 km (35 mi) northwest of Guanajuato.

Best known as the shoemaking capital of Mexico, León is also an important center for industry and commerce. With more than 1 million people, it is the state's most populous urban area.

If you know footwear and have the time (and patience) to browse through the downtown shops, you might find some good buys in León. First try the **Plaza del Zapato,** a mall with 70 stores on Boulevard Adolfo López Mateos, roughly one block from the bus station. From here take a taxi west (about a 10-minute ride) to the **Zona Peatonal,** a pedestrian zone with several shoe stores. On **Calle Praxedis Guerrero,** various artisans' stands sell leather goods.

Flecha Amarilla **buses** leave Guanajuato's Central Camionera every 15 minutes for León; the ride takes about 45 minutes and costs less than $1. **Taxis** cost about $17 one way. Pick up a map of León at the tourist office in Guanajuato.

Guanajuato A to Z

AIR TRAVEL

León's Guanajuato International Airport is 40 km (25 mi) west of the city of Guanajuato. The taxi ride from the airport to Guanajuato costs about $17 and takes around 45 minutes.

BUS TRAVEL

Direct bus service is available between the Central del Norte (North Bus Station) in Mexico City and Guanajuato's Central Camionera. Flecha Amarilla offers hourly service. For frequent first-class service use Estrella Blanca. Travel time is about five hours. Deluxe buses, including those of ETN and Primera Plus connect Guanajuato to Mexico City, San Miguel, and Guadalajara. There are several departures daily. Taxis to downtown Guanajuato from the Camionera cost $2–$3.

➤ Bus Information: **Estrella Blanca** (☎ 4/733–1344). **ETN** (☎ 4/733–1579). **Flecha Amarilla** (☎ 4/733–1332 or 4/733–1333). **Primera Plus** (☎ 4/733–1332 or 4/733–1333).

CAR RENTAL

Avis will drop a car at your hotel in Guanajuato.

➤ Major Agencies: **Avis** (✉ Hotel Fiesta Americana, Los Gabilanes, León, ☎ FAX 47/13–60–40).

CAR TRAVEL

Guanajuato is 365 km (226 mi), about five hours, northwest of Mexico City via Route 57 (to Querétaro), then via Route 45.

Don't bother with a car in Guanajuato. Many of the attractions are within strolling distance of one another and located between Avenida Juárez and Calle Pocitos, the city's two major north–south arteries. The twisting subterranean roadway—El Subterráneo—also has a primarily north–south orientation.

EMERGENCIES

Few people in Guanajuato have a good command of English, so in an emergency it's best to contact your hotel manager or the tourist office. El Fénix (pharmacy) is open Monday–Saturday 8 AM–9:45 PM, Sunday 9–9.

➤ Contacts: **Ambulance–Red Cross** (☎ 4/732–0487). **El Fénix** (✉ Av. Juárez 104, ☎ 4/732–6140). **Hospital General** (☎ 4/733–1577). **Police** (☎ 4/732–0266).

INTERNET

Redes Internet, open weekdays 9:30–8 and Saturday 10–3, charges $3 an hour for Internet access.

➤ Internet Cafés: **Redes Internet** (✉ Alonso 70, ☎ 4/732–0611).

TAXIS

You can find taxis at *sitios* (taxi stands) near the Jardín Unión, Plaza de la Paz, and Mercado Hidalgo.

TOURS

The following tour operators give half- and full-day tours with English-speaking guides. These tours typically include the Museum of Mummies, the church and mines of Valenciana, the monument to Pípila, the Panoramic Highway, subterranean streets, and residential neighborhoods. Night tours often begin at the Pípila Monument for a nighttime city view and end at a dance club. Estudiantinas usually perform during the weekend tours.

Transporte Exclusivo de Turismo has several tours of Guanajuato and its environs. Transporte Turísticos de Guanajuato also has a kiosk at the main bus terminal.

➤ Tour Operator Recommendations: **Transporte Exclusivo de Turismo** (✉ Av. Juárez and Calle 5 de Mayo, ☎ 4/732–5968). **Transporte Turísticos de Guanajuato** (✉ Plaza de la Paz 2, by Basílica de Guanajuato, ☎ 4/732–2134 or 4/732–2838).

TRAVEL AGENCIES

Viajes Georama is the local American Express representative. Viajes Frausto is reliable for hotel and airline reservations.

➤ Local Agent Referrals: **Viajes Frausto** (✉ Calle González Obregón 10, ☎ 4/732–3580, FAX 4/732–6620). **Viajes Georama** (✉ Plaza de la Paz 34, ☎ 4/732–5909, FAX 4/732–1954).

VISITOR INFORMATION

The Guanajuato tourist office is open daily 9–7.

➤ TOURIST INFORMATION: **Guanajuato tourist office** (✉ Plaza de la Paz 14, ☎ 4/732–1574 or 4/732–1982, FAX 4/732–4251).

ZACATECAS

In colonial days Zacatecas was the largest silver-producing city in the world, sending great treasures of the precious metal to the king of Spain. Still a large silver-mining center, with factories producing silver jewelry and trade schools training apprentices in the fine art of handmade silver craft, Zacatecas is relatively undiscovered by foreigners. Although it is a state capital with a population of some 300,000, it has the feel of a much smaller place. Zacatecas is kept spotlessly clean, thanks to civic pride and a mandate by the governor of the state of Zacatecas. This city is rightly famous for its historic role as the scene of one of Pancho Villa's most spectacular battles and for its 18th-century colonial architecture.

One of the town's unique charms is the *tambora*, a musical walk up and down the streets and alleyways led by a *tamborazo*, a typical local band that shatters the evening quiet with merriment. Also known as a callejoneada (*callejón* means "alley"), the tambora is a popular free-for-all, in which everyone along the way either joins in the procession or leans from balconies and doorways to cheer the group on. During the December *feria* (festival), the tamborazos play night and day as they serenade the Virgin of Zacatecas.

Exploring Zacatecas

Most of Zacatecas's colonial sights are near the city center, making it an easy place to explore on foot—and there is rarely much traffic in town. For an overview of Zacatecas, you can walk or taxi up to the mine, catch an elevator to a nearby hilltop, take the cable car across the city, then return to your starting point below by taxi or bus.

A Good Walk

Start your tour at the Plaza de Armas, in the center of the city. Here you'll find the stunning **Catedral de Zacatecas** ㉓ and the **Palacio del Gobierno** ㉔. Across the street from the plaza are two beautiful colonial buildings worth exploring; one is known as the **Palacio de la Mala Noche** ㉕ because of a local legend. Go to the Plaza Santo Domingo, two blocks west of the cathedral, to see the art in the **Pedro Coronel Museum** ㉖ and the baroque **Templo de Santo Domingo** ㉗ right next door. To visit the museum of the other Coronel brother—both were equally fanatical art collectors—return to the cathedral, turn left on Avenida Hidalgo, and walk about 1 km (½ mi) north of the plaza to the **Rafael Coronel Museum** ㉘.

For a longer walk, head south on Avenida Hidalgo until you come to Juárez, then go right (roughly west) up the hill, passing the several-block-long Alameda park and the Social Security Hospital to get to **La Mina Eden** ㉙. After touring the mine, you can take an elevator up to Cerro del Grillo (Cricket Hill) and catch the **Teleférico** ㉚ cable car across the city to **Cerro de la Bufa** ㉛, the site of Pancho Villa's famous battle.

Sights to See

㉓ **Catedral de Zacatecas.** This is one of Mexico's finest interpretations of baroque style. Each of the facades tells a different legend. According to one of them, an anticlerical governor of the state used the cathedral's silver cross and baptismal font to mint Zacatecas's first silver coins. ✉ *South side of Plaza de Armas on Av. Hidalgo.*

Zacatecas

....

NEED A
BREAK?

El Teatro Caffé (Av. Hidalgo 501, inside Teatro Caldreon, ☎ 4/922–8620), in a restored 100-year-old theater adorned in celestial murals, is a hopping coffee shop where students swap ideas over a cappuccino or a *Neive Opera* (vanilla ice cream topped with chocolate syrup, espresso, and cream).

....

③① Cerro de la Bufa. The city trademark, this rugged hill is the site of Pancho Villa's definitive battle against dictator Victoriano Huerta in June 1914. The spacious **Plaza de la Revolución,** paved with the three shades of pink Zacatecan stone, is crowned with three huge equestrian statues of Villa and two other heroes, Felipe Angeles and Panfilo Natera. Also on the site are the **Sanctuary of the Virgin of Patrocinio,** a chapel dedicated to the patron of the city, and the **Museo de la Toma de Zacatecas,** which has nine rooms filled with historic objects such as guns, newspapers, furniture, and clothing from the days of Pancho Villa. ⌧ *If driving, follow Av. Hidalgo north from town to Av. Juan de Tolosa; turn right and continue until you come to a fountain; take 1st immediate right off retorno (crossover) onto Calle Mexicapan, which leads to Carretera Panorámica. Turn right to signposted Carretera La Bufa, which leads to the top of the hill.* ☎ *Museum 4/922–8066.* ⌧ *$1.* ⊙ *Tues.–Sun. 10–4:30.*

② La Mina Eden. Now a tourist attraction, the Eden Mine supplied most of Zacatecas's silver from 1586 until 1960. An open mine train runs down into the underground tunnels. The tour is in Spanish, but you'll have no trouble imagining what the life of the miners was like. Be sure to wear sturdy shoes. Remember that mines are dark; through much of the tour, your only light may be the guide's flashlight. Farther down the train track there is another stop at, of all places, a discotheque. There's a small gift shop at the entrance. ⌧ *Entrance on Antonio Dovali off*

Av. Torreon beyond Alameda García de la Cadena, ☎ *4/922–3002.* ▣ *$2.* ◷ *Daily 10–6.*

㉕ **Palacio de la Mala Noche.** The Palace of the Bad Night is one of two beautiful 18th-century colonial buildings across from the downtown plaza. Both declared national monuments, they are built from native pink stone and have lacy ironwork balconies. One of them now houses the Continental Plaza hotel, and the other is a municipal building known as El Palacio de la Mala Noche. Legend has it that this was the home of a silver-mine owner who was called upon so often to help the needy that he built a hidden door from which he could enter and leave the palace undisturbed. Up the hill along the side of the palace, you will find the so-called hidden door. ⊠ *Av. Hidalgo 639.* ▣ *Free.* ◷ *Weekdays 7–3.*

㉔ **Palacio del Gobierno.** The Governor's Palace is an 18th-century mansion with flower-filled courtyards and, on the main staircase, a powerful mural painted in 1970 by António Pintor Rodríguez that depicts the history of Zacatecas. ⊠ *East side of Plaza de Armas.* ▣ *Free.* ◷ *Daily 9–2 and 5–8.*

★ ㉖ **Pedro Coronel Museum.** Originally a Jesuit monastery, this building was used as a jail in the 18th century. The museum houses the work of Zacatecan artist and sculptor Pedro Coronel and his extensive collection of works by Picasso, Dalí, Miró, Braque, and Chagall, among others, as well as art from Africa, China, Japan, India, Tibet, Greece, and Egypt. ⊠ *Av. Fernando Villalpando at Plaza Santo Domingo,* ☎ *4/922–8021.* ▣ *About $2.* ◷ *Fri.–Wed. 10–5.*

★ ㉘ **Rafael Coronel Museum.** The museum is in the Ex-Convento de San Francisco, northeast of the town center toward Lomas del Calvario. Its mellowed pink 18th-century facade conceals a rambling structure of open, arched corridors, all leading through garden patios to rooms that contain an amazing collection of some 4,500 *máscaras* (masks)—saints and devils, wise men and fools, animals and humans—used in regional festivals all over Mexico. There is also an outstanding display of puppets. ⊠ *Off Vergel Nuevo between Chaveño and Garcia Salinas,* ☎ *4/922–8116.* ▣ *About $2.* ◷ *Thurs.–Tues. 10–5.*

㉚ **Teleférico.** The only cable car in the world that crosses an entire city, the Teleférico runs from **Cerro del Grillo** (Cricket Hill) above the Eden Mine to Cerro de la Bufa and operates daily from 10 until dusk, except when there are high winds. True, it crosses at the narrowest point, but it presents a magnificent panoramic view of the city and its many baroque church domes and spires. It's also well worth the cost to get the ride up to Cerro de la Bufa, which is quite a climb otherwise. ⊠ *Cerro del Grillo station is off Paseo Díaz Ordaz, a steep walk from Plaza de Armas,* ☎ *4/922–5694.* ▣ *About $2.* ◷ *Daily 10–6.*

㉗ **Templo de Santo Domingo.** This 18th-century Jesuit church has an ornamented facade and a rich interior that includes gold-leaf religious paintings. The sacristy also contains an impressive collection of religious art. ⊠ *Av. Fernando Villalpando at Plaza Santo Domingo.* ◷ *Daily 7:30–3 and 5:30–8:30.*

Dining and Lodging

Several of Zacatecas's better restaurants are in hotels, and many of the best lodgings are in beautiful, well-preserved 18th- and 19th-century buildings. Other popular restaurants are on Avenida Juárez, which intersects Avenida Hidalgo.

$$$ ✕ **La Cuija.** Regional food is the strength of this large restaurant,
★ whose name means "the gecko." Start off with an appetizer of three
quesadillas: one each of squash blossoms, cheese, and *huitlacoche* (a
corn fungus delicacy). Also recommended are the *sopa campera* (a cream
soup with corn and squash blossoms) and asado de boda (pork in a
semisweet and spicy sauce). The decor approximates a wine cellar, and
in addition to fine food, the restaurant serves wine from the owner's
Cachola Vineyards in Valle de las Arsinas. A traditional Mexican trio
plays Thursday–Sunday afternoons. ✉ *Centro Commercial El Mer-
cado, bottom level,* ☎ *4/922–8275. AE, V.*

$$ **Café y Nevería Acrópolis.** This quaint diner is trimmed with paintings
and sketches given to the owner by some of the famous people who
have eaten here, including a small acrylic by Rafael Coronel. Enjoy a
strong Turkish coffee and watch the locals flood in for breakfast. The
chiliquiles verdes (strips of fried tortilla smothered in a tangy green sauce
and white cheese) is served with an alluring basket of pastries and bread.
Traditional café fare like hamburgers, sandwiches, and fruity shakes
are available for lunch. ✉ *Av. Hidalgo at Plazuela Candelario Huizar,
alongside the cathedral,* ☎ *4/922–1284. No credit cards.*

$$ **El Paraiso.** The fashionable cantina for the Zacatecano elite over 100
years ago, El Paraiso is still a town favorite today. Rich burgundy walls,
green velvet curtains, and brass accents impart a wealthy Old West–
saloon look. The extensive *botanas Zacatecano* (traditional Zacate-
cas appetizers) menu offers an ideal opportunity to sample various tra-
ditional dishes. The *platillo Zacatecano* for two people is a seasoned
filet served with quesadillas, guacamole, and beans. *Enchiladas de
ayer* (yesterday's enchiladas) may sound like leftovers, but the friendly
waiters promise that the flavor is enhanced by the second day. ✉ *Av.
Hidago y Plaza Goitia,* ☎ *4/922–6164. AE, MC, V.*

$$$ 🏨 **Quinta Real.** This hotel must be one of the most unusual in the world:
★ it is built around Mexico's oldest bullring, the second one constructed
in the Western Hemisphere. The terrazzo-paved ring provides a unique
view for the guest suites, each with a balcony overlooking the *plaza
de toro* (bullring) itself. Large and bright, the plush rooms are decorated in pastel fabrics that complement the dark traditional furniture.
The bar occupies some of the former bull pens, and an outdoor café
with bright-white umbrella tables takes up two levels of the spectator
area. Fine Continental cuisine is served in the elaborate, formal restaurant, with an awesome view of the bullring and the aqueduct beyond.
✉ *Av. Rayon 434, 98000,* ☎ *4/922–9104,* FAX *4/922–8440. 49 suites.
Restaurant, bar, shop, free parking. AE, MC, V.*

$$ ✕🏨 **Continental Plaza.** This beautiful old colonial building faces the
Plaza de Armas and the cathedral in the heart of the city. The pink-
stone facade dates from the 18th century; unfortunately the modern
interior is rather stark and charmless. Rooms are fitted with new but
unexceptional furniture. Those facing the plaza are within earshot of
late-night and early morning tamborazo music during festivals. That
said, you'll get a great view of the goings-on from your small balcony.
The hotel's restaurant, Candiles, offers both Continental and regional
dishes, and there is a daily breakfast buffet. ✉ *Av. Hidalgo 703, 98000,*
☎ *4/922–6183,* FAX *4/922–6245. 86 rooms, 13 suites. Restaurant, bar,
convention center, free parking. AE, MC, V.*

$$ 🏨 **Hostal del Vasco.** For a truly Zacatecano hotel, consider the clean,
cozy, and quiet Hostal del Vasco. Spacious brown-carpeted suites are
decorated in ponderous antiques and include telephones, cable TV, and
marble bathrooms; some are equipped with a small kitchen (but no
cookware). Sprawling plants and singing birds—Pepe the parrot leads
the choir—enliven the two-story interior courtyard. ✉ *Alameda y Ve-*

lasco 1, 98000, ☎ FAX 4/922–0428. 18 suites. Kitchenettes, beauty salon, laundry service. AE, MC, V.

$$ ⊞ **Mesón de Jobito.** This early 19th-century apartment building stood
★ for well over a hundred years before its recent conversion to a four-star hotel. The two levels of guest rooms are done in tasteful modern decor, with wall-to-wall carpet and striped drapes. All rooms have cable TV and phones. The restful atmosphere is enhanced by the Mesón's perfect location on a blissfully quiet little plaza a few blocks from the cathedral. ⊠ Jardín Juárez 143, 98000, ☎ FAX 4/924–1722. 53 rooms, 6 suites. 2 restaurants, bar. AE, MC, V.

$ ⊞ **Posada de la Moneda.** This very Mexican hotel in the middle of downtown is adequate if you're on a budget. Everything is highly polished, especially the lobby's tile floor. If the room furnishings are a bit threadbare, they are clean, and the carpet is relatively new. Each room has a phone and cable TV. ⊠ Av. Hidalgo 413, 98000, ☎ FAX 4/922–0881. 34 rooms, 2 suites. Restaurant, bar. AE, MC, V.

Nightlife and the Arts

There's live music in the lobby bar of the **Continental Plaza.** A must-see if only for its uniqueness, **El Malacate** (⊠ La Mina Eden, ☎ 4/922–3002), the discotheque in the Eden Mine, is more than 1,000 ft underground. It's best to make reservations at this popular place, which is both crowded and noisy. It's open Thursday–Saturday night; the cover charge is about $7. **Quinta Real** features a nightly band in a romantic bar located to one side of the old bullring.

Shopping

Don't expect to find quality crafts in Zacatecas; souvenirs are more along the line of tacky knickknacks than handicrafts. There is some decent silver jewelry, although not as much as one would expect.

Crafts

Opposite the east end of Plaza de Armas is **La Cazzorra** (⊠ Av. Hidalgo 713, ☎ 4/924–0484), a collectibles shop with authentic antiques, books about Zacatecas, wood furniture, Huichol art, ceramics, and a fine selection of jewelry from the local silver factory. The owners are a good source of information about the city.

Silver

The **Centro Comercial El Mercado** (⊠ Calle Hidalgo, next to cathedral) has a few shops with silver goods. **Centro Platero Zacatecas** (☎ 4/923–1007) sells silver jewelry with regional designs, made in its factory in nearby Guadalupe. **Sa Pe Ca** (☎ 4/922–0273) sells a large selection of silver jewelry and accessories for women and men.

Side Trips from Zacatecas

Guadalupe

7 km (4½ mi) southeast of Zacatecas.

If you are interested in colonial art and architecture, don't miss this small town. Its centerpiece is the **Ex-Convento de Guadalupe,** founded by Franciscan monks in 1707. It currently houses the **Museo de Arte Virreinal** (virreinal means "viceregal," or "colonial"), run by the Instituto Nacional de Antropología e Historia. The convent is itself a work of art, with its baroque **Templo de Guadalupe** and the **Capilla de Nápoles,** but even more impressive is the stunning collection of religious art under its roof. Works by Miguel Cabrera, Nicolás Rodríguez Juárez, Cristóbal de Villalpando, and Andrés López are included. ⊠ Jardín Juárez s/n, ☎ 4/923–2386. ☜ $3, free Sun. ☽ Daily 10–4:30.

In the 18th-century mansion of don Ignacio de Bernárdez, the **Centro Platero Zacatecas** is a school and factory for handmade silver jewelry and other items. Stop in to watch student silversmiths master this fine tradition. ⊠ *Casco de la Ex-Hacienda Bernárdez,* ☎ 4/923–1007. ☼ *Weekdays 10–6:30, Sat. 10–3.*

Zona Arqueológica La Quemada

50 km (31 mi) southwest of Zacatecas on Hwy. 54, 3 km (2 mi) off highway.

This ancient city was already a ruin before the Spaniards arrived in the 16th century. The site's original name, "Chicomostoc," means "place of the seven tribes." Although it was once believed that seven different Indian cultures built here, one community atop the other, this theory is currently under scrutiny. The remaining edifices appear to be constructed of thin slabs of stone wedged into place. The principal draw is a group of rose-color ruins containing 11 large, round columns built entirely of the same small slabs of rock seen in the rest of the ruins. An impressive site museum has a scale model of the ruins and some interesting artifacts. To get here, take a bus toward Villanueva, get off at the entrance to La Quemada, and walk in 3 km (2 mi). The bus ride takes about an hour. Alternatively, take a taxi or guided tour. ☎ *no phone.* ⌨ *$3, free Sun.* ☼ *Site and museum daily 10–4:30.*

Zacatecas A to Z

AIR TRAVEL

Mexicana has direct service to Zacatecas from Chicago, Denver, and Los Angeles. In Zacatecas, the Mexicana office is at Av. Hidalgo 406. The airport is 29 km (18 mi) north of town. Aerotransportes makes the trip for about $5; private taxis cost about $15.

➤ AIRLINES AND CONTACTS: **Aerotransportes** (☎ 4/922–5946). **Mexicana** (⊠ Av. Hidalgo 406, ☎ 4/922–7470 or 4/922–3248).

BUS TRAVEL

Major bus lines run several first- and second-class buses daily from Mexico City to Zacatecas. The trip takes eight to nine hours.

➤ BUS INFORMATION: **Futura** (☎ 4/922–0042). **Omnibus de México** (☎ 4/922–5495). **Turistar** (☎ 4/922–0042).

CAR TRAVEL

Zacatecas is 603 km (375 mi), about 7½–8 hours, northwest of Mexico City via Route 57 (to Querétaro and San Luis Potosí) and Route 49.

EMERGENCIES

English is not generally spoken in Zacatecas, so it's best to contact your hotel manager or the tourist office in case of an emergency.

Pharmacies are abundant; try Farmacia Isstezac, which is open daily 8 AM–10 PM.

➤ CONTACTS: **Emergency Service** (☎ 066). **Farmacia Isstezac** (⊠ Tacuba 153, ☎ 4/924–0690). **Hospital General** (☎ 4/923–3004). **Police** (☎ 4/922–0180). **Red Cross** (☎ 4/922–3005).

INTERNET

Cronos, open Monday–Saturday 9–8, Sunday 10:30–8, charges $2 an hour for Internet access.

➤ INTERNET CAFÉ: **Cronos** (⊠ Av. Rayon 212, ☎ 4/922–1548).

TOURS

Viajes Mazzoco, a well-established travel agency and the local American Express representative, gives a four-hour tour of the city center, the Eden Mine, the Teleférico, and La Bufa for about $12 a person. There are also tours to La Quemada ruins and environs ($16).

Operadora Zacatecas is recommended by the tourism office, and offers tours of the city center and elsewhere in the area.
➤ TOUR OPERATOR RECOMMENDATIONS: **Operadora Zacatecas** (✉ Av. Hidalgo 630, ☎ 4/924–0050). **Viajes Mazzoco** (✉ Calle Satima 115, ☎ FAX 4/922–0859).

TRANSPORTATION AROUND ZACATECAS
You can get to most of the town-center attractions on foot, although you might want to hire a taxi if you want to tour a mine or take a ride on the Teleférico (cable car) to the top of Cerro de la Bufa. The city has an excellent and inexpensive bus system.

VISITOR INFORMATION
The tourist information office is open weekdays 9–8, weekends 9–7.
➤ TOURIST INFORMATION: **Tourist information office** (✉ Av. Hidalgo 403, 2nd floor, ☎ 4/924–4047 or 4/924–0552).

QUERÉTARO

In 1810 the first plans for independence were hatched at the Querétaro home of Josefa Ortiz de Domínguez—known as La Corregidora, wife of El Corregidor, Querétaro's mayor of the time. She was a heroine of the independence movement. In 1848 the Mexican–American War was concluded in this city with the signing of the Treaty of Guadalupe Hidalgo. Emperor Maximilian made his last stand here in 1867 and was executed by firing squad on the *Cerro de las Campanas* (Hill of the Church Bells), north of town. A small memorial chapel, built by the Austrian government, marks the spot. A gigantic statue of Benito Juárez crowns a park on the crest of the hill just above it. Also, in 1917, the Mexican Constitution, which is still in force, was signed here. Now Querétaro is a state capital and an industrial center of nearly 1 million people.

Throughout Querétaro are markers, museums, churches, and monuments that commemorate the city's heroes and historic moments. A prevailing sense of civic pride is evident in the impeccably renovated mansions, the flower-draped cobblestone pedestrian walkways, and the hospitable plazas, which are softly lighted at night. On Sunday evening couples dance to live *danzón* music in the main plaza, or simply chat and enjoy the company of their friends. The people are among the most congenial in central Mexico and are quick to share their favorite sites and tales with travelers.

Querétaro is also renowned for opals—red, green, honey, and fire stones. Caveat emptor: some street vendors sell opals so full of water that they crumble shortly after purchase. Buy from reputable dealers.

Exploring Querétaro

Although Querétaro extends for some distance, the historic district is in the heart of town. You can easily spend a day or two here visiting museums, admiring architecture, and taking in local history.

A Good Walk
Most sights are near the **Plaza de la Independencia** ㉜. The **Palacio del Gobierno del Estado** ㉝ is on the plaza's northwest corner. If you walk around the square counterclockwise, you'll come to the Palacio de Justicia, originally built as a mansion for the wealthy Domingo Iglesia and,

beside it, the **Casa de Ecala** ㉞. Just past the Casa de Ecala is Avenida Libertad Oriente, one of the city's bougainvillea-draped pedestrian walk-ways. Turn west here and walk two blocks to reach Calle Corregidora. Bear right again, and in the middle of a long block you'll find the en-trance to the **Museo Regional de Querétaro** ㉟. Cross the street to Avenida Madero, another "pedway," this one lined with shops. The city's main square, Jardín Obregón, will be on your right.

One block past Avenida Juárez on the corner of Calle Allende Sur and Madero you'll see the former **Casa de la Marquesa** ㊱, an 18th-cen-tury mansion converted into a hotel. Across Allende, next to the Church of Santa Clara, is the neoclassical **Fountain of Neptune** ㊲. From the fountain, make a left on Calle Allende and walk almost a block to a fine example of baroque architecture, the **Museo de Arte de Querétaro** ㊳. Retrace your steps to Calle Corregidora. Make a left and walk one block to Calle 16 de Septiembre. Across the street is the **Jardín de la Corregidora** ㊴.

Sights to See

㉞ **Casa de Ecala.** Currently housing the offices of DIF, a family-services organization, this Mexican baroque palace has its original facade. As the story goes, its 18th-century owner adorned his home elaborately in order to outdo his neighbor, starting a remodeling war in which the Casa de Ecala eventually triumphed. Visitors are welcome to walk around the courtyard when the offices are open. ✉ *Pasteur Sur 6, Plaza de la Independencia.* ☺ *Daily 9–2 and 4–7.*

㊱ **Casa de la Marquesa.** Today a five-star hotel, this beautifully restored 18th-century house was built by the second Marqués de la Villa del Villar del Aguila. Most of the legends about the house's construction suggest that it was built to impress a nun with whom the marquis was terribly smitten. But he didn't live to see the casa completed in 1756, and its first resident was his widow, who had a penchant for things Arabic. The interior is *mudéjar* (Moorish) style, with lovely tilework. Stop in for a drink and the elegant atmosphere of **Don Porfirio's Bar.** ⊠ *Madero 41.*

NEED A BREAK?
Cafeteria El Naranjo (Av. Madero 48, ☎ 4/224–0136, ext. 109) has a wide selection of specialty coffee, including the Sexy Coffee (coffee, rum, Kahlúa, and whole cream). The outdoor patio is comfortable for people-watching.

㊲ Fountain of Neptune. Built in 1797 by Eduardo Tresguerras, the renowned Mexican architect and a native of the Bajío, the fountain originally stood in the orchard of the Monastery of San Antonio. According to one story, when the monks faced serious economic problems, they sold part of their land and the fountain along with it. It now stands next to the Church of Santa Clara. ⊠ *Calle Allende at Madero.*

㊴ Jardín de la Corregidora. This plaza is prominently marked by a statue of the War of Independence heroine—Josefa Ortiz de Domínguez—whose moniker it bears. Behind the monument stands the **Arbol de la Amistad** (Tree of Friendship). Planted in 1977 in a mixture of soils from around the world, the tree symbolizes Querétaro's hospitality to all travelers. This is the calmest square in town, with plenty of choices for patio dining. ⊠ *Calle Corregidora and Andador 16 de Septiembre.*

㊳ Museo de Arte de Querétaro. A fine example of baroque architecture, the museum is housed in an 18th-century Augustinian monastery. Its collection focuses on European and Mexican paintings from the 17th through 19th centuries, and there are rotating exhibits of 20th-century art. Note the elegant and fascinating baroque patio, and ask for an explanation of the symbolism of its columns and the figures in the conch shells at the top of each arch. ⊠ *Calle Allende 14 Sur,* ☎ *4/212–2357.* 🎟 *About $1.50, free Tues.* ☉ *Tues.–Sun. 10–6.*

㉟ Museo Regional de Querétaro. This bright-yellow, 17th-century Franciscan monastery displays the works of colonial and European artists in addition to historic memorabilia, including early copies of the Mexican Constitution and the table on which the Treaty of Guadalupe Hidalgo was signed. ⊠ *Calle Corregidora 3, at Av. Libertad Oriente,* ☎ *4/212–2031.* 🎟 *About $3, free Sun.* ☉ *Tues.–Sun. 10–7.*

㉝ Palacio del Gobierno del Estado. Also known as La Casa de la Corregidora, in 1810 this was the home of Querétaro's mayor-magistrate (El Corregidor) and his wife, Josefa Ortiz de Domínguez (La Corregidora). On many evenings, conspirators—including Ignacio Allende and Father Miguel Hidalgo—came here under the guise of participating in La Corregidora's literary salon. When El Corregidor learned that they were actually plotting the course for independence, he imprisoned his wife in her room. La Corregidora managed to whisper a warning to a coconspirator, who notified Allende and Hidalgo. A few days later, on September 16, Father Hidalgo tolled the bell of his church to signal the beginning of the fight for freedom. A replica of the bell can be seen atop the building. Now the Palacio houses municipal government offices. ⊠ *Northwest corner of Plaza de la Independencia.* 🎟 *Free.* ☉ *Weekdays 9–8, Sat. 9–2.*

㉜ Plaza de la Independencia. Bordered by carefully restored colonial mansions, this immaculate square, also known as Plaza de Armas, is especially lovely at night, when the central fountain is lighted. Built in 1842, the fountain is dedicated to the Marqués de la Villa del Villar, who constructed Querétaro's elegant aqueduct and provided the city with drinking water. The old stone aqueduct with its 74 towering arches still stands at the east end of town. ⊠ *Bounded by Av. 5 de Mayo on the north, Av. Libertad Oriente on the south, Luis Pasteur on the east, and Vergara Sur on the west.*

Dining

Many of Querétaro's dining spots are near the main plaza (Jardín Obregón), along Calle Corregidora, near the Teatro de la República, and particularly in the Jardín de la Corregidora. There are more-up-scale restaurants in hotels on the Plaza de la Independencia and off Route 57, north of the city.

$$$$ ✕ **Restaurante Josecho.** Bullfight aficionados and other sports fans fre-
★   quent this highway road stop next to the bullring at the southwest end of town as much for the lively atmosphere as for the food. Wood-paneled walls are hung with hunting trophies, including peacocks, elk, bears, and lions; waiters celebrate patrons' birthdays by banging on pewter plates and blasting a red siren. The place quiets down at night, when a classical guitarist or pianist performs. House specialties include *filete Josecho* (steak with cheese and mushrooms) and *filete Chemita* (steak sautéed in butter with onions). Save room for the coconut ice cream served in a real coconut shell. ⊠ *Dalia 1, next to Plaza de Toros Santa María,* ☎ *4/216–0229 or 4/216–0201. AE, MC, V.*

$$$ ✕ **El Mesón de Chucho el Roto.** Named after Querétaro's version of Robin Hood, this restaurant is on the quiet Plaza de Armas. The interesting menu highlights regional cooking, including exotic tacos of either steamed goat, shrimp with nopal cactus, or squash blossoms. You can enjoy a variety of breakfast foods here as well, either overlooking the plaza from the café tables outside, indoors, or on the back patio. ⊠ *Plaza de Armas,* ☎ *4/212–4295. AE, MC, V.*

$$$ ✕ **La Nueva Fonda del Refugio.** Situated in the Jardín de la Corregidora, this restaurant offers intimate indoor and outdoor dining. Inside, fresh flowers adorn white-clothed tables; outside, comfortable *equipale* chairs face the surrounding gardens. Seafood and beef fillets are the specialties; consider ordering the mustard fillet of beef. Cocktails are served on the terrace at night, when diners are often serenaded by guitar-playing trios. ⊠ *Jardín de la Corregidora 26,* ☎ *4/212–0755. AE, MC, V.*

$ ✕ **Bisquets Bisquets.** Mexican families flock to this friendly spot after church for good and hearty inexpensive food. The specialty of the house is—you guessed it—biscuits, made fresh on the premises, with such traditional toppings as butter and jelly or with more unusual ones such as mole or tuna. There are good enchiladas *Queretanas,* with cheese, potatoes, carrots, and cream, and *huevos al albañil* (eggs with red sauce and beans). ⊠ *Av. Pino Suarez 7,* ☎ *4/214–1481. No credit cards.*

$ ✕ **La Mariposa.** Celebrating more than 50 years in business, La Mariposa is easily recognized by the wrought-iron butterfly (*mariposa*) over the entrance. This is the place for coffee and cake or a light Mexican lunch: enchiladas, tacos, tamales, and *tortas* (sandwiches). It's a favorite among locals despite its very plain, cafeteria-like appearance. ⊠ *Angela Peralta 7,* ☎ *4/212–1166 or 4/212–4849. No credit cards.*

Lodging

Several new hotels in various price ranges have opened in Querétaro in the past 10 years. Lower-price hotels are located near the main plaza and thus tend to be noisy; restored colonial mansions are on or near the city's many plazas in the heart of town; and deluxe properties are on the outskirts of town.

$$$$ ⊞ **Hotel Señorial.** This sprawling four-story property has plain but clean, large, and modern rooms with telephones and cable TV. Rooms in front face a narrow, busy street, but traffic slows in the evening. There are purified-water dispensers in the hallways. The restaurant serves a Sunday buffet lunch. ⊠ *Guerrero Nte. 10-A, 76000,* ☎ *4/214–3700,* FAX *4/214–1945. 54 rooms. Restaurant. MC, V.*

$$$ ⊞ **Casa de la Marquesa.** This beautifully restored property, originally
★ an 18th-century private home, is perfectly situated in the heart of Querétaro. The central courtyard of the main building is a beautifully decorated sitting room. Each large guest room is furnished differently with antique furniture, tasteful art, parquet floors, and area rugs, and each has a direct-dial telephone. Rooms in the main building are more elegant and expensive than those in La Casa Azul (children under 12 are not admitted in the main building). The property's award-winning restaurant, Comedor de la Marquesa, is elegant and a bit austere. It specializes in such regional rarities as boar, venison, and *escamole* (ant eggs) in season, as well as more-traditional international cookery. ⊠ *Madero 41, 76000,* ☎ *4/212–0092,* FAX *4/212–0098. 6 rooms, 19 suites. 2 restaurants, bar, room service, shops. AE, MC, V.*

$$$ ⊞ **Hacienda Jurica.** A favorite getaway for Mexico City families, this
★ sprawling 16th-century ex-hacienda has nearly 30 acres of grassy sports fields, topiary gardens, a horse stable, and heated pool, and you can play golf at a nearby course. The grounds and courtyards are dotted with antique horse-drawn carriages, and the spacious earth-tone rooms have substantial dark-wood furniture, satellite TVs, and minibars. The hacienda is in Jurica, an upscale residential neighborhood 13 km (8 mi) northwest of the city off Highway 57 and is easiest to reach by car. ⊠ *Carretera Mexico–San Luis Potosí, Km 229, Apdo. 338, 76100,* ☎ *4/218–0022,* FAX *4/218–0136. 176 rooms, 6 suites. Restaurant, bar, minibars, pool, 2 tennis courts, horseback riding, billiards, travel services, free parking. AE, MC, V.*

$$$ ⊞ **Holiday Inn Querétaro.** This gracious, well-run establishment has a lot more charm than others in the chain. Located 3 km (about 2 mi) west of the historic district off Highway 57, the contemporary building incorporates many colonial touches such as stone archways and domed *boveda* (vaulted) ceilings. Sunny, ample rooms are comfortably appointed with rustic Mexican furnishings, cheery pastel bedspreads, satellite TVs, and minibars. ⊠ *Av. 5 de Febrero 110, 76000,* ☎ *4/216–0202,* FAX *4/216–8902. 171 rooms, 4 suites. 2 restaurants, piano bar, minibars, no-smoking room, pool, exercise room, baby-sitting, travel services, free parking. AE, MC, V.*

$$ ⊞ **Hotel Mirabel.** A favorite among business travelers and conventioneers, this modern high-rise hums with activity. Its carpeted rooms are insulated and quiet and have cable TV, telephones, wooden desks, and air-conditioning. Some double rooms have views of the Alameda Hidalgo park; some singles overlook a soccer stadium. ⊠ *Av. Constituyentes Ote. 2, 76000,* ☎ *4/214–3099 or 4/214–3444,* FAX *4/214–3585. 170 rooms, 10 suites. Restaurant, bar, free parking. AE, MC, V.*

$$ ⊞ **Mesón de Santa Rosa.** Located on the quiet Plaza de la Indepen-
★ dencia, this elegant property was used almost 300 years ago as a stopover for travelers to the north. Rooms are clustered around a quiet courtyard; lace-hung glass doors and wood-beam ceilings maintain the colonial charm. Amenities such as satellite TVs, minibars, and a heated pool make this lovely hotel comfortable as well. ⊠ *Pasteur Sur 17, 76000,* ☎ *4/224–2623,* FAX *4/212–5522. 5 rooms, 17 suites. Restaurant, bar, minibars, pool. AE, MC, V.*

Nightlife and the Arts

Band concerts are held in the **Jardín Obregón,** Querétaro's main square, every Sunday evening at 6. A monthly publication called *Tesoro Turístico,* available at the tourist office, provides information about current festivals, concerts, and other cultural events.

Shopping

A number of stores around town sell opals (not milky white, like Australian opals, but beautiful nonetheless) and other locally mined gems. If you're in the market for loose stones or opal jewelry, do some comparison shopping, as you're apt to find better prices here than in the United States. **Villalone y Artesanos** (✉ Av. Libertad 24-A, ☎ 4/212–8414) offers friendly service and authentic stones. **Lapidaria Querétaro** (✉ Corregedora 149 Nte., ☎ 4/212–0030) is a reputable dealer of loose stones and opals.

Side Trips from Querétaro

San Juan del Río and Tequisquiapan are both within an hour's drive of Querétaro. The highway between Querétaro and San Juan del Río is paved with factories, and San Juan is a bustling manufacturing center whose only real appeal is the semiprecious gems—especially opals, topaz, and amethyst—sold here, both loose or in settings. Tequisquiapan, on the other hand, is a tranquil and pretty *pueblo* (town) drenched in sun and bougainvilleas and flowering trees, and known as a producer of wicker and other handicrafts. Once frequented by harried Mexican urbanites who came to soak in the area's thermal waters, Tequis (as the locals call it) now suffers a dearth of hot water.

A car is the best means to get around. Buses serve both towns from Querétaro, but the trip is longer. If you go to both towns, shop first in San Juan del Río, then head to Tequisquiapan to look around, shop a bit, and perhaps have a meal or a snack. A taxi between the two towns costs about $4.50.

San Juan del Río
51 km (32 mi) southeast of Querétaro via Rte. 57.

Most of San Juan's gem shops are located near the main plaza downtown, and along Avenida Juárez and Calle 16 de Septiembre. **Lapidaria Guerrero** (✉ Av. Juárez Pte. 4, ☎ 4/272–1481) has an exceptionally large collection of opal, amethyst, turquoise, and topaz jewelry. The store is open daily 10–2 and 3–7:30.

Tequisquiapan
19 km (12 mi) east of San Juan del Río, off Rte. 120.

This town, famous for centuries for its restorative thermal waters, has in recent years lost much of its thermal flow, reportedly due to the extraordinary water consumption of a paper mill in the area. Many spas struggle on as simple swimming pools/recreation areas, but as the main tourist draw has receded with the once-warm waters, most are deserted midweek. Things do liven up on hot weekends, however. The **tourist office** (✉ Andador Independencia 1, Plaza Miguel Hidalgo, ☎ 4/273–0295), open daily 9–7, will cheerfully direct you to one or more of the spas, most of which are outside of town.

After lunch or a snack, head to the shops or to the **Mercado de Artesanías** (✉ Calzado de los Misterios s/n, ☎ no phone), where woven goods, jewelry, and locally made furniture are sold. The **Templo de Santa María de la Asunción,** on the main plaza, was begun in 1874 in the neoclassical style, but not completed until the beginning of the 20th century. In late May or early June, the city hosts a weeklong **wine and cheese festival.**

Xilitla

Approximately 320 km (198 mi) northeast of Querétaro.

Feel the ordinary world fade away with a trip to the decidedly off-the-beaten-path **Las Pozas** (The Pools), the extraordinary sculpture garden of the late, eccentric English millionaire Edward James (1907–84). Friend of artists Dalí and Picasso and rumored to be the illegitimate son of King Edward VII, James spent 20 years building 36 surrealist concrete structures deep in the waterfall-filled Xilitla jungle. These amazing structures are half-finished fantasy castles, gradually falling to ruin as the rain forest slithers in to claim them. It's like the ultimate child's fort. The castles don't have walls—just vine-entwined pillars, secret passageways, and operatic staircases leading nowhere.

It is a six- to seven-hour thrilling but exhausting mountainous drive to Xilitla, with hairpin turns and spectacular desert, forest, and jungle vistas. Plan on staying at least two nights, as you'll want time to soak up the jungle magic. If you choose not to drive, you can take a bus to Ciudad Valles (1½-hour drive from Xilitla) or fly to Tampico (3½-hour drive from Xilitla), and arrange ahead for the staff of Posada El Castillo to pick you up. ⊠ *From Querétaro, head north on Hwy. 57 (Carretera Mexico–San Luis Potosí). Take the* PEÑA DE BERNAL *turnoff, marked on a bridge overpass and also on a smaller sign at the Cadareyta exit. Continue north through Bernal, after which the road will join Rte. 120. Take 120 through Jalpan and then on to Xilitla, just across the border in the state of San Luis Potosí. The turnoff to Las Pozas is just beyond Xilitla on the left after passing a small bridge.* 🖼 *$1.50.* ◷ *Daily dawn–dusk.*

LODGING

$$ 🏨 **Posada El Castillo.** When he wasn't living in his jungle hut, Edward James stayed in town (a 10-minute drive away) in a whimsical house that feels like an extension of the garden structures at Las Pozas—except that it has walls. That house, El Castillo (the castle), is now a quirky inn run by Lenore and Avery Danziger, who have made an award-winning documentary film about James that they happily screen for guests. Rooms are adorned with simple wooden furnishings; the best rooms have huge Gothic windows and panoramic mountain views. You can arrange to have meals here; otherwise there are few dining options in the area. ⊠ *Ocampo 105, San Luis Potosí 79900,* ☎ *136/5–00–38,* FAX *136/5–00–55,* WEB *www.junglegossip.com. 7 rooms. Pool. No credit cards.*

Querétaro A to Z

BUS TRAVEL

Daily buses run direct between Mexico City's Central del Norte (North Bus Station) and Querétaro's Central de Autobuses. Major lines have frequent service; travel time is about three hours. Buses also leave several times a day for Guanajuato, San Miguel de Allende, and Morelia.
➤ BUS INFORMATION: **ETN** (☎ 4/229–0078 or 4/229–0019). **Flecha Amarilla** (☎ 4/211–4001). **Futura** (☎ 4/229–0022). **Omnibus de México** (☎ 4/229–0029).

CAR RENTAL

Two major car rental agencies are available in Querétaro. Both are located downtown.

➤ MAJOR AGENCIES: **Avis** (✉ Prol. Corregidora Nte. 318, Col. Alamos, 3a sección, ☎ 4/224–1785 or 4/224–1786, FAX 4/224–1786). **Budget** (✉ Av. Constituyentes Ote. 73, ☎ FAX 4/213–4498).

CAR TRAVEL
Querétaro is 220 km (136 mi) northwest of Mexico City, a three-hour drive on Route 57.

EMERGENCIES
Dial **066** for medical, fire, and theft emergencies. Oficinas Para la Seguridad de la Turista offers a country-wide 24-hour toll-free hot line to provide legal and medical help for tourists.
➤ CONTACTS: **Ambulance–Red Cross** (☎ 4/229–0545 or 4/229–0665). **Emergency** (☎ 066). **Fire Department** (☎ 4/212–3939 or 4/212–0627). **Oficinas Para la Seguridad de la Turista** (☎ 01–800/903–9200 **Police** (☎ 4/220–8383 or 4/220–8503). **Sanatorio Alcocer Pozo (Hospital)** (✉ Calle Reforma 23, ☎ 4/212–0149 or 4/212–1787). **Traffic Police** (☎ 4/213–8424).

MONEY MATTERS
Casa de Cambio Acueducto is open weekdays 9–2 and 4–6, Saturday 9–1.
➤ EXCHANGE SERVICES: **Casa de Cambio Acueducto** (✉ Av. Juárez Sur 58, ☎ 4/212–9304).

INTERNET
Web Café, open Monday–Saturday 10–10, Sunday 4–10, charges $3 an hour for Internet access.
➤ INTERNET CAFÉS: **Web Café** (✉ Ezequiel Montes Sur 67, ☎ 4/216–0250 or 4/216–7272).

TOURS
The tourist office conducts hour-long trolley tours of the city's historic landmarks at 9, 10, and 11 AM and at 4, 5, and 6 PM Tuesday–Sunday. To arrange a city tour in English, call the office—one day in advance if possible. The cost is about $1.50.

TRANSPORTATION AROUND QUERÉTARO
Most of Querétaro's historic sites are within walking distance of one another in the downtown district and can be reached by a series of walkways that are closed to automobile traffic most of the day. If you want to venture farther afield, you will find that buses and taxis run frequently along the main streets and are inexpensive.

TRAVEL AGENCIES
Turismo Beverly offers full travel services.
➤ LOCAL AGENT REFERRALS: **Turismo Beverly** (✉ Av. Tecnologia 118, ☎ 4/216–1500 or 4/216–1260, FAX 4/216–8524).

VISITOR INFORMATION
Dirección de Turismo del Estado is open weekdays 8–8, weekends 9–8.
➤ TOURIST INFORMATION: **Dirección de Turismo del Estado** (✉ Plaza de Armas, ☎ 4/212–1412 or 4/212–0907, FAX 4/212–1094).

MORELIA

With its long, wide boulevards and earth-tone colonial mansions, Morelia is the gracious capital of the state of Michoacán. Founded in 1541 as Valladolid (after the Spanish city), it changed its name in 1828 to honor José María Morelos, the town's most famous son. The legendary mule skinner–turned–priest took up the battle for independence after its early leaders were executed in 1811.

Morelos began with an ill-equipped army of 25 but soon organized a contingent of 9,000 that nearly gained control of the country. Although he was defeated and executed in 1815, he left behind a long-standing reformist legacy that called for universal suffrage, racial equality, and the demise of the hacienda system. The city today still pays tribute to Morelos—his former home has been turned into a museum, and his birthplace is now a library.

Morelianos love music, and several annual festivals are designed to indulge them. Each May the city celebrates the International Organ Festival in the cathedral, giving voice to its outstanding 4,600-pipe organ. The last two weeks in July are given to the Festival International de Música, featuring baroque and chamber music, with orchestras participating from throughout Mexico.

Morelia has the delicious distinction of being the candy capital of Mexico. So strong is the sweet-eating tradition that the city has a **Mercado de Dulces**—a sweets market. Morelia is also the home of writers, artists, philosophers, and poets, as well as American retirees.

Exploring Morelia

To explore Morelia and its surrounding hillside neighborhoods thoroughly would take some time. However, if you stroll through the historic plazas and frequent the cafés (as many locals do), you will begin to feel the city's vitality. Although the vehicle and sidewalk traffic can get a little heavy at times, Morelia is a pedestrian-friendly city.

A Good Walk

Begin your walk in Morelia's tree-lined downtown **Plaza de Armas** ⑩, on the east side of which is the city's famed **Catedral** ⑪. As you leave the cathedral, cross Avenida Madero Oriente to the **Palacio de Gobierno** ⑫, a former seminary. From the palace it's four blocks east along Avenida Madero Oriente to Calle de Belisario Domínguez. Make a right and walk one block south to the Church of San Francisco. To the rear of the church, in the former convent of San Francisco, is the entrance to the **Casa de las Artesanías del Estado de Michoacán** ⑬, a virtual cornucopia of crafts from around the state.

Walk two blocks south on Calle Vasco de Quiroga, a street lined with vendors, until you come to Calle del Soto Saldaña. Head west another two blocks to Avenida Morelos Sur. The corner building on the right is the **Casa Museo de Morelos** ⑭, which displays memorabilia of the independence leader. It's one block north from the museum to Calle Antonio Alzate and then one block west (where the street name changes to Calle Corregidora) to Calle García Obeso. On this corner stands the **Museo Casa Natal de Morelos** ⑮, Morelos's birthplace. Continue west on Calle Corregidora until you reach Calle Abasolo. On Calle Allende, one block to the north, you'll find the **Museo Regional Michoacano** ⑯.

After leaving the museum take Calle Abasolo back to the plaza; 2½ blocks to the north, you'll see the **Museo del Estado** ⑰ on the right side of the street (which changes to Calle Guillermo Prieto at Avenida Madero Oriente). Return to Avenida Madero Oriente and then go two blocks to the right to the corner of the Valentín Gómez Farías, to the **Mercado de Dulces** ⑱.

For a longer stroll, take Avenida Madero Oriente east a dozen blocks or so to where it forks. Stay to the right; you'll see the **Fountain of the Tarascans** on a traffic island to your left. Just past the fountain, Morelia's mile-long **aqueduct** begins. This 1875 structure, which consists of 253 arches, once carried the city's main source of drinking water. It's particularly beautiful at night when its arches—some rising to 30 ft—are illuminated. Two blocks farther along (Madero is now called Avenida Acueducto) is the entrance to **Bosque Cuauhtémoc,** Morelia's largest park. If you happen by during the week, you may encounter university students studying (or lounging) beneath the palms and evergreens. On weekends, especially Sunday, families on outings take over. Two blocks past the park entrance, you'll see the **Museo de Arte Contemporáneo** ⑲, also on the right side of the street.

Sights to See

⑬ **Casa de las Artesanías del Estado de Michoacán.** In the 16th century, Vasco de Quiroga, the bishop of Michoacán, helped the Purépecha Indians develop artistic specialties so they could be self-supporting. At this two-story museum and store, you can see the work that the Purépechas still produce: copper goods from Santa Clara del Cobre, lacquerware from Uruapan, straw items and pottery from Pátzcuaro, guitars from Paracho, fanciful ceramic devil figures from Ocumicho. At the **Museo Michoacana de las Artesanías** in the two main floors around the courtyard, some of these items are showcased behind glass while artists demonstrate how they are made. ⌧ *Calle Fray Juan de San Miguel 129,* ☎ *4/312–2486 museum; 4/312–1248 store.* ☒ *Free.* ☼ *Mon.–Sat. 10–3 and 5–8, Sun. 10–4:30.*

⑭ **Casa Museo de Morelos.** What is now a two-story museum was acquired in 1801 by José María Morelos and served as home to generations of the Mexican independence leader's family until 1934. Owned by the Mexican government, it contains family portraits, a copy of Morelos's birth certificate, various artifacts from the independence movement (such as a camp bed used by Ignacio Allende), and the blindfold Morelos wore for his execution. The excellent free tour is in Spanish only. ⊠ *Av. Morelos Sur 323,* ☎ *4/313–2651.* ⌷ *About $2, free Sun.* ☉ *Daily 9–7.*

㊶ Catedral. Morelia's cathedral is a majestic structure built between 1640 and 1744. It is known throughout Mexico for its 200-ft baroque towers, among the tallest in the land, and for its 4,600-pipe organ, one of the finest in the world. The organ is the vehicle for the international organ festival held here each May. ⊠ *Av. Madero between Plaza de Armas and Av. Morelos.*

㊽ Mercado de Dulces. If you have a sweet tooth, don't miss Morelia's famous candy market, just behind the tourist office. All sorts of local sweets are for sale, such as *ate* (a candied fruit) and *cajeta* (heavenly caramel sauce made from goat's milk). ⊠ *Av. Madero Pte. and Valentín Gómez Farías.* ☉ *Daily 10–9.*

㊺ Museo Casa Natal de Morelos. José María Morelos's birthplace is now a library and national monument housing mostly literature and history books (as well as two murals by Moreliano Alfredo Zalce). Be sure to visit the courtyard in back: it's a tranquil square, adjacent to the Church of San Agustín; a marker and an eternal flame honor the fallen hero. ⊠ *Calle Corregidora 113,* ☎ *4/312–2793.* ⌷ *Free.* ☉ *Weekdays 9–7, weekends 9–1.*

㊾ Museo de Arte Contemporáneo. The works of contemporary Mexican and international artists are on view at this well-lighted museum near the Bosque Cuauhtémoc. ⊠ *Av. Acueducto 18,* ☎ *4/312–5404.* ⌷ *Free.* ☉ *Tues.–Sun. 10–2 and 4–8.*

㊼ Museo del Estado. Just across from a small plaza with statues of Bishop Vasco de Quiroga and Spanish writer Miguel de Cervantes, this history museum is located in a stately mansion that was once the home of the wife of Agustín de Iturbide, Mexico's only native-born emperor. A highlight of the collection is a complete Morelia pharmacy dating from 1868. ⊠ *Guillermo Prieto 176,* ☎ *4/313–0629.* ⌷ *Free.* ☉ *Weekdays 9–2 and 4–8, weekends 9–2 and 4–7.*

㊻ Museo Regional Michoacano. An 18th-century former palace, the museum traces the history of Mexico from its pre-Hispanic days through the Cardenista period, which ended in 1940. President Lázaro Cárdenas, a native of Michoacán, was one of Mexico's most popular leaders because of his nationalization of the oil industry and his support of other populist reforms. The ground floor contains an art gallery, plus archaeological exhibits from Michoacán. Upstairs is an assortment of colonial objects, including furniture, weapons, and religious paintings. ⊠ *Calle Allende 305,* ☎ *4/312–0407.* ⌷ *About $3, free Sun.* ☉ *Tues.–Sat. 9–7, Sun. 9–4.*

NEED A BREAK? When you've finished your tour of the Museo Regional Michoacana, walk across the street to the colonial stone *portales* (arcades). The portales on one side of the square contain popular sidewalk cafés. For a sandwich or a fruit cocktail, or a good selection of juices, coffees, and teas, try **Café Catedral** (⊠ Portal Hidalgo 213, ☎ 4/312–3289). No one will mind if you linger over a book or newspaper for the better part of an hour sipping an excellent café americano—in fact, you might have to wait that long just to get the bill.

㊷ Palacio de Gobierno. This former Tridentine seminary, built in 1770, has had such notable graduates as independence hero José María

Morelos, social reformer Melchor Ocampo, and the first emperor of Mexico, Agustín de Iturbide. Striking murals decorate the stairway and second floor. Painted by local artist Alfredo Zalce in the early 1960s, they depict dramatic, often bloody scenes from Mexico's history. ☒ *Av. Madero 63,* ☎ *4/312–8598.* ☎ *Free.* ⊘ *Weekdays 8 AM–10 PM.*

❹ Plaza de Armas. During the War of Independence, several rebel priests were brutally murdered on this site, and the plaza, known as Plaza de los Mártires, is named after them. Today, however, the square belies its violent past: sweethearts stroll along the tree-lined walks, vendors sell mounds of roasted peanuts, placards announce cultural events, and lively recorded music blasts from a silver-dome band shell. ☒ *Bounded on the north by Av. Madero, on the south by Calle Allende, on the west by Calle Abasolo, and on the east by the cathedral.*

Dining

Some of Michoacán's tastiest dishes—tomato-based Tarascan soup, corn products such as *huchepos* (sweet tamales) and *corundas* (savory triangular tamales), and game (rabbit and quail)—are served at Morelia restaurants. Traditional chicken and beef fare are also available, as are international dishes. As a rule, more-upscale restaurants are in hotels near the plaza and on the outskirts of town.

$$$ ✕ **Fonda Las Mercedes.** This delightful restaurant's arty, modern fur-
★ nishings somehow fit perfectly in the plant-filled stone patio of this restored colonial mansion. The ambience is intimate yet airy, with a lovely soft natural light during the day. The inside dining room, which is equally pleasant, may be cozier on chilly days or evenings. Offerings from the eclectic menu include lots of soups and six kinds of crepes. If you dare, try the sinfully rich pasta with pistachios and pine nuts in cream sauce. ☒ *León Guzmán 47,* ☎ *4/312–6113. AE, MC, V. No dinner Sun.*

$$$ ✕ **Boca del Río.** Large picture windows opening onto a busy intersection provide ample light for this cheerful yet cafeteria-like restaurant, which claims to have fresh fish and seafood trucked in daily from Sinaloa and Veracruz. There are light snacks such as *coctel de camarones* (shrimp cocktail), along with heartier fare, such as the *jaiba rellena* (mushroom-and-cheese-stuffed crabs liberally seasoned with garlic). Beef and chicken dishes and a vegetarian sandwich are also offered. After lunch, head to the sprawling Mercado de Dulces, just across the street, for dessert. ☒ *Valentín Gómez Farías 185,* ☎ *4/312–9974. MC, V.*

$$ ✕ **Cenaduría Lupita II.** This restaurant is outside the city center in the
★ financial district near the Gigante supermarket and cinema. Although the name labels it a dinner spot (*cena* means dinner), enormous buffets are served for all three meals. The lunch buffet offers unlimited access to salads, soup, meats, desserts, coffee, juices, and beer or tequila. Dinner is built around *antojitos* (appetizers), but it's still a huge amount and assortment of foods. Eating here is a great way to try different regional specialties and find your favorites. ☒ *Av. Camelinas 3100, Col. Jardines del Rincón,* ☎ *4/324–4067. AE, MC, V.*

$ ✕ **Taquería Pioneros.** There's a reason the tables are full at lunch at
★ this positively plain taco shop: it has delicious grilled meats, served Michoacán style with salsas and mountains of fresh, hot tortillas made on site. The *pionero* (beef, ham, bacon, onions, and cheese, all grilled) is the only style served in a half portion, which is plenty for most appetites. Quesadillas, *sincronizadas* (quesadillas with ham), and beans are also served, as is beer and soda. ☒ *A. Serdán 7, at Ocampo,* ☎ *4/ 313–4938. No credit cards.*

Lodging

Morelia offers a number of pleasant colonial-style hotels both in the downtown and outlying areas. Generally, the cheapest properties are near the bus station, moderately priced selections are clustered around the plaza (or on nearby side streets), and deluxe resort hotels are in or near the Santa María hills.

$$$–$$$$ ⊞ **Hotel Virrey de Mendoza.** Built in 1565 to house a Spanish noble-
★ man, this downtown hotel still radiates plenty of Old World atmosphere. The elegant lobby lounge is fitted with an enormous stone fireplace and cushy black leather couches. Guest rooms have dark colonial-style furnishings, lace curtains, soaring ceilings, and creaking hardwood floors, as well as cable TVs and telephones. The bathrooms have porcelain tubs. ⊠ *Av. Madero Pte. 310, 58000,* ☎ *4/312–0633 or 4/312–4940,* FAX *4/312–6719,* WEB *www.hotelmex.com/hotelvirrey. 48 rooms, 9 suites. Restaurant, bar, coffee shop, laundry service, free parking. AE, MC, V.*

$$$ ⊞ **Villa Montaña.** French count Philippe de Reiset has fitted this villa
★ with all the trappings of a wealthy Mexican estate. High above More-lia in the Santa María hills, its five impeccably groomed acres are dot-ted with a pool, tennis court, and stone sculptures. Each individually decorated unit has at least one piece of antique furniture, and most have a fireplace and private patio. The hotel's renowned restaurant serves North American, French, and Mexican cuisine, and huge windows af-ford a marvelous view of Morelia, especially at night. Children under age eight are discouraged from dining in the restaurant, but the hotel can provide baby-sitters if requested a day in advance. ⊠ *Calle Patz-imba 201, 58000,* ☎ *4/314–0231 or 4/314–0179,* FAX *4/315–1423,* WEB *www.villamontana.com.mx. 15 rooms, 25 suites. Restaurant, piano bar, in-room safes, pool, tennis court, baby-sitting, laundry service, meet-ing room, business services, free parking. AE, MC, V.*

$$ ⊞ **Hotel Catedral.** Located in a restored colonial mansion, this three-story property began operating as a hotel some 30 years ago. Its mod-ern rooms are clustered around a skylighted courtyard; eight of them overlook the main plaza and cathedral on Avenida Madero. Interior quarters have less dramatic views but are less noisy. All rooms have dark-wood furnishings, telephones, and cable TV. The beds are rather soft. ⊠ *Iturbe 37, 58000,* ☎ *4/313–0783 or 4/313–0467,* FAX *4/313–0406. 43 rooms, 2 suites. Restaurant, bar, baby-sitting, dry cleaning. AE, MC, V.*

$$ ⊞ **Hotel Mansión Acueducto.** An elaborate wood and wrought-iron stair-case leads from the elegant lobby to more-modest quarters upstairs. Rooms have dark, colonial-style furniture, telephones, and color cable TV. Older rooms overlook the aqueduct and nearby park. Rooms in the motel-like wing have views of the garden, pool, and surrounding city. At times, student groups book the entire property. ⊠ *Av. Acue-ducto 25, 58000,* ☎ *4/312–3301,* FAX *4/312–2020. 36 rooms, 1 suite. Restaurant, bar, pool, free parking. MC, V.*

$$ ⊞ **Hotel Posada de la Soledad.** Set in a restored private mansion built
★ in the late 17th century, the Posada de la Soledad is conveniently lo-cated one block from the Plaza de Armas. All rooms have cable TVs, but otherwise vary in size, decoration, amenities, and price. The rooms in the original section surround an elegant patio with a large fountain and massive bougainvilleas. Rooms in a newer section are smaller and plainly furnished but quiet; rooms on Calle Ocampo get loud traffic noise from the street. If you're not impressed with the room you are shown, ask to see another. ⊠ *Ignacio Iturbe 90, 58000,* ☎ *4/312–1888,* FAX *4/312–2111,* WEB *www.hsoledad.com. 48 rooms, 9 suites. Restau-rant, bar. AE, MC, V.*

$ 🔲 **Hotel Valladolid.** Right on the Plaza de Armas, this sister property of the slightly more impressive Hotel Catedral has plain but clean rooms with brick floors and striped bedspreads. Twenty of the rooms have cable TV (none have phones), and the price includes coffee and juice. ✉ *Portal Hidalgo 245, 58000,* ☎ *4/312–0027,* 𝔽𝔸𝕏 *4/312–4663. 25 rooms. Restaurant. AE, MC, V.*

Nightlife and the Arts

Morelia has two lively folk-music clubs, both in beautiful locations downtown. **Colibri** (✉ Galeana 36, ☎ 4/312–2261) has folk music from throughout Latin America every night from 9:30 PM to 1 AM. **La Porfiriana** (✉ Calle Corregidora 694, ☎ 4/312–2663) presents spirited salsa music Tuesday–Saturday from 7 PM to 3 AM.

Side Trip to Santuario de Mariposas el Rosario

Approximately 115 km (71 mi) east of Morelia.

Every year 100 million monarch butterflies migrate from the United States and Canada to winter in the easternmost part of Michoacán, near the border of México state. A visit to the **Santuario de Mariposas el Rosario** (El Rosario Monarch Butterfly Sanctuary) between early November and early March is an awesome sensory experience. Caked with orange and black butterflies, the pine forest looks like it's on fire. Listen closely and you'll hear the rustle of nearly a billion wings beating. The hike to the groves is a steep climb, and the high altitude (10,400 ft) will require that you take it slowly.

This day trip takes about 10 hours, but it's well worth the effort. If you choose not to drive the rough roads, catch a guided tour in Morelia. ✉ *Hwy. 15 east to Zitácuaro, then take marked but unnumbered road north to Angangueo, and on to sanctuary entrance.* 🎟 *$2 (plus tip for guide).* ☉ *Daily 10–5.*

Morelia A to Z

AIR TRAVEL
There are daily flights between Francisco Mujica International Airport and Mexico City's International Airport on Aeroméxico.

CARRIERS
Mexicana has direct flights to and from Los Angeles, San Francisco, and Chicago. Flights are subject to cancellation; flight times change often and must be confirmed one day in advance. The 45-minute taxi ride from the airport to Morelia costs about $20.
➤ AIRLINES AND CONTACTS: **Aeroméxico** (☎ 01–800/021–4000). **Mexicana** (☎ 4/324–3808 or 4/324–3818).

BUS TRAVEL
Direct bus service is available daily between the Terminal Poniente (West Terminal, commonly referred to as the Observatorio) in Mexico City and Morelia's Central de Autobuses. Several bus lines have frequent service; the most direct trip ($18) takes four hours on ETN. Herradura de Plata is another bus line. Buses leave every hour or two around the clock.
➤ BUS INFORMATION: **Central de Autobuses** (✉ Eduardo Ruiz, between Valentín Gómez Farías and Guzmán, ☎ 4/312–5664). **ETN** (☎ 4/313–7440 or 4/313–4137). **Herradura de Plata** (☎ 4/312–2988).

CAR RENTAL

Budget has an office at the Francisco Mujica International Airport. National's office is located beside the airport on Acueducto.

➤ MAJOR AGENCIES: **Budget** (✉ Francisco Mujica International Airport, ☎ 4/313–3399). **National** (✉ Francisco Mujica International Airport and Av. Acueducto 3891, ☎ 4/324–6747).

CAR TRAVEL

The drive from Mexico City to Morelia (302 km [187 mi]) on the toll road through Toluca, Atlacamulco, Contepec, and Maravatio takes about four hours.

EMERGENCIES

Dial 070 for medical, fire, and theft emergencies.

➤ CONTACTS: **Ambulance–Red Cross** (☎ 4/314–5151). **Consumer Protection Office** (☎ 4/315–6202). **Fire Department** (☎ 4/312–1235). **Green Angels** (☎ 4/312–7777). **Hospital de la Cruz Roja** (☎ 4/314–5025). **Hospital Memorial** (☎ 4/315–1047 or 4/315–1099). **Police** (☎ 4/326–8522).

INTERNET

Chat Room Cyber Café, open Monday–Saturday 9 AM–10 PM and Sunday noon–9, charges $2 an hour for Internet access.

➤ INTERNET CAFÉS: **Chat Room Cyber Café** (✉ Nigromante 132-A, ☎ 4/312–9222).

MONEY MATTERS

Consultoría Internacional Casa de Cambio is open weekdays 9:30–5:30, Saturday 9:30–2:30.

➤ CONTACT: **Consultoría Internacional Casa de Cambio** (✉ Prieto 48, ☎ 4/313–8308).

TOURS

Several worthy operators conduct tours of Morelia and the butterfly sanctuary. Contact Ayangupani through David Saucedo Ortega at the Villa Montaña front desk.

➤ TOUR OPERATOR RECOMMENDATIONS: **Ayangupani** (✉ Calle Patzimba 201, ☎ FAX 4/315–4045). **Explora Viajes** (✉ Av. Madero Ote. 493B, ☎ 4/312–7766, FAX 4/312–7660). **Morelia Operadores de Viajes** (✉ Valentín Gómez Farías 131, ☎ 4/312–8723 or 4/312–8747, FAX 4/312–9591).

TRANSPORTATION AROUND MORELIA

As in many Heartland cities, Morelia's major sights are near the center of town and easy to get to on foot. Street names in Morelia change frequently, especially on either side of Avenida Madero, the city's main east–west artery. Taxis in Morelia can be hailed on the street or found near the main plaza. Buses run the length of Avenida Madero.

TRAVEL AGENCIES

Gran Turismo is the American Express representative.

➤ LOCAL AGENCY: **Gran Turismo** (✉ Edificio Ejecutivo Camelinas, Av. Camelinas 3233, Int. 102–103, ☎ 4/324–0484, FAX 4/324–0495).

VISITOR INFORMATION

Secretaría Estatal de Turismo is open weekdays 9–8, weekends 9–7.

➤ TOURIST INFORMATION: **Secretaría Estatal de Turismo** (✉ Palacio Clavijero, Calle Nigromante 79, ☎ 4/317–2371, FAX 4/312–9816).

PÁTZCUARO

Pátzcuaro, the 16th-century capital of Michoacán, exists in a time warp. A bit more than an hour by car from Morelia, this beautiful lakeside community set at 7,250 ft in the Sierra Madre is home to the Purépecha Indians, who fish, farm, and ply their crafts as they have for centuries. Women wrapped tightly in their striped wool *rebozos* (shawls) hurry to market in the chilly morning air. Men in traditional straw hats wheel overburdened carts down crooked, dusty backstreets.

The architecture, too, has remained largely unchanged over the years. In the 16th century, under kindly Bishop Vasco de Quiroga, Pátzcuaro underwent a building boom. After he died in 1565, the state capital was moved to Morelia, and the town became a cultural (and architectural) backwater for hundreds of years. These days 16th-century mansions surround the downtown plazas; one-story whitewashed houses with sloping red tile roofs line the side streets and hills.

Despite the altitude, the weather in Pátzcuaro is temperate year-round. (Autumn and winter nights, however, are cold; sweaters and jackets are a must.) On November 1 the town is inundated with tourists en route to Janítzio, an island in Lake Pátzcuaro, where one of the most elaborate Day of the Dead graveyard ceremonies in all of Mexico takes place. Go to the island of Yunuen for an authentic glimpse of daily island life, and you can stay overnight. At numerous small towns around the lake you can buy craft items from their makers, in the process absorbing a bit of small-town rural Mexico. These towns are just beginning to attract tourism, and several new dining and lodging venues are opening up outside Pátzcuaro. The Delegación de Turismo can share suggestions for adventures outside Pátzcuaro, as can expert local tour guides Francisco Castilleja and Marilyn Mayo.

Exploring Pátzcuaro

Most of Pátzcuaro's sights can be seen in a few hours, but the town and outlying areas deserve to be explored at a leisurely pace. There can be some traffic in the Plaza Bocanegra and on the main road coming into town, but elsewhere it is blissfully quiet.

A Good Walk

Start your stroll at the **tourist office** (Plaza Vasco de Quiroga 50A), where you can pick up maps and brochures. Walk across the large **Plaza Vasco de Quiroga** ㊿ to the east side of the square and turn right on Calle Dr. José María Coss; in less than a block you'll see a long cobblestone walkway leading to **La Casa de los 11 Patios** �51, a former convent now housing a number of crafts shops. As you leave the complex, continue up a stone walkway to Calle Lerín. To the north (past Calle Portugal) is the **Templo de la Compañia** �52, the state's first cathedral. After visiting the church, continue another half block along Calle Lerín to the **Museo de Artes Populares** �53 on your right.

Directly down Calle Lerín and across a cobblestone courtyard is **La Basílica de Nuestra Señora de la Salud** �54. Walk downhill from the basilica (take Buenavista to Libertad and turn left) to reach the **Biblioteca Pública Gertrudis Bocanegra** �55. For a nice detour from the library, continue for a half block to the large outdoor **mercado** sprawled along Calle Libertad and its side streets. At times the road is so crowded with people and their wares—fruit, vegetables, beans, rice, herbs, and other necessities of daily life—that it is difficult to walk. If you press on for about a block, you'll see an indoor market to your left, filled with more produce, large hanging slabs of meat, hot food, and a variety of cheap

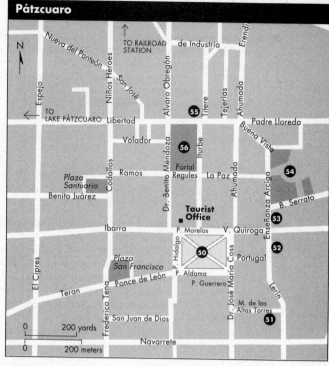

trinkets. When you're done with your market tour, retrace your steps down Calle Libertad. Across the street from the library, you can rest at **Plaza Bocanegra** ⑤⑥, just one block north of your starting point, Plaza Vasco de Quiroga.

Sights to See

⑤④ **La Basílica de Nuestra Señora de la Salud** (Basilica of our Lady of Health). The church was begun in 1554 by Vasco de Quiroga, and throughout the centuries others—undaunted by earthquakes and fires—took up the cause and constructed the church in honor of the Virgin of Health. Near the main altar is a statue of the Virgin made of derivatives of cornstalks and orchids. Several masses are still held here daily; the earliest begins shortly after dawn. Out front, Purépecha women sell hot tortillas, herbal mixtures for teas, and religious objects. You can glimpse Lake Pátzcuaro in the distance. ✉ *Enseñanza Arciga, near Calle Benigno Serrato.*

⑤⑤ **Biblioteca Pública Gertrudis Bocanegra.** In the back of this library, a vast mural painted by Juan O'Gorman in 1942 depicts in great detail the history of the region and of the Purépecha people. In the bottom right of the mural, you can see Gertrudis Bocanegra, a local heroine who was shot in 1814 for refusing to divulge the revolutionaries' secrets to the Spaniards. ✉ *North side of Plaza Bocanegra.* ⊙ *Weekdays 9–7, Sat. 10–2.*

⑤① **La Casa de los 11 Patios.** An 18th-century convent, 11 Patios houses a number of high-quality shops featuring Purépecha handiwork. As you meander through the shops and courtyards, you'll encounter weavers producing large bolts of cloth, artists trimming black lacquerware with gold, and seamstresses embroidering blouses. If you plan to shop in Pátzcuaro, this is a good place to start. You can view the selection of regional goods and begin to compare prices. ⊠ *Calle Madrigal de las Altas Torres s/n.* ⊙ *Daily 10–2 and 4–8.*

㊾ Museo de Artes Populares. Home to the Colegio de San Nicolás Obispo in the 16th century, the building today houses displays of colonial and contemporary crafts, such as ceramics, masks, lacquerware, paintings, and ex-votos in its many rooms. Behind this building is a *troje* (traditional Purépecha wooden house) braced atop a stone platform. ⊠ *Enseñanza Arciga,* ☎ *434/2–10–29.* 🎟 *About $3, free Sun,* ⊙ *Tues.–Sat. 9–7, Sun. 9–2:30.*

㊽ Plaza Bocanegra. The smaller of the city's two squares (it's also called Plaza Chica), this is the center of Pátzcuaro's commercial life. Bootblacks, pushcart vendors, and bus and taxi stands are all in the plaza, which is embellished by a statue of the local heroine, Gertrudis Bocanegra. ⊠ *Bounded by Av. Libertad on the north, Portal Regules on the south, Dr. Benito Mendoza on the west, and Iturbe on the east.*

㊿ Plaza Vasco de Quiroga. A tranquil courtyard surrounded by ash and pine trees and 16th-century mansions (since converted into hotels and shops), the larger of the two downtown plazas commemorates the bishop who restored dignity to the Purépecha people. During the Spanish conquest, Nuño de Guzmán, a lieutenant in Hernán Cortés's army, committed atrocities on the local population in his efforts to conquer western Mexico. He was eventually arrested by the Spanish authorities, and in 1537 Vasco de Quiroga was appointed bishop of Michoacán. Attempting to regain the trust of the indigenous people, he established a number of model villages in the area and promoted the development of artesanía commerce among the Purépechas. Quiroga died in 1565, and his remains were consecrated in the **Basílica de Nuestra Señora de la Salud.** ⊠ *Bounded by Calle Quiroga on the north, Av. Ponce de León on the south, Portal Hidalgo on the west, and Dr. José María Coss on the east.*

NEED A BREAK? Before heading to Lake Pátzcuaro, sit in **Plaza Vasco de Quiroga** for a moment and enjoy a rich Michoacán ice cream you can buy under the portals on the west side of the plaza. Or sip a warming Doña Paca cappuccino spiked with *rompope* (egg liqueur) at the sidewalk café in front of **Mansión Iturbe.**

㊼ Templo de la Compañia. Michoacán's first cathedral was begun in 1540 by order of Vasco de Quiroga and completed in 1546. When the state capital was moved to Morelia some 20 years later, the church was taken over by the Jesuits. Today it remains much as it was in the 16th century. Moss has grown over the crumbling stone steps outside; the dank interior is planked with thick wood floors and lined with bare wood benches. ⊠ *Calle Lerín s/n, near Calle Alcantaría.*

OFF THE BEATEN PATH   **LAKE PÁTZCUARO –** Just a 10-minute taxi ride from downtown are the tranquil shores of Lake Pátzcuaro. A few lakeside restaurants here serve fresh whitefish and other local catches. Amble along the dock or peek into the waterfront crafts shops. A boat trip to Janítzio (the largest of Lake Pátzcuaro's five islands), or to tiny Yunuen, which offers a clear-eyed view of island life, is recommended. Wooden launches, with room for 25 people, depart for Janítzio and the other islands daily 9–6. Purchase round-trip tickets for $3 at a dockside office (prices are controlled by the tourist department). The ride to Janítzio takes about 30 minutes and is particularly beautiful in late afternoon, when the sun is low in the sky. Once you're out on the lake, fishermen with butterfly nets may approach your boat. The nets are no longer used for fishing, but for a small donation these locals will let you take their picture.

On most days (November 1 being the exception), Janítzio is a quiet albeit touristy island inhabited by Purépecha Indians. It is crowned by a huge statue of independence hero José María Morelos, which is accessible by a cobblestone stairway. Although the road twists past many souvenir stands as it ascends, don't be discouraged. The view from the summit—of the lake, the town, and the surrounding hills—is well worth the climb. Inside the statue are some remarkable murals that spiral up from the base to the tip of the monument.

Although Janítzio has succumbed to tourism, the small island of Yunuen is just beginning to attract visitors. This tranquil town has just 21 families, and provides a more accurate picture of island life than does Janítzio. You can get a boat to here from the ferry landing, or arrange to stay overnight in simple yet clean cabins available for visitors. The office of tourism can provide information.

Dining

Many restaurants in Pátzcuaro specialize in seafood. In addition to whitefish, look for *trucha* (trout) and *charales* and *boquerones* (two small, locally caught fish served as appetizers). Purépecha dishes, such as *sopa tarasca*, are also common. As a rule, restaurants are located around the two plazas and in hotels. Since the large meal is served at midday, many dining establishments are shuttered by 9.

Note: Many Pátzcuaro restaurants and hotels do not accept traveler's checks, although some will take major credit cards.

$$$ ✕ **El Primer Piso.** This second-floor restaurant overlooks Plaza Vasco
★ de Quiroga, and on warm nights you can watch the comings and goings from a balcony table. There's plenty to look at inside as well; the restaurant doubles as an art gallery. The eclectic menu provides a break from the rather monotonous Pátzcuaro fare: try the pear salad with goat cheese, walnuts, and watercress, or the white-chocolate mousse with blackberries and melon cream. ⊠ *Plaza Vasco de Quiroga 29,* ☎ *434/2–01–22. AE, MC. Closed Tues.*

$$ ✕ **El Patio.** Although this low-key restaurant features mouthwatering whitefish platters (including salsa, vegetables, and french fries, it's possible to duck in at midday for just a strong cappuccino or glass of Mexican wine. For a late-afternoon snack, a plate of quesadillas with a side order of guacamole is highly recommended, and the *sopa tarasca* is superb. ⊠ *Plaza Vasco de Quiroga 19,* ☎ *434/2–04–84. MC, V.*

$$ ✕ **El Viejo Gaucho.** Join the crowd for a festive night of live music from North, Central, and South America performed on stage in front of a mural, repainted each season. Try the *Churrasco Argentino* (seasoned steak) and don't forget to top it with *chimichurri* (an Argentine sauce made with fresh herbs and olive oil). Most entrées are pseudo-Argentinian, but pizza, hamburgers, and American-style french fries are also available. The menu includes a myriad of imported and domestic drinks. ⊠ *Iturbe 10,* ☎ *434/2–36–27. AE, MC, V. No lunch.*

Lodging

Although Pátzcuaro has no deluxe hotels, there is an ample number of clean, moderately priced properties. Most are on or within a few blocks of the Plaza Vasco de Quiroga. Several more-expensive hotels are on Avenida Lázaro Cárdenas, the road to Lake Pátzcuaro. If you're planning to be in town on or near November 1–2, the Day of the Dead, make hotel reservations at least six months in advance.

$$ 🏨 **Hotel Posada de Don Vasco.** Located several minutes out of town on the road to Lake Pátzcuaro, this sprawling resort hotel offers a wide range of amenities, including satellite TV. Its 30 newer rooms are thickly carpeted and have either balconies or patios; the older quarters, which are oddly decorated with gold and brown patterned rugs and bright checkered bedspreads, are smaller and open onto a courtyard. The lovely, manicured grounds are relatively quiet despite the occasional rumbling of a passing bus or truck. The restaurant is decorated like a prosperous country estate, with a large fireplace that blazes on cold nights. At the Saturday buffet dinner, the regional Dance of the Old Men is performed at 8:30 PM. Unfortunately, the food is uninspired. ✉ *Av. Las Americas 450, 61600,* ☎ *434/2-39-71 or 434/2-24-90,* FAX *434/2-02-62. 99 rooms, 4 suites. Restaurant, pool, tennis court, badminton, bowling, billiards. AE, MC, V.*

$$ 🏨 **Mansión Iturbe.** This hotel, housed in a 17th-century mansion, still
★ retains much of its colonial charm. Both the rooms and corridors are frailly lighted, giving the impression of a true 17th-century home. Plant-filled courtyards are ringed by stone archways. Rooms, with large wood-and-glass doors, are partially carpeted. Bicycles are lent to guests for a few hours per stay, and every fourth night is free. Breakfast at Café Dona Paca is included in the room rate. The family is an excellent source of information regarding Pátzcuaro and the surrounding areas. ✉ *Portal Morelos 59, 61600,* ☎ *434/2-03-68 or 434/2-36-28,* FAX *4/313-45-93 in Morelia,* WEB *www.mexonline.com/iturbe.htm. 10 rooms, 4 suites. 3 restaurants, bicycles, travel services. AE, MC, V. BP.*

$ 🏨 **Cabañas Yunuen.** This complex was built in 1993 on the island of Yunuen in collaboration with the Department of Tourism to promote visits to some of the area's more authentic communities. There are six cabins in all: two each for 2, 4, and 16 people; each has a kitchenette with small refrigerator. Breakfast or dinner and round-trip transportation by boat is included in the price, about $38 for two people. Be sure to call ahead for reservations. ✉ *Domicilio Conocido, Isla de Yunuen,* ☎ *434/2-44-73. 6 cabins. Dining room, kitchenettes, Ping-Pong, billiards. No credit cards.*

$ 🏨 **Los Escudos.** Today a cozy hotel, this property was originally a 16th-century home. Its courtyards bloom with potted plants, and guest rooms contain small murals. Ten rooms situated in back and shielded from street noise open onto an outdoor patio. All rooms have color cable TVs and telephones; five have fireplaces. The adjoining restaurant has a varied menu, ranging from club sandwiches to multicourse midday meals. Particularly tempting is the *pollo especial Los Escudos* (chicken sautéed in tomato sauce and vegetables). ✉ *Portal Hidalgo 73, 61600,* ☎ *434/2-01-38 or 434/2-12-90,* FAX *434/2-06-49. 31 rooms, 2 suites. Restaurant. MC, V.*

$ 🏨 **Hotel Posada La Basílica.** This colonial-style inn, housed in a 17th-
★ century building, faces the Basílica de Nuestra Señora de la Salud, and on some mornings strains from a postdawn mass filter softly into the hotel. The property has comfortable, individually decorated rooms, some with fireplaces. Thick wood shutters cover floor-to-ceiling windows, and walls are trimmed in hand-painted colonial designs. The restaurant has views of the mountains, the lake, and tile-roof homes. Open for breakfast and lunch only, it offers such regional specialties as broiled trout with garlic and tamales with sweet cream. Service can be slow. ✉ *Calle Arciga 6, 61600,* ☎ *434/2-11-08,* FAX *434/2-06-59. 12 rooms. Restaurant. MC, V.*

$ 🏨 **Mesón del Gallo.** On a fairly quiet side street near the Casa de los 11 Patios, this two-story property is beginning to look a bit shabby. Beds have wood-and-tile headboards and grey wool spreads and curtains. Suites are furnished in more lively hues. All rooms have telephones but no TV. There is a grassy patio encircled by bougainvillea and fruit trees with a few lonely lounge chairs. Rates include breakfast. ⊠ *Calle Dr. Coss 20, 61600,* ☎ *434/2–14–74,* FAX *434/2–15–11. 20 rooms, 5 suites. Restaurant, bar. MC, V.*

Nightlife and the Arts

The **Danza de los Viejitos** (Dance of the Little Old Men), a widely known regional dance, is performed during Saturday dinner at Hotel Posada de Don Vasco for approximately $12 (includes dinner). The dance is also performed Saturday night at 9 PM at Los Escudos:, on Plaza de Quiroga.

Shopping

Pátzcuaro has some of Mexico's finest folk-art shopping. **Artesanias El Naranjo** (⊠ Plaza Vasco de Quiroga 29-2), an intimate group of stores, offers a variety of ceramics, clothing, and folk art. **Bordados Santa Cruz** (⊠ Calle Dr. Coss 3, ☎ 433/8–14–25) is a women's embroidery collective. Since 1898, the family-run **Chocolate Casero Joaquinita** (⊠ Enseñanza 38, ☎ 434/2–45–14) has been concocting delectable homemade cinnamon-spiced hot-chocolate tablets. High-quality ceramics, furniture, and silver jewelry can be found at **Galería del Arcángel** (⊠ Arciga 30, ☎ 434/2–17–74). And don't miss the stands in front of the basilica and at the daily mercado west of Plaza Chica. **Galería Iturbe** (⊠ Portal Morelos 59), at Mansión Iturbe, has an assortment of copper jewelry and the work of local painters. Ask the hotel desk clerk to open the store for you as it's often closed. **Mantas Tipicas** (⊠ Calle Dr. Coss 5, ☎ 434/2–13–24) sells hand-loomed tablecloths and more. **Santa Teresa Velas y Cirios** (⊠ Portugal 1, ☎ 434/2–09–18) sells handsome handmade candles in a rainbow of colors.

Side Trips from Pátzcuaro

Tzintzuntzan

 17 km (10½ mi) northeast of Pátzcuaro.

When the Spanish came to colonize the region in the 16th century, some 40,000 Purépechas lived and worshiped in this lakeshore village, which they called "place of the hummingbirds." The ruins of the pyramid-shape temples, or *yacatas,* found in the ancient capital of the Purépecha kingdom still stand today and are open to the public for $2. There are also vestiges of a 16th-century Franciscan monastery where Spanish friars attempted to convert the Indians to Christianity. Although Tzintzuntzan lost some prominence when Bishop Vasco de Quiroga moved the seat of his diocese to Pátzcuaro in 1540, the village is still well known for the straw and ceramic handicrafts made by the Purépecha Indians and sold in numerous shops along the main street of town. The bus marked QUIROGA takes a half hour to get from Pátzcuaro's Central Camionera to Tzintzuntzan.

Santa Clara del Cobre

20 km (12½ mi) south of Pátzcuaro.

Since before the conquest, Santa Clara del Cobre has been a center for copper arts. Now the local copper mines are empty, but the artisans still make gorgeous vessels, plates, napkin rings, and jewelry using the traditional method of pounding out each piece of metal by hand. For an introduction to quality and range of styles available, visit the **Museo del Cobre** (⊠ Calles Morelos and Pino Suárez, near the plaza), open Tuesday–Sunday 10–3 and 5–7. Admission is 50¢. Then explore the

50-some little shops and factories in town. The bus to Santa Clara del Cobre from Pátzcuaro's Central Camionera takes 40 minutes.

Uruapan

64 km (40 mi) west of Pátzcuaro.

The subtropical town of Uruapan is distinctly different from its lakeside neighbor: some 2,000 ft lower than Pátzcuaro, although still at an elevation of 5,300 ft, it is a populous commercial center with a warm climate and lush vegetation. The town's name is derived from the Purépecha word *urupan,* meaning "where the flowers bloom." Uruapan celebrates Palm Sunday with a lively procession through the streets, brass bands, and a spectacular, bargain-filled crafts market in the central plaza—one of the best in all of Mexico.

You can get to Uruapan from Pátzcuaro by car or bus. Route 14 and the new toll road are the most direct routes between the two cities. There is also frequent bus service on the Flecha Amarilla and other major lines; travel time is about 70 minutes.

You can see several points of interest within a few hours. The **Mercado de Antojitos,** an immense, sprawling market, begins in back of the Museo Regional de Arte Popular and extends quite a distance north along Calle Constitución. Along the road, Purépecha Indians sell large mounds of produce, fresh fish, beans, homemade cheese, and a variety of cheap manufactured goods. If you travel south along Calle Constitución, you'll come to a courtyard where vendors sell hot food.

The **Museo Regional de Arte Popular,** opposite the north side of Uruapan's Plaza Principal, was a 16th-century hospital known as La Huatápera before its conversion. It houses a collection of crafts from the state of Michoacán, including an excellent display of lacquerware made in Uruapan. ☎ *4/524–3434.* ☒ *Free.* ☉ *Tues.–Sun. 9:30–1:30 and 3:30–6.*

★ **Parque Nacional Eduardo Ruiz** (about six long blocks from the Plaza Principal off Calle Independencia) is a gem of an urban park. Its paved paths meander through verdant tropical acreage past abundant waterfalls, fountains, and springs to the source of the Río Cupatitzio. There also is a trout farm here and a popular playground.

Eleven km (7 mi) south along the Río Cupatitzio is the magnificent waterfall at **Tzaráracua.** At this point the river plunges 150 ft off a sheer rock cliff into a riverbed below; a rainbow seems to hang perpetually over the site. Buses marked TZARÁRACUA leave sporadically from the Plaza Principal in Uruapan. You can also take a taxi for about $3, or drive there via Avenida Lázaro Cárdenas.

Farther afield, about 32 km (20 mi) north of Uruapan, lies the dormant **Paricutín volcano.** Its initial burst of lava and ashes wiped out the nearby village of San Juan Parangaricútiro in 1943. Today travelers can visit this buried site by hiring gentle mountain ponies and a Purépecha guide in the town of Angahuan. To reach Angahuan, take the Los Reyes bus from Uruapan's Central Camionera or go by car via the Uruapan–Carapan highway.

DINING

For good comida casera, try **El Rincón del Burrito** (☒ Portal Matamorros 7, ☎ no phone). In the national park at the mouth of the Río Cupatitziothe is the restaurant at **Mansión de Cupatitzio** (☒ Parque Nacional s/n, ☎ 4/523–2070 or 4/523–2100).

Pátzcuaro A to Z

BUS TRAVEL

Buses run daily between the Terminal Poniente (West Terminal, commonly referred to as the Observatorio) in Mexico City and Pátzcuaro's Central Camionera on El Libramiento, on the southwestern outskirts of town. Several lines offer frequent service; the most direct trip, which takes five hours, is on either Herradura de Plata, Pegasso Plus, or ETN. Transportation coming from most heartland cities goes to Morelia; buses leave about every 15 minutes from there on the 45-minute trip to Pátzcuaro.

➤ Bus Information: **ETN** (☎ 434/2–10–60). **Herradura de Plata and Pegasso Plus** (☎ 434/2–10–45).

CAR TRAVEL

The Mexico City–Guadalajara tollway cuts driving time to Pátzcuaro to 4½ or 5 hours, and the trip on to Guadalajara to 4 hours by car. From Morelia, the excellent free road to Pátzcuaro takes just over an hour. You'll have to rent a car in Mexico City or Morelia, as there are no rental outlets in Pátzcuaro.

EMERGENCIES

Pharmacies are plentiful; Farmacia Gems is popular with residents. Pátzcuaro offers medical services through Hospital Civil.

➤ Contacts: **Farmacia Gems** (✉ Benito Mendoza 21, ☎ 434/2–03–32). **Hospital Civil** (✉ Romero 10, ☎ 434/2–02–85). **Police** (☎ 434/2–00–04). **Rescue** (☎ 434/2–02–09). **Traffic Police** (☎ 434/2–05–65).

MONEY MATTERS

Bancomer and Banca Promex have 24-hour ATMs. Banamex has an ATM for use during business hours.

➤ Exchange Services: **Banamex** (✉ Portal Juárez 32, ☎ 434/2–15–50 or 434/2–10–31). **Banca Promex** (✉ Portal Regules 9, ☎ 434/2–24–66). **Bancomer** (✉ Benito Mendoza 23, ☎ 434/2–03–34).

INTERNET

Informatica Integral de Pátzcuaro, open daily 9–9, charges $1.20 an hour for Internet access.

➤ Internet Cafés: **Informatica Integral de Pátzcuaro** (✉ Plaza Vasco de Quiroga 64).

TOURS

Marilyn Mayo designs custom tours based on your interests. She can take you to exuberant fiestas in tiny villages, to the home studios of master artisans, to the butterfly sanctuary, or any other place you want to go.

Guide Francisco Castilleja is highly knowledgeable about pre-Hispanic philosophy, history, archaeology, and medicinal herbs. He speaks fluent English, German, French, and Spanish.

➤ Tour Operator Recommendations: **Francisco Castilleja** (✉ Centro Eronga, Profr. Urueta 105, ☎ 434/4–01–67). **Marilyn Mayo** (✉ Apdo. 416, 61600, ☎ 434/2–23–01, 𝖥𝖠𝖷 434/2–27–56).

TRANSPORTATION AROUND PÁTZCUARO

Many of Pátzcuaro's principal sights are near the Plaza Vasco de Quiroga and Plaza Bocanegra in the center of town. Taxis and buses to the lake can also be found at the latter square. If you want to visit surrounding villages, taxi drivers will drive you for a reasonable rate. Be sure to agree on a fee before setting out.

VISITOR INFORMATION

Delegación de Turismo is the official tourism office and, although you may not find anyone here who speaks English, it will do its best to provide information regarding excursions outside Pátzcuaro. It's open Monday–Saturday 9–2 and 4–7, Sunday 9–2.

Dirección de Orientación y Fomento al Turismo offers maps and can answer basic questions about tourist facilities in Pátzcuaro. It's open daily 9–3 and 5–7.

➤ TOURIST INFORMATION: **Delegación de Turismo** (✉ Plaza Vasco de Quiroga 50A, ☎ FAX 434/2–12–14). **Dirección de Orientación y Fomento al Turismo** (✉ Portal Hidalgo 1, on Plaza de Quiroga, ☎ 434/2–02–15 or 434/2–02–16, FAX 434/32–09–67).

8 PACIFIC COAST RESORTS

Hollywood introduced us to two of the Mexican Riviera's most popular towns: Ava Gardner and Richard Burton's sleepy, steamy Puerto Vallarta in *The Night of the Iguana* and the sparkling Manzanillo coast that served as the backdrop to Bo Derek—and Dudley Moore's antics—in *10*. These days both places are prime stops, as is Mazatlán, a bustling port that attracts sportfishing enthusiasts, surfers, and snowbirds. Ixtapa/Zihuatanejo has two-for-one appeal, one of Mexico's most charming fishing villages adjoining a pristine resort.

Updated by
Jane Onstott

A CROSS THE GULF OF CALIFORNIA from the Baja California Peninsula lies Mazatlán, Mexico's largest Pacific port and the major Mexican resort closest to the United States, some 1,200 km (745 mi) south of the Arizona border. This is the beginning of "the Gold Coast," what cruise-ship operators now call the Mexican Riviera: with ports-of-call at Mazatlán, Puerto Vallarta, Manzanillo, and Ixtapa/Zihuatanejo. The coastline for the next 1,400 km (870 mi) is Mexico's tropical paradise. The Gulf of California, or the Sea of Cortez, as it is also called, ends just below the Tropic of Cancer, leaving the Pacific coastline open to fresh sea breezes. The farther south you travel, the warmer both air and water temperatures become.

Although Mexico's Pacific Coast cultures were in some ways as fascinating as that of the better known Aztecs, they left behind no major monuments, and so have been largely ignored by archaeological research teams. Not the place to see ruins, museums, and cathedrals, it's a gathering spot for sun worshipers, sportfishing enthusiasts, surfers, and swimmers. Not far from the resort regions are jungle streams and ocean coves, but the majority of visitors never venture to these isolated sites, preferring instead to immerse themselves in the simultaneously bustling and restful resort lifestyle, where great dining, shopping, and sunbathing are the major draws.

Thanks to its excellent port and the fertility of the surrounding countryside, **Mazatlán** is a busy commercial center. More than 600,000 acres of farmland near Mazatlán produce tomatoes, melons, cantaloupes, wheat, and cotton. Many of these products—along with tens of thousands of tons of shrimp, tuna, and sardines hauled in annually—are processed and frozen for the American and Japanese markets.

Proximity to the United States and excellent sportfishing account for Mazatlán's popularity as a resort. The port sits at the juncture of the Pacific and the Sea of Cortés, forming what has been called the world's greatest natural fish trap. Hunters are drawn to the quail, duck, and dove that thrive in the hillsides, and surfers find great waves on nearby beaches. Another draw is that accommodations are about half the cost of those in Cancún or Los Cabos. Additionally, downtown Mazatlán has several charming plazas and some beautifully restored buildings, among them a lovely opera house.

Some 323 km (200 mi) south of Mazatlán, **Puerto Vallarta** is the best-known resort on the upper Pacific Coast. Late film director and sometime resident John Huston put the town on the map when he filmed Tennessee Williams's *The Night of the Iguana* on the outskirts of the village in 1963. Elizabeth Taylor accompanied Richard Burton during the filming, and the gossip about their romance (both were married at the time, but not to each other) brought this quaint Mexican fishing village to the public's attention. Before long, travel agents were deluged with queries about Puerto Vallarta.

Today the fabled cobblestone streets can become clogged with bumper-to-bumper traffic, but Puerto Vallarta is still picturesque. For a sense of the Eden that once was, travel south of town to where the Río Tomatlán tumbles over boulders into the sea, or north to Punta de Mita on the northern tip of Bahía de Banderas (Bay of Flags).

Conquistador Hernán Cortés envisioned **Manzanillo** as a gateway to the Orient: from these shores, Spanish galleons would bring in the riches of Cathay to be trekked across the continent to Veracruz, where they would fill vessels headed for Spain. But Acapulco, not Manzanillo, be-

Navolato
Culiacán
DURANGO
Lázaro Cárdenas

TO LA PAZ
El Dorado
SINALOA
Santiago Papasquiaro

La Cruz
15
Canatlán

Estación Dimas

Tropic of Cancer
Presidio
El-Salto
40
Durango

Mazatlán
Copala
Villa Unión
Concordia

Golfo de California
El Caimanero
Rosario

Escuinapa de Hidalgo
Mezquital

Tecuala

Agua Brava

Islas Marías
Tuxpan
NAYARIT

San Blas
Bahía Matachén
Tepic

Rincón de Guayabitos
Río Grande de Sa ntiago

Punta de Mita
Sayulita
Lo De Marcos

Bahía de Banderas
San Francisco
Cruz de Huanacaxtle

Playa Las Ánimas

Cabo Corrientes
Boca de Tomatlán
Puerto Vallarta
Mismaloya
15

PACIFIC OCEAN
200
Ameca
Guadalajara

N
Tomatlán
80

Chamela
Ayotitlán
JALISCO
Lake Chapala

Armería

KEY
— Rail Lines
- - - Ferry Lines
Ciudad Guzmán

San Patricio Melaque
54
Barra de Navidad
COLIMA

0   100 miles
0   150 km
Manzanillo
110
Colima

Tecomán
Cerro de Ortega

Aquila

TO ZIHUATANEJO, IXTAPA ↓

came the port of call for the Manila galleons that arrived each year with riches from beyond the seas. Pirates are said to have staked out Manzanillo during the colonial era, and chests of loot are rumored to be buried beneath the sands.

With the coming of the railroads, Manzanillo became a major port of entry. It is now Mexico's second busiest port, and the lights of freighters at anchor can be seen along the southern beaches. Fifty years ago, a few seaside hotels opened up on the outskirts of town, which vacationers reached by train. The jet age, however, seemed to doom the port as a sunny vacation spot. Then Bolivian tin magnate Antenor Patiño built **Las Hadas** (The Fairies), a lavish Moorish-style resort inaugurated in 1974. It attracted the beautiful people, and for a while Las Hadas was better known than Manzanillo itself.

In recent years there's been a push to develop for tourism the pristine coast between Manzanillo and Puerto Vallarta. A four-lane toll road now cuts the driving time between Manzanillo and Guadalajara, Mexico's second-largest city, to three hours. Older hotels have been spruced up, and all-inclusive resorts constructed. About an hour north of Manzanillo, at the Jalisco state line across from Barra de Navidad, the **Grand Bay hotel** resort was built in 1998. The complex spreads over some 1,200 acres on a peninsula between the Pacific Ocean and the Navidad Lagoon, 20 minutes west of the Manzanillo airport.

Of the Gold Coast resorts, **Ixtapa/Zihuatanejo,** some 500 km (300 mi) south of Manzanillo, is the new kid on the block. Like Cancún, Ixtapa was the brainchild of the Mexican government in the early 1970s. With an offshore island and many beautiful beaches, this resort comprises two distinct destinations only 7 km (4½ mi) from each other. Ixtapa is the glitzier of the two, with international chain hotels lining its hotel zone, but it's far smaller and more low-key than resorts such as Puerto Vallarta and Cancún. Its development put neighbor Zihuatanejo, a sleepy fishing village virtually unknown even among Mexicans, on the tourist map. In Zihuatanejo, La Casa Que Canta is one of the finest small hotels in the world.

Pleasures and Pastimes

Beaches
Mexico's Pacific Coast doubtless has some of North America's most inviting beaches, with deliciously warm waters and spectacular sunsets. There are beaches for every taste: long stretches of creamy sand, crescents of soft gold and black volcanic grains, secluded coves, and pristine shores accessible only by boat.

Dining
Up and down the coast, the emphasis is on delicious seafood. Visitors savor traditional *pescado sarandeado* (whole fish marinated and grilled over hot coals) as well as elaborate dishes devised by imported European chefs. Shrimp, octopus, oysters, and fresh fish are the highlights; be sure to have a seafood cocktail along the beach. Mazatlán has a number of casual, lively restaurants serving surf-and-turf and traditional Mexican favorites, and prices are reasonable. Puerto Vallarta has the widest array of restaurants, some with spectacular views, others hidden in the small, romantic patios of former homes, and still others as popular for people-watching as they are for their great seafood. Several Manzanillo dining spots have scenic views of the jungle and water that compensate for their lack of culinary excitement. In Ixtapa/Zihuatanejo, restaurants range from open-air *palapas* on the beach to deluxe establishments with international chefs.

Some hotel restaurants add 15% IVA (value-added tax) as well as a service charge to your tab. Many more humble establishments charge neither, so check your bill and tip accordingly.

CATEGORY	COST*
$$$$	over $35
$$$	$25–$35
$$	$15–$25
$	under $15

per person for a three-course meal including 15% sales tax, and excluding drinks and service

Fishing

Mazatlán is tops in the Mexican Pacific for billfishing. Sailfish run from March through December, blue and black marlin from May through December, and swordfish and striped marlin from December through April. Other sportfish include rooster fish, wahoo, yellowfin tuna, bonito, mahimahi, and shark. Light-tackle fishing in the lagoons and just off the beach in *pangas* (small boats) for *huachinango* (red snapper) is also popular. Bass anglers will be pleased with the freshwater lakes in the foothills of the Sierra Madre.

Sportfishing is good off Puerto Vallarta most of the year, particularly for billfish, rooster fish, mahimahi, yellowtail, and bonito. Manzanillo claims to be the sailfish capital of the world; the season runs from mid-October through March. Blue marlin and dorado are also abundant. Ixtapa/Zihuatanejo is becoming Mexico's new sportfishing destination. Anglers revel in the profusion of sailfish (November through March), black and blue marlin (February through May), yellowfin tuna (November through June), and mahimahi (November through January). In November, Mazatlán, Puerto Vallarta, and Manzanillo host international fishing tournaments. More and more anglers each year are choosing to catch and release their prey.

Horseback Riding

In most Pacific Coast resorts, horseback riding along the shore is popular, and horses can be rented by the hour at major beaches. Most resorts have at least one stable offering half-day or even overnight rides to colonial villages in the Sierra Madre.

Lodging

Although not known for its upscale resorts, Mazatlán has its share of comfortable beachfront hotels, and one of the highest concentrations of trailer parks in the country. In Puerto Vallarta, accommodations range from tiny inns to luxury waterfront hotels and spectacular resorts on secluded coves. Big beachfront properties are the norm in Ixtapa; Zihuatanejo has budget hotels and several of the most exclusive small hotels in Mexico.

Most hotels raise their rates for the high season (December 15 through Easter Week); rates are lowest in May, June, September, and October). Though less common than in the Caribbean, hurricanes may crop up between late September and early November. Despite the rain and humidity, rates rise somewhat during July and August when Mexican families take advantage of the warm waters and swarm the beaches for their summer vacations. Price categories are based on high-season rates; expect to pay at least 25% less during the off-season.

CATEGORY	COST*
$$$$	over $200
$$$	$100–$200
$$	$50–$100
$	under $50

*All prices are for a standard double room, excluding 17% tax.

Shopping

You can spend as much time shopping in Puerto Vallarta as you can lazing in the sun. Shops selling excellent crafts from around the country vie with upscale art galleries and clothing and jewelry boutiques for buyers' attention, especially in the downtown area. Mazatlán and Ixtapa/Zihuatanejo also have some colorful markets and folk art shops. Look for masks from Jalisco and Guerrero states, and beaded masks, bowls, and statuettes made by the Huichol Indians.

Water Sports

Parasailing, swimming, windsurfing, sailing, kayaking, and waterskiing are popular at Pacific Coast resorts. Manzanillo, Mazatlán, and San Blas have some of the finest surfing in Mexico, and the best diving spots in this area are found around the islands off Puerto Vallarta, Ixtapa, and Mazatlán. Puerto Vallarta hosts Mexico's annual boat show each November, as well as various sailing regattas in winter.

Exploring the Pacific Coast Resorts

Resorts on this coastal stretch are at their best in winter, with temperatures in the 70s and 80s (a bit higher in Ixtapa/Zihuatanejo). The off-season brings humidity, mosquitoes, and higher temperatures (northernmost Mazatlán remains coolest), but also emptier beaches, warmer water (well into the 70s), and less-crowded streets—plus 25%–35% lower room rates and cheaper rental-car costs. Toward the end of the rainy season, which involves mostly brief daily showers, the countryside and the mountainous backdrop of the Sierra Madre del Sur turn a brilliant green.

MAZATLÁN

Mazatlán is the Aztec word for "place of the deer," and long ago its islands and shores sheltered far more deer than humans. Today it is a city of almost 700,000 residents and draws about 1 million tourists a year. Sunning, surfing, fishing, and sailing are the primary attractions, and in the winter months visitors from inland Mexico, the United States, and Canada flock to Mazatlán for a break in the sun. Hotel and restaurant prices are substantially lower than elsewhere on the coast. While the ambience downtown is that of a dignified port city, the Zona Dorada—lined with hotels, shops, and tourist-oriented restaurants—certainly has the feel of a tourist town.

Hunting and fishing were the original draw for visitors. At one time, duck, quail, pheasant, and other wildfowl fed in the lagoons, and mountain lions, rabbits, and coyotes roamed the surrounding hills. Today the more popular sport—at least among visitors—is deep-sea fishing. Mazatlán has one of Mexico's largest sportfishing fleets, and anglers haul in some of the coast's biggest catches: both in size and number. Approximately 12,000 billfish are caught and released each year, including some of gargantuan proportions.

The Spanish settled in the Mazatlán region in 1531 and used the indigenous people as a labor force to create the port and village. In the ensuing centuries, the center of Mazatlán gradually moved north. The original site is now the village of Villa Unión, 24 km (15 mi) southeast of the harbor.

In the early 1600s, the colonial government built a small fort and watchtowers atop the hills in the city to discourage attacks on the rich Spanish galleons by English and French pirates. The buccaneers were gone by 1800, but legends of buried treasure in the caves along the coast still circulate.

The port has a history of blockades. In 1847, during the Mexican–American War, U.S. forces marched down from the border through northeast Mexico and closed it. In 1864, the French bombarded the city and then controlled it for several years. The British occupied the port for a short period in 1871. Mexico's own internal warring factions took over from time to time. And after the Civil War in the United States, a group of Southerners tried to turn Mazatlán into a slave city.

Exploring Mazatlán

Downtown Mazatlán is a fun place to walk and explore, though many visitors never leave the Zona Dorada (Golden Zone), a broad avenue lined with hotels, shops, and party-down restaurants.

Numbers in the text correspond to numbers in the margin and on the Mazatlán map.

A Good Tour

Start from the **Zona Dorada** ①, Mazatlán's tourist area, at Punta Camarón (Shrimp Point). Stretching north from there along Avenida Camarón Sábalo are the stuff resorts are made of: bars and restaurants, shell and souvenir shops, and beachfront hotels. This route affords a good view of Mazatlán's three Pacific islands—Isla de los Pájaros, Isla de los Venados, and Isla de los Chivos. Just past the Playa Real resort, Avenida Camarón Sábalo becomes Avenida Sábalo Cerritos and crosses over the Estero del Sábalo lagoon. The area north of here is being developed as "la Zona Platinum," an exclusive resort area.

South of the Zona Dorada, the main road changes names frequently. Mazatlán's main highway begins at Punta Camarón and is here called Avenida del Mar. About halfway between Punta Camerón and downtown and a few blocks inland is the city's highly recommended aquarium, **Acuario Mazatlán** ②, on Avenida de los Deportes. Avenida del Mar continues past beaches popular with residents and travelers staying at the budget hotels across the street. You're sure to notice the avenue's main landmark, the Monumento al Pescador: an enormous statue of a voluptuous, nude woman reclining on an anchor, her hand extended toward a nude fisherman dragging his nets.

After the monument, Avenida del Mar becomes Paseo Claussen. Calles Juárez and Cinco de Mayo lead from the coast-hugging road to Mazatlán's busy downtown. The heart of the city is **Plaza República** ③, also called el *zócalo* (main square) or Plaza Revolución. On the north side of the square you'll see the twin-spired **Mazatlán Catedral** ④; on facing streets are the City Hall, banks, and post office. About three blocks south of the zócalo, the Teatro Angela Peralta, built in 1860 and now beautifully restored, was declared a historic monument in 1990. Stop for a drink or a bite at any one of the establishments around the nearby Plazuela Machado, known for its lively neighborhood fiestas. Head three blocks west to the **Museo de Arte de Mazatlán** ⑤, as well as the simple **Instituto Nacional de Antropología e Historia** ⑥.

Back along the waterfront, Paseo Claussen and the malecón continue past El Fuerte Carranza, an old Spanish fort built to defend the city

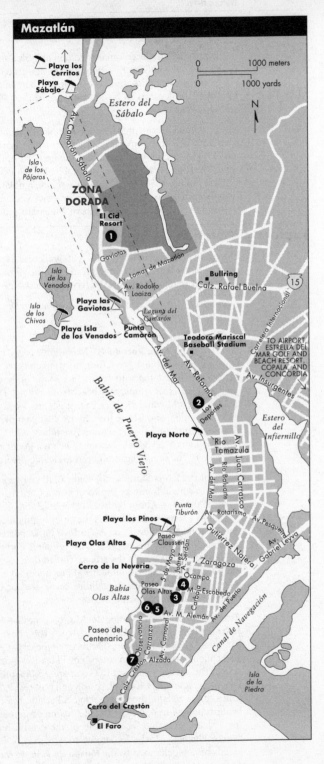

Mazatlán

0   1000 meters
0   1000 yards

N

Playa los
Cerritos

Playa
Sábalo

*Estero del
Sábalo*

Av. Camarón Sábalo

*Isla
de los
Pájaros*

**ZONA
DORADA**

El Cid
Resort

❶

Gaviotas

Av. Lomas de Mazatlán

Bullring

Calz. Rafael Buelna

15

*Isla
de los
Venados*

Av. Rodolfo
T. Loaiza

*Isla
de los
Chivos*

**Playa las
Gaviotas**

*Laguna del
Camarón*

**Playa Isla
de los Venados**

**Punta
Camarón**

**Teodoro Mariscal
Baseball Stadium**

Carretera Internacional

TO AIRPORT,
ESTRELLA DEL
MAR GOLF AND
BEACH RESORT,
COPALA, AND
CONCORDIA

Av. Insurgentes

Av. del Mar

Av. Reforma

Bahía de Puerto Viejo

Los
Deportes

❷

*Estero
del
Infiernillo*

Playa Norte

Río
Tamazula

Av. Juan Carrasco

Av. del Mar

Río Baluarte

Av. Pesqueira

Punta
Tiburón

Av. Rotarismo

Av.
Gabriel Leyva

Playa los Pinos

Paseo
Claussen

Gutiérrez Nájera

Playa Olas Altas

5 de Mayo

A. Serdán

Juárez

I. Zaragoza

Cerro de la Nevería

Ocampo

*Bahía
Olas Altas*

Paseo
Olas Altas

❹

M. J.
Escobedo

❸

Carbajal

Av. del Puerto

❻❺

Av. M. Alemán

Canal de Navegación

Paseo del
Centenario

Observatorio

Carranza

Av. Carnaval

❼

Alzada

Calz. Crestón

*Isla
de la
Piedra*

■ **Cerro del Crestón**

■ **El Faro**

against the French. Next you'll come to Playa Olas Altas, where at High-Divers Park, young men plunge into the sea, Acapulco-style, from a small white platform. It's spectacular at night, when the divers leap carrying flaming torches. Continuing south you'll see La Mazatleca, a bronze nymph, and across the street, a small bronze deer, the symbol of Mazatlán. Just down the road is the Monument to the Continuity of Life, a large fountain with a handsome couple on top of a large conch shell and a school of porpoises leaping from the water. Looming above the Olas Altas area is **Cerro de Vigía** ⑦ (Lookout Hill).

Sights to See

🖐 ❷ **Acuario Mazatlán.** A perfect child-pleaser, Mazatlán's aquarium features tanks of sharks, sea horses, and multicolor salt- and freshwater fish. Kids will also enjoy the skating macaw and penny-pinching parrot at bird shows held four times daily, as well as the sea-lion show and diving exhibition. There are botanical gardens, a large playground, an aviary, gift shop, and snack bars. ⊠ *Av. de los Deportes 111,* ☎ *6/ 981–7815.* 🎟 *$4.50.* ⊙ *Daily 9:30–6.*

❼ **Cerro de Vigía** (Lookout Hill). The view from this windy hill above Olas Altas is fantastic: you can see both sides of Mazatlán, the harbor, and the Pacific. The steep road up is better suited for a private car or taxi than for walking. At the top of the hill you'll see a rusty cannon and the **Centenario Pérgola,** built in 1848 to celebrate the end of the U.S. invasion. Order a beer, soda, or a snack at Restaurant el Mirador before heading back down the hill.

❻ **Instituto Nacional de Antropología e Historia.** The town's archaeological museum houses a small but interesting collection of artifacts from the region. Among these are exquisite black and red pottery left behind by the Totorames, an indigenous tribe that inhabited the area up until 200 years before the Spanish arrived. ⊠ *Sixto Osuna 76, off Paseo Olas Altas,* ☎ *6/981–1455.* 🎟 *Free.* ⊙ *Weekdays 10–3.*

NEED A BREAK? | The sidewalk tables at **Copa de Leche** and **Fonda Santa Clara** (⊠ Paseo Olas Altas, near Sixto Osuna) are perfect for watching sunsets.

❹ **Mazatlán Catedral.** The bright yellow spires of the downtown cathedral are a city landmark. Begun in 1855, the church was not completed until the end of the century, and embraces a variety of architectural styles. Made a basilica in 1935, it has a gilded and ornate triple altar, with murals of angels overhead and many small altars along the sides. ⊠ *Calles Juárez and 21 de Marzo.*

❺ **Museo de Arte de Mazatlán.** This small museum shows the work of local, regional, and national artists, including Gerardo Santamarino, José Luis Cuevas, and Armando Nava. Daily painting classes are offered. ⊠ *Sixto Osuna and Venustiano Carranza,* ☎ 🖷 *6/985–3502.* 🎟 *90¢.* ⊙ *Tues.–Sun. 10–2 and 4–7.*

❸ **Plaza República.** At the center of downtown, this city square hosts one of the most fascinating gazebos in Mexico—what looks like a '50s diner inside the lower level and a wrought-iron bandstand on top. The multicolor tiles on floors and walls, ancient jukebox, and soda fountain serving shakes, burgers, and hot dogs couldn't make a more surprising sight. Tourists and locals surround the bandstand Sunday afternoon to hear local musicians play. ⊠ *Bounded by 21 de Marzo to the north, Flores to the south, Benito Juárez to the east, and Nelson to the west.*

❶ **Zona Dorada.** Marking the beginning of Mazatlán's tourist zone is **Punta Camarón,** the rocky outcropping on which Valentino's disco sits, resembling a Moorish palace perched above the sea. To the north,

Avenida Rodolfo T. Loaiza splits off from Avenida Camarón Sábalo, running closer to the beach before rejoining Camarón Sábalo. In this four-block pocket are many hotels, shops, and restaurants. This is the place to souvenir-shop, hit the discos, and check out the hotel bars.

NEED A
BREAK?

No Name Café (✉ Av. Rodolfo T. Loaiza 417, ☎ 6/913–2031), in the Mazatlán Arts and Crafts Center, is a good spot for barbecued ribs and beer. At the **Panadería Panamá** (✉ Av. Camarón Sábalo across from Las Palmas hotel, ☎ 6/913–6977), you can sit at a table and enjoy fragrant cinnamon-flavored coffee with fresh-baked pastries.

Around Mazatlán

CONCORDIA
48 km (30 mi) east of Mazatlán.

A pleasant yet relatively unexceptional small town, Concordia is known for its furniture makers, its 18th-century church, and its unglazed clay pottery. Lined with organ cactus and mango trees, the drive is especially pretty after the summer rains cover nearby hills and distant mountains in green.

COPALA
25 km (15 mi) east of Concordia.

Huddled at the foot of the Sierra Madre Occidental, Copala's single cobblestone street winds through town to the tiny town square and 18th-century church, which perches above a gorge. As you amble about this small but picturesque former mining town, you'll pass old homes with colorful facades enlivened with flowering vines and trees and embellished with ironwork balconies and window coverings. Refresh yourself at one of the town's simple yet charming restaurants before heading back down the hill.

TEACAPAN
25 km (15 mi) south of Mazatlán.

A serene drive into cattle and coconut country is a great way to see the countryside outside Mazatlán. Tour companies such as Marlin Tours visit en route the 17th-century mining town of El Rosario, including the Spanish cemetery and lovely old church and a visit to nearby thermal springs, before visiting the Haas hacienda in Teacapan, with many exotic plants.

Beaches

Playa los Cerritos and Playa Bruja. A long stretch of sand running for several miles from the Marina Mazatlán to Punta Cerritos, Playa los Cerritos is still relatively unpopulated, although the construction of condos along its length may change that. A steep drop-off and undertow make it less than ideal for swimming. Around Punta Cerritos are thatch-roof eateries frequented by locals on weekends and by surfers relaxing after a day of surfing the point break.

Playa Isla de la Piedra. Sixteen kilometers (10 miles) of unspoiled beaches allow enough room for all visitors to spread out and claim their own space. This is the place to rent a horse for a good long ride on the beach. On Sunday, the beach looks like a small village, with lots of music and fun. Many of the small palapas set up along the north end of the beach serve a tasty smoked marlin and other seafood treats.

Playa Isla de los Venados. Boats make frequent departures from the Zona Dorada hotels for this beach on Deer Island. It's only a 10-minute ride, but the difference in ambience is striking. The beach is pretty, uncluttered, and clean, and you can hike around the southern point of the island to small, secluded coves covered with shells. El Cid hotel employs a 1964 army surplus amphibious vehicle, affectionately known as *el tiburón* (the shark), to take you to the island and back.

Playa Norte. This strand begins at Punta Camarón (Valentino's is a landmark) along Avenida del Mar and runs to the Fisherman's Monument. The dark brown sand is dirty and rocky at some points, but clean at others, and is popular with those staying at hotels across the avenue. Palapas selling cold drinks (including whole chilled coconuts), tacos, and fresh fish line the beach. Fishermen land their skiffs on the south end of this beach, sometimes referred to as Los Pinos (the pines).

Playa Olas Altas. This beach, whose name means "high waves," was the first tourist beach in Mazatlán, running south along the malecón from the Fisherman's Monument. Surfers congregate here during the summer months, when the waves are at their highest.

Playa Sábalo and Playa las Gaviotas. Mazatlán's two most popular beaches parallel la Zona Dorada. Both are crowded with vendors selling pottery, lace tablecloths, and silver jewelry and renting boats, windsurfers, and other toys. The beach is protected from heavy surf by the three islands—Venados, Pájaros, and Chivos. When you tire of sand and sun, repair to one of the many beachfront hotel restaurants willing to accommodate skimpily clad and somewhat sandy customers.

Dining

$$$ ✕ **Angelo's.** With its fresh flowers, cream-and-beige decor, gentle
★ piano music, and soft candlelight, this is by far the most elegant restaurant in Mazatlán. The Italian and Continental cuisine is outstanding—try the veal scallopini with mushrooms or shrimp marinara on pasta—and the service is impeccable. ✉ *Pueblo Bonito, Av. Camarón Sábalo 2121,* ☎ *6/914–3700. AE, MC, V. No lunch.*

$$$ ✕ **Sr. Peppers.** Elegant yet unpretentious, with ceiling fans, lush foliage, and candlelit tables, Sr. Peppers serves choice steaks and lobsters cooked over a mesquite grill. This is the place locals go for a fancy night out, and to enjoy the dance floor and live music. ✉ *Av. Camarón Sábalo across from Playa Real,* ☎ *6/914–0101. AE, MC, V. No lunch.*

$$ ✕ **La Casa Country.** This festive restaurant across from the Holiday Inn serves a variety of steaks and Mexican dishes to a country-loving crowd. Steaks are grilled over charcoal or fire wood—the *arrachera* (skirt steak) served with kettle beans and guacamole is a good bet, as is the rib-eye with baked potato. Margaritas and piña coladas are served by the pitcher; at night, country-music fans are brought to their feet for dancin' and carousin' until 2 AM. ✉ *Av. Camarón Sábalo s/n,* ☎ *6/916–5300. AE, MC, V.*

$$ ✕ **La Concha.** One of the prettiest waterside dining spots, La Concha
★ is a large enclosed palapa with three levels of seating, including a spacious dance floor adorned with twinkling lights and tables by the sand. Adventurous types might attempt the stingray with black butter or calamari in its ink, and the more conservative can try a thick filet mignon. During the winter season there's live music in the evenings. La Concha is also open for breakfast as well as lunch and dinner. ✉ *El Cid Megaresort, Av. Camarón Sábalo s/n,* ☎ *6/913–3333. AE, MC, V.*

$$ ✕ **El Paraíso Tres Islas.** With a good view of the three islands, this wonderful palapa on the beach is a favorite with families. Entire Sunday afternoons can be spent feasting on fresh fish; try the smoked marlin, oysters diablo, octopus, or the seafood platter. The waiters are friendly and eager to help. ✉ *Av. Rodolfo T. Loaiza 404,* ☎ *6/914–2812. MC, V.*

$$ × **Pedro & Lola.** Authentic Mexican seafood is served in this 19th-cen-
★ tury building in the heart of the historic center, decorated with con-
temporary art. Try the *papillot,* the day's fresh catch cooked in foil with
white wine, shrimp, and mushrooms. Named after Mexican *ranchera*
singers Pedro Infante and Lola Beltrán, the restaurant hosts excellent
live music in the evening, sometimes featuring jazz sax or oldies rock.
Reservations recommended Thursday through Saturday. ⊠ *Carnaval
1303, next to Plazuela Machado,* ☎ 6/982–2589. AE, MC, V. No lunch.

$$ × **El Shrimp Bucket.** In Old Mazatlán, facing the water, this was the
original Carlos 'n' Charlie's. The garden patio restaurant (part of the
inexpensive Hotel Siesta) is much quieter than its predecessors—some
would call it respectable. This is the in spot for Mazatlán businessmen
and social mavens at breakfast (from 6 AM). For lunch or dinner, best
bets are fried shrimp served in clay buckets and barbecued ribs. Portions are large, and there's live music at night. ⊠ *Paseo Olas Altas 11–
126 Sur,* ☎ 6/981–6350. AE, MC, V.

$ × **Karnes en Su Jugo.** A small family-run café on the malecón, with
a few outdoor tables and a large indoor restaurant, this establishment
specializes in *karnes en su jugo* (literally, "beef in its juice"), a Mexican stew with chopped beef, onions, beans, and bacon. It's a satisfying meal, especially when eaten with a basket of homemade tortillas.
⊠ *Av. del Mar 550,* ☎ 6/982–1322. No credit cards.

$ × **Restaurante Pancho's.** Upstairs or down, inside or out, seafood is
the specialty at this bustling, casual, and friendly seaside restaurant.
Choose from enormous seafood platters to share, seafood soup, ceviche,
or many other dishes. You can also order fresh salads, hearty tortilla
soup, and filet mignon smothered in mushrooms and served with rice,
steamed veggies, baked potato, and thick Texas-style toast. Portions
are generous, and the food is so good that you'll most likely clean your
plate. ⊠ *Rodolfo T. Loaiza 408, Centro Comercial Las Cabanas,
Local11-B,* ☎ 6/914–0911. MC, V.

Lodging

Most of Mazatlán's hotels are in the Zona Dorada, along the beaches.
Less expensive places are in Old Mazatlán, the original tourist zone
along the malecón on the south side of downtown.

$$$ ⊞ **El Cid Megaresort.** Mazatlán's largest resort, El Cid has 1,320 rooms
★ on four different properties, three of which are here. The fourth, the
upscale Marina El Cid Hotel and Yacht Club, is at the north end of
town and has 210 suites and a 100-slip marina; a free shuttle connects
the properties. Suites in the El Moro tower overlooking the ocean are
closest to the action and nicer (but more expensive) than rooms in the
older Castilla tower. All guests can enjoy such perks as a full-service
spa and fitness center, golf school and 27-hole course, deep-sea fish-
ing fleet, and aquatic sports center. The spacious rooms overlook the
pool and beach, and the hotel is popular with convention groups as
well as individual travelers. The glass-enclosed arcade has nice bou-
tiques, and La Concha is one of the most romantic spots on the beach.
⊠ *Av. Camarón Sábalo s/n, 82110,* ☎ 6/913–3333 or 800/525–1925,
FAX 6/914–1311, WEB *www.elcid.com. 1,320 rooms, suites, and studios.
8 restaurants, 5 bars, no-smoking rooms, 8 pools, spa, 27-hole golf
course, 11 tennis courts, gym, beach, marina, shops, dance club, chil-
dren's programs (ages 4–12), business services, meeting rooms, travel
services, car rental. AE, DC, MC, V.*

$$$ ⊞ **Fiesta Inn.** One of Mazatlán's newer hotels, the Fiesta Inn is oper-
ated by the Mexican hotel chain Posadas, and attracts primarily busi-
ness travelers. The nine-story tower is on a nice stretch of beach
between the Holiday Inn and Radisson hotels. Guest rooms are rather

plain, with tile floors, light-wood furniture, and tiny balconies. Public areas are pleasant, however, and the gym is roomy and well equipped. ⊠ *Av. Camarón Sábalo 1927, 82110,* ☎ *6/989–0100, 01–800/504–5000, or 800/343–7821,* FAX *6/989–0130. 117 rooms. 2 restaurants, bar, no-smoking rooms, 2 pools, gym, beach, business services, meeting rooms, travel services, car rental. AE, MC, V.*

$$$ 🏨 **Holiday Inn Sunspree Resort.** A consistently good hotel, the Holiday Inn has been drastically improved in recent years. Tour and convention groups fill the rooms and create a party mood by the pool and on the beach. The Kid's Spree program provides activities to keep children busy; adults can play bingo, attend tennis clinics, or borrow snorkel equipment or boogie boards. Rooms are done in whites and pastels, with large sliding doors that open to pretty views of the islands. Standard amenities now include remote-control cable TV, hair dryer, refrigerator, and coffeemaker. ⊠ *Av. Camarón Sábalo 696, 82110,* ☎ *6/913–2222 or 800/465–4329,* FAX *6/914–1287. 160 rooms, 23 suites. 3 restaurants, 2 bars, no-smoking rooms, pool, gym, volleyball, beach, children's programs (ages 6–15), business services, meeting rooms. AE, MC, V.*

$$$ 🏨 **Pueblo Bonito.** One of the comeliest properties in Mazatlán, this all-
★ suites hotel and time-share resort has an enormous lobby with chandeliers and beveled-glass doors; terra-cotta-color rooms have domed ceilings. An arched doorway leads from the tile kitchen into the elegant seating area, which is furnished with pale pink and beige couches and glass tables. Pink flamingos stroll manicured lawns, golden koi swim in small ponds, and bronzed sunbathers repose on padded white lounge chairs by the crystal-blue pool. Drawbacks are the time-share solicitors, additional 5% service charge, and inconvenient check-in and -out times (4 PM and 10 AM, respectively). Angelo's is a dining must—as elegant as Mazatlán gets. ⊠ *Av. Camarón Sábalo 2121, 82110,* ☎ *6/914–3700 or 800/990–8250,* FAX *6/914–1723,* WEB *www.pueblobonito.com. 250 suites. 3 restaurants, bar, 2 pools, massage, sauna, gym, beach, children's programs, travel services, car rental. AE, MC, V.*

$$$ 🏨 **Royal Villas Resort.** Panoramic elevators transport you from the cool
★ marble atrium lobby of this pyramid-shape, 12-story structure to the upper floors. More ample and functional than elegant, one- and two-bedroom suites have ocean views, remote-control TVs, direct-dial phones, balconies, and kitchenettes. Access to the inviting pool is by a bridge that crosses over a fish-filled pond. ⊠ *Av. Camarón Sábalo 500, 82110,* ☎ *6/916–6161 or 800/898–3564,* FAX *6/914–0777,* WEB *www.royalvillas.com.mx. 125 suites. 2 restaurants, bar, no-smoking rooms, pool, hot tub, exercise room, beach, business services, meeting rooms, travel services. AE, MC, V.*

$$$ 🏨 **Los Sábalos.** Smack in the center of the Zona Dorada, this white high-rise perches on a long clean beach. Rooms are boldly decorated in bright blue and stark white, and have such perks as satellite TV, coffeemakers, and hair dryers. You'll be in the thick of the action here, and it's the home of Joe's Oyster Bar, one of the most popular dance venues in town. ⊠ *Av. Rodolfo T. Loaiza 100, 82110,* ☎ *6/983–5333; 800/528–8760; 877/756–7532 in the U.S.,* FAX *6/983–8156,* WEB *www.lossabalos.com. 85 rooms, 100 suites. 3 restaurants, 2 bars, pool, spa, 2 tennis courts, gym, beach, dance club. AE, MC, V.*

$$ 🏨 **Azteca Inn.** At the low end of this price category, this hotel across the street from the Playa Mazatlán hotel is a great find for budget travelers who like to be in the center of things. The brown-and-white exterior color scheme isn't carried over into the rooms, which are decorated in bright reds and yellows. Rooms in the three-story low-rise—all with satellite TV and direct-dial phones—surround the courtyard pool and hot tub. The staff couldn't be friendlier. ⊠ *Av. Rodolfo T. Loaiza 307,*

82110, ☎ *6/913–4477,* ℻ *6/913–7476,* 🕸 *www.aztecainn.com.mx.*
74 rooms. Bar, cafeteria, pool, hot tub. AE, MC, V.

$$ ⌕ **Casa Contenta.** A small surprise on the beach one block north of
★ Las Flores, this property has seven one-bedroom apartments in a colo-
nial-style building. The large beachfront house boasts three bedrooms,
three baths, living and dining room, and even servants' quarters; it ac-
commodates eight people. All units have equipped kitchens and TVs,
but no phones. The bargain prices bring many repeat clients, so book
this one well in advance. ⊠ *Av. Rodolfo T. Loaiza 224, 82110,* ☎ *6/*
913–4976, ℻ *6/913–9986. 8 units. Kitchenettes, pool. MC, V.*

$$ ⌕ **Hotel Plaza Marina.** Near the Fisherman's Monument downtown,
all suites at this hotel have ocean views as well as kitchenettes, bed-
rooms with king-size beds, and bathtubs. Rooms face the pool and have
pastel color schemes. Don't be frightened by the lifelike, 4-ft-tall
wooden cobra in the lobby. ⊠ *Av. del Mar 73, 82110,* ☎ *6/982–3622*
or 01–800/711–9465, ℻ *6/982–3499. 56 rooms, 43 suites. Restau-*
rant, bar, pool, gym, travel services. AE, MC, V.

$$ ⌕ **Playa Mazatlán.** Palapas are set up on the patios by the rooms in
★ this casual low-rise hotel on Gaviotas Beach, popular with Mexican
families and laid-back singles more concerned with comfort than style.
The bright, sunny rooms have comfy beds with tile headboards, tile
tables by the windows, and terraces or balconies. At night candles flicker
in the breeze at the open-air restaurant right on the beach. Mazatlán's
first resort is known for its thrice weekly Mexican Fiesta. ⊠ *Av.*
Rodolfo T. Loaiza 202, 82110, ☎ *6/913–7989 or 800/762–5816,* ℻
6/914–0366, 🕸 *www.playamazatlan.com.mx. 425 rooms. Restaurant,*
bar, 3 pools, hot tub, gym, beach, shops, meetings rooms, travel ser-
vices. AE, MC, V.

$$ ⌕ **El Quijote Inn.** A great bargain on the beach in the midst of the hotel
zone, this five-story inn is a tranquil alternative to some of the more
frenzied facilities. A range of accommodations includes mainly one-
and two-bedroom suites with full kitchens. All units have tile floors,
rattan furnishings, satellite TV, and patios or balconies. The outdoor
bar and restaurant overlook both the beach and the nicely landscaped
pool area with large hot tub. ⊠ *Avs. Camarón Sábalo and Tiburón,*
82110, ☎ *6/914–1134,* ℻ *6/914–3344. 18 rooms, 52 suites. Restau-*
rant, bar, pool, hot tub, shop, meeting room, car rental. AE, MC, V.

$ ⌕ **Hotel Siesta.** At well below $50 per double, you can't beat the price
of this comfortable budget hotel. The beach across the street is rocky,
but the hotel's location in the Olas Altas is great for those who want
to explore the "real" Mazatlán, downtown. Rooms are plainly furnished,
but do have cable TV and air-conditioning. Interior-facing rooms overlook the courtyard and the Shrimp Bucket restaurant, where live music
is played nightly in high season until 11. ⊠ *Paseo Olas Altas 11 Sur,*
82110, ☎ *6/981–2640,* ℻ *6/982–2633,* 🕸 *www.lasiesta.com.mx. 57*
rooms. Restaurant, travel services, car rental. AE, MC, V.

$ ⌕ **Plaza Gaviotas.** You don't get a whole lot of perks here, but the lo-
cation across from Gaviotas Beach, for which it is named, is good, and
the salmon-color rooms in this clean, colonial-style budget hotel have
small balconies, although without chairs or table. ⊠ *Av. Rodolfo T.*
Loaiza 100 and Bugambilias, 82110, ☎ *6/913–4322,* ℻ *6/913–6685.*
67 rooms. Restaurant, bar, pool. MC, V.

Nightlife

Marking the southern edge of the Golden Zone, Valentino's, Bora Bora,
Pepe's & Joe, and Sheik are all part of the complex known as **Fiesta**
Land (⊠ Av. Camarón Sbalo at Calzada Rafael Buelna, ☎ 6/984–1006
or 6/984–1666). Valentino's, with its stark white towers rising above

Punta Camarón, has two dance clubs—one geared toward a younger crowd, the other with more tranquil, romantic music—as well as a karaoke salon. Bora Bora is a palapa restaurant and bar renowned for its raucous disco music and table-dancing; like Valentino's, it opens after 9 PM. Pepe's & Joe is a microbrew-beer factory with American-style burgers and dogs. Extravagant Sheik restaurant delights diners with waterfalls, ocean views, Moorish-inspired stained-glass windows, marble floors, and a central domed skylight; this place shouldn't be missed, if only for an early evening drink.

In the historic center near the Angela Peralta theater, **Café Pacífico** (⊠ Constitución 501, ☎ 6/981–3972) sometimes hosts jazz, bohemian guitarists, or other musicians Thursday through Saturday. **El Caracol Disco Club** (⊠ Av. Camarón Sábalo s/n, ☎ 6/913–3333), at El Cid Megaresort, has a high-tech disco, billiards, board and arcade games, and different theme nights throughout the week. A hefty $20 cover includes all drinks and games. **El Cid Megaresort** also has excellent theme nights throughout the week. Almost all hotel travel desks can provide you with information on days and times. **Joe's Oyster Bar** (⊠ Los Sábalos hotel, Av. Rodolfo T. Loaiza 100, ☎ 6/983–5333) is a popular beachfront spot where the dancing starts at noon and lasts until 2 AM.

The **Mexican Fiesta,** held Tuesday, Thursday, and Saturday 7–10:30 at the Playa Mazatlán is a good entertainment bet. The $25 fee includes a Mexican buffet dinner, open bar, entertainment, and live music for dancing. A favorite with young revelers bent on belting down tequila shooters and generally whooping it up is **Señor Frog** (⊠ Av. del Mar, ☎ 6/982–1925). This member of the Carlos Anderson chain is a restaurant as well, serving good barbecued ribs and chicken with corn on the cob. Bandidos carry tequila bottles and shot glasses in their *bandoliers,* Revolution-era ammunition belts. The drinking, dancing, and carousing go on well into the night.

Outdoor Activities and Sports

Participant Sports

ECOTOURS

Mazatleco Sport Center (⊠ Av. Rodolfo T. Loaiza s/n, next to Hotel Flores, ☎ 6/916–5933) leads Hobie Cat sailing tours and kayaking tours to Isla de los Venados, where paddlers can then hike or snorkel (4 hours, $37). They also lead kayaking trips (best in winter) to bird-watch among the mangroves south of town ($45, includes lunch). If you prefer to go solo, Mazatleco rents kayaks, snorkel gear, and ice chests. **Pronatura** (⊠ Av. Camarón Sábalo s/n, Centro Comercial de El Cid, Local 2627, ☎ 6/916–7720), in the El Cid complex, offers a variety of tours, including daily adventure tours via trimaran to Isla de los Venados ($37, includes lunch and open bar) for snorkeling and kayaking, and five-hour tours to El Verde ($32) to learn about marine tortoise protection programs. **Robert Hudson** (☎ 6/913–1764, WEB www.hudsontours.com), an American who has lived in Mazatlán for many years, offers spearfishing, snorkeling, kayaking, and other tours tailored to fit your needs.

FISHING

More than a dozen sportfishing fleets operate from the docks south of the lighthouse. Hotels can arrange charters, or you can contact the companies directly. Charters include a full day of fishing, bait, and tackle. Prices range from $80 to $100 per person on a party boat, or from $200 to $300 to charter a boat for 1–5 passengers. Charter companies include **Bill Heimpel's Star Fleet** (☎ 6/982–2665), **Flota Bibi** (☎ 6/981–3640), **Flota Faro** (☎ 6/981–2824), and **De Oro** (☎ 6/982–3130).

GOLF

The spectacular 27-hole course at **El Cid Megaresort** (☎ 6/913–3333), with 9 holes designed by Lee Trevino, is reserved for members of the resort, hotel guests, and their guests. Arthur Martori and Merv Griffin are two of the investors in the **Estrella del Mar and Beach Resort Complex** (☎ 6/982–3300), south of Mazatlán proper, off the airport highway on Isla de la Piedra (Stone Island). Here you'll find a championship 18-hole Robert Trent Jones golf course open to the public.

HORSEBACK RIDING

You can rent horses on **Isla de la Piedra** for about $5 per hour, guide included, unless you ask to go it alone.

TENNIS

Many of the hotels have courts, some of which are open to the public, and there are a few public courts not connected to the hotels. Call in advance for reservations at **El Cid Megaresort** (☎ 6/913–3333), which has 9 courts. Three courts are available at **Costa de Oro** (☎ 6/913–5344). The **Racket Club** (☎ 6/913–5939) has 6 courts.

WATER SPORTS

Jet Skis, Hobie Cats (a two-person catamaran), and windsurfers are available for rent at most beachfront hotels, and parasailing is popular along the Zona Dorada. Scuba diving and snorkeling are catching on, but there are no really great diving spots; the best are around Isla de los Venados. For rentals and trips, contact one of the many operators. **Centro Aquatico El Cid** (✉ Av. Camarón Sábalo s/n, ☎ 6/913–3333, ext. 3341) has parasailing and rents Wave Runners, kayaks, boogie boards, sailboats, and banana boats. They also arrange four-hour boat trips to Isla de los Venados aboard *el Colonage*, docked at Hotel Marina el Cid.

Parque Acuático Mazaguas (✉ Av. Sábalo Cerritos and Entronque Habal Cerritos, ☎ 6/988–0041 or 6/988–0152) has water slides, wading pools, and a pool with man-made waves—a total of 20 water activities on 4 acres. Entrance is about $8 per person.

Spectator Sports

BASEBALL

The people of Mazatlán loyally support their team, **Los Venados** (☎ 6/981–1710), a Pacific League Triple A team. Regular season games are played at the Teodoro Mariscal Baseball Stadium (✉ Blvd. Justo Sierra, Zona Estadio) October through December.

BULLFIGHTS AND CHARREADAS

Bullfights are held most Sunday afternoons at 3:30 from December through May at the bullring on Calzada Rafael Buelna. *Charreadas* (rodeos) take place year-round. Tickets (about $10–$20) are available at the **bullring** (☎ 6/986–4949), through most hotels and travel agencies, and from Valentino's.

Shopping

Zona Dorada

Mazatlán may not be a shopper's mecca, but like most Mexican resort towns, it has a range of souvenirs and folk art from around the country. Some of the best shops are located in the Zona Dorada, particularly along Avenidas Camarón Sábalo and Rodolfo T. Loaiza, where you can buy everything from piñatas to silver jewelry from Taxco.

CRAFTS

A good place for browsing is the **Mazatlán Arts and Crafts Center** (✉ Av. Rodolfo T. Loaiza 417, ☎ 6/913–2120), originally designed as a place to view artisans at work. The center, open 9–6, has a good sampling of the city's souvenir selection—onyx chess sets, straw sombreros, leather jackets, sandals, coconut masks, and Mickey Mouse piñatas.

Possibly Mazatlán's most beautiful shop is **Gallery Michael** (⊠ Camarón Sábalo 19, ☎ 6/916–7816), with several rooms of tastefully chosen folk art, religious icons, and jewelry.

Dealers Ron and Teresa Tammekand represent a number of top artists at **Mazatlán Art Gallery** (⊠ Plaza Balboa, Av. Camarón Sábalo 4480, ☎ 6/914–3612) and hold one-person shows in winter.

If seeing floor-to-ceiling shells that have been glued, strung, and molded into every imaginable form—from lamps to necklaces to kitschy statuettes—interests you, you'll love **Sea Shell City** (⊠ Av. Rodolfo T. Loaiza 407, ☎ 6/913–1301), a rather tacky seashell emporium.

JEWELRY

Madonna (⊠ Av. Las Garzas 1 at Calle Laguna, ☎ 6/914–2389) displays an extensive collection of silver and gold jewelry as well as masks and handicrafts.

Rubio Jewelers (⊠ Costa de Oro hotel, Av. Camarón Sábalo s/n, ☎ 6/914–3167) carries fine gold, silver, and platinum jewelry as well as ceramics. It's also Mazatlán's exclusive distributor of Sergio Bustamante's whimsical sculptures of ceramics and bronze.

Downtown

The gigantic **Mercado Central,** between Calles Juárez, Ocampo, Serdán, and Leandro Valle, is open daily and filled with produce, pungent meat and fish, and a sprinkling of handicrafts. While the latter are more along the lines of souvenirs than fine folk art, it's fun to search the market for great buys.

Nidart gallery and workshop (⊠ Libertad 45 and Carnaval, ☎ 6/981–0002) shows and sells handcrafted leather masks, ceramic figurines and sculptures, contemporary black-and-white photos, and other Mexican arts and crafts in a beautiful setting. Artisans can be seen producing these wares in open workshops. The gallery and workshop are open Monday–Saturday 10–2.

Mazatlán A to Z

AIR TRAVEL

You can fly to Mazatlán from major U.S. cities including Houston, Los Angeles, and Denver, or from Mexico City or other cities in Mexico.

CARRIERS

Aeroméxico has daily flights from multiple U.S. and Mexican cities. Alaska Airlines flies direct daily from Los Angeles. Continental flies daily, direct from Houston. AeroCalifornia has direct flights twice weekly from Los Angeles, and daily from La Paz, Guadalajara, and Mexico City. Mexicana flies in daily from Mexico City; twice weekly direct from Denver, and daily from Los Angeles with a stop in Los Cabos. America West links Mazatlán with Phoenix.
➤ AIRLINES AND CONTACTS: **AeroCalifornia** (☎ 6/913–2042). **Aeroméxico** (☎ 6/982–3444). **Alaska Airlines** (☎ 6/985–2730 or 001-800/426–0333). **America West** (☎ 01-800/363–2597). **Continental** (☎ 001-800/525–1700). **Mexicana** (☎ 6/982–5666).

AIRPORTS AND TRANSFERS

Mazatlán's Rafael Buelna International Airport is served by several airlines. The airport is a good 40-minute drive from town.

➤ AIRPORT INFORMATION: **Rafael Buelna International Airport** (☎ 6/982–2177).

AIRPORT TRANSFERS

Autotransportes Aeropuerto charges about $19 for a private car and $5 per person on its Volkswagen van shuttles into town. Private taxis charge approximately $19.

➤ TAXIS AND SHUTTLES: **Autotransportes Aeropuerto** (☎ 6/981–5554).

BOAT AND FERRY TRAVEL

Ferry service between La Paz and Mazatlán is fairly reliable. The car-and-passenger ferry takes about 17 hours to reach La Paz. One-way fares start at $37.50 for regular passage and $300 per car. Check the schedule and purchase tickets in advance, as the schedule is subject to change.

Royal Caribbean, Holland America, and Princess, among other cruise lines, include Mazatlán on their 7-day Mexican Riviera cruises.

➤ BOAT AND FERRY INFORMATION: **Ferry service** (✉ Prong. Carnaval s/n, Fracc. Playa Sur, ☎ 6/981–7020 or 01–800/696–9600).

BUS TRAVEL

The Mazatlán bus terminal is on Carretera Internacional 1203, three blocks behind the Sands Hotel. Elite, one of the area's best bus lines, has service to the U.S. border and south to Guadalajara and Mexico City. Estrellas del Pacífico serves western Mexico.

Buses and minibuses run frequently along all main avenues. Fares start at about 30¢ and increase slightly depending on the destination.

➤ BUS INFORMATION: **Elite** (☎ 6/981–3811). **Estrellas del Pacífico** (☎ 6/984–2817).

CAR RENTAL

The following rental firms have desks at Rafael Buelna International Airport as well as the addresses given here. Hertz rents cars and trucks. Budget has the usual assortment of vehicles. National has cars at the cruise ship terminal (no phone) as well as two Zona Dorada locations. They rent everything from VW Beetles and compacts without air-conditioning to Suburbans and 4x4s.

➤ MAJOR AGENCIES: **Hertz** (✉ Av. Camarón Sábalo 314, ☎ 6/913–4955). **Budget** (✉ Av. Camarón Sábalo 402, ☎ 6/913–2000). **National** (✉ Av. Camarón Sábalo 7000, ☎ 6/913–6000, ✉ El Camar shopping center, Av. Camarón Sábalo s/n, ☎ 6/984–4077).

CAR TRAVEL

Mazatlán is 1,212 km (751 mi) from the border city of Nogales, Arizona, via Mexico Route 15, either on the good but quite expensive toll road or on the federal highway. At least one overnight stop is recommended.

EMBASSIES

Agents of the U.S. Consul can be reached weekdays 9–1. The Canadian Consulate is also open weekdays 9–1.

➤ CANADA: **Canadian Consulate** (✉ Av. Rodolfo T. Loaiza 202, ☎ 6/913–7320).

➤ UNITED STATES: **U.S. Consul** (✉ Av. Rodolfo T. Loaiza 202, ☎ 6/916–5889).

EMERGENCIES

Dial **060** for all emergencies. Sharp Hospital, at Calzada Rafael Buelna at Avenida Dr. Jesus Cumate, has English-speaking doctors.

➤ CONTACTS: **Toll-free medical or travel advice** (☎ 01–800/903–9200). **Sharp Hospital** (☎ 6/986–5676).

ENGLISH-LANGUAGE MEDIA

The best place for English-language paperbacks, dictionaries, and maps is Mazatlán Book and Coffee Company, across from the Costa de Oro Hotel behind Banco Santander Mexicano. The store is open daily 9–7 and has copies of Mazatlán's English newspaper, *Pacific Pearl*.
➤ BOOKSTORE: **Mazatlán Book and Coffee Company** (☎ 6/916–7899).

MAIL, INTERNET, AND SHIPPING

The main post office is downtown, across from the main plaza. However, if you are in the Zona Dorada, it's easier to go to Mail Boxes Etc., which offers fax and e-mail services in addition to regular postal services.
➤ MAIL SERVICES: **Mail Boxes Etc.** (✉ Av. Camarón Sábalo 310, ☎ 9/916–4009). **Post office** (✉ Juárez at 21 de Marzo, ☎ 6/981–2121).

TAXIS

Most tourist hotels are located in the Zona Dorada, about 3 km (2 mi) north of downtown, but taxis cruise the strip regularly. Fares start at $3. A fun way to get around is on the *pulmonías* (VW Beetles without tops), so you can sunbathe and take pictures as you cruise along, although there are no windows to raise against rain or automobile fumes. The fare, for up to three passengers, starts at about $3 and increases according to the distance of the trip.

TOURS

Two- or three-hour city tours, which generally cost $15–$25, are a good way to get the lay of the land; the historical section downtown is small but interesting.

Bay cruises are available daily (except Monday) aboard *Costalegre* at 11 AM. Tickets are $14 and include round-trip transportation from Zona Dorada hotels and two drinks aboard. Centro Aquatico El Cid offers tours to Isla de los Venados including lunch and, for those who wish, snorkeling and kayaking (4 hours, $35). Viajes el Sábalo runs a five-hour bay tour ending at Isla de la Piedra, with time for lunch and a swim. Included in the $28 price are a choice of two activities; choose from snorkeling, horseback riding, or banana boats.

Also available are country tours to Concordia and Copala (about $28–$35, including lunch). Marlin Tours runs an eight-hour excursion ($42) ending in Teacapan, near the Nayarit border. The bus tour makes stops in towns, ranches, and sometimes a thermal spring, and includes Continental breakfast and drinks. Lunch at a seaside restaurant and an optional boat ride of the estuary are not included in the price.
➤ TOUR OPERATOR RECOMMENDATIONS: **Centro Aquatico El Cid**, ☎ 6/913–3333, ext. 3341). **Costalegre** (☎ 6/916–5747).

TRAVEL AGENCIES

American Express offers local tours and sells airline tickets. Marlin Tours offers a variety of city, bay, and country tours. Viajes el Sábalo is another longtime tour operator. Agencies are generally open weekdays 10–2 and 4–7, Saturday 10–2.
➤ LOCAL AGENT REFERRALS: **American Express** (✉ Av Camarón Sbalo s/n, Plaza Balboa, ☎ 6/913–0600). **Marlin Tours** (✉ Calle Laguna 300, ☎ 6/913–5301). **Viajes el Sábalo** (✉ Los Sábalos shopping center, ☎ 6/983–1933 or 6/913–1111; ✉ Hotel Los Sbalos, ☎ 6/981–3009).

VISITOR INFORMATION

The State Tourism Office is open weekdays 9–5.
➤ TOURIST INFORMATION: **State Tourism Office** (✉ Av. Camarón Sábalo, Banrural Bldg., 4th floor, ☎ 6/916–5160 through 6/916–5165).

PUERTO VALLARTA

On the edge of the Sierra Madre range sits one of the most popular vacation spots in Mexico. When Puerto Vallarta first entered the public's consciousness, with John Huston's 1964 movie *The Night of the Iguana,* it seemed an almost mythical paradise. At the time it was a quiet fishing and farming community in an exquisite tropical setting.

Puerto Vallarta's Bahía de Banderas attracted pirates and explorers as early as the 1500s; it was used as a stopover on long trips as a place for the crew to relax (or maybe plunder and pillage). Sir Francis Drake apparently stopped here. In the mid-1850s, Don Guadalupe Sánchez Carrillo developed the bay as a port for the silver mines by the Río Cuale. Then it was known as Puerto de Peñas and had about 1,500 inhabitants. In 1918 it was made a municipality and renamed for Ignacio L. Vallarta, a governor of Jalisco. "Puerto" is Spanish for port.

In the 1950s Puerto Vallarta was essentially a pretty hideaway for those in the know—the wealthy and some hardy escapists. After the publicity brought on by *The Night of the Iguana,* tourism began to boom. PV—as the former fishing village is called these days—is now a city with some 250,000 residents. Airports, hotels, and highways have supplanted palm groves and fishing shacks. About 3 million people visit each year, and from November through April cobblestone streets are clogged with pedestrians and cars. There are now more than 16,000 hotel rooms in Puerto Vallarta, with another 4,000 in Nuevo Vallarta, on the northern edge of the enormous bay, in Nayarit state.

Despite the transformation, every attempt has been made to keep the town's character and image intact. City ordinances require houses in town to be painted white, with restrictions on number of floors and architectural details. Houses with red-tile roofs perch on hills above the glistening blue bay and line the streets downtown, where pack mules still occasionally clop down the cobblestone streets. Within 16 km (10 mi) of town are rocky coves, rushing rivers, and steep mountain roads that curve and twist through jungles of pines and palms.

Exploring Puerto Vallarta

Central Puerto Vallarta has several major components. North of town, hotels and resorts surround Marina Vallarta, a public marina sharing space with restaurants, condos, and stores. Downtown, aka Viejo Vallarta, is the heart of the old city, where many two- and three-story houses have been converted to shops, galleries, and restaurants. Dividing downtown in two is el Río Cuale. This river—which ranges from ebullient to anemic, depending on the rains—embraces a sliver of an island with cultural center, museum, restaurants, and shops. Beginning just south of the river, Playas Olas Altas and Los Muertos are two beaches backed by lively outdoor restaurants and modest hotels.

A cab or rental car is helpful to fully explore the hotel zone—a long stretch of shopping centers, restaurants, and hotels—although buses cruise continually up and down as well. A car is a serious hindrance, however, downtown and in the Río Cuale area. Most of the interesting sights can be covered on foot—just be sure you wear comfortable shoes for the cobblestone streets.

Numbers in the text correspond to numbers in the margin and on the Puerto Vallarta map.

A Good Walk

When you start seeing cobblestone streets, you're in the downtown area, also known as **Old Town,** or Viejo Vallarta. This is the heart of PV, a vestige of old Puerto Vallarta. Start your walk at the northern end of the delightful **malecón** ⑧, which runs parallel to Díaz Ordáz beginning at 31 de Octubre. Nine blocks south, Díaz Ordáz merges with Calle Morelos at the old lighthouse tower. Two blocks farther south is the town's main square, Plaza de Armas. On the northern side of the busy, tree-shaded plaza you'll see the **Palacio Municipal** ⑨ (City Hall), and one block east, **La Iglesia de Nuestra Señora de Guadalupe** ⑩, which is topped by a distinctive crown. Los Arcos Amphitheater, across the street from the plaza on the malecón, is host to a number of concerts and other open-air performances. Local artists show their wares here in the evenings.

Head south a few blocks and turn left on A. Rodríguez. After a few blocks you'll come to the bustling **Mercado Municipal** at the foot of the upper bridge over the Río Cuale. The steep hillside above, dotted with vine-drenched villas, is called **Gringo Gulch** ⑪. Reach it by climbing the steps on Calle Zaragoza. In the middle of the Río Cuale lies the **Isla Río Cuale** ⑫ (accessible by bridges for both pedestrians and autos), an inviting place for dining, strolling, and shopping.

Sights to See

⑨ **Palacio Municipal** (City Hall). The late Manuel Lepe's 1981 mural depicting Puerto Vallarta as a fanciful seaside fishing and farming village hangs above the stairs on city hall's second floor. Puerto Vallarta's most famous artist, Lepe is known for his blissful, primitive-style scenes of the city, filled with smiling angels. The tourism office is on the first floor. ⊠ *Av. Juárez by zócalo.* ☉ *Weekdays 9–5.*

⑪ **Gringo Gulch.** Named after the hundreds of U.S. expats who settled here in the 1950s and '60s, this neighborhood's most famous attraction is Elizabeth Taylor's former home, **Casa Kimberly.** It's connected to Richard Burton's former home across the street by a pink-and-white "love bridge" he had constructed. Part of the house has been converted into an unattractive bed-and-breakfast, but its other areas can be toured daily 9–6. Burton bought the 24,000-square-ft home for Taylor's 32nd birthday after their much-publicized romance during his filming of *The Night of the Iguana* with Ava Gardner, Deborah Kerr, and Sue Lyon. Taylor owned the house for 26 years, and left 98 percent of her possessions behind (all on display) when she sold it in 1990. ⊠ *Calle Zaragoza 445,* ☎ 𝖥𝖠𝖷 *3/222–1336.* 🖼 *$6.*

⑩ **La Iglesia de Nuestra Señora de Guadalupe** (Church of Our Lady of Guadalupe). The town's main church is topped by an ornate crown that replicates the one worn by Carlota, the empress of Mexico in the late 1860s. The crown toppled during the earthquake that shook this area of the Pacific Coast in October 1995, and was quickly replaced with a fiberglass version in time for the celebration of the Feast of the Virgin of Guadalupe (December 12). ⊠ *Calle Hidalgo, 1 block east of zócalo.* ☉ 7:30 AM–8 PM.

⑫ **Isla Río Cuale** (Cuale River Island). Surrounded by the Río Cuale, this island effectively slices the downtown area in two. It has an outdoor marketplace as well as trendy restaurants and inexpensive cafés. A bronze statue of film director John Huston dominates the central plaza. Just beyond the statue at the east end of the island, the **Casa de la Cultura** sells the work of local artists, offers art and dance classes, and hosts cultural events. The **Museo Arqueológico** (⊠ western tip of island, ☎ no phone) hosts a small collection of pre-Columbian figures and In-

340

Puerto Vallarta

TO AIRPORT,
MARINA VALLARTA,
NUEVO VALLARTA, AND
BEACHES OF NAYARIT

200

Bahía de Banderas

Díaz Ordáz
Jesús Langarica
31 de Octubre
Allende
Pípila
L. Vicario
Matamoros
Miramar
Morelos
Abasolo
Aldama
Corona
E. Carranza

8

9

Plaza de
Armas

Juárez
Z. Hidalgo Galeana
Zaragoza
Iturbide
Guerrero

10

Casa
Kimberly

Libertad
A. Rodríguez
Encino

11

Río Cuale

12

Aquiles
Serdán
Madero
Ignacio Vallarta
Lázaro
Constitución
Av. Insurgentes
Cárdenas
Carranza
Basilio
Aguacate
Badillo

Venustiano
Calle
Francisca Rodríguez

Playa
Olas Altas

Olas Altas

Pier

El
Púlpito

Púlpito

Cafeta

Playa de
los Muertos

Amapas

TO SAN SEBASTIÁN
DEL OESTE

Carretera a Mismaloya

N

TO PLAYA LAS ÁNIMAS,
BOCA DE TOMATLÁN,
MANZANILLO, QUIMIXTO,
YELAPA

0   500 meters

0   500 yards

dian artifacts. The museum is open daily 10–6. ⊠ *To reach Isla Río Cuale from north side of town, cross bridge at Encino and Juárez or at Libertad and Miramar. From the south, cross at Ignacio L. Vallarta and Aquiles Serdán, or at Insurgentes and Aquiles Serdán.*

❽ Malecón. The malecón is downtown's main drag, a nice place to rest on a white wrought-iron bench. A seawall and sidewalk run along the bay, and restaurants, cafés, and shops are across the street. You'll see some interesting sculpture along the walkway—among other pieces, the bronze sea horse that has become Puerto Vallarta's trademark, and *La Nostalgia,* a bronze statue of a seated couple, inspired by the love life of author Ramiz Barquet. The latest sculptural addition is **Rotunda del Mar,** a collection of whimsical statues by artist Alejandro Colunga. ⊠ *Parallel to Díaz Ordáz, extending about 16 blocks from Río Cuale northeast to 31 de Octubre.*

Beaches

Puerto Vallarta's stellar attraction is its amazing beaches: crescents of golden sand fringed with palms along the hotel zone; endless stretches of gloriously unpopulated beaches to the north; and soft creamy beaches on craggy coves to the south. Near downtown, Olas Altas and Los Muertos—popular with visitors, families, and vendors—are closest to all that downtown has to offer, including shops, budget hotels, and sidewalk cafés. Beaches below are described in order from the southern part of the bay to the north.

Playa Las Ánimas and beyond. Yelapa, Quimixto, and Playa de Las Ánimas are three secluded fishing villages accessible by boat. Yelapa is approximately an hour southeast of downtown; Quimixto and Las Ánimas are a bit to the north. From the beach at Yelapa, take a 20-minute hike into the jungle to see the waterfalls. Quimixto's beautiful beach boasts calm, clear waters. Horses can be rented for a 15-minute ride to a spectacular large clear pool under a waterfall for swimming. Day excursions visit these beaches daily from the Marina Vallarta cruise ship terminal; or, hire a motor launch from Tomatlán ($43 round trip for 1–6 people to Playa Las Ánimas; about $86 to Yelapa). Water taxis ($6.50 round-trip) depart the pier at Los Muertos at 10:30 and 11 AM for Yelapa and return to pick you up at 3 or 4 PM.

Boca de Tomatlán. This small village at the mouth of the Río Tomatlán (Tomatlán River) is about 17 km (10½ mi) south of Puerto Vallarta and 4 km (2½ mi) south of Mismaloya. Just off the coast road down a short but bumpy dirt driveway is a beautiful, generally uncrowded cove. Both locals and visitors enjoy the scene while relaxing at one of several palapa restaurants on the sand. Water taxis leave from Boca to Los Arcos and the more secluded beaches of Playa Las Ánimas and Yelapa. About halfway between Boca and Playa de Mismaloya, Chee Chee's, a massive, terraced restaurant and swimming-pool complex, spreads down a steep hillside like a small village. Next door, similarly terraced Le Kliff restaurant is a great spot for a sunset cocktail. Just south of Boca is Chico's Paradise, and a bit farther on, Las Orquidias. Both are riverfront restaurants where you can swim in clear river pools and delight in the tropical vegetation.

Playa de Mismaloya. This once pristine cove is where "the movie" was made. The 13-km (8-mi) drive south from the center of town on Highway 200 passes spectacular houses, some of PV's oldest and quietest resorts, and a slew of condo and time-share developments. You can take a taxi or one of the bright green Mismaloya buses from Calles Vallarta and Badillo, in downtown PV. Although the jungle-fringed cove was spoiled by the construction of La Jolla de Mismaloya (a huge hotel complex), it still affords a good view of Los Arcos, an offshore rock formation popular with skin and scuba divers. From Mismaloya you can catch a cab inland 2 km (1 mi) on the dirt road to the jungle restaurant Chico's Paradise.

Playa Olas Altas and Playa de los Muertos. These two contiguous beaches south of the Río Cuale have long been a budget traveler's domain, although they have some of the more expensive restaurants and shops. Proximity to lively sidewalk bars and cafés here have made them the most popular and crowded beaches in Puerto Vallarta. Long ago, Playa de los Muertos was the site of a battle between pirates and Indians, hence the name, which means "Beach of the Dead." The area around the beach is now promoted as the Zona Romántica, but locals still call it Los Muertos. Strolling vendors selling lace tablecloths, wooden statues, kites, and jewelry are almost as abundant as sunbathers. Beach toys for rent include everything from rubber inner tubes to windsurfers. To the south, Playa de los Muertos ends at a rocky point called El Púlpito. Walking up the steps (more than 100) at the east end of Púpito street leads to a lookout with a great view of the beach and the bay.

La Zona Hotelera. Stretching north from downtown to the marina and cruise-ship terminal area is a string of beaches often collectively called "la zona hotelera," or hotel zone. The beach changes a bit with the character of each hotel it fronts, but it is particularly nice by the Fiesta Americana and the Krystal hotels.

Nuevo Vallarta and Nayarit. When PV swells with tourists, local families head out of town to relax and play on the unpopulated beaches at the north end of Bahía de Banderas, in the state of Nayarit. Twelve kilometers (7 miles) north of Nuevo Vallarta (Puerto Vallarta's newest hotel and marina development, which is actually in Nayarit), on yet another beautiful beach, is the simple town of **Bucerías,** where a loyal flock of snowbirds has encouraged the growth of small hotels and restaurants. Beyond Bucerías there are long stretches of deserted beach around **Cruz de Huanacaxtle** and **La Manzanilla,** where kids play in the shallow waters while their parents sip beer or soft drinks at beachfront restaurants. **Destiladeras** is a long, semi-rocky beach with good surf. The coast road continues to the popular beach at **El Anclote,** with simple restaurants. Just beyond El Anclote is **Punta de Mita,** on the northern tip of Bahía de Banderas. Home of the posh Four Seasons Resort, Punta de Mita has blue bay water that's nice for swimming; around the bend are waves for surfing. This is a prime spot for viewing a sunset and, during the winter months, the whales that come here to mate in the warm waters of the Mexican Pacific. Scuba divers like the fairly clear waters and abundance of tropical fish and coral on the bay side of the Isla Marietas, about a half hour offshore.

From Punta de Mita, a dirt road can be slowly traversed in dry weather to **Sayulita** (which can also be reached in about 45 minutes from Puerto Vallarta by staying on Highway 200 past Bucerías). In addition to hotels and restaurants, Sayulita has excellent surfing and a great beach hidden behind a hill only 10 minutes on foot north of the town center. Some say Sayulita is like Puerto Vallarta 40 years ago. Fifteen minutes north of Sayulita is **San Francisco,** unofficially known as San Pancho, with modest rental bungalows and eateries and a 1½-km- (1-mi-) long, barely developed stretch of beach. A half hour beyond San Francisco, the pretty beach at **Lo de Marcos** is popular with surfers.

Dining

Wonderful restaurants are concentrated downtown, especially along the part of Calle Basilio Badillo known as "restaurant row," one block south of Parque Lázaro Cárdenas in the Olas Altas area.

$$$$ ✕ **Café des Artistes.** A beautiful garden with a breathtaking view of the Pacific, this is Puerto Vallarta's most sophisticated—and expensive—dining spot. Owner/chef Thierry Blouet, formerly head chef at Hotel Camino Real's La Perla Restaurant, blends Mexican ingredients with European techniques to produce such interesting combinations as cream of prawn and pumpkin soup, mussels in a scallop mousse, and roast duck with soy and honey. A piano/flute duo provides musical accompaniment. ⊠ *Guadalupe Sánchez 740,* ☎ *3/222–3228. Reservations essential. AE, MC, V. No lunch.*

$$$$ ✕ **River Cafe.** Candles flicker at romantic tables lining the riverbank, and tiny white lights wrap the palm trees surrounding the restaurant's multilevel terrace. Attentive waiters serve such international dishes as steak, lobster, and pasta to a well-dressed crowd. If you're not into a romantic dinner, stop in for breakfast, or belly up to the intimate bar for a drink. ⊠ *Isla Río Cuale, Local 4,* ☎ *3/223–0788. AE, MC, V.*

$$$ ✕ **Adobe Café.** Minimalist decor in shades of white and earth tones, stark trees, and fresh flowers make for a delightful dining experience. The menu is interesting and varied, and dishes are cleverly presented. Specialties include black bean soup, pork tenderloin in rum, and one of the best desserts in town: a sinfully rich chocolate mousse between two layers of chocolate cake and chocolate icing. ⊠ *Calle Basilio Badillo 252,* ☎ *3/222–6720. MC, V. Closed Tues. Closed June–Sept. No lunch.*

$$$ ✕ **Café Maximilian.** Efficient and fluid service accompanied by genuine smiles from both diners and staff make this a top spot to eat around Olas Altas. Viennese and other European entrées dominate the menu, including braised baby lamb strips with rosemary and an excellent pork loin escallop with homemade noodles. These items can also be ordered from the delightful, European-style coffee house next door, open all day and specializing in desserts and sandwiches. ⊠ *Olas Altas 380,* ☎ *3/223–0760. AE, MC, V. Closed Sun. No lunch.*

$$$ ✕ **Chef Roger.** The cozy patio of a typical Puerto Vallarta house is the ★ unpretentious setting for one of the best restaurants in town. Roger Dreier, the Swiss owner and chef, combines his European training with Mexican ingredients, and the results are superb. Don't leave town without trying the pork tips "Zurich style," served in a light mushroom sauce with rosti potatoes (a grated-potato pancake), and for dessert, the fried apples with vanilla sauce. ⊠ *Calle Basilio Badillo 180,* ☎ *3/222–5900. AE, MC, V. Closed Sun. No lunch.*

$$$ ✕ **Daiquiri Dick's.** The beachside patio dining room of this longtime *vallartense* favorite frames one of the best views of the bay at Playa de los Muertos. It's especially popular for the lively Sunday brunch. The Caesar salad explodes with flavor, and the medallions of beef tenderloin demi-glacé and the lobster tacos are superb. Finish off with a hazelnut daiquiri. ⊠ *Olas Altas 314,* ☎ *3/222–0566. MC, V. Closed Wed. May–Nov.*

$$$ ✕ **Trio.** Two young German chefs, Bernhard Guth and Peter Lodes, have ★ become the favorites of local diners with their avant-garde Mediterranean creations—such as orange-crusted sea bass with a sweet purée of garbanzo, dates, olives, and cider, or the rack of lamb and ravioli with lamb ragout, vegetables, and mint sauce. The artsy crowd and professional staff make for a wonderful dining experience (not to mention the air-conditioning, live jazz during dinner, and great downtown location). The kitchen often stays open until midnight, and there's a

rooftop terrace on which to dine or have drinks. ⊠ *Guerrero 264,* ☎ *3/222–2196. AE, DC, MC, V.*

$$ ✕ **Archie's Wok.** Although the lumpia can be limp and the salads overdressed, the Asian-fusion cuisine here is a great break from Continental and Mexican food. International music at a discreet level permits conversation, and ceiling fans rustle the lacy limbs of potted ferns and palms. There are plenty of choices for noncarnivores, including stir-fry pastas with green veggies and mushrooms, Chinese sesame cucumber salad, and Vietnamese fish in banana leaves. ⊠ *Francisca Rodriguez 130,* ☎ *3/222–0411. AE, MC, V. Closed Sun.*

$$ ✕ **Don Pedro's.** Everything is a treat at this giant beachfront palapa
★ in Sayulita, a half hour north of the airport, where European-trained chef and co-owner Nicholas Parrillo serves an array of fish, seafood, and poultry sprinkled with herbs and grilled over mesquite. From the crusty herbed breads and pizzas to the rich mango ice cream, everything is fresh as can be and made on the premises. ⊠ *Calle Marlin 2, midway along Sayulita town beach, 35 km (22 mi) north of Puerto Vallarta airport,* ☎ *3/275–0229. AE, MC, V. Closed Aug.–Oct.*

$$ ✕ **Felipe's.** Sitting high on a hill, Felipe Palacio's gracious family home has the charm of old Vallarta mixed with spectacular views of the bay and town from its multilevel terraces. Try the grilled seafood, or the superbly prepared steaks served with baked potato and veggies. ⊠ *Av. Insurgentes 466, Col. Alta Vista,* ☎ *3/222–3820. AE, MC, V. Closed Sun. No lunch.*

$$ ✕ **Flaming Sombrero.** Grill your own marinated beef, lamb, chicken, pork, marlin, or prawns on a huge searing brass sombrero at the table with vegetables sizzling on the rim. The drink of the house is a Nicholashka: chew a slice of lime with ground coffee and sugar and take a shot of vodka. ⊠ *31 de Octubre 380–D,* ☎ *3/222–5595. MC, V. Closed Mon. No lunch.*

$–$$ ✕ **Chico's Paradise.** It's easy to while away hours—or even the day—
★ under the huge, multilevel palapa, enjoying the sound of the waterfall, taking a dip in the river, or watching tortillas being made by hand. Seafood, including fresh jumbo shrimp and stuffed crab, is a specialty, but *chiles rellenos* (stuffed chili peppers) and chicken burritos are also popular. Or just come for some of the huge tropical drinks. In the off season, Chico's closes just after sunset. ⊠ *Carretera a Manzanillo Km 20,* ☎ *3/222–0747. No credit cards.*

$ ✕ **Andale.** An Olas Altas hangout and a good spot for an afternoon beer with the locals, this restaurant serves giant shrimp, great herb-garlic bread, and delicious black-bean soup as well as nightly drink specials at the chummy bar. Despite the open storefront, the inside is cool, dark, and informal; two rows of tables line the narrow outdoor patio. ⊠ *Olas Altas 425,* ☎ *3/222–1054. MC, V.*

$ ✕ **La Bodeguita del Medio.** Near the north end of the malecón, this attractive, relatively new restaurant/bar has a view of the sea from the second-floor dining room. Like its Havana namesake (established in 1942), La Bodeguita del Medio sells Cuban rum and cigars, while the music, naturally, is pure Caribbean. The menu changes seasonally—try the roast pork shank or chicken with new potatoes and broccoli in wine sauce. ⊠ *Paseo Díaz Ordaz 858,* ☎ *3/223–1584 or 3/223–1585. No credit cards.*

$ ✕ **Cafe de Olla.** This is the place for cheap, down-to-earth Mexican food—
★ enchiladas, *carne asada* (grilled strips of marinated meat), and chiles rellenos. Service is excellent and the atmosphere inviting: trees extend from the dining-room floor through the roof, local artwork adorns the walls, and salsa music often plays in the background. The restaurant is hugely popular and you may need to wait a short while for a table. ⊠ *Calle Basilio Badillo 168-A,* ☎ *3/223–1626. No credit cards. Closed Tues.*

$ ✕ **Really Rosie's Restaurant and Cantina.** This is where to go if you want a taste of home. With a menu listing homemade corned-beef hash, biscuits and gravy, and cheese blintzes for breakfast—and meat loaf and country-fried steak and mashed potatoes among other dinner favorites—Rosie Sorrenson's food will soothe you if you're wearying of the exotic. Its new, expanded upstairs digs also includes a welcoming bar. Don't feel like going out? Rosie's delivers. ⊠ *Olas Altas 307,* ☎ *3/223–2048. AE, MC, V.*

Lodging

Most of PV's deluxe resorts are to the north of downtown. Many are concentrated in the Marina Vallarta complex, practically a town unto itself with a 355-slip marina, hundreds of condominiums, shopping centers, an 18-hole golf course, the Royal Pacific Yacht Club, and the cruise ship pier. Farther north is Nuevo Vallarta, just over the state line in Nayarit, at the mouth of the Río Ameca. This beautiful community with beachfront houses and condos on canals with direct access to the bay is home to several all-inclusive resorts. South of downtown and the Río Cuale, around Olas Altas and Playa de los Muertos, the rates are lower. If you head farther south still, the prices go up again: some spectacular properties are tucked away on hidden coves on the road to Manzanillo.

Rates at most hotels usually go down 25%–30% just after Easter week through December 15, although they may rebound during July and August when nationals take a two-week vacation. Reservations are a must at Christmas, New Year's, Easter, and in July and August.

$$$$ 🏨 **Camino Real.** One of PV's first hotels, this property sits on a lovely
★ small bay south of town. Rooms have cool marble floors with white furniture and bright pink, yellow, and purple highlights against stark white walls. The hotel has all the five-star touches—from plush robes in the rooms to the palapas on the beach and the fragrant white jasmine blooming along the natural waterfall. La Brisa restaurant serves superb seafood lunches; elegant, upscale La Perla has excellent international food and inspired desserts accompanied by a concert pianist. A newer 11-story tower houses the Camino Real Club, where guests receive upgraded amenities and breakfast on a terrace overlooking the ocean. ⊠ *Playa Las Estacas Km 3.5, 48300,* ☎ *3/221–5000 or 800/ 722–6466,* FAX *3/221–6000,* WEB *www.caminoreal.com. 326 rooms, 11 suites. 4 restaurants, 2 bars, 2 pools, wading pool, 2 tennis courts, gym, beach, children's programs (ages 5–10), meeting rooms, travel services. AE, DC, MC, V.*

$$$$ 🏨 **Continental Plaza Beach and Tennis Club.** This Mexican colonial complex went all-inclusive beginning 2001. There's a shopping plaza, several restaurants and bars, and a large swimming pool with little shade. Ideal for tennis lovers, it has a tennis club with eight courts and daily tennis clinics. Furnishings, however, are simple and motel-like, and few rooms in this four-story low-rise have an ocean view. ⊠ *Blvd. Francisco Medina Ascencio s/n, Zona Hotelera Las Glorias, 48300,* ☎ *3/ 224–0123 or 800/515–4321,* FAX *3/224–3932. 430 rooms. 3 restaurants, 2 bars, pool, gym, 8 tennis courts, beach. AE, DC, MC, V.*

$$$$ 🏨 **Fiesta Americana.** The dramatically designed terra-cotta building rises above a deep-blue pool that flows under bridges, palm oases, and palapa restaurants; a seven-story palapa covers the lobby and a large round bar. The ocean-view rooms have a modern pink and terra-cotta color scheme, and each has beige marble floors, tile bath with powerful shower, and balcony. The beach bustles with activity and equipment rentals. Located in the hotel zone, it's about halfway between the

Marina Vallarta complex and downtown. ⊠ *Blvd. Francisco Medina Ascencio Km 2.5, 48300,* ☎ *3/224–2010 or 800/343—7821,* ℻ *3/224–2108. 255 rooms, 36 suites. 2 restaurants, 3 bars, pool, beach, concierge, meeting rooms, travel services, car rental. AE, DC, MC, V.*

$$$$
★ **Four Seasons Resort.** Ensconced at the northern end of Bahía de Banderas, at Punta de Mita (a 40-minute drive northwest of the Puerto Vallarta International Airport), this hotel has been designed for exclusivity. Rooms (beginning at $600 per night) are housed in red-tile-roof Mexican-style casitas of one, two, and three stories. Furnished like luxurious Mexican homes and fitted with traditional Four Seasons amenities, rooms are spacious and feature private terraces or balconies with sweeping sea views. Most of the suites have private plunge pools as well as fax machines. The Jack Nicklaus–designed 18-hole championship golf course has a challenging, optional 19th island hole. Other sports facilities include tennis courts, a beautiful health club, and beach activities. ⊠ *Punta de Mita, Bahía de Banderas, Nayarit 63732,* ☎ *3/291–6000 or 800/819–5053,* ℻ *3/291–6060,* WEB *www.fourseasons.com. 140 rooms, 27 suites. 3 restaurants, 2 bars, in-room data ports, pool, wading pool, 18-hole golf course, 4 tennis courts, gym, horseback riding, snorkeling, windsurfing, children's programs (ages 5–12), concierge, meeting rooms, car rental. AE, DC, MC, V.*

$$$$ **La Jolla de Mismaloya.** Although the overpowering design of this resort has virtually ruined Mismaloya Bay for visitors, hotel guests have half the bay to themselves, as well as a fabulous view of Puerto Vallarta's famous Los Arcos rock formations. In its favor, the hotel's huge, brightly decorated one- and two-bedroom suites have terraces and well-equipped kitchens, and the many activities for children make it an ideal family getaway. Booked on the European Plan or as an all-inclusive, this hotel consistently gets high marks from guests. ⊠ *Zona Hotelera Sur Km 11.5, 48300,* ☎ *3/228–0660 or 800/322–2343,* ℻ *3/228–0853,* WEB *www.lajollademismaloya.com. 303 suites. 5 restaurants, bar, 4 pools, hot tub, spa, tennis court, exercise room, beach, dive shop, snorkeling, children's programs (ages 5–11), concierge, convention center, travel services, car rental. AE, MC, V.*

$$$$ **Krystal Vallarta.** A full-service resort that sprawls like a small town, the Krystal has pretty, bright hotel rooms and villas, many with private pools. The accommodations exude Mexican character, with tile floors and Spanish colonial-style furnishings. Not all rooms are by the ocean, but the secluded beach can accommodate all sunseekers. ⊠ *Carretera Aeropuerto, 48300,* ☎ *3/224–0202 or 800/231–9860,* ℻ *3/224–0111. 291 rooms, 114 villas. 5 restaurants, 3 bars, 3 pools, 2 tennis courts, beach, dance club, travel services. AE, DC, MC, V.*

$$$$ **Marriott Casa Magna.** Located on the beach in Marina Vallarta, this is one of Vallarta's largest and most glamorous hotels. The vast, plant-filled marble lobby is hung with wrought-iron chandeliers, the adjacent bar is wide open to the sea air and view, and the huge infinity pool is right on the beach. Rooms have polished and unpolished marble, blond woods, and floral-print spreads. And if the water sports, kid's club, and other hotel amenities aren't enough, you also have access to the facilities of the Marina Vallarta complex, including a huge shopping center, a yacht club, and more restaurants. ⊠ *Paseo de la Marina 5, 48354,* ☎ *3/221–0004 or 800/228–9290,* ℻ *3/221–0760,* WEB *www.marriott.com. 433 rooms, 29 suites. 4 restaurants, 3 bars, no-smoking rooms, pool, spa, 3 tennis courts, gym, beach, baby-sitting, children's programs (ages 5–12). AE, DC, MC, V.*

$$$$ **Meliá Puerto Vallarta.** On the beach in Marina Vallarta, this sprawling, top-of-the-line all-inclusive resort is only two blocks from the marina's 18-hole golf course. The soaring lobby is an odd blend of cool marble and tile floors, industrial-strength rust-and-marine-blue paint with lilac accents, and wicker furniture. The large rooms are more pleasingly decorated in soft natural tones of blue, cream, and sand; all have balconies with chairs. Amenities include the largest pool in the area, the Mini Club (for kids), an outdoor theater, and nightly shows. Two children under age seven can stay free (including meals and activities) if they share a room with their parents. ⊠ *Paseo de la Marina Sur 7, 48354,* ☎ *3/221–0200 or 800/336–3542,* FAX *3/221–0118. 380 rooms, 3 suites. 3 restaurants, 3 bars, pool, 2 tennis courts, archery, exercise room, beach, shops, video games, children's programs (ages 4–12), meeting room. AE, DC, MC, V.*

$$$$ 🏨 **Sierra Hotel Nuevo Vallarta.** Situated on a long, wide expanse of creamy sand beach in Nuevo Vallarta, the Sierra is a deluxe all-inclusive property. The rooms are light and airy, with tile floors, light-wood and wicker furniture, and the ubiquitous pastel bedspreads. Activities are nonstop: cookouts, beach parties, Mexican fiestas, disco blasts, theme nights, musicals, and karaoke. Daytime activities include aerobics, volleyball, tennis, minigolf, windsurfing, and kayaking, as well as jungle and city tours. A golf course is minutes away. ⊠ *Paseo de los Cocoteros 19, Nuevo Vallarta 63732,* ☎ *3/297–1300 or 800/448–5028,* FAX *3/297–1162. 350 rooms and suites. 3 restaurants, 3 bars, 2 pools, tennis court, aerobics, horseback riding, volleyball, beach, windsurfing, bicycles, billiards. AE, MC, V.*

$$$$ 🏨 **Westin Regina.** Architecturally dramatic, this elegant yet spare and ★ modern 14-story hotel sits on a choice 21-acre site in Marina Vallarta. In addition to four pools (one with semi-submerged tile "chaise lounges"), a long stretch of beach, and a full range of facilities and activities, the Westin has spacious balconied rooms with marble bathrooms and brightly colored, handwoven spreads and drapes. Rooms above the sixth floor have ocean views; those below face the 600 palm trees surrounding the beautiful pools. Cement-and-stone floors massage bare feet, and top-of-the-line mattresses with whisper-soft duvets make for heavenly siestas. Most suites have Jacuzzis. ⊠ *Paseo de la Marina Sur 205, 48321,* ☎ *3/221–1100 or 800/228–3000,* FAX *3/221–1121,* WEB *www.westin.com. 266 rooms, 14 suites. 2 restaurants, 3 bars, no-smoking rooms, 4 pools, spa, 3 tennis courts, gym, beach, baby-sitting, children's programs (ages 3–7), concierge, car rental. AE, DC, MC, V.*

$$$ 🏨 **Paradise Village.** Built like an Aztec pyramid, this Nuevo Vallarta hotel and time-share property has its own marina and hosts an international sailing regatta each March. All suites have tile floors and balconies with either marina or ocean views. Furnishings are functional: there are sofa beds and a full kitchen—including stove, microwave, coffeemaker, refrigerator, and plenty of cookware. Locals come by to visit the spa, which is noted for its massages and facials. ⊠ *Paseo de los Cocoteros 18, Nuevo Vallarta, 63732,* ☎ *3/297–0770,* FAX *3/297–0980. 510 suites. 2 restaurants, 4 bars, snack bar, 3 pools, spa, 4 tennis courts, aerobics, basketball, gym, volleyball, beach, jet skiing, windsurfing, travel services, car rental. AE, DC, MC, V.*

$$ 🏨 **Buenaventura.** An excellent value, this hotel has an ideal location ★ on the northern edge of downtown, about 10 blocks from the *malecón* and, in the opposite direction, the shops, hotels, and restaurants on the airport highway. The bright, cheerful rooms have beam ceilings and pale-wood furnishings. Many rooms have views of both arms of the bay, and some have equipped kitchenettes. A new seven-story luxury tower has six different styles of suites, many with Jacuzzis. An all-inclusive plan, adding just about $50 more per couple per night, includes food, drinks, room tax, and tip. ⊠ *Av. México 1301, 48350,* ☎ *3/222–3737 or 888/859–9439,* FAX *3/222–6242,* WEB *www.buenaventurahoteles.com. 199 rooms, 37 suites. 3 restaurants, 2 bars, 2 pools, hot tub, massage, beach, travel services, car rental. AE, DC, MC, V.*

$$ ▥ **Dulce Vida.** Popular with family groups as well as solo travelers,
★ this hidden villa four blocks off the bustling malecón has seven suites
of various sizes decorated with Mexican art and comfortable furniture.
All have well-equipped kitchens and most have ocean-view terraces;
the largest has two bedrooms, two baths, and a separate dining room.
There's a red-tile pool, tropical gardens, and Continental breakfast daily.
✉ *Calle Aldama 295, 48300,* ☎ *3/222–1008 or 800/600–6026,* FAX *3/
222–5815,* WEB *www.dulcevida.com. 7 suites. Pool. MC, V.*

$$ ▥ **Playa Los Arcos.** By far the most popular hotel on the beach near
the Río Cuale, the five-story Los Arcos has a friendly, casual air, and
an open central courtyard with pool. A glass elevator rises to the simple yet adequate and comfortable rooms, which are fitted with rustic
light-wood and pastel furnishings and have small balconies. There's
live music nightly until 11:30, and a Mexican fiesta on Saturday
evenings. ✉ *Olas Altas 380, 48380,* ☎ *3/222–0583,* FAX *3/222–2418.
170 rooms, 5 suites. Restaurant, bar, pool, beach. AE, MC, V.*

$$ ▥ **Villa Amor.** What began as a home on top of a hill transformed into
luxury palapa suites among the trees, with more outdoor than indoor
living and beautiful views of Sayulita's coast. Prices range from $50
for the least expensive (with hot plate and small fridge) to two-bed-
room suites with terrace and plunge pool for $250. The restaurant is
good and has live music on weekends. The hotel staff is quite friendly,
and a beautiful beach is just a short walk away. ✉ *Playa Sayulita,
Sayulita, Nayarit 63842,* ☎ *3/275–0196 or 888/295–1667,* FAX *3/275–
0263,* WEB *www.villaamor.com. 18 villas. Restaurant, snorkeling, surf-
ing. No credit cards.*

$ ▥ **Hotel Rosita.** Its lobby and oldest rooms remodeled in late 2000,
the city's first official hotel opened its doors in 1948. Since then, this
family-run business has served many repeat guests. On the northern
edge of the malecón, it's a great spot for budget travelers who want
to be close to the action. All rooms have air-conditioning. ✉ *Paseo Díaz
Ordaz 901, 48380,* WEB *www.hotelrosita.com,* ☎ FAX *3/223–2000 or
3/222–1033. 112 rooms. Restaurant, bar, pool. AE, MC, V.*

$ ▥ **Posada de Roger.** You'll enjoy the company of savvy budget trav-
elers from Europe and Canada hanging around the pool—an inter-
national meeting spot. The spare, simple rooms have telephones, TVs,
and air-conditioning; the showers are hot, the beds comfortable—if
you like a very firm mattress. The location a few blocks from Los Muer-
tos beach (and from "restaurant row") is a plus. ✉ *Basilio Badillo
237, 48380,* ☎ *3/222–0836 or 3/222–0639,* FAX *3/223–0482,* WEB
*www.puerto-vallarta.com/posada. 48 rooms. Restaurant, bar, pool.
AE, MC, V.*

En Route to Manzanillo

The coastline south of Puerto Vallarta is sprinkled with some of the Mex-
ican Riviera's most exclusive and secluded one-of-a-kind resorts. But
you'll never see them from Highway 200 as you head south—it's a rugged,
twisting road a short distance from the coast that runs through a trop-
ical forest of pines and palms. Most resorts are on unpaved roads. To
get there, fly to Puerto Vallarta or Manzanillo and take a taxi or hotel
van to your resort (which can run well over $100). Having arrived, you're
likely to stay put for a week or more, leaving only for the requisite shop-
ping spree in PV—or, for the well heeled, a chartered-plane shopping
spree to Tlaquepaque and Tonalá, outside Guadalajara.

Lodging

$$$$ ▥ **Las Alamandas.** Las Alamandas is defined by its personalized, at-
★ tentive service, and by its exclusivity. High prices lure movie stars and
Danish princes in search of a lovely but low-key environment far from

the hoi polloi. Surrounded by a nature preserve with abundant wildlife, the property's villas and suites are decorated with folk art and traditional Mexican furnishings. Among the outdoor activities are golf, horseback riding, fishing, and boat rides along the Río San Nicolás. Many guests fly in via the small airstrip; others take the hotel's limo from either the airport at Puerto Vallarta or Manzanillo —each about 1½ hours away. There's a two-night minimum; meal packages are available. ⊠ *A.P. 201, San Patricio Melaque, Jalisco 48980 (3525 Sage Rd., Houston, TX 77056);* ☎ *3/285–5500 or 888/882–9616,* ℻ *3/285–5027,* WEB *www.las-alamandas.com. 8 suites, 4 villas. 2 restaurants, 2 bars, pool, tennis court, croquet, exercise room, Ping-Pong, volleyball, beach, snorkeling, mountain bikes, shops, meeting room. AE, MC, V.*

$$$$ 🏨 **Hotelito Desconocido.** This isolated hotel on a long stretch of beach is an idyllic escape for Robinson Crusoes willing to pay a high price for simple pleasures. Individual *casitas* incorporate local building materials and styles, including plank floors, reed mats, bamboo walls, and palm frond roofs. Rustic-style bathrooms have tile floors; some overlook the estuary running through the property. Solar power runs essential equipment, but rooms are cooled only by battery-powered fans and lit by lanterns and candles, with no TV or telephone. In the morning, signal for coffee and croissants by running the flag up the flagpole. Meals (but not alcoholic beverages), bird-watching, yoga, horseback riding, kayaks, and other adventures included; massage, facials, and reflexology cost extra. ⊠ *Cruz de Loreto Tomatlán,* ☎ *3/222–2526 or 877/486–3372,* ℻ *3/223–0293,* WEB *www.hotelito.com, 19 rooms, 10 suites. 2 pools, spa, massage, beach, billiards. AE, MC, V.*

$$$$ 🏨 **El Tamarindo.** This magical resort, nestled in palm groves and sur-
★ rounded by more than 2,000 acres of ecological reserve and jungle, lies on 16 km (10 mi) of private coast. The 28 secluded villas, all with private plunge pools and outdoor living rooms, have been designed of regional materials and natural textures. Decorated in nubby fabrics, oiled wood, and other classy elements, the warm and casually elegant hotel embodies the "Careyes style" of architecture that first appeared in the 1960s, rendering simple design elements in local building materials. Activities include an oceanfront 18-hole golf course, a tennis club, and three secluded beaches. At night, the gracious staff lights more than 1,500 candles around the villas to create a truly enchanting setting. ⊠ *Melaque-Puerto Vallarta Hwy. Km 7.5, Cihuatlán, Jalisco 48970,* ☎ *3/351–5032,* ℻ *3/351–5070. 28 villas. Restaurant, bar, pool, 18-hole golf course, 2 tennis courts, beach, dive shop, snorkeling. AE, DC, MC, V.*

$$$ 🏨 **Careyes.** Resembling a boldly painted village nestled on a gorgeous bay, this pioneering resort is situated on Mexico's "Turtle Coast," 98 km (60 mi) north of Manzanillo airport and 172 km (107 mi) south of Puerto Vallarta. There are 51 recently renovated rooms and suites (some with private plunge pools) decorated in warm tones—yellow ochre, coral, and sapphire blue. The full-service spa features European beauty and body treatments and has a deli/snack bar selling fine wines, prosciutto, and other necessities of the good life. At the beach await a full range of water-sports equipment. Excursions can be made to lagoons, tropical forests, and Teapa Beach to see turtles breeding between July and October. ⊠ *Barra de Navidad Hwy. Km 53.5, Costa Careyes, Jalisco 48970,* ☎ *3/351–0000,* ℻ *3/351–0100,* WEB *www.careyes.com.mx. 48 rooms, 4 suites, 100 condominiums. Restaurant, bar, pool, spa, 2 tennis courts, gym, beach, snorkeling, boating, fishing. AE, DC, MC, V.*

$$$ 🏨 **Playa Blanca.** This Club Med has all the services the pioneer all-inclusive chain is known for, as well as fishing and horseback riding. The food, usually served buffet style, is ample and good, and there's a dinner-only restaurant with waiter service. The resort doesn't exactly feel isolated: with almost 300 rooms, a disco, and dance and aerobics classes, the ambience is more celebratory than somnolent. Guests, who tend to be earthy, active people in their late twenties to early forties, enjoy the rock-climbing wall, scuba diving, and even trapeze lessons. ✉ *Off Hwy. 200, Playa Blanca, Costa de Careyes, 48980,* ☎ *3/351–0001, 3/351–0002, or 800/258–2633,* FAX *3/351–0004. 295 rooms. 2 restaurants, 3 bars, pool, 6 tennis courts, gym, horseback riding, beach, kayaking, snorkeling, boating, windsurfing. AE, MC, V.*

Nightlife and the Arts

Puerto Vallarta is a party town, where the discos open at 10 PM and stay open until at least 3 or 4 AM. A $20 cover charge is not uncommon (at least for men) in the popular discos, many of which are at hotels. Motorcycle fans can let loose at **The American Legend Bar** (✉ Ignacio L. Vallarta 237, ☎ 3/222–2400), where live rock mixes with Harley Davidson rentals and T-shirt sales. **Cactus Club** (✉ Ignacio L. Vallarta 399, ☎ 3/222–6037) attracts a youngish crowd. The Krystal Vallarta hotel has **Christine's** (☎ 3/224–0202), which features a spectacular light show set to music from disco to techno. Near Marina Vallarta, **J.B.** (✉ Carretera al Aeropuerto Km 2.5, ☎ 3/224–3476), pronounced "Jota Bay," is popular with both locals and visitors for dancing to live salsa. Downtown, **Tropigala** (✉ Paseo Diaz Ordaz 920, ☎ 3/222–3875 or 3/222–3935) dance club offers live and canned music nightly. **The Zoo** (✉ Paseo Díaz Ordaz 630, ☎ 3/222–4945), facing the boardwalk near Olas Altas, attracts a youngish crowd.

As its name implies, **Collage** (☎ 3/221–0505), on the highway at the Marina Vallarta complex, has several restaurants, a bowling alley, billiards, two bars, shuffleboard, a video arcade, and a disco. **El Faro** (✉ Royal Pacific Yacht Club, Marina Vallarta, ☎ 3/221–0541) is a romantic spot from which to watch a lightning storm roll into the bay in hurricane season, or just to admire the bay and marina from the top of the 110-ft lighthouse. Formerly called Cuiza, the **Texas Grill** (✉ Isla Río Cuale, Local 3, ☎ 3/222–5646) has live jazz, blues or other music Sunday through Thursday.

Mexican fiestas are popular at the hotels and can be lavish affairs with buffet dinners, folk dances, and even fireworks. Reservations may be made with the hotels or travel agencies. The **Camino Real** (☎ 3/221–5000) hosts cultural events, such as music concerts or folkloric dances, on the first Thursday of every month at 9 PM.

Outdoor Activities and Sports

Swimming, sailing, windsurfing, and parasailing are popular sports at the beachfront hotels, which have stands on the beach offering boat trips and equipment. You needn't be a guest to rent these services.

Biking

B-B-Bobby's Bikes (✉ Miramar 402 at Iturbide, ☎ 3/223–0008) rents mountain bikes, beach cruisers, and "shopper's bikes" (with carrier racks) by the day or week and leads guided tours.

Bike Mex (✉ Guerrero 361, ☎ 3/223–1680) provides the gear (21-speed mountain bikes and helmets) and snacks for several different bike tours, which can be tailored to riders' experience and fitness level. The most popular is a three- to four-hour trip inland to bathe in an impressive waterfall.

Fishing

The sailfishing tournament in November draws dedicated fisherman from all over the world. Canadian Candice Shaw runs a bilingual-crewed boat, *Fishing with Carolina* (☎ 3/224–7250), with three chairs; an all-day trip costs $300. Throughout the year, the **Progreso Fishermen's Cooperative** offers a variety of fishing trips from its shack on the north end of the malecón; most hotels can arrange your reservations. Large group boats cost about $60 per person for a day's fishing. Cruisers may be chartered for $150–$350 a day, and include a skipper, fishing license, bait, and tackle; some also include lunch.

Golf

The 18-hole course at **Los Flamingos Country Club** (⊠ 12 km [8 mi] north of airport, ☎ 3/298–0280), designed by Percy Clifford, has a putting green, driving range, and tennis courts. There is a Joe Finger–designed 18-hole course at the **Marina Vallarta** complex (☎ 3/221–0545 or 3/221–0773), with caddies, carts, pro shop, lessons, and driving range. Make reservations for both through your hotel a day in advance.

Horseback Riding

Horseback riding along the shore is popular, and horses can be rented by the hour at area beaches. **Rancho Charro** (⊠ Poblano de Playa Grande, ☎ 3/224–0114) provides transportation to and from your hotel for three- to five-hour rides to area rivers and waterfalls. **Rancho El Ojo de Agua** (⊠ Cerrada de Cardenal 227, ☎ 3/224–8240 or 3/224–0607) also runs horseback sunset and half-day rides, some including lunch and time for a swim in a mountain stream. Excursions of up to five nights can be arranged to some of the colonial villages in the Sierra Madre.

Tennis

Most of the larger hotels have tennis courts for their guests' use. Courts are also available at the **Los Flamingos Country Club.**

Water Park

Children love **Splash** (⊠ Carretera a Tepic Km 155, Nayarit, ☎ 3/297–0723 or 3/297–0724, ☞ $13) where they can swim with dolphins, slide down enormous water slides, swim, and play on playground equipment and carnival rides. There are restaurants and bars as well as sea lion shows. The park is open daily 9–7.

Water Sports

Snorkeling and diving are most common at Los Arcos, a natural underwater preserve off Mismaloya beach. Quimixto Bay, about 32 km (20 mi) south of PV and accessible only by boat, has some good diving spots, as does Punta de Mita, about 80 km (50 mi) north. Experienced divers head for Las Marietas and El Morro islands, off Punta de Mita.

Many of the larger resort hotels rent snorkeling and diving equipment and offer short diving courses at their pools. For intensive certification courses, dive trips, and equipment rentals, contact **Chico's Dive Shop** (⊠ Paseo Díaz Ordaz 772, ☎ 3/222–1895). **Pacific Scuba** (⊠ Juárez 722, ☎ 3/222–4741) also rents equipment and arranges trips.

Shopping

Puerto Vallarta has been described as a shopper's paradise punctuated with hotels and beaches. There are plenty of shopping malls and small shops selling folk art, as well as more than 20 fine-art galleries. Prices in the shops are fixed, and U.S. dollars and credit cards are accepted. Bargaining is expected in the markets and by the vendors on the beach, who also freely accept American money. Most stores are open 10–8. A few close for siesta at 1 or 2, then reopen at 4.

Art

As its name implies, **Arte de las Américas** (✉ Marina las Palmas II–16, in Marina Vallarta, ☎ 3/221–1985) displays the work of celebrated and emerging contemporary artists from throughout Latin America. **Galería Arte Latinoamericano** (✉ Josefa Ortiz Domínguez 155, ☎ 3/222–4406) is the area's newest gallery, featuring contemporary art, sculptures, and lithographs. One of PV's best-known artists is the late Manuel Lepe, whose primitive-style prints can be seen in the galleries around town, including the one run by his family, **Galería Lepe** (✉ Juárez 533, ☎ 3/222–5515). Contemporary paintings and sculpture are displayed in **Galería Pacífico** (✉ Calle Aldama 174, ☎ 3/222–1982), a pioneer gallery nearly 20 years old. **Galería Rosas Blancas** (✉ Juárez 523, ☎ 3/222–1168) combines fine art with folk art. Wonderful, varied art in many media is found at **Galería Uno** (✉ Calle Morelos 561, ☎ 3/222–0908). Owners Jan Lavender and Martina Goldberg love to showcase local talent. Internationally known Sergio Bustamante—the creator of life-size brass, copper, and ceramic animals—has several galleries: **Sergio Bustamante** (✉ Av. Juárez 275, ☎ 3/222–1129; ✉ Paseo Díaz Ordaz 716, ☎ 3/223–1407; ✉ Paseo Díaz Ordaz 542, ☎ 3/222–5480).

Clothing

Most of the brand-name sportswear shops are located along the malecón and down its side streets. **La Bohemia** (✉ Constitución at Basilio Badillo, ☎ 3/222–3164; ✉ Plaza Neptuno Interior, Marina Vallarta, ☎ 3/221–2160) displays contemporary resortwear, designer artwear, unique jewelry, and accessories. **Express–Guess** (✉ Paseo Díaz Ordaz 660, ☎ 3/222–6470) carries its own line of quality sportswear. **Güeros** (✉ Calle Zaragoza 160, ☎ 3/222–0633) carries contemporary clothing for men, women, and children, as well as shoes, handbags, straw, leather, and home furnishings.

María de Guadalajara (✉ Puesta del Sol condominiums in Marina Vallarta, ☎ 3/221–2566; ✉ Plaza Malecón and Paseo Díaz Ordaz, ☎ 3/222–4735; ✉ Calle Morelos 550, ☎ 3/222–2387) carries easy-to-wear clothing for women in gauzy fabrics dyed in luscious colors. **Nina & June** (✉ Hidalgo 227–8, ☎ 3/222–3099) sells handwoven, originally designed fashions, fanciful accessories, and silver jewelry as well as outfits from Indonesia, Guatemala, New York, Mexico City, and Guadalajara. Tropical-print dresses, gauzy resortwear, and boxy cotton blouses and pants can be found at **Sucesos Boutique** (✉ Libertad and Hidalgo, ☎ 3/222–1002).

Folk Art

Puerto Vallarta is known for the variety of handicrafts sold, both from the region and throughout Mexico. Masks, pottery, lacquerware, clothing, mirrors, glass dishes, lamps, carved-wood animals, antiques and modern art, hand-dyed woven rugs, and embroidered clothing are all available in shops and markets, but look before you buy, as quality varies. **Galería de Ollas** (✉ Calle Morelos 101, ☎ 3/223–1045) has the wondrous pottery of Mata Ortiz exclusively. Highly prized beaded masks and statuettes, yarn art, and other folk crafts are found downtown at the **Huichol Collection Gallery** (✉ Morelos 490, ☎ 3/222–0182) or its sister store at Marina Vallarta. **Mundo de Azulejos** (✉ Carranza 374, ☎ 3/222–2675) sells a line of decorative tiles and will re-create your favorite scene or work of art in a series of tiles in 24 to 48 hours. Glassblowers at **Mundo de Cristal** (✉ Av. Insurgentes 333, at Basilio Badillo, ☎ 3/222–4157) factory create both avant-garde and classic designs to be sold in their store.

Olinalá (✉ Lázaro Cárdenas 274, ☎ 3/222–4995) specializes in painted ceremonial masks from throughout Mexico and sells contemporary paintings. **Puerco Azul** (⊠ Marina Las Palmas II promenade, ☎ 3/221–1985) carries one-of-a-kind items for the home, including furniture, ceramics, antiques, glassware, and whimsical pig figurines. **Querubines** (⊠ Juárez 501–A, ☎ 3/222–2988) sells a wealth of utilitarian and decorative folk art, especially woven goods: linens, placemats, and Guatemalan fabrics as well as painted gourds from Michoacán, tin, and ceramics. **Talavera Etc.** (⊠ Ignacio L. Vallarta 266, ☎ 3/222–4100) has a small but fine selection of majolica ceramics and handcrafted jewelry. Original hand-loomed rugs, fabrics, and hand-painted furniture are on display at **Tamacani** (⊠ Plaza Marina D-2, ☎ 3/221–0982).

Jewelry

There's a good selection of Mexican silver in Puerto Vallarta, but watch out for *chapa*, a combination of alloys. Real silver carries the 925 stamp required by the government. **Joyas Finas Suneson** (⊠ Calle Morelos 593, ☎ 3/222–5715) specializes in silver jewelry and objets d'art by some of Mexico's finest designers. At **Ric Taxco** (⊠ Pueblo Viejo shopping center, ☎ 3/224–4598; ⊠ Villa Vallarta shopping center, ☎ 3/223–0143), much of the sterling silver and gold jewelry is inspired by pre-Hispanic designs. **Viva** (⊠ Basilio Badillo 274, ☎ 3/222–4078) represents jewelers from around world, and has a large inventory of jewelry in silver, gold, and gemstones, as well as shoes and purses.

Markets

The **Mercado Municipal,** at Avenida Miramar and Libertad, is a typical market plopped down in the busiest part of town. Flowers, piñatas, produce, and plastics are all shoved together in indoor and outdoor stands that cover a full city block. The strip of **shops along Isla Río Cuale** is an outdoor market of sorts, with souvenir stands and exclusive boutiques interspersed with restaurants and cafés.

Shopping Centers

The highway on the north side of town is lined with small arcades and large shopping centers that are occupied by handicrafts and sportswear shops. The best selections are at the **Gigante Plaza,** by the Fiesta Americana hotel; **Plaza Malecón,** at the beginning of Paseo Díaz Ordaz; **Plaza Marina,** on the highway at Marina Vallarta; and **Villa Vallarta,** by the Plaza las Glorias hotel.

Puerto Vallarta A to Z

AIR TRAVEL

Puerto Vallarta's Gustavo Díaz Ordaz International Airport is 7½ km (4.5 mi) north of town, not far from the resorts at Marina Vallarta. Volkswagen vans provide economical transportation from the airport to PV hotels.

CARRIERS

Mexicana has direct service from Chicago, Denver, and Mexico City. Aeroméxico has flights from multiple U.S. and Mexican cities. Alaska Airlines serves the Western United States, with direct flights from Los Angeles, San Francisco, and Phoenix. American has daily nonstop flights from Dallas/Fort Worth. Continental flies direct from Houston. America West has direct flights from Phoenix.

➤ AIRLINES AND CONTACTS: **Aeroméxico** (☎ 3/221–1030 or 3/224–1799). **Alaska Airlines** (☎ 3/221–1353 or 3/221–1350). **American** (☎ 3/221–1799). **America West** (☎ 3/235–9292 or 3/221–1025). **Continental** (☎ 3/221–2213 or 3/221–1025). **Mexicana** (☎ 3/221–1266 or 3/224–8900).

➤ AIRPORT INFORMATION: **Gustavo Díaz Ordaz International Airport** (⊠ Hwy to Tepic Km 7.5, ☎ 3/221–1298 or 3/221–1325).

BOAT AND FERRY TRAVEL

Several cruise lines, including Carnival, Holland America Line, Princess Cruises, and Royal Caribbean Cruises sail to Puerto Vallarta, most frequently during the winter months.

BUS TRAVEL

One km (½ mi) north of the airport is PV's new Central Camionero, or central bus station. ETN has the most luxurious service to Guadalajara and Mexico City, with roomy, reclining seats. Transportes del Pacífico serves the region. Elite, which incorporates three lines (Estrella Blanca, Tres Estrellas de Oro, and Norte de Sonora), has first-class service to Guadalajara, Aguascalientes, and Mexico City. Primera Plus serves destinations throughout Mexico.

City buses serve downtown, the northern hotel zone, and the southern beaches. Bus stops—marked by blue-and-white signs—are located every two or three blocks along the highway (Carretera Aeropuerto) and in town. Buses to Playa Mismaloya and Boca de Tomatlán run about every 15 minutes from the corner of Avenida Insurgentes and Basilio Badillo, downtown.

➤ Bus Information: **Central Camionero** (✉ Puerto Vallarta–Tepic Hwy. Km 9, ☎ 3/221–0739). **Elite** (☎ 3/223–1117 or 3/221–0848). **ETN** (☎ 3/221–0550). **Primera Plus** (☎ 3/221–0095). **Transportes del Pacífico** (☎ 3/222–1015 or 3/221–0021).

CAR RENTAL

During the high season, rentals start at $50 per day, including mileage; always ask about special promotions. All the car-rental agencies below have desks at the airport; some have offices along the highway.

Alamo offers free pickup. Prices at Budget range from $50 to $78 a day. Dollar has branches at the Krystal and Buenaventura hotels. National is another well-known international chain.

➤ Major Agencies: **Alamo** (✉ Blvd. Francisco Medina Ascencio 1851, ☎ 3/224–1071). **Budget** (✉ Av. Paseo de las Palmas 1004, ☎ 3/222–2980). **Dollar** (✉ ☎ 3/223–1354). **National** (✉ Carretera Aeropuerto Km 1.5, ☎ 3/222–0515).

CAR TRAVEL

Puerto Vallarta is about 1,900 km (1,200 mi) south of Nogales, Arizona, at the U.S.–Mexico border, 354 km (220 mi) from Guadalajara, and 167 km (104 mi) from Tepic.

Driving in the city can be very unpleasant. From December through April—peak tourist season—traffic clogs the small cobblestone streets. During the rainy season, from July through October, the streets become flooded and the city's steep hills are muddy and slippery. Parking is nearly nonexistent.

EMBASSIES

The U.S. and Canadian consulates are in the same building on the main plaza.

➤ Canada: **Canadian Consulate** (✉ Calle Zaragoza 160, ☎ 3/222–5398).
➤ United States: **U.S. Consulate** (✉ Calle Zaragoza 160, 2nd floor, ☎ 3/222–0069).

EMERGENCIES

Dial 060 in emergency situations.

➤ Contacts: **Ambulance** (☎ 3/225–0386). **Farmacia California** (✉ Francisco Villa 880, ☎ 3/225–0635). **Hospital** (✉ Plaza Neptuno, Marina Vallarta, ☎ 3/221–0023). **Police** (✉ City Hall, Calles Morelos and Iturbide, ☎ 3/221–2586). **Red Cross** (☎ 3/222–1533).

ENGLISH-LANGUAGE MEDIA

There's no shortage of printed English-language information in PV. In addition to lots of slick (and truly helpful) map guides, check out the ad-driven but informative *PV Tribune*. The newest English-language rag, *Vallarta Voice*, is a monthly paper.

MAIL, INTERNET, AND SHIPPING

For sending and receiving mail and packages, go to Mail Boxes Etc., which also offers fax and e-mail services. The Net House is open from dawn to the wee hours, and has computers with English-language keyboards.

➤ INTERNET CAFÉS: **The Net House** (✉ Ignacio L. Vallarta 232, ☎ 3/222–6953).

➤ MAIL SERVICES: **Mail Boxes Etc.** (✉ Blvd. Francisco Medina Ascencio, Edificio Andrea Mar Local 7, ☎ 3/224–9434).

TAXIS

The ride from the north-side hotels to downtown costs about $10; within downtown, a ride is $2; from Marina Vallarta to downtown, about $4. Be sure to agree on a fare before embarking.

TOURS

The five-hour city tour is a good way to get the lay of the land, from Marina Vallarta and Gringo Gulch to the Río Cuale and Playa Mismaloya. Almost everyone goes on at least one daytime or sunset cruise of the bay. Daytime cruises go to Los Arcos, Yelapa, Quimixto, and Playa Las Ánimas, and to Isla Marietas for whale-watching (during winter months), snorkeling, swimming, and lunch, departing from the Terminal Marítima at around 9 AM.

Local fishermen at Punta de Mita have formed the Sociedad Cooperativa Corral de Risco, offering fishing, whale-watching, and snorkel trips around the Marieta islands at reasonable rates. Intermar Vallarta offers a dinner cruise to movie director John Huston's former home, on a private bay south of the city, with dancing on the return trip. Vallarta Adventure arranges transportation and tours to destinations such as San Sebastián del Oeste, an interesting old mining town high in the Sierra Madre, 62 km (38 mi) from Puerto Vallarta; or to shopping or tequila-tasting expeditions outside Guadalajara. Harris Tours offers city tours for about $16; tours to Yelapa run about $30; and tours to Las Ánimas and Quimixto cost approximately $40. It's worth the few extra dollars to go on a private tour (small groups) in a van rather than with a large group on a tour bus. Natura Tours offers numerous types of nature-oriented excursions, including bass and deep-sea fishing, hiking, scuba diving, and biking. Their subsidiary, Viva Tours, books cruises and air travel.

Tropical tours visit mango and banana plantations in Nayarit. These often include stops in Nayarit's capital, Tepic, and a boat ride on the scenic Río Tovara, through jungle thick with tropical birds, with a stop for a refreshing swim in a natural spring.

➤ TOUR OPERATOR RECOMMENDATIONS: **Harris Tours** (☎ 3/223–2972). **Natura Tours** (✉ Carr. Aeropuerto Km 5.5, ☎ FAX 3/224–0410). **Sociedad Cooperativa Corral de Risco** (✉ Av. el Anclote, Manzana 17, No. 1, ☎ 3/291–6298). **Vallarta Adventure** (✉ Av. de las Palmas at Nayarit, Nuevo Vallarta, ☎ 3/221–0657).

Travel Agencies

➤ LOCAL AGENT REFERRALS: **American Express** (✉ Morelos 660, ☎ 3/223–2955). **Intermar Vallarta** (✉ Paseo de la Marina s/n, Condominio Via Golf, ☎ 3/221–0734).

VISITOR INFORMATION
The municipal tourist office, open weekdays 9–5, is on the Plaza Principal. The state tourism office is open weekdays 9–7, Saturday 9–1.
➤ TOURIST INFORMATION: **Municipal Tourist Office** (✉ Independencia 123, ☎ 3/223–2500, ext. 230 or 231). **State Tourism Office** (✉ Plaza Marina shopping center, Local 144 & 146, ☎ 3/221–2676 or 3/221–2677).

MANZANILLO

Manzanillo is not your typical resort destination. Crystal blue waters lap the black and gold volcanic sand on its twin bahías, Manzanillo and Santiago, which host not only resort hotels but a major industrial port. Twin towns of the same name, with little polish, have a dearth of shops, museums, or other tourist attractions. Still, it's the very lack of sophistication combined with inviting beaches and some great resorts that attract a certain type of tourist year after year. In the July–September rainy season, rivers and lagoons swell, forming waterfalls and ponds.

La Península de Santiago, which separates Bahía de Santiago and Bahía de Manzanillo, is a spit of land on which perches Las Hadas resort. From the water or points above the beach, the resort seems a mirage, a mass of white domes and peaks that radiate pink in the midday heat. When Bolivian tin magnate Antenor Patiño conceived of this dazzling palace in the early 1960s, Manzanillo was easier to reach by sea than by land, a rugged, primitive port that attracted hardy sailors and beachcombers bent on creating their own tropical paradise. When Patiño's retreat was completed in 1974, the international social set began to visit Manzanillo. Even then, Manzanillo remained essentially a port city with only a few tourist attractions.

Manzanillo is still relatively undeveloped, a sleeper compared with other Pacific Coast resorts. Many shops and hotel desks close for afternoon siesta, and on Sunday most businesses (including restaurants) shut down and everyone heads for the beach.

Along with the rest of the Gold Coast, this area is being developed. The latest prize to be carved out of the wilderness by big-time investors is Isla Navidad, a 1,230-acre resort complex on a peninsula about 20 minutes north of the Manzanillo international airport and an hour north of Manzanillo proper. Robert Von Hagge designed the 27-hole golf course, and other amenities include a full-service marina.

Exploring Manzanillo

A vacation in Manzanillo is not spent shopping and sightseeing. There's little in the way of folk art to buy, and visitors generally stay put and relax on the beach, venturing out to survey the local scene only when boredom or sunstroke strike.

A Good Tour

The **Santiago** area, on Santiago Bay between the Santiago and Juluapan peninsulas, offers little indication that it's a tourist destination save a string of hotels and restaurants along the beach. The next area to the east, **Salahua,** is residential, with a baseball field and restaurants. Farther southeast on Manzanillo Bay, past the traffic circle and Avenida Morelos, you'll see **Las Brisas** beach, where some of the cheaper hotels are located.

Downtown is busy and jam-packed, but of little tourist interest, except for the bustling seaport and, just north of downtown, the **Archaeological Museum.** The museum displays 5,000 of its more than

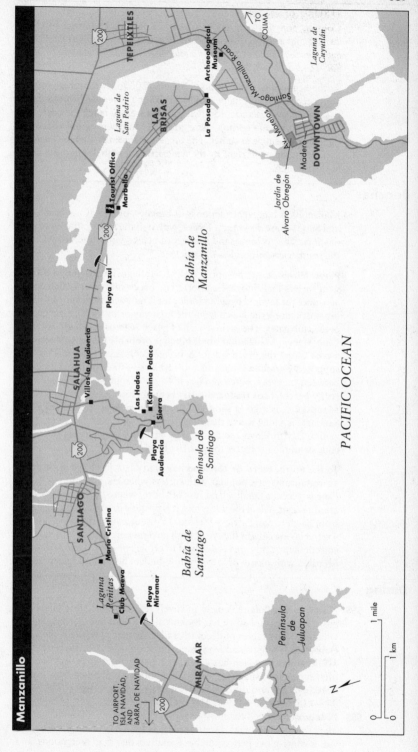

Manzanillo

PACIFIC OCEAN

Bahía de Manzanillo

Bahía de Santiago

Laguna de Cuyutlán

Laguna de San Pedrito

Laguna Penitas

TO COLIMA

Santiago-Manzanillo Road

Av. Morelos

Madero

DOWNTOWN

Jardín de Alvaro Obregón

Archaeological Museum

La Posada

LAS BRISAS

TEPEIXTLES

Tourist Office

Marbella

Playa Azul

SALAHUA

Villas la Audiencia

Las Hadas

Karmina Palace

Sierra

Playa Audiencia

Península de Santiago

SANTIAGO

María Cristina

Club Maeva

Playa Miramar

MIRAMAR

TO AIRPORT, ISLA NAVIDAD, AND BARRA DE NAVIDAD

Península de Juluapan

0   1 mile
0   1 km

18,000 artifacts, which come from the immediate region, the state of Colima, and throughout Mesoamerica. Chamber music, folkloric dance, and other cultural events are sometimes presented Friday evenings. ⊠ *San Pedrito traffic circle,* ☎ *3/332–2256.* ⚏ *$1.* ⊙ *Tues.– Sat. 10–2 and 5–8, Sun. 10–1.*

At the beginning of the harbor, Highway 200 jogs around downtown and intersects with Highway 110 to Colima. Avenida Morelos leads past the shipyards and into town. Just before you reach the port, stop at **Laguna de San Pedrito,** where graceful white herons and vivid pink flamingos assemble at sunset. The zócalo, or **Jardín de Alvaro Obregón,** is right on the main road by the waterfront. It's small but quite lively in the evening.

Beaches

Manzanillo's biggest attraction is its beaches. Every day is a beach day, and Sundays are downright festive, with half the town gathered to play onshore. The volcanic sand is a mix of black, white, and brown, with the southernmost beaches the blackest.

Playa Miramar, at the north end of Santiago Bay, is populated by windsurfers and boogie-boarders. The beach in front of Club Santiago, once the favored hangout for locals, is now accessible only by walking north along the beach from the highway or by passing the guards at the club gates. The main stretch of beach is across the highway from Club Maeva. Manzanillo's best beach is probably **Playa Audiencia,** in a cove along the north side of Santiago Peninsula. The local Indians supposedly granted Cortés an audience here—thus the name. Located between two rock outcroppings, it's a good spot for snorkeling. The rocky beach at **Las Hadas,** directly behind Hotel La Sierra on Bahí de Manzanillo, is a good snorkeling spot. **Playa Azul,** also called Playa Santiago, is a long strand that runs from Santiago Peninsula along Manzanillo Bay to Playa Las Brisas. The surf gets rough along the north end; swimming is better toward Las Brisas.

To the north, **Barra de Navidad** has pretty beaches lined with open-air restaurants; it's popular with surfers when the autumn swells hit. Pangas access a small island just offshore, where unbroken seashells are abundant. When the tide is low, it is possible to walk along the beach from Barra to San Patricio Melaque, a distance of about 6 km (almost 4 mi). Having caught the eye of both government tourism officials and entrepreneurs, this area is destined to grow. For now, Barra is a smallish town with plenty of low-key, low-budget hotels and restaurants.

Dining

$$$ ✕ **Colima Bay Café.** A comely and lively seaside venue, the Colima Bay has a large second-story bar looking down onto another bar below, which has low tables of decorative tiles, leather *equipale* chairs, and giant plaster hippos and frogs for decoration. The cheerful restaurant overlooking the beach has cardboard menus in English and Spanish offering nachos, spaghetti, barbecued pork accompanied by a stuffed baked potato, and other familiar dishes. ⊠ *Blvd. Costero 921,* ☎ *3/ 333–1150 or 3/334–0700. MC, V.*

$$$ ✕ **Legazpi.** Named for the navigator who put the Philippines on the map, this international restaurant at Las Hadas is beautiful. The service is white-glove perfection, but friendly rather than pretentious, and the food is decidedly elegant. The emphasis is on Continental cuisine with a Mexican touch, including Tulum salad (lettuce with crabmeat, avocado, and quail eggs) and grilled salmon with hibiscus-flower

sauce. The only drawback is the difficulty of finding the restaurant open. ⊠ *Las Hadas, Av. de los Riscos,* ☎ *3/334–0101. AE, DC, MC, V. Closed Wed., Fri., Sun. Closed Mar.–Nov. No lunch.*

$$$ ✕ **Toscana.** When the popular restaurant Willy's closed due to storm damage, the owners transferred customers' favorite dishes to their other restaurant, Toscana. Most tables at this French-Italian restaurant sit on the charming outdoor terrace adjacent to the beach. Specialties include smoked-salmon quiche, the San Remo salad (with tomatoes, onions, black olives, and Italian dressing), shrimp tempura, and a seafood assortment with scallop ceviche, shrimp, clams, and calamari. Live guitar music is offered nightly after 7 PM. (Don't be surprised if the name reverts to Willy's.) ⊠ *Blvd. Costero Miguel de la Madrid 3177,* ☎ *3/333–2515. MC, V. No lunch.*

$$ ✕ **El Bigotes.** Good seafood is served at a leisurely pace in this chain's two restaurants, both under open-air palapas on the beach. With no decoration save the oceanscape in front, the ambience comes from the lively patrons and canned music. The house specialty is the spicy Jalisco favorite *pescado sarandeado* (whole fish marinated and grilled over hot coals). Also recommended is Camerón Mustache: butterfly shrimp breaded in shredded coconut and sautéed. ⊠ *Blvd. Costero Miguel de la Madrid 3157,* ☎ *3/334–0831;* ⊠ *Puesta del Sol 3,* ☎ *3/ 333–1236. MC, V.*

$$ ✕ **Guadalajara Grill.** The liveliest restaurant in town doubles as a bardisco, since it is attached to Carlos 'n' Charlie's. Very popular with English-speaking tourists, Guadalajara Grill even has its own line of clothing. Mexican plates include enchiladas, fajitas, and a variety of fish dishes. Most people come for the lively ambience rather than the food. They congregate to watch sports, drink at the bar, and after 10:30 PM, to dance. Mariachi singers entertain on Tuesday and Thursday. ⊠ *Av. Audiencia Plaza Pacifico,* ☎ *3/334–1272. AE, MC, V.*

$$ ✕ **L' Recife.** A huge palapa set on a cliff with waves crashing on the
★ rocks below, and a pool/bar to one side, this is undoubtedly the best dinner-with-a-view in the area, and around March, a great place to see migrating whales. Beef is the specialty, but also popular is the *camaron L'Recife,* shrimp sautéed with corn, zucchini, and carrots, served with mango sauce on a bed of mashed potatoes. ⊠ *Cerro del Cenicero s/n, El Naranjo, Condominio Vida del Mar,* ☎ *3/335–0900. MC, V. Closed May–Oct. No lunch.*

$$ ✕ **El Vaquero Campestre.** Its name means "the country cowboy," so it's no surprise to find a setting reminiscent of a ranchland saloon. The menu at this restaurant en route to Las Hadas resort emphasizes fine cuts of beef—grilled without embellishment or marinated and seasoned carne asada. There are also burgers and shrimp; or try the *carne tampiqueña,* thin strips of grilled beef served with guacamole, beans, and quesadillas. ⊠ *Av. la Audiencia Lote 2,* ☎ *3/334–1548. MC, V.*

$ ✕ **Juanito's.** Owned by an American who settled in Manzanillo in 1976, Juanito's is the spot to watch U.S. football in good company. It's the most popular place in town for breakfast, and also specializes in great burgers, malts, fries, barbecued ribs, and fried chicken. Decoration is minimal, but the service is quick and the coffee strong and hot. It's also one of Manzanillo's only Internet cafés. ⊠ *Blvd. Costero Km 14,* ☎ *3/333–1388. Reservations not accepted. AE, MC, V.*

Lodging

Although the $10 room is a thing of the past, there are still several decent places where you can lay your head for less than $40. Travelers on a tighter budget usually head to Barra de Navidad and Melaque, about an hour north. As with the rest of the Pacific Coast, Manzanillo is in the midst of a building boom, mainly condominiums, to accommodate the growing number of Canadian snowbirds and Guadalajara residents buying vacation homes here. The resorts are spread out along the Santiago–Manzanillo Road.

$$$$ 🏨 **Grand Bay.** Set on a 1,200-acre peninsula between the Pacific and
★ the Navidad lagoon, 30 minutes north of Manzanillo airport, this no-holds-barred resort cascades down a hill to a delightful stretch of private beach. Rooms in this luxurious hotel, with Spanish arches, shady patios, fountains, and lush gardens, have mountain or sea views, imported-marble baths, original art, deluxe amenities, and balconies. Three striking tiered pools dot the gardens. Guests may play the adjacent 27-hole Robert Von Hagge–designed golf course; boat service is available to Barra de Navidad, across the bay. ⊠ *Isla Navidad (A.P. 20), Jalisco 48987,* ☎ *3/355–5050 or 888/472–6229,* ℻ *3/355–6071,* WEB *www.grandbay.com. 158 rooms, 41 suites. 3 restaurants, 3 bars, 3 pools, golf privileges, 3 tennis courts, gym, volleyball, beach, dive shop, snorkeling, jet skiing, waterskiing, marina, fishing, shops, baby-sitting, children's programs (ages 4–12), concierge. AE, MC, V.*

$$$$ 🏨 **Las Hadas.** For many years Manzanillo's premier resort, Las Hadas still delights with its exotic, "nouveau-Moorish" buildings set among six hectares of beautiful, flower-and-vine-covered grounds. Room rates are high considering the lackadaisical maintenance, however, and the resort no longer attracts the jet-set crowd of its glory days. Taken over in December 2000 by the new Grupo Hotelero Las Brisas, maintenance will hopefully improve. The hotel has its own golf course and looks over a gorgeous bay and marina, and Legazpi restaurant is the city's most elegant. ⊠ *Av. De los Riscos y Vista Hermosa s/n, Península de Santiago, 28867,* ☎ *3/331–0101 or 888/559–4329,* ℻ *3/331–0125,* WEB *www.brisas.com.mx. 184 rooms, 36 suites. 4 restaurants, 3 bars, 2 pools, beauty salon, massage, 18-hole golf course, 10 tennis courts, beach, shops, baby-sitting, laundry service, travel services. AE, DC, MC, V.*

$$$$ 🏨 **Karmina Palace.** Manzanillo's newest all-inclusive, all-suites hotel is just a short walk from neighboring Las Hadas. Punctuating Karmina's spacious lawns are cascades, fountains, eight multitier lagoon-pools, and a beautiful palapa restaurant at the ocean's edge. Junior suites have two TVs, marble floors, refrigerator, air-conditioning and fans, balcony or terrace, and large tubs with separate shower facilities and double vanities in the bathrooms. The seven-story resort hotel has 24-hour concierge service and a well-equipped business center, but service is only average. ⊠ *Av. Vista Hermosa 13, Fracc. Península de Santiago, Santiago, Colima 28200,* ☎ *3/334–1313 or 877/527–6462,* ℻ *3/334–1915. 325 suites. 3 restaurants, 8 pools, spa, gym, beach, shops, video games, children's programs (ages 4–12). AE, V.*

$$$ 🏨 **Sierra.** This 19-story white stucco giant is popular with families (up to two children under age six stay free in their parents' room) and conventioneers. All of the 350 inviting rooms and suites have private balconies; many have a bay view. A large free-form pool, four tennis courts, and several bars and restaurants round out the property. Light-wood and pastel colors dominate the pleasant decor. The all-inclusive resort includes buffet meals, snacks, dinners at a gourmet restaurant, domestic drinks, tennis, and water sports such as kayaking and windsurfing. ⊠ *Av. de la Audiencia 1, 28200,* ☎ *3/333–2000 or 800/448–5028,* ℻ *3/333–2272. 328 rooms, 11 suites. 3 restaurants, 4 bars, pool, 4 tennis courts, beach, children's programs (ages 4–12), meeting rooms. AE, MC, V.*

$$ 🏨 **Marina Puerto Dorado.** There are excellent views of the bay and har-
★ bor from this family hotel, which looks a lot like condos. With 40 suites, 10 of them penthouse suites with Jacuzzis and wet bars, this is a good bet for large families. Continental breakfast included in the reasonable

room price makes this a great bargain. ⊠ *Av. Lázaro Cárdenas 101, Fracc. Las Brisas Playa Azul, 28200,* ☎ ℻ *3/334–1480. 40 suites. Restaurant, 2 bars, pool, beach. AE, MC, V.*

$$ 🏨 **La Posada.** This "passionate pink" hotel has been a favorite with
★   North Americans since 1957. With only 24 rooms, most guests get to know each other well, mingling in the *sala*, a large, open-air living-dining area with a communal coffeepot. Rooms are comfortable but not at all fancy; there's one on the beach. Old iron keys work the antique locks. The room rate includes a complete breakfast; beer and soft-drink service is on the honor system. ⊠ *Las Brisas, at the end of the Old Hwy to Santiago, 28200,* ☎ ℻ *3/333–1899. 24 rooms. Bar, snack bar, pool, beach. MC, V.*

$$ 🏨 **Villas la Audiencia.** A block from the Las Hadas turnoff and about 1 km (½ mi) from the beach, this small white-and-red hotel and villa complex overlooks the Mantarraya golf course. Clean, air-conditioned rooms are motel-like, yet comfortable; special deals often make the one-, two-, and three-bedroom "villas" just a bit more expensive than the small, plain rooms. Free transportation is provided to the beach. The lack of an elevator means lots of trudging up and down stairs. ⊠ *Av. de la Audiencia and Las Palmas, off Santiago–Manzanillo Rd., 28860,* ☎ *3/333–0861,* ℻ *3/333–2653. 20 rooms, 26 villas. Restaurant, pool. AE, MC, V.*

$ 🏨 **María Cristina.** A clean but drab two-story motel in the Santiago area, it's just four blocks from the beach. All rooms have limited cable TV, but only three—they call them "bungalows"—are air-conditioned; they're well worth the difference in price. ⊠ *Calle 28 de Agosto 36, 28860,* ☎ *3/333–0966,* ℻ *3/334–1430. 21 rooms. Pool. MC, V.*

$ 🏨 **Marbella.** This hotel is one of the few reasonably priced places on the beach, which faces the open ocean, not the bay. The best rooms are on the beach; each has a tiny balcony under the palms. The accommodations are color-coordinated and have tile floors, air-conditioning, and TV. The Marbella has a good Spanish/seafood restaurant, El Marinero. ⊠ *Santiago–Manzanillo Rd. Km 9.5, 28869,* ☎ *3/333–1103,* ℻ *3/333–1222. 92 rooms. Restaurant, bar, pool. AE, MC, V.*

Nightlife and the Arts

For a rowdy drinking and dancing scene, head for **Carlos 'n' Charlies** (⊠ Av. Audencia Plaza Pacífico, ☎ 3/334–1272). To dance to live, authentic salsa and other tropical tunes, your best bet is **Tropigala** (⊠ Boulevard Miguel de la Madrid Km 14, ☎ 3/333–2474 or 3/333–2475). Some nights there are specials such as free dinner buffets or dance performances. Friday is ladies' night: no cover until 11 PM. **VOG** (⊠ Santiago–Manzanillo Rd. Km 9.2, ☎ 3/333–1875) plays disco music Thursday through Saturday.

Outdoor Activities and Sports

Fishing

Billed the "Sailfish Capital of the World," Manzanillo has fleets that regularly hook marlin, dorado, roosters, and tuna. Sportfishing charters are available at major hotels and through tour agencies. Contact **Ocean Pacific Tours** (⊠ ☎ ℻ 3/335–0605) to charter a 26-ft boat (1–5 persons) for $195, or a 40-ft cruiser (1–10 persons) for $245. Both tours last five hours and include a case of beer as well as the usual ice, bait, and tackle.

Golf

The nine-hole course at **Club Santiago** (☎ 3/335–0410), designed by Larry Hughes, has the usual amenities, including carts, caddies, pro shop, and restaurant. Robert Von Hagge mapped out the 27-hole course on **Isla Navidad** (☎ 3/335–6439). **La Mantarraya** (☎ 3/331–0101), the 18-hole golf course designed by Roy Dye at Las Hadas, has been rated among the world's 100 best courses by *Golf Digest*.

Water Sports

The rocky points off Manzanillo's peninsulas and coves make for good snorkeling and scuba diving. Kayaks, paddleboats, windsurfers, and snorkel and scuba gear can be rented at the Las Hadas and other major hotels and at La Audiencia beach.

Shopping

Most of the hotels offer a small selection of folk art and beachwear, but, in general, shopping in Manzanillo is poor. There are some shops around the main square, hardly worth the trip downtown, and others at Plaza Manzanillo, a shopping center at Km 7.5 on the Santiago–Manzanillo Road. Most of the shops are closed 2–4; many are open Sunday 10–2. **Centro Artesenal Las Primaveras** (⊠ Juárez 40, Santiago, ☎ 3/333–1699) has a huge assortment of handicrafts of so-so quality.

Side Trip

Colima

98 km (61 mi) northeast of Manzanillo.

Colima, the capital of the eponymous state, is about an hour from Manzanillo via an excellent toll road that continues on to Guadalajara. An easygoing provincial city, Colima is most famous for the pre-Hispanic "Colima dog" figurines, which originated in this region and which are on display—along with other archaeological pieces—at the **Museo de las Culturas del Occidente** (Museum of Western Cultures; ⊠ Casa de la Cultura, Calzada Galván and Av. Ejército Nacional, ☎ 3/312–3155; closed Mon.). The **Museo Universitario de Culturas Populares** (University Museum of Popular Culture; ⊠ Calle Gabino Barreda and Manuel Gallardo, ☎ 3/312–6869) has a large collection of pre-Hispanic and contemporary Indian costumes, masks, instruments, and other artifacts. Entry to the museum, which is open Tuesday–Sun 10–2 and 5–8, is free. The town of **Comala,** a 15-minute ride north of Colima, is noted for hand-carved furniture and ironwork.

Manzanillo A to Z

AIR TRAVEL

You can fly to Manzanillo from several United States cities as well as Mexico City.

CARRIERS

Aeroméxico has daily flights from Houston, Los Angeles, and Atlanta, with a plane change in Mexico City. Mexicana serves via Mexico City. Alaska Airlines flies out of Los Angeles. America West has twice weekly flights from Phoenix. AeroCalifornia flies in from Mexico City and Los Angeles daily.

➤ AIRLINES AND CONTACTS: **AeroCalifornia** (☎ 3/334–1414). **Aeroméxico** (☎ 3/333–0151). **Alaska Airlines** (☎ 800/426–0333). **America West** (☎ 01–800/363–2597). **Mexicana** (☎ 3/333–2323 or 3/334–0800).

AIRPORTS AND TRANSFERS

Manzanillo's Aeropuerto Internacional Playa de Oro is 32 km (20 mi) north of town, on the way to Barra de Navidad. Volkswagen vans transport passengers from the airport to major resorts; these shuttles are less expensive than taxis.

➤ AIRPORT INFORMATION: **Aeropuerto Internacional Playa de Oro** (☎ 3/333–2525).

BUS TRAVEL

The resorts in the Manzanillo area are several miles from the main bus stop (✉ Blvd. Costero Miguel de la Madrid Km 13.5). Elite and Estrella Blanca serve Manzanillo; the former has a longer list of destination cities. Primera Plus serves Puerto Vallarta, Guadalajara, Tijuana, Mexico City, Acapulco, and smaller coastal towns. ETN has comfortable buses with wide, almost totally reclining seats, to Guadalajara, Colima, Morelia, and Mexico City.

➤ BUS INFORMATION: **Elite** (☎ 3/332–0432). **Estrella Blanca** (☎ 3/332–0432). **ETN** (☎ 3/334–1050). **Primera Plus** (☎ 3/332–0515).

CAR RENTAL

Hertz has compact and mid-size cars with and without air-conditioning. Dollar has no airport booth but will pick customers up there; they offer sedans, VW bugs, and minivans. National has a desk at the airport as well.

➤ MAJOR AGENCIES: **Dollar** (✉ Hotel Karmina Palace, ☎ 3/334–1313). **Hertz** (✉ Blvd. Costero Miguel de la Madrid 1246-B, ☎ 3/333–3141). **National** (✉ Blvd. Costero Miguel de la Madrid 1070, ☎ 3/333–1140).

CAR TRAVEL

The trip south from the Arizona border to Manzanillo is about 2,419 km (1,500 mi); from Guadalajara, it is 332 km (206 mi) over mostly well-kept highways; from Puerto Vallarta, 242 km (150 mi) on Highway 200, which winds through the mountains beginning in Tepic, in the state of Nayarit.

A car is almost essential for exploring the area on your own. Considering the high cost of rental cars, some folks opt to hire a taxi—about $13 per hour, or $50–$80 per day, depending on your destination. Agree on a price beforehand.

EMERGENCIES

There is no general emergency number in Manzanillo, so call the police, hospital, or fire department directly.

➤ CONTACTS: **Police** (☎ 3/334–0557). **Fire Department** (☎ 3/312–5858). **Red Cross** (☎ 3/336–5770). **Public Security** (☎ 3/332–1004). **Hospital de Manzanillo** (☎ 3/336–7272).

TOURS

Manzanillo is spread out; you might consider a guided tour to get the lay of the land. More appealing, though, than the city tours are the sportfishing trips, sunset cruises, horseback outings, and excursions to Colima, Comala, and the volcanoes that can be arranged through area travel agencies.

Bahías Gemelas Agencia de Viajes offers city, walking, fishing, and horseback riding tours. Viajes Héctur offers the same tours as Bahía Gemelas, plus shopping, bay cruises, tours on four-wheelers, and day excursions to the beach or area banana plantations.

➤ TOUR OPERATOR RECOMMENDATIONS: **Bahías Gemelas Agencia de Viajes** (✉ Blvd. Costero Miguel de la Madrid 1556, ☎ 3/333–1000). **Viajes Héctur** (✉ Blvd. Costero Miguel de la Madrid 3147, ☎ 3/333–1707).

VISITOR INFORMATION

The State Tourism Office is open weekdays 9–3 and 5–7, Saturday 10–2.

➤ Tourist Information: **State Tourism Office** (✉ Blvd. Costero Miguel de la Madrid 1033, ☎ 3/333–2277).

IXTAPA/ZIHUATANEJO

One of the most appealing of the Pacific Coast destinations, Ixtapa/Zihuatanejo is a taste of Mexico present and past. Ixtapa (pronounced eesh-*tah*-pa), where most Americans stay—probably because they can't pronounce Zihuatanejo (see-wa-ta-*nay*-ho)—is young and glitzy. Exclusively a vacation resort, it was created in the 1970s by Mexico's National Fund for Tourism Development, which also dreamed up Cancún and Huatulco, and developed Los Cabos. High-rise chains in the hotel zone rent water-sports equipment, and rocky islets offshore help to protect the ocean-facing beach from rough surf. Across the road from the hotel zone are clusters of commercial plazas housing cafés, restaurants, and shops.

Zihuatanejo, only 7 km (4 mi) down the coast (southeast) from Ixtapa, is an old fishing village on a picturesque sheltered bay. Until the advent of Ixtapa, it was hardly known. But long before Columbus sailed to America, Zihuatanejo was a retreat for indigenous nobility. Figurines, ceramics, stone carvings, and stelae verify the presence of civilizations dating as far back as the Olmecs (3000 BC). Weaving was likely the dominant industry, as evidenced by pre-Hispanic figurines, bobbins, and other related artifacts found in the area. The original Nahuatl name, Cihuatlán, means "place of women."

In 1527, Spanish conquistadors launched a trade route from Zihuatanejo Bay to the Orient. Galleons returned with silks, spices, and, according to some historians, the Americas' first coconut palms, brought from the Philippines. But the Spaniards did little colonizing here. A scout sent by Cortés reported back to the conquistador that the place was nothing great, tagging the name Cihuatlán with the less-than-flattering suffix "ejo"—hence "Zihuatanejo."

With the arrival of Highway 200 in the 1960s and the construction of Ixtapa the following decade, Zihuatanejo began to grow, and now its streets have been paved in brick. The place has managed to retain its charm, even if its malecón and narrow streets are lined with hotels, restaurants, and shops. Zihuatanejo is also home to some of Mexico's most exclusive boutique hotels, attracting discerning clients who prefer the intimacy of these secluded settings to the comfortable but more mainstream high-rises in neighboring Ixtapa.

Exploring Ixtapa/Zihuatanejo

Ixtapa and Zihuatanejo have few sights per se, but they're both pleasant places to stroll—the former especially if you enjoy a modern beach ambience and shops, the latter if you prefer local color.

A Good Tour

The hotel zone in **Ixtapa** extends along a 3-km (2-mi) strip of wide, sandy beach called Playa del Palmar, on the open Pacific. It's fun to walk along the beach to check out the various hotel scenes and water-sports activities. Alternatively, you can stroll the length of the zone on Paseo Ixtapa, a nicely landscaped and immaculate thoroughfare lined with a series of Mexican village–style shopping malls. At one end of the hotel zone (when you enter from Zihuatanejo) is the 18-hole Ixtapa Golf Club, while on the other (generally described as being "up the coast," but actually lying to the northwest) you'll come to the Marina Ixtapa development, with a 600-slip yacht marina, a promenade

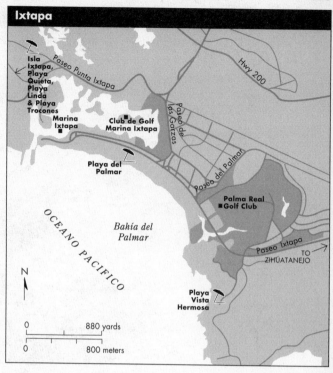

Ixtapa

with restaurants and shops, and the 18-hole Marina Golf Course. If you want to venture out of this compact resort area, take a taxi 15 minutes up the coast to **Playa Linda.** It's a 10-minute boat ride from here to **Ixtapa Island,** where you can spend the day eating, sunning, and swimming.

The town of **Zihuatanejo** (population, about 37,000 souls) lies near the back of a deep, enclosed bay with calm beaches. A simple way to tour the town is to take a taxi to the municipal pier (*muelle*), from which skiffs continually depart for the 10-minute ride to **Playa las Gatas,** most easily accessible by water. The sportfishing boats depart from this pier, too, and it's the beginning of the **Paseo del Pescador** (Fisherman's Walk), or malecón, which runs along the main beach, the most picturesque part of the town itself. The brick-paved seaside path, only ½ km (⅓ mi) long, is lined with small restaurants and overflowing shops; you'll pass a basketball court that doubles as the town square. The malecón ends at the **Museo Arquelógico** (⊠ east end of Paseo del Pescador, ☎ 7/553–2552), where pre-Hispanic murals, maps, and archaeological pieces describing the Olmec, Tarascan, and Aztec cultures are on permanent display. It's open Tuesday–Sunday 10–6. If you continue beyond the museum, you can take a footpath cut into the rocks to **Playa la Madera.**

Beaches

Ixtapa

Ixtapa Island. The most popular beach on Ixtapa Island (and closest to the boat dock) is Playa Cuachalalate, named for a local tree whose bark has been used as a remedy for kidney ailments since ancient times. This beach is lined with seafood eateries and water equipment concessions and is excellent for swimming. A short walk across to the

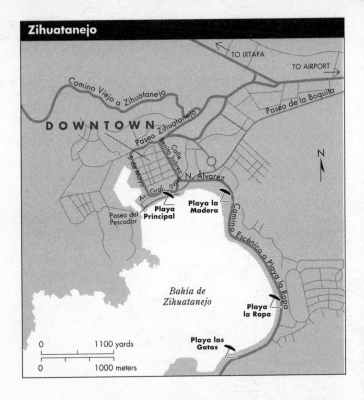

Zihuatanejo

other side of the island takes you to the gorgeous Varadero Beach, also with informal eateries and water-sports equipment rentals. Just behind the restaurants is Playa Coral, with crystal-clear water that's ideal for snorkeling. Playa Carey, toward the south end of the island, is small and isolated. Pangas run between the boat landings at both Cuacha-lalate and Varadero beaches and Playa Linda on the mainland.

Playa del Palmar. Ixtapa's main beach, this 3-km- (2-mi-) long broad sandy stretch runs along the hotel zone. Water-sports equipment is rented at many hotel concessions to guests and others. Since this is essentially open sea, the surf can be quite strong.

Playa Linda and Playa Quieta. About 10 minutes north of the Ixtapa hotel zone, thatch-roof restaurants dispense beer, sodas, and the catch of the day. The beach is protected by Ixtapa Island offshore, as is pretty Playa Linda, just beyond. Playa Linda is bordered at one end by an estuary with birds and gators, horses can be rented, and boats ($4 round-trip) run continually to Ixtapa Island.

Zihuatanejo

Playa la Madera. Across Zihuatanejo Bay from la Playa Principal, tiny Playa la Madera can be reached via a seaside footpath cut into the rocks. Also accessible by car, this pancake-flat beach has a sprinkling of small hotels and restaurants. It was named madera, or "wood," beach because it was a Spanish port for shipping oak, pine, cedar, and mahogany cut from the nearby Sierra Madre Sur.

Playa la Ropa. On the other side of a rocky point, Playa la Ropa is the most beautiful beach in the area; it's a five-minute taxi ride from town. Along this 1-km (½-mi) stretch of soft sand are open-air restaurants (complete with hammocks for post-meal siestas), a few hotels, and rental of wave runners, banana boats, and snorkel equipment. It got its name ("clothes beach") when a cargo of Oriental silks and clothing washed ashore from a Spanish galleon shipwrecked offshore.

Playa las Gatas. Named for the *gatas* (nurse sharks) that used to linger here, this beach has a long row of hewn rocks just offshore that serves as a breakwater. Legend has it that a Tarascan king built it to shelter his royal daughter's private beach, now lined with simple seafood eateries that provide lounge chairs for sunning. The clear waters are ideal for swimming, snorkeling, and diving. You can walk to Las Gatas in about 20 minutes from La Ropa beach; most folks come in pangas that run continuously to and from the municipal pier 8–5 PM. Purchase your round-trip ticket (about $3.50) at the Cooperativa office at the pier; keep the ticket stub for your return trip.

Playa Principal. At the edge of town, the town's picturesque main beach (aka Playa Municipal) is rimmed by the Paseo del Pescador. Here local fishermen keep their skiffs and gear, used for nightly fishing journeys out to sea. They return here in the early morning to sell their catch to the local townspeople and to restaurateurs.

Dining

Ixtapa

$$$$ ✕ **Bogart's.** Anyone who's been to any of the links in the Krystal hotel chain is familiar with the strikingly Moroccan flavor of this exotic (and expensive) eatery. Tables are separated by palm trees, and a Moorish fountain and piano music add to the movie-theme atmosphere. The international menu includes Suprema Casablanca, breaded chicken breasts stuffed with lobster. ⊠ *Krystal Ixtapa, Blvd. Ixtapa,* ☎ *7/553–0303. Reservations essential. MC, V. No lunch.*

$$$ ✕ **Beccofino.** This marina-side restaurant is always crowded, even
★ when its neighbors are empty. That's partly due to the elegant yet accessible atmosphere. Dark, polished wood contrasts nicely with bright white linens; outside, there's alfresco seating on a canopied deck adjacent to the water. Among the best dishes on the Northern Italian menu are minestrone soup, *caprese* salad (with tomatoes, basil, and mozzarella), fish fillet (usually red snapper or mahimahi) with a champagne sauce, salmon ravioli in cream, and chicken cacciatore. ⊠ *Plaza Marina Ixtapa,* ☎ *7/553–1770. Reservations essential. AE, MC, V.*

$$$ ✕ **El Galeón.** Seafood lovers and people-watchers like to settle in at Marina Ixtapa's nautical-decor bar, strewn with lots of rope and rigging, a ship's wheel, and other maritime knicknacks. Sit at the outdoor terrace or on a simulated galleon right on the water. The fresh tuna steak is outstanding, as are the pastas; upscale Mexican fare is also available. ⊠ *Plaza Marina Ixtapa,* ☎ *7/553–2150. AE, MC, V.*

$$ ✕ **Casa Morelos.** Positioned next to party-hearty Señor Frog, Casa Morelos offers excellent Mexican seafood on the patio or inside, where hand-loomed spreads, ochre walls, and wood furnishings give a homey feel. The *chile relleno de mariscos* (roasted chili stuffed with seafood), fish and octopus fajitas, and tuna steak topped with seven kinds of dry chilies are all filling and delicious. Save room for a margarita and a dance next door at Señor Frog. Or, come for breakfast: la Casa opens at 7:30 AM. ⊠ *La Puerta shopping center,* ☎ *7/553–0578. AE, MC, V.*

$$ ✕ **El Infierno y la Gloria.** "Hell and Paradise" is a Mexican cantina and restaurant, serving an array of dishes from throughout Mexico. The food is good, and you'll admire the walls, hand-painted with extravagant scenes and allegories. It opens early (8 AM) and closes around midnight. ⊠ *La Puerta shopping center,* ☎ *7/553–0304. AE, MC, V.*

$$ ✕ **La Valentina.** This relatively new and successful restaurant has
★   been built around Mexican gourmet recipes, many from celebrities such
as artist Martha Chapa. Truly memorable is the *pollo en mole de
tamarindo* (chicken in a spicy sauce flavored with tamarind and choco-
late). The decor is as Mexican as the menu. Also on the premises are
a video bar and disco. ⌧ *Blvd. Ixtapa next to the Radisson hotel,* ☏
7/553–1190. AE, MC, V. No lunch.

$–$$ ✕ **Mamma Norma & Deborah.** You can dine indoors or alfresco at this
lively, casual restaurant/bar, which has the best pizzas in town as well
as tasty seafood, hummus with pita bread, vegetarian dishes, and whole-
some salads. ⌧ *La Puerta shopping center,* ☏ *7/553–0274. MC, V.*

$ ✕ **Nueva Zelanda.** Although open all day, this sparkling little coffee
shop is best known for its tasty breakfasts. This location opened after
the success of the initial eatery in downtown Zihuatanejo. Both kitchens
produce fresh tropical fruit juices, fruit salads, and a variety of *tortas,*
sandwiches on large, crusty rolls. ⌧ *Los Patios shopping center, behind bandstand,* ☏ *7/554–2340;* ⌧ *Calle Cuauhtémoc 23, Zihuatanejo,* ☏ *7/553–0838. Reservations not accepted. No credit cards.*

Zihuatanejo

$$$ ✕ **Coconuts.** Its name reminiscent of Ixtapa's previous status as a co-
conut plantation, this downtown venue has become one of the top restau-
rants in Zihuatanejo. Under the direction of Chef Patricia Cummings,
Coconuts serves a variety of dishes including roast pork loin, seafood
tacos, sweet and zesty coconut shrimp, and a number of vegetarian items.
Five different dessert coffees are prepared flaming at your table. Lunch
is served noon–4, dinner 6–11. ⌧ *Agustín Ramírez 1,* ☏ *7/554–2518.
AE, DC, MC, V. Closed mid-Oct.–mid-May.*

$$–$$$ ✕ **Paul's.** Like many of Mexico's other high-end eateries, Paul's does-
n't open until 2 PM, but it's got some of the best food in town. The
zany Swiss-German owner seems to have created an eclectic lifestyle
here, and he may well greet you dressed in shorts and an unbuttoned
Hawaiian shirt. Notwithstanding his fashion choices, Paul has crafted
a small international menu of wonderful dishes. Start with a fresh ar-
tichoke or escargot appetizer or the lentil soup, followed by quail, pork
chops, or poached mahimahi served with a dill sauce. ⌧ *Benito Juárez
23,* ☏ *7/554–6528. MC, V. Closed May.*

$$ ✕ **Casa Elvira.** Named for the owner and onetime chef, this Zihuatanejo
institution near the town pier has a pleasant dining room and serves
a variety of consistently good seafood and Mexican dishes. Lobster is
the house specialty. ⌧ *Paseo del Pescador 8,* ☏ *7/554–2061. MC, V.*

$$ ✕ **Kau-Kan.** Opened in the mid-1990s, this restaurant quickly became
a local favorite. Owner-chef Ricardo Rodriguez, previously of Casa Que
Canta, serves imaginative, exquisitely prepared seafood, including fil-
let of sea bass, melt-in-your-mouth abalone, and grilled mahimahi
under a sweet, spicy pineapple sauce. Kau-Kan enjoys a gorgeous lo-
cation overlooking Zihuatanejo Bay and is probably the most elegant
restaurant in town. ⌧ *Carretera Escénica, Playa la Ropa Lote 7,* ☏
7/554–8446. AE, MC, V. No lunch.

$$ ✕ **Rossy.** A local favorite for dining on the roof terrace or right on the
beach, Rossy specializes in Mexican-style seafood, including a tempting
shrimp-and-pineapple brochette. Musicians usually serenade diners on
weekends. ⌧ *South end of Playa la Ropa,* ☏ *7/554–4004. MC, V.*

$ ✕ **Casa Puntarenas.** Talk about homey: Casa Puntarenas is not only
family-owned and -operated, but run out of the family residence. Select from a paper menu of seafood and Mexican specialties, which later
becomes your check. To get here, cross the footbridge over the lagoon
at the west end of town near the pier (or take a taxi). Come for breakfast until 11:30, or for the evening meal 6:30–9 PM. ⌧ *Noria 12,* ☏

7/554–2109. Reservations not accepted. No credit cards. Closed mid-Mar.–mid-Dec. No lunch.

$ ✕ **La Mordida.** Join the throngs after 4 PM at this simple, popular eatery for pizza and tasty charcoal-broiled burgers. Although in Mexico "una mordida" usually refers to a bribe or a payoff, here it refers to its more literal meaning: "a bite." ⊠ *Paseo de la Boquita 20,* ☎ *7/554–8216. No credit cards. No lunch.*

$ ✕ **La Perla.** Eat indoors if you want sports-bar action, or begin your day at the beach with an omelet or invigorating ceviche in the al fresco patio overlooking gorgeous Playa la Ropa. Among the seafood specialties, *filete La Perla* (fish fillet baked with cheese) is a favorite. ⊠ *Playa la Ropa,* ☎ *7/554–2700. AE, MC, V.*

$ ✕ **La Sirena Gorda.** Oil paintings and a bronze statue depict the namesake "fat mermaid" at this friendly restaurant near the pier. Specialties include seafood tacos and octopus kebab. The setting is casual, with an outdoor patio and a lively bar that's a popular local hangout. ⊠ *Paseo del Pescador 20,* ☎ *7/554–2687. Reservations not accepted. MC, V. Closed Wed. Mar.–mid-Dec.*

Lodging

Pricier Ixtapa specializes in deluxe, beachfront properties located along Playa del Palmar. Most of the budget accommodations are in Zihuatanejo, where the most glamorous hotels are on or overlooking La Madera or La Ropa beach, and the least expensive are downtown. For out-of-the-way seclusion, venture to the tiny beach of Troncones, about 30 minutes northwest of Zihuatanejo by car.

Ixtapa

$$$$ 🏨 **Presidente Inter-Continental Ixtapa.** One of Ixtapa's best all-inclusive properties, the Presidente has 24-hour beverage service, and various recreational activities—most of them centered on the pool. Rooms are attractively decorated in creams and whites, and rates include all meals. If you want tranquility, request a room near the east pool, away from where the action is. ⊠ *Blvd. Ixtapa s/n, 40880,* ☎ *7/553–0018 or 800/327–0200,* FAX *7/553–2312,* WEB *www.interconti.com. 420 rooms and suites. 4 restaurants, bar, no-smoking rooms, 2 pools, sauna, steam room, 2 tennis courts, basketball, exercise room, volleyball, beach, snorkeling, children's programs (ages 3–10), meeting rooms, car rental. AE, DC, MC, V.*

$$$$ 🏨 **Westin Brisas Ixtapa.** This immense, pyramid-shape architectural ★ wonder slopes down a hillside to its own secluded cove and beach, Playa Vista Hermosa. The grounds are lush with jungle vegetation; fresh flowers decorate your room. Every unit has a private balcony with a hammock, ocean view, and a table for room-service dining; junior suites have larger balconies with hot tubs. (Although this is Ixtapa's top hotel, accommodations are not as luxurious as what you might find at a Westin elsewhere.) Guests and nonguests enjoy the hotel's excellent Portofino and El Mexicano restaurants. ⊠ *Playa Vista Hermosa, Apdo. 87, 40880,* ☎ *7/553–2121 or 800/228–3000,* FAX *7/553–1031,* WEB *www.westin.com. 423 rooms and 19 suites. 5 restaurants, 2 bars, no-smoking rooms, 4 pools, beauty salon, 4 tennis courts, exercise room, children's programs (ages 3–7), concierge floor, business services, meeting rooms, travel services, car rental. AE, DC, MC, V.*

$$$ 🏨 **Dorado Pacífico.** This privately owned beachfront hotel is known for its fine food and good service. The huge pool, with two water slides, makes it a favorite with youngsters. Modern rooms are decorated in soft colors, and all have ocean views. Glass elevators look out on the dramatic atrium lobby. Try the beachside Cebolla Roja restaurant for dinner. ⊠ *Blvd. Ixtapa, 40880,* ☎ *7/553–2025 or 888/738–4205,* FAX

7/553–0126, WEB *www.doradopacifico.com. 285 rooms and suites. 4 restaurants, 2 bars, pool, massage, 2 tennis courts, shop, children's programs (10+), meeting rooms, travel services, car rental. AE, MC, V.*

$$$ 🏨 **Krystal Ixtapa.** Shaped like a boat with its bow pointing to the sea, this beachfront hotel is comfortable if lacking in charm. Rooms are standard contemporary style with a view to the ocean. The Club Krystalito provides recreational activities for children, and because of its meeting facilities, the hotel is often filled with conventioneers. The Krystal is home to Christine, Ixtapa's most popular disco, and Bogart's. ⊠ *Blvd. Ixtapa, 40880,* ☎ *7/553–0333 or 800/231–9860,* FAX *7/553–0336. 254 rooms, 20 suites. 4 restaurants, coffee shop, no-smoking floor, pool, beauty salon, 2 tennis courts, exercise room, dance club, children's programs (ages 3–10), meeting rooms, travel services, car rental. AE, DC, MC, V.*

$$ 🏨 **Best Western Posada Real.** Rooms were redecorated and the lobby remodeled between 1998 and 2000, maintaining the charm that has made this pleasant hotel more intimate than most of the others in Ixtapa. A good value, the beachfront low-rise has amenities such as a swim-up bar and putting green; rooms have remote-control satellite TV. ⊠ *Blvd. Ixtapa, 40880,* ☎ *7/553–1745 or 800/528–1234,* FAX *7/ 553–1805,* WEB *www.bestwestern.com. 110 rooms. Restaurant, bar, 2 pools, hot tub, putting green, volleyball, shop, travel services, car rental. AE, MC, V.*

Troncones

$$ 🏨 **El Burro Borracho.** Six comfortable stone cottages sit right on the 5-km- (3-mi-) long beach. Relax in a hammock on your private patio, or go beachcombing, boogie-boarding, hiking, or cave exploring. Afterwards, retreat to the congenial bar-restaurant, with menu options ranging from cheeseburgers to fresh lobster. The cost is near the low end of its price range; for cheaper digs, trailer spaces are available. Owners Dewey and Carolyn also own Casa de la Tortuga B&B, just up the beach. ⊠ *Troncones Beach, Apdo. 277, Zihuatanejo 40880,* ☎ *7/553– 2834,* FAX *7/553–2807. 6 bungalows. Restaurant, hiking, beach. No credit cards. Closed Aug. 1–Oct. 30.*

$$ 🏨 **Casa Ki.** Bungalows at this homey haven in the wilds of Troncones have tiny refrigerators, but guests may also use the fully equipped kitchen and barbecue, and breakfast is included in the rates. The house has a full kitchen as well as two bedrooms, living room, and larger bath. ⊠ *Troncones Beach, Apdo. 405, Zihuatanejo 40880,* ☎ *7/553–2815,* FAX *7/553–2417. 3 bungalows, 1 house. Beach. No credit cards.*

Zihuatanejo

$$$$ ✕🏨 **Casa Cuitlateca.** The smallest of Zihuatanejo's boutique hotels opened high above the bay, with spectacular views from three of the four individually decorated rooms. Rooms have handmade furnishings and arts and crafts from four Mexican states. A beautiful infinity pool is surrounded by a small fish pond, and there's a cool-water whirlpool on the villa's rooftop. The patio restaurant, open to the public for dinner only, serves a fixed, multicourse meal each night for $50 per person. The hotel's staff offers personalized attention and will arrange nearly any excursion you can think of. Unless one group books the entire hotel, children under 16 are not permitted. ⊠ *Calle Playa la Ropa, Apdo. 124, 40880,* ☎ *7/554–2448 or 877/541–1234,* FAX *7/554–2157,* WEB *www.casacuitlateca.com. 3 rooms, 1 suite. Restaurant, pool, hot tub. AE, MC, V.*

$$$$ ✕🏨 **La Casa Que Canta.** One of the loveliest small hotels in the world, ★   "The House That Sings" clings to a cliffside above Playa La Ropa. The multilevel palapa-topped lobby is adorned with folk-art furnishings, as are the individually decorated suites. Each boasts gorgeous bay views

from both the bedroom balcony and living-room terrace; 10 have private infinity pools. Bathrooms are huge, and fresh flower petals are arranged each day on your freshly made bed. Because of the stepped architecture, the main swimming pool seems to be airborne; below, a saltwater pool features a sea Jacuzzi (the beach is just a two-minute walk away). The romantic outdoor restaurant serves authentic Mexican and seafood dishes and opens to the public after 7 PM (reservations required). Children under 16 are not accepted at the hotel. ⊠ *Camino Escénico a Playa la Ropa, 40880,* ☎ *7/554–6529, 01–800/71–09345, or 888/523–5050,* FAX *7/554–7900,* WEB *www.casaquecanta.com. 25 suites. Restaurant, 2 pools, gym. AE, DC, MC, V.*

$$$$ 🏨 **Puerto Mío.** Within walking distance of downtown Zihuatanejo, this upscale resort nonetheless has a secluded, maritime air. Most guest rooms are in Casa del Mar, a home-cum-hotel on a 25-acre lot with a great bay view. The fanciest suites have an open-air living area as well as a terrace; in-room massage, facials, and pedicures are available. The hotel has a number of facilities near the water, including a romantic international restaurant, terrace bar, pool, two junior suites, a marina, and a rocky beach. Children under 16 are not accepted during the high season. ⊠ *Playa del Almacén, 40880,* ☎ *7/554–3344, 01–800/711–2080, or 888/633–3295,* FAX *7/554–3535,* WEB *www.puertomio.com.mx. 25 rooms and suites. Restaurant, bar, 2 pools, dive shop. AE, MC, V. Closed Sept.*

$$$$ ✕🏨 **Villa del Sol.** Zihuatanejo's first luxury hotel sits on 6 acres of coconut palms, lush tropical gardens, fountains, and meandering paths leading to lovely Playa la Ropa. Because the property is German-owned and -run, it is popular with European travelers. Rooms and baths are artistically designed, with king-size beds draped in gauzy canopies, colorful folk-art furnishings, and terraces or balconies. Beachfront and lagoon suites are considerably nicer than lower-price rooms. In the evening, try resisting one of Chef Fabrice's Mexican or international specialties, such as apple-and-cinnamon tacos. Elegant, romantic meals are served at the Villa del Sol restaurant, while casualwear is acceptable at the Cantina Bar and Grill. The Modified American Plan (including breakfast and dinner) is required in high season, when children under 14 are not accepted. ⊠ *Playa la Ropa, Apdo. 84, 40880,* ☎ *7/554–2239 or 888/389–2645,* FAX *7/554–2758,* WEB *www.hotelvilladelsol.com. 54 suites. 2 restaurants, no-smoking rooms, 4 pools, 2 tennis courts, beach, travel services. AE, MC, V.*

$$ 🏨 **Ávila.** Although somewhat institutional in character, this hotel is well situated in the center of town facing the beach at Paseo del Pescador. The large, clean rooms have TVs, air-conditioning, and ceiling fans. Visiting fisherfolk like to stay here during the March tournaments. ⊠ *Calle Juan N. Álvarez 8, 40880,* ☎ *7/554–2010,* FAX *7/554–8592. 26 rooms. AE, MC, V.*

$$ 🏨 **Bungalows Pacíficos.** Perched on three terraces above Playa la Madera, spacious but plain bungalows have no air-conditioning or TV, but do offer a sweeping view of the bay from the veranda, equipped with hammock, table, and chairs. Walk to Zihuatanejo's restaurants, just 10 minutes away, or cook in the room's fully equipped kitchen. The owner, who speaks Spanish, English, and German, enjoys sharing her knowledge of prime birding sites with her guests. ⊠ *Cerro de la Madera, Apdo. 12, 40880,* ☎ FAX *7/554–2112,* WEB *www.zihuatanejo-ixtapa.com.mx/bungalowspacificos. 6 units. No credit cards.*

$$ 🏨 **Catalina-Sotavento.** Really two hotels in one, this multilevel oldie-but-goodie sits on a cliff overlooking the bay. Below, accessible by extensive stairs, are Playa la Ropa and the hotel's beach bar and lounge chairs. Rooms are large and well maintained, with ceiling fans (but no air-conditioning) and ample terraces sporting hammocks and a chaise lounge. ⊠ *Playa la Ropa, Apdo. 2, 40880,* ☎ *7/554–2032,* FAX *7/554–2975. 126 rooms. Restaurant, 2 bars, pool. AE, DC, MC, V.*

$$ ⊞ **Irma.** One of Zihuatanejo's originals, this simple but comely colonial-style hotel sits on a bluff overlooking Madera Beach (accessible by a stairway). Rooms have both air-conditioning and fans, gleaming red-tile floors, and whitewashed walls with hand-painted headboards; those on the sixth floor have been remodeled. Ask for a room with a balcony and ocean view. ⊠ *Playa la Madera s/n, Apdo. 4, 40880,* ☎ *7/554–2105,* FAX *7/554–3738,* WEB *www.ixtapazihuatanejo.com.mx/irma. 72 rooms. Restaurant, bar, 2 pools. AE, MC, V.*

$$ ⊞ **Solimar Inn Suites.** Located on a quiet plaza four blocks from the main beach, this family-owned hotel has 12 suites with separate bedroom and both air-conditioning and fan. Thick white walls, tile floors, and bright accent colors give the rooms a distinctly Mediterranean flavor. Living/dining rooms have equipped kitchenettes, cable TV, and built-in couches that double as beds. Long-term guests receive discounts; some rent a blender, microwave, or coffee pot and stay for weeks. ⊠ *Plazas los Faroles, 40880,* ☎ FAX *7/554–3692. 12 rooms. Bar, pool. AE, MC, V.*

$$ ⊞ **Villas Miramar.** Most of the rooms have views of the exuberant gardens; a few overlook Madera Beach. All have a small balcony and are decorated in Mexican folk art and cooled by ceiling fans as well as air-conditioning. An extra $50 gets you a two-bedroom suite with equipped kitchenette, living/dining room, and a larger terrace overlooking the sea. ⊠ *Playa la Madera, Apdo. 211, 40880,* ☎ *7/554–2106,* FAX *7/554–2149. 16 rooms, 2 suites. Restaurant, bar, 2 pools. AE, MC, V.*

Nightlife

A good way to start an evening is a happy hour at one of Ixtapa or Zihuatanejo's hotel bars. Sunset is an important daily ritual, and plans should be made accordingly. Tops for sunset viewing (with live music) is the Westin's beachfront **Bar La Brisa. Christine** (☎ 7/553–0333), at the Krystal in Ixtapa, is the town's most expensive disco, featuring varied music and high-tech light shows. You'll get a gorgeous nighttime view from atop the 85-ft-high faux-lighthouse tower of **El Faro** (☎ 7/553–2090), attached to El Galeón restaurant, in Marina Ixtapa. There's live piano music nightly, and if you sing well, Raymundo will invite you to croon a tune as he tickles the ivories. Or head over to often-rowdy **Señor Frog** (⊠ Centro Comercial Ixtapa, opposite the Hotel Riviera Beach, ☎ 7/553–0692) for tequila shots and dancing.

Carlos 'n' Charlie's (⊠ Paseo del Palmar s/n, next to the Best Western Posada Real, ☎ 7/553–0085) has a party atmosphere, with late-night dancing on a raised platform by the beach. There's a desert-inspired disco, complete with blue sky and cactus, at **La Valentina** restaurant-video-bar-disco complex (⊠ Blvd. Ixtapa next to the Radisson hotel, ☎ 7/553–1190). Except for the casual spots like Señor Frog and Carlos 'n' Charlie's, most discos have dress codes, and may turn you away if you're wearing shorts or tennis shoes (also for men, tank tops or sandals).

A number of hotels feature **Mexican Fiesta** nights with buffets and folkloric dance performances. In high season you'll find Mexican Fiesta night Monday at the Hotel Krystal, Tuesday at the Dorado Pacífico, and Wednesday at the Barceló.

Outdoor Activities and Sports

Fishing

The area is best known for its feisty sailfish, hooked year-round. Seasonally one finds yellowfin tuna and yellowtail jacks, dorado, blue and black marlin, as well as mackerel, barracuda, bonito, and others. **Cooperativo Benito Juárez** (⊠ Paseo del Pescador 20, Zihuatanejo municipal pier, ☎ 7/554–3758) offers day trips in boats from 26 to 36 ft. Prices range from $150 for up to four for close-to-shore fishing in a motor launch to $270 for deep-sea fishing. Another Zihuatanejo cooperative venture with similar prices is **Cooperativo de Pescadores** (⊠ Paseo del Pescador 81, ☎ 7/554–2056). Bookings and information about sportfishing can be obtained through **Ixtapa Sportfishing Charters** (⊠ 19 Depue Ln., Stroudsburg, PA 18360, ☎ 570/688–9466, ℻ 570/688–9554). Cost ranges from $190 for 1–2 persons to a luxury yacht accommodating 6 people, at $900.

Golf

There are two 18-hole championship courses in Ixtapa. Each par-72 course has its own clubhouse with a restaurant, tennis courts, and pool. Part of the Marina Ixtapa complex, the challenging **Club de Golf Marina Ixtapa** (☎ 7/553–1410) was designed by Robert Von Hagge. Greens fees are $61 (including caddie or cart). The **Palma Real Golf Club** (☎ 7/553–1062), designed by Robert Trent Jones Jr., is on a wildlife preserve that runs from a coconut plantation to the beach. A round costs $48, plus cart ($25) and/or caddie ($6).

Horseback Riding

You can rent horses with guides at **Rancho Playa Linda** (☎ 7/554–3085) just up the coast from Ixtapa. **VIPSA** (☎ 7/553–2214 or 7/553–1858) tour operators also can arrange riding tours.

Scuba Diving

More than 30 dive sites in the area range from deep canyons to shallow reefs. The waters here are teeming with sea life, and visibility is generally excellent. On Ixtapa Island, **Centro de Buceo Oliverio** (⊠ Playa de Cuachalalate, ☎ 7/554–3992) provides rental equipment, instruction, and guided dives ($50 per tank). Owned and operated by NAUI (National Association of Underwater Instructors) master diver and marine biologist Juan Barnard, the **Zihuatanejo Scuba Center** (⊠ Centro Comercial Ixtapa, behind Restaurant Rafaello's, ☎ 7/553–0288) in Ixtapa runs one- and two-tank dives as well as five-day certification courses.

Tennis

All major Ixtapa hotels have lighted tennis courts. At the **Club de Golf Marina Ixtapa** (☎ 7/553–1410), fees are $10–$12 and equipment rentals are available. Fees are $10–$12 at the **Palma Real Golf Club** (☎ 7/553–1062 or 7/553–1163), where you can also rent equipment. In Zihuatanejo, **Villa del Sol** (☎ 7/554–2239) has courts available to nonguests.

Water Park

A treat for children is a trip to **Magic World** (⊠ Paseo de las Garzas s/n, next to Ixtapa Palace Hotel, ☎ 7/553–1359), with wave pools, water slides, an artificial lake for boating, a pirate ship, and several restaurants. It's open 10:30–5:30 pm Tuesday–Sunday and costs about $6.50 per person.

Water Sports

You'll find a variety of water sports along Playa del Palmar in Ixtapa. Parasailing costs about $22 for an eight-minute ride or $32 for 15 minutes; waterskiing runs about $38 per half hour; banana-boat rides are about $5.50 per person for a 20-minute trip. On Playa la Ropa, next to La Perla restaurant, Hobie Cats rent for about $27 an hour depending on the size of the boat, and classes cost $25 per half hour. Windsurfers—when you can find them—rent for $20 per hour; classes, which include six hours over four days, cost $40.

Shopping

Ixtapa

As you enter Ixtapa from the airport or from Zihuatanejo, you'll see a large handicrafts market, **Mercado de Artesanía Turístico,** on the right side of Boulevard Ixtapa. The result of an ordinance banning vendors from the beach, this market is open weekdays 10–10 and hosts some 150 stands, selling handicrafts, T-shirts, and kitschy souvenirs.

Across the street from the hotel zone, the shopping area is loosely divided into *centros comerciales,* or malls. These clusters of pleasant colonial-style buildings feature patios containing boutiques, restaurants, cafés, and grocery minimarkets.

Zihuatanejo

Downtown Zihuatanejo has a colorful **municipal market** with a labyrinth of small stands on the east side of the town center, on Calle Benito Juárez between Nava and González. On the western edge of town along three blocks of Calle Cinco de Mayo is the **Mercado de Artesanía Turístico,** similar to the craft and souvenir market in Ixtapa, but larger, with 255 stands. Good purchases include hand-painted wooden masks and ceramics made in small towns throughout the state, huaraches, and silver jewelry. Near the mercado, across from the Aeroméxico office and facing the waterfront, **Casa Marina** (⊠ Paseo del Pescador 9, ☎ 7/554–2373) is a two-story building with individual boutiques selling folk art, hammocks, and hand-loomed rugs.

In addition to these shops, the tiny three-block nucleus of central Zihuatanejo has several worthwhile shops. Shop for silver and gold jewelry at **Alberto's** (⊠ Calle Cuauhtémoc 12 and 15, ☎ 7/554–2161). **Coco Cabaña** (⊠ Agustín Ramírez 1, ☎ 7/554–2518) is a fascinating folk-art shop at Coconuts restaurant. Over at Playa la Ropa, **Gala Art** (⊠ Villa del Sol, ☎ 7/554–7774) exhibits and sells paintings, jewelry, and bronze, wood, and marble sculptures crafted by artists from throughout Mexico. **Galería Maya** (⊠ Calle Nicolás Bravo 31, ☎ 7/554–4606) is very browseable for its folk art and women's clothing. **Lupita's** (⊠ Juan N. Álvarez 5, ☎ 7/554–2238) has a good selection of colorful women's apparel, including handmade items from Oaxaca, Yucatán, Chiapas, and Guatemala.

Arte Mexicano Nopal (⊠ Av. Cinco de Mayo 56, ☎ 7/554–7530) sells Mexican handicrafts and natural pine furniture that can be finished according to the client's tastes.

Ixtapa/Zihuatanejo A to Z

AIR TRAVEL

You can fly to Ixtapa from Houston, Los Angeles, and other major cities. From the airport, the taxi fare to the Ixtapa hotel zone is about $20; the trip takes about 20 minutes. To Zihuatanejo, the 15-minute trip costs about $15.

CARRIERS

Mexicana has daily flights from the U.S. and Mexican cities. Aeroméxico flies from multiple U.S. and Mexican cities. Alaska Airlines has direct flights three times a week from Los Angeles. America West has direct service three times a week from Phoenix. Houston is the hub for Continental, which offers daily direct flights.

➤ AIRLINES AND CONTACTS: **Aeroméxico** (☎ 01–800/021–4010). **Alaska Airlines** (☎ 01–800/426–0333). **America West** (☎ 01–800/235–9292 or 01–800/356–6611). **Continental** (☎ 01–800/900–5000). **Mexicana** (☎ 7/554–2208 in Zihuatanjeo or 7/553–2208 in Ixtapa).

BOAT AND FERRY TRAVEL

Several cruise lines, including Holland America Lines and Royal Cruise Lines, sail to Ixtapa/Zihuatanejo as part of their seven-day Riviera Mexicana trips.

BUS TRAVEL

Various bus companies run from the Central de Autobuses. Estrella de Oro has deluxe service to Acapulco, Cuernavaca, Taxco, and Mexico City. Estrella Blanca offers first-class service to the same destinations as well as Querétaro, Aguascalientes, and León.

➤ BUS INFORMATION: **Central de Autobuses** (✉ Paseo Zihuatanejo at Paseo de la Boquita). **Estrella Blanca** (☎ 7/554–3476 or 7/554–8477). **Estrella de Oro** (☎ 7/554–2175 or 7/554–3802).

CAR RENTAL

Hertz has desks in the airport and in Zihuatanejo. Quick Rent-A-Car, in the Riviera Beach hotel, rents cars and Jeeps, and Suburbans with or without air-conditioning.

➤ MAJOR AGENCIES: **Hertz** (☎ 7/554–2590; 7/554–2255 in Zihuatanejo). **Quick Rent-A-Car** (✉ Blvd. Ixtapa s/n, ☎ 7/553–1830).

CAR TRAVEL

The new Autopista del Sol connects Ixtapa/Zihuatanejo to Mexico City passing Acapulco en route; tolls total around $55. Otherwise, the trip from Mexico City takes about eight hours. Acapulco is a 3½-hour drive on Highway 200, which passes through small towns and coconut groves and has some spectacular ocean views. The drive from Manzanillo takes about 12 hours, so you might want to stop along the way.

EMERGENCIES

There is no general emergency number, so call the police or the hospital directly. Hospital de la Armada is next to the Mercado de Artesanía Turístico, across from Los Patios Shopping Center.

➤ CONTACTS: **Hospital de la Armada** (✉ Paseo del Palmar s/n, ☎ 7/554–3099). **Police** (☎ 7/554–2040). **Red Cross** (☎ 7/554–2009). **Tourist Protection** ☎ 7/554–2207.

INTERNET

CDNET Internet Provider in Zihuatanejo offers inexpensive Internet access.

➤ INTERNET CAFÉS: **CDNET Internet Provider** (✉ Av. La Boquita 205, ☎ 7/554–7384).

TAXIS AND MINIBUSES

Unless you plan to travel great distances or visit remote beaches, taxis and buses are by far the best way to get around. Taxis are plentiful, and fares are reasonable and fixed. The fare from the Ixtapa hotel zone to Zihuatanejo begins at a little more than $3. To order a cab, call APAAZ. A second radio cab company is UTAAZ. Minibuses run every 10–15 minutes between the Ixtapa hotels and downtown Zihuatanejo; fare is about 30¢.

➤ TAXI COMPANIES: **APAAZ** (☎ 7/554–3680). **UTAAZ** (☎ 7/554–4583).

TOURS

Moderate and high-end hotels will arrange tours for their guests. Two-and-a-half-hour sunset cruises ($49) and four-hour swim and snorkel cruises aboard the 65-ft trimaran *Tri-Star* set sail from Zihuatanejo Bay. Both include open bar (domestic drinks); the snorkel cruise includes lunch. Other half-day cruises access Ixtapa Island or Playa las Gatas (both $20). Details on all these cruises are available from Yates del Sol.

You can hire a fisherman's boat from Zihuatanejo's municipal pier to go to scenic, remote Playa Manzanillo—great for snorkeling—or to Los Moros de Potosí, a group of large white rocks in the ocean where rare web-footed brown boobies congregate with cormorants, egrets, frigates, pelicans, and long-tailed white terns. To see pink flamingos and other wading birds, take a bus or taxi to Barra de Potosí (15 minutes past the airport), where a beautiful *laguna* (lake) is an unofficial bird sanctuary. You can arrange a cruise with the small fishing launches in front of the palapa restaurants there, but the fishermen probably don't speak English. Organized tours to Barra de Potosí are also available.

➤ Tour Operator Recommendations: **Yates del Sol** (☎ 7/554–2694).

TRAVEL AGENCIES

American Express in Ixtapa is open Monday–Saturday 9–6. In Zihuatanejo, TIP arranges snorkel and dive tours to beaches in and around Ixtapa/Zihuatanejo.

➤ Local Agent Referrals: **American Express** (✉ Krystal Ixtapa arcade, Blvd. Ixtapa, ☎ 7/553–0853, FAX 7/553–1206). **TIP** (✉ Juan N. Álvarez at Calle Benito Juárez, ☎ 7/554–7510).

VISITOR INFORMATION

The Municipal Tourism Office is open weekdays 8–4. The Guerrero State Tourism Office is open weekdays 8–9, Saturday 8–3.

➤ Tourist Information: **Guerrero State Tourism Office** (✉ La Puerta shopping center, across from Presidente Inter-Continental, Ixtapa, ☎ 7/553–1967). **Municipal Tourism Office** (✉ Zihuatanejo City Hall, Plaza Principal, ☎ 7/554–2355 or 7/554–7523).

To research prices, get advice from other travelers, and book travel arrangements, visit www.fodors.com.

9   ACAPULCO

After a half century, Acapulco endures at the top of the glitterati top-10 list as a sentimental favorite and a party-hearty resort town, with miles of beaches and some of the glitziest discos this side of the Pacific. A delightful three-hour drive from Acapulco is Taxco, a colonial treasure, where the Baroque towers of Santa Prisca church overlook cobblestone streets lined with silversmiths.

Updated by
Patricia Alisau

A CAPULCO IS A VIBRANT PORT CITY with one of the most beautiful bays in the world. Famed Mexican muralist Diego Rivera is said to have been so awestruck by the sunsets here that he re-created them on canvas. This beauty, no doubt, is what attracted the Hollywood celebrities of the 1950s who built homes and hotels as hideaways and places for entertaining their friends. The celebrity status continued. This is where John and Jackie Kennedy spent their honeymoon. Likewise, Bill and Hillary Clinton. And it's where Liz Taylor and Michael Todd ventured after tying the knot. In fact, Acapulco still ranks as one of the top honeymoon spots worldwide. Entertainers such as Placido Domingo come to give yearly benefit concerts and singers such as Julio Iglesias and a host of others maintain residences here, carrying on the Hollywood tradition that started long ago.

Acapulco has managed to age gracefully over the years even as it's grown into a town of a million inhabitants. Care is especially lavished on its upkeep. The city fathers initiated a multimillion-dollar beautification program some time ago, which is renewed annually to keep the bay, beaches, and streets landscaped and clean.

Of course, anyone who ventures to this stretch of the Pacific, 433 km (268 mi) south of Mexico City, does so to relax. Translate that as swimming, shopping, and enjoying the nightlife. Everything takes place against a staggeringly beautiful backdrop. The natural harbor of Acapulco Bay is the city's centerpiece. By day the water looks temptingly deep blue; at night it flashes and sparkles with the city lights.

The weather is Acapulco's major draw—warm waters, almost constant sunshine, and year-round temperatures in the 80s. It comes as no surprise, then, that most people plan their day around laying their towel on some part of Acapulco's many kilometers of beach. Both tame and wild water sports are available—everything from waterskiing to snorkeling, diving, and parasailing. Less strenuous possibilities are motorboat rides and fishing trips. Championship golf courses, tennis courts, and the food and crafts markets also lure some visitors away from the beach.

Most people rise from their hammocks, deck chairs, or towels only when impelled by hunger, and eating is one of Acapulco's great pleasures. In addition to the showy places, there are plenty of good no-frills, down-home Mexican restaurants. Eating at one of these joints takes you to the real Mexico.

At night Acapulco rouses itself from the day's torpor and prepares for the long hours ahead. Though Acapulco's heyday is past, its nightlife is legendary, and the constant opening of new and ever more spectacular dance clubs is proof positive that this remains the disco capital of the world. Perpetually crowded, the discos are grouped in twos and threes, and most people go to several places in one night.

Since the late 1940s, Acapulco has expanded eastward so that today it is one of Mexico's largest cities, with a population of approximately one million. Former President Miguel Alemán Valdés bought up miles of the coast just before the road and airport were built—as his namesake Avenida Costera Miguel Alemán testifies. Under development is a 3,000-acre expanse known as Acapulco Diamante, which encompasses the areas known as Punta Diamante and Playa Diamante and some of the city's most sparkling hotels and residential developments.

Pleasures and Pastimes

Beaches

The lure of sun and sand in Acapulco is legendary. Every sport is available, and you can eat in a beach restaurant, dance, and sleep in a *hamaca* (hammock)—all without leaving the water's edge. There are also plenty of quiet and even isolated beaches within reach.

Dining

Dining in Acapulco is more than just eating out—it is the most popular leisure activity in town. Every night the restaurants fill up, and every night the adventurous diner can sample a different cuisine. The variety of styles matches the range of cuisines: from greasy spoons that serve regional favorites to gourmet restaurants with gorgeous views of Acapulco Bay. Most restaurants fall somewhere in the middle, and on the Costera Miguel Alemán are dozens of beachside restaurants with *palapa* (palm frond) roofs, as well as wildly decorated rib and hamburger joints popular with visitors under 30—not necessarily in age, but definitely in spirit. Most establishments that cater to tourists purify their drinking water and use it to cook vegetables.

Lodging

Accommodations in Acapulco run the gamut from sprawling, big-name complexes with nonstop amenities to small, family-run inns where hot water is a luxury. Wherever you stay, however, prices will be reasonable compared with those in the United States, and service is generally good, as Acapulqueños have been catering to tourists for over half a century.

Nightlife

Acapulco has always been famous for its nightlife, and justifiably so. For many visitors the discos and restaurants are just as important as the sun and the sand. The minute the sun slips over the horizon, the Costera comes alive with people milling around window-shopping, deciding where to dine, and generally biding their time till the disco hour. The legendary Acapulco discos are open 365 days a year from about 10:30 PM until they empty out. Obviously you aren't going to find great culture here; theater efforts are few and far between, but Placido Domingo gives the occasional benefit concert and the Acapulco Symphonic Orchestra rates as one of the best in the country. International pop-music fests and several film events such as black- and French-cinema festivals are gaining popularity.

Shopping

The abundance of air-conditioned shopping malls and boutiques makes picking up gifts and souvenirs a snap. Malls in Acapulco range from the shopping arcades at several of the more lavish hotels to the huge, completely enclosed Plaza Bahía and Gran Plaza.

The State of Guerrero is especially known for hand-painted ceramics, items made from *palo de rosa* wood, primitive bark paintings depicting scenes of village life and local flora and fauna, and embroidered textiles. There are several good shops specializing in Mexican crafts, and the mercado municipal also is a good source of local handicrafts. Taxco is one of the silver capitals of the world.

Sports and the Outdoors

Acapulco has lots for sports lovers to enjoy. Most hotels have pools, and many have private tennis clubs and gyms. Acapulco's waters are teeming with sailfish, marlin, shark, and mahimahi, and although the waters aren't as clear as in the Caribbean, waterskiing is popular as are windsurfing, kayaking, and bronco riding (one-person jet skis). Scuba diving is best December, January, and February when the water is the most transparent. The city sunk a Canadian warship at the beginning of 2001 to make diving more appealing. Golfers can tee off at the 9-hole municipal course, in town, or at one of the five 18-hole championship courses in Acapulco Diamante.

EXPLORING

It's possible to get a feel for Acapulco during a short stay if you take in some downtown sights along with your beach activities. Those who have a longer time to spend can really soak up the ambience of the place and can enjoy excursions to some isolated beaches as well as to Taxco.

Numbers in the text correspond to numbers in the margin and on the Acapulco and Taxco maps.

Great Itineraries

IF YOU HAVE 3 DAYS

Spend the first day enjoying your favorite beach activity, be it parasailing, waterskiing, or simply sunning. That evening, to get the lay of the land, take a sunset cruise that includes a ringside view of Acapulco's daredevil *clavadistas* (divers) at **La Quebrada** ⑨. The following day, experience Acapulco at its most authentic, paying an early visit to the **Mercado Municipal** ④, the **waterfront** ⑦, and the **zócalo** (town square) ⑧. Head for the beach for some rays after all that activity and later take in some late-afternoon shopping in the boutiques and handicrafts markets along the Costera Miguel Alemán. Come nightfall, "shake off the dust" (as they say in Mexico) at one of the city's glitzy discos. The next day you'll want to try to land a sailfish, take in the Mexican Fiesta at the **Acapulco International Center,** and bid farewell to Acapulco with a late candlelit dinner at one of the city's romantic dining spots.

IF YOU HAVE 5 DAYS

Add on to the three-day itinerary a visit to the newly renovated **El Fuerte de San Diego** ⑥, built in the 18th century to protect Acapulco from pirates, and today home of the Anthropology Museum. Then swing down the street to the new **Casa de Mascaras** ⑤, with its collection of Guerrero masks. For a taste of the 1950s Acapulco of John Wayne and Johnny Weissmuller, hire a taxi to take you into the hills above Caleta and Caletilla; make it a point to drop into Los Flamingos Hotel, which Weissmuller once owned with others from the Hollywood gang. Head out to Pie de la Cuesta for a late lunch and boat ride or waterskiing on Coyuca Lagoon, and then cross the road and park your body under a palm-frond umbrella for a spectacular sunset on the beach. Save one morning for the thrilling **Shotover Jet** boat ride on the Papagayo River. Especially if you're traveling with children, devote a few hours to **Mágico Mundo Marino** ⑩.

IF YOU HAVE 7 DAYS

Follow the five-day itinerary above and then, for a complete change of pace, rent a car or arrange for a tour to **Taxco,** a colonial treasure of twisting cobblestone streets and some 2,000 silver shops, about a three-hour drive from Acapulco; plan to spend the night. For a change from shopping for silver, visit the **Iglesia de San Sebastián y Santa Prisca** ⑪, Taxco's most important landmark, on Plaza Borda, and the **Casa Humboldt** ⑬, which now houses a museum of viceregal art. Try to get a front-row seat at one of the bars or restaurants on the square and spend an hour watching the constant activity: weddings, funerals, baptisms, and vendors selling baskets and animal figurines. The following day, tour the **Grutas de Cacahuamilpa** ⑮, an amazing expanse of subterranean chambers.

Acapulco

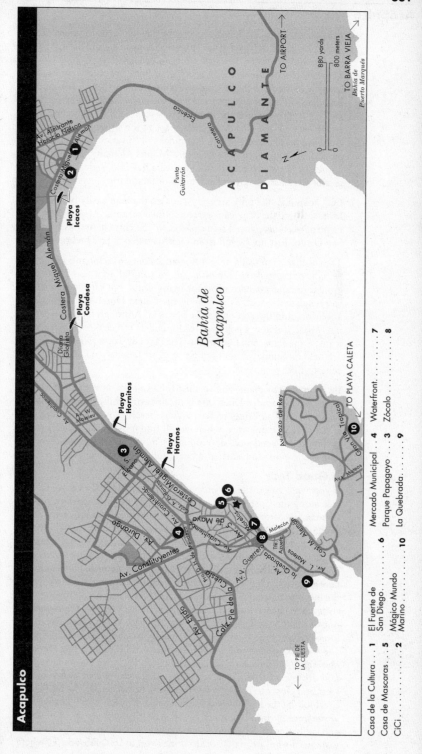

Bahía de Acapulco

Playa Icacos

Playa Condesa

Playa Hornitos

Playa Hornos

Punta Guitarrón

ACAPULCO DIAMANTE

TO AIRPORT →

TO BARRA VIEJA

TO Bahía de Puerto Marqués

880 yards
800 meters

TO PIE DE LA CUESTA

TO PLAYA CALETA

Casa de la Cultura....**1**

Casa de Máscaras....**5**

CiCi..................**2**

El Fuerte de San Diego......**6**

Mágico Mundo Marino......**10**

Mercado Municipal...**4**

Parque Papagayo....**3**

La Quebrada........**9**

Waterfront.........**7**

Zócalo............**8**

Acapulco

Acapulco is easily explored. During the day the focus for most visitors is the beach and the myriad activities that happen on and off it. At night the attention shifts to the restaurants and discos. The Avenida Costera Miguel Alemán, the wide boulevard that hugs Acapulco Bay from the Scenic Highway to Playa Caleta (about 8 km, or 5 mi), is central to both day and night diversions. All the major beaches, shopping malls, and big hotels—minus the more exclusive Acapulco Diamante properties—are off the Costera. Hence most of the shopping, dining, and clubbing takes place within a few blocks of this main drag, and many an address is listed only as "Costera Miguel Alemán." Because street addresses are not often used and streets have no logical pattern, directions are usually given from a major landmark.

Old Acapulco, the only area of Acapulco that can easily be visited on foot, is where the Mexicans go to run their errands. Also known as El Centro, it's where you'll find the zócalo, the church, and El Fuerte de San Diego. Just up the hill from Old Acapulco is La Quebrada.

The southern peninsula of Old Acapulco contains remnants of the first version of Acapulco. This primarily residential area was prey to dilapidation and abandonment for many years, but efforts were made to revitalize it—such as reopening the Caleta Hotel and opening the aquarium and the zoo on Isla la Roqueta. Although its prime is definitely past, it is now a popular area for budget travelers, especially Mexicans, Canadians, and Europeans. The **Plaza de Toros**, where bullfights are held on Sunday from the first week of January to Easter, is in the center of the peninsula.

If you arrived by plane, you've already had a royal introduction to Acapulco Bay. **Acapulco Diamante** is the area stretching east of Acapulco proper from Las Brisas to Barra Vieja beach. You'll need a car or a taxi to explore this area, where you'll find most of Acapulco's poshest hotels and residential developments, as well as several exclusive private clubs, pounding surf, and beautiful beaches.

A Good Tour

If you want to get the lay of the land, you might take a drive or taxi ride along the Costera Miguel Alemán, starting on its eastern edge at **La Base,** the Mexican naval base south of Playa Icacos. When you come to Playa Icacos, you'll see the **Casa de la Cultura** ① cultural complex on the beach side (just past the Hyatt Regency hotel); a little farther down is **CiCi** ②, a children's amusement park. About 1 km (½ mi) past CiCi, on the right side of the Costera, lies the **Acapulco International Center** (often called the Convention Center); you might return here in the evening to attend a Mexican Fiesta. Continue along through the commercial heart of the Costera until you reach **Parque Papagayo** ③, one of the top municipal parks in the country. When you arrive at the intersection of the Costera with Diego Hurtado de Mendoza, detour a few blocks inland to find Old Acapulco and the sprawling **Mercado Municipal** ④. You'll want to take the bus marked MERCADO or have your taxi drop you off; it's best to navigate this area by foot. A few blocks west and closer to the water, **El Fuerte de San Diego** ⑥ sits on the hill overlooking the harbor next to the army barracks. You'll next see the **waterfront** ⑦ (locally known as the *malecón*) with its series of docks and, adjoining it, the **zócalo** ⑧, the center of Old Acapulco. A 15-minute walk up the hill from the zócalo brings you to **La Quebrada** ⑨, where the famous cliff divers perform their daredevil stunts daily.

Sights to See

1 **Casa de la Cultura.** This cultural complex includes a small archaeological museum, an exhibit of Mexican and international crafts, and the Ixcateopan art gallery. ✉ *Costera Miguel Alemán 4834,* ☎ *7/ 484-4004.* ✍ *Free.* ☉ *Weekdays 9–2 and 5–8, Sat. 9–2.*

5 **Casa de Mascaras.** A private home has been turned into a gallery for a stunning collection of 550 ceremonial masks, most from the state of Guerrero. Some represent traditional ritualistic dances, such as "Moors and the Christians" and "Battle of the Tigers." ✉ *Calle Morelos S/N, ex-zona militar B, a half block from the Fuerte de San Diego,* ☎ *7/ 486-5577.* ✍ *Free (donation suggested).* ☉ *Mon.–Sat. 10–6.*

2 **CiCi** (Centro Internacional para Convivencia Infantil). A water-oriented theme park for children, CiCi has dolphin and seal shows, a freshwater pool with wave-making apparatus, a water slide, miniaquarium, and other attractions. Swim with the dolphins for $77 for an hour, $43 for a half hour, including transportation to or from your hotel. ✉ *Costera Miguel Alemán, across from Hard Rock Cafe,* ☎ *7/484-8210.* ✍ *$6.* ☉ *Daily 10–6.*

6 **El Fuerte de San Diego.** Acapulco was originally an important port for the Spanish—who used it to trade with Asian countries, notably the Philippines—and they erected this fortress in the 18th century to protect the city from pirates. Their original fort, destroyed in an earthquake, was built in 1616; it was restored in 2000. The pentagon-shape fort, restructured into 15 salons, now houses the **Museo Historico de Acapulco.** Bilingual videos and text explain the exhibits, which trace the city's history from the first settlements 3,000 years ago, to the exploits of famous pirates like Sir Francis Drake, through the era of the missionaries, and up to Mexico's independence from Spain in 1821. Air-conditioning makes the museum pleasant even in the heat. ✉ *Calle Hornitos and Morelos,* ☎ *7/482-3828.* ✍ *$2.70, free Sun.* ☉ *Tues.–Sun. 10–5.*

10 **Mágico Mundo Marino.** In addition to an aquarium, the Magic Marine World has a sea lion show, swimming pools, a toboggan, scuba diving, and (for rent) Jet Skis, inner tubes, and kayaks—not to mention clean rest rooms. From **Playa Caleta,** you can take the glass-bottom boat to **Isla la Roqueta** (about 10 minutes each way) for a visit to the small zoo. ✉ *Playa Caleta,* ☎ *7/483-1215.* ✍ *Aquarium $3; round-trip ferry service to Isla la Roqueta, including zoo, $3.* ☉ *Mágico Mundo daily 9–6, zoo daily 9–5.*

4 **Mercado Municipal.** Locals come to this sprawling municipal market to purchase their everyday needs, from fresh vegetables and candles to plastic buckets and love potions. The stalls within the mercado are densely packed together, but things stay relatively cool despite the lack of air-conditioning. There are baskets, pottery, hammocks, even a stand offering charms, amulets, and talismans. Come as early as possible to avoid the crowds. ✉ *Diego Hurtado de Mendoza and Av. Constituyentes, a few blocks west of Costera.* ☉ *Daily 7–7.*

3 **Parque Papagayo.** Named for the hotel that formerly occupied the grounds, the park sits on 52 acres of prime real estate on the Costera, just after the underpass that begins at Playa Hornos. Youngsters enjoy the life-size model of a Spanish galleon, made to look like the ones that sailed into Acapulco when it was Mexico's capital of trade with the Orient. There is an aviary, a roller-skating rink, a racetrack with mite-size race cars, a replica of the space shuttle *Columbia,* bumper boats in a lagoon, and other rides. ✉ *Costera Miguel Alemán,* ☎ *7/485-9623.* ✍ *No entrance fee, rides 70¢–$1.80, 10-ride package $4.* ☉ *Daily 10–8, rides section 4–11 nightly.*

❾ La Quebrada. High on a hill above downtown Acapulco, La Quebrada (literally "gorge"; in this case cliffs) is home to the Mirador Hotel, *the* place for tourists in the 1940s. These days most visitors come here to see the famous cliff divers jump from a height of 130 ft daily at 1 PM and evenings at 7:30, 8:30, 9:30, and 10:30. The dives are thrilling, so be sure to arrive early. Before they take the plunge, the divers say a prayer at a small shrine near the jumping-off point. Sometimes they dive in pairs; often they carry torches. The hotel's La Perla supper club is the traditional and most comfortable viewing spot, but you will be obligated to buy a drinks-show-tips ($13) or buffet-show-tips package ($23). Be forewarned: the tequila, rum, and brandy drinks are watered down. By all means, don't let this dissuade you from seeing the show. The divers can also be seen from a general observation deck next to the hotel (about $2). When you exit, some of the divers may also be waiting to greet you—and to ask for tips.

❼ Waterfront. A stroll by the docks will remind you that Acapulco is still a lively commercial port and fishing center. The cruise ships anchor here, and at night Mexicans bring their children to play on the small tree-lined promenade. Farther west, by the zócalo, are the docks for the sightseeing yachts and smaller fishing boats, a good spot for people-watching. ⊠ *Costera Miguel Alemán, between Calle Escudero on the west and El Fuerte de San Diego on the east.*

❽ Zócalo. You'll find the hub of downtown and Old Acapulco at this shaded plaza, overgrown with dense trees. All day it's filled with vendors, shoeshine men, and people lining up to use the pay phones. After siesta, they drift here to meet and greet. On Sunday evening there's often music in the bandstand. The zócalo fronts **Nuestra Señora de la Soledad,** the town's modern but unusual church, with its stark-white exterior and bulb-shape blue and yellow spires. ⊠ *Bounded by Calle Felipe Valle on the north, Costera Miguel Alemán on the south, Calle J. Azueta on the west, and Calle J. Carranza on the east.*

NEED A BREAK?	Just off the zócalo, **Sanborns** attracts locals and tourists alike; many linger for hours over a newspaper and a cup of coffee. **Cafetería Astoria** is a little outdoor café on the zócalo where businesspeople stop in for breakfast before work or meet midmorning for a cappuccino and a sweet roll.

Beaches

The bay has been considerably cleaned up over the past few years due to the efforts of city officials, and maintaining it continues to be a top priority. However, some beaches, such as Revolcadero and Pie de la Cuesta, have very strong undertows and surf, so swimming isn't advised. In addition, although vending on the beach has been officially outlawed, you'll still be approached by souvenir hawkers. You can always follow the lead of the Mexican cognoscenti and enjoy the waters at your hotel pool.

Beaches in Mexico are public, even those that seem to belong to a big hotel.

Barra Vieja

About 27 km (17 mi) east of Acapulco, between Laguna de Tres Palos and the Pacific, this long stretch of uncrowded beach is somewhat more inviting than Pie de la Cuesta because the drive out is much more pleasant. Most people make the trip out here for the solitude and to feast on *pescado à la talla* (fish marinated in spices and grilled over hot coals).

Caleta and Caletilla

On the peninsula in Old Acapulco, these two beaches once rivaled La Quebrada as the main tourist area in Acapulco's heyday. Now they attract families. Motorboats to Isla la Roqueta leave from here.

Condesa

Facing the middle of Acapulco Bay, this stretch of sand has more than its share of tourists, especially singles, and the beachside restaurants are convenient for bites between parasailing flights.

Hornos and Hornitos

Running from the Plaza las Glorias Paraíso to Las Hamacas hotel, these beaches are packed shoulder to shoulder on the weekends with locals and Mexican tourists who know a good thing: graceful palms shade the sand, and there are scads of casual eateries within walking distance.

Icacos

Stretching from the naval base to El Presidente hotel, away from the famous strip, this beach is less populated than others on the Costera. The morning waves are especially calm.

Pie de la Cuesta

You'll need a car or cab to reach this relatively unpopulated spot, about a 25-minute drive west of Acapulco's downtown, through one of the least picturesque parts of town. A string of rustic restaurants and new, rustic inns border the wide beach, and straw palapas provide shade. What attracts people to Pie de la Cuesta, besides the long expanse of beach and spectacular sunsets, is beautiful Coyuca Lagoon, a favorite spot for waterskiing, freshwater fishing, and boat rides. The boats will ferry you to La Laguna restaurant, where, some people claim, the pescado à la talla is even better than at Barra Vieja.

Puerto Marqués

Tucked below the airport highway, this strand is popular with Mexican tourists, so it tends to get crowded on weekends.

Revolcadero

A wide, sprawling beach next to the Vidafel Mayan Palace, Pierre Marqués, and Princess hotels, its water is shallow and its waves are fairly rough. People come here to surf and ride horses.

DINING

The top restaurants in Acapulco can be fun for a splurge and provide very good value. Even at the best places in town, a main dish of meat or fish rarely exceeds $35, and the atmosphere and views are fantastic. Ties and jackets are out of place, but so are shorts or jeans. Unless stated otherwise, all restaurants are open daily for lunch and dinner; dinner-only places open around 6:30 or 7.

Note: Loud music blares from many restaurants along the Costera, and proprietors will aggressively try to hustle you inside with offers of drink specials. If you're looking for a hassle-free evening, it's best either to avoid this area or decide in advance precisely where you want to dine.

CATEGORY	COST*
$$$$	over $35
$$$	$25–$35
$$	$15–$25
$	under $15

*per person for a main course at dinner

American

$$ ✕ **Carlos 'n' Charlie's.** An Acapulco landmark, this is still one of the most popular restaurants in town. Part of the Anderson group (with restaurants in the United States and Spain as well as Mexico), Carlos 'n' Charlie's cultivates an atmosphere of controlled craziness. Prankster waiters, a jokester menu, and eclectic decor add to the chaos. The crowd is mostly young and relaxed, seemingly oblivious to the rush-hour traffic noise that filters up to the covered balcony where people dine. The menu straddles the border, with ribs, stuffed shrimp, and oysters among the best offerings. ⊠ *Costera Miguel Alemán 112,* ☎ *7/484–1285 or 7/484–0039. AE, DC, MC, V.*

$$ ✕ **Hard Rock Cafe.** This link in the international Hard Rock chain is one of the most popular spots in Acapulco, and with good reason. The famous hamburgers and brownies plus southern-style food—fried chicken, ribs—are well prepared, and the portions are more than ample. The taped rock music begins at noon, and a live group starts playing at 11 PM (except Tuesday). ⊠ *Costera Miguel Alemán 37,* ☎ *7/484–6680. AE, MC, V.*

Belgian

$$$ ✕ **La Petite Belgique.** Mexican-born Yolanda Brassart, who spent
★ years in Europe studying the culinary arts, reigns in the kitchen of this small bistro. Guy, her Belgian husband, makes certain that the customers are happy. Diners are greeted by the enticing aromas of goose-liver pâté, home-baked breads, and apple strudel. The menu changes every three months but usually includes boned duck stuffed with almonds and mushrooms and served with a white wine and mushroom sauce. ⊠ *Plaza Marbella,* ☎ *7/484–7725. AE, MC, V.*

French

$$$ ✕ **Le Jardin des Artistes.** This chic garden hideaway, once a scruffy parking lot, is thoroughly French: the tables bear fresh flowers and Tiffany lamps, and discreet waiters deliver deliciously rich dishes with classic cream and butter sauces. Swiss chef Richard has a local following for his escargots in garlic butter, red-snapper fillet with savory mustard sauce, and smoked trout soufflé. After dinner, stroll through the snazzy art gallery adjoining the garden. ⊠ *Vicente Yañez Pinzón 11,* ☎ *7/484–8344. Reservations essential. AE, DC, MC, V.* ☉ *Closed Sun.–Wed. in Sept. and Oct. No lunch.*

Health Food

$ ✕ **100% Natural.** Along the Costera Miguel Alemán are several of these 24-hour restaurants that specialize in light, healthful food—yogurt shakes, fruit salads, and sandwiches made with whole-wheat bread. You can order soy burgers or dishes with chicken, about the only meat you'll find on the menu. The service is quick, and the food is a refreshing alternative to heavy meals. You can recognize these eateries by the green signs with white lettering. The original—and best—is across from the Acapulco Plaza hotel. ⊠ *Costera Miguel Alemán 200, near Acapulco Plaza,* ☎ *7/485–3982 or 7/484–8440;* ⊠ *Next to Oceanic 2000, at Costera Miguel Alemán 3111,* ☎ *7/485–3982 or 7/484–8440. MC, V.*

International

$$$$ ✕ **Bella Vista.** This alfresco restaurant in the exclusive Las Brisas area has fantastic sunset views of Acapulco. Its large menu includes items that range from Asian appetizers to Italian and seafood entrées. Try the delicious (and spicy) Thai shrimp, sautéed in sesame oil, ginger, Thai

Acapulco Dining & Lodging

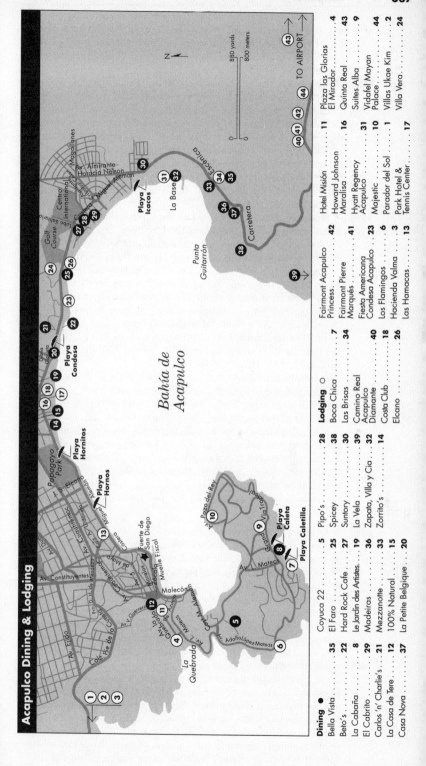

Dining ●

Bella Vista	35
Beto's	22
La Cabaña	8
El Cabrito	29
Carlos 'n' Charlie's	21
La Casa de Tere	12
Casa Nova	37
Coyuca 22	5
El Faro	25
Hard Rock Cafe	27
La Jardín des Artistes	19
Madeiras	36
Mezzanotte	33
100% Natural	15
La Petite Belgique	20
Pipo's	28
Spicey	38
Suntory	30
La Vela	39
Zapata, Villa y Cía	32
Zorrito's	14

Lodging ○

Boca Chica	7
Las Brisas	34
Camino Real Acapulco Diamante	40
Costa Club	18
Elcano	26
Fairmont Acapulco Princess	42
Fairmont Pierre Marqués	41
Fiesta Americana Condesa Acapulco	23
Los Flamingos	6
Hacienda Valma	3
Las Hamacas	13
Hotel Misión	11
Howard Johnson Maralisa	16
Hyatt Regency Acapulco	31
Majestic	10
Parador del Sol	1
Park Hotel & Tennis Center	13
Plaza las Glorias El Mirador	4
Quinta Real	43
Suites Alba	9
Vidafel Mayan Palace	44
Villas Ukae Kim	2
Villa Vera	24

chili, and hoisin sauce; or the red snapper étouffée, cooked in chardonnay, tomato, herbs, basil, and oyster sauce. Part of the restaurant has been enclosed and air-conditioned for those who like it cool. ⊠ *Carretera Escénica 5255,* ☎ *7/469–6900, ext. 500. Reservations essential. AE, DC, MC, V.*

$$$$ ✕ **Coyuca 22.** This is Acapulco's most beautiful restaurant, and more
★ celebrities have eaten here than you can shake a stick at. On hilltop terraces that overlook the bay from Old Acapulco, the understated decor includes Doric pillars and statuary; diners gaze down on an enormous illuminated obelisk and a small pool. It's like eating in a partially restored Greek ruin without the dust. Diners can choose from two fixed menus or order à la carte; either way, the food presentation is a work of art. Seafood and prime ribs are house specialties. ⊠ *Av. Coyuca 22 (10-min taxi ride from the zócalo),* ☎ *7/482–3468 or 7/483–5030. Reservations essential. AE, DC, MC, V. Closed Apr. 30–Nov. 1.*

$$$$ ✕ **Madeiras.** A local favorite, Madeiras is very difficult to get into, es-
★ pecially on weekends and during the Christmas and Easter holidays. The bar-reception area is decorated with dramatic coffee tables whose glass tops rest on carved wooden animals; the dishes and flatware were created by silversmiths in nearby Taxco; and all tables afford views back across the bay toward Acapulco. Dinner is served from a four-course, prix-fixe menu and costs about $38 without wine. Specialties include a delicious red snapper baked in sea salt (a Spanish specialty), tasty chilled soups, and a choice of steaks and other seafood. Seatings are every 30 minutes from 7 PM to 10:30 PM. ⊠ *Carretera Escénica 33-B, just past La Vista shopping center,* ☎ *7/484–7776. Reservations essential. AE, DC, MC, V. No lunch.*

$$ ✕ **Spicey.** In addition to another spectacular view of Acapulco's dia-
★ mond-studded bay from the air-conditioned dining room or the terrace, this restaurant has an innovative menu of dishes that blend international techniques and spices. The results are delicious, as well as a delight to the eye: spring rolls filled with smoked salmon, cream cheese, and vegetables, served with a Chinese plum sauce, and whole red snapper flavored with star anise and rosemary, glacéed with honey. ⊠ *Carretera Escénica, Fracc. Marina Las Brisas,* ☎ *7/481–1380. Reservations essential. AE, MC, V.*

Italian

$$$$ ✕ **Casa Nova.** Another ultraromantic spot created by Arturo Cordova,
★ the man behind Coyuca 22, Casa Nova is carved out of a cliff that rises up from Acapulco Bay. The views, both from the terrace and the air-conditioned dining room, are spectacular, the service impeccable, and the Italian cuisine divine. Diners at this dinner-only spot can choose the fixed-price menu (called *menu turístico*) or order à la carte. Favorites include antipasto, fresh pastas, a delightful *costoletta di vitello* (veal chops with mushrooms), lobster tail, and linguini *alle vongole* (with clams, tomato, and garlic). ⊠ *Carretera Escénica 5256, just past Madeiras,* ☎ *7/446–6237. Reservations essential. AE, DC, MC, V.*

$$$ ✕ **Mezzanotte.** If you want to dance with your waiter or take to the tabletops, this is the place. Attracting the who's who of Acapulco, Mezzanotte sits atop a rise off the Acapulco highway. The elegant and stylish interior features a large sunken dining area, original sculptures, and humongous bay windows looking out to sea. The menu offers a full compliment of fish, meat, and pasta dishes including fettuccine with smoked salmon in avocado sauce and the meatier charcoaled sea bass with shrimp and artichokes in a citrus sauce. Italian gelato and sumptuous homemade desserts add the final touches to the meal. The waiters are personable and efficient and, Friday and Saturday after midnight,

mix and dance with diners. ⊠ *Carr. Escenico 28–1, in the La Vista commercial center,* ☎ *7/446–5727. AE, DC, MC, V. Closed Sun.–Wed.*

Japanese

$$$$ ✕ **Suntory.** At this traditional Japanese restaurant, you can dine either in a blessedly air-conditioned interior room or in the delightful Asian-style garden. It's one of the few Japanese restaurants in Acapulco and one of the only deluxe restaurants open for lunch. Specialties are the sushi and the teppanyaki, prepared at your table by skilled chefs. ⊠ *Costera Miguel Alemán 36, across from La Palapa hotel,* ☎ *7/484–8088. AE, DC, MC, V.*

Mexican

$$ ✕ **Zapata, Villa y Cia.** The music and the excellent food at this Mexican version of the Hard Rock Cafe are strictly local, and the memorabilia recalls the Mexican Revolution—with guns, hats, and photographs of Pancho Villa. The highlight of an evening here is a visit from a sombrero-wearing baby burro, so be sure to bring your camera. (If per chance the burro is missing, it's likely that the staff is searching for a younger version.) The menu features tacos and grilled chicken and meats. ⊠ *Hyatt Regency Acapulco, Costera Miguel Alemán 1,* ☎ *7/469–1234. AE, DC, MC, V. No lunch.*

$$ ✕ **Zorrito's.** When Julio Iglesias is in town, this is where he heads in the wee hours of the morning, after the discos close. The menu of this simple, open-air streetside eatery, which is open almost all the time, includes a host of steak and beef dishes, Acapulco's famous green-and-white *pozole* (pork and hominy soup), and the special, *filete tampiqueña* (a strip of tender grilled beef), which comes with tacos, enchiladas, guacamole, and beans. ⊠ *Costera Miguel Alemán and Anton de Alaminos, next to Banamex,* ☎ *7/485–3735. AE, MC, V. Closed 7 AM–9 AM and Tues. 7 AM–2 PM.*

$ ✕ **El Cabrito.** This is a local favorite for true Mexican cuisine and ambience. The name—"The Goat"—is also its specialty. In addition, you can choose among chicken in *mole* (spicy chocolate-chili sauce); shrimp in tequila; jerky with egg, fish, and seafood; and other Mexican dishes. ⊠ *Costera Miguel Alemán between CiCi and Centro Internacional,* ☎ *7/484–77–11. AE, MC, V.*

$ ✕ **La Casa de Tere.** Hidden in a commercial district downtown (signs point the way), La Casa de Tere is in a league of its own—expect beer-hall tables and chairs, colorful Mexican decorations, and photos of Acapulco of yore. But that's part of the mix at this spotlessly clean, open-air Bohemianlike establishment. And so is its small but varied menu, which includes an outstanding *sopa de tortilla* (tortilla soup), chicken mole, and flan. ⊠ *Alonso Martín 1721, 2 blocks from Costera Miguel Alemán,* ☎ *7/485–7735. No credit cards. Closed Mon.*

Seafood

$$$$ ✕ **La Vela.** Set on a wharf that juts out into Pichilingue Bay, this open-
★ air dining spot is protected by a dramatic roof that simulates a huge white sail. It's very atmospheric after dark, when a stillness hangs over the bay and the lights of Puerto Marqués flicker in the distance. A variety of fish and shellfish dishes are on the menu, but the specialty of the house is the red snapper *à la talla* (basted with chili and other spices and broiled over hot coals). ⊠ *Camino Real Acapulco Diamante, Carretera Escénica, Km 14,* ☎ *7/466–1010. AE, DC, MC, V.*

$$$ ✕ **Beto's.** By day you can eat right on the beach and enjoy live music; by night this palapa-roof restaurant is transformed into a dim and romantic dining area lighted by candles and paper lanterns. Whole red snapper, lobster, and ceviche are recommended. At the Barra Vieja Beach branch, the specialty is pescado à la talla. ⊠ *Beto's, Costera Miguel Alemán at Playa Condesa,* ☎ *7/484–0473;* ⊠ *Beto's Barra Vieja, Barra Vieja Beach,* ☎ *7/444–6071. AE, MC, V.*

$$$ ✕ **El Faro.** Set on the Costera a few hundred yards from the Elcano Hotel, the sleek, classy El Faro resembles a lighthouse down to its nautical interior, with portholes and gleaming sculptures that evoke anchors and giant waves. Spanish chef Jorge Pereira adds touches of Basque and Mediterranean cooking to his original creations for a knockout menu. For starters, there's a lettuce salad mixed with goat cheese, dried wild fruits, and balsamic olive oil. Favorite main dishes are haddock with clams and seared tuna medallions with baby onions. Chicken, veal, and rib-eye steaks are also on the menu. A pianist tickles the ivories Tuesday through Sunday from 9 PM to midnight. ⊠ *Costera Miguel Alemán 75,* ☎ *7/484–3100. AE, MC, V.*

$ ✕ **La Cabaña.** This humble seaside restaurant run by the Alvarez family was a Bohemian hangout that attracted famous bullfighters and the likes of Mexican songwriter Agustín Lara and his lady love María Feliz in the 1950s. Other notables craving good seafood have stopped here ever since. You can see their photo over the bar and sample the same dishes that made the place famous then, such as baby-shark tamales. For heartier appetites, there's steaming seafood casserole or shrimp prepared with sea salt, curry, or garlic. The restaurant is smack in the middle of Playa Caleta, where vendors stroll the beach with peeled mangoes and shells, and has free lockers if you've dropped in for breakfast, lunch, or dinner. ⊠ *Playa Caleta Lado Ote. s/n, Fracc. Las Playas (a 5-min taxi ride east of town square),* ☎ *7/482–5007. AE, MC, V.*

$ ✕ **Pipo's.** Situated on a rather quiet part of the Costera, this old, fam-
★ ily-run seafood restaurant doesn't have an especially interesting view, but diners come here for the fresh fish, good service, and reasonable prices. *Huachinango veracruzano* (red snapper baked with tomatoes, peppers, onion, and olives) and fillet of fish in *mojo de ajo* (garlic butter) are about as sophisticated as the food preparation gets. The original location downtown is extremely popular, also with locals. ⊠ *Costera Miguel Alemán and Nao Victoria, across from Acapulco International Center,* ☎ *7/484–0165;* ⊠ *Almirante Bretón 3, downtown,* ☎ *7/482–2237. Reservations not accepted. AE, MC, V.*

LODGING

In Acapulco, geography is price, so where you stay determines what you pay. The most exclusive area is the Acapulco Diamante, home to some of the most luxurious hotels in Mexico—so lush and well equipped that most guests don't budge from the minute they arrive. The minuses: Playa Revolcadero is too rough for swimming (although great for surfing), and this area is a 15- to 25-minute (expensive) taxi ride from the heart of Acapulco.

There is much more activity on Avenida Costera Miguel Alemán, where the majority of large hotels, discos, American-style restaurants, and airline offices may be found, along with Acapulco's most popular beaches. All the Costera hotels have freshwater pools and sun decks, and most have restaurants and/or bars overlooking the beach, if not on the sand itself. Hotels across the street are almost always less expensive than those directly on the beach; because there are no private beaches in Acapulco, all you have to do is cross the road to enjoy the sand.

Moving west along the Costera leads you to downtown Acapulco. The beaches and restaurants here are popular with Mexican vacationers; the hotels attract Canadian and European bargain-hunters.

You can assume that accommodations that cost more than $50 (double) will be air-conditioned and will include a telephone, TV, and a view of the bay. If you can't afford air-conditioning, don't panic. Even the cheapest hotels have cooling ceiling fans.

Note: Most hotels are booked solid Christmas, Easter week, and during school vacations in July and August, so if you plan to visit then, it's wise to make reservations months in advance. Prices during Christmas week are 10% to 20% higher than the rest of the year.

CATEGORY	COST*
$$$$	over $250
$$$	$150–$250
$$	$75–$150
$	under $75

*All prices are for a standard double room, excluding 15% sales (called IVA) tax and 2% room tax.

Acapulco Diamante

$$$$ ★ 🏨 **Camino Real Acapulco Diamante.** This stunning hotel is set at the foot of a lush tropical hillside on exclusive Pichilingue Beach, far from the madding crowd. All rooms are done in luscious pastels, with tile floors, balcony or terrace, luxurious baths, ceiling fans, and air-conditioning. Each has a view of peaceful Puerto Marqués bay. Eleven extra-spacious club rooms have their own concierge and extra amenities. Some rates include a buffet breakfast. ⊠ *Carretera Escénica, Km 14, Calle Baja Catita, 39867,* ☎ *7/466–1010 or 800/722–6466,* FAX *7/466–1111,* WEB *www.caminoreal.com/acapulco. 145 rooms, 11 suites. 2 restaurants, 2 bars, room service, 3 pools, tennis court, gym, baby-sitting, concierge, meeting room, travel services, car rental. AE, DC, MC, V.*

$$$$ 🏨 **Vidafel Mayan Palace.** This all-suites resort will knock your socks off. Guests are welcomed in a 100,000-square-ft lobby that's sheltered under 75-ft palapa roofs. The rooms, on the other hand, are surprisingly subdued. Airy and spacious, they are beautifully appointed with marble floors, light-wood furniture, and luxurious baths. Canoes and paddleboats are available to paddle around the man-made, fish-filled canal, there's a new water park for kids, and you can swim in the 850-yard pool. ⊠ *Playa Revolcadero, 39000,* ☎ *7/466–2393 or 800/843–2335,* FAX *7/466–0038,* WEB *www.mayan-palace.com.mx. 366 suites. 4 restaurants, 3 bars, pool, 18-hole golf course, 12 tennis courts, beach, shops, billiards, video games, meeting rooms, travel services, car rental. AE, DC, MC, V.*

$$$ ★ 🏨 **Las Brisas.** Set high on a hillside, Las Brisas remains distinct in Acapulco for the secluded haven it provides its guests. This self-contained luxury complex has accommodations that range from one-bedroom units to deluxe private casitas, complete with small private pools. All have beautiful bay views and a few have TVs. Attention to detail is Las Brisas's claim to fame: fresh hibiscus blossoms are set afloat in the pools each day. Transportation is by white-and-pink Jeep. You can rent one for about $70 a day; or, if you don't mind a wait, the staff will do the driving. And transport is necessary—it is a good 15-minute walk to the beach restaurant, and all the facilities are far from the rooms. The rate includes Continental breakfast stylishly delivered to your room each morning. Each Saturday night, the hotel puts on a rousing Fiesta Mexicana. ⊠ *Carretera Escénica 5255, 39868,* ☎ *7/469–6900*

or 888/559–4329, FAX 7/484–2269. 300 rooms. 2 restaurants, 2 bars, in-room data ports, 3 pools, beauty salon, hot tub, sauna, 5 tennis courts, laundry service, dry cleaning, concierge, meeting room, travel services, car rental. AE, DC, MC, V.

$$$ ⌘ **Fairmont Acapulco Princess.** Acquired by Fairmont Hotels of Canada
★ at the end of 1999, the Princess is one of those megahotels that is always holding at least three conventions. But more rooms equal more facilities (several of the restaurants and bars close during the off season, May–October), including tennis, golf, and shopping in a cool arcade. The pool near the reception desk is sensational—fantastic tropical ponds with little waterfalls and a slatted bridge leading into a swimming-sunning area. The large rooms are light and airy, with cane furniture and rugs and curtains in earth-tone prints. A new gym and salsa dance club were added in 2000 as part of a $7 million hotelwide renovation. The optional Modified American Plan (breakfast and dinner) costs $38 per person. ⌧ *Playa Revolcadero (A.P. 1351), 39300, ☎ 7/469–1000 or 800/223–1818, FAX 7/469–1016. 927 rooms, 92 suites. 7 restaurants, 7 bars, room service, 5 pools, barbershop, beauty salon, 18-hole golf course, 7 tennis courts, basketball, gym, shops, dance club, baby-sitting, laundry service, concierge, meeting room, travel services, car rental. AE, DC, MC, V.*

$$$ ⌘ **Fairmont Pierre Marqués.** This hotel, built as a beach hideaway for
★ J. Paul Getty in 1958, is especially blessed because guests have access to all the Princess's facilities without the crowds. In addition, the Pierre Marqués offers guests an 18-hole golf course, three pools, and five tennis courts. Rooms are furnished identically to those at the Princess, but villas and duplex bungalows with private patios are also available. The hotel may obligate guests to participate in an all-inclusive plan ($299 per person with three meals, including taxes); check before booking. ⌧ *Apdo. 1351, Playa Revolcadero, 39907, ☎ 7/466–1000 or 800/223–1818, FAX 7/466–1046, WEB www.pierremarques.com. 274 rooms, 70 suites. 2 restaurants, bar, 3 pools, 18-hole golf course, 5 tennis courts, shops, baby-sitting, laundry service, concierge, meeting room, travel services, car rental. AE, DC, MC, V.*

$$$ ⌘ **Quinta Real.** In summer 1998, one of Mexico's most prestigious hotel chains inaugurated this exclusive low-slung resort in the posh Punta Diamante section, about a 10-minute drive from downtown Acapulco. The 74 suites built on a hillside overlooking the sea have Mexican-made hardwood furniture and earth-tone drapes, rugs, and bedcovers. All have balconies, climate control, satellite TVs, marble floors, and closet door handles shaped like iguanas—the hotel's signature motif. Guests take advantage of the large freshwater pools and the endless stretch of lovely beach. ⌧ *Paseo de la Quinta Lote 6, Desarrollo Turmstico Real Diamante, 39907, ☎ 7/469–1500 or 800/457–4000, FAX 7/469–1515, WEB www.summithotels.com. 74 suites. Restaurant, bar, 4 pools, exercise room, baby-sitting, laundry service, concierge, car rental. AE, DC, MC, V.*

The Costera

$$$$ ⌘ **Villa Vera.** A five-minute drive north of the Costera leads to what was once one of Acapulco's most exclusive hotels. This is where Elizabeth Taylor married Mike Todd and where Lana Turner put down roots for three years. Although it has many rivals, the name sells. Some of the villas, which were once private homes, have their own pools, and some standard rooms have been converted into suites. Units have coffeemakers, video-cassette players, and other amenities, but are otherwise unremarkable. The main pool, with its swim-up bar, is the hotel's hub. A 1,500-square-ft spa offering the latest in beauty treatments and massage opened at the end of 1999. Two championship ten-

nis courts host the Veterans tennis tournament. There's no beach but there are more than a dozen pools on the premises. Children under 16 are not allowed. ⊠ *Apdo. 560, Lomas del Mar 35, 39690,* ☎ *7/484–0333 or 888/554–2361,* FAX *7/484–7479. 24 rooms, 25 suites, 6 villas. Restaurant, piano bar, 15 pools, beauty salon, massage, sauna, 4 tennis courts, exercise room, laundry service, meeting room, travel services, car rental. AE, MC, V.*

$$$ 🏨 **Costa Club.** This resort hotel (the former Acapulco Plaza) still has more facilities than many Mexican towns: four bars, five restaurants, tennis, a sauna, three pools, and a location next to the Plaza Bahía, Acapulco's largest shopping mall. The La Jaula bar, at the mezzanine level, is most extraordinary—a wooden hut, suspended by a cable from the roof, reached by a gangplank and overlooking a garden full of exotic birds. Guest rooms have tile floors, rose and white decor, large desks, closet safes, cable TV, and bathtubs. The very popular all-inclusive option ranks as one of the best in Acapulco. For $180 per person guests get free meals in all restaurants, all domestic drinks, room service, themed shows, pool and beach sports, a private club on an open terrace for adults only (where topless sunbathing is common), plus discounts at local discos. Loud music plays in the lobby until 1 AM, so ask for a room far away from the atrium if you plan to turn in earlier. ⊠ *Costera Miguel Alemán 123, 39670,* ☎ *7/485–9050 or 800/537–8483,* FAX *7/485–5493,* WEB *www.travelweb.com. 506 rooms. 5 restaurants, 4 bars, 3 pools, barbershop, beauty salon, outdoor hot tub, massage, sauna, 3 tennis courts, aerobics, gym, scuba diving, snorkeling, boating, waterskiing, fishing, billiards, children's programs (ages 4–12), meeting rooms. AE, DC, MC, V.*

$$$ 🏨 **Hyatt Regency Acapulco.** A megahotel that you never have to leave, this property is popular with business travelers and conventioneers. The decor is striking, with strong Caribbean colors; in fact, the hotel's glamorous setting has appeared in many Mexican soap operas. Tennis courts, four outstanding eateries (including a kosher restaurant), three bars, and a lavish shopping area are among the reasons for staying put. The Hyatt is also the only hotel in Latin America with an on-site synagogue, supervised by the orthodox rabbinate of Mexico City. The Hyatt is a little out of the way, a plus for those who seek quiet. To avoid the noise of the maneuvers at the neighboring naval base, ask for a room on the west side of the hotel. Mexicana Airlines passengers can now check their luggage at the new on-site check-in counter before heading for the airport. ⊠ *Costera Miguel Alemán 1, 39869,* ☎ *7/469–1234 or 800/233–1234,* FAX *7/484–3087,* WEB *www.hyatt.com. 607 rooms, 17 suites. 4 restaurants, 3 bars, snack bar, 2 pools, massage, 5 tennis courts, exercise room, shops, baby-sitting, laundry service, meeting room, travel services, car rental, parking (fee). AE, DC, MC, V.*

$$ 🏨 **Elcano.** One of Acapulco's traditional favorites, this boutique hotel
★ has been completely remodeled while still (thankfully) maintaining its '50s flavor. The rooms are snappily done in nautical white and navy blue, with white-tiled floors and beautiful modern bathrooms. There's a beachside restaurant with an outstanding breakfast buffet, a more elegant indoor restaurant, and a gorgeous pool that seems to float above the bay, with whirlpools built into its corners. ⊠ *Costera Miguel Alemán 75, 39690,* ☎ *7/48–1950 or 800/972–2162,* FAX *7/484–2230,* WEB *www.hotel-elcano.com. 163 rooms, 17 suites. 2 restaurants, bar, pool, golf privileges, gym, scuba diving, snorkeling, boating, waterskiing, fishing, video games, baby-sitting, travel services. AE, DC, MC, V.*

$$ 🏨 **Fiesta Americana Condesa Acapulco.** The Condesa is right in the thick of the main shopping and restaurant district, and it is ever popular with tour operators. And no wonder—it's on one of the best beaches in town. Guest rooms were recently (1998) renovated in pastels. ⊠ *Costera*

Miguel Alemán 97, 39690, ☎ *7/484–2828 or 800/343–7821,* FAX *7/484–
1828,* WEB *www.fiestaamericana.com. 492 rooms, 8 suites. 2 restaurants,
bar, 2 pools, baby-sitting, children's programs (ages 4–12), meeting room,
travel services, car rental. AE, DC, MC, V.*

$$ ⭐ 🏨 **Howard Johnson Maralisa.** Formerly the sister hotel of the Villa Vera,
this property, on the beach side of the Costera, is now part of the Howard
Johnson chain. The rooms are light, decorated in whites and pastels.
This is a small, friendly place; all rooms have TVs, some have balconies,
and the price is right. The penthouse suite with a refrigerator goes for
$180. ✉ *Apdo. 721, Calle Alemania, 39670,* ☎ *7/485–6677 or 800/
446–4656,* FAX *7/485–9228,* WEB *www.acapulco-travel.com/hotels/
maralis.html. 85 rooms, 5 suites. Restaurant, bar, 2 pools, beach, dry
cleaning, laundry service. AE, DC, MC, V.*

$ 🏨 **Las Hamacas.** Las Hamacas is a friendly, old-fashioned Acapulco
hotel built in the 1950s with rooms surrounding a large inner court-
yard. Across the street from the beach, it has a lovely garden of co-
conut palms from its former days as a plantation, as well as two pools
and a large parking lot. Tile floors, updated bathrooms, and air-con-
ditioners are in all of the spacious, light-filled cream and white guest
rooms. Junior suites can sleep two adults and two children. Twenty
second-story rooms have bay views, but also lie above the busy Costera;
rooms facing the leafy courtyard are the quietest. The hotel is about a
three-minute ride from downtown. A new beach club was added in 2000.
✉ *Costera Miguel Alemán, 39670,* ☎ *7/483–7006 or 800/448–8355,*
FAX *7/483–0575,* WEB *www.hamacas.com.mx. 100 rooms, 20 suites.
Restaurant, bar, 2 pools, beauty salon, meeting room, travel services,
free parking. MC, V.*

$ 🏨 **Park Hotel & Tennis Center.** A helpful staff and prime location make
this hotel an appealing, intimate, and cordial place. In the recent past,
rooms were uninspired; now colonial-style wood furniture has been
refinished, walls painted, and quiet, individually controlled air-condi-
tioning units installed. Rooms are well-situated around a garden with
a good-size pool. Other assets include refrigerators, TVs (Spanish
channels only), and plenty of hot water; some rooms have kitchenettes
(for a small fee) and some have balconies, but all are spotlessly clean
and well priced. The Park has excellent tennis facilities, and it's only
a block to the beach. Since the hotel is right on the Costera, ask for a
room overlooking the tennis courts in the back, if you'd prefer quiet.
✉ *Apdo. 269, Costera Miguel Alemán 127, 39670,* ☎ *7/485–59–92,*
FAX *7/485–54–89. 88 rooms. Bar, pool, 3 tennis courts. MC, V.*

Old Acapulco

$$$ 🏨 **Plaza las Glorias El Mirador.** The old El Mirador has been taken
over by the Plaza las Glorias chain, which is part of the Sidek con-
glomerate responsible for marina and golf developments all over Mexico. Very Mexican in style—white with red tiles and hand-carved
Mexican furniture—Plaza las Glorias exudes nostalgia for a bygone
era. The hotel is set high on a hill with a knockout view of Acapulco
Bay and La Quebrada, where the cliff divers perform. Many of the suites
have hot tubs and stunning ocean vistas. ✉ *Quebrada 74, 39300,* ☎
7/483–1155 or 800/342–2644, FAX *7/482–4564. 72 rooms, 58 suites.
2 restaurants, bar, 3 pools, beauty salon, sauna, meeting room, travel
services, free parking. AE, DC, MC, V.*

$$ 🏨 **Boca Chica.** This Old Acapulco mainstay may have peeling paint
on the facade and an antique switchboard, but its old-time Mexican
ambience is the best at a price that's hard to beat. It's a few short steps
from a natural swimming cove, and the open-air lobby has lovely
views of Caletilla Bay. Rooms are small—with old-fashioned slats on

the door, little balconies, tile bathrooms, and nondescript furnishings—but they're very clean and air-conditioned and received a new coat of paint in 2001. The property, which also has a pretty palapa restaurant with sushi bar, landscaped jungle garden, and pool, attracts German tourists. An abundant Mexican breakfast is included in the price. ⊠ *Playa Caletilla, across the bay from Isla la Roqueta and Mágico Mundo Marino, 39390,* ☎ *7/483–6388 or 800/346–3942,* WEB *acapulco-travel.web.com.mx/hotels/bocachica. 42 rooms, 3 suites. Restaurant, bar, pool, shops, free parking. AE, MC, V.*

$$ 🗓 **Suites Alba.** On a quiet hillside, the Alba is a resort-style hotel with bargain prices, especially for groups (prices are the same for two or four). All suites sleep four and have a kitchenette, private bath, and terrace. There's no extra charge for up to two children under 12 sharing a room with relatives, which makes it especially popular with families. A cable car takes guests to the hotel's beach club on the bay, next door to the Club de Yates, with a 330-ft-long toboggan. During the high season (mid-December–mid-April) transportation from the hotel to Playa Caleta and downtown is free with more than one night's stay. ⊠ *Grand Via Tropical 35, 39390,* ☎ *7/483–0073,* FAX *7/483–8378,* WEB *www.acapulco-cvb.org/suites-alba. 244 suites. 3 restaurants, bar, 3 pools, tennis court, beach, shops, free parking. AE, MC, V.*

$ 🗓 **Los Flamingos.** Almost a historical monument, this hot-pink hotel was the favored hangout of John Wayne, Johnny ("Tarzan") Weissmuller, Errol Flynn, and the rest of the "Hollywood gang" back in the '50s, and their photographs adorn the walls of the lobby. The hotel is strung along a cliff that has some of the finest views in Acapulco—from Pie de la Cuesta all across Acapulco Bay. Los Flamingos attracts plenty of Europeans who come to bask in the ambience of Old Hollywood and toss down the *coco locos,* which barman Esteban Castañeda will tell you were invented here in the 1960s. The rooms feature bright pink walls and flowered print spreads; baths are spartan (shower only), but adequate. The circular two-bedroom master suite, set apart on a small rise, was once Johnny Weissmuller's digs. The hotel offers free transportation to the beach and downtown. ⊠ *Av. López Mateos,* ☎ *7/482–0690,* FAX *7/483–9806,* WEB *www.acapulco-cvb.org/losflamingos. 234 rooms, 2 suites. Restaurant, bar, pool, laundry service, free parking. MC, V.*

$ 🗓 **Majestic.** The stunning decor of the spacious rooms—tile floors, cool
★ colors, and good lighting—is completely unexpected in a hotel in this price range. Entrance is through the seventh-floor lobby, and the rest of the hotel is terraced down a rocky cliff. Many of the rooms in the main building have private terraces and each has a double bed and two studio couches; the villa rooms are smaller. There is no beach at the hotel, but free transportation is provided to the hotel's beach club, next to the Club de Yates (Yacht Club). An all-inclusive plan is sometimes available. ⊠ *Av. Pozo del Rey 73, 39390,* ☎ *7/483–2713,* FAX *7/484–2032,* WEB *www. acapulco-cvb.org/majestic. 72 rooms, 58 suites. 2 restaurants, 2 bars, 2 pools, tennis court, dance club, parking (fee). AE, MC, V.*

$ 🗓 **Hotel Misión.** Two minutes from the zócalo, this charming, colonial-style hotel surrounds a greenery-rich courtyard with an outdoor dining area that functions only on Thursday. (Ask for the green-and-white pozole.) The rooms are small and by no means fancy, with wrought-iron beds, tile floors, painted brick walls, and ceiling fans (no air-conditioning). Every room has a shower, and there's plenty of hot water. The best rooms are on the second and third floors; the top-floor room is large but hot in the daytime. ⊠ *Calle Felipe Valle 12, 39300,* ☎ *7/ 482–3643,* FAX *7/482–2076. 20 rooms. No credit cards.*

Pie de la Cuesta

$$$ ★ **Parador del Sol.** If you want to get away from it all, this is the perfect place. Traversing both the lagoon and the Pacific Ocean sides of the Pie de la Cuesta road, this all-inclusive property gives the impression that it was designed as a luxury resort. The 150 rooms are distributed among pink villas scattered over gardens. Spacious, with tile floors and baths, each room is air-conditioned and equipped with color TV, phone, and a fan-cooled terrace complete with hammocks. The rate includes all meals and refreshments, domestic drinks, tennis, dance class, shows, aerobics, and nonmotorized water sports. ⊠ *Carretera Pie de la Cuesta–Barra de Coyuca, Km 5, Apdo. 1070, 39300,* ☎ *7/444–4050 or 800/515–4321,* FAX *7/444–4051. 150 rooms. Restaurant, 2 bars, 2 pools, miniature golf, 4 tennis courts, exercise room, fishing, dance club, children's programs (ages 4–12), meeting rooms, free parking. AE, DC, MC, V.*

$$ ★ **Villas Ukae Kim.** You can't miss the bright colors of this rustic seaside lodge. The spacious rooms are tastefully painted in bright Mexican hues, and all have overhead fans (four have air-conditioning), mosquito nets slung over large double beds, and terraces. A perfect hideaway for a short or long stay, the hotel has 22 rooms including a honeymoon suite with a private hot tub for $130. The price of a room includes $21 credit a day in the restaurant, which is expensive but good and overlooks the beach. Don't expect phones or TVs—come here to get away from them. ⊠ *Av. Fuerza Aerea Mexicana 356, 39300,* ☎ FAX *7/460–2187. 21 rooms, 1 suite. Restaurant, bar, pool, waterskiing, fishing, laundry service, free parking. No credit cards.*

$ **Hacienda Valma.** Congenial hosts Philippe and Parwin run the place with European flair. It has become so popular that a whole new luxury wing was added in 2001. Twenty white stucco bungalows (six with air-conditioning), named after famous musicians and painters, line the beachfront property. The plain and small rooms, which accommodate two, three, or five people, have huge beds protected by mosquito nets and tiny bathrooms but no hot water. The rates go up on weekends when the hotel fills with embassy personnel from nearby Mexico City. Horseback riding or waterskiing can easily be arranged, and there's volleyball and boccie courts on the grounds. The restaurant features fish and meat dishes as well as pizza, burgers, and crepes. The new section has a spa with hot tub, massages, and the largest pool in Pie de la Cuesta. ⊠ *Av. Fuerza Aereo Mexicana 356, 39300,* ☎ *7/460–2882,* FAX *7/460–0697,* WEB *www.vayma.com.mx. 20 rooms. Restaurant, bar, pool, boccie, horseback riding, volleyball, waterskiing, laundry service, free parking. No credit cards.*

NIGHTLIFE AND THE ARTS

The companies listed in the Acapulco A to Z can organize evening jaunts to most of the dance and music places listed below. And don't forget the nightly entertainment at most hotels. The big resorts have live music to accompany the early evening happy hour, and some feature big-name bands from Mexico. Many hotels sponsor theme parties—Italian Night, Beach Party Night, and similar festivities.

Cultural Shows

Acapulco International Center (⊠ Costera Miguel Alemán, ☎ 7/484–32–18), also known as the Convention Center, has a Mexican Fiesta Wednesday and Friday (and Monday December–April), where you can take in mariachi bands, singers, and the *voladores* (flyers) from Papantla. The show with open bar and buffet costs about $47; entrance to the show alone is $30. The performance starts at 8. On Saturday at **El Mexi-cano** restaurant (⊠ Carretera Escénica 5255) in Las Brisas hotel, the Mexican Fiesta starts off with a *tianguis* (marketplace) of handicrafts and ends with a spectacular display of fireworks.

Dance

Salon Q (⊠ Costera Miguel Alemán 23, ☎ 7/484–3252), referred to as the "Cathedral of Salsa," is a combination dance hall and disco where the bands play salsas, merengues, and other Latin rhythms for young and old. There's a live show weekends—mostly impersonations of Mexican entertainers—as well as dance contests.

Discos

Reservations are advisable for a big group; late afternoon or after 9 PM are the best times to call. New Year's Eve requires planning.

Except for Palladium, Zucca, and Enigma, the discos are clustered on the Costera.

Alebrije is enormous, with seating for 1,200 people in love seats and booths. The most popular night is Friday, when everyone is bathed in foam, with a kind of wet-T-shirt effect. From 10:30 (opening time) to 11:30, the music is slow and romantic; then the disco music and the light show begin, and they go on till dawn. ⊠ *Costera Miguel Alemán 3308, across from Hyatt Regency,* ☎ 7/484–5902.

Andromeda is proof that Acapulco remains the disco capital of the world. Quite spectacular, even for a city known for its splendiferous discos, this one will impress even the most jaded discoers. Entrance to the Queen of the Sea's "castle" is over a torchlit moat; once inside, the impression is of being in a submarine, with a window to the sea where live "mermaids" swim about. There are supposedly two dance floors, but the 18–25 crowd dances everywhere to the latest techno and techno-pop sounds. ⊠ *Costera Miguel Alemán 15, at Fragata Yucatán,* ☎ 7/484–8815.

Baby O is a private club that is known to open its doors to a few select nonmembers. Eschewing the glitz and mirrors of Acapulco's older discos, Baby O resembles a cave in a tropical jungle. The crowd is 25 to 35, mostly well-dressed, wealthy Mexicans. ⊠ *Costera Miguel Alemán 22,* ☎ 7/484–7474.

Discobeach, right on the beach, is Acapulco's only alfresco disco and its most informal one. The under-30 crowd sometimes even turns up in shorts. The waiters are young and friendly—some people find them overly so. (In fact, this is one of Acapulco's legendary pickup spots.) One night they're all in togas carrying bunches of grapes; the next they're in pajamas. Every Wednesday, ladies' night, all the women receive flowers. During the day, you can try the new bungee jump on the beach. ⊠ *Playa Condesa,* ☎ 7/484–8230.

★ **Enigma** (formerly called Extravaganzza) claims to have the ultimate in light and sound and is Acapulco's answer to the Luxor hotel in Las Vegas with its lavish, New Egyptian theme. It accommodates 700 at a central bar and in comfortable booths, and a glass wall provides an unbelievable view of Acapulco Bay, which includes fireworks on weekends. No food is served, but there are several restaurants nearby. The music (which is for all ages) starts at 10:30. ⊠ *On Carretera Escénica to Las Brisas,* ☎ 7/484–7164.

Hard Rock Cafe, filled with rock memorabilia, is part bar, part restaurant, part dance hall, and part boutique.

Palladium is another spectacular production of Tony Rullán, creator of Enigma. A waterfall that cascades down the hill from the dance-floor level makes this place hard to miss. As at Enigma, the dance floor is nearly surrounded by 50-ft-high windows, giving dancers a wraparound view of Acapulco. ✉ *On Carretera Escénica to Las Brisas,* ☎ 7/481–0330.

★ **Zucca** attracts a 25–50 crowd—mainly couples—and is one of the few discos where people really dress up, with the men in well-cut pants and shirts and the women in racy outfits and cocktail dresses. Singles gravitate toward the two bars in the back. Zucca is quite snug, to put it nicely, and people tend to come here earlier than they do to other places to dance to music from the '60s, '70s and '80s. At 2 AM there is a fireworks display. A glassed-in elevator provides an interesting overview of the scene and leads upstairs to a little shop that stocks T-shirts and lingerie. ✉ *On Carretera Escénica to Las Brisas,* ☎ 7/484–6727.

OUTDOOR ACTIVITIES AND SPORTS

Participant Sports

Fishing
Fishing trips can be arranged through your hotel, downtown at the Pesca Deportiva near the *muelle* (dock) across from the zócalo, or through travel agents. At the docks near the zócalo you can hire a boat for $30 a day (two lines). It is safer to stick with one of the reliable companies whose boats and equipment are in good condition. Boats accommodating 4–10 people cost $200–$500 a day, $45–$60 by chair. Excursions usually leave about 7 AM and return at 1 PM or 2 PM. You are required to get a fishing license ($8–$10, depending on the season) from the Secretaría de Pesca; you'll find their representative at the dock. Don't show up during siesta, between 2 and 4 in the afternoon.

Small boats for freshwater fishing can be rented at **Cadena's** and **Tres Marías** at Coyuca Lagoon.

Fitness and Swimming
Most of the time, Acapulco weather is like August in the warmest parts of the United States. This means that you should cut back on your workouts and maintain proper hydration by drinking plenty of water.

Villa Vera Spa and Fitness Center in the Villa Vera hotel is equipped with exercise machines (including step machines), free weights, and benches. Masseuses and cosmetologists give facials, herbal wraps, algae marina treatments, and shiatsu, reflexology, and Swedish massages. Both the beauty center and the gym are open to nonguests.

Golf
There is a public golf course at the **Club de Golf** (☎ 7/484–0781) on the Costera across from the Acapulco Malibú hotel. Greens fees are $35 for nine holes, $52 for 18. Two 18-hole championship golf courses are shared by the **Fairmont Acapulco Princess** and **Fairmont Pierre Marqués** hotels. Reservations should be made in advance (☎ 7/469–1000). Greens fees are $65 for guests and $85 for nonguests. At **Tres Vidas** (Carretera al Aeropuerto, domicilio conocido, ☎ 7/444–5135), which is open to the public at large, greens fees are $70 for 18 holes. A round at the 18-hole **Vidafel Mayan Palace** (☎ 7/466–1879) course is $87 for guests, $98 for nonguests.

Jogging
If you don't like beach jogging, the only real venue for running in the downtown area is along the sidewalk next to the Costera Miguel Alemán at the seafront, but you'll have to go very early, before traffic fumes set in. Away from the city center, the best area for running is out at the Acapulco Princess hotel, on the airport road. A 2-km (1-mi)

loop is laid out along a lightly traveled road, and in the early morning you can also run along the asphalt trails on the golf course.

Rollerblading

For a change of pace from sand and sea activities, come to **Roller Gran Prix** (⊠ Brisamar, east of Costera Miguel Alemán, just before Los Rancheros restaurant, ☎ 7/484–93–13) for rollerblading to disco music and racing Formula One–style go-carts. The $4 fee includes blades, and instruction is available. Go-carts cost $3.50 for five minutes.

Scuba Diving

Arnold Brothers (⊠ Costera Miguel Alemán 205, near El Fuerte de San Diego, ☎ 7/482–18–77), one of the best in town, has been running scuba-diving excursions and snorkeling trips for almost 50 years. Scuba trips cost $30; snorkeling costs $15. Lessons are included.

Tennis

Court fees range from about $8 to $25 an hour during the day and double in the evening. At the hotel courts, nonguests pay about $5 more per hour. Lessons with English-speaking instructors start at about $10 an hour; ball boys get a $2 tip.

There are several places in town to play tennis. **Costa Club** (☎ 7/485–9050) has three hard-surface courts, two lighted. In addition to five outdoor courts, the **Fairmont Acapulco Princess** (☎ 7/469–1000) has two air-conditioned indoor courts. The **Fairmont Pierre Marqués** (☎ 7/466–1000) has five courts. The **Hyatt Regency** (☎ 7/484–1225) has three lighted courts at the Municipal Golf Club. There are three lighted courts at the **Park Hotel & Tennis Center** (☎ 7/485–5992). You'll find five courts at **Tiffany's Racquet Club** (⊠ Av. Villa Vera 120, ☎ 7/484–7949). At **Vidafel Mayan Palace** (☎ 7/469–1879), there are 12 lighted courts. **Villa Vera** (☎ 7/484–0333) has two outdoor lighted clay courts and two hard-surface courts.

Water Sports

Waterskiing, broncos (one-person jet skis), and parasailing can all be arranged on the beach. Parasailing is an Acapulco highlight; a five-minute trip costs $120. Waterskiing is about $35 an hour; broncos cost $35–$90 for a half hour, depending on the size. Windsurfing can be arranged at Caleta and most beaches along the Costera but is especially good at Puerto Marqués. The main surfing beach is Revolcadero.

Acapulco's latest attraction, the **Shotover Jet,** is an import from the rivers around Queenstown, New Zealand. For $54, you're driven via air-conditioned coach from the outfit's Acapulco offices to a site near the town of Tierra Colorado (35 minutes each way). There you climb aboard the 12-passenger craft for an exciting 30-minute boat ride on the Papagayo River, complete with several thrilling 360-degree turns—one of the Shotover Jet's trademarks—and vistas of local flora and fauna (cacti, bats, and iguanas). A new addition: shooting the rapids ($54 for an hour of rafting with a guide). For both rides, you pay $86. Rock climbing can be included in either for the same price. After the ride, you can return directly to Acapulco or take a later shuttle bus and linger at the riverside property, which has a new swimming pool plus restaurant, souvenir shop, and an iguana nursery. ⊠ *Continental Plaza, Costera Miguel Alemán, Locale 3,* ☎ 7/484–11–54.

Spectator Sports

Bullfights

The season runs from about the first week of January to Easter, and *corridas* (bullfights) are held on Sunday at 5:30. Tickets are available through your hotel or at the **Plaza de Toros** ticket window (⊠ Av. Cir-cunvalación, across from Playa Caleta, ☎ 7/482–11–81) Monday–Sat-urday 10–2 and Sunday 10:30–5. Tickets in the shade (*sombra*)—the only way to go—cost about $16. Preceding the fight are performances of Spanish dances and music by the Chili Frito band.

Jai Alai

The **Jai Alai Acapulco Race & Sports Book** (⊠ Costera Miguel Alemán 498, ☎ 7/484–31–95) has two restaurants and a bar, and capacity for 1,500 spectators. The fast-paced games take place Thursday through Sunday at 9 PM, mid-December through January 6, Easter week, and throughout July and August. Entrance is $6. The slower-paced game of bingo is played year-round, and Sports Book, or betting on major U.S. sporting events, is also a 365-day activity.

SHOPPING

The main shopping strip is on the Costera Miguel Alemán from the Costa Club to the El Presidente Hotel. Here you can find Guess, Peer, Aca Joe, Amarras, Polo Ralph Lauren, and other fashionable sportswear boutiques. Downtown (Old) Acapulco doesn't have many name shops, but this is where you'll find the inexpensive tailors patronized by the Mexicans, lots of little souvenir shops, and a vast flea market with crafts. Also downtown is Sanborns. Most shops are open from 10 to 7 Mon-day through Saturday and are closed on Sunday.

Department Stores and Supermarkets

Except for the waitresses' uniforms, the food, and a good handicrafts selection, **Sanborns** is very un-Mexican. Still, it is an institution through-out Mexico. It sells English-language newspapers, magazines, and books, as well as a line of high-priced souvenirs. The Calinda branch (⊠ Costera Miguel Alemán 1226, ☎ 7/484–4413), the Oceanic 2000 branch (⊠ Costera Miguel Alemán 3111, ☎ 7/484–2025), and the downtown branch (⊠ Costera Miguel Alemán 209, ☎ 7/482–6167) are open 7 AM to midnight during the high season and 7:30 AM–11 PM the rest of the year.

Branches of **Aurrerá, Gigante, Price Club, Sam's, Wal-Mart** (in case you don't get enough of them back home), **Comercial Mexicana,** and the new upscale **Liverpool** department store (called Fabricas de Francia) are all on the Costera and sell everything from liquor and fresh and frozen food to light bulbs, clothing, medicines, garden furniture, and sports equipment.

Malls

Malls in Acapulco range from the delightful air-conditioned shopping arcade at the Princess hotel to rather gloomy collections of shops that sell cheap jewelry and embroidered dresses. Malls are listed below from east to west.

Aca Mall, which is next door to Marbella Mall, is all white and mar-ble; here you'll find Tommy Hilfiger, Peer, and Aca Joe. The multilevel **Marbella Mall,** at the Diana Glorieta, is home to Martí, a well-stocked sporting-goods store; a health center (drugstore, clinic, and lab); the Canadian Embassy; and Bing's Ice Cream, as well as several restau-rants. **Plaza Bahía,** next to the Costa Club hotel, is an air-conditioned mall with boutiques such as Dockers, Mossimo, Nautica and Aspasia.

Markets

Not to be missed is the **Mercado Municipal. El Mercado de Artesanías El Parazal,** a conglomeration of every souvenir in town, is a 15-minute walk from Sanborns downtown. You'll find fake ceremonial masks, the ever-present onyx chessboards, $20 hand-embroidered dresses, imitation silver, hammocks, and even skin cream made from turtles (don't buy it, because turtles are endangered and you won't get it through U.S. Customs). ✉ *From Sanborns downtown, head away from the Costera to Vásquez de León and turn right 1 block.* ☉ *Daily 9–9.*

In an effort to get the itinerant vendors off the beaches and streets, the local government set up a series of **flea markets** along the Costera, mostly uninviting dark tunnels of stalls that carry a large supply of inexpensive collectibles and souvenirs. The selections of archaeological-artifact replicas, bamboo wind chimes, painted wooden birds ($5 to $30 each), shell earrings, and embroidered clothes begin to look identical. Prices at the flea markets are often quite low, but it's a good idea to compare prices of items you're interested in with prices in the shops, and bargaining is essential. It's best to buy articles described as being made from semiprecious stones or silver in reputable establishments, lest you end up with cleverly painted paste or a silver facsimile called *alpaca.* One large market with a convenient location is La Diana Mercado de Artesanías, a block from the Continental Plaza hotel, close to the Diana monument.

Specialty Shops

Art

Edith Matison's Art Gallery (✉ Av. Costera Miguel Alemán 2010, across from Club de Golf, ☎ 7/484–3084) shows the works of renowned international and Mexican artists, including Calder, Dalí, Siqueiros, and Tamayo, and a large line of Mexican crafts. **Galería Rudic** (✉ Vicente Yañez Pinzón 9, across from Continental Plaza and adjoining the Jardín des Artistes restaurant, ☎ 7/484–1004) is one of the best galleries in town, with a good collection of top contemporary Mexican artists, including Armando Amaya, Leonardo Nierman, Gastón Cabrera, Trinidad Osorio, and Casiano García.

Pal Kepenyes (✉ Guitarrón 140, ☎ 7/484–3738) gets good press for his sculpture and jewelry (some of it rather racy), on display in his workshop. The whimsical, painted papier-mâché and giant ceramic sculpture of **Sergio Bustamente** (✉ Costera Miguel Alemán 120–9, across from Fiesta American Condesa hotel, ☎ 7/484–4992) can be seen at his gallery and at the Hyatt Regency Hotel.

Boutiques

Armando's (✉ Costera Miguel Alemán at the Hyatt Regency, ☎ 7/484–5111; ✉ Costera Miguel Alemán 1252–7, in La Torre de Acapulco, ☎ 7/469–1234) carries its own line of women's dresses, jackets, and vests with a Mexican flavor, as well as some interesting Luisa Conti accessories. **Nautica** (✉ Plaza Bahía, ☎ 7/484–1650; smaller shop at ✉ Las Brisas hotel, Carretera Escénica 5255, ☎ 7/485–7511) is stocked with stylish casual clothing for men. **Pit** (✉ Princess arcade, Playa Revolcadero, ☎ 7/469–1000) has a smashing line of beach cover-ups and hand-painted straw hats, as well as bathing suits and light dresses. **St. Germaine** (✉ Costera Miguel Alemán, outside the entrance to Fiesta Americana Condesa hotel, ☎ 7/485–2515; ✉ Costa Club, Costera Miguel Alemán 123, ☎ 7/487–3712) carries a sensational line of swimsuits for equally sensational bodies.

Custom-Designed Clothes

Esteban's (✉ Costera Miguel Alemán 2010, across from Club de Golf, ☎ 7/484–3084) is the most glamorous shop in Acapulco, boasting a clientele of international celebrities and many of the important local families. Esteban's opulent evening dresses range from $200 to $3,000, although daytime dresses average $100. There's a men's clothing section on the second floor. If you scour the sale racks, you can find some items marked down as much as 80%.

Handicrafts

Alebrijes & Caracoles (✉ Plaza Bahía, ☎ 7/485–0490) comprises two shops designed to look like flea-market stalls. Top-quality merchandise is on display, including papier-mâché fruits and vegetables, Christmas ornaments, wind chimes, and brightly painted wooden animals from Oaxaca. **Arte Para Siempre** (✉ Costera Miguel Alemán 4834, near Hyatt Regency, ☎ 7/484–3624), in the Acapulco Cultural Center, sparkles with handicrafts from the seven regions of Guerrero including hand-loomed shawls, painted gourds, hammocks, baskets, Olinala boxes, and silver jewelry. **Marielena** (✉ Hyatt Regency, Costera Miguel Alemán 1, ☎ 7/469–1234, ext. 8986) has handcrafted candles, dressy women's cocktail jackets, and sculptures of the human form by Mexican Imelda Bravo.

Silver and Jewelry

Antoinette (✉ Princess arcade, Playa Revolcadero, ☎ 7/469–1000) has gold jewelry of impeccable design, set with precious and semiprecious stones, that you wouldn't be surprised to find on Fifth Avenue. Also on display is Emilia Castillo's line of brightly colored porcelain ware, inlaid with silver fish, stars, and birds. **Suzett's** (✉ Hyatt Regency, Costera Miguel Alemán 1, ☎ 7/469–1234), a tony shop that's been around for years, has a laudable selection of gold and silver jewelry. **Tane** (✉ Hyatt Regency, Costera Miguel Alemán 1, ☎ 7/469–1234; ✉ Las Brisas hotel, Carretera Escénica 5255, ☎ 7/469–6900) carries small selections of the exquisite flatware, jewelry, and objets d'art created by one of Mexico's most prestigious (and expensive) silversmiths.

SIDE TRIP TO TAXCO, THE SILVER CITY

275 km (170 mi) north of Acapulco.

This is Mexico's most medieval-looking city—marvelously preserved colonial buildings nuzzle cobblestone streets that wind up and down the foothills of the Sierra Madre in the state of Guerrero. You could say that its white stucco buildings, red-tile roofs, and quaint inns and cafés make it a centuries-old Mexican town at its best—which is why the government declared the city a national monument in 1928. The city Taxco (pronounced *tahss*-ko) is a living work of art. For centuries its silver mines drew foreign mining companies here. Now its charm, mild temperatures, abundant sunshine, flowers, and silversmiths make Taxco a popular getaway.

Hernán Cortés discovered Taxco's mines in 1522. The silver rush lasted until the next century, when excitement tapered off. Then, in the 1700s, a Frenchman who Mexicanized his name to José de la Borda discovered a rich lode that revitalized the town's silver industry and made him exceedingly wealthy. After Borda, however, Taxco's importance faded, until the 1930s and the arrival of William G. Spratling, a writer-architect from New Orleans. Enchanted by Taxco and convinced of its potential as a silver center, Spratling set up an apprentice shop, where his artistic talent and his fascination with pre-Columbian design combined to produce silver jewelry and other artifacts that soon earned Taxco its worldwide reputation as the Silver City. For the first time, Taxco became known for its silver artisans. Spratling's inspiration lives on in his students and their descendants, many of whom are the city's current silversmiths.

Getting around Taxco is easy, especially if you're a sturdy walker. But be advised that Taxco's altitude is 5,800 ft, so if you've come from sea level, you might want to take it easy on your first day.

11 The **Iglesia de San Sebastián y Santa Prisca** has dominated Plaza Borda—one of the busiest and most colorful town squares in all Mexico—since the 18th century. Usually just called Santa Prisca, it was built by French silver magnate José de la Borda in thanks to the Almighty for his having literally stumbled upon a rich silver vein. According to legend, St. Prisca appeared to workers during a storm and prevented a wall of the church from tumbling to the ground. Soon after, the church was named in her honor. The style of the church—sort of Spanish Baroque meets rococo—is known as churrigueresque, and its pale pink exterior is a stunning surprise. This is one of Mexico's most beautiful colonial churches and Taxco's most important landmark, and its facade, naves, and *bovedas* (vaulted ceilings), as well as important paintings by Mexican Juan Cabrera, are slowly being restored. ⊠ *Southwest side of Plaza Borda,* ⊙ *Daily 6 AM–9 PM.*

NEED A
BREAK?

Around Plaza Borda are several *neverías* (ice cream stands) where you can treat yourself to ice cream in exotic flavors such as tequila, corn, avocado, or coconut. **Bar Paco,** directly across the street from Santa Prisca, is a Taxco institution; its terrace is the perfect vantage point for watching the comings and goings on the zócalo while sipping a margarita or a beer.

12 The former home of William G. Spratling houses the **Spratling Museum.** This small gallery explains the working of colonial mines and displays Spratling's collection of pre-Columbian artifacts. ⊠ *Porfirio Delgado 1*, ☎ *7/622–1660.* ☞ *$3.* ⊙ *Tues.–Sat. 9–6, Sun. 9–3.*

❸ **Casa Humboldt** was named for the German adventurer Alexander von Humboldt, who stayed here in 1803. The Moorish-style 18th-century house has a finely detailed facade. It now houses a wonderful little museum of colonial art. ⊠ *Calle Juan Ruíz de Alarcón 6*, ☎ *7/622–5501.* ☞ *$2.* ⊙ *Tues.–Sat. 10–5, Sun. 10–3.*

❹ If you want to experience a typical Mexican market, with everything from peanuts to electrical appliances, the **Mercado Municipal** is worth a visit. Saturday and Sunday mornings, when locals from surrounding towns come with their produce and crafts, the market spills out onto the surrounding streets. You'll find it directly down the hill from the Church of San Sebastián and Santa Prisca. Look for the market's chapel to the Virgin of Guadalupe.

❺ The largest caverns in Mexico, the **Grutas de Cacahuamilpa** (Caves of Cacahuamilpa) are about 15 minutes northeast of Taxco. These 15 large chambers encompass 12 km (7½ mi) of geological formations. All the caves are illuminated, and a tour takes around two hours. ☞ *$3 (includes tour).*

Dining and Lodging
Gastronomes can find everything from tagliatelle to iguana in Taxco restaurants, and meals are much less expensive than in Acapulco. Dress is casual, but less so than at Acapulco resorts. There are several categories of hotel to choose from within Taxco's two types: the small inns nestled on the hills skirting the zócalo and the larger, more modern hotels on the outskirts of town.

$$ ✕ ★ **Pagaduría del Rey.** This restaurant has a long-standing reputation for international fare served in comfortable surroundings. ⊠ *Calle H. Colegio Militar 8 (Col. Cerro de la Bermeja, south of town)*, ☎ *7/622–3467. MC, V.*

$$ ✕ **Señor Costilla.** That's right, the name of this whimsical restaurant translates as "Mr. Ribs." The Taxco outpost of the zany Anderson chain serves barbecued ribs and chops in a restaurant with great balcony seating. ⊠ *Plaza Borda 1*, ☎ *7/622–3215. MC, V.*

$$ ✕ **Toni's.** Prime rib and lobster are the specialties. There's also a great view and a romantic setting. ⊠ *Monte Taxco Hotel*, ☎ *7/622–1300. AE, MC, V. Closed Sun. No lunch.*

$ ✕ **Cielito Lindo.** This charming restaurant has a Mexican-international menu. Give the Mexican specialties a try—for example, *pollo en pipian verde* (chicken simmered in a mild, pumpkin seed–based sauce). ⊠ *Plaza Borda 14*, ☎ *7/622–0603. MC, V.*

$ ✕ ★ **Hostería el Adobe.** The lack of view (there are only two window tables) is more than made up for by the original decor—for example, hanging lamps made of a cluster of masks—and the excellent food. Favorites include garlic-and-egg soup and the *queso adobe*, fried cheese on a bed of potato skins, covered with a green tomatillo sauce. ⊠ *Plazuela de San Juan 13*, ☎ *7/622–1416. MC, V.*

$ ✕ ★ **El Mural.** This is one of the nicest restaurants in town, with seating indoors or on a poolside terrace, where there's a view not only of a Juan O'Gorman mural but of the stunning Santa Prisca church. The chef prepares classic international favorites—filet mignon and surf and turf—and some delicious Mexican specialties, including cilantro soup, and huitlacoche crepes. The daily three-course fixed price meal is $13. ⊠ *Posada de la Misión, Cerro de la Misión 32*, ☎ *7/622–2198. AE, DC, MC, V.*

$ ✕ **Santa Fe.** Mexican family-type cooking at its best is served in this simple place. Puebla-style mole, Cornish hen in garlic butter, and enchiladas in green or red chili sauce are among the tasty offerings. There's a daily *comida corrida* (fixed price) meal for $5. ⊠ *Hidalgo 2,* ☎ *7/622–1170. AE, MC, V.*

$$$ 🏨 **Posada de la Misión.** Laid out like a colonial-style village, this hotel
★ is within walking distance of town. Rooms range from standard doubles to two-bedroom suites with kitchenettes, fireplaces, cable TV, hair dryers, and terraces. The pool area is adorned with a mural by noted Mexican artist Juan O'Gorman. Rates include breakfast and dinner; two children under 12 can stay with their parents at no extra charge. ⊠ *Apdo. 88, Cerro de la Misión 32, 40230,* ☎ *7/622–0063,* FAX *7/622–2198. 120 rooms, 30 suites. Restaurant, bar, pool, golf privileges, tennis court, dance club, meeting rooms, free parking. AE, DC, MC, V.*

$$ 🏨 **De la Borda.** Long a Taxco favorite, De la Borda is a bit worn, but the large and comfortable rooms were recently painted, and the staff couldn't be more hospitable. Ask for a room overlooking town. There's a restaurant, and many bus tours stay here overnight. ⊠ *Apdo. 6, Cerro del Pedregal 2, 40200,* ☎ *7/622–0025,* FAX *7/622–0617. 98 rooms, 4 suites. Restaurant, bar, pool, free parking. AE, MC, V.*

$$ 🏨 **Monte Taxco.** A colonial style predominates at this hotel, which has a knockout view, a funicular, three restaurants, a disco, and nightly entertainment. It is a few miles from town, so plan to take taxis to get back and forth. ⊠ *Apdo. 84, Lomas de Taxco, 40210,* ☎ *7/622–1300,* FAX *7/622–1428. 153 rooms, 6 suites, 32 villas. 3 restaurants, 9-hole golf course, 3 tennis courts, horseback riding, dance club. AE, DC, MC, V.*

$ 🏨 **Agua Escondida.** Popular with some regular visitors to Taxco, this small hotel has simple rooms decorated with Mexican-style furnishings. ⊠ *Guillermo Spratling 4, 40200,* ☎ *7/622–1166,* FAX *7/622–1306. 50 rooms. Restaurant, bar, café, pool, free parking. MC, V.*

$ 🏨 **Posada de los Castillo.** This in-town inn is straightforward, clean, and good for the price. The Emilia Castillo silver shop is off the lobby. ⊠ *Juan Ruíz de Alarcón 7, 40200,* ☎ *7/622–1396. 14 rooms. MC, V.*

$ 🏨 **Posada de San Javier.** Set somewhat haphazardly around a garden
★ with a pool and a wishing well is this sprawling, very private establishment. In addition to the rooms, there are seven one-bedroom apartments with living rooms and kitchenettes (generally monopolized by wholesale silver buyers). ⊠ *Estacas 32 or Exrastro 6, 40200,* ☎ *7/622–3177,* FAX *7/622–2351. 18 rooms, 7 apartments. Pool. No credit cards.*

$ 🏨 **Rancho Taxco-Victoria.** This hotel is under the same management as De la Borda. Like De la Borda, it is past its prime but exudes a certain charm. The rooms are always freshly painted, and the Mexican decor is simple but attractive. There's also the requisite splendid view. ⊠ *Apdo. 83, Carlos J. Nibbi 5, 40200,* ☎ *7/622–0210,* FAX *7/622–0010. 60 rooms, 4 suites. Restaurant, bar, pool. AE, MC, V.*

Nightlife and the Arts

FESTIVALS

Taxco's biggest single cultural event is the Jornadas Alarconianos in May. But it is also known for its abundance of fiestas, which are an integral part of the town's character. These fiestas provide an opportunity to honor almost every saint in heaven with music, dancing, marvelous fireworks (Taxco is Mexico's fireworks capital), and lots of fun. The people of Taxco demonstrate their pyrotechnic skills with set pieces—wondrous blazing "castles" made of bamboo. (Note: Expect high occupancy at local hotels and inns during fiestas.)

January 18–20, the feast of Santa Prisca and San Sebastián, the town's patron saints, is celebrated with music and fireworks.

Holy Week, from Palm Sunday to Easter Sunday, brings processions and events that blend Christian and Indian traditions; the dramas involve hundreds of participants, images of Christ, and, for one particular procession, brown-hooded penitents who flagellate themselves with boughs of thorns following a colonial custom. Most events are centered on Plaza Borda and the Santa Prisca Church. You must reserve a hotel months in advance for Easter week.

The **Jornadas Alarconianos,** during the third week of May, honors one of Mexico's greatest dramatists with theater, dance, and concerts.

September 29, Saint Michael's Day (Dia de San Miguel), is celebrated with regional dances and pilgrimages to the Chapel of Saint Michael the Archangel, on Calle José María Morelos.

In **early November,** on the Monday following the November 1–2 Day of the Dead celebrations, the entire town takes off to a nearby hill for the Fiesta de los Jumil. The *jumil* is a crawling insect, said to taste strongly of iodine, that is considered a great delicacy. Purists eat them alive, but others prefer them stewed, fried, or combined with chili in a hot sauce.

In **late November or early December,** the National Silver Fair (Feria Nacional de la Plata) draws hundreds of artisans from around the world for a variety of displays, concerts, exhibitions, and contests.

NIGHTLIFE

You should satisfy your appetite for fun after dark in Acapulco. Taxco has a few discos, a couple of bars, and some entertainment, but the range is limited.

Still, you might enjoy spending an evening perched on a chair on a balcony or in one of the cafés surrounding the Plaza Borda. The **Bar Paco** (✉ Plaza Borda 12, ☎ 7/622–0064) is a traditional favorite. At **Bertha's** (✉ Plaza Borda 9, ☎ 7/622–0172), Taxco's oldest bar, a tequila, lime, and club soda concoction called a Bertha is the house specialty. It is supposedly the forerunner of today's margarita cocktail. In addition, some of the town's best restaurants have music on weekends.

Or immerse yourself in the thick of things, especially on Sunday evening, by settling in on a wrought-iron bench on the zócalo to watch the action and fellow people-watchers.

La Pachanga discotheque (✉ Cerro de la Misión 32) at Posada de la Misión is open Tuesday–Sunday and is popular with townsfolk and tourists. **Passagge** (✉ Av. de los s/n, ☎ 7/627–1177) is a popular disco. Much of Taxco's nighttime activity is at the Monte Taxco hotel's **Windows** discotheque (✉ Lomas de Taxco) on weekends. Or, on Saturday night, the hotel has a buffet and a terrific fireworks display.

Outdoor Activities and Sports

You can play golf or tennis, swim, and ride horses at a few hotels around Taxco. Call to see if the facilities are open to nonguests, because the policy seems to change from time to time. Bullfights are occasionally held in the small town of Acmixtla, 6 km (4 mi) from Taxco. Ask at your hotel about the schedule.

Shopping

CRAFTS

Lacquered gourds and boxes from the town of Olinalá and masks, bowls, straw baskets, bark paintings, and many other handcrafted items native to the state of Guerrero are available from strolling vendors and are displayed on the cobblestones at "sidewalk boutiques."

Arnoldo (✉ Palma 2, ☎ 7/622–1272) has an interesting collection of ceremonial masks; originals come with a certificate of authenticity as well as a written description of origin and use. For $100 per person, Arnoldo will take you on a tour of the villages where the dances using the masks are performed on February 2, May 15, and December 12.

D'Elsa (✉ Plazuela de San Juan 13, ☎ 7/622–1683), owned by Elsa Ruíz de Figueroa, carries a selection of native-inspired clothing for women, and a wide and well-chosen selection of arts and handicrafts.

Sunday is market day, which means that artisans from surrounding villages descend on the town, as do visitors from Mexico City. It can get crowded, but if you find a seat on a bench in **Plaza Borda,** you're set to watch the show and peruse the merchandise that will inevitably be brought to you.

SILVER

Most of the people who visit Taxco come with silver in mind. Many of the more than 2,000 silver shops carry almost identical merchandise, although a few are noted for their creativity. Three types are available: sterling, which is always stamped .925 (925 parts in 1,000) and is the most expensive (and desirable); plated silver; and the inexpensive alpaca, which is also known as German or nickel silver. Sterling pieces are usually priced by weight according to world silver prices. Fine workmanship will add to the cost. Work is also done with semiprecious stones and rosewood.

Bangles start at $4, and bracelets and necklaces range from $10 to $200 and higher depending on where you buy them. William Spratling, Andrés Mejía, and Emilia Castillo, daughter of renowned silversmith Antonio Castillo, are some of the more famous design names. Designs range from traditional bulky necklaces (often inlaid with turquoise) to streamlined bangles and chunky earrings. Just about every hotel has an in-house silver shop or one next door, so you don't have to go far to shop.

Emilia Castillo (✉ Juan Ruíz de Alarcón 7, in the Posada de los Castillo hotel, ☎ 7/622–3471) is the most famous and decidedly one of the most exciting silver shops; it's especially renowned for innovative designs and for combining silver with porcelain (Neiman Marcus sells the wares in its U.S. stores).

The stunning pieces at **Galería de Arte en Plata Andrés** (✉ Av. de los Plateros 113A, near the Posada de la Misíon Hotel, ☎ 7/622–3778) are created by the talented Andrés Mejía. He showcases his own fine designs and copies those sent to him by Tiffany's, Elsa Piretti, and Paloma Picasso, which are them sold abroad.

Spratling Ranch (✉ south of town on the Mexico–Acapulco highway, Km 177, ☎ 7/622–6108) is where the heirs of William Spratling turn out designs using his original molds.

Talleres de los Ballesteros (✉ Florida 14, ☎ 7/622–1076) and their branch, Joyería San Agustín (✉ Cuauhtémoc 4, ☎ 7/622–3416), carry a large collection of well-crafted silver jewelry and serving pieces. They have three additional branches in Mexico City and one in San Antonio, Texas.

TAXCO A TO Z

BUS TRAVEL TO AND FROM TAXCO

First-class Estrella de Oro buses leave Acapulco for Taxco five times a day from 7 AM to 6:40 PM from the Terminal Central de Autobuses de Primera Clase. The cost for the approximately 4½-hour ride is about $12 one-way for first-class service. Sistema Estrella Blanca buses

depart Acapulco several times a day from the Terminal de Autobuses. Purchase your tickets at least one day in advance at the terminal. The one-way ticket is about $11 for first-class service. Buses depart from Taxco just about every hour starting at 6 AM.
➤ BUS INFORMATION: **Estrella de Oro** (✉ Av. Cuauhtémoc 158, ☎ 7/485–87–05 or 7/622–0648; Taxco terminal: ✉ Av. de los Plateros 126, ☎ 7/485–8705 or 7/622–0648). **Sistema Estrella Blanca** (✉ Ejido 47, ☎ 7/469–2028; Taxco terminal: Av. de los Plateros 104, ☎ 7/622–0131).

CAR TRAVEL
It takes about three hours to drive to Taxco from Acapulco, using the expensive (about $38) toll road. Overnight tours are common; check with your hotel for references and prices.

TAXIS
Minibuses travel along preset routes through Taxco and charge only a few cents, and Volkswagen "bugs" provide inexpensive (average $11.50) taxi transportation.

TELEPHONES
Taxco's area code, used when dialing a Taxco number from outside the city, has been changed from 762 to just 7. The 62 has been incorporated into the local phone number, which now has seven digits.

TRANSPORTATION AROUND TAXCO
Because of the byways, alleys, and tiny streets, maneuvering anything bigger than your two feet through Taxco will be difficult. Fortunately, almost everything of interest is within walking distance of the zócalo. Wear sensible shoes for negotiating the hilly streets.

VISITOR INFORMATION
The tourism office is open weekdays 9–2 and 5–8; Saturday 9–3.
➤ TOURIST INFORMATION: **Tourism Office** (✉ Av. de los Plateros 1, ☎ 7/622–6616).

ACAPULCO A TO Z

To research prices, get advice from other travelers, and book travel arrangements, visit www.fodors.com.

AIR TRAVEL
There are several airlines that fly directly to Acapulco from major United States cities. From New York via Dallas, the flying time to Acapulco is 4½ hours; from Chicago, 4¼ hours; from Los Angeles, 3½ hours.

CARRIERS
From the United States, American has nonstop flights from Dallas, with connecting service from Chicago and New York. Continental has nonstop service from Houston. Delta's direct flights are from Los Angeles and Atlanta. Mexicana's flights from Chicago and Los Angeles stop in Mexico City before continuing on to Acapulco. Aeroméxico's flight from New York to Acapulco stops in Mexico City. The carrier also has one-stop or connecting service from Atlanta, Chicago, Houston, Los Angeles, New York, Miami, and Orlando. America West has a flight from Phoenix.
➤ AIRLINES AND CONTACTS: **Aeroméxico** (☎ 7/466–9109). **American** (☎ 7/466–9227). **America West** (☎ 7/466–9257). **Continental** (☎ 7/466–9063). **Delta** (☎ 01–800–902–2100). **Mexicana** (☎ 7/486–7586).

AIRPORTS AND TRANSFERS
The Juan N. Alvarez International Airport is located about 20 minutes east of the city.

➤ AIRPORT INFORMATION: **Juan N. Alvarez International Airport** (☎ 7/466–9434).

AIRPORT TRANSFERS

Private taxis aren't permitted to carry passengers from the airport to town, so most people rely on Transportes Aeropuerto, a special airport taxi service. The system looks confusing, but there are dozens of helpful English-speaking staff members to help you.

Look for the name of your hotel and its zone number on the overhead sign on the walkway in front of the terminal. Then go to the desk designated with that zone number and buy a ticket for an airport taxi. The ride from the airport to the hotel zone on the strip costs about $8 per person for the *colectivo* (shared minivan) and starts at $25 for a nonshared cab. The drivers are usually helpful and will often take you to hotels that aren't on their list. Tips are optional.
➤ TAXIS AND SHUTTLES: **Transportes Aeropuerto** (☎ 7/462–1095).

BOAT AND FERRY TRAVEL

Many cruises include Acapulco as part of their itinerary. Most originate from Los Angeles. Celebrity Cruises is popular with tourists. Crystal P&O is a reliable operator. Cunard Line also offers cruises that include Acapulco. Krystal Cruises plies the Riviera Mexicana, which includes Acapulco. Princess Cruises offers trips several times a year. Royal Caribbean has added Acapulco to its Mexican itinerary. Bookings are generally handled through a travel agent.
➤ BOAT AND FERRY INFORMATION: **Celebrity Cruises** (☎ 800/437–3111). **Crystal P&O** (☎ 310/785–9300). **Cunard Line** (☎ 800/528–6273). **Krystal Cruises** (☎ 800/446–6640). **Princess Cruises** (☎ 800/421–0522). **Royal Caribbean** (☎ 800/327–6700).

BUS TRAVEL TO AND FROM ACAPULCO

Bus service from Mexico City to Acapulco is excellent. First-class buses, which leave every hour on the hour from the Tasqueña station, are comfortable and in good condition. The trip takes 5½ hours, and a one-way ticket costs about $22. There is also deluxe service, called *Servicio Diamante*, with airplanelike reclining seats, refreshments, rest rooms, air-conditioning, movies, and hostess service. The deluxe buses leave four times a day, also from the Tasqueña station, and cost about $37. *Plus* service (regular reclining seats, air-conditioning, and a rest room) costs $25.

BUS TRAVEL WITHIN ACAPULCO

The buses tourists use the most are those that go from Puerto Marqués to Caleta and stop at the fairly conspicuous metal bus stops along the way. Yellow air-conditioned tourist buses, marked ACAPULCO, now run about every 15 minutes along this route. If you want to go from the zócalo to the Costera, catch the bus that says LA BASE (the naval base near the Hyatt Regency). This bus detours through Old Acapulco and returns to the Costera just east of the Ritz Hotel. If you want to follow the Costera for the entire route, take the bus marked HORNOS. Buses to Pie de la Cuesta or Puerto Marqués say so on the front. The Puerto Marqués bus runs about every 10 minutes and is always crowded.

CAR RENTAL

Acapulco has franchises of major U.S. car rental companies. Avis is a good bet. Budget was one of the first agencies in Acapulco. Dollar has air-conditioned models. Hertz deals with all car sizes. Quick is a local company. All have offices at the airport.
➤ MAJOR AGENCIES: **Avis** (☎ 7/466–9190). **Budget** (☎ 7/481–2433). **Dollar** (☎ 7/466–9493). **Hertz** (☎ 7/485–8947). **Quick** (☎ 7/486–3420).

CAR TRAVEL

The trip to Acapulco from Mexico City on the old road takes about six hours. A privately built and run four-lane toll road connecting Mexico City with Acapulco is expensive (about $48 one way) but well maintained, and it cuts driving time between the two cities to 4½ hours. Many people go via Taxco, which can be reached from either road.

If you plan to visit some of the more remote beaches or decide to visit Taxco on your own, renting a car is convenient but fairly expensive. Prices start at about $54 a day for a Volkswagen sedan without air-conditioning. Don't expect a full tank; your car will have just about enough gas to get you to the nearest Pemex station.

CONSULATES

➤ CONSULATE INFORMATION: **Canadian Consulate** (⊠ Marbella Mall, Suite 23, ☎ 7/484–1305). **U.S. Consulate** (⊠ Continental Plaza Hotel, Costera Miguel Alemán 121–14, ☎ 7/484–0300.

EMERGENCIES

Your hotel can locate an English-speaking doctor, but they don't come cheap—house calls are about $100. The U.S. consular representative has a list of doctors and dentists, but it's against the consulate's policy to recommend anyone in particular.

Call the police or the Red Cross in case of an emergency. The Hospital Privado Magallanes and the Hospital del Pacífico are reliable.
➤ CONTACTS: **Hospital del Pacífico** (⊠ Fraile y Nao 4, ☎ 7/487–7180). **Hospital Privado Magallanes** (⊠ Wilfrido Massieu 2, ☎ 7/485–6544). **Police** (☎ 7/485–0650). **Red Cross** (☎ 7/485–4100).

ENGLISH-LANGUAGE MEDIA

English-language books and periodicals can be found at **Sanborns,** a reputable American-style department-store chain, and at the newsstands in some of the larger hotels. Many small newsstands carry the Mexico City *News*.

HORSE CARRIAGE TRAVEL

Buggy rides up and down the Costera are available evenings. There are two routes: from Parque Papagayo to the zócalo and from Playa Condesa to the naval base. Each costs about $10 (be sure to agree on the price beforehand).

INTERNET

More and more Internet facilities are cropping up in Acapulco to keep you connected while traveling. Smart PCs is in a shopping arcade next to Carlos 'n' Charlie's restaurant. iNternet Cyber Café is near the Marbella Hotel on the Costera Miguel Alemán.
➤ INTERNET CAFÉS: **iNternet Cyber Café** (⊠ Horacio Nelson 40–7A, ☎ 7/484–8254). **Smart PCs** (⊠ Costera Miguel Alemán 112–4, ☎ 7/484–2877).

SIGHTSEEING TOURS

There are organized tours everywhere in Acapulco, from the red-light district to the lagoon. Tour operators have offices around town and desks in many of the large hotels. Contact Mexico Travel Advisors at La Torre de Acapulco for tours of Acapulco. Viajes Acuario is another reliable tour company.

BOAT TOURS

The famous cliff divers at La Quebrada give one performance in the afternoon and four performances every night. The *Bonanza*'s sunset cruise, with open bar and live and disco music, costs about $16. All boats leave from downtown near the zócalo at 4:30 and 10:30. Many hotels and shops sell tickets, as do the ticket sellers on the waterfront.

➤ FEES AND SCHEDULES: *Bonanza* (☎ 7/482–4947). **Mexico Travel Advisors** (✉ Costera Miguel Alemán 1252, ☎ 7/484–7400). **Viajes Acuario** (✉ Costera Miguel Alemán 186–3, ☎ 7/485–6100).

TAXIS

How much you pay depends on what type of taxi you get. Hotel taxis are the most expensive, the roomiest, and in the best condition. A price list that all drivers adhere to is posted in hotel lobbies. Fares in town are usually about $3 to $7; to go from downtown to the Princess Hotel is about $15; to go from the hotel zone to Playa Caleta is about $8.

Cabs that cruise the streets usually charge by zone, with a minimum charge of $2. Before you go anywhere by cab, find out what the price should be and agree with the driver on a fare. A normal fare is about $3 to go from the zócalo to the International Center. Rates are about 30% higher at night, and although tipping isn't expected, Mexicans usually leave small change.

You can also hire a taxi by the hour or the day. Prices vary from about $10 an hour for a hotel taxi to $8 an hour for a street taxi. Never let a taxi driver decide where you should eat or shop, since many get kickbacks from some of the smaller stores and restaurants.

TRANSPORTATION AROUND ACAPULCO

Getting around in Acapulco is quite simple. You can walk to many places, and the bus costs less than 50¢. Taxis cost less than they do in the United States.

TRAVEL AGENCIES

American Express offers tours of Acapulco. Viajes Wagon-Lits has a wide variety of excursions.

➤ LOCAL AGENT REFERRALS: **American Express** (✉ La Gran Plaza shopping center, Costera Miguel Alemán 1628, Suites 7–9, ☎ 7/469–1166). **Viajes Wagon-Lits** (✉ Las Brisas, Carretera Escénica 5255, ☎ 7/484–1650, ext. 392).

VISITOR INFORMATION

Procuraduría del Turista, the State Attorney General's Tourist Office, is open 9 AM–11 PM daily. It's also the place to report a crime or voice a complaint.

➤ TOURIST INFORMATION: **Procuraduría del Turista** (✉ Acapulco International Center, Costera Miguel Alemán, ☎ 7/484–4416).

10 OAXACA

The geographic, ethnic, and culinary
diversity of Oaxaca has made the state a
favorite of Mexico aficionados. The majority
of residents are descendants of Zapotec
and Mixtec peoples, who centuries ago
built the Monte Albán and Mitla complexes
near Oaxaca City. Their contemporary
crafts and festivals are extremely colorful.
Although less exotic than Oaxaca City,
the state's coastal developments of Puerto
Escondido and Bahías de Huatulco are
beloved by surfers and beach bums.

Updated by
Barbara
Kastelein

O**AXACA** (pronounced wah-*hah*-kah) is both a pre-Columbian and a colonial treasure. The state has a vast geographic and ethnic diversity. Together with neighboring Chiapas, Oaxaca has the largest Indian population in the country, which explains its richness and variety in handicrafts, folklore, culture, and gastronomy. Two out of three Oaxaqueños descend from Zapotec or Mixtec Indians, whose villages dot the valleys, mountainsides, and coastal lowlands. They come from one of 17 distinct ethnic groups and speak 52 dialects—each very different from the other. If they speak Spanish—which many now do—it is a second language to them.

Indigenous civilizations flourished in the area thousands of years ago, and the archaeological ruins of Monte Albán, Mitla, and Yagul are among the vivid remnants of their cities. Located within a 40-km (25-mi) radius of the city of Oaxaca, the ruins bear witness to highly religious, artistic, and advanced cultures.

The Zapotec and Mixtec centers were conquered by the irrepressible Aztecs, who in the 15th century gave Oaxaca its name: *Huaxyaca*. In the Nahuatl language it probably means "by the acacia grove," referring to the location of the Aztec military base. Then came the Spanish conquest in 1528. The Spanish monarch Charles V gave Hernán Cortés the title of *Marqués del Valle de Oaxaca* as a reward for his conquest of Mexico. Cortés preferred to live elsewhere, so an estate was never built on the lands conferred with the title, but Cortés's descendants kept the property until Mexico's bloody 1910 Revolution.

Oaxaca's legacy to Mexican politics has been two presidents: Benito Juárez, the first full-blooded Indian to become chief of state, and Porfirio Díaz, a military dictator who declared himself president-for-life. Juárez, a Zapotec, was a sheepherder from San Pablo Guelatao, a settlement about 64 km (40 mi) north of Oaxaca. As a child he spoke only his native Zapotec tongue. Often referred to as Mexico's Abraham Lincoln, Juárez was trained for the clergy but later studied law and entered politics. He was elected governor of the state (1847), chief justice of the Supreme Court of Mexico (1857), and then president (1858–72), defeating a French effort in 1867 to install Hapsburg Archduke Ferdinand Maximilian of Austria as emperor. Porfirio Díaz, one of Juárez's generals, seized the presidency in his 1877 coup and held office until he was kicked out in 1911.

Oaxaca sits on the vast, fertile, 1½-km- (1-mi-) high plateau of the Oaxaca Valley, encircled by the majestic Sierra Madre del Sur mountain range. Mexico's fifth-largest state, it lies in the southwest, bordered by the states of Chiapas to the east, Veracruz and Puebla to the north, and Guerrero—whose touristic claims to fame are Acapulco and Ixtapa—to the west. The south of Oaxaca state spans 509 km (316 mi) of lush tropical Pacific coast with magnificent beaches. Until recently, these beaches had been relatively unexploited and unknown by tourism, except for the long-established small fishing town and seaside hideaway of Puerto Escondido and the even smaller town of Puerto Ángel. But now Bahías de Huatulco (Huatulco Bays), 125 km (77 mi) east of Puerto Escondido, is on the map—thanks to the government working to turn it into a world-class resort.

Note: Assaults and highway banditry still occur in Mexico, although the problem is less severe in recent years. First-class buses have sometimes been the target of highway robbery, especially the route between Juchitan, on the Oaxaca coast, and San Cristóbal de las Casas in Chiapas. Night buses are most vulnerable; you should travel by day and in buses that go directly to your destination, without stops. Although this is cause for concern, occurrences are infrequent.

Pleasures and Pastimes

Dining

One highlight of Oaxaca is its traditional cookery, one of the finest and most elaborate in all Mexico. Oaxaca is known as "the land of seven moles" because of its seven distinct kinds of multispiced mole sauces. One of them, mole *negro*, rivals that of neighboring Puebla in thickness and flavor because of the outstanding local chocolate from which it is made. Tamales, either sweet or stuffed with chicken, are another treat. The home- and factory-made mezcal, the alcoholic drink derived from the maguey cactus, differs in flavor with each maker and can be as high as 80 proof. The cream variety, thick and sweet, is flavored with orange, lime, or other fruits or nuts.

Oaxacan cuisine—the cheeses, mole sauces, and meats that make dining in the capital memorable—is in short supply along the coast, which has its own seafood-based cuisine. Huatulco's restaurants are making a name for themselves, and some of the places in Puerto Escondido are very good. With a few exceptions, cooking in Puerto Ángel is mediocre. Dress is casual and reservations are unnecessary at all restaurants unless otherwise noted. Prices are quite inexpensive throughout the state, with the exception of Huatulco.

CATEGORY	COST*
$$$$	over $15
$$$	$10–$15
$$	$5–$10
$	under $5

per person for a three-course meal, excluding drinks and tip

Lodging

Oaxaca City has few luxury resorts, but it does have some magnificently restored properties, including a 16th-century convent and dozens of smaller, moderate-price accommodations, most downtown. These smaller hotels are very popular around December and January, and some require six months to a year advance booking. Day of the Dead celebrations (October 31–November 2) and Holy Week are also times of high occupancy, so plan accordingly.

Hotel rates vary considerably in the coastal area. In Puerto Escondido and Puerto Ángel, most of the accommodations fall into the $$ or $ price range. Those in Huatulco, where you'll find luxury compounds, are considerably pricier, with the exclusive Quinta Real topping the scale. The high season along the coast runs from mid-December through Holy Week; rates increase 20% or more during this time. Budget accommodations are scarce in Huatulco, although more moderately priced rooms are becoming available, especially in La Crucecita.

CATEGORY	COST*
$$$$	over $120
$$$	$70–$120
$$	$30–$70
$	under $30

All prices are for a standard double room, including 17% tax.

Shopping

Oaxaca City is a magnet for both *mestizos* (people of mixed European and Indian descent) and indigenous people who live in the valley and nearby mountains. They come to town to buy and sell, especially on

Saturday. The market attracted the attention of D. H. Lawrence who wrote about it in *Mornings in Mexico,* and it remains an exotic spectacle. Mercado 20 de Noviembre is a feast for the senses, with cheap and authentic regional breakfasts and a cacophony of competing marimba and mariachi music. El Central de Abastos is the largest Indian market in Mexico, and only Michoacán and Chiapas have Oaxaca's variety and quality of crafts. Expect hectic activity and bright colors. At markets, listen for the singsong, tonal Zapotec and Mixtec languages, in which changes in the pitch of the voice change the meanings of words. In town, galleries exhibit the pottery, textiles, and fanciful wooden animals called *alebrijes* that have drawn international attention to Oaxaca's artisans.

Surfing

Oaxaca's Puerto Escondido is a household name for serious surfers who migrate to this sunny port for surfing championships each year. These challenging waves have been attracting surfers from all parts of the globe since word first got out in the 1960s.

Exploring Oaxaca

Travelers tend to gravitate toward two parts of Oaxaca: Oaxaca City, the state capital, spread over a valley in the Sierra Madre mountains; and the Pacific Coast area due south of the capital.

Numbers in the text correspond to numbers in the margin and on the Oaxaca City and Oaxaca Coast maps.

Great Itineraries

If you only have three days to spend in the state, choose between Oaxaca City and the coast. Go to Puerto Escondido for unspoiled beaches and wildlife, or if you'd rather pamper yourself, consider the luxurious resorts of Huatulco. Oaxaca City is food for the soul for history and folk-art aficionados, with its magnificent colonial buildings, world-famous crafts, and the ancient temples just outside the city. For a culture-beach combination, plan at least seven days—Oaxaca City and the coast merit three days apiece.

IF YOU HAVE 3 DAYS IN OAXACA CITY

Explore downtown to see the stunning colonial monuments that have been declared World Heritage structures by the United Nations. The first day, take in the **Catedral Metropolitana de Oaxaca** ④, the **Museo de Arte Contemporáneo de Oaxaca** ⑤, the **Iglesia y Ex-Convento de Santo Domingo** ⑦, and the adjoining **Museo de las Culturas** ⑧. On Day 2, beat the crowds by catching a tour or bus right after breakfast for **Monte Albán,** the ruins of an ancient, mountaintop Zapotec capital. After returning to the city and a late lunch, enjoy coffee at the 16th-century **Ex-Convento de Santa Catalina** ⑥, now the Hotel Camino Real, and take in the patio garden with the stone tub where the nuns washed clothes. Visit the **Museo de Arte Prehispánico Rufino Tamayo** ⑪ on Day 3, then shop for regional arts and crafts at the **Central de Abastos** and the **Mercado de Artesanías.** Watch the sun set over Oaxaca from the terrace bar of the **Hotel Victoria,** just above the city proper.

IF YOU HAVE 5 DAYS IN OAXACA CITY

Follow the three-day itinerary, and on Day 4 add a visit to the Mixtec ruins at **Mitla,** stopping on the way or back to see the 2,000-year-old *ahuehuete* cypress in Tule (or, on a Sunday, to experience a country market day in **Tlacolula**). Alternatively, spend the rest of the afternoon wandering up and down the **Calle Macedonio Alcalá,** checking out the boutiques full of high-quality crafts and the **IAGO** (Institute of Graphic Arts) ⑨. Dine on the same street or back in the **zócalo** ①. Day 5, head to the villages near Oaxaca City, where beautiful handicrafts are made before your eyes. Back in the city, visit the **Basílica de Nuestra Señora de la Soledad** ⑫.

IF YOU HAVE 3 DAYS IN THE COASTAL BEACH RESORTS

Using **Bahías de Huatulco** ⑮–⑰ as your base, take a boat tour of the bays on the first day, followed by a spell at the beach for a blazing sunset finale. Day 2, tour the small beaches and hidden bays between Huatulco and **Puerto Escondido** ⑬. On Day 3, laze on the beach and, in late afternoon, taxi to **La Crucecita** ⑱ for some strolling, followed by dining at one of the small restaurants on the main square.

IF YOU HAVE 5 DAYS IN THE COASTAL BEACH RESORTS

Follow the three-day itinerary, then sign up for bird-watching on the **Manialtepec Lagoon** on Day 4. Day 5, head inland for a special lunch on the **Coffee Plantation tour.** If you choose laid-back **Puerto Escondido** ⑬ as your base, you might spend Day 4 touring the **Lagoon of Chacahua,** and Day 5 riding horses on the beach in the morning, then relaxing with a soothing Temescal steam bath (a pre-Hispanic–style sauna) and massage in the afternoon.

IF YOU HAVE 7 DAYS OR MORE

You can immerse yourself in the cultural treasures of **Oaxaca City** ①–⑫ and **Monte Albán,** before kicking back with some sea and sun; spend Days 1–4 at the sights outlined in the first four days of the city itinerary. On Day 5, fly to **Bahías de Huatulco** ⑮–⑰ and, on arrival, sign up for a boat tour of the bays. Take Days 6 and 7 on the beach, or bird-watching and exploring **La Crucecita** ⑱. If you're staying longer, don't miss the **Museum of the Sea Turtle** tour.

When to Tour Oaxaca

Oaxaca celebrates Mexican holidays and its own state's fiestas with an intensity of tradition, color, and enthusiasm that attracts hordes. *El Día de los Muertos* (Day of the Dead) begins with graveyard celebrations in the city and nearby villages on October 31 and ends in the cemeteries on November 2, when families partake of the favorite food of those they are honoring. The most frequently visited village is Xoxo, but many others, including Atzompa and Xochimilco, also have colorful festivities.

December is full of festivities, starting with the miraculous *Virgen de Juqila* on December 8 in the village of Juquila, continuing with Mexico's patron Saint Guadalupe on 12, and Oaxaca state's patron *la Virgen de La Soledad* on December 18, where regional and indigenous dances are performed outside the Basilica on Independencia and Galeana streets. On December 23, *Noche de Rábanos* (Night of the Radishes), the zócalo is packed with growers and artists displaying their hybrid radishes carved and arranged in tableaux that depict everything from Nativity scenes to space travel. Prizes are awarded for the biggest and the best, and competition is fierce. Other arrangements are made with *flores inmortales* ("eternal flowers"; small dried flowers) or *totomoxtl* (corn husks, pronounced to-to-*mosh*-tl). Be prepared to line up for a long time to enter the square, and bring plenty of film. December 24 is *la Noche de Calendas* with street processions of bright papier-mâché figures.

Oaxaca's other major celebration is the *Guelaguetza* (Zapotec for "offering" or "gift"), held on the last two Mondays in July. Dancers from all the mountain and coastal communities converge on the city bearing tropical fruits, coffee, and other regional products. They perform elaborate dances in authentic costumes from early morning until early afternoon at the Guelaguetza Auditorium, an open-air amphitheater in the hills just northwest of the city center.

DIA DE LOS MUERTOS

DIA DE LOS MUERTOS, Day of the Dead, which actually takes place over three days (October 31–November 2), is one of Mexico's most passionately celebrated fiestas—equal to Christmas in terms of its sacred importance and ritual splendor.

The roots of the fiesta are a tangle of pre-Hispanic indigenous Mexican beliefs and post-Conquest Spanish Catholic influence. For the Aztecs, religion and art were inextricably bound together. A central component of their religion was ritual sacrifice of human beings and animals, and so death imagery abounds in their sculpture, painting, architecture, and poetry. They believed that a soul's destiny was determined not by the moral correctness of one's behavior while living, but rather by the cause of a person's death. People who died in battle, perished during childbirth, or were sacrificed to the gods went to a heaven called the Dwelling Place of the Sun. If they died of drowning, dropsy, gout, or lightning, they went to Tlalocan, a heaven ruled by the rain god Tlaloc. Infant souls went to a heaven called Chichihuacuauhco, where a wet-nurse tree fed them milk from its branches. Those unfortunate enough to die of natural causes went to a hell called Mictlán, where they underwent a series of trials that included trekking eight deserts and eight hills, and facing wild animals and obsidian-bladed winds. The dead were buried with goods—food and drink, clothing, toys, pottery, arrows—and sacrificed servants to take with them on their journey.

The Aztecs celebrated two major fiestas in honor of the dead. The first, the Little Feast of the Dead, occurred in the ninth month and was dedicated to deceased children; the other, the Great Feast of the Dead, in honor of adults, took place in the tenth month. These festivals included music, dancing, and graveside offerings of flowers, tamales, and figurines of deities sculpted from a dough of amaranth seeds and human blood.

After the Spanish Conquest of 1521, 12 Franciscan friars were charged with the spiritual conversion of the Indians. The friars burned pagan icons, destroyed sacred shrines, and imprisoned priests. However, because the Aztec feasts for the dead somewhat mirrored the Catholic feast days honoring All Souls and All Saints, the friars merged these holidays to facilitate the conversion process. All Souls Day, on November 1, commemorates all the faithful departed, and All Saints Day, on November 2, honors all Christian saints and martyrs. While the Indians observed the new holidays, many of them secretly clung to their native religion. The result is Day of the Dead, a creative fusion of Catholicism and indigenous beliefs.

Celebrated throughout the country, by people from all walks of life, the Day of the Dead festivities of the Purépecha Indians in Michoacán and the Zapotec Indians in Oaxaca are especially beautiful. Both at home and in cemeteries, families construct elaborate altars called *ofrendas* to honor their ancestors. They adorn these altars with fragrant marigold blossoms, candles, photos, favorite foods and belongings of the deceased, copal incense, and candy skulls. The vibrant mix of colors, smells, flavors, and potent nostalgia are meant to lure and guide the spirits back to earth for a family reunion.

Families lovingly prepare, in abundance, the favorite foods of the deceased. Care is taken to make the food and drinks especially rich and spicy: souls absorb the essence of offerings rather than physically consume them.

— Gina Hyams

Easter week and Independence Day (September 15 and 16) are also
very busy. Keep in mind that if you plan to come for these celebrations,
you'll need to book far in advance.

OAXACA CITY

Oaxaca City is traditionally Indian, and although cosmopolitan touches
are everywhere, women and children still peddle everything from
wooden combs to chili-seasoned grasshoppers, and men and boys
offer shoe shines around the city's many parks. Although poverty and
unemployment are severe problems and you'll see families playing ac-
cordions along the city streets for spare change, levels of destitution
in the state capital are far less harsh than in Mexico City.

The city is officially called Oaxaca de Juárez, and it is decidedly the
state's major attraction, with a population of about 400,000 and
around a million visitors a year.

Exploring Oaxaca City

The colonial heart of Oaxaca is laid out in a simple grid, with all major
attractions within walking distance of one another. Most of the streets
in the city's core change names once they pass the zócalo.

A Good Walk

Begin your exploration of Oaxaca at the shady **zócalo** ①, the heart of
the city and its pedestrian-only main square. On the south side of the
square visit the **Palacio de Gobierno** ②—step inside and check out the
mural by Arturo García Bustos stretching from the first to the second
floor. Upon leaving the government palace, go to the northwest corner of the zócalo and you'll reach **El Alameda** ③, a second square that
abuts the zócalo. On the east side of the Alameda, you can't miss the
Catedral Metropolitana de Oaxaca ④. After visiting the cathedral,
turn right on Avenida Independencia and left at the next corner. This
puts you on the pedestrian mall on Calle Macedonio Alcalá, where you'll
see restored colonial mansions in a palate of pastels, and some of Oaxaca's best galleries, shops, museums, and restaurants. It's also lively
and well lighted at night, and there are frequent outdoor arts-and-crafts
exhibitions. After a short 1½ blocks you'll see the **Museo de Arte Contemporáneo de Oaxaca** ⑤ on your right. Continue north on Calle Macedonio Alcalá, turn right on Calle Murguía, and left on the first street,
Calle 5 de Mayo. Taking up the entire block on the east side of the
street is the **Ex-Convento de Santa Catalina** ⑥, now the Hotel Camino
Real. Catercorner from the Camino Real is Parque Labastida, where
indigenous artists sell their wares, and musicians sometimes entertain.
Continue north until Calle 5 de Mayo ends at Calle Gurrión and the
beautifully restored **Iglesia y Ex-Convento de Santo Domingo** ⑦. You
can enter the church from its southern entrance and leave via the front
door onto Calle Macedonio Alcalá; but to enjoy the main entranceway and its elaborate ceiling, it's worth walking around to the superb
garden of succulents at the front. Adjacent to the church is the mammoth **Museo de las Culturas** ⑧, which contains priceless artifacts taken
from Tomb 7 of Monte Albán, interactive computer explanations of
Oaxacan history and biodiversity, a fabulous old library, and an informative ethnographic exhibit.

Continue north on Calle Macedonio Alcalá half a block and pop into
the gallery and library of the **Instituto de Artes Gráficas de Oaxaca** ⑨.
Then walk up the steps of La Plazuela del Carmen Alto, where Triqui
women in red, beribboned *huipiles* (tunics) sell embroidered blouses,
dresses, and other handicrafts. Take a right on Calle García Vigil, and

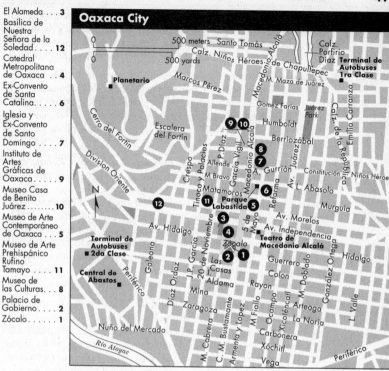

Oaxaca City

just a half block up, on the left side of the street, you'll find the **Museo Casa de Benito Juárez** ⑩, a museum honoring Oaxaca's most revered statesman. Upon leaving, return south on García Vigil 4½ blocks and turn right on Avenida Morelos. One and a half blocks up on the right, in a tranquil colonial home, is the **Museo de Arte Prehispánico Rufino Tamayo** ⑪. After seeing its elegant presentation of pre-Hispanic art, continue west on Morelos 2½ blocks. Descend the steps and cross the large plaza to the massive **Basílica de Nuestra Señora de la Soledad** ⑫, cracked and crooked with earthquake damage. On the left side of the church is a small museum housing items related to Oaxaca's patron saint. Go east on Avenida Independencia past the telegraph office and you'll be back at El Alameda, where you can stop and watch the daily parade of Oaxaqueños.

Sights to See

❸ **El Alameda.** This shady square is home to the Catedral Metropolitana de Oaxaca and the post office. Vendors here sell Che Guevara T-shirts, huge balloons, cassette tapes, snacks, and myriad souvenirs and crafts.

⑫ **Basílica de Nuestra Señora de la Soledad.** The Baroque basilica houses the statue of the Virgin of Solitude, Oaxaca's patron saint. According to legend, this statue was found in the pack of a mule that had mysteriously joined a mule train bound for Guatemala; when the mule perished at the site of the present church and the statue was discovered in its pack, the event was construed as a miracle, and the church was built in 1682 to commemorate it. The Virgin, who is believed to have supernatural healing powers, remains the object of fervent piety for the devout populace. She now stands in a gilded shrine. A small museum at the side of the church displays devotional items left by the faithful over the years. ⊠ *Av. Independencia 107, at Calle Galeana,* ☎ *no phone.* ☉ *Daily 7–7.*

4   **Catedral Metropolitana de Oaxaca.** Begun in 1544, the cathedral was destroyed by earthquakes and not finished until 1733. The king of Spain gave the city the wooden-cog clock that you can see in the facade. ⊠ *Av. Independencia 700,* ☎ *no phone.* ⊘ *Daily 8 AM–9 PM.*

6   **Ex-Convento de Santa Catalina.** This building is now the Hotel Camino Real and, like everything in downtown Oaxaca, is a National Heritage Site. Even if you're not staying here, it's worthwhile to explore the hotel's three courtyards; a large stone basin where the nuns did the convent's laundry 400 years ago still stands in the center of one of the patios. ⊠ *Calle 5 de Mayo 300.*

★ **7**   **Iglesia y Ex-Convento de Santo Domingo.** The most brilliantly decorated church of the city, this 16th-century wonder has an ornately carved facade that stands between two high bell towers. The interior is a profusion of white and gold—real gold leaf—typical of the energy with which Mexico seized on the Baroque style. The cultural complex of the Ex-Convento is all the more splendid, owing to a loving 1997–99 renovation. There are now botanical gardens (open for free afternoon tours), and a library of antiquarian books, in addition to the beautifully augmented **Museo de las Culturas.** ⊠ *Calles Macedonio Alcalá and Gurrión,* ☎ *no phone.* ⊘ *Daily 7 AM–8 PM.*

9   **Instituto de Artes Gráficas de Oaxaca** (El IAGO), across the street and north of the Ex-Convent of Santo Domingo, was established in 1988 by renowned Mexican painter Francisco Toledo, who can often be seen lurking in its shady haunts. The museum and library have an important collection of engravings, including works by Goya and Ensor. Temporary exhibitions feature local and international art, and you can relax and fine-tune your esthetic sensibility in the well-stocked art library. ⊠ *Calle Macedonio Alcalá 507,* ☎ *9/51–66980,* ⅢX *9/51–62045.* ⊠ *Free.* ⊘ *9:30–9. Exhibitions closed Tues.*

10   **Museo Casa de Benito Juárez.** Benito Juárez lived in this house as a servant during his youth. The museum re-creates a typical 19th-century house; none of the furnishings or memorabilia belonged to Juárez or his employer/benefactor. ⊠ *Calle García Vigil 609,* ☎ *9/51–61860.* ⊠ *$2.50, free Sun.* ⊘ *Tues.–Sat. 10–7, Sun. 10–5.*

★ **5**   **Museo de Arte Contemporáneo de Oaxaca.** This museum, also known as the MACO, is housed in an attractive colonial residence. It exhibits works in a variety of media; the permanent collection has that of some of Oaxaca's native sons, including Rufino Tamayo, Rodolfo Morales, and Francisco Toledo. Be sure to check out what remains of the frescoes in the second-floor front gallery. There's an excellent litle restaurant on one of the front patios that is ideal for lunch. ⊠ *Calle Macedonio Alcalá 202,* ☎ *9/51–42228,* ⅢX *9/51–42818.* ⊠ *$1.* ⊘ *Wed.–Mon. 10:30–8.*

★ **10**   **Museo de Arte Prehispánico Rufino Tamayo.** You'll find a beautifully displayed collection of pre-Hispanic pottery and sculpture at this carefully restored colonial mansion. Originally it was the private collection of the late painter-muralist Rufino Tamayo, who presented it to his hometown in 1979. ⊠ *Av. Morelos 503,* ☎ *9/51–64750.* ⊠ *$2.* ⊘ *Mon. and Wed.–Sat. 10–2 and 4–7, Sun. 10–3. Closed Tues.*

★ **8**   **Museo de las Culturas.** Laid out in a series of galleries around the cloister of the **Ex-Convento de Santo Domingo,** this museum, along with the entire ex-convent, has been totally refurbished. The ground floor now contains temporary galleries, a gift shop, and administrative offices. On the second floor you'll find 14 excellent thematic rooms, including those dedicated to Oaxacan music, medicine, indigenous languages, pottery, and more. Another gallery is dedicated to the treasure taken from the tombs at Monte Albán. The stunning gold jewelry from Tomb 7 was one of the greatest archaeological finds of all time. Tours (in Spanish) of the new botanical gardens are available Tuesday–Saturday at 1 PM for no additional cost. ⊠ *Plaza Santa Domingo,* ☎ *9/51–62991.* 🔊 *$3, free Sun.* 🕓 *Tues.–Sun. 10–8.*

★ ❷ **Palacio de Gobierno.** The splendid 19th-century neoclassical state capitol sits on the south side of the zócalo. Completed in 1988 and painted in fresco, the mural inside is a treasure for history buffs. In it, altars to the dead, painters of codices, fruit sellers, gods, Triqui children, and musicians crowd together to catalog the customs and legends of Oaxaca's indigenous people. ⊠ *Portal del Palacio,* ☎ *9/51–63850.* 🕓 *Daily 9–8.*

★ ❶ **Zócalo.** During the day, everyone comes to Oaxaca's shady main plaza, with its green wrought-iron benches and matching bandstand. At night, mariachi and marimba bands play under colonial archways or in the bandstand. ⊠ *Bounded by Portal de Clavería on the north, Portal del Palacio on the south, Portal de Flores on the west, and Portal de Mercaderes on the east.*

Dining and Lodging

The open-air cafés surrounding the zócalo are good for drinks, snacks, and people-watching, with the scene changing from serene early mornings to crowded parades with brass bands, floats, and *monos* (giant papier-mâché dolls) on holiday evenings. Most serve the economical *comida corrida* (midday set menu) after 1:30 PM. But you won't be very much out of pocket wherever you choose to dine.

Hotels here fill up quickly during Easter, July, November, and December, so book as far ahead as possible if you'll be visiting then.

$$$ ✕ **El Asador Vasco.** Basque (*vasco*) cuisine is served in this distinguished restaurant, where diners can overlook the main square. Try the lamb or sumptuous gratiné of oysters in chipotle chili sauce. From 8 to 9 PM, serenading by *tuna* (traditionally dressed student minstrels) evokes medieval Spain. Later, marimba music floats up from the restaurant below. ⊠ *Portal de Flores 10-A (west side of zócalo, upstairs),* ☎ *9/51–44755,* FAX *9/51–44762. AE, DC, MC, V.*

$$$ ✕ **El Colibrí.** Favored by upscale Mexican families and beeper-toting businesspeople, El Colibrí is quiet and air-conditioned, with romantic background music, free refills of super hot coffee, and fresh rolls and butter on the table. The menu is extensive: in addition to Oaxacan specialties, there are 10 different salads and five spaghetti dishes, plenty of appetizers, and burgers with fries. ⊠ *Calzada Niños Héroes de Chapultepec 903,* ☎ *9/51–58087. AE, MC, V.*

$$ ✕ **Catedral.** This elegant yet accessible local favorite takes up an entire original colonial house. Favorite dishes include mushroom soup flavored with *epazote* (a pungent local herb), chicken in squash-blossom sauce, served with rice and a squash blossom stuffed with cheese, and the *lechon* (suckling pig). You can feast at the lavish Sunday lunch buffet, served 2–6, ending with some of Catedral's great strong coffee. There's dancing in the bar Thursday, Friday, and Saturday nights after 9:30. ⊠ *Calle García Vigil 105, at Av. Morelos (1 block north of Catedral Metropolitana de Oaxaca),* ☎ *9/51–63285 or 9/51–63988. AE, DC, MC, V.*

$$ ✕ **El Naranjo.** A large, covered interior patio with melodic music in the background welcomes diners to this popular place, which specializes in contemporary Oaxacan cuisine. Each of Oaxaca's seven moles is featured once a week, and there are many delicious variations of *chiles rellenos* (stuffed peppers)—from mild to hot. Unusual dishes include a cream soup of smoky chipotle chili and nuts, and a spinach salad with a lovely, light dressing over fresh spinach leaves, jicama, bacon, and red hibiscus flowers. ⊠ *Calle Trujano 203*, ☎ *9/51–41878*, WEB *www.elnaranjo.com.mx. AE, MC, V.*

$$ ✕ **La Olla.** The name of this friendly restaurant means "the pot." It doubles as a gallery, and exhibitions of work by local artists change every month. The menu is varied—its strengths are the large, delicious, and healthy salads and regional dishes that the owner creates herself. A second-floor dining room doubles the restaurant space, and although the rustic rooftop terrace, complete with hammocks, is meant mainly for the adjoining hotel's guests, you can also take a drink up there for a good view of the city. Service tends to be slow. ⊠ *Calle Reforma 402*, ☎ *9/51–66668*, WEB *www.mexonline.com/laolla.htm. MC, V.*

$$ ✕ **Restaurant Casa Oaxaca.** This is doubtless the most exciting recent arrival on Oaxaca's culinary scene. Gifted young chef Alejandro creates his imaginative version of nouvelle Mexican cuisine with a light but sure touch. Dining is on the elegant patio of the hotel of the same name and in a small room by the kitchens. Creative entrées may include squash blossom stuffed with fresh cheese and honey; a superb main dish is pork with *mancha manteles* (stained tablecloth) mole. Alejandro also conjures up mouthwatering concoctions with fresh sea-bass. ⊠ *Calle García Vigil 407, 68000*, ☎ *9/51–44173*, FAX *9/51–64412. AE, MC, V.*

$$ ✕ **Terranova.** For delicious mole tamales and a good *caldo tlalpeño* (chicken-based soup with rice, avocado, chili, and tomato), make your way to the east side of the zócalo. One or more musicians are usually on hand 8:30–10:30 PM for some contemporary electric Latin sounds. ⊠ *Portal B. Juárez 116*, ☎ *9/51–40533*, FAX *9/51–40522*, WEB *www. terranova-oaxaca.com.mx. AE, MC, V.*

$ ✕ **Coffee Beans.** This coffeehouse is a great place for a cup of java, and there's a small selection of cakes and quiches. Different types and roasts of Mexican coffee beans are also on sale. ⊠ *Calle 5 de Mayo 205*, ☎ *no phone. No credit cards.*

$ ✕ **El Gecko.** The mustard-color courtyard of this tranquil coffeehouse is drenched in purple flowering vines. A variety of coffee drinks—including a fabulous iced cappuccino—are offered, as well as light food. You can use the Internet services at Axis, in the same plaza, as you sip your coffee. ⊠ *Calle 5 de Mayo 412, in Plaza Gonzalo Lucero*, ☎ *9/51–48024. No credit cards. Closed Sun.*

$ ✕ **El Mesón.** Mesón's inviting, inexpensive buffet is right off the zócalo. Stop by for a snack or full meal from the paper menu, where you check off your choices. Tortillas are made fresh in the evenings, and there are a variety of tacos, as well as *pozole* (hominy soup) and other Mexican dishes. For a sugar fix, have a cup of rich Oaxacan chocolate and a slice of nut or cheese pie. ⊠ *Av. Hidalgo 805, at Calle Valdivieso*, ☎ *9/51–62729*, FAX *9/51–44762. AE, MC, V.*

$$$$ ✕▣ **Hotel Camino Real Oaxaca.** A monastic air lingers in the breezy
★   patios and enclosed gardens of this beautifully restored former convent (1576), and Gregorian chants float softly through the hotel in the morning hours. The rooms themselves are far from austere, but there is nonetheless a touch of the divine in the atmosphere here. The massive buffets are the main draws at El Refectorio restaurant: the Saturday night spread, accompanied by mariachi music; the elaborate Sunday *comida* (late lunch); and the breakfast buffet. If you missed the Guelaguetza dance festival in July, you can watch a miniversion here on Friday night. ⊠ *Calle 5 de Mayo 300, 68000*, ☎ *9/51–60611*, FAX *9/51–60732*, WEB *www.caminoreal.com/oaxaca. 84 rooms, 7 suites.*

Restaurant, 2 bars, in-room safes, minibars, room service, pool, baby-sitting, laundry service, travel services. AE, DC, MC, V.

$$$ ✕🍴 **Casa Oaxaca.** A trio of eccentric Europeans poured their hearts
★ and souls into creating this most unusual bed-and-breakfast. They spent two years restoring a 200-year-old downtown house, combining colonial scale and traditional materials (adobe, cantera stone, etc.) with a distinctly contemporary minimalist sensibility. There is a beautiful indigo-blue-tile pool and a shaman-sanctioned *temazcal* (pre-Hispanic-style sweat lodge). Rooms have fresh flowers, 100% cotton sheets, and marble bathrooms, and serve as a rotating showcase for Oaxaca's modern artists. Breakfasts are included in the rate. ✉ *Calle García Vigil 407, 68000,* ☎ *9/51–44173,* 🆋 *9/51–64412,* 🆆🅴🅱 *www.casaoaxaca.com.mx. 5 rooms, 2 suites. Restaurant, bar, room service, pool, massage, sauna, laundry service. AE, MC, V.*

$$$ ✕🍴 **Hostal de la Noria.** The comfortable rooms in this restored colonial mansion two blocks off the zócalo are decorated with unique folkloric touches—some with carved wooden headboards, others with wrought-iron or hammered-tin ones. All have marble bathrooms, telephones, and cable TV. Among the house favorites at the hotel's elegant Restaurante Asunción are chicken mole, and foil-wrapped fish fillets steamed in a mezcal sauce. ✉ *Av. Hidalgo 918, 68000,* ☎ *9/51–47844,* 🆋 *9/51–63992,* 🆆🅴🅱 *www.lanoria.com. 46 rooms, 4 suites. Restaurant, bar, room service, baby-sitting, laundry service, free parking. AE, MC, V.*

$$$ 🍴 **Hacienda Los Laureles.** Situated in a quiet, green oasis but still not far from Oaxaca's historical center, this new resort hotel offers all modern amenities and is surrounded by a huge garden. The pool, hot tub, and spa, which includes temazcal steam baths and massage, help guests regain their inner balance. The adventurous can try horseback, bicycle riding, or ecological tours to the nearby mountains. A library with a selection of international magazines and newspapers is available, as is a business center with computer, fax, and Internet. ✉ *Av. Hidalgo 21, San Felipe del Agua 68020,* ☎ *9/50–15300,* 🆋 *9/52–00890,* 🆆🅴🅱 *www.haciendaloslaureles.com. 14 rooms, 3 suites. Restaurant, bar, room service, pool, massage, steam room, gym, jogging, baby-sitting, laundry service, free parking. AE, MC, V.*

$$$ 🍴 **Hotel Victoria.** Surrounded by terraced grounds and well-kept gardens, this sprawling salmon-color complex is perched on a hill overlooking the city. Draw back your curtains at dawn and catch your breath at the view of Oaxaca awakening under the Sierra Madre. Rooms, bungalows, and suites are available; be sure to request one with a view. You can take a shuttle bus on the half hour to the city center, 10 minutes away. ✉ *Calle Lomas del Fortín 1, 68070,* ☎ *9/51–52633,* 🆋 *9/51–52411,* 🆆🅴🅱 *www.hotelvictoriaoax.com.mx. 59 rooms, 57 suites, 34 bungalows. Restaurant, bar, in-room safes, minibars, room service, pool, tennis court, baby-sitting, laundry service, travel services, free parking. AE, MC, V.*

$$$ 🍴 **Misión de los Angeles.** Although this resort-style hotel is a long way from the zócalo, its peaceful gardens and relaxed ambience make it a good choice. It's much closer to El Llano, a city park frequented more by locals than by tourists. The hotel's commodious dining room is popular with tour groups. ✉ *Calzada Porfirio Díaz 102, 68050,* ☎ *9/51–51500,* 🆋 *9/51–51680,* 🆆🅴🅱 *www.misiondelosangeles.com. 155 rooms, 19 suites. 2 restaurants, 2 bars, room service, pool, tennis court, jogging, recreation room, free parking. AE, MC, V.*

$$ 🍴 **Las Golondrinas.** This intimate hotel is tastefully ablaze with color,
★ from the profusion of flowering plants to the walls—painted pink, blue, mustard, and rust. Guests read or lounge around the blissfully tranquil patios. Plain but cheerful rooms have red-tile floors and comfortable

beds; none has TV or phone, but there's a TV in the common sitting room. Breakfast (not included in room rates) is served 8–10 AM. ⊠ *Calle Tinoco y Palacios 411, 68000,* ☎ *9/51–43298 or 9/51–42126. 24 rooms. Laundry service. V.*

$$ 🏨 **Hotel Cazomalli.** Even the baked-earth floor tiles shine in this lovable hostelry, 15 minutes from downtown Oaxaca in the sleepy, cobblestone barrio of Jalatlaco. The hotel lives up to its name, which in Nahuatl means "house of tranquility." Clean, bright, quiet rooms have blond-pine furnishings and handwoven bedspreads and curtains. Rooms have no TVs—there's one in a small second-floor salon—but they do have phones. Owner Marina Flores and her family make the ambience friendly, and serve breakfast 8–10 AM. Head up to the roof to jump into the small whirlpool or to wash your own clothes. ⊠ *Calle El Salto 104, at Calle Aldama, Jalatlaco, 68080,* ☎ ᖴᗩX *9/51–38605. 15 rooms. Breakfast room, hot tub. AE, MC, V.*

$$ 🏨 **Hotel Rivera del Angel.** This large, plain-looking hotel is a favorite with Mexican families, groups, and traveling salesmen. Southwest of the zócalo near the markets, it has a huge garden pool. The attractive rooms have wide terraces, orthopedic mattresses, desk fans, and phones. Tourist buses to Monte Albán leave from here every hour on the half hour until 3:30 PM. ⊠ *Calle F. J. Mina 518, 68000,* ☎ *9/51–66666,* ᖴᗩX *9/51–45405. 62 rooms. Restaurant, room service, pool, free parking. MC, V.*

$$ 🏨 **Hotel Señorial.** It's a little worn around the edges, but still a good choice if you want a relatively inexpensive hotel right on the zócalo; the seven rooms that overlook the square have tiny balconies. Uncarpeted rooms have TVs and phones, and the beds are fairly comfortable, although far from firm. The clean bathrooms are tiled in cheerful light blue. ⊠ *Portal de Flores 6, 68000,* ☎ *9/51–63933,* ᖴᗩX *9/51–63668. 126 rooms, 8 suites. Restaurant, café, room service, pool, free parking. No credit cards.*

$$ 🏨 **Suites Colibri.** The suites in this business-oriented hotel are a good value. Large rooms have firm beds, cable TV, and phones. The three newest units have tile floors and painterly frescoes on the walls. All rooms have bathtubs. ⊠ *Privada de las Flores 109, off Calzada Niños Héroes de Chapultepec, 68050,* ☎ ᖴᗩX *9/51–36211. 22 suites. Restaurant, bar, room service, free parking. AE, MC, V.*

Nightlife and the Arts

Oaxaca has plenty of entertainment in evening hours. On almost any night you'll find live marimba, Andean music, or nouveau flamenco in the open-air cafés surrounding the zócalo. There's a slew of discotheques playing salsa or rock, and Sunday at 12:30 PM the **Oaxaca State Band** sets up under the Indian laurel trees in the main square. The **Teatro Macedonio Alcalá** has orchestral and theatrical performances sporadically—even the occasional opera. See the monthly *Guía Cultural* (free at the MACO and Sedetur information booth on Av. Independencia) for information in Spanish and English on these and other events.

El Sol y La Luna is *the* place to listen to live music, often jazz or jazzy Mexican and American ballads. You can sit over drinks or order dinner on the outside patio or inside at the residence-turned-restaurant, directly across from the Oaxaca Institute of Culture. A cover is charged ($2–$4, depending on the band) when the music begins at 9–9:30 PM. Off-season, there is usually music Thursday–Saturday only. ⊠ *Calle Reforma 502, at Calle Constitución,* ☎ *9/51–48069.*

Every Friday night—and Monday and Wednesday in busier seasons— the **Hotel Camino Real** (⊠ Calle 5 de Mayo 300, ☎ 9/51–60611) hosts the Guelaguetza, a smaller version of the pre-Hispanic Oaxacan dance fête displaying regional dances from throughout the state. The $25 price includes buffet dinner (beginning at 7 PM) and show (8:30 PM) in the former convent's 16th-century chapel. Drinks aren't included in the price. Reservations are recommended. If you want to see a less expensive Guelaguetza show, check with the tourist office for recommendations.

Shopping

Prospective folk-art buyers in Oaxaca City and surrounding villages should heed one major caveat: be sure you have a receipt showing that you paid the 15% sales tax on all items purchased. It isn't too difficult to ship your purchases home from many of the city's shops and shipping services, provided you have this. Many artisans have begun giving out official government tax receipts, but if you buy from one who doesn't, you may have a hard time finding someone to ship your goods for you. Ask for receipts and for referrals to shipping agents if you plan to buy more than you can carry home. Also, check out the displays at the shops in town and learn about quality and design before you start spending lots of pesos.

Markets

The Saturday market is held at the functionally named **Central de Abastos** (Supply Center) on the southern edge of the town center. By noon on Saturday the enormous covered market is swarming with thousands of sellers and shoppers—both from Oaxaca and the surrounding villages—and the experience can be quite overwhelming. Don't burden yourself with a lot of camera equipment or purses and bags; you'll have a hard enough time keeping track of companions in the crowd. If you see something you really like, purchase it on the spot because you might never find your way back. The market is active during the rest of the week, too. If you go then, you can check out the mounds of multicolored chilies and herbs, the piles of tropical fruit, and the aisles of baskets, rugs, and fragile green or black pottery. But it's on Saturday that you see the best handicrafts: huipiles that vary with the village of origin; *rebozos* (shawls) of cotton and silk; distinctive pottery from many villages; colorful woven baskets; and wooden and tin toys. Bargaining isn't unexpected, although some sellers quote the actual price these days.

Several other markets in Oaxaca are active daily. **Mercado Benito Juárez** is south of the zócalo between Calles 20 de Noviembre and Miguel Cabrera at Colón. Handicrafts can be found here, as well as cheese, mole, chocolate, fruits, and much more. Locals, budget travelers, and other adventurers eat regional food in the mornings at the intriguing stalls of the **Mercado 20 de Noviembre** (⊠ between Calles 20 de Noviembre and Miguel Cabrera at Calle Aldama). **Mercado de Artesanías** (⊠ Calle J. P. García near Calle Ignacio Zaragoza) sells mostly textiles. Triqui Indian women and children weave wall hangings with simple back-strap looms while they tend their stands.

Each neighborhood has its own market day in a nearby square or structure, although these don't generally sell handicrafts. If you're interested in seeing neighborhood markets, check out **Mercado de Conzatti** (⊠ Calle Reforma at Calle Humboldt) Friday until 4 PM. Sunday is market day for the **Mercado de Merced** (⊠ Calzada de la República at Calle Morelos).

Shops and Galleries

Besides having a mother lode of markets, Oaxaca has some spectacular shops and galleries; some are closed Sunday and others close at midday, so plan your shopping days accordingly.

FINE ARTS

Galería Quetzalli (⊠ Calle Constitución 104, ☎ 9/51–42606) features both established and up-and-coming Oaxacan artists. Prices are high, but the work is excellent. **Galería Arte Mexicano** (⊠ Plaza Santo Domingo, Calle Macedonio Alcalá 407–16, ☎ 9/51–63255) displays local artists' work, and in adjoining rooms, folk art, antiques, and silver jewelry.

HANDICRAFTS

ARIPO (⊠ Calle García Vigil 809, ☎ 9/51–44030) is a government-run artist cooperative with competitive prices and much exclusively Oaxacan work. It's one of the few craft stores open Sunday. The **Fonart** store (⊠ Crespo 114, ☎ 9/51–65764) has a representative selection of quality arts and crafts from elsewhere in Mexico. **La Mano Mágica** (⊠ Calle Macedonio Alcalá 203, ☎ 9/51–64275) is a crafts and fine-arts gallery with a large inventory of interesting pieces. You'll support the women artists' co-op (open daily) by shopping at the huge warren of shops that makes up **Mujeres Artesanas de las Regiones de Oaxaca** (⊠ Calle 5 de Mayo 204, ☎ 9/51–60670). Selection and quality are good, and prices are reasonable. **Artesanías Chimalli** (⊠ Calle García Vigil 513-A, ☎ 9/51–42101) has an excellent selection of alebrijes—brightly painted copal-wood animals with comical expressions and fantasy shapes. There's also a large assortment of quality crafts from throughout Mexico. Chimalli will cheerfully ship what you buy here, or what you've bought elsewhere. The two-story **Corazón del Pueblo** (⊠ Calle Macedonio Alcalá 307, ☎ 9/51–30547) sells beaded Huichol Indian masks, mystical tapestries from Nayarit state, *papel picado* (colorful cutout paper flags), and a good selection of English-language books on Mexican art and history.

JEWELRY

Oro de Monte Albán (⊠ Calle Macedonio Alcalá 403, ☎ 9/51–43813) is one of several branches of this store, which sells gold and silver reproductions of pre-Columbian jewelry found in the tombs of royalty at Monte Albán (there's also a shop at the archaeological site). Plenty of other fine shops sell jewelry in both traditional and modern styles, many of them along Calle Macedonio Alcalá and adjacent streets, as well as the streets west of Mercado 20 de Noviembre.

Side Trips from Oaxaca City

A trip to the colonial city of Oaxaca isn't complete without heading out to see the area's ancient past and the local village life that connects it with the present. The dramatic settings of the Zapotec and Mixtec ruins of Monte Albán, Mitla, and Yagul date back some 2,600 years. And the nearby towns that produce the wares sold in the Oaxaca City market give a taste of traditional regional lifestyles. All of these places are easily reached by public transportation, collective taxi, or on a tour. Recently, Sedetur, the state tourism board, developed the Tourist Yu'u project, which provides opportunities to experience life outside the city. The project makes available basic, comfortable, clean accommodations in artisan villages and near natural phenomena such as the cold-water springs and fossilized waterfalls at Hierve el Agua. Contact the tourism department for details and reservations.

Monte Albán

9 km (5½ mi) southwest of Oaxaca.

The onetime holy city of more than 30,000 Zapotecs, Monte Albán is arguably the most interesting and well-preserved ruin in the state. Experts estimate that a mere 10% of the site is uncovered—excavations are constantly taking place to unearth more knowledge about the fascinating culture of the Zapotec people who lived here.

Monte Albán overlooks the Oaxaca Valley from a flattened mountaintop 1,300 ft high. Either Zapotecs or their predecessors leveled the site around 600 BC. The Zapotecs did construct the existing buildings along a north–south axis, with the exception of one structure thought to have been an observatory, which is more closely aligned with the stars than with the earth's poles. And the varying heights of the site follow the contours of distant mountain ranges. The oldest of the four temples is the **Gallery of the Dazantes** (dancers), so named for the elaborately carved stone figures that once covered the building—the originals are now in the site museum. Experts are unsure whether the figures, mostly male nudes, represent captives, medical cases, or warriors; the theory that they were dancers has been discarded.

Another major point of interest is the **ball court,** where one or more ball games were played. Hips, shoulders, knees, and elbows were probably used to hit a wooden or rubber ball. Some insist the captain of the winning team was sacrificed as an honor, others condemn the losers—the exact outcome of these games is unknown. There is some speculation that the games were a means of solving disputes among factions or villages within the domain.

No one knows for sure whether the Zapotecs abandoned the site gradually or suddenly, but by AD 1000 they had vacated it. Until then, they had expanded the city and taken on Maya influences in buildings and stelae, as had other cultures in the region. The Mixtecs, who took over the site years after the Zapotecs' departure, used Monte Albán as a lofty necropolis, a massive cemetery of lavish tombs. More than 200 tombs and 300 burial sites have been explored to date; in 1932 **Tomb 7** yielded a treasure unequaled in North America. Inside were more than 500 priceless Mixtec objects, including gold breastplates; jade, pearl, ivory, and gold jewelry; and fans, masks, and belt buckles of precious stones and metals. Many of these treasures are now on view at the Museo de las Culturas. Here, there's a small **site museum** with an excellent bookstore–gift shop (☎ 9/51–61215). The cafeteria isn't half bad and has a great view of the valley of Oaxaca.

Special buses go to Monte Albán from the Hotel Rivera del Angel every hour on the half hour from 8:30 to 3:30; the last bus back is at 6 PM. The round-trip fare is about $2; to stay longer than two hours you must pay a 80¢ surcharge. A taxi from the zócalo costs about $10. ☞ *$3, free Sun. and holidays.* ☉ *Daily 8–6.*

Mitla

 40 km (25 mi) southeast of Oaxaca.

Mitla, like Monte Albán, is a complex of structures started by the Zapotecs and later taken over by the Mixtecs. In fact, the site of these palaces grew even as Monte Albán declined. Mitla's architecture is striking—and unique in the area—for the elegance of its geometric patterns and the brilliance of its stone. Unlike other ancient buildings in North America, there are no human figures or mythological events represented—only abstract designs. The name, from the Aztec word *mictlan,* means "place of the dead," and you can enter one of the underground tombs. The journey takes about 50 minutes from Oaxaca, and it's cheaper to grab a *colectivo* (collective taxi) at the side of the second-class bus station. ☞ *$2.50, free Sun. and holidays.* ☉ *Archaeological zone daily 8–5.*

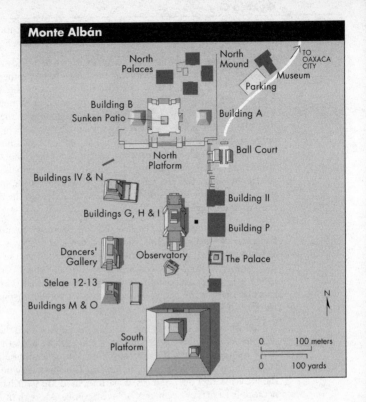

Monte Albán

*(map labels)* North Palaces · North Mound · TO OAXACA CITY · Museum · Parking · Building B · Sunken Patio · Building A · North Platform · Ball Court · Buildings IV & N · Building II · Buildings G, H & I · Building P · Dancers' Gallery · Observatory · The Palace · Stelae 12-13 · Buildings M & O · South Platform · 0 100 meters · 0 100 yards · N

Yagul

36 km (22 mi) southeast of Oaxaca.

Although the palace ruins at Yagul aren't nearly as elaborate as those at Monte Albán or Mitla, they stand handsomely atop a hill and are certainly worth a visit, especially if you're interested in Oaxaca's ancient cultures. This city was predominantly a fortress set slightly above a group of palaces and temples; it includes a ball court and more than 30 uncovered underground tombs. *$2.20, free Sun. and holidays. Archaeological zone daily 8–5.*

Traditional Villages

Many of the dozen or more villages around Oaxaca City are known for the skills of their artisans, who use both ancient and modern techniques to create their folk-art pieces; they often live among generations of families who have their own special designs for pottery, woven rugs, and wood carvings.

A west-to-south counterclockwise route from the city takes in **Atzompa,** 8 km (5 mi) from the city, where you can find fanciful clay pots and sculptures. Potters make the region's traditional green-glazed plates, bowls, and cups, and groups of 10 or more can watch the creative process in the *mercado artesanal* from 8 to 7. In **Arrazola,** artists carve alebrijes. On Thursday, **Zaachila** has the most authentic livestock and food market in the area. Located 17 km (11 mi) from Oaxaca, it also boasts an archeological zone and restaurants serving typical regional fare. The southern route goes to **San Bartolo Coyotepec,** the center for glossy, unglazed black pottery sold in people's homes and from a multistall cooperative next to the town square. In **Santo Tomás Jalietza,** women sell belts and table runners from pastel cotton made on small, back-strap looms. **San Martín Tilcajete,** south of Santo Tomás Jalietza on the road to Ocotlán, also is a town full of painted wooden animals. Friday's colorful market in **Ocotlán** is known for its handi-crafts, especially handcrafted machetes and knives, famous through-out Mexico.

An eastward route includes **Teotitlán del Valle,** where giant rug looms sit in the front rooms of many houses. One of the town's most respected rug makers is Isaac Vásquez. The small **Museo Comunitario** (closed Monday) on the main square focuses on the anthropology, crafts, and culture of the area. In **Santa Ana del Valle,** Lucio Aquino is the most famous rug maker, although there are many skilled artisans in town. In nearby **Tlacolula,** the Sunday market spreads for blocks around the Baroque 16th-century chapel. On Sunday it seems that all of Oaxaca takes this route, starting at the Tule Tree, moving to the ruins of Mitla, and then on to the crafts centers and market.

North of the city center, off the road to Mexico City, is **Etla;** its Wednes-day market is known for cheeses, mole, bread, and chocolates.

The markets on other routes are held on special days throughout the week, and you can easily fill a week with tours and never see the same sight twice. If you have to budget your time, use tour guides for these trips so you don't miss out on the fascinating details.

The Tule Tree
14 km (8½ mi) east of Oaxaca.

In the town of Santa María del Tule stands a huge ahuehuete cypress estimated to be more than 2,000 years old. One of the largest in the world, it is some 140 ft high, with roots buried more than 60 ft in the earth. It weighs nearly 640,000 tons and takes 35 adults with their arms outstretched to embrace it. The tree is the traditional center of the town of Santa María and is larger than the church behind it. 🖼 20¢.

OAXACA CITY A TO Z

AIR TRAVEL
You can fly to Oaxaca City's Benito Juárez Airport, 8 km (5 mi) south of town, from several U.S. cities, always making a stop in Mexico City. There is also service for triangle flight itineraries, including the Oax-acan coastal resorts of Bahías de Huatulco or Puerto Escondido.

CARRIERS
Mexicana flies from various U.S. cities (including Chicago, Los An-geles, San Francisco, Miami, and New York) to Oaxaca City with a stop in Mexico City. You'll have to change planes in Mexico City on other flights from the United States Aeroméxico or Mexicana. Domestic service to Oaxaca includes Aviacsa from Tuxtla Gutiérrez; Aero Vega for charters to and from Puerto Escondido; Aerocalifornia from Mex-ico City, Puebla, Mazatlán and Los Cabos; and Aerocaribe from Puerto Escondido and Huatulco.
➤ AIRLINES AND CONTACTS: **Aerocalifornia** (☎ 9/51–48570 or 800–237–6225). **Aerocaribe** (☎ 9/51–60266 or 9/51–60229). **Aeroméxico** (☎ 9/51–61066). **Aero Vega** (☎ 9/51–62777). **Aviacsa** (☎ 9/51–45304). **Mexicana** (☎ 9/51–68414 or 9/51–67352).

AIRPORT TRANSFERS
Transportes Aeropuerto will trundle you into the soonest available van and drop you off at your hotel for $2. There are usually no taxis in sight. From town, buy a ticket ahead of time for inexpensive airport transportation or hail a regular cab for about $6.
➤ TAXIS AND SHUTTLES: **Transportes Aeropuerto** (✉ Alameda de León, ☎ 9/51–44350).

BUS TRAVEL TO AND FROM OAXACA

Deluxe buses make the six-hour nonstop run from Mexico City to Oaxaca for about $23. Oaxaca City's first-class terminal is called the ADO, from which the ADO and Cristóbal Colón bus lines provide service. The second-class bus station, Central de Autobuses, serves intermediate towns within the state. Other lines have desks at one or both terminals.

➤ BUS INFORMATION: **ADO** (✉ Calzada Niños Héroes de Chapultepec 1036, at Calle Emilio Carranza, ☎ 9/51–51703). **Central de Autobuses** (✉ Prolongación de Trujano at the Periférico, ☎ 9/51–65824). **Cristóbal Colón** (☎ 9/51–51214).

CAR RENTAL

Cars are available for rent at the airport, in town, and through travel agencies at various hotels. Hertz has two convenient locations.

➤ MAJOR AGENCIES: **Alamo** (✉ 5 de Mayo 203, ☎ 9/51–48534). **Hertz** (✉ La Bastida 115–4, ☎ 9/51–62434, FAX 9/51–60009; ✉ Benito Juárez Airport, ☎ 9/51–15478).

CAR TRAVEL

From Mexico City, you can take Mexico 190 (Pan American Highway) south and east through Puebla and Izúcar de Matamoros to Oaxaca City—a distance of 546 km (338 mi) along a rather curvy road. This route takes six–seven hours. The toll road (*cuota*) that connects Mexico City to Oaxaca City via Tehuacan costs about $30 one way. It cuts driving time to four hours.

You won't need a car in Oaxaca City, which is fairly compact. Even outlying sights are easily accessible by taxi or on a tour. That said, a car is a great way for adventurous souls to see the countryside.

EMBASSIES

The Canadian Consulate is open weekdays 11–2. The U.S. Consulate is open weekdays 10–3.

➤ CANADA: **Canadian Consulate** (✉ Calle Pino Suarez 700, Local 11-B, ☎ 9/51–33777).

➤ UNITED STATES: **U.S. Consulate** (✉ Calle Macedonio Alcalá 201, Int. 204, ☎ FAX 9/51–43054).

EMERGENCIES

Dial 060 locally for all emergencies, including police and hospital.

➤ CONTACTS: **Police** (☎ 9/51–62224). **Hospital–Red Cross** (☎ 9/51–64455).

INTERNET

There are several Internet cafés downtown. Axis, open weekdays 10–8 and Saturday 10–6, charges $2 an hour.

➤ INTERNET CAFÉS: **Axis** (✉ Calle 5 de Mayo 412, ☎ 9/51–48024).

TAXIS

Taxis are plentiful, clearly marked, and reasonably priced. You can usually find them at any hour of the day cruising on downtown streets. There are also taxi stands on Avenida Independencia at Calle García Vigil, on one side of Alameda Park, and on Calles Abasolo and Cinco de Mayo, near the Hotel Camino Real. Cabs aren't metered. Determine the fare ahead of time (in town, usually $2–$2.50); for outlying destinations, ask the driver to show you the tariff card.

TOURS

Unless you're on a strict budget, take advantage of the many tour companies that offer guided trips to the archaeological sites, colonial churches and monasteries, outlying towns (some of which have weekly

market days), and folk-art centers. Prices start at $10. Licensed guides
are available as well through travel agencies for approximately $5 per
hour for a minimum of three persons. Viajes Turísticos Mitla and
Agencia Marqués del Valle are among the most established agencies.
For environment-friendly tourism, contact Expediciones Sierra Norte
or TierrAventura. Tierra Dentro specializes in bird-watching, and
groups are run in English.

➤ TOUR OPERATOR RECOMMENDATIONS: **Agencia Marqués del Valle** (✉
Portal de Clavería s/n, ☎ 9/51–46970 or 9/51–46962, FAX 9/51–69961).
Expediciones Sierra Norte (✉ Garcia Vigil 406, ☎ 9/51–48271, FAX 9/
51–67745, WEB www.sierranorte.org.mx). **Tierra Dentro** (✉ Reforma
528-B, ☎ 9/51–49284, WEB www.welcome.to/tierradentro). **TierrAventura** (✉ Boca del Monte 110, ☎ 9/51–43843, WEB www.
tierraventura.com). **Viajes Turísticos Mitla** (✉ Calle F. J. Mina 518,
in the Hotel Rivera del Angel, ☎ 9/51–66175, FAX 9/51–43152).

VISITOR INFORMATION

The Oficina de Turismo is open daily 9–8. It also has a booth in Oaxaca airport, which is open daily 6 AM–8 PM.

➤ TOURIST INFORMATION: **Oficina de Turismo** (✉ Av. Independencia
607, at Calle García Vigil, ☎ 9/51–64828 or 9/51–60123; airport booth
9/51–15040, WEB www.oaxaca.gob.mx/sedetur).

THE OAXACA COAST

Oaxaca's 520-km (322-mi) coastline is mainland Mexico's last Pacific
frontier. Huatulco, a project of Fonatur (the government's tourism developers), was launched in the early 1980s. Bahías de Huatulco, as the
entire area is called, covers 51,900 acres of mountain lowlands and
coastal stretches, 40,000 acres of which is supposed to remain a nature reserve. The focal point of the master-planned development is a
string of nine sheltered bays that stretches across 35 km (22 mi) of some
of the Pacific's prettiest coastline.

Huatulco's beauty is arguably best seen from a boat, even though some
of the bays are accessible by road. Bahía Tangolunda is the site of the
area's most exclusive hotels, whereas Bahía Santa Cruz has midrange
hotels, a marina, and a small plaza. Bahía Chahué has been developed
in the past few years, with some moderate-price hotels; a parking lot
makes the beach here quite accessible. The town of La Crucecita, originally built to house the construction crews and workers building Huatulco, has come along nicely: it has a pretty plaza and a recently
frescoed church, as well as some budget hotels and plenty of restaurants.

Puerto Escondido has long been prime territory for international
surfers. The town has the coast's first airport (not international) and
has grown up to tourism in a much more natural, and, some say,
pleasant, way than Huatulco. Although the four-block pedestrian
walkway—crowded with open-air seafood restaurants, shops, and
café bars—is lively, the "real" town above the strip, with its busy market and stores, provides a look at local life and a dazzling view of the
coast. The tiny port town of Puerto Ángel, midway between the Puerto
Escondido airport and the Bahías de Huatulco airport, has a limited
selection of hotels and bungalows tucked into the hills.

Puerto Escondido

⑬ *310 km (192 mi) south of Oaxaca City.*

A coffee-shipping port in the 1920s, Puerto Escondido is the first
tourist town on the Oaxaca coast, southeast of Acapulco on Highway

200. The town market, **Mercado Benito Juárez,** is a long walk (but a short cab or bus ride) from most hotels, and it's worth checking out (Saturday and Wednesday). If you want a bit of pampering, cleanse body and soul according to ancient traditions at the **Villa Temazcalli** (✉ Av. Infraganti, esq. Calle Temazcalli, ☎ 9/58–21023), which claims to combine "the energy of wood, fire, rock, and medicinal herbs." Massages are also offered, and afterward you can watch the sunset from the cliffs above the ocean. Back in town, at the north end of the main beach, you can hire a driver from among the *panga* (small boat) fleet for bay tours. It's around $5 per person or $28 for your own boat to tour all the bays. Fishing trips are a little steep at about $30 per hour. **La Playa Principal** (main beach) and the **Laguna Agua Dulce** are at the south end of the tourist strip, followed by **Marinero Beach,** a sharp outcropping of rocks, and, finally, the most famous—and dangerous—beach of all, **Zicatela.**

The main intersection in Puerto Escondido is at Highway 200 (also called the *carretera costera,* or coast highway) and Avenida Alfonso Pérez Gasga, which meanders south into the tourist zone. On the north side of the highway this street is called Avenida Oaxaca. Traveling down a steep hill, Avenida Gasga passes many of the tourist hotels; at the bottom, traffic is prohibited and the street becomes a four-block-long pedestrian mall lined with shops, restaurants, and lodgings that spread to the sands of the main beach.

The airport is on the northern edge of town, as are the hotels favored by charter groups. **Playa Bacocho,** just south of the airport, is an upscale housing-and-hotel development. The beach is not safe for swimming so don't be tempted. Some inviting bars, discos, and restaurants have opened in this area, although most of the action still centers around the tourist zone to the south.

Beaches
One of the top 10 surfing beaches in the world, **Zicatela** is a long stretch of cream-color sand battered by the Mexican Pipeline, as this stretch of mighty surf is called by those in the know. In November international surfing championships are held here, and the town fills with sun-bleached aficionados of both sexes intent on serious surfing and hard partying. The water is only for professional swimmers and, even then, a lifeguard must be on duty. Do *not* swim in these waters even if it looks calm, as the undertows and rip currents are deadly. Instead, watch the surfers at sunset from the *palapa* (thatch-roof) restaurant at the Arco Iris Hotel.

Of the seven beaches in Puerto Escondido, the safest for swimming and snorkeling are **Puerto Angelito** and **Carrizalillo;** both can be reached on foot, but more easily by cab or by boat from the town beach. Transportation is available from the many fishermen who park their pangas on the sand near town and use them as water taxis. The ride should cost about $2.

Dining and Lodging
Understandably, coastal cuisine focuses on fresh seafood dishes, although some savvy townspeople are introducing Italian and vegetarian food for variety. For such a small town, Puerto Escondido has more than its share of good restaurants.

$$ ✕ **Mario's Pizzaland.** The proprietor is a courtly, generous Italian who produces in short-order pizzas with many exotic toppings, including seafood. Also on the abbreviated menu are vegetarian and meat lasagna, enormous salads, and *bistec alla pizzaiola* (steak smothered in melted cheese and pizza sauce). ✉ *Av. Gasga east of the tourist zone,* ☎ *9/58–20570. No credit cards.*

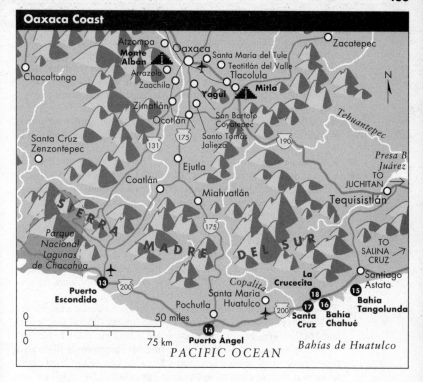

Oaxaca Coast

Atzompa
Oaxaca
Zacatepec
Monte Albán
Santa María del Tule
Arrazola
Teotitlán del Valle
Tlacolula
Chacaltongo
Zaachila
Yagul
Mitla
Zimatlán
Ocotlán
San Bartolo
Coyotepec
Santo Tomás
Jalieza
Tehuantepec
Santa Cruz
Zenzontepec
131
175
190
Presa B
Juárez
Ejutla
TO
JUCHITAN
Coatlán
Miahuatlán
SIERRA
Tequisistlán
175
MADRE
DEL
SUR
Parque
Nacional
Lagunas
de Chacahua
TO
SALINA
CRUZ
La
Crucecita
Santiago
Astata
13
200
Copalita
18
15
Puerto
Escondido
Santa María
Huatulco
17
16
Bahía
Tangolunda
Pochutla
Santa
Cruz
Bahía
Chahué
0
50 miles
200
0
75 km
14
Puerto Ángel
PACIFIC OCEAN
Bahías de Huatulco
N

$$ ✕ **La Perla.** Because it's in the "real" town uphill from the tourist zone, this excellent seafood restaurant has some of the best prices in town. *Pulpo* (octopus) is wonderfully tender. An excellent ceviche comes in a spicy cocktail sauce. It's a bit of a walk but a short, cheap cab ride. ⊠ *Calle 3a Poniente s/n, Sector Juárez,* ☎ *9/58–20461. No credit cards.*

$$ ✕ **Perla Flameante.** Fresh dorado, shark, tuna, and pompano come with teriyaki, Cajun, or garlic seasonings at this second-story bamboo restaurant. The deep-fried onion rings and zucchini are terrific. Perla is open for dinner only. ⊠ *Av. Gasga near end of tourist zone,* ☎ *9/58–20167. MC, V.*

$ ✕ **Art 'n' Harry's.** Only open during high season, this surfer hangout overlooking the Pipeline is the place to relax with a drink and watch videos or zone out on heavy-metal CDs. The menu offers various stir-fry and spaghetti dishes, salads, and seafood. ⊠ *South end of Zicatela beach,* ☎ *no phone. No credit cards.*

$ ✕ **Carmen's Bakery.** A long-standing favorite for great coffee, whole-★ grain breads, and sinful pastries, this bakery (a.k.a. La Patisserie) is on the main drag on Zicatela beach. The breakfast of fruit salad with yogurt and granola is sublime. The same owner runs Cafecito, a happening surfers' hangout down the beach and equally worthy of a visit. ⊠ *Calle del Morro s/n, Zicatela beach,* ☎ *no phone. No credit cards. No dinner.*

$ ✕ **La Gota de Vida.** This small vegetarian café and health-food store on Zicatela beach has all sorts of delicious salads, vegetable soups, tofu and tempeh dishes, and *licuados* (milk shakes made with yogurt and papaya, mango, or banana) as well as fresh vegetable and fruit juices at very reasonable prices. It's often packed with surfers and health-conscious travelers. ⊠ *Calle del Morro s/n,* ☎ *no phone. No credit cards.*

$$$ ✕⊡ **Hotel Santa Fe.** Framed by exuberant tropical plants at the north end of Zicatela beach, this pretty hotel has colonial furnishings and curtains and spreads of woven Mexican cloth. Some rooms have balconies overlooking the pools and patios or the beach. The hotel also manages the eight one-bedroom Bungalows Santa Cruz next door, which have well-stocked kitchenettes, cozy furnishings, and wide verandas. By all means treat yourself to at least one meal at the hotel restaurant—whether or not you're a guest. The menu is divided between seafood, vegetarian, and traditional Mexican dishes, and tables overlooking the surf have wonderful views. ⊠ *Calle del Morro s/n, 71980,* ☎ *9/58–20170,* FAX *9/58–20260. 59 rooms, 2 suites, 8 bungalows. Restaurant, bar, 2 pools, wading pool, shops, laundry service, free parking. AE, MC, V.*

$$ ✕🏨 **Flor de María.** Hand-painted birds, flowers, and tropical scenes
★ adorn this bright, attractive hotel a half block up from Playa Marinero. Crisp sheets cover firm beds, and rooms are bright and immaculate—with powerful ceiling fans, but no TV or phone. On the roof, you can swing in a row of hammocks, or cool off in the small pool or at the rooftop bar. Like all Zicatela beach hotels, Flor de María is a short but very dark walk from the tourist esplanade. In the outstanding restaurant, Canadian owner Joanne brings Italian and Peruvian touches to the dishes. ⊠ *Entrance to Playa Marinero s/n, 71980,* ☎ FAX *9/58–20536. 24 rooms. Restaurant, bar, fans, pool, laundry service. MC, V.*

$$$ 🏨 **Hotel Aldea del Bazar.** This sparkling white hotel sits on a bluff overlooking Playa Bacocho, just south of the airport. The restaurant and some of the rooms have a view of the beach below, which can be reached by a ramp—a long walk back up the hill. All the tastefully decorated rooms have small living rooms and color TVs. One of the hotel's best features is the pre-Hispanic–style eucalyptus sauna; the massages are mediocre. ⊠ *Av. Benito Juárez 7, Fracc. Bacocho, 71980,* ☎ FAX *9/58–20508. 47 rooms. Restaurant, bar, pool, massage, spa. AE, MC, V.*

$$–$$$ 🏨 **Paraíso Escondido.** Hidden halfway up the steps of Calle Union, this colonial-style hotel has the charm of a wealthy, eccentric, and somewhat dotty relative's house. No two rooms are alike, and all are furnished with a folkloric mixture of wood dressers, tin mirrors, and brightly colored curtains and spreads. It's just opened five new third-floor suites with kitchenettes and private, ocean-view terraces. ⊠ *Calle Union 10, 71980,* ☎ *9/58–20444. 20 rooms, 5 suites. Restaurant, bar, pool. No credit cards.*

$$ 🏨 **Studios Tabachín del Puerto.** Special touches such as clocks, vases, and shelves with books give these wonderfully furnished studio apartments a homey feel. Especially wonderful is the fourth-floor "penthouse," with its awesome view of the coast. Each of the six studios, behind the Hotel Santa Fe near Zicatela beach, has a kitchenette stocked with necessities and includes a splendid breakfast on the patio restaurant with the room rate. Owner Don Pablo also manages a small country inn, Posada Nopala, about two hours north of town, which is open October 31 to April 30. It sits in the pine forests of the Oaxaca mountains, amid coffee plantations and crystal-clear rivers. If you have a self-sufficient streak, this comfortable yet rustic lodge is perfect for experiencing life in rural Mexico. ⊠ *Calle de Morro s/n, Playa Zicatela, Apdo. 210, 71980,* ☎ FAX *9/58–21179,* WEB *www.tabachin.com.mx. 6 apartments. Breakfast room. MC, V.*

$–$$ 🏨 **Cabañas de Playa Acali.** A variety of sizes and styles of accommodations is available at this cluster of *cabañas* (cabins) and bungalows on Zicatela beach. Guests mingle around the large central pool. The least expensive rooms are in small, rustic cabañas without air-conditioning; the most expensive, though still a bargain, are eight bungalows with terraces, kitchens, air-conditioning, and dining areas. This is a good choice for groups of four or six who are sharing expenses and preparing their own meals. ⊠ *Calle del Morro s/n, 71980,* ☎ *9/ 58–20754,* FAX *9/58–20055. 8 cabañas, 6 bungalows. Kitchenettes, pool. No credit cards.*

$ 🏨 **Hotel Arco Iris.** This sprawling, three-story hotel on Zicatela beach
★ resembles a gracefully aging, old-fashioned guest house. The rooms are simple yet clean, with firm beds and worn but comfortable furnishings. Some rooms have kitchenettes; most have wide verandas (bring a hammock) that overlook the surfing beach just beyond. There's a large pool, a video salon, and a second-story restaurant with a wonderful ocean breeze. ⊠ *Calle del Morro s/n, Col. Marinero, Apdo. 105, 71980,* ☎ FAX *9/58–20432 or 9/58–21494. 32 rooms, 4 suites. Restaurant, bar, pool, laundry service. MC, V.*

Outdoor Activities and Sports

RIVER TRIPS

Behind El Cafecito restaurant on Calle del Morro at Zicatela beach, **Big Jim's River Trips** (☎ 9/58–21026) organizes 2½-hour trips down the Colotepec River. A half-hour truck ride takes clients to the drop-off point, and a kayak-paddling guide will accompany you downriver as you float idyllically in a truck inner tube. A minimum of two clients is required, and life jackets are provided. Excursions usually depart at 9:30 AM and 2:30 PM and cost about $25. Also ask about trips to La Reforma waterfall.

WATER SPORTS

You can rent boogie boards and surfboards at **Las Olas** (⊠ Calle del Morro s/n, ☎ no phone) for about $6.50 a day. You must pay a deposit of about $80, which will be refunded at the end of the day unless the equipment is damaged.

Puerto Ángel

⑭ *81 km (50 mi) southeast of Puerto Escondido.*

The leading seaport of the state 100 years ago, Puerto Ángel today is a dusty village on a beautiful bay. It has managed to stave off much of the development and commercialization of Puerto Escondido and will appeal to those who like a more rustic atmosphere.

The navy has its installations on the central town beach. The most popular swimming-and-sunning territory is at **Playa Panteón,** just past the oceanfront cemetery (*panteón* means "cemetery"). Other good (and less populated) swimming and snorkeling beaches are nearby. Six kilometers (4 miles) west of town is **Zipolite,** a bay known for its nude sunbathing. It's a favorite with surfers, wild young things, and travelers content with a hammock on the beach and little else in the way of creature comforts; it's not really a favorite with families. Moreover, the undertow is extremely dangerous here, and more than a few foolishly brave swimmers die in these waters every year.

The **Centro Mexicano de la Tortuga** (Museum of the Sea Turtle) in Mazunte makes an interesting side trip (about 13 km or 8 mi) from Puerto Ángel. It was born as a center of exploitation of the golfina turtle and even had its own slaughterhouse for their meat. A 1990 government ban on turtle hunting has for the most part stopped the carnage, and Mazunte is now devoted to protecting the species. The name derives from the nahuatl *Maxonteita,* which means "please come and spawn" and indeed four of the nine species of marine turtles that exist worldwide come to spawn on Oaxaca's shores. A dozen aquariums are filled with turtle specimens that once again flourish in the nearby ocean. From Puerto Ángel, take Highway 200 toward San Pedro Pochutla; about 15 km (9 mi) past town, follow the turnoff marked SAN AGUSTÍN. A few kilometers later at the sign for PLAYA MAZUNTE, ask for directions to the *museo,* which is on the beach. ⊠ *Playa Mazunte,* ☎ *9/58–43055,* FAX *9/58–43063.* 🎫 *$2.* ⊙ *Tues.–Sat. 10–4:30, Sun. 10–2:30.*

Dining and Lodging

$–$$ ✗🏨 **Posada Cañon Devata.** California comes to Puerto Ángel in this ecological hideaway carved into a wooded canyon. Simple bungalows on the hill offer private quarters; other rooms and buildings are scattered on the hillsides. At the top, the bar El Cielo (Heaven) is a good place to take in the sunset. Windows have screens, and the only drawback to this tranquil space is that there's no hot water. Boat trips and occasional hatha yoga retreats are available. The cool palapa restaurant—open to nonguests (you must reserve ahead for the 7 PM dinner, about $8)—is a find for vegetarians. Meals are healthy and creative, and portions are very generous. ⊠ *Past the cemetery, off Blvd. Virgilio Uribe (Apdo. 10), 70902,* ☎ FAX *9/58–43137. 16 rooms, 6 bungalows. Restaurant, bar, massage. No credit cards. Closed May–June.*

$ ✗🏨 **La Buena Vista.** Some of the clean, simple accommodations here have balconies, some have hammocks just outside, but none have hot water. The third-floor restaurant has one of the most dependable kitchens in town, and rooms at the top level of the hotel have a great view as well as the best breezes. There are a lot of steps to negotiate here, and no elevator. ⊠ *Calle la Buena Compañia (Apdo. 48), 70902,* WEB *www.labuenavista.com,* ☎ FAX *9/58–43104. 23 rooms. Restaurant. No credit cards.*

$ 🏨 **La Cabaña de Puerto Ángel.** This plain but adequate hotel is the closest to Playa Panteón, ideal if you want to roll right out of bed in the morning and walk on the beach. Rooms have louvered windows with screens and ceiling fans; six have small, shadeless balconies. It's worth the extra $5 a night to rent one of the three triple rooms, which have fantastic ocean views. ⊠ *Calle Pedro Sainz de Barranda s/n, across from Playa Panteón, 70902,* ☎ *9/58–43105. 24 rooms. No credit cards.*

Bahías de Huatulco

277 km (172 mi) south of Oaxaca City, 111 km (69 mi) east of Puerto Escondido, 48 km (30 mi) east of Puerto Ángel.

Bahías de Huatulco continues to march forward toward its completion date sometime in the next few years. Three of its nine bays have been developed to date, a fourth (Cacaluta Bay) is under way as a national park, and Conejos Bay is next in line for hotels and restaurants. Huatulco's pristine bays encompass a total of 36 tropical beaches. Because of the fits and starts of its construction, Huatulco has an unfinished look, a lack of polish that contrasts, to many minds favorably, with Cancún and Ixtapa. Environmentalists may prefer it, for being Mexico's only resort that does *not* pump sewage into the ocean. If you have a car at your disposal, you can drive to several bays that so far haven't been developed and play Robinson Crusoe to your heart's content.

Another popular option is to tour the bays by boat. Standard four- to eight-hour trips—depending on how many bays you visit—might include a lunch of freshly caught fish (which costs extra). Fishing, diving, and snorkeling tours visit the beaches or reefs most suitable for those activities.

⓯ The Huatulco of the future is most evident at **Bahía Tangolunda,** where the poshest hotels are in full swing and the sea is abob with sightseeing *lanchas* (small motorboats), kayaks, and small sailboats. The site was chosen by developers because of its five beautiful beaches. There is a challenging 18-hole golf course here, the Campo de Golf Tangolunda (☎ FAX 9/58–10059), designed by Mario Schetjnan. A small shopping-restaurant center is across from the entrance to the Barceló, but most of the shopping and dining take place in the towns of Santa Cruz and La Crucecita, each about 10 minutes from the hotels by taxi, or, for the economy-minded, by buses or cooperative taxis.

🔟 **Bahía Chahué** is a pleasant place to spend a relaxing beach day. The beach parking lot includes a veranda lookout point; the club here charges $2 for use of the pool, games, and palapas. Several moderate-price hotels and restaurants line the beach.

🔟 **Santa Cruz,** on the bay of the same name, was the center of a 30-family fishing community until the development of the Huatulco bays forced the community inland. Today, for better or worse, the bay is the perfect spot for swimming, snorkeling, and boating. Arrange a glass-bottom-boat or sightseeing tour, or a fishing trip from the marina. Or spend the day at **Tipsy's** beach club (⊠ Paseo Mitla beach, ☎ FAX 9/58–70576), where you can rent water toys, take waterskiing lessons, or play volleyball. A central zócalo with a wrought-iron gazebo has been built nearby; tourists and locals mingle in the little plaza, where you can sip a cool drink or cappuccino in the Café Huatulco, a showcase for the region's best *Pluma* coffee.

🔟 **La Crucecita,** just off Highway 200, is the only place in Huatulco that resembles—in a prefab way—a real Mexican town, with its central plaza and church which is covered inside with frescoes. Modern buildings with arches and balconies have gone up along the streets by the park, and this is becoming *the* place for hanging out at sidewalk cafés and shopping in boutiques. The bus station, tourism office, ice-cream shop, Internet café, and long-distance telephone office are here, along with a smattering of smaller, less expensive, and more intimate hotels.

Dining and Lodging

$$$ ✕ **Don Porfirio.** You can dine inside or out on the covered patio in this Tangolunda restaurant. There's a good variety of seafood and international dishes; try the combination shish kebab sautéed in tequila, served on a bed of rice with steamed veggies and potato. There is no air-conditioning, and the outdoor patio is loud with street noise, but the food and service are good. ⊠ *Zona Hotelera Tangolunda, across from Hotel Gala, Bahía Tangolunda,* ☎ 9/58–10001. AE, MC, V.

$$ ✕ **Restaurant de Doña Celia.** Although the official name of this long-
★ time favorite beachfront restaurant is Avalos, everyone knows it by the owner's name: Doña Celia. Even Presidente Ernesto Zedillo has stopped by for a seafood feast. Make your selection from the large menu, and prepare for large portions as well. Tables face the sand and sea at Santa Cruz Bay, just beyond the marina. ⊠ *Bahía Santa Cruz,* ☎ 9/58–70128. *No credit cards.*

$$ ✕ **Restaurant Ve El Mar.** The owner, Leonarda, has been here 21 years
★ and can tell tales about the transformation of Huatulco. She converted her snack-by-the-sea place into this friendly restaurant where you can wiggle your toes in the soft sand by the water's edge. Quieter than Doña Celia's, this is a good spot for a romantic candlelit dinner. ⊠ *Bahía Santa Cruz,* ☎ 9/58–70364. *No credit cards.*

$$ ✕ **Restaurante María Sabina.** Strangely named for a Oaxaca medicine woman immortalized for her use of magic (hallucinogenic) mushrooms, this is a great place for watching locals and tourists mingle in La Crucecita's pretty plaza. Grill orders are prepared on the outdoor *parrilla* (grill) and served with grilled onion, baked potato, and sour cream. A favorite is *reboso María Sabina,* steak with melted cheese, guacamole, and fresh salsa. ⊠ *Calle Flamboyan, west side of plaza, La Crucecita,* ☎ 9/58–70219. MC, V.

$$$$ ★ ✕▥ Barceló. Formerly the Sheraton, this cheerful resort hotel now offers appealing all-inclusive rates, and is the most user-friendly of the upscale hotels on Bahía Tangolunda. The rooms have bathtubs—a real luxury in these parts. Water sports and equipment—including kayaks and sailboats, (all-inclusive guests have free use of these)—are considered top notch here, and dive masters are on hand with dive equipment. The Casa Real restaurant is one of the most glamorous dining options in Huatulco. The menu emphasizes northern Italian dishes, the pianist is superb, and flickering candles are set out at night. Prices are remarkably accessible, and reservations must be made well ahead of time. ✉ *Blvd. Benito Juárez, Bahía Tangolunda 70989,* ☎ *9/58–10055,* ⅲ *9/58–10113,* 🔲 *www.barcelo.com 347 rooms, 9 suites. 3 restaurants, 3 bars, 2 pools, wading pool, massage, sauna, 4 tennis courts, exercise room, beach, dive shop, boating, shops, children's programs (ages 5 and up), travel services. AE, DC, MC, V.*

$$$$ ★ ▥ Camino Real Zaashila. This contemporary stucco Mexican-cum-Mediterranean palace overlooks a secluded lagoon with its own beach and a large, sleek pool, which has built-in chairs around the rim. The resort has 27 landscaped acres of gardens, fountains, and waterfalls; going from one end of the hotel to the other is a dreamy nature walk. All rooms have ocean views; 10 luxurious suites and 41 rooms have small private pools. Chez Beni, one of the restaurants, serves meals on a patio just off the beach. Paradise has a price tag, though: rates are high and are not all-inclusive. ✉ *Blvd. Benito Juárez 5, Bahía Tangolunda 70989,* ☎ *9/58–10460 or 800/722–6466,* ⅲ *9/58–10461,* 🔲 *www.caminoreal.com/zaashila. 120 rooms, 10 suites. 3 restaurants, 2 bars, in-room safes, minibars, 2 pools, wading pool, tennis court, exercise room, beach, baby-sitting, travel services. AE, DC, MC, V.*

$$$$ ★ ▥ Quinta Real. This hilltop resort takes Huatulco luxury to new and exclusive—and almost excessive—heights. A combination of Moorish domes and thatch palapas, the property's 27 tranquil suites are airy and plush, each with creamy white leather furnishings, exquisite Guatemalan tapestries, a Jacuzzi, terrace, and spectacular ocean views. Nine suites have private pools, and a few are equipped with telescopes for dolphin- and star-gazing. Nonguests should pop in for breakfast. ✉ *Blvd. Benito Juárez 2, Bahía Tangolunda 70989,* ☎ *9/58–10428 or 800/445–4565,* ⅲ *9/58–10429,* 🔲 *www.quintareal.com. 28 suites. 2 restaurants, bar, in-room safes, minibars, 2 pools, wading pool, tennis court, beach, baby-sitting, laundry service. AE, DC, MC, V.*

$$$–$$$$ ▥ Club Med. The nearly 500 rooms cut a pastel swath on a hillside overlooking Bahía Tangolunda. The colored cylinders are not exactly a pretty sight, but they come with three beaches and an endless list of amenities. Weeklong fitness programs are particularly popular, although enthusiasts should note that the Club is only open in peak season, from November through April. Packages with airfare included are usually available. This is one of the area's least expensive all-inclusives, but only nonalcoholic beverages come with the deal. ✉ *Bahía Tangolunda 70900 (40 W. 57th St., New York, NY 10019),* ☎ *9/58–10033 or 800/258–2633,* ⅲ *9/58–10101. 483 rooms. 4 restaurants, 3 bars, in-room safes, 4 pools, 11 tennis courts, exercise room, beach, dance club, children's programs (ages 4–17), playground. AE, MC, V.*

$$–$$$ ▥ Posada Flamboyant. This is the classiest option if you want to stay in the town of La Crucecita, about a five-minute cab ride from Bahía Tangolunda. The ivy-covered, four-story edifice has a vaguely European feel. All rooms have firm beds, cable TVs, and phones, and both the pool and surrounding area are large and inviting. Four comfortable two-bedroom, two-bath suites with well-furnished living rooms and kitchens are available for $100–$200 each per night (depending on the season) for up to six people. ✉ *Calle Gardenia esq. Tamarindo,*

La Crucecita 70989, ☎ 9/58–70113 or 9/58–70105, ℻ 9/58–70121. 66 rooms, 4 suites. Restaurant, bar, coffee shop, pool, wading pool, baby-sitting, playground, travel services. AE, MC, V.

$$ 🏨 **Marina Resort Huatulco.** This all-suites resort overlooking the marina on Santa Cruz Bay has plenty of amenities. Each comfortable suite's ample living area contains a small dining table, cable TV, and kitchenette. Upper-floor rooms have the best bay views; all rooms have bathtubs. There's also a disco and a beach club with water sports and a playground. ⊠ *Calle Tehunatepec 112, Bahía Santa Cruz,* ☎ *9/58–70963,* ℻ *9/58–70830. 47 suites. Restaurant, 2 bars, kitchenettes, 2 pools, wading pool, dance club, playground. AE, MC, V.*

$ 🏨 **Hotel Begonias.** Catercorner from the plaza in La Crucecita, this sweet, simple hotel has colonial-style furnishings, ceiling fans, comfortable beds, and color TVs. The hotel's popular restaurant, Oasis, serves an extensive menu of Oaxacan and Japanese dishes. ⊠ *Calle Bugambilias 503, La Crucecita 70989,* ☎ *9/58–70390 or 9/58–70018,* ℻ *9/58–71390. 9 rooms, 3 suites. Restaurant, bar. AE, MC, V.*

$ 🏨 **Hotel Las Palmas.** Plain but acceptable furnishings and rock-bottom prices (for Huatulco) are what you'll find at this small second-story hotel just a block from the plaza in La Crucecita. The cramped rooms have TVs, hot water, and both fans and air-conditioning. ⊠ *Calle Guamuchil 206, La Crucecita 70989,* ☎ *9/58–70060,* ℻ *9/58–70057. 8 rooms. Restaurant, bar. AE, MC, V.*

Outdoor Activities and Sports

BICYCLING

You can rent mountain bikes from **Eco-Discover Tours Huatulco** (⊠ Plaza las Conchas, Tangolunda Bay, ☎ 9/58–10002 or 9/58–10254, ℻ 9/58–70678). **Aventuras Huatulco** (⊠ Erasto Rojas H, Carrizal 504, La Crucecita, ☎ 9/58–71695) is recommended for guided or unguided mountain-bike tours. **Motor Tours Huatulco** rents chunky four-wheel motorbikes for the beach. **Jungle Tour** (⊠ In the Hotel Gala, Blvd. Benito Juárez 227, Bahía Tangolunda 70989, ☎ 9/58–10000, ext. 729) offers guided four-wheel motorbike tours.

FISHING

Sportfishing for sailfish, tuna, dorado, and other fish can be arranged through **Sociedad Cooperative Tangolunda,** the boat-owners' cooperative at the marina on Santa Cruz Bay (☎ 9/58–70081).

HORSEBACK RIDING

Arturo Casillas at **Rancho Caballo de Mar** (☎ 9/58–70530 or 9/58–70531) will collect you from your hotel. Rates are about $30 per morning.

WATER SPORTS

The PADI-certified dive masters at **Hurricane Divers** (⊠ Plaza Junior, Bahía de Chahué, ☎ 9/58–71107) in Chahué are among the most reliable in Huatulco. Roberto Kraak offers certification courses and dive trips (approximately $50 for one tank, $70 for two) and 1½-hour snorkeling trips ($20).

RIVER RAFTING

Rafting has become popular in recent years in the area. Try out your skills in this adventure sport or kayak with **Piraguas Aventuras.**

Shopping

Although Huatulco isn't exactly a shopper's paradise, there are several places worth mentioning. In La Crucecita, **Paradise** boutique (⊠ Calle Gardenia esq. Guarumbo, ☎ 9/58–70268), open daily, has an excellent selection of casual, stylish beach and resort wear, much of which comes from Bali and India. The Mexican crafts, including silver jewelry, coconut masks from Guerrero, and black pottery make great gifts.

The **Museo de Artesanías Oaxaqueñas** (⊠ Calle Flamboyan 216, La Crucecita, ☎ 9/58–71513) is really a store, not a museum, but the artisans who create the fanciful wooden alebrijes, the woven tablecloths, typical pottery, painted tinware, and rugs from throughout the state are on hand to demonstrate how they make their traditional crafts. It's open daily; avoid going at lunchtime, when the artisans take a break. La Crucecita's **Mercado Municipal** (municipal market; ⊠ Calle Guanacaste con Bugambilias, ☎ no phone) is a fun place to shop; in addition to leather sandals, postcards, and other tourist items, you'll see mountains of fresh fruits and vegetables.

OAXACA COAST A TO Z

AIR TRAVEL
You can fly into Puerto Escondido from Oaxaca, and into Huatulco from Oaxaca as well as several other Mexican and U.S. cities.

CARRIERS
Aero Vega has daily service to Puerto Escondido from Oaxaca's International Airport. Mexicana subsidiary AeroCaribe connects Puerto Escondido and Oaxaca City five times a week, with daily connections to Huatulco. Mexicana flies to Huatulco from Mexico City, Guadalajara, Cancún, Monterrey, and several other Mexican and U.S. gateways, all with connections in Mexico City.
➤ AIRLINES AND CONTACTS: **AeroCaribe** (☎ 9/58–22024 in Puerto Escondido; 9/58–71220 in Huatulco). **Aero Vega** (☎ 9/58–20151). **Mexicana** (☎ 9/58–70243; 9/58–70223 in Huatulco).

AIRPORTS AND TRANSFERS
Aeropuerto Puerto Escondido is a 10-minute taxi ride from town on Highway 200. Aeropuerto Bahías de Huatulco is about 16 km (10 mi) from Tangolunda on Highway 200.
➤ AIRPORT INFORMATION: **Aeropuerto Puerto Escondido** (⊠ Carretera Costera Km 3, ☎ 9/58–20492 or 9/58–20491). **Aeropuerto Bahías de Huatulco** (☎ 9/58–19008).

BUS TRAVEL
Cristóbal Colón has three first-class buses per day leaving from Oaxaca's first-class bus terminal, frequently referred to as the ADO, as well as a luxury bus *Servicio Plus* leaving just before midnight to Huatulco (7½ hours; $14). The first-class bus continues on to Puerto Escondido (9 hours; $16). There are several first-class buses each day to Pochutla (8 hours; $15), where you can connect to Puerto Ángel, but none are direct. The second-class buses to Acapulco stop in Huatulco and take 10 hours. They're only recommended by day.

Direct service between Oaxaca City and Puerto Escondido is available on first-class Autotransportes Turísticos. Buses leave from Oaxaca City and Puerto Escondido twice a day.

Frequent, inexpensive second-class buses connect Puerto Escondido, Puerto Ángel, and Huatulco, but you must stop at Pochutla, just off the highway near Puerto Ángel. These buses roar down the highway every 15 minutes or so, and each costs about $1.25. Do not travel at night. If you're going to Huatulco, be sure to specify that your final destination is the bus terminal in La Crucecita, which is closest to the bays.
➤ BUS INFORMATION: **Autotransportes Turísticos** (⊠ Calle Armenta y López 721, Oaxaca City, ☎ 9/51–40806, 9/58–20953, or 9/58–20050; ⊠ Av. Hidalgo between 16 de Septiembre and 4a Nte., Puerto Escondido, ☎ 9/51–40806, 9/58–20953, or 9/58–20050). **Cristóbal Colón** (⊠ Booking office: Calle 20 de Noviembre 204A, Oaxaca City, ☎ 9/

51–46655). **Huatulco bus stations** (✉ Calle Gardenias esq. Ocotillo, La Crucecita, ☎ 9/58–70261; ✉ Calle Jazmin s/n, behind Corona beer warehouse, ☎ 9/58–70193). **Puerto Escondido bus station** (✉ Calle Primera Nte. 201, ☎ 9/58–21073). *Servicio Plus* (✉ Calzada Niños Héroes 1036, Oaxaca City, ☎ 9/51–51703).

CAR RENTAL

Cars can be rented at the Huatulco airport, in Puerto Escondido, and in the Huatulco Bays area. International firms include Budget and Dollar. Rental cars are expensive, starting at $45 a day for a Volkswagen Beetle, for example, and there is an additional drop-off fee if you don't return the car where you picked it up. Nonaffiliated local firms often quote lower rates, but their vehicles may be in questionable condition.

➤ MAJOR AGENCIES: **Budget** (✉ Hotel Posada Real, Av. Benito Juárez 11, Puerto Escondido, ☎ 9/58–20312). **Dollar** (✉ Barceló Hotel, Blvd. Benito Juárez, Huatulco, ☎ 9/58–10055, ext. 787; 9/58–10480; Huatulco airport ☎ 9/58–10055, ext. 787; 9/58–19004).

CAR TRAVEL

The drive from Oaxaca City to the isthmus on Highway 190 is challenging despite good paving, with plenty of curves and hairpin turns. Highway 175 is best avoided. Highway 131, to Puerto Escondido via Sola de Vega, is an obstacle course of potholes. Do *not* attempt any of these roads at night. Plan on taking about eight hours, and leave early enough to arrive before dark. At the coast, Highway 200 links Huatulco, Puerto Ángel, and Puerto Escondido; it should be relatively hassle-free, if potholed. Having a car allows you to turn off the main road onto unmarked dirt roads leading to secluded beaches.

EMERGENCIES

In case of an emergency call either the Red Cross or the police at the local number in Puerto Escondido or Huatulco.

➤ CONTACTS: **Police** (☎ 9/58–70020 in Bahías de Huatulco; 9/58–2021786 in Puerto Escondido). **Red Cross** (☎ 9/58–71188 in Bahías de Huatulco; 9/58–20550 in Puerto Escondido).

INTERNET

In Huatulco, Choco Latté is the most attractive place for a coffee and Internet use.

➤ INTERNET CAFÉS: **Choco Latté** (✉ Gardenia 902, La Crucecita, ☎ 9/58–70165.).

TOURS

BIRD-WATCHING TOURS

In Puerto Escondido the most exciting tours are run by ornithologist Michael Malone, who offers dawn and sunset excursions (December–April) into the Manialtepec Lagoon, a prime bird-watching area. Arrange tours (about $35 per person) through your hotel or through Turismo Rodimar, the most reliable and comprehensive agency in town.

BIKING TOURS

Proximity to jungle flora and fauna is one of the appeals of a bicycle tour. Edgar Jiménez offers 4-hour trips to the mountain in 18-gear aluminum bikes with Eco-Discover Tours Huatulco. Protective helmet, water, and English-speaking guide are included in the price of around $20.

COFFEE PLANTATION TOURS

Visiting the coffee plantations is newly popular activity in Huatulco. Prices average around $60 per day. Call Max Scherenberg (✉ Resi-

dencial Chahué, Casa 31, ☎ 9/58–70697) to join his 8-hour trip to
Río Capalitilla, 45 miles from Huatulco at **Finca La Gloria.** Marco Antonio (✉ San Miguel del Puerto, ☎ 9/58–71771) takes people to see
the **Finca San Antonio.**

SIGHTSEEING TOURS

Bahías Plus, with offices in La Crucecita, is one of the most comprehensive travel agencies in Huatulco; it has tours to Puerto Ángel and
Puerto Escondido (van tours start at a bit less than $20 a person in a
group of six), as well as plane tours to Oaxaca ($337 a person). Most
major hotels also have travel agencies.

Daylong tours into the Sierra Madre are available with the bilingual
guides of Motor Tours Huatulco. One of the tours includes a visit to
a working coffee plantation, with an elaborate lunch. The cost is approximately $110, to be divided between one to three people. This agency
also arranges horse, all-terrain vehicle (ATV), and mountain-bike treks.

Paraiso Huatulco has all-day bay cruises for $30 a person, excluding
food. It also offers eco- and fishing tours. Piraguas Tours has great kayak
and raft tours. A quirky mud bath in the river is included in Lauro Carillo's "Bio Tour."

➤ Tour Operator Recommendations: **Bahías Plus** (✉ Calle Carrizal
704, Suite 1, Huatulco 70989, ☎ 9/58–70216 or 9/58–70932). **Lauro
Carillo** (☎ 9/58–70715 or 9/58–70714). **Eco-Discover Tours Huatulco**
(✉ Plaza las Conchas, Tangolunda Bay, ☎ 9/58–10002 or 9/58–
10254, ℻ 9/58–70678). **Motor Tours Huatulco** (✉ Blvd. Benito
Juárez, Lote 23, in the Hotel Club Plaza, Huatulco, ☎ 9/58–10024).
Paraiso Huatulco (✉ Barceló Hotel, Blvd. Benito Juárez, Bahía Tan-
golunda, ☎ 9/58–10218, ℻ 9/58–10200). **Piraguas Tours** (✉ Plaza
Oaxaca, Local 19, La Crucecita, ☎ 9/58–71333, ℻ 9/58–71339, ⓦⒺⒷ
www.piraguas.com). **Turismo Rodimar** (✉ Av. Pérez Gasga 905–B,
Puerto Escondido, ☎ 9/58–20734, ℻ 9/58–20737).

VISITOR INFORMATION

Puerto Escondido tourism office is open weekdays 9–3 and 4–6, Saturday 10–1. The small information desk at the north end of the pedestrian walkway is often more helpful than the main tourism office. It's
usually open weekdays 10–2 and 4–6, Saturday 10–1. Oficina de Convenciones y Visitantes offers friendly help in English from 9–6. The Sedetur Huatulco state tourism office is open weekdays 8–5, Saturday 9–1.
➤ Tourist Information: **Puerto Escondido tourism office** (✉ Blvd.
Benito Juárez, about a block from Aldea del Bazar Hotel at Playa Bacocho development, ☎ ℻ 9/58–20175). **Oficina de Convenciones y
Visitantes** (✉ Convention and Visitor's Bureau: Plaza San Miguel 1B,
Santa Cruz, ☎ ℻ 9/58–71037, www.baysofhuatulco.com.mx). **Sedetur** (✉ Blvd. Benito Juárez s/n, Bahía Tangolunda, in front of Restaurante Misió Fa-Sol, ☎ 9/58–10177, ℻ 9/58–10176).

11 CHIAPAS AND TABASCO

The state of Chiapas is a study in contrasts, with the luxuriant tropical lowlands around Palenque—one of the country's most brilliant Mayan ruins—giving way to gorgeous valleys and finally the highlands, home to many of Mexico's most traditional indigenous peoples.

Updated by
Cynthia
Hawes

K NOWN TO MANY foreigners only for the ruins of Palenque and the colonial town of San Cristóbal de las Casas, Chiapas and Tabasco have typically drawn trekkers and travelers rather than tourists. If you're looking for an outstanding travel experience, a well-planned trip to this area can be very satisfying, particularly if you come during a local festival. Unlike the country's popular beach resorts, Chiapas and Tabasco aren't an easy flight a few hours from major U.S. cities. Substantial ground transportation, either by bus or car, is usually required, although Tuxtla Gutiérrez and Villahermosa have international airports, and Palenque and San Cristóbal de las Casas have national airports with limited routes. Tourist information can be more difficult to obtain in Tabasco than in Chiapas.

World attention was drawn to off-the-beaten-path Chiapas in early 1994 when guerrillas staged a brief but potent rebellion, launching what has turned out to be a long-term struggle for equal rights for Mexico's indigenous groups. A bloody past of exploitation by and fierce confrontation with outsiders remains vividly present, as already impoverished indigenous communities in Chiapas are forced to compete for their lands with developers and new settlers. In fact, Chiapas has been at the margin of the nation's development and is one of the poorest states in Mexico. Land distribution, too, is skewed: 1% of landowners holds 15% of the territory—about 50% of the arable land—keeping the colonial system nearly intact, and repression is rampant. It was the indifference of the Mexican government to their plight that helped bring the anger of the indigenous people to a boil in 1994, leading the Zapatista National Liberation Army (EZLN is the Spanish acronym) to an armed uprising. Even though peace talks with the government have been stalled for years, the national and international interest sparked by the indigenous movement bodes well for the possibility of change in the region, as does the interest of President Vicente Fox in resolving the issue. The pipe-smoking Zapatista spokesperson, Subcomandante Marcos, has become a cult figure in Mexico, his ski-masked image appearing on everything from magazine covers to children's toys, and he puts his poetic communiqués on the Internet for worldwide consumption.

Nominally enriched a half century ago with the discovery of oil in the Gulf of Mexico on its northern border, Tabasco also has a bloody past. During the 1920s and '30s, Tomás Garrido Canabal, a vehemently anticlerical governor, outlawed priests and had all the churches either torn down or converted to other uses. Riots, deportations, and property confiscations were common. That said, you won't find much evidence of Tabasco's turbulent past today; the spirit that prevails here is wholly different from that of Chiapas.

Although the Mexican economic crisis has delayed plans for a stronger tourism infrastructure, travel to Chiapas is getting a boost from a government promotion program—a segment of the Mundo Mayan travel circuit. The circuit was created by the Mexican government in the early 1990s to showcase its Maya ruins and colonial cities, all in the name of regional development and ecotourism. However, this development has done little to help the environment or the indigenous groups in the region. The Lacandon jungle is disappearing, its Maya inhabitants being driven to live in a smaller portion of their ancestral lands. Massive erosion and deforestation are taking their toll as new settlers, forced off communal farmlands in the highlands, try unsuccessfully to farm the rain forest with highland farming techniques: after a couple years, the soil loses its nutrients, and the settlers must clear fresh plots. The soil is further depleted by ranchers who move into the abandoned lands to raise their cattle.

When you set out along tortuous mountain roads, however—full of dramatic hairpin turns along the edges of mist-filled ravines—you'll still find remote clusters of huts and cornfields planted on near-vertical hillsides. You'll pass traditional women wrapped in deep-blue shawls and coarsely woven wool skirts, and Indian children selling fruit and flowers by the roadside. Chiapas has nine distinct linguistic groups, primarily the highland-dwelling Tzotzils and the Tzeltals, who live in both highland and lowland areas. In more isolated regions, many villagers speak only their native language, or a rudimentary Spanish necessary for interaction with the outside world.

Business travelers make up the majority of those who visit Villahermosa, Tabasco's capital. But the city has a superb museum of pre-Columbian archaeology at the CICOM complex and a collection of massive Olmec heads and altars at Parque Museo La Venta. Both provide a good introduction to the Indian heritage of Tabasco and Chiapas. Palenque, with its incredible Maya ruins, is culturally and geographically linked with the lowlands in Tabasco. Geographically stunning, Tabasco has lakes, lagoons, caves, and wild rivers surging through the jungle.

Note: Although travel in the area is reasonably safe, at press time the U.S. State Department was advising travelers to "exercise caution" in Chiapas because of the presence of armed rebels and armed civilian groups in some areas of the state. Although sporadic confrontations haven't been near the main tourist destinations—and may be resolved by the time you visit—contact the State Department or any of the Mexican Government Tourist Offices in the United States before you go for the current status. Carry your visa and passport even on day trips throughout the region, as there may be military checkpoints along both main and secondary roads.

Pleasures and Pastimes

Archaeological Sites
Ruins of Mayan cities in mysterious, overgrown jungles are a big draw in this area. Unparalleled Palenque has the most appeal, and the lesser-known sites of Toniná, Bonampak, and Yaxchilán (pronounced yash-chee-*lan*) are attracting more attention than ever.

Dining
Chiapas has regional specialties but borrows heavily from Yucatán and Oaxaca. Culinary adventurers should try *atole* (a cornmeal drink), the many local variations of tamales, locally smoked pork called *cochito horneado,* candied fruit, and any dishes that contain the tasty Mexican herbs *chipilín* and *yerba santa* (or *mumu,* as locals call it). San Cristóbal's restaurants have an ample choice of Mexican and international cuisines, and most of them have added vegetarian dishes to their menus. Restaurants are generally not outstanding compared to those in other regions of Mexico.

Prices, however, are quite reasonable: a filling dinner (helped out by tortillas in one of their myriad forms) won't usually cost more than $10 a person. There's no dress code to speak of in this part of Mexico, and reservations aren't necessary. San Cristóbal closes down early, so unlike in other parts of Mexico, it is a fairly common practice to eat dinner before 8 PM. As is the case throughout Mexico, lunch is the main meal of the day, served between 1 and 4 PM.

Tabasco saves some of its export beef for the Villahermosa restaurants, which also serve lots of fresh fish from the Gulf and freshwater lakes and rivers. Local specialties include *pejelagarto,* an ancient fish with the head of an alligator and a strong, sweet flavor. Also try *puchero,* beef stew with vegetables and plantains; river shrimp; *tostones* (fried plantain chips); baked bananas with cream; banana liqueur; and the region's fresh, white cheese.

Generally speaking, the food served in the town of Palenque is modest in both quality and price. Many restaurants are open-air, which is where you want to be in this hot, humid part of Mexico. You'll spend more in the higher-price hotels; most moderate and inexpensive restaurants don't bother to charge sales tax.

CATEGORY	COST*
$$$$	over $15
$$$	$10–$15
$$	$5–$10
$	under $5

*per person for a three-course meal, excluding drinks, service, and 15% sales tax

Lodging

Almost all the hotels in San Cristóbal are within walking distance of the major attractions. Most of those we list are colonial—historically and architecturally—in keeping with the rest of the town. All rooms, unless otherwise stated, have showers; air-conditioning isn't necessary at this high altitude and, in fact, fireplaces are welcome.

Tuxtla Gutiérrez lodgings tend to be more functional than frilly; this town is the no-nonsense business and transportation hub of Chiapas. An exception to the rule is the Camino Real, which resembles a small palace perched on a hilltop.

Palenque is no longer the jungle outpost it used to be, fit only for those who consider rustic amenities colorful. This is a growing town with modern, comfortable hotels. The best and newest are strung along the Palenque–Pakalná highway that goes to the Palenque ruins just outside town; most have lush gardens, inviting pools, and air-conditioning or ceiling fans. There are quite a few *posadas* (guest houses) downtown and a couple of agreeable hotels and restaurants in the quiet neighborhood of La Cañada, between the downtown area and the highway.

Villahermosa hotels are relatively expensive, especially when compared with those in San Cristóbal. Fancy hotels geared to business travelers tend to be away from the city center, near Tabasco 2000 and Parque La Venta. But there are comfortable and economic hotels downtown, near the Grijalva River, or in the nearby, pedestrian-friendly Zona Luz (Light Zone), or Zona Remodelada (Remodeled Zone).

Many hotels (especially budget and moderate lodgings) quote prices that already include the 15%–17% tax, which varies from county to county; others do not. Be sure to ask.

CATEGORY	COST*
$$$$	over $90
$$$	$60–$90
$$	$30–$60
$	under $30

*All prices are for a standard double room, excluding tax (15%–17%).

Shopping

The artisans of Chiapas, especially in and around San Cristóbal, produce some of the most striking indigenous folk art of Mexico. Best are the embroidered blouses, *huipiles* (tunics), bedspreads and tablecloths, and leather goods. Lacandon bows and arrows and the beribboned ceremonial hats worn by local indigenous officials also make good souvenirs.

Chiapas is one of the few places in the world that has amber mines, so finely crafted jewelry made from this prehistoric resin is easy to find in San Cristóbal—as are plastic imitations sold by street vendors (stores usually sell amber and street vendors commonly have the fakes, although there is some crossover). San Cristóbal is also known for the quality wrought-iron crosses that bless its rooftops. Although many of the iron-working shops have closed, you can still find the crosses in crafts stores. Tuxtla Gutiérrez and Palenque, although not known for handicrafts, have a few shops selling quality crafts from throughout the state.

Exploring Chiapas and Tabasco

The abode of the ancient Olmecs who gave Mexico its mother culture, Tabasco is lush, green, and pastoral; Chiapas is for the most part mountainous, its Maya ruins and villages isolated from modern Mexico by sinuous roads and footpaths. The colonial city of San Cristóbal de las Casas once dominated both regions when the Spanish conquistadores held sway over the country. Modern Villahermosa is now the economic force in the two regions because of the petroleum industry.

The highlights of a trip to Chiapas and Tabasco are still the ruins of Palenque and the colonial town of San Cristóbal. These and all other major sights are accessible by road from either Tuxtla Gutiérrez or Villahermosa, the only cities with international airports. The once-isolated ruins of Yaxchilán and Bonampak are now more accessible—by paved roads or via bush planes that fly from the two internationally connected cities as well as from Palenque, Ocosingo, and Comitán. Palenque and San Cristóbal de las Casas have small new airports that land small-body jets on a limited basis. If you're a first-time visitor, and especially if you don't speak Spanish, it's faster, more efficient, and more comfortable to take tours to the area's major attractions.

Numbers in the text correspond to numbers in the margin and on the Chiapas and Tabasco and San Cristóbal de las Casas maps.

Great Itineraries

The farther you wander into the region, the more you'll be fascinated with its natural diversity and its remnants of Mayan and Spanish-colonial cultures. A three-day trip gives only a superficial glance at what the region has to offer, but it will give you a chance to visit Palenque and San Cristóbal de las Casas, two of Mexico's outstanding attractions. Stays of five to eight or more days will allow you to cover greater distances and get to the lesser-known wonders of Chiapas and Tabasco.

IF YOU HAVE 3 DAYS

Spend the first day and night at the Mayan ruins at **Palenque** ㉒, and consider going the proverbial extra mile to the lovely jungle waterfalls at **Misol-Há** ㉑ and **Agua Azul** ⑳. Tours from Palenque are the best way to pack it all into one day. The next day, drive south to **San Cristóbal de las Casas** ①–⑧, the oldest city in Chiapas. Spend at least two hours on a walking tour of town, starting at the centuries-old **zócalo** ① (town square). Overnight at San Cristóbal and, on Day 3, visit the Mayan villages of **San Juan Chamula** ⑭, known for its Catholic church where pre-Hispanic rituals are performed, and **Zinacantán** ⑮, famous for its

Chiapas and Tabasco

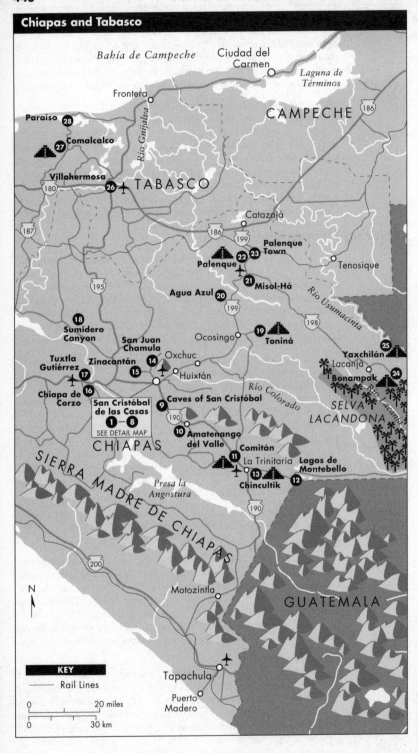

Bahía de Campeche

Ciudad del Carmen

Laguna de Términos

Frontera

CAMPECHE

186

Paraíso 28

Comalcalco 27

Villahermosa 26

TABASCO

180

187

195

Catazajá

186   199

Palenque Town

Palenque 22   23

Tenosique

21 **Misol-Há**

Río Usumacinta

Agua Azul 20

199

198

18 **Sumidero Canyon**

San Juan Chamula

Ocosingo

19 **Toniná**

25 **Yaxchilán**

Tuxtla Gutiérrez 17

Zinacantán 15   14

Oxchuc

Lacanjá

Bonampak 24

Chiapa de Corzo 16

Huixtán

Río Colorado

SELVA LACANDONA

San Cristóbal de las Casas

1 — 8

SEE DETAIL MAP

9 **Caves of San Cristóbal**

190

CHIAPAS

10 **Amatenango del Valle**

Comitán

11   **La Trinitaria**   **Lagos de Montebello**

13   12

Chincultik

Presa la Angostura

190

SIERRA MADRE DE CHIAPAS

200

Motozintla

GUATEMALA

N

KEY

Rail Lines

0   20 miles

0   30 km

Tapachula

Puerto Madero

handwoven tunics and pink shawls. Return to San Cristóbal to visit the market, shop for Indian crafts, and spend the night.

IF YOU HAVE 5 DAYS

Spend the first day and night in **Villahermosa** ㉖, exploring the giant Olmec heads, the river walkway, and the anthropology museum. Day 2, drive to **Palenque** ㉒, visit the ruins, and stay overnight in Palenque. Day 3, drive to **San Cristóbal de Las Casas** ①–⑧, stopping off at two or more of these sights along the way: the waterfalls at **Misol-Há** ㉑ or **Agua Azul** ⑳, or the Mayan site of **Toniná** ⑲, near Ocosingo. Spend the night in San Cristóbal. Day 4, see **San Juan Chamula** ⑭ and **Zinacantán** ⑮ in the morning and then return to San Cristóbal to shop for native crafts and spend another night. On Day 5, drive south on Highway 190 to see the **Lagos de Montebello** ⑫. After seeing the lakes, visit on the return trip as many of the following as your schedule permits: the small Maya sites of **Chincultik** ⑬ and **Tenam Puente;** the charming town of **Comitán** ⑪; the pottery-producing town of **Amatenango del Valle** ⑩; and the stalactite- and stalagmite-graced **Caves of San Cristóbal** ⑨. For a less rushed visit, plan to spend the night in Comitán and return early the next morning for San Cristóbal or Tuxtla.

IF YOU HAVE 8 DAYS

Spend the first day and night in **Villahermosa** ㉖, as in the five-day itinerary. Next day, drive north of the city to visit the unusual Maya temples at **Comalcalco** ㉗ and then to **Puerto Ceiba** near **Paraíso** ㉘ for a seafood lunch. Return to Villahermosa for a dinner cruise on the *Capitán Buelo* along the Grijalva River and overnight here again. Spend the next four days as on Days 2–5 of the five-day itinerary— seeing **Palenque** ㉒, **Misol-Há** ㉑, **Agua Azul** ⑳, and **Toniná** ⑲ on the way to **San Cristóbal de Las Casas** ①–⑧, from which you can take day trips north and southeast. On Day 7, head west, touring colonial **Chiapa de Corzo** ⑯ and the impressive **Sumidero Canyon** ⑱ by boat en route to **Tuxtla Gutiérrez** ⑰. Spend that night and the next in Tuxtla. On Day 8, visit Tuxtla's zoo, shop at the **Casa de las Artesanías,** and stroll in the **Parque Jardín de la Marimba** in the late afternoon.

If you want to go all out seeing Maya sites, add a day trip to **Bonampak** ㉔ and **Yaxchilán** ㉕—the paved highway from Palenque makes for a good road trip (chartered planes to the ruins are also sometimes available from Tuxtla Gutiérrez). You can arrange to spend the night at the ecotourism site Escudo Jaguar, on the Usumacinta River near the boat launch for Yaxchilán, or in Palenque. From San Cristóbal, you can still squeeze in a long day trip to **Comitán** ⑪, the **Lagos de Montebello** ⑫, and **Chincultik** ⑬. There's also a new paved road connecting Bonampak with the Lagos de Montebello, but check with the tourist office first before venturing out. Certain safety precautions may be advised.

When to Tour

Scheduling your visit to coincide with local festivals is worthwhile. Just make hotel reservations well in advance. Important holidays are January 15–23 for Chiapa de Corzo's San Sebastian festival (also held January 20–22 in Zinacantán); Carnival and Easter Week in San Juan Chamula, where villagers walk over hot coals; every Friday during Lent in Zinacantán; June 22–24 for Chamula's San Juan festival; the July 24–25 festival of the patron saint of San Cristóbal, when brightly decorated trucks, buses, and taxis parade up a hilltop to the San Cristóbal Church; the August 6–11 celebration of San Lorenzo in Zinacantán; the November 1–2 Día de los Muertos (Day of the Dead) celebrations in Zinacantán, with spirited graveside festivals; and the feast of the Virgin of Guadalupe (celebrated for a week in Tuxtla Gutiérrez) on December 12. Several indigenous highland villages hold celebrations on

December 31 to install new civil officials. Remember that it's beastly hot in the lowlands most of the year, but especially just prior to the rainy season, February–April.

SAN CRISTÓBAL DE LAS CASAS

San Cristóbal is a pretty town of about 150,000 in a valley of pine forests interspersed with maize fields and orchards—all at an altitude of 6,888 ft above sea level. It's the most touristic city of the Chiapas highlands; here indigenous women with babies tied tightly in colorful shawls share the plaza with backpackers. Travelers who come to San Cristóbal aren't put off by headlines about government troops and the EZLN— or are even intrigued by the political ramifications. In truth, the rival sides are more likely to snipe at each other via newspaper editorials or the Internet, than in hostile confrontations.

San Cristóbal is beautiful and inexpensive, the perfect hub for exploring some of the region's lakes, villages, and archaeological sites. Small enough to take in on foot in the course of a day, the town is also captivating enough to invite a stay of three days, a week, or even longer. In addition to viewing colonial monuments, consider planning an early morning visit to the *mercado* (market) to check out local culture and browse for crafts, or explore one of the traditional villages in the vicinity (Sunday is the best day for visiting village markets). Just soaking up the ambience in one of San Cristóbal's little cafés or unpretentious restaurants is a pleasure.

San Cristóbal is among the finest colonial towns in Mexico, and its cool climate is a refreshing change from the sweltering heat of the lower altitudes. On chilly evenings, smoke from chimney fires curls lazily over the red-tile roofs of small, brightly painted stucco houses and elegant colonial mansions. The mystical atmosphere here is intensified by the fog and low clouds that hover over the town and by the remarkable quality of the early morning and late-afternoon light.

The highlands were originally inhabited by Maya peoples who, along with most of Mesoamerica, harvested maize and had no centralized government; they also resisted the Spanish conquest more forcefully than the indigenous groups of northern Mexico, who either welcomed the conquistadors as gods or as allies in their opposition to the dominant Aztecs. In 1526 the Spaniards under Diego de Mazariegos finally defeated the Chiapan Indians at a battle outside town. Mazariegos founded the city, which was called Villareal de Chiapa de los Españoles, in 1528. For most of the viceroyalty, or colonial era, Chiapas, with its capital at San Cristóbal, was a province of Guatemala. Lacking the gold and silver of the north, it was of greater strategic than economic importance to the Spaniards.

Under Spanish rule the region's agricultural resources became entrenched in the *encomienda* system, in which wealthy Spanish landowners forced natives to work as slaves. "In this life all men suffer," lamented a Spanish friar in 1691, "but the Indians suffer most of all." The situation improved only slightly through the efforts of Bartolomé de las Casas, the bishop of San Cristóbal, who in the mid-1500s protested the torture and massacre of the native peoples; they protested in another way, murdering priests and other *ladinos* (Spaniards) in infamous uprisings.

Mexico, Guatemala, and the rest of New Spain declared independence in 1821. Chiapas remained part of Guatemala, until electing by plebescite to join Mexico on September 14, 1824—the date is still cel-

"A VOICE OF MANY VOICES"

IN THE EARLY HOURS of January 1, 1994, while most of Mexico was sleeping off the New Year's festivities, the Zapatista National Liberation Army (EZLN) took the world by surprise when it captured the colonial tourist center of San Cristóbal de las Casas and several surrounding towns, demanding land redistribution and equal rights for Chiapas's indigenous peoples.

The Zapatista military triumph was short-lived. The mostly Tzotzil and Tzeltal troops soon departed San Cristóbal, and on January 12, President Carlos Salinas de Gortari called for a unilateral ceasefire. According to government figures, 145 lives were lost during the 12-day struggle. But hundreds have been killed in eight years of clashes between rebel supporters and paramilitary groups; thousands have been displaced. "We did not go to war on January 1 to kill or to have them kill us," declared Subcomandante Marcos, the EZLN's charismatic leader and spokesperson. "We went to make ourselves heard."

The social, economic, and political factors that led to the Zapatista uprising are many and complex. Centuries of land appropriation, first by the Spanish and then by the Mexican aristocracy, repeatedly uprooted Chiapas's Maya-descended indigenous groups. The North American Free Trade Agreement (NAFTA), which went into effect on January 1, 1994, symbolized Mexico's entry into the First World for its political and business elite. But, as the Zapatista movement forced Mexico to recognize, much of the nation, and much of Chiapas, remained mired in the Third World. Despite its natural resources—Chiapas provides nearly half of Mexico's electricity and has extensive oil and gas reserves—the state's indigenous residents suffer appallingly high rates of illiteracy, malnutrition, and infant mortality.

In 1995 President Ernesto Zedillo sent troops into the Lacandon jungle to capture the Zapatista leadership, including Marcos, whom the government identified as former Mexico City communications professor Rafael Sebastian Guillen. The am-

bush failed. The following year negotiations with the rebels resulted in the so-called San Andrés Accords, which called for a constitutional amendment recognizing indigenous rights and limited autonomy. However, President Zedillo refused to implement the Accords and instead pursued a policy of low-intensity warfare throughout the rest of his administration. The policy led to disastrous results, including the massacre of 45 unarmed Zapatista supporters at the hands of pro-government paramilitary forces in the village of Acteal, Chenalho, in December 1997.

During his presidential campaign, Vicente Fox insisted that he could resolve the Zapatista conflict in 15 minutes, an example of Foxspeak frequently chided by his critics. Nevertheless, during his inaugural address the President announced that he was ordering partial troop withdrawals and would submit legislation to Congress based on the San Andrés Accords. In turn, Subcomandante Marcos announced three conditions for the restoration of negotiations—further military withdrawals, the release of Zapatista prisoners, and implementation of the Accords. Fox continues to be engaged in a protracted media war with Marcos, who began to express doubts about the president's desire to pursue peace in Chiapas. In early 2001, a Zapatista caravan took to the streets, traveling through twelve Mexican states and into the capital to demand negotiations. More than 100,000 supporters gathered in the city's zócalo in a dramatic culmination of the two-week procession.

Fox, who welcomed the Zapatistas to the capital, has come under attack from members of the Institutional Revolutionary Party (PRI) as well as members of his own National Action Party (PAN), who have criticized the indigenous movement and indicated they would not support the President's legislation. The restoration of negotiations would be a triumph for Fox, but hardly a solution to centuries-old problems in southern Mexico.

ebrated in San Cristóbal and all over Chiapas as the *día de la mexi-canidad* (Day of Mexicanization) of Chiapas. In 1892, because of San Cristóbal's allegiance to the Royalists during the War of Independence, the capital was moved to Tuxtla Gutiérrez. With that went all hope that the town would keep pace with the rest of Mexico. It wasn't until the 1950s that the roads into town were paved and the first automobiles arrived. Modern times came late to San Cristóbal, for which many locals and visitors are thankful.

Because of the altitude, it gets cold here at night, and can be chilly during the day as well; pack a warm sweater and layer your clothing. When the sun does appear, it can get quite hot, but most restaurants keep doors open even during cold weather, and hotels are for the most part unheated. The cobblestone and flagstone streets are best suited to comfortable, flat shoes.

Exploring San Cristóbal de las Casas

San Cristóbal is laid out in a grid pattern centered on the zócalo, with street names changing on either side of the square. For example, Calle Francisco Madero to the east of the square becomes Diego de Mazariegos to the west.

The town was originally divided into several *barrios* (neighborhoods), which now blend together into a city center that is easily negotiated. In colonial times, Indian allies of the triumphant Spaniards were moved onto lands on the outskirts of the nascent city. Each barrio was dedicated to a different occupation. There were weavers, Tlaxcala fireworks manufacturers, and pig butchers from Cuxtitali. Although these divisions no longer exist, other customs have been kept alive. For example, each Saturday certain houses downtown will put out red lamps to indicate that fresh homemade tamales are for sale.

A Good Walk

Head for the heart of downtown, the Plaza 31 de Marzo, or **zócalo** ① and take in the colonial buildings around the square, many of them homes of the Spanish conquistadores. Note the 16th-century **Casa de Diego de Mazariegos** ② on its southeast corner (now the Hotel Santa Clara). Continue in a northwesterly direction around the square to the neoclassical **Palacio Municipal** ③—which gets painted a different color according to the whim of each new governor—with its numerous arcades. **La Catedral** ④ (cathedral), on the north side of the zócalo, has a fascinating facade. Continue north five blocks along Avenida General Utrilla to the 16th-century **Templo de Santo Domingo** ⑤ with its ornamental baroque facade; walk around the complex to its museum and famous textiles cooperative amid the Indian families selling goods in the large exterior courtyard. Head for Avenida General Utrilla again and walk north three blocks to the **mercado** ⑥ to visit the stalls filled with fruits, vegetables, candles, and other necessities. You can catch a cab, or walk the nine long blocks east on Comitán, to the **Museo Na Bolom** ⑦, a great local repository of Indian artifacts. As the museum is shown by tour only, you'll probably want to time your arrival for the 4:30 tour. To end the day, catch another taxi (or walk five blocks south on Av. Vicente Guerrero and eight blocks west on Calle Real de Guadalupe) back downtown to see the gorgeous regional costumes on display at the **Museo Sergio Castro** ⑧.

Sights to See

❷ **Casa de Diego de Mazariegos.** One of the most accessible pieces of colonial architecture in San Cristóbal is now the **Hotel Santa Clara.** The stone mermaid and lions outside it are typical of the period's plateresque style—as ornate and busy as the work of a silversmith. ⊠ *Av. Insurgentes 1.*

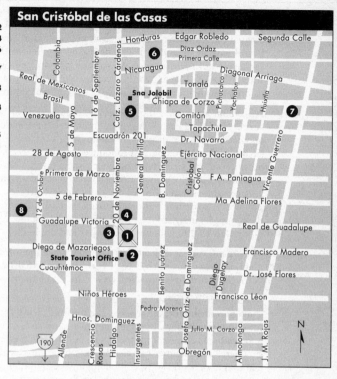

San Cristóbal de las Casas

NEED A
BREAK?

Cozy and relaxing, **La Galería Café** (⊠ Calle Hidalgo 3, ½ block south
of the zócalo, ☎ 967/8–15–47) is the favorite haunt of local intellectuals and poets who drink their way through cappuccinos, espressos, or
beers until midnight. Appetizers, pizza, and hard liquor are also served,
and an excellent art gallery and craft store are located inside. Live
music is played every day.

❹ **La Catedral.** Dedicated to San Cristóbal Mártir (St. Christopher the Martyr), the cathedral was built in 1528, then demolished, and rebuilt in
1693, with additions during the 18th and 19th centuries. The Baroque
facade, recently repainted in ochre with dark red, black, and white accents, is unforgettable. Inside, don't miss the painting *Nuestra Señora
de Dolores* (Our Lady of Sorrows) to the left of the altar, the gold-plated
retablo de los reyes (altarpiece), the Chapel of Guadalupe, and the gold-
washed pulpit. ⊠ *Calle Guadalupe Victoria between 20 de Noviembre and Av. Gral. Utrilla; entrance on south side.* ☉ *Daily 7:30–2 and
4–8:30, daily mass at 8* PM.

❻ **Mercado.** This municipal market occupies an eight-block area. Best visited early in the morning—especially on the busiest day, Saturday—
the market is the social and commercial center for the Indians from
surrounding villages. Stalls overflow with local produce, turkeys,
medicinal herbs, flowers, firewood, and wool, as well as huaraches (sandals), grinding stones, candles, and candied fruit. Do not carry anything of value: robberies at the market are common. If you must bring
your camera, be discreet, and, as always, ask permission before photographing people. ⊠ *Between Av. Gral. Utrilla, Nicaragua, Honduras, and Belisario Domínguez.*

★ **❼** **Museo Na Bolom.** Set aside an afternoon to tour this nonprofit organization, housed in a handsome 22-room neoclassical building built

as a Christian seminary in 1891. Frans (a Danish archaeologist) and Gertrude (a Swiss social activist) Blom bought the house in 1950, and created the institute for ethnological and ecological advocacy, which is still carried on today. It got its name, Na Bolom (House of the Jaguar), from the Lacandon Maya with whom Trudi worked: Blom sounds like the Mayan word for jaguar. Both Frans and Trudi fought to preserve and publicize the disappearing Maya cultures in the area.

Na Bolom showcases the Bloms' small collection of religious treasures, which had been hoarded in attics during the anticlerical 1920s and 1930s. Also on display are Franz Blom's findings from the Classic Maya site of Moxviquil (pronounced mosh-vee-*keel*), found on the outskirts of San Cristóbal, and his personal effects. Trudi's bedroom contains her jewelry, shawls, canes, collection of indigenous handicrafts, and wondrous wardrobe of 95 embroidered dresses. Also on the premises is a room full of objects from the daily life of the Lacandon; the Bloms documented their traditions and way of life. A library holds more than 10,000 volumes on Chiapas and the Maya.

The organization is dedicated to reforestation of the surrounding area, planting thousands of trees each year. Its own extensive nursery/garden is filled with firs, fruit trees, vegetables, and other flowering plants.

Revenue from Na Bolom's guest house, tours, restaurant, and gift shop goes to support the work of the institute. The gift shop sells Lacandon crafts such as flutes and bows and arrows, as well as black-and-white photos. Arrange for a meal at Na Bolom, even if you don't stay here. The facilities can also be used by groups as a base for special events or workshops, combining any permutation of accommodations, meals, and organized tours. Na Bolom's staff is well connected within San Cristóbal and can arrange tours to artisans' co-ops, villages, and nature reserves that are a bit off the beaten path. ☒ *Av. Vicente Guerrero 31, between Comitán and Chiapa de Corzo,* ☎ *967/8–14–18.* ⌑ *Museum and tour $3.* ☽ *Library weekdays 10–1:30, store daily 9:30–1:30 and 3–7. The only way to visit the museum is on a tour, conducted daily in English and Spanish at 11:30 and 4:30.*

❽ Museo Sergio Castro. Sergio Castro, an agronomist from northern Mexico who has dedicated himself to building schools in the highlands of Chiapas, has spent around 40 years working with the Indians; many of the ceremonial costumes were given to him as payment for his work in the communities. There are around 1,000 pieces in the collection, including textiles, weavings, and carved wooden saints, musical instruments, and toys. Sergio gives tours and slide shows in English, Spanish and French every evening, but you must make reservations in the morning. ☒ *Calle Guadalupe Victoria 61,* ☎ *967/8–42–89.* ⌑ *$2.50, including tour and slide show. Donations toward educational and health projects for indigenous communities are also welcome.* ☽ *Daily 5–9.*

❸ Palacio Municipal (Municipal Palace). Perhaps the most famous mansion in San Cristóbal is this building, with its wide colonial arches and tile patio. It was the seat of the state government until 1892, when Tuxtla Gutiérrez became the capital. It now houses municipal government offices. ☒ *Av. Hidalgo between Calles Diego de Mazariegos and Guadalupe Victoria.*

❺ Templo de Santo Domingo. This three-block-long complex houses a church, former convent, regional history museum, and the **Templo de la Caridad** (Temple of the Sisters of Charity). A two-headed eagle—emblem of the Hapsburg dynasty that once ruled Spain and its American dominions—broods over the pediment of the church, which was built between 1547 and 1569. The pink stone facade (which needs a good cleaning) is carved in an intensely ornamental style known as Baroque Solomonic: saints' figures, angels, and grooved columns overlaid with vegetation motifs abound. The interior is dominated by lavish altarpieces, an exquisitely fashioned pulpit, a sculpture of the Holy Trinity, and wall panels of gilded, carved cedar—one of the precious woods of Chiapas that centuries later lured the woodsmen of Tabasco to the obscure highlands surrounding San Cristóbal. At the southeast corner of the church park lies the tiny and much more humble Templo de la Caridad, built in 1715 to honor the Immaculate Conception. Its highlight is the finely carved altarpiece. Indians from San Juan Chamula are often lighting candles and making offerings here. (Do *not* take photos of the Chamulas.)

The Ex-Convento de Santo Domingo, adjacent to the Santo Domingo church, now houses **Sna Jolobil,** an Indian cooperative selling an excellent selection of rather expensive local weavings, embroidered clothing, and colorful postcards. The shop is open Tuesday through Saturday 9–2 and 4–7. The small **Regional History Museum** (☎ 967/8–16–09), also part of the complex, displays archaeological pieces and textiles and is open Tuesday–Sunday 10–5. Admission is $2, free Sunday. ⊠ *20 de Noviembre s/n, near Real de Mexicanos.*

❶ **Zócalo.** This main square around which the colonial city was built has in its center a gazebo used by musicians most evenings and weekend afternoons. You can have a coffee on the top or middle floor of the gazebo; be prepared for small children and women hawking their wares. Surrounding the square are a number of 16th-century buildings, many former mansions of the conquistadores, with wood-beam ceilings and plant-filled central patios. Don't be afraid to go into buildings whose doors are open. ⊠ *Between Avs. Gral. Utrilla and 20 de Noviembre and Calles Diego de Mazariegos and Guadalupe Victoria.*

Outside San Cristóbal. Surrounding San Cristóbal are many small and seldom-visited Indian villages celebrated for the exquisite colors and embroidery work of their inhabitants' costumes. Huixtán (hweesh-*tan*) and Oxchuc (osh-*chuc*) are about 28 km and 43 km (17 mi and 27 mi), respectively, on the road to Ocosingo. Neither is known for its market, although they are visited during their town festivals; Huixtán venerates San Miguel (Saint Michael) on September 29, and Oxchuc celebrates patron San Tomás (Saint Thomas) on July 3. The Thursday market in Tenejapa, 27 km (17 mi) northeast of San Cristóbal, is worth seeing.

Dining

$$$ ✕ **Paris-Mexico.** A cozy, laid-back atmosphere makes this a local fa-
★ vorite for breakfast, lunch, and dinner. Attentive waiters who speak French and Spanish (but no English) serve a range of traditional Mexican and French entrées, soups, and desserts topped off with your choice of a fine French wine or a margarita. ⊠ *Calle Madero 20, corner of Francisco León,* ☎ *967/8–06–95. AE, MC, V.*

$$$ ✕ **Restaurant L'Eden.** Local expats rave about the steaks at this small,
★ charming chalet-style restaurant within the Hotel El Paraíso. It has eight cozy dining tables, piped-in classical music, a fireplace, and friendly service. The margaritas are the biggest in San Cristóbal. Swiss delights include classic raclette—melted cheese and potato—and beef fondue for two. Homemade lime or raspberry pie makes a perfect finish to a meal. ⊠ *Av. 5 de Febrero 19,* ☎ *967/8–00–85. AE, MC, V.*

$$ ✕ **La Casa del Pan.** Organically grown fruits, vegetables, and coffee
★ get top billing at this vegetarian restaurant. The tasty tamales *chiapanecos* with a spicy cheese filling, hot bean soup, and the best salads in town

draw return visits, and the four-course special of the day, which includes variations on traditional Mexican cooking, really shines. The bakery sells homemade breads, bagels, coffee, cookies, and fruit preserves. You can also buy Chiapan organic coffee and handicrafts here. Musical groups with repertoires from jazz to pop perform every night. ⊠ *Dr. Navarro 10 at Av. Belisario Domínguez,* ☎ *967/8–58–95. MC, V. Closed Mon.*

$$ ✕ **Emiliano's Moustache.** Handmade tortillas with a wide variety of meat, chicken, and vegetarian fillings make this a popular spot among locals and tourists. A large selection of other typical Mexican dishes is also available. There's an upstairs bar that overlooks the nicely decorated restaurant named after Mexican peasant revolutionary hero Emiliano Zapata. Live music plays Monday through Saturday 9–11:30. ⊠ *Crescencio Rosas 7, a couple of blocks from the zócalo,* ☎ *967/8–72–46. V.*

$$ ✕ **Na Bolom.** Doña Bety, the late Trudi Blom's adopted daughter, heads the kitchen at this famous ethnological/ecological museum. Home-cooked meals emphasizing vegetarian and chicken dishes are the norm here—with foods such as roast chicken, coleslaw, avocado strips, and Mexican *chayote* (a mild green squash). The communal dining table is shared by international volunteers, Lacandon Indians, resident scholars, travelers, and artists in residence. Breakfast is served 7–11 and a five-course dinner at 7 (no lunch). If you're not staying at the institute, call at least two hours ahead for a reservation. ⊠ *Av. Vicente Guerrero 33,* ☎ *967/8–14–18. MC, V.*

$$ ✕ **Restaurante Continental.** The large enclosed courtyard of this converted neo-classic colonial home is an ideal setting for this family-style restaurant. Every day between 2:30 and 4:30 live marimba music makes it a pleasant place to spend an hour or two after a long morning tour of the city. On Sunday, there's a buffet with regional dishes, and you might catch the folkloric dancers who perform from 3 to 3:30 PM. Try the *trenzado Chamula* (strips of grilled beef and pork) and the delicious *guacamole* served with *tostadas*. If you're looking for good cigars, one of the stores facing the courtyard may be the only place in town where you'll find them. ⊠ *Real de Guadalupe 24,* ☎ *967/8–48–61. MC, V.*

$$ ✕ **Restaurante el Teatro.** Sunshine streams in the second-story windows here during the day, warming yellow walls decorated with European and local artwork. At night, candlelight presides. The French owner keeps the atmosphere unhurried and makes most everything himself, including the fresh pasta and chocolate mousse. The menu features primarily French and Italian dishes—including chateaubriand and crêpes. The wood-fired pizzas and shish kebab are also delicious; a few Mexican dishes are served. ⊠ *Av. 1 de Marzo 8, at Av. 16 de Septiembre,* ☎ *967/8–31–49. MC, V. Closed Mon.*

$ ✕ **La Selva Café.** This coffee shop has more than a dozen organic javas and assorted coffee-flavored concoctions. The odd menu features no egg dishes, but mostly sandwiches and cold plates, with exceptions such as codfish pie, chopped-meat pie, and Chiapas tamales. There's a separate no-smoking section, and a few tables are in the lush garden out back. ⊠ *Crescencio Rosas 9, at Calle Cuauhtémoc,* ☎ *967/8–72–44. No credit cards.*

Lodging

$$$ 🏨 **Hotel Casa Mexicana.** This beautifully designed hotel in a restored colonial mansion is colorful, clean, and friendly. Good beds, beam ceilings, and attractive artwork all help make this an outstanding hostelry. All rooms have phones and satellite TV, and the suites have hot tubs. The restaurant, which surrounds a lovely, plant-filled courtyard with a bubbling fountain in the middle, serves international dishes, such as chicken in pistachio sauce and eggplant Parmesan. ☒ *28 de Agosto 1, 29200,* ☎ *967/8–06–98, 967/8–06–83, or 967/8–13–48,* FAX *967/8–26–27,* WEB *www.casamexicana.com.mx. 52 rooms, 2 junior suites, 1 master suite. Restaurant, bar, room service, massage, sauna, baby-sitting, free parking. AE, MC, V.*

$$$ ⚑ **Posada Diego de Mazariegos.** This quaint hotel has fine colonial
★ details, beautiful gardens, and skylights throughout. Rooms have high ceilings and lovely tile bathrooms; some rooms have fireplaces the staff will light for you. ☒ *5 de Febrero 1, corner of Av. Gral. Utrilla, 29200,* ☎ *967/8–08–33,* FAX *967/8–08–27,* WEB *www.diegodemazariegos.com. 71 rooms, 3 suites. Restaurant, bar, cafeteria, travel services, car rental, free parking. AE, MC, V.*

$$ ⚑ **Casavieja.** Three blocks east of the zócalo, this spectacular hotel maintains the architectural style of the original colonial house, built in 1740. Each comfortable room is charmingly decorated in Mexican furnishings and has large windows looking out onto one of the three interior courtyards. All rooms have phones and TVs with English channels; suites also have hot tubs. Some rooms are heated. The Espinosas, who run and own the hotel, are warm and knowledgeable hosts. ☒ *Ma. Adelina Flores 27, 29230,* ☎ *967/8–03–85,* ☎ FAX *967/8–68–68,* WEB *www.casavieja.com.mx. 38 rooms, 2 suites. Restaurant, bar, free parking. AE, MC, V.*

$$ ⚑ **Hostal Flamboyant Español.** With its three lovely courtyards, arch-
★ ways, and lots of colorful Mexican tile, this refurbished mansion in the heart of the city retains its beautiful colonial style. The carved wooden furniture and other Mexican furnishings add charm to the three-story hotel, built in 1917. The traditionally decorated rooms all have tile baths, phones, cable TV, and heaters. During the day, you can soak up the sun in one of the plant-filled courtyards; sit near the fireplace in the cozy restaurant as the evening sets in. ☒ *1 de marzo 15, 29200,* ☎ *967/8–00–45,* FAX *967/8–05–14,* WEB *www.flamboyant.com.mx. 82 rooms. Restaurant, bar, gym, free parking. AE, MC, V.*

$$ ⚑ **Hotel Arecife de Coral.** Just four blocks from the zócalo, this colonial-style hotel has a gorgeous interior courtyard with a resident peacock and paradisiacal fruit trees. Rooms have cable TV and phones. ☒ *Av. Crescencio Rosas 29, corner of Alvaro Obregón,* ☎ *967/8–21–25,* FAX *967/8–20–98. 50 rooms. Restaurant, bar, free parking. MC, V.*

$$ ⚑ **Hotel El Paraíso.** The 13 guest rooms in this charming colonial home have beam ceilings; some rooms have lofts and carpeting; eight have phones. Comfortable leather-backed chairs in the guest lounge overlook a sunny, plant-filled, indoor/outdoor patio area with tables for breakfasting. The bar-restaurant offers the personal attention of owners Daniel and Teresa Suter, who met as students in Switzerland. For more solitude, request a room away from the street and lounge. ☒ *Av. 5 de Febrero 19, 29200,* ☎ *967/8–00–85,* FAX *967/8–51–68. 13 rooms. Restaurant, bar. AE, MC, V.*

$$ ⚑ **Hotel Santa Clara.** Once the home of city founder Diego de Mazariegos, this rambling 16th-century mansion is now a hotel overlooking the action in the main plaza. It has a tangible air of past grandeur: beam ceilings, antique furnishings, time-worn hardwood floors, and a slightly damp smell throughout. Six of the nine extra-roomy units with balconies overlook the zócalo. There is a tiny round pool in the courtyard. For entertainment, Bar Cocodrilos has live Latin rock and pop most nights. ☒ *Av. Insurgentes 1, 29200,* ☎ *967/8–08–71 or 967/8–11–40,* FAX *967/8–10–41,* WEB *www.hotelstaclara.com. 39 rooms. Restaurant, bar, coffee shop, pool, travel services, free parking. AE, MC, V.*

$$ ⚑ **Mansión del Valle.** A few blocks from the zócalo, this 19th-century property has been converted into a modest yet comfortable hotel with tasteful Spanish colonial design details. There is a rather plain sitting room

for card-playing or socializing in the large inner atrium. Rooms on the first floor are dark; the seven second-story rooms with patios overlooking La Merced church across the street are nicer. ✉ *Calle Diego de Mazariegos 39, corner of Calle Guadalupe Victoria, 29240,* ☎ *967/8–25–82 or 967/8–25–83,* FAX *967/8–25–81. 40 rooms, 7 suites. Restaurant, bar, coffee shop, meeting room, car rental, free parking. AE, MC, V.*

$$ ⊞ **Na Bolom.** Each of the rustic but cozy rooms available at this cen-
★ ter for the study and preservation of the Lacandon Maya and the rain forest is decorated with the accoutrements of a specific indigenous community—including crafts, photographs, and books. About half the rooms have bathtubs; all have fireplaces. Guests staying at Na Bolom receive a free tour of the house (including a documentary presentation) and access to the library. Book well in advance; ask for a garden view. You can share the dining room with staff and volunteers for a separate charge. Groups are welcome, and staff will make travel and tour arrangements for a small fee. ✉ *Av. Vicente Guerrero 33, 29200,* ☎ *967/8–14–18,* FAX *967/8–55–86,* WEB *www.ecosur.mx/nabolom. 13 rooms. Restaurant, library, free parking. MC, V.*

$$ ⊞ **Rincón del Arco.** The charming touches at this recently remodeled hotel include a freestanding fireplace in each room. Room 11 is secluded and has a pretty view of the garden. Rooms on the top floor share a wide balcony from which you can sit and enjoy the cityscape: a view of the Church of Guadalupe and ancient houses with red-tile roofs. Since each of the rooms is different, ask to see several until you find the one you like best. The cheerful dining room has a fireplace and wrought-iron wagon-wheel chandeliers. There's also a textile workshop on the premises you can visit. ✉ *Calle Ejército Nacional 66, 29200,* ☎ *967/8–13–13,* FAX *967/8–15–68,* WEB *www.mundomaya.com.mx/hernanz. 48 rooms, 2 junior suites. Restaurant, bar, free parking. V.*

Nightlife and the Arts

The number of cultural offerings in San Cristóbal is on the rise. Ask at the tourist office, La Pared book shop, and El Puente coffee house and cultural center about upcoming lectures or concerts.

Museo Na Bolom occasionally sponsors talks and film presentations. The elegant **Teatro Hermanos Domínguez** (✉ Diagonal Hermanos Paniagua s/n, just outside the city limits, ☎ 967/8–36–37) features programs such as folkloric dances from throughout Latin America. **El Puente** (✉ Real de Guadalupe 55, ☎ 967/8–37–23), a casual, hip restaurant-cum-social-center, serves breakfast all day, shows videos most nights, offers Internet access, and hosts occasional art exhibitions. It's a good place to hear what's happening around town.

Although nightlife hasn't traditionally been one of San Cristóbal's main draws, there are now several good clubs with live music. **Latinos** (✉ Francisco y Madero 23, corner of Benito Juárez, ☎ 967/8–20–83) serves up live Latin jazz, salsa, or tropical music after 9:30 daily. Flamenco guitar players perform Thursday through Saturday 9–11 at **Restaurant Bar Margarita** (✉ Real de Guadalupe 34, ☎ 967/8–09–57), followed by a small salsa band until 1. **El A-Dove** (✉ Miguel Hidalgo 2, ☎ 967/8–66–66) is the town's hippest club, with a firehouse design and deejay world music until 4 Thursday through Sunday. **Bar Cocodrilos** (✉ Av. Insurgentes 1, ☎ 967/8–08–71 or 967/8–11–40), part of the Hotel Santa Clara, on the zócalo, has a more mellow tavern feel but also hosts live rock and salsa bands most nights from 9:30 to midnight. **Las Velas Danza-Bar** (✉ Francisco I. Madero 14, ☎ 967/8–04–17, is a popular disco with live rock and reggae music, open daily 8 PM until 4 AM.

Outdoor Activities and Sports

A horseback ride into the neighboring indigenous villages is good exercise for mind and body. Most hotels can arrange for rentals of horses. Guides working through some travel agencies can also hire horses and will accompany tourists. Five or six hours are needed to visit area villages or the nature reserve at Huitepec. Novices should be aware, however, that several hours on a horse can be, well, a pain in the ass. Many outfitters do *not* take experience into account when assigning mounts.

Shopping

The market in San Cristóbal, although picturesque, sells more produce than handicrafts. The shops on Avenida Gral. Utrilla, south of the market, have a large selection of goods from Guatemala—but not always those of the highest quality. Guatemalan textiles often sell for less than Chiapan textiles, and the Mexican government is considering barring their import because of unfair competition with local producers. Nevertheless, make sure to bargain for these textiles to get a good price. Most Guatemalan cloth is dark-blue cotton with multicolor cotton needlepoint or trim.

Shops are generally open 9–2 and 4–8. Indian women and children will often approach you on the streets with their wares—mostly fake amber, woven bracelets, and small dolls—but their selections aren't as varied as those in the shops, and prices won't necessarily be better. On the other hand, you can be assured that the proceeds go directly to the craftspeople.

Among its excellent selection of wares, **Sna Jolobil** (Weaver's House in Tzotzil; ⊠ Ex-Convento de Santo Domingo, Calzada Lázaro Cárdenas 42, ☎ 967/8–71–78), the regional crafts cooperative, sells hand-dyed woolen sweaters and tunics, embroidered pillow covers, and pre-Hispanic-design wall hangings. It's closed Sunday and lunchtime.

Among the smart shops clustered along Real de Guadalupe are two subsidiaries of **El Arbol de la Vida** (⊠ Real de Guadalupe 27 and 28-A, ☎ 967/8–40–85 or 967/8–50–50), one block apart. They specialize in attractive designer amber jewelry mixed with silver and gold. There's a small museum inside the shop displaying the different types of amber found around the world. A video explains how this prehistoric resin is extracted from the mines and later transformed into this precious natural gem. Open daily 8:30–8:30.

Artesanías Chiapanecas (⊠ Calle Real de Guadalupe 46C, at Diego Dugelay, ☎ no phone) has an excellent selection of embroidered blouses, huipiles, tablecloths, and bags. The government-run **Instituto de las Artesanías** (⊠ Calle Niños Héroes and Av. Hidalgo, ☎ FAX 967/8–11–80, ☉ Mon.–Sat. 10–2, 4–8; Sun. 10–2) has wooden toys, ceramics, embroidered blouses, bags, and handwoven textiles from throughout the state, and a tiny ethnographic museum in back. At the Rincón del Arco Hotel, **Textiles Soriano** (⊠ Calle Ejército Nacional 66, ☎ 967/8–13–13, ☉ Mon.–Sat. 10–2, 4–8) specializes in handwoven bedspreads and other cloth, which can be made to order in a few days.

Taller Leñateros (⊠ Flavio A. Paniagua 54, ☎ 967/8–51–74), a unique indigenous co-op in an old colonial San Cristóbal home, has original top-quality crafts as well as free informal tours to observe artisans at work. Run by expat Ambar Past, the co-op sells handmade books, boxes, postcards, and writing paper fashioned on the premises out of recycled flower petals, plants, and bark.

SOUTH AND EAST OF SAN CRISTÓBAL

Southeast of San Cristóbal lies one of the least explored and most exotic regions of Chiapas: the Selva Lacandona, said to be the second-largest rain forest in the western hemisphere. Incursions of developers, settlers, controversial government development projects, and refugees from neighboring Guatemala are transforming Mexico's last frontier, which for centuries has been the homeland of the Lacandon, a small tribe descended from the Maya of Yucatán. Some of their people still maintain their ancient customs, living in huts and wearing long, plain tunics. However, their custom of not marrying outside the tribe is causing serious problems, and their numbers, never large to begin with, have been reduced to about 350. The fabulous Caves of San Cristóbal (also known as Las Grutas de Rancho Nuevo) are in this region.

The Caves of San Cristóbal

❾ *13 km (8 mi) south of San Cristóbal off Rte. 190.*

Spectacular limestone stalactites and stalagmites are illuminated along a 2,475-ft cement walkway inside these labyrinthine caves, which were discovered in 1960. But the caves were fully explored more recently, prompting the creation of the **San Cristóbal Recreational Park.** The Spanish-speaking gatekeeper (or his kids) is usually available to guide visitors for a small fee. The caves may be closed in inclement weather; if in doubt, check with the San Cristóbal tourist office first. Horses can be rented ($3 per hour) for a ride around the surrounding pine forest, and there is a small restaurant and picnic area on the site. To get here, catch a Teopisca-bound microbus at Boulevard Juan Sabines Gutiérrez, across from the San Diego church. Make sure to tell the driver to let you off at the "grutas." Get off at the signed entrance, and walk about 1 km (½ mi) along the dirt road. Alternatively, catch a taxi from town for about $4. For about twice that price, you can ask him to wait while you explore the caves. ☎ *No phone.* 🎫 *50¢.* ☼ *Daily 9–5.*

Amatenango del Valle

❿ *37 km (23 mi) southeast of San Cristóbal.*

Amatenango del Valle is a Tzeltal village known for the handsome, primitive pottery made principally by the town's women, whose distinctive red and yellow huipiles are also much remarked upon. On the road to Comitán, the village currently has no signage; watch closely for the ocher, black, and natural-clay flowerpots and animal figurines—primarily gray doves—sitting by the side of the road. You can stop at any of these roadside houses, or turn into the town; almost every household has wares to sell. If you go during the dry season, you might get to see some of the pots being fired over open flames (not stoves) outside, as long as rain isn't a threat. Spanish is definitely a second language here, and women negotiate without a lot of chitchat, or use younger children as interpreters.

Comitán

⓫ *55 km (34 mi) southeast of Amatenango del Valle.*

Comitán, whose Maya name, Balún-Canán, means "nine stars" or "guardians," is a pleasant commercial center and agricultural town of about 120,000. It's also the base from which many visitors tour the Lagos de Montebello and the small archaeological sites nearby. Built by the Spaniards, the city flourished early on as a major center linking the lowland temperate plains to the edge of the Maya empire on the Pacific. Even today it serves as the principal trading point for the Tzeltal Indians; such Guatemalan goods as sugarcane liquor and orchids come through here. One of the "Hundred Colonial Cities," Comitán was renovated with a federal government grant, and its pretty plaza and surrounding streets were all refurbished in colonial style.

Two notable churches are **Santo Domingo de Guzmán**, with architecture showing a Moorish influence, and **San Caralampio**, whose Spanish Baroque style shows the influence of Guatemalan artisans.

The **Casa-Museo Dr. Belisario Domínguez,** the lovely former home of a martyr of the revolution, opened as a museum in 1985. It houses a fascinating collection of medical instruments, pharmaceuticals, and late-19th-century furnishings, as well as photographs, documents, and letters from the Mexican revolution, during which the doctor was assassinated for his outspoken criticism of President Victoriano Huerta. ⊠ *Av. Central Sur Dr. Belisario Domínguez 35,* ☎ *963/2–13–00.* ⊠ *$1.* ⊘ *Tues.–Sun. 9–7.*

The centrally located **Museo de Arte Hermila Castellanos** shows work by modern Mexican artists, including master painters Rufino Tamayo and Francisco Toledo, both from Oaxaca (many of the painters represented here are Oaxaqueños). The subject matter deals largely with mestizo and indigenous people, most often in stylized, contemporary depictions. ⊠ *Av. Central Sur Dr. Belisario Domínguez 51,* ☎ *962/2–20–82.* ⊠ *$2.* ⊘ *Mon.–Sat. 10–6, Sun. 10–1.*

🔺 Some 7 km (4 mi) from Comitán, **Tenam Puente** is on a hill with a spectacular view of the valley. The Mayan site, primarily a ceremonial center, was built around the same time as Chincultik and occupied during the Classic and post-Classic period. Archaeologists Franz Blom and Oliver LeFarge discovered the site, and restoration began in 1993, with the unearthing of a royal tomb in 1996. There are three ball courts, apparently one each for the lower, middle, and upper classes. Most of the site has yet to be explored. ⊠ *Free.* ⊘ *Daily 9–4.*

Lagos de Montebello

⑫ *64 km (40 mi) southeast of Comitán.*

The 56 lakes and surrounding pine forest of the Lagos de Montebello (Lakes of the Beautiful Mountain) constitute a 2,437-acre park that is shared with Guatemala. A different color permeates each lake, whose waters glow with vivid emerald, turquoise, amethyst, azure, and steel-gray tints, caused by various oxides. The setting is serene and majestic, with clusters of oak, pine, and sweet gum. Practically the only denizens of the more accessible part of the forest are the clamorous goldfinches and mockingbirds. To the east roam puma, jaguar, deer, bear, and the rare quetzal bird.

At the park entrance, the paved road forks. The left fork leads to the Lagunas Coloradas (Colored Lakes). At Laguna Bosque Azul, the last lake along that road, there is a humble sit-down café in addition to the food and beverage stalls that crop up near every lake with a parking lot. Small boys will approach and offer a 45-minute horse-riding expedition to a cave and two cenotes within the forest. You can also tour the lake in a rowboat for $4 (up to four people).

Back at the park entrance, the right fork leads past various groupings of lakes to Tziscao Lake and, just outside the park boundaries, a village of the same name. There is a new restaurant with a spectacular view of the lake. A 30-minute boat ride costs $2.50 a person, and Tziscao and Montebello are the only lakes the tourist board recommends for swimming. Check with the Comitán tourist offices if you'd like to stay in the park; the recently remodeled Tziscao Lodge has several small cabins and a community hostel (about $5 per person).

You can pick up a helpful map of the lakes at the tourist office in Comitán. La Angostura (☎ 963/2–60–00) and Transportes Cuxtepeque (☎ 963/2–17–28) buses leave about every half hour from the Comitán bus station (✉ 2da Av. Pte. Sur 17-B, between 2a and 3a Calles Sur Pte.) to both Laguna Bosque Azul and Tziscao. If you take the bus, you can either walk or catch the same bus between lakes; check the map and time your forays to catch the bus on the half hour. To get to Tziscao from Laguna Bosque Azul you must go to the fork in the road, catch the Bosque Azul bus to the next fork in the road, and then board a Tziscao bus.

The tourist office recommends that you take a tour to save time and lots of walking. It's also safer. Tourists have been assaulted while walking from one lake to another. Police checkpoints are now dispersed throughout the area, but it's still best to be careful. If you travel on your own, stay on the paved roads. Don't wander off onto the dirt paths.

Chincultik

🔺 ⑬   *56 km (35 mi) southeast of Comitán.*

You can visit the small, Late Classic Maya site of Chincultik on the way to or from the Lagos de Montebello. It's a steep hike of about 10 or 15 minutes to the top of a restored pyramid (as well as a walk from the highway if you don't come by car). From the top you're rewarded with a fabulous view of the Montebello Lakes and the surrounding countryside. The Cenote Agua Azul, the large sinkhole on the site (ask the guard to point you in the right direction, as signage is poor). The ruins, which are only partially restored, also include a ball court and stelae. 🎟 *About $2, free Sun.* ☉ *Tues.–Sun. 9–5.*

To get to Chincultik from Comitán, continue south 15 km (9 mi) on Route 190, and turn left at the sign LAGOS DE MONTEBELLO outside of La Trinitaria. After 39 km (24 mi), there's a road on the left leading to the ruins, which are 5 km (3 mi) off the highway. A bus runs from Comitán: you have to get off at the road that leads to the ruins and walk to the site.

Dining and Lodging

$$ ✕🏨 **Museo Parador Santa María.** Built around the remains of a hacienda from the 1830s, this hotel has an excellent restaurant and six well-appointed rooms. Each room is decorated with a different period of antiques, including plateresque, Chiapas, and French; some have lovely sunken-tile bathtubs, a few have fireplaces. The regional food here is known throughout the state, and the restaurant's special fixed three-course meal is the perfect way to end your visit to the lakes or the ruins. You can also browse through the small museum that has a collection of religious art from the 16th to 19th centuries. It's open daily 10–6. ✉ *Km 22 on the road to the Lagos de Montebello,* ☎ ᶠᴬˣ *963/2–51–16,* ᵂᴱᴮ *www.santamaria.chiapas.net.mx. 6 rooms. MC, V.*

NORTH AND WEST OF SAN CRISTÓBAL

San Juan Chamula and Zinacantán are traditional villages in the scenic western outskirts of San Cristóbal. The small colonial town of Chiapa de Corzo will be the first major town you come to when you drive west from San Cristóbal along Route 190. Tuxtla Gutiérrez, the modern state capital, is about 15 km (9 mi) beyond Chiapa de Corzo. Sumidero

Canyon is north of Tuxtla; the farthest lookout point is 22 km (14 mi) from the capital.

San Juan Chamula

14 *12 km (7½ mi) northwest of San Cristóbal de las Casas.*

The spiritual and administrative center of the Chamula Indians is justly celebrated, as much for its rich past as for its turbulent present. The Chamula are a Tzotzil-speaking Maya group of nearly 52,000 individuals (of a total 300,000 Tzotzils) who live in hamlets throughout the highlands; several thousand of them live in San Juan Chamula.

The Chamula are fiercely religious, a trait that has played an important role in their history. The Chamula uprising of 1869 started when some tribesmen were imprisoned for crucifying a boy in the belief that they should have their own Christ. Some 13,000 Chamula then rose up to demand their leaders' release and massacred scores of ladino villagers in the process. More recently, the infiltration of Protestant evangelists into the community led to the expulsion of the Indian converts by Chamula authorities. In the past 20 years, more than 30,000 have been forced to abandon their ancestral lands and now live on the outskirts of San Cristóbal de las Casas, dressing in conventional clothing and often selling handicrafts in San Cristóbal's street markets. The Human Rights Commission is trying to mediate their return to the Chamula community.

Physically and spiritually, life in San Juan Chamula revolves around the church, a white stucco building whose doorway is decorated with a flower motif. To get permission to enter the church, pay a token fee (about 50¢) at the tourist office on the main square. A pamphlet gives guidelines about how to conduct yourself in the church and the village.

Extreme discretion must be exercised inside the church. Taking photographs and videos is absolutely prohibited and strictly enforced. There are no pews, and the floor is strewn with fragrant pine needles. The Chamula sit praying silently or chanting while facing colorfully attired statues of saints. For the most part, worshipers appear oblivious to intruders, continuing with their rituals: they burn candles of various colors, drink soft drinks, and may have a live chicken or eggs with them for healing the sick. They "pass" the illness to the chicken or egg, which then gets disposed of outside the church. The church is named after Saint John the Baptist, the main god of the universe, according to Chamulan belief; Jesus Christ is revered as his younger brother.

Outside the church there is no taboo against photography, but it is illegal to photograph Chamulan authorities, who wear black ponchos and carry a baton. Flocks of children will pester you to buy small trinkets and to photograph them for money (about 50¢ a shot). The best time to visit San Juan Chamula is on Sunday, when the market is in full swing and more formal religious rites are performed.

To get here from San Cristóbal, head west on Calle Guadalupe Victoria, which forks to the right onto Ramón Larrainzar. Continue 4 km (2½ mi) until you reach the entrance to the village. Most of these roads are paved. Because of the threat of robbery, walking between San Cristóbal, San Juan Chamula, and Zinacantán isn't recommended.

Zinacantán

15 *4 km (2½ mi) west of San Juan Chamula.*

The village of Zinacantán (Place of the Bats) is even smaller than San Juan Chamula and is reached via a paved road west just outside San

Juan Chamula (from San Cristóbal, take the Tuxtla road about 8 km [5 mi] and look for the signed turnoff on your right). Here photography is totally forbidden, except for the row of village weavers on view along the main street. It's the scenery en route to Zinacantán—terraced hillsides with cornfields and orchards—that draws visitors. There isn't much to see in the village except on Sunday, when people gather from the surrounding parishes, or during religious festivals. The men wear bright pink tunics embroidered with flowers; the women cover themselves with bright pink *rebozos* (shawls). If you take a tour you'll visit the homes of back-strap loom weavers. Watch for the plethora of crosses around the springs and mountains on the way to Zinacantán: they mark a Christian Chamulan cemetery.

The **Museo Ik'al Ojov,** on the *calle principal* (main street) behind the church, is in a typical home and displays Zinacantán costumes through the ages. ☎ *No phone.* 🖂 *Donation encouraged.* ⊘ *Tues.–Sun. 9–5.*

Chiapa de Corzo

16 *70 km (43 mi) northwest of San Cristóbal; 15 km (9 mi) east of Tuxtla Gutiérrez.*

Chiapa de Corzo was founded in 1528 by Diego de Mazariegos, who one month later fled the mosquitoes and transported all the settlers to San Cristóbal (then called Chiapa de los Españoles, to distinguish it from Chiapa de los Indios, as Chiapa de Corzo was originally known). The mosquitoes are still here.

Life in this small town on the banks of the Grijalva revolves, inevitably, around the **zócalo,** which is lorded over by *la pila,* a bizarre 16th-century Mozarabic fountain that resembles a crown. The interior is decorated with stories of indigenous peoples. Several handicraft shops line the square, selling huaraches, ceramics, lacquerware, elaborately carved wooden Parachico masks (used in ceremonial dances), and regional costumes.

The **Centro Cultural Ex-Convento de Santo Domingo de Guzmán,** in front of the public market one block from the zócalo, has a permanent exhibition of Chiapa de Corzo engraver Franco Lázaro Gomez, who died in a tragic accident at 27 in 1949. The center also houses Chiapa's **lacquerware museum,** which has a modest collection of delicately carved and painted *jícaras* (gourds). "The sky is no more than an immense blue jícara, the beloved firmament in the form of a cosmic jícara," explains the *Popul Vuh,* a 16th-century chronicle of the Quiché Maya. The lacquerware here is both local and imported—from Michoacán, Guerrero, Chiapas, Guatemala, and Asia. Free lacquerware workshops are held weekdays 3–7. 🖂 *Calle Mexicanidad de Chiapas 10,* ☎ *961/6–00–55.* 🖃 *Free.* ⊘ *Museum open Tues.–Sun. 10–5.*

Dining

$ ✕ **Jardines de Chiapa.** Sample an excellent and inexpensive variety of regional cuisines in this lovely patio setting. Try the *tasajo* (sun-dried beef served with pumpkin-seed sauce) and the *chipilín con bolita* soup, made with balls of ground corn paste cooked in a creamy herbal sauce and topped with cheese. A marimba band sometimes enlivens the afternoon meal. It's open daily from 9–8. 🖂 *Av. Francisco I. Madero 395,* ☎ *961/6–01–98,* ☎ FAX *961/6–00–70. AE, MC, V.*

Tuxtla Gutiérrez

17 *289 km (179 mi) southwest of Villahermosa, 15 km (9 mi) northwest of Chiapa de Corzo, 85 km (53 mi) northwest of San Cristóbal.*

Tuxtla Gutiérrez is the thriving capital city of the state of Chiapas. In 1939 Graham Greene characterized it as "not a place for foreigners— the new ugly capital of Chiapas, without attractions." That bleak description is slowly changing, but Tuxtla Gutiérrez is still a city most visitors will pass through unnoticing, even if it is of vital economic and political importance. It's the state's transportation hub, and it has what is probably the most innovative zoo in Mexico. It's also convenient for its proximity to Chiapa de Corzo and the Sumidero Canyon, where there is little in the way of accommodations.

Tuxtla's first name derives from the Nahuatl word *tochtlan,* meaning "abundance of rabbits." Its second name, Gutiérrez, honors Joaquín Miguel Gutiérrez, who fought for the state's independence from Spain and incorporation into newly independent Mexico.

The highway into town is endless. Tuxtla (population 550,000), the state capital since 1892, doesn't have many conveniences for tourists, but you can get your bearings best by staying on the main drag, which will run you smack into the zócalo, known locally as the *parque central* and fronted by huge government buildings.

All the species at the ✪ **Miguel Alvarez del Toro Zoo** (a.k.a. ZooMAT) are native Chiapans, and the more docile creatures roam free. The 100-plus species on display include jaguars, marsupials, iguanas, quetzal birds, boa constrictors and other snakes, tapirs, eagles, and monkeys. Nature videos are often shown Saturday at 11 AM, and you can visit the tiny museum and the well-stocked gift shop. Admission is free, although the zoo was considering a $6 fee at press time. ⊠ *Calzada Cerro Hueco s/n, southeast of town off Libramiento Sur,* ☎ *961/4–47–01 or 961/4–47–65.* 🖭 *Free.* ☉ *Tues.–Sun. 9–5.*

Amateur archaeologists and botanists should head for **Parque Madero,** which includes the **Botanical Garden,** the free **Botanical Museum,** and the **Regional Museum of Chiapas.** The Regional Museum actually houses an excellent history museum, an ethnological museum, and a salon for revolving cultural exhibits. The botanical museum is unimpressive, but the garden is pleasant and has labels showing the native plant species. ⊠ *Northeast of downtown, between Av. Nte. 5a and Calle Ote. 11a,* ☎ *961/3–44–79 or 961/3–45–54.* 🖭 *Regional Museum $3, free Sun. and holidays.* ☉ *Garden Tues.–Sun. 9–6, museums Tues.–Sun. 9–5.*

The government-run **Casa de Artesanías** has a fine small museum of indigenous Indian cultures in Chiapas, as well as a good selection of regional handicrafts for sale. Among the local specialties: amber fashioned into necklaces, earrings, and pendants; hand-embroidered and brocaded table mats, blouses, and huipiles; leather bags; gold filigree jewelry; and lacquerware. ⊠ *Blvd. Dr. Belisario Domínguez 2035,* ☎ *961/2–22–75.* 🖭 *Free.* ☉ *Mon.–Sat. 10–3, 5–8.*

As its name suggests, the **Parque Jardín de la Marimba** (⊠ Av. Central and 8 Pte.) hosts marimba bands, which play regional dancing music. You can grab a partner and join in—every evening 7–9.

Dining and Lodging

$$$$ ✕ **Montebello.** Prime rib and Mexican specialties headline the menu at this intimate restaurant at the Camino Real—where every roll, cake, dessert, and tortilla is made on the premises. Montebello is most romantic at night, when the city lights shimmer into view. The elegance of the earth-tone decor is set off by an unusual white mural of the Sumidero cliffs sculpted into a wall. Live, unobtrusive violin and piano music plays after 2 PM. ⊠ *Blvd. Dr. Belisario Domínguez 1195,* ☎ *961/7–77–77. AE, DC, MC, V. Closed Sun.*

$$$ ✕ **El Asador Castellano** (The Castillian Grill). Mouthwatering Span-
★ ish dishes such as *calamares a la romana* (Roman calamari) and *poches
   estofadas con chistorra* (navy beans with sausage) as well as imported
   choice U.S. beef cuts can be paired with one of more than 50 imported
   wines difficult to find in Mexico City, let alone Chiapas. Service is very
   attentive and the presentation flawless. Make a reservation on week-
   ends. ⊠ *Blvd. Dr. Belisario Domínguez 2320-A,* ☎ *961/3–90–00.
   AE, DC, MC, V. Closes at 7 PM Sun.*

$$$ ✕ **Restaurant Algarabia.** Choose from a wide array of savory seafood
   dishes—some prepared at your table—at this spacious palapa. Try the
   camarones en salsa de queso (shrimp in cheese sauce) or any other of
   the Mexican-style shrimp dishes. Service is excellent, and a marimba
   band plays Tuesday through Sunday 2–6. ⊠ *Blvd. Dr. Belisario
   Domínguez 1440,* ☎ *961/4–71–48. AE, DC, MC, V.*

$$ ✕ **Las Pichanchas.** An outstanding variety of regional dishes, includ-
   ing tamales and cochito horneado, is available here, as well as live
   marimba music in the afternoon and evening, and folkloric dances 9
   PM–11 PM. The restaurant is a favorite among Mexican families. ⊠ *Av.
   Central Ote. 837,* ☎ *961/2–53–51. AE, DC, MC, V.*

$$$$ ▦ **Camino Real.** This hilltop oasis of luxury sets a standard for accom-
★ modations in Chiapas. Rooms surround a huge open-air pool and bar
   area with exotic vegetation. A concierge floor, business center with com-
   puter rentals, and meeting facilities draw business travelers; they enter-
   tain clients in the Azulejos restaurant, enclosed in a sky-blue glass dome
   (the delicious daily breakfast and lunch buffets are well worth the price),
   or at the upscale Montebello. All rooms have a view of the mountains,
   satellite TVs, safes, minibars, phones, and full bathroom amenities. This
   member of the Camino Real chain offers more services and amenities
   than others charging twice as much. ⊠ *Blvd. Dr. Belisario Domínguez
   1195, 29060,* ☎ *961/7–77–77, 01–800/272–1107, or 800/722–6466,*
   FAX *961/7–77–99,* WEB *www.caminoreal.com/tuxtla. 174 rooms, 36 suites.
   2 restaurants, bar, in-room safes, minibars, pool, beauty salon, sauna,
   2 tennis courts, health club, concierge floor, business services, meeting
   room, travel services, car rental. AE, DC, MC, V.*

$$$ ▦ **Hotel Arecas.** The Arecas is a haven of quiet gardens and tasteful colo-
   nial decor, with fruit trees, flowering plants, a secluded swimming pool,
   and bungalow-style junior suites. Both restaurants, the elegant Los Can-
   diles for international cuisine and the more informal La Calabaza for
   regional dishes, offer relaxing environments and good service. All rooms
   have air-conditioning and cable TV. Like the Flamboyant, the Arecas is
   10 minutes by car from the city center. ⊠ *Blvd. Dr. Belisario Domínguez
   1080, 29020,* ☎ *961/5–11–22 or 961/5–11–28,* FAX *961/5–11–21,* WEB
   *www.hotelarecas.com.mx. 44 rooms, 16 suites. 2 restaurants, bar, pool,
   dance club, meeting room, free parking. AE, DC, MC, V.*

$$$ ▦ **Hotel Flamboyant.** The rooms in this luxury hotel have a restful atmo-
   sphere and Moorish touches; all are air-conditioned and have TVs with
   some channels in English. Twenty-four rooms face the large garden,
   and a dozen more are off a smaller, tranquil inner garden. Capacious
   is the byword here: the pool is huge and the public areas vast. The restau-
   rant is light and airy, and the food is good, but the service is poor; the
   bar is dark and tacky. A disadvantage is the location—a 10-minute drive
   west of the town center. ⊠ *Blvd. Dr. Belisario Domínguez, Km 1081,
   29000,* ☎ *961/5–08–88 or 961/5–09–99,* FAX *961/5–00–87,* WEB *www.
   flamboyant.com.mx. 120 rooms, 2 suites. Restaurant, coffee shop, bar,
   pool, tennis court, travel services. AE, MC, V.*

$$ ▦ **Hotel María Eugenia.** Although a touch sterile, this air-conditioned
   downtown hotel has clean rooms with floral spreads as well as a flo-
   ral scent. There's cable TV and a nice pool surrounded by white
   wrought-iron furniture. ⊠ *Av. Central Ote. 507, 29000,* ☎ *961/3–37–*

67 or 961/3–37–70, FAX 961/3–28–60, WEB *www.mariaeugenia.com.mx.*
*83 rooms. Restaurant, bar, pool, meeting room, travel services, free
parking. AE, DC, MC, V.*

Sumidero Canyon

🔞 *23 km (14 mi) north of Tuxtla Gutiérrez.*

Sumidero Canyon came into being about 36 million years ago, with
the help of the Grijalva River, which flows north along the canyon's
floor. The fissure meanders for some 23 km (14 mi); its near-vertical
walls, partly obscured by vegetation, rise 3,500 ft at the highest point.
You can admire it from above, as there are five lookout points along
the highway; one of them, La Atalaya, has a restaurant.

Viajes Miramar (✉ Camino Real, Local 2, Tuxtla Gutiérrez, ☎ 961/
7–77–77 ext. 7230) offers a five-hour minivan trip for about $7 a per-
son. You can also take a taxi or bus to the Cahuare[ac] dock, 20 minutes from Tuxtla, just before Chiapa de Corzo, and then a boat trip to
the Chicoasen hydroelectric dam. The best time of day is 10–2, when
you won't have to wait long for your boat to fill up. The trip there and
back takes approximately two hours and costs about $7 a person
(there's a 10-person minimum). Boats also leave from Chiapa de Corzo
dock between 8 AM and 4 PM daily. From the boat you can admire the
canyon's steep, striated walls, some odd rock formations, and the animals—including crocodiles, ducks, pelicans, herons, raccoons, iguanas, and butterflies—that live inconspicuously at its base. As you visit
the canyon, consider the fate of the Chiapa Indians, who in the 16th
century jumped into it rather than face slavery at the hands of the
Spaniards.

THE ROAD TO PALENQUE
AND BEYOND

The road from San Cristóbal to Palenque veers slightly east on Highway 190 upon leaving town, then links up to Highway 199, which heads
north to Palenque. You'll pass Ocosingo and the turnoff to Toniná along
the first half of the journey, then Agua Azul and Misol-Há before reaching the ruins. It's sierra country most of the way until the mild valleys
around Ocosingo; the climate will get progressively hotter and more
humid as you descend from the highland and approach Palenque. The
vegetation will also change, from mountain pine to thick, green tropical foliage. To get to Villahermosa from Palenque, head north for 56
km (35 mi) on Highway 199, and then turn left onto Highway 186 at
Catazajá for a leisurely drive on a fairly straight road. Frequent buses
are available for all routes.

Toniná

🔺 ⑲ *98 km (61 mi) northeast of San Cristóbal; 118 km (73 mi) south and
east of Palenque.*

Between San Cristóbal and Palenque, on a paved road running along
the Jataté River in the mild Ocosingo Valley, is the archaeological site
of Toniná. The name means "house of stone" in Tzeltal. Excavations
indicate that the vanquished rulers of Palenque and Yaxchilán were
brought here as prisoners for execution. Several ball courts and the main
pyramid platform (taller than those of Tikal and Teotihuacán) have
been uncovered; a small, on-site museum exhibits many relics from the
site. Toniná, with its monumental architecture and noteworthy sculptures, is thought to be the last major Mayan ceremonial center to

flourish in this area. To get to the site, follow the road from Ocosingo, off Route 199. ⬚ *$2.50.* ⊙ *Daily 9:30–4.*

Lodging

$ 🏠 **Rancho Esmeralda.** This macadamia-nut farm has eight comfort-
★ able wooden cabins just a 15-minute walk from the ruins. The accommodations are rustic, with limited electricity and no phones; there
are clean latrines and a common bathhouse from which you can savor
the view as you soak in the extra-long claw-foot tub. The help is
friendly, and you could spend an afternoon just talking with the young
barman in the thatch-roof, communal dining area. Delicious, filling meals
(especially the buffet breakfast and dinner) are served at extra cost; the
coffee is organic—grown, roasted, and ground on the premises. The
congenial hosts can help arrange an air excursion to the Bonampak
and Yaxchilán ruins (about $100) and white-water rafting trips on the
Shumulja River (about $85 a day). Resident cowboy Valentín can take
you on a three- to four-hour horseback excursion ($20) through the
beautiful Ocosingo Valley, where more than 50 species of exotic birds
live year-round. Tent camping is also permitted. ⊠ *Turnoff about 8
km (5 mi) along road from Ocosingo to Toniná ruins, Apdo. 68,* ☎
no phone, FAX *967/3–07–11,* WEB *www.ranchoesmeralda.net. 8 cabins.
Restaurant, horseback riding, camping, free parking. No credit cards.*

Agua Azul

❷⓿ *68 km (42 mi) northwest of Toniná, 64 km (40 mi) southwest of
Palenque.*

The series of waterfalls and crystalline blue pools at Agua Azul is
breathtaking to behold during the dry season—from about November
through March (the water is murky in the rainy season). The site has
lost its sense of isolation since the road was paved in the 1980s; food
shacks and camping facilities sprang up, and the natural beauty has
been somewhat marred. Still, it's a breathtaking spot, and you can swim
in a series of interconnected pools. The falls are surrounded by giant
palm fronds and tropical flowers; monkeys and toucans frolic in the
vicinity. Six-hour trips, which include a visit to Misol-Há, cost about
$10 per person and include the entrance fees (50¢ per person or $2
per car); you can book with most any travel agency in Palenque. For
about $7 a person (including the entrance fee), you can ride with So-
ciedad Cooperative Chambalum (⊠ *Calle Allende at Av. Juárez s/n,
Palenque,* ☎ *no phone*) to both sites. Their service runs every 30 minutes, 6–6.

Misol-Há

❷❶ *46 km (29 mi) northeast of Agua Azul, 18 km (11 mi) southwest of
Palenque.*

If the single cascade at Misol-Há is smaller than those at Agua Azul,
the area surrounding it is also less peopled with vendors and less lit-
tered with trash. You can swim in the pool formed by the 100-ft cascade, or explore behind the falls, where a cave leads to another,
subterranean pool. Surrounded by oversize tropical vegetation, the site
has rustic rest rooms, restaurants, and campgrounds. *See* Agua Azul,
above, for how to get there.

Palenque

★ ⛰ ❷❷ *191 km (118 mi) northeast of San Cristóbal de las Casas, 150 km (93
mi) southeast of Villahermosa.*

THE ROUTE OF THE MAYA: A MESOAMERICAN GIZA

THE MAYA WERE OUTSTANDING architects, without compare in the Americas. They erected immense palaces and towering pyramids in less-than-hospitable climates without the aid of metal tools, the wheel, or beasts of burden. Their ancient cities still resound with the magnificence of their cultures, even though the civilizations have faded.

Río Usumacinta. Builders of pyramids of this style typically gave them additional height by placing them on hillsides or crests—as you'll see at the otherworldly Palenque—and the principal structures were covered with exquisite bas-reliefs carved in stone. The small one-story pyramid-top temples characteristically had vestibules and rooms adorned with vault ceilings. The wide, spacious chambers inside the pyramids had smaller, attached rooms filled with bas-relief carvings of important events that occurred during the reign of the ruler who built the pyramid. Río Usumacinta friezes slope inward, rather than standing perpendicular under the large roof combs. Finest examples: Palenque, Yaxchilán.

Río Bec. Influenced by Guatemala's Petén style, the pitch of these pyramids is rather steep, and the foundations elaborately decorated. The stairways on the outside of some pyramids were built for aesthetic rather than practical purposes, and were "false" (unclimbable). The principal structures were long, one-story affairs containing two or sometimes three tall towers. Each was capped by a large roof comb emboldened with a dramatic stucco facade. Río Bec is found only in what is now the state of Campeche. Finest examples: Calakmul, Xpuhil, Río Bec.

Chenes. Found mainly in Campeche, this style likewise had long, single-story structures. In this case they were divided into three distinct sections, each with its own doorway charmingly surrounded by a face of the rain god, Chaac, whose mouth is the entrance. Facades were smothered in serpentlike embellishments. Finest examples: Hochob, Chicanná.

Puuc. Uxmal is the most striking illustration of the beautifully proportioned Puuc style. Commonly found in the state of Yucatán, it of all styles looks like the "typical" Maya style. The buildings were designed in a low-slung, quadrangle shape and had many, many rooms. Exterior walls were probably kept plain in order to show off the friezes above, which were lavishly embellished with stone-mosaic deities surrounded by geometric and serpentine motifs. The corners of buildings were characteristically lined with the curl-nosed Chaac. Pyramids here didn't have roof combs. Finest examples: Uxmal, Labná, Kabah, Sayil.

Northeast Plains. The fusion of two Maya groups—the early Chichén Maya and later Itzá Maya—produced this Late Classic (AD 600–900) style famously exemplified by Chichén Itzá. Here new forms such as columns and grand colonnades were introduced. Palaces with row upon row of columns carved in the form of serpents looked over private patios, platforms were dedicated to the planet Venus, and pyramids were offered to Kukulcán (the plumed serpent god borrowed from the Toltecs, who called him Quetzalcóatl). Chichén Itzá is also famous for its temple-top, reclining, carved stone chacmool (a reclining figure with an offering tray carved in its middle)—another Itzá addition. Finest examples: Chichén Itzá, Mayapán.

Quintana Roo Coast. Although somewhat influenced by the Itzá Maya, a style entirely different eventually evolved here. The large, squat-looking, one-story buildings have interior columns, wood-beam-supported ceilings, and numerous figures of the descending or Upside Down god that began appearing in the Post-Classic era (900–1530). Friezes were distinctively decorated with small niches. Finest examples: Tulum, El Rey, San Gervasio.

— Patricia Alisau

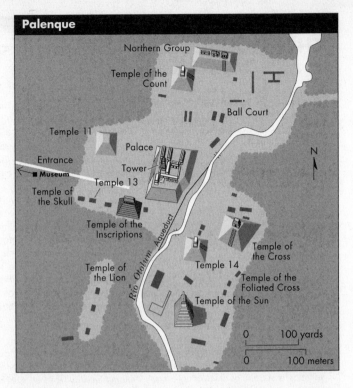

Palenque

Of all the Mayan ruins, none is more sublime than Palenque—only Tikal in Guatemala is its equal. Teotihuacán might be more monumental and Chichén Itzá more expansive, but Palenque possesses a mesmerizing quality, in part because of the intimacy that the surrounding jungle creates. In early morning or late afternoon, sunlight illuminates the structures in a hazy, iridescent glow. Birds call shrilly, and the local descendants of the Maya wander about collecting banana leaves, oranges, and avocados. You may even see a spider monkey or two, or hear their wild cries.

Antonio de Solis, a Spanish priest, accidently dug into a buried wall here in 1740 while he was trying to plant crops. In 1805 a royal Spanish expedition ventured here to follow up on the discovery. In 1832 an eccentric German count, Jean-Frederic Maximilien de Waldeck, set up house with his mistress for a year in a building known today as the Templo del Conde (Temple of the Count). Explorers John Lloyd Stephens and Frederick Catherwood lived briefly in the palace during their 1840 expedition. Serious excavations began in 1923, under the direction of Franz Blom, cofounder of the Na Bolom foundation in San Cristóbal. Work continued intermittently until 1952, when Alberto Ruz Lhuillier, a Mexican archaeologist, uncovered the tomb of the 7th-century ruler Pakal beneath the Temple of the Inscriptions. Since the early 1970s, groundbreaking work has been done on the Maya by archaeologists, linguists, and astronomers.

Palenque's elegance makes clear why archaeologist Sylvanus Morley called the Maya the "Greeks of the New World"—not only for their remarkable buildings, but also for the supple naturalism of the culture's art. The masters at work here shaped stone, stucco, and ceramics into ornate, lyrical designs. Artisans also took liberties here: relief sculpture of great expressiveness replaces the freestanding stelae of other Mayan cities.

The most important buildings of the site date from the Mid- to Late Classic period (AD 6th–9th centuries), although Palenque was inhabited as early as 1500 BC. At its zenith, the city dominated the greater part of Tabasco and Chiapas. The site was abandoned around AD 800, making it one of the earliest Mayan sites to be deserted in what was a west-to-east pattern of abandonment. The reasons for the Mayans' departure are still in debate.

Palenque's graceful tower—one of the site's signature structures—sets it apart from other Mayan settlements. The Temple of the Inscriptions, a 75-ft pyramid, is another. It was dedicated to Pakal, who took Palenque to its most glorious heights during his 28- to 38-year reign. He died around AD 692, having become the ruler at age 12 and living into his forties.

The ruling priest-kings communicated life at Palenque in elaborate glyphs and reliefs on the temples. The deciphering of a good portion of Palenque's hieroglyphics in 1988 has revolutionized scholars' understanding of both the Maya and the bloody history of Palenque. Only 800 of the thousands of glyphs have been deciphered, but they have already revealed the complex history of the Palenque dynasties. Exciting finds by archaeologists from the University of Texas in 1998 introduced a new character, Uc-Pakal-Kinich, into the lineage of Palenque rulers. Other clues unearthed at Temple 19 point to a probable liaison between rulers of Palenque and of Copán, in what is now Honduras.

In its heyday, Palenque encompassed an astonishing 128-plus square km (49 square mi). Artificial terraces were built to support the temples, which surrounded plazas, a ball court, altars, and burial grounds. The temples themselves had a complex array of corridors, narrow subterranean stairways, and galleries. And they served as fortresses in time of war. Only about 30% of the site has been excavated. Since late 1994, a huge portion of the ruins around the Temple of the Inscriptions has been reconstructed and is open. Explanations in Spanish, English, and Tzotzil have been placed at all major buildings.

As you enter the site, the first temple on your right is the reconstructed **Temple of the Skull,** which the Maya had painted red and blue in their time. A skull-shape stucco relief, presumed to be that of a rabbit, was found at the small entrance to the temple. It's now at the top of the stairs.

The **Temple of the Inscriptions** is just past Temple 13; its nine tiers correspond to the nine-level Mayan underworld. Atop this temple and the smaller ones around it are vestiges of roof combs—delicate vertical extensions that are among the features of southern Mayan cities. From the top, you'll get the best view of Palenque and an excellent orientation to its other buildings. Reaching the tomb inside involves a relatively easy, if slow, climb. Once at the summit, turn and take a long look back toward the once-mighty palace on the right. From the top of the Temple of Inscriptions, down the steep, damp flight of stairs 80 ft below is the **tomb of Pakal,** one of the first crypts found inside a Mexican pyramid. The tomb is no longer open to the public, but Pakal's remains along with his diadem and majestic jade, shell, and obsidian mask are on display at Mexico City's Museum of Anthropology. The intricately carved sarcophagus lid, weighing some 5 tons and measuring 10 by 7 ft, however, remains. A psychoduct—a stone tube in the shape of a snake through which Pakal's soul was thought to have passed to the netherworld—leads up to the temple. It can be difficult to make out the carvings on the slab, but they depict the ruler, prostrate beneath a sacred ceiba tree, who is still revered by the Maya today. The lords of the nine underworlds are carved into stucco reliefs on the walls around him.

In 1994, the small and unassuming **Temple 13**, attached to the Temple of the Inscriptions, revealed a royal tomb hidden in its depths. The tomb, which probably belonged to Pakal's mother or grandmother, is under investigation and isn't currently open to the public.

The patios, galleries, and other buildings that make up the **palace** are set on a 30-ft-high plinth. Stucco work adorns the pillars of the galleries and the inner courtyards. Inside are numerous friezes and masks, most of them depicting Pakal and his dynasty. Steam baths in the southwestern patio suggest that priests once dwelled in the adjoining cellars. The palace's iconic tower was built on three levels, representing the three levels of the universe as well as the movement of the stars.

To the east of the palace is the tiny Otulum River, which in ancient times was roofed over to form a 9-ft-high vaulted aqueduct. Cross the river and climb up 80 easy steps to arrive at the reconstructed **Plaza of the Cross,** which contains the Temple of the Foliated Cross, Temple of the Sun, Temple 14, and the Temple of the Cross, the largest of the group. Inside Temple 14, there's an underworld scene in stucco relief, done 260 days after Pakal died. The most exquisite roof combs are found on these buildings, which are open to the public.

To reach the cluster called the **Northern Group,** walk north along the river, passing the palace and then the unexcavated ball court on your left. There are five buildings here in various states of disrepair; the largest and best preserved is the **Temple of the Count.**

A short hike northeast of the Northern Group lies **Group C,** an area containing remains of the homes of Maya nobles and a few small temples shrouded in jungle. In order to maintain the natural setting in which the ruins were found, minimal restoration is being done. Human burials, funeral offerings of Jaina figurines, ceramics, and kitchen utensils have been found here as well as in the **Group B** area, which lies on the 20-minute "Ecological Path" hike through the jungle. On the way, you'll pass a small waterfall called El Baño de la Reina (The Queen's Bath). The path is poorly marked; be sure to veer left through the Grupo B ruins when you reach them.

The on-site **museum** has a remarkable collection of finely preserved heads of Maya deities in elaborate zoomorphic headdresses, discovered in front of the Temple of the Foliated Cross. The group includes 13 figures of the sun god Kinich Ahau. Also noteworthy are the handsome, naturalistic stucco faces of Maya men. Displays are labeled in English, Spanish, and Tzotzil. There's also a snack bar and a handicrafts store with weavings, hand-embroidered fabrics, leather, ceramics, amber jewelry, hand-painted wooden crosses, and children's toys. The museum can be reached from the main road leading to the ruins.

Since explanatory signs inside the ruins are scant and in Spanish, you may want to hire a multilingual guide at the ticket booth. They charge about $35 for a group of up to seven people. ⌧ *Ruins and museum $3. ☉ Ruins daily 8–4:45, museum Tues.–Sun. 9–3:45.*

Palenque Town

㉓ *8 km (5 mi) north of the ruins.*

Whereas cool highlander San Cristóbal has a polite but reserved exterior, Palenque Town wraps you in a warm tropical embrace. Its days as a sleepy cattle town are far behind, as the city swells with newcomers and longtime residents rush to turn family homes into rent-paying posadas. In only the past few years, thanks to tourism, upgraded services like e-mail servers have arrived; likewise ATMs and 24-hour long-distance phone service. Women and children from San Juan Chamula hawk crafts and souvenirs in front of restaurants and pharmacies along the principal downtown streets.

The principal landmark in Palenque Town is the chalk-white "cabeza Maya," a giant sculpture of the head of a Maya chieftain that graces the town's one traffic circle. West of downtown is the quiet neighborhood of La Cañada.

Dining and Lodging

$$$ ✕ **Maya Cañada.** This restaurant in La Cañada is the comely baby sis-
★ ter to the aging but still popular (and less expensive) Maya downtown. Sixties rock enlivens the atmosphere in the round, thatch-roof restaurant. Try the $3.50 set lunch menu, consisting of soup, a main dish, and dessert, or choose something from the extensive appetizer menu, which includes tacos and tostadas. Mexican wines are served, and there's a full bar. A trio plays music Thursday through Sunday 9–midnight. ⊠ *Calle Merle Green s/n, La Cañada,* 934/5–02–16. Downtown branch: ⊠ Av. Hidalgo and Independencia, ☎ 934/5–00–42. AE, MC, V.

$$$ ✕ **La Selva.** Although a stop on the tour-group route, this spacious *palapa*
★ (thatch-roof) restaurant is still popular with locals. The setting, surrounded by luxuriant jungle gardens, is superb, and so is the food, including the chips and salsa. There is a scrumptious Sunday brunch buffet after 1 PM for about $9. ⊠ *Carretera Ruinas Km 5,* ☎ 934/5–03–63. MC, V.

$$ ✕ **El Arbolito.** On the main road to the ruins, this fun and funky restaurant is full of souvenirs of old ranch life. There's a wall full of hats, each inscribed with a different Mexican proverb. Other walls have mounted animal heads and pelts. It's no surprise that the house specialty is meat. Favorites include the spicy *consomé de borrego especial,* a broth with barbecued sheep, onions, and fresh cilantro. Beef tips in smoky chipotle sauce or other, mild chili sauces are served with beans, rice, garnish, and piping hot tortillas. ⊠ *Carretera Palenque–Pakalná Km 1.5, across from Days Inn,* ☎ 934/5–09–00. MC, V.

$$ ✕ **Casa Grande.** This pleasant, art-filled café has an upstairs terrace overlooking Palenque's zócalo. Typical Mexican fare such as tacos and fried bananas complement the more exotic seafood dishes, which are expertly seasoned with Chiapan spices. This is the perfect place to perk up with an espresso or wind down with a glass of wine. ⊠ *Av. Hidalgo 6, corner of Jiménez,* ☎ 934/5–01–25. No credit cards.

$ ✕ **Pizzería Palenque.** This favorite spot of travelers has thin-crust pizzas (with a Mexican touch) that are so good, even Italians rave about them. It's not far from the downtown bus station. ⊠ *Av. Juárez 168,* ☎ 934/5–03–32. No credit cards.

$$$$ ▥ **Misión Palenque.** Four blocks from the zócalo in the downtown area, this hotel is fronted by a huge green lawn and pretty grounds but has plain, motel-like rooms. All are air-conditioned and have cable TV and phones; the tiny patios lack furniture. The terraced restaurant glows nightly with candlelight. Off Route 199, it has a free shuttle bus to the ruins. Tour groups, which constitute a large percentage of the clientele, rotate in and out daily. Note that you'll be quoted a higher price if you call the 800 number. ⊠ *Rancho San Martín de Porres, 29960,* ☎ 934/5–02–41 or 800/448–8355, FAX 934/5–03–00, WEB *www.hotelesmision.com.mx. 208 rooms, 2 suites. Restaurant, bar, pool, steam room, 2 tennis courts, shops, travel services, free parking.* AE, DC, MC, V.

$$$ ▥ **Chan Kah.** Four kilometers (2½ miles) from the ruins in a paradisi-
★ acal jungle setting that is also a forest reserve, Chan Kah shouldn't be confused with the sister hotel of the same name in downtown Palenque. There's a stone-lined, lagoon-style pool, aromatic jasmine bushes, and a stream flowing around the back. The outdoor restaurant is average,

and meals are accompanied by recorded Mexican music. But the very comfortable bungalows have wide terraces, mahogany furnishings, and ceiling fans and/or air-conditioning. Bungalows 6–10 have views of the pool and stream. The emphasis here is on tranquility: there are no TVs or phones in the rooms. ⊠ *Carretera Ruinas Km 3.5, 29960,* ☎ 𝖥𝖠𝖷 *934/5–11–00 or 934/5–11–34,* 𝖶𝖤𝖡 *www.chan-kah.zl.com.mx. 76 bungalows. Restaurant, bar, pool, free parking. AE, MC, V.*

$$$ ▦ **Ciudad Real Palenque.** This yellow and white colonial-style hotel sits amid glorious jungle gardens of the type only possible in Palenque. A small waterfall and creek run through the grounds. All rooms have cable TV and air-conditioning as well as a balcony facing the gardens. ⊠ *Carretera Pakal-Na Km 1.5, 29960,* ☎ 𝖥𝖠𝖷 *934/5–12–85, 934/5–13–15, or 934/5–13–43,* 𝖶𝖤𝖡 *www.ciudadreal.com.mx. 69 rooms, 3 suites. Restaurant, bar, pool, travel services, free parking. AE, MC, V.*

$$$ ▦ **Hotel Calinda Nututún Palenque.** This property has plain, ample rooms with tile floors. There is a $7 difference between rooms with a small, furnitureless terrace and TV and those without. The real draw is the large natural pool formed from a bend in the Nututún River, which runs through the grounds. Camping is permitted near the river for about $5.50 a person. ⊠ *Carretera Palenque–Ocosingo Km 3.5, Apdo. 74, 29960,* ☎ *934/5–01–00, 934/5–01–61, or 800/221–2222,* 𝖥𝖠𝖷 *934/5–06–20,* 𝖶𝖤𝖡 *www.reservhotel.com. 55 suites, 12 rooms. Restaurant, bar, pool, camping, playground, free parking. AE, MC, V.*

$$ ▦ **Casa Inn Tulijá.** You can't beat the price or location of this cheerful little hotel, which is about a 10-minute walk from downtown. It has the basics for a comfortable stay: color cable TV, air-conditioning, and firm beds, although rooms are smallish. The 25-m-long pool is a great boon for swimmers. The tequila bar boasts more than 35 brands of the distilled agave liquor. ⊠ *Apdo. 57, Carretera Ruinas Km 27.5, 29960,* ☎ *934/5–01–04 or 800/900–1400,* 𝖥𝖠𝖷 *934/5–01–63,* 𝖶𝖤𝖡 *www.tulija.mx. 48 rooms. Restaurant, bar, pool, billiards, laundry service, meeting room, travel services, free parking. AE, MC, V.*

Bonampak

🔺 ㉔ *183 km (113 mi) southeast of Palenque.*

Bonampak, which means "painted walls" in Mayan, is renowned for its courtly murals of ancient Maya life. The settlement was built on the banks of the Lacanjá River during the 7th and 8th centuries and was uncovered again in 1946. Explorer Jacques Soustelle called it "a pictorial encyclopedia of a Mayan city." In remarkable ocher and faience colors, the scenes portrayed in the three rooms of the **Templo de las Pinturas** graphically recall subjects such as life at court and the prelude and aftermath of battle. It's open daily 8–5; admission is $2.50. For an extra $5 a Lacandon guide will join you near the park entrance. Segments of the murals are deteriorating because the high humidity in the area eats away at the colors, and thick white deposits of calcium from dripping water have covered some of the paintings completely. In 1984 Mexican experts devised a technique for cleaning and restoring the murals, and with the help of the National Geographic Society—and computerized, digital amplification techniques—remarkable details and color have come to light. It stands to reason that the reproductions at the archaeological museums in Mexico City and Villahermosa are more legible than the on-site specimens.

Until recently, only the most devoted fans of the Maya attempted the trip to the ruins of Bonampak and Yaxchilán. Now, however, you can drive or take a three-hour bus ride from Palenque on the newly paved Highway 198 directly to Bonampak. If you drive, hook up with the tour groups that meet around 6 AM in Palenque and travel together for added safety. They are escorted by a highway patrolman and a Green Angel truck that can assist you in case of a mechanical problem. Buses or tour vans will take you all the way to the ruins, or drop you at Lacanjá and let you hike the last 3 km (2 mi) into Bonampak, as was done before the road was built.

Getting to Yaxchilán still requires a one-hour jungle boat ride on the Usumacinta River; you must first drive or take a bus to the small town of Frontera Corozal, just off Highway 198, where boats depart for the ruins and Guatemala. This is best arranged through travel agencies or state tourist offices in Mexico City, Palenque, or San Cristóbal de Las Casas, which can also arrange for you to stay at the wonderful Tzeltal Indian cooperative Escudo Jaguar. Be sure to wear sturdy shoes, and bring insect repellent, good sunglasses, and a hat to protect yourself from mosquitoes, ticks, sand flies, undergrowth, and the jungle sun.

Yaxchilán

★ ▲ ㉕ *50 km (31 mi) northeast of Bonampak, 190 km (118 mi) southeast of Palenque.*

Excavations at Yaxchilán (yash-chee-*lan*), on the banks of the Usumacinta River, have uncovered stunning temples and delicate carvings in an isolated jungle setting. Spider monkeys and toucans are, at this point, more prolific than tourists, and howler monkeys growl like lions from the towering *chico zapote* (fruit tree) and hundred-year-old ceiba trees. Yaxchilán, which means "place of green stones," reached its cultural peak during the Late Classic period, from about AD 680 to 770. It is dominated by two acropolises containing a palace, temples with finely carved lintels, and great staircases. Until recently, the Lacandon, who live in the vicinity, made pilgrimages to this site in the heart of the jungle, leaving behind "god pots" (incense-filled ceramic bowls) in honor of ancient deities. They were particularly awed by the headless sculpture of Yaxachtun (ya-sha-*tun*) at the entrance to the temple (called Structure 33) and believed that the world would end when its head was replaced on its torso.

Yaxchilán was situated on the trade route between Palenque and Tikal, and the existence of a 600-ft bridge crossing the Usumacinta River to connect Yaxchilán to Guatemalan territory has been discovered. The engineering know-how of the people of Yaxchilán is still being deciphered by modern-day engineers. The site was once threatened with destruction by a huge dam to be built by Mexico and Guatemala. Thankfully, plans seem to have been put off indefinitely due to lack of funds. 🎟 *Free.* ☉ *Daily 9–5.*

Lodging

$$ 🏨 **Escudo Jaguar.** This ecotourism project 144 km (89 mi) south of
★ Palenque is run by the local Tzeltal people and is designed to bring people closer to the Maya ruins of Bonampak and Yaxchilán. If you don't mind going a bit rustic, it's the ideal place to stay while you take in the jungle and both archaeological sites. There are 13 comfortable wooden cabins. Each has a wide cement veranda with two large, colorful hammocks for lounging. Inside, the thatch-roof cabins have screened windows, mosquito nets, and fans. The restaurant serves sandwiches and shakes in addition to full breakfasts, lunches, and dinners. It's best to book trips to Bonampak and Yaxchilán ahead of time, mentioning that you want to stay overnight at Escudo Jaguar. You must call the Miditel operator in Mexico City for reservations. ⊠ *Frontera Corozal, Ocosingo; reservations: Miditel operator,* ☎ *5/147–*

93–00, ext. 52–01–64–41 FAX *ext. 52–01–64–40. 13 cabins. Restaurant, free parking. No credit cards.*

VILLAHERMOSA AND TABASCO

Graham Greene's succinct summation of Tabasco in *The Power and the Glory* as a "tropical state of river and swamp and banana grove" captures its essence. Although the state played an important role in the early history of Mexico, its past is rarely on view. Instead, it's Tabasco's modern-day status as a supplier of oil that defines it. Set on a humid coastal plain and crisscrossed by 1,930 km (1,197 mi) of rivers, low hills, and unexplored jungles, the land is still rich in banana and cacao plantations. Shantytowns and refineries are for the most part invisible to the visitor, who on bus trips passes small ranches with pastures of tall, green grass feeding horses and beef cattle. The capital city of Villahermosa epitomizes the mercurial development of Tabasco (the airplane was here before the automobile). Thanks to oil and urban renewal, the cramped and ugly neighborhoods in the mosquito-ridden town of the 1970s have been replaced by spacious boulevards, lush green parks, and cultural centers. Sandwiched between the Grijalva River and the historic downtown, the Zona Luz has been redone as a brick-paved pedestrian zone housing galleries and museums in addition to restaurants, ice cream shops, and a Howard Johnson hotel.

This is not to say that the rest of Tabasco has nothing to offer. There are beaches, lagoons, caves, and nature reserves, but the tourism infrastructure is minimal. The fired-brick Mayan ruins of Comalcalco attest to the influence of Palenque. Probably the most interesting region is the one to the south and east of Villahermosa, where rivers and canyons are home to jaguars, deer, and alligators.

Tabasco—specifically the mouth of the Grijalva River—lay along the route of the Spanish explorations of Mexico in 1518–19. At that time, the state's rivers and waterways, along which the Maya lived, served as a trade route between the peoples of the north and those of the south. When the Spaniards came to Tabasco, they had to bridge 50 rivers and contend with swarms of mosquitoes, beetles, and ants—as well as the almost unbearable heat. At the same time, the region was so lush that one early chronicler termed it a Garden of Eden.

The Spanish conquest was made easier by the extreme antipathy and tribal warfare between the Tabascans and their Aztec overlords. Among the 20 slave women turned over to the Spaniards upon their arrival in the Aztec capital was a Chiapan named Malintzín (or Malinche), who was singled out by the Spaniards for her ability to speak both the Maya and the Nahuatl languages. Called Doña Marina by the Spaniards, she learned Spanish and became not only Cortés's mistress and the mother of his illegitimate son but also an interpreter of Indian customs. Malinche's cooperation helped the conquistador vanquish both Moctezuma and Cuauhtémoc, the last Aztec rulers. Even today, "La Malinche" is synonymous with "traitor" throughout Mexico.

Until the early 20th century, Tabasco slumbered. It didn't become a state until 1924. After the American Civil War, traders from the southern United States began operating in the region and on its rivers, hauling the precious mahogany trees upstream from Chiapas and shipping them north from the small port of Frontera. This was Tabasco's most prosperous era until the discovery of oil some 50 years ago and the oil boom of the 1980s.

Villahermosa

26 *821 km (509 mi) southeast of Mexico City, 632 km (392 mi) southwest of Mérida.*

There are a good many ways to spend your time in Tabasco's capital. The Zona Luz (a.k.a. Zona Remodelada) is a grid of pedestrian-only streets with restored colonial buildings, sidewalk cafés, galleries, and museums. Most people make a beeline for the **Carlos Pellicer Museo Regional de Antropología** (Regional Museum of Anthropology). Named after the man who donated many of the artifacts and whom the locals call the "poet laureate of Latin America" (1897–1978), the museum is on the right bank of the Grijalva and is part of the huge CICOM cultural complex dedicated to research on the Olmec and Maya (which is what the Spanish acronym CICOM stands for). It provides one of the last tranquil vistas of Villahermosa as it might have looked 50 years ago. Note that all the explanations are in Spanish.

Much of the collection is devoted to Tabasco and the Olmec, or "inhabitants of the land of rubber," who flourished in Tabasco as early as 1200 to 1300 BC and disappeared about AD 800. The Olmecs have long been honored as inventors of the numerical and calendrical systems that spread throughout the region. The pyramid is also attributed to them. Some of the most interesting artifacts of the Olmec, apart from the remarkable stone sculptures and giant stone heads on view at Parque Museo La Venta, are the remnants of their jaguar cult displayed here. The jaguar symbolized the earth fertilized by rain (i.e., procreation), and many Olmec sculptures portray half-human, half-jaguar figures, and jaguar babies. Other sculptures portray human heads emerging from the mouth of a jaguar, bat gods, bird-headed humans, and female fertility figurines.

Many of Mexico's ancient cultures are represented on the upper two floors, from the red-clay dogs of Colima and the nose rings of the Huichol Indians of Nayarit to the huge burial urns of the Chontal Maya, who built Comalcalco. The CICOM complex also houses a theater, restaurant, public library, and handicrafts shop. ⊠ *Periféico Carlos Pellicer 511, an extension of the malecón (boardwalk),* ☎ *93/12–63–44.* 🎟 *About $1.* ⊘ *Tues.–Sun. 9–8.*

The giant stone heads and other figures carved by the Olmec were salvaged from the oil fields of La Venta, on the western edge of Tabasco near the state of Veracruz. They are on display in the 8-hectare **Parque Museo La Venta,** in a tropical garden on the beautiful Lago de las Ilusiones (Lake of Illusions)—also founded by Carlos Pellicer, in 1958. The 6-ft-tall, bold-featured carved stone heads, wearing what look like helmets and weighing up to 20 tons, have sparked endless scholarly debate. It has been theorized that they depict ancient Phoenician slaves or space invaders. The latest and least outlandish (or offensive) theory is that the faces on the sculptures—very similar to today's Tabasco Maya—are actual portraits of successful Olmec athletes, war heroes, and other public figures. La Venta contains 33 sculptures, including jaguars, priests, monsters, stelae, and stone altars. Within the park is a **zoo** with creatures such as Tabascan river crocodiles, deer, jaguars, coatimundi, monkeys, and wild parrots. There's also a gift shop and several outdoor stands selling embroidered blouses, T-shirts, and souvenirs. ⊠ *Blvd. Ruíz Cortines near Paseo Tabasco,* ☎ *93/14–16–52.* 🎟 *$1.50.* ⊘ *Daily 8–5 (ticket booth closes at 4), zoo closed Mon.*

The small **Museo de la Historia Natural** (Natural History Museum) is just outside the entrance to the park. Of most interest are the displays of Tabasco's native plants and animals, many of which are now under government protection. Other rooms are dedicated to geology, evolution, and the solar system. ⊠ *Blvd. Ruíz Cortines next to Parque Museo La Venta,* ☎ *no phone.* 🎫 *$1.* ☉ *Tues.–Sun. 9–4.*

One of Villahermosa's newest attractions is **Yumká,** which means "the spirit that looks after the forest" in Chontal Maya. It's a nature reserve spread over 250 acres of jungle, savannah, and wetlands. Half-hour guided walking tours take you over a hanging bridge and past free-roaming endangered or threatened species such as spider monkeys, red macaws, toucans, crocodiles, turtles, and native *tepezcuintles* (a giant rodent). Next comes a longer aerial tram ride past Asian and African species such as elephant and zebra. Optional $1 boat tours glide past birds wading or taking flight. ⊠ *16 km (10 mi) from downtown, before the airport at Poblado Dos Montes,* ☎ *93/56–01–19 or 93/56–01–15,* FAX *93/56–01–07.* 🎫 *$2.* ☉ *Daily 9–5 (ticket window closes at 4).*

Dining and Lodging

$$$$ ✕ **El Mesón del Duende.** This restaurant, whose name translates as the House of the Elf, adds a regional accent to standard meat and fish dishes. Try the house favorites, *filete en salsa de espinaca y queso* (beef fillet in a spinach and cheese sauce) and *la posta de robalo* (grilled snook). The modest decor is in keeping with the family-style atmosphere. ⊠ *Gregorio Méndez 1703,* ☎ *93/15–13–24. AE, MC, V.*

$$$ ✕ **Los Tulipanes.** Tucked between the Esperanza Iris Theater and the
★ Carlos Pellicer Regional Museum of Anthropology in the CICOM complex, spacious Los Tulipanes specializes in seafood and has a soothing river view. Try the regional appetizers, including stuffed tortillas and *empanadas* (turnovers stuffed with crab or shrimp), or the Tabasco specialty pejelagarto, a succulent fish. The same owners run the Capitán Buelo ($$$), a small cruiser that runs 1½-hour dining trips on the Grijalva River twice daily ($5 minimum consumption). Board on the malecón at the foot of Lerdo de Tejada, or call Los Tulipanes for reservations. Daily (except Monday) at 3:30 and 9:30 PM; Sunday 1:30 and 3:30. ⊠ *Periférico Carlos Pellicer 511,* ☎ *93/12–92–09,* FAX *93/12–92–17. AE, MC, V.*

$$ ✕ **La Hacienda Azul.** This popular spot for scrumptious oysters (cooked just about any way you like them) and other seafood has live traditional musicians on weekend nights in the large, air-conditioned section of the restaurant. ⊠ *Av. Ruíz Cortines 1506,* ☎ FAX *93/15–34–94. AE, DC, MC, V.*

$$ ✕ **La Fontana Italiana Trattoria.** If you're tiring of Mexican cuisine, enjoy Italian fare (including pizza) at this air-conditioned restaurant near the Parque Museo La Venta. It's a favorite among locals. ⊠ *Av. Ruíz Cortines 1410, Col. Lopez Mateos,* ☎ FAX *93/14–32–83. AE, MC, V.*

$$$$ 🏨 **Calinda Viva & Spa Villahermosa.** This attractively remodeled five-story hotel has all the amenities you'd ever possibly need. There's an enormous square pool with two hot tubs, surrounded by lounge chairs and umbrella-shaded tables. All rooms have air-conditioning, FM stereos, color satellite TV, and small balconies. They're also equipped with coffeemakers, ironing boards, and irons. You can use the computer room to check e-mail and later go to the gym and work out, ending the day with a relaxing massage and sauna. The restaurant serves many regional dishes, with a daily breakfast and lunch buffet. ⊠ *Av. Ruíz Cortines at Paseo Tabasco s/n, Col. Linda Vista, 86050,* ☎ *93/15–00–00 or 800/711–5555,* FAX *93/15–30–73. 239 rooms, 1 suite. Restaurant, 2 bars, pool, massage, sauna, steam room, exercise room, dance club. AE, MC, V.*

$$$$ 🏨 **Camino Real.** This inviting nine-story resort property at the fringe of the Tabasco 2000 shopping complex has air-conditioned rooms with carpet, bathtubs, cable TV, and minibars. The rambling lobby, with rat-

tan furniture in attractive niches, leads to the Tabasco 2000 mall, which has the largest number of upscale stores in Villahermosa. Shaded by bamboo curtains, the restaurant's floor-to-ceiling windows overlook a lovely garden. There's live entertainment in the lobby lounge nightly. Continental breakfast and an appetizer hour are offered for those staying in the more capacious rooms on the executive floor. ⊠ *Paseo Tabasco 1407, 86030,* ☏ *93/16–44–00 or 800/722–6466,* FAX *93/16–44–00,* WEB *www. caminoreal.com. 180 rooms, 16 suites. Restaurant, bar, coffee shop, room service, pool, beauty salon, exercise room, travel services, car rental, free parking. AE, DC, MC, V.*

$$$$ 🏨 **Hyatt Regency Villahermosa.** This American-style luxury hotel offers the amenities of the worldwide Hyatt chain: air-conditioned rooms with cable TV, voice mail, and minibars, and two executive floors with concierge service. Rooms have marble floors and polished wood furnishings. The La Ceiba Café has pleasing tropical decor and a superb daily breakfast buffet ($10) to which local families flock on Sunday. In the lobby, El Plataforma video bar is decked out like the inside of an offshore oil platform with photos of oilmen at work; there is live music nightly at 8 in the El Flamboyant bar. ⊠ *Av. Juárez 106, Zona Hotelera, 86050,* ☏ *93/15–12–34 or 800/228–9000,* FAX *93/15–12–35,* WEB *www.hyatt.com. 166 rooms, 9 suites, 32 Regency Club rooms. 2 restaurants, 2 bars, pool, 2 tennis courts, travel services, car rental. AE, DC, MC, V.*

$$$ 🏨 **Cencali.** This two-story hotel, across from La Venta museum and park, sits on a lagoon and is surrounded by lush greenery; it has the best view in town. Most of the cheerfully decorated rooms have lots of light; 30 of the best also have balconies overlooking the lagoon, which is fringed with coconut-palm, mango, and cacao trees. All rooms have bathtubs, air-conditioning, phones, and cable TV. Don't miss the fabulous lobby mural of pre-Columbian indigenous life (inspired by the *Popol Vuh*) by Tabascan master Daniel Montúy (1925–). The airy La Isla restaurant, overlooking the pool and the lagoon, has a daily breakfast buffet ($8.50). ⊠ *Av. Juárez and Paseo Tabasco, 86040,* ☏ FAX *93/ 15–19–99,* WEB *www.cencali.com.mx. 112 rooms, 8 suites. Restaurant, bar, pool. AE, DC, MC, V.*

$$$ 🏨 **Maya Tabasco Best Western.** A few blocks from the first-class (ADO) bus station, the Maya Tabasco has rooms with air-conditioning, cable TV, and phones; a rather plain lobby; and an energetic staff. This hotel is outclassed by others of similar price range, but it will do if your first choices are booked. You can check out open-mike night in the new Belle Epoque Trova Bar Café, smack in the middle of the swimming pool. ⊠ *Av. Ruíz Cortines 907, 86000,* ☏ *93/12–11–11 or 01–800/237–7700,* FAX *93/12–10–97,* WEB *www.bestwestern.com. 149 rooms, 3 suites. Restaurant, bar, café, pool, dance club, travel services, car rental. AE, DC, MC, V.*

$$ 🏨 **Howard Johnson.** This five-story hotel is conveniently located in the pedestrian-only Zona Luz area, not far from the historic downtown and the malecón. It has lots of conveniences for its price range, including cable TV, complimentary newspaper, room service, and an Internet café. Weekend rates offer a substantial discount (as do most business-oriented hotels here). The coffee shop's attentive waiters serve mugs of hot coffee with real cream and refills. ⊠ *Aldama 404, 86000,* ☏ FAX *93/14–46–45,* WEB *www.hojo.com.mx. 93 rooms, 6 suites. Coffee shop, bar, room service, free parking. AE, DC, MC, V.*

$$ 🏨 **Plaza Independencia.** There's a lot to recommend this attractive hotel besides an excellent location between the Grijalva River and the Plaza de Armas. Common areas are overwashed in Mexican pink, sky blue, and sunny yellow paint, and there's a midsize pool in the back patio. Some of the rooms have wacky decorations, with mint-green and

orange furnishings that clash with cotton bedspreads in other bright colors. Others rooms are more subdued. All have room safes, closets, cable TV, and air-conditioning. Ask for a room with a balcony overlooking the river. ⊠ *Av. Independencia 123, 86000,* ☎ *93/12–12–99,* FAX *93/14–47–24,* WEB *www.hotelesplaza.com.mx. 88 rooms, 1 jr. suite. Restaurant, bar, in-room safes, pool, free parking. AE, DC, MC, V.*

Comalcalco

 ㉗   *60 km (37 mi) northwest of Villahermosa off Rte. 187.*

Comalcalco, which means "place of the clay griddles" (bricks) in Nahuatl, is the most-important Mayan site in Tabasco. The abundant cacao trees in the region provided food and livelihood for a booming population during the Late Classic period (AD 600–900); it was founded approximately in the 1st century BC. The site marks the westernmost reach of the Maya, and descendants of its builders, the Chontal, still live in the vicinity. This site is unique among Maya cities for its use of fired brick (made of sand, seashells, and clay), as the Tabasco swamplands lacked the stone for building that was found elsewhere in the empire. The bricks were inscribed and painted with figures of reptiles and birds, geometric figures, and drawings of hands and feet before being covered with stucco. The major pyramid on the Great Eastern Acropolis, is decorated with large stucco masks of the sun god Kinich Ahau and carvings. The burial sites are another radical departure from Mayan custom: the dead were placed in cone-shaped clay urns, in a fetal position. Some have been left in situ, others are on display in the site **museum,** which houses many of the artifacts that were uncovered here. ⊠ *About $2.50, free Sun.* ☼ *Daily 10–4:30.*

Paraíso

㉘   *19 km (12 mi) north of Comalcalco.*

As you head toward the Gulf of Mexico coast and Paraíso, stop at one of the cacao plantations and chocolate factories. To visit **Hacienda Cholula,** about 2 km (1¼ mi) from Comalcalco, call ahead (☎ 933/4–38–15) to arrange a free tour in English. You'll learn everything about cocoa, from the plant to the chocolate stage. The cocoa bean was used as currency here in Pre-Hispanic times.

From here, continue on to the coast where you'll get a glimpse of small-town life. Climb nearby **Teodomiro Hill** for a spectacular view of Las Flores lagoon and coconut plantations. Small seafood restaurants and several small hotels dot the shore here; others are a few kilometers inland, in town. To take a boat ride around a mangrove-lined lagoon, go to **Puerto Ceiba,** a fishing community whose inhabitants breed and harvest oysters, just 15 km (8 mi) southeast of Paraíso. As you cross the bridge over Mecoacán Lagoon, you'll see **La Posta** restaurant on the right, where you can take a boat ride (about $10 for up to 10 people) around the lagoon. Afterwards, eat some of the freshest seafood you've ever tasted at this restaurant that overlooks the water.

CHIAPAS AND TABASCO A TO Z

To research prices, get advice from other travelers, and book travel arrangements, visit www.fodors.com.

AIR TRAVEL

The San Cristóbal Airport serves Mexico City daily on Aeromar. The closest major airport to San Cristóbal is in Tuxtla Gutiérrez, 85 km (53 mi) to the west. Villahermosa is the only international gateway in

Tabasco, with one flight arriving daily from Atlanta, Georgia. You can fly into Villahermosa, Tuxtla Gutiérrez, or San Cristóbal from Mexico City, or from smaller Mexican cities to Villahermosa and Tuxtla Gutiérrez.

CARRIERS

Aeroméxico has three daily nonstop flights to Villahermosa from Mexico City and one flight daily to Atlanta, Georgia. Mexicana has five daily nonstop flights to Mexico City from Villahermosa. Both airlines have connecting flights to other Mexican cities. Aviacsa flies to Villahermosa nonstop from Mexico City. AeroCalifornia has one daily nonstop flight from Villahermosa to Mexico City. Aerocaribe, Mexicana's regional line, serves southwest Mexico, Palenque, Campeche, Merida, and Flores/Tikal from Villahermosa.

From Tuxtla Gutiérrez, Aerocaribe flies nonstop to Mexico City, Oaxaca, and Villahermosa; from Villahermosa, the flight continues on to Palenque. Aerocaribe also flies between Palenque and Flores, Guatemala (near the Tikal ruins), and Tuxtla Gutiérrez (with connections to Oaxaca and Mexico City). Aviacsa also has direct flights to Tuxtla Gutiérrez from Mexico City, Oaxaca, and Tapachula; from Cancún, Guadalajara, and other cities you have to connect through Mexico City.

➤ AIRLINES & CONTACTS: **AeroCalifornia** (☎ 93/16–80–00 in Villahermosa). **Aerocaribe** (☎ 93/16–50–46 in Villahermosa; 961/2–16–92 or 961/2–00–20 in Tuxtla Gutiérrez). **Aeromar** (☎ 961/4–30–03 in Tuxtla Gutiérrez). **Aeroméxico** (☎ 93/12–15–28 or 93/12–95–54 in Villahermosa). **Aviacsa** (☎ 93/16–57–33 in Villahermosa; 961/2–80–81 or 961/1–20–00 in Tuxtla Gutiérrez). **Mexicana** (☎ 93/16–31–32, 93/16–31–33, 93/16–31–34, or 93/16–31–35 in Villahermosa).

AIRPORTS AND TRANFERS

Two airports serve Tuxtla: Llano San Juan Airport, which is in the town of Ocozocoautla, 22 km (14 mi) west of the city, and Terán Airport, 8 km (5 mi) southwest of the city center. Flights are routed to one of these two airports depending on meteorological conditions, as fog is frequently a problem.

The Capitan Carlos A. Rovirosa Airport, 15 km (9 mi) to the south, in Rancheria Dos Montes, serves Villahermosa.

The San Cristóbal Airport opened in October 1999; it has daily flights to Mexico City.

➤ AIRPORT INFORMATION: **Capitan Carlos A. Rovirosa Airport** (☎ 93/56–01–57 or 93/56–01–56). **Llano San Juan Airport** (☎ 961/2–29–20 or 961/3–50–74). **San Cristóbal Airport** (✉ Corazón de María Km 17, ☎ 967/4–30–16). **Terán Airport** (☎ 961/5–04–98 or 961/5–14–37).

AIRPORT TRANSFERS

You can catch a *colectivo* (shared minivan) to San Cristóbal at either of the two airports in Tuxtla Gutiérrez: from the Llano San Juan Airport, it costs about $6 a person; from the Terán Airport, $4.

You can catch a colectivo taxi from San Cristóbal to Tuxtla at the corner of Boulevard Juan Sabines Gutiérrez and Avenida Ignacio Allende, across from the second-class bus station. The taxi ($5 per person) will leave when it has four passengers.

BUS TRAVEL

From Palenque, first- and luxury-class service is available to Ocosingo (two hours), Villahermosa (2½ hours), San Cristóbal (four hours), Campeche (six hours), Tuxtla Gutiérrez (seven hours), Mérida (eight hours), Cancún (11 hours), and Mexico City (12 hours) on the first-class ADO and Cristóbal Colón. Buses leave from the ADO bus terminal. If you can't get a first-class bus, many of the same destinations can be reached on the second-class buses Omnibus de Chiapas and Express Plus, both a few doors away from the ADO bus terminal.

From San Cristóbal, Cristóbal Colón bus station has deluxe and first-class buses to major destinations in Chiapas and beyond. Suburbans and vans of Corazón de María (no phone) leave next door to the Cristóbal Colón terminal for Tuxtla Gutiérrez as soon as they fill up (about every 20 minutes) 5 AM–10 PM and cost about $4. From the same location, you can also take a suburban or van of Tres Estrellas (no phone) to Comitáfor about $2.50. Second-class service on Transportes Tuxtla Express Plus to Tuxtla, Palenque, and Comitán departs from the terminal at Avenida Ignacio Allende, ½ block from Boulevard Juan Sabines Gutiérrez, about four blocks to the west. You can purchase bus tickets without going to the bus terminal at Ticket Bus.

From Tuxtla Gutiérrez, Cristóbal Colón bus station offers deluxe and first-class service between Tuxtla and Oaxaca, Palenque, Villahermosa, Tapachula, Mérida, Mexico City, San Cristóbal, Cancún, Puerto Escondido, and Playa del Carmen. First- and second-class transportation within the state is available on Sociedad de Transportes Dr. Rodulfo Figueroa. You can get from Tuxtla to San Cristóbal by first-class bus, which leaves several times each day (two hours; about $3.50).

From Villahermosa, deluxe and first-class service to Campeche, Chetumal, Mérida, Mexico City, Palenque, San Cristóbal, Tapachula, Tuxtla Gutiérrez, Veracruz, and elsewhere is available from the ADO bus terminal, which is served by UNO and G. L. and Cristóbal Colón. There is frequent second-class service to the same cities from the Central Camionera de 2a Clase.

➤ Bus Information: **ADO bus terminal** (⊠ Av. Juárez near Av. de la Vega, Palenque, ☎ 934/5–13–44; ⊠ Calle F. J. Mina 297, corner of Lino Merino, Villahermosa, ☎ 93/12–76–92 or 93/12–14–46). **Central Camionera de 2a Clase** (⊠ Av. Ruíz Cortines s/n, Villahermosa, ☎ 93/12–29–77 or 93/12–10–91). **Cristóbal Colón** ☎ (93/12–29–37 or 93/12–89–00 in Villahermosa). **Cristóbal Colón bus station** (⊠ Av. Insurgentes and Blvd. Juan Sabines Gutiérrez, San Cristóbal, ☎ 967/8–02–91; ⊠ Av. 2a Nte. Pte. 268, Tuxtla Gutiérrez, ☎ 961/2–16–39 or 961/2–26–24). **Express Plus** (☎ 934/5–10–12 in Palenque). **G. L.** (☎ 93/12–76–92 in Villahermosa). **Omnibus de Chiapas** (☎ 934/5–13–22). **Sociedad de Transportes Dr. Rodulfo Figueroa** (⊠ 4a Pte. Sur 1060, ☎ 961/3–65–92 in Tuxtla Gutiérrez). **Ticket Bus** Av. Real de Guadalupe 5-E, San Cristóbal, ☎ 967/8–85–03. **Transportes Tuxtla Express Plus** (☎ 967/8–48–69 in San Cristóbal). **UNO** (☎ 93/12–76–27 in Villahermosa).

CAR RENTAL

In San Crisóbal, Budget is inside the Mansión del Valle hotel. Excellent is near the zócalo. Budget and Alamo are represented at both Tuxtla airports. Internationally known companies with offices at the airport and downtown Villahermosa include Advantage, Budget, Dollar, and Hertz.

➤ Major Agencies: **Advantage** (☎ 93/15–58–33 or 93/15–50–48). **Budget** (⊠ Calle Diego de Mazariegos 36, San Cristóbal, ☎ FAX 967/8–18–71 or 967/8–31–00; ☎ 93/14–37–90 or 93/56–01–18 in Villahermosa; ☎ 961/5–13–82 or 961/5–06–83 in Tuxtla). **Dollar** (☎ 93/56–02–11). **Hertz** (☎ 93/16–44–00 or 93/56–02–00).
➤ Local Agencies: **Excellent** (Real de Guadalupe 5-E, San Cristóbal, ☎ 967/8–76–56).

CAR TRAVEL

From Tuxtla Gutiérrez, Highway 190 goes east through Chiapa de Corzo to San Cristóbal before continuing southeast to Comitán and the Guatemala border. Highway 199 to Highway 186 (the turnoff is at Catazajá) is the preferred route from San Cristóbal to Villahermosa; it'll take you via Toniná, Agua Azul, and Palenque. The drive from San Cristóbal to Palenque takes about five hours along a winding paved road, and it's another two hours from Palenque to Villahermosa along a fairly straight road.

On the map, Highway 195 may look like the most direct way to travel between San Cristóbal and Villahermosa, but it entails hours of hairpin curves—it's only for the stalwart and absolutely not to be traveled at night because of seasonal fog as well as a lack of reflectors, illumination, and other cars to help in case of emergency.

To get to Villahermosa from Coatzacoalcos and Veracruz, take Highway 180. In all cases, exercise caution during the rainy season (June through October), when roads are slick. Although expensive, car rentals are available at the Tuxtla and Villahermosa airports as well as in San Cristóbal.

EMERGENCIES

In larger cities such as Tuxtla Gutiérrez and Villahermosa, dial 060 for fire, theft, and medical emergencies. If you don't speak Spanish, it might be better to call hotel personnel or the tourist office (during open hours) and ask for an English-speaking representative.

For tourist-related problems in Palenque contact the Agencia del Ministerio Público at the tourist office. Travelers in Villahermosa are advised to call the state tourist office for all emergencies. Visit the Centro de Salud in Palenque, weekdays 7 AM–8 PM, for medical consultation. In an emergency, the Hospital General, next door, is open 24 hours a day, as is Farmacia Lastra. In San Cristóbal, Farmacia Bios is open 7 AM–11 PM. In Tuxtla, Farmacia del Ahorro is open 24 hours and offers delivery services. Farmacia Unión in Villahermosa is open 24 hours.

➤ CONTACTS: **Cruz Roja** (Red Cross, ⊠ Prolongación Ignacio Allende 55, San Cristóbal, ☎ 967/8–07–72 or 967/8–65–65). **Federal Highway Police** (⊠ Blvd. Juan Sabines Gutiérrez, s/n, San Cristóbal, ☎ 967/8–64–66). **Municipal police** (⊠ Blvd. Juan Sabines Gutiérrez, s/n, near Unidad Deportiva, San Cristóbal, ☎ 967/8–05–54).

➤ HOSPITALS & CLINICS: **Centro de Salud** (⊠ Prolongación Juárez s/n, Palenque, ☎ 934/5–00–25). **Red Cross Hospital** (⊠ Av. Sandino, s/n, Col. Primero de Mayo, Villahermosa, ☎ 93/15–55–55 or 93/15–62–63). **Hospital General** (Prolongación Juárez s/n, Palenque, ☎ 934/5–07–33). **Hospital General** (⊠ Av. Insurgentes 24, San Cristóbal, ☎ 967/8–07–70).

➤ PHARMACIES: **Farmacia Bios** (⊠ Av. Hidalgo at Av. Cuauhtémoc, San Cristóbal, ☎ 967/8–18–18). **Farmacia del Ahorro** (⊠ Av. Central Pte. 874 Tuxtla, ☎ 961/3–88–18). **Farmacia Lastra** (⊠ Av. Juárez s/n at Abasolo, downtown Palenque, ☎ 934/5–11–19). **Farmacia Unión** (⊠ Av. 27 de Febrero 1205, Villahermosa, ☎ 93/15–47–17).

ENGLISH-LANGUAGE MEDIA

In San Cristóbal, Chilam Balam has the latest editions of travel, archaeology, and art books along with posters and maps of Mexico. There's a second store at Avenida Insurgentes 18. La Mercantil has the best selection of English- and Spanish-language periodicals.

➤ BOOKSTORES: **Chilam Balam** (⊠ Casa Utrilla at Av. Gral. Utrilla 33 and Dr. Navarro, ☎ 967/8–04–86). **La Mercantil** (⊠ Calle Diego de Mazariegos 21).

INTERNET

Cibernet in Palenque is packed with eager elementary-school students and the occasional traveler. At only $1.50 an hour, the Internet access here is fast enough. Cibernet is open Monday–Saturday 8–2 and 4–9.

In San Cristóbal you can choose between CyberC@fe or Café Azteca Internet. CyberC@fe is in a small shopping center near the zócalo. You can have beer, coffee, or dessert while you surf the Web for $4 per hour. It's open 9 AM–9:30 PM daily. Café Azteca Internet, open 8 AM–10 PM daily, is fast and less-expensive at $1.50 an hour.

There's a great Internet café in Villahermosa at the coffee shop of the Howard Johnson's hotel, in the popular Zona Luz district. It's open weekdays 8 AM–10 PM, Saturday 8–8, and Sunday noon–8, and charges $2 an hour.

The CyberCafe is about 10 blocks from the Cristóbal Colón bus station, in Tuxtla Gutiérrez, but the price is right: $1.50 an hour for Internet access. It's open daily 9–9.

➤ INTERNET CAFÉS: **Café Azteca Internet** (✉ 5 de mayo 10-A, San Cristóbal, ☎ 967/8–00–99). **Cibernet** (✉ Calle Independencia s/n, at Av. 5 de Mayo, Palenque, ☎ 934/5–1710). **CyberC@fe** (✉ Real de Guadalupe 7, San Cristóbal, ☎ 967/8–7488). **CyberCafe** (✉ 3a Nte. Pte. 1346, Tuxtla Gutiérrez, ☎ 961/2–3900). **Howard Johnson's** (✉ Aldama 404, Villahermosa, ☎ 93/12–96–59).

TAXIS

In Palenque the local *sitio* (taxi stand) is at the town park. In San Cristóbal, taxis can be taken off the street. There is colectivo service to outlying villages, departing from and returning to the sitio at Blvd. Jaime Sabines and Insurgentes near the Cristóbal Colón bus station. In Villahermosa, there is both *special* (individual) and collective taxi service. Call for a radio taxi.

You can take a taxi from Tuxtla to San Cristóbal (1½ hours; $15 for one person, $4 each with four passengers). Many travel agencies in both cities provide private taxi service.

➤ TAXI COMPANIES: **Palenque taxi stand** (☎ 934/5–03–79 or 934/8–23–53). **Villahermosa radio taxi** (☎ 93/15–83–33 or 93/15–84–33).

TOURS

From the town of Palenque, most tour operators offer half-day guided tours of Palenque ruins for about $6, which includes guide, entrance to the ruins, hotel pickup, and lunch. Also offered are six-hour tours to the waterfalls at Misol-Há and Agua Azul, at about $10 per person—a good deal as it includes entrance to both sites and transportation. Longer trips to San Cristóbal, Toniná, and the Sumidero Canyon are also available. Reliable, recommended tour operators include Turismo Quetzal and Kukulcán. Both have one- and two-day trips to Bonampak and Yaxchilán by land. A one-day trip costs $30–$40 via land and boat, including transportation, Spanish-speaking guide, and lunch. Two-day trips overnight in tents at the Lacandon village of Lacanjá and cost about $60, including five meals, transportation, and guide services. Both companies can arrange river trips to the Mayan ruins at Tikal, in Guatemala, as well as day trips to Misol-Há and Agua Azul waterfalls near Palenque.

Ceiba Adventures has guided adventure tours throughout the Ruta Maya, including excursions to Palenque, Bonampak, Yaxchilán, and Tikal. Available are cave explorations and river rafting along several Chiapan waterways sunk deep in the jungle.

Pepe Santiago and his partner lead tours ($10) daily to San Juan Chamula and Zinacantán, leaving from Na Bolom at 10 AM and returning about 3:30. Gabriela Gudiño, who has more than 20 years experience as a guide specializing in history, archaeology and ethnography of the Maya Route and southeast Mexico, can be reached at 967/8–65–70. She charges about $11. Mercedes Hernández leaves from the zócalo at approximately 9 AM; look for her colorful umbrella. She charges about $5 per person. These guides speak English.

A.T.C., Viajes Pakal, Viajes "Chincultik," and Viajes Navarra offer local tours around San Cristóbal and beyond, as well as tours of Bonampak, Yaxchilán, Palenque, Agua Azul, Lagos de Montebello, Amatenango, Chincultik and Sumidero Canyon; some arrange transportation to Guatemala, the Yucatán, and Belize. Pronatura offers day trips to the tropical cloud forests of Reserva Huitepec; profits go to Chiapas conservation and reforestation programs. Most tour operators transport passengers in minibuses and can arrange hotel pickup. DANA offers low-impact four-day guided hiking tours to Laguna Miramar, the largest natural lake in southwestern Mexico, in the Lacandon rain forest. Here you'll experience camping, swimming, snorkeling, fishing, horseback riding, and visits to small area ruins and indigenous communities. A three-night stay (the minimum) costs about $180 if you go by land.

Viajes Lido and Viajes Miramar, run by the Castillo sisters, offer city tours of Tuxtla Gutiérrez, plus five-hour excursions to Chiapa de Corzo and Sumidero Canyon for $10.

Agencia de Viajes Tabasco has city tours of Villahermosa as well as trips to Comalcalco, Palenque, and San Cristóbal. Rutas del Usumasinta specializes in tours to Chiapas and Guatemala, including Bonampak and Yaxchilán.

➤ TOUR OPERATOR RECOMMENDATIONS: **Agencia de Viajes Tabasco** (⊠ Hyatt Regency, Av. Juárez 106, Zona Hotelera, Villahermosa, ☎ ℻ 93/16–10–58 or 93/16–44–54; ⊠ Galería Tabasco 2000, Local 173, Villahermosa, ☎ 93/15–12–34, 93/15–57–90, or 93/16–40–88, ℻ 93/16–40–90). **A.T.C.** (⊠ Av. 16 de Septiembre 16, San Cristóbal, ☎ 967/8–25–50 or 967/8–25–57, ℻ 967/8–31–45). **Ceiba Adventures** (⊠ Box 2274, Flagstaff, AZ 86003, ☎ 520/527–0171, ℻ 520/527–8127). **DANA** (⊠ Dr. Navarro 10, San Cristóbal, ☎ ℻ 967/8–43–07). **Kukulcán** (⊠ Av. Juárez s/n at Calle Allende, Palenque, ☎ 934/5–15–06). **Pronatura** (⊠ Av. Juárez 11-B, San Cristóbal, ☎ 967/8–50–00). **Rutas del Usumasinta** (⊠ Calle Remo 215, Residencial Cuidad Deportiva, Villahermosa, ☎ 93/51–04–05, ℻ 93/51–05–35. **Turismo Quetzal** (⊠ Av. Juárez 135, Palenque, ☎ 934/5–06–01).**Viajes "Chincultik"** (⊠ Real de Guadalupe 34, San Cristóbal, ☎ 967/8–09–57, ℻ 967/8–78–32). **Viajes Lido** (⊠ Av. Central Pte. 861-A, Tuxtla Gutiérrez, ☎ 961/3–66–71, ℻ 961/2–11–30). **Viajes Miramar** (⊠ Camino Real, Local 2, Tuxtla Gutiérrez, ☎ 961/7–77–77, ext. 7230, ℻ 961/5–59–25). **Viajes Navarra** (⊠ Real de Guadalupe 15-D, San Cristóbal, ☎ 967/8–11–43). **Viajes Pakal** (⊠ Calle Cuauhtémoc 6A, San Cristóbal, ☎ ℻ 967/8–28–19).

TRANSPORTATION AROUND CHIAPAS AND TABASCO

A car or a tour arranged through a local travel agency is the easiest way to reach Palenque's surrounding attractions, although the ruins themselves can easily be reached via private taxi or inexpensive colectivo service from downtown (corner of Av. Hidalgo and Calle Allende) or from the ADO bus station. The downtown itself is small enough to traverse on foot.

As with many other colonial towns, the most enjoyable and thorough way to explore San Cristóbal is on foot. If you do come to town with a car, leave it in the hotel garage until you're ready to take an excursion outside San Cristóbal.

Of the three rivers surrounding it, Villahermosa is oriented toward the Grijalva River to the east, which is bordered by a malecón. The city is huge, and driving can be tricky. The main road through town, Ruíz Cortines, is almost a highway; exit ramps are about 1 km (½ mi) apart, and tourist destinations aren't clearly marked. Information about city buses can be difficult to find.

VISITOR INFORMATION

The state of Chiapas has a toll-free tourist information number, which can be dialed from anywhere in Mexico, but which isn't always answered.

The people in the tourist office in Comitán are very knowledgeable and helpful. The office is open weekdays 9–4 and 6–9, weekends 9–2. Palenque tourist information is open weekdays 9–3 and 6–9.

The people at the municipal tourist office in San Cristóbal have some information about San Cristóbal proper. You can get information about attractions throughout the state at the state tourist office. Both are open Monday through Saturday 9–8, Sunday 9–2.

The folks at the state tourist office in Tuxtla Gutiérrez are extremely helpful; they're there weekdays 9–9, Saturday 9–8, Sunday 9–3.

The state tourist office in Villahermosa, Tabasco 2000, next to the municipal palace, is open weekdays 9–3 and 6–9, Saturday 9–1. The auxiliary office at Parque Museo La Venta is open daily 9–4; the information booth at the airport open daily 7 AM–9 PM.

➤ TOURIST INFORMATION: **Chiapas tourist information hot line** (☎ 01–800/280–3500). **Palenque Tourist information** (✉ Av. Juárez and Abasolo, at Plaza de Artesanías, Palenque, ☎ 934/5–01–41 or 934/5–00–13). **Municipal tourist office–San Cristóbal** (✉ Palacio Municipal [City Hall], ground floor, on the zócalo, San Cristóbal, ☎ 967/8–06–65 or 967/8–01–35). **State tourist office–San Cristóbal** (✉ Miguel Hidalgo 1-B, ½ block from zócalo, San Cristóbal, ☎ FAX 967/8–65–70). **State tourist office–Tuxtla** (✉ Edificio Plaza de las Instituciones, ground floor, Blvd. Dr. Belisario Domínguez 950, Tuxtla Gutiérrez, ☎ 961/3–44–99 or 01–800/280–3500). **State tourist office–Villahermosa** (✉ Av. Los Ríos at Calle 13 S/N, Villahermosa, ☎ 93/16–36–33 or 93/16–28–89). **Tourist office–Comitán** (✉ ground floor of Municipal Palace, facing zócalo, Comitán, ☎ 963/2–40–47).

12 VERACRUZ AND THE NORTHEAST

The superb but little-explored pyramids of El Tajín and the raffish charm of Veracruz, the first European city established on the North American mainland, are among Mexico's indisputable highlights. Many Texans get their first taste of Mexico in the northeastern border towns of Nuevo Laredo, Reynosa, and Matamoros. Texan or otherwise, if you venture farther down to Monterrey, you'll find far more sophisticated dining, shopping, and cultural attractions in the country's third-largest city.

T**HERE ARE PLENTY** of reasons to make your way to the state of Veracruz, not least of which are its culture and history. You can explore El Tajín—its Temple of the Niches is one of the most enchanting pre-Columbian buildings in Mexico. Or wander the venerable port of Veracruz, where the Spanish first landed in 1519; witness the fascinating aerial ritual of the *voladores* (fliers) of Papantla; and enjoy an archaeological museum second only to the one in Mexico City. You can also stroll the plazas of quaint mountain villages, laze on sandy beaches, and dine on some of the best seafood in Mexico, prepared in the famous Veracruz style.

Updated by
Amy Mansell

Hybrids of Mexican and U.S. culture, the three border cities of Nuevo Laredo, Reynosa, and Matamoros are busy industrial areas that lure American day-trippers with moderate-price handicrafts and authentic Mexican dishes. Improved roads have also led more people to take advantage of the opportunity to visit Monterrey, Mexico's third-largest city. With its cultural attractions, five-star hotels and restaurants, and, of course, shops, it's a highlight of the region. In Monterrey, you can arrange horseback rides, mountain-biking excursions, and treks into the pine forests of the nearby Sierra Madre.

Pleasures and Pastimes

Dining

The state of Veracruz is famous for its signature dish, *huachinango a là veracruzana* (red snapper in the Veracruz style, covered in tomatoes, onions, olives, and herbs). Leaving Veracruz without sampling this would be both a shame and a bit of a feat, as every chef has his own version, which he will insist you try.

In Veracruz, as befits a hot, breezy port town, the emphasis is on simple, fresh food, mostly *pescado* (fish) and *mariscos* (shellfish). Whether at night or during the day, a stop at one of the town's cafés is de rigueur— the 19th-century Café del Portal is known internationally for its atmosphere and its fantastic coffee. Jalapa probably has the best restaurants in the state; the cookery is just as creative as the town's arts and music scene. It's not uncommon to hear the pat-pat of tortillas being hand-formed as you eat, and beans, rice, cheese, and occasionally chilies (this is, after all, the hometown of the jalapeño) are cleverly integrated into main dishes of meat and river fish such as trout. You can eat cheaply and heartily in Papantla, but with little variation. Just as Tuxpán's best attractions are its pretty river and nearby beaches, some of the best places to eat here are the small, family-run seafood *palapas* (thatch-roof huts) lining the beach as well as the river, as it makes its way to the gulf at Playa Tuxpán. If you ask for the *platillo del día* (daily dish), most likely you'll be treated to a cold shrimp, calamari, or crab cocktail, or a plate of fried fish or shrimp with Mexican rice and tortillas.

Although the Northeast isn't especially renowned for its cuisine, you'll find a nice variety of dishes from around the country. Among the regional specialties are *cabrito* (roast kid), *carne asada* (grilled fillet of beef), and *café de olla* (a delicious blend of coffee, cinnamon, and brown sugar brewed in a clay pot).

Very little in the state of Veracruz or the Northeast is truly formal. Even in the cities of Veracruz and Monterrey reservations are almost never necessary, and a jacket and tie would look out of place almost anywhere (unless we note otherwise). In a town such as Papantla, to say that dress is casual would be an understatement: shorts and a T-shirt won't get a second glance even in the town's fanciest dining room.

CATEGORY	COST*
$$$$	over $40
$$$	$25–$40
$$	$15–$25
$	under $15

per person for a three-course meal, excluding drinks and service

Fishing

Northeastern Mexico is a popular place for American anglers. You're likely to hook something at La Pesca—as the name would indicate—on the Tamaulipas coast between Matamoros and Tampico east of Ciudad Victoria and Soto La Marina.

Lodging

The state of Veracruz is just starting to get world-class hotels such as the super-deluxe Fiesta Americana. The port city also has a number of inexpensive hotels with plenty of atmosphere, and the moderately priced and more expensive places offer good value for your money—especially in comparison with their counterparts in areas of Mexico that see more foreign tourists.

Although there are plenty of clean, comfortable, and inexpensive options in downtown Jalapa, more upscale choices are limited. Many people choose to see El Tajín as a day trip from the more developed city of Tuxpán, only passing through Papantla. If you decide to spend a night or two here, your options are limited: Papantla has few hotels, and none are exceptional. Fortunately, they're concentrated in a five-block radius and almost never fill up. Tuxpán also has a five-star hotel, as well as plenty of safe and comfortable budget rooms. Tuxpán sees few foreigners, and aside from during Semana Santa (Holy Week) and July and August, when middle-class Mexicans head en masse for the beach, its hotels are usually empty.

Catering mostly to business travelers and short-term tourists, the hotels in the border towns are what you'd expect—not luxurious but reasonably priced and mostly well kept. Monterrey affords more choices in all price ranges, and new hotels keep popping up to keep pace with the increase in corporate travelers.

CATEGORY	COST*
$$$$	over $160
$$$	$90–$160
$$	$40–$90
$	under $40

All prices are for a standard double room, excluding tax.

Exploring Veracruz and the Northeast

The lively port city of Veracruz was of vital importance in the history of the Spanish conquest of Mexico. The lush coastal state of Veracruz also has its share of colonial history, as well as native ruins and newly established adventure-tourism routes.

Northeastern Mexico consists of a string of border towns across from the United States, the city of Monterrey, and some surrounding natural wonders. Although the border towns are worth a visit to sample Mexican cuisine and buy handicrafts, their charm is limited. You might prefer to linger in Monterrey, a major city with elegant hotels, cutting-edge art at the Museum of Contemporary Art, a phenomenal 100-acre city square, and a variety of natural wonders in the surrounding areas, including Horsetail Falls.

Numbers in the text correspond to numbers in the margin and on the Veracruz and East Central Mexico, Veracruz, Northeastern Mexico, and Monterrey maps.

Great Itineraries

The state of Veracruz and Northeast Mexico are separate regions, which is how most travelers approach them when planning a trip. Veracruz is closer to Mexico City and more appealing. Northeast Mexico is closer to Texas and is more often frequented by Texans hopping across the border than by people using Mexico City as a gateway. Our approach to the northeast is therefore from Texas. The drive up the coast from Veracruz is possible, but the distances—502 km (311 mi) between Veracruz and Tampico and 1,005 km (623 mi) from Veracruz to Monterrey—may be daunting from behind the wheel.

IF YOU HAVE 3 DAYS

If you are flying, head straight for the port of **Veracruz** ①–⑤, the most Caribbean of the Gulf of Mexico cities. You'll have no problem spending two days here: in addition to the excellent aquarium and the museums you'll find some of the country's best cafés, music, and seafood restaurants. On Day 3, take a day trip to the state capital, **Jalapa** ⑧, and its Museum of Anthropology; stop on the way at **La Antigua** and at the archaeological site of **Cempoala** ⑦, a major Totonac city.

If you're driving down from Texas and have limited time, you could simply explore the area around **Monterrey** ⑮–㉒, the cultural and industrial giant of the northeast, to get a feeling for Mexico. Spend the first day walking around the Gran Plaza area, where the modern-art and history museums are outstanding, and then drive to the **Cuauhtémoc Brewery** ⑳ on the outskirts of town. Devote the next two days to enjoying some of the region's natural attractions, including the **Barranca de la Huasteca** ㉓, an impressive gorge; the ancient **Grutas de García** ㉔; and the **Parque Nacional Cumbres de Monterrey** ㉕, with its spectacular waterfall.

IF YOU HAVE 5 DAYS

Start in **Veracruz** ①–⑤. On the second day make your way out of the city to the cool hill towns of **Los Tuxtlas** ⑥, where you can consult a *curandero* (healer) for whatever ails you. On Day 3 make your way to the city of **Jalapa** ⑧. Plan to spend the two remaining days at **El Tajín** ⑨, overnighting in the nearby town of **Papantla de Olarte** ⑩. Make your way back down the coast to Veracruz, and consider stopping on the way at **La Antigua** and **Cempoala** ⑦.

For five days in the northeast, add an excursion to **Tampico** ㉖, on the Gulf of Mexico, to the three-day jaunt. Check out sculptures of Tlazoltéotl, the pre-Hispanic Huastecan Goddess of Love, at the **Museo de la Cultura Huasteca,** and relax with picnicking Mexican families at Playa Miramar.

IF YOU HAVE 7 DAYS

In east central Mexico, follow the five-day itinerary above, but extend the trip to include more time around **Jalapa** ⑧ and visit the magnificent falls at **Xico,** overnighting nearby in the picturesque colonial town of Coatepec. The next day, go river rafting on the Río Pescados southeast of Jalapa. If you drive, consider adding a visit to **Los Tuxtlas** ⑥; if you don't have a car, spend a leisurely extra day enjoying the beaches and seafood restaurants of **Boca del Río,** a small fishing village that is quickly turning into a suburb of Veracruz, or visiting more of the sights you missed in the port's downtown.

When to Tour

In Veracruz, the weather is balmy between November and April. The notorious *nortes*—gusty, chilly winds that blow in off the Gulf of Mexico—usually appear between October and February, and especially in December. Pack a sweater and light coat or jacket if you plan to travel during these months. In summer, both the temperature and humidity soar, but the frequent rains afford a respite from the heat.

A great time to visit Veracruz is the week before Ash Wednesday for Carnaval, Mexico's pre-Lenten bash. It's wild and merry but has a small-town ambience that makes it saner and safer than the better-known celebrations in Río or New Orleans. The biggest problem at such times is finding a room (reserve well in advance). The same is true during Christmas as well as Easter week, when all of Mexico goes on vacation and heads for the beach.

The hottest months in the northeast are April through June. The cooling rains arrive in July and last through August. There are never any crowds at the border towns or in Monterrey except during major U.S. holidays, when Americans head south for a day or weekend.

THE STATE OF VERACRUZ

A long, skinny crescent of land bordering the Gulf of Mexico, the state of Veracruz is often ignored by travelers, many of whom do no more than glimpse it through the window of a bus barreling toward the Yucatán Peninsula. Although Veracruz's ruins and beaches don't quite compare with those on the Yucatán, the state is popular with vacationing Mexicans, drawn to the cool hill towns of the Sierra de Los Tuxtlas and the liveliness of Veracruz City.

Descending from the volcanic Sierra, the Veracruz coast consists of flat lowlands that have their share of terrible heat and swamps and are pockmarked by noisome oil refineries. As you head inland a ways—Veracruz is only 140 km (87 mi) across at its widest point—the land rises to meet the Sierra Madre Oriental range, with its 6,100-m (20,130-ft) Pico de Orizaba (also called Citlaltépetl), Mexico's highest peak. In the foothills of this range, you'll find the university town and state capital Jalapa, where students share the colonial streets with local farmers marketing their crops. Jalapa is a favored place for foreigners to study Spanish, and the nearby town of Jalcomulco is a base for river-rafting explorations on the Río Pescados. The state does have some good beaches along the coast, particularly around the northern city of Tuxpán, but the real reasons to come are the atmosphere, the history, and the people. All these are at their best in the city of Veracruz, a working port with so many marimba bands in the *zócalo* (main square) on weekend evenings that they have to compete to be heard.

Olmec civilization thrived in Veracruz long before the rise of the Maya. The state's best-preserved ruins, at El Tajín near Papantla, are thought to have been the work of yet another (unidentified) civilization, which had its heyday later, between AD 550 and 1100. By the time Hernán Cortés landed in Veracruz in 1519, the Aztecs held sway, but within a very short time the Indian population was decimated by war and European diseases.

The state of Veracruz played a pivotal role in Cortés's march to Tenochtitlán. A government-sponsored circuit called the Ruta de Cortés (Route of Cortez) traces the Spanish conquistador's footsteps, from his Veracruz landing to his arrival in Mexico City, where he defeated the Aztec rulers. It's a mélange of soft adventure excursions, such as river rafting, combined with visits to colonial cities, old haciendas, and archaeological zones.

In modern times, the discovery of oil in Veracruz caused a population explosion that saw the number of *veracruzanos* go from about 1 million at the beginning of the century to more than 7 million today. For most visitors, the occasional sulfurous stench of a coastal refinery is an unpleasant intrusion on their tropical reverie, but for many of the state's residents, oil is their bread and butter.

Veracruz

502 km (311 mi) south of Tampico, 345 km (214 mi) west of Mexico City.

In 1519 Cortés landed in La Antigua, a tiny slip of a place, but it was Veracruz that became the major gateway for Spanish settlement of Mexico. Its name, which appears throughout Latin America, means "true cross." To more fruitfully profit from their conquest, the Spanish brought a large number of Africans to Veracruz as slaves. Later, Cuban immigrants flooded the port. This mix in modern days has created an open-minded city, where visitors of all cultural extractions are generously welcomed.

Veracruz's diverse influences can be seen in its music and dance. Veracruz is the hometown of "La Bamba," a song that dates back to the 17th century. The city has a special brand of music, played by lively trios outfitted in white and slapping away at tiny guitars and portable harps. In the evening, mariachis entertain outside sidewalk cafés around the main plaza.

The *danzón,* a languorous two-person dance with lots of subtle hip movement, was brought to the city by refugees fleeing Cuba in 1879 following its Ten Years' War. Most ended up living outside the city walls (only Veracruz aristocrats were allowed to live inside), but the sons of the Mexican elite sneaked into the poor neighborhoods at night and eventually introduced the danzón to high society. Sensuous compared with the stiff and formal dance that had been the norm until this time, the danzón was at first considered scandalous, but it soon won the hearts of even its detractors and became the most popular dance in the city. It later spread throughout the country.

Veracruz was Mexico's premier seaside resort and the port of entry for most foreign visitors until a few decades ago; travelers arrived by ship, then boarded a train to Mexico City, often looking back wistfully. Today relatively few foreigners find their way to Veracruz's beaches, which are polluted, but domestic vacationers are lured to the fun-loving town by excellent seafood and a lively nightlife.

Sights to See

❶ Museo de la Ciudad. This museum is a good place to get oriented to the Veracruz port. The region's history is narrated through artifacts and displays, and scale models of the city help you get the lay of the land. Also exhibited are copies of pre-Columbian statues and contemporary art. Tours in English are available on Monday, Wednesday, and Friday mornings. ⊠ *Zaragoza at Morales,* ☎ *29/31–84–10, 29/89–88–72, or 29/89–88–73.* �她 *Free.* ☉ *Wed.–Mon. 10–6.*

❷ Fort of San Juan de Ulúa. During the Viceregal era, Veracruz was the only east-coast port permitted to operate in New Spain. As a result, it was frequently attacked by pirates. The great fort, built shortly after the conquest and the last territory in Mexico to be held by the Spanish Royalists, is a monument to that swashbuckling era. A miniature

Veracruz and East Central Mexico

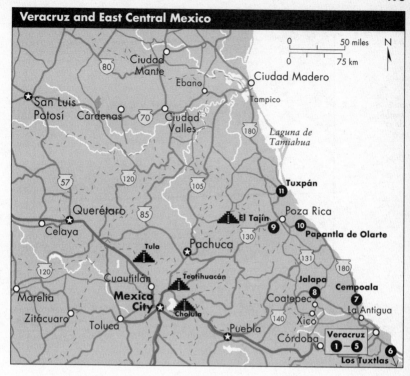

city in itself, the island fort is a maze of moats, ramparts, and draw-bridges smack in the middle of the busy port area (it's now connected to the mainland by a causeway). Fortification of the island began in 1535 under the direction of Antonio de Mendoza, the first viceroy of New Spain. Ground coral, sand, and oyster shells were used for the original walls. A few centuries later, the fort was used as a prison, housing such figures as Benito Juárez, who was held here by conservative dictator Santa Anna before being exiled to Louisiana in 1853. After Independence, it was used in unsuccessful attempts to fight off first the invading French, the Americans, the French again, and, in 1914, the Americans yet again. ⊠ *Via causeway from downtown Veracruz,* ☎ *29/38–51–51.* ⊡ *$2.50, free Sun.* ⊙ *Tues.–Sun. 9–5.*

❸ **Baluarte de Santiago.** The fortress and museum is all that's left of the old city walls; like the Fort of San Juan de Ulúa, the colonial bulwark was built as a defense against pirates (but some 100 years later, in 1635). The structure is impressively solid from the outside and romantically lighted at night. Inside is a small museum that has an exquisite permanent exhibition of gold pre-Columbian jewelry—definitely Spanish plunder—which was discovered by a fisherman 25 years ago. ⊠ *Canal at 16 de Septiembre,* ☎ *no phone.* ⊡ *$1.75, free Sun.* ⊙ *Tues.–Sun. 10–4:30.*

★ ☕ ❹ **Acuario de Veracruz.** Veracruz is home to one of the three most important aquariums in the world. In addition to its public displays, the complex also houses a marine research center. The main exhibits include a tank with 2,000 species of marine life native to the Gulf of Mexico, including nurse sharks, manta rays, barracudas, sea turtles, and the prehistoric *pejelagartos,* which look like a combination of crocodile and fish. Check out the 18-ft-long outline on the far wall, above the caption THIS IS THE ACTUAL SIZE OF A GREAT WHITE SHARK CAUGHT OFF

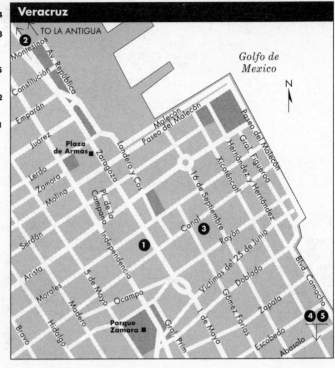

THE COAST OF TUXPÁN, VERACRUZ. ⊠ *Plaza Acuario, Blvd. Manuel Avila Camacho s/n,* ☎ *29/32–79–84 or 29/32–80–06.* 🎟 *$2.* ☯ *Weekdays 10–7, weekends 10–7:30.*

❺ **Casa Museo Agustín Lara.** Lara is one of Mexico's most beloved songwriters and singers. Among his occupations were piano player in a house of ill repute and bullfighter; he is also famous for marrying seven women, including Mexican screen goddess Maria Félix. He died in 1970 at age 73, having spent the last years of his life writing and recording music in this house. Among his most famous songs are "Maria Bonita," which he dedicated to Félix, and "Granada." Newspaper clippings, caricatures, and a replica of the radio station where Lara went on the air nightly with "La Hora Azul" (The Blue Hour) are on view. ⊠ *Adolfo Ruíz Cortines s/n, at Av. Manuel Avila Camacho, Boca del Río,* ☎ *29/37–02–09 or 29/31–40–78.* 🎟 *$2.* ☯ *Tues.–Sat. 10–7, Sun. 10–5.*

. . . .

OFF THE
BEATEN PATH

LA ANTIGUA – This town, given its name by the Spaniards after they abandoned it, was the site of the first European landing in the New World and the conquistadors' capital for 75 years. The customshouse, which once had 22 rooms surrounding a huge courtyard, lies abandoned on the northern edge of the village. It's worth seeing if only for its crumbling masonry, taken over by clinging vines and massive tree roots. La Antigua also has the first church of New Spain, Ermita del Rosario, a little white stucco structure that's been restored (and changed) many times over the years. La Antigua is 25 km (16 mi) northwest of Veracruz, off Highway 180 (toward Poza Rica). The turnoff is just past the toll booth. You can also take the "San Juan De Ulúa" bus from Av. República; it costs about $1.

. . . .

Beaches

Veracruz City's beaches are much less inviting than you might expect: most are somewhat dirty, and the water is polluted. Good beaches begin south of town in **Mocambo,** about 7 km (4½ mi) from downtown, and get better even farther down: about 4 km (2½ mi) south of Playa Mocambo, **Boca del Río** is a small fishing village at the mouth of the Río Jamapa that is quickly getting sucked into Veracruz's orbit.

Dining and Lodging

In addition to the restaurants in Veracruz, you'll want to also visit Boca del Río. Many of the village's restaurants—they seem to turn up between every other house—are modest but serve some of the finest seafood in Mexico. Boca del Río holds a spot in *The Guinness Book of Records* for the largest fish fillet stuffed with shellfish—it was 408 ft long and weighed almost two tons, and was prepared at Pardiño's restaurant.

$$$ ✕ **La Casita Blanca.** In the same building as the Agustín Lara, this elegant restaurant is decorated with colorful murals and photographs of the popular singer. The menu consists of seafood dishes and thick cuts of steak, and includes a wonderful rendition of a local favorite— *pampano huachinango* (red snapper topped with tomatoes, onions, and herbs). ⊠ *Adolfo Ruíz Cortines s/n, at Av. Manuel Avila Camacho, Boca del Río,* ☎ *29/37–13–38 or 29/37–13–63. AE, MC, V.*

$$$ ✕ **Che Tango.** The elegant atmosphere (expressed in clean lines, arches, and embedded soft-hued lights) at this Argentine steak house encourages guests to linger. If the sun and surf has gone to your head, try the refreshing house cocktail—*Rosita* (a blended anise cocktail)—guaranteed to cool throbbing temples. For starters, order any of the flaky empanadas topped with a secret-recipe *chimchuri* (sauce made with olive oil and parsley). Select your cut of rib eye, tenderloin, top sirloin or strip steak from the chilled display plate that is brought to your table; all are charcoal grilled to order. The white-jacketed waiters are accommodating and happy to make suggestions. ⊠ *Calle 16 de Septiembre 1938, at Calle Enríquez,* ☎ *29/32–17–45 or 29/32–17–56. AE, MC, V.*

$$$ ✕ **El Gaucho Restaurante.** Since 1983, meat lovers have packed this cavernous family-friendly ranch-style restaurant morning, noon, and night. The epic menu lists nearly 100 dishes—from spicy chorizo and Veracruz-style tongue to chicken fajitas. The house specialty drink, *jarra de clericot* (red wine with chewy bits of watermelon, pineapple, and cantaloupe), is delicious. ⊠ *Bernal Díaz del Castillo 187, at Colón,* ☎ *29/35–04–11. AE, MC, V.*

$$$ ✕ **Pardiño's.** This modest eatery, a local favorite, is the star of Boca
★ del Río's many seafood restaurants. Its fame has even spread abroad— it's not unusual for the chef to be invited to gastronomic festivals in France. Plain tables in a nondescript storefront belie the elegant preparation of such dishes as crabs *salpicón* (finely chopped with cilantro, onion, and lime), grilled sea bass, and of course, huachinango à la veracruzana (for $17 a kilo). Also delicious are the simple, fresh appetizers, such as shrimp cocktail with generous chunks of avocado. ⊠ *Zamora 40, Boca del Río,* ☎ *29/86–01–35. AE, DC, MC, V.*

$$ ✕ **Mariscos Villa Rica Mocambo.** This casual, open-air palapa restau-
★ rant on the seafront is worth the small effort to find it. Hidden on a small street that runs parallel to Playa Mocambo, the Villa Rica is a favorite with locals in the know but sees almost no tourists. The menu consists almost entirely of seafood; specialties include mussels, shark, grouper, and octopus prepared as you wish. There are a few meat and poultry dishes, including prime rib and chicken Cordon Bleu. The beverage of choice among loyal patrons is cold Sol (beer) with lime. There's live music Thursday through Sunday, 3 PM–7 PM. ⊠ *Calzada*

Mocambo 527 (near Hotel Mocambo), Boca del Río, ☎ 29/22–21–13 or 29/22–37–43. AE, DC, MC, V.

$$ ✕ **Villa Marina Shrimp and Steak House.** You'll find this laid-back restaurant sitting on stilts above the water just off the *malecón* (boardwalk). Waiters bring platters of the day's catch to the table for you to choose from—fresh lobster, shrimp, clams, and sea bass. Then you get to ponder the 18 *al gusto* ways your selection can be cooked—breaded, grilled, sautéed in garlic, with cheese sauce, and so on. The menu also lists prime rib, rib eye, and T-bone steaks, as well as a number of pasta dishes. Enjoy live music Friday and Saturday, 3 PM to closing. ✉ *Av. Manuel Avila Camacho s/n,* ☎ *29/35–10–34. MC, V.*

$ ✕ **Gran Café de la Parroquia.** Don't be confused if someone tells you this is the wrong Gran Café de la Parroquia: the coffeehouse that long held that name is now called Gran Café del Portal. This eatery is run by a faction of the Fernandez family (kicked out of del Portal after a 20-year lawsuit). The menu and music tend to draw local families. La Parroquia occupies one full side of the city block on the malecón. ✉ *Gómez Farías 34, at the corner of 16 de Septiembre,* ☎ *29/32–25–84. No credit cards.*

$ ✕ **Gran Café del Portal.** Opened by a Spanish immigrant in 1835 in a
★ former monastery, this most famous of Veracruz's sidewalk cafés eventually grew to cover an entire city block. Formerly Gran Café de la Parroquia, it resumed its original name after a family feud in 1995. Every Mexican president since Benito Juárez has been here; it's lively from dawn to dusk with the animated babble of customers, the tapping of spoons against glasses to summon waiters, and live marimba music played by the best musicians in town. The menu has a wide selection of egg dishes, as well as soups, sandwiches, a traditional version of huachinango à la veracruzana, and hearty steak and chicken entrées. But the *café lechero* (coffee with hot milk)—made using well-guarded family secrets—is the real draw. ✉ *Independencia 1185, across from cathedral,* ☎ *29/31–27–51. No credit cards.*

$$$$ ⚑ **Fiesta Americana.** This splashy hotel on Playa Costa de Oro, inaugurated by the president in 1996, has the best business facilities in the state of Veracruz. It has seven floors and miles of marble corridors, all of which seem to lead to the giant serpentine pool and lush gardens facing the ocean. Rooms have terraces; voice mail; closet safes; and luxurious bathrooms with tubs, phones, audio systems, and hair dryers. Fiesta Club floors have a business center, concierge service, and a bilingual staff. Guests have access to a nine-hole golf course 20 minutes away. No-smoking rooms and wheelchair-accessible units are available. ✉ *Blvd. Manuel Avila Camacho at Boca del Rio, Fracc. Costa de Oro 94299,* ☎ *29/89–89–89 or 800/343–7821,* FAX *29/89–89–07. 211 rooms, 22 suites. 4 restaurants, 2 bars, in-room safes, no-smoking rooms, room service, indoor-outdoor pool, 3 hot tubs, massage, tennis court, dive shop, shops, baby-sitting, children's programs (ages 4 and up), meeting rooms, business center, free parking. AE, DC, MC, V.*

$$$$ ⚑ **Hotel Lois.** For those with a sense of humor, this swanky Boca del Río hotel is an over-the-top mishmash of art deco, '50s kitsch, and riotous neon colors. The coffee shop alone has sparkling ceilings, lavender Naugahyde chairs, etched-glass windows, several random Roman columns, and lots of gleaming chrome. Guest rooms are more conventional, with a subdued pastel palette, rattan furniture, and cable color TVs. ✉ *Adolfo Ruíz Cortines 10, Boca del Río 94249,* ☎ *29/37–82–90 or 01–800/712–9136,* FAX *29/37–80–89. 112 rooms, 4 suites. Restaurant, 2 bars, coffee shop, in-room safes, minibars, room service, pool, beauty salon, sauna, exercise room, squash, billiards, baby-sitting, children's programs (ages 3–9), meeting room, car rental, free parking. AE, MC, V.*

$$$$ 🏨 **Torremar.** The lobby in this deluxe high-rise resort on Playa Mocambo is adorned with glass sculptures and pastel oil paintings. Suites have small balconies with fantastic views of the Gulf of Mexico. An executive floor, with special concierge service and complimentary breakfast, is also available. Children will like the cascading poolside fountain and the organized activities in the children's play area. ⊠ *Adolfo Ruíz Cortines 4300 (Playa Mocambo), Boca del Río 94260,* ☎ *29/89–21–00 or 01–800/712–9900,* 🅵🅰🆇 *29/89–21–21. 231 rooms, 18 suites. 2 restaurants, bar, room service, 2 pools, exercise room, baby-sitting, children's programs (ages 3–11), laundry service, concierge floor, car rental, free parking. AE, DC, MC, V.*

$$$–$$$$ 🏨 **Hotel Emporio.** The lobby of this large, elegant hostelry on the
★ malecón is a dramatic sweep of marble and potted palms. Some of the immaculate, light-filled rooms have sea views; all have marble bathrooms with bathtubs (those in the suites are hot tubs), satellite color TVs, and air-conditioning. Dine in the popular restaurant, which is decorated in neoclassical French style, or in the shade of an umbrella at any of the hotel's three pools (one is equipped with a waterfall, slides, and a miniature "ship" nearby for kids). ⊠ *Paseo del Malecón 244, 91700,* ☎ *29/32–22–22, 29/32–00–20, or 01–800/295–2000,* 🅵🅰🆇 *29/ 32–57–52. 182 rooms, 22 suites. Restaurant, bar, coffee shop, room service, 3 pools, sauna, exercise room, shops, children's programs (ages 5–8), meeting room, car rental, free parking. AE, MC, V.*

$$$ 🏨 **Calinda Veracruz.** The rooftop patio (with a pool) at the Calinda has a fantastic view of the zócalo. Immaculate rooms have cool marble floors, bright-peach walls, cable TVs, and phones. Downstairs, Sanborns offers a variety of foreign magazines, candies, and toiletries. ⊠ *Av. Independencia s/n, at the corner of Miguel Lerdo 91700,* ☎ *29/ 31–22–33 or 01–800/290–0000,* 🅵🅰🆇 *29/31–51–34. 116 rooms, 5 master suites, 5 junior suites. Restaurant, cafeteria, room service, pool, laundry service, free parking. AE, MC, V.*

$$$ 🏨 **Villa del Mar.** This unassuming hotel, just across from one of the nicer sections of the downtown beach, is an ideal place to bring children. The standard, motel-style rooms are spacious and comfortable and surround a large, pretty garden with a tennis court, pool, and small playground. All accommodations have color TVs, phones, and air-conditioning. The staff is very helpful, and some English is spoken at the reception desk. A number of bungalows (accommodating up to five people) are also available: they aren't air-conditioned and are a bit gloomy, but some have kitchenettes. Breakfast is included in the room rate. ⊠ *Blvd. Avila Camacho at Bartolomé de las Casas, 91910,* ☎ *29/31–33–66,* 🅵🅰🆇 *29/32–71–35. 91 rooms, 14 bungalows. Restaurant, bar, pool, hot tub, tennis court, playground, laundry service, free parking. MC, V.*

$$ 🏨 **Hotel Hawaii.** This little jewel of a hotel with a prime location on
★ the malecón is one of the best deals in town, offering comfort, class, and personalized service at a reasonable price. All rooms are impeccably maintained and come with air-conditioning, phone, color cable TV, and marble bathrooms with hair dryers. The staff is eager to please, and there's always a bowl of flowers at the check-in desk. You can have all the free coffee and ice cream you want at the snug ground-floor coffee shop; maps are available for the asking; and everyone gets a free pair of beach sandles. The management also sees to it that each guest receives a bag of Veracruz coffee to take home. ⊠ *Paseo del Malecón 458, 91700,* ☎ *29/31–04–27,* 🅵🅰🆇 *29/32–55–24. 30 rooms. Coffee shop, room service, in-room safes, indoor pool, laundry service, free parking. AE, MC, V.*

$$ 🏨 **Hotel Ruiz Milan.** This multistory waterfront hotel is a good value. Guest rooms, although on the small side, are clean, comfortable, and modern. (Ask for a newly remodeled one.) All have color TVs (local stations only), phones, air-conditioning, balconies, ample closet space, and sizable bathrooms. The invitingly cool marble-floor lobby is usually crowded with Mexican businesspeople, and the hotel itself has the amenities of a more expensive establishment, including an indoor pool, a pleasant restaurant, and free covered parking. ⊠ *Paseo del Malecón 432, 91700,* ☎ *29/32–67–07,* ℻ *29/32–37–77, ext. 106. 69 rooms, 19 suites. Restaurant, room service, indoor pool, meeting room, free parking. AE, DC, MC, V.*

$ ⊞ **Hotel Concha Dorada.** The basically characterless Concha Dorada has the cheapest accommodations on the zócalo. Rooms are cramped but brightly painted, and all have color cable TVs, phones, and air-conditioning. Ask for an inside room to avoid the marimba battles that last until the wee hours. The downstairs restaurant–sidewalk café serves simple fare and is especially popular (read noisy) at lunchtime and on weekend nights. ⊠ *Miguel Lerdo 77, near Zaragoza, 91700,* ☎ *29/31–29–96 or 01–800/712–5342,* ℻ *29/31–32–46. 46 rooms, 2 suites. Restaurant, bar, room service, laundry service. AE, MC, V.*

Nightlife and the Arts

Every Tuesday, Friday, and Saturday night after 8 at the **Plaza de Armas** (zócalo), a local troupe dressed in white performs danzón on stage, then hits the street to involve the townsfolk in this traditional Veracruz dance, accompanied by live marimba music. On Sunday night, there's danzón at **Parque Zamora** 6–9. The **Instituto Veracruzo de Cultura** (Veracruz Cultural Institute; ⊠ Calles Canal and Zaragoza, ☎ 29/31–69–67) offers danzón classes for a minimal fee.

For authentic Cuban music, head for the unpretentious **El Rincón de la Trova** (⊠ Callejón de Lagunilla 59, ☎ no phone), where people of all ages gather Thursday through Saturday to dance to famous tropical bands until the wee hours; the floors are cement and the ambience is fun and strictly local. El Rincón de la Trova's six-day Cuban music festival in November draws performers and fans from all over Mexico and the Caribbean.

Discos and video bars are plentiful along the waterfront. Most are packed Friday and Saturday nights with a young, largely local crowd. **Ocean** (⊠ Adolfo Ruíz Cortines 8, at Avila Camacho, ☎ 29/35–23–90) is a flashy, modern discotheque. **Carioca** (⊠ Adolfo Ruíz Cortines 10, at Avila Camacho, ☎ 29/37–82–90) is in the wildly decorated Hotel Lois and has salsa dancing and live music nightly starting at 9. **Blue Ocean** (⊠ Avila Camacho 9, ☎ 29/22–03–55) is a tropical-theme video bar replete with rock sculptures, waterfalls, and a light show.

Outdoor Activities and Sports

Deep-sea fishing is popular in Veracruz, and you'll find places to windsurf in the coastal areas a few miles south of Boca del Río. An annual **regatta** from the port of Galveston in Texas to the port of Veracruz takes place at the end of May. Check with the Mexican Government Tourist Office (☎ 713/780–3740 in Houston) for details.

Shopping

Stands lining the **malecón** sell a variety of ocean-related items: seashells and beauty creams and powders derived from them, black-coral jewelry, ships-in-a-bottle. You'll also find Coatepec coffee, T-shirts, bloody crucifixes, and tacky stuffed frogs, iguanas, and armadillos. The **Plaza de las Artesanías** market on the malecón purveys higher-quality goods, including leather and jewelry—with higher prices to match. For an authentic slice of Mexican daily life, head for the wildly vibrant and chaotic **Mercado Hidalgo** (⊠ bounded by Calles Cortés, Soto, Madero, and Hidalgo), where you'll find artful displays of strawberries and chilies beside heaps of mysterious medicinal herbs and platters of cow eyeballs and chicken feet. One of the more unusual shops in town is in the aquarium: **Fiora** (⊠ Plaza Acuario, Blvd. Manuel Avila Camacho s/n, ☎ 29/32–99–50) sells beautiful jewelry designed from miniature flowers grown in Veracruz.

Veracruzanos have adopted the fashion of neighboring Yucatán, and its famous embroidered *guayabera* shirts are as popular here as mariscos. For the best quality guayabera shirts in the area, visit **Guayaberas Fina Cab** (⊠ Av. Zaragoza 233, between Calles Arista and Serdán, ☎ 29/31–84–27). This family-run shop has a great selection of hand-stitched shirts and dresses, with embroidery ranging from basic interlocking cables to elaborate floral designs. **El Mayab** (⊠ Calle Zamora 78, at Av. Zaragoza, ☎ no phone) has machine-produced guayaberas, which go for less than the hand-embroidered variety.

With its sizable Cuban population, Veracruz does a brisk business in cigars. Around Plaza de Armas, there are plenty of streetside stands that specialize in both Mexican and Caribbean tobacco. For the largest variety of cigars, try the small kiosk on Avenida Independencia, in front of Gran Café del Portal; it sells Cuban Cohibas for less than a buck. Although Cuban smokes are the big draw for cigar-puffing tourists, keep in mind that Veracruz upholds its own proud tradition in the tobacco trade. **Cubahi** (⊠ Av. Sarmiento 59, ☎ 29/33–97–10) offers the finest local-tobacco products, and owner José Antonio Sarmiento is happy to make a house call to your hotel.

Los Tuxtlas

❻ *140 km (87 mi) south of Veracruz.*

A small volcanic mountain range, the Sierra de Los Tuxtlas, meets the sea at Los Tuxtlas. The area has lakes, waterfalls, rivers, mineral springs, and access to beaches, making it a popular stopover for travelers heading east from Mexico City to the Yucatán. The region's three principal towns—**Santiago Tuxtla, San Andrés Tuxtla,** and **Catemaco**—are carved into the mountainsides some 600 ft above sea level, lending them a coolness even in summer that's the envy of the perspiring masses on the coastal plain. The Tuxtlas gain an air of mystery from the cool, gray fog that slips over the mountains and lakes and the whisperings among the townspeople about the *brujos* (witches), also called curanderos, who read tarot cards, prescribe herbal remedies, and cast spells here. Los Tuxtlas is also known for its cigars (the town of San Andrés Tuxtla makes a famous hand-rolled variety, which comes in several sizes). Tours of the cigar factories can be arranged just by showing up. **Te-Amo** (⊠ Blvd. 5 de Febrero 10) is just outside San Andrés Tuxtla on the highway to Catemaco and Santa Clara, on the bypass road. All the factories have stores open to the public.

Although much of the architecture here in Los Tuxtlas is of the 1960s school of looming cement, all three towns are laid out in the colonial style around a main plaza and a church, and all have a certain amount of charm. Santiago Tuxtla has managed to retain more of its colonial character than the other two Tuxtla towns. The region was also a center of Olmec culture, and Olmec artifacts and small ruins abound. A huge stone Olmec head dominates the zócalo at Santiago Tuxtla, and 21 km (13 mi) east are the ruins of **Tres Zapotes,** now decidedly unspectacular but once an important Olmec ceremonial center believed to have been occupied as early as AD 100. The town also has an informative museum, where you can learn about the region's indigenous heritage and contemporary local cultures.

The largest of the three towns, and the only one with an ATM, is San Andrés, but Catemaco is by far the most picturesque and relaxing place to stay. Many of Catemaco's lodgings are on the lake shore; others are grouped around the small square. Catemaco is popular among Mexicans as a summer and Christmas resort and is also the place to go for a *consulta* (consultation) with a brujo, should you require any spiritual clarity or supernatural intervention. Tours of Lake Catemaco, which was formed from the crater of a volcano and which harbors a colorful colony of fish-eating baboons, can be arranged through most local hotels. Beyond Catemaco, a paved road continues over the hills and down to a lovely stretch of undeveloped coastline. Twenty km (12½ mi) from Catemaco is the village of **Sontecomapan,** where you can take a *lancha* (launch) across the lagoon to a desolate beach. A bumpy dirt road follows the coast 19 km (12 mi) north of Sontecomapan to the sleepy fishing village of **Montepío,** which has a wide beach and a couple of inexpensive, basic hotels.

Cempoala

 42 km (26 mi) northwest of Veracruz.

Cempoala (often spelled Zempoala) was the capital of the Totonac nation, whose influence spread throughout Veracruz in pre-Hispanic times. The name means "place of 20 waters," after the sophisticated irrigation system the Totonacs used. The site gained its role in history as the place where, in 1519, Cortés formed his first alliance with a native chief. At the time, the population of Cempoala was around 20,000. The alliance with the Totonacs enlarged Cortés's paltry army of 200 men and encouraged the Spaniard to push on to Mexico City and fight the Aztecs. In his turn, the leader of the Totonacs—dubbed Fat Chief by his own people because of his enormous girth—was an avowed enemy of the powerful Aztecs, who forced his people to perform human sacrifices to the Aztec war god and put military garrisons on Totonac land.

Cempoala was rediscovered by Francisco del Paso y Troncoso in 1891. Ten of the 60–90 structures at Cempoala have been excavated and can be visited. All are built of river stones, shells, sand, and "glue" made from the whites of turtle and bird eggs. As the story goes, when Cortés first sighted Cempoala at night, the buildings glowed white under a full moon. Cortés thought he had discovered a city of silver.

Upon entering the ruins, you see **Circulo de los Gladiadores,** a small circle of waist-high walls to the right of center. This was the site of contests between captured prisoners of war and Totonac warriors: each prisoner was required to fight two armed warriors. One such prisoner, the son of a king from Tlaxcala, won the unfair match and became a national hero. His statue stands in a place of honor in Tlaxcala. Another small structure to the left of the circle marks the spot where an eternal flame was kept lighted during the sacred 52-year cycle of the Totonacs.

The **Templo Mayor,** the main pyramid, is the largest structure on the site. Follow the dirt path that lies straight ahead when you enter. Cortés, after gaining the allegiance of Fat Chief, placed a Christian cross atop this temple—the first gesture of this sort in New Spain—and had mass said by a Spanish priest in his company.

At the smaller **Templo de la Luna** (Temple of the Moon), to the far left of Templo Mayor, outstanding warriors were honored with the title "Eagle Knight" or "Tiger Knight" and awarded an obsidian nose ring to wear as a mark of their status. Just to the left of the Moon Temple is the **Templo del Sol** (Temple of the Sun), where the hearts and blood of sacrificial victims were placed.

Back toward the dirt road and across from it is the **Templo de la Diosa de la Muerte** (Temple of the Goddess of Death), where a statue of the pre-Hispanic deity was found along with 1,700 small idols.

A small on-site **museum** (housed in a palapa). The voladores of Papantla usually give a performance on weekends. Well-trained guides are available, but tours are mainly in Spanish. ☎ *No phone.* ✆ *$2, free Sun.* ☉ *Tues.–Sun. 10–5.*

Jalapa

❽ *90 km (56 mi) northwest of Veracruz.*

Jalapa, which was a Totonac ceremonial center when Cortés arrived, is perched on the side of a mountain, between the coastal lowlands of Veracruz and the high central plateau. More than 4,000 ft above sea level, the city has a bizarre climate—sun, rain, and fog are all likely to show themselves in the course of a day. However, for perspiration-soaked escapees from the coast, it's a nice change. The capital and cultural hub of the state of Veracruz, Jalapa is a university town with a diverse population; you're as likely to see young hippies sitting around in cafés as you are wizened campesinos walking to work. The town is also home to a symphony orchestra, a ballet company, and a state theater that attracts big-name performers. Jalapa is filled with pretty parks and lakes and stately government buildings.

Much of the city seems to have been built haphazardly, and that's the source of its charm. The hills here pose intriguing engineering problems, and major avenues tend to make 180-degree turns, following level surfaces rather than adhering to a strict grid system. In some places, the twisting cobblestone streets are bordered by 6-ft-high sidewalks to compensate for sudden sharp inclines. Locals refer to the city as a *plato roto* (broken dish) because of this scattered, logic-defying layout.

You'll often see the name of the city spelled Xalapa: Jalapa is the Hispanicized version of the original Nahuatl word. Residents of Jalapa call themselves *jalapeños.*

The town's prime cultural attraction is the **Museo de Antropología de Jalapa.** With 3,000 of 29,000 pieces on display, it is second only to Mexico City's archaeological museum and is a treasure trove of artifacts from the three main pre-Hispanic cultures of Veracruz: Huastec, Totonac, and most important, Olmec. Its three sections are filled with magnificent stone Olmec heads; carved stelae and offering bowls; terra-cotta jaguars and cross-eyed gods; cremation urns in the forms of bats and monkeys; lovely Totonac murals; and, most touching of all, life-size sculptures of women who died in childbirth (the ancients elevated them to the status of goddesses). At a burial site, you can see ritually deformed skulls and ceremonial figurines. Tours by English-speaking students are available daily 11–4, but it's best to call in advance and make an appointment, as the tour schedule is unpredictable. ✉ *Av. Jalapa s/n,* ☎ *28/15–09–20 or 28/15–07–08.* ✆ *$1.50, $10 for tour in English.* ☉ *Daily 9–5.*

Dining and Lodging

$$ ✕ **La Casa de Mamá.** This very popular restaurant is on a busy thor-
★ oughfare just east of the town center. The dark, antique furnishings and lazy ceiling fan almost succeed in giving this place the feel of a northern Mexican hacienda, but the incessant street noise reminds you that you're in a busy capital city. Never mind; you'll be focusing on the generous portions of charcoal-broiled steaks and the succulent shrimp and fish dishes, served with *frijoles charros* (black beans cooked in a spicy

sauce) or Mexican rice. The place is known for its desserts, which include flan with caramel and bananas flambéed in brandy. ⊠ *Avila Camacho 113,* ☎ *28/17–31–44,* FAX *28/17–31–44. AE, MC, V.*

$$ ✕ **La Estancia de los Tecajetes.** For fine regional dishes with a dash of
★ creativity, try this rustic, lodgelike restaurant overlooking the lushly tropical Parque los Tecajetes (tucked into a small strip mall, the restaurant can be a bit difficult to find). Inside, it's cozy and relaxing, always buzzing with diners feasting on *cecina* (paper-thin beef fillet) with enchiladas, beans, and avocado; *crepa consentida* (crepes filled with chicken and smothered in poblano chilies and cheese); or *pollo manzana* (a boneless chicken breast cooked in butter, cream, and white wine). Corn tortillas are made on the premises, and the walls are filled with charming sepia-tone photos of Jalapa's past. ⊠ *Plaza Tecajetes, Avila Camacho 90–12,* ☎ *28/18–07–32. MC, V.*

$ ✕ **La Casona del Beaterio.** In contrast to the cafeteria-style eateries along Avenida Zaragoza, La Casona dishes up fine local fare in a comfortable setting. The restaurant's two spacious rooms, surrounding a courtyard garden with a fountain, are set with sturdy wooden furniture, stained-glass windows, historical photos, and hanging plants. Breakfast specials are a steal, and a typical morning finds locals and business travelers wallowing away a few hours over a cup of strong coffee and *huevos rancheros* (fried eggs with chili sauce, raw onion, grated cheese, and tortillas). The generous steak and seafood dinners, including the house specialty—*cazuela de mariscos* (stew of shrimp, octopus, and clams cooked with chipotle chilies)—draw crowds. This is java country, so the menu has a dozen different coffee and espresso concoctions. ⊠ *Av. Zaragoza 20,* ☎ *28/18–21–19. AE, MC, V.*

$ ✕ **La Fonda.** The entrance to this traditional breakfast-and-lunch restaurant is hidden on a small pedestrian walkway off busy Calle Enríquez, a block from Parque Juárez. Brightly colored streamers, baskets, flowers, and paintings of Jalapa churches adorn the walls, and the warm corn tortillas served with every meal are made before your eyes. The food is hearty northern Veracruzan fare: beef or chicken and beans, *nopales* (cactus strips), and/or chili are essential elements of almost every dish. ⊠ *Callejón del Diamante 1, at Calle Enríquez,* ☎ *28/ 18–72–82. No credit cards. Closed Sun. No dinner.*

$ ✕ **La Sopa.** Modest as it may look, this restaurant draws hearty eaters from all walks of life—local politicians, students, and blue-collar workers—who make a beeline for the bargain *comida corrida* (fixed-price lunch). One of the best-kept secrets in town, La Sopa's four-course attraction might include carrot-and-potato soup, chicken with rice and fresh corn tortillas, and vanilla pudding served with coffee or tea. The menu features Mexican *antojitos* (appetizers) in the evening, including *chiles rellenos* (green chili peppers stuffed with meat or cheese and fried in egg batter) and tamales. Live music fills the air Thursday (Huastec folk music), Friday (danzón), and Saturday (a harpist), about 7:30–11:30. ⊠ *Antonio M. de Rivera 3-A (also known as Callejón del Diamante),* ☎ *28/17–80–69. No credit cards. Closed Sun.*

$$$ 🛏 **Fiesta Inn Xalapa.** This attractive chain hotel has the fresh look of a beach property in tropical climes (perhaps to offset Jalapa's rather gloomy weather), and it has the most upscale amenities. It's a bit out of the way—in a primarily residential neighborhood 10 minutes by car from the center of town—but a good bet if you are looking for a comfortable, quiet, secure, and well-equipped base. The modern guest rooms in the two-story, colonial-style structure have satellite color TVs, phones, air-conditioning, bathtubs, and plenty of morning sunlight. Airport transfers from the port of Veracruz are available for a fee. ⊠ *Carretera Xalapa–Veracruz Km 2.5, Fracc. Las Animas 91000,* ☎ *28/12–79–20 or 01–800/504–5000,* FAX *28/12–79–46. 119 rooms,*

4 suites. Restaurant, bar, coffee shop, in-room data ports, room service, pool, exercise room, free parking. AE, DC, MC, V.

$$$ ★ 🏨 **Posada Coatepec.** Specializing in fine food (but slow service) and catering to French and German travel groups, the Posada (built in 1890) is the former villa of a coffee baron. It has homey guest rooms, each with original tile floors, satellite color TV, and a heater for Coatepec's chilly, rainy winters; ask for one away from the murmur of street noise. The lobby and courtyard are splendidly decorated with a fine collection of antiques; a bar framed by lead-crystal windows is cozy and clubby. The hotel can arrange tours to nearby coffee plantations. The Posada is a 15-minute drive from Jalapa. ✉ *Hidalgo 9, Coatepec 91500,* 🕿 *28/16–05–44,* FAX *28/16–00–40. 7 rooms, 16 suites. Restaurant, bar, room service, pool, laundry service. AE, MC, V.*

$$ 🏨 **Hotel Xalapa Finca Real.** The Hotel Xalapa, which sits on a hill above Parque Los Tecajetes, is the most well-equipped downtown hotel, with many of the amenities of a more expensive establishment: phones, color TVs, air-conditioning (in most units), and bathtubs; free covered parking; and a disco. A 1960s institutional behemoth, the building isn't particularly attractive, and the gaudy pink-and-orange paint job can be tough on the eyes, but the rooms are large, sunny, and quiet. The hotel staff is well meaning, if not particularly competent, and the hot-water supply can be dicey. ✉ *Victoria at Bustamante, Zona Centro 91000,* 🕿 *28/18–22–22 or 28/17–70–64,* FAX *28/18–94–24. 170 rooms, 28 suites, 2 villas. 2 restaurants, bar, room service, pool, dance club, baby-sitting, playground, laundry service, meeting rooms, car rental, free parking. AE, DC, MC, V.*

$ ★ 🏨 **Mesón del Alférez.** A royal lieutenant of the Spanish Viceroy lived in this colonial house some 200 years ago. Now it's a reasonably priced gem of a hotel, restored with earthenware tiles, rustic wood, and lime pigment washes on the walls in such luminous hues as lilac, sky blue, and magenta. Rooms surround three small bougainvillea-drenched courtyards and have lovely hand-carved wood headboards, Talavera lamps, and hand-loomed bedspreads, as well as phones and color TVs (local channels only). ✉ *Sebastián Camacho 2, at Zaragoza, 91000,* 🕿 *28/18–63–51; 28/18–01–13; 01–800/715–5172; 877/867–9943 in the U.S.,* FAX *28/12–47–03. 15 rooms, 6 suites. Restaurant, room service, laundry service, free parking. AE, MC, V.*

$ 🏨 **Hotel Principal.** This spiffy hotel is a short walk from Parque Juárez. The rooms are big and comfortable, with phones, cable TVs, and high ceilings. The bathrooms, on the other hand, are small, with curtainless showers. Be sure to get a room facing the courtyard, or the traffic will set your teeth to rattling. ✉ *Zaragoza 28, 3½ blocks east of Parque Juárez, 91000,* 🕿 *28/18–61–00. 40 rooms. Restaurant, laundry service. No credit cards.*

Nightlife and the Arts

The **Agora** (✉ Parque Juárez, 🕿 28/18–57–30) cultural center has art exhibitions and the occasional folk-music performance and shows classic and avant-garde films in its cinema club. Stop by during the day to see what's planned. The **Teatro del Estado** (✉ Ignacio de la Llave s/n, 🕿 28/17–31–10) is the big, modern state theater of Veracruz. The Orquesta Sinfónica de Jalapa performs here, often giving free concerts during the off-season (early June–mid-August). Check *Diario Xalapa* (the Jalapa city newspaper in Spanish, available at newsstands) for dates and times of performances, or stop by the Agora. You might find someone who speaks English.

La 7a Estacion (✉ 20 de Noviembre near Central Camionera, 🕿 28/17–31–55) is packed with salsa dancers Wednesday night; Thursday through Saturday it's rock and alternative music. **Tempo Libero** (✉ Av.

Camacho 101, ☏ no phone) is a video dance bar that attracts mostly university students with thumping house-music rhythms Tuesday through Sunday. The **Bar Lovento** (✉ 20 de Noviembre Ote. 641, ☏ 28/17–83–34) heats up with a salsa beat for dancing Wednesday through Saturday night. A good mix of locals, tourists, and expats jams **Bar Boulevard 93** (✉ Av. Camacho 93, ☏ 28/46–27–93), a tony, neon-lit all-night club across from Parque Los Tecajetes.

Outdoor Activities and Sports

RIVER RAFTING

River rafting along the Río Pescados is gaining in popularity. Most of the operators who run these trips are trained in Canada and are highly professional. Base camps with tents, rafting equipment, and dining facilities are near the river at Jalcomulco, 42 km (26 mi) southeast of Jalapa.

Shopping

Mexico's finest export coffee is grown in this region, specifically in the highlands around the picturesque colonial towns of Coatepec and Xico, less than 10 km (6 mi) from Jalapa. Shops selling the prized *café de altura* (coffee of the highlands) abound in the main squares of both places. **Cafécali** (✉ Callejón del Diamante 2, ☏ 28/18–13–39) offers a wide selection of excellent coffee at competitive prices. **Café Colón** (✉ Calle Primo Verdad 15, between Avs. Zaragoza and Enríquez, ☏ 28/17–60–97) in Jalapa sells 20 varieties of coffee for about $2 a pound.

Callejón del Diamante, also known as Antonio M. Rivera, is a charming pedestrian street with vendors hawking a variety of wares: cheap jewelry, keepsakes, books, and fleece-lined slippers among them.

The **Mercado Juaregui** (✉ Av. Revolución and Calle Altamirano), open daily, is a wild indoor bazaar with everything from jewelry, blankets, and fresh vegetables to some rather dubious-looking natural "healing" potions and supposedly aphrodisiacal body pastes.

Side Trip to Xico

19 km (12 mi) south of Jalapa on road to Coatepec.

If you close your eyes and try to imagine the ideal Mexican small town, it couldn't be any more perfect than Xico. Aside from the occasional passing automobile, this village seems untouched by time; donkeys hauling burlap sacks of fresh beans clip-clop along the quaint cobblestone streets, followed by coffee-picking locals, machetes tied to their waists with red sashes. Lying in Mexico's premier coffee-growing region at the base of the mist-filled Perote foothills, Xico is famous for its native cuisine (*mole xiqueno,* a tasty mix of poblano chili and chocolate sauce) and its raucous summer festival (beginning July 22) celebrating the town's patron saint, Mary Magdalene.

But Xico is perhaps even better known for its natural wonders, notably the **Cascada de Texolo,** a majestic waterfall set in a deep gorge of tropical greenery. The setting for much of the 1984 film *Romancing the Stone,* this lush, scenic area is great for exploring; numerous paths lead off from the main falls through forests of banana trees to smaller cascades and crystal-blue pools, perfect for a refreshing swim. There's also a steep staircase that will take you from the observation deck to the base of the falls, a favorite spot for picnicking locals.

The falls are about 3 km (2 mi) from the center of town. To reach them, start from the red-and-white church where Calles Zaragosa and Matamoros meet and follow the cobblestone street downhill, bearing right when you reach the small roadside shrine to the Virgin Mary. Continue through the coffee plantations, following the signs for "La Cascada" until you reach the main observation deck, which includes a small restaurant (and a view of the nearby hydroelectric dam). Entry is free.

El Tajín

★ ▲ ❾ *13 km (8 mi) west of Papantla.*

The extensive ruins of El Tajín—the Totonac word means "thunder"—express the highest degree of artistry of any ancient city in the coastal area. The city remained hidden until 1785, when a Spanish engineer came upon it. Early theories attributed the complex—believed to be a religious center—to a settlement of Maya-related Huastecs, one of the most important cultures of the Veracruz area. Because of its immense size and unique architecture, however, scholars now believe it may have been built by a distinct El Tajín tribe related to the Maya. Although much of the site has been restored, many structures are still hidden under thick jungle growth.

El Tajín is thought to have reached its peak between AD 600 and 1200. During this time, hundreds of structures of native sandstone were built here, including temples, double-storied palaces, ball courts, large retaining walls, and hundreds of houses. But El Tajín was already an important religious and administrative center during the first three centuries AD. Its influence is in part attributed to the fact that it had large reserves of cacao beans, used as money in pre-Hispanic times.

Evidence suggests that the southern half of the uncovered ruins—the area around the lower plaza—was reserved for ceremonial purposes. Its centerpiece is the 60-ft-high **Pyramid of the Niches,** surely one of the finest pre-Columbian buildings in Mexico. The finely wrought seven-level structure has 365 coffers—one for each day of the solar year—built-in around its seven friezes. The reliefs on the pyramid depict the ruler, 13-Rabbit—all the rulers' names were associated with sacred animals—and allude also to the El Tajín tribe's main god, the benign Quetzalcóatl. One panel on the pyramid tells the tale of heroic human sacrifice and of the soul's imminent descent to the underworld, where it is rewarded with the gift from the gods of sacred *pulque,* a milky alcoholic beverage made from cactus.

Just south of the pyramid is a series of 10 I-shape **ball courts**—more than at any other site in Mesoamerica—where the sacred pre-Columbian ball game was played. The walls are covered with relief sculpture. The game, played throughout Mesoamerica, is similar in some ways to soccer—players used a hard rubber ball that could not be touched with the hands, and suited up in knee pads and body protectors—but far more deadly. Intricate carvings at this and other complexes indicate that the games ended with human sacrifice. It's still a subject of debate whether the winner or loser of the match was the sacrificial victim. It is surmised that the players may have been high-standing members of the priest or warrior classes.

El Tajín Chico, to the north, is thought to have been the secular part of the city, administrative and residential. It was likely the location of the elite's living quarters. Floors and roofing were made with a pre-Columbian cement of volcanic rock and limestone. The most important structure here is the Complejo de los Columnos (Complex of the Columns). The columns once held up the cement ceilings, but early settlers in Papantla removed the ceiling stones to construct houses.

A small museum at the entrance displays some pottery and sculpture and tells what little is known of the site. But because guided tours of

El Tajín aren't available, the rest is left to your imagination. The area outside the entrance is lined with covered stalls that sell inexpensive meals and tacky souvenirs, and there's a large, cafeteria-style restaurant at the site. If you're prepared to work your way through the thick jungle, you can see some more recent finds along the dirt paths that lead over the nearby ridges. ⌑ $2.50, free Sun. ☉ Daily 9–5.

Papantla de Olarte

❿ *250 km (155 mi) northwest of Veracruz.*

Papantla de Olarte sits amid tropical hills, the center of a vanilla-producing region (vanilla products are sold in every corner store and restaurant). A distinctive mix of Spanish colonial and indigenous influence can be seen here: Totonac men in flowing white pants lead their donkeys through the crowded streets, and palm trees shade the traditional, tile zócalo. The relaxed pace of the town is conducive to easygoing afternoons of reading, strolling, and people-watching; but the town is best known for its *voladores* (fliers), who twirl off an 82-ft pole next to Papantla's ornate cathedral. This ritual was originally performed as a tribute to the god of sun and rain. The four voladores begin the dance on a platform at the top of the ceremonial pole, each facing one of the cardinal directions. They start their descent from the side of the platform facing east—where the sun rises and the world awakes—twisting left for 13 full rotations each. Between them, the four fliers circle the pole 52 times, representing the sacred 52-year cycle of the Totonacs (the Maya calendar had the same 52-year cycle). A fifth man, the prayer giver, sits atop the pole, playing a small flute while keeping rhythm on a drum as the fliers descend. Originally the ceremony was held on the vernal equinox, but now the voladores fly for the crowds every Saturday and Sunday at 12:45 PM and give special shows on Corpus Christi.

Dining and Lodging

$ ✕ **Plaza Pardo.** From the balcony of this colorful second-story café and gift shop, you can watch the happenings in the zócalo. Bright yellow tablecloths adorn the tables where house specialties—including *tampiqueña* (Tampico-style filet of beef), *bocoles* (chicken- or cheese-stuffed gordita), and *rellenos al gusto* (green chilies stuffed with your choice of chicken, cheese, or beef)—are served. ⌑ *Enríquez 105 Altos A,* ☎ *784/2–00–59. No credit cards.*

$ ✕ **Restaurante Sorrento.** With more than 200 items on the menu, this
★ is the most popular restaurant in Papantla, crowded with locals who come to enjoy the cheap regional seafood and to catch a few minutes of the *telenovela* (soap opera) on the corner set. Large picture windows overlook the zócalo (ideal for people-watching) and the voladores ceremonial pole. ⌑ *Enríquez 105,* ☎ *784/2–00–67. No credit cards.*

$ ☷ **Hotel Premier.** Right on Papantla's pretty, lively zócalo, the Premier is the town's swankiest hotel and a real bargain. The lobby is lined with mirrors and etched glass and furnished with small purple chairs. The rooms are spotless and good-sized and have tiny balconies overlooking the square. Amenities include tile bathrooms, air-conditioning, phones, and satellite color TVs. ⌑ *Enríquez 103, 93400,* ☎ *784/2–16–45, FAX 784/2–42–13. 16 rooms, 4 suites. Room service, free parking. MC, V.*

$ ☷ **Hotel Tajín.** The trick at the Tajín is getting the right room; be sure to ask for the "superior" rooms, which come with air-conditioning (and possibly a less lumpy bed). The phones don't always work, but the rooms are spotless and have cable TVs. The hillside perch makes for nice views, and there's usually an English-speaking staff member at the reception desk. ✉ *Nuñez y Domínguez 104, 93400,* ☎ *784/2–01–21,* FAX *784/ 2–10–62. 59 rooms. Hair salon, free parking. AE, V.*

Shopping
A half block downhill from the zócalo, along Avenida 20 de Noviembre, is a teeming **street market** selling native Totonac costumes, carvings, woven baskets, handbags, cassettes, and food. The quality is not great, but if you poke around, you can find some good deals. The real draw is vanilla, the chief product of this region, which is sold in every conceivable form—beans and extract are common, but for a real souvenir, pick up a box of vanilla-flavored cigars.

Tuxpán

⓫ *193 km (120 mi) south of Tampico, 309 km (192 mi) northwest of Veracruz, 89 km (55 mi) north of Papantla.*

Tuxpán is a peaceful riverside town with graceful winding streets—and the Río Tuxpán is even clean enough to swim in. **Juárez,** the main street, running parallel to the river, is lined with diners, hotels, and shops. The **Parque Reforma** is the center of social activity in town, with more than a hundred tables set around a hub of cafés and fruit stands. It has a memorial to Fausto Vega Santander, a member of the 201st Squadron of the Mexican Air Force and the first Mexican to be killed in combat during World War II. Lanchas shuttle passengers across the river to the **Casa de Fidel Castro,** where Castro lived for a time while planning the overthrow of Fulgencio Batista. A replica of the *Granma,* the ship that carried Fidel's men from Tuxpán to Cuba, molders outside. Inside, the casa is bare save some black-and-white photos of Fidel.

Beaches
Tuxpán's main appeal is the untouristed miles of beaches that begin just 7 km (4½ mi) east of town. The first, and most accessible beach from Tuxpán, is **Playa Tuxpán.** The surf here isn't huge, but there's enough action to warrant breaking out your surf or boogie board. Of the palapas on Playa Tuxpán, the most established is Restaurant Miramar, which has an extensive menu and also provides umbrellaed beach chairs for customers.

Dining and Lodging
$$ ✗ **Antonio's.** Antonio's is a quiet, comparatively elegant eatery with a varied menu. The *cazuela de mariscos* is excellent, as are the prawns, served grilled or in garlic sauce. A number of beef dishes and sandwiches are also available. Enjoy a cocktail from the full bar. ✉ *Av. Juárez 25, at Garizurieta,* ☎ *783/4–16–02. AE, MC, V.*

$$ ✗ **Berra de Mariscos.** This unpretentious, open-air eatery on Tuxpán's busy Avenida Juárez is an ideal place to spend a relaxing lunch people-watching. Don't be fooled by the white plastic tables and the bare-bones decor: the quality of the seafood dishes here easily rivals fancier places in town. Hunker down with a cold beer and a plate of *pulpos* (octopus and squid cooked with onions, butter, and garlic) or the house specialty, *camarones a la diabla* (a spicy concoction of grilled prawns and chilies). The wait staff is friendly and prompt, and all meals are preceded by a generous serving of freshly made tortilla chips. ✉ *Av. Juárez 44, at Calle Mina,* ☎ *783/4–10–61. No credit cards.*

$$ ▥ **Hotel May Palace.** The most luxurious lodgings in Tuxpán are at this hotel in the center of town. The modern five-story property is geared to a business clientele. The rooms are swathed in pastels and set off by rattan furniture designed for the hotel. All units have phones, satellite TVs, and air-conditioning. Guest services include a small video bar, a restaurant specializing in seafood and regional dishes, a rooftop

pool, and meeting salons. ⊠ *Av. Juárez 44, facing Parque Reforma, 92800,* ☎ FAX *783/4–88–82 or 783/4–44–61. 68 rooms, 2 suites. Restaurant, bar, room service, pool, exercise room, laundry service, meeting room, free parking. AE, MC, V.*

$$ 🏨 **Hotel Plaza Palmas.** In a sleepy suburban neighborhood five min-
★ utes from the city center, this sprawling bi-level hostelry is a welcome respite from Tuxpán's riverfront bustle. And although the mounted stag heads overseeing the spare lobby give the Palmas a rather incongruous tropical-motel-cum-hunting-lodge quality, the quirkiness ends there. Quaint cobblestone paths lead to the accommodations, which are housed in two U-shape buildings surrounding a large palm-lined pool area with tables and a small seafood bar. Rooms are spacious and clean with blue-tile floors, brick and stucco walls, two double beds, air-conditioning, phone, and cable TV. ⊠ *Libramiento Carretera s/n, 92800,* ☎ *783/4–35–29 or 783/4–35–74,* FAX *783/4–35–35 or 783/4–27–42. 98 rooms, 3 suites. Restaurant, bar, room service, pool, 2 tennis courts, playground, laundry service, meeting room, free parking. AE, MC, V.*

$ 🏨 **Hotel Florida.** Don't be deceived by the harsh fluorescent light in
★ the lobby: this is the best hotel deal in downtown Tuxpán. The rooms, all with phones, cable TV, and air-conditioning, are decorated in soft pastels; most have ample light and space as well as immaculate bathrooms. Outer rooms have terraces and views of the cathedral and waterfront. The amicable staff may be the best in northeast Mexico. ⊠ *Av. Juárez 23, across from cathedral, 92800,* ☎ *783/4–02–22 or 783/4–06–02,* FAX *783/4–06–50. 75 rooms. Restaurant, bar, room service, meeting room, free parking. DC, MC, V.*

Outdoor Activities and Sports

WATER SPORTS

For scuba diving, head to **Tamiahua,** a small village just north of Tuxpán, where you can hire a fishing boat for the 45-minute journey to the prime diving around **Isla Lobos** (Wolf Island), a protected eco-reserve that shares its space with a military outpost and a lighthouse. In the shallow water offshore are a few shipwrecks and colorful reefs that host a large variety of sea life, including puffer fish, parrot fish, damselfish, and barracuda. **Aquasport** (☎ 783/7–02–59), just west of Playa Tuxpán, arranges scuba diving trips to Isla Lobos (most enjoyable May–August) and also has deep-sea fishing excursions. Other outfits run trips to the island, which include permits, scuba gear, lunch, and transportation.

VERACRUZ A TO Z

AIR TRAVEL TO AND FROM VERACRUZ

There are nonstop flights on Mexicana and Aeroméxico from Mexico City to Heriberto Jara International Airport about 8 km (5 mi) south of downtown Veracruz.

➤ AIRLINES & CONTACTS: **Aeroméxico** (☎ 29/35–08–33 or 29/35–02–83). **Mexicana** (☎ 29/32–22–42 or 29/32–86–99).

AIRPORTS AND TRANSFERS

➤ AIRPORT INFORMATION: **Heriberto Jara International Airport**(☎ 29/34–37–74).

AIRPORT TRANSFERS

A cab to the city center costs $8.50. No city bus serves the airport. An air-conditioned private car ($10) runs between the airport and the downtown office of Transavion.

➤ TAXIS & SHUTTLES: **Transavion** (⊠ Av. Diaz Miron 3008, ☎ 29/37–89–78).

BUS TRAVEL TO AND FROM VERACRUZ

Veracruz's main bus terminal is about 4 km (2½ mi) south of the zócalo. The main bus company is ADO, with daily service to Jalapa every 20 minutes from 6 AM to 11:30 PM and round-the-clock departures for Mexico City. ADO also offers first-class all-day service to Reynosa, on the Texas border. If you're headed north and east, the deluxe bus line UNO goes to Jalapa, Puebla, and Mexico City. Cristóbal Colón offers daily first-class service to Oaxaca, and Autobuses Unidos has second-class service to Los Tuxtlas.

➤ BUS INFORMATION: **ADO** (☎ 29/37–29–22 or 29/35–07–83). **Autobuses Unidos** (☎ 29/37–57–32). **Bus Terminal** (✉ Díaz Mirón 1698, ☎ 29/37–57–44). **Cristóbal Colón** (☎ 29/37–57–44). **UNO** (☎ 29/35–07–83 or 29/37–29–22).

CAR RENTAL

Sun del Golfo is the only rental agency in Jalapa. Avis is the only service in the Herberto Jara International Airport, but Dollar and National are both close to the center of Veracruz. Hertz has service in Boca del Río.

➤ MAJOR AGENCIES: **Avis** (✉ Heriberto Jara International Airport, ☎ 29/32–16–76). **Dollar** (✉ Víctimas del 5 y 6 de Julio 883, ☎ 29/35–52–31 or 29/35–33–77). **Hertz** (✉ Hotel Costa Verde, Avila Camacho 3797, Boca del Río, ☎ 29/37–47–76). **National** (✉ Díaz Mirón 1036, ☎ 29/31–17–56 or 29/31–33–12). **Sun del Golfo** (✉ Ignacio de la Llave 14, Jalapa, ☎ 28/17–70–46, 28/41–17–78, or 28/41–17–79).

CAR TRAVEL

The city of Veracruz can be reached in about eight hours by traveling south from Tampico via Mexico 180, or in six hours from Mexico City via Mexico 150. The highways throughout the state, paved and kept up with oil money, are generally very good.

EMERGENCIES

Dial 060 in Veracruz for medical, fire, and theft emergencies. Should you find yourself in a medical emergency situation, call the local Red Cross (Cruz Roja) for ambulance service. The local police can handle small incidences, but if you feel the situation could escalate, contact the Oficinas Para La Seguridad de la Turista, which offers a country-wide 24-hour toll-free hot line to provide legal and medical help for tourists.

➤ HOSPITALS: **Hospital General de Veracruz** (✉ 20 de Noviembre s/n, ☎ 29/31–78–48).

➤ EMERGENCY SERVICES: **Jalapa Cruz Roja** (☎ 28/18–42–81 or 28/17–81–58). **Jalapa Police** (☎ 28/18–74–90 or 28/18–71–99). **Oficinas Para la Seguridad de la Turista** (☎ 01–800/903–9200). **Papantla Cruz Roja** (☎ 784/2–01–26). **Papantla Police** (☎ 784/2–00–75). **Tuxpán Cruz Roja** (☎ 783/4–01–58). **Tuxpán Police** (☎ 783/4–02–52). **Veracruz Cruz Roja** (☎ 29/37–55–00). **Veracruz Police** (✉ Playa Linda 222, ☎ 29/38–06–64 or 29/38–06–93).

HEALTH

PHARMACIES

In Jalapa, Calle Enríquez is lined with pharmacies. For 24-hour service, the Farmacia Plus is your best option. Farmacia de Descuento, the largest pharmacy in Papantla, is open daily 7:30 AM–10 PM. In downtown Tuxpán, Farmacia El Fenix is open daily 8 AM–10 PM. In Veracruz, Farmacia del Ahorro is a big, convenient drugstore downtown; it closes at 10:30 PM daily. For 24-hour home delivery in Veracruz, call Las Torres Pharmacy.

➤ PHARMACY INFORMATION: **Farmacia del Ahorro** (✉ Paseo del Malecón 342, at Calle Fariaz, Veracruz, ☎ 29/37–35–25). **Farmacia de Descuento**

(✉ Gutiérrez Zamora 103, Jalapa, ☎ 784/2–19–41). **Farmacia El Fenix** (✉ Calle Morelos1, at Av. Juárez, Tuxpán, ☎ 783/4–30–23). **Farmacia Plus** (✉ Revolución 173, at Sagayo, Papantla, ☎ 28/17–27–77 or 28/17–27–97). **Las Torres Farmacia** (✉ Diaz Mirón 165, Veracruz, ☎ 29/32–63–63).

MAIL AND SHIPPING

Mail and fax services in Jalapa are available at the main post office. Caseta Telefonica has three computers for e-mail and Internet access, charges $1.50 an hour, and is open weekdays 7 AM–10 PM and weekends 8 AM–9 PM. Compupapel has eight computers; it's open daily 9–8:30 and charges $1 an hour.

Several blocks from the Papantla zócalo, PC's Palafox has 10 computers with Internet access for $1.50 an hour 8 AM–9 PM weekdays, 8–7 Saturday, and 8–5 Sunday.

The Tuxpán post office is a half block from Avenida Juárez. Internet cafés in the downtown area all charge about $1.50 an hour. Sesico, which has 10 computers, is open Monday–Saturday 9–8:30 and Sunday 10–3.

In Veracruz, the main post office is a five-block walk from the zócalo. For Internet access, Web Café has the fastest machines, for $1.80 an hour, with slightly cheaper rates for students. It's open 10–10 daily. Netcha Boys, open weekdays 9–9 and weekends noon–8, will run you $1.50 an hour for Internet access.

➤ POST OFFICES: **Jalapa post office** (✉ Av. Zamora 70, at Calle Diego Leno). **Tuxpán post office** (✉ Calle Morelos 12). **Veracruz post office** (✉ Plaza República 213).

➤ INTERNET SERVICES: **Caseta Telefonica** (✉ Av. Enríquez 16, Jalapa, ☎ 28/17–36–86 or 28/12–24–62). **Compupapel** (✉ Calle Primo Verdad 23, at Av. Zaragoza, Jalapa, ☎ 28/17–23–22). **PC's Palafox** (✉ Aquiles Serdán 500, at Calle Galeana, Papantla, ☎ 784/2–13–57). **NetchaBoys** (✉ Calle Miguel Lerdo 369, Veracruz, ☎ no phone). **Web Café** (✉ Calle Rayon 579-A, between Avs. Independencia and Zaragoza, Veracruz, ☎ no phone). **Sesico** (✉ Av. Juárez 52, off Parque Reforma, Tuxpán, ☎ 783/4–45–05).

MONEY MATTERS

About seven blocks from Jalapa's Parque Juárez, Casa de Cambio Monendes Internacional has good rates; it's open 9–3 and 5–7:30 weekdays. You can also change money in the morning at several banks on Parque Juárez. Most have 24-hour ATMs.

There are plenty of banks surrounding the Papantla zócalo, most of which change money weekday mornings. Banamex changes both cash and traveler's checks weekdays 9–noon and has a 24-hour ATM that accepts Cirrus, Plus, Visa, and MasterCard.

The Tuxpán Banamex changes cash and traveler's checks 9–5 weekdays; it has a 24-hour ATM. Bancomer has a 24-hour ATM and changes cash and traveler's checks weekdays 8:30–2:30.

The best rates in Veracruz are at Bancomer, but money-changing hours are limited to 9–noon weekdays, so you'll have to arrive early to make it through the lines. The Casa de Cambio Puebla is open weekdays 9–6. Or use the ATMs that are readily available downtown.

➤ BANKS: **Banamex** (✉ Enríquez 102, Papantla; ✉ Av. Juárez at Calle Corregidora, Tuxpán). **Bancomer** (✉ Av. Juárez at Escuela Médico Militar, Tuxpán, ☎ 783/4–00–09; ✉ Av. Juárez at Independencia, Veracruz, ☎ 29/31–00–95 or29/89–80–00). **Casa de Cambio Monendes Inter-**

nacional (⊠ Elustres 48, Jalapa, ☎ 28/17–20–60). **Casa de Cambio Puebla** (⊠ Av. Juárez 112, Veracruz, ☎ 29/31–24–50).

SIGHTSEEING TOURS

Jalapa. Expediciones Mexico Verde has river rafting along the Río Pescados near Jalapa. One-day or overnight excursions are available. All equipment, including life jackets, helmets, and oars, is provided. The outfit also runs 7- or 10-day trips on the Cortés Route, which includes Veracruz City, La Antigua, Cempoala, Jalapa, and Coatepec (in the state of Veracruz) and continues on to conquistador-related sites in the states of Tlaxcala, Puebla, and Mexico. English is spoken.

Veracruz. Boat tours of the bay depart from the malecón daily 7–7. Boats leave whenever they're full, and the $2.50 half-hour ride includes a (Spanish-language) talk on Veracruz history. Longer trips to nearby Isla Verde (Green Island) and Isla de Enmedio (Middle Island) leave daily from the shack marked PASEO EN LANCHITA near Plaza Acuario. Boats wait until they're full to set off, so it's best to be in a group. The cost should be about $3–$5 per person, but feel free to bargain.

Martin Sandoval Tours has city tours as well as trips to El Tajín and Papantla, Los Tuxtlas, and Jalapa. Diving and fishing trips are available, too. There are also travel desks at the Torremar and Emporio.
➤ FEES & SCHEDULES: **Expediciones Mexico Verde** (⊠ Homero 526, Int. 801, Col. Polanco, Mexico, D.F. 11560, ☎ 5255–44–00 or 01/800–362–8800, ☎ 𝖥𝖠𝖷 5/255–4465). **Martin Sandoval Tours** (⊠ Balboa 327, between Washington and Martí, ☎ 29/37–19–84, ☎ 𝖥𝖠𝖷 29/35–31–72). **Veraventuras** (⊠ Santos Degollado 81, Int. 8, ☎ 28/18–97–79, 28/18–96–80, or 01–800/2–65–72).

VISITOR INFORMATION

The Jalapa tourist office is in the large office building on the way out of town toward Veracruz (known as Torre Animas) and is open weekdays 9–9. There's also a Jalapa tourist information booth in front of the Palacio Municipal; it's open daily 9–9.

The Tuxpán tourist office is open daily 8–3 and 4–6.

The Veracruz Dirección Municipal de Turismo is open Monday–Saturday 9–9, Sunday 10–1.
➤ TOURIST INFORMATION: **Jalapa tourist information booth** (⊠ Calle Enríquez 14). **Jalapa tourist office** (⊠ Blvd. Cristóbal Colón 5, Jardines de las Animas, ☎ 28/12–85–00, ext. 130, 𝖥𝖠𝖷 28/12–59–36). **Tuxpán tourist office** (⊠ Av. Juárez 26, ☎ 783/4–01–77). **Veracruz Dirección Municipal de Turismo** (⊠ Palacio Municipal on zócalo, ☎ 29/22–23–14, 𝖥𝖠𝖷 29/32–75–93).

THE NORTHEAST

Few travelers go out of their way to visit northeastern Mexico. The arid area is becoming increasingly industrial as more and more multinational companies establish *maquiladoras* (foreign-owned factories in duty-free zones) along the border, creating more and more air pollution and often horrible living conditions for the maquila workers, who come from all over Mexico.

But day- and weekend-trippers from Texas enjoy the foreign color and cuisine of border towns such as Nuevo Laredo, Matamoros, and Reynosa. And only about three hours from the border is Monterrey, a fast-paced city that's home to Mexico's major brewery, some good museums, and one of Latin America's finest universities.

Nature lovers can enjoy the Parque Nacional Cumbres de Monterrey, northwest of the city, with its impressive Cola de Caballo waterfall. Also near Monterrey is the dramatic cut of the Barranca de la Huasteca, as well as the Grutas de García, caves with an underground lake and a stalactite and stalagmite forest. Tampico is known both for its seaside appeal and its interesting architectural sights.

Nuevo Laredo

⑫ *1½ km (1 mi) south of Laredo, Texas.*

Of all the eastern border towns, Nuevo Laredo receives the largest onslaught of American souvenir-seekers. Shopping is the primary pursuit here, and you'll find a warren of stalls and shops as well as a large crafts market concentrated on Avenida Guerrero in a seven-block stretch that extends from the International Bridge to the main plaza. In addition to the standard border-town curios, Nuevo Laredo shops stock a good selection of high-quality handicrafts from all over Mexico, at somewhat inflated prices. Wander a few blocks off the main drag in any direction for better prices and smaller crowds.

Nuevo Laredo was founded after the Treaty of Guadalupe Hidalgo in 1848, which ended the Mexican-American War. The treaty established the Río Bravo (or Rio Grande) as the border between the two countries and forced Mexico to give up a substantial amount of territory. Many of Laredo's Mexican residents, who suddenly found themselves living in the United States, crossed the river and founded Nuevo Laredo on what had been the outskirts of town. Today, Nuevo Laredo's economy depends greatly on gringos who head south for a few days of drunken revelry, returning home with a bottle of tequila and suitcases full of souvenirs.

Dining and Lodging

$$$ ✕ **Restaurant Victoria 3020.** Set back from the street and surrounded
★ by a garden, the Victoria offers the swankiest dining in town. In the pastel-hue main room, amid abstract paintings and sculptures by Mexico's top artists, diners feast on such rich creations as broiled New York steak topped with demiglace burgundy and marrow butter, frog legs sautéed in garlic and white-wine sauce, and rainbow trout in a sweet almond sauce. The white-jacketed waiters won't let you get away without trying the *tunas borrachas victoria* (prickly pear and kiwi served with tequila and vanilla ice cream) for dessert. The candlelit courtyard in back is perfect for a quiet, romantic dinner. ✉ *Victoria 3020, at Matamoros,* ☎ *87/12–69–00 or 87/13–30–20. AE, MC, V.*

$$ ✕ **El Dorado.** Dating from the Prohibition era, this spot is a favorite with the Texas crowd—a hangout better known for its atmosphere than for its cuisine. Try the combination plate of grilled meat, which includes two selections of either goat, quail, or frogs' legs. ✉ *Ocampo at Calle Belden,* ☎ *87/12–00–15. AE, MC, V.*

1$: ✕ **México Típico.** This establishment, decorated in murals from various Mexico cities, offers indoor and outdoor dining, with mariachis coming in from the street to entertain. The patio, partially covered, has a fountain. Specialties are carne asada and cabrito. True to its name, México Típico serves the typical Mexican plate of beef or chicken enchiladas with rice and refried beans. ✉ *Av. Guerrero 934,* ☎ *87/12–15–25. MC, V.*

$$$ 🏨 **Hotel Hacienda Real.** A carved wooden statue of *San Judas* and another of *San Miguel* guard the tiled lobby here. It's the small touches—the wrought-iron balconies, the European-style streetlamps along the walkways—that make the Hacienda Real well worth the 15-minute trip from the city center. The bright, immaculate rooms, overlooking a central garden and palm-lined pool area, all have hand-carved wooden furniture, embroidered bedspreads, large tile bathrooms, air-conditioning, and cable TV. ✉ *Av. Reforma 5530, 88280,* ☎ *87/17–00–00 or 01–800/718–7470,* 🆅 *87/17–04–20. 72 rooms, 2 suites. Restaurant, bar, room service, pool, beauty salon, tennis court, basketball, meeting room, free parking. AE, MC, V.*

$$ 🏨 **Hotel Reforma.** An older hotel just a half block south of Plaza Hidalgo, Reforma has a restaurant, marble lobby, and secure parking. Rooms in the older section, although somewhat small and rather nondescript, are comfortable; the junior suites in the newer section are slightly bigger and have fresh carpets and curtains, although the hallways smell musty. All units come with shower, air-conditioning, cable color TVs, and phones. ✉ *Av. Guerrero 822, 88000,* ☎ *87/12–62–50,* 🆅 *87/12–67–14. 45 rooms. Restaurant, bar, room service, free parking. MC, V.*

Nightlife and the Arts

All of the popular dance clubs are on Avenida Guerrero in the heart of the shopping district. **Victoria's,** (☎ 84/12–69–00), three blocks from International Bridge 1, is a noisy favorite; the **El Dorado** (☎ 87/12–00–15) is somewhat more sedate. The new **Plaza San Miguel** (☎ 87/14–44–44; $20–$30 cover for shows) is the local disco.

Shopping

On the stretch where International Bridge 1 leads into Avenida Guerrero, you'll find most of Nuevo Laredo's shops—classy and junky alike. Most stores stay open until 8 PM. **Granada** (✉ Av. Guerrero 504, ☎ 87/12–86–44) has better-quality items than many of the other vendors, including lead crystal and serapes. Artisan shops selling lots of leather goods and ceramics are in the **Nuevo Mercado de la Reforma,** a market three blocks south of International Bridge 1, at Avenida Guerrero and Calle Belden. The **Maria Cristina** mall, at Avenida Guerrero 631, houses about three dozen curio outlets.

Reynosa

🔞 *16 km (10 mi) south of McAllen, Texas.*

Because of its manageable size and mellow attitude, Reynosa is one of the most pleasant points of entry into Mexico. It is also a convenient starting point if you're bound for Mexico City, Monterrey, or Veracruz. That said, Reynosa is still an industrial border town of limited charm, driven economically by the petrochemicals industry, agriculture, and the ever-present tourist trade. As you enter town, you'll see the **Zona Rosa** (Pink Zone) tourist district, with a few curio shops and a couple of bars and restaurants. The heart of the city, around **Plaza Principal,** is about five blocks from the International Bridge. In the downtown area, sidewalks are wide, parks have new benches, and the cobblestone streets have tidy street signs. After leaving downtown, Reynosa is a jumble of tacky border-town urban sprawl.

Plaza Principal is in many ways a typical Mexican town center, but its original colonial church has been joined like a Siamese twin to an ultramodern newer addition with arches and stained-glass windows, bordered on one side by a movie theater and on the other by a Nike outlet store. **Hidalgo Street,** a colorful pedestrian mall of shops and street vendors, leads off from the plaza. Many Texans save money by having their teeth fixed south of the Rio Grande—which explains the many dental offices you'll see in this area.

Dining and Lodging

$$ ✕ **La Fogata.** Baby goat, stuffed goat intestines, lamb ribs, and a variety of beef cuts are all prepared on a smoky open grill at the back of this popular cabrito joint. The Herculean portions of slow-roasted meat are served in the classic northern style, with side dishes of guacamole, lime, jalapeños, and tortillas. The menu also includes chicken fajitas, quail, and Cornish hen. ⊠ *Matamoros 750, at Chapa,* ☎ *89/22–47–72 or 89/22–82–16. AE, MC, V.*

$$ ✕ **Sam's.** Wild game such as quail and dove (served from November–January) and seafood are the reasons to come here. Desserts include ice cream, flan, and cheesecake. In winter, Sam's is frequented by Americans from the Rio Grande Valley and snowbirds from Minnesota. ⊠ *Allende 1100,* ☎ *89/22–00–34 or 89/22–34–34. AE, MC, V.*

$ ✕ **Café Paris.** Grab a coffee and a pastry or the spicy *comida corrida* (lunch special) and watch the action in this boisterous café. Decorated in cool white-tile floors and equipped with strong air-conditioning, the Café Paris is an oasis from the heat; friends and lovers flock here for an afternoon of visiting amidst clanging silverware and walk-in music trios (which often include a harp). ⊠ *Hidalgo 815,* ☎ *89/22–55–35. No credit cards.*

$$$–$$$$ 🏨 **Hacienda.** Along the highway to Monterrey about 16 km (10 mi) from the U.S. border, this sparkling hotel is luxurious by Reynosa standards. Its tile lobby is decorated with colonial-style furniture and handicrafts, which carry over into the light-filled, cheerful rooms; all have color cable TVs, air-conditioning, and direct-dial phones. ⊠ *Blvd. Hidalgo 2013, 88650,* ☎ *89/24–60–10,* 🆉🆇 *89/23–59–62. 20 rooms, 13 suites. Restaurant, bar, room service, meeting room, free parking. AE, MC, V.*

$$ 🏨 **Astromundo.** Downtown and close to the market and the few good local restaurants, this popular hotel gets a lot of traffic from weekending Texans. Rooms are clean with strong air-conditioning units, and each floor is painted a different bright color. ⊠ *Juárez 675, 88500,* ☎ *89/22–56–25,* 🆉🆇 *89/22–98–88. 90 rooms, 6 suites. Restaurant, bar, room service, free parking. AE, MC, V.*

$$ 🏨 **San Carlos.** This five-story hotel on the square has air-conditioned rooms with colonial-style furniture and satellite TVs. Business travelers and tourists appreciate its central location, close to the square and shopping center, and the friendly staff. ⊠ *Hidalgo 970, 88500,* ☎ *89/ 22–12–80 or 89/22–40–00,* ⊡ *89/22–40–00. 66 rooms, 10 suites. Restaurant, room service, laundry service, free parking. MC, V.*

Nightlife and the Arts

The **Imperial** (⊠ Av. Virreyes 1087, entrance at the back of gift shop, ☎ no phone) offers slow-dance music on weeknights and disco on weekends; don't get too close to the live chained monkey on the patio—he bites! The Zona Dorada (along Emilio Portés Gel) has the most popular discos, including **Frida's** (⊠ Emilio Portés Gel 1410, ☎ 89/22–22–33); it's decorated with Frida Kahlo memorabilia.

Shopping

Treviño's (⊠ Av. Virreyes 1075, ☎ 89/22–14–44) has a good selection of Mexican arts and crafts, sculpture, papier-mâché, perfumes, liquors, and clothing.

Matamoros

⓮ *1 km (about ½ mi) south of Brownsville, Texas.*

Matamoros, across from Brownsville, Texas, is the most historic of the border towns, dating from the 18th century. It actually is named H. Matamoros, or Heroic Matamoros, for one of the many rebellious priests who were executed by the Spanish during the War of Independence (1810–21). The first major battle of the Mexican-American War was fought here when guns in Matamoros began shelling Fort Brown on the north side of the Rio Grande. Shortly afterward, troops of Zachary Taylor occupied Matamoros and began their march south.

Today Matamoros is the commercial center of a rich agricultural area and a manufacturing center for multinational corporations. Of the three border towns, Avenida Alvaro Obregón makes the prettiest entryway. The town's best shops, restaurants, and accommodations are here.

The **Casa Mata Museum** is in the remains of Fort Mata, built in 1845 to defend the city against American invasion. The fortress wasn't completed in time, and Zachary Taylor's troops were able to capture Matamoros easily. Casa Mata now displays photos and artifacts, mostly from the Mexican Revolution. ⊠ *Guatemala and Santos Degollado,* ☎ *88/ 13–59–29.* ⊡ *Free.* ☼ *Mon.–Sat. 9:30–5, Sun. 9:30–3.*

Dining and Lodging

$$ ✕ **Garcia's.** Rebuilt and redecorated over its own parking garage, this
★ is a romantic place for dancing and dining on lobster or steak and your choice of a dozen fine tequilas. An elevator from the garage takes you up to a gift shop with wares from all over Mexico as well as to the restaurant and a bar. ⊠ *Av. Alvaro Obregón 82,* ☎ *88/12–39–29 or 88/13–18–33. AE, MC, V.*

$ ✕ **Los Norteños.** A goat slow-roasting over hot coals in the window is the not-so-subtle advertisement for the best cabrito in town. Don't let the mixed decor of rich wooden columns and tables beneath harsh flourescent lights drive you away from a tender 12-ounce T-Bone steak or Tampequeño Fajitas. All meals are served with a tasty black-bean soup and a heaping pile of tortillas. ⊠ *Calle Matamoros between 8 and 9,* ☎ *88/13–00–37. No credit cards.*

$$$ 🏨 **Gran Hotel Residencial.** The best hotel in the city, this pleasant low-
★ rise built along Spanish colonial lines is near the center of Matamoros. All rooms have terraces, two queen- or one king-size bed, and color

cable TVs. There's also a large pool and a children's play area in the lush garden. ⊠ *Av. Alvaro Obregón 249, at Amapola, 87330,* ☎ *88/13–98–11 or 01–800/718–8230,* FAX *88/13–27–77. 109 rooms, 5 suites. Restaurant, bar, room service, pool, playground, meeting room, travel services, car rental, free parking. AE, MC, V.*

$$ 🔟 **Hotel Plaza Matamoros.** This member of the Best Western chain has
★ comfortable, clean rooms near the center of town. All have heavy wooden furniture, thick burgundy carpeting, air-conditioning, phones, and cable TVs, and look out over a central indoor restaurant. ⊠ *Calle 9 No. 1421, at Bravo, 87330,* ☎ *88/16–16–96 or 88/16–16–02,* FAX *88/16–16–87. 40 rooms. Restaurant, bar, room service, shops, laundry service, meeting room, free parking. AE, MC, V.*

Nightlife and the Arts

The **Teatro Reforma** (⊠ Calle 6 and Abasolo, ☎ 88/16–62–07 or 88/12–51–20), Matamoros's cultural hub, presents music and dance performances from around the country.

Garcia's offers live music in a dimly lit bar. The **Gran Hotel Residencial** is an elegant and relaxed place to stop for a drink. If you're looking for some dance action, head out to Avenida Alvaro Obregón toward the International Bridge, where you'll find several discos, including **Crazy Lazy, Zero Zone,** and **Mr. Lee's Dragon Club.**

Shopping

The most appealing shops are on Avenida Alvaro Obregón, which leads from the border bridge to the center of town. The salmon-color building that houses **Garcia's** restaurant also contains a huge gift shop, where you can buy everything from big sombreros to quality tequila, silver, Oaxacan wedding dresses, and leather jackets. Across from Garcia's, **Aztlan** (⊠ Av. Alvaro Obregón 75, ☎ 88/16–29–47) has high-quality jewelry, pewter, clothes, some contemporary artwork, and wooden and stone carvings. **Barbara** (⊠ Av. Alvaro Obregón 37, ☎ 88/16–54–56) sells attractive craft items, home furnishings, good costume jewelry, and imported cosmetics. It's also the only store that prepares free margaritas for shoppers. The covered, block-long **Mercado Juárez** downtown, between Calle 9 and Matamoros, is the place to haggle for bargains on souvenirs and pottery.

Monterrey

235 km (146 mi) southwest of Nuevo Laredo, 225 km (140 mi) west of Reynosa, 325 km (201 mi) west of Matamoros.

Monterrey is a favorite with weekenders and "winter Texans" from the Rio Grande Valley (it's a three-hour drive from the border or a short flight from Dallas, Houston, or San Antonio). The top hotels are clustered downtown in the Zona Rosa or Barrio Antiguo (Old Quarter). Several streets, including Avenida Morelos—the main drag—are pedestrian malls.

In 1996 Monterrey celebrated the 400th anniversary of its founding. It's Mexico's third-largest city and the capital of the state of Nuevo León. This industrial center is a brewer of beer and forger of steel, with nothing in the way of a laid-back lifestyle. Some of the country's most powerful captains of industry hold sway here—a fact that earned the city its nickname, the Sultan of the North. Monterrey also has the country's most sophisticated convention center—a high-tech facility called Cintermex—and built a gigantic sports arena to host international events.

The impressive **Gran Plaza**—at 100 acres, one of the country's largest squares—was part of a 1985 urban renewal project that included sev-

Monterrey

N

KEY

—— Metro
—— Rail Lines

TO AIRPORT →

1 mile

1 km

Río Santa Catarina

Gómez García

Av. Colón

Av. Madero

Av. Chapultepec

Revolución

Marquez

Av. de la Constitución

Av. Ignacio M. Prieto

Luis Elizonda

Gral Treviño

Felix U. Gómez

E. Garza Sada

Morelos

Ayutla

J.I. Ramón
Allende

Av. Zuazua

Av. Zaragoza

Mariano Escobedo

Galeana

Gran
Plaza

Morelos

Hidalgo

16 de Septiembre

Leon

Jalisco

Zacatecas

Garibaldi

Juarez

Av. Washington

15 de Mayo

Av. Padre Mier

J.M. Morelos

Hidalgo Plaza

Ocampo

Av. J. M. Pino Suárez

Av. Cuauhtémoc

Universidad

Av. Colón

Av. Madero

Gral Treviño

Villagómez

Alvarez

Díaz

Corona

Arramberi

América

Mariano Matamoros

5 de Mayo

Av. Hidalgo

Av. V. Carranza

Río Santa Catarina

Colima

Tlaxcala

5 de Febrero

2 de Abril

Bolívar

Av. P. Gonzalez

Av. Gonzalitos

Gral P. Gonzalez

Av. de la Constitución

Av. I. Morones Prieto

Av. Gral.
FCO Naranjo

Av. Manuel
Gómez Morín

⑰

⑮

⑱ ⑯

⑳

⑲

㉑

㉒

eral grand fountains, curio shops, and museums. The plaza is within walking distance of the downtown hotels. Better known as Macroplaza, it extends from the modernistic Palacio Municipal (City Hall) several blocks past the newly painted cathedral, the old City Hall, and the Legislative Palace to the Palacio de Gobierno (State House).

⑮ Towering above the plaza, opposite the neoclassical **Palacio de Gobierno,** is a giant orange concrete slab topped by the Beacon of Commerce, a laser beam that flashes from 8 to 11 nightly. It was designed by Luis Barragán to commemorate the 100th anniversary of the founding of the city's Chamber of Commerce. Handsome Saddle Mountain and the craggy Sierra Madre provide a majestic backdrop to this austere modern monument. The grandly lighted Palacio de Gobierno stays open all night, piping out soft classical music over a loudspeaker, and makes for a wonderful evening visit. ✉ *Between 5 de Mayo, 15 de Mayo, and Avs. Zaragoza and Zuazua.*

★ **⑯** The opulent **Museo de Arte Contemporaneo** (Museum of Contemporary Art) is the principal sight on the Gran Plaza. Designed in the style of a Moorish palace by renowned Mexican architect Ricardo Legorretta, it has 11 galleries that display cutting-edge art of Mexico and Latin America and sometimes other parts of the world. There's an outstanding collection of art books for sale at the gift shop. Listen to live music alongside a reflecting pool on the beautiful marble patio Wednesday evening (6–8) and watch the candlelit tables fill up with culture vultures sipping coffee and nibbling on pie. ✉ *Gran Plaza at Av. Zuazua and Jardón,* ☎ *8/342–4820.* ✑ *About $3, free Wed.* ☉ *Tues. and Thurs.–Sun. 10–6, Wed. 10–8.*

⑰ The **Museo de Historia Mexicana** (Mexican History Museum) has a mini riverwalk with cafés and a boat ride on its grounds. It displays the country's most complete history of its 1910–20 Revolution. Battles, marches, and political protagonists come to life in the newsreels of the period, part of a sophisticated multimedia show held inside a railroad car that served as a troop carrier for the insurgents. Life-size plaster-of-paris casts of the Villistas (soldiers under the command of Pancho Villa) sit shotgun on the roof of a car that has just been "liberated" from the Mexican army. Other exhibits include the first bottle-capping machine used by Coca-Cola, a history of Mexican cinema, and pre-Columbian Huastec artifacts. Free guided tours are available in English (call ahead to confirm that an English-speaking guide is available). ✉ *Dr. Coss 445 Sur,* ☎ *8/345–9898.* ✑ *$1, free Tues., 50¢ Sun.* ☉ *Tues.–Thurs. 11–7, Fri.–Sun. 11–8.*

⑱ Monterrey's Spanish history began in 1596, and for its first couple of centuries it was little more than an outpost. Construction of the **Catedral de Monterrey** began in 1600 but took some 250 years to finish. As a result, a Baroque facade is set off by neoclassical columns and two huge ornate plateresque medallions on the main door. Murals by local artists frame the main altar. ✉ *Gran Plaza at Av. Zuazua and Jardón.*

⑲ The **Obispado** (Bishop's House) is the only landmark to be completed in the colonial era (1788). Built on a hilltop as a home for retired prelates, it was used as a fort during the Mexican-American War (1847), the French Intervention (1862), and again during the Mexican Revolution (1915). Today it houses the **Museo Regional de Nuevo León El Obispado,** with exhibits that focus on the history of the entire area. The museum's major appeal, however, is its splendid view of Monterrey. ✉ *Far west end of Av. Padre Mier, at Rafael José Berger,* ☎ *8/346–0404.* ✑ *$3.* ☉ *Tues.–Sun. 10–5.*

❷⓿ The explosion of the popularity of Mexican beer in recent years owes much to the **Cuauhtémoc Brewery,** which opened a century ago. Named after a famous Aztec chief, the brewery is the heart of an industrial empire that produces Carta Blanca and Tecate beer. The brewery complex includes the Mexican Baseball Hall of Fame, a sports museum, the Museo de Monterrey Electronic Arts Gallery, and a beer garden with free beer—obviously the big draw. ⊠ *Av. Alfonso Reyes 2202 Nte.,* ☎ *8/328–5746; 8/328–5745 to book a tour.* ☎ *Free.* ☉ *Tues.–Fri. 9:30–5:45, weekends 10:30–6. Brewery tours by request, weekdays 9–1 and 3–6.*

❷⓵ The Cuauhtémoc Brewery spawned a glass factory for bottles, a steel mill for caps, a carton factory, and, eventually, several industrial conglomerates. One of the last, Alfa, gave Monterrey the **Centro Cultural Alfa** (Alfa Cultural Center), probably the best museum of science and technology in the country. The museum has many hands-on exhibits and an IMAX theater. Free buses to the museum run from the downtown *alameda* (main square) hourly 3–8 daily. ⊠ *Roberto Garza Sada 1000,* ☎ *8/303–0002.* ☎ *$6; two people for $6 on Wed.* ☉ *Tues.–Fri. 3–8:30, Sat. 2–8:30, Sun. noon–8:30.*

❷❷ The newest recreational/educational play area for children is the cleverly designed **Parque Plaza Sesamo** (Sesame Plaza Park), a sprawling theme park built on the grounds of Parque Fundidora that also houses the city's Cintermex convention complex. There are three main areas. One has a world of water sports with 17 water toboggans, pint-size pools, interactive games, and minirivers. A second area has a computer center where children can plug into the Internet and play (nonviolent) video games. The last section is taken up by restaurants and theaters where the park's own personalities put on musical shows. Families can easily spend an entire day here. ⊠ *Calle Agricola 3700–1 Ote., Col. Agricola in Parque Fundidora,* ☎ *8/354–5400.* ☎ *$12.* ☉ *June–Aug., daily 11–9:30; Sept.–May, daily 3–8.*

Dining and Lodging

$$$$ ✕ **Luisiana.** Perhaps the most elegant dining room downtown, this is ★ a taste of how New Orleans is imagined in Mexico. There are no Cajun specialties on the menu, but the deepwater crawfish are divine. Wonderfully prepared steak and seafood dishes make this one of the best restaurants in the country. The waiters wear tuxedos, and there's always soft piano music playing at dinnertime. ⊠ *Av. Hidalgo Ote. 530,* ☎ *8/340–3753 or 8/343–1561. AE, MC, V.*

$$$ ✕ **Residence.** A clubby meeting place for Monterrey's high-powered ★ industrialists and executives, Residence has a menu featuring both Mexican specialties and Continental dishes such as prime rib. The "tasting menu" provides six small portions from some of the restaurant's best specialty dishes. ⊠ *Degollado 605 Sur, at Matamoros,* ☎ *8/342–7230, 8/345–5040, or 8/345–5478. AE, DC, MC, V.*

$$$ ✕ **Vitrales.** Join the friendly staff at Vitrales for an elegant night of din- ★ ing under a grand stained-glass ceiling. The sizeable smoked salmon appetizer is served with fresh herbs, bermuda onions, and hard-boiled eggs. For an entrée, choose from a selection of freshly prepared pastas, *arrachera* steak, and the broiled salmon fillet served with rice and fresh steamed vegetables. Enjoy an after-dinner coffee and dessert while listening to live piano music. ⊠ *Hidalgo 310 Ote., inside the Sheraton Ambassador,* ☎ *8/380–7000. AE, DC, MC, V.*

$$ ✕ **El Rey de Cabrito.** The restaurant's name ("King of Kid") is no lie: this is *the* place to try what is probably the best roast kid you'll ever eat. (The owner keeps his own goat herds.) The hunting lodge–theme restaurant covers half a city block and has become so well known that it's constantly filling out-of-town orders. ⊠ *Constitución 817, at Dr. Coss,* ☎ *8/345–3232 or 8/345–3292. MC, V.*

$ ✕ **Las Monjitas.** Cruise down tiled steps into the bustling dining room of the little nuns (waitresses are in full habits). Murals of peacefully cooking nuns adorn the walls of this hopping Mexican diner. Choose from three commida corridas, or for a casual dinner try "La Pecadora" (thinly sliced grilled chicken topped with melted asadero cheese, fried onions, and mushrooms and served with guacomole, refried beans and lettuce). ⊠ *Escobedo 903 Sur,* ☎ *8/344–6713. AE, MC, V.*

$$$$ 🏨 **Fiesta Americana Centro Monterrey.** In the center of the Zona Rosa, this spiffy pink sandstone building has a striking atrium lobby that is abuzz with business travelers. The light-filled units (all of them two-room suites) are tastefully decorated and have burgundy carpets. Each suite has cable TV and a fold-out sofa, and the bathroom is stocked with specialty lotions and soaps. Rooms facing the plaza have fabulous mountain views. ⊠ *Av. Corregidora Ote. 519, Zona Rosa, 64000,* ☎ *8/319–0900 or 01–800/504–5000,* FAX *8/319–0980. 207 suites. Restaurant, bar, minibars, no-smoking rooms, room service, indoor pool, exercise room, baby-sitting, laundry service, concierge, parking (fee). AE, DC, MC, V.*

$$$$ 🏨 **Quinta Real.** This elegant all-suites business hotel holds sway among
★   Monterrey's financial elite and exudes the aura of a prosperous hacienda of bygone days. The high-dome lobby is set with French furnishings in soothing colors, huge bowls of flowers, and carvings of classic Mexican handicrafts, many of them one-of-a-kind works. A collection of finely executed indigenous weavings and embroideries lines the long lobby corridors. The suites have either two double beds or one king, robes, color TVs, and luxury bathroom soaps and lotions. The hotel's restaurant serves excellent French and Mexican cuisine and has built up quite a local following. ⊠ *Av. Diego Rivera 500, Fracc. Valle Ote., San Pedro Garza García 66260,* ☎ *8/368–1000 or 800/445–4565,* FAX *8/368–1070. 125 suites. Restaurant, bar, minibars, no-smoking rooms, room service, sauna, exercise room, baby-sitting, laundry service, concierge, travel services, car rental, free parking. AE, DC, MC, V.*

$$$$ 🏨 **Radisson Plaza Gran Hotel Ancira.** Built in 1912, this hotel is rem-
★   iniscent of the grand hotels of Europe: an elegant spiral staircase dominates an expansive art deco lobby accented by a black-and-white tile floor and crystal chandeliers. Legend has it that Pancho Villa, taken with the place, settled in and stabled his horse in the lobby. Rooms are conservatively decorated with tasteful pastel walls and matching furnishings. All have minibars, cable TVs, and large marble baths. The Plaza Club business-floor suites have impeccable concierge service. ⊠ *Ocampo No. 443, Ote. Centro or Hidalgo at Escobedo, 64000,* ☎ *8/150–7000 or 800/830–6000,* FAX *8/345–7875. 236 rooms, 26 suites. Restaurant, 2 bars, minibars, no-smoking rooms, pool, beauty salon, outdoor hot tub, sauna, exercise room, shops, baby-sitting, laundry service, concierge floor, travel services, car rental, free parking. AE, DC, MC, V.*

$$$$ 🏨 **Sheraton Ambassador.** This downtown landmark has spacious
★   rooms decorated in burgundy and forest green and equipped with cable TVs, phones in the room and the bathroom, and feather pillows. The concierge floor has secretarial and fax service, and a comfortable executive lounge. A health club, a restaurant, and a piano bar with a stained-glass ceiling are among the other amenities. The staff is friendly and professional. ⊠ *Hidalgo 310 Ote., 64000,* ☎ *8/380–7000 or 800/325–3535,* FAX *8/380–7039. 223 rooms, 16 suites. Restaurant, bar, minibars, no-smoking rooms, room service, pool, massage, tennis court, health club, racquetball, laundry service, concierge floor, meeting room, travel services, free parking. AE, DC, MC, V.*

$$$ 🖬 **Hotel Chipinque.** If you have a car, this hilltop resort overlooking
the city on 700 acres of forest land is a tranquil choice. The view from
the restaurant is extraordinary, especially at night. All rooms have ei-
ther a king or two queen-size beds, satellite TVs, and phones; some
have fireplaces. ⊠ *Meseta de Chipinque 1000, San Pedro Garza Gar-
cía, 66297,* ☎ *8/378–1100, 8/378–6600, or 888/237–3316,* FAX *8/
378–6759. 58 rooms, 13 suites. Restaurant, bar, air-conditioning,
room service, pool, outdoor hot tub, tennis court, billiards, meeting
room, free parking. AE, MC, V.*

$$ 🖬 **Colonial.** This no-frills hotel—the oldest in Monterrey—has an ideal
central-downtown location and budget-price rooms. The small lobby
is stocked with sturdy, ranch-style chairs and large tables filled with
magazines. Rooms have cable TVs, carpeting, and air-conditioning units.
At night, rooms facing the street get an earful from the noisy men's
club next door. ⊠ *Hidalgo 475 Ote., 64000,* ☎ *8/343–6791,* ☎ FAX
*8/342–1169. 100 rooms. Laundry service, dry cleaning, free parking.
AE, MC, V.*

Nightlife and the Arts

Fashionable residents and visitors flock to downtown hotels for after-
dark action. The pianist at the **Sheraton Ambassador** (⊠ Hidalgo 310
Ote., ☎ 8/340–7000) performs soothing pieces that provide the perfect accompaniment to a restful cocktail and visit with friends. The **Fiesta Americana Centro Monterrey** (⊠ Av. Corregidora Ote. 519, ☎ 8/
319–0900) features a lobby bar, complete with a talented jazz pianist.
Monasterio (⊠ Calle Escobedo 913, ☎ no phone), presents an eclectic mix of live music—from rock to romantic Mexican ballads—Tuesday through Saturday nights. **Vat–Kru,** (⊠ Blvd. Constitución 3050 Pte.,
☎ 8/333–5241), bizarre name and all, is one of the hottest discos in
town.

The charming Barrio Antiguo has a number of live music bars; a local
favorite is **Fonda San Miguel** (⊠ Morelos 924 Ote., ☎ 8/342–6659),
where you'll find an eclectic mix of locals and visitors.

Shopping

Top-quality shops center on Plaza Hidalgo, near the major hotels.
Leather and cowboy boots are the local specialties. Owner Porfirio Sosa
handpicks all the items he sells at the upscale **Carápan** (⊠ Hidalgo 305
Ote., ☎ 8/345–4422) and loves to talk about them. His array of Mexican antiques, hand-loomed rugs, shawls, clay figures from Michoacán,
metal sculptures, and handblown glassware rivals that of stores anywhere in the country. **Sanborns** (⊠ Escobedo 920, off Plaza Hidalgo,
☎ 8/343–1834) offers a standard selection of silver, onyx, and other
Mexican craft items. **Plaza Fiesta San Agustín** (⊠ Av. Real de San Agustín
at Lázaro Cárdenas, San Pedro Garza García) is an enormous mall where
Monterrey socialites shop for evening gowns, precious gems, and imported perfumes. The **Mercado Indio** (⊠ Bolivar Nte. 1150) is a typical Mexican market with dozens of stalls, although the selections are
a little monotonous.

Outdoor Activities and Sports

ICE SKATING

Pista de Hielo San Pedro (⊠ Plaza San Pedro Local 10, ☎ 8/356–7293)
is a popular ice-skating rink. It's open weekdays 10–3 and 4:30–8, weekends 10–8.

ROCK CLIMBING

Antonio Rodriguez Tours (☎ 8/134–8164) runs climbing and hiking
tours to Barranca de la Huasteca and Las Grutas de García.

Barranca de la Huasteca (Huastec Canyon)

☺ ㉓ *23 km (14 mi) southwest of Monterrey.*

The Barranca de la Huasteca, with its 1,000-ft-deep gorge, is spectacular for the striated grooves etched into its walls that make it resemble a giant piece of Lalique glassware. A children's play area has a miniature train ride and two pools. ⊠ *From Monterrey, 20 km (12 mi) west on Hwy. 40 to Santa Catarina, then 3 km (2 mi) south on marked road to canyon,* ☎ *no phone.* ⊒ *$1 per car and 10¢ per person.* ☉ *Daily 9–6.*

Grutas de García (García Caves)

㉔ *49 km (30 mi) northwest of Monterrey.*

The Grutas García are an estimated 50–60 million years old and at one time were submerged by an ocean. Petrified sea animals are visible in some of its walls. From the entrance, you can hike the steep 1 km (½ mi) to the caves or hop on a swaying funicular. Guides lead the way through a strenuous mile of underground grottoes and caverns. ⊠ *From Monterrey, Hwy. 40 west for 40 km (25 mi) to Saltillo, then 9 km (5½ mi) on marked road to caves,* ☎ *8/347–1599.* ⊒ *$3, $5 with funicular.* ☉ *Daily 9–5.*

Parque Nacional Cumbres de Monterrey

㉕ *90 km (56 mi) northwest of Monterrey.*

One of the highlights of a trip to the Parque Nacional Cumbres de Monterrey, tucked into the Sierra Madre, is a view of **La Cascada Cola de Caballo** (Horsetail Falls), a dramatic 75-ft-high waterfall that tumbles down from the pine-forested heights. The waterfall is about 1 km (½ mi) from the park's entrance, up a cobblestone road. You can rent a docile horse or burro for about $3 an hour from the local kids who hang out by the ticket booth, or hop on a horse-drawn carriage for $2. ⊠ *From Monterrey, Hwy. 85 northwest 90 km (56 mi) to falls,* ☎ *no phone.* ⊒ *$1.50.* ☉ *Daily 9–7.*

Tampico

㉖ *504 km (312 mi) south of Matamoros, 583 km (361 mi) southeast of Monterrey.*

Tampico is a picturesque port adjoining Ciudad Madero, now an oil-refining center. In 1828 the Spaniards attempted to reconquer then-independent Mexico by landing troops at Tampico, but they were soundly defeated. After later invasions by the Americans and the French, the port languished until oil was discovered in the region about a century ago. The British and Americans developed the industry until it was nationalized in 1938. Petroleum helped Tampico to prosper, but it isn't the kind of thing to enhance tourism. And the Río Pánuco is so polluted that it no longer attracts tarpon fishermen, although the big ocean freighters are an impressive sight.

Still, because of its relative proximity to the border, Tampico gets a smattering of U.S. visitors. (Usually a low-profile place, Tampico made big news in 1995 when it was discovered to be the hometown of the elusive Subcomandante Marcos, spokesperson for the Chiapas-based Zapatista movement.) And it is a fascinating place to wander around for a spell—the old part of town has something of the feel of a run-down New Orleans French Quarter. **Plaza de la Libertad,** near the harbor, is surrounded by old colonial buildings. A block away is the regal **Plaza**

de Armas, its majestic City Hall guarded by towering palms. The **cathedral** here, started in 1823, was completed with funds donated by Edward L. Doheny, an oil magnate implicated in the U.S.'s Teapot Dome scandal of the 1920s.

In Ciudad Madero (between Tampico and the coast), the small **Museo de la Cultura Huasteca** (Museum of Huastec Culture) houses an exquisite collection of pre-Hispanic ceramics, shellwork and costumes, and some pots dating as far back as 1100 BC. ✉ *Instituto Tecnológico, 1 de Mayo at Sor Juana Inés de la Cruz, Ciudad Madero,* ☎ *12/10–22–17.* 🎫 *By donation.* ☉ *Weekdays 10–5, Sat. 10–3.*

Beaches

Playa Miramar, about 5 km (3 mi) from town, is a favorite with locals. For a fee, lounge chairs, towels, and showers are available from the hotels and restaurants along the beach. Public transportation from Tampico consists of public buses marked "Playa," which cost about $1, and colectivos (the old bright-yellow cars and vans), which take groups for about $5 per person.

Dining and Lodging

$$ ✕ **Papa Cuervo Restaurant and Bar.** Enter an underwater fantasy world where the bar is a pirate ship equipped with sails, crates, and a monkey hanging off the stern (he doesn't bite) and each wall is a three-dimensional mural of the undersea world. Try the *pollo San Miguelito,* a rolled chicken breast stuffed with cheese, spinach, and mushrooms and drizzled with pecan sauce. Servings tend to be small but satisfying. Save some energy for live music and dancing on the weekends. ✉ *Morelos 779 Centro,* ☎ *12/22–01–80. No credit cards.*

$$ ✕ **Restaurant La Troya.** Exceedingly rich meat and seafood dishes are the focus of this restaurant in one of Tampico's oldest buildings, the Hotel Posada del Rey. House specialties include *paella a la troya* (a saffron-flavored stew of chicken, pork, seafood, and vegetables) and *caldo gallego* (Spanish broth with pork, sausage, beans, potatoes, and chard). The best tables are out on the balcony, overlooking the Plaza de la Libertad. Downstairs, in the hotel lobby, is where Brigadier General Don Isidor Barrados surrendered to Mexican troops September 11, 1829, ending Spain's final attempt to reconquer Mexico. ✉ *Calle Madero 218 Ote., at Av. Juárez,* ☎ *12/14–11–55. AE, MC, V.*

$ ✕ **Café y Nevería Elite.** This is a popular gathering spot for breakfast, coffee, and ice-cream treats. Don't be put off by the noise and the rather worn Formica tables; it's all part of the local color. ✉ *Av. Díaz Mirón 211 Ote.,* ☎ *12/12–03–64. MC, V.*

$$$ 🏨 **Camino Real.** Attractively decorated, this low-rise property 20 minutes from the city center is a resort hotel—the best you'll find in Tampico (in spite of the name, it's not part of the Camino Real chain). Its rooms and bungalows surround a huge garden overflowing with tropical trees and flowers. Rooms contain Chippendale-style furniture, minibars, cable color TVs, and direct-dial phones. Fishing excursions can be booked through the hotel's travel agency. ✉ *Hidalgo 2000, 89140,* ☎ *12/13–88–11 or 01–800/570–0000,* 📠 *12/13–92–26. 100 rooms, 3 suites. Restaurant, bar, room service, minibars, pool, tennis court, laundry service, travel services, car rental. AE, DC, MC, V.*

$ 🏨 **Posada del Rey.** The art nouveau facade of this fourth-oldest building in Tampico faces the Plaza de la Libertad. Rooms are clean, air-conditioned, carpeted, and have TVs and phones; lighting is somewhat dim, but the effect is cozy and charming. ✉ *Francisco 1 Medero 218 Ote., 89000,* ☎ *12/14–11–55 or 12/14–10–24,* 📠 *12/12–10–77. Restaurant, bar. AE, MC, V.*

Nightlife and the Arts

Byblos (⊠ Byblos 1, ☎ 12/13–08–27) is a popular disco. The bar at the **Camino Real** hotel (⊠ Hidalgo 2000, ☎ 12/13–88–11) has evening piano music every night except Sunday. **Papa Cuervo Restaurant and Bar** (⊠ Morelos 779 Centro, ☎ 12/22–02–80) has live music and dancing on Friday and Saturday night 10–1 with a $4 cover charge.

Outdoor Activities and Sports

FISHING

Although the river is polluted, tarpon and snapper fishing is still popular at **Chairel Lagoon,** with boats and equipment available for rent (just don't plan to eat what you hook). You can arrange for a boat, guide, and equipment through the **Camino Real** hotel (⊠ Hidalgo 2000, ☎ 12/13–88–11 or 01–800/570–0000).

GOLF

Lagunas de Miralta Country Club (☎ 12/24–00–03) sells day passes at Centro Commercial Tres Arcos on Hidalgo for its golf course at Km 26.1 on the Carretera Tampico–Altamira. Ask at your hotel about passes or special discounts at other local clubs.

THE NORTHEAST A TO Z

To research prices, get advice from other travelers, and book travel arrangements, visit www.fodors.com.

AIR TRAVEL

The airport in Monterrey is the only international one in the region, but you can fly to Tampico, Nuevo Laredo Matamoros, and Reynosa on various Mexican airlines.

CARRIERS

From Mexico City, Aeroméxico has service to Matamoros andReynosa. Mexicana flies to Nuevo Laredo. Aerolitoral has nonstop flights to Tampico from Mexico City. Aeroméxico has flights between Tampico and Mexico City. As well, Mexicana has flights between Tampico and Mexico City.

From the United States, Mexicana has flights from Chicago, Denver, Los Angeles, New York, San Antonio, and San Francisco to Monterrey, via Mexico City. Aeroméxico has direct service to Houston and Los Angeles and flights to New York via Mexico City. Continental flies from Chicago, Las Vegas, Los Angeles, Miami, and New York, via Houston. American has six flights a day to Monterrey from Dallas. Aerolitoral has service from McAllen and San Antonio, Texas.

➤ AIRLINES & CONTACTS: **Aerolitoral** (☎ 8/386–2070 in Monterrey; 12/28–41–97 or 12/28–08–57 in Tampico). **Aeroméxico** (☎ 88/12–24–60 in Matamoros; 8/343–5560 in Monterrey; 89/22–11–15 in Reynosa; 12/13–96–00 in Tampico). **American** (☎ 8/340–3031 in Monterrey). **Continental** (☎ 8/348–4282 in Monterrey). **Mexicana** (☎ 8/124–2500 in Monterrey; 87/12–20–52 in Nuevo Laredo; 12/13–96–00 in Tampico).

AIRPORTS

Monterrey's Aeropuerto Internacional Mariano Escobedo has luggage storage ($4 a day) and a money-exchange booth and is 6 km (4 mi) northeast of downtown. The only way to get here is by taxi, which will cost about $14.

➤ AIRPORT INFORMATION: **Aeropuerto Internacional Mariano Escobedo** (☎ 8/345–4432).

BUS TRAVEL

Northeastern Mexico is well connected by buses, which are becoming downright luxurious, with fares remaining low. Information on Mexican bus service is available from Transportes del Norte in Laredo, McAllen, and Brownsville. In conjunction with Greyhound, Transportes del Norte runs from San Antonio, Dallas, and Houston to Monterrey.

➤ BUS INFORMATION: **Transportes del Norte** (☎ 8/372–4965 in Monterrey); Laredo (Valley Transit, ☎ 956/723–4324); McAllen (Valley Transit, ☎ 956/686–5479); Brownsville (Valley Transit, ☎ 956/546–7171).

CAR TRAVEL

Downtown Nuevo Laredo is reached by two bridges: International Bridge 1 in town, and the Columbia–Laredo Bridge (42 km, or 26 mi, northwest of Laredo). Both have facilities for clearing you for travel to the interior of Mexico. (When parking your vehicle in Nuevo Laredo, use only parking lots with attendants on duty—there have been a number of reports of theft of luggage and car stereos.)

The New Bridge is the best route from Brownsville to Matamoros. U.S. 281 leads down to Hidalgo, Texas, and the bridge into Reynosa. For brief excursions across the border, consider leaving your car in Texas and walking over. This eliminates the long wait—often a half hour or more—to bring a car back into the United States.

From Matamoros, Mexico 180 runs down the Gulf coast to Tampico, Veracruz, and beyond. Mexico 97 leads from Reynosa to Mexico 101/ 180, which meet up for a bit. From Reynosa, you can drive the free routes Mexico 40 to Mexico 35 to Linares; here Mexico 58 will lead you across to San Roberto (and Mexico 57) via a spectacular road with a most unusual mural by Frederico Cantú chiseled out of the side of a mountain.

From Laredo, the old Pan-American Highway, Mexico 85 Libre (free), and the four-lane Mexico 85 Cuota (toll) both lead to Monterrey, some 242 km (150 mi) south. The latter road, which ends in Monterrey, is a much better one, although the toll is expensive (about $15). It's around the same price to take the toll road Mexico 40 to Monterrey from Reynosa. Although the Laredo route is more scenic, traversing some nice mountains, Laredo itself is more congested to get through than Reynosa. The Reynosa road, although flat and dull, is more convenient to downtown Monterrey.

The port of Tampico is roughly a seven-hour drive from Matamoros on Mexico 180, or eight hours from Monterrey via Mexico 85, which connects with Mexico 80.

Distances are deceiving in this part of Mexico because of mountainous driving in the Sierra Madre Oriente. It generally takes three hours to drive from the border to Monterrey. From Monterrey to Ciudad Victoria, it's another four hours.

A car trip is not without its red tape. Sanborn's Mexican Insurance can help you complete the paperwork in advance—free if you buy insurance there, otherwise for a fee.

➤ CONTACTS: **Sanborn's Mexican Insurance** (✉ 2009 S. 10th St., McAllen, TX 78503, ☎ 800/222–0158, FAX 956/686–0732).

EMBASSIES

➤ CONSULATES: **Canadian Consulate (Monterrey)** (✉ Edificio Kalos, 108-A Calle Mariano Escobedo and Av. Constitución, ☎ 8/344–3200, FAX 8/344–3048). **U.S. Consulate (Matamoros)** (✉ Calle 1 No. 232, ☎ 88/12–44–02). **U.S. Consulate (Monterrey)** (✉ Av. Constitución 411 Pte., ☎ 8/343–7124 or 8/345–2120, FAX 8/343–9399).

EMERGENCIES
Call the local Red Cross for ambulance service in a medical emergency situation. The local police can handle small incidences, but if you feel the situation could escalate, contact the Oficinas Para La Seguridad de la Turista, which offers a country-wide 24-hour toll-free hot line to provide legal and medical help for tourists.

➤ CONTACTS: **Hospital Santander in Reynosa** (✉ Fco. Madero and Ortiz Rubyo, ☎ 89/22–96–22 or 89/22–93–97). **Matamoros Cruz Roja Hospital** (✉ García and L. Caballero, ☎ 88/12–00–44). **Matamoros Police** (✉ Pedro Cárdenas and Soledad, ☎ 88/17–22–05). **Monterrey Cruz Roja** (✉ Av. Alfonso Reyes 2503, ☎ 8/375–1212). **Monterrey Police** (✉ Gonzalitos 2300, at Lincoln, ☎ 8/151–6000). **Nuevo Laredo Cruz Roja** (✉ Independencia 1619 and San Antonio, ☎ 87/12–09–49 or 87/12–09–89). **Nuevo Laredo Police** (✉ Maclovio Herréra and Ocampo, ☎ 87/12–30–25). **Reynosa Cruz Roja** (☎ 89/22–13–14 or 89/22–62–50). **Reynosa Police** (✉ Morelos between Veracruz and Nayarit, ☎ 89/22–00–08 or 89/22–07–90). **Tampico Cruz Roja Hospital** (✉ Tamaulipas and Colegio Militar, Zona Centro, ☎ 12/12–13–33). **Tampico Police** (✉ Sor Juana Inés de la Cruz and Tamaulipas, ☎ 12/12–10–32).

PHARMACIES
Pharmacy Benavides, near the international bridge in Matamoros, is open daily 8 AM–10 PM. Farmacia El Fenix, downtown, is open daily 8 AM–10 PM.

In Monterrey, Farmacia Benavides is open daily 8 AM–10 PM. For 24-hour service in Nuevo Laredo, use Farmacia Calderón.

Reynosa's Farmacia Sucursal Aduana is open 24 hours.

Off Plaza de la Libertad in Tampico, Farmacia Droguería del Pueblo, is open daily 8 AM–9:30 PM. For service until 11 PM, use Farmacia El Fenix, near Plaza de Armas.

➤ CONTACTS: **Farmacia Benavides** (✉ Morelos 499, at Escobedo, Monterrey, ☎ 8/345–0257). **Farmacia Calderón** (✉ Guerrero 704, Nuevo Laredo, ☎ 87/12–51–77). **Farmacia Droguería del Pueblo** (✉ Juárez 308 Sur, Tampico, ☎ 12/12–15–42). **Farmacia El Fenix** (✉ Abosolo 806, Matamoros, ☎ 88/12–29–09). **Farmacia El Fenix** (✉ Díaz Mirón at Olmos, Tampico, ☎ 12/12–43–51). **Farmacia Sucursal Aduana** (✉ Av. Alemán 115-B, Reynosa, ☎ 87/12–51–77). **Pharmacy Benavides** (✉ Av. Obregón 65, Matamoros, ☎ 88/12–53–78).

MAIL AND INTERNET
Monterrey's central post office is at the far northern end of Macro Plaza. Ships 2000, above the video arcade, offers the only Internet service in the Zona Rosa; the rates are steep at $3.50 an hour. It's open daily 10–10.

The Reynosa post office is on the corner of Díaz and Colón. Cyberspace Internet Café is generally open weekdays 9–9, weekends until 4, and charges about $1.50 per hour. Computadores has Internet services for $1.50 an hour. It's open weekdays 9–9, weekends until 4.

In Tampico, there's a post office just off the Plaza de la Libertad. Coffee Net has 10 computers with Internet access for $1.50 an hour; it's open Monday–Saturday 9–9.

➤ POST OFFICES AND INTERNET SERVICES: **Coffee Net** (✉ Carranza 106 Pte., Tampico, ☎ 12/14–13–90). **Computadores** (✉ Allende and Av. Juárez, Reynosa, ☎ 89/22–55–73). **Cyberspace Internet Café** (✉ Hidalgo and Allende, Reynosa, ☎ no phone). **Monterrey post office** (✉ Washington, between Zaragoza and Zuazua). **Ships 2000** (✉ Escobedo

819 Sur, Monterrey, ☎ 8/343–2568). **Tampico post office** (✉ Madero 309 Ote.).

MONEY MATTERS
Some banks won't cash traveler's checks, but most have ATMs.

There are plenty of banks in downtown Matamoros, mostly around Plaza Hidalgo, that change money and traveler's checks. Money-changing hours at banks generally end at 3 PM weekdays, so if you arrive late, try Turismo Axis, which stays open until 5 PM.

Banks in Monterrey's Zona Rosa generally change money and traveler's checks weekdays 9–3. For later money-changing and traveler's check services, try Eurodivisas; it stays open until 8 PM Sunday through Friday, 9 PM Saturday.

In Reynosa, many casas de cambio line Avenida Alemán at the entrance to town via the International Bridge. Most banks change money only, but Citibank will change traveler's checks weekdays 9–2. The best exchange rates are closer to the city center, around Plaza Principál and along Calle Hidalgo.

Citibank in Tampico changes money and traveler's checks weekdays 9–3. Banamex changes money and traveler's checks until 5 PM. Casa de Cambio is open weekdays 9–6, Saturday 9–1:30.
➤ EXCHANGE SERVICES: **Banamex** (✉ Madero 403 Ote., Tampico, ☎ 12/14–02–30). **Casa de Cambio** (✉ Juárez 215 Sur, Tampico, ☎ 12/12–90–00). **Citibank** (✉ Av. Alemán 100, Reynosa, ☎ 89/22–56–19 or 89/22–56–60). **Citibank** (✉ Aduana 309 Sur, Tampico, ☎ 12/12–92–40). **Eurodivisas** (✉ Morelos 359 Ote., Monterrey, ☎ 8/340–1683). **Turismo Axis** (✉ Morelos 94–107, at Calle 5, Matamoros).

TOURS AND PACKAGES
Various sightseeing excursions are available through Tours Gray Line, Osetur Tours, and Sanborn's Viva Tours, which run shopping and sightseeing excursions to border towns and the interior, including to El Tajín.
➤ TOUR-OPERATOR RECOMMENDATIONS: **Osetur Tours** (✉ Calles San Francisco and Loma Larga, Monterrey, ☎ 8/347–1599 or 8/347–1614). **Sanborn's Viva Tours** (✉ 2015 S. 10th St., McAllen, TX 78503, ☎ 800/395–8482; 956/682–9872 in the U.S.). **Tours Gray Line** (✉ Av. Eugenio Garza Sada 2256, Monterrey, ☎ 8/369–6472 or 8/369–6473).

TRAIN TRAVEL
There is no first-class train service from the border to Monterrey or Tampico. Information about schedules and prices for second-class service is available from Mexico by Train in Laredo, Texas.
➤ TRAIN INFORMATION: **Mexico by Train** (☎ FAX 956/725–3559 in the U.S.; ☎ 800/321–1699).

TRANSPORTATION IN MONTERREY
METRO TRAVEL
The Monterrey metro, which runs along elevated tracks across the city, is modern and efficient. There are only two lines. Magnetic cards are used to enter the station. Buy them from station vending machines in units of one, three, or five rides. Each ride costs less than 50¢. The metro runs 6 AM–midnight daily.

TAXIS
Taxis are pretty scarce and expensive in border towns but plentiful and moderately priced in Monterrey. In Monterrey, Metrotaxi provides reliable on-call service.
➤ CONTACT: **Metrotaxi** (☎ 8/342–2069).

VISITOR INFORMATION

In the United States, the best information about this part of Mexico is found in Texas border towns, especially at places that sell the (mandatory) Mexican automobile insurance. The Brownsville Chamber of Commerce, one block from International Bridge, is open daily from 9–5.

In Mexico, Matamoros Tours-Transport, a few blocks from International Bridge, is open daily 8–6. The Nuevo Laredo office is open daily 8–8, and the Reynosa office weekdays 7:30 AM–8 PM. Also near the International Bridge, cab drivers and roving tourist-department representatives are glad to dispense free information to travelers. Monterrey Infotour is open Tuesday through Sunday 10–5. The Tampico office is open weekdays 9–7.

➤ TOURIST INFORMATION NORTH OF THE BORDER: **Bravo Insurance** (✉ 2212 Santa Ursula St., Laredo, TX,☎ 956/723–3657, FAX 956/723–0000). **Brownsville Chamber of Commerce** (✉ 1600 E. Elizabeth St., ☎ 956/542–4341). **Johnny Ginn's Travel** (✉ 1845 Expressway 77, Brownsville, TX, ☎ 956/542–5457, FAX 956/504–2919). **Sanborn's Mexican Insurance** (✉ 2009 S. 10th St., McAllen, TX 78503, ☎ 800/222–0158, FAX 956/686–0732). **Sanborn's Viva Tours** (✉ 2015 S. 10th St., McAllen, TX 78503, ☎ 800/395–8482 or 956/682–9872).

➤ TOURIST INFORMATION SOUTH OF THE BORDER: **Nuevo Laredo office** (✉ Calles Herrera and Juárez, ☎ 87/12–73–97). **Matamoros Tours-Transport** (✉ Tamaulipas and Av. Alvaro Obregón, ☎ 88/12–21–18). **Monterrey Infotour** (✉ Hidalgo 441 Ote., ☎ 8/345–0870, 8/345–0902, 01–800/83–222, or 800/235–2438). **Reynosa office** (✉ Puente Internacional/International Bridge, ☎ 89/22–11–89 or 89/22–24–49). **Tampico office** (✉ 20 de Noviembre 218 Ote., ☎ 12/12–26–68 or 12/12–00–07).

13 THE YUCATÁN PENINSULA

The Yucatán Peninsula is Mexico's perennial favorite for more reasons than you can count—the high-profile sparkle of Cancún, the laid-back beachcombing of Isla Mujeres, the spectacular seas around Cozumel, the fascinating Spanish-Maya mix of Mérida, and the evocative Maya ruins of Tulum, Chichén Itzá, and Uxmal. And if the heart of nature moves your blood, there are two huge coastal eco-zones: Sian Ka'an Biosphere Reserve and Parque Natural Río Lagartos, migration stopovers for thousands of flamingos and other birds.

F OR MOST PEOPLE, Mexico's great appeal is its beaches and its ancient ruins. Cancún and the Yucatán have the best of both. Cancún is Mexico's most popular tourist mecca, and it rises against a backdrop of Maya culture—both ancient ruins and modern villages. Although much of the Yucatán Peninsula is vast, scrubby desert with a smattering of jungles and hills, its eastern coastline on the clear, turquoise waters of the Caribbean has superb natural features. In addition to a semitropical climate, the Caribbean coast has unbroken stretches of beach and the world's second-longest barrier reef, starting off the coast of Cancún and extending in its entirety down into South America. Isla Mujeres (Isle of Women) and Cozumel are also part of the Yucatán. And on the west side of the peninsula, Mérida, one of Mesoamerica's first Spanish cities, has colonial atmosphere rare in this part of Mexico.

In its entirety, the 113,000-square-km (43,600-square-mi) peninsula encompasses the Mexican states of Yucatán, Campeche, and Quintana Roo, as well as Belize and part of Guatemala. Within its bounds are tremendous bird-watching, water sports, archaeology, handicrafts, and savory Yucatecan cuisine. Above all, there are the friendly and open Yucatecos themselves.

As many activities as there are on the Yucatán, there is an equal range of accommodations, from the never-leave-the-site resorts of Cancún to more modest properties near the ruins and humble but adequate beach shacks. That means that you'll see a broad range of travelers: package-tour groups, backpackers, people tripping around in rental cars. International airports at Cancún and Cozumel provide nonstop service from several North American cities. The Mérida airport handles primarily domestic flights. Cruise ships call at Cozumel and Playa del Carmen.

Pleasures and Pastimes

Beaches

Cancún and the rest of the Yucatán have a wonderful variety of beaches: Those who thrive on the resort atmosphere will probably enjoy Playa Chacmool and Playa Tortugas on the bay side of Cancún, which is calmer than the windward side. On the north end of Isla Mujeres, Playa Norte (or Playa Cocoteros) offers handsome sunset vistas. Beaches on the sheltered leeward side of Cozumel are wide and sandy. The Caribbean Coast abounds with hidden and not-so-hidden beaches. There are also long stretches of white sand, usually filled with sunbathers, at Playa del Carmen, Akumal, and Tulum. Around Campeche, the gulf waters are deep green, shallow, and tranquil.

Bird-Watching

The Yucatán Peninsula is one of the finest areas for birding in Mexico. Habitats range from wildlife and bird sanctuaries to unmarked lagoons, estuaries, and mangrove swamps. Frigates, tanagers, warblers, and macaws inhabit Isla Contoy (off Isla Mujeres) and the Laguna Colombia on Cozumel. There is an even greater variety of species in the Sian Ka'an Biosphere Reserve on the Boca Paila Peninsula south of Tulum. Along the north and west coasts of Yucatán, flamingos, herons, ibis, cormorants, pelicans, and peregrine falcons thrive.

Dining

The mystique of Yucatecan cooking has a lot to do with generous doses of local spices and herbs, although generally the spices aren't too fiery hot. Among the specialties are *cochinita pibíl* and *pollo pibíl* (succulent pork or chicken baked in banana leaves with a spicy, pumpkin-seed-and-chili sauce), *poc chuc* (Yucatecan pork marinated in sour-orange sauce with pickled onions), *tikinchic* (fried fish prepared with sour orange), *panuchos* (fried tortillas filled with black beans and topped with turkey, chicken, or pork, pickled onions, and avocado), *papadzules* (tortillas stuffed with hard-boiled eggs and drenched in a sauce of pumpkin seed and fried tomato), and *codzitos* (rolled tortillas in pumpkin-seed sauce). *Achiote* (annatto), cilantro, and the fiery chili habañero are heavily favored condiments.

Restaurants in Cancún, Isla Mujeres, Cozumel, and the North Caribbean Coast are more expensive than in the states of Yucatán and Campeche.

CATEGORY	CANCÚN, ISLA MUJERES, COZUMEL, AND THE CARIBBEAN COAST	YUCATÁN AND CAMPECHE STATES
$$$$	over $30	over $15
$$$	$21–$30	$11–$15
$$	$10–$20	$6–$10
$	under $10	under $6

*per person for a main course at dinner

Fishing

The rich waters of the Caribbean and the Gulf of Mexico support hundreds of species of tropical fish, making the Yucatán coastline and the outlying islands a paradise for deep-sea fishing, fly-fishing, and bone-fishing. Particularly between April and July, the waters off Cancún, Cozumel, and Isla Mujeres teem with sailfish, marlin, red snapper, tuna, barracuda, and wahoo. Bill fishing is so rich around Cozumel, Isla Mujeres, Puerto Morelos, and Puerto Aventuras that each holds its own annual tournament.

Farther south, along the Boca Paila Peninsula, banana fish, bonefish, mojarra, shad, permit, and sea bass provide great sport for flat fishing and fly-fishing, while oysters, shrimp, and conch lie on the bottom of the Gulf of Mexico near Campeche and Isla del Carmen.

Lodging

Accommodations in the Yucatán range from the ultraglitzy megaresorts of Cancún to the charming colonial mansions in Mérida and the rustic but character-filled lodgings near the ruins. The following sets of price categories are for accommodation in the more expensive Cancún, Isla Mujeres, Cozumel, and the state of Campeche, and for the North Caribbean Coast and the state of Yucatán. Prices are based on nondiscounted rates in the peak winter season, December to early May.

CATEGORY	CANCÚN, ISLA MUJERES, COZUMEL, AND CAMPECHE STATE	CARIBBEAN COAST AND YUCATÁN STATE
$$$$	over $200	over $100
$$$	$120–$200	$70–$100
$$	$50–$120	$30–$70
$	under $50	under $30

*All prices are for a standard double room, excluding 12% tax.

Ruins

Amateur archaeologists will find heaven in the Yucatán. Pick your period and your preference, whether for well-excavated sites or overgrown, out-of-the-way ruins barely touched by scholars' shovels. The major Maya sites are Cobá and Tulum on the Caribbean Coast and Chichén Itzá and Uxmal in the state of Yucatán, but smaller ruins scattered throughout the peninsula are often equally fascinating.

Scuba Diving and Snorkeling

The clear turquoise waters of Cozumel, Akumal, Puerto Morelos, Isla Mujeres, and other parts of Mexico's Caribbean Coast are filled with exquisitely colored fish swimming in the brilliant coral formations. Currents allow for drift diving, and there are both reefs and offshore wrecks to dive to, many of which are safe enough for neophytes. The peninsula's cenotes (natural sinkholes) also provide unusual dive experiences.

Exploring the Yucatán Peninsula

Numbers in the text correspond to numbers in the margin and on the Cancún, Isla Mujeres, Cozumel, North Caribbean Coast, State of Yucatán, Mérida, and Campeche City maps.

Great Itineraries

If you go to the major beach resorts of Cancún and Cozumel, you're likely to settle in for the entire stay, perhaps taking side trips to the ruins of Tulum or Chichén Itzá or the city of Mérida. As for beach experiences, Cancún has a higher profile and is more expensive. Isla Mujeres tends to be more relaxed. The following itineraries are designed to keep you on the move from a base either in one of the Caribbean Coast towns or in Mérida. The first is ideal for water sports, the others for steeping yourself in Maya civilization.

IF YOU HAVE 3 DAYS

If you want to base yourself on the Caribbean Coast, get a room in **Playa del Carmen** ⑳ and relax on the white-sand beach or go diving around the nearby reefs. Day 2, visit the ruins of the Maya city of **Tulum** ㉒. Afterward, climb down to the small beach alongside it for a dip in the ocean. Day 3, head for **Akumal** ㉑ for diving, deep-sea fishing, snorkeling, or swimming. Later in the day visit the tiny lagoon of **Yalkú,** which was around during the time of the Maya traders.

An alternative is to spend two days in **Mérida** ㉕–㊱, savoring the city's unique character as you make your way among its historic churches and mansions, and enjoy its parks and restaurants. You can easily devote a day to exploring the heart of downtown, including the **zócalo** (main square) ㉕ and its surrounding buildings. Take a second, more leisurely day to visit the Museum of Anthropology and History in the **Palacio Cantón** ㊱ and, perhaps, the **Museo de Arte Contemporáneo** ㉛. On Day 3, drive or take a tour to one of Yucatán's most famous Maya ruins—**Chichén Itzá** ㊲ or **Uxmal** ㊶. Each is within about two hours of Mérida.

IF YOU HAVE 7 DAYS

Again basing yourself in **Playa del Carmen** ⑳, spend Day 2 visiting **Tulum** ㉒. Day 3, tour the Maya ruins of **Cobá** ㉓. Day 4, head for **Akumal** ㉑ and its water sports. Day 5, sign up for a tour of the **Sian Ka'an Biosphere Reserve** ㉔. On Days 6 and 7, head west for the colonial city of **Mérida** ㉕–㊱. Spend one day in the city and the next out at **Chichén Itzá** ㊲ or **Uxmal** ㊶.

On a weeklong trip in and around Mérida, take in the city's sights first and then take two separate overnight excursions. First, head for Uxmal and overnight at one of the nearby archaeological hotels. The next day explore the Ruta Puuc, the series of lost cities south of Uxmal that includes **Kabah, Sayil,** and **Labná,** as well as the fascinating **Loltún Caves.** On the second excursion, to Chichén Itzá, allow as much as a full day en route to explore some of the present-day Maya villages along the way. An alternate side trip—go north of **Valladolid** ㊲ to see the flamingo nesting grounds at **Parque Natural Río Lagartos** ㊵.

IF YOU HAVE 9 DAYS

With even more time, consider continuing from **Mérida** ㉕–㊱ to **Campeche City** ㊸–㊾. After spending a day seeing the city's sights—almost all those of interest are within the compact historic district—head inland the next morning to **Edzná,** a magnificently restored ceremonial center an hour's drive from the city.

When to Tour the Yucatán Peninsula

Thousands of people swarm to Chichén Itzá for the vernal equinox on the first day of spring to see the astronomical phenomenon that makes a shadow resembling a snake—which represented the plumed serpent god Kukulcán—appear on the side of the main pyramid. The phenomenon also occurs on the first day of fall, but the rainy autumnal weather tends to discourage visitors. Both the capital and outlying villages of Campeche state celebrate the Day of the Dead (November 1–2) with special fervor because it corresponds to a similar observance in ancient Maya tradition.

High season in the states of Yucatán and Campeche generally corresponds to high season in the rest of Mexico: Christmastime, Easter week, and July and August. Rainfall is heaviest and—humidity most uncomfortable—from May to October or November. On the Caribbean Coast, including Cancún, Cozumel, and Isla Mujeres, the peak tourist times are mid-December through late March. In less visited towns, levels of service differ drastically between the high and low seasons (when staff and activities may be cut back), so be prepared for the trade-off. The rainy season isn't a bad time to visit if you don't mind the afternoon showers and the sometimes reduced tourist attentions. On the coast, hurricane season is September–October.

CANCÚN

FLYING INTO CANCÚN, you see nothing but green treetops for miles. It's clear from the air that this resort was literally carved out of the jungle. When development began here in 1974, the beaches were deserted except for birds and iguanas. Now luxury hotels, shopping malls, and restaurants line Cancún's oceanfront. More vacationers come here than to any other part of Mexico, and many come again and again for the white-sand beaches, crystalline turquoise waters, sizzling nightlife, numerous restaurants, and the proximity of Maya ruins throughout the Yucatán peninsula.

Updated by
Shelagh
McNally

Cancún has two very different sides. On the mainland is the actual Ciudad Cancún (Cancún City), the commercial center that is also informally known as El Centro. The other half, the Zona Hotelera (Hotel Zone), is the tourist mecca. The Zone is actually a 22½-km (14-mi) barrier island off the Yucatán Peninsula. A separate northern strip called Punta Sam, located north of Puerto Juárez (where the ferries to Isla Mujeres depart), is sometimes considered part of the Zone, unofficially referred to as the Northern Hotel Zone. Both areas have been designed to please average American tastes: most people speak English, and there are fast-food outlets, brand-name stores, and cable TV. Shopping, eating, and lounging in the year-round tropical warmth are the main activities. (The sun shines an average of 240 days a year, reputedly more than at almost any other Caribbean spot. Temperatures linger at about 80°F.) At night you can enjoy a variety of activities, such as knocking back tequila slammers at a bar, listening to great music at clubs, watching folkloric dance performances, and sampling Yucatecan food.

But there is more to Cancún than plopping yourself down under a *palapa* (thatch roof). Downtown offers a more authentic glimpse into the sights and sounds of Mexico. For diving and snorkeling, the reefs off Cancún and nearby Cozumel, Puerto Morelos, and Isla Mujeres are among the best in the world. Cancún also makes a relaxing base for venturing to the stupendous ruins of Chichén Itzá, Tulum, and Cobá, remnants of the area's rich Maya heritage.

As for Cancún's history, not much was written about it before its birth as a resort. The Maya people did settle the area during the Preclassic era, around AD 200, and remained until the 14th or 15th century, but little is known about them. The overlooked barrier island doesn't appear on early navigators' maps. It was never heavily populated, perhaps because its terrain of mangroves and marshes (and resulting swarms of mosquitoes) discouraged settlement. Some minor Maya ruins were discovered in the mid-19th century, but archaeologists didn't get around to studying them until the 1950s.

In 1967, the Mexican government, under the leadership of Luis Echeverría, commissioned a study to pinpoint the ideal place for an international Caribbean resort. The computer chose Cancún, and the transformation began. At the time the area's only residents were the three caretakers of a coconut plantation. In 1972 work began on the first hotel, and the island and city grew from there.

But Cancún's success has not come without a price. Its lagoons and mangrove swamps have been polluted (the area's waste is pumped directly into the sea), and a number of species, such as conch and lobster, are dwindling. Parts of the coral reef are dead. And although the beaches still appear pristine for the most part, an increased effort will have to be made in order to preserve the physical beauty that is the resort's prime appeal.

Exploring

Cancún is divided into two parts: the hotel zone, Zona Hotelera, a numeral 7–shaped island; and Cancún City or downtown Cancún, known as El Centro, 4 km (2½ mi) west of the hotel zone on the mainland. The hotel zone consists entirely of hotels, restaurants, shopping complexes, marinas, and time-share condominiums, with few residential areas. It's not the sort of place you can get to know by walking, although there is now a bicycle/walking path that starts at the Convention Center, ending downtown.

A Good Tour

Cancún's scenery consists mostly of its beautiful beaches and crystal-clear waters, but there are also a few intriguing historical sites tucked away among the modern hotels. In addition to the attractions listed below, two modest vestiges of the ancient Maya civilization are worth a visit, but only for dedicated archaeology buffs. Neither is identified by name. On the 12th hole of Pok-Ta-Pok golf course (Blvd. Kukulcán, Km 6.5)—the name means "ball game" in Maya—stands a ruin consisting of two platforms and the remains of other ancient buildings. And the ruin of a tiny Maya shrine is cleverly incorporated into the architecture of the Hotel Camino Real, on the beach at Punta Cancún.

You don't need a car in Cancún, but if you've rented one to make extended trips, start in the Southern Hotel Zone at **Ruinas del Rey** ① and **San Miguelito** ②, drive north to **Yamil Lu'um** ③, and then stop in at the **Cancún Convention Center** ④ before heading west to **El Centro** ⑤.

Cancún

TO PUNTA SAM

TO ISLA MUJERES

Puerto Juárez
180

CANCÚN CITY
Av. Uxmal
Av. Lopez Portillo
Av. Bonampak
Av. Tulum
Av. Yaxchilán
5
Blvd. Kukulcán
Av. Cobá
Paseo Kukulcán
Aviary Park
307

Bahía de Mujeres

Laguna Morales

Playa Linda

Playa Langosta

Playa Tortugas

Punta Cancún

4

HOTEL

Laguna Bojórquez

Playa Chacmool

3

Playa Merlin

Laguna Nichupté

ZONE

Caribbean Sea

Av. Tulum

307

Playa Ballenas

1 2

N

Laguna Río Inglés

Playa Delfines

Punta Nizuc

KEY

🚢 Ferry

0   2 miles

0   3 km

Paseo Kukulcán

TO TULUM

Sights to See

4 **Cancún Convention Center.** This strikingly modern venue for cultural events is the jumping-off point for a 1-km (½-mi) string of shopping malls that extends west to the Presidente Inter-Continental Cancún. In the Convention Center complex itself, **Inter Plaza** contains 15 restaurants, 21 boutiques, a bank, and several airline offices.

The **National Institute of Anthropology and History** (☎ 9/883–0305), a small museum on the ground floor of the Convention Center, traces Maya culture with a fascinating collection of 1,000- to 1,500-year-old artifacts collected throughout Quintana Roo. Admission to the museum is about $3 (free Sunday); it's open Tuesday through Sunday 9–7. Guided tours are available in English, French, German, and Spanish. ⊠ *Blvd. Kukulcán, Km 9,* ☎ *9/883–0199.*

5 **El Centro** (Downtown Cancún). Markets, instead of malls, offer a glimpse into a more provincial Mexico. The main street, **Avenida**

Tulum, is easily recognizable for the huge seashell sculpture in the round-about, which is dramatically lit up at night. Many restaurants and shops are along this street; **Ki Huic** is the largest crafts market in Cancún. If you're looking for shopping bargains, however, the parallel **Avenida Yaxchilán** usually has better prices, particularly in the Mercado Veinteocho (Market 28). Just off Avenida Yaxchilán and Sunyaxchén, this is the hub of downtown, filled with shops and restaurants frequented by locals.

① Ruinas del Rey (Ruins of the King). Large signs on the Zone's lagoon side, roughly opposite the Playa de Oro and El Pueblito hotels, point out these small ruins, which have been incorporated into the Caesar Park Beach & Golf Resort complex. The ruins were explored by archaeologists in 1910, though excavations did not begin until 1954. In 1975 archaeologists, along with the Mexican government, began the restoration of the Ruinas del Rey and San Miguelito.

Del Rey may not be particularly impressive when compared to major archaeological sites such as Tulum or Chichén Itzá, but it is the largest ruin in Cancún, and it's definitely worth a look. Dating from the 3rd to 2nd century BC, del Rey is notable for its unusual architecture: two main plazas bounded by two streets—most other Maya cities contained only one plaza. The pyramid here is topped by a platform, and inside its vault are paintings on stucco. Originally named Kin Ich Ahau Bonil, Maya for "king of the solar countenance," the site was linked to astronomical practices in the ancient Maya culture. ⊠ *Blvd. Kukulcán, Km 17,* ☎ *no phone.* ⊡ *About $3, free Sun.* ☼ *Daily 8–5.*

② San Miguelito. On the east side of Boulevard Kukulcán are the remains of a Maya site—a very small stone building with a number of columns each about 4 ft high. Local archaeologists have plans to do more work on this site. ⊠ *Blvd. Kukulcán, Km 16.5,* ☎ *no phone.*

③ Yamil Lu'um. A small sign at the Sheraton will direct you to a dirt path leading to this site, which stands on the highest point of Cancún—the name Yamil Lu'um means "hilly land." Although it comprises two structures—one probably a temple, the other probably a lighthouse—this is the smallest of Cancún's ruins. The remains date from the late 13th or early 14th century. ⊠ *Blvd. Kukulcán, Km 12,* ☎ *no phone.*

Dining

With more than 1,200 restaurants in Cancún, finding the right dining spot might be the hardest work you do while on vacation. Both the Hotel Zone and downtown have plenty of great places to eat. There are some pitfalls: restaurants that line noisy Avenida Tulum often have tables spilling onto pedestrian-laden sidewalks with gas fumes and hordes of people detracting from the romantic outdoor-café ambience. In the Hotel Zone, restaurants often cater to what they assume is a tourist preference for bland, not-too-foreign-tasting food.

Most of the local haunts are in the downtown area. Parque de las Palapas, just off Avenida Tulum, is where locals go for Yucatecan-style food prepared by experts. Farther into the city center, you can find the freshest seafood and other traditional Mexican fare at Mercado 28. There are dozens of small restaurants there that serve great food at reasonable prices.

Dress is casual in Cancún, but many restaurants do not allow bare feet, short shorts, bathing suits, or no shirt. At upscale restaurants, pants, skirts, or dresses are favored over shorts at dinnertime. Unless otherwise stated, restaurants serve lunch and dinner daily.

Hotel Zone

Hotel Zone restaurants are located on the Cancún Hotel Zone Dining and Lodging map.

$$$–$$$$ ✕ **Ruth's Chris Steak House.** With its cream-color interior and stained-glass accents, this restaurant goes beyond what you'd expect at your typical neighborhood steak house. The steak here—whether fillet, porterhouse, or rib eye—is so tender it can be cut with a fork. The blackened tuna and barbecue shrimp are also well prepared, and the accompanying wine list is excellent. ⊠ *Kukulcán Plaza, Blvd. Kukulcán, Km 13.5,* ☎ *9/885–3301. AE, MC, V.*

$$–$$$$ ✕ **Club Grill.** The dining rooms of Cancún's Ritz-Carlton are the hands-down favorite for exceptional food and romantic dining. Everything is quietly elegant: rich wood trimmings, fresh flowers, tall windows overlooking a courtyard fountain. Classic dishes have been given a distinctly Mexican flavor. The sautéed foie gras with caramelized mango is a good starting point, followed by the bean and lentil soup with *habañero* chili. If you're having trouble deciding, try the tasting menu, a selection of dishes paired with wines. Don't forget the wickedly delicious desserts. Cynthia Davis, one of Cancún's top jazz vocalists, entertains nightly. ⊠ *Blvd. Kukulcán (Retorno del Rey 36),* ☎ *9/885–0808. AE, MC, V. No lunch.*

$$–$$$$ ✕ **Côté Sud.** Dining is relaxed and stylish in this main restaurant of
★ the Le Meridien hotel. Decorated with fresh green-and-taupe plaids, white linen, and contemporary table settings, it offers spectacular views of the ocean. The menu features dishes from France's Provence region with creative twists, such as duck breast in a potato *galette* (a flat cake) and lavender sauce or rack of lamb Moroccan style. Fresh fish is grilled to perfection, and the bread is baked daily on the premises. A new dessert called "The Fifth Element"—a chocolate extravaganza in the shape of the planet Mars, dripping with strawberry sauce—has become the most-talked-about dessert in the Hotel Zone. All of this is complemented by an extensive wine list and an attentive staff that cares about the details. ⊠ *Le Meridien, Blvd. Kukulcán, Km 14 (Retorno del Rey 37),* ☎ *9/881–2260. AE, DC, MC, V.*

$$–$$$ ✕ **Blue Bayou.** The first Cajun restaurant in Mexico, Blue Bayou was an immediate success that continues to be popular with locals and visitors alike. Five levels of intimate dining areas are decorated in wood, rattan, and bamboo against a backdrop of cascading waterfalls and a tropical garden. Specialties include Cancún jambalaya, blackened grouper, herb crawfish Louisiana, plantation duckling, and chicken Grand Bayou. There's live jazz every night and dancing on the weekends. ⊠ *Hyatt Cancún Caribe, Blvd. Kukulcán, Km 10.5,* ☎ *9/883–0044. Reservations essential. AE, DC, MC, V. No lunch.*

$$–$$$ ✕ **Lorenzillo's.** Named after a 17th-century pirate, this is one of the handsomest waterfront restaurants in the Hotel Zone. Built on the lagoon underneath a giant palapa roof, its indoor-outdoor terrace is the perfect spot to watch the sunset. It has its own lobster farm, so the delicacy is offered year-round and is fresh. Also good is the "Treasure Chest," shrimp stuffed with lobster. ⊠ *Blvd. Kukulcán, Km 10.5,* ☎ *9/883–1254. AE, MC, V.*

$–$$$ ✕ **Iguana Wana.** This upbeat, contemporary Mexican café decorated with art from around Mexico offers an extensive, inexpensive all-you-can-eat breakfast buffet along with special vegetarian and children's menus. During the day, televised sports provide the entertainment; in the evening, there's live music. Choose from the extensive "zizzling" fajitas menu or from the "wana grill." There is also a tempting selection of beers and tequilas. ⊠ *Plaza Caracol, Blvd. Kukulcán, Km 8.5,* ☎ *9/883–0829. AE, MC, V.*

Cancún Hotel Zone Dining and Lodging

$–$$$ ✕ **Maria Bonita.** Here is authentic Mexico in food, music, and atmo-
★ sphere. This delightful restaurant overlooking the water is divided
into sections named after three states of Mexico: Jalisco, Michoacán,
and Oaxaca. The menu includes food from these areas, as well as other
Mexican specialties. Worth trying are the various mole dishes, such as
chicken almond mole (with chocolate, almonds, and chilies), *la dona*
(poblano chilies stuffed with lobster and mushrooms), or any of the
various Tex-Mex or grilled entrées. The menu, which explains the dif-
ferent chilies used by the kitchen, makes this a great place to learn about
Mexican cuisine. Attentive service matches the wonderful food. ⊠ *Hotel
Camino Real, Punta Cancún, Blvd. Kukulcán, Km 9,* ☎ 9/848–7000.
AE, MC, V. No lunch.

$$ ✕ **La Destileria.** Be prepared to have your perceptions about tequila
★ changed forever at this combination restaurant–tequila museum. Ta-
bles are centered on a huge antique still from a tequila distillery. Enjoy
one of 100 tequilas to taste, or try the amazing margaritas (be warned—
you may never again be able to enjoy cheap tequila drinks). The tasty,
traditional food from northern Mexico (served by seriously charming
waiters) includes *sopa de elote* (spiced corn soup) and *pescado con flor
de calabaza* (fish with pumpkin flowers). The title of the dessert menu,
"Favorite Sins," says it all. Afterward, you can drop by the restaurant's
tequila shop and pick up your favorite brand. ⊠ *Blvd. Kukulcán, Km
12.65 (across from Kukulcán Plaza),* ☎ 9/883–1087. *AE, MC, V.*

$–$$ ✕ **Cenacolo.** Italian art and stained glass fill the relaxed interior of this
★ charming neighborhood restaurant, where musicians serenade you
throughout your meal. Outside is a bustling, plant-filled patio overlooking Boulevard Kukulcán. The food is consistently excellent, especially the salad of mixed greens, the ricotta ravioli, the lasagna with
béchamel, and the sliced filet mignon in balsamic vinegar. The staff spoils
you completely. ⊠ *Kukulcán Plaza, Blvd. Kukulcán, Km 13.5,* ☎ 9/
885–3603. *AE, MC, V.*

$ ✕ **100% Natural.** Looking for something light and healthy? Head to
one of the four locations of this cheery open-air restaurant, done up
with plenty of plants and modern Maya sculptures. The menus em-
phasize soups, fruit and veggie salads, fresh fruit drinks, and other non-
meat items. Also look for egg dishes, sandwiches, grilled chicken and
fish, and Mexican and Italian specialties. The branch at Plaza Terramar is open around the clock. ⊠ *Hotel Zone: Kukulcán Plaza, Blvd.
Kukulcán, Km 8.5,* ☎ 9/885–2903; ⊠ *Forum Plaza, Blvd. Kukulcán,
Km 9.5,* ☎ 9/883–1180; ⊠ *Downtown: Av. Sunyaxchén 62,* ☎ 9/884–
3617. *Reservations not accepted. AE, DC, MC, V.*

Downtown

*Downtown restaurants are located on the Downtown Cancún Dining
and Lodging map.*

$$–$$$ ✕ **La Habichuela** (The Green Bean). Once an elegant home, this en-
★ chanting, much-loved garden restaurant is decorated with local trees,
flowers, and plants and accented by Maya sculpture. The garden, lit
up at night, is bewitching. In the 24 years since the Pezzotti family
took over, there have been very few unhappy customers. Don't miss
the famous *crema de habichuela* (a rich, cream-based seafood soup)
or the *cocobichuela* (lobster and shrimp in a light curry sauce served
inside a coconut). The grilled seafood, chicken, and steaks are also
sensational. Finish off your meal with Xtabentun, a Maya liqueur made
with honey and anise. ⊠ *Av. Margaritas 25, Sm 22,* ☎ 9/884–3158.
AE, DC, MC, V.

$$–$$$ ✕ **Lacanda Paolo.** Southern Italian cuisine is brought to new heights
★ of excellence in this sophisticated, innovative restaurant—considered
by many to be the best Italian in Cancún. Don't even think of passing

up the black pasta in calamari sauce, or the penne with basil and tomato sauce. Also delicious are the steamed lobster in garlic sauce and the lemon fish. Fresh flowers, artwork on the walls, and attentive service combine for an atmosphere that's Old World–warm without being fussy. ⊠ *Av. Uxmal 35, Sm 3,* ☎ *9/887–2627. AE, DC, MC, V.*

$–$$ ✕ **El Cejas.** Located in the heart of the bustling, lively Mercado 28, this
★ is a neighborhood restaurant with an international reputation. The seafood is the freshest there is and cheaper than in the Hotel Zone. If you've had a wild night, try the *vuelva la vida,* or "return to life," (conch, oysters, shrimp, octopus, calamari, and fish with a hot tomato sauce). Equally wonderful is the ceviche and hot, spicy shrimp soup. ⊠ *Mercado 28, Av. Sunyaxchén,* ☎ *9/887–1080. AE, DC, MC, V.*

$–$$ ✕ **Mesón del Vecindario.** This sweet little restaurant tucked away from the street resembles an A-frame house in the woods. The menu specializes in all kinds of cheese and beef fondues along with terrific salads, fresh pasta, and baked goods. Breakfasts are hearty and economical. It makes a pleasant change from the usual downtown fare. ⊠ *Av. Uxmal 23, Sm 3,* ☎ *9/884–8900. AE.*

$–$$ ✕ **Sasha's Bistro.** This 10-table, not-to-be-missed bistro is where the
★ executive chefs from the Hotel Zone come to eat. Owner Alexander (Sasha) Rudin is a Swiss master chef who serves the most original and inspired menu found in Cancún (or anywhere along the Riviera Maya)— a fusion of Asian, Thai, and Vietnamese flavors with French undertones. The menu changes monthly so it's always fresh, but Sasha is so accommodating you can virtually custom-order your food. Past masterpieces have included grilled lamb chops in a pecan and macadamia-nut crust over Moroccan couscous and baked Chilean sea bass stuffed with Thai mushrooms and tempura duck tenderloins over sticky rice. The back room is a smoking lounge where Sasha's own brand of cigars is available along with the perfect drink. Fridays and Saturdays are prime-

rib nights. ⊠ *Av. Nader 118, Sm 3 (at Av. Mojarro)*, ☎ 9/887–9105. *No credit cards. Closed Sun. and Mon. No lunch.*

$ ✕ **Los Almendros.** Illustrations take some of guesswork out of the to-
★ tally Yucatecan menu at this modest spot. Specialties include lime soup and *poc chuc* (Yucatecan pork marinated in a sour-orange sauce with pickled onions), *papadzules* (tortillas piled with hard-boiled eggs and drenched in a pumpkin-seed sauce), and *pollo pibíl* (chicken baked in banana leaves). The staff has that genuine Yucatán warmth often miss-ing in the larger places. This is the best introduction to Maya food you will find in these parts. ⊠ *Av. Bonampark and Sayil, opposite the bull ring*, ☎ 9/887–1332. *AE.*

$ ✕ **Bisquets Obregon.** With its cheery colors, two levels of tables, and
★ sit-down luncheon counter, this cafeteria-style spot is *the* place to have breakfast downtown. Begin your day with hearty Mexican classics such as *huevos rancheros* (eggs sunny-side up on tortillas, covered with tomato sauce) or *huaraches* (thick tortillas with a variety of toppings). There is fresh-squeezed orange or carrot juice, but do try the *cafe con leche* (cof-fee with hot milk)—just watching the waiters pour it is impressive. The place opens early (7 AM). ⊠ *Av. Nader 9*, ☎ 9/887–6876. *MC, V.*

$ ✕ **Navajos.** Just behind the Parque de las Palapas, this outdoor restau-rant serves simple, light food. Breakfast features yogurt, sweetbreads, and fruit plates. Lunch and dinner offerings include soups, sandwiches, and salads, all fresh and filling, with daily specials offered at great prices. The decor, as the name suggests, honors Native Americans. It's a great place to watch all the action in this busy downtown neighborhood. ⊠ *Av. Alcatraces 18*, ☎ 9/887–7269. *AE, MC, V.*

Lodging

You might find it bewildering to choose among the variety of hotels in Cancún. For luxury and amenities, the Hotel Zone is the place to stay. For the most part the downtown hotels don't offer anything near the luxury or amenities of the Hotel Zone properties. They will, how-ever, give you the opportunity to stay in a popular resort without pay-ing resort prices, and many places have free shuttle service to the beach. Downtown hotels are also closer to Ki Huic, Cancún's crafts market, and restaurants that are more authentic—and less costly—than those that are in the Zone.

Expect minibars, satellite TV, laundry and room service, private safes (check to see if there is an extra charge for safe use), and bathroom hair dryers in hotels in the $$$$ category; in addition, almost every major hotel has suites, rooms for people with disabilities, no-smoking rooms, an in-house travel agency and/or a car-rental concession, guest parking, water-sports facilities, beauty salon and spa, fully equipped gym, and a daily schedule of planned games and activities for guests. Unless otherwise noted, all hotels have air-conditioning and private baths. Hotel Zone hotels have a beach unless otherwise indicated.

For most of the hotels, it's best to make reservations at least one month in advance and up to three months in advance for the Christmas sea-son. Many of the larger chain hotels also offer special Internet deals, with room rates dropping considerably when reserved on line.

Hotel Zone

Hotels in this section appear on the Cancún Hotel Zone Dining and Lodging map.

$$$$ ▥ **Baccará.** Each suite of this gorgeous Yucatán Resort property, a per-
★ fect example of a boutique hotel, is decorated differently, with a vari-ety of Mexican paintings, sculptures, ceramics, textiles, and furniture.

All have fully equipped kitchens, living and dining rooms, and private hot tubs that overlook either the ocean or the lagoon. Downstairs is a lobby and beach bar centered on an artfully designed pool area. You can dine at the elegant Avanti restaurant or grab a hamburger downstairs at Studebaker's. The attentive staff adds to the hotel's warmth. ⊠ *Blvd. Kukulcán, Km 11.5, 77500,* ☎ *9/883–2077 or 800/713–8170,* FAX *9/883–2173,* WEB *www.yucatanresorts.com. 34 rooms. 3 restaurants, 3 bars, pool, car rental. AE, DC, MC, V.*

$$$$ 🏨 **Hilton Cancún Beach & Golf Resort.** Hilton has taken over the for-
★ mer Caesar Park Beach & Golf Resort, combining the best of the old with the best of the new. The lobby has been refurbished in cheerful Caribbean colors, and the rooms brightened up in yellows and greens that complement the terra-cotta floors and rattan furniture. All rooms have a balcony or terrace with an ocean view; some have views of the resort's championship 18-hole, par-72 golf course across Boulevard Kukulcán. Seven lavish, interconnecting pools wind through palm-dotted lawns, ending at the magnificent beach. For total luxury consider staying at the Beach Club, with its 80 oceanfront villas. During the day, Spices restaurant serves excellent international fare. In the evening enjoy incredible Asian fare at the romantic seaside restaurant, Sirenita. The hotel staff's warmth and efficiency are added bonuses. ⊠ *Blvd. Kukulcán, Km 17 (Retorno Lacandones), 77500,* ☎ *9/881–8000,* FAX *9/881–8082,* WEB *www.hilton.com. 426 rooms, 4 suites. 3 restaurants, 3 bars, lobby lounge, 7 pools, beauty salon, hot tubs, saunas, 18-hole golf course, 2 tennis courts, aerobics, gym, shops, children's programs. AE, DC, MC, V.*

$$$$ 🏨 **Le Meridien.** The architecture of this refined yet relaxed resort hotel
★ is updated Art Deco with subtle Maya influences; there's lots of wood, glass, and mirrors. High on a hill, the property offers rooms with spectacular views, furnished tastefully in French provincial style. The many thoughtful extras—a complimentary shopping bag, different temperature in each of the three swimming pools—make a stay here special. The Spa del Mar is the best in the area, offering the newest European techniques and state-of-the-art equipment, along with a modern gym that overlooks an outdoor hot tub and waterfall. The spa is open to the public for a modest fee, so it's worth a visit even if you're not a hotel guest. Gourmet dining can be found at the wonderful Côté Sud. ⊠ *Blvd. Kukulcán, Km 14 (Retorno del Rey, Lote 37), 77500,* ☎ *9/881–2200 or 800/543–4300,* FAX *9/881–2201,* WEB *www.meridiencancun.com.mx. 213 rooms, 28 suites. 3 restaurants, 2 bars, 3 pools, hot tub, spa, 2 tennis courts, gym, children's programs, shops. AE, MC, V.*

$$$$ 🏨 **Presidente Inter-Continental Cancún.** It's hard to miss the striking yellow entrance of this hotel, five minutes from Plaza Caracol. Inside, lavish marble with accents of Talavera pottery decorates the hotel throughout. It has a quiet beach and a waterfall in the shape of a Maya pyramid by the pool. Larger-than-average rooms are done in royal blue or beige color schemes with light wicker furniture and area rugs on stone floors. Rooms on the first floor have patios and outdoor hot tubs. The suites have contemporary furnishings, in-room video equipment, and spacious balconies. ⊠ *Blvd. Kukulcán, Km 7.5, 77500,* ☎ *9/883–0200 or 800/327–0200,* FAX *9/883–2515,* WEB *www.interconti.com. 290 rooms, 6 suites. 2 restaurants, bar, 2 pools, beauty salon, hot tubs, tennis court, gym, shops. AE, MC, V.*

$$$$ 🏨 **Ritz-Carlton Cancún.** Ultraposh, ornate, and sumptuous, the Ritz radiates old-world elegance. The lobby, richly appointed with thick carpets, plush furniture, and European and American antiques and oil paintings, evokes the Ritz atmosphere so strongly that you may forget you are in Mexico. Rooms are decorated in shades of teal, beige, and rose; all offer wall-to-wall carpeting and large balconies overlooking the Caribbean. Travertine marble bathrooms are fitted with telephones and separate tubs and showers. The hotel's elegant restaurants, especially the Club Grill and Fantino (which serves northern Italian dinners), are standouts. ⊠ *Blvd. Kukulcán, Km 14 (Retorno del Rey 36), 77500,* ☎ *9/885–0808 or 800/241–3333,* FAX *9/885–1048,* WEB *www.ritzcarlton.com. 365 rooms, 40 suites. 3 restaurants, 2 bars, 3 pools, hot tub, spa, 3 tennis courts, health club, pro shop, shops. AE, DC, MC, V.*

$$$ 🏨 **Park Royal Pirámides Cancún.** One of the most charming hotels in
★ Cancún, this twin pyramid property has a lobby that's compact but well laid out, with cool beige furnishings. Rooms are decorated in sea and sunset colors, and original artwork (some of it created with local sand) hangs on the walls. Standard suites have two double beds and full baths; Ambassador suites have fully equipped kitchens, living-dining rooms, three double beds, and full baths. Selected suites also have private jacuzzis and terraces either facing the lagoon or the ocean. The beachside presidential suite has a remarkable view of the Maya ruin Yamil Lu'um next door. The property has two pools joined by a waterfall, a lovely beach, and a well-stocked, reasonably priced grocery store. ⊠ *Blvd. Kukulcán, Km 12.5, 77500,* ☎ *9/885–1333,* FAX *9/ 885–0113,* WEB *www.pyramidescancun.com.mx. 232 rooms, 54 suites. Restaurant, bar, grocery, 2 pools, gym, children's programs (ages 4– 12), shops, travel services. AE, MC, V.*

$$$ 🏨 **Villas Tacul.** These 23 villas on 5 acres of land—including their own stretch of beach—are a great place to set up housekeeping. The grounds are beautifully landscaped with well-trimmed lawns, flowering shrubs, and trees. Inside, highlights include red-tile floors, authentic Mexican colonial–style furniture, wagon-wheel chandeliers, and tin-work mirrors. All villas have kitchens and from two to five bedrooms, making them ideal for families or couples traveling together. For an extra charge you can have a housekeeper who cleans and serves breakfast. There are also some less expensive rooms available without kitchen facilities. ⊠ *Blvd. Kukulcán, Km 5.5, 77500,* ☎ *9/883– 0000 or 800/842–0193,* FAX *9/883–0349,* WEB *www.vilastacul.com.mx. 23 villas. Restaurant, bar, pool, 2 tennis courts, basketball. AE, DC, MC, V.*

$$ 🏨 **Holiday Inn Express.** Located within easy walking distance of the Pok-ta-Pok golf course, this clean, pleasant hotel was built to resemble a Mexican hacienda—but with a pool instead of a courtyard at its center. Rooms are decorated in bright blues and reds with modern furniture and have either patios or small balconies that overlook the pool and deck. While not luxurious, it's perfect for families in which Dad wants to golf, Mom wants to shop, and the kids want to hit the beach. A complimentary shuttle bus takes guests to the shops and beaches five minutes away; taxis are inexpensive alternatives. ⊠ *Paseo Pok-ta-Pok, 77500,* ☎ *9/ 883–2200,* FAX *9/883–2532,* WEB *www.holidayinncancun.com.mx. 119 rooms. Restaurant, pool. AE, MC, V.*

$$ 🏨 **Suites Sina.** These economical suites are in the heart of the Hotel Zone in front of the Nichupté lagoon and close to the golf course. Each suite is equipped with comfortable furniture, kitchenette, dining-living room with sofa bed, balcony or terrace, television, and double beds. Outside is a central pool and garden. Perhaps the best deal in the Hotel Zone, these suites are particularly affordable if you rent for a few weeks or share with someone. ⊠ *Quetzal 33, Club de Golf, 77500,* ☎ *9/883–1017 or 877/666–9837,* FAX *9/883–2459,* WEB *www.cancunsinasuites.com.mx. 33 suites. Kitchenettes, pool. AE, MC, V.*

Downtown

Downtown hotels appear on the Downtown Cancún Dining and Lodging map.

$$ ⊞ **Antillano.** Right on the main strip, this pleasant hotel is beautifully ★ maintained and stands out from the others in its league. Each room is fitted with wood furnishings, one or two double beds, a sink area separate from the bath, red-tile floors, and a small television. There is a cozy little lobby bar and decent-size pool. The quietest rooms are those facing the interior—avoid the noisier rooms that face Avenida Tulum. ⊠ *Av. Tulum at Calle Claveles, 77500,* ☎ *9/884–1532,* ℻ *9/ 884–1878,* WEB *www.hotelantillano.com. 48 rooms. Bar, pool, shops, baby-sitting. AE, DC, MC, V.*

$$ ⊞ **Holiday Inn Centro Cancún.** This is the place to stay if you want to ★ pay modest rates and be near the restaurants and shops but still have luxury hotel amenities. The attractive, pink, four-story building is reminiscent of a hacienda and houses modern rooms with mauve and blue color schemes and appealing Mexican touches, like ceramics and textiles. All rooms overlook a large pool surrounded by tropical plants. Its sister hotel, **Margaritas Cancún** (⊠ Av. Yaxchilán 41, ☎ 9/884– 9333, ℻ 9/884–1324), also downtown, has prettier rooms with balconies and the same amenities and is a little less expensive. ⊠ *Av. Nader 1, Sm 2, 77500,* ☎ *9/887–4455 or 800/465–4329,* ℻ *9/884–7954,* WEB *www.holidayinn.com. 246 rooms. 2 restaurants, 2 bars, pool, beauty salon, tennis court, gym, nightclub, coin laundry, travel services, car rental. AE, DC, MC, V.*

$$ ⊞ **Hotel El Rey del Caribe.** A marvel in downtown Cancún, El Rey del ★ Caribe has been designed to have zero impact on the environment, in part by using solar energy for electricity, a water recycling plan, and special composting toilets. And its luxuriant garden, which blocks the heat and noise of downtown, makes it an oasis. Hammocks hang poolside, and wrought-iron tables and chairs are placed throughout the grounds. Rooms are on the small side but are pleasant and have convenient kitchenettes. The hotel is within walking distance of all downtown shops and restaurants. ⊠ *Corner of Avs. Uxmal and Nader Sm 2-A, 77500,* ☎ *9/884–2028,* ℻ *9/884–9857,* WEB *www.reycaribe.com. 26 rooms. Pool, hot tub. AE, MC, V.*

$$ ⊞ **Suites El Patio.** This charming inn has the feel of an old Mexican residence. The entrance leads off a busy street into a central patio, landscaped with trees, flowers, and a lovely tiled fountain. Off to one side is a comfortable dining-living room. Upstairs, the large, airy rooms are furnished with Spanish-style furniture and Mexican photos and ceramics. Downtown attractions are within walking distance, and the helpful owners, who live on site, will direct you to the best spots in the area. ⊠ *Av. Bonampak 51, Sm 2-A, 77500,* ☎ *9/884–3500,* ℻ *9/884–3540,* WEB *www.cancun-suites.com. 18 rooms. MC, V.*

$ ⊞ **Maria de Lourdes.** Renovated in 2000, this budget hotel offers a lot ★ of luxury for extremely reasonable rates. Basic rooms are furnished with two queen-size beds, television, and bath. A well-maintained, decent-size swimming pool is surrounded by tables, where guests gather to play cards and chat. The staff is as amiable as the surroundings. It's within walking distance of shops and restaurants along Tulum. ⊠ *Av. Yaxchilán 31, 77500,* ☎ *9/884–4744,* ℻ *9/884–1242. 50 rooms. Restaurant, bar, pool. MC, V.*

$ ⊞ **Mexico Hostels.** Only four blocks from the main bus terminal and ★ open 24 hours, this new hostel is absolutely *the* cheapest place to stay in Cancún. The pleasant, clean space offers beds (four per room), private lockers, access to a full kitchen, a lounge area, and Internet access. Those who want to sleep outdoors can share a space with 20 others under a palapa roof. ✉ *Calle Palmera 30 (off Av. Uxmal, beside the BMW dealership), 77500,* ☎ *9/887–0191, 212/699–3825 ext. 7860,* 🌐 *www.mexicohostels.com. 50 beds. No credit cards.*

Nightlife and the Arts

The Arts

The **Casa de Cultura** (✉ Prolongación Av. Yaxchilán, Sm 21, ☎ 9/884–8364) hosts local cultural events, such as art exhibits, dance performances, plays, and concerts throughout the year.

FESTIVALS

Cancún's **Jazz Festival** is an annual weeklong event in late May that draws a huge international crowd from the United States, South America, and Europe. The **Cancún Hotel Association** (✉ Av. Ign. García de la Torre, Sm 1, Lote 6, Cancún, Quintana Roo, 77500, ☎ 9/884–7083) can provide information about this popular gathering.

Each fall the city of Cancún hosts the **Caribbean Culture Festival.** Artists and musicians from all over the Caribbean come to participate in a series of events that range from dance to music to poetry readings. There are also exhibits by Latin American painters and sculptors. The real draw, however, is the variety of salsa music performed. Consult your hotel for details.

PERFORMANCES

The **Ballet Folklórico de Cancún** performs Monday through Saturday at the **Convention Center** (✉ Blvd. Kukulcán, Km 9, ☎ 9/883–0199). This popular ballet folklórico dinner show has upbeat music and dances from across Mexico. Cocktails are at 6:30; dinner, a typical Mexican buffet, is at 7; and the dance production goes on at 8. Tickets are $50. Every weeknight the **Teatro de Cancún** (✉ El Embarcadero, Blvd. Kukulcán, Km 4, ☎ 9/849–4848) presents two shows: *Voces y Danzas de Mexico* (*Voice and Dance of Mexico*), a colorful showcase of popular songs and dances from different cities in Mexico, as well as *Tradición del Caribe* (*Traditions of the Caribbean*), which highlights the rhythms, music, and dance of Cuba, Puerto Rico, and other Caribbean destinations. Tickets for each performance are $29. Downtown the nightclub **Backstage** (✉ Av. Tulipanes 30, Sm 22, ☎ 9/887–9106) offers a gay cabaret and floor show Tuesday to Sunday.

Nightlife

Nightlife happens all over Cancún and in a wide variety of places. Many restaurants do double duty as party centers; discos offer music (sometimes taped, sometimes live) and light shows; and most nightclubs have live music and dancing. Sometimes the lines between the three get blurred.

DISCOS

Cancún wouldn't be Cancún without its glittering discos, which generally start jumping about 10:30. The scene's grande dame is **Christine** (✉ Krystal Cancún Hotel, Blvd. Kukulcán, Km 9, Lote 9, ☎ 9/883–1793), which puts on an incredible light show. **Dady'O** (✉ Blvd. Kukulcán, Km 9.5, ☎ 9/883–3333) has been around for a while but is still very "in." The **Liquid Club** (✉ Party Center, Blvd. Kukulcán, Km 9.5, ☎ 9/883–3147) is a high-energy disco with high-tech lighting and sound. In La Isla Shopping Village, **The Myth** (El Alebrije; ✉ Blvd. Kukulcán, Km 1.5, ☎ 9/883–4525) has fantasy decorations and continual laser shows but a small dance floor. **Ma'Ax'O** (✉ Blvd. Kukulcán, Km 1.5, ☎ 9/883–5599), also in La Isla Shopping Village, is a club-bar with the latest music and a wild dance floor. **La Boom** (✉ Blvd. Kukulcán, Km 3.5, ☎ 9/883–1152) is always the last place to close; it has a video bar with a light show and regular weekly events.

MUSIC

To mingle with locals and hear great music for free, head down to the **Parque de las Palapas** (✉ in area bounded by Avs. Tulum, Yaxchilán, Uxmal, and Coba). Every Friday night at 7:30 there is live music that ranges from jazz to salsa to Caribbean.

Azucar (✉ Hotel Camino Real, Blvd. Kukulcán, Km 9, Punta Cancún, ☎ 9/883–7000) showcases the very best Latin American bands. Go just to watch the locals dance (the beautiful people don't turn up here until *really* late) and enjoy the hot salsa. Proper dress is required—no jeans or sneakers. **Batacha** (✉ Hotel Miramar Misión, Blvd. Kukulcán, Km 9.5, ☎ 9/883–1755) is a terrific, down-to-earth spot for Latin American and Mexican music, as well as a great place to practice your salsa moves—there's always some local willing to offer you tips. The **Blue Bayou Jazz Club** (✉ Hyatt Cancún Caribe, Blvd. Kukulcán, Km 10.5, ☎ 9/883–0044) has nightly jazz in the lobby bar. The classy downtown **Roots Bar** (✉ Av. Tulipanes 26, near Parque de las Palapas, ☎ 9/884–2437) is the place for jazz, flamenco, blues, and modern Brazilian music. **El Camarote** (✉ Avs. Uxmal and Nader, ☎ 9/884–3218) offers bohemian-style and alternative music.

Outdoor Activities and Sports

Golf

The main course is at **Pok-Ta-Pok** (✉ Blvd. Kukulcán, between Km 6 and Km 7, ☎ 9/883–1230), a club with fine views of both sea and lagoon, whose 18 holes were designed by Robert Trent Jones, Sr. The club also has a practice green, a swimming pool, tennis courts, and a restaurant. The greens fees are $70 ($55 after 2 PM); electric cart, $25; clubs, $15; caddies, $20; and golf clinics, $25 per hour. Playing hours are 6–6 (last tee-off is at 4). There is an 18-hole championship golf course at the **Hilton Cancún Beach & Golf Resort** (✉ Blvd. Kukulcán, Km 17, ☎ 9/881–8016); greens fees are $95 ($75 for hotel guests), carts are included, and club rentals run from $20 to $30. The 18-hole executive course (par 53) at the **Hotel Meliá Cancún** (✉ Blvd. Kukulcán, Km 12, ☎ 9/885–1160) forms a semicircle around the property and shares its beautiful ocean views. The greens fee is about $20.

Water Sports

There are lots of ways to play in the water in Cancún. You can find places to go parasailing (about $35 for eight minutes); waterskiing ($70 per hour); or jet-skiing ($70 per hour, or $60 for Wave Runners, double-seated Jet Skis). Paddleboats, kayaks, catamarans, and banana boats are readily available, too.

El Embarcadero, at Playa Linda, is the largest marina complex and is where most water tours depart. At the dock you will find the Garrafon Ferry, the Isla Mujeres Tour Boat, the Captain Hook Galleon, the Nautibus, Aquabus, and HeliTours. Inside the complex are Xcaret ticket booths, an artist's flea market, various snack bars, and the Teatro Cancún, where nightly acts are performed.

Aqua Fun (✉ Blvd. Kukulcán, Km 16.5, ☎ 9/885–2930) maintains a full-service marina with large fleets of water toys such as Wave Runners, Jet Skis, speedboats, kayaks, and windsurfers. **Parque Nizuc** (✉ Blvd. Kukulcán, Km 25, ☎ 9/881–3030) is the area's newest marine park. Your entry fee includes a visit to **Baxal-Há**, a snorkel area that's home to gentle sharks and manta rays; and **Wet n' Wild**, a water theme park offering seven different water slides and a chance to see dolphins at **Atlántida**, an interactive dolphin aquarium. There is an extra charge to swim with the dolphins. Visitors are asked not to bring food or beverages into the park. If you would like to swim with the dolphins or feed some sharks without leaving the Hotel Zone, head over to the **Interactive Aquarium** (⊠ Blvd. Kukulcán, Km 12.5, ☎ 9/884–8487). Prices start at $40 for a half-hour dip with the dolphins.

FISHING/MARINAS

Some 500 species of tropical fish, including sailfish, wahoo, bluefin, marlin, barracuda, and red snapper, live in the waters adjacent to Cancún. Deep-sea fishing boats and gear may be chartered from outfitters starting at about $350 for four hours, $450 for six hours, and $550 for eight hours. Charters generally include a captain and first mate, gear, bait, and beverages. The following all have charter boats for deep-sea fishing at competitive prices: **Aqua Tours** (⊠ Blvd. Kukulcán, Km 6, ☎ 9/883–0227); **Barracuda Marina** (⊠ Blvd. Kukulcán, Km 14, ☎ 9/885–3444); **Marina del Rey** (⊠ Blvd. Kukulcán, Km 15.5, ☎ 9/883–0554); and **Mundo Marina** (⊠ Blvd. Kukulcán, Km 5.5, ☎ 9/883–0442).

SNORKELING AND SCUBA DIVING

Snorkeling is best at Punta Nizuc, Punta Cancún, and Playa Tortugas, although you should be especially careful of the strong currents at the last. You can generally rent gear for $10 per day from many of the scuba-diving places, and most hotels and resorts have their own gear for rent. If you've brought your own snorkeling gear and want to save money, just take a city bus down to Club Med and walk along the resort's beach for less than 1 km (½ mi) until you get to Punta Nizuc.

Barracuda Marina (⊠ Blvd. Kukulcán, Km 14, ☎ 9/885–2444) has a two-hour Wave Runner jungle tour through the mangroves, which ends with snorkeling at the Punta Nizuc coral reef. The $38.50 fee includes snorkeling equipment, life jackets, and refreshments.

Scuba diving has gained in popularity in Cancún. A word of caution about one-hour "resort" courses offered as freebies by the resorts: this does not prepare you to dive in the ocean, no matter what the high-pressure concession operators tell you. A one-hour lesson in a controlled environment such as a pool differs vastly from one in the open ocean. If you have caught the scuba bug, invest in a few more lessons and prepare yourself properly so you can enjoy the experience.

The secret of a good scuba company is personal attention, which is more often found at the smaller companies. Ask to meet the dive master and check out the company's equipment and certifications thoroughly. As its name implies, **Scuba Cancún** (⊠ Blvd. Kukulcán, Km 5, ☎ 9/883–1011) specializes in diving trips and offers NAUI, CMAS, and PADI instruction. It's operated by Luis Hurtado, who has more than 35 years of experience. **Solo Buceo** (⊠ Blvd. Kukulcán, Km 9, ☎ 9/883–3979) offers two-tank dives for $50 with NAUI, SSI, and PADI instruction. The outfit goes to Cozumel, Akumal, Xpu-ha, and Isla Mujeres. Extended diving trips are available from $180.

Shopping

Resort wear and handicrafts are the most popular purchases in Cancún, but the prices are higher than in other cities and the selection is limited. If your vacation includes visits to other Mexican locales, it's best to postpone your shopping spree until then. Cancún is most noted for luxury items. Many stores are "duty-free," selling designer goods at reduced prices, sometimes as much as 30%–40% off the usual retail price.

A note of caution about tortoiseshell products: the turtles from which they're made are an endangered species. It's also illegal to bring tortoiseshell into the United States and several other countries.

Shopping hours are generally weekdays 10–1 and 4–7, although more and more stores are staying open throughout the day rather than closing for siesta between 1 and 4. Many shops keep Saturday morning hours, and some are now open on Sunday until 1. Shops in the malls tend to be open weekdays from 9 AM or 10 AM to 8 PM or 10 PM.

Downtown

There's a wide variety of shops downtown along Avenida Tulum (between Avenidas Cobá and Uxmal). **Fama** (⊠ Av. Tulum 105, ☎ 9/884–6586) is a department store that sells clothing, English reading matter, sports gear, toiletries, liquor, and *latería* (crafts made of tin). **Ultrafemme** (⊠ Av. Tulum and Calle Claveles, ☎ 9/885–1402) is another popular downtown store that carries duty-free perfume, cosmetics, and jewelry. It also has branches in the Hotel Zone at Plaza Caracol, Plaza Mayafair, Kukulcán Plaza, and La Isla Shopping Village. The oldest and largest of Cancún's crafts markets is **Ki Huic** (⊠ Av. Tulum 17, between Bancomer and Bital, ☎ 9/884–3347), which is open daily from 9 AM to 10 PM and houses about 100 vendors.

Hotel Zone

There is only one open-air market in the Hotel Zone. **Coral Negro** is located next to the **Convention Center** and is a collection of about 50 stalls selling crafts items. It's open daily until late evening. Everything here is overpriced, but bargaining works.

Kukulcán Plaza (⊠ Blvd. Kukulcán, Km 13, ☎ 9/885–2304) is a mall that never seems to end, with around 130 shops (including Benetton and Harley Davidson shops), 12 restaurants, a bar, a liquor store, a bank, a three-screen cinema, bowling lanes, and a video arcade. The plaza is also notable for the many cultural events and shows that take place in the main public area.

Leading off Plaza Caracol is the oldest and most varied commercial center in the Zone, **Mayafair Plaza** (⊠ Blvd. Kukulcán, Km 8.5, ☎ 9/883–2801). Mayafair has a large open-air center filled with shops, bars, and restaurants, including El Mexicano. An adjacent indoor shopping mall is decorated to resemble a rain forest, complete with replicas of Maya stelae.

Specialty Shops

GALLERIES

The **Renato Dorfman Gallery** (⊠ Avs. Sunyaxchén and Yaxchilán 63, Sm 25, ☎ 9/887–4615; ⊠ La Isla Shopping Village, Blvd. Kukulcán, Km 12.5, ☎ 9/883–0359 or 9/883–5573) carries Dorfman's original pieces as well as his hand-carved replicas of Maya art and stelae. The **Modern Art Café** (⊠ La Isla Shopping Village, Blvd. Kukulcán, Km 12.5, ☎ 9/883–4511) is decorated with a revolving exhibit of works by local and international artists, all for sale. The **Huichol Collection** has three locations: Plaza Kukulcán (⊠ Blvd. Kukulcán, Km 13, ☎ 9/883–6078), Plaza Caracol (⊠ Blvd. Kukulcán, Km 8.5, ☎ 9/883–5059), and La Isla Shopping Village (⊠ Blvd. Kukulcán, Km 12.5, ☎ 9/883–5025). Each store sells handcrafted beadwork and embroidery made by the Huichol Indians of the West Coast. You can also watch a visiting tribe member doing this amazing work.

Cancún A to Z

ADDRESSES

In Cancún addresses, "Sm" stands for Super Manzana. All neighborhoods are labeled with an Sm number (Sm 23, Sm 25, etc.). Each Sm has its own park or square, and the area streets are fashioned around the park.

AIR TRAVEL TO & FROM CANCÚN

Aeroméxico flies nonstop to Cancún from Houston, Miami, and New York. American has nonstop service from Dallas and Miami. Continental offers daily direct service from Houston. Mexicana's nonstop flights are from Los Angeles, Miami, and New York. From Cancún, Mexicana subsidiaries Aerocaribe and Aerocozumel fly to Cozumel, the ruins at Chichén Itzá, Mérida, and other Mexican cities.

CARRIERS

➤ AIRLINES & CONTACTS: **Aerocaribe** (☎ 9/884–2000 downtown; 9/ 886–0083 airport). **Aerocozumel** (☎ 9/884–2000 downtown; 9/886– 0162 airport). **Aeroméxico** (☎ 9/884–3571). **American** (☎ 9/904–6000). **Continental** (☎ 9/886–0006). **Mexicana** (☎ 9/887–4444 or 9/883– 4881).

AIRPORTS & TRANSFERS

Cancún International Airport is 16 km (9 mi) southwest of the heart of Cancún and 10 km (6 mi) from the southernmost point of the Hotel Zone.

➤ AIRPORT INFORMATION: **Cancún International Airport** (✉ Cancún– Puerto Morelos Hwy./Hwy. 307, Km 9.5, ☎ 9/886–0073).

AIRPORT TRANSFER

The public-transport options are taxis or *colectivos* (vans); buses are not allowed into the airport due to an agreement with the taxi union. A counter at the airport exit sells colectivo and taxi tickets; prices range from $15 to $40, depending on the destination. Getting back to the airport for your departure is less expensive; taxi rates to the airport range from $10 to $22. Hotels post current rates. Be sure to agree on a price before getting into the taxi.

BOAT & FERRY TRAVEL

From Playa Linda, Plaza Caracol, and Playa Tortuga on Cancún, you can take a shuttle boat to the main dock at Isla Mujeres. Municipal ferries carry vehicles and passengers between Cancún's Punta Sam and Isla's dock.

Aquabus, a water-taxi service in the Hotel Zone, travels from the hotels to various restaurants and shops; a one-way fare is $3.

➤ WATER-TAXI INFORMATION: **Aquabus** (☎ 9/883–3155).

BUS TRAVEL TO & FROM CANCÚN

First-class buses arrive at the downtown bus terminal from Mexico City; first- and second-class buses come from Puerto Morelos, Playa del Carmen, Tulum, Chetumal, Cobá, Valladolid, Chichén Itzá, and Mérida. Local public buses take Route 8 to Puerto Juárez and Punta Sam for the ferries to Isla Mujeres (or you can take a taxi from the bus station to Puerto Juárez for about $2).

➤ BUS INFORMATION: **Bus terminal** (✉ Avs. Tulum and Uxmal, ☎ 9/ 884–1378 or 9/884–3948).

BUS TRAVEL WITHIN CANCÚN

Public buses run between the Hotel Zone and downtown from 6 AM to midnight; the cost is 5 pesos. There are designated bus stops—look for blue signs with white buses in the middle—but you can also flag down drivers along Boulevard Kukulcán. The service is frequent and quite reliable. Buses from the Zone do not go into downtown Cancún but will drop you off anywhere along Avenida Tulum when you indicate you would like to get off the bus. From there you can catch a connecting bus that takes you into the downtown area. Taking the bus can save you a considerable amount of money on taxis, particularly if you are staying in the Hotel Zone. The buses are filled with a variety of people, and the driver often plays his favorite music as he barrels along the boulevard.

CAR RENTAL

Cars are available at Cancún International Airport or from any of a dozen agencies in town. Most of the agencies have several locations in the area: Avis, Thrifty, and Localiza Rent a Car have five each; Hertz has nine; and National has seven. The telephone numbers given here are for the airport locations.

Most rental cars are standard-shift subcompacts and Jeeps; air-conditioned cars with automatic transmissions should be reserved in advance (though bear in mind that some smaller car-rental places have only manual-transmission vehicles). Rates average around $55 per day but can be as high as $75 daily if you haven't reserved a car; you can save a great deal on a rental by booking before you leave home. It's also a good idea to shop around. In addition to the rental agencies, the Car Rental Association can help you arrange a rental.

➤ MAJOR AGENCIES: **Avis** (⊠ Cancún International Airport, ☎ 9/886–0222). **Hertz** (⊠ Cancún International Airport, ☎ 9/884–1326). **National** (⊠ Cancún International Airport, ☎ 9/886–0152). **Thrifty** (⊠ Cancún International Airport, ☎ 9/886–0333).

➤ LOCAL AGENCIES & CONTACTS: **Car Rental Association** (☎ 9/884–2039). **Executive** (⊠ Av. Yaxchilán 160, Sm 20, ☎ 9/884–2699). **Econorent** (⊠ Avs. Bonampak and Cobá, ☎ 9/887–6487). **Localiza Rent a Car** (⊠ Av. La Costa 128, Sm 30, ☎ 9/887–3109). **Zipp Rental Cars** (⊠ Baccará Hotel, Blvd. Kukulcán, Km 11.5, ☎ 9/883–2077).

CAR TRAVEL

Driving any kind of vehicle in Cancún is not for the faint of heart. Traffic moves at a breakneck speed; adding to the danger are the many one-way streets, traffic circles (*glorietas*), sporadically working traffic lights, ill-placed *topes* (speed bumps), numerous pedestrians, and large potholes. Be sure to observe speed limits in the Hotel Zone and downtown. The traffic police are quite vigilant and eager to hand out tickets. In addition, car travel becomes expensive, as it entails tips for valet parking as well as gasoline and rather costly rental rates.

Although driving in Cancún is not recommended, you might want a car to explore the surrounding areas on the peninsula. The roads are excellent within a 100-km (62-mi) radius.

Route 180 runs from Matamoros at the Texas border through Campeche, Mérida, Valladolid, and into Cancún. The trip from Texas can take up to three days. Route 307 runs south from Cancún through Puerto Morelos, Tulum, and Chetumal, then into Belize. There are few gas stations on these roads, so keep your tank full. Route 307 has two Pemex stations between Cancún and Playa del Carmen. When approaching any village, town, or city, watch out for the numerous speed bumps—hitting them at top speed can ruin your transmission and tires.

EMBASSIES & CONSULATES

The consulates in Cancún operate with skeleton staffs, and for complicated problems you need to contact the offices in Mérida. The U.S. Consulate, in the Hotel Zone, is open weekdays 9–1; the Mérida offices are open weekdays 7:30–4.

The Canadian Consulate is open daily 11–1. Should you have an emergency when the embassy is closed, contact the Canadian Embassy in Mexico City.

➤ CANADA: **Consulate** (✉ Plaza Caracol 11, 3rd floor, ☎ 9/883–3360;
01–800/706–2900 emergencies, ℻ 9/883–3232). **Embassy** (☎ 015/724–
7900 in Mexico City).
➤ UNITED STATES: **Consulate** (✉ Plaza Caracol, 3rd floor, ☎ 9/883–
0272; ✉ Blvd. Montejo 453, Mérida, ☎ 9/925–5011; 9/845–4364 after-
hours emergencies).

EMERGENCIES

Cancún is grossly lacking medical-care facilities that focus on the patient rather than the amount of money to be made. The safest bet is
the American Medical Centre, run by Drs. Michael and Lisa McFall,
from the United States.

Cancún has a lot of pharmacies. Among those that offer delivery service are Canto, Pharmacia Cancún, and Paris (all downtown) and, in
the Hotel Zone, Roxsanna's. Paris delivers around the clock.
➤ DOCTORS & DENTISTS: **American Medical Center** (✉ Blvd. Kukulcán, Km 8, ☎ 9/883–1001; 9/883–0113; 9/887–1455 pager, 10844 PIN).
➤ EMERGENCY SERVICES: **Emergencies** (☎ 06). **Fire Department** (☎ 9/
884–9480). **Highway Police** (☎ 9/884–2445). **Immigration Office** (☎
9/884–1749). **Municipal Police** (☎ 9/884–1913). **Red Cross** (✉ Avs.
Xcaret and Labná, Sm 21, ☎ 9/884–1616). **Traffic Police** (☎ 9/884–
0710).
➤ PHARMACIES: **Canto** (✉ Av. Yaxchilán 35, ☎ 9/884–9330). **Pharmacia
Cancún** (✉ Av. Tulum 17, ☎ 9/884–1283). **Paris** (✉ Av. Yaxchilán 32,
☎ 9/884–3005). **Roxsanna's** (✉ Plaza Kukulcán, Kukulcán Blvd.,
Km 13, ☎ 9/885–0860).

MAIL & SHIPPING

The post office (*correos*) is open weekdays 8–5 and Saturday 9–1; there's
also a Western Union office in the building and a courier service. Bear
in mind, however, that postal service to and from Mexico is extremely
slow and may take four weeks or more. Avoid sending or receiving
parcels—and never send checks or money through the mail. Invariably
they are stolen.

RECEIVING MAIL
You can receive mail at the post office if it's marked "Lista de Correos,
Cancún, 77500, Quintana Roo, Mexico." If you have an American Express card, you can have mail sent to you at the American Express Cancún office, which is open weekdays 9–6, Saturday 9–1.
➤ SERVICES: **American Express** (✉ Av. Tulum 208, at Calle Agua, ☎
9/884–4243). **Post Office** (✉ Av. Sunyaxchén at Av. Xel-há, ☎ 9/884–
1418).

MONEY MATTERS

Generally, banks in Cancún are open weekdays 9–5, with money-ex-
change desks open 9–1:30. Downtown locations are along Avenida
Tulum; some of the larger banks have branches in the Hotel Zone as
well. All have automatic teller machines that dispense Mexican money.
The ATMs at the smaller banks are often out of order, but the larger
banks generally have working machines. If your PIN (personal iden-
tification number) has more than four digits, you may have trouble using
the ATMs. Also, don't delay in taking your card out of the machine.
ATMs are quick to eat up cards, and it takes a visit to the bank and a
number of forms to get them back. If your transactions require a teller,
go early to avoid long lines.

Banamex, which has offices downtown and in the Hotel Zone, can exchange or wire money. Other banks include Bital, Banca Serfin, Banco
del Surestse, Bancomer, Inverlat, and Santander Mexicano.

➤ BANKS: **Banamex** (✉ Av. Tulum 19, next to City Hall, ☎ 9/884–
6402; ✉ Plaza Terramar, Blvd. Kukulcán, Km 37, ☎ 9/883–3100).
Banca Serfin (✉ Av. Cobá at Av. Tulum, ☎ 9/884–4850; ✉ Plaza Kukul-
cán, Blvd. Kukulcán, Km 9, Hotel Zone, ☎ 9/881–4809). **Bancomer**
(✉ Av. Tulum 20, ☎ 9/884–4400; ✉ Plaza Caracol, Blvd. Kukulcán,
Km 8.5, ☎ 9/883–1128). **Banco del Sureste** (✉ Avs. Yaxchilán and
Sunyaxchén, ☎ 9/884–4991). **Bital** (✉ Av. Tulum 15, ☎ 9/881–4113;
✉ Plaza Caracol, Blvd. Kukulcán, Km 8.5, ☎ 9/883–4652). **Inverlat**
(✉ Av. Tulum 26, ☎ 9/884–3130). **Santander Mexicano** (✉ Av. Tulum
173, ☎ 9/884–0629; ✉ Plaza Lagunas, Blvd. Kukulcán, Km. 8.5, ☎
9/883–0148).

TAXIS

Taxi rides within the Hotel Zone cost $5–$7; between the Hotel Zone
and downtown, $8 and up; and to the ferries at Punta Sam or Puerto
Juárez, $15–$20 or more. Prices depend on distance, your negotiating
skills, and whether you pick up the taxi in front of a hotel or decide
to save a few dollars by going onto the avenue to hail one yourself (look
for green city cabs). Most hotels list rates at the door; confirm the price
with your driver *before* you set out. If you lose something in a taxi or
have questions or a complaint, call the Sindicato de Taxistas (☎ 9/888–
6985).

TELEPHONES

Most hotels charge the equivalent of between 50¢ and $1 for each local
call you make from your room. In addition, there is usually a hefty
service charge on long-distance calls, and it can add up quickly. In order
to make a phone call—local or long distance—from any public phone,
you must purchase a Ladatel phone card, sold in blocks of about $3,
$5, $10, and $20. An alternative to the phone card is the *caseta de larga
distancia*—the long-distance telephone office. The offices have specially
designed booths where you take your call after the number has been
dialed by a clerk. A service fee of $3.50–$5 is added on top of the steep
long-distance charge. The booths do, however, offer more privacy and
comfort than many public-phone booths.

Cancún's area code is 98, and in the past it wasn't dialed for local calls.
Now, however, the 8 must be dialed even for local calls. The change
was made in order to accommodate a growing number of telephone
lines. Bear in mind that some of the older printed material on Cancún
does not reflect this change and shows the telephone written in the old
style.

TOURS
BOAT TOURS
Day cruises to Isla Mujeres are popular. They generally include snorkeling, shopping downtown, lunching at an open-bar buffet, and listening to music or lounging at Playa Norte. Plenty of tour operators offer
such trips. Captain Hook runs an Isla Mujeres day tour that departs
at 10 AM from the pier in front of Fat Tuesday, on Boulevard Kukulcán, and returns at 5 PM; it costs about $55. Dolphin Discovery sails
daily from Playas Langosta and Tortugas to the company's dock on
Isla Mujeres; its program includes an instruction video, a 30-minute
swim session with the dolphins, and time to explore the island. Tickets start at $75. Riviera Holiday Cruises offers a three-day, two-night
cruise from Cancún to Havana for $150.
➤ FEES & SCHEDULES: **Captain Hook** (✉ Blvd. Kukulcán, Km 4.5, ☎
9/883–3736). **Dolphin Discovery** (✉ Playa Langosta, Isla Mujeres, ☎
9/883–0777 or 9/883–0779). **Riviera Holiday Cruises** (✉ Calle Tierra
15, Local E, Sm 4, ☎ 9/884–7743, ⊞WEB www.rivieraholidaycruises.com).

While many claim to have ecological tours, few outfits actually deliver truly ecological experiences in authentic jungle settings. An exception is Reserva Ecológica El Eden, which was established in 1990 by one of Mexico's leading naturalists, Arturo Gómez-Pompa, and his nephew, Marco Lazcano-Barrero. The 500,000-acre reserve, 48 km (30 mi) northwest of Cancún, is dedicated to research for biological conservation in Mexico. It offers excursions for people interested in experiencing the reserve's wetlands, mangrove swamps, sand dunes, savannas, and tropical forests. "Eco-scientific" tours include bird-watching, animal-tracking, stargazing, crocodile ecology, and cenote and archaeological explorations. Prices include transportation between Cancún and the reserve, one to two nights' accommodation at La Savanna Research Station, meals, cocktails, guided nature walks, and all tours. Two-day, one-night excursions start at $235 per person, three-day, two-nights at $315.

➤ FEES & SCHEDULES: **Reserva Ecológica El Eden** (✉ A.P. 308, Postal 770, 77500, Cancún, Quintana Roo, ☎ FAX 9/880–5032).

PLANE TOURS

Promocaribe flies one-day tours between Cancún and Guatemala City, continuing on to Flores and the ruins at Tikal. A round-trip fare of $267 includes all ground transfers, departure taxes, entrance to ruins, a tour guide, and lunch.

➤ FEES & SCHEDULES: **Promocaribe** (✉ Plaza Centro, Av. Nader 8, Local 309, Sm 5, ☎ 9/884–4741, WEB www.promocaribe.com).

TRAVEL AGENCIES

American Express, Aviomar, Intermar Caribe, and Mayaland Tours all offer day trips. You can shop around for the best price or call the Travel Agency Association for further information.

➤ LOCAL AGENT REFERRALS: **Travel Agency Association** (✉ Plaza México, Av. Tulum 200, Suite 301, ☎ 9/887–1670, FAX 9/884–3738).

➤ LOCAL AGENTS: **American Express** (✉ Av. Tulum 208, ☎ 9/884–2001). **Aviomar** (✉ Av. Yaxchilán 82, ☎ 9/884–8831). **Intermar Caribe** (✉ Av. Tulum at Av. Cobá, ☎ 9/884–4266). **Mayaland Tours** (✉ 225 Party Center, Blvd. Kukulcán, Km 9, ☎ 9/883–0679).

VISITOR INFORMATION

The Mexican Ministry of Tourism has a toll-free 24-hour English-language help line for visitors.

➤ TOURIST INFORMATION: **Mexican Ministry of Tourism help line** (☎ 01–800/9–03–92). **State Tourism Information Center** (✉ Av. Tulum 23, ☎ 9/884–8073). **State Tourism Office—Quintana Roo** (SECTUR; ✉ Government Palace, Av. Tulum, ☎ 9/884–0437).

ISLA MUJERES

ISLA MUJERES (*ees*-lah moo-*hair*-ayce) has a magic of its own that seems to defy change. It makes this tiny, fish-shape island 8 km (5 mi) off Cancún a tranquil alternative to its bustling western neighbor. Only about 8 km (5 mi) long by 1 km (½ mi) wide, Isla has flat sandy beaches on its northern end and steep rocky bluffs to the south.

Updated by
Shelagh
McNally

The name means "Island of Women," although no one is exactly sure who dubbed it that. Many believe it was the ancient Maya, who used the island as a religious center for worshiping Ixchel (ee-*shell*), the Maya goddess of rainbows, the moon, and the sea, and the guardian of fertility and childbirth. Another popular legend has it that the Spanish conquistador Hernández de Córdoba named the island when he landed here in 1517 and found hundreds of female-shape clay idols dedicated to Ixchel and her daughters. Others say that the name dates from the 17th century, when Isla was a haven for buccaneers and smugglers. Pirates would stash their women here before heading out to rob the high seas.

After its popularity waned with brigands, Isla settled into life as a quiet fishing village. In the 1950s it became a favorite vacation spot for Mexicans. Americans discovered it shortly afterward, and in the '60s Isla became well known among hippies and backpackers. As Cancún grew so did Isla. During the late 1970s, the number of day-trippers coming over from the mainland increased, bringing Isla's hotel, restaurant, and shop owners more business than ever. Boatloads were streaming off the ferries for quick lunches followed by frenzied shopping, and thus the island became a small-scale tourist haven. Like the rest of the area, Isla is being developed, but it manages to keep its character as a peaceful retreat with its own local history and culture centered on the sea. And it continues to be a favorite of people who'd rather scuba dive, snorkel, and relax on the beach than watch TV, sample fast-food joints, and hang out at discos.

Exploring

To get your bearings, think of Isla Mujeres as an elongated fish, the head being the southeastern tip, the northwest prong the tail. The minute you step off the boat, you see how small Isla is. Directly in front of the ferry piers is the island's only town, known simply as El Pueblo. It extends the full width of Isla's northern "tail" and is sandwiched between sand and sea to the south, west, and northeast, with no high-rises to block the view.

A Good Tour

The best way to explore the entire island is to take a taxi or rent either a moped or golf cart. You can walk to Isla's historic **cemetery** ⑥ by going northwest from the ferry piers on Avenida López Mateos. Then head southeast (by car or other vehicle) along Avenida Rueda Medina past the piers to reach the Mexican naval base. It's off-limits to tourists—and the Mexican navy doesn't like anyone photographing the crew, base, or ships—but you can see the flag ceremonies from the road at sunrise and sunset. Continue southeast out of town; 2½ km (1½ mi) farther down the road is **Laguna Makax** ⑦, on the right.

At the southeast end of the lagoon, a dirt road to the left leads to the remains of the **Hacienda Mundaca** ⑧. About a block southeast of the hacienda, turn right off the main road at the sign that says SAC BAJO to a smaller, unmarked side road, which loops back northwest. Approximately ½ km (¼ mi) farther on the left is the entrance to the **Tortugranja** ⑨.

Return to Avenida Rueda Medina and continue southeast past Playa Lancheros to **El Garrafón National Park** ⑩. Slightly more than ½ km (¼ mi) farther along the same road, on the windward side of the tip of Isla Mujeres, sit the remains of a small Maya ruin dedicated to Ixchel, the **Santuario Maya a la Diosa Ixchel** ⑪. Although little of the ruin remains, the ocean and bay views from here are well worth seeing. Follow the paved eastern perimeter road northwest back into town. Known as the Corredor Panoramico (Panoramic Highway), this is a beautiful, scenic drive with a few pull-off areas along the way, perfect for a secluded picnic. Swimming is not recommended along this coast because of the strong currents and rocky shore.

Isla Mujeres

Punta Norte

TO ISLA CONTOY

Playa Norte

6

Guerrero
Hidalgo

El Cemeterio
Piers
Mexican Naval Base

Main Square

Bravo

TO PUNTA SAM

TO PUERTO JUÁREZ

Caribbean Sea

• **Playa Gaviota**

Av. Rueda Medina

Hotel Villa Rolandi Gourmet & Beach Club

7

Puerto Isla Mujeres Resort & Yacht Club

Laguna Makax

Bahía de Mujeres

Dolphin Discovery

Salina Grande

Corredor Panorámico (Panoramic Hwy.)

Cristalmar

Tortugranja
9
8
Hacienda Mundaca

Playa Paraíso

Playa Lancheros

Playa Indios

La Casa de los Sueños

Hotel & Beach Club Garrafón de Castilla

El Garrafón National Park
10

Santuario Maya a la Diosa Ixchel
11

Punta Sur

KEY

🚢 Ferry

0 ——— 1 mile
0 ——— 1 km

Sights to See

⑥ El Cemeterio. Isla's unnamed cemetery, with its century-old gravestones, is on Avenida López Mateos, the road that runs parallel to Playa Norte. Filled with carved angels and flowers, the most beautiful of the decorated tombs are those in memory of children. Hidden among them is the tomb of the notorious Fermín Mundaca. This 19th-century slave trader—who's often billed more glamorously as a pirate—carved his own skull-and-crossbones tombstone with the ominous epitaph: AS YOU ARE, I ONCE WAS; AS I AM, SO SHALL YOU BE. Mundaca's grave is empty, however; his remains lie in Mérida, where he died. The monument is not easy to find—ask a local to point out the unidentified marker. ⊠ *Av. López Mateos.*

⑩ El Garrafón National Park. This national marine park has undergone a major commercialization with the addition of a three-floor facility with restaurants, bathrooms, and gift shops. The fancy buildings and walkways don't change the sad fact that much of the coral reef here has died—a result of too many snorkelers. Because the reef is dead, the fish must be bribed with food; sometimes they don't bite and there isn't much for snorkelers to see except for some clownfish and the occasional starfish. (The Garrafón Beach Club, next door, is a much less expensive alternative and the snorkeling is equal to if not better than that in the park.) Marine-park tickets are available at any kiosk in Cancún and in Playa del Carmen; you can also get tickets at the park entrance. ⊠ *Carretera El Garrafón, 2½ km (1½ mi) southeast of Playa Lancheros,* ☎ *9/883–3233 in Cancún, 9/873–2801 in Playa del Carmen,* 🖳 *www.garrafon.com.* 🎫 *$19.95.* ⊙ *Daily 8:30–6:30.*

⑧ Hacienda Mundaca. A dirt drive and stone archway mark the entrance to the remains of the mansion that 19th-century slave trader–cum–pirate Fermín Mundaca de Marechaja built. When the British navy began cracking down on slavers, Mundaca settled on the island. He fell in love with a local beauty nicknamed La Trigueña (The Brunette). In order to woo her, Mundaca built a sprawling estate with verdant tropical gardens. Apparently unimpressed, La Trigueña married a young islander—and Mundaca went slowly mad waiting for her to change her mind.

There is little to see of the actual hacienda; locals say the government tore it down, or merely neglected its upkeep. The most interesting things to see here are the ruined stone archway and triangular pediment, which is carved with the following inscription: *HUERTA DE LA HACIENDA DE VISTA ALEGRE MDCCCLXXVI* (Orchard of the Happy View Hacienda, 1876). ⊠ *East off Av. Rueda Medina (take main road southeast from town to "S" curve at the end of Lugana Makax and turn left onto dirt road),* ☎ *no phone.* 🎫 *$1.* ⊙ *Daily dawn–dusk.*

⑦ Laguna Makax. Pirates are said to have anchored their ships in this lagoon as they lay in wait for the hapless vessels plying the Spanish Main (the geographical area in which Spanish treasure ships trafficked). These days the lagoon houses a local shipyard and is a safe harbor for boats during hurricane season. The lagoon is off of Avenida Rueda Medina about 2½ km (1½ mi) south of town, across the street from a Mexican naval base and some *salinas* (salt marshes), which are on the left.

⚓ ⑪ Santuario Maya a la Diosa Ixchel (Sanctuary of the Goddess Ixchel). The sad vestiges of a Maya temple once dedicated to Ixchel are about 1 km (½ mi) southeast of El Garrafón National Park, at Isla's tip. Though Hurricane Gilbert walloped the ruin and succeeded in blowing most of it away in 1988, part of it has since been restored. A lovely walkway around the remains continues down to a natural arch underneath the ruin. The view from here, of the open ocean on one side and the Bahía Mujeres (Bay of Women) on the other, is spectacular. Adjacent is a **lighthouse.** The official word is that climbing to the top is no longer allowed, but a small tip and your powers of persuasion may convince the keeper to let you up to see the incredible view. The ruin is at the point where the road turns northeast into the Corredor Panorámico.

❾ **Tortugranja** (Marina Turtle Farm). Run by an outfit called Eco Caribe, this facility is dedicated to the study and preservation of sea turtles. During hatching season, from May through September, upwards of 6,000 turtles hatch along the coast of Quintana Roo. Some are brought to the farm to be raised until they are large enough to survive at sea. Visitors can view hatchlings and young turtles of various species in outdoor tanks, go on a tour led by one of the biologists, and watch feedings. A small but well-designed museum explains the various stages of turtle life and different parts of the coral reef. ⊠ *Take Av. Rueda Medina south of town; about a block southeast of Hacienda Mundaca, take the right fork (the smaller road that loops back north); the entrance is about ½ km (¼ mi) farther, on the left.* ☎ 9/877–0595. ▣ *$3.* ☉ *Daily 9–5.*

Beaches

The superb **Playa Norte,** known for its congenial atmosphere, is easy to find: simply head north on any of the north–south streets in town until you hit it. The turquoise sea is as calm as a lake, and you can wade out for 40 yards in waist-deep water.

The beaches between Laguna Makax and El Garrafón National Park, including **Playa Paraíso,** are good spots for having lunch or for shopping at the small stands that sell local handicrafts, souvenirs, and T-shirts. Some pet sea turtles and harmless *tiburones gatos* (nurse sharks) are housed in sea pens at **Playa Lancheros. Playa Indios,** southeast of Laguna Makax, has a lovely beach with soft white sand, palm trees, and easy access to the water. However, it's also the staging point for the large and noisy *Atilla Bay,* where day-trippers throng for snorkeling, water sports, and other planned activities.

Dining

As in the rest of Mexico, locals eat their main meal during siesta hours, between 1 and 4, and then have a light dinner in the evening. Unless otherwise stated, restaurants are open daily for lunch and dinner.

$-$$$$ ✕ **Casa Rolandi.** Part of the Rolandi family of restaurants, this Casa
★ Rolandi features the Swiss–northern Italian menu that won high marks at its Cancún location. The *carpaccio di tonno alla Giorgio* (thin slices of fresh tuna with extra-virgin olive oil and lime juice) is particularly good, as are the pastas—including lasagna and shrimp-filled black ravioli—which are prepared daily by the chef. The restaurant extends from the Hotel Villa Rolandi lobby to an open-air deck that juts out over the beach, so the water views are spectacular, particularly at sunset. Stained-glass accents behind the bar and along the windows are a nice touch, as are the crisp green and white linens. The waitstaff is warm, friendly, and discreet. ⊠ *Hotel Villa Rolandi Gourmet & Beach Club, Fracc. Laguna Mar Makak, Sm 7,* ☎ 9/877–0100. AE, MC, V.

$-$$$ ✕ **Lo Lo Lorena.** The food here is simple yet innovative, with a menu
★ that changes daily according to what's available. Favorites include "Lover's Salad," with conch and ginger, and a fantastic tart Tatin. The chef puts on an entertaining show in the open kitchen. Wooden shut-

ters, a wide porch, wicker furniture, and pastel colors give the old wooden house a lovely Caribbean flavor. ✉ *Av. Guerrero 7,* ☎ *no phone. MC, V. No lunch*.

$–$$ ✕ **Tequila Sol.** With its high ceilings, wood beams, and tile floors, this
   ★   restaurant is reminiscent of the old haciendas found throughout colonial Mexico. The excellent vegetarian and Mexican menu includes soy burgers and vegetarian fajitas, soups, and salads. Desserts, especially the chocolate cake and the flan, are very good, and the bar is well stocked. The staff is young, energetic, and eager to please. ✉ *Avs. Hidalgo and Matamoros,* ☎ *no phone. MC, V.*

$ ✕ **All Natural Café.** This haven for vegetarians serves breakfast, lunch, and light dinners. The offerings include great combinations from the juice bar, such as the orange-carrot mix and the papaya-melon drink, along with fresh salads, soups, and veggie sandwiches served on baguettes. Owner Beatrix Ferasse is usually either here or next door, at Nauti Pete Bistro, which she also owns. ✉ *Centro Hidalgo, Plaza Karlita,* ☎ *9/877–0720. MC, V.*

$ ✕ **La Cazuela M&J.** At this oceanfront eatery next to the Roca Mar
   ★   Hotel, a fresh breeze and a spectacular Caribbean view are the backdrops for the terrific food. In addition to the freshly ground, dark Colombian coffee, breakfast offerings include fruit, crepes, and omelets. Or try "La Cazuela," the house specialty created by chef-owner Marco Fraga; it's somewhere between an omelet and a soufflé. Grilled chicken with homemade barbecue sauce and thick, juicy hamburgers are on the lunch menu. ✉ *Calle Nicolas Bravo, Zona Maritima,* ☎ 🖷 *9/877–0101. No credit cards. No dinner.*

$ ✕ **Velazquez.** This family-owned palapa-style restaurant on the beach
   ★   is open until dusk and serves the freshest seafood on the island. You haven't eaten Yucatecan until you've tried the regional specialty called *tikinchic*—fish marinated in a sour-orange sauce and achiote paste, wrapped in banana leaves, and cooked over an open flame. It's excellent here. Feasting on a fantastic fish meal while you sit outside and watch the boats go by is a true Isla experience. Watch your head going into the restaurant, as the ceiling is quite low. ✉ *Av. Rueda Medina (2 blocks northwest of the ferry docks),* ☎ *no phone. No credit cards.*

Lodging

Isla has plenty of hotels. Generally the older, more modest places are in town, and the newer, more expensive resorts tend to front the beach around Punta Norte or on the peninsula near the lagoon. Most hotels have ceiling fans, and some have air-conditioning, but few have TVs or phones. Local travel agents can provide information about luxurious, self-contained time-share condominiums, which are another option.

$$$–$$$$ 🏨 **La Casa de los Sueños.** Tucked away at Isla's south end, this daz-
   ★   zling residence turned (no-smoking) bed-and-breakfast is honeymoon-perfect. A large interior courtyard leads to a sunken, open-air living room decorated in sunset colors. The living room extends into an open-air terrace that ends with a two-tier swimming pool on a cliff overlooking the ocean. There's also a glassed-in dining room, a well-stocked kitchen (simple salad lunches are available), and a staircase down to the private dock. All nine rooms are individually decorated and have ocean-view balconies or terraces. The master suite has a whirlpool bath with a sunset view. Room rates include a full American breakfast; scuba lessons in the pool; and the use of bicycles, kayaks, and snorkeling equipment. ✉ *Carretera El Garrafón, 77400,* ☎ *9/877–0651 or 800/551–2558,* 🖷 *9/877–0708. 8 rooms, 1 suite. Dining room, air-conditioning, fans, pool, beach, dock, snorkeling, boating, bicycles. AE, MC, V.*

$$$–$$$$ ⊡ **Hotel Villa Rolandi Gourmet & Beach Club.** This compact hotel is
★ as plush as any Cancún property. A private yacht delivers you to the
island; a smart cocktail awaits in the hotel's elegant open-air lobby.
All 20 suites are decorated in bright colors and have either two dou-
ble beds or a single king-size bed. A small sitting area looks out on an
ocean-front balcony with a heated whirlpool bath. In the bathroom,
the showers have six adjustable heads, seats, and a window with water
views. Both the Casa Rolandi restaurant, which serves first-class cui-
sine, and the lovely garden pool overlook the Bahía Mujeres and lead
down to an intimate beach. Room rates include Continental breakfast
and lunch or dinner. Children under age 13 are discouraged from vis-
iting. Smoking isn't allowed. ⊠ *Fracc. Laguna Mar Makax, Sm 7, Mza
75, 77400,* ☎ *9/877–0100,* FAX *9/877–0700,* WEB *www.rolandi.com. 20
suites. Restaurant, air-conditioning, pool, spa, gym, beach, dock, boat-
ing. AE, MC, V.*

$$ ⊡ **Hotel Roca Mar.** The turquoise sea is the star here, one of the few
★ downtown hotels overlooking the water. You can see, smell, and hear
the ocean as soon as you step into your room. The private balcony,
the wooden slats on the windows, and the simple furnishings—all are
designed to be inconspicuous. Of course, the lovely courtyard and pool
overlook the ocean, too. ⊠ *Calle Nicolas Bravo, Zona Maritima
77400,* ☎ FAX *9/877–0101. 31 rooms. Restaurant, fans, pool, beach,
snorkeling. AE, MC, V.*

$$ ⊡ **Na Balam.** This intimate hotel on Playa Norte may satisfy all your
tropical-paradise fantasies. Each room in the main building has a
palapa roof, eating area, large bathroom, and either a patio or balcony
facing the ocean. Decorated with Mexican folk art or photographs, the
rooms are simple yet elegant. Across the street are eight more spacious
rooms, each with a balcony, sitting area, double bed, and palapa roof.
There's also a swimming pool, garden, and meditation room. Break-
fast at the restaurant is a delightful way to kick off the day. ⊠ *Calle
Zazil-Ha 118, 77400,* ☎ *9/877–0279 or 800/552–4550,* FAX *9/877–0446.
31 rooms. Restaurant, bar, air-conditioning, pool, beach. AE, MC, V.*

$ ⊡ **Playa Gaviota.** The real plus at this hilltop hotel sandwiched be-
★ tween a garden and the ocean is the private beach with its barbecue,
palapas, coconut trees, white sand, and gorgeous sunset views. Each
of the 10 suites, decorated in basic blue and white, has a fully equipped
kitchenette, two queen-size beds, a small eating area, and a large ter-
race facing the ocean. Three smaller, older (but still comfortable) cab-
ins on the beach are for rent as well. The owners, a quiet Mexican family,
live on site. ⊠ *Carretera El Garrafón, 77400,* ☎ FAX *987/7–02–16. 10
suites, 3 cabins. Air-conditioning, fans, kitchenettes, beach. No credit
cards.*

Nightlife and the Arts

The Arts

The island celebrates many religious holidays and festivals in El Pueblo's
main square, usually with live entertainment on the outdoor stage. Car-
nival is in February and is spectacular fun. Other popular events in-
clude the springtime regattas and fishing tournaments. Founding Day,
August 17, marks the island's official founding by the Mexican gov-
ernment. During the **Isla Mujeres International Music Festival,** held the
second week in October, the island fills with music and dancers from
around the world.

Casa de la Cultura (⊠ Av. Guerrero, ☎ 987/7–06–39), near the youth
hostel, offers art, drama, yoga, and folkloric-dance classes year-round.
It's open Monday through Saturday 9–1 and 4–8.

Nightlife

A pedestrian "Cancún corridor" set up along Plaza Isla Mujeres at Avenidas Hidalgo and Guerrerro includes a number of bars and restaurants open until the wee hours. One of the liveliest (and loudest) is **Koko Nuts** (⊠ Av. Hidalgo 85, ☎ 9/877–8787). **Chiles Loco** (⊠ Plaza Isla Mujeres, Local A-4, ☎ no phone), a holdover from quieter days, has a large bar and a huge television.

Outdoor Activities and Sports

For water sports, beaches on the north and west sides are the calmest.

Fishing

If you're interested in participating in the **Red Cross Billfish Tournament,** held in the spring, contact Michael Creamer (⊠ A.P. 54, Isla Mujeres, Quintana Roo 77400, ☎ FAX 9/877–0443).

Captain Ricardo Gaitan (⊠ ½ Av. Madero 16, ☎ FAX 9/877–0434) offers specialized fishing trips aboard his 29-ft vessel, starting at $600. **Sea Hawk Divers** (⊠ Calle Carlos Lazo, Playa Norte, ☎ 9/877–0296) runs fishing trips—for barracuda, snapper, and smaller fish—that start at $150 for a half day. The **Sociedad Cooperativa Turistica** (☎ 9/877–0274) offers four hours of fishing close to shore for $100; eight hours farther out is $240.

Marinas

Puerto Isla Mujeres Resort & Yacht Club (⊠ Puerto de Abrigo, Laguna Makax, ☎ 9/877–0093 or 800/960–4752), the only place along the coast to get your boat repaired, has a full-service marina for vessels up to 170 ft. Daily mooring costs are $1.50 for vessels up to 89 ft and $2 for vessels 90 ft and over. The marina offers a full-service fuel station, a 150-ton lift, customs assistance, 110/220 V single and three-phase hookups, crew services, 24-hour security, and laundry, interior cleaning, and boatyard services.

Snorkeling and Scuba Diving

DIVE SITES

The famous coral reefs at **El Garrafón** have suffered tremendously because of negligent snorkelers and divers, boats dropping anchors (now outlawed), and the effects of Hurricane Gilbert. Good snorkeling continues near Playa Norte on the north end. In the waters near the lighthouse is a partially buried but still visible statue of the Virgin Mary.

Offshore, there's excellent diving and snorkeling at **Xlaches** (pronounced *ees*-lah-chayss) reef, due north on the way to Isla Contoy. One of Contoy's most alluring dives is the **Cave of the Sleeping Sharks,** east of the northern tip. The caves were discovered by an island fisherman known as Vulvula and extensively explored by Ramon Bravo, a local diver, cinematographer, and Mexico's foremost expert on sharks. It's a fascinating 150-ft dive for experienced divers only.

At the extreme southern end of the island on the leeward side lies **Los Manchones.** At 30 ft–40 ft deep and 3,300 ft off the southwestern coast, this coral reef is a good dive site. During the summer of 1994, an ecology group hoping to divert divers and snorkelers from El Garrafón commissioned the creation of a 1-ton, 9¾-ft bronze cross, which was sunk here. Named the Cruz de la Bahía (Cross of the Bay), it is a tribute to all men and women who have died at sea. Most area dive spots are also described in detail in *Dive Mexico,* a colorful magazine readily available in local shops.

DIVE SHOPS

Coral Scuba Dive Center (✉ Av. Matamoros 13-A, ☎ 9/877–0371) offers two tank dives for $39; shipwreck dives or photo dives for $59; and snorkel trips for $14. **Mundaca Divers** (✉ Av. San Francisco y Madero 10, ☎ 9/877–0607, FAX 9/877–0601) rents tanks starting at $45 along with snorkeling gear for $5 a day. **Sea Hawk Divers** (✉ Calle Carlos Lazo, Playa Norte, ☎ 9/877–0296) rents two tanks for $40; it also has dive gear and snorkeling equipment. Mundaca Divers and Sea Hawk Divers both offer dive trips to the reefs and the Cave of the Sleeping Sharks.

Water Parks

Dolphin Discovery (✉ Playa Langosta, on the Caribbean side of Laguna Makax, ☎ 9/883–0777 or 9/883–0779) offers the chance to play with the delightful sea mammals in a small, supervised group in a pool. There are four swims daily, at 9, 11, 1, 3. Each session consists of a 30-minute instruction video and 30 minutes in the water. The cost is $134 and includes the boat ride from Cancún and an all-you-can-eat Mexican buffet.

Shopping

Shopping on Isla Mujeres is a mixture of stores selling T-shirts, suntan lotion, beer, and groceries and those that sell Mexican crafts, including silver and jewelry, folk art, textiles, and clothes. Most shops accept credit cards. Hours are generally Monday through Saturday 10–1 and 4–7, although quite a few stores stay open through siesta hours (1–4).

Many local artists display their works at the public **Artesanias Market** (✉ Av. Matamoros and Calle Carlos Lazo, ☎ no phone), which offers plenty of bargains. **Casa del Arte Mexica** (✉ Av. Hidalgo 6, ☎ 9/877–0459)has a good selection of fine limestone carvings along with silver jewelry, batiks, wood carvings, leather goods, and hammocks. **Cosmic Cosas** (✉ Av. Matamoros 82, ☎ 9/877–0806) is the only English-language bookstore on the island. The friendly shop offers two-for-one book trades, e-mail and computer services, and a message board.

Isla Mujeres A to Z

BIKE & MOPED TRAVEL

You can rent bicycles on Isla, but keep in mind that it's very hot here and the road conditions aren't great (especially those unexpected speed bumps). Don't ride at night; many roads don't have streetlights, so drivers have a hard time seeing you. David's Bikes for Rent and Rentadora El Zorro rent bicycles; rates start at about $3 an hour.

Rentals of mopeds, a favored mode of transportation on Isla, also are available. R Cárdenas offers mopeds at $20 per day. P'pe's Rentadora has fully automatic Honda Aeros starting at $5 per hour (two-hour minimum). Ciro's Motorent has 50 Honda Tact mopeds.
➤ RENTALS: **Ciro's Motorent** (Av. Guerrero Nte. 11, at Av. Matamoros, ☎ 9/877–0578). **David's Bikes for Rent** (✉ Av. Rueda Medina 15, ☎ no phone). **P'pe's Rentadora** (✉ Av. Hidalgo 19, ☎ 9/877–0019). **R Cárdenas** (✉ Av. Guerrero 105, ☎ 9/877–0079). **Rentadora El Zorro** (✉ Av. Guerrero 7, ☎ no phone).

BOAT & FERRY TRAVEL

Speedboats and passenger ferries run between the main dock on Isla and Puerto Juárez on the mainland. Shuttles to Isla's main dock leave from Playa Linda, Plaza Caracol, and Playa Tortuga on Cancún. Municipal ferries carry vehicles and passengers between Isla's dock and Cancún's Punta Sam.

The passenger ferries (*Sultana del Mar* and *Blanca Beatriz*) are the least expensive option. A one-way ticket is $1 and the trip takes at least 45 minutes. Delays and crowding aren't unknown, but often there is live music on board, which contributes to a partylike atmosphere. The speedboats *Caribbean Lady* and *Miss Valentina* are air-conditioned cruisers with bar service. A one-way ticket costs $3.50 and the crossing takes about 20 minutes. Passenger ferries and speedboats leave every half hour from Cancún and Isla Mujeres 5 AM–8 PM. Always check the times posted at the dock, as the schedule is subject to change.

Shuttles from Cancún cost about $15 round-trip and take approximately 30 minutes, depending on weather conditions. Colon Tours has a shuttle that leaves Playa Linda at 9:30 AM and Isla at 4 PM. Asterix Water Taxi departs from Plaza Caracol at 9, 11, 1, and 3; return trips leave Isla at 10, noon, 2, and 5. The Isla shuttle leaves Playa Tortuga at 9, 11, 1, and 3:45 and Isla at 10, 12:30, 2:30, and 5. Call ahead, as schedules change according to demand.

➤ BOAT & FERRY INFORMATION: **Asterix Water Taxi** (☎ 9/886–4847). *Caribbean Lady* and *Miss Valentina* (☎ 9/877–0254 or 9/877–0253). **Colón Tours** (☎ 9/884–5333). **Ferry office** (☎ 9/877–0065). **Isla shuttle** (☎ 9/883–3448).

BUS TRAVEL
Municipal buses run at 20- to 30-minute intervals daily between 6 AM and 10 PM, generally following the ferry schedule. The route goes from the Posada del Mar hotel on Avenida Rueda Medina out to Colonia Salinas on the windward side. Service is slow because the buses make frequent stops.
➤ BUS INFORMATION: **Municipal buses** (☎ 9/877–0529 or 9/877–4173).

CAR TRAVEL
There is little reason to bring a car to Isla Mujeres. Taxis are inexpensive and the island is small. In addition, driving can be slow going.

EMERGENCIES
The Centro de Salud offers 24-hour emergency service and accepts regular visits 8 AM–8 PM. Isla also has an excellent Red Cross Clinic, which is run by a British doctor. Payment is by donation (the clinic doesn't receive government funding and operates on a shoestring budget). Your hotel can also help you find an English-speaking doctor.

A couple of pharmacies are open late: Farmacia Isla Mujeres, 9 AM–10 PM Monday through Saturday and 9–3 on Sunday, and Farmacia La Gloria, daily 8 AM–11 PM, with 24-hour service available.
➤ CONTACTS: **Centro de Salud** (✉ Av. Guerrero 5, on the plaza, ☎ 9/877–0217). **Police** (☎ 9/877–0082). **Port Captain** (☎ 9/877–0095). **Red Cross Clinic** (✉ Colonia La Gloria, south side of the island, ☎ 9/877–0280).
➤ LATE-NIGHT PHARMACIES: **Farmacia La Gloria** (✉ Carretera El Garrafón, Mza 67, ☎ 9/877–0885). **Farmacia Isla Mujeres** (✉ Av. Juárez 8, ☎ 9/877–0178).

LODGING
Some of the private homes on Isla are available as long- and short-term rentals. Mundaca Travel & Real Estate handles many of the rentals.
➤ LOCAL AGENTS: **Mundaca Travel & Real Estate** (☎ 9/877–0025 or 9/877–0026, FAX 9/877–0076).

MAIL & SHIPPING

The post office is open weekdays 8–7 and Saturday 9–1. You can have mail for you sent to "Lista de Correos, Isla Mujeres, Quintana Roo, Mexico"; the post office will hold it for 10 days.

➤ POST OFFICE: ⊠ Av. Guerrero, ½ block from the market, ☎ 9/877–0085.

MONEY MATTERS

Bital, the only bank on the island, is open weekdays 8–7. The ATM often runs out of cash, especially at the end of the day (be sure to save some money for the ferry ride back to the mainland). Sunday is especially bad, with long lines and little available cash.

Bital changes currency weekdays 10–noon. You can also exchange money at Cunex Money Exchange, which is open weekdays 8:30–7 and Saturday 9–2.

➤ BANKS: **Bital** (⊠ Av. Rueda Medina 3, ☎ 9/877–0104 or 9/877–0005).

➤ EXCHANGE SERVICES: **Cunex Money Exchange** (⊠ Av. Hidalgo at Francisco Madero 12-A, ☎ 9/887–0421).

TAXIS

Taxis line up by the ferry dock around the clock. Fares run $1 to $2 from the ferry or downtown to the hotels on the north end, at Playa Norte. You can also hire a taxi for a private island tour at about $15 an hour.

➤ TAXI COMPANIES: **Taxi** (⊠ Av. Rueda Medina, ☎ 9/877–0066).

TELEPHONES

Isla's area code is 987, but the 87 must be dialed even when making local calls. Keep in mind that some of the printed material on Isla doesn't reflect this and shows the old style: 987/1–23–45.

Isla has plenty of phones. Those that encourage you to "just pick up and dial 0" charge ridiculously high prices. It's better to use the TelMex phones that take a Ladatel phone card. You can buy the cards from local stores in blocks equivalent to $3, $5, $10, and $20. Once connected, you can dial direct anywhere in the world.

To place a collect call, dial 090 for an international operator from any phone booth (no card is required) and ask for *para cobrar* (literally, "to pay").

TOURS

Cooperativa Lanchera runs four-hour trips to the submerged Virgin statue, the lighthouse, the turtles at Playa Lancheros, the coral reefs at Los Manchones, and El Garrafón, for about $25 including lunch. Cooperativa Isla Mujeres rents boats for a maximum of four hours and six people ($120). An island tour with lunch (minimum six people) costs $15 per person.

Sociedad Cooperativa Isla Mujeres and La Isleña launch boats to Isla Contoy daily at 8:30 AM and return at 4 PM. Groups are a minimum of 6 and a maximum of 12 people, depending on the size of the boat. Captain Ricardo Gaitan, a local Isla Contoy expert, offers an excellent tour aboard his *Keen M.*

The trip to Isla Contoy takes about 45 minutes, depending on the weather and the boat; the cost is $30–$40. Tour operators provide a fruit breakfast on the boat and stop at Xlaches reef on the way to Isla Contoy for snorkeling (gear is included). The tour of Contoy's leeward side includes views from the water of Bird Beach and Puerto Viejo Lagoon. Along the way your crew trolls for the lunch it cooks on the beach.

➤ FEES & SCHEDULES: **Captain Ricardo Gaitan** (⊠ ½ Av. Madero 16, ☎ FAX 9/877–0434). **Cooperativa Lanchera** (⊠ waterfront near dock, ☎ no phone). **Cooperativa Isla Mujeres** (⊠ Av. Rueda Medina, ☎ 9/877–0274). **La Isleña** (⊠ corner of Avs. Morelos and Juárez, ½ block from pier, ☎ 9/877–0578). **Sociedad Cooperativa Isla Mujeres** (⊠ Pier, ☎ 9/877–0500).

TRANSPORTATION AROUND ISLA MUJERES
Many places on Isla rent golf carts, a fun way to get around the island, especially when traveling with children. Ciro's Motorent has rates as low as $50 for 24 hours; it has more than 30 carts and accepts credit cards. El Sol and P'pe's Rentadora also rent carts.
➤ RENTALS: **Ciro's Motorent** (⊠ Av. Guerrero Nte. 11, at Av. Matamoros, ☎ 9/877–0578). **El Sol** (⊠ Av. Francisco Madero 5, entrance off Av. Guerrero and Playa Norte, ☎ 9/877–0068). **P'pe's Rentadora** (⊠ Av. Hidalgo 19, ☎ 9/877–0019).

TRAVEL AGENCIES
Mundaca Travel sells plane and bus tickets, offers Federal Express services, and arranges airport transfers, tours, and house rentals.
➤ LOCAL AGENCIES: **Mundaca Travel** (⊠ Av. Hidalgo, ☎ 9/877–0025, 9/877–0026, 888/501–4952, FAX 9/877–0076).

VISITOR INFORMATION
The Isla Mujeres tourist office is open weekdays 9–2 and 7–9 and has general information about Isla Contoy. Isla's offical Web site, www.isla-mujeres.net, offers excellent information about the island.
➤ TOURIST INFORMATION: **Isla Mujeres tourist office** (⊠ Plaza Isla Mujeres, ☎ 9/877–0767).

COZUMEL

Updated by
Shelagh
McNally

A 490-square-km (189-square-mi) island 19 km (12 mi) east of the Yucatán peninsula, Cozumel is mostly flat, with an interior covered by parched scrub, dense jungle, and marshy lagoons. White, sandy beaches with calm waters line the island's leeward (western) side, which is fringed by a spectacular reef system, while the windward (eastern) side, facing the Caribbean Sea, has powerful surf and rocky strands. A lot of Cozumel has been developed, but a good deal of the land and the shores has been set aside as national park; a few Maya ruins provide what limited sightseeing there is aside from the island's glorious natural attractions. San Miguel is the only town.

The island's name comes from the Maya word *Ah-Cuzamil-Peten,* which means "land of the swallows." For the Maya, Cozumel was the sacred site of the fertility goddess Ixchel, as well as a key center of trade and navigation. For the Spanish, it was useful as a naval base in the late 16th century. For pirates, its safe harbors and the catacombs and tunnels the Maya dug were ideal for their treasure-gathering and -storing needs. After cycles of settlement and abandonment that included an economic boom based on the island's abundant supply of zapote trees, which produce chicle, a chewing-gum industry staple, Jacques Cousteau discovered Cozumel's incredible reefs and diving opportunities in 1961, and the trajectory of its current life was set.

Despite the inevitable effects of cruise ships that dock here, the island's earthy charm remains largely intact, and the relaxing atmosphere remains typically Mexican—friendly and unpretentious. A mainstay of Cozumel's mood is the isleños, descendents of the Maya who have inhabited the island for centuries.

Exploring

Cozumel is 53 km (33 mi) long and 15 km (9 mi) wide and, aside from the road leading to Punta Molas, has excellent paved roads. Aside from the 15% of the island that has been developed, Cozumel is made up of expanses of sandy or rocky beaches, quiet little coves, palm groves, lagoons and swamps, scrubby jungle, and a few low hills. Several minor Maya ruins dot the eastern coast of the island. One of them, El Caracol, served as an ancient lighthouse. There are also a couple of minuscule ruins—El Mirador (The Balcony) and the El Trono (The Throne)—identified by roadside markers.

A Good Tour

Taxis have become so costly on the island that it's worth renting some kind of vehicle to explore Cozumel. Be forewarned that most car-rental companies have a policy that voids your insurance when you leave the southern roads and journey north to Punta Molas. This dirt road is not maintained, so proceed with great caution.

Head south from **San Miguel** ⑫ and in about 15 minutes you come to **Parque Chankanaab** ⑬. Continue past the park to reach the beaches: Playa Corona, Playa San Clemente, Playa San Francisco, and Playa Sol. If you stay on this road you eventually reach, on your left, the turnoff for the ruins of **El Cedral** ⑭. Look for the red arch alongside the road announcing the turnoff.

Back on the main coast road, continue south until you reach the turnoff for Playa del Palancar, where the famous reef lies offshore. Continue to the point where the road swings north—the most southern point of the island—and you come to the **Parque Punta Sur** ⑮ entrance. The park encompasses Laguna Colombia and Laguna Chunchacaab as well as an ancient Maya lighthouse, El Caracol, and the modern lighthouse, Punta Celerain Faro.

At Punta Sur the coast road turns north. Not far from the Parque Punta Sur entrance are the minuscule ruins of **El Mirador** and **El Trono.** This road also passes one beach after another: Punta Chiqueros, Playa de San Martín, and Punta Morena. At Punta Este, the coast road intersects with Avenida Benito Juárez, which crosses the island to the opposite coast. You can take this road back into San Miguel or continue toward Punta Molas.

The road to Punta Molas is quite rough and only half of it is accessible by car—you must walk the rest of the way. The beaches on this part of the island are marvelously deserted: Ixpal Barco, Los Cocos, Hanan Reef, Ixlapak, and then Playa Bonita, with the small **Castillo Real** ⑯, another Maya site. Farther north are a number of other minor ruins, including a lighthouse, **Punta Molas Faro** ⑰, at the island's northern tip.

If you take Avenida Benito Juárez from Punta Este, you come to the turnoff (just past the army airfield) for the ruins of **San Gervasio** ⑱. Turn right and follow this well-maintained road for 7 km (4½ mi) to get to the ruins. To return to San Miguel, return to Avenida Benito Juárez and continue driving west.

Sights to See

🔺 ⑯ **Castillo Real** (Royal Castle). A Maya site on the coast near the northern tip of the island, the *castillo* (castle) includes a lookout tower, the base of a pyramid, and a temple with two chambers capped by a false arch. The waters here harbor several shipwrecks, and it's a fine spot for snorkeling, because there are few visitors to disturb the fish. Note, however, that the surf can get quite strong, so pick a time when the sea is tranquil.

Cozumel

TO PUERTO MORELOS

Punta Molas

**Punta Molas
Faro**

17

16

Castillo Real

↟ **Playa
Bonita**

↟ **Ixlapak**

Sea

↟ **Hanan Reef**

Punta Norte

**Isla de
Pasión**

18

San Gervasio

↟ **Playa
Los Cocos**

Sea

↟ **Playa
Santa Pilar**

↟ **Playa Ixpal
Barco**

↟ **Playa
San
Juan**

✈ **Airport**

↟ **Playa Oriente**

Punta Este

TO PLAYA
DEL CARMEN

12 **San
Miguel**

La plaza

Av. Benito Juárez

■ **Punta Morena**

Av. Rafael Melgar

Caribbean

■ **La Ceiba**

↟ **Playa de
San Martin**

13 **Parque Chankanaab**

■ **Punta Chiqeros**

Playa Corona

▲ **El Trono**

↟ **Playa San
Clemente**

▲ **El Mirador**

**Playa San
Francisco**

Caribbean

**Playa
Sol**

14 **El Cedral**

↟ **Nachi-Cocom**

**Parque
Punta Sur**

↟ **Playa Paradiso**

R E E F S

15

**Playa del
Palancar**

▲ **El Caracol**

*Laguna
Colombia*

*Laguna
Chunchacaab*

■ **Punta Celerain
Faro**

KEY

🛳 Ferry

🚢 Cruise Ship

0   6 miles

0   9 km

🔺 ⑭ **El Cedral.** Once the hub of Maya life on Cozumel, this was the first site found by Spanish explorers in 1518. It was also the island's first official city, founded in 1847. These days it's a quaint farming community with small houses and gardens that show little evidence of its past glory. Conquistadors tore down much of the temple, and the U.S. Army Corps of Engineers destroyed the rest during World War II to make way for the island's first airport. All that remains of the ruins is a small structure with an arch. Alongside is a green-and-white cinderblock church, decorated inside with crosses shrouded in embroidered lace where, reportedly, the first Mass in Mexico was celebrated. Hidden in the surrounding jungle are other small ruins, but you need a guide to find them. A number of the locals might approach you and offer a tour on horseback. ⊠ *Turn at Km 17.5 off the main island road, then drive 3 km (2 mi) inland to the site,* ☎ *no phone.* 🎫 *Free.* ☉ *Daily dawn–dusk.*

🔺 🖐 ⑬ **Parque Chankanaab** (Chankanaab Park). A 15-minute drive south of San Miguel, Chankanaab (the name means "small sea") is a lovely saltwater lagoon that the government has made into a national park with an archaeological park, botanical garden, dolphin aquarium, and wildlife sanctuary.

Scattered throughout the archaeological park are 60 reproductions of Olmec, Toltec, Aztec, and Maya stone carvings from well-known sites in Mexico. Guides lead interesting, informative tours, explaining the history of the most significant pieces. Also on site is a good example of a typical Maya house.

The botanical garden has more than 450 species of plants from the region. Enjoy a cool walk through pathways leading to the lagoon, home to 60-odd species of marine life, including fish, coral, turtles, and various crustaceans. Unfortunately, swimming is no longer allowed in the lagoon; the area's ecosystem has become quite fragile since the collapse of the underwater tunnels linking the lagoon to the sea. But you can swim, scuba dive, or snorkel at the beach. There's plenty to see under the sea: a sunken ship, crusty old cannons and anchors, a Maya Chacmool (the revered rain god), and a beautiful sculpture of the Virgin del Mar (Virgin of the Sea).

A small but worthwhile museum near the beach has photographs illustrating the history of the park, coral and shell exhibits, and some sculptures. There's also a sea-lion park, where children can enjoy watching the sea lions perform at one of their daily shows. Come early, as the park fills up fast. ⊠ *Carretera Sur, Km 9,* ☎ *no phone.* 🎫 *$7; free after 5 PM.* ☉ *Daily 7–6.*

⑮ **Parque Punta Sur.** The 247-acre national preserve, at Cozumel's southernmost tip, is home to numerous birds and animals, including crocodiles, flamingos, foxes, egrets, and herons. Cars aren't allowed on the premises, so visitors must use park transportation: bicycles or public buses. From observation towers you can spot crocodiles and birds in **Laguna Colombia** or **Laguna Chunchacaab.** Or visit the ancient Maya lighthouse, **El Caracol,** constructed to whistle when the wind blows in a certain direction. At the southernmost point of the park is the **Faro de Celarain** (Celarain Lighthouse), now a navigational museum outlining the history of seamanship in the area. The beaches here are deserted and wide, and there's great snorkeling offshore. Snorkeling equipment is available for rent, as are kayaks. The park also has an excellent restaurant, information center, small souvenir shop, and rest rooms. If you don't rent a vehicle to get here, a round-trip taxi ride from San Miguel costs close to $60. ⊠ *Southernmost point on Car-*

retera Sur and the coastal road, ☎ *no phone.* 🎫 *$10; free after 3* PM. ⊙ *Daily 7–4.*

⑰ Punta Molas Faro (Molas Point Lighthouse). At the northernmost point of Cozumel, the lighthouse is an excellent spot for sunbathing, birding, and camping. The jagged shoreline and the open sea offer magnificent views, making it well worth the time-consuming and somewhat difficult trip. Be prepared to walk some of the way. Area car-rental companies actively discourage visitors from driving here. Access is easier by boat, or you may prefer to take a guided tour.

⑱ San Gervasio. Standing in a lovely forest, these remarkable ruins make up the largest existing Maya and Toltec site on Cozumel. San Gervasio was once the island's capital and ceremonial center, dedicated to the fertility goddess Ixchel. The Classic- and Postclassic-style buildings were continuously occupied from AD 300 to AD 1500. At the entrance there's a snack bar and some gift shops. If you want a rugged hike, take the 15-km (9-mi) dirt road that travels north to the coast and Castillo Real. ⊠ *From San Miguel, take Av. Benito Juárez east to San Gervasio access road; turn left and follow road for 7 km (4½ mi).* 🎫 *Access to road $1, ruins $3.50.* ⊙ *Nov.–Sept., daily 8–5.*

⑫ San Miguel. Although highly commercialized and packed with tourists, Cozumel's only town has retained some of the flavor of a Mexican village. Stroll along the malecón and take in the ocean breeze. The main square is where townspeople and visitors hang out, particularly on Sunday night, when musical groups join the assortment of food and souvenir vendors.

Beaches

Cozumel's beaches vary from long, treeless, sandy stretches to isolated coves and rocky shores. Most development is on the leeward (western) side, where the coast is relatively sheltered by the proximity of the mainland 19 km (12 mi) to the west. The best sand beaches lie along 5 km (3 mi) of the southern half of Cozumel's leeward side—from **Playa Corona** south to **Punta Celerain.** In between them are **Playa San Clemente,** which has wide, sandy beaches and shallow waters, **Playa San Francisco,** considered one of the longest and finest on Cozumel, and **Playa del Palancar,** which has kept its prices down in order to keep drawing divers to its famous Palancar Reef.

Reaching beaches on the windward (eastern) side is more difficult and requires transportation, but you'll be rewarded with solitude. Near El Mirador is **Playa Paradiso** (also known as Playa Bosh), the southernmost of the windward beaches. North of Playa Paradiso, **Punta Chiqueros** is a moon-shape cove sheltered from the sea by an offshore reef. Where the paved road toward Punta Molas Faro ends lies a long stretch of deserted beaches, including **Playa Bonita,** which extends to Punta Molas at the island's northern tip. It's unspoiled and quite beautiful—perfect for sunbathing and communing with nature.

Dining

Dining options on Cozumel reflect the nature of the place as a whole: breezy and relaxed with the occasional harmless pretensions. The downtown core has more than 80 restaurants, so you can choose among fast food, great regional dishes, and gourmet seafood. Many restaurants accept credit cards; café-type places generally don't. A dining tip: don't follow the suggestions of cab drivers, who are usually paid to recommend restaurants and don't discriminate.

$–$$$ ✕ **La Veranda.** This charming wooden Caribbean house oozes ro-
★ mance and is the obvious choice for that special dinner—or for the wed-
ding reception that follows. Inside, there's comfortable rattan furniture,
soft lighting, and good music. Outside, a terrace looks into a lush trop-
ical garden that extends back to a small gazebo where you can sit and
enjoy the evening. Choices might include poblano chilies stuffed with
goat cheese, cilantro ravioli with jalapeño pesto, and fillet of fish mar-
inated in strawberry beer. The French onion soup and Caesar salad are
classics, and the flambé desserts are sensational. ⊠ *Calle 4 Nte. 140,
between Avs. 5 and 10 Nte.,* ☎ *9/872–4132. AE, MC, V. No lunch.*

$$ ✕ **French Quarter.** This is the restaurant that introduced Louisiana-Cajun
cuisine to the island. Owner Mike Slaughter is here nightly making sure
that everyone is happy. The options include homestyle gumbo and jam-
balaya as well as the more exotic, like glazed frogs' legs in a Cajun mari-
nade. On the grill are the finest cuts of Canadian Black Angus. You
can dine outside on the spacious terrace or inside with the colorful murals. The bar is comfortable and well stocked. ⊠ *Av. 5-A Sur, one block
off the plaza,* ☎ *9/872–6321. AE, MC, V.*

$–$$ ✕ **Chen Río.** The best fish on Cozumel is served here, on the east side
★ of the island at Playa de San Martín. The restaurant is run by a Maya
family whose sons go out in the morning to catch the fish they serve
for lunch. Relax under the coconut trees, watch the surf, or go for a
swim while you wait for your meal to arrive. The combo plate—with
shrimp, lobster, fish, rice, and vegetables—is a phenomenal bargain.
⊠ *East-coast road, Km 28,* ☎ *no phone. No credit cards.*

$–$$ ✕ **La Cocay.** The name is Maya for "firefly," and, like its namesake,
★ this place is a bit magical. Atop a small hill, the restaurant offers some
of the most innovative and flavorful cuisine on the island. The chef
and manager create a menu every four to five weeks; dishes might include spiced-nut-and-tamarind-crusted chicken breast, pumpkin-stuffed
medialunas (half-moon pasta) with sage and Parmesan butter sauce,
and rack of lamb with a red-onion sauce. The decor is simple yet sophisticated, with wood tables, wrought-iron chairs, soft lighting, great
music, and an open-air kitchen that lets you watch the staff do its magic.
Desserts are phenomenal, and the wine list has a nice selection. ⊠ *Av.
17 Sur 1000, at Av. 25,* ☎ *9/872–5533. No credit cards. Closed Sun.
and Oct. No lunch.*

$–$$ ✕ **Prima.** On a breezy second-floor terrace, this is the best Italian
★ restaurant on the island. Everything here is fresh: the meat is flown in
daily from the United States, and the vegetables come from local gardens. The pastas are wonderful, salads exemplary, and the steaks divine. Try the salad with blue cheese, and then move on to pasta with
pesto sauce, seafood ravioli, veal scallopini, or an Angus steak. There
can be lines during the busy season, but you can wait for your table
downstairs in the cigar-sports bar. ⊠ *Calle Adolfo Rosado Salas 109-
A,* ☎ *9/872–4242. AE, MC, V. No lunch.*

$–$$ ✕ **Las Tortugas.** The motto at this simple eatery is "delicious seafood
at accessible prices," and Las Tortugas lives up to it in a big way. The
menu lists only the freshest fish, lobster, and conch caught by local fishermen. This means daily special changes according to what's available.
Fajitas and other traditional Mexican dishes also are available. This
is a great place to experience the hospitality of Cozumel. ⊠ *Av. 10 Nte.
82,* ☎ *9/872–1242. MC, V.*

$ ✕ **Plaza Leza.** The best fajitas and ceviche in town are served in this
unpretentious Mexican sidewalk café. You can let the hours slip away
while enjoying the great food and watching the action in the square.
For more privacy, go indoors to the somewhat secluded, cozy inner patio
for everything from *poc chuc* (pork chops grilled Yucatecan style with
hot spices), enchiladas, and lime soup to chicken sandwiches and co-

conut ice cream. You can get breakfast here, too. ✉ *South side of the main plaza,* ☎ *9/872–1041. AE, MC, V.*

$ ✕ **Rock 'n Java Caribbean Café.** Healthful is the key word here. The
★ extensive breakfast menu offers such delights as whole-wheat French toast and cheese blintzes. For lunch or dinner, consider the vegetarian tacos or lasagna, or choose from the selection of more than a dozen salads. To balance things out there are scrumptious pies, cakes, and pastries baked daily on the premises. Enjoy your healthy meal or your sinful snack while sitting on the wrought-iron studio chairs and watching the waterfront out back. ✉ *Av. Rafael E. Melgar 602-6,* ☎ *9/872–4405. No credit cards. Closed Sun.*

$ ✕ **El Turix.** Off the beaten track, about 10 minutes by cab from down-
★ town, this simple place is worth the trip for a chance to experience true Yucatecan cuisine served by the amiable owners, Rafael and Maruca. Don't miss the *pollo pibíl* (chicken baked in banana leaves with pumpkin-chili sauce) or the *poc chuc* (pork marinated in a sour-orange sauce and pickled onions). There are also daily specials, and paella on request. ✉ *Av. 20 Sur, between Calles 17 and 19,* ☎ *9/872–5234. No credit cards. No lunch.*

Lodging

All of Cozumel's hotels are on the leeward (west) side of the island. Hotels north and south of San Miguel tend to be the larger, all-inclusive resorts, while less expensive places are in town. Because of the proximity of the reefs, divers and snorkelers tend to congregate at the southern properties, while sailors and anglers prefer the hotels to the north, where the beaches are better.

North Hotel Zone

$$$–$$$$ 🏨 **Coral Princess Hotel & Resort.** Tasteful, elegant, and artistic, this is
★ one of the best hotels in the North Hotel Zone (Zona Hotelera Norte). The lobby, with its water fountain of leaping dolphins and sculptures of wrought iron and glass, resembles an art gallery. Rooms are decorated with Mexican furnishings and artwork. Princess Villas have two bedrooms, two bathrooms, a kitchen, a dining room, and private terrace; the Coral Villas have one bedroom with a combined kitchen-dining area and terrace. Except for 61 studios, all rooms overlook the ocean. There isn't much of a beach, but there's a wonderful pool and huge deck leading down to the ocean. Inside there's a game room, convention salon, and a pretty celestial-theme bar perfect for a romantic drink before dinner at El Galeón restaurant (off the main lobby). ✉ *Zona Hotelera Norte, Km 2.5, 77600,* ☎ *9/872–3200 or 800/253–2702,* ⅎᴬˣ *9/872–2800. 100 rooms, 37 villas, 2 penthouses. Restaurant, bar, air-conditioning, pool, volleyball, dock, dive shop, snorkeling, fishing, car rental. AE, MC, V.*

$$$ 🏨 **Playa Azul Hotel.** At this quiet, comfortable hotel, bright, airy rooms have either great ocean views or face beautiful tropical gardens. All have sliding doors leading to sun-filled terraces. Some of the rooms have couches that convert to beds, which is ideal for families. Along the beach, small palapas are set up with comfortable chairs. Snorkeling, scuba diving, and fishing trips depart daily from Playa Azul's own dock. The Palma Azul restaurant serves delicious meals centered on fresh fish. You can also eat at Mr. Sancho's beach club, at the south end of the island, and charge it to your room. ✉ *Carretera San Juan, Km 4, 77600,* ☎ *9/872–0199,* ⅎᴬˣ *9/872–0110. 31 rooms. Restaurant, 2 bars, air-conditioning, pool, massage, dive shop, dock, snorkeling, fishing, billiards, car rental. AE, MC, V.*

South Hotel Zone

$$$$ **Presidente Inter-Continental Cozumel.** Luxury, comfort, efficiency, and
★ privacy are hallmarks of the Presidente. The stylish rooms are done in
bright, contemporary colors with white cedar furnishings and private
terraces; a majority of the rooms overlook the ocean, while garden rooms
look into the beautifully kept grounds. Trees, plants, and shrubs along
the corridors contribute to the exotic, tropical feel of the hotel. The pool
is modest, but the beach is the nicest on the island and has great snorkeling: clown fish, angelfish, and parrot fish all swim in the waters a few
feet off the beach. There's also a professional dive and water-sports center, tennis courts, and a serene botanical garden. With the recent addition of a fitness center, meeting rooms, and new bar, the hotel is fully
equipped for a comfortable visit. The Arrecife restaurant is highly recommended. ⊠ *Carretera Chankanaab, Km 6.5, 77600,* ☎ *9/872–0322
or 800/327–0200,* 𝔽𝔸𝕏 *9/872–1360,* 𝕎𝔼𝔹 *www.interconti.com. 253 rooms.
2 restaurants, 3 bars, coffee shop, air-conditioning, pool, hot tub, 2 tennis courts, dive shop, motorbikes, shops, children's programs, car rental.
AE, DC, MC, V.*

$$$ **Fiesta Americana Cozumel Reef.** Hard to miss since it's painted a
blinding orange, this property is ideally situated for snorkeling and scuba
diving. Although the hotel building itself is across the road from the
water, a pedestrian walkway provides easy access to the dive shop, dock,
beach, pool, and restaurant. Standard rooms are large, with light-
wood furnishings; all have oceanfront balconies. There's also a 56-room
semicircular cluster of villas with patios and ocean views. Reasonable
prices and a good location have made the Fiesta Americana one of the
most popular hotels on the island. There are some great sailing pack-
ages as well. ⊠ *Carretera Chankanaab, Km 7.5, 77600,* ☎ *9/872–2622
or 800/343–7821,* 𝔽𝔸𝕏 *9/872–2666. 172 rooms, 56 villas. 3 restaurants,
3 bars, air-conditioning, 2 pools, 2 tennis courts, dive shop, dock, mo-
torbikes, travel services, car rental. AE, MC, V.*

$$$ **Iberostar.** This all-inclusive resort at the southernmost point of
Cozumel has managed to keep the local flora and fauna intact, so that
it has an exotic jungle setting. Rooms are small but pleasantly decorated with Mexican wrought iron and have either a king-size bed or
two queen-size beds; all have terraces or patios. The one drawback:
there isn't much privacy, since paths through the resort wind around
the rooms. The resort has so many activities for the whole family to
do that you may never make it to town (which is an expensive 20-minute
cab ride away). ⊠ *Carretera Chankanaab, Km 17, 77600 (past El Cedral turnoff),* ☎ *9/872–9900,* 𝔽𝔸𝕏 *9/872–9909. 292 rooms, 8 villas. 4
restaurants, 3 bars, air-conditioning, 2 pools, hair salon, spa, 2 tennis
courts, dive shop, dock, boating, theater, children's programs, car
rental. AE, MC, V.*

$$ **Villablanca Garden Beach Hotel.** Beautiful architecture and a refined
★ atmosphere set this apart from other divers' hotels. Standard rooms
have an open-air design, with a large double bed placed between two
pillars and an archway. On the other side of the arch is a separate sit-
ting area with doors opening onto the garden. Suites have refrigera-
tors, sunken bathtubs, and private terraces. Everything is done in
white, with flower arrangements providing the color. La Veranda, the
hotel restaurant, is very accommodating and can prepare special din-
ner menus for groups or for those with dietary restrictions. Outside
are a pool, a tennis court, and a huge garden. Excellent dive packages
are available at bargain prices. The on-site compressor is also a bonus.
⊠ *Carretera Chankanaab, Km 3, 77600,* ☎ *9/872–07300,* 𝔽𝔸𝕏 *9/872–
0865,* 𝕎𝔼𝔹 *www.villablanca.net. 25 rooms, 25 suites. Restaurant, air-
conditioning, fans, refrigerators (some), pool, tennis court, dock. AE,
MC, V.*

Downtown Hotels

$$ 🏨 **Casa Martillo Condos.** These luxury condos come equipped with every-
★   thing you need for a comfortable stay. All units face the pool and have
full kitchens, dining and living areas, sofa beds, and balconies or pa-
tios. Second-floor condos are split-level, with the bedroom and bath-
room upstairs. Other pluses include daily maid service, a laundry
facility, local phone service, individual dive-gear storage, and shopping
carts for visits to the local grocery store. It's three blocks from the beach
and a five-minute cab ride to town. If you share, these condos are a
great bargain. ⊠ *Calle 19 Sur and Av. 15 Sur, 77600,* ☎ *9/872–2629
or 877/627–8455,* FAX *530/623–2671. 6 apartments. Air-conditioning,
fans, pool, laundry service. AE, MC, V.*

$$ 🏨 **Tamarindo Bed & Breakfast.** The owners of this five-room charmer
have created a place that combines the flavor of Mexico with the ele-
gance of France. Rooms are gracefully decorated with individual touches.
Breakfasts consist of fresh breads, fruits in season, homemade yogurt,
and French pressed coffee. The staff arranges diving expeditions, and
there's a rinse tank and gear-storage facility on the premises. ⊠ *Calle
4 Nte. 421, between Avs. 20 and 25, 77600,* ☎ FAX *9/872–3614. 5 rooms.
Massage, bicycles, baby-sitting, laundry service. MC, V.*

$ 🏨 **Charrita's.** This charming bed-and-breakfast has a Western flavor
★   and is a great deal. Its quiet location in a residential neighborhood seven
blocks from the beach gives you a chance to experience a slice of Mexico you won't find at other hotels. Each of the five rooms is extremely
comfortable, with individual decorations and a private bath. Upstairs
there's a charming terrace for sunbathing or taking in sunsets. If this
place is full, ask to stay at Les Delphines, the delightful sister residence
on Calle 15 Sur; it has four luxurious guest rooms set up for maximum privacy. ⊠ *Calle 21 Sur, between Felipe Angeles and Av. 40 Sur,
77600,* ☎ FAX *9/872–4760. 5 rooms. Fans, deck. No credit cards.*

Nightlife and the Arts

The arts scene on Cozumel tends to focus on the local culture; every
Thursday there's a folkloric dance performance at the **Fiesta Americana** (☎ 9/872–2622). The whole island explodes with music, costumes,
dancing, parades, and parties for Carnival, which takes place just before the start of Lent in February. Visitors from around the world are
encouraged to dress up and catch the fever.

Bars

Cactus (⊠ Av. Rafael E. Melgar 145, ☎ 9/872–3045) has a disco, live
music, and a bar that stays open until 5 AM. Sports fiends can catch
all the news on ESPN at **Sports Page Video Bar and Restaurant** (⊠
Av. 5 Nte. and Calle 2, ☎ 9/872–1199).

Discos

The oldest disco on the island, **Neptune Dance Club** (⊠ Av. Rafael E.
Melgar at Av. 11, ☎ 9/872–1537) still lets you boogie into the night.
Viva Mexico (⊠ Av. Rafael E. Melgar, ☎ 9/872–0799) has a DJ who
spins dance music until the wee hours. There's also a terrific snack menu.

Live Music

For sophisticated jazz, smart cocktails, and great cigars, check out the
Havana Club (⊠ Av. Rafael E. Melgar, between Calles 6 and 8, second floor, ☎ 9/872–6599). The food isn't the draw at **Joe's Lobster
House** (⊠ Av. 10 Sur 229, between Calles Adolfo Rosada Salas and 3
Sur, ☎ 9/872–3275), but the reggae and salsa bring them in (nightly
from 10:30 until dawn). Sunday evenings 8–10, locals head for the *zócalo*
(plaza) to hear mariachis and island musicians playing tropical tunes.

Outdoor Activities and Sports

Most people come to Cozumel for the water sports—scuba diving, snorkeling, and fishing are particularly popular. Services and equipment rentals are available throughout the island, especially through major hotels and water-sports centers such as **Scuba Du** (✉ Calle 3 Sur 33, between Avs. Rafael E. Melgar and 5 Sur, ☎ 9/872–1994).

Fishing

Regulations forbid commercial fishing, sportfishing, spear fishing, and collecting any marine life in certain areas around Cozumel. It's illegal to kill certain species, including billfish, so be prepared to return prize catches back to the sea. For the past 22 years the annual **International Billfish Tournament** (✉ A.P. 442, 77600, ☎ 800/253–2701, FAX 9/872–0999), held the last week in April or the first week in May, has drawn anglers from around the world to Cozumel.

Charters

You can charter high-speed fishing boats for $400 for a half day or $500 for a full day (maximum six people). **Albatros Deep Sea Fishing** (☎ 9/872–5619 or 888/333–4643) is a local outfit specializing in fishing trips. **Marathon Fishing & Leisure Charters** (☎ 9/872–1986) is popular with fishermen. Your hotel can help you arrange daily charters—some hotels have special deals, with boats leaving from their own dock.

Scuba Diving

The options for divers in Cozumel include deep dives, drift dives, shore dives, wall dives, and night dives, as well as theme dives focusing on ecology, archaeology, sunken ships, and photography. With so many shops to choose from (there are now more than 100), divers should look for high safety standards and documented credentials. The best places are those that offer small groups and individual attention. Next to your equipment, your dive master is the most important aspect of your dive, particularly if you're new to diving.

The **Cozumel Recompression Chamber** (✉ San Miguel Clinic, Calle 6 between Avs. 5 and 10, ☎ 9/872–3070, 9/872–2387, or 9/872–1848) is a fully equipped recompression center. There's a reputable recompression chamber at the **Buceo Medico Mexicano** (✉ Calle 9 Sur 21-B, ☎ 9/872–2387). These chambers, which aim for a 35-minute response time from reef to chamber, treat decompression sickness, commonly known as "the bends." Recompression chambers are also used to treat nitrogen narcosis, collapsed lungs, and overexposure to the cold. Most of the dive shops in town offer complete dive-accident coverage for just $1 per day.

When diving, stay at least 3 ft above the reef, not just because the coral can sting or cut you but also because coral is easily damaged and grows very slowly: it has taken 2,000 years for it to reach its present size.

DIVE SHOPS AND TOUR OPERATORS

Most dive shops can provide you with all the incidentals you'll need, as well as with guides and transportation. You can choose from a variety of two-tank boat trips and specialty dives ranging from $45 to $60; two-hour resort courses cost about $50–$60, and 1½-hour night dives, $30–$35. Basic certification courses are available for about $350, while advanced certification courses cost as much as $700. Equipment rental is relatively inexpensive, ranging from $6 for tanks or a lamp to about $8–$10 for a regulator and BC vest; underwater camera rentals can cost as much as $35, video-camera rentals run about $75, and professionally shot and edited videos of your own dive are priced at about $160.

ANOAAT (Aquatic Sports Operators Association; ☎ 9/872–5955) has listings of affiliated dive operations. Before signing on, ask some experienced divers about the place, check credentials, and look over the boats and equipment.

Aqua Safari (⊠ Av. Rafael E. Melgar 429, between Calles 5 and 7 Sur, ☎ 9/872–0101). **Black Shark** (⊠ Av. 5 Sur, between Calles Adolfo Rosado Salas and 3 Sur, ☎ 9/872–0396). **Chino's Scuba** (⊠ Calle Adolfo Rosado Salas 16-A, ☎ 9/872–5836). **Cozumel Equalizers Scuba Centre** (⊠ Calle Adolfo Rosado Salas 72, ☎ FAX 9/872–3511. **Dive Cozumel** (⊠ Calle Adolfo Rosado Salas 72, at Av. 5 Sur, ☎ 9/872–4567. **Eagle Ray Dive School** (⊠ Avs. Chichén and Pamuul, ☎ 9/872–5735. **Flash Adventures** (⊠ Av. 5 Nte. between Calles 5 and 7, ☎ 9/872–0570. **Gran Azul** (⊠ Av. 25a No. 1081, ☎ FAX 9/872–3223 **Michelle's Dive Shop** (⊠ Av. 5 Sur 201, at Calle Adolfo Rosado Salas, ☎ 9/872–0947).

Snorkeling

Snorkeling equipment is available at the Presidente Inter-Continental hotel as well as at Chankanaab Bay, Playa San Francisco, and Playa Sol and directly off the beach near the Fiesta Americana Cozumel Reef and Playa Corona for less than $10 a day.

One option for snorkelers is to contact the dive shops to see if you can tag along when they go out to a suitable snorkeling reef. Official snorkeling tours run from $25 to $50, depending on the length, and take in the shallow reefs off Palancar, Colombia, and Yucab. **Fiesta Cozumel** (⊠ Calle 11 Sur 598, between Avs. 25 and 30, ☎ 9/872–0725, FAX 9/872–1389) runs snorkeling tours from the 45-ft catamarans *El Zorro* and *Fury*. Rates begin at about $50 per day and include equipment, a guide, soft drinks and beer, and a box lunch.

Shopping

Cozumel's main shopping area is **downtown** on the waterfront along Avenida Rafael E. Melgar, and on some of the side streets around the plaza (there are more than 150 shops in this area alone). There's a **crafts market** (⊠ Calle 1 Sur, behind the plaza) in town, which sells a respectable assortment of Mexican wares. In addition, small clusters of shops can be found at **Plaza del Sol** (on the east side of the main plaza), **Villa Mar** (on the north side of the main plaza), and **Plaza Confetti** (on the south side of the main plaza). As a general rule, the newer, trendier shops line the waterfront, while the area around Avenida 5a houses the better crafts shops. The crafts market **Puerto Maya,** where the cruise ships dock, has some crafts at good prices.

Specialty Stores

CLOTHING

Several trendy sportswear stores line Avenida Rafael E. Melgar between Calles 2 and 6. **Bikinis do Brasil** (⊠ Calle 1 Sur, between Avs. 10 and 15, ☎ 9/872–0260) features a collection of Brazilian swimwear and sundresses. **Poco Loco** (⊠ Av. Rafael E. Melgar 18 and Av. Benito Juárez 2-A, ☎ 9/872–5499) sells casual wear and beach bags.

JEWELRY

Jewelry on Cozumel is pricey, but it tends to be of higher quality than what you'll find in many other Yucatán towns. **Diamond Creations** (⊠ Av. Rafael E. Melgar Sur 131, ☎ 9/872–5330) lets you custom-design a piece of jewelry from its collection of loose diamonds, emeralds, rubies, sapphires, or tanzanite. Quality gemstones and striking designs are the strong point at **Rachat & Romero** (⊠ Av. Rafael E. Melgar 101, ☎ 9/872–0571).

Los Cinco Soles (✉ Av. Rafael E. Melgar Nte. 27, ☎ 9/872–0132) is the best bet for one-stop shopping for quality items. The nearly block-long store stocks an excellent variety of well-priced, well-displayed Mexican wares. **Talavera** (✉ Av. 5 Sur 349, ☎ 9/872–0171) carries beautiful ceramics from all over Mexico.

Cozumel A to Z

AIR TRAVEL

CARRIERS

Continental flies nonstop from Houston to Cozumel; Mexicana has nonstop service from Miami and San Francisco. Mexicana subsidiaries Aerocaribe and Aerocozumel fly between Cozumel and Cancún and other destinations in Mexico.

➤ AIRLINES & CONTACTS: **Aerocaribe** (☎ 9/872–0503). **Aerocozumel** (☎ 9/872–0928). **Continental** (☎ 9/872–0487). **Mexicana** (☎ 9/872–0157).

AIRPORTS

The Cozumel airport is 3 km (2 mi) north of town.
➤ AIRPORT INFORMATION: **Cozumel Airport** (☎ 9/872–0928).

AIRPORT TRANSFER

Because of an agreement between the taxi drivers' and bus drivers' unions, there is taxi service *to* the airport but not *from* the airport. The *colectivo,* a van that seats up to eight, takes arriving passengers to their hotels; the fare is about $7. If you want to avoid waiting for the van to fill or for other passengers to be dropped off, you can hire an *especial*—an individual van. A trip via an individual van to one of the hotel zones costs about $15; a trip to the city runs about $10. Taxis to the airport cost between $8 to $25 from the hotel zones and approximately $5 from downtown.

BOAT & FERRY TRAVEL

Passenger-only ferries to Playa del Carmen leave Cozumel's main pier approximately every hour on the hour from 6 AM to 11 PM (no ferries at noon, 2, 8, and 10 PM). They leave Playa del Carmen's dock also about every hour on the hour, from 4 AM to 10 PM (no service at 5 and 11 AM, 1, 7, and 9 PM). The trip takes 45 minutes. Call to verify the times. Bad weather often prompts cancellations.

➤ BOAT & FERRY INFORMATION: **Playa del Carmen dock** (☎ 9/872–1508).

BUS TRAVEL

Because of a union agreement with taxi drivers, public buses cannot operate in the North and South Hotel zones; local bus service runs mainly within the town of San Miguel, although there is a route from town to the airport. Service is irregular but inexpensive.

CAR RENTAL

A rental car is a great way to get around the island, particularly as taxi prices are high here. A vehicle with four-wheel drive (check to make sure that it hasn't been disconnected) is a must if you want to get to the more secluded beaches and ruins.

All the large hotels have rental offices, and most of the major car-rental companies have a location at the airport. Rental rates start at about $40 a day. Insurance doesn't cover trips off the main roads. Many of the smaller companies carry only standard transmission cars, so request an automatic in advance.

➤ MAJOR AGENCIES: **Avis** (☎ 9/872–0099 airport). **Hertz** (☎ 9/872–3888 airport).

➤ LOCAL AGENCIES: **Aguila Rentals** (✉ Calle 11 No. 101, ☎ 9/872–0729). **Cocodrilos Car Rental** (✉ Av. Rafael E. Melgar 601, ☎ 9/872–5030). **Rentadora Islena** (✉ Calle 7 No. 49, ☎ 9/872–0788).

CRUISE TRAVEL

At least a dozen cruise lines call at Cozumel and/or Playa del Carmen, including, from Fort Lauderdale, Celebrity Cruises, Cunard Line, and Princess Cruises; from Miami, Carnival Cruise Lines, Costa Cruise Lines, Norwegian Cruise Line, Premier Cruises, and Royal Caribbean; from New Orleans, Commodore Cruise Line; and from Tampa, Holland America Line.

➤ CRUISE LINES: **Carnival Cruise Lines** (☎ 800/327–9501). **Celebrity Cruises** (☎ 800/437–3111). **Commodore Cruise Line** (☎ 800/327–5617). **Costa Cruise Lines** (☎ 800/327–2537). **Cunard Line** (☎ 800/221–4770). **Holland America Line** (☎ 800/426–0327). **Norwegian Cruise Line** (☎ 800/327–7030). **Premier Cruises** (☎ 800/222–1003). **Princess Cruises** (☎ 800/568–3262). **Royal Caribbean** (☎ 800/327–6700).

EMERGENCIES

Both the Centro Medico de Cozumel (Cozumel Medical Center) and the Medical Specialties Center offer 24-hour air-ambulance service and a 24-hour pharmacy. The Centro de Salud clinic offers round-the-clock emergency care.

The Farmacia Dori is open daily 7 AM–midnight; Farmacia Joaquín is open Monday through Saturday 8 AM–10 PM and Sunday 9–1 and 5–9. Farmacias Canto, open 24 hours, delivers to hotels.

➤ CONTACTS: **Air Ambulance** (☎ 9/872–4070). **Centro Medico de Cozumel** (Cozumel Medical Center; ✉ 1A Sur 101, corner of Av. 50, ☎ 9/872–3545 or 9/872–5370). **Centro de Salud** (✉ Av. 20 Sur at Calle 11, ☎ 9/872–0140). The **Chiropractic Center** (✉ Av. 5 Sur 24-A, between Calles 3 and 5, ☎ 9/872–5099). **Medical Specialties Center** (✉ Av. 20 Nte. 425, ☎ 9/872–1419 or 9/872–2919). **Police** (✉ Anexo del Palacio Municipal, ☎ 9/872–0092). **Recompression Chamber** (✉ Calle 5 Sur 21-B, between Avs. Rafael E. Melgar and 5 Sur, ☎ 9/872–2387). **Red Cross** (✉ Calle Adolfo Rosada Salas at Av. 20 Sur, ☎ 9/872–1058).

➤ LATE-NIGHT PHARMACIES: **Farmacia Dori** (✉ Calle Adolfo Rosada Salas, between Avs. 15 and 20 Sur, ☎ 9/872–0559). **Farmacia Joaquín** (✉ north side of the plaza, ☎ 9/872–2520). **Farmacias Canto** (☎ 9/872–5377).

MAIL & SHIPPING

The local post office (*correos*), six blocks south of the square, is open weekdays 8–8, Saturday 9–5, and Sunday 9–1. Holders of American Express cards can receive mail at Fiesta Cozumel Holidays/American Express, which is open weekdays 8–1 and 5–8, Saturday 8–5.

➤ SERVICES: **Fiesta Cozumel Holidays/American Express** (✉ Calle 11 Sur 598, between Avs. 25 and 30, ☎ 9/872–0725). **Post office** (✉ Calle 7 Sur at Av. Rafael E. Melgar, ☎ 9/872–0106.

MONEY MATTERS

Most of the banks are in the main square and are open weekdays 9–1:30. Many change currency, but often only until noon.

➤ BANKS: **Banamex** (✉ Av. 5 Nte., at the plaza, ☎ 9/872–3411). **Bancomer** (✉ Av. 5 Nte., at the plaza, ☎ 9/872–0550). **Banco Serfín** (✉ Calle 1 Sur, between Avs. 5 and 10 Sur, ☎ 9/872–0930). **Bancrecer** (✉ Calle 1 Sur, between Avs. 5 and 10, ☎ 9/872–4750). **Bital** (✉ Av. Rafael E. Melgar 11, ☎ 9/872–0142).

CURRENCY EXCHANGE

If you need to exchange money after banking hours, go to Promotora Cambiaria del Centro, open Monday through Saturday 8 AM–9 PM.
➤ EXCHANGE SERVICES: **Promotora Cambiaria del Centro** (⊠ Av. 5 Sur between Calles 1 Sur and Adolfo Rosada Salas, ☎ no phone).

TELEPHONES

In order to accommodate a growing number of telephone lines, the last two digits of the 987 area code have been added as a prefix to local phone numbers. Some of the printed material on Cozumel does not reflect this change.

The least expensive way to make an international call is to buy a La-datel phone card (sold in blocks of $3, $5, $10, and $20) and use the TelMex public phones. An alternative to the phone card is the *caseta de larga distancia*—the long-distance telephone office. There's an office on Calle 1, on the south side of the plaza; it's open 8–1 and 4–9. These offices have specially designed booths where you take your call after the number has been dialed by a clerk.

A much more expensive but handy option is Calling Station, at Avenida Rafael E. Melgar 27 and Calle 3 Sur. It also offers video and cell-phone rentals, currency exchange, Internet access, and dry cleaning and is open 8 AM–11 PM daily during high season.

TOURS

BOAT & SUBMARINE TOURS

Fiesta Cozumel Holidays offers three-hour trips aboard the *Principe*, a glass-bottom boat, or *Nautilus IV*, a vessel that goes partially underwater. Tours cost $26 each, including soft drinks and beer. Atlantis Submarines runs 1½-hour submarine rides that explore the Chankanaab Reef and surrounding area; tickets for the tours are $74 for adults, $38 for children.
➤ FEES & SCHEDULES: **Atlantis Submarines** (⊠ Carretera Chankanaab, Km 4, across from Hotel Casa del Mar, ☎ 9/872–5671). **Fiesta Cozumel Holidays/American Express** (⊠ Calle 11 Sur 598, between Avs. 25 and 30, ☎ 9/872–0725).

HORSEBACK TOURS

Aventuras Naturales offers four-hour guided horseback tours. They start at $45 and visit Maya ruins and the beach. Rancho Buenavista offers four-hour horseback rides through the jungle. Tours run by Rancho Palmitas, near the turnoff to El Cedral village, take you through the jungle to the Maya ruins; they start at $35 a person. The small Rancho San Manuel has seven horses and offers jungle tours for $20 an hour.
➤ FEES & SCHEDULES: **Aventuras Naturales** (☎ 9/872–1628). **Rancho Buenavista** (☎ 9/872–1537). **Rancho Palmitas** (⊠ Carretera Chankanaab, Km 16.5, ☎ no phone). **Rancho San Manuel** (⊠ Playa Paraíso, Av. Rafael E. Melgar, Km 3.5, ☎ no phone).

ORIENTATION

Tours of the island's sights, including the San Gervasio ruins, El Cedral, Parque Chankanaab, and the Museo de la Isla de Cozumel, cost about $45 a person and can be arranged through travel agencies. Fiesta Cozumel Holidays, which has representatives in most major hotels, and Caribe Tours sell a number of similar tours. Another option is to take a private tour of the island via taxi, which costs about $50 to $70 for the day, depending on which parts of the island you visit.
➤ FEES & SCHEDULES: **Caribe Tours** (⊠ Av. Rafael E. Melgar at Calle 5 Sur, ☎ 9/872–3100). **Fiesta Cozumel Holidays/American Express** (⊠ Calle 11 Sur 598, between Avs. 25 and 30, ☎ 9/872–0725).

TAXIS

You can hail taxis on the street, and cabs wait at all the major hotels. The fixed rates (at press time but subject to change) run about $1.50 within town; $5–$8 between town and either hotel zone; $10 from most hotels to the airport; and about $20–$40 from the northern hotels or town to Parque Chankanaab or Playa San Francisco. The cost from the cruise-ship terminal to San Miguel is about $6. Prices quoted by the drivers should be in pesos. Tipping isn't necessary, as most drivers own their vehicles. Despite the established taxi fares, many of the aggressive cab drivers have begun charging double or even triple these rates. If you have to take a taxi, be firm on a price before getting into the car. Familiarize yourself with the established rates but be prepared to argue with some drivers.

TRAVEL AGENCIES

A number of local travel agencies offer tours. Fiesta Cozumel Holidays and Turísmo Aviomar are represented in the lobbies of several hotels.
➤ LOCAL AGENTS: **Caribe Tours** (✉ Av. Rafael E. Melgar at Calle 5 Sur, ☎ 9/872–3100). **Fiesta Cozumel Holidays/American Express** (✉ Calle 11 Sur 598, between Avs. 25 and 30, ☎ 9/872–0725). **IMC** (Calle 2 Nte. 101–8, ☎ 9/872–1535). **Turísmo Aviomar** (✉ Av. 5 Nte. 8, between Calles 2 and 4, ☎ 9/872–0588).

VISITOR INFORMATION

The island's official Web site is www.islacozumel.com.mx. The state tourism office is open weekdays 9–2:30, but the Cozumel Island Hotel Association also functions unofficially as the island's tourist-information bureau.
➤ TOURIST INFORMATION: **Cozumel Island Hotel Association** (✉ Calle 2 Nte. 15-A, ☎ 9/872–3132, FAX 9/872–2809). **State tourism office** (✉ upstairs in the Plaza del Sol mall, at the east end of the main square, ☎ FAX 9/872–0972).

THE NORTH CARIBBEAN COAST

Updated by
Shelagh
McNally

South of Cancún, the coast of the Yucatán Peninsula runs the gamut of tropical possibilities. Whereas Puerto Morelos retains the relaxed atmosphere of a Mexican fishing village, the once laid-back town of Playa del Carmen now has resorts as glitzy as those in Cancún and Cozumel. The beaches are beloved by scuba divers, snorkelers, birders, and beachcombers, and there are accommodations to suit every budget, from campsites and bungalows to condos and luxury hotels. Rustic but comfortable fishing and scuba diving lodges on the even more secluded Boca Paila in the Sian Ka'an Biosphere Reserve and on the Xcalak Peninsula have a well-deserved reputation for excellent bone fishing and superb diving on virgin reefs. At the same time this coast is one of the most threatened by development, and concerned environmentalists are supporting the rise of ecotourism programs such as the ones at Xcacel that get visitors involved in helping to save the threatened sea-turtle population.

Against this backdrop is the Maya culture. The modern Maya live in the cities and villages along the coast; the legacy of the ancient inhabits the ruins. The dramatic remains of Tulum stand on a bluff overlooking the Caribbean. A short distance inland, at Cobá, there are towering jungle-shrouded pyramids, a testament to the site's importance as a leading center of commerce in the ancient Maya world.

The coast is divided into two areas: Puerto Morelos to Tulum, which has the most ancient sites and places to lodge; and south of Tulum to Chetumal, where civilization thins out quite a bit. We detail the coast as far as the Sian Ka'an Biosphere Reserve just south of Tulum. If you want to venture farther, you'll be rewarded with remote beaches, coves, inlets, lagoons, and tropical landscapes.

Puerto Morelos

⑲ *36 km (22 mi) south of Cancún on Highway 307.*

For years, Puerto Morelos was known as the small, relaxed coastal town where the car ferry left for Cozumel. This lack of regard actually helped it to avoid the tidal wave of development that had engulfed other communites. However, the construction of two massive all-inclusive resorts (640 rooms in total) may spoil the fishing-village atmosphere. Still, more and more people are discovering that Morelos, exactly halfway between Cancún and Playa del Carmen, makes a great base for exploring the region.

In ancient times this was a point of departure for Maya women making pilgrimages by canoe to Cozumel, the sacred isle of the fertility goddess, Ixchel. Remnants of Maya ruins exist along the coast here, but nothing has been restored. The town itself is small, with a central plaza surrounded by shops and restaurants; its trademark is a leaning lighthouse. Puerto Morelos's greatest appeal lies out at sea: the superb coral reef only 1,800 ft offshore, which provides excellent grounds for snorkeling and scuba diving. The proximity of the reef creates an exceptionally calm and safe beach. In addition, the mangroves in back of town are home to 36 species of birds, making it a great place for birders.

Dining and Lodging

$ ✕ **Twin Delphines Taquería & Restaurant.** Two chefs run this outdoor
★ restaurant beside the fishing dock. In the morning you can have one of the best breakfasts in town, including great egg dishes and coffee at reasonable prices. In the evening it's a taquería that serves fresh tacos at bargain prices. Have an ice-cold beer and watch the moon over the water while your chicken-and-cheese, beef, or bean tacos are made fresh on the grill. When the weather is bad, the place is closed. ✉ *Twin Delphines Aquarium, Av. Rafael Melgar,* ☎ *no phone. No credit cards.*

$$ ⊡ **Casa Caribe.** This small, pretty hotel sits a few blocks from the town
★ center and five minutes from the beach. The breezy rooms have refrigerators, king-size beds, and roomy tile baths. Terraces have hammocks and views of the ocean or the mangroves. A large kitchen leading to a huge terrace is available for guests' use. The grounds include a walled courtyard and a fragrant tropical garden. Children under 10 stay free. ✉ *Av. Javier Rojo Gomez and Ejercito Mexicano (3 blocks north of town),* ☎ *9/871–0049; 763/441–7630 in the U.S.,* WEB *www.us-webmasters.com/Casa-Caribe. 6 rooms. Refrigerators, fans. No credit cards.*

Outdoor Activities and Sports

WATER SPORTS

Enrique at **Almost Heaven Adventures** (☎ 9/871–0230), in the main square by the currency exchange, can set up snorkeling and fishing trips. **Brecko's** (✉ Casita del Mar, Calle Heriberto Frias 6, ☎ 9/871–0301) offers snorkeling and deep-sea fishing in a 25-ft boat. Snorkeling trips start at $15–$20 and fishing trips at $200.

Playa del Carmen

⑳ *68 km (42 mi) south of Cancún.*

Playa del Carmen was once a fishing village with a ravishing, deserted beach. The villagers fished and raised coconut palms to produce copra,

North Caribbean Coast

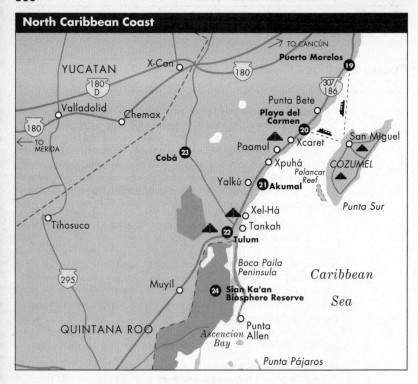

and foreigners were infrequent visitors. These days it's one of the fastest-growing cities in Mexico, with a population of more than 30,000, and it's as exciting and fast-paced as Cancún. The beach is still delightful—alabaster-white sand, turquoise-blue waters—it's just not deserted. For the past few years Playa's construction boom has transformed the city every few months. Hotels, restaurants, and shops are multiplying faster than you can say "Kukulcán."

Dining and Lodging

Playa's most luxurious rooms are at the 880-acre Playacar development. The most expensive hotels in town line the beach; the more modest rooms are farther north. Competition among the smaller hotels is fierce, so most ask for a deposit (usually the price of one night) before taking your reservation. As for the dining scene, mediocrity reigns, though most restaurants have great decor.

$–$$ ✕ **Zas.** The Canadian couple that runs this stylish restaurant has brought the best of Toronto's cuisine and combined it with Mexican flavors. Owner–chef Carla is in the kitchen daily, creating dishes such as chicken stuffed with sundried tomatoes. The breakfast menu includes delicious pancakes and omelets. A sister restaurant, Media Luna, on Avenida 5 at Calle 8 (no phone), offers a great vegetarian menu in a cozy place decorated with Mexican and Guatemalan accents. ⊠ *Av. 5 at Calles 12 and 14,* ☎ *no phone. No credit cards.*

$ ✕ **Sabor.** The prices have gone up and beer and wine are now on the menu, but the savory salads, sandwiches, and baked goods are still tasty. Seats at breakfast and lunch are hard to find. ⊠ *Av. 5, between Calles 3 and 4,* ☎ *no phone. No credit cards.*

$ ✕ **Yaxche.** This is the best restaurant along the Riviera Maya. The owner
★ shows his love of the Maya culture and cuisine; decorations include hand-carved stelae from famous ruins along with ceiling and wall mu-

rals of Maya gods and kings. The real knockout is the food; dishes such as *halach winic* (chicken in a spicy four-pepper sauce) and *tikinchic* (fish in a sour orange–onion sauce with achiote) bring Maya cuisine to gourmet levels. Finish off your meal with a Maya Kiss (Kahlúa and Xtabentun, a local liqueur flavored with anise and honey). Book a reservation for the backyard patio if you want to have your meal amid the fountain, plants, and Maya art. ⊠ *Calle 8 at Avs. 5 and 10,* ☎ *9/873–2502. AE, MC, V.*

$$$$ ⚇ **Baal Nah Kah.** True to its name, which means "home hidden among ★ the gum trees" in Maya, this small hotel is quite homey. Guests have the use of a large kitchen, common sitting room, and barbecue pit. The five bedrooms and one studio are on different levels, affording complete privacy. Two rooms have spacious balconies with a panoramic view of the ocean; all have tile baths, fans, double or king-size beds, and Mexican decor. A small café next door serves breakfast, snacks, and light meals. The beach is one block away. ⊠ *Calle 12 near Av. 5,* ☎ *9/873–0110,* FAX *9/873–0050,* WEB *www.cancunsouth.com/baalnahkah. 5 rooms, 1 apartment. Fans. No credit cards.*

$$$$ ⚇ **Royal Hideaway.** Sitting on a breathtaking stretch of beach, this ★ 13-acre, ultraluxurious adults-only resort offers exceptional amenities and superior service. The two- and three-story villas are a fusion of Spanish–Mexican colonial architecture set on grounds with winding rivers, waterfalls, and fountains. Each villa has its own concierge to take care of your needs. Deluxe rooms have two queen beds, sitting areas, and ocean-view terraces done in royal blue, cream, and yellow. Meals at the five restaurants are à la carte. This is also one of the few resorts that are wheelchair accessible. ⊠ *Fracc. Playacar, Lote 6,* ☎ *9/873–4500 or 877/284–0935,* FAX *9/873–4506,* WEB *www.allegroresorts.com. 192 rooms, 8 suites. 5 restaurants, 3 bars, airconditioning, in-room data ports, 2 pools, spa, 2 tennis courts, health club, travel services. AE, MC, V.*

$$$ ⚇ **Mosquito Blue.** This beautiful hotel has become a landmark in Playa ★ for its artistic design and architecture. The rooms and lobby, with their lovely mahogany furniture, Indonesian decor, and soft lighting, are at once casual, exotic, and elegant. King-size beds, great views, and kitchenettes round out the rooms. A cloistered courtyard has a garden, pool, and open-air bar. A dive shop is on site, the beach a five-minute walk away. Note that children under age 16 are not allowed. ⊠ *Calle 12 between Avs. 5 and 10,* ☎ FAX *9/873–1335,* WEB *www.mosquitoblue.com. 16 rooms, 8 suites. Restaurant, 2 bars, kitchenettes, 2 pools, massage, gym, dive shop. AE, MC, V.*

$$ ⚇ **Hotel Casa Tucan.** The owners have worked hard at creating a cozy community a short distance from the main drag. The peaceful gardens here are home to a small menagerie of rabbits, ducks, birds, and turtles, and there is a variety of clean and cheerful rooms geared to different budgets. The property also includes a restaurant, a billiards–game room, a meditation palapa, a TV bar, a language school, and a specially designed dive pool that is used by the on-site dive center. Families are welcomed here. ⊠ *Calle 4 between Avs. 10 and 15,* ☎ *9/873–0283. 20 rooms. Restaurant, bar, pool, dive shop, recreation room. MC, V.*

$$ ⚇ **Paraiso Azul's (Casa de Gopala).** For years this small hotel has been a favorite destination for travelers seeking clean, comfortable, and reasonably priced accommodations. Once you pass through the wooden doors, you enter a private jungle that is cool and tranquil. Rooms are spacious, bright, and airy, with large windows, two double beds, and Mexican accents. It's a great place to experience the laid-back rhythm of the old Playa. ⊠ *Calle 2 between Avs. 10 and 15,* ☎ FAX *9/873–0054. 16 rooms. Pool (next-door to Hotel Casa Tucan), fans. No credit cards.*

$$ ⊡ **Posada Mariposa.** One of the best hotels in Playa, the Mariposa is
★ in the quiet north section of town. Not only does it have impeccable
style, it's also comfortable and well priced. Rooms center on a tropi-
cal garden filled with plants, flowers, trees, and a small fountain. All
have ocean views, luxurious bathrooms with bidets, and shared pa-
tios, and are furnished with queen-size beds and wall murals each with
a different theme. Suites have full kitchens. Sunset on the rooftop is
quite spectacular and the beach is five minutes away down a private
road. ⊠ *Av. 5 No. 314, between Calles 24 and 26,* ☎ *9/876–4117 or*
800/416–2747, FAX *9/873–1054,* WEB *www.hotelmariposa.com. 16*
rooms, 8 suites. Air-conditioning, fans. No credit cards.

$ ⊡ **Posada Freud.** On the main strip behind the Media Luna restau-
rant (where guests get a discount) is this quirky little hotel with a Eu-
ropean flavor. Each room is decorated differently, with Mexican textiles
and wall murals. The bigger rooms have refrigerators and coffee mak-
ers. The inner courtyard and garden do a remarkable job of keeping
out the Avenida 5 noise. ⊠ *Av. 5 between Calles 8 and 10,* ☎ FAX *9/*
873–0601. 12 rooms. Refrigerators (some). No credit cards.

Nightlife and the Arts

Most of Playa closes down around 11 PM, but a growing number of
bars and discos stay open until the wee hours of the morning. Unfor-
tunately, Playa's drug culture sometimes surfaces in the clubs. Note that
travelers who have indulged have landed in jail and been robbed dur-
ing transactions.

The **Blue Parrot** (⊠ Calle 12 at Av. 1, ☎ 9/873–0083) has live music
every night until midnight; the bar sometimes stays open until 3 AM.
Capitán Tutix (⊠ Calle 4 Nte., ☎ no phone) is a lively party place with
food and music. To party off the beach check out **Requiem** (⊠ Calle
6 between Avs. 5 and 10, ☎ 9/973–3189), a dance club that plays the
latest in techno and house music.

Outdoor Activities and Sports

DIVING

Playa del Carmen's scuba scene has grown considerably in the past few
years. Most dive shops offer similar services, but the quality of the equip-
ment and dive instructors varies; shop around. The **Abyss** (☎ 9/873–
2164) offers training courses in addition to dive trips. The oldest shop
in town, **Tank-Ha Dive Shop** (☎ FAX 9/873–5037), runs diving and
snorkeling trips to the reefs and caverns. **Yucatek Divers** (☎ 9/873–
0283) specializes in cenote dives, diving packages, and works with divers
who have disabilities.

Shopping

Avenida 5 between Calles 4 and 10 is the best place to shop along the
coast. Unique shops and boutiques sell folk art and textiles from
around Mexico, and clothing shops carry original designs created
from hand-painted Indonesian batiks. Shops usually are open from about
10 in the morning to 9 or 10 at night.

Amber Museum Shop (⊠ Av. 5 between Calles 4 and 6, ☎ FAX 9/873–
0446) has elegantly crafted amber jewelry by a local designer who im-
ports the amber from Chiapas; there is also a small jewelry-making work-
shop for children. **Telart** (⊠ Av. Juárez 10, ☎ 9/873–0066) carries textiles
from all over Mexico.

Akumal

㉑ *37 km (23 mi) south of Playa del Carmen, 102 km (63 mi) south of Cancún.*

The Maya name means "place of the turtle," and for hundreds of years this beach has been a nesting ground for turtles. The place first attracted international attention in 1926, when explorers discovered the *Mantanceros,* a Spanish galleon that sank in 1741. In 1958, Pablo Bush Romero, a wealthy businessman who loved diving these pristine waters, created the first resort, which became the headquarters for the club he formed— the Mexican Underwater Explorers Club (CEDAM). Akumal soon became a gathering spot for wealthy underwater adventurers who flew in on private planes and searched the waters for sunken treasures, some of which you can see at the Museo CEDAM in Puerto Aventuras.

These days Akumal is probably the most Americanized community on the coast. Akumal consists of three distinct areas: Half Moon Bay, with some pretty beaches, the best snorkeling around, and the greatest concentration of rentals; Akumal Proper, a large resort with a market, grocery stores, laundry facilities, a pharmacy, and, farther up across the highway, the original Maya community; and Akumal Aventuras, to the south, with more condos and homes.

Devoted snorkelers may want to walk to **Yalkú,** a couple of miles north of Akumal along an unmarked dirt road. A series of small lagoons that gradually reach the ocean, Yalkú is home to schools of parrot fish in superbly clear water with visibility to 160 ft. It's now an "eco-park," which means it has a toilet, a small parking lot, and an entrance fee of about $6.

Dining and Lodging

$$ ✕ **La Lunita.** The breakfast and dinner menus change daily at this converted condo in Half Moon Bay, but not the quality; the food is consistently great, with service to match. Choices include fish, ceviche, and chicken. The atmosphere is friendly and inclusive, so you're likely to pick up some tips on local events. ✉ *Hacienda de la Tortuga (enter through Club Akumal Caribe and turn left, or north, at the dirt road to Half Moon Bay),* ☎ 987/59070. AE, MC, V.

$ ✕ **Restaurante Oscar y Lalo.** Outside of Akumal at nearby Bahías de Punta Soliman is this wonderful restaurant run by a local Maya couple. The seafood is excellent and the pizza divine. If you're inspired to sleep on the beach, campgrounds and RV hookups are available. ✉ *Hwy. 307 north of Akumal (look for faded white sign),* ☎ *no phone. No credit cards.*

$$$$ 🏨 **Club Oasis Akumal.** One of the all-inclusive pioneers, this hotel still remains intimate, sophisticated, and understated. The atmosphere is enhanced by the gorgeous mahogany railings, doors, furniture, and floors amid the tropical plants and flowers. Rooms are spacious, with nice terraces or balconies, king-size beds, and sitting areas. The bathrooms are exceptional: sunken tile showers with Moorish arches and windows with beach views. ✉ *South of Akumal off Hwy. 307,* ☎ *987/57300,* FAX *987/57302,* WEB *www.oasishotels.com.mx. 182 rooms. Restaurant, 2 bars, 4 pools, tennis court, beach, dive shop, bicycles, travel services, car rental. AE, MC, V.*

$$$ 🏨 **Club Akumal Caribe & Villas Maya.** On the edge of the cove, this
★ beachfront resort offers congenial accommodations and staff. Rooms in the hotel have rattan furniture; large, comfortable beds; lovely tile work; and harbor views. The quaint but rustic bungalows are surrounded by a tropical garden and have great kitchens and bathrooms. More-secluded options are the one-, two-, and three-bedroom condomini-

ums called the Villas Flamingo, on Half Moon Bay, with their own beach and pools (definite bargains). Diving, fishing, and other water sports are all within walking distance. The restaurant, Lol Ha, is a nice beach-side spot that offers tasty fare. ✉ *Hwy. 307, Km 104,* ☎ *987/59012; 800/351–1622; 800/343–1440 in Canada,* WEB *www.clubakumal.com. 21 rooms, 40 bungalows, 4 villas, 5 condos. 3 restaurants, bar, pool, beach, 2 dive shops, children's program (ages 5–14). AE, MC, V.*

Outdoor Activities and Sports

SCUBA DIVING

Akumal Dive Center (✉ about 10 mins north of Club Akumal Caribe, ☎ 987/59025), the oldest and most experienced dive operation in the area, offers reef or cenote diving, fishing, and snorkeling.

Tulum

 130 km (81 mi) south of Cancún.

One of the Caribbean coast's biggest attractions, Tulum is the Yucatán Peninsula's most visited Maya ruin, attracting more than 2 million people annually. Unfortunately, this means you have to share the site with roughly half of the tourist population of Quintana Roo on any given day, even if you arrive early. Its location by the blue-green waters of the Caribbean is indeed breathtaking.

At the entrance to the ruins you can hire a guide, but keep in mind that some of their information is more entertaining than historically accurate. (Disregard that stuff about virgin sacrifices atop the altars.) Because you are not allowed to climb or enter the fragile structures—only three really merit close inspection anyway—you can take in the ruins in two hours. You might, however, want to allow extra time for a swim or a stroll on the beach, where ancient Maya beached their canoes.

Tulum is the only Maya city known to have been inhabited when the conquistadors arrived in 1518. Its pre-Columbian name, Zama, from the word *zamul* (dawn), suggests "city of the dawn"; Tulum means "wall." When the Spaniards arrived, Juan de Grijalva and his men, who spotted Zama from their ships, were so intimidated by the enormity of its vivid 25-ft-high blue, white, and red walls that they were reluctant to land. What they had seen was four towns so close to one another that they appeared to be one continuous metropolis.

Tulum has long held special significance for the Maya. A key city in the League of Mayapán (AD 987–1194), it was never conquered by the Spaniards, although it was abandoned about 75 years after the Conquest. For 300 years thereafter, it symbolized the defiance of an otherwise subjugated people; it was one of the last outposts of the Maya during their insurrection against Mexican rule in the War of the Castes, which began in 1846. Uprisings continued intermittently until 1935, when the Maya ceded Tulum to the government.

The first significant structure is the two-story **Temple of the Frescoes**, to the left of the entryway. The temple's vault roof and corbel arch are examples of classic Maya architecture. Faint traces of blue-green frescoes outlined in black on the inner and outer walls refer to ancient Maya beliefs (the clearest frescoes are hidden from sight now that you can't walk into the temple). Reminiscent of the Mixtec style, the frescoes depict the three worlds of the Maya and their major deities and are decorated with stellar and serpentine patterns, rosettes, and ears of maize and other offerings to the gods.

The largest and most famous building, the **Castillo** (castle) looms at the edge of a 40-ft limestone cliff just past the Temple of the Frescoes. Atop

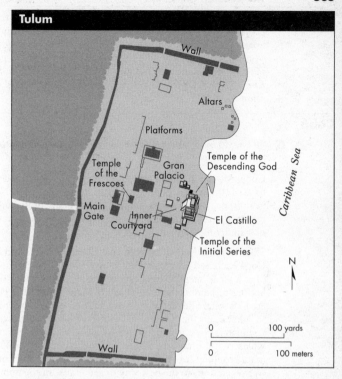

Tulum

Wall

Altars

Platforms

Temple of the
Descending God

Temple
of the
Frescoes

Gran
Palacio

Caribbean Sea

Main
Gate

Inner
Courtyard

El Castillo

Temple of the
Initial Series

N

Wall

0   100 yards

0   100 meters

the castle, at the end of a broad stairway, sits a temple with stucco ornamentation on the outside and traces of fine frescoes inside the two
chambers. The front wall of the Castillo has faint carvings of the Descending God and columns depicting the plumed serpent god, Kukulcán, who was introduced to the Maya by the Toltecs. To the left of the
Castillo is the **Temple of the Descending God**—so called for the carv-
ing of a winged god plummeting to earth over the doorway.

The tiny cove to the left of the Castillo and Temple of the Descending
God is a good spot for a cooling swim, but there are no changing rooms.
A few small altars sit atop a hill at the north side of the cove and have
a good view of the Castillo and the sea. ✉ *$2, free Sun.; parking $1;
use of video camera $4.* ☉ *Daily 8–5.*

Dining and Lodging

Tulum's official Web page for hotels and cabañas is www.hotels-
tulum.com.

$$$$ ✕🏠 **Las Ranitas.** Here is a perfect example of the self-sustaining ho-
★   tels springing up in Tulum that don't sacrifice comfort, style, and elegance to be ecologically correct. Las Ranitas (The Froggies) uses
wind-generated electricity, solar energy, and recycled water, but what
you really notice is how chic the rooms are. Each is decorated with
gorgeous tile and fabric from Oaxaca. Terraces overlook the gardens
and ocean, and jungle walkways lead down to the breathtaking beach.
The pool, tennis court, and terrace are spectacular as well. But the real
pièce de résistance is the French chef, who creates incredible food that
matches the hotel's magic (in the $$ price range). ✉ *Carretera Tulum–
Boca Paila (last hotel before Sian Ka'an Biosphere Reserve),* ☎ FAX *987/
78554,* WEB *www.lasranitas.com. 14 rooms. Restaurant, pool, tennis
court, beach. No credit cards.*

$$ 🏨 **Cabañas Tulum.** Idyllically set in a coconut grove on the beach, this property offers palapa bungalows with comfortable double beds and hot water. The rooms are basic and clean, with two large double beds, overhead fans, and private bathrooms. There is also a good indoor–outdoor restaurant with a large menu. ⊠ *Carretera Tulum–Boca Paila, Km 7,* ☎ *987/12009. 32 cabañas. Restaurant, bar, fans, beach, recreation room. No credit cards.*

Cobá

 ㉓ *49 km (30 mi) northwest of Tulum, 167 km (104 mi) southwest of Cancún.*

Cobá, Maya for "water stirred by the wind," flourished from AD 800 to AD 1100, with a population of as many as 55,000. Now it stands in solitude, with the jungle having taken many of its buildings. Cobá exudes a certain stillness, the silence broken by the occasional shriek of a spider monkey or the call of a bird.

Situated on five lakes between coastal watchtowers and inland cities, Cobá exercised economic control over the region through a network of at least 16 *sacbéob* (white stone roads), one of which measures 100 km (62 mi) and is the longest in the Maya world. The city once covered 70 square km (27 square mi), making it a noteworthy sister state to Tikal in northern Guatemala, with which it had close cultural and commercial ties. It is noted for its massive temple–pyramids, one of which is 138 ft tall, the largest and highest in northern Yucatán. The main groupings of ruins are separated by several miles of dense tropical vegetation, so the best way to get a sense of the immensity of the city is to scale one of the pyramids. It's easy to get lost here, so stay on the main road and don't be tempted by the narrow paths that lead into the jungle unless you have a qualified guide with you.

The first major cluster of structures, off the main path to your right as you enter the ruins, is the **Cobá Group,** whose pyramids are built around a sunken patio. At the near end of the group, facing a large plaza, you'll see the 79-ft-high Iglesia (church), where some Maya people still place offerings and light candles in hopes of improving their harvests. Farther along the main path to your left is the **Chumuc Mul Group,** little of which has been excavated. The principal pyramid here is covered with the remains of vibrantly painted stucco motifs (*chumuc mul* means "stucco pyramid"). A kilometer (½ mile) past this site is the **Nohoch Mul Group** (Large Hill Group), the highlight of which is the pyramid of the same name, the tallest at Cobá. The pyramid, which has 120 steps—equivalent to 12 stories—shares a plaza with **Temple 10.** The Descending God (also seen at Tulum) is depicted on a facade of the temple atop Nohoch Mul, from which the view is excellent.

Beyond the Nohoch Mul Group is the **Castillo,** with nine chambers that are reached by a stairway. To the south are the remains of a ball court. From the main route follow the sign to **Las Pinturas Group,** named for the still-discernible polychrome friezes on the inner and outer walls of its large, patioed pyramid. An enormous stela here depicts a man standing with his feet on two prone captives. Take the minor path for 1 km (½ mi) to the **Macanxoc Group,** not far from the lake of the same name. The main pyramid at Macanxoc is accessible by a stairway.

Cobá is a 35-minute drive northwest of Tulum along a well-marked and well-paved road that leads straight through the jungle. You can comfortably make your way around Cobá in a half day, but spending the night in town is highly advised as doing so will allow you to visit the ruins in solitude when they open at 8 AM. Even on a day trip, consider taking time out for lunch to escape the intense heat and mosquito-heavy humidity of the ruins. Buses depart from Cobá for Playa del Carmen and Tulum at least twice daily. Taxis to Tulum are still reasonable. ☒ *$1.75, free Sun.; use of video camera $4.* ☉ *Daily 8–5.*

Lodging

$$$ ▨ **Villa Arqueológica Cobá.** A 10-minute walk from the ruins, this Club Med property overlooks one of the region's vast lakes. There is a slightly Mediterranean feel to the place, which has high arches, white stucco, and red paint. But this is a hit-and-miss operation: *sometimes* the rooms are clean and comfortable, and *sometimes* the food is well prepared. Still, this is the only hotel in the area that offers any kind of amenities. ☒ *Lagoon road, west of the ruins,* ☎ *5/254–7077 for reservations,* FAX *5/255–3164,* WEB *www.clubmed.com. 40 rooms, 3 suites. Restaurant, bar, pool, tennis court, library. AE, MC, V.*

$ ▨ **El Bocadito.** The warmth of the family who owns and operates this hotel makes up for the lack of luxury here. Each of the extremely basic rooms has two double beds, a ceiling fan, toilet, and, if you are lucky, hot water. The ruins are a 10-minute walk away. Rooms here fill up quickly—if you're thinking of spending the night, stop here before visiting the ruins. The restaurant next door serves simple but tasty meals. ☒ *On road to ruins,* ☎ *987/42087. 10 rooms. AE, V.*

Sian Ka'an and the Boca Paila Peninsula

15 km (9½ mi) south of Tulum to Boca Paila turnoff, located within Sian Ka'an; 137 km (85 mi) south of Cancún.

Sian Ka'an ("where the sky is born") was first settled by the Maya in the 5th century AD. In 1986 the Mexican government established the ㉔ 1.3-million-acre **Sian Ka'an Biosphere Reserve** as an internationally protected area. The next year, it was named a World Heritage Site by the United Nations Educational, Scientific, and Cultural Organization (UNESCO). In 1996 the reserve was extended by 200,000 acres.

The Sian Ka'an reserve constitutes 10% of the land in Quintana Roo and covers 100 km (62 mi) of coast. Freshwater and coastal lagoons, mangrove swamps, watery cays, savannas, tropical forests, a barrier reef, hundreds of species of local and migratory birds, fish, other animals and plants, and fewer than 1,000 local residents (primarily Maya) share this area. There are approximately 27 ruins (none excavated) linked by a unique canal system—one of the few of its kind in the Maya world. This is one of the last undeveloped stretches of coastline in North America.

Many species of the once-flourishing wildlife have fallen into the endangered category, but the waters here still teem with rooster fish, bonefish, mojarra, snapper, shad, permit, sea bass, and crocodiles. Fishing the flats for wily bonefish is especially popular, and the peninsula's few lodges also run deep-sea fishing trips.

In order to see the sites you must take a guided tour offered by one of the private, nonprofit organizations, such as **Amigos de Sian Ka'an** (☒ Crepúsculo 18, at Amanecer, SM 44, Mza 13, Cancún, Quintana Roo 77506, ☎ 9/848–1618, 9/848–2136, 9/880–6024, FAX 9/887–3080). The four-hour boat tour includes bird-watching, a visit to the Maya ruins of Xlapak, and a tour of the mangroves. Tour groups depart from Cabañas Ana y José in Tulum every Wednesday and Saturday morning; the fee includes a bilingual guide and binoculars.

Lodging

$$$$ 🏨 **Boca Paila Fishing Lodge.** Home of the "grand slam" (fishing lingo
★ for catching three different kinds of fish at once), this charming lodge
sits amid the Sian Ka'an Biosphere Reserve. Nine spacious cottages
offer comfortable accommodations with two double beds, couches,
large bathrooms, and separate screened-in sitting areas. Catering principally to anglers, the lodge provides boats and guides for fly-fishing
and bonefishing; guests can bring their own tackle or rent some at the
lodge. Meals, included in the room rate, are excellent, ranging from
fresh fish to Maya specialties. The beach is exceptionally lovely and
tranquil. ⊠ *Boca Paila Peninsula (mailing address: Frontiers, Box 959,
Wexford, PA 15090),* ☎ *724/935–1577 or 800/245–1950, for reservations. 9 cottages. Restaurant, bar. No credit cards unless arranged
with Frontiers.*

$$$$ 🏨 **Casa Blanca Lodge.** Punta Pájaros, to which this remote fishing re-
★ sort provides unique access, is reputed to be one of the best places in
the world for light-tackle saltwater fishing. The American-managed,
all-inclusive lodge—100 ft from the ocean—is set on a rocky outcrop
covered with palm trees. Bonefish swarm in the mangrove swamps, flats,
and shallow waters. The lodge's 10 large, modern guest rooms, painted
white with turquoise trim, have slatted windows and tile and mahogany bathrooms and provide a pleasant tropical respite at dusk. Rates
include a charter flight from Cancún to the lodge, all meals, a boat,
and a guide. ⊠ *Punta Pájaros (mailing address: Frontiers, Box 959,
Wexford, PA 15090),* ☎ *724/935–1577 or 800/245–1950, for Frontiers; 713/526–3739 or 800/533–7299 for Outdoor Travel. 10 rooms.
Restaurant, bar, fishing. MC, V.*

The North Caribbean Coast A to Z

AIR TRAVEL
Almost everyone who arrives by air into this region flies into Cancún.
In Chetumal, however, there is an airport on the southwestern edge of
town, along Avenida Alvaro Obregón where it turns into Route 186.
In Playa del Carmen, there's an air strip across from Plaza Antiqua.
➤ AIRPORT INFORMATION: **Chetumal Airport** (⊠ Rte. 186, Chetumal).

BOAT & FERRY TRAVEL
Passenger-only ferries and two large speedboats depart from the dock
at Playa del Carmen for the 45-minute trip to the main pier in Cozumel.
They leave approximately every hour on the hour 5 AM–11 PM, with
no ferries at noon, 2, 8, or 10. Return service to Playa runs every hour
on the hour 4 AM–10 PM, with no ferries at 5, 11 AM, 1, 7, or 9 PM.
Call ahead to verify the schedule as it changes often.
➤ BOAT & FERRY INFORMATION: **Playa del Carmen passenger ferry** (☎
9/872–1508, 9/872–0588, 9/872–0477).

BUS TRAVEL
Playa del Carmen has two bus stops. Buses arriving from south of Playa
and continuing north to Cancún drop people off at the terminal on
the highway. All other buses leave from downtown. All three major
buslines—ADO, Oriente, and Mayab—run express, first-class, and second-class buses to major destination points. Service to Cancún is every
10–20 minutes and buses to Chetumal leave twice daily. It's always
best to check the times at the main bus terminal, at Juárez at Avenida
5. The scheduled times change frequently.
➤ BUS INFORMATION: **ADO** (☎ 983/29877). **Caribe Express** (☎ 983/
27889).

CAR RENTAL

Most first-class hotels in Akumal also rent cars. In Puerto Morelos you are better off renting from Cancún, as there aren't many bargains in town. In Playa del Carmen, it's best to stick with the bigger rental agencies: Hertz, Budget, and Thrifty. If you want air-conditioning or automatic transmission, reserve your car at least one day in advance.

➤ MAJOR AGENCIES: **Budget** (✉ Continental Plaza, Playa del Carmen, ☎ 9/873–0100). **Hertz** (✉ Plaza Marina, Local 40, Playa del Carmen, ☎ 9/873–0702). **Thrifty** (✉ Calle 8 between Avs. 5 and 10, Playa del Carmen, ☎ 9/873–0119).

CAR TRAVEL

The entire coast from Punta Sam near Cancún to the main border crossing to Belize at Chetumal is traversable on Highway 307. This straight road is entirely paved and has been widened into four lanes south to Xcaret. Drive with caution—there are lots of speed demons on this highway. Puerto Morelos, Playa del Carmen, and Tulum have one gas station.

Good roads that run into Highway 307 from the west are Route 180 (from Mérida and Valladolid), Route 184 (from central Yucatán), and Route 186 (from Villahermosa and, via Route 261, from Mérida and Campeche). There is an entrance to the *autopista* toll highway between Cancún and Mérida off Highway 307 just south of Cancún.

If you drive south of Tulum, keep an eye out for military and immigration checkpoints. Have your passport handy, be friendly and cooperative, and don't carry any items, such as firearms or drugs, that might land you in jail.

ECOTOURISM

You can visit the ruins of Cobá with Alltournative Expeditions. The group offers a variety of other ecotours as well.

ATV Explorer offers two-hour rides through the jungle on all-terrain vehicles; explore caves, see ruins, and snorkel in a cenote. Tours start at $38.50.

➤ CONTACTS: **Alltournative Expeditions** (✉ Av. 10 No. 1, Plaza Antigua, Playa del Carmen, ☎ 9/873–2036, WEB www.alltournative.com). **ATV Explorer** (✉ Hwy. 307, 1 km [½ mi] north of Xcaret, ☎ 9/873–1626).

EMERGENCIES

In Puerto Morelos, there are two drugstores in town on either side of the gas station on Highway 307.

In Playa del Carmen, there's a pharmacy at the Plaza Marina shopping mall; several others are on Avenida 5 between Calles 4 and 8. There are two pharmacies on Avenida Juárez between Avenidas 20 and 25.

➤ PLAYA DEL CARMEN: **Centro de Salud** (✉ Av. Juárez at Av. 15, ☎ 9/ 872–1230 ext. 147). **Police** (✉ Av. Juárez between Avs. 15 and 20, ☎ 9/873–0291). **Red Cross** (✉ Av. Juárez at Av. 25, ☎ 9/873–1233).

LODGING

You can arrange house and apartment rentals through Mary Lowers at Mayansites Bookings. Also, surf the Internet, where you can find good deals.

➤ CONTACTS: **Mayansites Bookings** (☎ 877/620–8715, WEB www.mayansites.com).

MAIL & SHIPPING

The Playa del Carmen post office is open weekdays 8–7.

➤ POST OFFICE: **Playa del Carmen** (✉ Av. Juárez, next to the police station, ☎ 9/873–0300).

MONEY MATTERS

Local banks in Playa del Carmen include Bital, Bancomer, Banamex, Inverlat, and Bancrecer.

➤ BANKS: **Bital** (⊠ Av. Juárez between Avs. 10 and 15, Playa del Carmen; ⊠ Av. 30 between Avs. 4 and 6, Playa del Carmen; ⊠ Av. Héroes 37, Chetumal). **Bancomer** (⊠ Av. Juárez between Calles 25 and 30, Playa del Carmen; ⊠ Av. Alvaro Obregón 222, at Av. Juárez, Chetumal). **Banamex** (⊠ Av. Juárez between Avs. 20 and 25, Playa del Carmen). **Inverlat** (⊠ Av. 5 between Av. Juárez and Av. 2, Playa del Carmen). **Bancrecer** (⊠ Av. 5 by the bus station, Playa del Carmen).

TELEPHONES

There are TelMex phones all over Playa del Carmen; several long-distance calling stations are on Avenida 5 as well as in front of the post office on Avenida Juárez and at the corner of Avenidas Juárez and 5.

TOURS

Although some guided tours are available in this area, the roads are quite good for the most part, so renting a car is an efficient and enjoyable alternative. Most of the sights you see along this stretch are natural, and you can hire a guide at the ruins. If you would like someone else to do the planning and driving for you, contact Maya Sites Travel Services, which offers inexpensive tours and the chance to create your own travel itinerary.

MAYA RUINS

Based in Playa del Carmen, Tierra Maya Tours runs trips to the ruins of Chichén Itzá, Uxmal, Palenque, and Tikal. It can also help you with transfers, tickets, and hotel reservations. Many first-class hotels in Playa del Carmen can arrange day tours to Tulum, Chichén Itzá, and Cobá.

➤ TOUR-OPERATOR RECOMMENDATIONS: **Maya Sites Travel Services** (☎ 719/256–5186 or 877/620–8715, WEB www.mayasites.com). **Tierra Maya Tours** (⊠ Av. 5 at Calle 6, Playa del Carmen, ☎ 9/873–1385, FAX 9/873–1386).

TRANSPORTATION AROUND THE CARIBBEAN COAST

You can hire taxis in Cancún to go as far as Playa del Carmen, Tulum, or Akumal, but the price is steep unless you have many passengers. Fares run about $65 or more to Playa alone; between Playa and Tulum or Akumal, expect to pay at least another $25. It's much cheaper from Playa to Cancún, with taxi fare running about $30; negotiate before you hop into the cab. Getting a taxi along Highway 307 can take a while. Ask your hotel to call one for you.

TRAVEL AGENCIES

There are more major travel agencies and tour operators along the coast than ever, and first-class hotels in Playa del Carmen and Akumal usually have their own in-house travel services.

➤ LOCAL AGENT REFERRALS: **Alltournative Expeditions** (⊠ Av. 10 No. 1, Plaza Antigua, Playa del Carmen, ☎ 9/873–2036). **IMC** (⊠ Plaza Antigua, Playa del Carmen, ☎ 9/873–1439, FAX 9/873–1439, WEB www.imcplay.com).

VISITOR INFORMATION

The Tourist Information Booth in Playa del Carmen is open Monday through Saturday, 8 AM–9 PM.

➤ TOURIST INFORMATION: **Playa del Carmen** (⊠ Av. Juárez by the police station, ☎ 9/873–2804).

THE STATE OF YUCATÁN

Updated by
Patricia Alisau

CULTURALLY, the Yucatán is one of the richest parts of Mexico. It is the heart of a fascinating juxtaposition of two powerful civilizations—that of the Maya and that of transplanted Europeans. Vestiges of the past are evident in this land of oval thatch-roof huts and stately old mission churches, and in its people. Mysterious "lost cities" lie hidden in the forests. Small fishing villages dot beaches that are so far unjaded by the tourist industry. In the midst of this exotic landscape stands the elegant city of Mérida, for centuries the main stronghold of Spanish colonialism in the land of the Maya.

It's the celebrated Maya ruins, Chichén Itzá and Uxmal above all, that bring most people to the State of Yucatán. Indeed, the Puuc hills south of Mérida have more archaeological sites per square mile than any other place in the hemisphere.

Mérida

There is a marvelous eccentricity about Mérida. Fully urban, with maddeningly slow-moving traffic, it has a self-sufficient, self-contented air that would suggest a small town more than a state capital. The Maya Indian presence is unmistakable: women wear *huipiles* (hand-embroidered, tuniclike white dresses), and craftspeople and vendors from the outlying villages come to town in their huaraches (woven leather sandals). Indeed, to this day the Maya in more remote or isolated villages speak no Spanish, or just enough to get by.

Mérida is the cultural and intellectual center of the peninsula, with museums, schools, and attractions that can greatly enhance your insights into the history and character of Yucatán. Indeed, the quality and number of its offerings make it one of Mexico's leading cultural centers. Consider making it one of the first stops in your travels, and make sure your visit includes a Sunday, when traffic is light and the city seems to revert to a more gracious era.

A Good Walk

Start at the **zócalo** ㉕: see the **Casa de Montejo** ㉖ (now a Banamex bank), on the south side; the **Palacio Municipal** ㉗ and the **Centro Cultural de Mérida Olimpo** ㉘, on the west side; the **Palacio del Gobierno** ㉙, on the northeast corner, and, catercorner, the **catedral** ㉚; and the **Museo de Arte Contemporáneo** ㉛ on the east side. Step out on Calle 60 from the cathedral and walk north to Parque Hidalgo and the **Iglesia de la Tercera Orden de Jesús** ㉜, which is across Calle 59. Continue north along Calle 60 for a short block to the **Teatro Peón Contreras** ㉝, which lies on the east side of the street; the entrance to the **Universidad Autónoma de Yucatán** ㉞ is on the west side of Calle 60 at Calle 57. A block farther north on the west side of Calle 60 is the Parque de Santa Lucía. From the park, walk north four blocks and turn right on Calle 47 for two blocks to **Paseo Montejo** ㉟. Once on this street, continue north for two long blocks to the **Palacio Cantón** ㊱. From here look either for a *calesa* (horse-drawn carriage) or cabs parked outside the museum to take you back past the zócalo to the Mercado Municipal—or walk if you're up to it.

Sights to See

㉖ **Casa de Montejo.** This stately palace sits on the south side of the plaza, on Calle 63. Francisco de Montejo—father and son—conquered the peninsula and founded Mérida in 1542; they built their "casa" 10 years

State of Yucatán

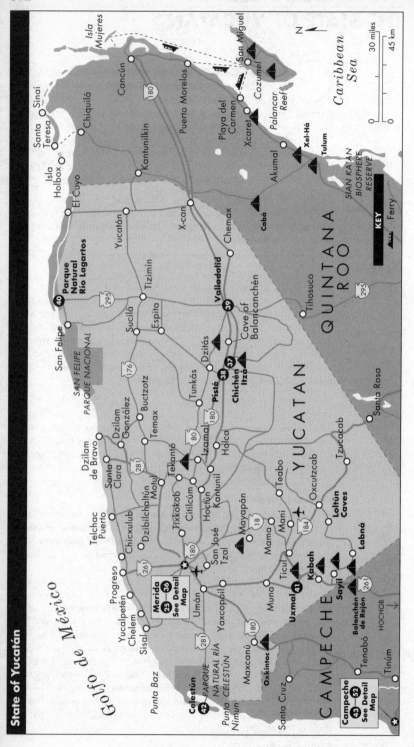

Golfo de México

Caribbean Sea

N

30 miles
45 km

Isla Mujeres

Santa Sinaí
Santa Teresa
Isla Holbox
El Cuyo
Chiquilá
Kantunilkín
Cancún
Puerto Morelos
Playa del Carmen
Xcaret
Palancar Reef
San Miguel
Cozumel
Akumal
Xel-Há
Tulum

Parque Natural Río Lagartos
40
Yucatán
X-can
Chemax
Cobá

SIAN KA'AN BIOSPHERE RESERVE

QUINTANA ROO

San Felipe
SAN FELIPE PARQUE NACIONAL
295
Tizimín
Sucilá
Espita
Valladolid
39
Cave of Balancanchén
Tihosuco
295

176
Dzitás
38 Pisté
37 Chichén Itzá
Santa Rosa

Dzilam de Bravo
Santa Clara
Dzilam González
Temax
Buctzotz
Tunkás
80
180
Izamal
Halcá
Santa Rosa

Telchac Puerto
Chicxulub
Dzibilchaltún
Motul
Tixkokob
Tekantó
Citilcúm
Hoctún
Kantunil
Mayapán
18
Teabo
Maní
YUCATAN
Tzucacab
Oxcutzcab
Loltún Caves

Progreso
Chelem
Yucalpetén
Sisal
281
Umán
Yaxcopoil
San José Tzal
Muna
Ticul
Mama
184
Labná

Merida
25—36
See Detail Map
180
261
Maxcanú
180
Oxkintoc
Sayil
Kabah
Uxmal
41

Punta Baz
42 Celestún
PARQUE NATURAL RÍA CELESTÚN
Punta Nimun
Santa Cruz
281
Tenabó

CAMPECHE
Bolonchén de Reijón
261
HOCHOB

Campeche
43—52
See Detail Map
Tinúm

KEY
---- Ferry

later. The property remained with the family until the late 1970s, when it was restored by banker Agustín Legorreta and converted to a bank. Built in the French style during Mérida's heyday as the world's henequen capital, it now represents the city's finest—and oldest—example of colonial Plateresque architecture. A bas-relief on the doorway—which is all that remains of the original house—depicts Francisco de Montejo the younger, his wife, and daughter as well as Spanish soldiers standing on the heads of the vanquished Maya. Even if you have no banking to do, step into the building weekdays between 9 and 5 to glimpse the leafy inner patio.

③⓪ Catedral. Begun in 1561 and dedicated to St. Idelfonso, this is the oldest cathedral in Mexico and the second-oldest on the North American mainland. It sits on the east side of the plaza. It took several hundred Maya laborers, working with stones from the pyramids of the ravaged Maya city, 36 years to complete it. Designed in the somber Renaissance style by an architect who had worked on the Escorial in Madrid, its facade is stark and unadorned, with gunnery slits instead of windows, and faintly Moorish spires. Inside, the black **Cristo de las Ampollas** (Christ of the Blisters) occupies a side altar to the left of the main one. The statue is a replica of the original, which was destroyed during the Revolution. According to one of many legends, the Christ figure burned all night yet appeared the next morning unscathed—except that it was covered with the blisters for which it is named. The crucifix above the side altar is reputedly the second-largest in the world. ⊠ *Calle 60 at Calle 61,* ☎ *no phone.* ⊗ *Daily 7–11:30 and 4:30–8.*

②⑧ Centro Cultural de Mérida Olimpo (Mérida Olimpo Cultural Center). Referred to as just Olimpo, this is the best venue for free cultural events in the city. The beautiful, porticoed cultural center was built adjacent to City Hall, occupying what used to be a parking lot. The marble interior is a showcase for international art exhibitions, classical music concerts, conferences, and theater and dance presentations. Next door, a movie house renovated to its 1950s look features film festivals, classics by such directors as Buñuel, Fellini, and Kazan, plus a Sunday family-movie series. The complex also includes a Librería Dante bookstore and El Via café. ⊠ *Calle 62 between Calles 61 and 63,* ☎ *9/928–2020.* ⊠ *Free.* ⊗ *Tues.–Sun. 10–10.*

③② Iglesia de la Tercera Orden de Jesús. To the north of Parque Hidalgo is one of Mérida's oldest buildings and the first Jesuit church in the Yucatán. The church was built in 1618 of limestone from a Maya temple that had stood on the site, and faint outlines of ancient carvings are still visible on the stonework of the west wall. Although it is a favorite place for society weddings because of its antiquity, the church interior is not very ornate. The former convent rooms in the rear of the building now host the small **Pinoteca Juan Gamboa Guzmán** (State Repository of Paintings). ⊠ *Calle 59 between Calles 58 and 60,* ☎ *9/924–7912.* ⊠ *$1; free Sun.* ⊗ *Tues.–Sat. 8–8, Sun. 8–2.*

③① Museo de Arte Contemporáneo (Museum of Contemporary Art). This enormous two-story building, originally designed as an art school, is full of light. It showcases the works of Yucatecan artists such as Gabriel Ramírez Aznar and Fernando García Ponce and has excellent international art exhibitions in the second-floor galleries. ⊠ *Pasaje de la Revolución 1907, between Calles 58 and 60 (on main square),* ☎ *9/928–3258 or 9/928–3236.* ⊠ *$2; free Sun.* ⊗ *Wed.–Mon. 10–5:30.*

③⑥ Palacio Cantón. The most compelling of the mansions on ☞ **Paseo Montejo,** the pale-peach palacio presently houses the air-conditioned **Museo de Antropología e Historia** (Museum of Anthropology and History).

Designed by Enrique Deserti, who also did the blueprints for the Teatro
Peón Contreras, the building has grandiose airs that seem more characteristic of a mausoleum than a home, but in fact it was built for a
general between 1909 and 1911. There is marble everywhere, likewise
Doric and Ionic columns and other Italianate Beaux Arts flourishes. From
1958 to 1967 the mansion served as the residence of the state governor. In 1977 it became a museum dedicated to the culture and history
of the Maya. Although it's not as impressive as its counterparts in other
Mexican cities, it can serve as an introduction to ancient Maya culture
before you visit nearby Maya sites. ⊠ *Calle 43 and Paseo Montejo,* ☎
9/923–0557. ☜ *$2; free Sun.* ⊙ *Tues.–Sat. 8–8, Sun. 8–2.*

㉙ **Palacio del Gobierno** (State House). Occupying the northeast corner
of the main square is this structure, built in 1885 on the site of the Casa
Real (Royal House). The upper floor of the State House contains Fernando Castro Pacheco's vivid murals of the bloody history of the conquest of the Yucatán, painted in 1978. On the main balcony (visible
from outside on the plaza) stands a reproduction of the **Bell of Dolores Hidalgo,** on which Mexican independence rang out on September 16, 1810, in the town of Dolores Hidalgo in Guanajuato. Every
September 16, the state governor tolls the bell to commemorate the
occasion. ⊠ *Calle 61 between Calles 60 and 62.* ☜ *Free.* ⊙ *Daily 8
AM or 9 AM–9 PM.*

㉗ **Palacio Municipal** (City Hall). The west side of the main square is occupied by this 17th-century building, which is painted pale yellow and
trimmed with white arcades, balustrades, and the national coat of
arms. Originally erected on the ruins of the last surviving Maya structure, it was rebuilt in 1735 and then completely reconstructed along
colonial lines in 1928. It remains the headquarters of the local government. ⊠ *Calle 62 between Calles 61 and 63.* ⊙ *Daily 9–8.*

③⑤ Paseo Montejo. North of downtown, this 10-block-long street exemplifies the Parisian airs the city took on in the late 19th century, when wealthy plantation owners were building opulent, impressive mansions. The broad boulevard, lined with tamarinds and laurels, is sometimes wistfully referred to as Mérida's Champs-Elysées. Inside the mansions the owners typically displayed imported Carrara marble and antiques, opting for the decorative and social standards of New Orleans, Cuba, and Paris over styles that were popular in Mexico City.

③③ Teatro Peón Contreras. This 1908 Italianate theater was built along the lines of the grand turn-of-the-20th-century European theaters and opera houses. In the early 1980s the marble staircase and the dome and frescoes were restored. Today, in addition to performing arts, the theater also houses temporary art exhibitions and the main **Centro de Información Turística**, which is to the right of the lobby. The information center distributes maps and brochures and can provide details about local attractions. ⊠ *Calle 60 between Calles 57 and 59,* ☎ *9/923–7354, 9/924–9290 tourist-information center.* ☉ *Theater daily 7 AM–1 AM; tourist-information center weekdays 8 AM–9 PM, weekends 8–8.*

③④ Universidad Autónoma de Yucatán. The arabesque university plays a major role in the city's cultural and intellectual life. The folkloric ballet performs on the patio of the main building Friday at 9 PM. The building, which dates from 1711, has crenellated Moorish ramparts and archways. Bulletin boards just inside the entrance announce upcoming cultural events. ⊠ *Calle 60 between Calles 57 and 59,* ☎ *9/924–8000 or 9/924–7260.*

②⑤ Zócalo (main square). The Meridanos also traditionally call this the Plaza Principal and Plaza de la Independencia, and it's a good spot from which to begin any tour of the city. Ancient, geometrically pruned laurel trees and *confidenciales* (S-shape benches designed for tête-à-têtes) invite lingering. The plaza was laid out in 1542 on the ruins of T'hó, the Maya city demolished to make way for Mérida, and is still the focal point around which the most important public buildings cluster. ⊠ *Bordered by Calles 60, 62, 61, and 63.*

Dining and Lodging

$–$$ ✕ La Bella Epoca. For a special dinner, nothing matches the elegance
★ and style of this second-story dining room, the former ballroom of an old mansion that has been restored beyond its original grandeur. Crystal chandeliers sparkle over tiny balcony tables overlooking Parque Hidalgo. You seem to pay for the ambience here, and the shills outside trying to entice customers inside take the image down a peg or two, but the food is still tops. An ambitious but almost unreadable handwritten menu includes French, Mexican, Middle Eastern, Yucatecan, vegetarian, and unusual Maya dishes. Arrive for dinner before 8 PM to claim one of the balcony tables overlooking the street. ⊠ *Hotel del Parque, Calle 60 between Calles 57 and 59,* ☎ *9/928–1928. AE, MC, V.*

$–$$ ✕ Habichuela. The food and service at this quietly elegant spot are ex-
★ cellent. Custom-made hardwood furniture, marble floors, and lots of leaded-glass accents contribute to its clubby feel. Local businessmen hold power lunches here; at night, it's filled with families and couples. For starters, try the seafood crepes or salmon pâté. Main dishes feature meat, fish, and fowl prepared with flair; choices include butterflied shrimp with ginger, tamarind, or fruit sauce, and chicken Veronica stuffed with Serrano ham and bananas with sweet gravy on the side. The chocolate-mousse cake is the star of the dessert menu. The chef welcomes special requests. ⊠ *Calle 1 No. 416, Col. Mexico Oriente (about 20 mins by car from main square),* ☎ *9/926–3626. AE, MC, V. No dinner Sun.*

$ ✕ **Los Almendros.** This Mérida classic takes credit for the invention of the regional specialty called *poc chuc* (slices of pork marinated in sour-orange juice and spices), although some dispute the claim. The food can be greasy, and local spices, such as achiote, can overwhelm the main ingredients. Still, Los Almendros is a good introduction to the variety of Yucatecan cuisine. The menu includes *cochinita pibíl* (pork baked in banana leaves), panuchos, pork sausage, *papadzules* (corn tortillas with chopped, hard-cooked egg and pumpkin-seed sauce), and *pollo ticuleño* (boneless, breaded chicken in tomato sauce filled with fried beans, peas, red peppers, ham, and cheese). ✉ *Calle 50 No. 493 (between Calles 57 and 59),* ☎ *9/923–8135 or 9/928–5459. AE, MC, V.*

$ ✕ **Café La Havana.** Old-fashioned ceiling fans and elegant wicker fur-
★ niture contribute to the Old Havana nostalgia at this overwhelmingly popular café—an outpost of a famous coffee house in Mexico City that Fidel Castro supposedly frequented. The aroma of fresh-ground coffee fills the air at this casual 24-hour place, where you can comfortably linger, chat with friends, or hammer out a business deal. Sixteen javas are offered, including Irish, frappé, espresso, and Arab. The menu has light snacks such as lime soup, as well as some entrées, including spaghetti, fajitas, and breaded shrimp. The café is a few blocks north of the main square. ✉ *Corner of Calles 59 and 62,* ☎ *9/928–6502. No credit cards.*

$$$$ ✕🔲 **Hacienda Katanchel.** This romantic, rambling 17th-century
★ henequin hacienda on 740 acres was brought back to its original splendor by Anibal Gonzalez and his wife Monica Hernandez. The guest suites are housed in spacious, freestanding pavilions built along a winding garden walkway. They have direct-dial telephones and are outfitted with overhead fans, hammocks, huge tile bathrooms, plunge pools, and double beds that look like pieces of modern sculpture. The former Casa de Máquina (Processing Plant) is now a gorgeous restaurant that serves contemporary Yucatecan cuisine. The menu makes liberal use of the hacienda's organically grown fruits and vegetables; offerings include cream of beet soup, chicken in *pipian* (pumpkin seed) and pistachio sauce, and desserts such as vanilla ice cream with sweet and tangy sour-orange sauce. Room rates include early-morning coffee or tea and biscuits, placed outside your door. Floral and herbal massages bring pampering to a new level. ✉ *25 km (15 mi) east of Mérida on Hwy. 180 (toward Cancún),* ☎ *9/923–4020 or 800/223–6510,* ℻ *888/882–9470,* WEB *www.hacienda-katanchel.com. 39 suites. Restaurant, bar, air-conditioning, pool, massage, chapel, travel services, car rental, free parking. AE, MC, V.*

$$$$ ✕🔲 **Hacienda Teya.** The draw at this beautiful henequen-era hacienda
★ 8 mi from the city is the fabulous regional food; reservations for Sunday lunch or dinner are essential. After a typical lunch of cochinita pibíl or baked chicken, you can stroll in the orchard or surrounding gardens, or swim in the huge rectangular pool. There are six rooms for rent here; the rates include Continental breakfast. ✉ *13 km (8 mi) east of Mérida on Hwy. 180,* ☎ *9/968–0800 or 9/968–5000,* ℻ *9/968–5001. 6 rooms. Restaurant, bar, pool, free parking. AE, MC, V.*

$$$$ 🔲 **Fiesta Americana Mérida.** This posh hotel and shopping/business cen-
★ ter caters to business travelers, conventions, and high-end travelers, but it also brings in locals who come to see and be seen. Its lovely pink facade mirrors the architecture of Paseo Montejo mansions on an epic scale. The colonial echoes carry into the spacious upper lobby with its massive columns, gleaming marble and brass work, and 300-ft-high stained-glass atrium. Floral prints, painted-wood furnishings, and slightly larger-than-life proportions maintain the theme of bygone elegance in the guest rooms, but the units have all the modern conveniences, including remote-control TVs concealed in armoires and three phones.

There are 12 concierges, and guests on the business floor have access to the Fiesta Room for morning breakfast and newspapers or afternoon appetizers. ✉ *Av. Colón No. 451, at Paseo Montejo, 97000,* ☎ *9/942–1111 or 800/343–7821,* FAX *9/942–1122,* WEB *www.fiestaamericana.com. 323 rooms, 27 suites. 2 restaurants, 2 bars, in-room data ports, minibars, no-smoking rooms, health club, 2 tennis courts, shops, concierge floor, travel services, car rental, free parking. AE, MC, V.*

$$$ 🏨 **Casa del Balam.** This very pleasant hotel on well-heeled Calle 60
★ was built more than 60 years ago as the home of the Barbachano family, pioneers of Yucatán tourism. Today the hotel—owned and managed by Carmen Barbachano—has a lovely courtyard ornamented with a fountain, arcades, ironwork, and a black-and-white tile floor. Rocking chairs in the hallways impart a colonial feeling, as do the mahogany trimmings and cedar doorways. The rooms are capacious and well maintained, with painted sinks, wrought-iron accessories, and refrigerator–minibars. All rooms have hair dryers and double-pane windows. Cocktails and light meals are served in the lobby courtyard; meals are served in the restaurant. Guests have access to a golf and tennis club about 15 minutes from the hotel. ✉ *Calle 60 No. 488 (Box 988), 97000,* ☎ *9/924–8844, 9/924–2150, 800/624–8451,* FAX *9/924–5011,* WEB *www.mayaland.com. 51 rooms, 3 suites. Restaurant, 2 bars, minibars, no-smoking rooms, pool, travel services, car rental, free parking. AE, DC, MC, V.*

$$$ 🏨 **Casa Mexilio.** Four block from the main square is this choice bed-
★ and-breakfast, run by partners Jorge and Roger. It has wonderfully eclectic decor—Middle Eastern wall hangings, French tapestries, colorful tile floors, tile sinks, and folk-art furniture. The exquisitely decorated rooms, each a private oasis in itself, along with the lush gardens and hidden terraces make it a romantic and serene escape. (The honeymooners' favorite is the Palomar Room.) Casa Mexilio lacks the amenities of the larger hotels—only five rooms have air-conditioning—but a stay here is more casual, like in a private home. A rooftop bistro offers creative cooking. ✉ *Calle 68 No. 495 (between Calles 57 and 59), 97000,* ☎ FAX *9/928–2505. Reservations in the U.S.:* ☎ *800/538–6802 or 303/674–9615,* FAX *303/674–8735,* WEB *www.mexicoholiday.com. 8 rooms. Restaurant, breakfast room, air-conditioning (some), pool. MC, V.*

$$ 🏨 **Casa San Juan.** This B&B is housed in a beautifully restored colonial mansion that was built by a Portuguese family in the 1860s. Designated a historical monument by the government, the house has many original components, such as high ceilings decorated with Belgium railroad ties—a fashion of the time—tile floors, a stone fountain, and 10-ft-tall mahogany doors. Three patios and a sitting room surround a lush interior garden. Most guest rooms are extra large, with double beds, firm mattresses, and ceiling and floor fans; two have air-conditioning. Room rates here include the tax, and there's a three-night minimum. ✉ *Calle 62 No. 545-A (between Calles 69 and 71), 97000,* ☎ *9/986–2937,* FAX *305/559–3564 in the U.S.,* WEB *www.casasanjuan.com. 6 rooms. Breakfast room, air-conditioning (some), fans, travel services. MC, V when booked from the U.S.*

$ 🏨 **Trinidad Galería.** Eccentricity holds sway at this impossibly original, slightly ramshackle, nearly unidentifiable little hotel. In its previous lives it has been a hacienda, a car-rental shop, and a furniture store, but in the late 1980s owner Manolo Rivero made it into what he calls "a post-contemporary museum hotel." An adjacent art gallery has four yearly expositions of young talent, to which all hotel guests receive formal invitations. The large, chaotic lobby is filled with art, plants, a fountain, and yellow wicker furniture. Making your way through the maze that is the rest of the hotel, you encounter painted wooden angels, curved columns, and all sorts of installation-style art. Rooms are small and

equally odd; rates are higher for the two that have air-conditioning ($$).
⊠ *Calle 60 No. 456, at Calle 51, 97000,* ☎ *9/923–2463,* FAX *9/924–2319. 33 rooms, 2 suites. Café, air-conditioning (some), pool, free parking. No credit cards.*

Nightlife and the Arts

Mérida has an unusually active and diverse cultural life, including free government-sponsored music and dance performances most nights, as well as sidewalk art shows in local parks. On Saturday check out the **Noche Mexicana,** a free, outdoor spectacle of music, dance, and regional handicrafts that draws more locals than tourists. It happens 8 PM–11 PM at the foot of Paseo Montejo at Calle 47. On Sunday, when six blocks around the zócalo are closed off to traffic, you can hear live music at Plaza Santa Lucía and Parque Hidalgo (usually at 11 AM); mariachis, marimbas, folkloric dance, and other treats at the main plaza (1 PM). For more information on performances, consult the tourist office, the local newspapers, or the billboards and posters at the **Teatro Peón Contreras,** on Calle 60 at Calle 57, or the **Universidad Autónoma de Yucatán** or **Café Pop,** both on Calle 57 between Calles 60 and 62.

DANCING

A number of restaurants have live music and dancing. **Ay Caray** (⊠ Calle 60 No. 482, between Calles 55 and 57, ☎ 9/924–2323) is a lively video bar with salsa music, rock shows, and song impersonators until 1 AM, after which there's two hours of dancing. It's open 9 PM–3 AM. **Pancho's** (⊠ Calle 59 No. 509, between Calles 60 and 62, ☎ 9/923–0942) attracts locals and foreigners for a mix of live salsa and Western music.

FOLKLORIC SHOWS

Paseo Montejo hotels such as the Fiesta Americana, Hyatt Regency, and Holiday Inn stage dinner shows with folkloric dances; check with concierges for schedules. The **Folkloric Ballet of the University of Yucatán** presents a combination of music, dance, and theater, every Friday at 9 PM at the Universidad Autónoma de Yucatán (⊠ Calle 57 between 60 and 62, ☎ 9/924–7260); tickets are $2. This includes the "University Serenade," with music, folkloric dance, and poetry. (There are no shows from August 1 to September 22 and during the last two weeks of December.)

Outdoor Activities and Sports

GOLF

The 18-hole championship golf course at **Club de Golf La Ceiba** (⊠ Carr. Mérida-Progreso, Km 14.5, ☎ 9/922–0053 or 9/922–054) is open to the public. It is about 16 km (10 mi) north of Mérida on the road to Progreso; greens fees are about $42; closed Mon.

Shopping

MARKETS

The second floor of the **Mercado Municipal** (⊠ between Calles 65 and 67 and Calles 54 and 56) has crafts, food, flowers, and live birds, among other items. If you're interested strictly in handicrafts, visit the government-run **Casa de Artesanías** (⊠ Calle 63 No. 503, between Calles 64 and 66, ☎ 9/923–5392). It sells folk art from throughout Mexico, including hand-painted wooden animals from Oaxaca, handmade candles and leather bags from Mérida, and hand-embroidered vests, shawls, and blouses from Chiapas. The streets north of the main square, especially **Calle 60,** are lined with crafts and jewelry stores.

SPECIALTY STORES

Clothing. Mexicanísimo (⊠ Calle 60 No. 496, at Calle 61, on Parque Hidalgo, ☎ 9/923–8132) sells expensive designer cotton clothing inspired by regional dress. For a good selection of guayaberas, try **Camis-ería Canul** (⊠ Calle 62 No. 484, between Calles 57 and 59, ☎ 9/923–0158).

Galleries. The **Galería Ateneo Peninsular** (⊠ Calle 60 between Calle 61 and Pasaje Revolución, ☎ 9/925–7952 or 9/925–8253) sponsors shows by international artists. The **Galería Casa Colón** (⊠ Av. Colón 507, ☎ 9/925–7952 or 9/925–8253) highlights modern-day Mexican painters in the setting of a colonial home.

The Scenic Route to Chichén Itzá

Although you can get to Chichén Itzá (120 km [74 mi] east of Mérida) along the shorter Route 180, it's far more scenic to follow Route 80 until it ends at Tekantó, then head south to Citilcúm, east to Dzitas, and south again to Pisté. These roads have no signs but are the only paved roads going in these directions. Be sure to stop in Izamal, 72 km (44 mi) southeast of Mérida, to see the enormous 16th-century Convento de San Antonio de Padua, perched on—and built from—the remains of a pyramid.

Chichén Itzá

🔺 �37 *116 km (72 mi) from Mérida.*

One of the four most magnificent Maya ruins—along with Palenque in Chiapas in Mexico, Tikal in Guatemala, and Copán in Honduras—Chichén Itzá was the most important city in Yucatán from the 10th through the 12th centuries. Its architectural mélange covers pre-Columbian Mesoamerican history and shows the influence of several different Maya groups. Because epigraphers have been able to read 85% of the Chichén inscriptions, the site's history has become clearer to archaeologists. Chichén was altered by each wave of inhabitants, and archaeologists date the arrival of these waves by the changes in the architecture and information contained in inscriptions. The site is believed to have been first settled in AD 432, abandoned for an unknown period of time, then rediscovered in 868 by the Maya-speaking Itzás, who came from the southern Maya region of the Petén rain forest around Tikal. The latest data point to the city's being refounded by not only the Itzás but also by two other foreign groups—one from the Valley of Mexico (present-day Mexico City) and another from Ek Balam. The trio formed a ruling triumvirate. The Itzás may have also abandoned the site, but they were the dominant group until 1224, when the site appears to have been abandoned for good.

Chichén Itzá means "the mouth of the well of the Itzás." The enormity and gracefulness of the site are unforgettable. Chichén Itzá encompasses approximately 6 square km (2½ square mi), though only 30 to 40 structures and buildings of the several hundred at the site have been fully explored. It's divided into two parts, called Old and New, although a more convenient distinction is topographical, since there are two major complexes of buildings separated by a dirt path.

The martial, imperial architecture of the Itzás and the more cerebral architecture and astronomical expertise of the earlier Maya are married in the 98-ft-tall pyramid called **El Castillo** (the Castle), which dominates the site and rises above all the other buildings. Atop the Castillo is a temple dedicated to Kukulcán, the legendary Toltec priest–king from Tula in the Valley of Mexico who was held to be an incarnation of the mystical plumed serpent. An open-jawed plumed serpent rests on the balustrade of each stairway, and serpents reappear at the top of the temple as sculptured columns. At the spring and fall equinoxes, the afternoon light strikes one of these balustrades in such a way as to form a shadow representation of Kukulcán undulating out of his temple and down the pyramid to bless the fertile earth. Each evening there's a sound-and-light show that highlights the architectural details in El Castillo and other buildings with a clarity the eye doesn't see in daylight, though its narrative has inaccuracies.

The temple rests on a massive trapezoidal square, on the west side of which is Chichén Itzá's largest **ball court,** one of seven on the site. The game played here was something like soccer (no hands were used), but it had a strictly religious significance. Bas-relief carvings at the court depict a player being decapitated, the blood spurting from his neck fertilizing the earth. Other bas-reliefs show two teams of opposing players pitted against each other during the ball game.

Between the ball court and El Castillo stands a **Tzompantli,** or stone platform, carved with rows of human skulls. In ancient times it was covered with stakes on which the heads of enemies were impaled. Legend has it that the **Sacred Well,** a cenote 65 yards in diameter that sits 1 km (½ mi) north of El Castillo at the end of a sacbé, was used for human sacrifices; another cenote at the site supplied drinking water. Many archaeologists believe that nonhuman sacrifices were carried out by local chiefs hundreds of years after Chichén Itzá was abandoned. Thousands of artifacts made of gold, jade, and other precious materials, most of them not of local provenance, have been recovered from the brackish depths of the cenote.

Returning to the causeway, you see on your left the **Group of the Thousand Columns** with the famous **Temple of the Warriors,** a masterful example of the Itzá influence at Chichén Itzá. The temple was used as a meeting place for the high lords of the council that ruled Chichén Itzá. The temple-top sculpture of the reclining Chacmool—its head turned to the side, the offertory dish carved into its middle—is probably the most photographed symbol of the Maya. Murals of everyday village life and scenes of war can be viewed here, and an artistic representation of the defeat of one of the Itzás' Maya enemies can be found on the interior murals of the **Temple of the Jaguar.**

To get to the less visited cluster of structures at **New Chichén Itzá**—often confused with Old Chichén Itzá—take the main road south from the Temple of the Jaguar past El Castillo and turn right onto a small path opposite the ball court on your left. Archaeologists have been restoring several buildings in this area, including the **Tomb of the High Priest,** where several tombs with skeletons and jade offerings were found, and the northern part of the site, which was used for military training and barracks for the army. The most impressive structure within this area is the astronomical observatory called **El Caracol.** The name, meaning "snail," refers to the spiral staircase at the building's core. Used for observing the heavens, it probably also served a religious function. After leaving El Caracol, continue south several hundred yards to the beautiful **La Casa de las Monjas** (The Nunnery) and its annex, which have long carved panels.

At Old Chichén Itzá, "pure Maya" style—a combination of Puuc and Chenes styles, with playful latticework, Chaac masks, and gargoyle-like serpents on the cornices—dominates. Highlights include the **Date Group,** so named because of its complete series of hieroglyphic dates; the **House of the Phalli;** and the **Temple of the Three Lintels.** Maya guides will lead you down the path by an old narrow-gauge railroad track to

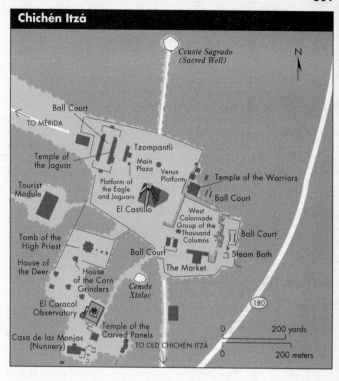

Chichén Itzá

Cenote Sagrado
(Sacred Well)

N

Ball Court

TO MÉRIDA

Tzompantli

Temple of
the Jaguar

Main
Plaza

Venus
Platform

Temple of the Warriors

Tourist
Module

Platform of
the Eagle
and Jaguars

Ball Court

El Castillo

West
Colonnade
Group of the
Thousand
Columns

Ball Court

Tomb of the
High Priest

Ball Court

Steam Bath

House of
the Deer

House
of the Corn
Grinders

The Market

Cenote
Xtoloc

180

El Caracol
Observatory

Temple of the
Carved Panels

0   200 yards

Casa de las Monjas
(Nunnery)

TO OLD CHICHÉN ITZÁ

0   200 meters

even more ruins, barely unearthed, if you ask. A fairly good restaurant and a great ice cream stand are in the entrance building, as is a gift shop where you can purchase film, bus tickets, postcards, and books. $8.50, free Sun.; sound-and-light show $4 in Spanish (English speakers have to rent translating earphones for another $4); parking $2; use of video camera $7. ☉ Daily 8–5; sound-and-light show Apr.–Oct. daily at 8 PM, Nov.–Mar. daily at 7 PM..

Lodging

$$$$
★
🏨 **Mayaland.** The hotel closest to the ruins, this charming 1920s lodging belongs to the Barbachano family, whose name is practically synonymous with tourism in Yucatán. In addition to a main hotel building, there are a wing and several bungalows set in a large garden on the 100-acre site. You can actually see part of "Old Chichen-Itza" from the gardens, and the hotel has a private walkway into the ruins. All guest rooms are colonial style and have decorative tiles, air-conditioning, and cable TV; five suites have hot tubs. Tour buses fill the road in front of the hotel, so choose a room at the back. The 24 bungalows at the rear of the hotel are the prettiest (and most expensive) accommodations, with hammocks out on the wide verandas, bright white tubs, and thatch roofs. Light meals served poolside and at tables overlooking the garden are a better choice than the expensive fixed-price meals served in the dining room. Guided horseback tours to Balanché are available at extra cost. ⊠ Carretera Mérida–Puerto Juárez, Km 120 (mailing address: ⊠ Mayaland Tours, Box 407, Mérida), ☎ 985/10127 or 800/235–4079, ℻ 985/10129, ⓦⒺⒷ www.mayaland.com. 91 rooms, 10 suites, 50 bungalows. 4 restaurants, 2 bars, air-conditioning, minibars, 3 pools, tennis court, shuffleboard, volleyball, meetings rooms, free parking. AE, DC, MC, V.

$$$ ★ 🏨 **Hacienda Chichén.** A converted 16th-century hacienda, this hotel once served as the home of U.S. Consul General Edward S. Thompson. Later it was the headquarters for the Carnegie expedition to Chichén Itzá. The rustic cottages have handwoven bedspreads, dehumidifiers, and air-conditioning. All rooms, which are simply furnished in colonial Yucatecan style, have private bathrooms and verandas but no phones or TVs. There's a color satellite TV in the library. An enormous old pool as well as an old family chapel now used for weddings sit in the midst of the landscaped gardens. Fairly good meals are served on the patio overlooking the grounds, and there's an air-conditioned restaurant; stick with the Yucatecan specialties. ⊠ *Carretera Mérida–Pto. Juárez, Km 120,* ☎ *985/10045 or 800/624–8451,* 🆅🆇 *9/924–5011. 24 rooms, 4 suites. Restaurant, bar, air-conditioning, pool, chapel, free parking. AE, DC, MC, V.*

Pisté

🔟 *1 km (½ mi) west of Chichén Itzá.*

The town of Pisté serves mainly as a base camp for travelers to Chichén Itzá. Hotels, campgrounds, restaurants, and handicrafts shops tend to be less expensive here than south of the ruins. On the outskirts of Pisté and a short walk from Chichén Itzá is **Pueblo Maya,** a pseudo-Maya village with a shopping and dining center for tour groups. The restaurant serves a bountiful buffet at lunch ($12). Across from the Dolores Alba hotel, in town, is the **Parque Ik Kil** (Place of the Winds). The park is built around a lovely cenote where you can swim between 8 AM and 6 PM for $3. The park includes the Restaurant el Jardín, which serves Mexican and international fare, a swimming pool, bungalows inspired by Maya dwellings, and a row of shops where artisans demonstrate their crafts. ⊠ *Carretera Libre Pisté–Cancún, Km 112,* ☎ *no phone.*

Lodging

$$ 🏨 **Dolores Alba.** This family-run hotel is a longtime favorite in the area south of Pisté. Twelve rooms were added in 2000 and existing rooms got a face-lift, with colonial-style furniture, tile bathroom floors, and air-conditioning. Hammocks hang by one of the two pools, and breakfast and dinner are served family-style in the main building. Free transportation to Chichén Itzá is provided, and there is a covered, guarded parking lot. ⊠ *Carretera Mérida–Cancún, Km 122, 3 km (2 mi) south of Chichén Itzá (mailing address: Calle 63 No. 464, Mérida),* ☎ *9/928–5650,* 🆅🆇 *9/928–3163,* 🆆🅴🅱 *www.doloresalba.com). 40 rooms. Restaurant, air-conditioning, 2 pools, free parking. AE.*

Valladolid

🔟 *44 km (27 mi) east of Chichén Itzá.*

The second-largest city in the State of Yucatán, Valladolid is a picturesque provincial town (pop. 70,000). It has been enjoying growing popularity among travelers en route to or from Chichén Itzá or Río Lagartos who want a change from the more touristy places. Montejo founded Valladolid in 1543 on the site of the Maya town of Sisal. The city suffered during the Caste War—when the Maya in revolt killed nearly all Spanish residents—and again during the Mexican Revolution.

Today, however, placidity reigns in this agricultural market town. The center is mostly colonial, although it has many 19th-century structures. The main sights are the colonial churches, principally the large **cathedral** on the central square and the 16th-century **San**

Bernardino Church and Convent three blocks southwest. Both were pillaged during the Caste War. A briny, muddy cenote in the center of town draws only the most resolute swimmers; instead, visit the adjacent **ethnographic museum.** West of the main square on the old highway to Chichén Itzá, you can swim with the catfish in **Cenote Dzitnup,** in a cave lit by a small, natural skylight; admission is $2.

Valladolid is renowned for its cuisine, particularly its sausages; try one of the restaurants within a block of the central square. You can find good buys on sandals, baskets, and the local liqueur, Xtabentún, flavored with honey and anise.

Lodging

$$ ☕ **Ecotel Quinta Real.** For a little luxury, this attractive salmon-color hotel dressed in Mexican colonial architecture fills the bill. Near a leafy park five blocks from downtown, the pretty rooms have cool tile floors, two double beds, cable TV, air-conditioning, and spacious balconies. You can wander the tree-filled garden and visit the pool, palapa bar, tennis court, or duck pond. The restaurant serves regional and some international dishes, but it's a bit more expensive than other places in town. ⊠ *Calle 40 No. 160–A, at Calle 27, 97780,* ☎ *985/63472 or 985/63473,* ℻ *985/62422,* ᴡᴇʙ *www.ecotelquintareal.com.mx. 48 rooms. Restaurant, bar, air-conditioning, pool, tennis court, Ping-Pong, travel services, car rental, free parking. MC, V.*

$$ ☕ **El Mesón del Marqués.** On the north side of the main square is this well-preserved hacienda built around a lovely courtyard. All rooms have air-conditioning, phones, and cable TV and are furnished with rustic and colonial touches. The 25 junior suites have large bathrooms with bathtubs. The restaurant, set under porticos surrounding the courtyard, serves Yucatecan specialties such as pollo pibíl and local sausage served in a variety of ways. It's open 7 AM–11 PM. ⊠ *Calle 39 No. 203, 97780,* ☎ *985/62073 or 985/63042,* ℻ *985/62280. 58 rooms, 25 suites. Restaurant, bar, air-conditioning, pool. AE.*

Parque Natural Río Lagartos

④⓪ *101 km (63 mi) north of Valladolid, 150 km (93 mi) northeast of Mérida.*

If the thought of a phenomenal flamingo spectacle appeals—flamingo season runs from June through March—don't miss Parque Natural Río Lagartos. Actually encompassing a long estuary, not a river, the park was developed with ecotourism in mind. In addition to seeing flamingos, birders can spot snowy egrets, red egrets, white ibis, great white herons, cormorants, pelicans, and even peregrine falcons flying over these murky waters. The protected hawksbill and green turtles lay their eggs on the beach at night.

To get here, you can drive or take a bus or a tour out of Mérida or elsewhere. Buses leave Mérida and Valladolid regularly from the second-class bus terminals to either Río Lagartos or, 10 km (6 mi) west of the park, San Felipe. A boat tour to see the flamingos is available from either point. About ½ km (¼ mi) from the entrance to Río Lagartos is an information station. The helpful people who work here can contact a guide with a boat for you. The boat glides up the estuary east of the dock and in 10 minutes is deep into mangrove forests; another hour and the boat is at the flamingo feeding grounds. For a bilingual birding guide ($10–$15 an hour), you must make arrangements at least three days in advance with the reserve office in Tizimín (☎ 986/3–43–90).

Uxmal, the Ruta Puuc, and the Coast

Passing through the large Maya town of Umán on Mérida's southern outskirts, you enter one of the least populated areas of the Yucatán. The highway to Uxmal and Kabah is a fairly traffic-free route through uncultivated woodlands. The forest seems to become more dense beyond Uxmal, which was connected to a number of smaller ceremonial centers in ancient times by *caminos blancos* (white roads). Several of these satellite sites, including **Kabah,** with its 250 Chaac masks; **Sayil,** with its majestic, three-story palace; and **Labná,** with its iconic, vaulted *Puerta* (gateway), are open to the public along a side road known as the Ruta Puuc, which winds its way eastward and eventually joins busy Highway 184, a major highway. Along this route you'll also find the **Loltún Caves,** the largest known cave system in the Yucatán, containing wall paintings and stone artifacts from Maya and pre-Maya times. You can make a loop to all of these sites, ending the loop in the little town of **Plaza,** which produces much of the pottery you'll see around the peninsula. **Ticul** is a convenient alternative to spending the night at the hotels just outside the Uxmal ruins, and the reasonable **Plaza** hotel (☎ 997/20026), a block from the town square, is a suitable place to stay.

Uxmal

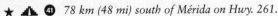

★ ▲ ㊶ *78 km (48 mi) south of Mérida on Hwy. 261.*

If Chichén Itzá is the most impressive Maya ruin in Yucatán, Uxmal is arguably the most beautiful. Where the former has a Maya Itzá grandeur, the latter seems more understated and elegant—pure Maya. The architecture reflects the Late Classical renaissance of the 7th–9th centuries and is contemporary with that of Palenque and Tikal, among other great Maya metropolises of the southern highlands.

The site is considered the finest and largest example of Puuc architecture, which embraces such details as ornate stone mosaics and friezes on the upper walls, intricate cornices with curled noses, rows of columns, and soaring vaulted arches. Lines are clean and uncluttered, with the horizontal—especially the parallelogram—preferred to the vertical. Although most of Uxmal hasn't been restored, three buildings in particular merit attention:

At 125 ft high, the **Pyramid of the Magician** is the tallest and most prominent structure at the site. Unlike most other Maya pyramids, which are stepped and angular, it has a strangely round-corner design. It was built five times at 52-year sequences to coincide with the ceremony of the new fire, each time over the previous structure. The pyramid has a stairway on its western side that leads through a giant open-mouthed mask of Chaac to two temples at the summit.

West of the pyramid lies the **Quadrangle of the Nuns,** considered by some to be the finest part of Uxmal. According to recent research, what is called the **Nunnery** was actually the palace and living quarters of a high lord of Uxmal by the name of Chaan Chak, which means "abundance of rain." You may enter the four buildings; each comprises a series of low, gracefully repetitive chambers that look onto a central patio. Elaborate decoration—masks, geometric patterns, coiling snakes, and some phallic figures—blankets the upper facades.

Continue walking south; you pass the ball court before reaching the **Palace of the Governor,** which archaeologist Victor von Hagen considered the most magnificent building ever erected in the Americas. Interestingly, the palace faces east while the rest of Uxmal faces west. Archaeologists believe this is because the palace was used to sight the planet Venus. Covering 5 acres and rising over an immense acropolis, the palace lies at the heart of what must have been Uxmal's administrative center.

Today a sound-and-light show recounts Maya legends. The artificial colored light brings out details of carvings and mosaics that are easy to miss when the sun is shining. The show is performed nightly in Spanish; earphones provide an English translation. ☜ *Site and museum $8.50, free Sun.; sound-and-light show $4; parking $2; use of video camera $8.* ☉ *Daily 8–5; sound-and-light show Apr.–Oct. nightly at 8 PM, Nov.–Mar. nightly at 7 PM.*

Dining and Lodging

$$$$ ⊞ **Hacienda Uxmal.** The oldest hotel at the Maya site, built in 1955 and still owned and operated by the Barbachano family, this pleasant colonial-style building has lovely floor tiles, ceramics, and iron grillwork. The rooms—all with ceiling fans, cable TV, and air-conditioning—are tiled and decorated with worn but comfortable furniture. All are fronted with wide, furnished verandas where you can enjoy the fresh air. The Uxmal ruins are across the road and about 100 yards south. ⊠ *Within walking distance of the ruins (mailing address: ⊠ Mayaland Tours, Calle 60 between Calles 59 and 61, Mérida),* ☎ *9/924–2099 or 800/235–4079,* ℻ *9/924–6290,* ⌨ *www.mayaland.com. 78 rooms, 2 suites. 2 restaurants, bar, air-conditioning, fans, room service, 2 pools, Ping-Pong, billiards, free parking. AE, MC, V.*

$$$$ ⊞ **Lodge at Uxmal.** The entrance to the Uxmal ruins is across from this luminous property owned and run by Mayaland Resorts. The rooms are housed in rustic-looking, two-story thatch-roof buildings. They have glossy red-tile floors, lots of carved and polished hardwood, and faux-stained-glass windows as well as cable TV, minibars, air-conditioning, and bathtubs. Simple furnishings and local weavings are used to create a seminative ambience in the midst of the luxury amenities. Rocking chairs on the wide verandas look out on green lawns or one of the swimming pools. ⊠ *Antigua Carretera Mérida–Campeche, Km 78, 97000,* ☎ *9/923–2202, 9/923–0275, 800/235–4079,* ℻ *9/923–4744,* ⌨ *www.mayaland.com. 30 rooms, 10 suites. 2 restaurants, bar, air-conditioning, 2 pools, free parking. AE, MC, V.*

$$ ⊞ **Villas Arqueológicas Uxmal.** Rooms at this Club Med down the street from the ruins are small and functional, with wooden furniture that fits the niches nicely and powerful but quiet air conditioners. Half of the rooms have garden views. The French and Continental food served in the restaurant—including niçoise salad, pâté, and filet mignon—can be a delightful change from regional fare. Day-trippers have free use of the pool—towels are provided for those who have a meal or drinks here. ⊠ *Carretera Uxmal, Km 76 (mailing address: Box 449, Mérida 97000),* ☎ *9/976–2018 or 800/258–2633,* ℻ *9/976–2018,* ⌨ *www.clubmed.com. 40 rooms, 3 suites. Restaurant, bar, air-conditioning, pool, tennis court, billiards, library, free parking. AE, MC, V.*

Celestún

㊷ *90 km (56 mi) west of Mérida on Routes 180 and 281.*

This tranquil fishing village, with its air of unpretentiousness and gulf-coast flavor, sits at the end of a spit of land separating the Celestún estuary from the Gulf on the western hump of the Yucatán. Celestún is the only point of entry to the **Parque Natural Ría Celestún,** a 100,000-acre wildlife reserve with extensive mangrove forests and salt flats and one of the largest colonies of flamingos in North America. From June through March, clouds of pink wings soar over the pale blue backdrop of the estuary, up to 18,000 at a time. It's also the fourth-largest wintering ground for ducks of the gulf-coast region, with more than 200 other species of birds and a large sea-turtle population.

Celestún Expeditions (☒ Calle 10 No. 97, between Calles 9 and 11, ☎ 991/62049) is a small company run by two natives of Celestún. In addition to the standard flamingo tours, they offer three-hour guided bike tours, jungle walks (day or night), crocodile tours at night, bird-watching excursions, and trips to the Maya ruins and haciendas. Tours range from $20 to $75 per person.

Dining and Lodging

$ ✕ **La Palapa.** A facade made entirely of conch shells leads you to the best seafood place in town, famous for its *camarones a la palapa* (fried shrimp smothered in a garlic and cream sauce). There's a roofed-in area plus an open-air terrace for lunching and watching the sea. The menu is full of fresh fish such as sea bass and red snapper, plus crab, squid, and other denizens of the deep. It's usually open 11 AM–7 PM. ☒ *Calle 12 No. 105, between Calles 11 and 13,* ☎ *991/62063. MC, V.*

$$$$ 🏨 **Hotel Eco Paraíso Xixim.** On an old coconut plantation in a nature reserve outside town, this hotel is a cut above the other Yucatán coast lodges. Rooms are in thatch-roof bungalows, with porches and hammocks, that stand right on the 5-km-long (3-mi-long) beach. Each small suite has two comfortable queen-size beds, tile floors, and attractive wicker, cedar, and pine furniture, some inlaid with hand-painted tiles. There's also a sitting area and writing desk—but no air-conditioning, TVs, or phones. Bring strong insect repellent, as mosquitoes can be vicious, especially in the rainy season. Room rates include ample breakfasts and dinners at the clubhouse. ☒ *Camino Viejo a Sisal, Km 10, 97367,* ☎ *991/62100 or 888/264–5792,* 🆅🆇 *991/62111,* 🕸 *www. mexonline.com. 15 cabañas. Restaurant, bar, fans, in-room safes, pool, beach, billiards, library. AE, MC, V.*

$ 🏨 **Hotel Sol y Mar.** A half block from the town beach, this is definitely the best hotel of this category around. Rooms are spare but clean, with two double beds, a small table and chairs, tile bathrooms, and either air-conditioning (in three rooms, for $6 more) or overhead fans. ☒ *Calle 12 No. 104, at Calle 10, 97367,* ☎ *991/62166. 8 rooms. Air-conditioning (some), fans (some). No credit cards.*

The State of Yucatán A to Z

AIR TRAVEL

Aeroméxico flies direct to Mérida from Miami with a stop (but no plane change) in Cancún. Mexicana has a connecting flight from Newark via Cancún and a number of other connecting flights from the United States via Mexico City. Delta has nonstop flights from Atlanta to Mérida and as well as connecting flights via Mexico City. Aerocaribe, a subsidiary of Mexicana, has flights from Cancún, Chetumal, Cozumel, Oaxaca City, Tuxtla Gutiérrez, and Villahermosa. It also offers service from Cozumel, Cancún, and Palenque to Chichén Itzá.

➤ AIRLINES & CONTACTS: **Aerocaribe** (☎ 9/928–6790). **Aeroméxico** (☎ 9/920–1260 or 9/920–1265). **Mexicana** (☎ 9/946–1332). **Delta** (☎ 800/241–4141).

AIRPORTS

The Mérida airport is 7 km (4½ mi) west of the city's zócalo, about a 20-minute ride.

A private taxi costs about $9; collective service, about $4, is only for groups (usually a Volkswagen minibus). For both, you pay the taxi-ticket vendor at the airport, not the driver. The inexpensive but irregular Bus 79 goes from the airport to downtown. If you're driving into town, take the airport exit road, make a right at the four-lane Avenida Itzaes (the continuation of Route 180), and follow it to the one-way Calle 59, just past El Centenario Zoological Park. Turn right on Calle 59 and go straight until you reach Calle 62, where you again turn right, and drive a block to the main square. (Parking is difficult here.)

➤ AIRPORT INFORMATION: **Mérida Airport** (☎ 9/946–1300).

BUS TRAVEL

Mérida's municipal buses run daily 5 AM–midnight, but service is somewhat confusing until you master the system. In the downtown area buses go east on Calle 59 and west on Calle 61, north on Calle 60 and south on Calle 62. You can catch a bus heading north to Progreso on Calle 56. Unfortunately, there is no direct bus service from the hotels around the plaza to the long-distance bus station.

There are many long-distance bus lines, including superdeluxe buses with air-conditioning and spacious seats. Many second-class bus lines now also have air-conditioning. All have at least one round-trip run daily to the main archaeological sites and colonial cities. Autotransportes del Sureste, at the second-class bus station, has the best coverage for out-of-the-way places, with daily service to the Guatemalan border, Palenque, and San Cristóbal de las Casas, and five buses daily to Uxmal.

First-class buses, including ADO and UNO, serve Akumal, Cancún, Chichén Itzá, Playa del Carmen, Tulum, Uxmal, Valladolid, and other major Mexican cities from the CAME Station. ADO also has a location at the Fiesta Americana Hotel.

Several other first-class lines go to CAME. ADO has its own terminal next door, the Terminal Unica. These lines have frequent buses to Cancún, Valladolid, and other places east of Mérida.

➤ BUS LINES: **ADO** (☎ 9/924–7868; 9/920–0126 or 9/925–0910 in Fiesta Americana). **Autotransportes del Sureste** (ATS; ☎ 9/923–2287 or 9/924–0830). **Super Expreso** (✉ Calle 70 No. 555, at Calle 71, ☎ 9/924–8391). **TRP** (☎ 9/923–2287 ext. 3412). **UNO** (☎ 9/924–8391).

➤ BUS STATIONS: **CAME Station** (✉ Calle 70 No. 555, at Calle 71, ☎ 9/924–8391 or 9/924–9263). **Second-class bus station** (✉ Calle 69 No. 544, between Calles 68 and 70, ☎ 9/922–2387 or 9/923–2287). **Terminal Unica** (✉ Calle 69 between Calles 68 and 70, ☎ 9/923–2287 or 9/924–0830).

CAR RENTAL

Mérida has almost 20 car-rental agencies, including Budget, Hertz, National, and Thrifty outlets. Prices are sometimes lower if you arrange your rental in advance.

➤ MAJOR AGENCIES: **Budget** (✉ Hyatt Regency, Calle 60 No. 344, at Av. Colón, ☎ 9/942–1226 or 9/925–5453; ✉ Holiday Inn, Av. Colón 498 and Calle 60, ☎ 9/925–5453; ✉ airport, ☎ 9/946–1380). **Hertz** (✉ , ☎ 9/925–7595; ✉ Calle 60 between Calles 55 and 57, ☎ 9/924–2834 or 9/984–0028; ✉ airport, ☎ 9/946–1355 or 9/946–2554). **National** (✉ Fiesta Americana, ☎ 9/925–7524; ✉ airport, ☎ 9/946–1394). **Thrifty** (✉ Calle 60 No. 446-C, between Calles 51 and 49, ☎ 9/923–3440; ✉ airport, ☎ 9/946–2515).

CAR TRAVEL

Driving in Mérida can be frustrating because of the one-way streets (many of which are in effect one-lane because of the parked cars) and because traffic is dense. But having your own wheels is the best way to take excursions from the city. Route 180, the main road along the gulf coast from the Texas border, passes through Mérida en route to

Cancún. Mexico City lies 1,550 km (961 mi) west, Cancún 320 km (198 mi) due east.

The *autopista* is a four-lane toll highway between Mérida and Cancún. Beginning at the town of Kantuníl, 55 km (34 mi) southeast of Mérida, it runs somewhat parallel to Route 180 and cuts driving time between Mérida and Cancún—around 4½ hours—by about one hour and bypasses about four dozen villages. Access to the toll highway is off old Highway 180 and is clearly marked. The highway has clearly marked exits for Valladolid and Pisté (Chichén Itzá), as well as rest stops and gas stations. Tolls between Mérida and Cancún total about $24.

CONSULATES

➤ CONTACTS: **United Kingdom** (⊠ Calle 58 No. 450, at Calle 53, ☎ 9/928–6152). **United States** (⊠ Paseo Montejo 453, ☎ 9/925–5011 or 9/925–5409).

EMERGENCIES

➤ DOCTORS & HOSPITALS: **Clínica Yucatán** (⊠ Calle 66 No. 528, at Calle 65, ☎ 9/924–9391). **Red Cross Hospital** (⊠ Calle 68 No. 533, between Calles 65 and 67, ☎ 9/928–5391).
➤ EMERGENCY SERVICES: **Fire** (☎ 9/924–9242). **General emergency** (☎ 06). **Police** (☎ 9/925–2555). **Red Cross** (⊠ Calle 68 No. 583, at Calle 65, ☎ 9/924–8913).
➤ LATE-NIGHT PHARMACIES: **Farmacia Canto** (⊠ San Fernando branch, Calle 60 at Av. Colón ☎ 9/925–8126). **Farmacia Canto Centro** (⊠ Calle 60 at Calle 63, ☎ 9/928–5027). **Farmacia Yza** (☎ 9/926–6666 delivery or for nearest branch).

MAIL & SHIPPING

Mérida has only one post office, open weekdays 8–6 and Saturday 9–2. However, you can buy postage stamps at handicrafts shops in town. If you must send mail from Mexico, the Mex Post service can speed delivery a bit, even internationally, for a higher fee than regular mail.
➤ POST OFFICE: ⊠ Calle 65 at Calle 56, ☎ 9/928–5404 or 9/924–3590.

MONEY MATTERS

Most banks throughout Mérida are open weekdays 9–5. Banamex has its main offices, open weekdays 9–5 and Saturday 9–1:30, in the handsome Casa de Montejo, on the south side of the main square, with branches at the airport and the Fiesta Americana Hotel. All have automatic teller machines that can be accessed with Cirrus, Plus, MasterCard, and Visa bank cards. Several other banks can be found on Calle 65, between Calles 62 and 60, and on Paseo Montejo, and most have the same automatic teller service.

CURRENCY EXCHANGE

There are several exchange houses in Mérida, including Casa de Cambio del Sureste, open weekdays 9–5 and Saturday 9–1; Centro Cambriano Canto, open weekdays 9–1 and 4–7; and two on the ground level of the Fiesta Americana Hotel, open weekdays 9–5.
➤ EXCHANGE SERVICES: **Casa de Cambio del Sureste** (⊠ Calle 56 at Calle 57, ☎ 9/928–2152). **Centro Cambriano Canto** (⊠ Calle 61 No. 468, between Calles 52 and 54, ☎ 9/928–0458).

TAXIS

Taxis charge beach-resort prices, which makes them a little expensive for this region of Mexico. They don't cruise the streets for passengers and instead are available at 13 taxi stands around the city, or in front of the Hyatt Regency, Holiday Inn, and Fiesta Americana hotels, which are strung out on the same block. The minimum fare is $2. Taxis operate around the clock.

➤ TAXI COMPANIES: **Sitio Parque de la Madre** (☎ 9/928–5322). **Sitio Mejorada** (☎ 9/928–5589).

TELEPHONES

Larger cities such as Mérida have seven-digit phone numbers. Smaller towns such as Ticul have three-digit area codes followed by five-digit numbers.

Mérida has many Ladatel phone booths: at the airport, at all bus stations, in the main plaza, at Avenidas Reforma and Colón, Calle 57 at Calle 64, Calle 59 at Calle 62, and Calle 60 between Calles 55 and 53. You can make local and international direct calls at these public phones. Coin-operated phones are history—these take only Ladatel cards, electronic phone cards you can buy at newsstands and pharmacies.

TOURS

Mérida has more than 50 tour operators, who generally go to the same places. What differs is the mode of transportation—and whether or not the vehicle is air-conditioned and insured.

A two- to three-hour group tour of the city, including museums, parks, public buildings, and monuments, costs $20 to $55 per person. Or you can pick up an open-air sightseeing bus at Parque de Santa Lucía for $6 (departures are Monday through Saturday at 10, 1, 4, and 7 and Sunday at 10 and 1). A day trip to Chichén Itzá, with guide, entrance fee, and lunch, costs approximately $53. For about the same price you can see the ruins of Uxmal and Kabah in the Puuc region; for a few more dollars you can add the neighboring sites of Sayil, Labná, and the Loltún Caves. Most tour operators take credit cards.

Juergen Kremer, a German anthropologist who worked as a rocket scientist earlier in his life, is one of the best guides to the Maya ruins, including Ek Balam, Chichén Ítza, and Uxmal. He speaks German, English, and Maya and can be contacted via the Casa San Juan. Diego Nuñez is an outstanding guide who conducts boat tours of Río Lagartos. He charges $42 for a 2½-hour tour, which accommodates five or six people. He can be found at the Tizimín restaurant called Isla de Contoy, which he runs. Occasionally, Pronatura, a wildlife conservation program, arranges guided one- or two-day trips for groups to Celustún or Rió Lagartos accompanied by a bilingual biologist.

➤ TOUR OPERATORS: **American Express** (⊠ Calle 56 No. 494, between Calles 43 and 45, ☎ 9/942–8200 or 9/924–4326, ℻ 9/942–8270). **Betanzos Internacional** (⊠ Calle 60 No. 463, between Calles 53 and 55, Depto. 1, ☎ 9/923–9966 or 9/923–8594, ℻ 9/923–9966). **Carmen Travel Service** (⊠ Hotel María del Carmen, Calle 63 No. 550, at Calle 68, ☎ 9/924–1212, ℻ 9/924–1288). **Diego Nuñez** (c/o Isla de Contoy, ⊠ Calle 19 No. 12, Tizimín, ☎ 986/20000). **Juergen Kremer** (☎ c/o Casa San Juan, 9/986–2937 or 9/950–1462). **Mayaland Tours** (⊠ Calle 57 between Calles 58 and 61, ☎ 9/928–3075 or 800/235–4079, ℻ 9/928–3077; ⊠ Fiesta Americana, Calles Colón and 60, ☎ ℻ 9/924–6290); request a Mayaland guide rather than a guide subcontractor, because the latter tends to be less professional. **Pronatura** (⊠ Calle 1-D No. 254-A, Campestra, ☎ ℻ 9/925–3787). **Turismo Aviomar** (⊠ Calle 58A No. 500-C, Glorieta San Fernando, ☎ 9/920–0444 or 9/920–0443, ℻ 9/925–5064).

VISITOR INFORMATION

Mérida has an information kiosk at the airport that's open daily 8–8. The City Tourist Information Center and the kiosk at Calle 39 and Paso de Montejo are open weekdays 8–2 and 5–7. The state tourist center is open daily 8–8.

➤ Mérida: **City Tourist Information Center** (✉ Calle 59 between Calles 60 and 62, ☎ 9/928–6547). **State Tourist Information Center** (✉ Teatro Peón Contreras, Calle 60 between Calles 57 and 59, ☎ 9/924–9290).

THE STATE OF CAMPECHE

Updated by
Shelagh
McNally

C AMPECHE, THE LEAST VISITED and most underrated corner of the Yucatán, is the perfect place for adventure. The people here are friendly and welcoming, the colonial cities and towns retain an air of history, and protected biospheres, farmland, and jungle traverse the remaining expanse. The forts of Campeche City have 300-year-old cannons pointing across the Gulf of Mexico, relics from pirate days. Beyond its walls, the ancient pyramids and ornate temples of ancient Maya kingdoms—some of the most important discoveries in the Maya empire to date—lie waiting in tropical forests. The terrain of the State of Campeche varies, from the northeastern flatlands to the rolling mountains of the south. More than 60% of the territory is covered by jungle. The Gulf Stream keeps temperatures at about 26°C (78°F) year-round, but the humid, tropical climate is eased by evening breezes.

Campeche City

The city of Campeche has a time-weathered and lovely feel to it—no contrived, ultramodern tourist glitz here—just a friendly city by the sea (population 270,000) that is proud of its heritage and welcomes all to share in it. This good-humored, open-minded attitude is described as *campechano*, an adjective that means "easygoing and cheerful."

Because it has been walled since 1686, most of the historic downtown is neatly contained in an area measuring just five blocks by nine blocks. The city is easily navigable—on foot, that is. With its narrow cobblestone roads and lack of parking spaces, driving here is a frustrating exercise. On strategic corners surrounding the old city, or Viejo Campeche, stand the seven remaining *baluartes* (bastions) in various stages of disrepair. These were once connected by a 3-km (2-mi) wall in a hexagonal fortification that was built to safeguard the city against the pirates who continually ransacked it. Only short stretches of the wall still stand, and two stone archways—one facing the sea, the other the land—are all that remain of the four gates that once provided the only means of access to Campeche.

A Good Walk

The Ciudad Viejo, the old city center, is the best place to start a walking tour, beginning with the **Baluarte de la Soledad** ㊸ and its small Maya stelae museum. From the nearby Parque Principal, the city's central plaza, take a short stroll to view some of the Yucatán Peninsula's most stately Spanish colonial architecture, including the **Catedral** ㊹ and the adjacent **Casa Seis** ㊺. On Calle 8 between Calles 51 and 53 is the Mansión Carvajal; **Baluarte de Santiago** ㊻ is about a block to the north. Head east on Calle 51 to the small, well-fortified **Baluarte de San Pedro** ㊼, on the corner of Circuito Baluartes and

Campeche City

Calle 18. Walk south along Calle 18 to **Puerta de Tierra** ㊽ and the Baluarte San Juan, and then turn down **Calle 59** ㊾ past the beautiful **Iglesia de San Francisquito** ㊿. Turn down Calle 10 to reach the **Ex-Templo de San José** �51 and the **Iglesia de San Román** �52. Both are considered masterpieces of colonial religious architecture. Proceed north along Calle 8 for a look at the contrasting, modernistic designs of the Congreso del Estado and the Palacio del Gobierno. Finish the walk along the beachfront malecón.

Sights to See

㊸ **Baluarte de la Soledad.** Originally built to protect the **Puerte de Mar** (sea door), one of the four city gates, through which all seafarers were forced to pass, this bastion is on the south side of Parque Principal. The largest of the bastions, this one has comparatively complete parapets and embrasures that offer a sweeping view of the cathedral, municipal buildings, and the 16th- to 19th-century houses along Calle 8. The **Museo de las Estelas** (Stelae Museum) is housed inside. ⊠ *Calles 8 and 57,* ☏ *no phone.* ▦ *$2.* ☼ *Mon. 8–2, Tues.–Sat. 8–8, Sun. 8–6.*

㊼ **Baluarte de San Pedro.** Built in 1686 to protect the city from land attacks by pirates, this bastion's thick walls, flanked by watchtowers, now house a handicrafts and souvenir shop and a satellite office for the Secretary of Tourism, where you can book an English tour guide. Many of the tours to ruins such as Calakmul and Edzná leave from this point. ⊠ *Av. Gobernadores and Circuito Baluartes,* ☏ *no phone.* ▦ *Free.* ☼ *Mon.–Sat. 9–9.*

㊻ **Baluarte de Santiago.** The last of the bastions to be built (1704) has been transformed into the **X' much Haltún Botanical Gardens.** More than 200 plant species from the region are house here, including the *ceiba, campeachy,* and *balche* trees. Although the original bastion was demolished at the turn of the 20th century, then rebuilt in the 1950s, architecturally this fort looks much the same as the others in Campeche. ⊠ *Calles 8 and 59, Circuito Baluartes,* ☎ *no phone.* 🖘 *Donation.* ⊙ *Weekdays 9–4 and 6:30–8:30, Sat. 9–1 and 5–8, Sun. 9–1.*

㊾ Calle 59. On this city street, between Calles 8 and 18, once stood some of Campeche's finest homes, many of them two stories high, with the ground floors serving as warehouses and the upper floors as residences. The richest inhabitants built as close to the sea as possible, in case escape became necessary. To see the oldest houses in Campeche, walk south along Calle 10 past Circuito Baluartes to where it meets the malecón into the San Roman neighborhood.

Ⓒ ㊺ Casa Seis (House No. 6). One of the first colonial homes built in Campeche, this is now the city's Cultural Center. It has been beautifully restored—the rooms are furnished with original antiques and a few reproductions to create a replica of a typical 19th-century colonial house. The original frescoes bordering the tops of the walls remain, some dating from 1500. The courtyard has Moorish architecture offset by lovely 18th-century stained-glass windows; it's used as an exhibit area, with displays of various sites in the city. The two largest bedrooms have been converted into an art gallery and a bookstore. There's a small restaurant off the original kitchen area that serves excellent local specialities. ⊠ *Calle 57, across from main plaza,* ☎ *9/816–1782.* 🖘 *Free.* ⊙ *Daily 9–9.*

㊹ Catedral. It took two centuries (from 1650 to 1850) to finish this grand building, and as a result, it incorporates both neoclassical and Renaissance elements. The present cathedral occupies the site of Montejo's original church, which was built in 1540 on what is now Calle 55, between Calles 8 and 10. The simple exterior is capped with two bulbous towers rising on each side of the gracefully curved stone entrances, the fluted pilasters echoing those of the towers. Sculptures of saints in niches recall French Gothic cathedrals. The interior is no less impressive, with a single limestone nave, supported by Doric columns set with Corinthian capitals, arching toward the huge octagonal dome above a black-and-white marble floor. The pièce de résistance, however, is the magnificent Holy Sepulchre, carved from ebony and decorated with a multitude of stamped silver angels. ⊠ *North side of the Plaza Principal.* ⊙ *Daily 6–noon and 5:30–7.*

㊿ Ex-Templo de San José. The Jesuits built this fine Baroque structure in 1756, and today it is the most beautiful of the city's churches. It has a block-long facade and a portal that is completely covered with blue-and-yellow Talavera tiles and crowned with seven narrow stone finials that resemble both the roof combs on many Maya temples and the combs Spanish women used to wear as part of their elaborate hairdos. ⊠ *Calle 10 at Calle 65.*

Ⓒ Fuerte de San Miguel. The scenic Avenida Ruíz Cortines near the south end of the city winds its way to a hilltop, where this fort commands one of the grandest views overlooking the city and the Gulf of Mexico. Built in 1771, the fort was positioned to bombard enemy ships with cannonballs. But as soon as it was completed, pirates stopped attacking the city. Its impressive cannons were fired only once, in 1842, when General Santa Anna used Fuerte de San Miguel to put down a revolt by Yucatecan separatists seeking independence from Mexico. The fort houses the **Museo de la Cultura Maya,** which was renovated in 2001. The museum has some world-class exhibits that include Maya mummies and funeral masks, as well as jewelry and pottery found at various tombs in the Calakmul ruins. ⊠ *Av. Francisco Morazán s/n, north of town center,* ☎ *no phone.* ⌦ *$1.70.* ⊙ *Daily 8–8.*

🕲 **Fuerte de San José "el Alto."** This lofty fortress—*el alto* means "the tall"—at the opposite end of town from Fuerte de San Miguel, is home to the **Museo de Armas y Barcos** (Museum of Arms and Boats). The displays focus on 18th-century weapons of siege and defense used in the many wars fought against the pirates. Also look for scale ships-in-a-bottle, manuscripts, and religious art. ⊠ *Av. Escénica s/n, south of downtown,* ☎ *no phone.* ⌦ *$1.70.* ⊙ *Tues.–Sun. 8–8.*

㊿ **Iglesia de San Roque or San Francisquito.** With its elaborately carved altars, Baroque columns adorned with gold leaf, and carved, wooden pews and creches with statues of San Francisco, this long, narrow church—built as a convent in 1565—adds to historic Calle 59's old-fashioned beauty. ⊠ *Calle 12 at Calle 59.* ⊙ *Daily 8:30–noon and 5–7.*

㉒ **Iglesia de San Román.** Just outside the intramural boundary in the barrio of the same name, at Calles 10 and Bravo, San Román, with its bulbous bell tower typical of other Yucatán churches, was built to house the *naboríos* (Indians brought by the Spaniards to aid in the conquest). The barrio, like other neighborhoods, grew up around the church. Built in the early part of the 16th century, the church became central to the lives of the Indians when an ebony image of Christ, the "Black Christ," was brought from Italy in about 1575. The Indians had been skeptical about Christianity, but this Christ figure came to be associated with miracles. The legend goes that a ship that refused to carry the tradesman and his precious statue was wrecked, while the ship that did take him on board reached Campeche in record time. ⊠ *Calles 10 y Bravo.* ⊙ *Daily 7–1 and 3–7.*

🕲 **㊽** **Puerta de Tierra (Land Gate).** Old Campeche ends here, at the only one of the four city gates with its basic structure intact. The walls, arches, and gates were refurbished in 1987. The stone arch intercepts a stretch of the partially crenulated wall, 26 ft high and 10 ft thick, that once encircled the city. You can walk along the full length of the wall to the **Baluarte San Juan,** where there are some excellent views of both the old and new city. The staircase leads down to an old well, underground storage area, and dungeon. There is a two-hour light show offered at Puerta de Tierra in Spanish and English, Tuesday through Saturday at 8:30 PM, that includes a torchlight walk along the wall and a visit to the underground chambers at Baluarte San Juan. The schedule is sometimes reduced in low season, so check with the tourist office. ⊠ *Calles 18 and 59.* ⌦ *$1.70.* ⊙ *Daily 8–5.*

Dining and Lodging

$$–$$$
★ ✕ **La Pigua.** A favorite with local professionals lingering over long lunches, La Pigua is arguably the best seafood restaurant in town, with the most pleasant ambience. The restaurant's two long glass walls form a terrarium of trees and plants. A truly ambitious lunch would start with a seafood cocktail or plate of cold crab claws, followed by *camarones al coco* (fried shrimp with a layer of crispy coconut) and, for dessert, local peaches drenched in sweet liqueurs. ⊠ *Av. Miguel Alemán 197-A,* ☎ *9/811–1365. MC, V. No dinner.*

$–$$
★ ✕ **Chez Fernando.** In an old colonial house, this café-style restaurant offers French-style fresh pastas, salads, fish, chicken, and steak. The lasagna Florentine, pollo Dijon, and fettuccine gambetti are all excellent. The chocolate mousse is the best in the state. The decor, like the food, is a departure from Campechano tradition—the purple walls are decorated with watercolor sketches of France and the music is French. ⊠ *Calle 12, between Calles 51 and 53,* ☎ *9/816–3972. No credit cards.*

$-$$ ✕ **El Guacamayo.** One of the oldest restaurants in Campeche (1947), this eatery is popular with locals and tourists. It serves regional specialties such as *cochinita pibíl* (coconut shrimp) and excellent cream soups on the outdoor patio or indoors in the hacienda-style dining room. After your dinner be sure to visit the mascot—a colorful Guacamayo bird. ☒ *Av. Miguel Alémán 143,* ☎ *9/816–4636. AE, MC, V.*

$-$$ ✕ **Marganzo.** Traditional Campeche cuisine is served by a tradi-
★ tionally attired waitstaff at this colorful and rustic restaurant a half block south of the plaza. Recommended is the *pompano en escabeche* (grilled fish with chiles and orange juice), as well as the fresh shrimp dishes. ☒ *Calle 8 No. 267, between Calles 57 and 59,* ☎ *9/811–3898. AE, MC, V.*

$$ ▥ **Del Mar Hotel.** This is the fanciest hotel in town, even if by inter-
★ national standards it is quite average. It has many amenities, includ-ing bathtubs. Rooms are fairly large, with tasteful drapes and floor tiles, rattan furniture, color cable TV, and balconies that overlook the pool or the bay across the street. The lobby coffee shop, El Poquito, serves excellent meals, and Lafitte's, the bar-restaurant, offers room service until AM. ☒ *Av. Ruíz Cortines 51 (on the waterfront) 24000,* ☎ *9/816–2233,* FAX *9/811–1618,* WEB *www.delmar.com. 138 rooms, 11 suites. Restaurant, coffee shop, air-conditioning, pool, travel services, free parking. AE, MC, V.*

$$ ▥ **Hotel America.** A colonial home converted into a hotel, this hotel has three levels of rooms that open onto large corridors with a dramatic black-and-white checked floor offsetting the white Moorish arches. The rooms all have two double beds, ceiling fans, local television, and bamboo furniture. Rooms facing the street have balconies but are noisier. This is one of the few hotels in the center with parking. ☒ *Calle 10 No. 252, 24000,* ☎ *9/816–4588,* FAX *9/816–4576,* WEB *www.hotelamerica.com. 52 rooms. Fans, parking (fee). AE, MC, V.*

$ ▥ **Colonial.** The former home of a high-ranking army lieutenant, this
★ building dates back to 1812 but was converted into a hotel in the 1940s, when its wonderful colorful tiles were added. All rooms are delight-fully different, as befits a colonial mansion, with ceiling fans or air-conditioning (in four of the rooms), cool cotton bedding, good mattresses, tile bathrooms, and window screens. Most rooms still have the origi-nal telephones and antique plumbing (which works quite well), adding to the romance of the hotel. Rooms 16, 18, 27, and 28 have wonder-ful views of the cathedral and city at night. Public areas include two leafy patios, a small sun roof, and a sitting room on the second floor. ☒ *Calle 14 No. 122, between Calles 55 and 57, 24000,* ☎ *9/816–2222. 30 rooms. Air-conditioning, fans. No credit cards.*

Nightlife and the Arts

KY8 (☒ Calle 8 between Calles 59 and 61, ☎ no phone) plays dance music popular with locals. The high-tech **Millenium** (☒ Av. Resurgimiento 112, ☎ 9/818–4555) has laser shows and dance music on Friday and Saturday. The largest dance club in Campeche is **Platform 21** (☒ Av. López Mateos, ☎ no phone), north of the city and open Wednesday through Saturday nights. You need to take a taxi to get here.

Outdoor Activities and Sports

Fishing and birding are popular throughout the state of Campeche. Con-tact **Don José Sansores** at the Snook Inn in Champotón (☒ Calle 30 No. 1, ☎ FAX 9/828–0018) to arrange sportfishing or wildlife photo excursions in the Champotón area. **Francisco Jávier Hernandez Romero** (☒ La Pigua restaurant, Av. Miguel Alemán 179–A, ☎ 9/811–3365) can arrange boat or fishing trips to the Peténes Ecological Reserve.

Shopping

Because Campeche is a seaport, ships-in-a-bottle, tacky statues made of seashells, and mother-of-pearl and black coral jewelry are everywhere. Buying black coral is environmentally harmful, since the harvesting of the coral destroys the reef that takes thousands of years to grow.

In a lovely old mansion, the government-run **Casa de Artesanía Tukulna** (✉ Calle 10 No. 333, between Calles 59 and 61, ☎ 9/816–9098) sells well-made embroidered dresses, blouses, regional dress for men and women, hammocks, jewelry, and baskets. The house is beautiful; it's worth a visit if only to admire the interior. The shop is open Monday through Saturday 9–8 and Sunday 10–2.

From Campeche City to Mérida on Highway 261

This is the long way to reach the Yucatán capital of Mérida, passing by the Chenes ruins of southeastern Campeche. Chenes-style temples are easily recognized by their elaborate stucco facades decorated with geometric designs and giant masks of jaguars, and birds. Also characteristic of the style are doorways shaped like the open mouth of a monster. It is a scenic route, leading through green hills with tall dark forests and valleys covered by low scrub, cornfields, and citrus orchards.

Edzná

 55 km (34 mi) southeast of Campeche City.

The Maya ruin of Edzná deserves more fame than it has. Archaeologists consider it one of the peninsula's most important ruins because of the crucial transitional role it played among several architectural styles. Occupied from around 300 BC to AD 1450, Edzná reached its pinnacle between AD 600 to AD 900. Over the course of several hundred years, Edzná grew from a humble agricultural settlement into a major political-religious center. It's now known that Edzná was the collection point for agricultural products grown in the region. Some products were sent to the Peté in Guatemala in exchange for hand-carved ritual objects and adornments for the site.

Commanding center stage in the **Great Acropolis** (Gran Acrópolis) is the **Five-Story Pyramid** (Pirámide de los Cinco Pisos), which rises 102 ft. The structure consists of five levels, terminating in a tiny temple crowned by a roof comb. Hieroglyphs have been carved into the vertical face of the 15 steps between each level, and numerous stelae depict the opulent attire and adornment of the ruling class—quetzal feathers, jade pectorals, and skirts of jaguar skin. The **House of the Moon, Southwest Temple, Northwest Temple, Temezcal** (steam bath), **Puuc Courtyard,** and **Platform of the Knives** are within this complex. In 1992 Campeche archaeologist Antonio Benavides discovered that the Five-Story Pyramid was so constructed that, during certain dates of the year, the setting sun would illuminate the mask of the sun god, Itzamná, inside one of the pyramid's rooms. This happens annually on May 1, 2, and 3, the beginning of the planting season for the Maya, and on August 7, 8, and 9, the days of harvesting and thanking the god for his help. South of the Great Acropolis lies the **Small Acropolis,** whose four buildings each face a cardinal point in the compass. Carved into the **Temple of the Masks (Building 414),** adjacent to the Small Acropolis, are some masks of the sun god with huge protruding eye sockets and crossed eyes.

If you're not driving, consider taking one of the inexpensive day trips offered by most travel agencies in Campeche; this is far easier than trying to get to Edzná by municipal buses. **Servicios Turísticos Picazh** (✉ Calle 16 No. 348, between Calles 57 and 59, ☎ 9/816–4426) offers transportation only or guided service to Edzná at reasonable prices. ✉ *Rte. 261 east from Campeche City for 44 km (27 mi) to Cayal, then Rte. 188 southeast for 18 km (11 mi),* ☎ *no phone.* 🎟 *$2, free Sun.* ☉ *Daily 8–5.*

The State of Campeche A to Z

AIR TRAVEL
Aeroméxico has one flight daily from Mexico City to Campeche City.
➤ CONTACT: **Aeroméxico** (☎ 981/65678).

BUS TRAVEL
ADO, a first-class line, runs buses to Campeche City from Mérida almost every hour, and to Ciudad del Carmen, Mexico City, Tampico, Veracruz, and Villahermosa regularly, but less frequently. Adjacent to the ADO station, the second-class bus station has service on Autobuses del Sur to intermediate points throughout the Yucatán Peninsula. A half block from the ADO station, Nuevos Horizontes has first-class service to Mérida, Ciudad del Carmen, Mexico City, Veracruz, Cancún, Jalapa, Puebla, and Villahermosa at least once a day. Try to book your bus tickets to avoid an extended stopover in Escárcega, along Route 261. Though the government has beefed up security—Escárcega was an unsafe spot for tourists, with bus passengers the targets of robberies and assaults—and things have calmed down quite a bit, it is still not a place to linger.

Within Campeche City, buses run along Avenida Ruíz Cortines and cost about 30¢.
➤ BUS INFORMATION: **ADO** (✉ Av. Gobernadores 289, at Calle 45, along Rte. 261 to Mérida, ☎ 981/14334 or 981/63445). **Autobuses del Sur** (☎ 981/63445 or 981/62802, ext. 2405). **Nuevos Horizontes** (✉ Av. Gobernadores 575, between Calles 15 and 17, ☎ 981/10261).

CAR RENTAL
Reliable rental agencies are AutoRent—which charges $45 a day including insurance and allows 200 km (120 mi) per day—and the slightly more expensive Maya Rent a Car, which rents small Chevys for $59 a day, including insurance and unlimited mileage.
➤ MAJOR AGENCIES: **AutoRent** (✉ Hotel del Paseo, Calle 8 No. 215, ☎ 981/1–01–00). **Maya Rent a Car** (✉ Del Mar Hotel, Av. Ruíz Cortínez, at Calle 59, ☎ 981/62233, ✉AX 981/11618), which rents small Chevys for $59 a day, including insurance and unlimited mileage.

CAR TRAVEL
Campeche City is about 1½ hours from Mérida along the 160-km (99-mi) *via corta* (short way), Route 180. The alternative route, the 250-km (155-mi) *via larga* (long way), Route 261, takes at least six hours but passes the major Maya ruins of Uxmal, Kabah, and Sayil. Villahermosa is about six hours away if you drive inland via the town of Francisco Escárcega but longer if you hug the Gulf and cross the bridge at Ciudad del Carmen.

EMERGENCIES
Dial **06** throughout Campeche state for emergencies.
➤ DOCTORS: **Social Security Clinic** (✉ Av. López Mateos and Talamantes, ☎ 981/61855 or 981/65202).

➤ EMERGENCY SERVICES: **Green Angels** (☎ 981/60934 or 981/12544). **Police** (✉ Av. Resurgimiento 77, Col. Lazareto, ☎ 981/62309). **Red Cross** (✉ Av. Las Palmas, at Ah-Kim-Pech s/n, Campeche City, ☎ 981/52411). ➤ HOSPITALS: **Hospital General** (✉ Av. Central, at Circuito Baluartes, ☎ 981/60920 or 981/64233). ➤ 24-HOUR PHARMACIES: **Clínica Campeche** (✉ Av. Central 65, near the Social Security Clinic, Campeche City, ☎ 981/65612).

MAIL & SHIPPING
The post office (*correos*) in Campeche City is open weekdays 8–8, Saturday 9–1. ➤ POST OFFICE: **Campeche City** (✉ Av. 16 de Septiembre, between Calles 53 and 55, ☎ 981/62134).

MONEY MATTERS
Campeche City banks are open weekdays 9–1. Those where you can exchange money include Banamex and Bancomer.

➤ BANKS & EXCHANGE SERVICES: **Banamex** (✉ Calle 53 No. 15, at Calle 10, ☎ 981/65251). **Bancomer** (✉ Av. 16 de Septiembre 120, ☎ 981/66622).

TAXIS
Taxis can be hailed on the street in Campeche City or, more reliably, commissioned from the main taxi stand, or at stands by the bus stations and market. Because of the scarcity of taxis, it's quite common to share them with other people headed in the same direction as you. Don't be surprised to see one already occupied slow down to where you are standing, or flash its lights to indicate that the cab driver thinks he can pick up another fare. A shared cab ride costs under $1. If you have one to yourself, it's $1.50–$3. ➤ TAXIS: **Main taxi stand** (✉ Calle 8 between Calles 55 and 53, ☎ 981/53036).

TELEPHONES
TelMex phones that take the electronic Ladatel cards are found throughout the city. Intertel has phone booths for long-distance calls. Another *larga distancia* (long distance) store can be found at the corner of Calles 10 and 59. ➤ SERVICES: **Intertel** (✉ Calle 57 No. 1, ☎ 981/66863, FAX 981/67334).

TOURS
Trolley tours of Campeche City leave from the Plaza Principal daily at 9:30, 6, and 8. The one-hour, bilingual tour costs 70¢. On weekends there is an additional tour at 7 PM. You can buy tickets on board the trolley, or ahead of time in the municipal tourist office right next to the cathedral, also on the plaza. One route takes you through the city and another goes to the forts—check to see which route is being offered before boarding.

TRAVEL AGENCIES
➤ LOCAL AGENTS: **American Express/VIPs** (✉ Prolongación Calle 59, Edificio Belmar, Depto. 5, ☎ 981/11010 or 981/11000, FAX 981/68333). **Destinos Maya** (✉ Av. Miguel Alemán 162 [altos], Locale 106, ☎ 981/10934; 713/440–0291 in the U.S., FAX 981/10934). **Viajes Campeche** (✉ Calle 10 No. 329, between Calles 61 and 63, ☎ 981/65233, FAX 981/62844).

VISITOR INFORMATION
The tourist office is open daily 9–3 and 5–8. On weekends a guard hands out maps and literature but has little knowledge. The municipal tourist

office is open daily 8–2:30 and 4–8. The staff speaks very little English, but you can pick up a map. City trolley tours are booked here.

➤ TOURIST INFORMATION: **Tourist office** (✉ Av. Ruíz Cortines s/n, Plaza Moch-Couoh, across the street from the Palacio del Gobierno, ☎ 981/65593, ☎ 🅵🅰🆇 981/66767). **Municipal tourist office** (✉ Calle 55, just west of the cathedral, ☎ 981/13989 or 981/13990).

14 BACKGROUND AND ESSENTIALS

Maps of Mexico

Chronology

Spanish Vocabulary

Further Reading

Smart Travel Tips A to Z

Mexico

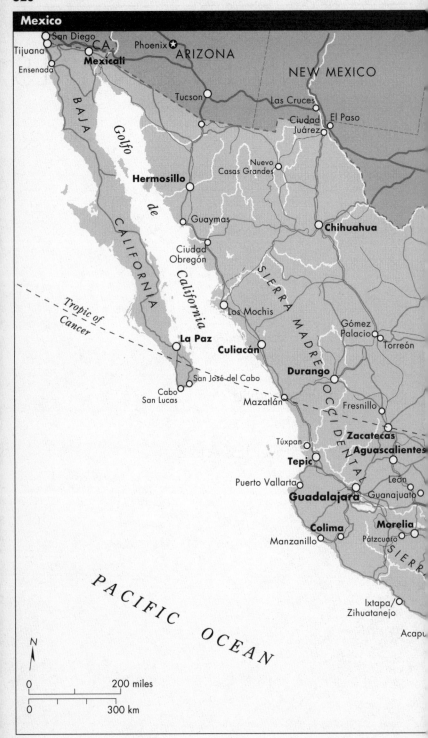

San Diego
Tijuana
Ensenada
CA
Phoenix ☆
ARIZONA
Mexicali
NEW MEXICO
Tucson
Las Cruces
El Paso
Ciudad
Juárez
BAJA
Golfo
Nuevo
Casas Grandes
Chihuahua
Hermosillo
de
Guaymas
CALIFORNIA
Ciudad
Obregón
California
SIERRA
Tropic of
Cancer
Los Mochis
Gómez
Palacio
Torreón
La Paz
Culiacán
MADRE
San José del Cabo
Durango
Cabo
San Lucas
Mazatlán
Fresnillo
OCCIDENTAL
Túxpan
Zacatecas
Aguascalientes
Tepic
Puerto Vallarta
León
Guadalajara
Guanajuato
Colima
Morelia
Manzanillo
Pátzcuaro
SIERRA
PACIFIC
Ixtapa/
Zihuatanejo
Acapu
OCEAN
N

0   200 miles

0   300 km

Mexican States and Capitals

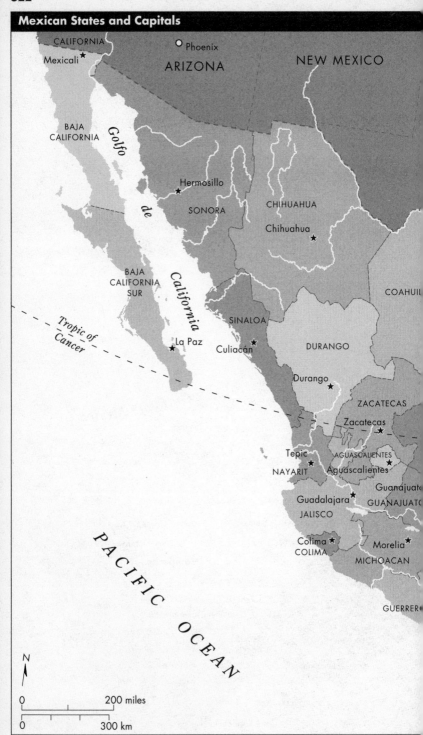

CALIFORNIA

Mexicali ★

○ Phoenix

ARIZONA

NEW MEXICO

BAJA CALIFORNIA

Golfo

de

California

Hermosillo ★

SONORA

CHIHUAHUA

Chihuahua ★

COAHUIL

BAJA CALIFORNIA SUR

Tropic of Cancer

La Paz ★

SINALOA

Culiacán ★

DURANGO

Durango ★

ZACATECAS

Zacatecas ★

Tepic ★

NAYARIT

AGUASCALIENTES

Aguascalientes ★

Guanajuate

Guadalajara ★

JALISCO

GUANAJUATO

Colima ★

COLIMA

Morelia ★

MICHOACAN

PACIFIC OCEAN

GUERRER

N

0   200 miles

0   300 km

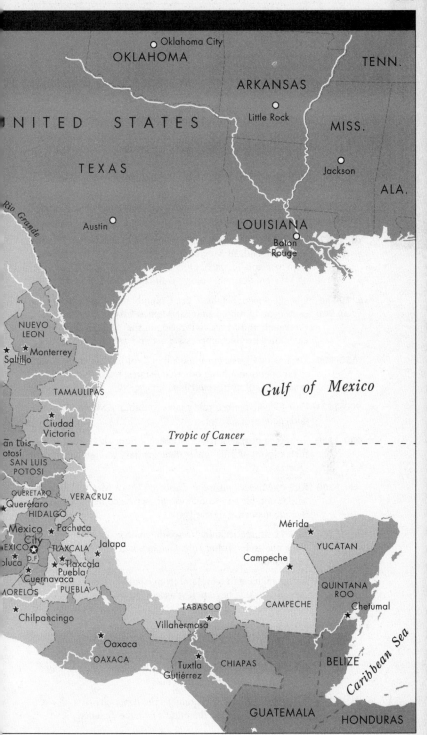

OKLAHOMA

Oklahoma City

ARKANSAS

TENN.

UNITED STATES

Little Rock

MISS.

TEXAS

Jackson

ALA.

Rio Grande

Austin

LOUISIANA

Baton Rouge

NUEVO LEON

Monterrey

Saltillo

Gulf of Mexico

TAMAULIPAS

Ciudad Victoria

Tropic of Cancer

San Luis Potosí

SAN LUIS POTOSI

QUERETARO

VERACRUZ

Querétaro

HIDALGO

Mérida

Mexico City

Pachuca

YUCATAN

MEXICO

TLAXCALA

Jalapa

Campeche

oluca

D.F.

Tlaxcala

Puebla

QUINTANA ROO

Cuernavaca

PUEBLA

Chetumal

MORELOS

TABASCO

CAMPECHE

Chilpancingo

Villahermosa

Caribbean Sea

Oaxaca

OAXACA

Tuxtla Gutiérrez

CHIAPAS

BELIZE

GUATEMALA

HONDURAS

MEXICO AT A GLANCE

Pre-Columbian Mexico

ca. 50,000 BC Asian nomads cross land bridge over the Bering Strait to North America, gradually migrate south.

ca. 5000–2000 BC Archaic period, which marked the beginnings of agriculture and village life.

ca. 2000–200 BC Formative or pre-Classic period: development of pottery, incipient political structures.

ca. 1500–900 BC The powerful and sophisticated Olmec civilization develops along the Gulf of Mexico in the present-day states of Veracruz and Tabasco. Olmec culture, the "mother culture" of Mexico, flourishes along Gulf coast.

ca. 200 BC–AD 900 Classic period: height of pre-Columbian culture. Three centers at Teotihuacán (near Mexico City), Monte Albán (Oaxaca), and Maya civilization in the Yucatán. Priest-run city-states produce impressive art and architecture.

650–900 Decline of Classic cultures: fall of Teotihuacán ca. 650 leads to competition among other city-states, exacerbated by migrations of northern tribes.

ca. 900–1521 Post-Classic period: rule passes to military; war and war gods gain prominence.

ca. 900–1150 Toltecs, a northern tribe, establish a flourishing culture at their capital of Tula under the legendary monarch Topiltzin-Quetzalcóatl.

ca. 1200 Rise of Mixtec culture at Zapotec sites of Monte Albán and Mitla; notable for production of picture codices, which include historical narratives.

ca. 1000–1450 Maya culture, declining in south, emerges in the Yucatán; under Toltec rule, Chichén Itzá dominates the peninsula.

1111 Aztecs migrate to mainland from island home off the Nayarit coast. They are not welcomed by the peoples of central Mexico.

1150–1350 Following the fall of Tula, first the Chichimecs, then the Tepanecs assert hegemony over central Mexico. The Tepanec tyrant Tezozómoc (1320–1426), like his contemporaries in Renaissance Italy, establishes his power with murder and treachery.

1376 Tezozómoc grants autonomy to the Aztec city of Tenochtitlán, built in the middle of Lake Texcoco.

1420–1500 Aztecs extend their rule to much of central and southern Mexico. A warrior society, they build a great city at Tenochtitlán.

1502 Moctezuma II (1466–1520) assumes throne at the height of Aztec culture and political power.

1517 Spanish expedition under Francisco Hernandez de Córdoba (1475–1526) lands on Yucatán coast.

1519 Hernán Cortés (1485–1547) lands in Cozumel, founds Veracruz, and determines to conquer. Steel weapons, horses, and smallpox, combined with a belief that Cortés was the resurrected Topiltzin-Quetzalcóatl, minimize Aztec resistance. Cortés enters Tenochtitlán and captures Moctezuma.

The Colonial Period

1520–21 Moctezuma is killed; Tenochtitlán falls to Cortés. The last Aztec emperor, Cuauhtémoc, is executed.

1528 Juan de Zumarraga (1468–1548) arrives as bishop of Mexico City, gains title "Protector of the Indians"; conversion to Catholicism begins.

1535 First Spanish viceroy arrives in Mexico.

1537 Pope Paul III issues a bull declaring that native Mexicans are indeed human and not beasts. First printing press arrives in Mexico City.

1546–48 Silver deposits discovered at Zacatecas.

1547 Spanish conquest of Aztec Empire—now known as "New Spain"—completed, at enormous cost to native peoples.

1553 Royal and Pontifical University of Mexico, first university in the New World, opens.

1571 The Spanish Inquisition established in New Spain; it is not abolished until 1820.

1609 Northern capital of New Spain established at Santa Fe (New Mexico).

1651 Birth of Sor (Sister) Juana Inés de la Cruz, greatest poet of colonial Mexico (d. 1695).

1718 Franciscan missionaries settle in Texas, which becomes part of New Spain.

1765 Charles III of Spain (1716–88) sends José de Galvez to tour New Spain and propose reforms.

1769 Franciscan Junípero Serra establishes missions in California, extending Spanish hegemony.

1788 Death of Charles III; his reforms improved administration, but also raised social and political expectations among the colonial population, which were not fulfilled.

1808 Napoléon invades Spain, leaving a power vacuum in New Spain.

The War of Independence

1810 September 16: Father Miguel Hidalgo y Costilla (1753–1811) preaches his *Grito de Dolores,* sparking rebellion.

1811 Hidalgo is captured and executed; leadership of the movement passes to Father José Maria Morelos y Pavón (1765–1815).

1813 Morelos calls a congress at Chilpancingo, which drafts a Declaration of Independence.

1815 Morelos is captured and executed.

The Early National Period

1821 Vicente Guerrero, a rebel leader, and Agustín de Iturbide (1783–1824), a Spanish colonel converted to the rebel cause, rejuvenate the Independence movement. Spain recognizes Mexican independence with the Treaty of Córdoba.

1822 Iturbide is named Emperor of Mexico, which stretches from California through Central America.

1823 After 10 months in office, Emperor Agustín is turned out.

1824 A new constitution creates a federal republic, the Estados Unidos Mexicanos; modeled on the U.S. Constitution, the Mexican version retains the privileges of the Catholic Church and gives the president extraordinary "emergency" powers.

1829 President Vicente Guerrero abolishes slavery. A Spanish attempt at reconquest is halted by General Antonio López de Santa Anna (1794–1876), already a hero for his role in the overthrow of Emperor Agustín.

1833 Santa Anna is elected president by a huge majority; he holds the office for 11 of its 36 changes of hands by 1855.

1836 Although voted in as a liberal, Santa Anna abolishes the 1824 constitution. Already dismayed at the abolition of slavery, Texas—whose population is largely American—declares its independence. Santa Anna successfully besieges the Texans at the Alamo. But a month later he is captured by Sam Houston following the Battle of San Jacinto. Texas gains its independence as the Lone Star Republic.

1846 The U.S. decision to annex Texas leads to war.

1848 The treaty of Guadalupe Hidalgo reduces Mexico's territory by half, ceding present-day Texas, New Mexico, Arizona, California, Nevada, Utah, and part of Colorado to the United States.

1853 Santa Anna agrees to the Gadsden Purchase, ceding a further 48,000 square km (30,000 square mi) to the United States.

The Reform and French Intervention

1855 The Revolution of Ayutla topples Santa Anna and leads to the period of The Reform.

1857 The liberal Constitution of 1857 disestablishes the Catholic Church, among other measures.

1858–61 The Civil War of the Reform ends in liberal victory. Benito Juárez (1806–72) is elected president. France, Spain, and Britain agree jointly to occupy the customs house at Veracruz to force payment of Mexico's huge foreign debt.

1862 Spain and Britain withdraw their forces; the French, seeking empire, march inland. On May 5, General Porfirio Díaz repulses the French at Puebla.

1863 Strengthened with reinforcements, the French occupy Mexico City. Napoléon III of France appoints Archduke Ferdinand Maximilian of Austria (1832–67) as Emperor of Mexico.

1864 Maximilian and his empress Charlotte, known as Carlotta, land at Veracruz.

1867 With U.S. assistance, Juárez overthrows Mexico's second empire. Maximilian is executed; Carlotta, pleading his case in France, goes mad.

1872 Juárez dies in office. The Mexico City–Veracruz railway is completed, symbol of the new progressivist mood.

The Porfiriato

1876 Porfirio Díaz (1830–1915) comes to power in the Revolution of Tuxtepec; he holds office nearly continuously until 1911. With his advisors, the *cientificos,* he forces modernization and balances the budget for the first time in Mexican history. But the social cost is high.

1886 Birth of Diego Rivera (d. 1957).

1890 José Schneider, who is of German ancestry, founds the Cerveceria Cuauhtémoc, brewer of Carta Blanca.

1900 Jesús, Enrique, and Ricardo Flores Magón publish the anti-Díaz newspaper *La Regeneración.* Suppressed, the brothers move their campaign to the United States, first to San Antonio, then to St. Louis.

1906 The Flores Magón group publish their Liberal Plan, a proposal for reform. Industrial unrest spreads.

The Second Revolution

1907 Birth of Frida Kahlo (d. 1954).

1910 On the centennial of the Revolution, Díaz wins yet another rigged election. Revolt breaks out.

1911 Rebels under Pascual Orozco and Francisco (Pancho) Villa (1878–1923) capture Ciudad Juárez; Díaz resigns. Francisco Madero is elected president; calling for land reform, Emiliano Zapata (1879–1919) rejects the new regime. Violence continues.

1913 Military coup: Madero is deposed and murdered. In one day Mexico has three presidents, the last being General Victoriano Huerta (1854–1916). Civil war rages.

1914 American intervention leads to dictator Huerta's overthrow. Villa and Zapata briefly join forces at the Convention of Aguascalientes, but the Revolution goes on. Birth of poet-critic Octavio Paz.

1916 Villa's border raids lead to an American punitive expedition under Pershing. Villa eludes capture.

1917 Under a new constitution, Venuziano Carranza, head of the Constitutionalist Army, is elected president. Zapata continues his rebellion, which is brutally suppressed.

1918 CROM, the national labor union, is founded.

1919 On order of Carranza, Zapata is assassinated.

1920 Carranza is assassinated; Alvaro Obregón (1880–1928), who helped overthrow dictator Huerta in 1914, is elected president, beginning a period of reform and reconstruction. Schools are built and land is redistributed. In the next two decades, revolutionary culture finds expression in the art of Diego Rivera and José Clemente Orozco (1883–1949), the novels of Martin Luis Guzmán and Gregorio Lopez y Fuentes, and the music of Carlos Chavez (1899–1978).

1923 Pancho Villa is assassinated. The United States finally recognizes the Obregón regime.

1926–28 Catholics react to government anticlericalism in the Cristero Rebellion.

1934–40 The presidency of Lázaro Cárdenas (1895–1970) leads to the fullest implementation of revolutionary reforms.

1938 Cárdenas nationalizes the oil companies, removing them from foreign control.

1940 On August 20, exiled former Soviet leader Leon Trotsky murdered in his Mexico City home.

Post-Revolutionary Mexico

1951 Mexico's segment of the Pan-American Highway is completed, confirming the industrial growth and prosperity of post-war Mexico. Culture is increasingly Americanized; writers such as Octavio Paz and Carlos Fuentes express disillusionment with the post-revolution world.

1968 The Summer Olympics in Mexico City showcase Mexican prosperity, but massive demonstrations indicate underlying social unrest.

1981–82 Recession and a drop in oil prices severely damage Mexico's economy. The peso is devalued.

1985 Thousands die in the Mexico City earthquake.

1988 American-educated economist Carlos Salinas de Gortari is elected president; for the first time since 1940, support for the PRI, the national political party, seems to be slipping.

1993 North American Free Trade Agreement (NAFTA) is signed with United States and Canada.

1994 Uprising by the indigenous peoples of Chiapas, led by the Zapatistas and their charismatic ski-masked leader, Subcomandante Marcos; election reforms promised as a result.

Popular PRI presidential candidate Luis Donaldo Colosio assassinated while campaigning in Tijuana. Ernesto Zedillo, generally thought to be more of a technocrat and "old boy" PRI politician, replaces him and wins the election.

Zedillo, blaming the economic policies of his predecessor, devalues the peso in December.

1995 Recession sets in as a result of the peso devaluation. The former administration is rocked by scandals surrounding the assassinations of Colosio and another high-ranking government official; ex-President Carlos Salinas de Gortari moves to the United States.

1996 Mexico's economy, bolstered by a $28 billion bailout program led by the United States, turns upward, but the recovery is fragile. The opposition National Action Party (PAN), which is committed to conservative economic policies, gains strength. New details of scandals of the former administration continue to emerge.

1997 Mexico's top antidrug official is arrested on bribery charges. Nonetheless, the United States recertifies Mexico as a partner in the war on drugs. The Zedillo administration faces midterm party elections.

1998 Death of Octavio Paz.

1999 Raúl Salinas, brother of the former president Carlos Salinas de Gortari (in exile in Ireland), sentenced for the alleged murder of a PRI leader.

2000 Spurning long-ruling PRI, Mexicans elect opposition candidate Vicente Fox president.

Chronology

WORDS AND PHRASES

English	Spanish	Pronunciation
Basics		
Yes/no	Sí/no	see/no
Please	Por favor	pore fah-*vore*
May I?	¿Me permite?	may pair-*mee*-tay
Thank you (very much)	(Muchas) gracias	(*moo*-chas) *grah*-see-as
You're welcome	De nada	day *nah*-dah
Excuse me	Con permiso	con pair-*mee*-so
Pardon me/what did you say?	¿Como?/Mánde?	ko-mo/*mahn*-dey
Could you tell me?	¿Podría decirme?	po-*dree*-ah deh-*seer*-meh
I'm sorry	Lo siento	lo see-*en*-toe
Good morning!	¡Buenos días!	*bway*-nohs *dee*-ahs
Good afternoon!	¡Buenas tardes!	*bway*-nahs *tar*-dess
Good evening!	¡Buenas noches!	*bway*-nahs *no*-chess
Goodbye!	¡Adiós!/¡Hasta luego!	ah-dee-*ohss*/ *ah*-stah-*lwe*-go
Mr./Mrs.	Señor/Señora	sen-*yor*/sen-*yore*-ah
Miss	Señorita	sen-yo-*ree*-tah
Pleased to meet you	Mucho gusto	*moo*-cho *goose*-to
How are you?	¿Cómo está usted?	*ko*-mo es-*tah* oo-*sted*
Very well, thank you.	Muy bien, gracias.	*moo*-ee bee-en, grah-see-as
And you?	¿Y usted?	ee oos-*ted*
Hello (on the telephone)	Bueno	*bwen*-oh
Numbers		
1	un, uno	oon, *oo*-no
2	dos	dos
3	tres	trace
4	cuatro	*kwah*-tro
5	cinco	*sink*-oh
6	seis	sace
7	siete	see-*et*-ey
8	ocho	*o*-cho
9	nueve	new-*ev*-ay
10	diez	dee-*es*

11	once	*own*-sey
12	doce	*doe*-sey
13	trece	*tray*-sey
14	catorce	kah-*tor*-sey
15	quince	*keen*-sey
16	dieciséis	dee-es-ee-*sace*
17	diecisiete	dee-*es*-ee-see-*et*-ay
18	dieciocho	dee-*es*-ee-o-cho
19	diecinueve	dee-*es*-ee-new-*ev*-ay
20	veinte	*bain*-tay
21	veinte y uno/ veintiuno	*bain*-te-oo-no
30	treinta	*train*-tah
32	treinta y dos	train-tay-*dose*
40	cuarenta	kwah-*ren*-tah
43	cuarenta y tres	kwah-*ren*-tay-*trace*
50	cincuenta	seen-*kwen*-tah
54	cincuenta y cuatro *kwah*-tro	seen-*kwen*-tay
60	sesenta	sess-*en*-tah
65	sesenta y cinco	sess-*en*-tay *seen*-ko
70	setenta	set-*en*-tah
76	setenta y seis	set-*en*-tay *sace*
80	ochenta	oh-*chen*-tah
87	ochenta y siete	oh-*chen*-tay see-*yet*-ay
90	noventa	no-*ven*-tah
98	noventa y ocho	no-*ven*-tah o-cho
100	cien	see-*en*
101	ciento uno	see-en-toe *oo*-no
200	doscientos	doe-see-*en*-tohss
500	quinientos	keen-*yen*-tohss
700	setecientos	set-eh-see-*en*-tohss
900	novecientos	no-veh-see-*en*-tohss
1,000	mil	meel
2,000	dos mil	dose meel
1,000,000	un millón	oon meel-*yohn*

Colors

black	negro	*neh*-grow
blue	azul	ah-*sool*
brown	café	kah-*feh*
green	verde	*vair*-day
pink	rosa	*ro*-sah
purple	morado	mo-*rah*-doe
orange	naranja	na-*rahn*-hah

red	rojo	*roe*-hoe
white	blanco	*blahn*-koh
yellow	amarillo	ah-mah-*ree*-yoh

Days of the Week

Sunday	domingo	doe-*meen*-goh
Monday	lunes	*loo*-ness
Tuesday	martes	*mahr*-tess
Wednesday	miércoles	me-*air*-koh-less
Thursday	jueves	who-*ev*-ess
Friday	viernes	vee-*air*-ness
Saturday	sábado	*sah*-bah-doe

Months

January	enero	eh-*neh*-ro
February	febrero	feh-*brair*-oh
March	marzo	*mahr*-so
April	abril	ah-*breel*
May	mayo	*my*-oh
June	junio	*hoo*-nee-oh
July	julio	*who*-lee-yoh
August	agosto	ah-*ghost*-toe
September	septiembre	sep-tee-*em*-breh
October	octubre	oak-*too*-breh
November	noviembre	no-vee-*em*-breh
December	diciembre	dee-see-*em*-breh

Useful Phrases

Do you speak	¿Habla usted	*ah*-blah oos-*ted*
English?	inglés?	in-*glehs*
I don't speak	No hablo español	no *ah*-blow
Spanish		es-pahn-*yol*
I don't understand (you)	No entiendo	no en-tee-*en*-doe
I understand (you)	Entiendo	en-tee-*en*-doe
I don't know	No sé	no *say*
I am American/	Soy americano(a)/	soy ah-meh-ree-*kah*-no(ah)/
British	inglés(a)	in-*glace*(ah)
What's your name?	¿Cómo se llama usted?	*koh*-mo say yah-mah oos-*ted*
My name is . . .	Me llamo . . .	may *yah*-moh
What time is it?	¿Qué hora es?	keh *o*-rah es
It is one, two,	Es la una; son las	es la *oo*-nah/sone
three . . . o'clock.	dos, tres	lahs dose, trace
Yes, please/No,	Sí, por favor/No,	*see* pore fah-*vor*/no

thank you	gracias	*grah*-see-us
How?	¿Cómo?	*koh*-mo
When?	¿Cuándo?	*kwahn*-doe
This/Next week	Esta semana/ la semana que entra	*es*-tah seh-*mah*-nah/ lah say-*mah*-nah keh *en*-trah
This/Next month	Este mes/el próximo mes	*es*-tay mehs/el *proke*-see-mo mehs
This/Next year	Este año/el año que viene	*es*-tay *ahn*-yo/el *ahn*-yo keh vee-*yen*-ay
Yesterday/today/ tomorrow	Ayer/hoy/mañana	ah-*yair*/oy/mahn- *yah*-nah
This morning/ afternoon	Esta mañana/tarde	*es*-tah mahn-*yah*- nah/*tar*-day
Tonight	Esta noche	*es*-tah *no*-cheh
What?	¿Qué?	keh
What is it?	¿Qué es esto?	keh es *es*-toe
Why?	¿Por qué?	pore *keh*
Who?	¿Quién?	kee-*yen*
Where is . . . ? the train station?	¿Dónde está . . . ? la estación del tren?	*dohn*-day es-*tah* la es-tah-see-*on* del *train*
the subway station?	la estación del Metro?	la es-ta-see-*on* del *meh*-tro
the bus stop?	la parada del autobús?	la pah-*rah*-dah del oh-toe-*boos*
the post office?	la oficina de correos?	la oh-fee-*see*- nah day koh-*reh*-os
the bank?	el banco?	el *bahn*-koh
the . . . hotel?	el hotel . . . ?	el oh-*tel*
the store?	la tienda . . . ?	la tee-*en*-dah
the cashier?	la caja?	la *kah*-hah
the . . . museum?	el museo . . . ?	el moo-*seh*-oh
the hospital?	el hospital?	el ohss-pea-*tal*
the elevator?	el ascensor?	el ah-*sen*-sore
the bathroom?	el baño?	el *bahn*-yoh
Here/there	Aquí/allá	ah-*key*/ah-*yah*
Open/closed	Abierto/cerrado	ah-be-*er*-toe/ ser-*ah*-doe
Left/right	Izquierda/derecha	iss-key-*er*-dah/ dare-*eh*-chah
Straight ahead	Derecho	der-*eh*-choh
Is it near/far?	¿Está cerca/lejos?	es-*tah sair*-kah/ *leh*-hoss
I'd like . . . a room	Quisiera . . . un cuarto/una habitación	kee-see-*air*-ah oon *kwahr*-toe/ oo-nah ah-bee- tah-see-*on*
the key	la llave	lah *yah*-vay
a newspaper	un periódico	oon pear-ee-*oh*- dee-koh
a stamp	un timbre de correo	oon *team*-bray day koh-*reh*-oh
I'd like to buy . . .	Quisiera comprar . . .	kee-see-*air*-ah kohm-*prahr*
cigarettes	cigarrillo	ce-gar-*reel*-oh
matches	cerillos	ser-*ee*-ohs

a dictionary	un diccionario	oon deek-see-oh-*nah*-ree-oh
soap	jabón	hah-*bone*
a map	un mapa	oon *mah*-pah
a magazine	una revista	*oon*-ah reh-*veess*-tah
paper	papel	pah-*pel*
envelopes	sobres	*so*-brace
a postcard	una tarjeta postal	*oon*-ah tar-*het*-ah post-*ahl*
How much is it?	¿Cuánto cuesta?	*kwahn*-toe *kwes*-tah
It's expensive/cheap	Está caro/barato	es-*tah kah*-roh/bah-*rah*-toe
A little/a lot	Un poquito/mucho . . .	oon poh-*kee*-toe/*moo*-choh
More/less	Más/menos	mahss/*men*-ohss
Enough/too much/too little	Suficiente/demasiado/muy poco	soo-fee-see-*en*-tay/day-mah-see-*ah*-doe/*moo*-ee *poh*-koh
Telephone	Teléfono	tel-*ef*-oh-no
Telegram	Telegrama	teh-leh-*grah*-mah
I am ill/sick	Estoy enfermo(a)	es-*toy* en-*fair*-moh(ah)
Please call a doctor	Por favor llame un médico	pore fa-*vor ya*-may oon *med*-ee-koh
Help!	¡Auxilio! ¡Ayuda!	owk-*see*-lee-oh/ah-*yoo*-dah
Fire!	¡Encendio!	en-*sen*-dee-oo
Caution!/Look out!	¡Cuidado!	kwee-*dah*-doh

On the Road

Highway	Carretera	car-ray-*ter*-ah
Causeway, paved highway	Calzada	cal-*za*-dah
Route	Ruta	*roo*-tah
Road	Camino	cah-*mee*-no
Street	Calle	*cah*-yeh
Avenue	Avenida	ah-ven-*ee*-dah
Broad, tree-lined boulevard	Paseo	pah-*seh*-oh
Waterfront promenade	Malecón	mal-lay-*cone*
Wharf	Embarcadero	em-bar-cah-*day*-ro

In Town

Church	Templo/Iglesia	*tem*-plo/e-*gles*-se-*ah*
Cathedral	Catedral	cah-tay-*dral*
Neighborhood	Barrio	*bar*-re-o
Foreign exchange shop	Casa de cambio	*cas*-sah day *cam*-be-o
City hall	Ayuntamiento	ah-yoon-tah-mee-*en*-toe
Main square	Zócalo	*zo*-cal-o

Traffic circle	Glorieta	glor-e-*ay*-tah
Market	Mercado (Spanish)/ Tianguis (Indian)	mer-*cah*-doe/ tee-*an*-geese
Inn	Posada	pos-*sah*-dah
Group taxi	Colectivo	co-lec-*tee*-vo
Group taxi along fixed route	Pesero	pi-*seh*-ro

Items of Clothing

Embroidered white smock	Huipil	whee-*peel*
Pleated man's shirt worn outside the pants	Guayabera	gwah-ya-*beh*-ra
Leather sandals	Huaraches	wah-*ra*-chays
Shawl	Rebozo	ray-*bozh*-o
Pancho or blanket	Serape	seh-*ra*-peh

Dining Out

A bottle of . . .	Una botella de . . .	*oo*-nah bo-*tay*-yah deh
A cup of . . .	Una taza de . . .	*oo*-nah *tah*-sah deh
A glass of . . .	Un vaso de . . .	oon *vah*-so deh
Ashtray	Un cenicero	oon sen-ee-*seh*-roh
Bill/check	La cuenta	lah *kwen*-tah
Bread	El pan	el pahn
Breakfast	El desayuno	el day-sigh-*oon*-oh
Butter	La mantequilla	lah mahn-tay-*key*-yah
Cheers!	¡Salud!	sah-*lood*
Cocktail	Un aperitivo	oon ah-pair-ee-*tee*-voh
Dinner	La cena	lah *seh*-nah
Dish	Un plato	oon *plah*-toe
Dish of the day	El platillo de hoy	el plah-*tee*-yo day oy
Enjoy!	¡Buen provecho!	bwen pro-*veh*-cho
Fixed-price menu	La comida corrida	lah koh-*me*-dah co-*ree*-dah
Fork	El tenedor	el ten-eh-*door*
Is the tip included?	¿Está incluida la propina?	es-*tah* in-clue-*ee*-dah lah pro-*pea*-nah
Knife	El cuchillo	el koo-*chee*-yo
Lunch	La comida	lah koh-*me*-dah
Menu	La carta	lah *cart*-ah
Napkin	La servilleta	lah sair-vee-*yet*-uh
Pepper	La pimienta	lah pea-me-*en*-tah
Please give me	Por favor déme	pore fah-*vor* *day*-may

Salt	La sal	lah sahl
Spoon	Una cuchara	*oo*-nah koo-*chah*-rah
Sugar	El azúcar	el ah-*sue*-car
Waiter!/Waitress!	¡Por favor	pore fah-*vor* sen-
	Señor/Señorita!	*yor*/sen-yor-*ee*-tah

FURTHER READING

Considering how little most U.S. citizens know about Mexico, there is a world of reading available with which to educate yourself about the country. Fiction written both in and outside of Mexico is a great place to start. The best nonfiction on Mexico blends history, culture, commentary, and travel description. Some may be out of print and available only in libraries.

Pre-Columbian and Colonial Works and Histories

If the pre-Columbian way of thinking has any appeal to you, Dennis Tedlock's superb translation of the Maya creation myth, *Popol Vuh*, is essential reading.

Good general reference works that can deepen your understanding of Mexico's indigenous peoples (and enrich your trips to the many marvelous archaeological sites in Mexico) include *The Conquest of the Yucatán* by celebrated ethnographer and champion of indigenous cultural survival Frans Blom; *A Rain of Darts: The Mexican Aztecs,* by Burr Cartwright Brundage; *In the Land of the Aztec* and *The Maya and Mexico,* by Michael D. Coe; *The Toltec Heritage,* by Nigel Davies; *The Last Lords of Palenque: The Lacandon Mayas of the Mexican Rain Forest,* by Victor Perera and Robert D. Bruce; *The Blood of Kings: Dynasty & Ritual in Maya Art,* by Linda Schele and Mary Ellen Miller; and the colorful *Ancient Mexico,* by Maria Longhena. Mary Miller has also collaborated with Karl Taube to produce a useful glossary-style handbook called *The Gods and Symbols of Ancient Mexico and the Maya.*

A number of fascinating first-hand accounts of the colonial period by some of its most important figures have been translated and published. Of these, the most compelling may be *Letters from Mexico,* by conquistador Hernán Cortés, and *Tears of the Indians,* an unsparing account of Spanish brutality toward the native population by the outspoken Catholic priest Bartolomé de las Casas. While no 19th-century history of the conquest of Mexico could be reconciled with our contemporary view of the conquistadores barbarism, Prescott's *The Conquest of Mexico* is no less intriguing for its dated conceits.

For decades, the standard texts written by scholars for popular audiences have been *A History of Mexico,* by Henry B. Parkes; *Many Mexicos,* by Lesley Byrd Simpson; and *A Compact History of Mexico,* an anthology published by the Colegio de México. Michael C. Meyer and William L. Sherman's *The Course of Mexican History* and Eric Wolf's *Sons of the Shaking Earth* are also good survey works.

Contemporary Histories

Most people's understanding of Mexico is such that an absorbing history of the country is the best reading to start with. Enrique Kraus's ambitious *Mexico: Biography of Power* begins its romantic sweep with the Insurgent priests of the early 1800s. Jorge Castañeda's 1995 *The Mexican Shock* is an important study of the financial and political crisis in Mexico and its ramifications for United States-Mexico relations. His previous works, *Utopia Unarmed* and, with American political scientist Robert A. Pastor, *Limits to Friendship: The United States and Mexico,* are also excellent resources.

A number of journalists have made important contributions to the literature on historical and contemporary Mexico. William Langewiesche's *Cutting for Sign* examines life along the 1,951-mile-long Mexican–U.S. border. And Alan Riding's *Distant Neighbors: A Portrait of the Mexicans* and Jonathan Kandell's

La Capital: The Biography of Mexico City are both notable. Elena Poniatowska, better known in the English-speaking world for her fiction, is one of Mexico's most highly respected journalists. Massacre in Mexico, her account of government repression of a demonstration in Mexico City in 1968, is an enlightening and disturbing work. Bill Weinberg writes of oppression and rebellion in one of Mexico's poorest states in Homage to Chiapas. Setting Chiapas's indigenous movement of resistance in a broad historical context, it's also an education in Mexican politics, economics, and traditional culture. More academic works on Mexico's modern history include Hector Aguila Camín's In the Shadow of the Mexican Revolution, Roderic A. Camp's Politics in Mexico, and Merilee Grindle's Bureaucrats, Politicians and Peasants in Mexico.

Culture/Ethnography
Excellent ethnographies include Oscar Lewis's classic works on the culture of poverty The Children of Sanchez and Five Families; Juan the Chamula, by Ricardo Pozas, about a small village in Chiapas; Mexico South: The Isthmus of Tehuantepec, by Miguel Covarrubias, which discusses Indian life in the early 20th century; Gertrude Blom's Bearing Witness, on the Lacandones of Chiapas; and Maria Sabina: Her Life and Chants, an autobiography of a shaman in the state of Oaxaca.

Food
Perhaps one of the most unusual and delightful books published on Mexican cookery in recent years is Recipe of Memory: Five Generations of Mexican Cuisine (New Press, 1995). Written by Pulitzer Prize–winning food journalist Victor Valle and his wife, Mary Lau Valle, this book reproduces recipes the couple found in an antique chest passed down through the Valle family and in the process weaves an intriguing family and social history. Two lushly photographed cookbooks capturing the culinary history and culture of Mexico are Patricia Quintana's The Taste of Mexico (Stewart, Tabori & Chang, 1993) and Mexico the Beautiful Cookbook (Harper-Collins, 1991). Diane Kennedy's culinary works are also popular; one is The Art of Mexican Cooking (Bantam, 1989). Marita Adair's The Hungry Traveler Mexico, with descriptions of Mexican foods and their origins, goes beyond the typical food list.

Travelogues
Two of the more straightforward accounts from the early 19th century are the letters of Frances Calderón de la Barca (Life in Mexico) and John Lloyd Stephens's Incidents of Travel in Central America, Chiapas and Yucatán. Foreign journalists have described life in Mexico during and after the revolution: John Reed (Insurgent Mexico); John Kenneth Turner (Barbarous Mexico); Aldous Huxley (Beyond the Mexique Bay); and Graham Greene (The Lawless Roads, a superbly written narrative about Tabasco and Chiapas, which served as the basis for The Power and the Glory). In much the same vein, but more contemporary, are works by Patrick Marnham (So Far from God), about Central America and Mexico, and Hugh Fleetwood, whose A Dangerous Place is informative despite its cantankerousness. Alice Adams's 1991 Mexico: Some Travels and Some Travelers There, which includes an introduction by Jan Morris, is available in paperback; James A. Michener's 1992 novel, Mexico, captures the history of the land and the personality of the people. Probably the finest travelogue-cum-guidebook is Kate Simon's Mexico: Places and Pleasures. Into a Desert Place chronicles Graham Mackintosh's trek along the Baja coast. So entranced by San Miguel de Allende that he decided to stay, Tony Cohen recounts a gringo's daily life there in On Mexican Time. James O'Reilly and Larry Habegger have edited a diverse collection of articles and essays by contemporary authors in Travelers' Tales Mexico.

Contemporary Literature
The late poet-philosopher Octavio Paz was the dean of Mexican intellectuals. His best works are Labyrinth of Solitude, a thoughtful, far-reaching dissection of Mexican culture, and the biography of Sor Juana Inés de la Cruz, a 17th-century nun and poet. For more

on Sor Juana, including her own writings, see Alan Trueblood's *A Sor Juana Anthology*. Other top authors include Carlos Fuentes (*The Death of Artemio Cruz* and *The Old Gringo* are among his most popular novels), Juan Rulfo (his classic is *Pedro Páramo*), Jorge Ibarguengoitia, Elena Poniatowska (*Dear Diego* and *Fleur de Lis,* among others), Rosario Castellanos (*The Nine Guardians* and *City of Kings*), Elena Garros (*Recollections of Things to Come*), Gregorio López y Fuentes (*El Indio*), Angeles Mastretta (*Mexican Bolero*), and José Emilio Pacheco (*Battles in the Desert and Other Stories*).

Recent biographies of the artist couple Frida Kahlo and Diego Rivera (by Hayden Herrera and Bertram D. Wolfe, respectively) provide glimpses into the Mexican intellectual and political life of the '20s and '30s. Laura Esquivel's novel-cum-cookbook, *Like Water for Chocolate,* captures the passions and palates of Mexico during the revolution. Edited by Juana Ponce de Léon, *Our Word Is Our Weapon* contains writings by the articulate Subcomandante Insurgente Marcos. They range from communiqués made on behalf of the Zapatista movement to Marcos's own stories and poetry.

English Literature

D. H. Lawrence's *The Plumed Serpent* is probably the best-known foreign novel about Mexico, although its noble savage theme is quite offensive. Lawrence recorded his travels in Oaxaca in *Mornings in Mexico*. A far greater piece of literature is Malcolm Lowry's *Under the Volcano*. The mysterious recluse B. Traven, whose fame rests largely on his *Treasure of the Sierra Madre,* wrote brilliantly and passionately about Mexico in *Rebellion of the Hanged* and *The Bridge in the Jungle*. Also noteworthy is John Steinbeck's *The Log from the Sea of Cortez. The Reader's Companion to Mexico,* edited by Alan Ryan, includes material by Langston Hughes, D. H. Lawrence, and Paul Theroux.

Books

ESSENTIAL INFORMATION

ADDRESSES

The Mexican method of naming streets can be exasperatingly arbitrary, so **be patient when searching for street addresses.** Streets in the centers of many colonial cities (those built by the Spanish) are laid out in a grid surrounding the *zócalo* (main square) and often change names on different sides of the square. Other streets simply acquire a new name after a certain number of blocks. Numbered streets are usually designated *norte/sur* (north/south) or *oriente/poniente* (east/west) on either side of a central avenue. (Three of these are abbreviated: Nte., Ote., and Pte. Sur is spelled out.)

In many cities, streets that have proper names, such as Avenida Benito Juárez, change names when they cross some other street—and only a map will show where one begins and the other ends.

Blocks are often labeled numerically, according to distance from a chosen starting point, as in "la Calle de Pachuca," "2a Calle de Pachuca," etc.

Many Mexican addresses have "s/n" for *sin número* (no number) after the street name. This is common in small towns where there aren't many buildings on a block. Similarly, many hotels give their address as "Km 30 Carr. a Querétaro," which indicates that the property is at the 30th kilometer on the *carretera* (main highway) to Querétaro.

In Mexico City (and other cities), most addresses include their *colonia* (neighborhood), which is abbreviated as Col. Other abbreviations used in addresses include: Av. (*avenida*, or avenue); Calz. (*calzada*, or road); Fracc. (*fraccionamiento*, or housing estate); and Int. (interior).

Addresses in Mexico are written with the street name first, followed by the street number. A five-digit *código postal* (postal code) precedes, rather than follows, the name of the city. (Note that in this book, however, cities precede postal codes for the sake of clarity.) Apdo. (*apartado*) means box; Apdo. Postal, or A.P., means post-office box number. Here is a sample address: *Hacienda Paraíso, Calle Allende 211, 68000 Oaxaca, Oax.*

AIR TRAVEL

BOOKING

When you book **look for nonstop flights** and **remember that "direct" flights may stop at least once.** Try to avoid connecting flights, which require a change of plane. For more booking tips and to check prices and make on-line flight reservations, log on to www.fodors.com.

CARRIERS

Domestic plane travel costs about four times as much as the bus, but it will save you considerable travel time.

➤ FROM THE U.S.: **AeroCalifornia** (☎ 800/237–6225) to Mexico City, Guadalajara, Hermosillo, La Paz, Loreto, Los Cabos, Manzanillo, Mazatlán, Monterrey, Tijuana. **Aeroméxico** (☎ 800/237–6639) to Mexico City, Acapulco, Cancúun, Cozumel, Guadalajara, Guaymas/San Carlos, Ixtapa/Zihuatanejo, León/El Bajío, Los Cabos, Mérida, Monterrey. **Alaska Airlines** (☎ 800/426–0333) to Los Cabos, Puerto Vallarta. **America West** (☎ 800/235–9292) to Mexico City, Acapulco, Guaymas, Ixtapa/Zihuatanejo, Los Cabos, Manzanillo, Mazatlán, Puerto Vallarta. **American** (☎ 800/433–7300) to Mexico City, Acapulco, Cancún, Guadalajara, León/ El Bajío, Los Cabos, Monterrey, Puerto Vallarta. **Continental** (☎ 800/231– 0856) to Mexico City, Cancún, Chihuahua City, Cozumel, Guadalajara, Ixtapa/Zihuatanejo, León/El Bajío, Los Cabos, Mazatlán, Mérida, Monterrey, Puerto Vallarta, Veracruz, Tampico. **Delta** (☎ 800/241–4141) to Mexico City, Acapulco, Cancún, Guadalajara, Guaymas, Hermosillo, Ixtapa/Zihuatanejo, León/El Bajío, Los Cabos, Los Mochis, La Paz, Mérida, Puerto Vallarta. **Mexicana** (☎ 800/531–7921) to Mexico City, Acapulco, Cancún, Guadalajara, Ixtapa/Zihuatanejo, León/El Bajío, Los Cabos, Mazatlán, Mérida, Morelia, Puerto Vallarta, Zacatecas **Northwest** (☎ 800/225–2525) to Mexico City, Cancún, Cozumel, Puerto Vallarta. **United** (☎ 800/241–6522) to Mexico City. **US Airways** (☎ 800/428–4322) to Cancún.

➤ FROM THE U.K.: **British Airways** (☎ 0845/773–3377) has a nonstop flight from London to Mexico City. **Air France** (☎ 0181/742–6600), via Paris. **American** (☎ 020/8572–5555; 0345/789–789 outside London), from London via Chicago, Dallas, or Miami. **Continental** (☎ 01293/776–464), from London via Houston, and from Birmingham and Manchester via Newark. **Delta** (☎ 0800/849–1111), via Atlanta. **Iberia** (☎ 0171/830–0011), via Madrid. **KLM** (☎ 0181/750–9820), via Amsterdam. **Lufthansa** (☎ 0181/750–3535), via Frankfurt. **United** (☎ 0181/990–9900), via Chicago or Washington, D.C.

➤ DOMESTIC AIRLINES: **AeroCalifornia** (☎ 5207–1392 or 800/237–6225) serves Guadalajara, Loreto, Mérida, Oaxaca, Puebla, Tepic, Tijuana, Veracruz, Villahermosa, and several other gateways. **Aerocaribe** (reserve through Mexicana) serves the Yucatán and the South. **Aerolitoral** (reserve through Aeroméxico or Mexicana) serves northeastern Mexico. **Aeromar** (reserve through Mexicana or Aeroméxico) serves central Mexico. **Aeroméxico** (☎ 5133–4000 or 800/237–6639) serves most major cities. **Aviacsa** (☎ 961/2–80–81 in Chiapas; 5448–8900 in Mexico City) serves Cancún, Chetumal, and Mérida. **Mexicana** (☎ 5448–0990 or 800/531–7921) serves most major cities.

CHECK-IN & BOARDING

Assuming that not everyone with a ticket will show up, airlines routinely overbook planes. When everyone does, airlines ask for volunteers to give up their seats. In return, these volunteers usually get a certificate for a free flight and are rebooked on the next flight out. If there are not enough volunteers, the airline must choose who will be denied boarding. The first to get bumped are passengers who checked in late and those flying on discounted tickets, so **get to the gate and check in as early as possible,** especially during peak periods.

Always **bring a government-issued photo I.D. to the airport;** a passport is best. You may be asked to show it before you are allowed to check in.

CUTTING COSTS

The least expensive airfares to Mexico must usually be purchased in advance and are nonrefundable. It's smart to **call a number of airlines, and when you are quoted a good price, book it on the spot**—the same fare may not be available the next day. Always **check different routings** and look into using different airports. Travel agents, especially low-fare specialists, are helpful.

Consolidators are another good source. They buy tickets for scheduled international flights at reduced rates from the airlines, then sell them at prices that beat the best fare available directly from the airlines, usually without restrictions. Sometimes you can even get your money back if you need to return the ticket. Carefully read the fine print detailing penalties for changes and cancellations, and **confirm your consolidator reservation with the airline.**

When you **fly as a courier,** you trade your checked-luggage space for a ticket deeply subsidized by a courier service. There are restrictions on when you can book and how long you can stay.

➤ CONSOLIDATORS: **Cheap Tickets** (☎ 800/377–1000). **Discount Airline Ticket Service** (☎ 800/576–1600). **Unitravel** (☎ 800/325–2222). **Up & Away Travel** (☎ 212/889–2345). **World Travel Network** (☎ 800/409–6753).

➤ COURIERS: **Air Courier Association** (☎ 800/693–8333, WEB www.aircourier.com). **Air Facility** (☎ 718/

712–1769, WEB www.airfacility.com).
Now Voyager (☎ 212/431–1616).

ENJOYING THE FLIGHT

For more legroom, **request an emergency-aisle seat.** Don't sit in the row in front of the emergency aisle or in front of a bulkhead, where seats may not recline. If you have dietary concerns, **ask for special meals when booking.** These can be vegetarian, low-cholesterol, or kosher, for example. On long flights, try to maintain a normal routine to help fight jet lag. At night, **get some sleep.** By day, **eat light meals, drink water** (not alcohol), and **move around the cabin** to stretch your legs. For additional jet-lag tips consult *Fodor's FYI: Travel Fit & Healthy* (available at bookstores everywhere).

FLYING TIMES

Mexico City is 4½ hours from New York, 4 hours from Chicago, and 3½ hours from Los Angeles. Cancún is 3½ hours from New York and from Chicago, 4½ hours from Los Angeles. Acapulco is 6 hours from New York, 4 hours from Chicago, and 3½ hours from Los Angeles.

From London, Mexico City is a 12½-hour flight, Cancún 11¾ hours.

HOW TO COMPLAIN

If your baggage goes astray or your flight goes awry, complain right away. Most carriers require that you **file a claim immediately.**

➤ AIRLINE COMPLAINTS: U.S. Department of Transportation **Aviation Consumer Protection Division** (✉ C-75, Room 4107, Washington, DC 20590, ☎ 202/366–2220, WEB www.dot.gov/airconsumer). **Federal Aviation Administration Consumer Hotline** (☎ 800/322–7873).

AIRPORTS

The main gateway to Mexico is **Aeropuerto Internacional Benito Juárez** in Mexico City.

➤ AIRPORT INFORMATION: **Mexico City** (Aeropuerto Internacional Benito Juárez, ☎ 5571–3600). **Acapulco** (General Juan Alvarez airport, ☎ 74/66–9434). **Cancún** (Cancún airport, ☎ 98/860–049). **Cozumel** (Cozumel airport, ☎ 987/2–04–85). **Guadala-** jara (Ramón F. Quintanilla García airport, ☎ 3/688–51–20). **Ixtapa** (Manuel Zúrita Gallegos airport, ☎ 755/42–070). **Los Cabos** (Licenciado Alberto de la Mora airport, ☎ 114/2–03–41). **Manzanillo** (Playa de Oro airport, ☎ 333/32–525). **Mazatlán** (Juan Buelna airport, ☎ 69/82–23–99). **Mérida** (Hector José Navarrete Muñoz airport, ☎ 99/46–13–40). **Puerto Vallarta** (Gustavo Díaz Ordaz airport, ☎ 322/1–12–98).

BIKE TRAVEL

Bike travel in Mexico is a rough-and-ready proposition. Some roads have never seen a bicycle, and drivers are not accustomed to cyclists. In addition, most Mexican roads lack shoulders and are often pitted. Despite these drawbacks, cycling in Mexico can be fun if you plan ahead, and bikes are especially useful for travel to places where there are only dirt roads or tracks, or where public transportation is scant. In the Yucatán, for example, bikes are a primary form of transportation for locals, and bike-repair shops are common even in smaller towns. When planning your trip, consult an up-to-date AAA, Pemex, or Guía Roji map. You can find Pemex and Guía Roji maps in Mexico at most Sanborns restaurant/shops and major supermarket chains—such as Superama, Aurrera, and Commercial Mexicana—for less than $10. Be sure to carry plenty of water and everything you might need to repair your bike. Pack extra patch kits, as shards of glass often litter the roads. If you can take your bike apart and fold it up, buses will allow you to store it in the cargo space; likewise on trains in the Copper Canyon.

Bicycling Mexico (Hunter Publishing Inc.), by Ericka Weisbroth and Eric Ellman, is the bicyclist's bible, complete with maps, color photos, historical information, and a kilometer-by-kilometer breakdown of every route possible. For a list of companies that run organized bike tours of Mexico, *see* Tours & Packages, *below.*

BIKES IN FLIGHT

Most airlines accommodate bikes as luggage, provided they are dismantled and boxed. Airlines sell bike boxes, which are often free at bike shops, for about $5 (it's at least $100 for bike bags). International travelers can sometimes substitute a bike for a piece of checked luggage at no charge; otherwise, the cost is about $100. Domestic and Canadian airlines charge $25–$50.

BUS TRAVEL

Getting to Mexico by bus is no longer for just the adventurous or budget-conscious. In the past, bus travelers were required to change to Mexican vehicles at the border, and vice versa. Now, however, in an effort to bring more American visitors and their tourist dollars to off-the-beaten-track markets and attractions, the Mexican government has removed this obstacle, and a growing number of trans-border bus tours are available.

Gateway cities in Texas, such as El Paso, Del Rio, Laredo, McAllen, Brownsville, and San Antonio, along with Tijuana, are served by several small private bus lines as well as by Greyhound. If you'll be leaving Mexico by bus, you can buy tickets from the Greyhound representative in Mexico City.

The Mexican bus network is extensive, far more so than that of the railroads. Buses go where trains do not, service is more frequent, tickets can be purchased on the spot (except during holidays and on long weekends, when advance purchase is crucial), and first-class buses are punctual, faster, and much more comfortable than trains. On all overnight bus rides, **bring something to eat** in case you don't like the restaurant where the bus stops, and **carry toilet paper,** as rest rooms might not have any.

In large cities, bus stations are a good distance from the center of town. Though there's a trend toward consolidation, some towns have different stations for each bus line. Bus service in Mexico City is well organized, operating out of four terminals.

CLASSES

For travel within Mexico, buses run the gamut from comfortable air-conditioned coaches with bathrooms, movies, reclining seats with seat belts, and refreshments (premier or deluxe) to dilapidated "vintage" buses (second- and third-class) on which pigs and chickens travel and frequent stops are made. A lower-class bus ride can be interesting if you're not in a hurry and want to see the sights and experience the local culture—and the fares are generally up to 30% cheaper than those in the premium categories. Still, you should be prepared for cracked windows and litter in the aisles. But for comfort's sake alone, if you're planning a long-distance haul, **buy tickets for first-class or better when traveling by bus within Mexico.** Smoking is prohibited on all first-class and deluxe buses.

There are several first-class bus lines. ADO serves Cancún, Oaxaca, Tampico, Veracruz, Villahermosa, and Yucatán from Mexico City; ADO GL offers deluxe service to the same destinations. Cristóbal Colón goes to Chiapas, Oaxaca, Puebla, and the Guatemala border from Mexico City. Estrella Blanca goes from Mexico City to Manzanillo, Mazatlán, Monterrey, and Nuevo Laredo. ETN goes to Mexico City, Manzanillo, Morelia, Puerto Vallarta, and Toluca. Estrella Blanca has first-class and deluxe service to all states but Yucatán, Quintana Roo, and Chiapas. You can take Estrella de Oro from Mexico City to Acapulco, Cuernavaca, Ixtapa, and Taxco.

➤ BUS INFORMATION: **ADO** (☎ 5785–9659, 01–800/702–8000). **ADO GL** (☎ 5785–9659). **Cristóbal Colón** (☎ 5133–2444). **Estrella Blanca** (☎ 5729–0707). **ETN** (☎ 5273–0251, 01–800/715–5519). **Estrella Blanca** (☎ 5729–0707). **Estrella de Oro** (☎ 5549–8520). **Greyhound** (☎ 800/231–2222; ✉ Amores 707-102, Col. del Valle, Mexico City, ☎ 5669–0986).

PAYING

For the most part, you should plan to pay in pesos, although some of the deluxe bus services have started accepting credit cards such as Visa and Mastercard.

RESERVATIONS

Tickets for first-class or better—unlike tickets for the other classes—can and should be reserved in advance.

BUSINESS HOURS

BANKS & OFFICES

Banks are generally open weekdays 9–3. In larger cities, most are open until 5 or 7. Many of the larger banks keep a few branches open Saturday from 9 or 10 to 2:30 and Sunday 10–1:30; however, the extended hours are often for deposits or check cashing only. Banks will give you cash advances in pesos (for a fee) if you have a major credit card. Government offices are usually open to the public 8–3; along with banks and most private offices, they're closed on national holidays.

GAS STATIONS

Gas stations are normally open 7 AM–10 PM. Those near major thoroughfares in big cities stay open 24 hours, including most holidays.

MUSEUMS & SIGHTS

Along with theaters and most archaeological sights, museums are closed on Monday, with few exceptions. Museums across the country have free admission on Sunday. Hours are normally 9 to 5 or 6.

SHOPS

Stores are generally open weekdays and Saturday from 9 or 10 AM to 7 or 8 PM; in resort areas, shops may also be open on Sunday. In some resort areas and small towns, shops may close for a two-hour lunch break—about 2–4. Airport shops are open seven days a week.

CAMERAS & PHOTOGRAPHY

You should **always ask permission before taking photos of people.** They may ask you for a *propina,* or tip, in which case a few pesos is customary. Some churches in Chiapas and elsewhere forbid cameras.

The *Kodak Guide to Shooting Great Travel Pictures* (available at bookstores everywhere) is loaded with tips.

➤ PHOTO HELP: **Kodak Information Center** (☎ 800/242–2424).

EQUIPMENT PRECAUTIONS

Don't pack film and equipment in checked luggage, where it is much more susceptible to damage. X-ray machines used to view checked luggage are becoming much more powerful and therefore are much more likely to ruin your film. Always **keep film and tape out of the sun.** Carry an extra supply of batteries, and **be prepared to turn on your camera or camcorder** to prove to security personnel that the device is real. Always **ask for hand inspection of film,** which becomes clouded after repeated exposure to airport X-ray machines, and **keep videotapes away from metal detectors.**

FILM & DEVELOPING

Film—especially Kodak and Fuji brands—is fairly easy to find in many parts of Mexico. If purchased in a major city, a roll of 36-exposure print film costs about the same as in the United States; the price is slightly higher in tourist spots and in more remote places, where finding film might not be as easy. Advantix is now available in Mexico, although developing may take one or two days. It's a good idea to **pack more film than you think you'll need** on your trip. One-hour and overnight film developing is fairly common in Mexico.

VIDEOS

Videotapes are good quality and are easy to find in urban areas. A 120-minute tape costs about $3.

CAR RENTAL

When you think about renting a car, bear in mind that you may be sharing the road with bad local drivers—sometimes acquiring a driver's license in Mexico is more a question of paying someone off than of having tested skill. In addition, the highway system is very uneven from state to state: in some regions, modern, well-paved superhighways prevail; in others—particularly the mountains—potholes, untethered livestock, and dangerous, unrailed curves are the rule. Check on local road conditions before you rent.

Mexico manufactures Chrysler, Ford, General Motors, Honda, Nissan, and Volkswagen vehicles. With the exception of Volkswagen, you can get the same kind of midsize and luxury cars in Mexico that you can rent in the United States and Canada. Economy usually refers to a Volkswagen Beetle, which may or may not come with air-conditioning.

Rates begin at $45 a day and $245 a week in Mexico City and $40 a day and $240 a week in Acapulco for a compact car with air-conditioning, manual transmission, and unlimited mileage. This doesn't include tax on car rentals, which is 15%, or insurance, which runs about $100 a week. Avoid local car-rental agencies; **stick with the major companies** because they tend to be more reliable.

You can also hire a car with a driver; they're normally available through hotels and charge around $20 an hour within town, with a three-hour minimum requirement. Limousine service runs about $50 an hour within town, with a five-hour minimum. Rates for out-of-town trips are higher. **Negotiate a price beforehand** if you'll need the service for more than one day. If your hotel can't arrange limousine or car service, ask the concierge to refer you to a reliable *sitio* (cab stand); the rate will be lower.

➤ MAJOR AGENCIES: **Alamo** (☎ 800/ 522–9696; 020/8759–6200 in the U.K.). **Avis** (☎ 800/331–1084; 800/ 879–2847 in Canada; 02/9353–9000 in Australia; 09/525–1982 in New Zealand; 0870/606–0100 in the U.K.). **Budget** (☎ 800/527–0700; 0870/607–5000 in the U.K., through affiliate Europcar). **Dollar** (☎ 800/ 800–6000; 0124/622–0111 in the U.K., through affiliate Sixt Kenning; 02/9223–1444 in Australia). **Hertz** (☎ 800/654–3001; 800/263–0600 in Canada; 020/8897–2072 in the U.K.; 02/9669–2444 in Australia; 09/256– 8690 in New Zealand) **National Car Rental** (☎ 800/227–7368; 020/8680– 4800 in the U.K., where it is known as National Europe).

INSURANCE

When driving a rented car you are generally responsible for any damage to or loss of the vehicle as well as for any property damage or personal injury that you may cause. Before you rent, see what coverage your personal auto-insurance policy and credit cards provide.

REQUIREMENTS & RESTRICTIONS

In Mexico your own driver's license is acceptable. An International Driver's Permit is a good idea; it's available from the U.S. and Canadian automobile associations, and, in the United Kingdom, from the Automobile Association or Royal Automobile Club. These international permits are universally recognized, and having one in your wallet may save you a problem with the local authorities.

SURCHARGES

Before you pick up a car in one city and leave it in another, **ask about drop-off charges or one-way service fees,** which can be substantial. Note, too, that some rental agencies charge extra if you return the car before the time specified in your contract. To avoid a hefty refueling fee, **fill the tank just before you turn in the car,** but be aware that gas stations near the rental outlet may overcharge.

CAR TRAVEL

There are two absolutely essential points to remember about driving in Mexico. First and foremost is to **carry Mexican auto insurance.**

Point No. 2: **if you enter Mexico with a car, you must leave with it.** In recent years, the high rate of U.S. vehicles being sold illegally in Mexico has caused the Mexican government to enact stringent regulations for bringing a car into the country—at great inconvenience to motoring American tourists. In order to drive into the country, **you must cross the border with the following documents:** title or registration for your vehicle; a birth certificate or passport; a credit card (AE, DC, MC, or V); a valid driver's license with a photo. The title holder, driver, and credit-card owner must be one and the same—that is, if your spouse's name is on the title of the car and yours isn't, you cannot be the one to bring the car into the country. For financed, leased, rental, or company cars, you must **bring a notarized letter of permission** from the bank, lien holder, rental agency, or company.

When you submit your paperwork at the border and pay a $15 charge on your credit card, you'll receive a car permit and a sticker to put on your vehicle, all valid for up to six months. Be sure to **turn in the permit and the sticker** at the border prior to their expiration date; otherwise you could incur high fines.

One alternative to going through this hassle when you cross is to **have your paperwork done in advance** at a branch of Sanborn's Mexican Insurance; look in the Yellow Pages for an office in almost every town on the U.S.–Mexico border. You'll still have to go through some of the procedures at the border, but all your paperwork will be in order, and Sanborn's express window will ensure that you get through relatively quickly. There's a $10 charge for this service. The fact that you drove in with a car is stamped on your tourist card, which you must give to immigration authorities at departure. If an emergency arises and you must fly home, there are complicated customs procedures to face.

If you bring the car into the country you must **be in the vehicle at all times when it is driven.** You cannot lend it to another person.

For day trips and local sightseeing, **consider hiring a car and driver** (who often acts as a guide) for a day; this can be a hassle-free, more economical way to travel than renting a car and driving yourself. Hotel desks will know which taxi companies to call, and you can negotiate a price with the driver.

EMERGENCY SERVICES

To help motorists on major highways, the Mexican Tourism Ministry operates a fleet of more than 350 pickup trucks, known as the Angeles Verdes, or Green Angels. The bilingual drivers provide mechanical help, first aid, radio-telephone communication, basic supplies and small parts, towing, tourist information, and protection. Services are free, and spare parts, fuel, and lubricants are provided at cost. Tips are always appreciated (figure $5–$10 for big jobs, $2–$3 for minor repairs). The Green Angels patrol fixed sections of the major highways twice daily 8–8 (later on holiday weekends). If you break down, **pull off the road as far as possible,** lift the hood of your car, hail a passing vehicle, and ask the driver to **notify the patrol.** Most bus and truck drivers will be quite helpful. If you witness an accident, do not stop to help—inform the nearest official.

➤ CONTACTS: **Green Angels, Mexico City** (☎ 5250–8221).

GASOLINE

Pemex franchises all gas stations in Mexico. Stations are located at most road junctions and in cities and towns; gas is measured in liters instead of gallons. Gas stations usually do not accept U.S. or Canadian credit cards or dollars. Fuel prices vary from region to region. They tend to be on the lower end in Mexico City and surroundings and near the U.S. border, increasing the farther you get from these areas. Overall, prices run slightly to moderately higher than in the United States. Premium unleaded gas (called Magna Premio) and regular unleaded gas (Magna Sin) are available nationwide, but it's still a good idea to **fill up whenever you can.** Fuel quality is generally lower than that in the United States and Europe. Vehicles with fuel-injected engines are likely to have problems after driving extended distances.

Gas-station attendants pump the gas for you and may also wash your windshield and check your oil and tire air pressure. A five- or 10-peso tip is customary depending on the number of services rendered. **Keep a close eye on the gas meter** to make sure the attendant is starting it at "0" and that you're charged the correct price.

INSURANCE

You must **carry Mexican auto insurance,** which you can purchase near border crossings on either the U.S. or Mexican side. If you injure anyone in an accident, you could well be jailed—whether it was your fault or not—unless you have insurance. Guilty until proven innocent is part of the country's Code Napoléon. Purchase enough Mexican automobile insurance at the border to cover your estimated trip. It's sold by the day, and if your trip is shorter than your original estimate, some companies might issue a prorated refund for the

unused time upon application after
you exit the country.

➤ CONTACTS: **Instant Mexico Auto
Insurance** (✉ 223 Via de San Ysidro,
San Ysidro, CA 92173, ☎ 619/428–
3583). **Oscar Padilla** (✉ 4330 La
Jolla Village Dr., San Diego, CA
92122, ☎ 800/258–8600). **Sanborn's
Mexican Insurance** (✉ 2009 S. 10th
St., McAllen, TX 78503, ☎ 210/
686–0711).

ROAD CONDITIONS

There are several well-kept toll roads
in Mexico—most of them four lanes
wide. However, these *carreteras*
(major highways) don't go too far out
of the capital into the countryside.
(*Cuota* means toll road; *libre* means
no toll, and such roads are two lanes
and usually not as smooth.) Some
excellent new roads have opened in
the past decade or so, making car
travel safer and faster. These include
highways connecting Acapulco and
Mexico City; Cancún and Mérida;
Nogales and Mazatlán; León and
Aguascalientes; Guadalajara and
Tepic; Mexico City, Morelia, and
Guadalajara; Mexico City, Puebla,
Teotihuacán, and Oaxaca; Mexico
City and Veracruz; and Nuevo Laredo
and Monterrey. However, tolls as
high as $40 one way can make using
these thoroughfares prohibitively
expensive. Approaches to most of the
large cities are also in good condition.

In rural areas, roads are quite poor:
**use caution, especially during the
rainy season,** when rock slides and
potholes are a problem, and watch
out for animals. Driving in Mexico's
central highlands may also necessitate
adjustments to your carburetor. Generally, driving times are longer than
for comparable distances in the United
States. *Topes* (speed bumps) are also
common; it's best to slow down when
approaching a village.

Common sense goes a long way: if
you have a long distance to cover,
start early and fill up on gas; don't let
your tank get below half-full. Allow
extra time for unforeseen occurrences
as well as for the trucks that seem to
be everywhere. By day, **be alert to
animals,** especially cattle and dogs.

Traffic can be horrendous in cities,
particularly in Mexico City. As you
would in metropolitan areas anywhere, **avoid rush hour** (7–9 AM and
6–8 PM) and when schools let out (2–
3 PM). Signage is not always adequate
in Mexico, so **travel with a companion and a good map.** Always lock
your car, and never leave valuable
items in the body of the car (the trunk
will suffice for daytime outings, but
don't pack it in front of prying eyes).

ROAD MAPS

The Mexican Tourism Ministry
distributes free road maps from its
tourism offices outside the country.
Guía Roji and Pemex (the government petroleum monopoly) publish
current city, regional, and national
road maps, which are available in
bookstores and big supermarket
chains for under $10; gas stations
generally do not carry maps.

RULES OF THE ROAD

When you sign up for Mexican car
insurance, you should receive a booklet on Mexican rules of the road.
Read this booklet in order to avoid
breaking laws that differ from those
of your country.

Illegally parked cars are either towed
or have wheel blocks placed on the
tires, which can require a trip to the
traffic-police headquarters for payment of a fine. When in doubt, **park in
a lot instead of on the street**; your car
will probably be safer there anyway.

If an oncoming vehicle flicks its lights
at you in daytime, slow down: it could
mean trouble ahead. When approaching a narrow bridge, the first vehicle to
flash its lights has right of way. One-
way streets are common. One-way
traffic is indicated by an arrow; two-
way, by a double-pointed arrow. A
circle with a diagonal line superimposed on the letter *E* (for *estaciona-
miento*) means "no parking." Other
road signs follow the now-widespread
system of international symbols, a
copy of which will usually be provided
when you rent a car in Mexico.

In Mexico City, **watch out for "Hoy
no Circula" notices.** Because of pollution, all cars in the city without a
Verification "0" rating (usually those
built before 1994) are prohibited

from driving one day a week (two days a week during high-alert periods). Posted signs show certain letters or numbers paired with each day of the week, indicating that vehicles with those letters or numbers in their license plates are not allowed to drive on the corresponding day. Foreigners are not exempt.

Mileage and speed limits are given in kilometers: 100 kph and 80 kph (62 and 50 mph, respectively) are the most common maximums. A few of the newer toll roads allow 110 kph (68 mph). In cities and small towns, **observe the posted speed limits,** which can be as low as 20 kph (12 mph).

Seatbelts are now required by law throughout Mexico.

SAFETY ON THE ROAD

Never drive at night in remote and rural areas. *Banditos* are one concern, but so are potholes, free-roaming animals, cars with no working lights, road-hogging trucks, and difficulty in getting assistance. It's best to use toll roads whenever possible; although costly, they are much safer.

If you're driving from Manzanillo to Ixtapa/Zihuatanejo—about 8–10 hours with a meal stop—make the trip only during daylight hours, due to reports of car jackings around the area of Playa Azul. Military and police patrols have been increased on Highway 200 and the number of incidents has dramatically decreased; still, exercise caution.

Some of the biggest hassles on the road might be from police who pull you over for supposedly breaking the law, or for being a good prospect for a scam. Remember to **be polite**—displays of anger will only make matters worse—and be aware that a police officer might be pulling you over for something you didn't do. Although efforts are being made to fight corruption, it's still a fact of life in Mexico, and the $5 it costs to get your license back is definitely supplementary income for the officer who pulled you over with no intention of taking you down to police headquarters.

If you are stopped for speeding, the officer is supposed to take your license and hold it until you pay the fine at the local police station. But the officer will always prefer a *mordida* (small bribe) to wasting his time at the police station. If you decide to dispute a charge that seems preposterous, do so with a smile, and tell the officer that you would like to talk to the police captain when you get to the station. The officer usually will let you go rather than go to the station.

When crossing the streets by foot, **look both ways for oncoming traffic,** even with the light. Although pedestrians have the right of way by law, drivers disregard it. And more often than not, if a driver hits a pedestrian, he'll drive away as fast as he can without stopping, to avoid jail. Many Mexican drivers do not carry auto insurance, so you'll have to shoulder your own medical expenses.

CHILDREN IN MEXICO

Mexico has one of the strictest policies about children entering the country. All children, including infants, must have proof of citizenship for travel to Mexico. All children up to age 18 traveling with a single parent must also have a notarized letter from the other parent stating that the child has his or her permission to leave their home country. If the other parent is deceased or the child has only one legal parent, a notarized statement saying so must be obtained as proof. In addition, parents must now fill out a tourist card for each child over the age of 10 traveling with them.

If you are renting a car, don't forget to **arrange for a car seat** when you reserve.

For general advice about traveling with children consult *Fodor's FYI: Travel with Your Baby* (available in bookstores everywhere).

FLYING

If your children are two or older, **ask about children's airfares.** As a general rule, infants under two not occupying a seat fly at greatly reduced fares or even for free. When booking, **confirm carry-on allowances** if you're traveling with infants. In general, for babies charged 10% of the adult fare you are allowed one carry-on bag and a collapsible stroller; if the flight is full, the stroller may have to be checked or you may be limited to less.

Experts agree that it's a good idea to use safety seats aloft for children weighing less than 40 pounds. Airlines set their own policies: U.S. carriers usually require that the child be ticketed, even if he or she is young enough to ride free, since the seats must be strapped into regular seats. Do **check your airline's policy about using safety seats during takeoff and landing.** And since safety seats are not allowed everywhere in the plane, get your seat assignments early.

When reserving, **request children's meals or a freestanding bassinet** if you need them. But note that bulkhead seats, where you must sit to use the bassinet, may lack an overhead bin or storage space on the floor.

FOOD & SUPPLIES

Fresh milk isn't always readily available, though necessities such as disposable diapers can be found in almost every town.

LODGING

Most hotels in Mexico allow children under a certain age to stay in their parents' room at no extra charge, but others charge for them as extra adults; be sure to **find out the cutoff age for children's discounts** before booking accommodations.

Many hotel chains in Mexico offer services that make it easier to travel with children. They include connecting family rooms, play areas such as kiddie pools and playgrounds, and kids' clubs with special activities and outings. Check with your hotel before booking to see if the services are included in the price or if there is an extra charge.

SIGHTS & ATTRACTIONS

The larger tourist areas have plenty of activities for children. Places that are especially appealing to children are indicated by a rubber-duckie icon (🐤) in the margin of this book.

COMPUTERS ON THE ROAD

Internet cafés have sprung up all over Mexico, making e-mail by far the

easiest way to get in touch with people back home.

If you have a Toshiba or Macintosh laptop, bear in mind that having it serviced might be hopeless. Parts for these machines are hard to come by in Mexico.

Carry a spare battery because replacement batteries are expensive and difficult to find. Always check with your hotel about surge protection, especially if the property isn't part of a major chain and/or is in an out-of-the-way place. Extreme electrical fluctuations and surges can damage or destroy your computer. Check with IBM for its pen-size modem tester that plugs into a telephone and jack to test if the line is safe.

CONSUMER PROTECTION

Whenever shopping or buying travel services in Mexico, **pay with a major credit card,** if possible, so you can cancel payment or get reimbursed if there's a problem. If you're doing business with a particular company for the first time, **contact your local Better Business Bureau and the attorney general's offices** in your state and (for U.S. businesses) the company's home state as well. Have any complaints been filed? Finally, if you're buying a package or tour, always **consider travel insurance** that includes default coverage.

➤ BBBs: Council of Better Business Bureaus (✉ 4200 Wilson Blvd., Suite 800, Arlington, VA 22203, ☎ 703/276–0100, ℻ 703/525–8277, 🌐 www.bbb.org).

CUSTOMS & DUTIES

When shopping, **keep receipts** for all purchases. Upon reentering the country, **be ready to show customs officials what you've bought.** If you feel a duty is incorrect or object to the way your clearance was handled, note the inspector's badge number and ask to see a supervisor. If the problem isn't resolved, write to the appropriate authorities, beginning with the port director at your point of entry.

IN MEXICO

Upon entering Mexico, you'll be given a baggage declaration form and asked to itemize what you're bringing into the country. You are allowed to bring in 2 liters of spirits or wine for personal use; 400 cigarettes, 50 cigars, or 250 grams of tobacco; a reasonable amount of perfume for personal use; one movie camera and one regular camera and 12 rolls of film for each; and gift items not to exceed a total of $300. If driving across the U.S. border, gift items must not exceed $50. You are not allowed to bring firearms, meat, vegetables, plants, fruit, or flowers into the country.

IN AUSTRALIA

Australian residents who are 18 or older may bring home $A400 worth of souvenirs and gifts (including jewelry), 250 cigarettes or 250 grams of tobacco, and 1,125 ml of alcohol (including wine, beer, and spirits). Residents under 18 may bring back $A200 worth of goods. Prohibited items include meat products. Seeds, plants, and fruits need to be declared upon arrival.

➤ INFORMATION: **Australian Customs Service** (Regional Director, ✉ Box 8, Sydney, NSW 2001, Australia, ☎ 02/9213–2000, ℻ 02/9213–4000, WEB www.customs.gov.au).

IN CANADA

Canadian residents who have been out of Canada for at least seven days may bring home C$500 worth of goods duty-free. If you've been away fewer than seven days but more than 48 hours, the duty-free allowance drops to C$200; if your trip lasts 24–48 hours, the allowance is C$50. You may not pool allowances with family members. Goods claimed under the C$500 exemption may follow you by mail; those claimed under the lesser exemptions must accompany you. Alcohol and tobacco products may be included in the seven-day and 48-hour exemptions but not in the 24-hour exemption. If you meet the age requirements of the province or territory through which you reenter Canada, you may bring in, duty-free, 1.14 liters (40 imperial ounces) of wine or liquor *or* 24 12-ounce cans or bottles of beer or ale. If you are 16 or older you may bring in, duty-free, 200 cigarettes and 50 cigars. Check ahead of time with Revenue Canada or the Department of Agriculture for policies regarding meat products, seeds, plants, and fruits.

You may send an unlimited number of gifts worth up to C$60 each duty-free to Canada. Label the package UNSOLICITED GIFT—VALUE UNDER $60. Alcohol and tobacco are excluded.

➤ INFORMATION: **Revenue Canada** (✉ 2265 St. Laurent Blvd. S, Ottawa, Ontario K1G 4K3, Canada, ☎ 613/993–0534; 800/461–9999 in Canada, ℻ 613/991–4126, WEB www.ccra-adrc.gc.ca).

IN NEW ZEALAND

Homeward-bound residents 17 or older may bring back $700 worth of souvenirs and gifts. Your duty-free allowance also includes 4.5 liters of wine or beer; one 1,125-ml bottle of spirits; and either 200 cigarettes, 250 grams of tobacco, 50 cigars, or a combination of the three up to 250 grams. Prohibited items include meat products, seeds, plants, and fruits.

➤ INFORMATION: **New Zealand Customs** (Custom House, ✉ 50 Anzac Ave., Box 29, Auckland, New Zealand, ☎ 09/300–5399, ℻ 09/359–6730, WEB www.customs.govt.nz).

IN THE U.K.

From countries outside the EU, including Mexico, you may bring home, duty-free, 200 cigarettes or 50 cigars; 1 liter of spirits or 2 liters of fortified or sparkling wine or liqueurs; 2 liters of still table wine; 60 ml of perfume; 250 ml of toilet water; plus £136 worth of other goods, including gifts and souvenirs. If returning from outside the EU, prohibited items include meat products, seeds, plants, and fruits.

➤ INFORMATION: **HM Customs and Excise** (✉ Dorset House, Stamford St., Bromley, Kent BR1 1XX, U.K., ☎ 020/7202–4227, WEB www.hmce.gov.uk).

IN THE U.S.

U.S. residents who have been out of the country for at least 48 hours (and who have not used the $400 allowance or any part of it in the past 30 days) may bring home $400 worth of foreign goods duty-free. U.S. residents

21 and older may bring back 1 liter of alcohol duty-free. In addition, regardless of your age, you are allowed 200 cigarettes and 100 non-Cuban cigars. Antiques, which the U.S. Customs Service defines as objects more than 100 years old, enter duty-free, as do original works of art done entirely by hand, including paintings, drawings, and sculptures.

You may also mail or ship packages home duty-free: up to $200 worth of goods for personal use, with a limit of one parcel per addressee per day (except alcohol or tobacco products or perfume worth more than $5); label the package PERSONAL USE and attach a list of its contents and their retail value. Do not label the package UNSOLICITED GIFT or your duty-free exemption will drop to $100. Mailed items do not affect your duty-free allowance on your return.

➤ INFORMATION: **U.S. Customs Service** (✉ 1300 Pennsylvania Ave. NW, Washington, DC 20229; WEB www. customs.gov; inquiries ☎ 202/354–1000; complaints c/o ✉ 1300 Pennsylvania Ave. NW, Room 5.4D, Washington, DC 20229; registration of equipment c/o ✉ Resource Management, ☎ 202/927–0540).

DINING

Mexican restaurants run the gamut from humble hole-in-the-wall shacks, street stands, *taquerías,* and American-style fast-food joints to internationally acclaimed gourmet restaurants. Prices, naturally, follow suit. To save money, **look for the fixed-menu lunch** known as *comida corrida* or *menú del día,* which is served 1–4 almost everywhere in Mexico.

The restaurants we list are the cream of the crop in each price category. Price categories are based on either a full three-course meal or the main course alone. For more information on local foods throughout Mexico, *see* "La Cocina Mexicana" in Mexico City (Chapter 1) and the Dining sections that appear under Pleasures and Pastimes at the beginning of each chapter.

MEALTIMES

In Mexico, lunch is the big meal; dinner is rarely served before 8 PM.

Unless otherwise noted, the restaurants listed in this guide are open daily for lunch and dinner.

PAYING

Credit cards—especially American Express, MasterCard, and Visa—are widely accepted at pricier restaurants. Bargains are usually cash only.

RESERVATIONS & DRESS

Reservations are always a good idea: we mention them only when they're essential or not accepted. Book as far ahead as you can, and reconfirm as soon as you arrive. We mention dress only when men are required to wear a jacket or a jacket and tie.

DISABILITIES & ACCESSIBILITY

Mexico is poorly equipped for travelers with disabilities. There are no special discounts or passes for such travelers in Mexico, nor is public transportation, including the Mexico City Metro, wheelchair accessible. An exception is the city of Veracruz, where street corners have ramps in the downtown area. Roads and sidewalks are most often crowded and without ramps—in colonial cities cobblestone sidewalks and streets are unnavigable—and people on the street will not usually assist you unless expressly asked. You cannot rent vehicles outfitted for travelers with disabilities in Mexico, so your best bet for exploring comfortably is to **bring a car or van.**

Most hotels and restaurants have at least a few steps, and while rooms considered "wheelchair accessible" by hotel owners are usually on the ground floor, the doorways and bathroom may not be maneuverable. It's a good idea to call ahead to find out what a hotel or restaurant can offer. Despite these barriers, Mexicans with disabilities manage to negotiate places that most travelers outside Mexico would not consider accessible.

LODGING

The best choices of accessible lodging are found in major resort towns such as Acapulco, Cancún, and Mazatlán, and big cities such as Mexico City and Guadalajara.

RESERVATIONS

When discussing accessibility with an operator or reservations agent, **ask hard questions.** Are there any stairs, inside *or* out? Are there grab bars next to the toilet *and* in the shower/tub? How wide is the doorway to the room? To the bathroom? For the most extensive facilities meeting the latest legal specifications, **opt for newer accommodations.**

➤ COMPLAINTS: **Aviation Consumer Protection Division** for airline-related problems. **Civil Rights Office** (✉ U.S. Department of Transportation, Departmental Office of Civil Rights, S-30, 400 7th St. SW, Room 10215, Washington, DC 20590, ☎ 202/366–4648, FAX 202/366–9371, WEB www. dot.gov/ost/docr/index.htm) for problems with surface transportation. **Disability Rights Section** (✉ U.S. Department of Justice, Civil Rights Division, Box 66738, Washington, DC 20035-6738, ☎ 202/514–0301 or 800/514–0301; 202/514–0383 TTY; 800/514–0383 TTY, FAX 202/307–1198, WEB www.usdoj.gov/crt/ada/adahom1.htm) for general complaints.

TRAVEL AGENCIES

In the United States, the Americans with Disabilities Act requires that travel firms serve the needs of all travelers. Some agencies specialize in working with people with disabilities.

➤ TRAVELERS WITH MOBILITY PROBLEMS: **Access Adventures** (✉ 206 Chestnut Ridge Rd., Scottsville, NY 14624, ☎ 716/889–9096, dltravel@prodigy.net), run by a former physical-rehabilitation counselor. **CareVacations** (✉ 5-5110 50th Ave., Leduc, Alberta T9E 6V4, Canada, ☎ 780/986–6404 or 877/478–7827, FAX 780/986–8332, WEB www.carevacations.com), for group tours and cruise vacations. **Flying Wheels Travel** (✉ 143 W. Bridge St., Box 382, Owatonna, MN 55060, ☎ 507/451–5005 or 800/535–6790, FAX 507/451–1685, WEB www.flyingwheelstravel.com).

DISCOUNTS & DEALS

Be a smart shopper and **compare all your options** before making decisions. A plane ticket bought with a promotional coupon from travel clubs, coupon books, and direct-mail offers or on the Internet may not be cheaper than the least expensive fare from a discount ticket agency. And always keep in mind that what you get is just as important as what you save.

DISCOUNT RESERVATIONS

To save money, **look into discount reservations services** with toll-free numbers, which use their buying power to get a better price on hotels, airline tickets, even car rentals. When booking a room, always **call the hotel's local toll-free number** (if one is available) rather than the central reservations number—you'll often get a better price. Always ask about special packages or corporate rates.

When shopping for the best deal on hotels and car rentals, **look for guaranteed exchange rates,** which protect you against a falling dollar. With your rate locked in, you won't pay more, even if the price goes up in the local currency.

➤ AIRLINE TICKETS: ☎ **800/FLY–ASAP.**

➤ HOTEL ROOMS: **Players Express Vacations** (☎ 800/458–6161, WEB www.playersexpress.com). **Steigenberger Reservation Service** (☎ 800/223–5652, WEB www.srs-worldhotels.com). **Turbotrip.com** (☎ 800/473–7829, WEB www.turbotrip.com).

PACKAGE DEALS

Don't confuse packages and guided tours. When you buy a package, you travel on your own, just as though you had planned the trip yourself. Fly/drive packages, which combine airfare and car rental, are often a good deal.

ELECTRICITY

For U.S. and Canadian travelers, electrical converters are not necessary because Mexico operates on the 60-cycle, 120-volt system; however, many Mexican outlets have not been updated to accommodate three-prong and polarized plugs (those with one larger prong), so to be safe **bring an adapter.**

If your appliances are dual-voltage, you'll need only an adapter. Don't use 110-volt outlets marked FOR SHAVERS

ONLY for high-wattage appliances such as blow-dryers. Most laptops operate equally well on 110 and 220 volts and so require only an adapter.

EMBASSIES

Australia, Canada, New Zealand, the United Kingdom, and the United States all have embassies in Mexico City. If you need assistance in an emergency, you can go to your country's embassy. Proof of identity and citizenship are generally required to enter.

➤ AUSTRALIA: **Australian Embassy** (✉ Rubén Darío 55, Col. Polanco, ☎ 5531–5225).

➤ CANADA: **Canadian Embassy** (✉ Schiller 529, Col. Polanco, ☎ 5724–7900).

➤ NEW ZEALAND: **New Zealand Embassy** (✉ José Luis LaGrange 103, 10th fl., Col. Polanco, ☎ 5281–5486).

➤ UNITED KINGDOM: **British Embassy** (✉ Río Lerma 71, Col. Cuauhtémoc, ☎ 5207–2089).

➤ UNITED STATES: **U.S. Embassy** (✉ Paseo de la Reforma 305, Col. Cuauhtémoc, ☎ 5209–9100).

EMERGENCIES

You're not protected by the laws of your native land once you're on Mexican soil. If you get into a scrape with the law, you can call the Citizens' Emergency Center in the United States. You can also call the 24-hour English-language hot line of the Procuraduría de Protección al Turista (Attorney General for the Protection of Tourists) in Mexico City; it can provide immediate assistance as well as general, nonemergency guidance. **In an emergency, dial 080 from any phone in Mexico City.**

➤ CONTACTS: **Citizens' Emergency Center**(☎ 202/647–5225 weekdays 8:15 AM–10 PM EST, Sat. 9AM–3 PM; 202/634–3600 after hours and Sun.). **Procuraduría de Protección al Turista** (Attorney General for the Protection of Tourists; ☎ 01–800/903–9200; 800/482–9832 from the U.S.).

ENGLISH-LANGUAGE MEDIA

English-language magazines and books can be found at some of the larger grocery stores in Mexico, but they're expensive—usually at least double what you'd pay back home. Several stores in Mexico City sell English-language publications and you can probably find at least one place in other major cities to buy them. However, in most smaller towns, you won't have much luck.

NEWSPAPERS & MAGAZINES

Mexico has one major English-language newspaper: *The News,* available at hotels and newsstands in the tourist areas.

ETIQUETTE & BEHAVIOR

In the United States, for example, being direct, efficient, and succinct is highly valued. But in Mexico, where communication tends to be more subtle, this style is often perceived as curt and aggressive. Mexicans are extremely polite, so losing your temper over delays or complaining loudly will get you branded as rude and make people less inclined to help you. **Remember that things move at a slow pace** here and that there's no stigma attached to being late; accept this gracefully. Learning basic phrases in Spanish such as "please" and "thank you" will make a big difference in how people respond to you.

BUSINESS ETIQUETTE

Personal relationships always come first here, so developing rapport and trust is essential. A handshake and personal greeting is appropriate along with a friendly inquiry about family, especially if you have met the family. In established business relationships, do not be surprised if you're greeted with a kiss on the cheek or a hug. Always be respectful toward colleagues in public and keep confrontations private. Meetings may or may not start on time, but you should be patient. When invited to dinner at the home of a client or associate, bring a gift and be sure to send a thank-you note afterward.

GAY & LESBIAN TRAVEL

Mexican same-sex couples keep a low profile, and foreign same-sex couples may want to do the same. Two people of the same gender can often have a hard time getting a *cama matrimonial* (double bed), especially in smaller hotels. This could be attributed to the influence of the Catholic Church—Mexico is a devoutly Catholic country. The same rule that applies all over the world holds in Mexico as well: alternative lifestyles in general are more accepted in cosmopolitan areas, such as Mexico City, Acapulco, Ajijic, Cancún, Cuernavaca, Guadalajara, Puerto Vallarta, San Miguel de Allende, and Veracruz City.

➤ GAY- & LESBIAN-FRIENDLY TRAVEL AGENCIES: **Different Roads Travel** (✉ 8383 Wilshire Blvd., Suite 902, Beverly Hills, CA 90211, ☎ 323/651–5557 or 800/429–8747, FAX 323/651–3678, lgernert@tzell.com). **Kennedy Travel** (✉ 314 Jericho Turnpike, Floral Park, NY 11001, ☎ 516/352–4888 or 800/237–7433, FAX 516/354–8849, WEB www.kennedytravel.com). **Now Voyager** (✉ 4406 18th St., San Francisco, CA 94114, ☎ 415/626–1169 or 800/255–6951, FAX 415/626–8626, WEB www.nowvoyager.com). **Skylink Travel and Tour** (✉ 1006 Mendocino Ave., Santa Rosa, CA 95401, ☎ 707/546–9888 or 800/225–5759, FAX 707/546–9891, WEB www.skylinktravel.com), serving lesbian travelers.

HEALTH

AIR POLLUTION

Air pollution in Mexico City can pose a health risk. The sheer number of cars and industries in the capital, thermal inversions, and the inability to process sewage have all contributed to the high levels of lead, carbon monoxide, and other pollutants in Mexico City's atmosphere. Though the long-term effects are not known, children, the elderly, and those with respiratory problems should avoid jogging, outdoor sports, and being outdoors more than necessary on days of high smog alerts. If you have heart problems, keep in mind that Mexico City is, at 7,556 ft, the highest metropolis on the North American continent. This compounded with the smog may pose a serious health risk, so check with your doctor before planning a trip.

The Australian, British, Canadian, New Zealand, and U.S. embassies in Mexico City can provide lists of English-speaking doctors.

DIVERS' ALERT

Do not fly within 24 hours of scuba diving.

FOOD & DRINK

In Mexico the major health risk, known as *turista*, or traveler's diarrhea, is caused by eating contaminated fruit or vegetables or drinking contaminated water. So **watch what you eat.** Stay away from ice, uncooked food, and unpasteurized milk and milk products, and **drink only bottled water** or water that has been boiled for at least 10 minutes (ask: *quiero el agua hervida por diez minutos*), even when you're brushing your teeth. Mild cases may respond to Imodium (known generically as loperamide or Lomotil) or Pepto-Bismol (not as strong), both of which can be purchased over the counter; keep in mind, though, that these drugs can complicate more serious illnesses. Drink plenty of purified water or tea; chamomile tea (*te de manzanilla*) is a good folk remedy and it's readily available in restaurants throughout Mexico. In severe cases, rehydrate yourself with Gatorade or a salt-sugar solution (½ teaspoon salt and 4 tablespoons sugar per quart of water).

When ordering cold drinks at untouristed establishments, **skip the ice:** *sin hielo.* (You can usually identify ice made commercially from purified water by its uniform shape and the hole in the center.) Hotels with water-purification systems will post signs to that effect in the rooms. *Tacos al pastor*—thin pork slices grilled on a spit and garnished with the usual cilantro, onions, and chili peppers—are delicious but dangerous. It's also a good idea to pass up *ceviche*, raw fish cured in lemon juice—a favorite appetizer, especially at seaside resorts. The Mexican Department of Health warns that marinating in lemon juice does not constitute the "cooking" that would make the shellfish safe to eat. Also, be wary of hamburgers sold from street stands, because you can never be certain what meat they are made with (horse meat is common).

MEDICAL PLANS

No one plans to get sick while traveling, but it happens, so **consider signing up with a medical-assistance company.**

Members get doctor referrals, emergency evacuation or repatriation, hot lines for medical consultation, cash for emergencies, and other assistance.

➤ MEDICAL-ASSISTANCE COMPANIES: **International SOS Assistance** (WEB www.internationalsos.com; ✉ 8 Neshaminy Interplex, Suite 207, Trevose, PA 19053, ☎ 215/245–4707 or 800/523–6586, FAX 215/244–9617; ✉ 12 Chemin Riantbosson, 1217 Meyrin 1, Geneva, Switzerland, ☎ 4122/785–6464, FAX 4122/785–6424; ✉ 331 N. Bridge Rd., 17-00, Odeon Towers, Singapore 188720, ☎ 65/338–7800, FAX 65/338–7611).

PESTS & OTHER HAZARDS

Caution is advised when venturing out in the Mexican sun. Sunbathers lulled by a slightly overcast sky or the sea breezes can be burned badly in just 20 minutes. To avoid overexposure, **use strong sunscreens and avoid the peak sun hours** of noon to 2 PM. Sunscreen, including many American brands, can be found in pharmacies, supermarkets, and resort gift shops.

SHOTS & MEDICATIONS

According to the U.S. National Centers for Disease Control and Prevention (CDC), there is a limited risk of malaria and dengue fever in certain rural areas of Mexico. In most urban or easily accessible areas you need not worry. However, if you plan to visit remote regions or stay for more than six weeks, **check with the CDC's International Travelers Hotline.** In areas where malaria and dengue, both of which are carried by mosquitoes, are prevalent, use mosquito nets, wear clothing that covers the body, apply repellent containing DEET, and use spray for flying insects in living and sleeping areas. Repellents (*repelentes contra moscos*) and sprays (*repelentes de sprie contra moscos*) can be purchased at pharmacies. In some places you see mosquito coils (*espirales contra moscos*) used; they can be purchased in hardware stores (*ferretería*) as well as in pharmacies. Also **consider taking antimalarial pills** if you are doing serious adventure activities in subtropical areas. There is no vaccine to combat dengue, which if you are reasonably healthy is usually not serious (only dengue hemmorrhagic fever is potentially fatal).

➤ HEALTH WARNINGS: **National Centers for Disease Control and Prevention** (CDC; National Center for Infectious Diseases, Division of Quarantine, Traveler's Health Section, ✉ 1600 Clifton Rd. NE, M/S E-03, Atlanta, GA 30333, ☎ 888/232–3228 or 800/311–3435, FAX 888/232–3299; WEB www.cdc.gov).

HOLIDAYS & FESTIVALS

Banks and government offices close on January 1, February 5 (Day of the Constitution), March 21 (Benito Juárez's birthday), May 1 (Labor Day), September 16 (Independence Day), November 20 (Day of the Revolution), December 25. They may also close on unofficial holidays, such as Day of the Dead (November 2), and during Holy Week (the days leading to Easter Sunday). Government offices usually have reduced hours and staff from Christmas through New Year's Day.

INSURANCE

The most useful travel-insurance plan is a comprehensive policy that includes coverage for trip cancellation and interruption, default, trip delay, and medical expenses (with a waiver for preexisting conditions).

Without insurance you will lose all or most of your money if you cancel your trip, regardless of the reason. Default insurance covers you if your tour operator, airline, or cruise line goes out of business. Trip-delay covers expenses that arise because of bad weather or mechanical delays. Study the fine print when comparing policies.

If you're traveling internationally, a key component of travel insurance is coverage for medical bills incurred if you get sick on the road. Such expenses are not generally covered by Medicare or private policies. U.K. residents can buy a travel-insurance policy valid for most vacations taken during the year in which it's purchased (but check preexisting-condition coverage). British and Australian citizens need extra medical coverage when traveling overseas.

Always **buy travel policies directly from the insurance company**; if you buy them from a cruise line, airline, or tour operator that goes out of business you probably will not be covered for the agency or operator's default, a major risk. Before making any purchase, **review your existing health and home-owner's policies** to find what they cover away from home.

➤ TRAVEL INSURERS: In the U.S.: **Access America** (✉ 6600 W. Broad St., Richmond, VA 23230, ☎ 804/285–3300 or 800/284–8300, FAX 804/673–1586, WEB www.previewtravel.com), **Travel Guard International** (✉ 1145 Clark St., Stevens Point, WI 54481, ☎ 715/345–0505 or 800/826–1300, FAX 800/955–8785, WEB www.noelgroup.com).

➤ INSURANCE INFORMATION: In the U.K.: **Association of British Insurers** (✉ 51–55 Gresham St., London EC2V 7HQ, ☎ 020/7600–3333, FAX 020/7696–8999, WEB www.abi.org.uk). In Canada: **Voyager Insurance** (✉ 44 Peel Center Dr., Brampton, Ontario L6T 4M8, ☎ 905/791–8700; 800/668–4342 in Canada). In Australia: **Insurance Council of Australia** (✉ Level 3, 56 Pitt St., Sydney NSW 2000, ☎ 03/9614–1077, FAX 03/9614–7924). In New Zealand: **Insurance Council of New Zealand** (✉ Box 474, Wellington, ☎ 04/472–5230, FAX 04/473–3011, WEB www.icnz.org.nz).

LANGUAGE

Spanish is the official language of Mexico, although Indian languages are spoken by approximately 8% of the population and some of those people speak no Spanish at all. Basic English is widely understood by most people employed in tourism, less so in the less-developed areas. At the very least, shopkeepers will know the numbers for bargaining purposes.

As in most other foreign countries, knowing the mother tongue has a way of opening doors, so **learn some Spanish words and phrases.** Mexicans welcome even the most halting attempts to use the language.

Castilian Spanish—which is different from Latin American Spanish not only in pronunciation and grammar but also in vocabulary—is most widely taught outside Mexico. Words or phrases that are harmless or everyday in one country can offend in another. Unless you are lucky enough to be briefed on these nuances by a native coach, the only way to learn is by trial and error.

A phrase book and language-tape set can help get you started. *Fodor's Spanish for Travelers* (available at bookstores everywhere) is excellent.

LANGUAGE-STUDY PROGRAMS

Language institutes are pretty widespread in Mexico, and attending one is an ideal way not only to learn Mexican Spanish but also to acquaint yourself with the customs and the people of the country. For total immersion, most language schools offer boarding with a Mexican family, but your choice of lodgings and of length of stay is generally flexible.

We recommend the places listed below for learning Spanish and living with a Mexican family. AmeriSpan Unlimited, based in the United States, can arrange for language study and homestays. Special programs include those at the Centro de Idiomas de la Universidad Autónoma Benito Juárez, which offers classes in Mixtec and Zapotec as well as in Spanish, and at Cemanáuac, which has an emphasis on Latin American studies as well as language acquisition.

➤ LANGUAGE INSTITUTES: **AmeriSpan Unlimited** (✉ Box 40513, Philadelphia, PA 19106, ☎ 800/879–6640, FAX 215/985–4524). **Centro de Idiomas de la Universidad Autónoma Benito Juárez** (✉ Burgoa at Bustamante, Oaxaca 68000, ☎ FAX 9/51–65922). **Centro Internacional de Estudios para Estranjeros** (✉ Tomás V. Gómez 125, Guadalajara, Jalisco 44600, ☎ 3/616–4399; ✉ Libertad 42, Local 1, Puerto Vallarta, Jalisco 48360, ☎ 322/3–20–82, FAX 322/3–29–82). **Cemanáuac** (✉ San Juan 4, Col. Las Palmas Cuernavaca, Morelos, CP 62051, ☎ 73/18–64–07, FAX 73/12–54–18). **Iberoamerican University Programs for Foreign Students** (✉ Prolongación Paseo de la Reforma 880, Lomas de Santa Fe, Mexico, D.F. 01210, ☎ FAX 5267–4000 ext. 4017). **Instituto**

Allende (⊠ Ancha de San Antonio 20, San Miguel de Allende, Guanajuato 37700, ☎ 415/2–01–90 or 415/2–02–26, FAX 415/2–45–38). **Instituto Falcon** (⊠ Callejón de la Mora 158, Guanajuato 36000, ☎ 4/731–0745, WEB www.institutofalcon.com). **Instituto de Lenguas Jovel, A.C.** (⊠ A.P. 62, Ma. Adelina Flores 21, San Cristóbal de las Casas, Chiapas 29200, ☎ FAX 967/8–40–69). **National Autonomous University of Mexico School for Foreign Students** (⊠ A.P. 70, Taxco, Guerrero 40200, ☎ FAX 7/622–01–24). **SLI–Spanish Language Institute** (⊠ Bajada de la Pradera 208, Col. Pradera, Cuernavaca, Morelos 62170, ☎ FAX 73/17–52–94; in the U.S. contact Language Link Inc. ⊠ Box 3006, Peoria, IL 61612, ☎ 800/552–2051, FAX 309/692–2926).

LODGING

The price and quality of accommodations in Mexico vary about as much as the country's restaurants: from super-luxurious, international-class hotels and all-inclusive resorts to modest budget properties, seedy places with shared bathrooms, *casas de huéspedes* (guest houses), youth hostels, and *cabañas* (beach huts). You may find appealing bargains while you're on the road, but if your comfort threshold is high, **look for an English-speaking staff, guaranteed dollar rates, and toll-free reservation numbers.**

The lodgings we list are the cream of the crop in each price category. We always list the facilities that are available—but we don't specify whether they cost extra; when pricing accommodations, **always ask what's included and what costs extra.** Lodgings are denoted in the text with a house icon, ☂ ; establishments with restaurants that warrant a special trip have ✕☂ .

APARTMENT & VILLA RENTALS

If you want a home base that's roomy enough for a family and comes with cooking facilities, **consider a furnished rental.** These can save you money, especially if you're traveling with a group. Home-exchange directories sometimes list rentals as well as exchanges.

➤ INTERNATIONAL AGENTS: **At Home Abroad** (⊠ 405 E. 56th St., Suite 6H, New York, NY 10022, ☎ 212/421–9165, FAX 212/752–1591, WEB www.athomeabroadinc.com). **Hideaways International** (⊠ 767 Islington St., Portsmouth, NH 03801, ☎ 603/430–4433 or 800/843–4433, FAX 603/430–4444, WEB www.hideaways.com; membership $129). **Vacation Home Rentals Worldwide** (⊠ 235 Kensington Ave., Norwood, NJ 07648, ☎ 201/767–9393 or 800/633–3284, FAX 201/767–5510, WEB www.vhrww.com). **Villas and Apartments Abroad** (⊠ 1270 Avenue of the Americas, 15th floor, New York, NY 10020, ☎ 212/897–5045 or 800/433–3020, FAX 212/897–5039, WEB www.vaanyc.com). **Villas International** (⊠ 950 Northgate Dr., Suite 206, San Rafael, CA 94903, ☎ 415/499–9490 or 800/221–2260, FAX 415/499–9491, WEB www.villasintl.com).

B&BS

The B&B craze hasn't missed Mexico, and the same delights that you find elsewhere in the world apply here, too—personable service, interesting local furnishings and decorative talent, and tasty morning meals. San Miguel de Allende and other Heartland cities have their share of charming places, as do Mexico City and parts of the Yucatán. If you arrive in Mexico City without a reservation, the Mexico City Hotel and Motel Association operates a booth at the airport that will assist you.

➤ RESERVATION SERVICES: **Mexico City Hotel and Motel Association** (☎ 5571–3268, 5571–3262).

CAMPING

A host of camping opportunities exist in Mexico, but don't expect the typical U.S.-style campground. Mexico's are usually trailer parks with running water, cooking areas, and room to pitch tents; sites can cost $1–$10. To enjoy more-rustic surroundings, you can set up camp off the road or on the beach in relative safety, and save loads of money. Usually, you can camp at an *ejido* (farming community) or on someone's land for free as long as you ask permission first; **ask locals about the safest and best spots.** The beaches at night aren't as safe as they once were; **be alert and don't camp alone.** And don't camp at archaeological sites.

Camping supplies are scarce in Mexico. Before you begin packing loads of camping gear, however, consider how much camping you'll actually do versus how much trouble it will be to haul around your tent, sleeping bag, stove, and accoutrements. Finding a place to store your gear can be difficult—lockers tend to be small.

In many towns along the Pacific and Caribbean coasts, beachside *palapas* (thatch-roof huts) are an excellent alternative to tent camping. All you'll need for a night in a palapa is a hammock (they don't cost much in Mexico), some mosquito netting, and a padlock for stashing your belongings in a locker.

HOME EXCHANGES

If you would like to exchange your home for someone else's, **join a home-exchange organization,** which will send you its updated listings of available exchanges for a year and will include your own listing in at least one of them. It's up to you to make specific arrangements.

➤ EXCHANGE CLUBS: **HomeLink International** (✉ Box 47747, Tampa, FL 33647, ☎ 813/975–9825 or 800/638–3841, FAX 813/910–8144, WEB www.homelink.org; $98 per year).

HOSTELS

No matter what your age, you can **save on lodging costs by staying at hostels.** In Mexico, however, high-school and college students are more often the norm at hostels than older travelers. In some 5,000 locations in more than 70 countries around the world, Hostelling International (HI), the umbrella group for a number of national youth-hostel associations, offers single-sex, dorm-style beds and, at many hostels, rooms for couples and family accommodations. Membership in any HI national hostel association, open to travelers of all ages, allows you to stay in HI-affiliated hostels at member rates; one-year membership is about $25 for adults (C$26.75 in Canada, £9.30 in the U.K., $30 in Australia, and $30 in New Zealand); hostels run about $10–$25 per night. Members have priority if the hostel is full; they're also eligible for discounts around the world, even on rail and bus travel in some countries.

➤ ORGANIZATIONS: **Hostelling International—American Youth Hostels** (✉ 733 15th St. NW, Suite 840, Washington, DC 20005, ☎ 202/783–6161, FAX 202/783–6171, WEB www.hiayh.org). **Hostelling International—Canada** (✉ 400–205 Catherine St., Ottawa, Ontario K2P 1C3, Canada, ☎ 613/237–7884, FAX 613/237–7868, WEB www.hostellingintl.ca). **Youth Hostel Association of England and Wales** (✉ Trevelyan House, 8 St. Stephen's Hill, St. Albans, Hertfordshire AL1 2DY, U.K., ☎ 0870/8708808, FAX 01727/844126, WEB www.yha.org.uk). **Australian Youth Hostel Association** (✉ 10 Mallett St., Camperdown, NSW 2050, Australia, ☎ 02/9565–1699, FAX 02/9565–1325, WEB www.yha.com.au). **Youth Hostels Association of New Zealand** (✉ Box 436, Christchurch, New Zealand, ☎ 03/379–9970, FAX 03/365–4476, WEB www.yha.org.nz).

HOTELS

It's essential to **reserve in advance** if you're traveling during high season or holiday periods. Overbooking is a common practice in some parts of Mexico, such as Cancún and Acapulco. Travelers to remote areas will encounter little difficulty in obtaining rooms on a walk-in basis unless it's during a holiday season.

Hotel rates are subject to the 15% value-added tax (it's 10% in the states of Quintana Roo, Baja California, and Baja California Sur). In addition, many states charge a 2% hotel tax, and the revenue is being used for tourism promotion. Service charges and meals generally are not included in the hotel rates. The Mexican government categorizes hotels, based on qualitative evaluations, into *gran turismo* (super-deluxe, or six-star, properties, of which there are only about 50 nationwide); five-star down to one-star; and economy class. Keep in mind that many hotels that might otherwise be rated higher have opted for a lower category to avoid higher interest rates on loans and financing.

High- versus low-season rates can vary significantly. Hotels in this guide have private bathrooms with showers, unless stated otherwise; bathtubs are not common in inexpensive hotels and properties in smaller towns.

If you're particularly sensitive to noise, you should **call ahead to learn if your hotel of choice is located on a busy street.** Many of the most engaging accommodations in Mexico are on downtown intersections that experience heavy automobile and pedestrian traffic. And large hotels are known to have lobby bars with live music in the middle of an open-air atrium leading directly to rooms. When you book, **request a room far from the bar.**

➤ TOLL-FREE NUMBERS: **Best Western** (☎ 800/528–1234, WEB www.bestwestern.com). **Choice** (☎ 800/221–2222, WEB www.hotelchoice.com). **Days Inn** (☎ 800/325–2525, WEB www.daysinn.com). **Doubletree and Red Lion Hotels** (☎ 800/222–8733, WEB www.doubletree.com). **Forte** (☎ 800/225–5843, WEB www.forte-hotels.com). **Four Seasons** (☎ 800/332–3442, WEB www.fourseasons.com). **Hilton** (☎ 800/445–8667, WEB www.hilton.com). **Holiday Inn** (☎ 800/465–4329, WEB www.basshotels.com). **Howard Johnson** (☎ 800/654–4656, WEB www.hojo.com). **Hyatt Hotels & Resorts** (☎ 800/233–1234, WEB www.hyatt.com). **Inter-Continental** (☎ 800/327–0200, WEB www.interconti.com). **Marriott** (☎ 800/228–9290, WEB www.marriott.com). **Le Meridien** (☎ 800/543–4300, WEB www.lemeridien-hotels.com). **Nikko Hotels International** (☎ 800/645–5687, WEB www.nikkohotels.com). **Omni** (☎ 800/843–6664, WEB www.omnihotels.com). **Radisson** (☎ 800/333–3333, WEB www.radisson.com). **Ramada** (☎ 800/228–2828, WEB www.ramada.com). **Ritz-Carlton** (☎ 800/241–3333, WEB www.ritzcarlton.com). **Sheraton** (☎ 800/325–3535, WEB www.starwood.com). **Westin Hotels & Resorts** (☎ 800/228–3000, WEB www.westin.com). **Wyndham Hotels & Resorts** (☎ 800/822–4200, WEB www.wyndham.com).

MAIL & SHIPPING

The Mexican postal system is notoriously slow and unreliable; **never send packages** or expect to receive them, as they may be stolen. (For emergencies, use a courier service or the express-mail service, with insurance). If you're an American Express cardholder, your best bet is to have packages sent to the nearest AmEx office.

Post offices (*oficinas de correos*) are found in even the smallest villages. International postal service is all airmail, but even so your letter will take anywhere from 10 days to six weeks to arrive. Service within Mexico can be equally slow.

OVERNIGHT SERVICES

Federal Express, DHL, and United Parcel Service are available in major cities and many resort areas, but Federal Express is the most widespread. They offer office or hotel pickup with 24-hour advance notice and are very reliable. From Mexico City to anywhere in the United States, the minimum charge is around $22 for a package weighing about one pound. Starting prices are higher for Australia, Canada, New Zealand, and the U.K., and deliveries take longer.

➤ MAJOR SERVICES: In Mexico City: **Federal Express** (☎ 5228–9904); **DHL** (☎ 5345–7000); and **United Parcel Service** (☎ 5228–7900).

POSTAL ABBREVIATIONS

Mexican states have postal abbreviations of two or more letters. To send mail to Mexico, use the following Mexican state postal codes: **Baja California**: B.C.; **Baja California Sur**: B.C.S.; **Campeche**: Camp.; **Chiapas**: Chis.; **Chihuahua**: Chih.; **Distrito Federal (Mexico City)**: D.F.; **Guanajuato**: Gto.; **Guerrero**: Gro.; **Jalisco**: Jal.; **Estado de Mexico**: Edo. de Mex.; **Michoacán**: Mich.; **Morelos**: Mor.; **Nuevo Leon**: N.I.; **Oaxaca**: Oax.; **Querétaro**: Qro.; **Quintana Roo**: Q. Roo; **Sinaloa**: Sin.; **Sonora**: Son.; **Tabasco**: Tab.; **Veracruz**: Ver.; **Yucatán**: Yuc.; **Zacatecas**: Zac.

POSTAL RATES

It costs 4.20 pesos to send a postcard or letter weighing under 20 grams to the United States or Canada; it's 5.30 pesos to Europe and 6 pesos to Australia.

RECEIVING MAIL

To receive mail in Mexico, you can have it sent to your hotel or use *poste restante* at the post office. In the latter case, the address must include the words "a/c Lista de Correos" (general delivery), followed by the city, state, postal code, and country. To use this service, you must first register with the post office at which you wish to receive your mail. The post office posts and updates daily a list of names for whom mail has been received. Holders of American Express cards or traveler's checks can have mail sent to them in care of the local American Express office. For a list of offices worldwide, write for the *Traveler's Companion* from **American Express** (✉ Box 678, Canal Street Station, New York, NY 10013).

MONEY MATTERS

Prices in this book are quoted most often in U.S. dollars. We would prefer to list costs in pesos, but because the value of the currency fluctuates considerably, what costs 90 pesos today might cost 120 pesos in six months.

Mexico is less expensive than other North American vacation spots, such as the Caribbean. In general, costs will vary with the when, where, and how of your travel in Mexico. If you travel only by air or package tour, stay at international hotel-chain properties, and eat at tourist restaurants, you might not find Mexico such a bargain. If you want a closer look at the country and are not wedded to standard creature comforts, you can spend as little as $25 a day on room, board, and local transportation. Speaking Spanish is also helpful in bargaining situations and when asking for dining recommendations.

Cancún, Puerto Vallarta, Mexico City, Monterrey, Acapulco, Ixtapa, Los Cabos, Manzanillo, and, to a lesser extent, Mazatlán and Huatulco are the most expensive places to visit in Mexico. All the beach towns, however, offer budget accommodations, and the smaller, less accessible ones are often more moderately priced, examples being the Gulf coast and northern Yucatán, parts of Quintana Roo, some of the less developed spots north and south of Puerto Vallarta in the states of Jalisco and Nayarit, Puerto Escondido, and the smaller Oaxacan coastal towns as well as those of Chiapas and Tabasco.

Average costs in major cities vary, although less than in the past because of an increase in business travelers. A stay in one of Mexico City's top hotels can cost more than $200 (as much or more than at the coastal resorts), but you can get away with a tab of $45 for two at what was once an expensive restaurant.

Probably the best value for your travel dollar is in smaller, inland towns, such as San Cristóbal de las Casas, Mérida, Morelia, Guanajuato, and Oaxaca, where tourism is less developed. Although Oaxaca lodging can run more than $150 a night, simple colonial-style hotels with adequate accommodations for under $40 can be found, and tasty, filling meals are rarely more than $15.

Prices throughout this guide are given for adults. Substantially reduced fees are almost always available for children, students, and senior citizens.

ATMS

ATMs (*caja automática*) are becoming commonplace in more and more Mexican towns and cities. Cirrus and Plus are the most commonly found networks in Mexico. Before you leave home, **ask what the transaction fee will be** for withdrawing money in Mexico. (It's usually $3 a pop.) Many Mexican ATMs cannot accept PINs (personal identification numbers) that have more than four digits; if yours is longer, **ask your bank about changing your PIN (*número de clave*) before you leave home,** and keep in mind that processing such a change often takes a few weeks.

If your transaction still cannot be completed—an annoyingly common occurrence—chances are that the computer lines are busy or that the machine has run out of money or is being serviced.

For cash advances, plan to use Visa or MasterCard, as many Mexican ATMs don't accept American Express. The ATMs at Banamex, one of the oldest nationwide banks, tend to be the most reliable. Bancomer is another bank with many ATM locations, but they usually provide only cash advances. The newer Serfín banks have reliable ATMs that accept credit cards as well as Plus and Cirrus cards.

See Safety, *below,* on avoiding ATM robberies.

CREDIT CARDS

Traveler's checks and all major U.S. credit cards are accepted in most tourist areas of Mexico. Smaller, less expensive restaurants and shops, however, tend to take only cash. In general, credit cards aren't accepted in small towns and villages, except for tourist-oriented hotels. Diner's Club is usually accepted only in major hotel chains; the most widely accepted cards are Mastercard and Visa. When shopping, you can usually get better prices if you **pay with cash.**

At the same time, when traveling internationally you'll **receive wholesale exchange rates** when you make purchases with credit cards. These exchange rates are usually better than rates that banks give you for changing money. In Mexico the decision to pay cash or use a credit card might depend on whether the establishment in which you are making a purchase finds bargaining for prices acceptable. To avoid fraud, it's wise to **make sure that "pesos" is clearly marked on all credit-card receipts.**

Throughout this guide, the following abbreviations are used: **AE,** American Express; **DC,** Diner's Club; **MC,** MasterCard; and **V,** Visa.

➤ REPORTING LOST CARDS: Before you leave for Mexico, be sure to **find out your credit-card companies' toll-free card-replacement numbers** that work at home as well as in Mexico; they could be impossible to find once you get to Mexico, and the calls you place to cancel your cards can be long ones. **Carry these numbers separately from your wallet** so you'll have them if you need to call to report lost or stolen cards.

CURRENCY

At press time, the peso was still "floating" after the devaluation enacted by the Zedillo administration in late 1994. While exchange rates have been as favorable as 9.92 pesos to US$1, 6.40 pesos to C$1, 15.40 pesos to £1, 6.10 pesos to A$1, and 4.85 pesos to NZ$1, the market and prices continue to adjust. **Check with your bank or the financial pages of your local newspaper for current exchange rates.** For quick estimates of how much something costs in U.S. dollar terms, divide prices given in pesos by 10. For example, 50 pesos would be about $5.

Mexican currency comes in denominations of 10-, 20-, 50-, 100-, 200-, 500-, and 1,000-peso bills. Coins come in denominations of 20, 10, 5, and 1 pesos and 50, 20, 10, and 5 centavos. Many of the coins and bills are very similar, so check carefully.

U.S. dollar bills (but not coins) are widely accepted in many parts of the Yucatán, particularly in Cancún and Cozumel, where you'll often find prices in shops quoted in dollars. However, you'll get your change in pesos. Many tourist shops and market vendors as well as virtually all hotel service personnel also accept dollars.

CURRENCY EXCHANGE

ATM transaction fees may be higher abroad than at home, but ATM currency-exchange rates are the best of all because they're based on wholesale rates offered only by major banks. And if you take out a fair amount of cash per withdrawal, the transaction fee becomes less of a strike against the exchange rate (in percentage terms). However, most ATMs allow only up to $300 a transaction. Banks and *casas de cambio* (money-exchange houses) have the second-best exchange rates. The difference from one place to another is usually only a few centavos.

Most banks change money on weekdays only until 1 (though they stay open until 5), while casas de cambio generally stay open until 6 and often operate on weekends. Bank rates are regulated by the federal government and are therefore invariable, while casas de cambio have slightly more variable rates. Some hotels also exchange money, but for providing you with this convenience they help themselves to a bigger commission than banks.

You can do well at most airport exchange booths, except in Cancún, but not necessarily at rail and bus stations, in hotels, in restaurants, or in stores.

When changing money, count your bills before leaving the bank or casa de cambio, and don't accept any partially torn or taped-together notes; they won't be accepted anywhere. Also, many shop and restaurant owners are unable to make change for large bills. Enough of these encounters may compel you to request *billetes chicos* (small bills) when you exchange money.

➤ EXCHANGE SERVICES: **International Currency Express** (☎ 888/278–6628 for orders, WEB www.foreignmoney. com). **Thomas Cook Currency Services** (☎ 800/287–7362 for telephone orders and retail locations, WEB www. us.thomascook.com).

TRAVELER'S CHECKS

Do you need traveler's checks? It depends on where you're headed. If you're going to rural areas and small towns, go with cash; traveler's checks are best used in cities. Lost or stolen checks can usually be replaced within 24 hours. To ensure a speedy refund, buy your own traveler's checks—don't let someone else pay for them: irregularities like this can cause delays. The person who bought the checks should make the call to request a refund.

OUTDOORS & SPORTS

Mexico offers golf, waterskiing, diving, and hiking. Mexico City, Guadalajara, Monterrey, and smaller cities as well as beach resorts all have golf facilities. Courses abound in Los Cabos, an area that's been gearing up to become Mexico's premier golf resort.

Waterskiing is very popular at beach resorts, while the scuba diving in Cozumel, the Caribbean coast, and Cancún is excellent. Renting equipment isn't a problem in the larger resort areas.

Mexico's volcanoes and mountains provide many hiking opportunities. The Copper Canyon is a favorite destination for this.

PACKING

When traveling internationally, it's always a good idea to pack a change of clothes in your carry-on bag in case your other luggage is lost. Take at least a change of underwear, essential toiletries, and a shirt—add to that a bathing suit if you're heading to a beach resort. Also, **pack an extra pair of eyeglasses or contact lenses** in your carry-on luggage, and **enough of any medication you take** to last the entire trip. You may also ask your doctor to write a spare prescription using the drug's generic name, since brand names may vary from country to country. In luggage to be checked, **never pack prescription drugs or valuables.** To avoid customs delays, carry medications in their original packaging. And don't forget to carry with you the addresses of offices that handle refunds of lost traveler's checks.

For resorts, bring lightweight sportswear, bathing suits, and cover-ups for the beach. Bathing suits and immodest clothing are inappropriate for shopping and sightseeing, both in cities and beach resorts. Mexico City is a bit more formal than the resorts and, because of its high elevation, cooler. Men will want to bring lightweight suits or slacks and blazers for fancier restaurants; women should pack tailored dresses or pants suits. Many Mexico City restaurants require jacket and tie; jeans are acceptable for shopping and sightseeing, but shorts are frowned upon for men and women. You'll need a lightweight topcoat for winter and an all-weather coat and umbrella in case of sudden summer rainstorms. Lately the rains have been appearing at other times of the year, so always **pack a small umbrella** at least.

Cancún and Acapulco are both casual and elegant; you'll see high-style sportswear, cotton slacks and walking shorts, and plenty of colorful sundresses. The sun can be fierce; **bring a sun hat and sunscreen** for the beach and for sightseeing. You'll need a sweater or jacket to cope with hotel and restaurant air-conditioning, which can be glacial, and for occasional cool spells. Few restaurants require a jacket and tie.

Check *Fodor's How to Pack* (available in bookstores everywhere) for more tips.

Luggage carts are free at the Mexico City airport, practically the only airport where you'll find them; bus and train stations do not have carts.

CHECKING LUGGAGE

How many carry-on bags you can bring with you is up to the airline. Most allow two, but not always, so make sure that everything you carry aboard will fit under your seat or in the overhead bin, and get to the gate early. Note that if you have a seat at the back of the plane, you'll probably board first, while the overhead bins are still empty.

If you are flying internationally, note that baggage allowances may be determined not by piece but by weight—generally 88 pounds (40 kilograms) in first class, 66 pounds (30 kilograms) in business class, and 44 pounds (20 kilograms) in economy.

Airline liability for baggage is limited to $1,250 per person on flights within the United States. On international flights it amounts to $9.07 per pound or $20 per kilogram for checked baggage (roughly $640 per 70-pound bag) and $400 per passenger for unchecked baggage. You can buy additional coverage at check-in for about $10 per $1,000 of coverage, but it excludes a rather extensive list of items, shown on your airline ticket.

Before departure, **itemize your bags' contents** and their worth, and label the bags with your name, address, and phone number. (If you use your home address, cover it so potential thieves can't see it readily.) Inside each bag, **pack a copy of your itinerary.** At check-in, **make sure that each bag is correctly tagged** with the destination airport's three-letter code. If your bags arrive damaged or fail to arrive at all, file a written report with the airline before leaving the airport.

PASSPORTS & VISAS

When traveling internationally, **carry your passport** even if you don't need one (it's always the best form of I.D.) and **make two photocopies of the data page** (one for someone at home and another for you, carried separately from your passport). If you lose your passport, promptly call the nearest embassy or consulate and the local police.

ENTERING MEXICO

For stays of up to 180 days, Americans must prove citizenship through either a valid passport, certified copy of a birth certificate, or voter-registration card (the last two must be accompanied by a government-issue photo ID). Minors traveling with one parent need notarized permission from the absent parent. For stays of more than 180 days, all U.S. citizens, even infants, need a valid passport to enter Mexico. Minors also need parental permission.

Canadians need only proof of citizenship to enter Mexico for stays of up to six months.

U.K. citizens need only a valid passport to enter Mexico for stays of up to three months.

Mexico has instituted a $17 visitor fee that applies to all visitors—except those entering by sea at Mexican ports who stay less than 72 hours, and those entering by land who do not stray past the 26–30-km (16–18-mi) checkpoint into the country's interior. For visitors arriving by air, the fee, which covers visits of more than 72 hours and up to 30 days, is usually tacked on to the airline-ticket price. You must pay the fee each time you extend your 30-day tourist visa.

PASSPORT OFFICES

The best time to apply for a passport or to renew is in fall and winter. Before any trip, check your passport's expiration date, and, if necessary, renew it as soon as possible.

➤ AUSTRALIAN CITIZENS: **Australian Passport Office** (☎ 131–232, WEB www.dfat.gov.au/passports).

➤ CANADIAN CITIZENS: **Passport Office** (☎ 819/994–3500; 800/567–6868 in Canada, WEB www.dfait-maeci.gc.ca/passport).

➤ NEW ZEALAND CITIZENS: **New Zealand Passport Office** (☎ 04/494–0700, WEB www.passports.govt.nz).

➤ U.K. CITIZENS: **London Passport Office** (☎ 0870/521–0410, WEB www.ukpa.gov.uk) for fees and documentation requirements and to request an emergency passport.

➤ U.S. CITIZENS: **National Passport Information Center** (☎ 900/225–5674; calls are 35¢ per minute for automated service, $1.05 per minute

for operator service; WEB www.travel.
state.gov/npicinfo.html).

REST ROOMS

Expect to find clean flushing toilets,
toilet tissue, soap, and running water
in the major tourist destinations.
Other places should have simple but
clean toilets. The more primitive rest
rooms, usually in public areas with
little tourist traffic, will have no paper, no water at times, and no toilet
seats. Some public places, like bus
stations, charge one or two pesos to
use the facility, but toilet paper is
included in the fee. Keep tissues with
you, just in case.

SAFETY

The U.S. State Department has
warned of "critical levels" of crime
against tourists in Mexico, noting an
increase in the level of violence of the
crimes committed and what appeared
to be a significant incidence of sexual
assaults against women. Reports indicated that uniformed police officers
were on occasion perpetrating the
nonviolent crimes, sometimes stopping cars and seeking money.

The largest increase in crime has taken
place in Mexico City, where the age-
old problem of pickpocketing has been
overshadowed by robberies at gun-
point. Another development has been
abductions and robberies in taxicabs
hailed from the street (as opposed to
hired from a hotel or taxi stand).

Many foreigners are aware of Mexico's reputation for corruption. The
patronage system is a well-entrenched
part of Mexican politics and industry,
and workers in the public sector—
notably policemen and customs officials—are notoriously underpaid.
Everyone has heard some horror story
about highway assaults, pickpocketing, bribes, or foreigners languishing in
Mexican jails. These reports of crimes
apply in large part to Mexico City and
more-remote areas of Oaxaca and
Chiapas. So far, crime is not such a
problem in the Heartland (cities like
San Miguel de Allende), Puerto Vallarta, Cancún, and much of the rest of
the country. Pickpocketing is usually
the biggest concern.

Use common sense everywhere, but
**exercise particular caution in Mexico
City.** In addition, **avoid remote, less-
traveled areas of Oaxaca and Chiapas**
as crime in these areas can be more
life-threatening. Do not pick up hitch-
hikers or hitchhike yourself. Also, try
to use luxury buses (rather than sec-
ond- or third-class vehicles), which
use the safer toll roads—and it's best
to travel only during the day. For the
time being, **women should not venture
alone onto uncrowded beaches,** and
everyone should **avoid urges to get
away from it all** on your own (even as
a couple) to go hiking in remote
national parks.

In Mexico City, **don't wear any
valuables, including watches,** and try
not to act too much like a tourist.
Wear a money belt, put valuables in
hotel safes, avoid driving on untrav-
eled streets and roads at night, and
carry your own baggage whenever
possible, unless in a luxury hotel.
Also, you won't need your passport
in the city, so leave it in the hotel
safe—replacing it would be more
trouble than you need.

Take only registered hotel taxis or
have a hotel concierge call a *sitio*
(stationed cab)—**do not hail taxis on
the street under any circumstances.**
Use ATMs during the day and in big,
enclosed commercial areas. Avoid the
glass-enclosed street variety of banks
where you may be more vulnerable to
thieves who force you to withdraw
money for them; abduction is also
possible. This cannot be stressed
strongly enough.

Bear in mind that reporting a crime to
the police is often a frustrating experience unless you speak excellent Spanish and have a great deal of patience. If
you are the victim of an assault, contact your local consular agent or the
consular section of your country's embassy in Mexico City, especially if you
need medical attention. For more-de-
tailed information on travel safey, consult the Mexican Ministry of Tourism's
Web site at www.safemexico.com.

WOMEN IN MEXICO

Women traveling alone are likely to
be subjected to *piropos* (catcalls). To
avoid this, don't wear tight or
provocative clothes or enter street
bars or cantinas alone; in some very
conservative rural areas, even sleeve-

less shirts or Bermuda shorts may seem inappropriate to the locals. Your best strategy is always to ignore the offender, do not speak to him, and go on about your business. If the situation seems to be getting out of hand, don't hesitate to ask someone for help. Piropos are one thing, but more aggressive harassment of women is not considered acceptable behavior. If you express outrage, you should find no shortage of willing defenders.

SENIOR-CITIZEN TRAVEL

To qualify for age-related discounts, **mention your senior-citizen status up front** when booking hotel reservations (not when checking out) and before you're seated in restaurants (not when paying the bill). When renting a car, ask about promotional car-rental discounts, which can be cheaper than senior-citizen rates.

Mexican senior citizens must present a special government-issued credential to obtain discounts at any facility; foreign-issued credentials (such as from AARP) are not recognized in the country, and it's not enough to mention that you are a senior citizen.

➤ EDUCATIONAL PROGRAMS: **Elderhostel** (✉ 11 Ave. de Lafayette, Boston, MA 02111-1746, ☎ 877/426–8056, FAX 877/426–2166, WEB www.elderhostel.org). **Interhostel** (✉ University of New Hampshire, 6 Garrison Ave., Durham, NH 03824, ☎ 603/862–1147 or 800/733–9753, FAX 603/862–1113, WEB www.learn.unh.edu).

SHOPPING

At least three varieties of outlets sell Mexican crafts: indoor and outdoor municipal markets, shops run by Fonart (a government agency to promote Mexican crafts), and tourist boutiques in towns, shopping malls, and hotels. If you buy in the municipal shops or markets, you can avoid the value-added tax (*impuesto de valor agregado,* or IVA), but you should pay in pesos because paying in dollars won't give you a good exchange rate most of the time. Be sure to **take your time and inspect merchandise closely**: you'll find bargains, but quality can be inconsistent. Fonart shops are a good reference for quality and prices (the latter are fixed), and they accept credit

cards. Boutiques also accept credit cards if not dollars; although their prices may be higher, they are convenient and sometimes carry one-of-a-kind items. (You may be asked to pay up to 10% more on credit-card purchases; savvy shoppers with cash have greater bargaining clout.) The 15% IVA (10% in the states of Quintana Roo, Baja California, and Baja California Sur) is charged on most purchases but is often included in the price or disregarded by eager or desperate vendors.

It is not always true that the closer you are to the source of an article, the better the selection and price are likely to be. Mexico City, Guadalajara, Pátzcuaro, San Miguel de Allende, Puerto Vallarta, Oaxaca, San Cristóbal de las Casas, and Mérida have some of the best selections of crafts—and bargains as well. Prices are usually higher and selections more touristy at beach resorts.

Bargaining is widely accepted in markets, but you should understand that not all vendors will start out with outrageous prices. If you feel the price quoted is too high, start off by offering half the asking price and then slowly go up, usually to about 70% of the original price. Always **shop around.** In major shopping areas such as San Miguel, shops will wrap and send purchases back to the United States via a package-delivery company. Items made from tortoiseshell and black coral are not allowed into the United States.

STUDENTS IN MEXICO

➤ I.D.S & SERVICES: **Council Travel** (CIEE; ✉ 205 E. 42nd St., 15th floor, New York, NY 10017, ☎ 212/822–2700 or 888/268–6245, FAX 212/822–2699, WEB www.councilexchanges.org) for mail orders only, in the United States. **Travel Cuts** (✉ 187 College St., Toronto, Ontario M5T 1P7, Canada, ☎ 416/979–2406 or 800/667–2887 in Canada, FAX 416/979–8167, WEB www.travelcuts.com).

TAXES

Mexico charges an airport departure tax of US$18 or the peso equivalent for international and domestic flights. This tax is usually included in the price of your ticket, but check to be certain. Traveler's checks and credit cards are not accepted at the airport as payment for this.

Many states are charging a 2% tax on accommodations, the funds from which are being used for tourism promotion.

VALUE-ADDED TAX

Mexico has a value-added tax of 15% (10% in the states of Quintana Roo, Baja California, and Baja California Sur), called IVA (*impuesto de valor agregado*), which is occasionally (and illegally) waived for cash purchases. Other taxes and charges apply for phone calls made from your hotel room.

TAXIS

Government-certified taxis have a license with a photo of the driver and a taxi number prominently displayed, a meter, and either an orange or green stripe at the bottom of the license plate. In many cities, taxis charge by zones. In this case, be sure to agree on a fare before setting off. For reasons of security, especially in Mexico City, it's always best to call a *sitio* (stationed) cab rather than to flag one on the street. Tipping is not necessary unless the driver helps you with your bags, in which case a few pesos are appropriate.

AT THE AIRPORT

From the airport, **take the authorized taxi service.** Purchase the taxi vouchers sold at stands inside or just outside the terminal, which ensure that your fare is established beforehand. However, before you purchase your ticket, it's wise to locate the taxi originating and destination zones on a map and make sure your ticket is properly zoned; if you only need a ticket to Zone 3, don't pay for a ticket to Zone 4 or 5. Don't leave your luggage unattended while making transportation arrangements.

IN CITIES & BEACH RESORTS

In Mexican cities, **take a taxi rather than public transportation,** which, though inexpensive, is frequently slow and sometimes patrolled by pickpockets. (The exceptions are the air-conditioned buses in Acapulco, Cancún, and Mérida.) Always **establish the fare beforehand,** and **count your change.** In most of the beach resorts, there are inexpensive fixed-route fares, but if you don't ask, or your Spanish isn't great, you may get taken. In cities, especially the capital, be certain that the meter runs before getting in, and remember that there is usually an extra charge after 10 PM. For out-of-town and hourly services, negotiate a rate in advance; many drivers will start by asking how much you want to pay to get a sense of how street-smart you are. In all cases, if you are unsure of what a fare should be, ask your hotel's front-desk personnel or bell captain.

Hire taxis only from hotels and taxi stands *(sitios),* **or use those that you have summoned by phone.** Street taxis might be the cheapest, but an alarming increase in abductions and violent crime involves street cabs—for safety's sake, under no circumstances should you take one. And never leave luggage unattended in a taxi.

In addition to private taxis, many cities have bargain-price collective taxi services using Volkswagen minibuses (called *combis*) and sedans. The service is called *colectivo* or *pesero*. Peseros run along fixed routes, and you hail them on the street and tell the driver where you are going. The fare—which you pay before you get out—is based on distance traveled. We recommend that you take only the *colectivos* (special airport taxis) that transport passengers from—and sometimes to—airports. In places like Cozumel you'll find that colectivos only—not taxis—are permitted to take passengers from airport terminals into town.

TELEPHONES

Thanks to its 1991 privatization, Teléfonos de México (Mexico's phone service)—which for so long was exasperatingly inefficient—is gradually being overhauled. As of January 1997, Teléfonos de México's monopoly ended, enabling competition from several long-distance services, including MCI and AT&T. Many phones, especially in the better city hotels, have Touch-Tone (digital) circuitry. If you think you'll need to access an automated phone system or voice mail in the United States or elsewhere and you don't know what phone service will be available, it's a good idea to take along a Touch-Tone simulator (you can buy one for about $17 at most electronics stores). With the increased installation of new phone and fax lines in major Mexican cities, many phone numbers are in the process of being changed; a recording may offer the new number.

AREA & COUNTRY CODES

The country code for Mexico is 52. When calling a Mexico number from abroad, dial the country code and then all of the numbers listed for the entry.

DIRECTORY & OPERATOR ASSISTANCE

Directory assistance is 040 nationwide. For international assistance, dial 00 first for an international operator and most likely you'll get one that speaks English; tell the operator in what city, state, and country you require directory assistance, and he or she will connect you with directory assistance there.

INTERNATIONAL CALLS

To make an international call, **dial 00 before the country code, area code, and number.** When calling home, the country code for the U.S. and Canada is 1, the U.K. 44, Australia 61, New Zealand 64, and South Africa 27.

LOCAL & LONG-DISTANCE CALLS

The number of digits you need to dial for local calls varies. Numbers preceding the slash in our listings are the area or city codes, to be dialed when calling long distance within Mexico. However, in some cities, even when calling locally you now must dial the area code as well as the regular number.

For local or long-distance calls, one option is to find a *caseta de larga distancia*, a telephone service usually operated out of a store such as a *papelería* (stationery store), pharmacy, restaurant, or other small business; look for the phone symbol on the door. Casetas may cost more to use than pay phones, but you have a better chance of immediate success. To make a direct long-distance call, tell the person on duty the number you'd like to call, and she or he will give you a rate and

dial for you. Rates seem to vary widely, so shop around. Sometimes you can make collect calls from casetas, and sometimes you cannot, depending on the individual operator and possibly your degree of visible desperation. Casetas will generally charge 50¢–$1.50 to place a collect call (some charge by the minute); it's usually better to call *por cobrar* (collect) from a pay phone.

LONG-DISTANCE SERVICES

AT&T, MCI, and Sprint access codes make calling long distance relatively convenient, but you may find the local access number blocked in many hotel rooms. First ask the hotel operator to connect you. If the hotel operator balks, ask for an international operator, or dial the international operator yourself. One way to improve your odds of getting connected to your long-distance carrier is to travel with more than one company's calling card (a hotel may block Sprint, for example, but not MCI). If all else fails, call from a pay phone.

➤ ACCESS CODES: **AT&T Direct** (☎ 01-800/288-2872 or 01-800/112-2020). **MCI WorldPhone** (☎ 01-800/021-8000 or 001-800/674-7000).

PHONE CARDS

In most parts of the country now, pay phones accept prepaid cards, called Ladatel cards, sold in 30-, 50- or 100-peso denominations at newsstands or pharmacies. Many pay phones in Mexico only accept these cards; coin-only pay phones are usually broken. Still other phones have two unmarked slots, one for a Ladatel (a Spanish acronym for "long-distance direct dialing") card and the other for a credit card. These are primarily for Mexican bank cards, but some accept Visa or MasterCard, though *not* U.S. telephone credit cards.

To use a Ladatel card, simply insert it in the appropriate slot, dial 001 (for calls to the States) or 01 (for calls in Mexico), and the area code and number you're trying to reach. Credit is deleted from the card as you use it, and your balance is displayed on a small screen on the phone.

TOLL-FREE NUMBERS

Toll-free numbers in Mexico start with an 800 prefix. To reach them, you need to dial 01 before the number. In this guide, Mexico-only toll-free numbers appear as follows: 01–800/12–345 (numbers can also have six or seven digits). The 800 numbers listed simply 800/123–4567 work in the U.S. only.

TIME

Mexico has three time zones; most of the country falls in Central Standard Time, which includes Mexico City and is in line with Chicago. Baja California is on Pacific Standard Time—the same as California. Baja Californa Sur and parts of the northwest coast, including Sonora, are on Mountain Standard Time.

TIPPING

When tipping in Mexico, remember that the minimum wage is the equivalent of $3 a day and that the vast majority of workers in the tourist industry live barely above the poverty line. However, there are Mexicans who think in dollars and know, for example, that in the United States porters are tipped about $2 a bag. Many of them expect the peso equivalent from foreigners and may complain if they feel they deserve more—you and your conscience must decide. Following are some guidelines. Naturally, larger tips are always welcome.

Porters and bellboys at airports and at moderate and inexpensive hotels: $1 per bag.

Porters at expensive hotels: $2 per person.

Maids: $1 per night (all hotels).

Waiters: 10%–15% of the bill, depending on service (make sure a 10%–15% service charge hasn't already been added to the bill, although this practice is more common in resorts).

Taxi drivers: Tipping is necessary only if the driver helps with your bags—5 pesos to 10 pesos should be sufficient, depending on the extent of the help.

Tour guides and drivers: at least $1 per half day, minimum.

Gas-station attendants: 3 pesos to 5 pesos; if they check the oil, tires, etc., tip more.

Parking attendants and theater ushers: 5 pesos to 10 pesos. Some restaurants and theaters charge for valet-parking service; it's still customary to tip the attendant at least 10 pesos.

TOURS & PACKAGES

Because everything is prearranged on a prepackaged tour or independent vacation, you'll spend less time planning—and often get it all at a good price.

BOOKING WITH AN AGENT

Travel agents are excellent resources. But it's a good idea to collect brochures from several agencies as some agents' suggestions may be influenced by relationships with tour and package firms that reward them for volume sales. If you have a special interest, **find an agent with expertise in that area**; ASTA has a database of specialists worldwide.

Make sure your travel agent knows the accommodations and other services of the place they're recommending. Ask about the hotel's location, room size, beds, and whether it has a pool, room service, or programs for children, if you care about these. Has your agent been there in person or sent others whom you can contact?

Do some homework on your own, too: local tourism boards can provide information about lesser-known and small-niche operators, some of which may sell only direct.

BUYER BEWARE

Each year consumers are stranded or lose their money when tour operators—even large ones with excellent reputations—go out of business. So **check out the operator.** Ask several travel agents about its reputation, and try to **book with a company that has a consumer-protection program.** (Look for information in the company's brochure.) In the United States, members of the National Tour Association and the United States Tour Operators

Association are required to set aside funds to cover your payments and travel arrangements in the event that the company defaults. It's also a good idea to choose a company that participates in the American Society of Travel Agents' Tour Operator Program (TOP); ASTA will act as mediator in any disputes between you and your tour operator.

Remember that the more your package or tour includes the better you can predict the ultimate cost of your vacation. Make sure you know exactly what is covered, and **beware of hidden costs.** Are taxes, tips, and transfers included? Entertainment and excursions? These can add up.

➤ TOUR-OPERATOR RECOMMENDATIONS: **American Society of Travel Agents** (☞ Travel Agencies, *below*). **National Tour Association** (NTA; ✉ 546 E. Main St., Lexington, KY 40508, ☎ 859/226–4444 or 800/682–8886, 🖳 www.ntaonline.com). **United States Tour Operators Association** (USTOA; ✉ 342 Madison Ave., Suite 1522, New York, NY 10173, ☎ 212/599–6599 or 800/468–7862, 🖷 212/599–6744, 🖳 www.ustoa.com).

THEME TRIPS

➤ ART & ARCHAEOLOGY: **Archaeological Conservancy** (✉ 5301 Central Ave. NE, #1218, Albuquerque, NM 87108-1517, ☎ 505/266–1540). **Crow Canyon Archaeological Center** (✉ 2339 Road K, Cortez, CO 81321, ☎ 970/565–8975 or 800/422–8975, 🖷 970/565–4859). **Far Horizons Archaeological & Cultural Trips** (✉ Box 91900, Albuquerque, NM 87199-1900, ☎ 505/343–9400 or 800/552–4575, 🖷 505/343–8076).

➤ BICYCLING: **Backroads** (✉ 801 Cedar St., Berkeley, CA 94710-1800, ☎ 510/527–1555 or 800/462–2848, 🖷 510/527–1444). **Edelweiss Bike Travel** (✉ 129 Hillside Ave., Williston Park, NY 11596, ☎ 516/746–6761 or 800/877–2784, 🖷 516/746–6690). **Imagine Tours** (✉ Box 123, Davis, CA 95617, ☎ 530/758–8782 or 888/592–8687, 🖷 530/758–8778).

➤ BIRDING: **Field Guides** (✉ 9433 Bee Cave Rd., Bldg. 1, Suite 150, Austin, TX 78733, ☎ 512/327–4953 or 800/728–4953, 🖷 512/327–9231). **Victor

Emanuel Nature Tours (✉ 2525 Wallingwood Rd., Bldg. 10, Austin, TX 78746, ☎ 512/328–5221 or 800/328–8368, 🖷 512/328–2919). **Wings** (✉ 1643 N. Alvernon Way, Suite 105, Tucson, AZ 85712, ☎ 520/320–9868, 🖷 520/320–9373).

➤ BUTTERFLY SANCTUARIES: **Natural Habitat Adventures** (✉ 2945 Center Green Ct., Boulder, CO 80301, ☎ 303/449–3711 or 800/543–8917, 🖷 303/449–3712). **Remarkable Journeys** (✉ Box 31855, Houston, TX 77231-1855, ☎ 713/721–2517 or 800/856–1993, 🖷 713/728–8334).

➤ HORSEBACK RIDING: **Equitour FITS Equestrian** (✉ Box 807, Dubois, WY 82513, ☎ 307/455–3363 or 800/545–0019, 🖷 307/455–2354).

➤ WALKING: **Backroads** (☞ Bicycling, *above*). **Butterfield & Robinson** (✉ 70 Bond St., Toronto, Ontario, Canada M5B 1X3, ☎ 416/864–1354; 800/678–1147 in the U.S. and Canada, 🖷 416/864–0541).

➤ WHALE-WATCHING: **American Cetacean Society** (✉ 801 Stanley Ave., Long Beach, CA 90804, ☎ 562/438–8960, 🖷 310/548–6950). **Planet Expeditions** (✉ 2549 Center Green Ct. S., Suite H, Boulder, CO 80301, ☎ 800/233–2433, 🖷 303/349–3712).

TRAIN TRAVEL

By late 1997 private companies operating the Mexican railroads decided that passenger service was not profitable enough, mainly because of the North American Free Trade Agreement, which rendered the freight service more valuable. Private rooms and berths were taken out, and only general first-class service, *clase única primera,* remained, entitling passengers to a reserved reclining seat. As first-class bus service proliferates throughout the country, however, first-class rail cars and schedules are practically nonexistent.

As a result, rail travel in Mexico is not recommended, excepting the spectacular train ride through the Copper Canyon (the train was privatized in 1998 and remodeled cars went into service in 1999), which you can do either on the Mexican train or on privately run trains that originate in the United States. Another new service is the limited Tequila Express, which runs between Guadalajara and Tequila.

At press time there was no central office in Mexico with train information. From the United States, you can get some information on trains and rail-hotel packages by contacting Mexico by Train.

➤ TRAIN INFORMATION: **Mexico by Train** (☎ FAX 956/725–3659, ☎ 800/ 321–1699).

TRAVEL AGENCIES

A good travel agent puts your needs first. Look for an agency that has been in business at least five years, emphasizes customer service, and has someone on staff who specializes in your destination. In addition, **make sure the agency belongs to a professional trade organization.** The American Society of Travel Agents (ASTA), with more than 26,000 agents in some 170 countries, is the largest and most influential in the field. Operating under the motto "Without a travel agent, you're on your own," it maintains and enforces a strict code of ethics and will step in to help mediate any agent-client disputes if necessary. ASTA also maintains a Web site that includes a directory of agents. (If a travel agency is also acting as your tour operator, *see* Buyer Beware *in* Tours & Packages, *above*.)

➤ LOCAL AGENT REFERRALS: **American Society of Travel Agents** (ASTA; ☎ 800/965–2782 24-hr hot line, FAX 703/739–7642, WEB www.astanet. com). **Association of British Travel Agents** (✉ 68–71 Newman St., London W1T 3AH, U.K., ☎ 020/7637–2444, FAX 020/7637–0713, WEB www. abtanet.com). **Association of Canadian Travel Agents** (✉ 130 Albert St., Ste. 1705, Ottawa, Ontario K1P 5G4, Canada, ☎ 613/237–3657, FAX 613/ 237–7502, WEB www.acta.net). **Australian Federation of Travel Agents** (✉ Level 3, 309 Pitt St., Sydney NSW 2000, Australia, ☎ 02/9264–3299, FAX 02/9264–1085, WEB www.afta.com. au). **Travel Agents' Association of New Zealand** (✉ Box 1888, Wellington 10033, New Zealand, ☎ 04/499–0104, FAX 04/499–0827, WEB www. taanz.org.nz).

VISITOR INFORMATION

➤ MEXICAN GOVERNMENT TOURIST OFFICES (MGTO): **United States** (☎ 800/446–3942 nationwide; ✉ 21 East 63rd St., 3rd fl., New York, NY 10021, ☎ 212/821–0314, FAX 212/ 821–0367; ✉ 300 North Michigan Ave., 4th fl., Chicago, IL 60601, ☎ 312/606–9306, FAX 312/606–9012; ✉ 2401 West 6th St., 5th fl., Los Angeles, CA 90057, ☎ 310/351–2069, FAX 310/351–2074; ✉ 10103 Fondren Ave., Suite 540, Houston, TX 77096, ☎ 713/772–2581, FAX 713/772–6058; ✉ 1200 NW 78th Ave., Suite 203, Coral Gables, FL 33126, ☎ 305/718–4091, FAX 305/718–4098).

Canada (✉ 1 Place Ville Marie, Suite 1526, Montréal, Québec H3B 2B5, ☎ 514/871–1052, FAX 514/871–3825; ✉ 2 Bloor St. W, Suite 1502, Toronto, Ontario M4W 33E2, ☎ 416/ 925–0704, FAX 416/925–6061; ✉ 110-999 W. Hastings St., Vancouver, British Columbia V6C 2W2, ☎ 604/669–2845, FAX 604/669–3498).

United Kingdom (✉ 42 Hertford St., London W1Y 7TF, ☎ 020/7488–9392, FAX 020/7265–0705).

Mexico (✉ Presidente Masaryk 172, Mexico, D.F. 11550, ☎ 5250–0123 or 01-800/903–9200).

➤ U.S. GOVERNMENT ADVISORIES: **U.S. Department of State** (✉ Overseas Citizens Services Office, Room 4811 N.S., 2201 C St. NW, Washington, DC 20520, ☎ 202/647–5225 for interactive hot line, WEB www.travel.state. gov); enclose a self-addressed, stamped, business-size envelope.

WEB SITES

Do check out the World Wide Web when planning your trip. You'll find everything from weather forecasts to virtual tours of famous cities. Be sure to **visit Fodors.com** (www.fodors.com), a complete travel-planning site. You can research prices, and book plane tickets, hotel rooms, rental cars, vacation packages, and more. Other planning tools include a currency converter and weather reports, and there are loads of links to other travel resources.

WHEN TO GO

Mexico is sufficiently large and geographically diverse enough that you can find a place to visit any time of year. October through May are generally the driest months; during the peak of the rainy season (June–September), it may rain for a few hours daily. But the sun often shines for the rest of the day, and the reduced off-season rates may well compensate for the reduced tanning time.

From December through the second week after Easter, the Mexican resorts—where the vast majority of tourists go—are the most crowded and therefore the most expensive. This also holds true for July and August, school-vacation months, when Mexican families crowd hotels. To avoid the masses, the highest prices, and the worst rains, **consider visiting Mexico during October, November, April, or May,** just not during the traditional holiday periods. Hotel rates at the beach resorts can fall as much as 30% in the shoulder season, 50% in the off-season.

Mexicans travel during traditional holiday periods—Christmas through Jan. 6, Three Kings Day, *Semana Santa* (Holy Week, the week before Easter), the week after Easter—and summertime school vacations as well as over extended national holiday weekends, called *puentes* (bridges). Festivals play a big role in Mexican national life. If you plan to travel during a major national event, reserve both lodgings and transportation well in advance.

CLIMATE

Mexico's coasts and low-lying sections of the interior are often very hot if not actually tropical, with temperatures ranging from 17°C to 31°C (63°F to 88°F) in winter and well above 32°C (90°F) in summer. A more temperate area ranging from 16°C to 21°C (60°F to 70°F) is found at altitudes of 1,220–1,830 m (4,000–6,000 ft). In general, the high central plateau on which Mexico City, Guadalajara, and many of the country's colonial cities are located is springlike year-round.

➤ FORECASTS: **Weather Channel Connection** (☎ 900/932–8437), 95¢ per minute from a Touch-Tone phone.

ACAPULCO (PACIFIC COAST)

Jan.	88F	31C	May	90F	32C	Sept.	90F	32C
	72	22		75	24		75	24
Feb.	88F	31C	June	90F	32C	Oct.	90F	32C
	72	22		77	25		75	24
Mar.	88F	31C	July	90F	32C	Nov.	90F	32C
	72	22		77	25		73	23
Apr.	90F	32C	Aug.	91F	33C	Dec.	88F	31C
	73	23		77	25		71	22

COZUMEL (CARIBBEAN COAST)

Jan.	84F	29C	May	91F	33C	Sept.	89F	32C
	66	19		73	23		75	24
Feb.	84F	29C	June	89F	32C	Oct.	87F	31C
	66	19		75	24		73	23
Mar.	88F	31C	July	91F	33C	Nov.	86F	30C
	69	21		73	23		71	22
Apr.	89F	32C	Aug.	91F	33C	Dec.	84F	29C
	71	22		73	23		68	20

ENSENADA (BAJA CALIFORNIA)

Jan.	66F	19C	May	70F	21C	Sept.	79F	26C
	45	7		52	11		59	15
Feb.	68F	20C	June	73F	23C	Oct.	75F	24C
	45	7		54	12		54	12
Mar.	68F	20C	July	77F	25C	Nov.	72F	22C
	46	8		61	16		48	9
Apr.	69F	21C	Aug.	79F	26C	Dec.	68F	20C
	48	9		61	16		45	7

LA PAZ (BAJA CALIFORNIA SUR)

Jan.	73F	23C	May	91F	33C	Sept.	95F	35C
	54	12		59	15		73	23
Feb.	77F	25C	June	95F	35C	Oct.	91F	33C
	54	12		64	18		66	19
Mar.	80F	27C	July	97F	36C	Nov.	84F	29C
	54	12		71	22		61	16
Apr.	86F	30C	Aug.	97F	36C	Dec.	77F	25C
	55	13		73	23		54	12

MEXICO CITY (CENTRAL MEXICO)

Jan.	70F	21C	May	79F	26C	Sept.	72F	22C
	44	6		54	12		52	11
Feb.	73F	23C	June	77F	25C	Oct.	72F	22C
	45	7		54	12		50	10
Mar.	79F	26C	July	73F	23C	Nov.	72F	22C
	48	9		52	11		46	8
Apr.	81F	27C	Aug.	73F	23C	Dec.	70F	21C
	50	10		54	12		45	7

MONTERREY (NORTHEAST MEXICO)

Jan.	68F	20C	May	88F	31C	Sept.	88F	31C
	48	9		68	20		70	21
Feb.	73F	23C	June	91F	33C	Oct.	81F	27C
	52	11		72	22		63	17
Mar.	79F	26C	July	91F	34C	Nov.	73F	23C
	57	14		72	22		55	13
Apr.	86F	30C	Aug.	93F	34C	Dec.	70F	21C
	64	18		72	22		50	10

SAN MIGUEL DE ALLENDE (HEARTLAND)

Jan.	75F	24C	May	88F	31C	Sept.	79F	26C
	45	9	59	15		59	15	
Feb.	79F	26C	June	88F	30C	Oct.	79F	26C
	48	9	59	15		54	12	
Mar.	86F	30C	July	82F	28C	Nov.	75F	24C
	54	12	59	15		50	10	
Apr.	88F	31C	Aug.	82F	28C	Dec.	75F	24C
	57	14	59	15		46	8	

FESTIVALS & SEASONAL EVENTS

Mexico is the land of festivals; if you reserve lodging well in advance, they're a golden opportunity to experience Mexico's culture. January is full of long, regional festivals. Notable are the **Fiesta de la Inmaculada Concepción** (Feast of the Immaculate Conception), which transforms the city of Morelia into a sea of lights and flowers for much of the month, and a series of folkloric dances in Chiapa de Corzo, Chiapas, that culminates in the **Feast of San Sebastian,** the third week in January.

➤ JAN. 1: **New Year's Day** is a major celebration throughout the country.

Agricultural and livestock fairs are held in the provinces.

➤ JAN. 6: **Feast of Epiphany** is the day the Three Kings bring gifts to Mexican children.

➤ JAN. 17: **Feast of San Antonio Abad** honors animals all over Mexico. Pets and livestock are decked out with flowers and ribbons and taken to church for a blessing.

➤ FEB. 2: **Día de la Candelaria,** or Candlemas Day, means fiestas, parades, bullfights, and lantern-decorated streets. Festivities include a running of the bulls through the streets of Tlacotalpan, Veracruz.

➤ FEB.–MAR.: **Carnaval** is celebrated throughout Mexico—most notably in Mazatlán and Veracruz, with parades of floats and bands.

➤ MAR. 21: **Benito Juárez's Birthday,** a national holiday, is most popular in Guelatao, Oaxaca, where Juárez, the beloved 19th-century president of Mexico and champion of the people, was born. This is also the day that Cuernavaca's **Fiesta de la Primavera** marks the beginning of spring.

➤ MAR.–APR.: **Semana Santa** (Holy Week), the week leading to Easter Sunday, is observed with parades and passion plays.

➤ APR.–MAY: **San Marcos National Fair,** held in Aguascalientes, is one of the country's best fairs. It features Indian *matachnes* (dances performed by grotesque figures), mariachi bands, and bullfights. Also during this time, the 10-day **Festival de las Artes** (Arts Festival) brings music, theater, and dance troupes from all over Latin America to San Luis Potosí.

➤ MAY 1: **Labor Day** is a day for workers to parade through the streets.

➤ MAY 5: **Cinco de Mayo** marks, with great fanfare countrywide, the anniversary of the French defeat by Mexican troops in Puebla in 1862.

➤ MAY 15: **Feast of San Isidro Labrador** is noted nationwide by the blessing of new seeds and animals. In Cuernavaca, a parade of oxen wreathed in flowers is followed by street parties and feasting.

➤ JUNE 1: **Navy Day** is commemorated in all Mexican seaports and is especially colorful in Acapulco, Mazatlán, and Veracruz. The **Feast of Corpus Christi** is celebrated in different ways. In Mexico City, children are dressed in native costumes and taken to the cathedral on the zócalo for a blessing. In Papantla, Veracruz, the Dance of the Flying Birdmen—a pre-Hispanic ritual to the sun—is held throughout the day.

➤ JUNE 24: **Saint John the Baptist Day,** a popular national holiday, sees many Mexicans observing a tradition of tossing a "blessing" of water on most anyone within reach.

➤ EARLY JULY: The **Feria Nacional** (National Fair) in Durango runs from the Day of Our Lady of Refuge (July 4) to the anniversary of the founding of Durango in 1563 (July 22). The old-time agricultural fair has become known across the country for its carnival rides, livestock shows, and music. The **Guelaguetza Dance Festival,** a pre-Columbian Oaxacan affair, usually falls on the first and third Monday of July.

➤ JULY 16: **Our Lady of Mt. Carmel Day** is celebrated with fairs, bullfights, fireworks, even a major fishing tournament.

➤ LATE JULY: The **Feast of Santiago** features *charreadas,* Mexican-style rodeos.

➤ AUG.: The **Feast of St. Augustine** brings a month of music, dance, and fireworks to Puebla. On August 26 (feast day) it is customary to prepare the famous *chiles en nogada.*

➤ AUG. 15: **Feast of the Assumption of the Blessed Virgin Mary** is celebrated nationwide with religious processions. In Huamantla, Tlaxcala, the festivities include a running of the bulls and a carpet of flowers laid out in front of the church.

➤ AUG. 25: **San Luis Potosí Patron Saint Fiesta** is the day the town honors its patron, San Luis Rey, with traditional dance, music, and foods.

➤ SEPT. 15–16: **Independence Day** is marked throughout Mexico with fireworks and parties that outblast those on New Year's Eve. The biggest celebrations are in Mexico City.

➤ SEPT. 29: **San Miguel Day** honors St. Michael, the patron saint of all towns with San Miguel in their names—especially San Miguel de Allende—with bullfights, folk dances, concerts, and fireworks.

➤ OCT.: **October Festival** means a month of cultural and sporting events in Guadalajara.

➤ OCT. 4: **Feast of St. Francis of Assisi** is a day for processions dedicated to St. Francis in parts of the country.

➤ OCT. 12: **Día de la Raza** (Day of the Race) is comparable to Columbus Day in the United States.

➤ OCT.–NOV.: **International Cervantes Festival** in Guanajuato is a top cultural event that attracts dancers, singers, and actors from various countries.

➤ Nov. 1–Nov. 2: On **All Souls' and All Saints' Day,** or Day of the Dead, families welcome back the spirits of departed relatives to elaborate altars and refurbished gravesites. Especially intriguing are the celebrations in Pátzcuaro and Oaxaca.

➤ Nov. 20: **Anniversary of the Mexican Revolution** is a national holiday.

➤ Nov.–Dec.: **National Silver Fair,** an annual Taxco event, is an occasion for even more silver selling than usual, the crowning of a Silver Queen, and jewelry and silver exhibitions.

➤ Dec. 12: On **Feast Day of the Virgin of Guadalupe,** Mexico's patron saint is feted with processions and native folk dances, particularly at her shrine in Mexico City. In Puerto Vallarta, 12 days of processions and festivities lead up to the night of Dec. 12.

➤ Dec. 16–25: **The Posadas and Christmas** include candlelight processions that lead to holiday parties and the breaking open of piñatas. Mexico City is brightly decorated, but don't expect any snow.

➤ Dec. 23: **Night of the Radishes,** a pre-Christmas tradition in Oaxaca, is one of the most colorful in Mexico: participants carve giant radishes into amusing shapes and display them in the city's main plaza.

INDEX

ABOUT OUR WRITERS

The more you know before you go, the better your trip will be. Mexico's most deserted beach or overgrown Maya ruin could be just around the corner from your hotel, but if you don't know it's there, it might as well be on the other side of the globe. That's where this book comes in. It's a great step toward making sure your next trip lives up to your expectations. As you plan, check out the Web as well. Guidebooks have been helping smart travelers find the special places for years; the Web is one more tool. Whatever reference you consult, be savvy about what you read, and always consider the source. Images and language can be massaged to make places appear better than they are. And one traveler's quaint is another's grimy. Here at Fodor's, and at our on-line arm, Fodors.com, our focus is on providing you with information that's not only useful but accurate and on target. Every day Fodor's editors put enormous effort into getting things right, beginning with the search for the right contributors—people who have objective judgment, broad travel experience, and the writing ability to put their insights into words. There's no substitute for advice from a like-minded friend who has just come back from where you're going, but our writers, having seen all corners of Mexico, are the next best thing. They're the kind of people you'd poll for tips yourself if you knew them.

So drawn to the surrealism of Mexico that she turned a one-week vacation into a 20-year sojourn, **Patricia Alisau** has traveled just about every inch of the country on assignment for Mexican and U.S. journals. She has written for Mexico's *Vogue* magazine and, as a foreign correspondent, for the *New York Times*, the *Chicago Tribune*, and the Associated Press. This year, she updated our Acapulco chapter and sections of the Yucatán Peninsula chapter.

Journalist **Cynthia Hawes**, who updated this edition's Chiapas and Tabasco chapter and Smart Travel Tips, has lived in Mexico for nearly 20 years. A native of Southern California, she first went to Mexico as a student and returned years

later to settle down and raise her two daughters, Nayeli and Itzel. Cynthia has worked for more than 25 years as a reporter and producer for major U.S., Canadian, and British media. Currently, she is an editor of the on-line edition of *The News*, the Mexico City English-language newspaper.

Barbara Kastelein made her way to Latin America from Holland via Great Britain, under whose gray skies she obtained a Doctorate in Literary Studies. A freelance writer with special interests in travel, environment, and politics, she has been living in Mexico's smoggy and sinful capital for five years. She enjoys her colorful country of choice with her partner, three-year-old daughter, and baby son. For this edition, Barbara updated the Mexico City, Side Trips from Mexico City, and Oaxaca chapters.

Berkeley-based **Denise M. Leto,** who edited parts of this book, longs to leave the rains of Northern California behind for a spin through the tropics of Mexico. In the meantime, she seeks consolation at her favorite Mexican restaurant. Her own work has appeared online, in the *San Francisco Bay Guardian*, and in many a Fodor's guidebook.

A decade after her first trip to Morelia, **Amy Mansell** plunged into the heart of Mexico and found a life of writing, travel, and adventure in colorful San Miguel de Allende. She's currently working on a collection of short stories that include a famous street dog named Lupita. Amy updated the Veracruz and the Northeast and The Heartland chapters for this edition.

Journalist–turned–travel writer **Shelagh McNally** has lived on the Yucatán Peninsula with her young daughter since 1987, when she left her native Canada for a four-month Mexican vacation that turned into a major life change. She has covered the Caribbean Coast and Campeche for us and also has written for the *Miami Herald*, *Mundo Maya* magazine, and other publications in Mexico, Canada, and the United States.

Recipient of the prestigious Pluma de Plata award for writing on Mexico, **Maribeth Mellin** lives in San Diego near the Tijuana border in a home filled with folk art and photos from Latin America—including a snapshot of the 140-pound marlin she caught in the Sea of Cortez. She has authored travel books on Mexico, Costa Rica, Argentina, and Peru and is currently creating a fictional account of her adventures. Maribeth updated this year's Baja California chapter.

Since earning a B.A. in Spanish language and literature, **Jane Onstott** has lived and traveled extensively in Latin America. She worked as Director of Communications and Information for the Darwin Research Station in the Galapagos Islands, and studied painting in Oaxaca between 1995 and 1998. Since 1986 Jane has contributed to Fodor's guides to Mexico and South America; this year, she updated the Guadalajara and Pacific Coast Resorts chapters.

We'd also like to acknowledge Mexicana for its considerable assistance with travel arrangements.

Don't Forget to Write

We love feedback—positive and negative—and follow up on all suggestions. So contact the Mexico editor at editors@fodors.com or c/o Fodor's, 280 Park Avenue, New York, New York 10017. Have a wonderful trip!

Karen Cure
Editorial Director

FODOR'S MEXICO 2002

EDITOR: Amy Karafin

Editorial Contributors: Patricia Alisau, David Bell, Cynthia Hawes, Gina Hyams, Barbara Kastelein, Denise M. Leto, Amy Mansell, Shelagh McNally, Maribeth Mellin, Jane Onstott

Editorial Production: Tom Holton

Maps: David Lindroth, *cartographer*; Rebecca Baer, Robert Blake, *map editors*

Design: Fabrizio La Rocca, *creative director*; Guido Caroti, *art director*; Jolie Novak, *senior picture editor*; Melanie Marin, *photo editor*

Cover Design: Pentagram

Production/Manufacturing: Angela L. McLean

COPYRIGHT

IMPORTANT TIP

Although all prices, opening times, and other details in this book are based on information supplied to us at press time, changes occur all the time in the travel world, and Fodor's cannot accept responsibility for facts that become outdated or for inadvertent errors or omissions. So always confirm information when it matters, especially if you're making a detour to visit a specific place.

SPECIAL SALES

Fodor's Travel Publications are available at special discounts for bulk purchases for sales promotions or premiums. Special editions, including personalized covers, excerpts of existing guides, and corporate imprints, can be created in large quantities for special needs. For more information, contact your local bookseller or write to Special Markets, Fodor's Travel Publications, 280 Park Avenue, New York, NY 10017. Inquiries from Canada should be directed to your local Canadian bookseller or sent to Random House of Canada, Ltd., Marketing Department, 2775 Matheson Boulevard East, Mississauga, Ontario L4W 4P7. Inquiries from the United Kingdom should be sent to Fodor's Travel Publications, 20 Vauxhall Bridge Road, London SW1V 2SA, England.

PHOTOGRAPHY